ENCYCLOPEDIA OF THE RENAISSANCE

ENCYCLOPEDIA OF THE

ENAISSANCE

Paul F. Grendler

Editor in Chief

PUBLISHED IN ASSOCIATION WITH
THE RENAISSANCE SOCIETY OF AMERICA

VOLUME 1

Abrabanel – Civility

CHARLES SCRIBNER'S SONS

An Imprint of The Gale Group

NEW YORK

Charles Scribner's Sons
1633 Broadway
New York, New York 10019

1 3 5 7 9 11 13 15 17 19   20 18 16 14 12 10 8 6 4 2

PRINTED IN THE UNITED STATES OF AMERICA

Library of Congress Cataloging-in-Publication Data
Encyclopedia of the Renaissance / Paul F. Grendler, editor in chief.
       p. cm.
    Includes bibliographical references and index.
    ISBN 0-684-80514-6 (set) — ISBN 0-684-80508-1 (v. 1) — ISBN 0-684-80509-X (v. 2)
— ISBN 0-684-80510-3 (v. 3) — ISBN 0-684-80511-1 (v. 4) — ISBN 0-684-80512-X (v.
5) — ISBN 0-684-80513-8 (v. 6)
    1. Renaissance—Encyclopedias.   I. Grendler, Paul F.   II. Renaissance Society of
America.
CB361.E52   1999
940.2′3′03—dc21   99-048290

The typeface used in this book is ITC Garamond, a version of a typeface attributed to the
French publisher and type founder Claude Garamond (c. 1480–1561).

Dedicated to the Memory of

Paul Oskar Kristeller
1905–1999

Charles Trinkaus
1911–1999

Editorial and Production Staff

CONTENTS

VOLUME 1

List of Maps   xix

List of Genealogical Tables   xix

Introduction   xxi

Chronology   xxv

List of Abbreviations   lxv

*Encyclopedia of the
Renaissance*

A

Abravanel, Isaac
Absolutism
Academies
Accounting
Achillini, Alessandro
Acoustics
Adrian VI (pope)
Africa, North
Africa, Sub-Saharan
Africanus, Leo
Agricola, Georgius
Agricola, Rudolf
Agriculture
Agrippa of Nettesheim, Heinrich
Agustín, Antonio
Alberti, Leon Battista
Albuquerque, Afonso de
Alcalá de Henares, University of
Alchemy
Alciato, Andrea
Aldine Press
Alemán, Mateo
Alemanno, Yohanan ben Isaac
Alexander VI (pope)
Alfonso the Magnanimous
Allegory
Almeida, Francisco de

Alvárez de Toledo, Fernando
Amboise, Georges d'
Amerbach Family
Americas
Amsterdam
Amyot, Jacques
Anatomy
Andreini, Isabella
Angelico, Fra
Anguissola, Sofonisba
Anjou, François de Valois, duc
    d'Alençon et d'
Anna of Saxony
Anne de Beaujeu
Anne of Brittany
Antiquarianism
Anti-Semitism
Antoninus
Antwerp
Arabic Literature and Language
Aragona, Tullia d'
Architecture
    Architecture in the Renaissance
    Architectural Treatises
Aretino, Pietro
Ariosto, Ludovico
Aristocracy
Aristotle and Aristotelianism
Aristotle and Cinquecento Poetics
Armada, Spanish
Arms and Armor
Art
    Renaissance Art
    Education and Training
    Women Artists
Artillery
Artisans
Ascham, Roger
Asia, East
Astronomy
Aubigné, Théodore-Agrippa d'
Augsburg

Augustine of Hippo
Austria
    Austria in the Renaissance
    Art in Austria

B

Bacon, Francis
Baïf, Lazare de
Balassi, Bálint
Baldung Grien, Hans
Baltic States
Bandello, Matteo
Banking and Money
Barbaro, Francesco
Barocci, Federico
Baronio, Cesare
Baroque, Concept of the
Bartolommeo della Porta, Fra
Basel
Basel, Council of
Basile, Giambattista
Bavaria
Bawdy, Elizabethan
Beatus Rhenanus
Beaufort, Margaret
Behn, Aphra
Bellarmine, Robert
Bellièvre, Pomponne de
Bellini Family
Bembo, Pietro
Benedetti, Giovanni Battista
Beni, Paolo
Bernardino of Siena
Berni, Francesco
Béroalde de Verville, François
Bessarion
Bèze, Théodore de
Bible
    Texts and Textual Criticism
    Christian Interpretation of the Bible
    Jewish Interpretation of the Bible
    Printed Bibles

German Translations
The English Bible
Bidermann, Jakob
Biography and Autobiography
Europe
England
Biondo, Flavio
Birth and Infancy
Boccaccio, Giovanni
Bodin, Jean
Bohemia
Böhme, Jakob
Boiardo, Matteo Maria
Bologna
Bologna, University of
Borgia, House of
Borgia, Cesare
Borgia, Lucrezia
Boscán, Juan
Bosch, Hieronymus
Botany
Botero, Giovanni
Botticelli, Sandro
Bourbon Family and Dynasty
Bourgeoisie
Bouts, Dirck
Bracciolini, Poggio
Brahe, Tycho
Bramante, Donato
Brandenburg
Brant, Sebastian
Brantôme, Pierre de Bourdeille,
seigneur de
Britain, Art in
Brittany
Browne, Thomas
Brueghel Family
Bruges
Brûlart de Sillery, Nicolas
Brunelleschi, Filippo
Brunfels, Otto
Bruni, Leonardo
Bruno, Giordano
Brunswick-Wolfenbüttel
Brussels
Bucer, Martin
Budé, Guillaume
Buonamici, Francesco
Burchiello
Burgundy
Burton, Robert
Busche, Hermann von dem

Bussa de' Ponziani, Francesca
Byrd, William

C

Cajetan, Thomas de Vio
Calderón de la Barca, Pedro
Calendars
Calligraphy
Calvin, John
Cambrai, League of
Cambridge, University of
Camerarius, Joachim
Camões, Luíz Vaz de
Campanella, Tommaso
The Life of Campanella
Campanella the Philosopher
Campanella the Literary Figure
Canter, Jacob
Capito, Wolfgang
Caravaggio, Michelangelo Merisi
da
Cardano, Girolamo
Carnival
Caro, Joseph ben Ephraim
Carpaccio, Vittore
Carracci Family
Carvajal y Mendoza, Luisa de
Casaubon, Isaac
Castiglione, Baldassare
Catalan Literature and
Language
Catherine de Médicis
Catherine of Aragon
Catherine of Bologna
Catherine of Genoa
Catherine of Siena
Catholic Reformation and
Counter-Reformation
Cavendish, Margaret
Caxton, William
Cecchi, Giovanni Maria
Cecil, William
Cellini, Benvenuto
Cellini the Writer
Cellini the Artist
Celtis, Conrad
Censorship
Censorship on the Continent
Censorship in England
Census
Ceramics
Cereta, Laura
Cervantes Saavedra, Miguel de

Cesalpino, Andrea
Champier, Symphorien
Charivari
Charles V (Holy Roman
Emperor)
Charles I (England)
Charles VIII (France)
Charles IX (France)
Charles the Bold
Charron, Pierre
Chateaux
Chemistry
Childhood
Chivalry
Knighthood and Chivalric Orders
Romance of Chivalry
English Arthurian Romance
Chivalry in Renaissance Art
Christianity
The Western Church
Orthodox Christianity
Christian Theology
Christina of Sweden
Chronicle, Elizabethan
Chrysoloras, Manuel
Cicero
Ciruelo, Pedro
Cisneros, Francisco Jiménez de
Cities and Urban Life
City-State
Civility

VOLUME 2

Classical Antiquity
Discovery of Classical Antiquity
Classical Antiquity in Renaissance
Art
Classical Scholarship
Clavius, Christopher
Clement VII (pope)
Clement VIII (pope)
Clergy
Catholic Clergy
Protestant Clergy
Cleve, Joos van
Clocks
Clothing
Cobos, Francisco de los
Coimbra, University of
Coins, Medals, and Plaquettes
Colet, John
Coligny, Gaspard II de
Collège de France

Cologne
Colonna, Francesco
Colonna, Vittoria
Columbus, Christopher
Commandino, Federico
Commedia dell'Arte
Commonplace Books
Communication and
    Transportation
Commynes, Philippe de
Complutensian Polyglot Bible
Comuneros, Revolt of the
Conciliarism
Concordats
Confraternities
Constance, Council of
Constantinople, Fall of
Constitutionalism
Contarini, Gasparo
Conversos
Copernicus, Nicolaus
Coquille, Guy
Cornaro Piscopia, Elena Lucrezia
Corner, Caterina
Correggio
Cortés, Hernán
Corvinus, Matthias
Court
Covarrubias y Leiva, Diego de
Cracow
Cranach, Lucas
Cranmer, Thomas
Crime and Punishment
Croatia and Dalmatia
    Croatia and Dalmatia in the
        Renaissance
    Art in Croatia and Dalmatia
Cromberger Press
Cromwell, Thomas
Crusade

D

Daily Life
Dance
Dante in the Renaissance
Dantiscus, Johannes
Datini, Francesco
Death
Decorative Arts
Dedekind, Friedrich
Dee, John
Della Casa, Giovanni
Della Porta, Giambattista

Della Valle, Federico
Delmedigo, Elijah
Demography
Des Périers, Bonaventure
Desportes, Philippe
Despotism
Des Roches, Catherine and
    Madeleine
Devotio Moderna
Diane de Poitiers
Diaries and Memoirs
Dictionaries and Encyclopedias
Diffusion of Ideas
Dignity of Man
Diplomacy
Dolet, Étienne
Donatello
Doni, Anton Francesco
Donne, John
Doria, Andrea
Dovizi, Bernardo
Drake, Francis
Drama
    Religious Drama
    Tragedy
    Erudite Comedy
Drama, English
    Elizabethan Drama
    Jacobean Drama
    Jacobean Court Masque
Drama, French
Drama, Spanish
Drawing
Du Bartas, Guillaume de Salluste
Du Bellay, Joachim
Dubrovnik
Dudley, Robert
Duel
Du Fail, Noël
Dufay, Guillaume
Du Guillet, Pernette
Dumoulin, Charles
Dunstaple, John
Dürer, Albrecht
Du Tillet, Jean
Du Vair, Guillaume
Dynastic Rivalry

E

Early Modern Period
East Central Europe, Art in
Eberlin, Johann von Guenzburg
Education

Edward VI (England)
Eguía Press
El Greco
Elizabeth I (England)
Elyot, Thomas
Elzevier Press
Emblem
Emilia, Art in
Encina, Juan del
England
English Literature and Language
Epernon, Jean-Louis de Nogaret,
    duc
Epic
Epicurus and Epicureanism
Erasmus, Desiderius
Erauso, Catalina de
Ercilla y Zúñiga, Alonso
Espionage
Este, House of
Este, Isabella d'
Estienne Family
Estrées, Gabrielle d'
Ethnography of the New World
Euclid
Eugenius IV (pope)
Europe, Idea of
Exploration
Eyck, Jan van and Hubert van

F

Fabricius of Aquapendente,
    Girolamo
Facezie
Faction
Fairs
Family and Kinship
Famous Men and Women
Farnese, House of
Fedele, Cassandra
Federico da Montefeltro
Feminism
Ferdinand I (emperor)
Ferdinand of Aragon
Fernández de Córdoba, Gonzalo
Ferrara
    Ferrara in the Renaissance
    Art in Ferrara
Ferreira, António
Festivals
Ficino, Marsilio
Fiction, Elizabethan
Field of Cloth of Gold

Filarete (Antonio Averlino)
Filelfo, Francesco
Finance and Taxation
Fiorentino, Niccolò
Firearms
Firenzuola, Agnolo
Fischart, Johann
Fisher, John
Flavius Mithridates
Florence
    Florence in the Renaissance
    Art of the Fifteenth Century
    Art of the Sixteenth Century
Florence, Council of
Folengo, Teofilo
Fonte, Moderata
Food and Drink
Forgeries
Fortifications
Fortune
Foxe, John
Fracastoro, Girolamo
France
    The Kingdom of France
    Art in France
Francesco di Giorgio
Francis I (France)
Francis II (France)
Francis Xavier
Franck, Sebastian
Franco, Veronica
French Literature and Language
Froben Press
Fugger Family
Furió Ceriol, Fadrique

VOLUME 3

G

Galen
Galilei, Galileo
Gallicanism
Gama, Vasco da
Gàmbara, Veronica
Gans, David ben Solomon
Gansfort, Wessel
Garcilaso de la Vega
Gardens
Gattamelata, Erasmo da Narni, il
Gattinara, Mercurino
Gaza, Theodore
Gelli, Giovanni Battista
Gemistus Pletho, George

Genoa: Genoa in the Renaissance
Genoa: Art in Genoa
Gentileschi, Artemisia
Geography and Cartography
Geology
George of Trebizond
German Literature and Language
Germany, Art in
Ghetto
Ghiberti, Lorenzo
Giannotti, Donato
Gibbons, Orlando
Gilbert, William
Giles of Viterbo
Ginés de Sepúlveda, Juan
Giocondo, Fra
Giolito Press
Giorgione
Giotto di Bondone
Giovio, Paolo
Giraldi, Giambattista Cinzio
Giulio Romano (Giulio Pippi)
Giunti Press
Glory, Idea of
Glueckel of Hameln
Goes, Hugo van der
Gómez de Silva, Ruy
Góngora y Argote, Luis de
Gonzaga, Giulia
Gonzaga, House of
González de Mendoza, Pedro
Gothic
Goulart, Simon
Gournay, Marie de
Granada, Luis de
Grand Tour
Grazzini, Anton Francesco
Greek Émigrés
Gregory XIII (pope)
Grey, Jane
Groningen
Grotesques
Grotius, Hugo
Grumbach, Argula von
Grünewald, Matthias
Guarini, Giovanni Battista
Guarini, Guarino
Guevara, Antonio de
Guicciardini, Francesco
Guilds
Guise-Lorraine Family
Gutenberg, Johann

H

Habsburg Dynasty
Hagiography
Hakluyt, Richard
Harriot, Thomas
Harvey, William
Hebrew Literature and Language
Helmont, Johannes Baptista van
Heltai, Gáspár
Henry VII (England)
Henry VIII (England)
Henry II (France)
Henry III (France)
Henry IV (France)
Heraldry
Herbert, George
Hermetism
Herrera, Fernando de
Herrera, Juan de
Hesse
Hessus, Helius Eobanus
Hilliard, Nicholas
Hippocrates of Cos
Historical Themes in Renaissance
    Art
Historiography, Classical
    Classical Historians
    Greek Historians
    Roman Historians
Historiography, Renaissance
    Italian Historiography
    French Historiography
    British Historiography
    German Historiography
    Jewish Historiography
    Spanish Historiography
Holbein, Hans the Elder
Holbein, Hans the Younger
Holy Roman Empire
Homilies, Book of
Homosexuality
Honor
Hooft, Pieter Corneliszoon
Hooker, Richard
Horace
Hospitals and Asylums
Hotman, François
Household
Huarte de San Juan, Juan
Human Body in Renaissance Art
Humanism
    The Definition of Humanism
    The Origins of Humanism

Italy
Spain
Portugal
Germany and the Low Countries
The British Isles
France
Legal Humanism
Humanity, Concept of
Humor
Hungary
Hungary in the Renaissance
Art in Hungary
Hurtado de Mendoza, Diego
Hutten, Ulrich von

I

Ignatius Loyola
Illumination
Immortality
Index of Prohibited Books
Individualism
Industry
Inns of Court
Inquisition
Roman Inquisition
Spanish Inquisition
Inquisition in the Americas
Portuguese Inquisition
Ireland
Isabella of Castile
Islam
Islamic Thought
Isserles, Moses
Italian Literature and Language
Italy

J

James I (England)
Jeanne d'Albret
Jerome
Jewel, John
Jewelry
Jewish Medicine and Science
Jewish Messianism
Jewish Philosophy
Jewish Thought and the
Renaissance
Jews
The Jewish Community
Jewish Women and Family Life
Jewish Religious Life
Court Jews
Jews and the Arts
Jews and Music

Print and Jewish Cultural
Development
Jews and the Catholic Church
John of Austria
John of the Cross
Jones, Inigo
Jonson, Ben
Josquin des Prez
Joyeuse, Anne de
Juan de Ávila
Judeo-Italian
Julius II (pope)

K

Kabbalah
Kepler, Johannes
Klonowic, Sebastian Fabian
Knox, John
Kochanowski, Jan
Krzycki, Andrzej

L

Labé, Louise
La Boderie, Guy Le Fèvre de
La Boétie, Étienne de
Ladino Literature and Language
Landino, Cristoforo
La Noue, François de
Lanyer, Aemilia
Lascaris, Constantine
Lascaris, Janus
Las Casas, Bartolomé de
Łaski Family
Lasso, Orlando di
Lateran V, Council of
Law
Lefèvre d'Étaples, Jacques
Leiden
Leipzig
Leo X (pope)
León, Luis de
Leonardo da Vinci
Leone Ebreo
Lepanto, Battle of
Le Roy, Louis
Leto, Pomponio
Letterbooks
L'Hôpital, Michel de
Libertinism
Libraries
Life Stages
Ligorio, Pirro
Linacre, Thomas

Lipsius, Justus
Lisbon
Literacy
Literary Theory, Renaissance
Liturgy
Livorno
Lodi, Peace of
Logic
London
Louis XI (France)
Louis XII (France)
Louis XIII (France)
Louise of Savoy
Louvain, University of
Love
Lucca
Lucian
Luria, Isaac
Luther, Martin
Luzzatto, Simone
Lyly, John
Lyon

VOLUME 4

M

Machiavelli, Niccolò
The Life of Machiavelli
The Political Theorist
The Literary Figure
Machiavelli's Influence
Madrid
Magellan, Ferdinand
Magic and Astrology
Magic and Astrology
Jewish Astrology and the Occult
Jewish Magic and Divination
Maharal of Prague
Major, John
Makin, Bathsua
Maldonado, Juan
Malherbe, François
Mannerism
Mantegna, Andrea
Mantua
Manuscripts
Margaret of Austria
Margaret of Navarre
Margaret of Parma
Margaret of Valois
Mariana, Juan de
Marie de Médicis
Marinella, Lucrezia

Marino, Giambattista
Marlowe, Christopher
Marot, Clément
Marriage
Marvell, Andrew
Mary I (England)
Mary Stuart
Masaccio
Material Culture
Mathematics
Matter, Structure of
Maurice of Nassau
Maximilian I (Holy Roman
    Emperor)
Maximilian II (Holy Roman
    Emperor)
Mazzoni, Jacopo
Mechanics
Medici, House of
Medici, Cosimo de'
Medici, Lorenzo de'
    Political Leader and Patron of the
      Arts
    The Literary Figure
Medici, Cosimo I
Medicine
Mediterranean Sea
Mehmed II (sultan)
Melanchthon, Philipp
Memling, Hans
Menassah ben Israel
Mercantilism
Mercenaries
Merici, Angela
Metaphysics
Michelangelo Buonarroti
    Michelangelo the Artist
    Michelangelo the Poet
Middle Ages
Midwives and Healers
Milan
    Milan in the Renaissance
    Art in Milan and Lombardy
Milton, John
Mining and Metallurgy
Missions, Christian
Modena
Modena, Leon
Molina, Tirso de
Monarchy
Montaigne, Michel de
Monte, Guidobaldo, marchese del
Montefeltro Family

Montemayor, Jorge de
Monteverdi, Claudio
Montluc, Blaise de Lasseran-
    Massencôme, seigneur de
Montmorency Family
Montmorency, Anne de
Moral Philosophy
Morata, Olympia
More, Thomas
Moriscos
Morison, Richard
Morra, Isabella di
Mostaert, Jan
Motherhood
Müntzer, Thomas
Muret, Marc-Antoine
Murner, Thomas
Museums
Music
    Renaissance Music
    Music in Renaissance Culture
    Music in Renaissance Society
    Music Treatises
    Transmission of Music
    Performance Practice
    Musical Instruments
    Instrumental Music
    Sacred Vocal Music
    Secular Vocal Music
    Intermedi
    Opera
Music in England
Music in France
Music in Italy
Music in Spain and Portugal
Music in the Holy Roman Empire
Music in the Low Countries
Myth

N

Naogeorgus, Thomas
Naples
    Naples in the Renaissance
    Art in Naples
Nation-State
Natural Philosophy
Naval Warfare
Nebrija, Antonio de
Neo-Latin Literature and Language
Neo-Stoicism
Nepotism
Netherlandish Literature and
    Language

Netherlands
    The Netherlands in the Renaissance
    Art in the Netherlands
Nicholas V (pope)
Nicholas of Cusa
Nifo, Agostino
Nogarola, Isotta
Nostradamus
Notaries
Novella
Numerology
Nürnberg
Nürnberg Chronicle

O

Obstetrics and Gynecology
Ockeghem, Johannes
Oecolampadius
Oligarchies
Optics
Orcagna, Andrea
Orphans and Foundlings
Orzechowski, Stanisław
Ottoman Empire
Ovid
Oxford, University of

P

Pacioli, Luca
Padua, University of
Paganism
Painting
Palaces and Townhouses
Palatinate
Palestrina, Giovanni Pierluigi da
Palladio, Andrea
Palmieri, Matteo
Pannonius, Janus
Papacy
Paracelsus
Parades, Processions, and
    Pageants
Paragone
Paré, Ambroise
Paris
Paris, University of
Parker, Matthew
Parma
Parmigianino
Parr, Katherine
Paruta, Paolo
Pasquier, Étienne
Pasquino

Pastoral
  Pastoral on the Continent
  Elizabethan Pastoral
Patristics
Patrizi, Francesco
Patronage
  Patrons and Clients in Renaissance
    Society
  Patronage of the Arts
  Literary Patronage in England
Paul III (pope)
Paul IV (pope)
Paul V (pope)
Pavia, Battle of
Pavia, University of
Pazzi Conspiracy
Peasantry
Peasants' War
Pérez, Antonio
Perugia
Perugino
Peruzzi, Baldassare
Petrarch
Petrarchism

VOLUME 5

Peucer, Kaspar
Peurbach, Georg
Peutinger, Conrad
Philip II (king of Spain)
Philip III (king of Spain)
Philosophy
Physics
Pibrac, Guy du Faur, sieur de
Picaresque Novel
Piccolomini, Alessandro
Pico della Mirandola, Giovanni
Piedmont-Savoy
Piero della Francesca
Pilgrimage
Pinturicchio
Piracy
Pirckheimer, Caritas
Pirckheimer Family
Pisa
Pisanello, Antonio Pisano, il
Pisano, Andrea
Pius II (pope)
Pius IV (pope)
Pius V (pope)
Pizan, Christine de
Pizarro, Francisco
Plague

Plantin, Christophe
Platina, Bartolomeo
Plato, Platonism, and
  Neoplatonism
Platter Family
Plautus, Titus Maccius
Pléiade
Pliny the Elder
Plotinus
Podestà
Poetics
  Survey
  French Poetics
Poetry
  Classical Poetry
  Religious Poetry
  The Sonnet outside England
  The English Sonnet
Poetry, English
  Neo-Latin Poetry in England
  Tudor Poetry before Spenser
  Elizabethan Poetry
  Early Stuart and Metaphysical
    Poetry
Poetry and Music
Poland
Pole, Reginald
Political Thought
Poliziano, Angelo
Pomponazzi, Pietro
Pontano, Giovanni
Popular Culture
Popular Revolts
Pornography
Portugal
Portuguese Literature and
  Language
Postel, Guillaume
Poverty and Charity
Prague
Prayer Book, English
Preaching and Sermons
  Christian Preaching and Sermons
  Jewish Preaching and Sermons
Pregnancy
Prince
Printing and Publishing
Printmaking
Professions
Prose, Elizabethan
Prosody, Elizabethan
Prostitution
Protestant Reformation
Psychology

Ptolemy
Pulci, Antonia
Pulci, Luigi
Puritanism

Q

Queens and Queenship
Querelle des Femmes
Quevedo, Francisco de
Quiroga, Vasco de

R

Rabbis
Rabelais, François
Ralegh, Walter
Ramus, Petrus
Ramusio, Giovanni Battista
Rape
Raphael
Ratio Studiorum
Reason of State
Regiomontanus
Régnier, Mathurin
Religious Literature
Religious Orders
  Orders of Men
  Orders and Congregations of
    Women
  New Religious Orders and
    Congregations in Italy
  The Jesuits
  New Religious Congregations in
    France
Religious Piety
Religious Themes in Renaissance
  Art
Renaissance
  The Renaissance in Historical
    Thought
  The English Renaissance in Literary
    Intepretation
  The Renaissance in Popular
    Imagination
  Influence of the Renaissance
  Renaissance Studies
Renaissance, Interpretations of the
  Giorgio Vasari
  Jules Michelet
  Jakob Burckhardt
  John Ruskin
  John Addington Symonds
  Walter Pater
  Bernard Berenson
  Aby Warburg
  Johan Huizinga

Erwin Panofsky
Hans Baron
Eugenio Garin
Remigio Sabbadini
Georg Voigt
Paul Oskar Kristeller
Economic Interpretations
Renée of Ferrara
Representative Institutions
Republicanism
Resistance, Theory of
Reuchlin, Johann
Reuchlin Affair
Rhetoric
Rhétoriqueurs
Ribadeneira, Pedro de
Ribeiro, Bernardim
Ricci, Matteo
Riccio, Andrea Briosco, il
Riemenschneider, Tilman
Ritual, Civic
Rojas, Fernando de
Rome
    The City of Rome
    Art in Rome and Latium
Rome, Sack of
Ronsard, Pierre de
Roper, Margaret More
Rossellino, Bernardo
Rouen
Royal Iconography, English
Rubens, Peter Paul
Rudolf II (emperor)
Ruiz de Alarcón y Mendoza, Juan
Russia
Ruzzante

S

Sachs, Hans
Sá de Miranda, Francisco de
Sadoleto, Jacopo
Sahagún, Bernardino de
Saint Andrews University
Saint-Gelais, Mellin de
Salamanca, University of
Salernitano, Masuccio
Salons
Salutati, Coluccio
Salviati, Leonardo
Sanches, Francisco
Sandoval y Rojas, Francisco
    Gómez
Sannazaro, Jacopo

Sardinia
Sarpi, Paolo
Satire
    Satire on the Continent
    Satire in England
    Satire in France
    Satire in Germany
    Satire in Italy
Satire Ménippée
Savonarola, Girolamo
Saxony
Scaliger, Joseph Justus
Scaliger, Julius Caesar
Scamozzi, Vincenzo
Scandinavian Kingdoms
Scève, Maurice
Schegk, Jakob
Scholasticism
Schongauer, Martin
Schurman, Anna Maria van
Science
Science, Epistemology of
Scientific Instruments
Scientific Method
Scotland
Sculpture
Secundus, Johannes
Seminaries
Serlio, Sebastiano
Servants
Servetus, Michael
Seville
Sexuality

VOLUME 6

Shakespeare, William
Ships and Shipbuilding
Sicily
Sickness and Disease
Sidney, Mary
Sidney, Philip
Siena
    Siena in the Renaissance
    Art in Siena
Signorelli, Luca
Sigonio, Carlo
Sixtus IV (pope)
Sixtus V (pope)
Skarga, Piotr
Skepticism
Slavery
Sleidanus, Johannes
Social Status

Soto, Domingo de
Space and Perspective
Spain
    The Spanish Kingdoms
    Art in Spain and Portugal
Spanish Literature and Language
Speght, Rachel
Spenser, Edmund
Spilimbergo, Irene di
Spirituali
Spirituality, Female
Sponde, Jean de
Sports
Stampa, Gaspara
Starkey, Thomas
Stoicism
Straparola, Gianfrancesco
Strasbourg
Strozzi, Alessandra Macinghi
Stuart Dynasty
Stunica, Jacobus Lopis
Sturm, Johann
Suárez, Francisco
Süleyman I (sultan)
Sully, Maximilien de Béthune, duc
    de
Sumptuary Laws
Switzerland
Szymonowic, Szymon

T

Tansillo, Luigi
Tarabotti, Arcangela
Tartaglia, Niccolò
Tasso, Bernardo
Tasso, Torquato
Technology
Telesio, Bernardino
Terence
Teresa of Ávila
Theaters
Thirty Years' War
Tinódi, Sebestyén
Tintoretto
Titian
Toledo
Toleration
Toletus, Franciscus
Tombs
Tornabuoni, Lucrezia
Torres Naharro, Bartolomé de
Toscanelli, Paolo dal Pozzo
Tournaments

Tournon, François de
Translation
    Overview
    Elizabethan Translations
    Jewish Translators
Travel and Travel Literature
Traversari, Ambrogio
Trent, Council of
Trissino, Gian Giorgio
Trithemius, Johann
Tudor Dynasty
Turnèbe, Adrien
Tyndale, William
Typography
Tyrannicide

U

Umbria, Art in
Universities
Urbanism
Urbino
Urfé, Honoré d'
Usury
Utopias

V

Vadianus, Joachim
Valdés, Alfonso de
Valdés, Juan de
Valla, Lorenzo
Valois Dynasty
Varchi, Benedetto
Varthema, Lodovico de
Vatican Library
Vega, Inca Garcilaso de la

Vega Carpio, Lope Félix de
Venice
    Venice in the Renaissance
    Art in Venice
Vergara, Juan de
Vergerio, Pierpaolo
Vergil, Polydore
Vernia, Nicoletto
Veronese, Paolo
Verrocchio, Andrea del
Vesalius, Andreas
Vespucci, Amerigo
Vicente, Gil
Victoria, Tomás Luis de
Vienna
Vignola, Giacomo Barozzi da
Villa I Tatti
Villalón, Cristóbal de
Villas
Villeroy, Nicolas de Neufville,
    seigneur de
Villon, François
Violence
Virgil
Virginity and Celibacy
Virtù
Visconti, Giangaleazzo
Vitoria, Francisco de
Vittorino da Feltre
Vives, Juan Luis
Vossius, Gerardus Joannes

W

Ward, Mary
Warfare

Wars of Italy
Wars of Religion (France)
Webster, John
Wechel Family
Weights and Measures
Weyden, Rogier van der
Wickram, Jorg
Widowhood
William the Silent
Wimpheling, Jacob
Witchcraft
Wolsey, Thomas
Women
    Women in the Renaissance
    Women and Protest
    Women and Literature
    Women and Philosophy
    Portrayal in Renaissance Art
    Women and Science
Wroth, Mary

Y–Z

Yiddish Literature and Language
Zabarella, Jacopo
Zell, Katharine
Zoology
Zumárraga, Juan de
Zwingli, Huldrych

Systematic Outline

Directory of Contributors

Index

List of Maps

VOLUME 1

Africa   16
The Americas   55
Asia and the Indian Ocean   147
Austrian Habsburg Lands   158
Baltic Lands   170
Burgundy   316

VOLUME 2

England   271
Republics of Florence and
    Siena   378
City of Florence   383
France   414

VOLUME 3

Habsburg Lands   113
Holy Roman Empire   190
Hungary   240
Ireland   277
Italy, 1500   294
Italy, 1559   297
London   448

VOLUME 4

Milan   140
Naples and Sicily   277
The Netherlands   305
The Ottoman Empire   350
The Papal States   381
The Papal States in Italy   382

VOLUME 5

Poland-Lithuania   103
Portugal   132
Rome   349
Russia   377
The Scandinavian Kingdoms   416
Scotland   438

VOLUME 6

Spain   55
Switzerland   106
Universities   190
Venetian Territories in Italy   224
Venetian Territories in the Eastern
    Mediterranean   226
Wars of Italy   292

List of Genealogical Tables

Genealogical tables appear in the following entries:

VOLUME 1

Borgia, House of   252–253
Bourbon Family and Dynasty
    266–267
Burgundy   318
Carracci Family   353

VOLUME 2

Este, House of   294
Farnese, House of   332

VOLUME 3

Guise-Lorraine Family   105
Habsburg Dynasty   110

VOLUME 4

Medici, House of   84–85
Milan   138
Montefeltro Family   175
Montmorency Family   180–181

VOLUME 5

Portugal   136

VOLUME 6

Spain   59
Stuart Dynasty   96
Tudor Dynasty   174
Valois Dynasty   214

INTRODUCTION

n the middle years of the fourteenth century, the Italian scholar and poet Petrarch looked at his world with fresh, often critical, eyes and found it wanting. In place of the scholastic learning and medieval values of his day, he looked back to the literature and philosophy of the pagan and Christian ancient world for inspiration and advice on how to live. By the time of his death in 1374, Petrarch had acquired followers who shared his vision. By about 1400 a group of Italian scholars and men from other walks of life had created an intellectual movement called humanism that was simultaneously ethical, philosophical, pedagogical, and rhetorical. They had begun to transform Italian and European civilization.

Over the next three centuries or so, a series of intellectual, artistic, political, and social initiatives that began in Italy about 1350 spread to the rest of Europe and to the wider world. These innovations had an enduring influence on modern civilization. The humanists and other men and women of the era believed that they were giving birth to a new age. They called it a renaissance, because they saw their own age as a rebirth of the best of the ancient world. By the late fifteenth century, their concerns and writings, indeed their preferences and prejudices, had spread to the rest of Europe in greater or lesser degree. In the sixteenth century no contemporary doubted that a new age had dawned, as Europe witnessed remarkable changes and developments. It was one of the most innovative periods in the history of mankind. The Renaissance affected every area of life and knowledge, from art to zoology, from commerce to philosophy. The age of the Renaissance transformed Europe and then the rest of the world that Europeans touched. And its influence endures to this day. Some of the major individuals, such as Michelangelo and Shakespeare, and terms, such as "Renaissance" and "Machiavellian," are instantly recognizable today, by scholars and by members of the general public.

Encyclopedia of the Renaissance presents a panoramic view of the cultural movement and the period of history called the Renaissance. The chronological coverage begins in Italy in approximately 1350, then broadens geographically to embrace the rest of Europe in the middle to late fifteenth century. Sometimes a chronological guidepost long recognized by scholars demarcates a useful starting point. Typical starting dates are the invention of movable type in the 1450s, the beginnings of the dual monarchy of Ferdinand of Aragon and Isabella of Castile between 1474 and 1479, and the beginning of the Tudor dynasty in England in 1485. Such dates are never absolute, but serve as useful guides. They recognize change while not denying continuity. The chronological coverage of this Encyclopedia ends in the seventeenth century, again with a number of key transitional events. Politically, the eve of the Thirty Years' War (1618–1648) and transformations of various monarchies in the first quarter of the century ushered in a new period in European political history. The artistic, intellectual, and literary Renaissance had mostly run its course by the early seventeenth century. Baroque art was different from Renaissance art, and Galileo Galilei made philosophy and science different from what went before. The great revival of the learning of ancient Greece and Rome through humanism had been integrated into the curricula of European schools and universities. The exceptions to these terminal dates and events are few and long recognized by scholars. The coverage of English literature, for example, includes John Milton, whose life and works are traditionally considered as concluding the era of the English Renaissance.

The conception behind the Encyclopedia is that the Renaissance was both a cultural movement and a period of history. There was considerable unity in the roughly three centuries covered. Indeed, Europe may have enjoyed greater cultural and social unity than it would experience again before the late twentieth century. In the sixteenth century, the Venetian noble and the English legist shared a common intellectual formation because both had attended Latin schools where they learned the classics of ancient Rome and Greece. Scholars in different parts of Europe communicated by means of Latin. Rulers of northern and southern Europe made peace and war on a common basis, because they practiced a common diplomacy in peace and employed the same firearms in war. Men and women in both northern and southern Europe often experienced a similar hard life and followed similar social customs. Urban residents may have had more in common with their counterparts in other parts of Europe than with the rural people who lived outside the gates of the city. *Encyclopedia of the Renaissance* concentrates on what European men and women did in Europe in all areas of life. Coverage of the rest of the world is limited to discussion of how Europeans found other continents and the European impact on them. These limitations are partly thematic and partly practical, because all reference works must fit into the available space. Fuller treatment of the Protestant and Catholic Reformations and European exploration can be found in other reference works.

The contributors to *Encyclopedia of the Renaissance* have attempted to understand the Renaissance as it was in its own time and in its own historical era, not as the end of the Middle Ages or the beginning of modern times. The Encyclopedia tries to incorporate as much as possible of recent scholarship. Probably the three most important developments in the study of the Renaissance in the latter half of the twentieth century have been the numerous studies of humanism throughout Europe, the increased concentration on the social history of the Renaissance period, and the study of women in the Renaissance. The majority of scholars recognize that humanism was the dominant intellectual influence on the Renaissance. Humanism crossed political and linguistic boundaries, influenced both the rhetoric and thought of individuals, and affected in greater or lesser degree practically all other learning. Social historians have explored in great detail the social conditions of life, the high and low, the merchant and the peasant, in the Renaissance. And scholars have examined the many roles that women played in the period. The Encyclopedia takes into account all three of these scholarly emphases.

There are nearly twelve hundred entries in *Encyclopedia of the Renaissance,* arranged in alphabetical order letter by letter. Each entry attempts to provide a learned and succinct account suitable for inquiring readers at several levels. The high school student and the general reader will find much that is new and fascinating. The college and university student will discover thoughtful analyses of both well-known and novel aspects of the Renaissance. And the scholar will find accurate information on topics outside his or her specialty.

The contributors have sought to write in clear language with a minimum of technical vocabulary. The articles give important terms and titles in their original languages with English translations when needed. Each article includes a selective bibliography of primary sources—preferably modern editions of literary works in the original languages and in English translation—when appropriate, as well as secondary works for the reader who wishes to pursue a topic in greater detail. For secondary sources, the most important scholarly works in any language, plus the most useful works in English, are included.

Composite entries gather together discussions of similar or related topics. For example, under the entry term "Florence" the reader will find three subentries: an overview of the history of Florence in the Renaissance, a discussion of Florentine art of the fifteenth century, and a discussion of Florentine art of the sixteenth century. Clustered under the entry term "Humanism" are a definition of humanism, a discussion of its origins, subentries on humanism in various countries, and a discussion of legal humanism. A headnote listing the various subentries introduces each composite entry.

There are three types of cross-references. Many entries are followed by end-references that direct the interested reader to discussions of related topics. There are cross-references within the body of a few articles. Blind entries direct the user from an alternate form of an entry term to the entry itself. For example, blind entries for "Da Vinci, Leonardo" and "Vinci, Leonardo da" tell the reader to look under "Leonardo da Vinci."

The frontmatter for volume 1 contains a chronological table. The Encyclopedia includes over 750 illustrations including full-color frontispieces and inserts in each volume, some thirty-five maps, and seventeen genealogical tables. The full-color inserts in each volume are cross-referenced to the articles in which they are mentioned. In volume 6 the backmatter includes the systematic outline (which shows how articles relate to one another and to the overall design of the Encyclopedia), the directory of contributors, and the index.

Many people have contributed their talents to the making of this Encyclopedia, and it is a pleasure to thank them. The publisher of Charles Scribner's Sons, Karen Day, strongly supported the project from the beginning. The most important collaborator throughout has been Stephen Wagley, who played a key role from the planning of the table of contents in 1996 to publication in 1999. Hannah Borgeson and Timothy J. DeWerff served ably and with great good will as senior project editors, supported by the associate project editors, Laura K. Smid, Deborah A. Gershenowitz, and Andrew McCarthy. The Scribner staff oversaw a large team of copyeditors, fact checkers, proofreaders, translators, and a cartographer who turned articles into smooth English prose, checked facts and bibliographical references, read proof, and made maps. Nina Whitney, Libby Taft, and Carole Frohlich tracked down illustrations from sources scattered across Europe and North America. The Scribner staff prepared the genealogical tables.

The Encyclopedia was conceived and produced in association with the Renaissance Society of America, which aided the project in various ways. A learned group of scholars served as associate editors. They worked throughout with great amicability and willingness, sometimes beyond their own areas of expertise and beyond the call of duty. Two senior scholars, Paul Oskar Kristeller and Charles Trinkaus, through their scholarship and example over the past sixty years helped make this reference work possible. Most important, 638 contributors have taken time from their busy schedules to write learned and informative articles. *Encyclopedia of the Renaissance* is the joint product of all these talented people.

As this work neared completion in 1999, the two distinguished consulting editors died. On 7 June Paul Oskar Kristeller, renowned scholar of Renaissance humanism and philosophy, died at the age of ninety-four. He was the last of a group of extra-ordinarily learned and influential scholars who, fleeing the terror engulfing Europe in the 1930s, came to North America, where they created the field of Renaissance studies. Through his writing, teaching, and humanity, he influenced every aspect of this new field. On 15 September Charles Trinkaus died at the age of eighty-seven. The most senior of American-born and American-trained scholars of the period, he was a distinguished historian of the Italian Renaissance and mentor to many younger scholars. It is fitting, therefore, that *Encyclopedia of the Renaissance* be dedicated to the memory of Paul Oskar Kristeller and Charles Trinkaus.

Paul F. Grendler
October 1999

CHRONOLOGY

Date	Politics and Society	Religion	Visual Arts and Architecture
1300			
1302			d. Cimabue
1303		d. Pope Boniface VIII; Pope Benedict XI, 1303–1304	
1304		Pope Clement V, 1305–1314	
1308		d. Duns Scotus	
1309		Pope Clement V moves papal seat to Avignon	
1311		Council of Vienne	
1316		Pope John XXII, 1316–1334; d. Raymond Lull (Llull)	
1318			d. Duccio di Buonsegna
1321			
1322	Galeazzo Visconti, lord of Milan, 1322–1328		
1324			
1328	Azzo Visconti, lord of Milan, 1328–1339; beginning of Valois dynasty in France		
1330			
1334		Pope Benedict XII, 1334–1342	
1337	Hundred Years' War between England and France begins		d. Giotto di Bondone
1339	Giovanni and Lucchino (d. 1349) Visconti, joint rulers of Milan		
1341			
1342		Pope Clement VI, 1342–1352	
1343			
1344			d. Simone Martini
1345			d. Pietro Lorenzetti
1346	Battle of Crécy		
1347			
1348			d. Ambrogio Lorenzetti; d. Andrea Pisano
1349	Giovanni Visconti, sole ruler of Milan, 1349–1354		

Abbreviations
d.   died
?d.   died (date uncertain)
HRE   Holy Roman Emperor

Performing Arts	Literature, Humanism, and Printing	Philosophy, Science, and Exploration	Date
	d. Guido Cavalcanti		1300
			1302
			1303
			1304
	Dante begins *Divine Comedy*		1308
			1309
			1311
			1316
Philippe de Vitry, *Ars nova*			1318
	d. Dante Alighieri		1321
			1322
		d. Marco Polo	1324
			1328
Liège, *Speculum musicae*	Juan Ruiz, *Libro de buen amor*		1330
			1334
			1337
			1339
	Petrarch crowned with laurel wreath in Rome		1341
			1342
	University of Pisa founded	d. Marsilius of Padua	1343
			1344
	Petrarch discovers Cicero's letters to Atticus in Verona		1345
			1346
		Plague begins to devastate Europe	1347
	University of Prague founded		1348
		d. William of Ockham	1349

Date	Politics and Society	Religion	Visual Arts and Architecture
1351			
1352		Pope Innocent VI, 1352–1362	
1353			
1354	Galeazzo II Visconti (d. 1378) and Bernabò Visconti (d. 1385), joint rulers of Milan		
1355	Charles IV, HRE, 1355–1378		
1357			
1358			
1360			Work begins on the Alcazar in Seville
1361			
1362		Pope Urban V, 1362–1370	
1363	Timur (Tamerlane) begins conquest of western Asia		
1364	Charles V, king of France, 1364–1380		
1365			
1366			
1368			d. Andrea Orcagna
1369			
1370		Pope Gregory XI, 1370–1378	
1374			
1375			
1377			
1378	Giangaleazzo Visconti becomes joint ruler of Milan with Bernabò Visconti	Roman Pope Urban VI, 1378–1389; beginning of Western Schism with election of Avignonese Pope Clement VII, 1378–1394	
1380		d. Catherine of Siena	
1381	Peasants' Revolt in England		
1384		d. John Wyclif	
1385	Giangaleazzo Visconti, sole ruler of Milan, 1385–1402		
1386			
1388			
1389		Roman Pope Boniface IX, 1389–1404	
1391		Persecution of Jews in Spain	

Performing Arts	Literature, Humanism, and Printing	Philosophy, Science, and Exploration	Date
	d. Juan Ruiz		1351
			1352
	Boccaccio, *Decameron*		1353
			1354
d. Jean Muris			1355
		d. Bartolo of Sassoferrato	1357
		d. Jean Buridan	1358
	Boccaccio begins *De claris mulieribus* (On famous women)		1360
d. Philippe de Vitry	University of Pavia founded		1361
			1362
			1363
			1364
	University of Vienna founded		1365
	Petrarch, *Canzoniere*		1366
			1368
	Chaucer, *Book of the Duchess*		1369
	Langland, *Piers Plowman*		1370
	d. Petrarch		1374
	d. Giovanni Boccaccio		1375
d. Guillaume de Machaut			1377
			1378
			1380
			1381
			1384
	Chaucer, *Troilus and Cryseide;* University of Heidelberg founded		1385
	Chaucer, *Canterbury Tales*		1386
	University of Cologne founded		1388
			1389
		Chaucer, *A Treatise on the Astrolabe*	1391

Date	Politics and Society	Religion	Visual Arts and Architecture
1392			
1393		d. John of Nepomuk	
1394		Avignonese Pope Benedict XIII, 1394–1423	
1395	Giangaleazzo Visconti created duke of Milan, 1395–1402		
1397	Union of Kalmar in Scandinavia		
1399	Henry IV, king of England, 1399–1413		
1400	Rupert III, king of Germany, 1400–1410		
1402	Giovanni Maria Visconti, duke of Milan, 1402–1412		
1403			
1404		Roman Pope Innocent VII, 1404–1406	
1405	d. Timur (Tamerlane)		
1406	James I, king of Scotland, 1406–1437	Roman Pope Gregory XII, 1406–1415	
1408			Donatello, *David*
1409		Council of Pisa elects Pope Alexander V, 1409–1410	
1410		Pisan Pope John XXIII, 1410–1415; d. Hasdai ben Abraham Crescas	
1411		Jan Hus excommunicated	
1412	Filippo Maria Visconti, duke of Milan, 1412–1447; Ferdinand I, king of Aragon, 1412–1416		
1413	Henry V, king of England, 1413–1422		
1414		Council of Constance (to 1418); Medicis become bankers to the papacy	
1415	Battle of Agincourt	Council of Constance deposes Benedict XIII and John XXIII; Jan Hus executed	

Performing Arts	Literature, Humanism, and Printing	Philosophy, Science, and Exploration	Date
	Salutati discovers Cicero's Familiar Letters in Verona		1392
			1393
			1394
			1395
d. Francesco Landino	Manuel Chysoloras begins teaching Greek in Florence		1397
			1399
	d. Geoffrey Chaucer		1400
	Vergerio begins *De ingenuis moribus et liberalibus studiis adulescentiae* (On noble customs and liberal studies of adolescents)		1402
	Leonardo Bruni begins *Laudatio florentinae urbis* (Praise of the city of Florence)		1403
			1404
	Christine de Pisan, *Livre de la cité des dames* (Book of the city of ladies)		1405
	d. Coluccio Salutati; d. Ibn Khaldūn		1406
			1408
	Leipzig University founded		1409
	d. Jean Froissart	d. Francesco Datini	1410
	St. Andrews University founded		1411
d. Johannes Ciconia			1412
	d. Bernat Metge		1413
			1414
	d. Manuel Chrysoloras		1415

Date	Politics and Society	Religion	Visual Arts and Architecture
1416	Alfonso the Magnanimous, king of Aragon, 1416–1458		
1417		Pope Martin V, 1417–1431	
1420		d. Pierre d'Ailly	
1421			d. Nanni di Banco
1422	Charles VII, king of France, 1422–1461; Henry VI, king of England, 1422–1461		
1423		Council of Pavia-Siena (to 1424)	
1424			
1425			d. Lorenzo Monaco
1426	John VIII Palaeologus, emperor of Eastern Roman Empire, 1425–1448		d. Hubert van Eyck
1427			d. Gentile da Fabbriano
1428	Treaty of Delft		d. Masaccio
1429	Joan of Arc raises siege at Orleans		
1430			
1431	Joan of Arc burned at Rouen	Council of Basel (to 1449); Pope Eugenius IV, 1431–1447	
1432			
1433	Sigismund, HRE, 1433–1437		
1434	Cosimo de' Medici, ruler of Florence, 1434–1464; Władysław III, king of Poland, 1434–1444		
1435	Treaty of Arras		
1436	Compact of Iglau		
1437	James II, king of Scotland, 1437–1460	Nicholas of Cusa, *De docta ignorantia* (On learned unkowing)	
1438		Council of Ferrara-Florence-Rome (to 1445); Pragmatic Sanction of Bourges	d. Jacopo della Quercia
1439		Basel Pope Felix V (1439–1449); *Laetantur coeli*	
1440	Frederick III, HRE, 1440–1493	Lorenzo Valla, *De falso credita* (On the donation of Constantine)	d. Cennino Cennini
1441			d. Jan van Eyck

Performing Arts	Literature, Humanism, and Printing	Philosophy, Science, and Exploration	Date
	Poggio Bracciolini discovers Quintilian's *Institutio oratoria* (Institutes of oratory)		1416
			1417
			1420
	Cicero's *De oratore* (On oratory) discovered		1421
			1422
	Vitorino da Feltre establishes his school at Milan		1423
	Leonardo Bruni, *De studiis et literis liber* (Book on studies and letters); d. Jordi de Sant Jordi		1424
			1425
	University of Louvain founded		1426
			1427
			1428
			1429
	d. Christine de Pisan		1430
			1431
	University of Poitier founded	Cabral's voyage to Azores	1432
			1433
			1434
			1435
Guillaume Dufay, *Nuper rosarum flores*			1436
			1437
			1438
	University of Caen founded ; d. Ambrogio Traversari		1439
			1440
			1441

Date	Politics and Society	Religion	Visual Arts and Architecture
1442			
1443	d. Erasmo da Narni, il Gattamelata		
1444	Mehmed II, sultan of Ottoman Empire, 1444–1446, 1451–1481	d. Bernardino of Siena	d. Ottaviano Nelli
1445			
1446			d. Filippo Brunelleschi
1447		Pope Nicholas V, 1447–1455	d. Masolino da Panicale
1448	Constantine XI Palaeologus, emperor of Eastern Roman Empire, 1448–1453	Concordat of Vienna between HRE and papacy	
1449			
1450	Francesco Sforza, ruler of Milan, 1450–1466		d. Stefano di Giovanni, il Sassetta
1451	Mohammed II, sultan of the Turks, 1451–1481		
1452		d. George Gemistus Pletho (or 1454)	Ghiberti, Gates of Paradise completed
1453	Hundred Years' War ends; Turks capture Constantinople		d. Niccolò Baroncelli
1454	Peace of Lodi		d. Arduino da Baiso
1455	Wars of the Roses begin	Pope Callistus III, 1455–1458	d. Fra Angelico; d. Lorenzo Ghiberti; d. Antonio Pisano, il Pisanello
1456	d. János Hunyadi		d. Angelo Macagnino
1457			d. Andrea del Castagno
1458	Turks sack the Acropolis at Athens; Matthias Corvinus, king of Hungary, 1458–1490; George of Podebrady, king of Bohemia, 1458–1471	Pope Pius II, 1458–1464	
1459		d. Antoninus of Florence	d. Antonio di Cristoforo
1460	James III, king of Scotland, 1460–1488	Pius II forbids appeals to general councils of the church	
1461	Edward IV, king of England, 1461–1470, 1471–1483; Louis XI, king of France, 1461–1483		
1462	Ivan III, grand duke of Moscow, 1462–1505		
1463		d. Catherine of Bologna	

Performing Arts	Literature, Humanism, and Printing	Philosophy, Science, and Exploration	Date
	University of Ferrara revived		1442
			1443
	d. Leonardo Bruni; d. Pier Paolo Vergerio		1444
			1445
d. Paul Rebhun	d. Vittorino da Feltre		1446
			1447
			1448
	d. Burchiello; d. Franz Pirckheimer		1449
	Vatican Library founded; chair of music instituted at University of Bologna		1450
	Glasgow University founded		1451
			1452
d. John Dunstable	Gutenberg begins printing Bible		1453
	d. Francesco Barbaro		1454
			1455
	d. Juan de Mena; d. Elisabeth von Nassau-Saarbrücken		1456
	d. Lorenzo Valla		1457
			1458
	d. Poggio Bracciolini; d. Ausiàs March		1459
Maistre Pierre Pathelin; d. Gilles Binchois	d. Guarino Guarini	d. Henry the Navigator	1460
		d. Georg Peurbach	1461
			1462
	d. Flavio Biondo; d. François Villon		1463

Date	Politics and Society	Religion	Visual Arts and Architecture
1464		Pope Paul II, 1464–1471; d. Nicholas of Cusa	d. Desiderio da Settignano; d. Michele Pannonino; d. Bernardo Rossellino; d. Rogier van der Weyden
1465			
1466	Galeazzo Maria Sforza, duke of Milan, 1466–1476		d. Donatello
1467	Charles the Bold, duke of Burgundy, 1467–1477		d. Hans Multscher
1468			
1469	Lorenzo de' Medici, ruler of Florence, 1469–1492		d. Filarete; d. Fra Filippo Lippi
1470	Henry VI, king of England, 1470–1471		
1471	Vladislav II, king of Bohemia, 1471–1516	Pope Sixtus IV, 1471–1484; d. Thomas á Kempis	
1472		d. John Bessarion	d. Michelozzo di Bartolomeo
1473			
1474	Federico da Montefeltro, duke of Urbino, 1474–1482; Isabella, queen of Castile, 1474–1504		
1475			d. Dirck Bouts; d. Paolo Uccello
1476	Giangaleazzo Sforza, duke of Milan, 1476–1494		
1477			
1478	Pazzi consipiracy in Florence	Inquisition established in Spain	Botticelli, *La Primavera;* d. Francesco del Cossa
1479	Ferdinand, king of Aragon, 1479–1516		d. Taddeo Crivelli; d. Luciano da Laurana; d. Antonello da Messina
1480			
1481	Bayezid II, sultan of the Turks, 1481–1512		d. Jean Fouquet
1482	Peace of Arras; d. Federico da Montefeltro		d. Luca della Robbia; d. Hugo van der Goes; d. Giovanni di Paolo; d. Franco dei Russi

Performing Arts	Literature, Humanism, and Printing	Philosophy, Science, and Exploration	Date
	First printing press in Italy, at Subiaco	Regiomontanus writes *De triangulis omnimodis* (On triangles; published 1533)	1464
			1465
	d. Isotta Nogarola		1466
			1467
	d. Johann Gutenberg		1468
	Printing begins in Venice	Marsilio Ficino translates Plato's dialogues (to 1469)	1469
d. Hans Rosenplüt	First printing press in Paris		1470
	d. Thomas Malory; d. Alessandra Macinghi Strozzi	Regiomontanus builds observatory in Nürnberg	1471
	First printing press in Spain; d. Janus Pannonius	d. Leon Battista Alberti	1472
	First printing press in Lyon		1473
d. Guillaume Dufay			1474
	d. Albrecht von Eyb; d. Theodore Gaza; d. Matteo Palmieri; d. Masuccio Salernitano; University of Copenhagen founded		1475
	Caxton sets up printing press in England	d. Regiomontanus	1476
Johannes Tinctoris, *Liber de arte contrapuncti* (On the art of counterpoint)			1477
	Amerbach Press established; d. Niklas von Wyle		1478
			1479
	d. Eleonore of Austria		1480
	d. Francesco Filelfo; d. Bartolommeo Platina		1481
Ramos, *Musica practica*	d. Lucrezia Tornabuoni	d. Paolo dal Pozzo Toscanelli; Campanus, translation of Euclid's *Elements*	1482

Date	Politics and Society	Religion	Visual Arts and Architecture
1483	Charles VIII, king of France, 1483–1498; Edward V, king of England, 1483; Richard III, king of England, 1483–1485		
1484	French Estates General meet at Tour	Pope Innocent VIII, 1484–1492	Botticelli, *Birth of Venus;* d. Mino da Fiesole
1485	Battle of Bosworth Field; Henry VII, king of England, 1485–1509		
1486	Maximilian I, king of Germany, 1486–1519		
1487		Institoris and Sprenger, *Malleus maleficarum* (Hammer of witches)	
1488	James IV, king of Scotland, 1488–1513		d. Andrea del Verrocchio
1489		d. Wessel Gansfort	
1490	Vladislav II, king of Hungary, 1490–1516		d. Guglielmo Giraldi del Magro
1491	Treaty of Pressburg		d. Martin Schongauer
1492	Spanish conquer Granada; d. Anne de Beaujeu	Pope Alexander VI, 1492–1503; Jews expelled from Spain	d. Piero della Francesca; d. Domenico Gagini; d. Baccio Pontelli
1493	Maximilian I, HRE, 1493–1519; Pope Alexander VI draws Line of Demarcation		
1494	French invasion of Italy; Ludovico Sforza, duke of Milan, 1494–1500		d. Carlo Crivelli; d. Melozzo da Forli; d. Domenico Ghirlandaio; d. Hans Memling
1495	Manuel I, king of Portugal, 1495–1521; d. Pedro González de Mendoza	Sebastian Brant, *Narrenschiff* (Ship of fools)	d. Cosmè Tura
1496	Frederick III, king of Naples, 1496–1501	Jews expelled from Portugal	d. Piero Pollaiuolo; d. Ercole de' Roberti
1497		Foundation of Confraternity of Divine Love	Leonardo da Vinci, *Last Supper;* d. Benozzo Gozzoli
1498	Louis XII, king of France, 1498–1515	Savonarola executed in Florence; d. Torquemada	d. Antonio Pollaiuolo

Performing Arts	Literature, Humanism, and Printing	Philosophy, Science, and Exploration	Date
	d. Katharina Pirckheimer	Alfonsine Tables published	1483
	d. Luigi Pulci	Chuquet writes *Triparty en la science des nombres* (Three-part treatise on the science of numbers); Portuguese reach Congo River	1484
d. Johannes Regis	d. Rudolf Agricola		1485
	Giovanni Pico della Mirandola, *Oration on the Dignity of Man;* d. George of Trebizond	Portuguese reach Angola	1486
			1487
		Bartolomeu Dias reaches Cape of Good Hope	1488
	Giunti Press established	Johann Widman, first use of plus and minus signs	1489
			1490
	d. William Caxton		1491
Gaffurio, *Theorica musicae;* d. Antoine Busnois	Antonio de Nebrija, *Gramática de la lengua castellana*	Columbus reaches Western Hemisphere; Martin Beheim makes first globe map of Europe; Leonardo da Vinci sketches flying machine	1492
	Nürnberg Chronicle	Columbus begins second voyage	1493
	Aldus Manutius begins publishing in 1494 or 1495; d. Matteo Maria Boiardo; d. Giovanni Pico della Mirandola; d. Poliziano	Pacioli, *Summa de aritbmetica;* Leonardo da Vinci sketches pendulum clock; Treaty of Tordesillas	1494
Johannes Tinctoris, *Terminorum musicae diffinitorium* (Dictionary of music); d. Johannes Ockeghem			1495
Gaffurio, *Practica musicae*			1496
	d. Roiç de Corella	Cabot's voyage to Canada; Vasco da Gama begins voyage to India; d. Elijah Delmedigo	1497
	d. Cristoforo Landino; d. Pomponio Leto	Columbus begins third voyage; d. John Cabot	1498

Date	Politics and Society	Religion	Visual Arts and Architecture
1499	French expel Ludovico Sforza from Milan; Perkin Warbeck executed		
1500			Hieronymus Bosch, *Ship of Fools;* Michelangelo, *Pietà*
1501	Peace of Trent		d. Matteo Civitali
1502			d. Francesco da Laurana; d. Francesco di Giorgio Martini
1503	Spanish rule in Naples begins	Pope Pius III, 1503; Pope Julius II, 1503–1513	d. Bartolomeo Caporali; d. Andrea di Christoforo Bregno
1504	Treaty of Lyon	d. Yohannan ben Isaac Alemanno	Michelangelo, *David;* d. Pedro Berruguete; d. Mauro Codussi; d. Filippino Lippi
1505	Treaty of Salamanca		
1506	Sigismund I, king of Poland, 1506–1548; Juana, queen of Castile, 1506–1555		Leonardo, *Mona Lisa;* d. Gian Francesco Maineri; d. Andrea Mantegna
1507	d. Cesare Borgia		
1508	League of Cambrai formed	d. Isaac Abravanel	Michelangelo begins painting Sistine Chapel ceiling; d. Antoniazzo Romano
1509	Henry VIII, king of England, 1509–1547; d. Margaret Beaufort		d. Adam Krafft
1510	d. Francisco de Almeida; d. Caterina Corner	Reuchlin affair; d. Georges d'Amboise; d. Catherine of Genoa	d. Sandro Botticelli
1511	d. Philippe de Commynes	Council of Pisa (to 1512)	d. Giorgione da Castelfranco
1512	Massimiliano Sforza, duke of Milan, 1512–1515; Selīm I, sultan of Turkey, 1512–1520	Council of Lateran V (to 1517)	Michelangelo completes Sistine Chapel ceiling
1513	Christian II, king of Denmark and Norway, 1513–1523; James V, king of Scotland, 1513–1542	Pope Leo X, 1513–1521	d. Pinturicchio
1514	d. Anne of Brittany		Raphael, *Sistine Madonna;* d. Donato Bramante

Performing Arts	Literature, Humanism, and Printing	Philosophy, Science, and Exploration	Date
	d. Laura Cereta	Vespucci voyage to America; d. Marsilio Ficino; d. Nicoletto Vernia	1499
		Jakob Nufer performs first recorded cesarean operation on a living woman; Cabral reaches Brazil; d. Bartolomeu Dias	1500
Ottaviano dei Petrucci publishes *Harmonice musices odhecaton A;* d. Antonia Pulci	d. Constantine Lascaris; d. Johannes Pirckheimer		1501
	Estienne Press established; University of Wittenberg founded	Columbus begins fourth voyage; d. Francesco di Giorgio Martini; Peter Henlein builds first pocket watch	1502
	Cromberger Press established; d. Giovanni Pontano		1503
	Sannazaro, *Arcadia*		1504
d. Jacob Obrecht			1505
	University of Frankfurt an der Oder founded	d. Christopher Columbus	1506
		Martin Waldseemüller first applies name "America" to Western Hemisphere; d. Martin Behaim	1507
d. Bernardo Buontalenti	d. Conrad Celtis		1508
	Teaching begins at University of Alcalá de Henares		1509
		Albuquerque captures Goa	1510
d. Johannes Tinctoris	d. Ambrosius Calepinus		1511
d. Antoine de Févin		d. Allesandro Achillini; d. Amerigo Vespucci	1512
	Machiavelli, *The Prince;* Machiavelli begins writing *Discourses on the First Ten Books of Livy;* d. Johann Amerbach	Balboa crosses Isthmus of Panama and reaches Pacific Ocean; Ponce de Leon explores Florida	1513
		Copernicus publishes his heliocentric theory; ?d. Luca Pacioli	1514

Date	Politics and Society	Religion	Visual Arts and Architecture
1515	Francis I, king of France, 1515–1547; d. Alfonso de Albuquerque; d. Gonzalo Fernández de Córdoba		d. Fra Gioconda
1516	Charles I, king of Spain, 1516–1556	Concordat of Bologna between France and the papacy; Erasmus publishes his Greek and Latin New Testament	Titian, *Assumption;* d. Jacopo de' Barbari; d. Hieronymus Bosch; d. Vincenzo Foppa; d. Biagio Rossetti; d. Giuliano da Sangallo
1517		Luther's Ninety-five Theses; d. Francisco Jiménez de Cisneros	d. Fra Bartolomeo della Porta
1518			d. Guido Mazzoni; d. Francesco Raibolini, il Francia
1519	Charles I of Spain becomes Charles V, HRE, 1519–1556; d. Lucrezia Borgia		Albrecht Dürer, *Virgin and Child with St. Anne;* d. Salmone da Sessa; d. Leonardo da Vinci
1520	Field of Cloth of Gold; Revolt of the Comuneros in Spain; Süleyman I, sultan of Ottoman Empire, 1520–1566	Luther, *Freedom of a Christian, Address to the German Nobility, Babylonian Captivity*	d. Raphael
1521	Cortes assumes control of Mexico; John III, king of Portugal, 1521–1557	Philipp Melanchthon, *Loci communes* (Commonplaces)	d. Piero di Cosimo
1522	Francesco Maria Sforza, duke of Milan, 1522–1535	Luther's translation of the Bible; Complutensian Polyglot Bible published; Pope Adrian VI, 1522–1523	
1523	Frederick I, king of Denmark and Norway, 1523–1533; Gustavus I, king of Sweden, 1523–1560	Pope Clement VII, 1523–1534	d. Perugino; d. Luca Signorelli; d. Pietro Vannucci
1524	Peasants' War begins in Germany	Clement VII approves Theatines	d. Hans Holbein the Elder
1525	Battle of Pavia	William Tyndale's translation of the Bible; d. Thomas Müntzer	
1526	Battle of Mohacs; d. Juan del Elcina		d. Vittore Carpaccio
1527	Sack of Rome		

Performing Arts	Literature, Humanism, and Printing	Philosophy, Science, and Exploration	Date
d. Hans Folz	Bote, *Till Eulenspiegel;* d. Aldus Manutius		1515
	Ariosto, *Orlando furioso;* More, *Utopia;* d. Batista Spagnuoli; d. Johann Trithemius	Pompanazzi, *De immortalitate animae* (On the immortality of the soul)	1516
d. Loyset Compère; d. Heinrich Isaac	d. Filippo Giunti	Girolamo Fracastoro explains fossils as remains of living organisms	1517
d. Pierre de La Rue	Erasmus, *Colloquies* (first edition)	Royal College of Physicians founded in London; ?d. Martin Waldseemüller	1518
	Claude de Seysell, *La monarchie de France;* d. John Colet	Magellan begins voyage around the world	1519
d. Antoine Brumel; d. Bernardo Dovizi	d. Hermann Bote; d. Henry Estienne the Elder; d. Claude de Seysell	Paracelsus introduces tincture of opium (laudanum)	1520
d. Josquin des Prez	Machiavelli, *Art of War;* d. Sebastian Brant	d. Ferdinand Magellan	1521
d. Franchino Gaffurio; d. Jean Mouton	d. Johann Reuchlin	Cuthbert Tunstall publishes first book on arithmetic in England	1522
	Eguía Press established; Juan Luis Vives, *De institutione feminae christianae* (Education of the Christian woman) and *De ratione studii puerilis* (On the right method of instruction for children); d. Ulrich von Hutten		1523
	Juan Luis Vives, *Introductio ad sapientiam* (Introduction to knowledge)	d. Vasco da Gama; d. Thomas Linacre	1524
d. Bartolomé de Torres Naharro	d. Jean Lemaire de Belges; d. Guillaume Cretin	d. Pietro Pomponazzi	1525
	Wechel Press established; Juan Luis Vives, *De subventione pauperum* (On aid to the poor)	d. Scipione del Ferro	1526
	d. Francesco Colonna; d. Niccolò Machiavelli		1527

Date	Politics and Society	Religion	Visual Arts and Architecture
1528			d. Albrecht Dürer; d. Matthias Grünewald; d. Lodovico Mazzolino
1529	Treaty of Cambrai; Reformation Parliament in England (to 1536); Turks besiege Vienna; d. Baldassare Castiglione		d. Andrea Sansovino
1530	d. Mercurino Gattinara; d. Margaret of Austria	Diocese of Mexico City established; d. Thomas Wolsey	d. Andrea del Sarto; d. Quentin Massys; d. Properzia de' Rossi
1531	d. Louise of Savoy	d. Diego López de Zúñiga; d. Oecolampadius; d. Huldrych Zwingli	d. Hans Burgkmair; d. Tilman Riemenschneider
1532		d. Giles of Viterbo	d. Andrea Briosco, il Riccio; d. Jan Gossaert; d. Bernardino Luini
1533	Ivan IV, tsar of Russia, 1533–1584	Clement VII approves Barnabites; d. Johann von Guenzburg Eberlin	Han Holbein the Younger, *The Ambassadors;* d. Veit Stoss
1534	Affair of placards in France	Foundation of Society of Jesus; Pope Paul III, 1534–1549	d. Correggio; d. Marcantonio Raimondi
1535	Thomas More executed; Charles V captures Tunis	John Fisher executed; John of Leiden executed; Inquisition established in Portugal	Holbein, *Henry VIII*
1536	d. Catherine of Aragon; execution of Anne Boleyn	d. Jacques Lefèvre d'Étaples; d. William Tyndale	d. Baldassare Peruzzi
1537	Cosimo I Medici, duke of Florence, 1537–1574	*Consilium de emendenda ecclesia* (Advice on reform of the church)	Serlio, *Trattato di Architettura*
1538			d. Albrecht Altdorfer
1539	d. Isabella d'Este	Clément Marot, French translation of Psalms	d. Giovanni Antonio, il Pordenone
1540	Treaty between Venice and Turkey signed; Thomas Cromwell executed	Paul III approves Society of Jesus; d. Angela Merici	d. Joos van Cleve; d. Jean Clouet; d. Parmigianino; d. Giovanni Battista di Jacopo, il Rosso Fiorentino

Performing Arts	Literature, Humanism, and Printing	Philosophy, Science, and Exploration	Date
	Castiglione, *The Courtier;* Juan Luis Vives, *De officio mariti* (On the duties of the husband); d. Jacob Wimpheling		1528
Fogliano, *Musica theorica;* d. John Skelton; d. Robert Fayrfax	Collège de France founded; Agrippa von Nettesheim, *De nobilitate et praecellentia foeminei sexus* (On the nobility and excellence of the female sex); d. Jacob Canter		1529
d. Juan del Encina; d. Niklas Manuel	d. Willibald Pirckheimer; d. Jacopo Sannazaro	Brunfels, *Herbarum vivae eicones* (Illustrations of plants; to 1536); Fracastoro, *Syphilis sive de morbo gallico* (Syphilis, or the French disease); d. Gian Giacomo Bartolotti	1530
	Juan Luis Vives, *De disciplinis* (On education)		1531
	Rabelais, *Pantagruel;* d. Caritas Pirckheimer; d. Alfonso de Valdés		1532
	d. Ludovico Ariosto	Gemma Frisius, *De principiis astronomiae et cosmographiae* (Principles of astronomy and cosmography); Pizarro captures Cuzco	1533
	Rabelais, *Gargantua;* d. Hermann von dem Busche	d. Otto Brunfels	1534
	d. Francesco Berni; d. Janus Lascaris	d. Heinrich Agrippa of Nettesheim; d. Leone Ebreo	1535
d. Gil Vicente	Giolito Press established; d. Desiderius Erasmus; d. Johannes Secundus; William Tyndale executed		1536
	d. Thomas Murner	Tartaglia, *Della nova scientia* (On the new learning)	1537
	Juan Luis Vives, *Linguae latinae exercitatio* (Latin exercises); d. Lucantonio Giunti; d. Thomas Starkey	Juan Luis Vives, *De anima et vita* (On the soul and life); d. Federico Grisogono (Chrysogonis); d. Agostino Nifo	1538
	First printing press in New World established in Mexico	Olaus Magnus produces a map of the world	1539
	d. Guillaume Budé; d. Giovanni Giolito; d. Francesco Guicciardini; d. Helius Eobanus Hessus; d. Juan Luis Vives		1540

Date	Politics and Society	Religion	Visual Arts and Architecture
1541	d. Francisco Pizarro	d. Wolfgang Capito; d. Juan de Valdés	
1542	Mary Stuart, queen of Scotland, 1542–1587	Paul III establishes Inquisition in Rome; d. Gasparo Contarini; d. Sebastian Franck	d. Dosso Dossi
1543		d. Johann Eck	d. Polidoro Caldara da Caravaggio; d. Hans Holbein the Younger
1544		Paul III approves Ursulines	
1545		First period of Council of Trent (to 1549)	d. Hans Baldung Grien
1546		d. Martin Luther; d. Francisco de Vitoria	d. Gaudenzio Ferrari; d. Giulio Romano; d. Antonio da Sangallo the Younger
1547	Moscow destroyed by fire; Edward VI, king of England, 1547–1553; Henry II, king of France, 1547–1559; d. Hernán Cortés	d. Thomas de Vio Cajetan; d. Jacopo Sadoleto	d. Sebastiano del Piombo; d. Perino del Vaga
1548	d. Katherine Parr	d. Juan de Zumárraga	Titian, *Charles V on Horseback;* d. Battista Dossi
1549	d. Margaret of Angoulême (Margaret of Navarre)	First Book of Common Prayer	d. Giovanni Antonio Bazzi, il Sodoma
1550		Pope Julius III, 1550–1555	Vasari, *Lives of the Artists*
1551		Second period of Council of Trent (to 1552); d. Martin Bucer	Titian, *Philip II;* d. Domenico Beccafumi; d. Joachim Vadianus
1552		d. Francis Xavier	Titian, *Self-Portrait*
1553	Jane Grey proclaimed queen of England and deposed; Mary I, queen of England, 1553–1558	Michael Servetus executed in Geneva	Titian, *Danaë;* d. Lucas Cranach

Performing Arts	Literature, Humanism, and Printing	Philosophy, Science, and Exploration	Date
d. Fernando de Rojas		d. Paracelsus	1541
d. Ruzzante	d. Juan Boscán; d. Thomas Wyatt	Francis Xavier arrives in India	1542
d. Ludwig Senfli	d. Agnolo Firenzuola	Copernicus, *De revolutionibus orbium coelestium* (On the revolutions of the heavenly spheres); Vesalius, *De humani corporis fabrica* (On the fabric of the human body); d. Nicolaus Copernicus	1543
	d. Bonaventure Des Périers; d. Teofilo Folengo; d. Clément Marot; d. Margaret More Roper	Sebastian Münster, *Cosmographia*	1544
d. Constanzo Festa; d. John Taverner	d. Pernette Du Guillet; d. Antonio de Guevara	Ambroise Paré's book on surgery; Girolamo Cardano, *Ars magna;* first university botanical gardens, Padua and Pisa	1545
	d. Étienne Dolet; d. Thomas Elyot	Girolamo Fracastoro, *De contagione* (On contagion); Georgius Agricola, *De natura fossilium* (On fossils)	1546
Henricus Glareanus (Heinrich Loris), *Dodecachordon*	d. Lazare de Baïf; d. Beatus Rhenanus; d. Pietro Bembo; d. Vittoria Colonna; Henry Howard executed; d. Conrad Peutinger		1547
	First Jesuit school founded, at Messina; d. Johannes Dantiscus		1548
	Joachim du Bellay, *Défense et illustration de langue française;* d. Elia Levita	Francis Xavier arrives in Japan	1549
	d. Veronica Gàmbara; d. John Major; d. Gian Giorgio Trissino; d. Andrea Alciato		1550
	Collegio Romano founded; universities of Lima and Mexico founded	Konrad Gesner, *Historia animalium* (History of animals), vol. 1	1551
	Pierre de Ronsard, *Les amours;* d. Paolo Giovio; d. Sebastian Münster; d. Bernardim Ribeiro	Bartolomeo Eustachio describes Eustachian tubes; d. Peter Appian	1552
Sachs, *Tristan und Isolde*	d. François Rabelais	d. Girolamo Fracastoro	1553

Date	Politics and Society	Religion	Visual Arts and Architecture
1554	Jane Grey executed		d. Sebastiano Serlio
1555	Peace of Augsburg; Charles V abdicates	Pope Marcellus II, 1555; Pope Paul IV, 1555–1559; d. Polydore Vergil	
1556	Philip II, king of Spain, 1556–1598	Thomas Cranmer executed; d. Ignatius Loyola	d. Girolamo da Carpi; d. Lorenzo Lotto; d. Jan Mostaert
1557	Sebastian I, king of Portugal, 1557–1578		d. Jacopo da Pontormo
1558	Ferdinand I, HRE, 1556–1564; Elizabeth I, queen of England; 1558–1603	d. Reginald Pole	
1559	Peace of Cateau-Cambrésis between France and Spain; Francis II, king of France, 1559–1560; Frederick II, king of Denmark, 1558–1588	Pope Pius IV, 1559–1565; first Roman index of prohibited books; Centuriators of Magdeburg, *Historiae ecclesiae Christi* (History of the church of Christ; to 1574); Elizabethan religious settlement in England	Brueghel, *Carnival and Lent*; d. Garofalo; d. Michele Sammicheli; d. Irene di Spilimbergo
1560	Charles IX, king of France, 1560–1574; French Estates General meets at Orléans; d. Andrea Doria	d. Melchior Cano; d. Philipp Melanchthon	Brueghel, *Children's Games*; d. Baccio Bandinelli
1561		Colloquy of Poissy in France	
1562	Wars of Religion in France begin; Jeanne d'Albret, queen of Navarre, 1562–1572; d. François de Tournon	Third period of Council of Trent (to 1563)	
1563	Peace of Amboise	First version of Thirty-nine Articles (England); Foxe, *Book of Martyrs*; Council of Trent ends	Brueghel, *Tower of Babel*; construction of El Escorial palace begins; d. Diego de Siloé
1564	Peace of Troyes; Maximilian II, HRE, 1564–1576	Tridentine Index of Prohibited Books issued; d. John Calvin	d. Michelangelo Buonarotti
1565		d. Vasco de Quiroga	Brueghel, *The Harvesters*; Tintoretto, *Flight into Egypt*; Veronese begins *The Family of Darius*

Performing Arts	Literature, Humanism, and Printing	Philosophy, Science, and Exploration	Date
	Wickram, *Der Goldfaden;* first printing of *Lazarillo de Tormes;* d. Juan Maldonado; d. Gaspara Stampa	d. Leo Africanus	1554
Nicola Vicentino, *L'antica musica ridotta alla musica pratica*	d. Hélisenne de Crenne; d. Olympia Morata; d. Johannes Sleidanus; d. Jacques Tahureau	d. Georgius Agricola; d. Reiner Gemma Frisius	1555
d. Sebestyén Tinódi; d. Burkhard Waldis	d. Pietro Aretino; d. Giovanni della Casa; d. Richard Morison; d. Nicholas Udall; d. Thomas, Lord Vaux	Georgius Agricola, *De re metallica* (On metallurgy); Pomponazzi's *De incantationibus* (On enchantments or spells) published; d. Luca Ghini	1556
	d. Gianfrancesco Straparola; d. Juan de Vergara	Robert Recorde introduces equal sign, plus sign, and minus sign to England; d. Giovanni Battista Ramusio; d. Niccolò Tartaglia	1557
Zarlino, *Le Institutioni harmoniche* (Introduction to harmony)	Margaret of Angoulême, *Heptaméron;* University of Jena founded; d. Cassandra Fedele; d. Francisco de Sá de Miranda; d. Mellin de Saint-Gelais; d. Julius Caesar Scaliger	d. Jean-François Fernel	1558
	Jacques Amyot, French translation of Plutarch's *Lives;* Genevan Academy founded; d. Robert Estienne	d. Realdo Colombo	1559
d. John Sheppard	d. Joachim Du Bellay; d. Philipp Melanchthon	Giambattista della Porta founds Academia Secretorum Naturae, first scientific society; d. Domingo de Soto	1560
d. Loys Bourgeois; d. Jorg Wickram	d. Matteo Bandello; d. Olivier de Magny; d. Jorge de Montemayor	Gabriele Falloppio describes Fallopian tubes and organs of inner ear	1561
d. Claudin de Sermisy; d. Adrian Willaert	d. Katherine Zell	Hawkins voyages to Africa; d. Gabriele Falloppio; d. Pierre Franco; d. Thomas Geminus (Lambert)	1562
	d. Giovanni Battista Gelli; d. Étienne de La Boétie; d. Thomas Naogeorgus		1563
	d. Charles Estienne; d. Maurice Scève	d. Georg Hartmann; d. Andreas Vesalius	1564
d. Cipriano de Rore	d. Adrien Turnèbe; d. Benedetto Varchi	Konrad Gesner, *De rerum fosillium* (On fossils); d. Konrad Gesner	1565

Date	Politics and Society	Religion	Visual Arts and Architecture
1566	d. Diane de Poitiers; d. Charles Dumoulin	d. Bartolomé de Las Casas; d. Giulia Gonzaga; Pope Pius V, 1566–1572	
1567	d. Anne de Montmorency		Brueghel, *Adoration of the Magi*
1568	Treaty of Longjumeau; John III, king of Sweden, 1568–1592	d. Miles Coverdale	
1569	Morisco revolt in Granada	Inquisition established in Mexico and Peru; d. Juan de Ávila	d. Pieter Brueghel the Elder; d. Giovanni Battista Castello, il Bergamasco
1570	Peace of St. Germain-en-Laye; Peace of Stettin; Turks declare war on Venice; d. Jean Du Tillet		Palladio, *I quattro libri dell' architettura* (Four books of architecture); d. Francesco Primaticcio; d. Jacopo Sansovino
1571	Battle of Lepanto	Pope Pius V establishes Congregation of the Index; d. John Jewel	d. Benvenuto Cellini
1572	St. Bartholomew's Day massacre in France; d. Gaspard de Coligny	Pope Gregory XIII, 1572–1585; d. Moses Isserles; d. John Knox; d. Isaac Luria	d. Galeazzo Alessi; d. Bronzino; d. François Clouet
1573	d. Ruy Gómez de Silva; d. Michel de L'Hôpital		d. Giacomo Barozzi da Vignola
1574	Henry III, king of France, 1574–1589; d. Renée of Ferrara		d. Giorgio Vasari
1575	Stephen Báthory, king of Poland, 1575–1586; d. Diego Hurtado de Mendoza	d. Joseph Karo; d. Matthew Parker	
1576	Rudolf II, HRE, 1576–1612		d. Nicholas Hilliard; d. Levina Teerlinc; d. Titian
1577	d. Diego de Covarrubias y Leiva; d. Blaise de Lasseran-Massencôme, seigneur de Montluc	Teresa of Avilà, *Interior Castle*; John of the Cross, *Dark Night of the Soul*	El Greco, *Assumption of the Virgin*
1578			d. Giulio Clovio; d. Giovanni Battista Moroni
1579	William the Silent, stadholder, 1579–1584		

Performing Arts	Literature, Humanism, and Printing	Philosophy, Science, and Exploration	Date
Gascoigne, *The Supposes;* d. Antonio Cabezón	d. Tullia d'Aragona; d. Pierre Boaistuau; d. Annibale Caro; d. Louise Labé; d. Stanisław Orzechowski	d. Nostradamus; d. Leonhard Fuchs	1566
		Pomponazzi's *De fato* (On fate) published; d. Michael Stifel	1567
	d. Roger Ascham; d. Luigi Tansillo		1568
	d. António Ferreira; d. Bernardo Tasso		1569
d. Jacques Grévin	Académie de Poésie et de Musique founded		1570
J.-A. de Baïf founds Académie de Poésie et de Musique	d. Robert Estienne the Younger; d. Jacques Yver		1571
	Luíz Vaz de Camões, *Os Lusíadas*	Rafael Bombelli, *Algebra;* d. Petrus Ramus	1572
d. Étienne Jodelle	François Hotman, *Francogallia;* d. Juan Ginés de Sepúlveda; d. Giambattista Cinzio Giraldi; d. Isabella Whitney	Tycho Brahe, *De nova stella* (On the nova of 1572); d. John Caius	1573
d. Domenico Maria Ferrabosco	Théodore de Bèze, *Du droit des magistrats* (The law of magistrates); d. Joachim Camerarius; d. Anton Francesco Doni; d. Gáspár Heltai	Tycho Brahe, *Oratio de disciplinis mathematicis* (Address on mathematics); d. Bartolommeo Eustachio	1574
	University of Leiden founded	Francesco Maurolico, *Arithmeticorum libri duo* (Two books on arithmetic); d. Federico Commandino	1575
d. Hans Sachs	Jean Bodin, *Six livres de la république* (Six books of the commonwealth); Innocent Gentillet, *Anti-Machivel;* University of Warsaw founded	Frobisher voyages to Canada begin; d. Giralamo Cardano; d. Jacques Gohory (Leo Suavius); d. Georg Joachim Rheticus	1576
d. Mattheus Le Maistre Walloon	Holinshed, *Chronicles of England, Scotlande and Irelande;* d. Rémy Belleau; d. George Gascoigne; d. Louis Le Roy	Drake begins voyage around the world	1577
	d. Gabriel Giolito; d. Alessandro Piccolomini		1578
	Lyly, *Euphues;* Spenser, *Shepheardes Calendar*	Francisco Vieta, *Canon mathematicus* (Mathematical rules)	1579

Date	Politics and Society	Religion	Visual Arts and Architecture
1580	Union of Portugal with Spain		d. Andrea Palladio
1581	Levant Company founded		
1582	d. Fernando de Alvárez de Toledo	Catholic translation of New Testament published at Reims; d. Teresa of Ávila	
1583		d. Thomas Erastus (Lüber)	d. Pirro Ligorio
1584	Fyodor I, tsar of Russia, 1584–1598; d. François de Valois, duc d'Alençon et Anjou; d. Guy du Faur, sieur de Pibrac		d. Anton Francesco Grazzini
1585	First English settlement in America	Pope Sixtus V, 1585–1590	d. Luca Cambiaso; d. Wenzel Jamnitzer
1586	d. Margaret of Parma	Robert Bellarmine, *Disputationes de controversiis Christianae fidei* (Disputation on controverted points of the Christian faith); d. Antonio Agustín	El Greco begins *The Burial of the Count of Orgaz;* d. Luis de Morales
1587	Sigismund III, king of Poland, 1587–1632; d. Anne de Joyeuse; Mary, queen of Scots, executed	d. John Foxe	d. Plautilla Nelli
1588	Spanish Armada; Christian IV, king of Denmark, 1588–1648; d. Robert Dudley	Baronius, *Annales ecclesiastici* (to 1607); d. Luis de Granada	d. Paolo Veronese
1589	Assassination of Henry III of France; Henry IV, king of France, 1589–1610; d. Catherine de Médicis	Lorenzo Scupoli, *The Spiritual Combat*	
1590	d. François Hotman; d. Francis Walsingham	Pope Urban VII, 1590; Pope Gregory XIV, 1590–1591; d. Bernardino de Sahagún	d. Leone Leoni; d. Diana Mantuana; d. Marietta Robusti; d. Alonso Sanchez Coello
1591	d. François de La Noue	Pope Innocent IX, 1591	

Performing Arts	Literature, Humanism, and Printing	Philosophy, Science, and Exploration	Date
	Montaigne, *Essais;* Sidney, *Arcadia;* d. Raphael Holinshed; d. Luíz Vaz de Camoẽs	d. Giovanni Filippo Ingrassia	1580
Beaujoyeux, Ballet comique de la Royne; Vincenzo Galilei, *Dialogo della musica antica;* d. Joachim Thibault de Courville	Tasso, *Gerusalemme liberata* (Jerusalem delivered); d. Guillaume Postel		1581
	Hakluyt, *Divers Voyages Touching the Discoverie of America;* University of Edinburgh founded; d. Jacques Peletier du Mans; d. Thomas Platter	Gregorian calendar adopted in Catholic countries	1582
Queen's Company of Players formed	Elzevier Press established; Garnier, *Les Juives;* d. François Belleforest	Matteo Ricci enters China	1583
d. Pietro Vinci	d. Jan Kochanowski; d. Carlo Sigonio	Davis voyage to Greenland	1584
d. Thomas Tallis	d. Marc-Antoine Muret; d. Pierre de Ronsard	d. Anna of Saxony	1585
d. Andrea Gabrieli	d. Bénigne Poissenot; d. Philip Sidney		1586
Marlowe, *Tamburlaine*	Volksbuch von Dr. Faustus; Tottel's *Miscellany;* d. Catherine and Madeleine des Roches	d. Leonardo Botallo ; d. Francisco Hernandez; d. Jakob Schegk	1587
Musica transalpina; Marlowe, *Dr. Faustus*		Camerarius, *Hortus Medicus;* d. Bernardino Telesio	1588
Shakespeare, *Henry VI, Part 1*	d. Jean-Antoine de Baïf; d. Bernard Palissy; d. Christophe Plantin; d. Leonardo Salviati; d. Johannes Sturm	d. Jacopo Zabarella	1589
Guarini, *Il Pastor fido;* Lodge, *Rosalynde;* Marlowe, *Jew of Malta;* d. Robert Garnier; d. Gioseffo Zarlino	Spenser, *Faerie Queen;* d. Dirck Volckertszoon Coornhert; d. Guillaume de Saluste Du Bartas; d. Johann Fischart; d. Étienne Tabourot	d. Giovanni Battista Benedetti; d. Ambroise Paré	1590
d. Vincenzo Galilei	Lyly, *Endymion;* Sidney, *Astrophel and Stella;* Trinity College, Dublin, founded; d. Noël Du Fail; d. Veronica Franco; d. John of the Cross; d. Luis de León		1591

Date	Politics and Society	Religion	Visual Arts and Architecture
1592		Pope Clement VIII, 1592–1605	d. Bartolommeo Ammannati; d. Jacopo da Ponte Bassano
1593	Henry IV of France abjures Protestantism		El Greco, *Crucifixion;* d. Giuseppe Archimboldo
1594		Edict of St. Germain-en-Laye	Giambologna, statue of Cosimo I de' Medici; d. Jean Cousin; d. Tintoretto
1595		d. Philip Neri	
1596		d. Franciscus Toletus	
1597			d. Juan de Herrera
1598	Peace of Vervins between France and Spain; Treaty of Ponts de Cé; Boris Godunov, tsar of Russia, 1598–1605; Philip III, king of Spain, 1598–1621; d. William Cecil	Edict of Nantes (France)	Brueghel, *Adoration of the Magi*
1599	d. Gabrielle d'Estrées		
1600	Henry IV and Marie de Médicis marry	d. Richard Hooker; d. Luis de Molina	El Greco, *View of Toledo;*
1601			Caravaggio, *Conversion of St. Paul*
1602			d. Agostino Carracci; d. Giacomo Della Porta; d. Sebastiano Filippi, il Bastianino
1603	James I, king of England, 1603–1625; d. Guy Coquille	d. Pierre Charron	

Performing Arts	Literature, Humanism, and Printing	Philosophy, Science, and Exploration	Date
Kyd, *Spanish Tragedy*; Shakespeare, *The Comedy of Errors, Richard III*; d. Robert Greene	d. Moderata Fonte; d. Fadrique Furió Ceriol; d. Michel de Montaigne	Galileo, *Della scienza mechanica* (On mechanics); d. Thomas Cavendish	1592
London theaters closed due to plague; Shakespeare, *Taming of the Shrew, Titus Andronicus, Venus and Adonis*; d. Christopher Marlowe	d. Jacques Amyot		1593
London theaters reopened; Peri, *Dafne*; Shakespeare, *Romeo and Juliet, Two Gentlemen of Verona; Love's Labor's Lost, The Rape of Lucrece*; d. Thomas Kyd; d. Orlando di Lasso; d. Giovanni Pierluigi da Palestrina	*Satire Ménippée*; d. Bálint Balassi; d. Guillaume Bouchet; d. Alonso Ercilla y Zuñiga; d. Barnaby Googe	d. Martin Frobisher; d. Gerardus Mercator	1594
Shakespeare, *Midsummer Night's Dream, Richard II*	d. Jan van der Noot; Robert Southwell executed; d. Jean de Sponde; d. Torquato Tasso; d. George Turbeville	Mercator's atlas published; d. John Hawkins	1595
Shakespeare, *Merchant of Venice, King John*; d. George Peele	d. Jean Bodin	d. Francis Drake	1596
Shakespeare, *Henry IV, Parts 1 and 2*	d. Fernando de Herrera; d. Aldus Manutius the Younger	d. Willem Barents	1597
Shakespeare, *Much Ado about Nothing, Henry V*; d. Friedrich Dedekind	d. Henry Estienne the Younger; d. Paolo Paruta	Hakluyt, *Principal Navigations, Voyages, Traffics, and Discoveries of the English Nation*; d. Jacopo Mazzoni	1598
Globe Theater opened; Shakespeare, *Julius Caesar, As You Like It*; d. Luca Marencio	d. Edmund Spenser		1599
Shakespeare, *Hamlet, Merry Wives of Windsor*; d. Andrea Amati; d. Claude Le Jeune	Moderata Fonte, *Il merito delle donne* (The worth of women)	English East India Company founded; telescope invented; Giordano Bruno executed; d. Sebastian Basso	1600
Shakespeare, *Twelfth Night, Troilus and Cressida*; d. Thomas Nashe	University of Parma founded; Lucrezia Marinella, *La nobilta et l'eccellenza delle donne* (The nobility and excellence of women)	d. Tycho Brahe	1601
Giulio Caccini, *Le nuove musiche*; Shakespeare, *All's Well That Ends Well*; d. Thomas Morley	d. Sebastian Fabian Klonowic	Dutch East India Company founded; d. Kaspar Peucer	1602
		d. Francesco Buonamici; d. Andrea Cesalpino; d. William Gilbert	1603

Date	Politics and Society	Religion	Visual Arts and Architecture
1604	Charles IX, king of Sweden, 1604–1611		d. Isabella Andreini
1605	Gunpowder Plot in England; d. Jan Zamoyski	Pope Leo XI, 1605; Pope Paul V, 1605–1621; d. Théodore de Bèze	
1606	Guy Fawkes executed		
1607	First permanent English colony in America; d. Cesare Baronio; d. Pomponne de Bellièvre		d. Domenico Fontana
1608		Francis de Sales, *Introduction à la vie dévote* (Introduction to the devout life)	d. Giambologna
1609		Expulsion of Moriscos from Spain; Catholic translation of Old Testament published at Douai; d. Maharal of Prague	d. Annibale Carracci
1610	Assassination of Henry IV of France; Louis XIII, king of France, 1610–1643	d. Matteo Ricci	d. Michelangelo Merisi da Caravaggio; d. Adam Elsheimerr
1611	Gustavus II Aldophus, king of Sweden, 1611–1632; d. Antonio Pérez	French Oratory founded; Authorized (King James) Version of the Bible (England); d. Pedro de Ribadeneira	Rubens, *Descent from the Cross*
1612	d. Robert Cecil	d. Piotr Skarga	El Greco, *Baptism of Christ;* d. Federico Barocci
1613	Peace of Knarod; Turks invade Hungary		d. Lodovico Cigoli
1614	Estates General in France	d. Luisa de Carvajal y Mendoza; d. Isaac Casaubon	d. El Greco; d. Lavinia Fontana
1615	d. Margaret of Valois; d. Étienne Pasquier		
1616			d. Vincenzo Scamozzi
1617	d. Nicolas de Neufville, seigneur de Villeroy	d. Francisco Suárez	

Performing Arts	Literature, Humanism, and Printing	Philosophy, Science, and Exploration	Date
Shakespeare, *Othello, Measure for Measure*		Kepler, *Optics*	1604
Shakespeare, *King Lear, Macbeth;* d. Jacob Ayrer; d. Pontus de Tayard	Cervantes, *Don Quixote*, Part 1		1605
Jonson, *Volpone;* Shakespeare, *Antony and Cleopatra;* d. John Lyly; d. Jean Vauquelin de la Fresnaye	d. Philippe Desportes; d. Justus Lipsius	d. Justus Lipsius	1606
Beaumont, *Knight of the Burning Pestle;* Shakespeare, *Coriolanus, Timon of Athens;* Urfé, *Astrée;* first performance of Monteverdi's *Orfeo*		d. Guidobaldo, marchese del Monte	1607
d. Jean de La Taille	d. Thomas Sackville	d. Alberico Gentili; d. John Dee	1608
Shakespeare, *Sonnets*	d. Joseph Justus Scaliger	Inca Garcilaso de la Vega, *History of the Conquest of Peru*	1609
Jonson, *The Alchemist*			1610
Shakespeare, *The Tempest;* d. Johannes Eccard; d. Tomás Luis de Victoria		d. Henry Hudson	1611
Shakespeare, *Two Noble Kinsmen, Henry VIII* (with Fletcher?); Webster, *The White Devil;* d. Giovanni Gabrieli; d. Pierre de Larivey	d. Giovanni Battista Guarini; d. Henric Laurenszoon Spieghel	d. Christopher Clavius	1612
Globe Theater burns; Webster, *Duchess of Malfi*	d. Thomas Bodley; d. Sebastián de Covarrubias y Orozco; d. Mathurin Régnier	d. David ben Solomon Gans	1613
Jonson, *Bartholomew Fayre*	Ralegh, *History of the World;* University of Groningen founded; d. Mateo Alemán; d. Pierre de Bourdeille, seigneur de Brantôme	Danish East India Company founded	1614
	Cervantes, *Don Quixote*, Part 2	Galileo faces Inquisition; d. Giambattista Della Porta	1615
d. Francis Beaumont; d. William Shakespeare	Chapman translation of *Odyssey;* d. Miguel de Cervantes Saavedra; d. Inca Garcilaso de la Vega	Galileo warned not to defend Copernican thesis as scientific truth; d. Richard Hakluyt	1616
	d. George Wither	d. Bernardino Baldi; d. John Napier	1617

Date	Politics and Society	Religion	Visual Arts and Architecture
1618	Thirty Years' War begins; Walter Ralegh executed	Synod of Dort (Dordrecht)	d. Antonio Carracci
1619	Ferdinand II, HRE, 1619–1637	Paolo Sarpi, *Istoria del Concilio Tridentino* (History of the Council of Trent)	d. Ludovico Carracci; d. Nicholas Hilliard
1620	Plymouth Colony founded in Massachusetts		
1621	Philip IV, king of Spain, 1621–1665	Pope Gregory XV, 1621–1623; d. Robert Bellarmine	
1622	Treaty of Montpellier	Congregation de Propaganda Fide founded; d. Francis de Sales	Rubens begins Medici cycle (to 1625); d. Francesco Carracci
1623	d. Francisco de Sandoval y Rojas	Pope Urban VIII, 1623–1644	
1624	d. Nicolas Brûlart de Sillery	d. Jakob Böhme	
1625	Charles I, king of England, 1625–1649; d. Maurice of Nassau		d. Sofonisba Anguissola; d. Paolo Carracci; d. Jan Brueghel the Elder
1626			
1627			d. Adriaen de Vries
1628			
1629		d. Pierre de Bérulle	
1630	d. Théodore-Agrippa d'Aubigné		
1631			
1632			
1633			Van Dyck, *Charles I*
1634			

Performing Arts	Literature, Humanism, and Printing	Philosophy, Science, and Exploration	Date
d. Giulio Caccini	d. Gerbrandt Adriaensz Bredero	Dutch West African Company founded	1618
d. Richard Burbage; d. Nathan Field	d. Giovanni Botero; d. Samuel Daniel; d. Ginés Pérez de Hita	d. Girolamo Fabricius of Aquapendente	1619
	d. Thomas Campion; d. Simon Stevin; d. Roemer Visscher	Bacon, *Instauratio magna*	1620
d. Antoine de Montchrestien; d. Michael Praetorius; d. Jan Pieterszoon Sweelinck	Burton, *Anatomy of Melancholy*; University of Strasbourg founded; d. Guillaume Du Vair; d. Mary Sidney	d. Thomas Harriot	1621
Middleton and Rowley, *The Changeling*	Marie de Gournay, *Égalité des hommes et femmes* (The equality of men and women)	January 1 adopted as beginning of new year; d. William Baffin	1622
d. William Byrd	d. Nicholas Breton; d. Jean de La Ceppède; d. Giles Fletcher	d. William Camden	1623
	d. Juan de Mariana		1624
d. John Fletcher; d. Orlando Gibbons; d. John Webster	Grotius, *De jure belli ac pacis* (Law of war and peace); d. Paolo Beni; d. Thomas Lodge; d. Giambattista Marino; d. Honoré de Urfé		1625
d. John Dowland; d. Jacob Pontanus; d. William Rowley; d. Tabarin; d. Théophile de Viau	Marie de Gournay, *Grief des dames* (The ladies' grievance); d. François Béroalde de Verville; d. John Davies	d. Francis Bacon	1626
Marin Mersenne, *Traicté de l'harmonie universelle*; d. Thomas Middleton	d. Luis de Gónzaga y Argote	Company of New France founded	1627
d. John Bull	d. Fulke Greville; d. François Malherbe	Harvey, *De motu cordis et sanguinis* (On the movement of the heart and blood)	1628
	d. Szymon Szymonowicz		1629
d. Johann Hermann Schein		d. Johannes Kepler	1630
d. Philipp Dulichius	d. John Donne; d. Michael Drayton		1631
d. Thomas Dekker; d. Alexandre Hardy	d. Giambattista Basile	Galileo, *Dialogo sopra i due massimi sistemi del mondo* (Dialogue on the two great world systems)	1632
d. Jacopo Peri	d. George Herbert	Condemnation of Galileo	1633
Oberammergau Passion Play first performed; d. George Chapman; d. John Marston	University of Utrecht founded		1634

Date	Politics and Society	Religion	Visual Arts and Architecture
1635			d. Jacques Callot
1637	Ferdinand III, HRE, 1637–1657		
1638			d. Pieter Brueghel the Younger; d. Adriaen Brouwer
1639	First Bishops' War		Rubens, *Judgment of Paris*
1640	Revolt of the Catalans in Spain begins (to 1652); Portuguese war of independence begins (to 1668); Long Parliament assembled in England; Second Bishops' War		d. Peter Paul Rubens
1641			d. Anthony Van Dyck
1642	English Civil War begins		d. Guido Reni
1643			
1644			d. Bernardo Strozzi
1645	d. Hugo Grotius	d. Mary Ward; execution of William Laud	
1647			
1648	Peace of Westphalia ends Thirty Years' War	d. Leon Modena	
1649	Charles I of England executed and Commonwealth established		
1651			
1652			d. Inigo Jones
1653	Cromwell becomes Lord Protector		d. Artemisia Gentileschi; d. Simon de Vlieger

Performing Arts	Literature, Humanism, and Printing	Philosophy, Science, and Exploration	Date
d. Lope Félix de Vega Carpio	Académie Française founded; University of Budapest founded; d. Alessandro Tassoni; d. Jean-Baptiste Chassignet; d. Thomas Randolph		1635
d. Ben Jonson	Milton, *Lycidas*	d. Daniel Sennert	1637
			1638
d. Jakob Bidermann; d. Elizabeth Cary; d. John Ford; d. Juan Ruiz de Alarcón y Mendoza		d. Tommaso Campanella	1639
d. Philip Massinger	d. Robert Burton; d. Thomas Carew		1640
Monteverdi, *Il Ritorno d'Ulisse;* d. Thomas Heywood	Anna Maria van Schurman, *De ingenii muliebris ad doctrinam et meliores litteras aptitudine* (On women's fitness for learning and aptitude for letters; or Whether a Christian woman should be educated)	Descartes, *Méditations métaphysiques*	1641
Monteverdi, *L'Incoronazione di Poppea;* theaters closed in England		Hobbes, *De cive* (On citizenship); d. Galileo Galilei	1642
d. Girolamo Frescobaldi; d. Claudio Monteverdi	d. William Browne	Barometer invented; Williams, *Key into the Language of America*	1643
	Milton, *Areopagitica;* d. Francis Quarles	Descartes, *Principia philosophicae* (Principles of philosophy); d. Johannes Baptista van Helmont	1644
	d. Marie de Gournay; d. Aemilia Lanyer; d. Francisco de Quevedo		1645
	d. Pieter Cornelisz Hooft	d. Francesco Cavalieri; d. Evangelista Torricelli	1647
d. Tirso de Molina; d. Johann Stadlmayr			1648
	d. Richard Crashaw; d. Maria Messelschade; d. Gerardus Vossius		1649
d. Heinrich Albert	d. Anna Visscher		1651
	d. Arcangela Tarabotti		1652
	d. Lucrezia Marinella; d. Mary Wroth		1653

Date	Politics and Society	Religion	Visual Arts and Architecture
1657		d. Menassah ben Israel	
1658			
1663		d. Simone Luzzatto	
1664			
1667			
1673			
1674			
1678			
1679			
1682			
1684			
1689			
1724			

Performing Arts	*Literature, Humanism, and Printing*	*Philosophy, Science, and Exploration*	*Date*
	d. Richard Lovelace		1657
	d. John Cleveland; d. Baltasar Gracián		1658
			1663
	d. Katherine Phillips		1664
	Milton, *Paradise Lost*		1667
	d. Margaret Cavendish		1673
	Wood, *Historia et antiquitates universitatis Oxoniensis;* d. Bathsua Makin; d. John Milton		1674
Aphra Behn, *Sir Patient Fancy*	d. Anna Maria van Schurman		1678
Aphra Behn, *The Feign'd Curtezan*			1679
Aphra Behn, *The Roundheads* and *The City Heiress*			1682
	d. Elena Lucrezia Cornaro Piscopia		1684
	Aphra Behn, *Oroonoko*		
d. Aphra Behn			1689
	d. Glueckel of Hameln		1724

COMMON ABBREVIATIONS
USED IN THIS WORK

A.D.	*Anno Domini,* in the year of the Lord
A.H.	*Anno Hegirae,* in the year of the Hegira
b.	born
B.C.	before Christ
B.C.E.	before the common era (= B.C.)
c.	*circa,* about, approximately
C.E.	common era (= A.D.)
cf.	*confer,* compare
chap.	chapter
d.	died
D.	Dom, Portuguese honorific
diss.	dissertation
ed.	editor (pl., eds.), edition
e.g.	*exempli gratia,* for example
et al.	*et alii,* and others
etc.	*et cetera,* and so forth
f.	and following (pl., ff.)
fl.	*floruit,* flourished
HRE	Holy Roman Empire, Holy Roman Emperor
ibid.	*ibidem,* in the same place (as the one immediately preceding)
i.e.	*id est,* that is
MS.	manuscript (pl. MSS.)
n.	note
n.d.	no date
no.	number (pl., nos.)
n.p.	no place
n.s.	new series
N.S.	new style, according to the Gregorian calendar
O.F.M.	*Ordo Fratrum Minorum,* Order of Friars Minor; Franciscan
O.P.	*Ordo Predicatorum,* Order of Preachers; Dominican
O.S.	old style, according to the Julian calendar
p.	page (pl., pp.)
pt.	part
rev.	revised
S.	*san, sanctus, santo,* male saint
ser.	series

S.J.	*Societas Jesu,* Society of Jesus; Jesuit
SS.	*sancti, sanctae,* saints; *sanctissima, santissima,* most holy
Sta.	*sancta, santa,* female saint
supp.	supplement
vol.	volume
?	uncertain, possibly, perhaps

ENCYCLOPEDIA OF THE RENAISSANCE

ABRABANEL. *See* **Leone Ebreo.**

ABRAVANEL, ISAAC (1437–1508), courtier and Hebrew writer. The offshoot of a distinguished Ibero-Jewish family, Isaac Abravanel spent forty-five years in Portugal, then passed the nine years immediately prior to Spanish Jewry's 1492 expulsion in Castile. At that time an important figure at the court of Ferdinand and Isabella, he chose Italian exile over conversion to Christianity and spent his remaining years in various centers in Italy (primarily Naples, Monopoli, and Venice), where he composed most of his works, a combination of prodigious biblical commentaries and involved theological tomes. Together these form one of the largest and most diverse Hebrew literary corpora of medieval or Renaissance times.

While the teachings, methods, and sources of Abravanel's writings are, in the main, those of the late Jewish Middle Ages, a range of nascent Renaissance themes and sensibilities are evinced in them as well, most explicitly in the works composed after 1492. In Iberia, Abravanel was exposed to humanist methods and intellectual concerns, first at the court of Portugal's Afonso V, where he was a leading figure, and later in Castile, where he spent much of his time in the service of grandees of the house of Mendoza, including Cardinal Pedro González de Mendoza, youngest son of the marquis of Santillana and a leading sponsor of Castilian Renaissance scholarship and architecture. Abravanel's commentaries on the books of Joshua, Judges, and 1 and 2 Samuel, written in Spain in 1483–1484, attest to novel inter-

ests in and approaches to questions of scriptural authorship, chronology, and the origins of biblical books, some of which imply the impress of a humanist sense of historicity and techniques of textual analysis on his exegetical thought processes. Seen from this vantage point they offer perhaps the earliest example of Renaissance stimulus in works of Hebrew literature composed beyond Italy.

After the 1492 expulsion Abravanel spent two years in Naples, where he presumably encountered figures reflective of the city's status as a major Renaissance center, among them the head of its renowned humanist academy, Giovanni Pontano, a senior member of the Neapolitan court's upper echelons, into which Abravanel was quickly inducted. Judah Messer Leon, foremost among a number of Judeo-Italian scholars receptive to Renaissance trends and the first of these to evince a strong interest in humanism, also resided in Naples at this time. Abravanel's early Italian Renaissance learning, however, was apparently most indebted to a Jewish colleague of the celebrated Florentine Neoplatonist Giovanni Pico della Mirandola, Yohanan Alemanno, though the debt goes unacknowledged in his writings. Most probably Abravanel became apprised of Alemanno's teachings by way of the latter's writings, but a degree of oral transmission via Abravanel's eldest son, Judah (alias Leone Ebreo), author of the famous Renaissance Neoplatonic tract *Dialogues on Love,* might have been another conduit. Abravanel's familiarity with Renaissance motifs appropriated by Alemanno concerning magic, music, and King Solomon as exemplar of the *homo universalis* appears in his commentaries on 1 and 2 Kings, completed but a year after his arrival in Italy. In later Italian works both Isaac and Judah Abravanel would espouse other distinctively Italian Renaissance conceptions, among them a Judeocentric version of Pico's notion of "the ancient theology" (*prisca theologia*), according to which a single truth could be found underlying diverse writings of antiquity.

Abravanel was read by later Jewish scholars who unfolded more fully Renaissance elements apparent in his works (for example, the late-sixteenth-century historian Azariah de Rossi) and by a large number of sixteenth- and seventeenth-century Christian savants.

BIBLIOGRAPHY

Lawee, Eric. "On the Threshold of the Renaissance: New Methods and Sensibilities in the Biblical Commentaries of Isaac Abarbanel." *Viator* 26 (1995): 283–319.

Netanyahu, B. *Don Isaac Abravanel: Statesman and Philosopher.* 5th ed. Ithaca, N.Y., 1998.

ERIC LAWEE

ABSOLUTISM.

"Absolutism" is a word used in at least two different, though connected, ways. It sometimes means a type of government in which the central authorities, usually kings in the Renaissance, exercise vast and almost untrammeled power over the inhabitants of a country. It also refers to a political theory in which the sovereign of a state is accountable neither to the people nor to the church, but only to God, and in which rulers can make law without the consent of their subjects, at least in a case of necessity. The period from the late sixteenth to about the mid-eighteenth century is often seen as an age of absolutism in both the practical and theoretical senses—an age when in France especially but also elsewhere governments increased their powers through a process of state-building, and when the theory of absolute sovereignty received classic expression in works by Jean Bodin, Jacques-Bénigne Bossuet, and others.

The Concept of Absolutism. The term "*absolutisme*" came into use in France only at the very end of the eighteenth century, and it was not until the 1830s that the English started talking about "absolutism." Arguably, it makes little sense to analyze the past in terms of categories that contemporaries did not themselves employ, and therefore we ought not to talk about absolutism in a work on the Renaissance. But this line should not be pressed too far. People in Renaissance Europe used few terms ending in "ism," but often possessed concepts very

like those to which such terms refer. They did frequently speak of "absolute power," "absolute monarchy," "absolute sovereignty," and so on. Nowadays, we often associate such notions with totalitarianism and dictatorship. But those who recommended "absolute" kingship in the sixteenth and seventeenth centuries did not want the ruler to act as a despot or tyrant, or to ride roughshod over the established rights of groups or individuals. Commonly, their main concern was to insist that kings can never be coerced or violently resisted by their subjects, and that they have whatever powers they need to govern well, including discretionary powers that they could employ to set aside customary restrictions in emergencies. The absolute king, they said, was freed from (*absolutus;* absolved from) the sanctions of the ordinary law of the land, but he was still under a moral obligation to govern justly, to obey the laws of God and nature, and to promote the public good.

A second concept of absolutism has been employed by historians and social theorists as a convenient means of referring to some major changes that took place in France and many other European countries from the late sixteenth century onward. Absolutism in this sense means the growth of state power at the expense of representative institutions, local elites, and the church. Typical aspects of this kind of absolutism, it is often said, were the use of Intendants (officials appointed by the central government and directly accountable to it) rather than local administrators to govern in the localities; the systematic curtailment of the powers of national and provincial estates and of other institutions (such as the high court known as the Parlement of Paris) that limited royal freedom of action; the growth of central bureaucracies; the formation of large standing armies; and the enforcement of the principle that taxation and legislation do not require the subject's consent. Absolutism defined in this way is sometimes regarded as a key stage on the road from the medieval world to modernity.

The Practice of Absolutism. During the late sixteenth century, France was ravaged by religious civil war. In 1576 Jean Bodin published his *Six livres de la république* (Six books of the commonwealth), advocating strong monarchical government as the solution to the country's problems. Many people came to share his views. Under Henry IV (1589–1610), the French crown increased its authority, and although there was a resurgence of noble particularism during the regency that followed his death, the state's power was further advanced under Cardinals Richelieu and Mazarin from 1624 to 1661. After meeting in 1614–1615, the Estates General was not summoned again until the eve of the French Revolution. During the Thirty Years' War, France was threatened with invasion by Spanish troops posted in the Netherlands, and the exigencies of war led the two cardinals to build up the French army, tax at very high levels, and employ emergency powers. Elsewhere in Europe, too, the growth of state power in the seventeenth century was often closely linked to warfare. In France, royal power suffered a setback during the Fronde (civil revolts between 1648 and 1653) but recovered once more thereafter, reaching its zenith in the period of Louis XIV's personal rule (1661–1715). In 1673 the Parlement of Paris was formally deprived of the right to remonstrate against royal edicts before registering them; in 1682 the French clergy endorsed royal claims to power over the French church; in 1685 the religious rights of Protestants were extinguished.

In Brandenburg-Prussia, Russia, Denmark, Sweden, and elsewhere, the ruler's powers were also strengthened during the course of the seventeenth century. In Brandenburg, for example, the Diet met for the last time in 1653, and the Great Elector Frederick William (1640–1688) expanded his power by building up the army and the bureaucracy. In Denmark, royal power reached new heights in the 1660s; in Sweden, in the 1680s; in Russia, at the end of the century under Peter the Great (1682–1725).

Whether these regimes and others should be described as absolutist is a highly debated question, especially in relation to the practical limitations on rulers' power. For instance, some scholars claim that Louis XIV governed by striking deals with local elites rather than by overthrowing them, and that his efforts to gain control over the church were only partially successful. In fact, venality of office and hereditary office-holding limited the king's control over his own bureaucracy. Nevertheless, the powers of the crown in France and many other countries were far greater at the end of the seventeenth century than they had been a hundred years earlier.

The Theory of Absolutism. In his *Six livres de la république,* Bodin argued that in every state there was and ought to be just one sovereign, who held supreme authority including the power to make law without the consent of the subject. Bodin asserted that sovereignty was necessarily indivisible and absolute. He claimed that sovereign power had to be held by a single person or assembly, arguing that if sovereignty were divided there would be constant conflict among those who possessed the different parts of it (for example, between whomever made law and whomever commanded the army). If the king were accountable to an assembly, or if he were subject to laws of which an assembly was the definitive interpreter, then it and not he would hold sovereignty. Bodin claimed that any state in which sovereignty was divided would be highly unstable and not really a state at all.

He insisted that subjects may never use force to resist their sovereigns, but claimed that the sovereign ought to respect the laws of God and nature and the property rights of individuals. Nor could the sovereign, according to Bodin, change "fundamental" laws, such as the laws of succession. Subjects could never actively resist their king, but they had a duty to disobey any royal order that conflicted with divine law. If the king punished them, they were obliged to accept their fate meekly. Bodin stressed that people held rights of property against the sovereign, and he urged rulers to honor these, and to abide by established customs. Ordinarily, he insisted, the sovereign should tax only with the subject's consent, expressed in representative institutions. However, in a case of necessity the sovereign was empowered to tax without consent and to alter any other settled arrangements. It was the sovereign who decided what constituted a case of necessity.

In the decades after Bodin, French absolutists dropped the requirement that kings should obtain the subject's consent before introducing new financial exactions. But they continued to insist that sovereigns ought not to depart from established ways, or impose new taxes except in emergencies. Cardin Le Bret and other apologists for Richelieu's policies stressed the wide emergency powers that the government could exercise for "reason of state"—to use the catchphrase of the time. They argued that the harsh demands that the Cardinal's regime made of the population were justified by the exigencies of wartime. The same claims were repeated under Mazarin and Louis XIV, and the notion that the king should summon the Estates General if he wanted new taxes—a principle on which Bodin had insisted—disappeared.

Absolutist ideas spread to most parts of Europe in the later sixteenth and seventeenth centuries. Many theorists accepted Bodin's doctrines on sovereignty, but commonly they gave rather more weight than did Bodin to the divine origins of royal government, using scripture and theology to show that kings derive their authority from God alone and not from a grant by the people. This theory of the "divine right of kings" was voiced by King James VI of Scotland and I of England, the French bishop Jacques-Bénigne Bossuet, and many others. In Germany, Bodin's views on indivisible sovereignty aroused criticism because they did not seem to provide a satisfactory account of the constitution of the Holy Roman Empire. Thinkers such as Henning Arnisaeus followed Bodin on many points—for instance asserting that subjects may never take up arms against their sovereign—but claimed that constitutions were possible in which sovereign powers were distributed among different officials or assemblies. The same argument had already been voiced by Bodin's Italian critic Fabio Albergati in 1602. Some theorists rejected Bodin's claim that all states must be governed by a single absolute sovereign but argued that absolute monarchy was nevertheless a perfectly feasible form of government. This was the line taken by the highly influential Dutch theorist Hugo Grotius in his *De jure belli ac pacis* (On the law of war and peace) of 1625.

In England, a variant of the divine right of kings was developed by thinkers including Sir Robert Filmer, whose most famous work was *Patriarcha*, written about 1630, revised a few years later, and first published only in 1680. Filmer's theory, known as patriarchalism, viewed the state as a family and the sovereign as a father. It was commonly acknowledged that a father's power over his wife and children is natural and therefore divine (since God was seen as the author of nature); fathers, people agreed, do not get their authority from a grant by family members. Filmer claimed that the first father of all—Adam—had ruled as a king over his descendants (of whom there were a great many, since he lived for many centuries). When Adam died, his heir inherited his fatherly (and kingly) powers, although unlike Adam he was not himself the progenitor of the whole kinship group. Filmer's essential point was that however sovereigns get power, their authority is the same as Adam's and is therefore independent of the consent of the subject.

Filmer's ideas were attacked by John Locke in the first of the *Two Treatises of Government* (1689). Filmer himself attacked the most famous of all English absolutists, Thomas Hobbes. The two thinkers agreed on the rights of sovereigns, endorsing Bodin's views. But while Filmer rejected the notion that rulers get power from their subjects, Hobbes argued that political power arises from consent, claiming that in a situation where there is no government (the state of nature) life would be so unpleasant that

people would voluntarily erect an absolute sovereign to rule them.

In the English-speaking world, it is commonly supposed that Locke refuted the ideas of thinkers like Filmer and Hobbes, and that the French finally recognized the poverty of absolutism in the Revolution of 1789. But it is not clear that it was the theoretical defects of absolutist thinking (or the abstract merits of Lockean liberalism) that led to the overthrow of James II and Louis XVI. The extent to which divine right thinking was abandoned even in England in the eighteenth century has been doubted, and one key absolutist doctrine—Bodin's doctrine of sovereignty—lived on in English legal thought: in the 1640s the parliamentarian pamphleteer Henry Parker portrayed not the king but parliament as sovereign, and the sovereignty of parliament became an established constitutional principle.

See also **Monarchy**; **Political Thought**; **Reason of State**; **Representative Institutions**; *and biography of Jean Bodin.*

BIBLIOGRAPHY

Beik, William. *Absolutism and Society in Seventeenth-Century France: State Power and Provincial Aristocracy in Languedoc.* Cambridge, U.K., 1985. Important local study of French absolutism in practice, revising earlier accounts.

Bodin, Jean. *On Sovereignty.* Edited by Julian H. Franklin. Cambridge, U.K., 1992. English translations of some of the most important sections of Bodin's *Six livres de la République.* It is part of Cambridge Texts in the History of Political Thought, an excellent series that also includes editions of many other key primary texts.

Brady, Thomas A., Heiko A. Oberman, and James D. Tracy, eds. *Handbook of European History, 1400–1600.* 2 vols. Grand Rapids, Mich., 1996. Good collection of essays, many on themes connected with absolutism.

Burns, J. H., and Mark Goldie, eds. *The Cambridge History of Political Thought 1450–1700.* Cambridge, U.K., 1991. A fine collection of essays, with a good bibliography.

Figgis, John Neville. *The Divine Right of Kings.* New York, 1965. With an introduction by G. R. Elton. First published in 1896, this remains a highly readable account.

Miller, John, ed. *Absolutism in Seventeenth Century Europe.* Houndmills, U.K., 1990. Useful, recent essays surveying theory and practice in a number of countries.

Skinner, Quentin. *The Foundations of Modern Political Thought.* 2 vols. Cambridge, U.K., 1978. The best introduction to early modern political thought.

Vierhaus, Rudolf. *Germany in the Age of Absolutism.* Translated by Jonathan B. Knudsen. Cambridge, U.K., 1988. Translation of *Deutschland im Zeitalter des Absolutismus* (1978). Good, brief, clear account.

JOHANN P. SOMMERVILLE

ACADEMIES. During the middle decades of the fifteenth century Italian humanists began to describe their informal scholarly congregations as "academies." Drawing inspiration from ancient models such as the Lyceum of Athens, Renaissance scholars envisioned the academy as an important part of their revival of the ideas and values of the ancients. The academy represented the collaborative project of knowledge; its reappearance in such centers as Florence and Rome, both important sites of early Renaissance humanism, testified to the birth of a broad intellectual community committed to the recuperation of the past.

Most well-known was the Platonic Academy, established in 1462–1463 under the patronage of Cosimo de' Medici at his villa at Careggi near Florence. Under the leadership of the Florentine humanist and physician Marsilio Ficino, the Platonic Academy played an important role in the transmission of Greek learning and the revival of Platonism in western Europe. Ficino had access to Byzantine Greek manuscripts that allowed him to translate into Latin the works of Plato as well as the elusive Hermetic Corpus, attributed to the Egyptian God Hermes Trismegistus and thought to be an important precursor to the teachings of Christianity. More locally, the Platonic Academy reflected the peculiar fusion of politics and culture that characterized many Renaissance academies. Its members counted themselves among the elite of Florentine society. This informal association made the pursuit of learning and the patronage of culture a central feature of patrician identity.

During the late fifteenth and early sixteenth centuries such associations continued to be fairly informal, ad hoc gatherings. Only twelve such groups have been officially identified as academies in Italy prior to 1530. The reasons why have to do with the relative lack of institutional identity when compared with the Renaissance universities. Many intellectual circles, such as the one that met regularly in Bernardo Rucellai's private gardens (the *Orti Oricellari*) and included among its members Niccolò Machiavelli, never even gave themselves an official name. Lacking any official criteria for membership, rules of governance, and archival records of their activities, it was hard to distinguish an academy from any other gathering of nobles and patricians devoted to conversation and culture.

Beginning in the 1540s, academies became a more visible and pervasive feature of cultural life. The city-states and principalities of Italy played a leading role in fostering this type of organization. Political decentralization, a relatively high level of urbanization, and a clear sense of the value of culture as a competitive investment helped to shape Italy's unique academic landscape. The vitality of university towns such as Padua, Bologna, and Pavia and the emergence of princely courts in cities such as Florence, Ferrara, Mantua, and Milan fostered numerous centers in which talented scholars, lawyers, physicians, engineers, artists, and musicians congregated.

By 1600, 377 academies had been founded in Italy; an additional 870 appeared in the following century. Most clustered in major cities in the dozens or even hundreds, though virtually every Italian town had at least one or two academies by the seventeenth century. Many of the Italian academies were of brief duration, sometimes closing within a year or two of their founding. In other instances, seeming continuity over the centuries masked a relatively somnolent existence punctuated by brief bursts of activity and renewal. Generally speaking, the peaks and valleys of academy life in a large city marked its changing status as a political and cultural center. For instance, during the sixteenth century cities such as Ferrara and Siena had almost as many academies as Rome; in the seventeenth century both displayed a marked decline in academy activities, while Rome's number of academies increased to 132, surpassing every other Italian city as it became one of the leading cultural capitals of Europe.

The function of the academy varied greatly by city and according to the inclinations of its founder. In many instances, the playful intentions of the academies are evident in the witty names academicians gave their organizations: Ardenti (the Impassioned), Addormentati (the Somnolent), Gelati (the Frigid), Confusi (the Confused), Infiammati (the Inflamed), Occulti (the Secret Ones). Each academician was identified by his (or occasionally her) pseudonym and often made use of a particular *impresa*—an emblematic device that combined the visual wit of the heraldic tradition with the humanist elegance of various Latin sayings—in public writings. Such rituals helped to create a distinctive communal identity for academicians.

The majority of academies were purely local. In some instances, they publicly celebrated the distinctive cultural contributions of a particular region. For instance, the Florentine Academy (founded c. 1540) devoted itself to the preservation and dissemination of the literature and language of Tuscany. Subsidized by the grand dukes of Tuscany, it and its successor, the Accademia della Crusca (1582), played an important role in making Tuscan the preferred written vernacular of all Italy. Its success led French humanists to encourage their monarchs to found princely academies that would make language, culture, and science important to the realm.

In its decision to focus on a particular subject, the Florentine Academy also belonged to the minority of Renaissance academies, most of which deliberately cultivated an eclectic, encyclopedic program of scholarship. The exceptions, however, played a significant role in developing new approaches to a variety of arts and sciences. Artistic academies such as Carracci academy in Bologna, the Accademia di San Luca in Rome, and the Accademia del Disegno in Florence publicized the work of artists in various cities and created a context in which patrons, masters, and aspiring students interacted. Scientific academies such as the Accademia dei Lincei in Rome (1603–1630) and the Accademia del Cimento (1657–1667) in Florence gave official sanction to anti-Aristotelian learning and new philosophical and experimental programs.

Prior to its success in creating a network of regional centers, the Accademia dei Lincei had dreamed of creating a network of colonies in the 1610s and 1620s, stretching from Germany to New Spain, but had only succeeded in establishing a second colony in Naples. The inability of the Italian academies to transcend their local origins helps us to understand why they were so plentiful and so transitory. By contrast, the academies in emerging nation-states such as France and England exhibited more distinctive patterns of centralization. Academies such as the Académie Française (founded 1634), Académie Royale des Sciences (founded 1666), and the Royal Society of London (founded 1660) aspired to attend to the cultural and scientific needs of a nation. They endured longer than any of their Italian counterparts while drawing inspiration from these earlier Renaissance models.

See also Italian Literature and Language; Plato, Platonism, and Neoplatonism.

BIBLIOGRAPHY

Cochrane, Eric. "The Renaissance Academies in Their Italian and European Setting." In *The Fairest Flower: The Emergence of Linguistic National Consciousness in Renaissance Europe.* Florence, 1985. Pages 21–39.

Field, Arthur. *The Origins of the Platonic Academy of Florence.* Princeton, N.J., 1988.

Maylender, Michele. *Storia delle Accademie d'Italia.* 5 vols. Bologna, Italy, 1926–1930.

Quondam, Amadeo. "L'Accademia." In *Letteratura italiana.* Vol. 1, *Il letterato e le istituzioni.* Edited by Alberto Asor Rosa. Turin, Italy, 1982. Pages 823–898.

Yates, Frances. *The French Academies of the Sixteenth Century.* London, 1988.

PAULA FINDLEN

ACCOUNTING.   The Renaissance was a period of marked improvement in accounting. The financially sophisticated urban centers of Italy were the centers for innovation, which culminated in the introduction of double-entry bookkeeping, the cornerstone of modern accounting. The procedure involved recording each transaction twice, as both debit and credit, and striking a balance between them. Real and nominal accounts were carefully integrated, with cross-referencing and calculation of changes in owner's equity. The method allowed a rational means of determining assets, liabilities, and profits. It constituted a great improvement over single-entry or "charge and discharge" accounting, which listed only the movement of money and goods over a period of time, without concern for measure of profit and loss. From Italy the new technique eventually spread to the rest of Europe.

The oldest known postclassical European commercial records date from twelfth-century Genoa. They are notarial registers in Latin, consisting of three small sheets of profit calculations made in 1157 for a business partnership. The oldest account book is also Italian: a Florentine bankbook, written in Tuscan dialect. Both documents reveal a high degree of sophistication in the bookkeeping, distinguishable from the rudimentary and primitive forms of tabulation used in medieval manorial accounts elsewhere in Europe.

Double-Entry Bookkeeping.   When these already advanced methods developed into double entry has been a matter of dispute, primarily because sources are fragmentary. Some scholars believe the new method first started in the account books of the Florentine merchants Rinieri Fini (1296–1305) and Giovanni Farolfi (1299–1300). Others point to the books of the London branch of the Gallerani bank (1305–1308). While all these account books possess many elements of the new technique, none possesses all. Opinions differ, too, about what precisely constitutes double entry, beyond the basic definition. Scholars, however, have agreed to disagree. It is now widely accepted that double entry most likely began in late thirteenth- or early fourteenth-century Tuscany.

The first accepted example of double entry is in the account book of the treasury officials (*massari* or stewards) of Genoa of 1340. The citations are in Latin, in bilateral form, with debits on the left side and credits on the right. Debits are indicated by the Latin phrase *debet/debent nobis* (he/they owe us), while credits are marked off by the phrase *recepimus in* (we received from). The entries include the date, the nature of the transaction, and the amount of money. The debits and credits were cross-indexed to their corresponding accounts in a ledger (see Table 1). Expenses were posted to an *avaria* (medieval Latin for brokerage) account, while losses on sales of commodities were listed in the account labeled *proventus cambii et dampnum de rauba vendita* (income from exchange and loss on sales). The balances of expense and income were transferred to the account of the Commune of Genoa, which functioned as the capital (or equity) account.

The accounts of Francesco Datini illustrate the evolution of double-entry technique in Tuscany. Datini's books survive intact, from those of his earliest independent concerns in Avignon in 1366 until his death in Prato in 1410. The Avignon accounts of 1366–1367 were kept in single entry. By 1383, however, Datini's method had changed. That year he incorporated into the books of his Pisan company a sort of modified bilateral form, with personal ac-

TABLE 1. Accounts of Massari of Genoa, 1340

26 August 1340	*26 August 1340*
Debit [*debet nobis*] Jacopo Bonica on behalf of Antonio Marino on page 61 for lire 49/soldi 4	Credit [*Recepimus in*] for expenses on behalf of the commune of Genoa, on page 231, made by the same Jacopo for the Army of Taxaroli in trabuchets (seige engines) and other necessities . . . lire 62/soldi 10
Debit the same Jacopo ["*Item*"] on 5 Sept. on behalf of Marzocco Pinello on page 92 for lire 12/soldi 10	
Debit the same Jacopo March 6 1341 for rest of his account in the new ledger page 41 soldi 16	
Sum: lire 62/soldi 10	

Source: Edward Peragallo, *The Origin and Evolution of Double-Entry Bookkeeping.* New York, 1938, p. 35. The present author has retranslated Peragallo's Latin, which was faulty. The page references correspond to those in the original ledger.

counts for receivables and payables listed side by side, but merchandise expense and profit-and-loss accounts arranged with credit beneath the debit. By the 1390s, Datini had undeniably implemented the new technique. He capped off his accounts by drawing up financial statements, which summarized and tallied assets, liabilities, and profits, to notify the home office and the principal investors (in this case Prato and Datini) of the status of business. The financial statements appear to have been the unique contribution of Tuscan merchants.

Accounts in Italy. By the fifteenth century, double entry had become common throughout Italy. In Florence, the Medici bank, among others, kept its accounts in double entry, while in Genoa the Bank of Saint George (1408–1444) did the same, as did some Milanese firms.

Regional differences in style, method, and terminology remained. Genoese and Milanese merchants, for example, maintained their accounts in Latin; Tuscan merchants used the vernacular. The Genoese showed from the first an inclination to arrange their accounts in bilateral form, while Tuscan merchants preferred a vertical arrangement until 1380. Florentines consistently drew up financial statements; the others did not. The Milanese called the ledger book a *liber tabulle;* the Genoese called it a *cartularium;* and the Tuscans referred to it as a *libro dei debitori e creditori*.

The most mature and nuanced form of double entry—the one that would become synonymous with the Italian achievement—belonged to the Venetians. The earliest examples are the mercantile account books of the Soranzo brothers (1406–1436), who specialized in trading cotton in Syria. Scholars often refer to the Venetian method as "venture accounting" because Venetians, who were primarily merchants engaged in import and export trade, recorded in their books the profit and loss on each commodity or "venture."

The most sophisticated of the fifteenth-century Venetian books are those of the merchant Andrea Barbarigo. Barbarigo books, which cover the period from 1431 to 1582, use a system of journal and ledger, carefully cross-indexed and coordinated to form a coherent whole. Like the Genoese, the form was bilateral, with debits facing credits. The simplicity, however, contrasts sharply with the contemporary Florentine practice, which used many books.

Accounts in the Rest of Europe. Both the diffusion and adoption of double entry were very uneven. The Milanese merchants Marco Serrainerio

Balancing the Books. The scales in *Allegory of Commerce* (detail), a 1585 woodcut by Jost Amman, represent the debit *(left)* and credit *(right)* sides of recording financial transactions in the double-entry method of bookkeeping.
©THE BRITISH MUSEUM, LONDON

and Giovannino da Dugnano arranged their accounts in double entry (indeed, "venture" accounting), but their contemporaries, the del Maino, did not. Datini used double entry in the 1390s, but the del Bene gave up the practice when monetary fluctuations made the routine cumbersome and difficult.

The Italian innovations radiated slowly to the rest of Europe. Despite the volume and sophistication of their trade, contemporary Hanseatic merchants did not use double entry, and their bookkeeping methods were unsystematic. The records of the Lübeck merchant Hermann Wittenborg and his son Johann (1329–1360), the earliest surviving Hanse account books, exemplify this. They are poorly organized and written in a medley of awkward Latin and Low German. The books of the Danzig merchant Johann Pisz (1421–1451) are somewhat better organized. The system nevertheless fell far short of the Italian model.

Dutch and French merchants also lagged. The surviving books of an anonymous trader from the town of Hoorn in Northern Holland (1457–1463) are messy, with credits and debits arranged in random

order. The accounts of Jacme Olivier of Narbonne, a Frenchman with extensive dealings in the Levant, list only investments in each enterprise, not the returns (although these may have been lost). The records of the Bonis brothers, fourteenth-century merchants from Montauban, display more sophistication. There is evidence that like contemporary Tuscans they drew up financial statements.

Accounting methods were more developed in southern German lands, where, by the middle of the fourteenth and fifteenth centuries, banks on the magnitude of those of the great Florentine firms had begun to spring up. Southern German firms did not, however, adopt double entry, preferring instead a well-ordered form of single entry. Their failure to adopt the new technique is surprising, in that their companies resembled Italian banks in internal structure and many features. Nevertheless, even the formidable Fugger bank did not use double entry, though its legendary leader, Jakob Fugger, had studied in Venice and surely encountered the method there.

As the southern German banks show, efficient and orderly accounting procedure was possible without double entry. This was also true of the famous fourteenth-century Bruges money changers, Collard de Marke and Guillaume Ruyelle. Their records reveal the use of a style of bilateral form and careful accounting of credit and debits, but no double entry.

The use of double entry became widespread throughout Europe after 1500, with the Spanish taking the lead. The books of the great Ruiz firm were, by the middle of the century, in double entry, as were those of the Miguel and Garcia firms of Salamanca. The first examples of English double entry also date from this time. As in Italy, however, the adoption was not uniform.

Diffusion and Significance. A major factor in the dissemination of the new method was the work of several fifteenth-century Italian writers, who set out the principals of double entry to larger audiences. The first, Benedetto Cotrugli, was not a bookkeeper but a judge at the court of King Alfonso in Naples. In 1458 Cotrugli wrote *Della mercatura et del mercante perfetto* (Of commerce and the perfect merchant). The book was devoted to commerce, with a short chapter on bookkeeping. The chapter in effect endorsed the double-entry method without actually using the term. The book, however, lay unpublished for one hundred years. Much more influential was Luca Pacioli's *Summa de arithmetica*

(Summary of arithmetic), which circulated widely after its publication in 1494. The book offered the clearest and most complete description of double entry to date, using the Venetian model.

The greater significance of double entry continues to be debated. Many, including Max Weber, Joseph Schumpeter, and Werner Sombart, saw it as a driving force in the transformation of feudal society into a capitalist one. Sombart argued that by allowing for more rational determination of profits and losses, the method rendered business as a whole more rational, more coldly impersonal, and thus more capitalistic. Others, however, have viewed double entry as little more than a business technique, a means to help manage business, with no broader significance. They point out that calculation of profits and rational financial planning could also be achieved by single entry. A third approach has stressed the reciprocal nature of the new method, arguing that the improved accounting technique was as much the result of the growing sophistication of trade as its cause. In any case, the debate, which involves dispute over the meaning of capitalism as much as double entry, remains unresolved.

BIBLIOGRAPHY

De Roover, Raymond. "The Development of Accounting prior to Luca Pacioli according to Account Books of Medieval Merchants." In *Business, Banking and Economic Thought in Late Medieval and Early Modern Europe*. Edited by Julius Kirshner. Chicago, 1974. Pages 119–180. A bit dated, but still the most comprehensive treatment of the subject

Edwards, J. R. *A History of Financial Accounting*. London, 1989.

Lane, Frederic C. "Double Entry Bookkeeping and Resident Merchants." *Journal of European Economic History* 6 (1977): 177–191.

Lane, Frederic C. "Venture Accounting in Medieval Business Management." In his *Venice and History*. Baltimore, 1966. Pages 99–108.

Parker, R. H., and B. S. Yamey. *Accounting History: Some British Contributions*. Oxford, 1994.

Peragallo, Edward. *The Origin and Evolution of Double-Entry Bookkeping*. New York, 1938.

Yamey, Basil S. "Scientific Bookkeeping and the Rise of Capitalism." *Economic History Review* 2, series 1 (1949): 99–113.

WILLIAM CAFERRO

ACHILLINI, ALESSANDRO (1463–1512), Italian philosopher. Alessandro Achillini was an important professor of philosophy and of medicine who used his knowledge of Aristotle and Aristotle's Greek commentators to develop his own views on the unity of the intellect and the immortality of the soul. His philosophical doctrines may also have been influenced by the work of the English Franciscan William of Ockham (c. 1285–?1349).

On 7 September 1484 Achillini received degrees in philosophy and medicine from the University of Bologna, where he then taught philosophy and medicine until 1506. In that year he succeeded Antonio Fracantiano (d. 1506) at the University of Padua, where he taught with the Mantuan philosopher Pietro Pomponazzi (1462–1525). Beginning in 1508 Achillini again taught at Bologna until early 1512, when the university was closed because the Spanish army was bombarding the walls of the city.

Achillini's anatomical notebook, *Annotationes anatomicae,* was published by his brother, Giovanni Filoteo, at Bologna, in 1520. Achillini is given credit by modern writers (for example, Alidosi and Sorbelli) for numerous anatomical discoveries, but not, it would seem, by his contemporaries (such as Paolo Giovio and Luca Gaurico). His notebook consists of observations made and structures seen. In at least six instances, Achillini records the year, from 1502 to 1506, when he noted certain anatomical features, some normal, some abnormal. Finally, he frequently criticizes medical authorities (including Galen, Avicenna, and Jacobus Foroliviensis), based in part on his own observations. Castiglioni, in a judicious paragraph, says that he studied the anatomy of the bladder, the cecum, and the bile ducts, and described the suspensory ligament of the liver.

Active in academic affairs, Achillini oversaw many doctoral examinations and students' arts disputations. His published writings reflect the "disputed question" model of these exams, an integral part of medieval and Renaissance university instruction. That is, his works are not, for the most part, single-subject monographs in the modern sense but instead address one question or a group of related questions.

Achillini left eleven works in twenty-four editions published between 1494 and 1568, including five collections of his writings published in 1508, 1545, 1548, 1551, and 1568. He also edited or revised four other items. Of these works, five are most important: *Quodlibeta de intelligentiis* (On intelligences or intellects; 1494); *De orbibus [coeli]* (On heavenly bodies; 1498), for which he used Aristotle's *De caelo* as his starting point; *De universalibus* (On universals; 1501); *De elementis* (On matter, form, and privation; 1505), in which he discussed the traditional Aristotelian principles of natural philosophy; and *De distinctionibus* (On distinctions; 1510), a handbook of metaphysical distinctions, especially the scholastic transcendentals, those made by Aristotle and his commentator Averroes, and those employed by the moderns, by whom he meant the Scotists.

Two main questions interested Achillini in the early sixteenth century and became even more prominent after Pope Leo X's encyclical *Apostolici Regiminis* of 19 December 1513 (as part of the Fifth Lateran Council): the unity of the intellect and the immortality of the soul. On the question of intellect, Achillini made a clear distinction between the opinions of philosophers and those of theologians. The question of immortality, however, he left to the theologians, apparently believing that, although immortality cannot be proved by "natural" reason, it must be accepted as an article of faith, a view that anticipated, in part, Pomponazzi's argument in *Tractatus de immortalitate animae* (On the immortality of the soul), published in 1516, four years after Achillini's death.

BIBLIOGRAPHY

Matsen, Herbert S. *Alessandro Achillini (1463–1512) and His Doctrine of "Universals" and "Transcendentals": A Study in Renaissance Ockhamism.* Lewisburg, Pa., 1974. See appendix 1, "Alessandro Achillini (1463–1512) as Professor of Philosophy in the 'Studio' of Padua (1506–1508)," pp. 185–197.

Matsen, Herbert S. "The Influence of Duns Scotus and His Followers on the Philosophy of Alessandro Achillini (1463–1512)." *Regnum Hominis et Regnum Dei.* Edited by Camille Bérubé. Vol. 2. Rome, 1978. Pages 229–247.

Matsen, Herbert S. "Students' 'Arts' Disputations at Bologna around 1500, Illustrated from the Career of Alessandro Achillini (1463–1512)." *History of Education* 6 (1977): 169–181.

HERBERT S. MATSEN

ACOUSTICS. The physics and mechanics of sound, its propagation, and reception by the human ear and mind were the subject of both speculative and experimental investigation during the fifteenth and sixteenth centuries.

Classical and Medieval Sources. Through much of the fifteenth century musicians, theorists, and philosophers depended on the music treatise of Boethius (480–524), *De institutione musica* (trans. *Fundamentals of Music*), for the science of sound and music. The theories presented there are not entirely consistent because, as evidence now shows, different parts of the five-book work followed several different Greek authorities. Sound is defined (book 1, chapter 3) as a percussion of air reaching the hearing, more frequent motion resulting in higher pitch, less frequent in lower. A tighter string produces faster motion and higher sound. When a string is struck, the air around it pulsates rapidly many times, but the hearing senses a continuous sound, higher or lower in pitch, depending on the speed of the motion. This plurality, Boethius con-

tends, is a quantity; so sounds can be compared as quantities or numbers, some equal, as in a unison, others unequal, as in the consonances and other intervals.

Boethius followed the Pythagoreans in admitting only unequal numbers from 1 to 4 in superparticular ($n + 1/n$) or multiple (mn/n) ratios as productive of consonances. In a later chapter (1.8), however, he defines consonance subjectively as a blend of high and low sound pleasing to the ear, and dissonance as a displeasing mixture. In book 5 (chapter 4), where Boethius paraphrases book 1 of Ptolemy's *Harmonica* (Harmonics), he cites the opinion of Aristoxenus, who held that the differences between pitches are qualitative, not quantitative as the Pythagoreans believed.

Since the number of pulsations was not measurable, investigation of quantity concentrated on the dimensions of the physical objects producing the sound. Boethius, rather than adducing more recent observations, cites the legend of Pythagoras hearing consonances issuing from a blacksmith shop (1.10) and his speculations on this experience (1.11). Pythagoras is said to have concluded that the consonant pitches he heard were caused by hammers of different weights hitting the anvil, and that the relation of these weights could be expressed in number ratios, such as 2:1 for the octave. He later found these same ratios in the consonances made by pipes of different lengths, glasses filled and partly filled when struck, weights attached to strings, and lengths and thickness of strings.

Boethius likens the communication of sound to waves caused by a stone thrown into quiet water, forming ever larger circles, except when the motion meets an obstacle and the motion rebounds, making new circles (1.14).

These views were elaborated, refined, and corrected during the fifteenth and sixteenth centuries. An important step was the coincidental publication in 1475 of two translations of the *Problems* of Aristotle (now believed to be partly by Aristotle, partly by his students), one a thirteenth-century Latin translation by Bartolomeo da Messina with a commentary by Pietro d'Abano (dated 1310) and the other by the fifteenth-century émigré Greek scholar Theodore Gaza.

In his commentary d'Abano states that to produce a sound a body must vibrate vigorously and rapidly so that the air is forcefully stretched (*Problems* 11.1). This motion is transmitted through the air not like a projectile but as air pushing air, so that the air reaching the ear is not the same as was stirred by the sounding body. Contrary to Plato's belief, high sounds do not travel faster, but the speed of the transmitted motion is faster (11.6), the air being broken up into smaller parts (11.19).

A significant insight into why the octave is heard as a consonance is the statement (19.39) that the higher note in an octave makes two percussions of the air for every one of the lower note: "the second impulse on the air of *nete* is *hypate*." (*Nete* and *hypate* are Greek names for notes that are an octave interval apart.) Problem 19.42 asks a question that Theodore Gaza rendered most clearly: "Why, if *nete* is struck and then dampened, does one seem to hear in response only *hypate?*" Although not adequately resolved until the late seventeenth century, this question inspired the study of sympathetic vibration.

Sixteenth-Century Theorists. Whether pitch differences were quantitative or qualitative exercised music theorists in the sixteenth century as it had the Greek philosophers. Lodovico Fogliano, a musician and Aristotelian scholar, took the middle road in his *Musica theorica* (Venice, 1529). Although he recognized that dividing a string through simple ratios such as 2:1, 3:2, 4:3, 5:4, 6:5, 5:3, and 8:5 yielded the consonances in their best sounding forms, he maintained, with Aristotle, that sound was a natural, not mathematical phenomenon. He concluded that the consonances should be defined and judged by purely sensory and practical criteria. He placed the thirds and sixths ahead of the fourth despite the latter's simpler ratio. Gioseffo Zarlino in *Le Istitutioni harmoniche* (The principles of harmony; Venice, 1558), although sympathetic to this view, insisted that the fourth was a perfect consonance and imposed a numerical limit of 6 on the consonant ratios, leaving out the minor sixth, 8:5. Vincenzo Galilei in *Dialogo della musica antica et della moderna* (Dialogue on ancient and modern music; Florence, 1581) uncoupled number from consonance again and declared that even sensitive musicians had no preference for the sound of simple ratios, and anyway they were impossible to maintain in polyphonic music.

Girolamo Fracastoro, trained in Padua, where Aristotelian natural science dominated instruction, studied the phenomenon of sympathetic vibration (*De sympathia et antipathia rerum;* Concerning the sympathy and antipathy of things; Venice, 1546) from a new angle. He reasoned that sound required a dense yet flexible medium that responded to the repeated blows of a vibrating object alternately compressing and decompressing the medium. The succession of compression or condensation (*addensatio*) and rarefaction (*distractio*) of the air behaved like a wave (*more undarum*) that spread around the sounding body in a circle. Fracastoro applied this theory to two strings tuned to the same pitch. When one string is plucked it impels the air to move the second string, first away from the first string, then returning toward its original position as the first string returns. Only strings tuned to a unison respond this way, because otherwise the second string impedes the motion of the air. Marin Mersenne (*Harmonicorum libri;* Books on harmonics; Paris, 1635), citing Fracastoro, applied the theory to strings not in unison but obtained invalid results that two Oxford physicists, William Noble and Thomas Pigot, corrected in 1673.

In an effort to explain the ear's preference for consonance, the mathematician and physicist Giovanni Battista Benedetti in a letter of around 1563 to the composer Cipriano de Rore (c. 1516–1565) and later published (*Diversarum speculationum mathematicarum et physicarum liber;* Book of diverse mathematical and physical theories; Turin, 1585) analyzed the motion of strings. He concluded that consonance arose from an equalization of percussion (*aequatio percussionum*) or from an equal concurrence of air waves (*aequali concursu undarum aeris*), or from the coincidence of their terminations (*conterminatio earum*). These terminations, or moments of no vibration, concur every two vibrations of the shorter string in an octave, every three in a twelfth, and so on. Benedetti arrives at an index of agreement by multiplying the two terms of the ratio of a consonance, for example 2 for an octave, 6 for a fifth, 30 for a minor third, 40 for a minor sixth, the numbers increasing but showing no break between "perfect" consonances (such as 12 for the fourth) and "imperfect" (such as 15 for the major sixth). He based his explanation on the assumption that the frequency of a sounding string under uniform tension varies inversely with its length. He had no experimental proof, since he could not determine the frequency, but once a means was found to count the vibrations he was proved correct.

Vincenzo Galilei challenged the legend of the Pythagoras hammers on two counts in his *Discorso intorno all'opere di Gioseffo Zarlino* (Discourse concerning the works of Gioseffo Zarlino of Chioggia; Florence, 1589). His experiments showed that weights in the ratio of 2:1 attached to strings do not produce an octave when the strings are plucked, because a proportion of 4:1 is needed, and pipe lengths in that ratio also cannot be depended on to produce an octave unless the diameter is taken into account, the required ratio of cubic volumes being 8:1. Mersenne confirmed these observations (*Traité de l'harmonie universelle;* Treatise on universal harmony; Paris, 1627) and further repudiated the blacksmith legend by proving through experiment that a glass half full of water makes a tritone against a full one and that when a hammer strikes an anvil or piece of metal the hammer's weight is not a factor in the pitch heard (*Harmonie universelle;* Paris, 1636).

The advances made in acoustic science, by discrediting Pythagorean mythology, liberated both music theory and composition from the tyranny of number ratios. Consonance and dissonance were now seen as qualities in a continuum of intervals, some more consonant, some more dissonant. The ear of the composer or musician judged their appropriateness to a particular musical context. This attitude is reflected in Italian secular music of the last decades of the sixteenth century.

See also **Music,** *subentry on* **Music Treatises.**

BIBLIOGRAPHY

Primary Works

Boethius, Anicius Manlius Severinus. *De institutione musica.* Edited by Gottfred Friedlein. Leipzig, Germany, 1867. Translated by Calvin M. Bower as *Fundamentals of Music.* New Haven, Conn., 1989.

Galilei, Vincenzo. "Three Scientific Essays." Edited by Claude V. Palisca. In *The Florentine Camerata.* New Haven, Conn., and London, 1989. Pages 152–207.

Secondary Works

Cohen, H. F. *Quantifying Music.* Dordrecht, Netherlands, 1984.

Dostrovsky, Sigalia, et al. *Geschichte der Musiktheorie.* Vol. 6, *Entstehung der Musikalischen Akustic, 1600–1750.* Darmstadt, Germany, 1987.

Drake, Stillman. "Renaissance Music and Experimental Science." *Journal of the History of Ideas* 31 (1970): 483–500.

Hunt, Frederick V. *Origins in Acoustics: The Science of Sound from Antiquity to the Age of Newton.* New Haven, Conn., 1978.

Palisca, Claude V. "Mersenne Pro Galilei Contra Zarlino." In *Essays in Honour of David Evatt Tunley.* Edited by Frank Callaway. Nedlands, Western Australia, 1995. Pages 61–72.

Palisca, Claude V. "Scientific Empiricism in Musical Thought." In *Seventeenth Century Science and the Arts.* Edited by H. H. Rhys. Princeton, N.J., 1961. Pages 91–137. Reprinted with prefatory note in Palisca, *Studies in the History and Theory of Italian Music,* Oxford, 1994, pp. 200–235.

Palisca, Claude V. "Was Galileo's Father an Experimental Scientist?" In *Music and Science in the Age of Galileo.* Edited by Victor Coelho. Dordrecht, Netherlands, 1992. Pages 143–151.

Walker, Daniel P. *Studies in Musical Science in the Late Renaissance.* London and Leiden, Netherlands, 1978.

CLAUDE V. PALISCA

ADOLESCENCE. *See* **Childhood.**

ADRIAN VI (Adrian Florenszoon Boeyens; 1459–1523), pope (1522–1523). Born in Utrecht into a middle-class family, Adrian studied Latin in Utrecht and Zwolle. He attended Louvain University, receiving an M.A. (1478) and Ph.D. (1491). He was ordained a priest in 1490. From 1490 to 1515 Adrian was a professor of scholastic theology in Louvain. In 1507 Maximilian I chose him as preceptor for his grandson, the future emperor Charles V. In 1515 Charles sent him as ambassador to secure his succession as king of Spain. During the king's absences he was entrusted with the regency in Spain. He was appointed bishop of Tortosa in 1516 and created cardinal in 1517. He became inquisitor general of Aragon (1516) and Castile (1518).

Because of the stalemate at the conclave of 1521, Adrian, though absent and little known, was elected pope on 9 January 1522, as a pious man acceptable to the emperor. He was crowned in Rome on 31 August. His efforts to foster peace in Europe and to organize a crusade against the Turks were in vain. In his dealings with Lutheranism he intervened at the Diet of Nürnberg (1522–1523) through his legate Francesco Chieregati, insisting on the implementation of the Edict of Worms (1521) against Luther while admitting the need for reform in the Catholic church.

Adrian was a studious and learned man, not in a humanistic, but in a traditional, scholastic sense. He maintained contact with humanists such as Desiderius Erasmus and Juan Luis Vives throughout his life. Because of his convictions about church reform he was not comfortable with the way of life led by his papal predecessors. The Romans disliked the ascetic, pious, and rather parsimonious Dutchman. His tomb in Santa Maria dell'Anima was commissioned by Cardinal Willem van Enkevoirt (1464–1534) and designed by Baldassare Peruzzi (1481–1536), a well-known Renaissance architect.

BIBLIOGRAPHY

Burmannus, Casparus. *Hadrianus VI sive analecta historica de Hadriano sexto trajectino papa romano.* Utrecht, Netherlands, 1727. A collection of older biographies, various documents, and some of Adrian's letters.

Ducke, Karl-Heinz. "Pope Adrian VI." In *Contemporaries of Erasmus*. Edited by Peter G. Bietenholz. Toronto, 1985. Vol. 1, Pages 5–9. On relations between Adrian and Erasmus, with a bibliography.

McNally, Robert E. "Pope Adrian VI (1522–23) and Church Reform." *Archivum historiae pontificiae* 7 (1969): 253–285.

Pastor, Ludwig. *The History of the Popes from the Close of the Middle Ages*. Vol. 9. Saint Louis, Mo., 1910. Pages 1–230. Still the most extensive treatment of Adrian's pontificate.

Jos E. Vercruysse

ADVICE BOOKS. *See* **Diaries and Memoirs.**

AFRICA, NORTH. One of the major questions for the history of the Mediterranean world is why Europe's Renaissance did not stimulate a creative exchange between Christian and Islamic civilizations. On this issue, the early modern history of Spain and North Africa provides some insight.

Western Islam and the Renaissance. Until the age of the Renaissance, the frontier of Islam in the Iberian Peninsula produced cultural exchanges between Islamic, Jewish, and Christian civilizations that transferred classical learning and values to Europe. The cultural experience that had characterized this frontier implied further exchanges between Mediterranean civilizations, but they did not happen. Rather, the Portuguese, Spanish, and Ottoman Empires jointly constructed a cultural barrier that sealed the Iberian spirit of the Renaissance within the new territorial boundaries of Europe.

From the middle of the fourteenth century to the beginning of the seventeenth century, the Muslim community was forced to leave the Iberian Peninsula, a region it had occupied since the eighth century. The uniqueness of this process was based not just upon the Christian control of all Iberia by 1492, but also on the decision of the Catholic kings to impose Christianity upon the peninsula's multiconfessional society. This act politicized religion, polarized the divisions between cultures, and ultimately led to the Spanish expulsion of the remaining Muslim and Jewish communities in 1609.

Such a divisive social event can hardly have created a hospitable environment during the sixteenth and seventeenth centuries for cultural exchanges between Europe and Islamic North Africa. The exclusionary social and religious relationships that separated North Africa from Spain were, however, not simply a Christian imposition. For as the balance of power against Islam shifted in the direction of the Christian states of Iberia, powerful Muslim empires ruled by Turks restored Islamic civilization in the east and then extended a conservative definition of Islamic culture into North Africa during the sixteenth century.

North Africa before the Turks. By the fourteenth century, North Africa had ceased to provide military energy for Spanish Islam. Yet despite the ultimate failure of the Holy War in the Iberian Peninsula, the regular mobilization of troops south of the Strait of Gibraltar had firmly implanted Islam throughout the Maghrib. Then, Muslim migrants fleeing from fifteenth-century Christian oppression simply consolidated what was an overwhelmingly Muslim identity for North Africa.

In Portugal and Spain the arrival of the Renaissance and the development of a homogeneous religious society went hand in hand with innovative acts of state building. Within North Africa, however, a widespread attachment to Islam did not bring on a new political order. Rather, the rulers of the three North African dynasties founded after the thirteenth-century collapse of Almohad rule—the Marinid, Hafsid, and Zayyanid—presided over a period of political decline. On the cultural plane during this same era, the educated elite neither challenged inherited religious thinking nor, with the exception of the brilliant sociologist of politics, Ibn Khaldun, infused the study of human affairs with a new spirit.

When the Spanish took Granada in 1492, the logic of events seemed bound to add North Africa to Christian territories. This did not take place. Christian rulers simply turned away from the Muslim world to form new seagoing empires on the basis of superior maritime technologies. The ensuing age of Iberian oceanic expansion then began a period of innovation that shifted the balance of power between European and Islamic civilizations in favor of Europe. While Muslim sailors informed Ottoman sultans of the pattern-breaking accomplishments of the Spanish and Portuguese navigators, this information provoked no effort at the heart of the Islamic world to acquire European innovations in maritime technology and science.

Turks and the Revival of Islam. From the eleventh to the fifteenth centuries, the rulers of Islamic lands confronted a challenge capable of destroying Islamic civilization. For them the great problem was how to tame and acculturate wave after wave of nomadic invaders who entered the Muslim world from the Eurasian steppe. By the beginning of the sixteenth century the emergence of powerful, agriculturally based Turkish empires—Ottoman, Safavid, and Mogul—signaled a recovery of Islamic military, political, and cultural power. The consequence of this success for the Mediterranean region of the Muslim world was the expulsion of the Christian crusaders from the Middle East, the defeat of the Byzantine Empire, and an assault on Eastern Europe that reached the gates of Vienna in 1529.

While the Ottomans borrowed powder weapons from Europeans, administrative techniques from Byzantine bureaucrats, and recruits from Balkan populations, the internal cultural context of their empire building rested on conservative foundations. Here the most important contrast with European cultural development was the absence of institutional support for innovative thought.

Between 1526 and 1580 the Ottoman Empire extended its imperial system to all of North Africa except Morocco, where the Saadians maintained a tributary relationship with Istanbul. Even though this placed a Muslim empire on the doorstep of Spain, the Ottomans and the Spanish agreed upon a truce in 1580. A subsequent unwillingness of the two empires to resume large-scale military operations along the coasts of the Mediterranean Sea cemented the cultural barrier between the two civilizations. When European sailors and merchants arrived off the coast of North Africa with new ships, weapons, and business techniques at the beginning of the seventeenth century, the Ottomans, absorbed with the effort of managing a huge agricultural empire, made little effort to acquire the latest technological advances of the Europeans.

The Renaissance and North Africa. What influence the Renaissance had upon North Africa depends upon one's historical perspective. From a Mediterranean point of view the impact of the Renaissance on North African institutions was slight. The Voyages of Discovery, internal European affairs, and the balance of power between differing Mediterranean empires did not encourage North Africans to participate in the creative initiatives that the Renaissance stimulated in Europe. However, viewed through modern, global lenses, the breakdown in cultural exchanges between the two civilizations contributed to the growth of unprecedented inequalities between European and Muslim states and peoples. Since the consequences of lagging behind Europe were, and are, so fraught with violence for the heirs of both civilizations, the Renaissance has in-

deed influenced both North African society and modern civilization.

See also Ottoman Empire *and* Spain, *subentry on* The Spanish Kingdoms.

BIBLIOGRAPHY

Primary Work

Ibn Khaldun. *The Muqaddima: An Introduction to History.* Translated by Franz Rosenthal. 3 vols. New York and London, 1958. An analytical introduction to an Islamic history written by the fourteenth-century North African historian Ibn Khaldun (1332–1406).

Secondary Works

Hess, Andrew C. *The Forgotten Frontier: A History of the Sixteenth Century Ibero-African Frontier.* Chicago, 1978. A comparative Ottoman-Habsburg history of the early modern Christian-Muslim frontier separating North Africa from Spain.

Huff, Toby E. *The Rise of Early Modern Science: Islam, China, and the West.* Cambridge, U.K., and New York, 1993. A study of why modern science emerged in Europe but not in the civilizations of Islam and China.

Lewis, Bernard. *The Muslim Discovery of Europe.* New York and London, 1982. A history of the sources and nature of Muslim knowledge concerning Europe with an emphasis on the early modern and modern periods.

ANDREW C. HESS

AFRICA, SUB-SAHARAN. European interest and knowledge of Africa in the fourteenth century was limited. Merchants involved in the trade of North Africa provided most of the information and none of it was firsthand. When the kingdom of Ethiopia sent a mission addressed to the "king of the Spains" in 1306, it was taken to be from Prester John, a legendary Christian monarch previously believed to rule in the Far East, India, or Ethiopia. From that point onward, most Europeans agreed that Prester John was the ruler of Ethiopia. Iberian diplomacy, especially Aragonese and Portuguese diplomacy, occasionally sought to develop strategic alliances with Ethiopia in order to outflank the Muslim powers of the Nile Valley, symbolized by negotiations for a dynastic union between Ethiopia and Aragon in 1428.

Ethiopia continued its own outreach to the west. Ethiopian monks traveled to Cyprus and to Italy and were present at the Council of Florence in 1414, when there was some talk of reconciling the Ethiopian Orthodox Church with the Roman Catholic Church. Ethiopian linguistic material was studied in Renaissance Italy, and commercial contacts, mediated especially by Catalans and various Italians, shaped an interest in the lands of the supposed Prester John, represented by an increasingly accurate portrayal of Ethiopian geography on European maps.

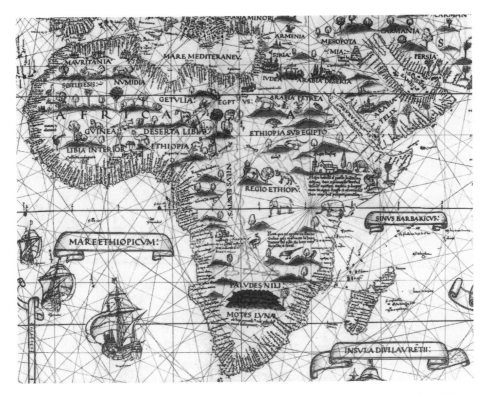

Africa. Africa and the Mediterranean from the world map of Diego Ribeiro (Seville, 1529).
MAP DIVISION, LIBRARY OF CONGRESS

While the relationship with Ethiopia was developing, Europeans began naval explorations into the Atlantic. Lanzarotto Malocello, a Genoese sailor, discovered the sea route to the Canaries, probably by accident, about 1312, and in the following years merchants and raiders from most western Mediterranean powers visited the islands. There were several attempts at colonization, the first successful one by Normans operating in Spanish service in 1405.

The frequent sailing in the seas around the Canaries resulted in the discovery of the uninhabited Atlantic islands of the Azores and Madeira as well as a solution to the age-old navigational problem of making a round-trip voyage to Senegal. Europeans were aware from trading contacts in North Africa that mines in western Africa produced the gold that the Muslim merchants offered them, and maps from the early fourteenth century show a substantial, detailed knowledge of the geography of the western Sudan. Ocean visits to the region, however, were bedeviled by the Canary current, which allowed voyages to the south, but not return trips. The settlement of the Atlantic islands made it possible to bypass the current, and by the mid-fifteenth century Portuguese ships were regularly visiting the Senegal area.

Most of the early Portuguese exploration was financed privately, and commercial motives prevailed. Consequently, as soon as the profitable trade of the Senegal and Gambia regions was attained, there was no motivation to explore farther. It was only when the Portuguese crown sought to monopolize and regulate trade that the private merchants pushed on along the coast in the 1470s, eventually entering the Gulf of Guinea, locating important new sources of gold in the Gold Coast (modern Ghana), and reaching the Kingdom of Benin.

When the Portuguese envoys to Benin met ambassadors from an unknown inland country bearing cross-shaped insignia, they concluded that they were close to the lands of Prester John. Acting on this belief, the Portuguese crown dispatched Diogo Cão on an exploration mission to locate the route to Prester John in 1482. At the same time that Cão left by sea, Pero de Corvilhão was sent to reach Ethiopia by land.

Cão's sailors discovered that Prester John's land was not near Benin, and moreover that the African coast stretched southward for many more miles. The length of the coast discouraged the crown's belief that its sailors could easily reach from Benin to "In-

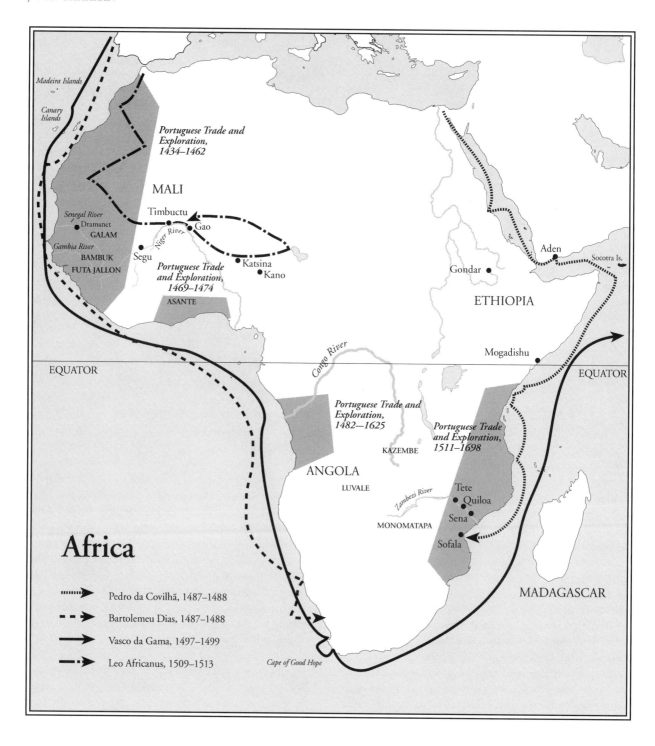

Africa

‣‣‣‣‣▶   Pedro da Covilhã, 1487–1488

- - -▶   Bartolemeu Dias, 1487–1488

——▶   Vasco da Gama, 1497–1499

–‧–‧▶   Leo Africanus, 1509–1513

dia" (which in the geography of the time included Ethiopia), and it was not until the end of the fifteenth century that Bartolomeu Dias (1488) and Vasco da Gama (1498) found the way around the southern tip of Africa. To some degree, their failure to reach Christian Ethiopia was compensated by the conversion of the king of Kongo to Christianity in 1491,

following up on contacts initiated by Cão's voyage. Moreover, Corvilhão did reach Ethiopia, and it was through his mediation that the Luso-Ethiopian alliance of 1520 was concluded.

The first relations between Portuguese and west Africans were hostile, born out of the Portuguese propensity to raid for slaves. But after African naval vessels inflicted a series of reverses on the Portuguese, the crown negotiated more peaceful relations through its emissary, Diogo Gomes, between 1456 and 1462. This was followed by the growth of trade in a variety of African commodities, including gold, pepper, ivory, and slaves (primarily prisoners of African wars after the initial period of raiding). The Portuguese crown entertained a number of emissaries from African countries, and a few toyed with the possibility of becoming Christian, though only in Kongo was the initial interest followed by permanent conversion.

See also biography of Leo Africanus.

BIBLIOGRAPHY

Thornton, John. *Africa and Africans in the Making of the Atlantic World, 1400–1800.* 2d ed. New York, 1998.

Winius, George D. *Portugal, the Pathfinder: Journeys from the Medieval toward the Modern World, 1300–ca. 1600.* Madison, Wisc., 1995.

JOHN K. THORNTON

AFRICANUS, LEO (al-Hasan ibn Muhammad al-Wassan az-Zayyati; c. 1490–c. 1554), geographer of Africa. Born to a Muslim family in Granada between 1489 and 1495, he was forced to emigrate to Morocco after the Spanish conquest of his native city. Well educated, he traveled widely in Morocco during his youth, performed some service in administration, and visited the western Sudan (West Africa) on two occasions between 1509 and 1513. In 1518 he was captured by Christian pirates and presented as a slave to Pope Leo X, who gave him the name of Leo Africanus when he was subsequently baptized as a Christian. Later in his life, and in spite of the favor he had been shown in Rome, Leo returned to North Africa and resumed his Muslim faith.

While in captivity in Rome, and sometime before 1529, Leo wrote *Della descrittione dell'Africa,* a detailed geography especially of Morocco but including several chapters on the western Sudan, where at the time the Songhai Empire was at its height. The original version may have been in Arabic, but it was published in Italian by Giovani Battista Ramusio, author and editor of travel literature, in 1550. It was frequently re-edited and translations were made into most European languages, including an English one by John Pory in 1600.

Upon its publication, *Descrittione* became the source for much of Europe's knowledge of the interior regions of West Africa, partly because of the popularity of Ramusio's collection of travels, but also because it was a vivid firsthand account of the area.

It was particularly influential in European cartography, especially for those regions of Africa which lay sufficiently far inland that they were unknown to coastal travelers from the Portuguese navigations of the fifteenth century and beyond. *Descrittione* continued to be favored by cartographers and even geographers until travelers' accounts of the eighteenth century gradually replaced it. It remains today an important primary source for historians of sixteenth-century West Africa.

See also **Africa, North**; **Africa, Sub-Saharan**.

BIBLIOGRAPHY

L'Africain, Jean-Léon (Leo Africanus). *Description de l'Afrique.* Edited and translated by A. Épaulard. 2 vols. Paris, 1956.

JOHN K. THORNTON

AGRICOLA, GEORGIUS (George Bauer; 1494–1555), German scholar and mineralogist. Born in Glauchau, Saxony, Georgius Agricola studied classical literature at the University of Leipzig between 1514 and 1518. Although he began to study medicine in 1522, until 1523 Agricola trained primarily as a grammarian, and he sought to deepen his classical education in Italy. In Basel in the autumn of 1523 he almost certainly met with Erasmus and with the printer Hieronymus Froben. In 1523 Agricola began to follow courses at the University of Bologna, and in August 1524 he took the degree in medicine. He then moved to Venice, where he found employment in the printing house of Aldo Manuzio. He collaborated on editions of medical works by Galen, Hippocrates, and Paulus da Egina.

Agricola developed an interest in mining and mineralogy after he became town physician in 1526 in Sankt Jochimsthal, a mining town, where he realized that Greek and Latin authors had not examined systematically the nature of the subterranean world. To fill this void Agricola published a dialogue entitled *Bermannus sive de re metallica* (Bermannus, on metals; 1530). This small booklet was the first publication concerning metallurgy and mining to be published in Latin. The dialogue presented itself as a work by a humanist addressed to an audience of learned scholars rather than to miners. Erasmus wrote an introduction praising Agricola's ability to describe clearly the complex world of mining.

In 1546 Agricola published, at Froben's press in Basel, a collection of mineralogical tracts, all written in Latin, in which he developed the ideas he set forth in the *Bermannus.* In the most important tract of this collection, *De natura fossilium* (On fossils), Agricola introduced the first classification of minerals (called

Metallurgy. An iron-smelting furnace and forge. From *De re metallica* by Georgius Agricola.

"fossils" at the time) based on their external characters. In 1553 Agricola sent to Hieronymus Froben the manuscript of his masterpiece, *De re metallica* (On metals), the preparation of which had been announced since 1530. *De re metallica* was published in 1556, just a few months after the death of its author. With its 292 woodcuts and twelve books it was the longest work on mining ever printed, and it was the first book on mining to be printed in a folio format.

In this work Agricola presented a systematic and thorough survey of metallurgical knowledge, the techniques employed to work metals, the laboratories and workshops used by miners, and the machines and tools used to excavate and maintain the shafts and the veins. *De re metallica* was a huge suc-

cess because it provided comprehensive information and clarified the nomenclature in metallurgy. It was translated into German (1557) and Italian (1563) and quickly became one of the most successful scientific works printed in the sixteenth century.

BIBLIOGRAPHY

Primary Work

Agricola, Georgius. *De re metallica*. Translated into English by Herbert Clark Hoover and Lou Henry Hoover. New York, 1950.

Secondary Works

Beretta, Marco. "Humanism and Chemistry: The Spread of Georgius Agricola's Metallurgical Writings." *Nuncius* 12 (1997): 17–47.

Wilsdorf, Helmut. *Georg Agricola und seine Zeit*. Berlin, 1956.

MARCO BERETTA

AGRICOLA, RUDOLF (Roelof Huisman; 1444–1485), Frisian scholar, humanist. Agricola was the pioneer of humanistic learning in the Low Countries and Germany, as well as an educational reformer and theoretician of dialectic and rhetoric.

Life and Career. Born in the countryside around Groningen, Agricola was the illegitimate son of a church official, and he grew up in the house of his mother and stepfather. He was not only intellectually talented but also musically gifted (both as a composer and a performer), and he enjoyed painting and drawing. He received his primary education at St. Martin's school in Groningen. Having gained financial independence in 1454 thanks to a prebend, or stipend, granted to his father by the bishop of Münster, Agricola studied arts from 1456 onward, first in Erfurt (B.A., 1458), then in Cologne and Louvain (M.A., 1465). In Louvain he also began to study law. Possibly encouraged by the circle of humanistic scholars gathered around the canonist Raimundus de Marliano, who taught in Louvain, he had crossed the Alps to Pavia by 1469, where he first continued his law studies but soon turned to the new *studia humanitatis*. From 1475 to 1479 he lived in Ferrara, where he was in the service of Duke Ercole I d'Este (1433–1505) as an organist and learned Greek with Giovanni Battista Guarini (1538–1612). During his Italian years Agricola not only attained a thorough knowledge of ancient Greco-Roman literature, history, and moral philosophy, he also acquired great competence as a Latinist and orator.

He returned to the north in 1479, spending that summer in Dillingen, where he completed his main work, *De inventione dialectica libri tres* (Three books on dialectical invention; printed 1515). In

1480 he was appointed secretary to the city of Groningen, then an important regional power. Although Agricola lived among a number of men who favored humanism, and though his office allowed him to visit libraries and meet like-minded people during business trips, he was not satisfied either with his function or with the intellectual climate in Groningen. In 1482, after having declined two offers of appointment elsewhere, he decided to take up the invitation to join his friend Johann von Dalberg in Heidelberg. Dalberg was bishop of Worms and chancellor of Heidelberg University. After his delayed arrival in 1484, Agricola was an active member of the intellectual community in Heidelberg, lecturing, delivering speeches, and participating in academic disputations. He also began to learn Hebrew. In 1485, Agricola and Dalberg went to Rome to attend the consecration of Pope Innocent VIII (1484–1492); Agricola wrote the speech that Dalberg delivered before the new pope. On the journey home Agricola fell sick. Although he interrupted his trip to recuperate, he arrived sick again in Heidelberg and died shortly afterward.

Agricola's Works. Agricola worked for the restoration of pure latinity, promoted educational reforms, and aspired to unite pagan learning with Christian piety. His works include eight orations (one containing an idealized biography of Petrarch), six Latin translations of short ancient Greek texts and one of a French letter by a contemporary, twenty-six poems, a correspondence of fifty-four letters (fifty by Agricola), the treatise *De inventione dialectica libri tres,* a brief monograph on the universals (transmitted in two versions, one still unpublished), and brief commentaries on a part of the late ancient excerpts from Seneca the Elder's rhetorical works and on Cicero's *De lege Manilia.* Finally, there exist two manuscripts written by Agricola, one containing works by Tacitus, one containing Pliny's letters, and also a manuscript of Pliny and three editions—Tacitus, Pliny, and Boethius—containing printed notes by Agricola or annotations in his hand. There are also some spurious and lost writings.

Agricola's greatest achievement is his *De inventione dialectica libri tres.* Starting from his discontent with contemporary scholastic dialectic, Agricola combined Aristotelian dialectic and rhetoric and thus provided a comprehensive theory of methodical thinking and reasoning. Book 1 contains a detailed account of twenty-four *loci argumentorum,* combining the traditional dialectical and rhetorical *loci,* or topics. Book 2 focuses on the different parts of dia-

Rudolf Agricola. CULVER PICTURES

lectic. These include the substance of dialectic (the *quaestio* and its subdivisions), and the instrument of dialectic (the *oratio* or ratiocination)—two basic forms of reasoning are discerned, namely *argumentatio,* addressed to an audience that resists or must be persuaded into assent, and *expositio,* setting matters out for an audience that follows willingly. Book 2 also discusses the treatment of the *loci,* that is, the method of recognizing *loci* in a given literary text, and of using the *loci* to find arguments.

In book 3, Agricola discusses the techniques of moving and pleasing the audience; he adds a section on *dispositio* and stresses in the concluding chapter the importance of constant training in writing. *De inventione dialectica* is a specialized but readable manual, mainly because the rules are frequently illustrated by means of detailed examples from classical authors. Despite its title, *De inventione* was a treatise on humanistic rhetoric, not logic, and it was enormously influential. During the sixteenth century it was evidently much read by advanced students, professors, and theoreticians, and thus influenced both teaching practices and scholarly research concerning rhetoric and dialectic.

Most of Agricola's works did not appear before the sixteenth century. Several went through numerous printings, especially in centers of humanistic culture and learning such as Louvain, Cologne, and Paris, and thus show the importance of Agricola's legacy for the development of humanism in northern Europe. These works include *De inventione dialectica*, the translations of Isocrates's *Praecepta ad demonicum* (Exhortation to Demonicus, on practical ethics) and of Aphthonius's *Progymnasmata* (Preliminary exercises), and letter 38 to Jacob Barbireau, *De formando studio* (On the organization of the program of studies). This letter provides a standard description of the humanistic arts curriculum and of its methodology. It owes its popularity especially to the fact that it includes a brief description of the method of collecting writing materials by means of commonplaces (*loci communes*).

Agricola was not only a guide for many of his friends (such as the Deventer schoolmaster Alexander Hegius [c. 1433–1498], whose Latin he corrected and to whom he taught Greek), but he also inspired Erasmus (c. 1466–1536)—who, as a schoolboy in Deventer, saw him once—and many other humanists of Erasmus's generation. Between 1492 and 1539 as many as six biographies of Agricola were written, bearing witness to the importance attached in that period to Agricola and his intellectual legacy.

BIBLIOGRAPHY

Primary Works

Agricola, Rudolf. *De inventione dialectica*. Edited by Lothar Mundt. Tübingen, Germany, 1992. Critical edition with German translation and commentary.

Agricola, Rudolf. *De inventione dialectica. Lucubrationes*. Nieuwkoop, Netherlands, 1967. A facsimile of the 1539 Cologne edition.

Agricola, Rudolf. *Écrits sur la dialectique et l'humanisme*. Edited by Marc van der Poel. Paris, 1997. Anthology with French translation and commentary.

Agricola, Rudolf. *Exhortatio ad clerum Wormatiensem*. Edited by Lewis W. Spitz and A. Benjamin. In *Archiv für Reformationsgeschichte* 54 (1963): 1–15.

Agricola, Rudolf. *Oratio de vita Petrarchae*. Edited by Ludwig Bertalot. In *La bibliofilia* 30 (1928): 382–404. Reprint in *Studien zum italienischen und deutschen Humanismus*. 2 vols. Edited by P. O. Kristeller. Rome, 1975. Vol. 2, pages 1–29.

Agricola, Rudolf. *Oratio in laudem philosophiae*. Edited by Hans Rupprich. In Hans Rupprich, *Humanismus und Renaissance in den deutschen Städten und an den Universitäten*. Darmstadt, Germany, 1964. Page 144–159.

Agricola, Rudolf. *Oratio rectoratus pro domino Paulo de Baenst*. Edited by Agostino Sottili. In *Ut granum sinapis: Essays on Neo-Latin Literature in Honour of Jozef IJsewijn*. Edited by Gilbert Tournoy and Dirk Sacré. Louvain, Belgium, 1997. Pages 87–130.

Agricola, Rudolf. *Scholia in orationem pro lege Manilia*. Edited by Marc van der Poel. In *Lias* 24 (1997): 1–35.

Dörfler-Dierken, Angelika, and Wolfgang Schibel. *Rudolf Agricolas Anna mater—Heiligenverehrung und Philosophie*. In *Rudolf Agricola, 1444–1485: Protagonist des nordeuro-*

päischen Humanismus, zum 550. Geburtstag. Edited by Wilhelm Kühlmann. Bern, Switzerland, 1994. Pages 293–354. Edition of poem 5.

Schoonbeeg, Pieter. "Agricola alter Maro." In *Proceedings of the International Conference at the University of Groningen, 28–30 October 1985*. Edited by Fokke Akkerman and Arjo Vanderjagt. Leiden, Netherlands, 1988. Page 190. Edition of poems 27 and 28.

Van der Laan, Adrie H. *Anatomie van een taal: Rodolphus Agricola en Antonius Liber aan de wieg van het humanistische Latijn in de Lage Landen (1469–1485)*. Groningen, Netherlands, 1998. Dissertation. Critical edition of Agricola's letters with introduction and linguistic commentary. A critical edition of the entire correspondence, with English translation, edited by Fokke Akkerman and Adrie H. van der Laan is forthcoming.

Waterbolk, Edzo Hendrik. "Deux poèmes inconnus de Rodolphe Agricola?" *Humanistica Lovaniensia* 21 (1972): 37–49. Edition of poems 25 and 26.

Wiegand, Hermann, ed. *Mentibus at vatum deus insidet . . . Zu Rudolf Agricolas lateinischer Dichtung*. In *Rudolf Agricola, 1444–1485: Protagonist des nordeuropäischen Humanismus, zum 500. Geburtstag*. Edited by Wilhelm Kühlmann. Bern, Switzerland, 1994. Page 261–291. Edition of poems 3 and 15.

Secondary Works

Akkerman, Fokke, and Arjo J. Vanderjagt, eds. *Rodolphus Agricola Phrisius, 1444–1485: Proceedings of the International Conference at the University of Groningen, 28–30 October 1985*. Leiden, Netherlands, 1988. Contains twenty-six articles and a full bibliography of works and studies, including information on old editions and the main manuscript sources.

Kühlmann, Wilhelm, ed. *Rudolf Agricola, 1444–1485: Protagonist des nordeuropäischen Humanismus, zum 550. Geburtstag*. Bern, Switzerland, 1994.

Mack, Peter. *Renaissance Argument: Valla and Agricola in the Traditions of Rhetoric and Dialectic*. Leiden, Netherlands, 1993.

Weiss, J. M. "The Six Lives of Rudolph Agricola: Forms and Functions of the Humanist Biography." *Humanistica Lovaniensia* 30 (1981): 19–39.

MARC VAN DER POEL

AGRICULTURE. The concept of "Renaissance agriculture" may be understood as the process by which the plants and the methods of cultivation that became the basis of the "agricultural revolution" of the eighteenth century were studied in books, gardens, and fields. The fact that modern European agronomy was first developed in the course of the deliberate retrieval of classical agronomy makes this a characteristically Renaissance endeavor. At the same time, the genetic plasticity of southern European cultivars ensured that Mediterranean gardens and farms became a laboratory for northern European agriculture. Therefore the agricultural revolution was the end result of the transfer of Mediterranean agricultural styles and experience to northern Europe.

The beginning of Renaissance agriculture is marked by the completion of Pietro de Crescenzi's *Liber cultus ruris* (Book of estate cultivation) around 1320. The period is punctuated by two events. First, the printing in 1472 of four Roman agricultural works—those of Cato, Columella, Palladius, and Varro—in one volume, *Rerum rusticarum scriptores* (Writers on rural subjects; Venice), made the agronomy of the ancients easily available to estate owners. Second, the discovery of America in 1492 brought a stream of new food plants to Europe, where they were studied by botanists and agriculturists and acclimatized in gardens for future use. The text of Palladius survived the early Middle Ages in only one manuscript, Columella in two; but by the fifteenth century copies of both proliferated.

The Significance of Forage Crops.

The key elements in agricultural change in this period were the planting of forage crops and the expansion of irrigation in order to water them. Growing fodder crops allowed farmers to keep more animals over the winter, thus increasing their supply of manure. Nitrogen-fixing crops like alfalfa and clover restored fertility to the soil, permitting the reduction or elimination of fallowing. The pivotal forage crop was alfalfa (also known as lucerne), a nitrogen-fixing grass that had been cultivated in antiquity, the knowledge of which had been lost in medieval Italy. A perennial crop that requires irrigation for seeding and reproduction, in many places it grew wild or as a weed in wheat fields or pastures. It continued to be cultivated in Spain, where the Arabs had reintroduced it as the crop they knew as *fiṣfiṣah* or *faṣfaṣah*. The recovery of alfalfa in Latin Europe was a complex process that involved the identification of the term "*herba medica*" in the texts of the Roman agronomists. *Medica* referred not to medicine but to the Middle Eastern provenance of this grass; it became *melica* or *meliga* in vulgar Latin; thus medieval readers confused it with *millica* (millet), which was in turn confused with sorghum, an African cereal that the Arabs diffused throughout their empire. Adding to the confusion, it was frequently mistaken for sainfoin (*Onobrychis spp.*), the same name denoting both crops in different vernacular nomenclatures.

Pietro de Crescenzi recommended sowing turnips as forage and rotating wheat and corn on irrigated fields without fallowing, but he did not mention either alfalfa or clover. Lucius Junius Moderatus Columella's first-century account of alfalfa became the standard treatment; indeed, even the Arab agronomists of Islamic Spain had perpetuated his system,

ascribing it simply to "Yunius." Rutilius Taurus Aemilianus Palladius (fourth–fifth century) adapted Columella's system to the kind of subsistence farming that became the norm in late Roman and medieval Europe. His *De re rustica* (On agriculture) was the most influential Roman text in the Middle Ages. In the sixteenth century, abridgments of Palladius that stressed grafting techniques were popular everywhere in Europe. Just such a shortened version known popularly as "Geoffrey upon Pallady," by Godfridus the Englishman, encouraged later English writers like Sir John Prise, a mid-sixteenth-century official and landowner, to focus on Mediterranean agriculture as a source of innovation for northern Europe. Palladian texts were often read together with that of Crescenzi, annotated, and compared with one another. According to Mauro Ambrosoli, the relationship between agronomic texts and practical experience changed in the course of the sixteenth century. Medieval writers did not reveal their sources because "they themselves constituted tradition and source," owing to the dominant model of scholarship as the transmission of authoritative texts (*The Wild and the Sown,* p. 242). But agricultural writers of the sixteenth century were obliged to defend their sources by checking them against information obtained from persons directly engaged in agriculture. These texts and editions were directed primarily at owners of manors or agricultural estates, although the abridgments they spawned and the low cost of books extended their social reach.

Alfalfa eventually made a comeback as a cultivated crop in Italy, where it was introduced as "Spanish grass" around 1540. At the same time, the availability of printed botanical works, particularly *De materia medica* (On medicine) of Dioscorides (from 1478), made possible the identification of wild alfalfa in various areas of Italy, particular the Veneto. The irrigation of alfalfa diffused through northern Italy during the second half of the sixteenth century, sometimes in tandem with rice cultivation, informed by the Italian translation (1557) of Gabriel Alonso de Herrera's *Obra de agricultura* (Book on agriculture).

Herrera (c. 1480–c. 1539) was a horticulturalist who worked mainly in Granada and a traveler who observed agricultural practices in Spain, France, and Italy. His *Obra de agricultura* (1513) was a typical Renaissance product, mixing classical citations (Pliny, cited 602 times), Palladius (529), Columella (517), and Varro (165) with the medieval compilation of Crescenzi (888) and the Muslim authors Ibn Sīnā (Avicenna) and the agronomist Ibn Wafid. Herrera states that the climatic and geographical unity of the Mediterranean basin is what make his sources authoritative and that he has confirmed theory with his own observations. Herrera's approach, based in part on the Hispano-Arab agronomists, was that water was the primary regulator of soil quality, of greater importance than fertilizer. The Italian translation of the *Obra* became the standard Italian authority on alfalfa, described as an irrigated crop. A decade later Camillo Tarello marked the beginning of modern Italian agronomy by suggesting the rotation of wheat with clover.

Interrelated processes taking place in sixteenth-century Provence illustrate the key features of the Renaissance agricultural tradition. First, meadows were enclosed so that alfalfa could be planted in them. Second, the viability of this practice had already been established by the growing of alfalfa by horticultural methods in small gardens. Gardens were, in this sense, laboratories in which wild plants could be tested under domestic conditions, where such plants could be identified using botanical texts, and whose cultivation could be perpetuated by the gathering of seed. Subsequently, Provence became a kind of agricultural emporium whose seeds were exported all over Europe.

Irrigation and Drainage.   Provence was also a center of large-scale irrigation plans in the second half of the sixteenth century. In 1558 an agricultural entrepreneur named Adam de Craponne built a large irrigation canal bearing his name, with water from the Durance River. In eastern Spain the irrigated agricultural area was vastly extended. In Alicante the completion of the Tibi Dam (1594) enabled the creation of a whole new layer of water rights assigned to proprietors of newly irrigated fields. Between 1401 and 1529 a series of plans were hatched to divert the water of the Júcar River to the Turia, which watered the *huerta* (market garden) of Valencia, or to effect a more southerly diversion of the Júcar, toward Elche. Between 1480 and 1600 the *huerta* of Murcia increased in size by about one-third, as crop specialization, particularly the white mulberry (for silkworms), became the norm throughout the lower Segura valley. Farther west, the Imperial Canal of Aragón (constructed 1529–1539) made possible a vast expansion of irrigation in the Ebro valley. Throughout northern Italy the expansion of irrigation systems was linked to the cultivation of both rice and forage crops planted on meadowlands, particularly during the last quarter of the sixteenth century. In temperate regions, such as England and Switzer-

land, irrigated "water meadows" were created on which to seed forage crops.

In Holland a hydraulic revolution took place in the fifteenth century with the draining of inland seas to form new polders (older polders had been reclaimed from the sea earlier). This new phase of drainage reclamation was accomplished with windmills (the first polder mill dating from 1408). The process was capital intensive and required the reorganization of water administration, involving the formation of a regional water court of seven dyke-reeves under the nominal directorship of a bailiff who represented the count of Holland. In the second half of the sixteenth century the English fenlands passed through a period of agricultural expansion midway between the assarts, or lands cleared for cultivation, of the late Middle Ages and the large-scale drainage reclamation plans of the seventeenth century, an advance of which was formulated in 1589 by Humphrey Bradley, a Dutchman who later formed a company for draining lakes and swamps in France.

Plants from the New World.   The first American food plant to diffuse in Europe was maize (sweet corn). As early as 1498 Columbus himself observed that it was abundant in Castile. The plant diffused so quickly that its origin was forgotten. Leonhard Fuchs (1501–1566) and other botanists called it "Turkish wheat" (*frumentum turcicum, grano turco*). Sweet potatoes were also grown in sixteenth-century Europe. The botanist Charles de L'Écluse (1526–1609) saw them in Málaga in 1544. They were cultivated in the Canary Islands, and in 1580 the physician and botanist Nicolás Monardes (c. 1493–1588) reported boatloads of sweet potatoes arriving in Seville from Vélez-Málaga. Most early citations of "potato" in fact refer to sweet potatoes. In the sixteenth century the white potato was grown in gardens as a medicinal plant or just as a curiosity. Tobacco was cultivated early as a medicinal plant; Monardes had some in his garden in Seville. It was grown commercially in Italy by the end of the century. In general, however, the commercialization of New World plants in European agriculture was a phenomenon of the seventeenth century.

Change in Early Modern Agriculture.   There were two models of agricultural improvement in this period. An early model sought to increase manuring and eliminate fallowing. Later, ridge and furrow plowing was replaced by cross plowing (a second plowing perpendicular to the first): forage crops had to be tilled flat in any case, so they could be

Agriculture. "The Labors of the Twelve Months" from *Le rustican* by Pietro de Crescenzi, c. 1460. MUSÉE CONDÉ, CHANTILLY, FRANCE/GIRAUDON/ART RESOURCE, NY

mowed. However, attention to the quality of the soil and its relation to plowing and irrigating was a hallmark of Renaissance agriculture. There was also a change in ideas on seeding. The classical wisdom that it was wasteful to sow thickly on poor soil was reversed in the Middle Ages, then retrieved in the Renaissance (possibly related to the experience of gardens, where seeds were planted in rows and spaced evenly).

It would be premature to generalize on the relationship between the social reorganization of farmland and agricultural change, because the patterns differed widely from region to region. It had been widely supposed since the sixteenth century that the "rationalization" of agriculture was furthered by the process of enclosing fields from commonly held pasture or open fields, because it gave each landowner freedom to decide which plants to grow. But forage plants could, and were, sown on open fields as well as on enclosed ones, and enclosure itself had less to do with increasing arable yields than did cross plowing, improvement of cultivating techniques, and the availability of high-quality seed.

Oddly enough, the "agricultural revolution" of the early Middle Ages as proposed by Lynn White Jr., and which featured the shift from ox- to horsepower, and a change from a two-course to a three-course rotation that permitted the growing of oats with which to feed the horses, may not, in fact, have been completed until the sixteenth century. Therefore, the changes discussed above may well have been taking place at the vanguard of European agriculture, primarily on enclosed fields, while the transformation of traditional agriculture was still proceeding in the open fields.

Finally, the development of a capitalist model of agriculture changed the way in which agricultural land was surveyed. Linear measurements by which metes and bounds were established in medieval Europe were supplemented, from mid-sixteenth century on, by square measures of area. Traditional measures of land (for example, according to how much a team could plow in a day or a year) and of irrigation water (for example, according to how much water could move a millstone) came increasingly to be quantified in standard measurement units.

See also **Peasantry.**

BIBLIOGRAPHY

Ambrosoli, Mauro. *The Wild and the Sown: Botany and Agriculture in Western Europe, 1350–1850.* Translated by Mary McCann Salvatorelli. Cambridge, U.K., 1997. Magisterial statement of both conceptual and practical aspects of Renaissance agriculture.

Brown, Virginia. "Columella, Lucius Junius Moderatus." In *Catalogus translationum et commentariorum. Medieval and Renaissance Latin Translations and Commentaries.* Vol. 3. Washington, D.C., 1976. Pages 173–193.

Ciriacono, Salvatore. *Acque e agricoltura: Venezia, l'Olanda e la bonifica europea in età moderna.* Milan, 1994. Detailed history of reclamation by drainage and irrigation in early modern Europe, with emphasis on Holland and Venice.

Fussell, G. E. *The Classical Tradition in West European Farming.* Newton Abbot, U.K., 1972. Classical study of the persistence of Roman agronomical ideas.

García Armendáriz, José Ignacio. *Agronomía y tradición clásica: Columela en España.* Seville, Spain, 1994. Columella's influence in medieval and Renaissance Spanish agronomy.

Glick, Thomas F. Introduction to *Obra de Agricultura,* by Gabriel Alonso de Herrera. 1513. Facsimile ed., Valencia, Spain, 1979.

Pardo Tomás, José, and María Luz López Terrada. *Las primeras noticias sobre plantas americanas en las relaciones de viajes y crónicas de Indias (1493–1553).* Valencia, Spain, 1993. Useful guide to New World plant species mentioned in Spanish descriptive literature of the fifteenth and sixteenth centuries.

Reynolds, L. D., ed. *Texts and Transmission: A Survey of the Latin Classics.* Oxford, 1983. See "Cato and Varro," "Columella," and "Palladius."

Rodgers, R. H. "Palladius Rutilus Taurus Aemilianus." In *Catalogus translationum et commentariorum. Medieval and Renaissance Latin Translations and Commentaries.* Vol. 3. Washington, D.C., 1976. Pages 195–199.

White, Lynn, Jr. *Medieval Technology and Social Change.* Oxford, 1962.

THOMAS F. GLICK

AGRIPPA OF NETTESHEIM, HEINRICH

(1486–1535), German humanist, occultist, polymath. Agrippa was born on 14 September 1486 in Cologne. He received a B.A. from the University of Cologne in 1502 and apparently studied at Dôle, Paris, and Pavia. He claimed doctorates in law and medicine. As a youth he traveled in Spain, southern France, and Italy.

Even in these early years a reputation for learning in the occult sciences attracted friends (and also enemies). In 1509 Agrippa lectured at the University of Dôle on the kabbalistic work *De verbo mirifico* (On the wondrous word; 1494) by the German Hebraist Johann Reuchlin (1455–1522). His inaugural lecture became his noted *Declamation on the Nobility and Preeminence of the Female Sex* (Antwerp, 1529). His choice of the Kabbalah as the subject of his lectures caused the local Franciscan provincial to denounce him as a "judaizing heretic," and he returned to Germany. In 1510 he visited another famous occultist, Johann Trithemius (1462–1516) of Sponheim, abbot of a Benedictine community at Würzburg; he later dedicated to Trithemius the earliest version of his major occultist work, *De occulta philosophia* (*Occult Philosophy*; first complete edition 1533).

A major influence on his intellectual development was the six years (1512–1518) he spent in Italy. Agrippa's subsequent works are strongly influenced by the Renaissance Neoplatonists Marsilio Ficino (1433–1499) and Giovanni Pico della Mirandola (1463–1494). Although Agrippa came to Italy in imperial service, by 1515 he was mainly engaged in the study of occultist learning. He embraced the Florentine Neoplatonists' belief in a secret body of ancient wisdom handed down through such ancient sages as the Jewish Kabbalists, Hermes Trismegistus, Pythagoras, Zoroaster, and Plato. In 1515–1516 he lectured at the University of Pavia on Platonic and Hermetic topics.

In 1518 Agrippa left Italy, spending brief periods at Metz (1518–1520), where he worked as legal counselor to the city council; at Geneva (1521–1523), where friends secured his appointment as medical director of the local hospital; and at Swiss Fribourg (1523–1524), where he became city physician. In these years he developed a vague sympathy for the Reformation but never fully embraced it. Many of his friends were openly sympathetic to Martin Luther (1483–1546), and he publicly defended the reformist humanism of Jacques Lefèvre d'Étaples (c. 1455–1536) against mendicant preachers at Metz. But although he adopted a vaguely reformist outlook, his circle of friends was more clearly defined by interest in magic, astrology, and other occult arts.

In 1524 he moved to Lyon as personal physician to the queen mother of France, Louise of Savoy. Unfortunately, the government's financial problems made payment of his salary unreliable; and his incessant complaints, joined to his brusque rejection of the queen mother's request to cast her son's horoscope (on the grounds that this was superstitious), led to his dismissal in the autumn of 1526. This period of disfavor and growing isolation produced his second major work, the pessimistic *De incertitudine et vanitate scientiarum* (On the vanity and uncertainty of arts and sciences; written in the summer of 1526, published in 1530). Here Agrippa denounces every human art and science as useless, even harmful, attacking not only the scholastic theologians and worldly clergy but also the learned fields of law, medicine, grammar, and natural philosophy, the practical and mechanical arts, and even the occult sciences, to which he had devoted his scholarly career. Although the work has often been classed as a social satire or a mere literary exercise, it does show some familiarity with ancient skepticism; and at the end he adopts a vaguely "evangelical" (Protestant) tone, declaring that there is no secure knowledge except for simple faith in scripture.

Agrippa explicitly retracted his own *Occult Philosophy,* and yet he continued to pursue occultist learning. A year after the publication of *Vanity* at Antwerp in 1530, he published book 1 of his *Occult Philosophy*. The first full edition (1533) contained as an appendix the chapters of *Vanity* in which he repudiates the occult arts. In 1528 he moved to the Netherlands, settling at Antwerp as imperial historiographer to the governor, Margaret of Austria (1480–1530). He now began publishing his accumulated writings. Once again the problems of a cash-starved royal court made payment of his salary insecure. In addition, as he began publishing his books, his anticlerical sentiments and unconventional theological ideas got him in trouble with the theological faculty of Louvain and with the governor herself. Hence he sought a new patron, the prince-archbishop of Cologne, Hermann von Wied (1477–1552), dedicating the partial edition of *Occult Philosophy* to him in 1531. The next year he moved to the archiepiscopal residence at Bonn, where he was still living in 1533. For reasons unknown, he moved to Lyon in 1535 and was promptly arrested because of his public criticisms of the French king's mother. Friends secured his release, and later in 1535 he died at Grenoble.

Heinrich Agrippa of Nettesheim. SOCIÉTÉ DE L'HISTOIRE DU PROTESTANTISME FRANÇAIS, PARIS

Agrippa's rich though disorderly learning in the occult sciences, his practice of alchemy and medicine, his puzzling attacks on his own occult learning in *Vanity,* and his turbulent and unstable career created a popular image of him: Agrippa as the scholarly expert in strange and perilous forms of learning; even Agrippa as the practitioner of diabolical magic. This image was reinforced by his publications, many of which, especially *Occult Philosophy, Vanity,* and his book on the superiority of women, were frequently reprinted and translated into several vernacular languages.

Far more than the obscure German charlatan Georg Faust (c. 1480–c. 1540), who gave his name to the literary Dr. Faustus, Agrippa had a career that truly exemplified the man who mastered all fields of learning and found all of them worthless. The puzzling and apparently polar opposition between his *Occult Philosophy* and his *Vanity* sharpened this image, and popular legends about his supposed dealings with the devil seemed to confirm it. These legends were transferred to the name of Faust but contained recognizable elements from Agrippa. Indeed, the diabolical black poodle that comes to claim Faust's soul is certainly Agrippan; and

Agrippa's pupil Johannes Wier explained in vain that the origin of this ridiculous legend was Agrippa's ownership of two poodles, one black and one white, whom he named Monsieur and Mademoiselle.

BIBLIOGRAPHY

Primary Works

Agrippa von Nettesheim, Heinrich Cornelius. *Declamation on the Nobility and Preeminence of the Female Sex.* Translated and edited by Albert Rabil Jr. Chicago, 1996. Agrippa's famous work on female superiority, ably translated and provided with a helpful introduction.

Agrippa von Nettesheim, Heinrich Cornelius. *De occulta philosophia libri tres.* Edited by Vittoria Perrone Compagni. Leiden, Netherlands, 1992. Excellent critical edition of Agrippa's major magical work, with useful introduction and bibliography.

Agrippa von Nettesheim, Heinrich Cornelius. *Opera.* 2 vols. Lyon, n.d. The publisher and place of publication given are fictitious; several different editions, never fully distinguished from one another, bear the same publication data. Virtually all of Agrippa's works and his extensive correspondence, all in Latin, appear here.

Secondary Works

Keefer, Michael H. "Agrippa's Dilemma: Hermetic 'Rebirth' and the Ambivalences of *De vanitate* and *De occulta philosophia.*" *Renaissance Quarterly* 41 (1988): 614–653.

Nauert, Charles G. *Agrippa and the Crisis of Renaissance Thought.* Urbana, Ill., 1965.

Walker, Daniel P. *Spiritual and Demonic Magic from Ficino to Campanella.* London, 1958. Reprint, Nendeln, Liechtenstein, 1969.

Yates, Frances A. *Giordano Bruno and the Hermetic Tradition.* Chicago, 1964.

Zambelli, Paola. "Magical and Radical Reformation in Agrippa of Nettesheim." *Journal of the Warburg and Courtauld Institutes* 39 (1976): 69–103.

CHARLES G. NAUERT

AGUSTÍN, ANTONIO (1517–1586), Spanish legal scholar and historian. Agustín was born on 26 February 1517; his father was vice-chancellor of Aragon and his sister Isabella was to marry the duke of Cardona. Studies at the universities of Alcalá and Salamanca were followed in 1535 by a move to the Spanish College at the University of Bologna, where he was a pupil of Andrea Alciato, among others, and where he took his doctorate in 1541.

In 1542, Agustín was joined by the French humanist Jean Matal (c. 1520–1586). He had already traveled widely in northern Italy and explored libraries for legal and other manuscripts, a labor shared by Matal, and Agustín now went to Florence to work on the Florentine codex of the Digest (part of the codification of Justinian). Although it had been used by scholars, notably Politian, Agustín's *Emendationum et Opinionum Libri IV* (Four books of

emendations and opinions; 1544) marked the moment at which the readings of the Florentine codex, as opposed to those of what is known as the Bologna tradition, first effectively entered the public domain. It was in this period that Agustín formed the project of collecting the sources of Roman and canon law, a project that was expounded in a famous letter to Diego Hurtado de Mendoza of 1 August 1544 and which led Agustín to begin working on the statutes and senatorial decrees of ancient Rome, a work published only in 1583. Agustín was appointed a judge in the papal court of the Rota, arriving in Rome late in 1544 and followed by Matal early in 1545.

Agustín's project also involved placing Roman legal enactments of different periods in their institutional context. It was apparent that Roman inscriptions provided critical evidence for the institutions of the Roman state, and the next five years saw Matal collecting texts of inscriptions. More importantly, both Agustín and Matal explored with other scholars how best to organize the vast bulk of material available and compiled indices of Roman offices, legions, and so on. The insistence on historicizing legal texts played a major part in the developing Renaissance sense of history and established for subsequent historians of antiquity the agenda of integrating history and antiquarianism.

Agustín was sent on papal diplomatic missions to Britain in 1555 and Germany in 1557 and by King Philip II of Spain to inspect Sicily in 1559. From 1561 to 1563 he was at the Council of Trent. He had been appointed bishop of Alife in 1557 and was appointed bishop of Lerida in 1561, arriving there in 1564. He became archbishop of Tarragona in 1576 and died there on 31 May 1586.

Agustín's increasing involvement in diplomacy and administration from 1555 left him less time for scholarly activity, but his interest in the literary evidence for Roman institutions issued in editions of Varro's *De lingua Latina* in 1557 and of the encyclopedia of Festus in 1559. His publishing activity after his return to Spain was largely devoted to late Roman law and canon law. But he was persuaded to publish his *De legibus et senatusconsultis* (On laws and decrees of the senate) in 1583, and a major work, *Dialogos de medallas, iscriciones, y otras antiguedades* (Discussions of medals, inscriptions, and other antiquities), appeared posthumously in 1587.

BIBLIOGRAPHY

Primary Work

Flores Sellés, Candido, ed. *Epistolario de Antonio Agustín.* Salamanca, Spain, 1980.

Secondary Works

Crawford, M. H., ed. *Antonio Agustín between Renaissance and Counter-Reform.* London, 1993.

Zulueta, Francis de. *Don Antonio Agustín.* Glasgow, Scotland, 1939.

MICHAEL HEWSON CRAWFORD

ALBERTI, LEON BATTISTA (1404–1472), Italian humanist and architect. Alberti was born in Genoa, the illegitimate son of Lorenzo Alberti, a Florentine banker whose family had been exiled from Florence as a result of the Ciompi Revolt of 1378. He was named Battista Alberti, after the patron saint of Florence, John the Baptist, and only assumed the name Leo or Leon as an adult.

Education. Between 1415 and 1418 Alberti studied in Padua with Gasparino Barzizza, and then he went to the University of Bologna to study civil and canon law. When his father died in 1421 Battista was cheated of his inheritance by unscrupulous cousins. Evidently preferring literary endeavors to legal studies, the twenty-year-old Alberti composed a Latin comedy titled *Philodoxeos* (The lover of glory), which he circulated as an ancient work written by the fictitious Lepidus. It may have been in Bologna that Alberti began to compose and collect what he called *Intercenales* (Dinner pieces), brief Latin dialogues and apologues illustrating moral themes. In Bologna Alberti met Tommaso Parentucelli, the future pope Nicholas V (reigned 1447–1455), and Francesco Filelfo (1398–1481), with whom he may have studied Greek. Alberti's *Intercenales* draw inspiration from the works of the Greek satirist Lucian. Yet by contrast to humanists like Filelfo, Alberti never translated ancient works from Greek but merely used them as models for his own original compositions.

In 1428 Alberti completed his law degree and, taking orders, sought employment in the papal Curia. While in Bologna Alberti composed at least two Italian works on the subject of love, to which he gave Greek names in the manner of Giovanni Boccaccio: the treatise *Ecatonfilea* and the dialogue *Deifira*. These two works enjoyed enormous success both in the original and in translation, and were in fact the only works of Alberti printed in his lifetime (Padua, 1471).

In 1431 Alberti became secretary to Biagio Molin, patriarch of Grado and a papal chancellor. When Molin asked his protégé to write a Latin biography of the obscure Saint Potitus, Alberti found the task uncongenial. As he later wrote in a letter to his col-

Leon Battista Alberti. *Self-portrait.* Bronze medal with black patina, c. 1435; 20 × 13.6 cm (7.9 × 5.4 in.). NATIONAL GALLERY OF ART, WASHINGTON, D.C., SAMUEL H. CRESS COLLECTION

league Leonardo Dati, he was forced to base his *Vita S. Potiti* (Life of St. Potitus) on such flimsy historical evidence that even the saint's existence appeared doubtful.

In 1428 the exile of the Alberti family from Florence was revoked, and in 1432 Battista visited his ancestral city, where he was named prior of the rural parish of San Martino a Gangalandi. Meeting with a cool reception by older Florentine humanists, Alberti composed the Latin essay *De commodis litterarum atque incommodis* (On the utility and futility of literary studies), in which he decries the low social status that attends the pursuit of learning. (On the basis of Alberti's autobiography the work was traditionally dated to 1428, but Luca Boschetto has proposed the later date.)

Early Vernacular Writings. If his Latin work met with little praise in Florence, Alberti was prepared to challenge the Tuscan humanists on their own linguistic ground. Leonardo Bruni and Poggio Bracciolini had recently revived the Latin philosophical dialogue following the model of Cicero. Inspired by their example, Alberti composed an Italian dialogue in three books to which he gave the Latin title *De familia* (The family). (Like many Renaissance authors, Alberti usually gave Latin titles to his vernacular writings.) The dialogue features distinguished men of the Alberti clan who discuss the principles of householding, including education, marriage, and estate management. To these three books Alberti in 1437 added a fourth book in which the topic of friendship is discussed. Curiously, the complete work enjoyed less popularity than a rewriting of his third book that circulated, and was even printed, as the *Governo della famiglia* (Managing the family) ascribed to Agnolo Pandolfini.

Despite the Florentine origins of his family, Alberti was raised in the north of Italy and found it difficult to write in idiomatic Tuscan prose. Following the linguistic suggestions of Tuscan friends, Alberti revised *De familia,* creating a versatile Italian prose that ranges from colloquial banter to formal disquisition. He became the century's most prominent champion of the vernacular and later composed the first grammar of the Italian language, the *Grammatica della lingua toscana* (Grammar of the Tuscan language). As in other fields, Alberti was an innovator as an Italian poet. He wrote the first eclogue in Italian, *Tirsi* (Thyrsis), and experimented with classical meters such as unrhymed hexameters.

In 1441, precisely a hundred years after Petrarch had been crowned in Rome for his Latin poetry, Alberti organized an Italian poetic competition in Florence that he called the *Certame Coronario* (Contest for the Crown). When the judges declined to award the prize, Alberti circulated an anonymous letter of protest in Italian and recorded the event in his Latin dinner pieces *Corolle* (Garlands) and *Invidia* (Envy). Such setbacks also inspired two Italian dialogues to which Alberti gave Latin titles, *Theogenius* and *Profugiorum ab erumna libri* (Remedies for misfortune). In both works a sage elder comforts a younger man who is overwhelmed by recent rejections and tribulations. Many of these writings reflect the disappointment that, in contrast to his reception among artistic circles, Alberti felt in the company of older and more prominent Florentine humanists like Leonardo Bruni, Niccolò Niccoli, and Gian Francesco Poggio Bracciolini. In this context, we may understand the note of defiance in his personal motto. While he adopted the winged eye as his personal emblem, symbolizing the swiftness of his intellectual

gifts, he chose as a motto the Latin phrase *Quid tum?* (So what?), which, as Guglielmo Gorni was the first to see, is a citation from Virgil's *Eclogues* 10.38 ("Quid tum, si fuscus Amyntas?") that makes light of Alberti's illegitimacy.

Florentine Environment. In Florence Alberti seems to have found the artistic environment particularly congenial and stimulating. In 1435 he composed a Latin treatise, *De pictura* (On painting), which he soon translated into Italian (*Della pittura;* 1436) with a dedication to Filippo Brunelleschi, hoping to make the work available to artists without a knowledge of Latin. In its three books Alberti sets forth the principles of optics and linear perspective, discusses the narrative subject (*istoria*), and advocates the value of humanist learning in the visual arts.

From 1436 to 1438 Alberti was in Bologna with the Curia, and the return to the city of his student days inspired a number of short compositions in Latin. He wrote the treatise *De jure* (On law), a dialogue on episcopal duties titled *Pontifex* (The bishop), and a hundred Aesopic fables, *Apologi,* which, as he proudly recorded in the manuscript, he composed during the week of 16–24 December 1437. The most influential composition of this period was his autobiography of 1437, a *Vita* that he modeled after the recently translated *Peri biōn dogmatōn kai apophthegmatōn tōn en philosophia eudokimēsantōn* (Lives of the philosophers) of Diogenes Laertius. Written in the third person, like the memoirs of Xenophon and Caesar, this "anonymous" life was to inspire Jakob Burckhardt's notion of the universal man of the Renaissance, an ideal by which the illegitimate Alberti legitimated his cultural identity. In 1437 Alberti also wrote two Italian works on love, the treatise *De amore* dedicated to Paolo Codagnello, and the brief dialogue *Sofrona*.

When the Council of Ferrara-Florence convened in 1438, the Este rulers of Ferrara gave Alberti his first artistic commission, a classical arch to support an equestrian statue of Nicolò III d'Este. The Estes of Ferrara thus became the first of the northern Italian rulers to foster Alberti's artistic and literary projects. To Leonello d'Este, Alberti dedicated first his Italian dialogue *Theogenius* and later his Latin treatise on the horse, *De equo animante*. To Leonello's brother Meliaduso d'Este he dedicated his *Ludi rerum mathematicarum* (Mathematical recreations; 1450–1452), an Italian handbook of twenty exercises in surveying and applied geometry. After Alberti's death some of his *Intercenales* circulated in Ferrara, where they were copied by Pandolfo Collenuccio

Alberti's Tempio Malatestiano. Church of San Francesco (called the Tempio Malatestiano), Rimini, Italy, built by Alberti between 1446 and 1455. ALINARI/ART RESOURCE

(1444–1504) and imitated by Ludovico Ariosto (1474–1533). During the summer of 1438, when a plague forced the Curia to leave Ferrara, Alberti used his leisure to write *Villa,* a brief set of Italian precepts on agriculture based on Hesiod and Cato the Elder, and *Uxoria* (Taking a wife), a Latin fable that he later translated into Italian.

From 1439 to 1443 Alberti was back in Florence. Around 1440 he wrote three Latin works in a lighter vein on the topic of animals: *Canis* (My dog), a eulogy for his deceased pet; *Musca* (The fly), a rewriting of Lucian's *Muscae encomium* (Encomium of the fly), which he had read in Guarino da Verona's translation; and *De equo animante.*

In 1443 the Curia returned to Rome, where Alberti produced his *Descriptio urbis Romae* (Survey of the city of Rome), a map of the city viewed from the Capitoline Hill and charted on polar coordinates. Alberti applied a similar method in a Latin treatise on statuary, probably dating from the same period, in which he described how a given statue can be copied using a series of measurements taken from a central vertical axis. During the pontificate of Nicholas V, a friend from his days in Bologna, Alberti participated in a number of projects involving restoration and city planning. Around 1450 Alberti published his most ambitious literary work in Latin, *Momus, o del principe* (Momus, or On the ruler), a prose novel in four books. Borrowing from Lucian's satirical dialogues of the gods, Alberti narrates how a feckless Jupiter wavers in his resolve to destroy the world and create a new one. Scenes set in heaven and on earth satirize the foolish ambitions and political machinations of both gods and men.

In 1452 Alberti completed *De re aedificatoria* (On the art of building), ten books in Latin on the theory and practice of architecture. Although the Roman treatise by Vitruvius served as a model, Alberti's books are largely original in their weighing of historical evidence and in their synthesis of building styles and their social context. Addressing every aspect of the subject—symmetry, proportion, ornamentation, restoration, and even urban planning—Alberti's books prove more comprehensive than the later architectural treatises of the high Renaissance. During the same period, Alberti wrote Latin and Italian versions of the treatise *Elementa picturae, Elementi di pittura* (Fundamentals of painting) and dedicated the Latin version to the Byzantine scholar Theodore Gaza, recently arrived in Rome from Ferrara. In 1453, after Stefano Porcari led an abortive plot against Pope Nicholas V, Alberti wrote a brief account of the event in a Latin epistle that is his only historical work.

Architectural Work. After 1450 Alberti increasingly devoted his spare time to architectural projects. In Rome he was apparently consulted in the restoration of Santo Stefano Rotondo, a circular fifth-century church. His first large-scale commission came from Sigismondo Malatesta, lord of Rimini, for whom Alberti attempted to convert the church of San Francesco into what became known as the Tempio Malatestiano (Malatesta Temple). To the existing structure Alberti applied an outer shell resting on a classical pediment: a facade patterned after the nearby Roman triumphal arch in Rimini, and exterior walls incorporating arched recesses. In this project as in later ones, Alberti supervised the work from a distance, writing to Matteo de' Pasti in Mantua to express his wishes.

In the 1460s and 1470s the Florentine merchant Giovanni Rucellai chose Alberti as the architect for a number of commissions. In the Rucellai palace and loggia Alberti successfully adapted classical elements to Florentine secular building. In his parish church of San Pancrazio, Rucellai had his own tomb built in the form of the Holy Sepulcher, which is the only architectural project that Alberti seems to have supervised personally. Rucellai also financed the completion of the facade of Santa Maria Novella, which had been begun in the Gothic style. Alberti's design effects a smooth transition from the Gothic angularity of the lower facade to the more serene geometric patterns of the upper portion. With great insight Alberti also solved the problem of reconciling the towering central nave with the lower side aisles. His solution, the aedicula, or temple-shaped, facade with sloping volutes (scroll buttresses) that join the two elevations, soon entered the common vocabulary of church architecture and remained in wide use even in the baroque.

The Gonzaga rulers of Mantua were important promoters of Alberti's artistic endeavors. Around 1438 Alberti sent the Latin version of his 1435 treatise *De pictura* to Giovan Francesco II Gonzaga with a letter of dedication. In 1460 Alberti was in Mantua with Pope Pius II, who was attempting to organize a crusade against the Turks. In the next twelve years Alberti received three important commissions from Marquis Ludovico Gonzaga: in Florence, the choir of the church of Santissima Annunziata; and in Mantua, the churches of San Sebastiano and Sant' Andrea. In their extant form, none of these works make clear Alberti's intentions. It is not even certain that Alberti designed the choir of Santissima Annunziata. But Giorgio Vasari (1511–1574) ascribed the work to Alberti, only to criticize the awkwardness of its design

The Palazzo Rucellai. Alberti built the palace and loggia for the Rucellai family of Florence. ALINARI/ART RESOURCE

as proof of Alberti's bookish inexperience. San Sebastiano, begun in the 1460s, represents an early example of the Renaissance fascination with centrally planned churches. In it, a larger square is set as a diamond over a smaller square half its size. Unfortunately, the church underwent later modifications, including a muddled restoration carried out in the 1920s. Sant' Andrea, which many consider Alberti's masterpiece, was begun in the 1470s, and much of the structure was completed only after his death. Alberti achieved the church's massive proportions by basing the elevations of nave and chapels on Roman barrel vaults that imitate those of the baths of Caracalla or the Basilica of Maxentius in Rome. The monumental vaults of Sant' Andrea provided inspiration for churches in Rome such as Saint Peter's and the Gesù.

Late Works. In his later years Alberti wrote only a few works. Around 1460 he compiled a brief Latin manual of rhetoric titled *Trivia senatoria* (Elements of civic oratory) which he dedicated to the young Lorenzo de' Medici (1449–1492). In 1462, he wrote a brief set of *Sentenze pitagoriche* (Pythagorean maxims), written in Italian and dedicated to his nephews.

In 1464, when Pope Paul II abolished the office of apostolic abbreviator (who reviewed the Latin in documents), Alberti found himself with time for new projects, both literary and architectural. In 1465 he composed a Latin treatise on cryptology *De componendis cyfris* (How to devise codes), dedicated to Leonardo Dati, his colleague in the Curia who may have been in charge of encoding papal correspondence. As David Kahn writes, "Alberti's three remarkable firsts—the earliest Western exposition of cryptanalysis, the invention of polyalphabetic substitution, and the invention of enciphered code—make him the Father of Western Cryptology" (*The Codebreakers,* p. 130). In his preface, Alberti mentions the recent invention of movable type, and one is tempted to speculate what he might have achieved if he had lived long enough to exploit the new technology. In 1470 he completed his last work, *De iciarchia* (The householder), a didactic Italian dialogue in which Alberti appears as the elderly Battista instructing young Florentines in the social responsibilities of the ideal householder. He died in Rome, but the location of his remains is unknown.

In the generation after his death Alberti's accomplishments were largely eclipsed, although Angelo Poliziano, editor of the books on architecture published in 1485 and dedicated to Lorenzo de' Medici, praised his learning and eloquence. In part, this temporary oblivion was the result of Alberti's own ambiguous and elusive role as an author and architect. Alberti often placed himself at a distance from his literary works, frequently using pseudonyms or describing himself in the third person. Such detachment is mirrored in the long-distance supervision of his architectural projects. (His Florentine patron Giovanni Rucellai never mentions Alberti in the *zibaldone,* or diary, that records his personal and civic projects.) Even today many of his written works, both in Latin and Italian, remain the scattered fragments of a prolific genius who died without a literary executor. Most of his works survive as single compositions or "occasional" experiments—even improvisations, as he boasts in *Musca* or in his dating of the *Apologi.* Alberti did not cultivate popular humanist genres such as historical tracts or epistolary collections, and his more ambitious compositions were often left incomplete. The ten books on architecture contain many lacunae that he apparently intended to fill in later. By 1499 the editor Girolamo Massaini lamented that he could find no complete collection of Alberti's *Intercenales.*

Given their scope and variety, Alberti's writings could only be rediscovered in a fragmentary fashion.

The first works to be printed ranged from the Italian treatises on love to the Latin books on architecture. Massaini's 1499 edition pointed the way toward anthologies of various genres. Two editions of *Momus* were printed in Rome in 1520, and by midcentury the work was translated into Spanish. A high point in the Tuscan revival of Alberti is marked by the years 1550 and 1568, when Giorgio Vasari published the first and second editions of his *Vite de' più eccelenti architetti, pittori, ed scultori italiani* (trans. *Lives of the Artists*) and Cosimo Bartoli printed his Italian translations of *De re aedificatoria, Momus,* and other works.

The versatility described in Alberti's autobiography inspired Burckhardt's notion of the "universal man of the Renaissance." But this individualistic notion of culture was less influential than Alberti's syncretic vision of learning and its applications. More than any of his contemporaries, Alberti succeeded in fusing ancient and modern elements in the double perspective of humanist endeavor. On the one hand, his systematic treatises on Italian grammar, painting, statuary, and architecture offered a theoretical basis for a new literary and artistic culture. On the other, he showed the practical utility of cross-fertilization by translating his Latin works into Italian and by designing innovative monuments that incorporate classical models and motifs. Yet Alberti's classicism is eclectic rather than dogmatic. The private structure of the Palazzo Rucellai adapts an elevation based on the public amphitheater, and his Christian churches feature both decorative motifs borrowed from Roman triumphal arches and structural units such as the barrel vault used in Roman baths.

See also **Architecture,** *subentry on* **Architectural Treatises; Humanism,** *subentry on* **Italy.**

BIBLIOGRAPHY

Primary Works

Alberti, Leon Battista. *L'architettura (De re aedificatoria; On the Art of Building).* Edited and translated by Giovanni Orlandi and Paolo Portoghesi. 2 vols. Milan, 1966.

Alberti, Leon Battista. *Dinner Pieces: A Translation of the "Intercenales."* Translated by David Marsh. Binghamton, N.Y., 1987.

Alberti, Leon Battista. *The Family in Renaissance Florence.* Translated by R. N Watkins. Columbia, S.C., 1969. Translation of *Della famiglia.*

Alberti, Leon Battista. *On the Art of Building in Ten Books.* Translated by Joseph Rykwert, Neil Leach, and Robert Tavernor. Cambridge, Mass., 1988.

Alberti, Leon Battista. *On Painting and On Sculpture: The Latin Texts of "De pictura" and "De statua."* Edited and translated by Cecil Grayson. London, 1972.

Alberti, Leon Battista. *Opere volgari.* Edited by Cecil Grayson. 3 vols. Bari, Italy, 1960–1973.

Secondary Works

Albertiana. An annual journal (1998–) published by the Société Internationale Leon Battista Alberti.

Baxandall, Michael. *Painting and Experience in Fifteenth-Century Italy: A Primer in the Social History of Pictorial Style*. Oxford, 1972. Useful for Alberti's theory of painting.

Borsi, Franco. *Leon Battista Alberti*. Translated by Rudolf G. Carpanini. New York, 1977. The best survey of Alberti's art and architecture.

Burroughs, Charles. *From Signs to Design: Environmental Process and Reform in Early Renaissance Rome*. Cambridge, Mass., 1990. Important for Alberti's Roman projects under Nicholas V.

Davies, Paul, and David Hemsoll. "Leon Battista Alberti." *Dictionary of Art*. Edited by Jane Turner. Vol. 1. London, 1996. Pages 555–569. Fine survey with ample bibliography.

Grafton, Anthony. *The Winged Eye*. New York, 2000. An intellectual biography of Alberti.

Grayson, Cecil. *Studi su Leon Battista Alberti*. Florence, 1998. Important essays and textual studies by the preeminent editor of Alberti's works.

Kahn, David. *The Codebreakers: The Story of Secret Writing*. New York, Rev. ed., 1996. Includes a discussion of Alberti's importance as cryptologist.

Kelly, Joan. *Leon Battista Alberti: Universal Man of the Early Renaissance*. Chicago, 1969. Useful survey of Alberti's life and achievements.

Mancini, Girolamo. *Vita di Leon Battista Alberti*. 2d ed. Florence, 1911. Reprint, Rome, 1971. The standard biography.

Marsh, David. *The Quattrocento Dialogue: Classical Tradition and Humanist Innovation*. Cambridge, Mass., 1980. Includes a chapter on Alberti's *On the Family*, pp. 78–99.

Rykwert, Joseph, and Anne Engel, eds. *Leon Battista Alberti*. Milan, 1994. Exhibition catalog with important essays in Italian.

Smith, Christine. *Architecture in the Culture of Early Humanism: Ethics, Aesthetics, and Eloquence, 1400–1470*. New York, 1992. An analysis of Alberti and humanist notions of aesthetics.

Tavernor, Robert. *On Alberti and the Art of Building*. New Haven, Conn., 1998. A richly illustrated survey of Alberti's architecture in the context of humanism.

DAVID MARSH

ALBUQUERQUE, AFONSO DE (1453?–1515), surnamed the Great, principal creator of the Portuguese empire in Asia (Estado da India). Albuquerque was born in the town of Alhandra near Lisbon, the second son of Gonçalo de Albuquerque, lord of Villa Verde, and Leonor de Menezes, the daughter of Alvaro Gonçalves de Ataíde, the first count of Atouguia. Educated at the court of Afonso V, "the African," he accompanied this king on two expeditions (1481 and 1489) against the Turks. In recognition of these services he obtained the post of chief equerry to the new king, John II. Following in the wake of the seminal voyages of Vasco da Gama and Pedro Cabral, Albuquerque first sailed to Asia in 1503, where he helped to obtain permission from the king of Cochin for the construction of a Portuguese fort; he returned to Lisbon in July 1504 with a rich cargo of pepper. In 1506, bearing secret letters patent naming him the next governor of India, Albuquerque returned to the Indian Ocean commanding five ships of the fleet of sixteen under Tristão da Cunha. After bombarding towns along the East African and Omani coasts, he began to implement part of his grand strategy for dominating the trade between Europe and Asia, by capturing the rich entrepôt of Hormuz at the mouth of the Persian Gulf in October 1507. Albuquerque's strategy was largely based on exploiting seapower and the control of strategic points in the Indian Ocean trading system.

Albuquerque and his small squadron reached Cannanore on the Malabar Coast of India in December 1508. There, relations between Albuquerque and Viceroy Francisco de Almeida, initially warm, quickly deteriorated and ultimately resulted in the viceroy's refusal to relinquish authority and the imprisonment of Albuquerque. The arrival of the grand marshal of Portugal, Fernando Coutinho, with a fleet of fifteen ships in late October 1509, ensured the release of Albuquerque and his assumption to power as captain-general and governor of India.

After the death of the grand marshal at the bungled sacking of Calicut in January 1510, Albuquerque finally had a free hand to undertake his grand plans for further establishing the Portuguese Empire as a geopolitical, religious, and economic power in the Indian Ocean basin. He first turned his attention to the rich city of Goa on India's Konkan coast, then under the control of the Adil Shah dynasty of Bijapur. Initially capturing Goa in March 1510, he lost it in May. Albuquerque definitively recaptured Goa in November 1510, thus providing a suitable capital for the Estado da India for the next four centuries. To provide the Portuguese with a strategic fortress to influence the rich Malaysian and Indonesian trade, Albuquerque then captured and fortified the notable entrepôt of Malacca (later Melaka) in August 1511.

Returning to Goa in September 1512, he repulsed another Bijapuri attack and in March 1513 led an unsuccessful attack on the town of Aden on the Red Sea. Albuquerque reversed this setback in May 1515 when he again captured Hormuz, a key possession the crown of Portugal would control until 1622. Fighting off illness and fatigue, Albuquerque nevertheless completed the fortress of Hormuz before sailing again for Goa. He died aboard ship in sight of his Asian capital on 16 December 1515, having established the basis for Portuguese dominance over the European share of the Indian Ocean trade for the next century.

See also **Asia, East**; *biography of Francisco de Almeida.*

BIBLIOGRAPHY

Primary Works

Albuquerque, Afonso de. *Cartas para el-rei d. Manuel I.* Edited by António Baião. Lisbon, Portugal, 1942.

Albuquerque, Afonso de. *The Commentaries of the Great Afonso Dalboquerque, Second Viceroy of India.* 4 vols. London, 1875–1884. Translation by Walter de Gray Birch of *Commentarios de grande Afonso Dalboquerque* (1774).

Secondary Works

Prestage, Edgar. *Afonso de Albuquerque, Governor of India: His Life, Conquests, and Administration.* Watford, U.K., 1929.

Sanceau, Elaine. *Indies Adventure: The Amazing Career of Afonso de Albuquerque, Captain-General and Governor of India (1509–1515).* London and Glasgow, 1936.

GLENN J. AMES

ALCALÁ DE HENARES, UNIVERSITY OF. Located nineteen miles (thirty-one kilometers) east of Madrid, the town of Alcalá was known as Complutum to both the Romans and the Goths. The university founded there was called both the Complutense and the University of Alcalá. The university was created by the archbishop of Toledo, Francisco Jiménez de Cisneros, who obtained a papal bull for establishing it from Pope Alexander VI in 1499. The main buildings were finished by 1508, and the university was inaugurated the same year; the first formal course of study began in 1509–1510. The constitutions of the Complutense authorized faculties in arts, philosophy, theology, languages, canon law, and medicine.

The University of Alcalá is connected to the Spanish Renaissance specifically in the first three decades of the sixteenth century, especially through its centerpiece, the College of San Ildefonso. San Ildefonso, a *colegio mayor* or "major college," was founded simultaneously with the university. One of six such institutions established in Spain between 1401 and 1521, like its analogues San Ildefonso was supposed to cultivate an academic elite: major colleges as a body admitted only mature scholars who already had attained their first degrees; their members were supposed to read in advanced subjects. The *colegios mayores* were always distinctive, but San Ildefonso was unique, for its rector was the highest authority in the entire university. This idiosyncrasy meant that the college and the university were thoroughly entwined, unlike their counterparts elsewhere in Spain. Moreover, Cisneros founded San Ildefonso and the university to revive theological studies: he consequently prohibited the study of civil law, banned jurists in canon law from San Ildefonso, and expected the members of that college to devote their time to the study of God.

The activities that arose from this religious focus are what link San Ildefonso, and the University of Alcalá, to the Renaissance. Cisneros advanced professorships in Hebrew and Greek and underwrote a multilingual edition of the Old and New Testaments. This proposed edition of scripture attracted Hebrew and Greek scholars to the university; the work that was printed between 1513 and 1517 was called the Complutensian Polyglot Bible, a six-volume colossus that involved parallel columns of Hebrew, Aramaic, Greek, and Latin. Yet notable as the Complutensian Polyglot was, recent scholars have pointed out that it did not evince as much textual criticism as we might have expected. Though the Polyglot looks as if it measured the Latin Bible against its Hebrew and Greek originals, Cisneros and his translators ensured that the Vulgate's authority, and the status of its purported translator, St. Jerome, remained intact. The Complutensian Polygot duplicated Jerome's prefaces to the books of the Bible, and its New Testament readings frequently followed the Latin text when the Greek one ought to have been the prototype; its New Testament editors even made the Greek conform to the Latin on eight different occasions. What compounds these subtleties is the fact that the university's chairs in Hebrew and Greek were filled only sporadically. While its theological faculty taught Thomas Aquinas as well as nominalism, its professors balanced more or less recent intellectual emphases. Such factors indicate that the university and its members participated in the Spanish Renaissance, but in intricate ways that call for further exploration.

See also **Complutensian Polyglot Bible; Universities.**

BIBLIOGRAPHY

Bentley, Jerry H. *Humanists and Holy Writ.* Princeton, N.J., 1983.

García Oro, José. *La Universidad de Alcalá en la etapu fundacional (1458–1578).* Santiago de Compostela, Spain, 1992.

Kagan, Richard L. *Students and Society in Early Modern Spain.* Baltimore, 1974.

Urriza, Juan. *La Preclara, Facultad de Artes y Filosofía de la Universidad de Alcalá de Henares, en el Siglo de Oro (1509–1621).* Madrid, 1941.

LU ANN HOMZA

ALCHEMY. Alchemical ideas and imagery permeate Renaissance society at many levels, from art and music to medicine and natural philosophy. Re-

Alchemy. *The Alchemist* painted by Jan van der Straat, called Giovanni Stradano (c. 1523–1605), a Flemish painter active in Florence; the work is in the Studiolo of the Palazzo Vecchio, Florence. SCALA/ART RESOURCE

membered by many scholars as the forefather of experimental chemistry, alchemical ideas in the Renaissance period were as important metaphysically as they were physically. The alchemy of the Renaissance was based on ancient ideas about the constitution and transformation of matter, which passed from antiquity into the hands of Arab philosophers and commentators such as Geber (Jābir ibn Hayyān; c. 721–c. 851). They drew together a corpus of ideas about the two generative qualities of matter (the sulfuric or inflammable quality and the mercurial or volatile quality) and their interaction with the four material elements (air, earth, fire, and water). As these ideas entered Christian Europe in the thirteenth century, they were again transformed by the translation of Arabic texts into Latin, the incorporation of Christian theological beliefs in transubstantiation and redemption, and the growth of an increasingly complicated symbolic system to explain alchemical ideas. By the Renaissance, therefore, alchemy was a combination of ancient, Islamic, and Christian ideas

fused with metallurgical and chemical skills. Alchemy thus struck a delicate balance between the elite "life of the mind," associated with literacy and learning, and the "life of the hands," enjoyed by craftsmen and other members of the lower orders of society.

Renaissance alchemy was based on the idea that metals "grew" in the "womb of the earth," undergoing an organic process that was likened to the growth of any other animate substance such as a plant or an animal. Metals where thus drawn into the vitalistic great chain of being in which every aspect of the divinely created world was joined to everything else according to God's ordered scheme. The great chain of being was not only ordered, it was also hierarchical, and the kingdom of metals was organized into a sequence that led from the rudest and most immature metals (lead, tin, iron, and copper) to the higher, more perfect metals (mercury, silver, and gold). Through natural generative processes, all metals were literally growing and changing in the earth until they reached the most pure and perfect gold, which did not tarnish, corrode, or otherwise decay.

The art and practice of alchemy hastened this natural, organic process. Alchemists argued that if the womb of the earth could serve as a vessel for the transformation of lead into gold, then a glass vessel containing lead could be subjected to heat and then led through the growth process. Other metals and chemicals were added to speed the process further and facilitate a successful outcome. Alchemists worked over hot charcoal fires for weeks (and often years) as they attempted to nurture the metals into higher and higher levels of perfection. When substances were added to the alchemical vessels it was often described as "feeding"; the substances in the vessels were then reduced through distillation and fed once more. This often caused spectacular changes in the color of the vessels' substances, and the alchemical practitioners who believed that the changes in color reflected other, more essential, material changes in the metals carefully noted these changes.

The work of alchemy was risky, however. All too often the charcoal fires would burn too hot and the glass vessels would explode, spilling the contents onto the fire and releasing noxious fumes. Weeks spent tending the fires would often result in singed eyebrows and eyelashes for the alchemist. Because there were no tests to determine the purity of metals, alchemists often unwittingly put toxic substances into their vessels. The free use of sulfur and mercury also endangered the health of the alchemists, who absorbed these substances through the skin and even ingested the results of their experiments to ascertain what metals were present.

For many alchemists the goal of this painstaking and dangerous work was gold and the lure of an inexhaustible supply of riches. For others, however, the goal of alchemical transformation was not gold but an elusive substance called the philosopher's stone. The philosopher's stone was the result of subjecting alchemically purified metals to more refined processes. The stone that was said to result was a universal medicine capable of both "healing" sick or imperfect metals and curing sick and imperfect human bodies. Some alchemists believed that the stone could make human beings immortal, redeeming their material bodies and transforming them into a spiritual and divine body. Because of the implications surrounding the possession and use of the philosopher's stone, alchemists interested in pursuing this more philosophical and metaphysical branch of alchemy kept their ideas and techniques as secret as possible during the Renaissance. While manuscripts and printed works on the philosopher's stone circulated through alchemical circles, their contents were often cloaked in obscure symbolism to keep a full knowledge of the alchemical art within a tight-knit circle of adepts and their apprentices.

In the sixteenth century, alchemy underwent many changes as print culture and higher levels of literacy began to threaten alchemy's well-guarded secrets. Increasing numbers of popular alchemical practitioners habituated the fairs and markets, and alchemical charlatans were investigated and imprisoned by civic and royal officials. In addition, the German alchemist and natural philosopher Paracelsus (1493–1541), who introduced a new principle (salt, or the fixed principle) into alchemy for the first time in centuries, challenged the ancient sulfur-mercury theory of metallic generation and transformation. Paracelsus's work was enormously influential in the sixteenth century as alchemists, physicians, and apothecaries began to experiment with his theories and with a considerable body of chemical medicines attributed to him.

Despite the proliferation of alchemical charlatans, alchemy retained its connections to royalty during the Renaissance, and many members of the nobility throughout Europe maintained alchemical laboratories and retained alchemical practitioners. The Medici family of Florence was interested in alchemy, as was Elizabeth I of England and James VI of Scotland (James I of England). The most well-known of the alchemical princes, however, was the Holy Roman Emperor Rudolf II, whose court at Prague served as an intellectual center for many European alchemists in the sixteenth century.

Apart from Paracelsus, alchemists who made significant contributions to understanding the structure of matter include Basil Valentine (b. 1394), a medieval author whose works were recovered and published in the Renaissance. Also important on the Continent were Leonhard Thurneysser (1531–1596), Andreas Libavius (c. 1560–1616), and Michael Sedzimir (Sendigovius, 1566–1636). Robert Fludd (1574–1637), the most prominent English Paracelsian, kept alchemical ideas alive in England well into the seventeenth century.

See also **Chemistry**.

BIBLIOGRAPHY

Debus, Allen G. *Chemistry, Alchemy, and the New Philosophy, 1550–1700: Studies in the History of Science and Medicine.* London, 1987. Contains articles published between 1961 and 1984.

Dobbs, Betty Jo Teeter. *The Foundations of Newton's Alchemy: Or, "The Hunting of the Greene Lyon."* Cambridge, U.K., and New York, 1975.

Webster, Charles. *From Paracelsus to Newton: Magic and the Making of Modern Science.* Cambridge, U.K., and New York, 1982.

DEBORAH E. HARKNESS

ALCIATO, ANDREA (1492–1550), legal scholar and humanist. Andrea Alciato was born in Milan on 8 May 1492, the only child of a wealthy merchant and his nobly born wife. Alciato studied Latin and Greek with some well-known humanists in Milan, then went to the University of Pavia about 1507 to study law. He also studied law at the University of Bologna from 1511 to 1514, and acquired a doctorate in civil and canon law at the University of Ferrara on 18 March 1516, although he attended few, if any, classes there. Alciato began to publish humanistic and legal works before receiving his degree, and he exchanged many letters with Desiderius Erasmus in the 1520s and 1530s.

Alciato had a distinguished legal career. He taught at the University of Avignon, 1518–1522, then spent the years from 1522 to 1527 practicing law in Milan. He returned to Avignon to teach 1527–1529, then taught law at the University of Bourges, 1529–1533. Political pressure from Emperor Charles V and the duke of Milan brought Alciato back to Italy. He taught civil law at the universities of Pavia (1533–1537), Bologna (1537–1542), Ferrara (1542–1546), and Pavia again (1546–1550), where he died in Jan-

Prudentes uino abstinent.

Quid me uexatis rami? sum Palladis arbor,
Auferte hinc botros,uirgo fugit Bromium.

An Emblem by Alciato. "The prudent abstain from wine."
From Andrea Alciato, *Emblematum liber,* 1531.

uary 1550. Alciato may have been the most famous and best paid professor of law in Italy. For example, at the University of Ferrara, his annual salary equaled those of the other forty-five professors combined and consumed 10 percent of the budget of the city of Ferrara.

Alciato became famous and received these high salaries because he was the founder of humanistic jurisprudence. He lectured directly from the ancient texts, correcting them when necessary. Alciato presented a historical and philological analysis of the text in place of what had until then been standard: a lengthy recitation of the opinions of medieval and Renaissance jurists. He lectured in excellent humanistic Latin, which boosted his reputation. As a legist with humanist training and inclinations, Alciato had a better understanding of the ancient legal texts in their historical context than did his traditional counterparts. The humanistic jurisprudence that Alciato pioneered was often called *mos gallicus* (French method) because the majority of the humanist juris-

prudents were French and had been his students. His French students and followers, especially from Bourges, created a historical school of law that greatly influenced French jurisprudence, politics, and religion.

At the same time, Alciato was a practical legal scholar. He did not sneer at the medieval commentators as the humanists often did, but added a historical perspective to traditional jurisprudence. Alciato wrote numerous legal works in the method of humanistic jurisprudence, of which *De verborum significatione libri quatuor* (Four books on the significance of words; 1530) may have been the best known in his day.

Alciato also wrote philological studies on nonlegal texts, such as his *Annotationes in Tacitum* (Annotations on Tacitus; 1517). He published the first Renaissance emblem book, *Emblematum liber* (Book of emblems; 1531). An emblem consisted of a title, such as a motto; a picture; and a short text, usually based on classical Latin and Greek material. The text explained the meaning and moral significance of the title and picture. Alciato's emblem book went into over 170 editions, including translations in English, French, German, Italian, and Spanish, and had many imitators. No other Renaissance figure combined expertise in law and humanistic studies so fruitfully and profitably as did Alciato.

See also **Emblem**; **Law**.

BIBLIOGRAPHY

Primary Work

Alciato, Andrea. *Emblemata. Lyons, 1550.* Translated and annotated by Betty I. Knott, with an introduction by John Manning. Aldershot, Hampshire, U.K., and Brookfield, Vt., 1996. Facsimile of the Latin edition with English translation.

Secondary Works

Abbondanza, Roberto. "Alciato, Andrea." In *Dizionario biografico degli italiani*. Vol. 2. Rome, 1960. Pages 69–77. Succinct biography with extensive bibliography.

Kelley, Donald R. *Foundations of Modern Historical Scholarship. Language, Law, and History in the French Renaissance.* New York and London, 1970. Chapter 4 discusses Alciato's humanistic jurisprudence and his followers.

PAUL F. GRENDLER

ALDINE PRESS. The Aldine press was an Italian publishing company, active in Venice and Rome from 1495 to 1597. The press was established by Aldus Manutius (c. 1449–1515), a scholar and printer who studied Latin under Domizio Calderini and Greek under Battista Guarino. He gained a sufficient reputation as a scholar to be accepted into the circle of Giovanni Pico della Mirandola and was employed as tutor to the count's nephews, princes Alberto and Lionello Pio of Carpi. Probably seeing an opportunity in the undeveloped market for Greek texts, he decided to move into printing some time in the late 1480s and had settled in Venice by 1490 to establish a company.

The Aldine Company. Though Aldus may have produced one or two editions independently in 1494, from 1495 the company consisted of two blocks of shares and was based near the church of Sant' Agostin. The late doge Marco Barbarigo's son Pier Francesco supplied capital, and Andrea Torresani, later Aldus's father-in-law, supplied capital and business experience; he had been printing in Venice since 1479 and published a *Musarum panegyris* (Celebration of the Muses) written by Aldus in 1491. Though the capital base of the company cannot be reconstructed in detail, it is evident that Aldus's investment was much the smallest, amounting to about one-fifth of Torresani's. But his friendship with the princes of Carpi gave Aldus the influence of social prestige, and he seems to have been able to turn to them for sponsorship with costly projects like the publication of Aristotle.

For the first five years Aldus concentrated on Greek texts, chiefly grammars, dictionaries, and a five-volume first edition of Aristotle. His Greek types, based on the cursive script of the time, have since been criticized by scholars as spidery and difficult to read, but they were probably intended, like his Latin italics, to blur the distinction between manuscript and print so as to raise the prestige of the new medium. Some Latin or Italian texts, including Pietro Bembo's *De Aetna* (On Etna; 1496) and Francesco Colonna's *Hypnerotomachia Poliphili* (The dream-battle of Poliphilo; 1499) were commissioned work, but the list also included scholarly and devotional editions, such as Angelo Poliziano's *Opera* (Works; 1498) and Catherine of Siena's *Epistole* (Letters; 1500). Aldus introduced the portable literary book "in octavo" (about seven inches tall) and the cursive or "italic" Latin type, both embodied in the edition of Virgil that appeared in 1501. The italic was modeled on the cursive script of the chancery schools and was fashionably classical in form. The following year he introduced the "dolphin and anchor" emblem, which was copied from a Roman coin of the first century A.D. and first used in volume 2 of the *Poetae Christiani veteres* (Early Christian poets). These octavos were new only in presenting literary texts in an unusual format and were no

cheaper than the same titles in larger size. But their convenience and the appeal of their types to contemporary taste made them an instant success, and the "brand image" of the anchor became attached personally to Aldus. Although he secured a ten-year monopoly on the right to print in cursive just before Virgil was published, his editions were so widely plagiarized that he petitioned twice in 1502 for sanctions to be more rigorously enforced.

The Aldine Academy and the Last Years. The Aldine press was most active between 1501 and 1503, producing forty-two editions in thirty-six months. Thereafter work slowed down, stopping entirely in 1505–1507 and 1509–1512. In 1502 Aldus printed *Neakademias nomos* (Statutes of the new academy) and hoped to link his work as a printer to the teaching of the ancient languages at an established institution. Between 1503 and 1505 Emperor Maximilian I had sent messages that may have encouraged Aldus to reduce his activity in Venice. He spent time between 1505 and 1507 reviving scholarly contacts in northern Italy. When his hopes for an academy were disappointed, he returned to Venice and strengthened his ties with with Andrea Torresani, whose daughter he had married in 1505. The company was rewarded by the success of Erasmus's *Adagia* in 1508.

Although Aldus was disappointed by the failure of his renewed efforts to found an academy between 1509 and 1512, the years from 1512 to 1514 were among his busiest. Regrouping an editorial team around Marcus Musurus, Andrea Navagero, and Giambattista Egnazio, he produced twenty-five editions, which included the first Greek texts of Plato, Pindar, and Hesychius, and improved versions of Latin authors such as Lucretius and Pliny the Younger. As the appeal of Greek spread through European universities, Aldus's reputation grew as well, and when he died he was laid in state like a military hero in the church of San Stefano, his books laid around him like trophies.

The Aldine Legacy and the Torresani. Aldus's father-in-law Andrea Torresani and Torresani's sons Gianfrancesco and Federigo were disliked by scholars for their caution with money, and Erasmus pilloried them in his dialogue *Opulentia sordida* (Penny pinching; 1531). But they traded on their relationship with Aldus, continued to employ his emblem, and faithfully pursued his program with the help of editors like Navagero and Egnazio. Gianfrancesco even tried to emulate Aldus's reputation as a Greek scholar. Between 1516 and 1529 they pro-

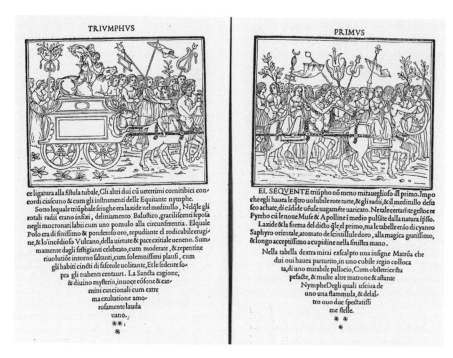

An Aldine Edition. *Hypnerotomachia Poliphili* by Francesco Colonna, printed by the Aldine Press in 1499. [For discussion of *Hypnerotomachia Poliphili,* see the article on Colonna in volume 2.] LIBRARY OF CONGRESS

duced sixty-nine Latin and thirty-seven Greek editions. The Greek texts included a Septuagint Bible (1518), which had been planned as a Polyglot since 1497, a first edition of Aeschylus (1518) to round off those of Sophocles and Euripides (1502, 1503), and a five-volume first printing of the complete works of Galen (1525). An important contemporary work, Baldassare Castiglione's *Il cortegiano* (*The Book of the Courtier*), was published on its author's instructions under the Aldine imprint in 1528, though the Torresani were no more interested in modern literature than Aldus had been.

Paulus Manutius.   The death of Andrea Torresani in 1528 cast doubts on the survival of the company. His sons, who now controlled the bulk of the capital, seemed content to act as booksellers or publish through other printers, and no editions appeared under the Aldine imprint between 1529 and 1533. But Aldus's immediate family and his admirers were determined to keep his name alive, and from 1533 his third son Paulus (1512–1574) began to issue books from "the house of the heirs of Aldus Manutius of Rome, and his father-in-law Andrea of Asola." Paulus was only twenty, and his assertive temperament soon alienated his uncles. Most of the later 1530s were taken up with litigation over the right to

use the company's types, or over the division of assets between the Torresani and Manutius interests. The two families were printing independently by 1539, and the original company was dissolved in 1542. Though the Torresani and Paulus's brothers, Antonius and Manutius, published occasionally under their own names, between 1533 and 1574 the driving force came from Paulus, and the 630 editions issued under the Aldine imprint during that time reflect his interests.

The bias differed greatly from that shown in the editions of Aldus's time. Greek, with only twenty-seven editions, was relegated to the sidelines. Aldus's preference for the plain text was also abandoned, for Paulus was one of the most respected Ciceronian scholars of the time, and his annotated six-volume edition of Cicero's complete works (1540 and 1541) proved most successful. Texts, commentaries on, or translations of the works of Cicero filled 101 of his editions. Classical (156 editions) and contemporary humanist Latin (163 editions) now outstripped even the rise of vernacular Italian texts, of which he printed seventy-eight. If such specialization narrowed the range of output, it consolidated the company's reputation for responsible editorship at a time when that would matter most. In 1556 Paulus received an offer of 600 ducats from the Protestant elector of the Rhenish Palatinate to shift his entire operation to Germany, and in 1558 he became official publisher to the Accademia Veneta. The fifty-seven scientific editions printed for the Accademia between 1558 and 1561, when the organization went bankrupt, were commissions issued to Paulus rather than his own choices. The same is true of the forty-nine theological and twenty-nine canon law texts that he printed in Rome between 1562 and 1566.

In 1561 Paulus accepted an invitation from Pius IV to move to Rome to become official printer to the papacy. In its original form this project was planned by the humanist cardinals Girolamo Seripando and Giovanni Morone to challenge the dominance of scholarly publishing established in Protestant centers such as Basel by Johannes Oporinus, or Geneva by the Estienne family. The list was to include "books of all kinds," and a Polyglot Bible was given priority. Paulus was so elated at the terms offered—an annual salary of 500 crowns and a palace of his own—that he felt his father's dreams of an academy were being realized. Between 1562 and 1566 the Aldine press was working at the highest capacity in its history, as the conclusion of the Council of Trent demanded the publication of its decrees while classical texts continued to pour from Venice. In 1566 Pius V demanded that all service books be reissued in accordance with the decisions of the council and awarded the monopoly to Paulus. Though the commercial opportunity was great, Paulus was disappointed by the deviation from the more humanist program that had tempted him to Rome and embarrassed by his lack of experience in the technique of printing in red and black, which was required for missals and breviaries. He delegated responsibility for sales in the Spanish dominions to Christopher Plantin, distanced himself even from work in Rome, and died in 1574.

Aldus the Younger. Paulus's son was born in 1547, and since he was supposed to have edited *Eleganze della lingua toscana* (Gems of the Tuscan language) by 1556, it is clear that much was expected of him. He assisted his father both in Venice and Rome during the 1560s, and his marriage to Francesca Giunta, of the Florentine Giunti family of publishers, in 1572 forged a link between two of the principal publishers in Italy. The Aldine press continued to publish during the plague years of 1575–1576, when Venice lost its leadership of Italian industry to Rome as the number of companies declined by nearly two-thirds. Acclaimed as a grammarian and expert on Roman antiquities, from 1583 to 1588 Aldus also held academic posts in Venice, Bologna, Pisa, and Rome. He followed his father in preparing a ten-volume annotated edition of the complete works of Cicero, which was completed in 1583. But, because the tension between publishing and teaching duties was more serious for him than it had been for his father or grandfather, much of the work was delegated, and it is difficult to determine the significance of Aldus's contribution. Some two hundred editions appeared over his name before 1598, 101 of them classical or humanist Latin. Greek had vanished entirely. The sixty-four Italian editions, which included important first printings of some of the works of Torquato Tasso (1581), demonstrate the growing importance of the vernacular. There are also some exotic items, like the Polish translation of Euripides's *Electra,* which appeared in 1598. But Aldus had died in the previous year, selling his library to the Vatican to cover a number of debts.

The Aldine Mystique. Aldus the Elder was the first to print a large majority of the classics of ancient Greece, and for most of the first fifteen years of the sixteenth century, when Greek studies were gaining in prestige throughout Europe, his was the only press from which Greek texts could be obtained. His octavo books linked study and recreation by their convenient size, and blurred the distinction between manuscript and print with their adaptation of a fashionable script form to type. Commissioned works such as *Hypnerotomachia Poliphili* involved Aldus in experiments with illustration and page design that had a delayed but profound effect. The roman font used for *Poliphili* achieved a clarity and precision that made it a model for printers in northern Europe, especially in Paris, after 1530. Aldus's dedications to dignitaries like Alberto Pio, his own grammatical writings, and his son's Latin scholarship gave their books a social and academic respectability that demolished lingering prejudice against printing as "vulgar" and established the concept of "scholarly publishing."

See also Colonna, Francesco; Giunti Press; Printing and Publishing.

BIBLIOGRAPHY

Primary Work

Manuzio, Aldo. *Aldo Manuzio editore*. Edited by Martin Lowry. 2 vols. Milan, 1975.

Secondary Works

Barberi, Francesco. *Paolo Manuzio e la stamperia del Populo romano (1561–1570), con documenti inediti*. Reprint, Rome, 1985.

Barker, Nicolas. *Aldus Manutius and the Development of Greek Script and Type in the Fifteenth Century.* Sandy Hook, Conn., 1985.

Fletcher, H. George. *New Aldine Studies.* San Francisco, 1988.

Lowry, Martin. *Facing the Responsibility of Paulus Manutius.* Los Angeles, 1995.

Lowry, Martin. *The World of Aldus Manutius.* Oxford, 1979.

Pastorello, Ester. *L'epistolario manuziano; Inventario cronologico-analitico, 1483–1597.* Florence, 1957.

Renouard, Antoine Augustin. *Annales de l'imprimerie des Alde.* 3d ed. Paris, 1834.

MARTIN J. C. LOWRY

ALEMÁN, MATEO (1547–1614), Spanish writer. Mateo Alemán was born in Seville, a great trading city, where his father, Hernando, possibly a converso (one descended from converted Jews), was appointed physician and surgeon to the Royal Prison. His mother's family were Florentine merchants. After receiving a thorough humanistic education and spending years in obscure business operations, law studies, and imprisonment for debt, he was appointed judge in the Royal Treasury (1582). He investigated suspected malfeasance by local officials and also working conditions in the mercury mines at Almadén, which were operated by Fugger, the German banking firm, with Spanish convict labor (1593). Shortly afterward he was in Madrid, failing in business, cultivating the friendship of writers and reformers, and writing his picaresque masterpiece *Guzmán de Alfarache* (part 1, 1599; part 2, 1604). In 1607 he emigrated with his family to Mexico and never returned to Spain. Alemán also wrote *La vida de San Antonio de Padua* (1607), *Ortografía castellana* (1609), and *Sucesos de fray García Guerra, arzobispo de México* (1613).

Guzmán is rooted in Alemán's experience of financial swindles, the lives of criminals and outcasts, and the destructive social effect of Spain's huge debt to foreign bankers. Its documentary realism is directed toward reform of individual and collective behavior. Compared with Spain's first picaresque narrative (the brief, ironic *Vida de Lazarillo de Tormes,* author unknown; 1554), *Guzmán* is huge and explicitly moralizing. The first-person narrator calls it his "general confession." The protagonist's careers—as vagrant, servant, page, buffoon, financial swindler, pimp, student of divinity, confidence artist—carry him through various social levels, from filthy inns to a Roman cardinal's palace, to four years at a university, and across Spain and Italy. He writes his story late in life as a convict sentenced to the royal galleys, awaiting a pardon after saving the ship from mutineers.

The extensive moralizing passages in *Guzmán* are not confined to Counter-Reformation doctrine, as has been thought (the book was a great success in Protestant England, translated by James Mabbe, 1622–1623). In context, the theological discourse in *Guzmán* is a vehicle for reflections on the place of the individual in society and on the economic, social, and ethical obligations of persons at all levels. Alemán's "new man" is marked by more than Christian repentance. His contrition is social, encompassing not only his years of cheating and trafficking in bills of exchange rather than productive work but his obsession with honor. Alemán and his mercantilist friends in the royal councils held an antiaristocratic concept of honor that privileged social virtues: work, industrial and commercial enterprise, and a tacitist idea of the welfare of the state. In his humanistic *Ortografía castellana,* published in Mexico, he reveals himself to be on the side of the "moderns," contemptuous of received ideas and an enthusiastic proponent of innovation.

In its time, *Guzmán* was more widely read than Cervantes's *Don Quixote,* and it influenced the writing of Hans Grimmelshausen, Tobias Smollett, and Daniel Defoe, among others. A spurious part 2 by Juan Martí appeared in 1602.

BIBLIOGRAPHY

Primary Work

Alemán, Mateo. *The Rogue; or, The Life of Guzmán de Alfarache.* Translated by James Mabbe. London, 1623. Reprint, New York, 1967.

Secondary Works

Cavillac, Michel. *Pícaros y mercaderes en el* Guzmán de Alfarache: *Reformismo burgues y mentalidad aristocratica en la España del siglo de oro.* Granada, Spain, 1994.

Cros, Edmond. *Mateo Alemán: Introducción a su vida y a su obra.* Salamanca, Spain, 1971.

PETER N. DUNN

ALEMANNO, YOHANAN BEN ISAAC (c. 1435–c. 1504), Italian Jewish exegete, philosopher and Kabbalist, author. Alemanno was born in Mantua—or, according to documents discovered in the 1990s, in Città di Castello, near Perugia—about 1435 to a French Ashkenazi family. Around 1456 we find him in Florence, where he lived in the house of the rich banker and patron of letters Yechiel da Pisa. After a period spent in northern Italy, where he attended Judah Messer Leon's yeshiva, he received in Padua the title of *Doctor artium liberalium et medicinae* (1469/70), granted to him by Messer Leon. In 1488 he returned to Florence, where he served as a tutor for Yechiel da Pisa's sons; in the same year he met Giovanni Pico della Mirandola, with whom he established a close intellectual relationship that lasted until Pico's death in 1494. He left Florence in 1494 or 1497, when the Jews were expelled from the Tuscan town, and, after wandering about in northern Italy, he finally settled in Mantua, where he died, probably after 1504.

Most of Alemanno's works were begun in Mantua around 1470 but were completed in Florence after meeting Pico. His extant treatises have reached us mostly in autograph manuscripts: a commentary on the Song of Songs, entitled *Heshek Shlomo* (Solomon's desire), which was completed on Pico's demand; the encyclopedic work *Hai ha-'olamim* (The immortal); an unfinished commentary on the Pentateuch, entitled *'Einei ha-'eidah* (The eyes of the community), which shows resemblances to Pico's *Heptaplus;* an untitled kabbalistic work; a supercommentary to Moses of Narbonne's commentary on Abu Bakr ibn Tufayl's *Hayy ibn Yaqzan* (this Arabic work could have been translated into Latin by Alemanno for Pico); and a notebook (*Likkutim*) containing useful autobiographical material. Some other minor works, quoted within Alemanno's treatises, were inserted by the author in the final version of *Heshek Shlomo* and *Hai ha-'olamim*.

Alemanno founded his philosophical system on Islamic and Jewish medieval traditions, but he seems to have been deeply influenced by Florentine fifteenth-century Neoplatonic thought. Most of Alemanno's theories on universal love, astrology, and magical medicine show affinities with Marsilio Ficino's views. According to Alemanno, humanity's love for God is the main factor allowing the human soul to return to its origin in the Godhead: the best model of such an itinerary is pointed out in the Song of Songs. In the introduction to *Heshek Shlomo* Alemanno describes the perfection of King Solomon— the alleged author of the Song of Songs—a universal sage, according to humanist standards. Alemanno addresses contemporary Jews, pointing out that the doctrines the humanists were trying to retrace in the Bible and in pagan sources (e.g., pseudo-Hermetic and Zoroastrian texts, the so-called *prisca theologia,* on ancient theology) actually derive from God's revelation to Abraham, Moses, the prophets, and all the people of Israel.

The theory of Israel's cultural primacy was widely diffused in the Middle Ages; what is new in Alemanno's approach is his decision to deal especially with Solomon, who didn't reach the prophetic level of Abraham or Moses but nevertheless could carry out, with God's help, a rational study program which allowed him to achieve an intellectual level that no other person had ever reached. Underscoring Solomon's human qualities, his virtues but also his vices, Alemanno accepts the reevaluation of humanity's role within creation central to Pico's view of human dignity and important to humanist thought in general. At the same time he shows that Jewish people are superior to other nations, not only for their special relationship to God, but also for their sciences, which had influenced all the nations of the earth since Solomon's time. The biblical king represents a model of cultural and ethical as well as political perfection which could constitute the basis for the restoration of the national identity of the Jews: even if the Jews are not granted a prophetic status, they can achieve a certain degree of knowledge which will enable them to unify their material intellect with the Active Intellect.

The aim of achieving *devekut* (cleaving) with God through a rational study program is the subject of *Hai ha-'olamim,* an encyclopedic compilation of the most influential Arabic (in their Hebrew versions) and Jewish scientific and philosophical medieval sources, reinterpreted in humanist garb. In its rhetorical introduction, which is reminiscent of Averroes, Moses Maimonides, and the Italian Scholastics, Alemanno explains that his audience is neither intellectuals nor common people but rather those people in between who have been granted by God the prerequisites to enlarge their knowledge since their birth, but for different reasons could not afford to carry out their studies. However, in order to achieve union with God, rational philosophy is not sufficient: talented individuals should devote themselves to a higher level of knowledge, represented by Kabbalah, which is interpreted by Alemanno as a superior form of Neoplatonic magic allowing humankind to control the terrestrial and celestial worlds. Aristotelian philosophy in Platonic garb is thus connected to Kabbalah and magic in a comprehensive system of thought which shows, in its syncretistic attitude, affinities with Pico as well as with Leone Ebreo. Alemanno's influence was probably greater upon Christian (through Pico's works) than upon Jewish thought; however, traces of his kabbalistic beliefs can be still found in the sixteenth century, mainly within the da Pisa family circle.

BIBLIOGRAPHY

Primary Works
Among Alemanno's works only the long introduction to his commentary on the Song of Songs, known by the separate title

Shir ha-ma`alot li-Shlomo* (The song of Solomon's ascents), has been printed: *Sha`ar ha-heshek (The gate of desire; Livorno, Italy, 1790; reprint, Halberstadt, Germany, 1860?). In 1976 the same work was published in a critical edition with an introduction: Arthur Michael Lesley Jr., *"The Song of Solomon's Ascents" by Yohanan Alemanno: Love and Human Perfection according to a Jewish Associate of Giovanni Pico della Mirandola* (Ann Arbor, Mich., 1976). See also Yohanan Alemanno, *Hay ha-`olamim (L'Immortale). Parte I: la Retorica,* edited by Fabrizio Lelli (Florence, 1995).

Secondary Works

Cassuto, Umberto. *Gli Ebrei a Firenze nell'età del Rinascimento.* Florence, 1918. See pp. 301–318.

Idel, Moshe. "The Magical and Neoplatonic Interpretations of the Kabbalah in the Renaissance." In *Jewish Thought in the Sixteenth Century.* Edited by Bernard Dov Cooperman. Cambridge, Mass., 1983. Pages 186–242.

Lelli, Fabrizio. "L'educazione ebraica nella seconda metà del '400. Poetica e scienze naturali nel *Hay ha-`olamim* di Yohanan Alemanno." *Rinascimento,* 2d ser., 36 (1996): 75–136.

Novak, B. C. "Giovanni Pico della Mirandola and Jochanan Alemanno." *Journal of the Warburg and Courtauld Institutes* 45 (1982): 125–147.

FABRIZIO LELLI

ALEXANDER VI (Rodrigo de Borja y Doms, or, in Italian, Rodrigo Borgia; 1431–1503), pope (1492–1503). The most controversial of all Renaissance popes, Alexander VI was long portrayed as a monster of perfidy and lust, although a few historians have attempted unconvincingly to exculpate him. Modern historians have tended to discount the more lurid tales about him and have stressed his political skill in defending his position and increasing the authority of the papacy within the Papal States, but they have had little effect on the popular image of the Borgia as iniquitous.

Borgia was born at Játiva in Valencia; both his father, Jofré, and his mother, Isabella, were members of the Borja family. He studied at the University of Valencia and later, in the early 1450s, studied canon law at the University of Bologna. His uncle Alonso was bishop of Valencia and a cardinal, and Rodrigo had been intended for an ecclesiastical career from childhood. Alonso was elected pope in 1455, taking the name Calixtus III; in 1456 he created Rodrigo a cardinal and in 1457 appointed him vice-chancellor of the church, which office Rodrigo held until he became pope. The many benefices he accumulated made him very wealthy. Although Rodrigo fathered at least seven illegitimate children as a cardinal, his behavior was not particularly scandalous for the times. He had little experience outside Rome (the major exception being a legation to Spain in 1472–1473), but he was keenly interested in politics and

became a major figure in the College of Cardinals, although he was not really trusted by his colleagues. His reputation for political acumen as well as his wealth overcame their doubts and secured his election as pope on 11 August 1492, taking the name Alexander VI.

Soon, however, he aroused considerable opposition among the cardinals; the major cause of their dissatisfaction was his nepotism. The scope of his ambitions for his family and the frankness with which he spoke of them disconcerted even seasoned observers at the papal court. During preparations for the conquest of Naples by the French king Charles VIII, it seemed his primary concern was to exploit the need of King Alfonso of Naples for support in order to gain land, titles, and marriage partners for some of his children. Nevertheless, he has been credited with concern to keep the French out of Italy and praised for his handling of negotiations with Charles when the king passed through Rome in December 1494–January 1495, accompanied by dissident cardinals, including Giuliano della Rovere (later Julius II), calling for his deposition. Alexander became a member of the Holy League against the French in 1495, until he came to an agreement with the new king, Louis XII, in 1499 in which he granted the king an annulment of his marriage in exchange for a French bride and lands for his son Cesare and military support for Cesare's conquests.

Cesare Borgia's duchy of Romagna was the most substantial of the endowments Alexander gave to his children; his daughter Lucrezia's marriage to Alfonso d'Este (after her two previous husbands had been disposed of when they no longer suited Alexander's plans) was intended to provide support for Cesare from Ferrara. Lucrezia and other Borgia children (including Giovanni, the son of Alexander's mistress Giulia Farnese, who bore him in 1498) were given lands taken from leading Roman baronial families. By the end of his pontificate, most of the barons were in exile and their lands in the possession of the Borgia, but they soon recovered them after his death. Again, some historians have argued that Alexander intended to impose order and increase the authority of the papacy, but his contemporaries regarded him as indifferent to disorder as long as it did not obstruct his personal plans.

Alexander was unpopular in the Curia, and not only because he was a Spanish pope in a court increasingly dominated by Italians. There was also genuine fear of him: He threatened those who crossed him, and there were suspicious deaths. Even some cardinals did not feel safe in Rome and went

Pope Alexander VI. Detail of *The Risen Christ* by Pinturicchio and his school in the Borgia Apartments in the Vatican. ALINARI

into exile. As head of the church, his act of most lasting significance was his division of the newly discovered lands between Spain and Portugal in 1493.

Alexander was a cultivated man and encouraged the University of Rome. His artistic projects mostly continued work begun by others. In the Vatican he had the Borgia apartments decorated by Pinturicchio in 1492–1494 and added the Torre Borgia. He had an elevated corridor built linking the Vatican with the papal fortress, the Castel Sant'Angelo, which he had strengthened by the architect Antonio da Sangallo the Elder and decorated by Pinturicchio. He also commissioned work on several churches in Rome and on fortresses in the Papal States, notably at Civita Castellana.

Alexander died of a fever, not, as was rumored, of poison prepared for a rich cardinal.

See also **Borgia, House of.**

BIBLIOGRAPHY

Mallett, Michael. *The Borgias: The Rise and Fall of a Renaissance Dynasty.* London, 1969. The most levelheaded of the biographies of the Borgia, portraying Alexander as a skilled politician.

Shaw, Christine. "Alexander VI, Cesare Borgia, and the Orsini." *European Studies Review* 11 (1981): 1–23. A more critical view of Alexander's policies in the Papal States.

CHRISTINE SHAW

ALFONSO THE MAGNANIMOUS (1396–1458), V of Aragon (ruled 1416–1458), IV of Catalonia (ruled 1416–1458), III of Valencia (ruled 1416–1458), I of Majorca (ruled 1416–1458), II of Sardinia (ruled 1420–1458), I of Naples (ruled 1442–1458), and I of Sicily (ruled 1416–1458).

Alfonso was warrior-monarch over a pan-Mediterranean dynastic confederation centered on his Naples kingdom, and patron-practitioner of Renaissance learning and arts, centered on the brilliant Naples pluricultural court. Born in 1396, his reign comprised some twenty years based in Arago-Catalonia and another twenty at Naples. His Spanish dominions were troubled by wars (with Castile and Genoa), peasant revolts (in Majorca and Catalonia), factionalism, and constitutional conflicts. Claiming succession to Giovanna II, Alfonso conquered the kingdom of Naples against Angevin, papal, Venetian, Florentine, and Milanese opposition and then built a "modern" bureaucratic state there as well as a commercial imperium in the Levant, especially via Egypt.

His wars against Florence, the papal states, Venice, and especially Genoa all ultimately foundered. His claims to Athens and Hungary made some headway, while his Balkan protectorate against the Ottomans was more successful: the rulers of Serbia, Bosnia, and Albania, including the great Scanderbeg, were vassals. Intrigues with Ethiopia (thought to be the home of the mythical Prester John), Burgundy, England, the Holy Roman Empire, Byzantium, and Trebizond failed to save Constantinople, which fell in 1453.

Witty, jovial, and athletic, Alfonso was deliberately temperate in food, clothing, and behavior, assiduous in piety, and discreet about his mistresses until in old age he became besotted (though platonically) with the scheming Lucrezia d'Alagno. Alfonso's illegitimate son Ferrante succeeded him in Naples, his brother Juan in Spain.

Fervent for all things classical, Alfonso singlehandedly brought Renaissance culture to southern Italy. He surrounded himself with humanists both in Greek (Theodore Gaza, George of Trebizond, and Giannozzo Manetti) and Latin (especially his feuding secretaries Lorenzo Valla and Antonio Beccadelli, or "Panormita"). He founded the "Academia Alfonsina" (also called Panormitana and later Pontaniana, after

Alfonso the Magnanimous. Allegorical depiction of the triumph of Alfonso as king of Naples. Illumination; second half of the fifteenth century. © BIBLIOTECA APOSTOLICA VATICANA, VATICAN CITY

its first two directors), an institution that survived to the mid-sixteenth century. Lavishly openhanded, he conducted lively soirées or literary circles around his imported luminaries both at home and in the field. He studied Latin daily with a humanist mentor. Through agents he systematically collected one of the best libraries in Europe; a library tent next to his on military expeditions allowed him to expand his reading. Alfonso supported a team of translators, scribes, miniaturists, and bookbinders, as well as a school to train boy classicists. Humanists elsewhere in Italy corresponded with and dedicated works to him (Leonardo Bruni, for example, and Poggio Bracciolini).

Alfonso enjoyed theological debate, the philosophical ruminations on the human condition then current, and all manner of personal participation in his round of cultural events. Castilian in speech and tastes, he welcomed Catalan (Ausies March, Joanot Martorell, Jordi de Sant Jordi) and Provençal literary influences, and found a place in his chancery for both Sicilian and south Italian dialects. Moorish en-

tertainers added to the exotic mix of this hybrid culture. Ancient coins and modern medals were a particular passion, especially with the services of Antonio Pisano ("Pisanello"). Alfonso also recruited eminent musicians from all over Europe, making Naples a distinguished musical center. In his building program, the triumphal arch built by Francesco Laurana at Castelnuovo stands out. Alfonso was also a conduit for humanism to Spain.

See also **Naples,** *subentry on* **Naples in the Renaissance; Spain,** *subentry on* **The Spanish Kingdoms.**

BIBLIOGRAPHY

Bisson, Thomas N. *The Medieval Crown of Aragon: A Short History.* Oxford, 1986.

XIV Congresso di storia della corona d'Aragona. *La Corona d'Aragona in Italia (secc. XIII–XVIII).* 9 vols. Sassari, Italy, 1993–1996.

Ryder, Alan. *Alfonso the Magnanimous: King of Aragon, Naples, and Sicily, 1396–1458.* Oxford, 1990.

Ryder, Alan. *The Kingdom of Naples under Alfonso the Magnanimous: The Making of a Modern State.* Oxford, 1976.

ROBERT I. BURNS, S.J.

ALLEGORY. Allegory is not easily defined. In a general sense, the word is used to describe fiction that uses symbolic figures or actions to express generalizations about life. Sometimes allegory is a genre in its own right (the book of Revelation, Aesopian fables, William Langland's *Piers Plowman* [c. 1360–1400], morality plays, and state pageantry—processions, masques, and tournaments). At other times it is a treatment of reality incorporated into works in another genre, such as the allegorical pastoral of the Italian poet "Mantuan" (Giovanni Battista Spagnoli; c. 1448–1516) or allegorical romance (Torquato Tasso's *Gerusalemme liberata,* 1581; Edmund Spenser's *Faerie Queene,* 1590, 1596). Moreover, in addition to writing allegorically, we can read or interpret allegorically (allegoresis) even if the author never intended us to do so. Often it is difficult, of course, to tell what meaning was or is "really there" in a text and what we are bringing to it. Allegory and allegoresis overlap in a gray area, which Jungians have ascribed to the cultural unconscious shared by poet and reader, while late-twentieth-century reader-response criticism claims that every meaning is more or less the contribution of the reader.

Renaissance Allegory and Allegoresis.
The Elizabethan critic, George Puttenham, author of *The Arte of English Poesie* (1589) wrote that allegory is "when we do speak in sense translative and wrested from the owne signification" and where a word no longer signifies its usual meaning, but is "nevertheless not altogether contrary but having much conveniencie with it." "Allegory" is thus an all-embracing conception. The Elizabethans used the term "symbol" only on rare occasions to designate an allegorical image; "figure" and "type" were more frequent. Elizabethan critics practiced allegoresis, as readers had in late antiquity and the Middle Ages, to find redeeming social value in seemingly frivolous, pagan, or secular stories, and lyrics. Renaissance poets rewrote or reinterpreted older poetry (such as the Song of Songs within the Bible) as if it were directed toward God.

Sir Philip Sidney in the *Defense of Poetry* (1595) and Spenser in his "Letter to Ralegh" (appended to the first instalment of the *Faerie Queene*) justify the creation of fictions as the allegorizing of moral truths. Sidney, however, appeals more frequently and more modishly to the Aristotelian doctrine of mimesis, which held that imaginative imitations of action could be not only entertaining but educational in themselves. In the Renaissance, mimesis could overlap with allegory if it included "doctrine by ensample"—a story that produced a discernible moral lesson ("Letter to Ralegh").

The ancient defense of literature as allegory both fostered and was fostered by the vogue of esoteric writing seen in the works of Dante, Marsilio Ficino, Giovanni Pico della Mirandola, George Chapman, and, on occasion, Spenser. Even so, allegory occurs in fact somewhat less frequently in the Renaissance than it did in the Middle Ages; and it contains more mythology, greater concern for this world, and a more detailed and individualized subjectivity. However, it is not radically different. The major change came later: with the obsolescence both of providential history, and of the notion that all things were governed by correspondences, allegory confined its themes and assumptions to politics and to theories of culture (as in Alexander Pope's *Dunciad,* 1728).

The Renaissance inherited personification from classical antiquity, especially from the Platonic tradition by way of the Middle Ages. The most abstract and philosophical kind of allegory, personification is the portrayal of an abstraction (for example, Disdain) or a group (for example, Britannia) as a person. Personification is by no means universal: it is rare in the Bible and virtually unknown in Chinese and Japanese literature. In pure personifications like Disdain, the abstraction means exactly what it says; only its actions are "wrested," as Puttenham would say, from human portraiture; for example, Spenser's Disdain walks on tiptoes and has unbending knees (*Faerie Queene* VI. vii. 42; viii. 15–16). When a personification has an ordinary proper name, especially a historical one, it is called a veiled personification and its name a cue-name (Dante's Beatrice and Spenser's Una stand for revealed truth, Dante's Virgil and the Palmer in Spenser stand for reason).

In three other kinds of allegory prevalent in the Renaissance, particularly *figura* or typology, the image is related to the meaning by way of analogy. A physical object often relates to its meaning in this way, as in sexual symbolism where a pointed weapon suggests a phallus. Alternatively, a physical object can relate to its meaning by metonymy or synecdoche (associated attribute or the part for the whole) as when a crown symbolizes rulership, or by mere convention as in heraldry. Also operating by analogy is typology or *figura*—the analogy, supposedly arranged by God, of historical persons, groups, or events to those in salvation-history past, present, or to come. *Figura* gained currency as part of the Christian allegoresis of the Old Testament: it was practiced by St. Paul and therefore even by the Reformers, who otherwise inclined to a literal interpretation. *Figura* constituted "allegory" in the restricted meaning "what you should believe" that it has in the second of the medieval four exegetical senses, used to guide biblical interpretation. These are defined in the mnemonic jingle, "Littera gesta docet, quid credas allegoria, / Moralis quid agas, quo tendas anagogia" ("The *letter* teaches the events, the *allegory* what you should believe, the *moral* what you should do, the *anagogy* where you should be going"). The four interpretive senses as a system had been affirmed in secular literature by Dante (*Epistle to Can Grande*) and by Giovanni Boccaccio (*De genealogia deorum,* 1351–1360). Though repudiated by Protestant Reformers, they were reaffirmed for secular literature by Spenser's contemporary and admirer and Queen Elizabeth's godson, Sir John Harington in both his preface and his notes to his translation of Ludovico Ariosto's *Orlando furioso* (1591).

Spenser, like Harington and many allegorists, believed that ordinary human authors could create typological allegory of a sort. Arthur rescuing Red Cross from Orgoglio's dungeon (I.viii) reenacts the Harrowing of Hell in the daily Creed; Red Cross's forestate of marriage (I.xii) prefigures the Marriage of the Lamb (Revelation 21); and Guyon lying apparently dead at the mouth of a cave guarded by an angel, parallels the entombed Christ (II.viii). Guyon is different from a biblical type, however, because he is an entirely fictional not a historical figure.

Thirdly, typology's literary equivalent is the roman à clef, or any passage that must be read as "historical allegory." Spenser assured Queen Elizabeth I that she could discern herself "in mirrours more than one" in *The Faerie Queene* (III Proem 5) "and thine own realmes in lond of Faery" (II Proem 5); early manuscript glosses were inclined to this reading (suggesting analogies to her, for instance, in Una). Marguérite de Navarre in her *Heptaméron* claims that her characters are thinly veiled real people; and the story of Argalus and Parthenia in Sidney's *Arcadia* reenacts an event in the life of his parents.

Haunting all allegorical interpretations of this period, however, were surely various words of St. Paul, above all the verse "For now we see as in a glass darkly; but then face to face; now I know in part; but then shall I know even as also I am known" (1 Corinthians 13). Witness Spenser's reference to his major work as "a continued Allegory, or darke conceit" ("Letter to Raleigh"). The belief that our life is a dark mirror accounts indeed for both the ubiquity and the force of Renaissance allegory.

BIBLIOGRAPHY

Primary Work

Puttenham, George. *The Arte of English Poesie* (1589). Edited by Gladys Doidge Willcock and Alice Walker. Cambridge, U.K., 1936.

Secondary Works

Auerbach, Erich. "Figura." In his *Scenes from the Drama of European Literature.* Translated by Willard Trask. New York, 1959. Pages 11–76.

Bloomfield, Morton. "A Grammatical Approach to Personification Allegory." In his *Essays and Explorations: Studies in Ideas, Language, and Literature.* Cambridge, Mass., 1970. Pages 243–260. Contains refutation of the once-standard opposition between allegory and symbolism.

Fletcher, Angus. *Allegory: The Theory of a Symbolic Mode.* Ithaca, N.Y., 1964. Bibliography.

Hough, Graham. *A Preface to the* Faerie Queene. London, 1962. Chapter 6 diagrams the kinds of allegory on a clock face.

Lubac, Henri de. *Medieval Exegesis.* Vol. 1: *The Four Senses of Scripture.* Translated by Mark Sebanc. Grand Rapids, Mich., 1998. Translation of *Exégèse médiévale.* Vol. 1: *Les quatre sens de l'écriture.* Paris, 1959.

MacQueen, John. *Allegory.* London, 1970. Good brief treatment of medieval background. Bibliography.

Teskey, Gordon. *Allegory and Violence.* Ithaca, N.Y., 1996.

Williams, Arnold. "Medieval Allegory: An Operational Approach." In *Poetic Theory/Poetic Practice: Papers of the Midwest Modern Language Association.* Edited by Robert E. Scholes. Iowa City, 1969. Pages 77–84. A brief, magisterial, but little-known taxonomy.

CAROL V. KASKE

ALMEIDA, FRANCISCO DE (1450?–1510), first viceroy of Portuguese Asia, or Estado da India. Almeida was born in Lisbon, the son of the first count of Abrantes. He earned his reputation as a skilled military commander in the wars against the "Moors" in both Castile and North Africa. In March 1505 he was named by King Manuel I as first viceroy for Portugal's rapidly expanding Asian empire and sailed for the Indian Ocean with a formidable fleet of some twenty-two ships and twenty-five hundred men, including fifteen hundred soldiers. Reaching the East African coast by July of that year, he captured Kilwa with little opposition and thereafter built a fort there "so strong that it would keep even the King of France at bay." He then captured and sacked Mombasa. Intent upon following his orders from King Manuel and solidifying the position of the Portuguese crown in the spice trade, he also fortified posts upon the island of Angediva near Goa and at Cannanore before establishing his viceregal office at Cochin, where Afonso de Albuquerque had secured a fortress in 1503.

During the next three years, Almeida accomplished much in his quest to establish the Portuguese

Empire as a dominant force in the Asian trade. He negotiated a successful commercial treaty with the rich entrepôt of Malacca (later Melaka) and his talented and much beloved son, Lourenço, made significant discoveries and inroads in the lucrative cinnamon trade located on the island of Ceylon, while Fernando Soarez was perhaps the first European to sight the island of Madagascar. When Lourenço was killed in a naval engagement in March 1508 with the Arab-Egyptian fleet then seeking to expel the Portuguese from their trade off Chaul, Almeida was determined to revenge his son, and in doing so to once and for all destroy Islamic naval and commercial power in the Indian Ocean.

In the midst of Almeida's preparation of a large high-seas fleet, Albuquerque reached the Malabar coast in late 1508 and produced "secret" letters patent from Manuel I empowering him to succeed Almeida. The viceroy flatly refused to accept this change in command and eventually imprisoned his rival. In the meantime, he inflicted a crushing defeat upon Islamic power in February 1509 off Diu, on the western coast of India. In a seminal encounter that demonstrated the superiority of European shipborne artillery at that time, the viceroy's fleet decimated the numerically superior Arab-Egyptian fleet, thus helping to ensure Portuguese power in the trade for the next century.

Returning to Cochin after this great victory, Almeida was forced to free Albuquerque and recognize his claim in November 1509 following the arrival of a large fleet from Lisbon carrying the grand marshal of Portugal, Fernando Coutinho. In early December of that same year, he sailed for Europe with three ships. Stopping for water and provisions at Table Bay (Cape Town), Almeida was killed on 1 March 1510 in a bloody attack on the Hottentots in which sixty-five of his men also perished. Portugal's first Asian viceroy, however, had already established the solid imperial footing upon which Albuquerque and others would build in the decades that followed, thrusting Portugal to the rank of world power by the mid-sixteenth century.

See also **Asia, East**; *biography of Afonso de Albuquerque.*

BIBLIOGRAPHY

Albuquerque, Afonso de. *Cartas para el-rei d. Manuel I.* Edited by António Baiáo. Lisbon, Portugal, 1942.

Albuquerque, Afonso de. *The Commentaries of the Great Afonso Dalboquerque, Second Viceroy of India.* 4 vols. London, 1875–1884. Translation by Walter de Gray Birch of *Commentarios de grande Afonso Dalboquerque* (1774).

Castanheda, Fernão Lopes de. *Historia do descobrimiento e conquista da Índia pelos Portugueses.* 9 vols. Edited by C. Wessels, S.J. Coimbra, Portugal, 1924–1933.

GLENN J. AMES

ALMSGIVING. *See* **Poverty and Charity.**

ALTARPIECES. *See* **Decorative Arts.**

ALVÁREZ DE TOLEDO, FERNANDO (third duke of Alba, or Alva; 1507–1582), Spanish general, statesman. Fernando Alvárez de Toledo was born at Piedrahita (Ávila) on 29 October 1507, to one of the largest and most powerful Castilian families. His father died three years later, and the boy's grandfather, Fadrique, second duke of Alba, supervised his upbringing aided by Juan Boscán, translator of Baldassare Castiglione's *Il cortegiano* (*The Book of the Courtier;* 1528). Instruction in theology and the classics leavened an otherwise military education. At sixteen, Fernando fought at Fuenterrabía, and in 1529 at Vienna. After inheriting his title in 1531 he went on to serve Charles V in the campaigns of Tunis, Provence, and Algiers, and emerged during the Schmalkaldic wars of 1546–1547 as the emperor's chief military adviser.

In 1548, Charles appointed Alba majordomo to Prince Philip, a position that enabled him to become head of an aristocratic faction that contended for influence with another group headed by the royal chamberlain Ruy Gómez de Silva. Alba accompanied Philip to England in 1554 but soon went to Italy, where he served briefly as viceroy of Milan and then of Naples. In 1556–1557 he commanded the royal forces in a successful campaign against Pope Paul IV, and in 1559 he played a major role in negotiating the treaty of Cateau-Cambrésis. By 1560 Alba was back in Spain as a member of Philip's Council of State. The king found Alba's overbearing personality difficult but valued his military advice and trusted his religious orthodoxy to the point that he often consulted him on religious appointments.

When the seventeen provinces of the Netherlands began to protest Philip's policies of reform, Alba opposed all compromise. He was therefore the logical choice to suppress the rioting and iconoclasm that broke out in 1566, and he marched to the Low Countries the following year with an army of Spanish and Italian veterans. Though peace had since been restored, Alba executed the counts of Egmont and Hoorne as rebels and organized the Council of Troubles, a political tribunal that became

Her nimpt mit gewalt dem rychtom von   Il prend par fortresse le richesse du pais
Dem land vnd hat vil ontschuldich blut   Et par finesse a respandu le sang
Laffen hervour gen vnd brennen   Inocent par grand triesse

Her hat auch egmont vnd horm das leben   Il a mis a mort egmont et horne et
Genomen vndem ganßen adel ßnderbracht   Tout gentils barons occis par infame que
Das maß vom borger vnd bauwr worten byd Bourgoys fun plaint et laboureurs

Fernando Alvárez de Toledo. Allegorical engraving of the duke of Alba, Spanish governor of the Netherlands. AKG LONDON

known somewhat unfairly as the Council of Blood. William of Orange then assumed leadership of the revolt, but the duke easily defeated his German mercenaries, and by Christmas 1568 Alba was in full control of the Netherlands. He used his position to reorganize the ecclesiastical hierarchy and reform the judicial code, but his regime was unpopular. When he sought to impose a perpetual tax known as the Tenth Penny in 1572, most of the country rebelled. Though Alba once again restored order, his policy of deliberate frightfulness led the king to recall him in the following year. Back at court the duke's position gradually weakened, and Philip briefly imprisoned him before recalling him to lead the successful invasion of Portugal in 1580. Alba died there at Tomar in 1582.

Contemporaries regarded Alba as the greatest soldier of his age. His ideas on warfare inspired an influential school of military writers, most of whom had served under him as officers. His political legacy, however, was almost entirely negative. Alba's poli-

cies in the Netherlands intensified the opposition to Spanish rule and probably made an already difficult situation irretrievable.

BIBLIOGRAPHY

Alvárez de Toledo, Fernando. *Epistolario.* Edited by Jacobo Stuart Fitz-James y Falco, duke of Berwick and Alba. 3 vols. Madrid, 1952.

Maltby, William S. *Alba: A Biography of Fernando Alvárez de Toledo, Third Duke of Alba, 1507–1582.* Berkeley, Calif., 1983.

WILLIAM S. MALTBY

AMBOISE, GEORGES D' (1460–1510), French cardinal and statesman. Born into a Norman noble family, Georges d'Amboise began royal service early in life. He was erected a bishop at age nineteen and moved on to the archbishopric of Rouen in 1493. He attached himself to Louis of Orléans's party during Louis's problems with the monarchy, and when Louis became king (as Louis XII) Amboise functioned as his chief minister and became a cardinal in 1498. When Louis XII occupied Milan in 1500, Amboise served as its governor for four years. In 1502 Pope Alexander VI made him legate *a latere,* with enormous authority in the French church. Amboise's service was so extensive that the saying "Let George do it!" supposedly referred to him.

The cardinal spent time in Italy, especially Milan, and became an enthusiastic supporter of Renaissance culture. He befriended Machiavelli, who served as Florentine ambassador to France while he was in power. Amboise patronized many Italian artists, including Leonardo da Vinci, whom he could not persuade to come to France. He engaged Italians to work on the reconstruction of his château of Gaillon, near Rouen. Fra Giocondo was the major designer, and the three Giusti brothers and Andrea Solari were involved in its decoration. Gaillon's Italianate features had considerable influence on art and architecture in Normandy.

Amboise exercised a restraining influence on Louis XII in his conflict with Pope Julius II, which began in 1509. His death the next year removed the one man who was capable of mediating between them, leading to the war with Julius's Holy League that clouded Louis's last years.

BIBLIOGRAPHY

Baumgartner, Frederic J. *Louis XII.* New York, 1994.

Bridge, John. *A History of France from the Death of Louis XI to 1515.* 5 vols. Oxford, 1921–1936.

Quilliet, Bernard. *Louis XII, père du peuple.* Paris, 1986.

FREDERIC J. BAUMGARTNER

AMERBACH FAMILY, publishers and legal scholars. The Amerbach family began with the printer-publisher Johann Amerbach (c. 1443–1513), who took the name of his birthplace, Amorbach in Franconia, instead of his family name, Welcker, when he established his press in Basel in around 1478. Amerbach studied with humanist professor Johann Heynlin von Stein at the University of Paris and by 1464 completed his baccalaureate and master's degrees there. Although his mentor Heynlin was a cofounder of the first press in Paris, Amerbach probably learned the craft in Venice. Soon after setting up shop in Basel, he became part of the community. He joined the merchants' guild (1481), purchased a house (now Rheingasse 23) in Klein Basel, married Barbara Ortenberg (1483), and became a citizen of Basel (1484). Four of the five Amerbach children survived to adulthood: Bruno (1484–1519), Basilius (1488–1535), Margarete (1490–1541), and Bonifacius (1495–1562).

Amerbach attracted many intellectuals of the northern Renaissance to his publishing projects. Heynlin was an editor and influential editorial advisor; Beatus Rhenanus, Johann Reuchlin, Conrad Pellican, and Sebastian Brant served as scholarly editors. Either alone or in partnership with Johann Petri and Johann Froben, Amerbach published many standard works of late Scholasticism, but his reputation rests on his humanist program to publish the first printed editions of the collected works of saints Ambrose, Augustine, and Jerome. These collected editions required long searches for manuscripts and took years to finish. The Jerome edition was completed after Amerbach's death by his junior partner Johann Froben, his sons Bruno and Basilius, and Desiderius Erasmus, who joined the project in 1514.

The Amerbach sons received a humanist education that emphasized mastery of classical Latin style, Greek, and Hebrew. After taking degrees at the University of Paris, Bruno and Basilius worked as editors in the family firm. Bonifacius pursued a career in law. He attended the University of Basel (B.A. 1511; M.A. 1512), then studied with two of the greatest jurists of the period, Johann Ulrich Zasius in Freiburg and Andrea Alciato in Avignon. Receiving his doctorate in Avignon, he returned to Basel as professor of civil law at the University in 1525.

In the first years of the Reformation Bonifacius embraced the prospect of Luther and Erasmus inaugurating a new age of theology. After seeing the radical social and political effects of the Reformation, however, Bonifacius withdrew his support. When Basel officially adopted reform in 1529, pressure to

Bonifacius Amerbach. Portrait by Hans Holbein the Younger, 1519. KUNSTMUSEUM BASEL/ARTOTHEK

conform to the new communion began to mount. Erasmus left the city. Bonifacius refused to accept the Reformers' position on the eucharist. The city council, reluctant to drive one of its most prominent citizens into exile, delayed taking action. In 1532 Bonifacius was offered a professorship at Dôle. At the urging of the council he remained in Basel. By 1534 Bonifacius reconciled his views with those of the Reformed Church of Basel, became a Protestant, and served the university and council the rest of his life.

Bonifacius assured his place in history as a jurist by his synthesis of two approaches to jurisprudence then current, the *mos italicus* and *mos gallicus*. The former relied on reference to medieval legal commentaries to illuminate the law; the latter, promoted by earlier humanists, emphasized the historical understanding of legal texts. Bonifacius employed both the medieval commentators (despite their unclassical Latin) and humanist philological criticism in juridical interpretation.

Bonifacius was in touch with the intellectual and scholarly community of Europe in a correspondence that continued regardless of religious differences. He maintained connections with Alciato, Zasius, Michel Montaigne, Philipp Melanchthon, Conrad Pellican, and others. He enjoyed a lifelong friendship with Erasmus, who named him heir and executor of his charitable trust. Bonifacius married Martha Fuchs, with whom he had five children; two reached adulthood, Faustina and Basilius. Like his father, Basilius became professor of law at the university and legal advisor to the council. After the death of his wife and infant son, Basilius turned his energy and resources into expanding the collection of art, books, coins, and curiosities inherited from his father. Basilius is chiefly responsible for the scope and magnitude of the cabinet that the city purchased in 1661.

The male line of the family ended with the death of Basilius's son Bonifaciolus, but continues today through descendants of Basilius's sister Faustina Iselin. The Amerbach family left two great legacies: the Amerbach correspondence and the Amerbach Cabinet. The correspondence contains letters written by and to three generations of the family from 1481 to 1591. The collections of the cabinet have been distributed to the Universitätsbibliothek, the Kunstmuseum, and Historisches Museum of Basel.

BIBLIOGRAPHY

Primary Work

Die Amerbachkorrespondenz. Edited by Alfred Hartmann and Beat R. Jenny. 10 vols. (in progress). Basel, 1942–1991. The volumes published to date cover 1481–1558. The letters are an unparalleled source for a picture of the daily life, business, and intellectual concerns of this prominent Renaissance family.

Secondary Works

Bietenholz, Peter G., ed. *Contemporaries of Erasmus: A Biographical Register of the Renaissance and Reformation.* Vol. 1. Toronto, 1985. Pages 42–48.

Gilmore, Myron P. *Humanists and Jurists: Six Studies in the Renaissance.* Cambridge, Mass., 1963. See chapter 6, "Boniface Amerbach," pp. 146–177.

Guggisberg, Hans R. *Basel in the Sixteenth Century: Aspects of the City Republic before, during, and after the Reformation.* St. Louis, Mo., 1982.

Halporn, Barbara. *Johann Amerbach's Correspondence: Early Printing in Its Social Context.* Ann Arbor, Mich., 2000.

Kabinettstücke der Amerbach im Historischen Museum Basel. Objets choisis de la Collection Amerbach. Show Pieces from the Amerbach Cabinet. Text by Elisabeth Landolt with contributions by Beatrice Scharli, Hans Chr. Ackermann. Basel, 1984.

BARBARA C. HALPORN

AMERICAS. In October 1492 Christopher Columbus and his men completed a transatlantic voyage that initiated European contact with the Americas, thereafter never to be broken. Although American societies were ancient, the continents of the Western Hemisphere represented a new world for the Europeans.

The Americas in 1492. Columbus's voyages opened to the ambitions of the states and peoples of western Europe vast territories that for millennia had existed in virtual isolation from the rest of the world. These lands were as varied culturally and linguistically as they were geographically. Hundreds of distinct peoples inhabited environments ranging from the woodlands and plains of North America, the semiarid plateau of present-day Mexico, and the jungles and highlands of Central America, to the great Amazonian basin, high Andean valleys, rain forests, and temperate pampas (grasslands) of South America.

Densely populated, socially and politically complex societies, which utilized intensive forms of agriculture, such as irrigation, terracing, and artificial construction of garden plots, had taken shape where climate and topography permitted. Important centers of civilization arose, especially in such areas as central and southern Mesoamerica and the Andean region, where higher altitudes mitigated tropical and semitropical temperatures, although some developed in lowland and coastal zones as well. The Mayas, for example, flourished in both the lowlands and highlands of present-day Yucatán, Chiapas, and Guatemala, and recent archaeological work indicates that advanced societies existed on the Pacific coast of Peru and the Caribbean coast of Honduras.

By the late fifteenth century many centers of civilization had undergone several cycles of rise and eventual fragmentation. One such center was the great Mexican metropolis of Teotihuacán, which at its height may have attained a population of nearly a quarter of a million and influenced other centers as far away as Monte Albán in Oaxaca. Although the Mayas were divided into a number of small city-states by the time Europeans arrived, larger states and confederations still flourished in the Americas—the Aztec and Tarascan states of central and western Mexico, the Inca empire of the Andean region, the Chibcha and other kingdoms of Columbia, and the Iroquois Confederation of northeastern North America.

The groups living in the Americas in the late fifteenth century nearly defy generalization by reason of their number and diversity (see table 1). Some basic features of life were widely shared, such as a diet that included maize (corn), which was cultivated throughout North and South America, even in areas such as the Andes and the Caribbean where tubers predominated. The weaving of textiles from cotton or wool (in the Andean region) and production of pottery of high aesthetic as well as functional value also were common, as were wood carving and metalworking, the latter mostly for ornamental purposes. Metallurgy apparently originated in South America and spread from there to Mesoamerica.

TABLE 1. Estimated Indigenous Population of America at the Time of European Contact.

	Estimated population	Percentage of total American population
North America	4,400,000	7.7
Mexico	21,400,000	37.3
Central America	5,650,000	9.9
Caribbean	5,850,000	10.2
Andes	11,500,000	20.1
Lowland South America	8,500,000	14.8
Total	57,300,000	100.0

SOURCE: *The Native Population of the Americas in 1492* by William M. Denevan, p. 291. Copyright © 1992. Reprinted by permission of the University of Wisconsin Press.

American peoples had developed perhaps the most varied and productive agriculture in the world. Maize and manioc (a starchy root also known as cassava and cultivated in the rain forest regions of South America as well as the Caribbean islands) were superior to any European staple in terms of caloric yield and productivity. In contrast to Europe, Africa, and Asia, however, the Americas had few domesticated animals. Only the Andeans had large domesticated animals—llamas, alpacas, vicuñas—that served as significant sources of food, wool, and transportation. In the North American plains, however, herds of wild bison provided subsistence for tribes that used the skins, pelts, and meat for shelter and clothing as well as food.

Indigenous Americans had strong notions of territoriality and close ties with the land where they lived, hunted, fished, or farmed. For them the land, with its mountains, lakes, streams, deserts, flora, and fauna, had profound spiritual meaning and power and was inextricably linked to a group's understanding of its origins and history. The nature of the relationship of people to land varied considerably, from forms of landholding and use that were rather similar to those of some Europeans to more flexible concepts of territorial rights that could be specific without necessarily being exclusive.

Europeans of the late fifteenth and sixteenth centuries also held a range of beliefs connected with the land and its cultivation and vested certain places in the countryside with particular spiritual significance, but on the whole the land and its features and products were probably less central to their beliefs than to those of Native Americans. For the most part, in the Americas the land held no special meaning for Europeans; rather they viewed it, and its inhabitants, in terms of their potential for generating profit.

Early Contacts. The first contacts of Europeans with people in the Americas were not with representatives of the most sophisticated civilizations but instead with simpler societies of agriculturalists, fishers, and hunters. The nature of these early encounters doubtless bolstered European notions of cultural superiority and allowed them to maintain such assumptions even later in the face of compelling evidence that at least some of the indigenous societies of the Americas could not reasonably be judged inferior.

One can but speculate how Europeans might have responded if they first had reached the dazzling Aztec metropolis of Tenochtitlan (Tenochtitlán; the site of the present-day Mexico City), with its great causeways, temples, gardens, and teeming but orderly marketplaces, rather than the farming villages of the Taino of the Greater Antilles. Had they done so, it seems unlikely that they would have formed the kind of impressions of indigenous people that Columbus did of the islanders, or Vaz de Caminha of the people of coastal Brazil, or Jacques Cartier of groups in Canada. These men described the people they met as docile and apparently lacking in religious beliefs; hence they concluded that they could readily be converted to Christianity. Had they seen the temples and priests of Tenochtitlan or Cuzco, they probably would not have been so quick to assume that their religion could easily be imposed on indigenous people, and indeed it was not long before the difficulty and complexity of the task became apparent.

Nonetheless, the unquestioning assumption of European cultural superiority, doubtless rooted in or bolstered by the seeming backwardness of the groups first encountered and the relative ease with which they intimidated and manipulated people like the Taino (who lived in the Bahamas and the Greater Antilles), was a powerful force. That confidence sustained them even through serious challenges to their claims to authority and underlay their singleminded and usually well-coordinated approach to conquest.

In those relatively rare instances where Europeans found themselves immersed in indigenous society and isolated from other Europeans, some alteration in perception could occur. Certainly that was the case for Álvar Núñez Cabeza de Vaca, survivor of a disastrous Spanish expedition to Florida in the mid-1530s, who lived among the tribes of the Gulf Coast and southwestern part of the present-day

Naming America. A 1589 Flemish ink drawing by Jan van der Straat, called Giovanni Stra-dano (c. 1523–1605), *Discovery of America: Vespucci Landing in America,* includes the allegorical personification of the Americas as a female figure. The European explorer, identi-fied as "Americus Vespucius," addresses the woman in the hammock as "America." THE METROPOLITAN MUSEUM OF ART, GIFT OF THE ESTATE OF JAMES HAZEN HYDE, 1959

United States for years and developed some degree of understanding of and empathy with the people he came to know. Yet even he never abandoned the almost universally held Spanish assumption that the Indians (as they called all indigenous people, despite the very real and perceptible differences among them) should be Christianized and incorporated into the framework of Spanish society as productive la-borers—that is, subjects. Nor did Bartolomé de Las Casas, the Dominican priest who protested and con-demned the Spanish settlers' ill treatment and ex-ploitation of the Indians.

The debate in which Las Casas participated con-cerned how the Indians should be converted and thereby civilized, not the objective itself. Christiani-zation justified conquest. Even those individuals who immersed themselves most deeply in the study of indigenous culture, language, and history, such as Fray Bernardino de Sahagún, never lost sight of the ultimate goal of conversion.

Men like Las Casas and Cabeza de Vaca belonged to the upper echelons of Spanish society, and not-withstanding both internal and external conflict they remained faithful to its general ethos and objectives. Not so those individuals who abandoned their ties

to European society and opted for life with the In-dians, usually leaving so little trace in the records that it is all but impossible to decipher their motives. Shipwrecked on the coast of Yucatán in the 1510s, Gonzalo Guerrero—unlike Jerónimo de Aguilar, also stranded there for years, who was poignantly grateful to be rescued, and who became Hernando Cortés's interpreter—not only rejected all invitations to rejoin his compatriots but for some years appar-ently led the Mayas in waging war on them.

While the phenomenon of Europeans opting for an indigenous lifestyle on the whole was marginal to the history of the colonization of the Americas, it nonetheless offers an intriguing counterpoint to and commentary on the prevailing model of European-indigenous relations. Furthermore, there were situ-ations that at least for a time seemed to occupy a middle ground. In the Spanish colony of Paraguay the small number of European settlers (who in-cluded Portuguese, Germans, and Italians as well as Spaniards) intermarried with Guarani clans, to the extent that the so-called Spanish sector in a genera-tion or two became largely mestizo (mixed), and in-digenous material culture, household structure, and even language prevailed. In Canada, French fur traders adopted indigenous ways and lived with Indian women, and to a great extent the success of early Portuguese and French ventures in the brazilwood trade in Brazil hinged on friendly relations that traders were able to form with local groups. Yet these cases primarily reflect pragmatic adaptations to particular circumstances, not any real ideological differences among Europeans.

Indigenous settlement patterns, lifestyles, and responses to Europeans had an enormous impact on what the newcomers could and could not do. Almost nowhere in the Americas did Europeans find themselves in empty wilderness. Even in the most sparsely occupied regions they usually found villages or encampments and towns, and in some places heavily urbanized areas where populations were larger. At the outset they depended almost entirely on their indigenous hosts for food and relied on them for information about geography, resources, and other groups. Indians offered hospitality and guided the newcomers from place to place.

Yet despite the extent of their dependence, Europeans more often than not failed to reciprocate with gratitude or respect, and even if initially they did so, over the long run they generally did not maintain balanced relations. From early on, if not from the very outset, they kidnapped hostages whom they hoped to use as interpreters and guides or to carry back home as curiosities and proof of their exploits; tried to coerce people into revealing stores of precious metals or gems (often nonexistent); commandeered carefully stored provisions that would have sustained a tribe or village through the lean months of the year; intimidated people through shows of force and actual violence; and took indigenous leaders captive and often executed them. They lied and deceived, ignored ceremony and protocol, and violated ritual. They waged all-out, destructive warfare. If some Native Americans initially thought that the newcomers might be divine, not surprisingly they quickly realized otherwise and began to retaliate and resist as best they could. While the refusal or inability of indigenous groups to aid Europeans could lead to frustration and even deprivation, contact could produce mutually beneficial relationships for trade and alliance. Ultimately, however, wherever they established a lasting presence Europeans usually managed to turn the situation in their favor.

Spanish Colonization.
The first century of European activity in the Americas was essentially a Spanish enterprise. Although other Europeans were also present and active, with the exception of the

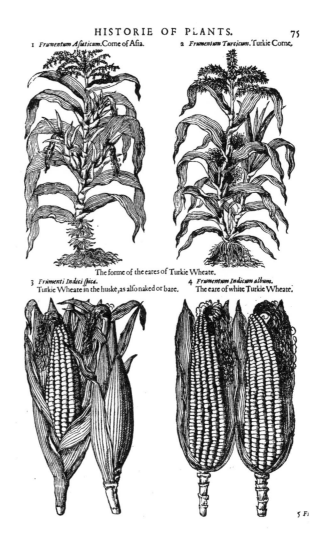

Maize. An engraving from J. Gerarde's *The Herball* (1597) depicts maize, a significant American contribution to European agriculture. COURTESY HERZOG AUGUST BIBLIOTHEK, WOLFENBÜTTEL

Portuguese, the ambitions and possibilities of other nations interested in the new territories hinged on what the Spanish claimed and accomplished in the first two generations after Columbus's voyages. The scope of the Spanish achievement was, in its own terms, enormous, but the beginnings in the Caribbean were modest.

The trajectory of conquest. For nearly twenty years after 1492, Spanish efforts focused almost exclusively on the island of Hispaniola (today shared by Haiti and the Dominican Republic). The Spanish did not conquer the other large islands of the Caribbean (Cuba, Puerto Rico, and Jamaica) until the years 1508–1511, although well before then they were familiar with the outlines of the circum-Caribbean mainland as a result of the voyages of Columbus and others.

The Spaniards established their basic mode of progressive settlement early on, consolidating control over an area and then using it as a base to organize a move to another. Hence Cuba was the starting point for the conquest of Mexico, Cuba and Puerto Rico for expeditions to Florida, and Hispaniola for the move into the isthmian region they called Tierra Firme. Panama in turn became the launching ground for the conquest of Peru. Following the conquest of central Mexico expeditions fanned out to the north—eventually taking Spaniards as far as New Mexico and the great plains of North America—and south to Honduras, just as Chile was reached from Peru. With some exceptions, such as the mostly disastrous expedition to the Río de la Plata, which was organized in Spain itself and resulted in the founding of Asunción in 1537, this pattern prevailed; even the settlement of the Philippines was largely accomplished from Mexico.

The Caribbean phase. Because of this pattern of settlement, Spanish activity on Hispaniola and the other large islands of the Caribbean, although experimental and in the end transitional, was crucial to future activities and successes. Although after the first voyage Columbus continued to search for the mainland of what he had expected to be Asia and for better opportunities for trade, real colonization began with his second voyage. By the time the Spanish crown sent Fray Nicolás de Ovando, accompanied by 2,500 people (among them Francisco Pizarro and Bartolomé de Las Casas), to govern Hispaniola in 1502 Spaniards had subdued the chiefdoms in the interior of the island and eliminated many of the caciques (indigenous chieftains). In the early years, when governmental authority was weak (Columbus himself was frequently absent), conflict (both factional and with the Taino) endemic, and settlement still tentative, many Spaniards went to live in Indian villages in order to survive.

They began to claim rights to the labor of the people with whom they lived. This system, known as *repartimiento,* was formalized legally under Ovando. It gave rise to the *encomienda,* which Spaniards would impose virtually everywhere that they found sedentary people who lived in towns and villages. In Spain itself the *encomienda* was an institution that arose during the reconquest of the peninsula from the Muslims, where it was an award of jurisdiction over a specified territory and its inhabitants that pro-

vided the holder with an income from rents and dues. In Spanish America the meaning of the institution was analogous, since it still represented an award for ostensible services to the crown. Its function and significance for the Indians, however, were quite distinct. Based on existing sociopolitical units and indigenous systems for organizing labor and collecting tribute (where there were such mechanisms), and relying on the authority of the traditional governing group or individual, *encomiendas* became the primary means for subordinating indigenous productivity and channeling it into the support of Spanish enterprises in the early decades of colonization. As such they could be highly disruptive of native life and society, although at the same time—because the *encomiendas'* successful operation depended on the maintenance of the sociopolitical units on which they were based, with their traditional authority figures—the preservation of these preconquest institutions was useful for the Spaniards.

In the islands, however, both intentional and unintentional destruction of indigenous society was far more common than preservation. Disruption of the agricultural cycle as men were taken away to work in gold mines, new diseases, the elimination of much of the cacique group, and nearly untrammeled abuse and mistreatment of the Indians in a frontier situation of minimal political control or clerical influence all spelled social and demographic disaster for the islanders. More settled and less warlike than the mobile Caribs of the smaller islands, the Taino were overwhelmed by the intruders from Europe and all but disappeared from the Caribbean. Relations between European men and indigenous women did guarantee a lasting genetic legacy in island populations, and the Taino left their imprint on diet, material culture, and language.

The brief period of economic success in the Caribbean hinged mainly on gold mining. Profits from gold financed further ventures to the mainland and allowed Spaniards to import the things they needed, which in the early years included a broad range of commodities, although they became self-sufficient in basic foodstuffs fairly quickly. By 1515 supplies of both gold and indigenous labor had dwindled notably, and settlers who stayed on the islands turned to sugarcane cultivation and cattle ranching and imported growing numbers of African slaves.

Despite the almost stunning rapidity of the cycle of boom and bust, a stable society nonetheless took hold. Hispaniola's capital, Santo Domingo, was laid out on a grid plan that probably reflected notions of

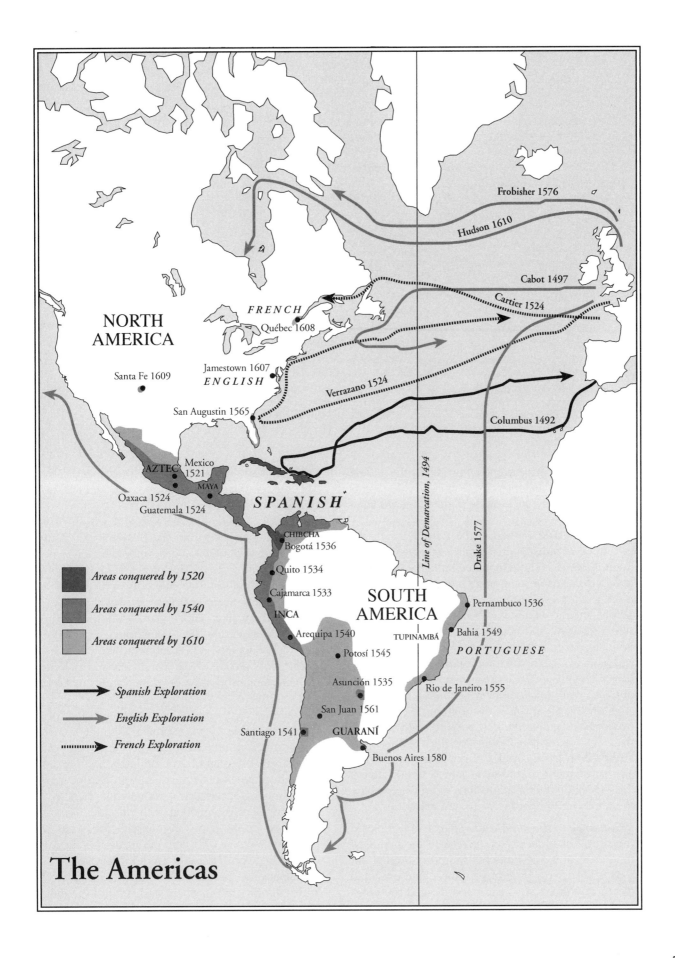

NORTH
AMERICA

FRENCH
Québec 1608

Santa Fe 1609

Jamestown 1607
ENGLISH

San Augustin 1565

Frobisher 1576

Hudson 1610

Cabot 1497

Cartier 1524

Verrazano 1524

Columbus 1492

AZTEC   Mexico
         1521
Oaxaca 1524   MAYA
Guatemala 1524   *SPANISH*

CHIBCHA
Bogotá 1536

Quito 1534

Cajamarca 1533

INCA

Arequipa 1540

Line of Demarcation, 1494

Drake 1577

SOUTH
AMERICA

TUPINAMBÁ

Pernambuco 1536

Bahia 1549

PORTUGUESE

Potosí 1545

Asunción 1535

Rio de Janeiro 1555

San Juan 1561

Santiago 1541   GUARANÍ

Buenos Aires 1580

Areas conquered by 1520

Areas conquered by 1540

Areas conquered by 1610

→ *Spanish Exploration*

→ *English Exploration*

·····▶ *French Exploration*

The Americas

55

TABLE 2. Estimated Population of the Spanish Indies in about 1570.

Region	Europeans	Indians	Blacks, Mixed Bloods	Totals
Mexico	30,000	3,500,000	25,000	3,555,000
Central America	15,000	550,000	10,000	575,000
Española	5,000	500	30,000	35,500
Cuba	1,200	1,350	15,000	17,550
Puerto Rico	1,000	300	10,000	11,300
Jamaica	300	. . .	1,000	1,300
Colombia	10,000	800,000	15,000	825,000
Venezuela	2,000	300,000	5,000	307,000
Ecuador	6,500	400,000	10,000	416,500
Peru	25,000	1,500,000	60,000	1,585,000
Bolivia	7,000	700,000	30,000	737,000
Paraguay	3,000	250,000	5,000	258,000
Argentina	2,000	300,000	4,000	306,000
Uruguay	. . .	5,000	. . .	5,000
Chile	10,000	600,000	10,000	620,000
Totals	118,000	8,907,150	230,000	9,255,150
Percentage of total	1.3	96.2	2.5	100.0

SOURCE: *Spain and Portugal in the New World, 1492–1700* by Lyle N. McAlister, p. 131. Copyright © 1984 by the University of Minnesota. Reprinted by permission of the publisher, the University of Minnesota Press.

town planning then current in Europe. By the middle of the sixteenth century Santo Domingo had a Gothic cathedral and was the location of the first *Audiencia* (high court).

Precedents established in the Caribbean shaped the course of much future Spanish activity elsewhere in the Americas. These included an initial search for precious metals or some other highly lucrative commodity; early establishment of municipalities, often before actual conquest had been completed or even started; seizing and frequently executing the traditional leader to establish control; progressive imposition of royal authority, often starting with fiscal officials who ensured that the crown would receive its due and with the *Audiencia* becoming the key institution for governance; distribution of *encomiendas* and land grants, the best ones normally going to those who participated in the conquest of an area or arrived with good social and political connections; and subsequent migration of people who, having missed out on the initial rewards, often were willing to participate in expeditions to new territories.

Advance to the mainland. Spaniards completed the conquest of Mexico in 1521 with the taking of the Aztec capital of Tenochtitlan and of Peru about a decade later (in 1532 they captured and executed the Inca emperor Atahualpa and divided the enor-

mous ransom he had amassed among themselves, although conflict and rebellion continued for some time). Spaniards relied on precedents established in the islands, but the greater size and wealth of the mainland societies meant the possibility of institutional and socioeconomic development on a new and impressive scale. The crown sent viceroys to serve as the highest royal authority in the new kingdoms of New Spain and Peru. Towns and cities—many of them, like Tenochtitlan, established on pre-existing indigenous sites—multiplied, and a flood tide of immigrants, representing a broad socioeconomic cross section of Spanish society and including an increasing proportion of women and families, began to arrive.

Spaniards imported large numbers of African slaves (see table 2), who, familiar with the technology and agriculture of their masters and resistant to diseases that wrought havoc on indigenous civilizations, became essential auxiliaries in European enterprises. An ecclesiastical framework, parallel to and sometimes competing with the administrative apparatus, took shape. Institutional responses occurred in Spain as well, with the creation of the Casa de Contratación (House of Trade) in Seville in 1503 to regulate the movement of ships, people, goods, and bullion between Spain and the Indies, and in

TABLE 3. Estimated Minimum Spanish American Bullion Production, 1571–1700 (in Millions of Pesos of 8 *Reales*).

Year	Registered Bullion Imports into Seville*	Estimated Minimum Silver Production by Amalgamation	Adjusted Total Minimum Bullion Production
1571–1575	19.7	17.3	21.6
1576–1580	28.5	35.5	44.4
1581–1585	48.6	39.2	49.0
1586–1590	39.4	49.2	61.5
1591–1595	58.2	47.4	59.3
1596–1600	57.0	41.3	51.6
1601–1605	44.9	31.6	39.5
1606–1610	52.0	34.5	43.1
1611–1615	40.6	49.3	61.6
1616–1620	49.8	50.5	63.1
1621–1625	44.7	62.3	77.9
1626–1630	41.3	39.1	48.9
1631–1635	28.3	46.3	57.9
1636–1640	27.0	51.9	64.8
1641–1645	22.8	49.2	61.4
1646–1650	19.5	36.8	45.0
1651–1655	12.1	49.7	62.1
1656–1660	5.6	37.5	46.9
1661–1665		32.6	40.8
1666–1670		31.9	39.9
1671–1675		42.6	53.3
1676–1680		33.8	42.3
1681–1685		15.2	19.4
1686–1690		26.5	33.1
1691–1695		34.5	43.1
1696–1700		31.9	39.9

*Figures in this column are based on Hamilton's statistics, which end in the five-year period 1656–1660.

SOURCE: David A. Brading and Harry C. Cross, "Colonial Silver Mining and Peru," Table 1: Estimated Minimum Spanish-American Bullion Production, 1571–1700, *Hispanic American Historical Review,* 52:4 (November 1972), p. 579. Copyright © 1972, Duke University Press. Reprinted with permission.

1524 with the establishment of the Consejo de Indias (Council of the Indies), which became the highest governing body for the Americas short of the king himself.

The Church in Spanish America. In the early sixteenth century the Spanish crown acquired from the pope in Rome remarkably broad powers over the church in America. These powers included the right to nominate (in effect, to appoint) candidates for church office and to use the income from tithes for evangelization, including the construction of churches, monasteries, and hospitals. Dominicans went to Hispaniola in 1510 and Franciscans began to arrive in the Caribbean soon after, but reasonably organized, sustained missionary efforts really got un-

der way with the arrival of twelve (after the Apostles) Franciscans in Mexico at Cortés's invitation in 1524. The secular branch of the church (that part organized into bishoprics and parishes and including the cathedral chapters) also grew rapidly; by 1550 there were already twenty-two dioceses, with the vice-regal capital of Mexico City and Lima achieving metropolitan status with archbishops in 1546.

The sheer size of the task of creating a functioning ecclesiastical apparatus to serve the needs of both Spanish and indigenous society meant that the regular orders would play the most important role in the early development of the church in Spanish America. A special dispensation allowed members of the orders to occupy positions normally held by the secular clergy, such as parish benefices, and regulars

TABLE 4. Approximate Numbers of European Emigrants to America, 1500–1783.

Country of Origin	Number	Date
Spain	437,000	1500–1650
Portugal	100,000	1500–1700
Britain	400,000	1607–1700
Britain[1]	322,000	1700–1780
France	51,000	1608–1760
"Germany"[2]	100,000	1683–1783
Total	1,410,000	1500–1783

[1] Includes between 190,000 and 250,000 Scots and Irish.
[2] Germany refers to emigrants from southwestern Germany and the German-speaking cantons of Switzerland and Alsace Lorraine.

SOURCE: *"To Make America": European Emigration in the Early Modern Period* ed. by Ida Altman and James Horn, p. 3. Copyright © 1991 by The Regents of the University of California. Reprinted by permission of the University of California Press.

occupied even high church offices, as in the case of the Franciscan Fray Juan de Zumárraga, who was bishop and later archbishop of Mexico.

Franciscans and Dominicans were followed by Augustinians, Mercedarians, and eventually members of the new Society of Jesus, who would play the most important role in the church of early Portuguese Brazil and in missionary efforts in French Canada. For the Franciscans especially the Americas represented an unprecedented opportunity to fulfill their utopian visions of the conversion of all the world's peoples. Early evangelization campaigns that included mass baptisms fairly soon gave way to more gradual approaches emphasizing education. The orders built impressive monastery complexes in the countryside and in indigenous towns. While the dichotomy of the secular clergy serving Spanish society and the regular clergy serving the Indians has some basis in reality, the lines were blurred: the orders established their headquarters in the Spanish cities, and *encomenderos* hired secular priests to serve as parish priests, or *doctrineros,* to fulfill their responsibility for the conversion of the Indians under their jurisdiction.

Economic Development. To a great extent what underlay and sustained the activities of both branches of the church, the establishment and elaboration of governmental institutions at all levels, and the immigration of Spaniards and importation of Africans to the Americas was the wealth generated by silver mining in Mexico and Peru (see table 3). Silver financed trade with Europe and later with Asia via the Philippines. As the colonies produced nearly all

they required in the way of foodstuffs and other bulky items, long-distance trade came to consist mainly of high-quality cloth and clothing (for the upper echelons of Spanish society) and iron, both worked and unworked.

In contrast to other parts of the Americas, where commercial agriculture brought the wealth that sustained colonization—sugar in Brazil and later the Caribbean, tobacco in the Chesapeake—few commodities in early Spanish America found a market in Spain. Colonists did export dyestuffs—cochineal from Mexico and later indigo from Central America—and some high-quality leather to Europe, but little else, although there was a flourishing intercolonial trade. Traditional products such as coca in the Andes, yerba maté (a kind of herb that could be made into a beverage) in Paraguay, or cacao and pulque (an alcoholic beverage) in Mesoamerica became increasingly commercialized in terms of production and marketing even if the market for them long remained largely indigenous. The precocious self-sufficiency of the Spanish American colonies rested largely on the agrarian base sustained by indigenous labor, notwithstanding the huge losses of population that occurred in the sixteenth century, and on the wealth from the mines.

Other Colonizers in the Americas. Compared to Spanish America the colonial enterprises of almost all other European countries up to the early seventeenth century were fairly tenuous, as in fact were Spanish efforts wherever they failed to find large sedentary populations and mineral wealth. Europeans attempting to settle in North America and the Atlantic side of South America progressed only slowly (see table 4). Frequently they faced competition with other Europeans or were rebuffed by Indians (the French and Portuguese were almost equally active in Brazil until around 1565, as were the French and the Spanish in Florida); they were restricted by Spanish claims reinforced by Spanish naval superiority; or they were unable to maintain friendly relations with local groups (as in the case of the English on the Atlantic coast). Although for much of the sixteenth century they were mainly concerned with their far-flung trading empire in Africa and Asia, after the middle of the century the Portuguese did begin to take a greater interest in colonizing Brazil and established their capital at Salvador da Bahia in 1549 in the northeast.

See also **Columbus, Christopher; Ethnography of the New World; Missions, Christian;** *and biographies of figures mentioned in this entry.*

BIBLIOGRAPHY

Primary Works

Burns, E. Bradford, ed. *A Documentary History of Brazil.* New York, 1966. Includes fascinating accounts of early Portuguese activity in Brazil.

Díaz del Castillo, Bernal. *The Conquest of New Spain.* Translated by J. M. Cohen. London, 1963. Classic account by one of the participants in the conquest, written many years later.

Lockhart, James, and Enrique Otte, eds. *Letters and People of the Spanish Indies.* Cambridge, U.K., 1976. Letters from sixteenth-century emigrants to Spanish America with analysis by the editors.

Nuñez Cabeza de Vaca, Alvar. *Castaways.* Edited by Enrique Pupo-Walker. Translated by Frances M. López-Morillas. Berkeley and Los Angeles, 1993.

Secondary Works

Altman, Ida. *Emigrants and Society: Extremadura and Spanish America in the Sixteenth Century.* Berkeley and Los Angeles, 1989. Considers the impact of emigration to the Indies on local Spanish society.

Chiappelli, Fredi, ed. *First Images of America: The Impact of the New World on the Old.* 2 vols. Berkeley and Los Angeles, 1976.

Elliott, J. H. *The Old World and the New, 1492–1650.* Cambridge, U.K., 1970. Considers the intellectual and economic impact of the Indies on Spain.

Foster, George. *Culture and Conquest: America's Spanish Heritage.* Chicago, 1960. Important work on the transference and transformation of Spanish culture in the Americas.

Gibson, Charles. *The Aztecs under Spanish Rule: A History of the Indians of the Valley of Mexico, 1519–1810.* Stanford, Calif., 1964. Classic study of change and development in central Mexico after the conquest.

Lockhart, James. *Spanish Peru, 1532–1560: A Colonial Society.* Madison, Wis., 1968. Key work on socioeconomic formation in early Peru.

Lockhart, James, and Stuart B. Schwartz. *Early Latin America: A History of Colonial Spanish America and Brazil.* Cambridge, U.K., 1983. Excellent overview.

Phelan, John Leddy. *The Millennial Kingdom of the Franciscans in the New World.* 2d rev. ed. Berkeley, Calif., 1970.

Ricard, Robert. *The Spiritual Conquest of Mexico: An Essay on the Apostolate and the Evangelizing Methods of the Mendicant Orders in New Spain, 1523–1572* (orig. ed. Paris, 1933). Translated by Lesley B. Simpson. Berkeley and Los Angeles, 1966. Classic study of missionary activities in early Mexico.

Sauer, Carl O. *The Early Spanish Main.* Berkeley and Los Angeles, 1966. Good overview of Spanish activity in the Caribbean based on the writings of Columbus and other chroniclers.

Sauer, Carl O. *Sixteenth Century North America: The Land and the People as Seen by the Europeans.* Berkeley and Los Angeles, 1971.

Schwaller, John F. *The Church and Clergy in Sixteenth-Century Mexico.* Albuquerque, N. Mex., 1987.

Spalding, Karen. *Huarochirí: An Andean Society under Inca and Spanish Rule.* Stanford, Calif., 1984. Important study tracing the evolution of indigenous society in Peru before and after the conquest.

Thornton, John. *Africa and Africans in the Making of the Atlantic World, 1400–1680.* Cambridge, U.K., 1992.

Wilson, Samuel. *Hispaniola: Caribbean Chiefdoms in the Age of Columbus.* Tuscaloosa, Ala., 1990. Detailed reconstruction of European-Indian interaction immediately after Columbus's first voyages.

IDA ALTMAN

AMSTERDAM. The Dutch city of Amsterdam rose rapidly in the late sixteenth and early seventeenth centuries to become the most important commercial center in northern Europe. Located at the conjunction of the Ij and Amstel Rivers on the Zuider Zee, Amsterdam became the principal port in the transfer of goods between the Baltic and northeastern Europe in the seventeenth century. The city's strong mercantile orientation produced an open and diverse society that attracted thousands of immigrants and made Amsterdam home for a variety of publishers, thinkers, and artists in the late baroque era.

Early History. Receiving its city charter around 1300, Amsterdam was a fairly young city in the Renaissance era. Amsterdammers had reshaped their environment by constructing dikes, draining marshes, and damming rivers. Like other cities in the province, Amsterdam received privileges from the counts of Holland that enabled municipal patricians to govern the city with little outside interference. From the early fourteenth to the late sixteenth century, Amsterdam's population grew from around three thousand in 1400 to eleven thousand by 1500. Eighty years later, Amsterdam boasted a population of thirty thousand, the largest city in Holland, one of the most urbanized provinces in Europe. By the 1540s, Amsterdam was a leading port of entry for grain in northern Europe.

Revolt and Reformation. The religious and political struggles in the Low Countries during the late sixteenth and early seventeenth centuries eventually led to independence from Habsburg domination and the establishment of Calvinism in the northern seven provinces. Armed rebellion broke out in 1568, and in the summer of 1572 the Dutch "Beggar" army captured large parts of Holland. With little enthusiasm for rebellion, the staunchly Catholic city government of Amsterdam remained loyal to Spain and became a refuge center for loyalists and Catholics throughout the province. The war isolated Amsterdam from the rest of Holland and had a deleterious effect on trade, making this a bleak period in the city's history. Amsterdam finally capitulated to the rebel forces in 1578, after the city militia revolted. It soon became clear that the Dutch victory in the northern provinces would be permanent, although

Amsterdam. Drawing by Peter Brueghel the Elder, 1562. MUSÉE DES BEAUX-ARTS, BESANÇON, FRANCE/GIRAUDON/ART RESOURCE, NY

Spain did not formally recognize the independence of the Dutch Republic until 1648.

Shortly after the surrender in 1578, a new regime composed of both Protestants and Catholics loyal to the republic took the reins of power in Amsterdam. For most of the seventeenth century, the Amsterdam city government pursued a fairly moderate religious policy, favoring the official Dutch Reformed Church but also overlooking the private worship of Catholics and other religious dissidents. Amsterdam came down firmly on the side of Prince Maurice and the strict Calvinists (Counter-Remonstrants) against the Arminians (Remonstrants) and Johan van Oldenbarnevelt in the infamous Remonstrant controversy. This conflict originated as a fierce theological dispute over predestination among Calvinists and Arminians, but from 1609 to 1621 it became part of a broad political struggle between Prince Maurice and Oldenbarnevelt. Eventually, though, the Remonstrants came to power in Amsterdam in 1628 and maintained control of the city government throughout most of the seventeenth century. They strongly promoted a policy of religious tolerance; it was un-

der their auspices that Amsterdam became such a lively intellectual and cultural center.

The Golden Age. The Dutch Republic reached the height of its economic hegemony and cultural influence during its "golden age" from 1620 to 1700. By the 1590s, commercial and industrial activity in Amsterdam had surpassed the output of its southern rivals, chiefly Antwerp, in part because of the closing of the Scheldt estuary. Amsterdam merchants became the driving force behind the far-flung merchant empires in both Asia and America, controlled by the well-known joint stock companies, the Dutch East India Company (VOC) and the Dutch West India Company (WIC), respectively. As a result of its commercial dominance, Amsterdam became one of the most important financial centers in Europe at this time. The city's population grew from 50,000 in 1600 to 150,000 in 1650 and 205,000 in 1700. Although Amsterdam would retain a meaningful place in European culture down to modern times, the prosperous golden age was relatively brief. By the end of the seventeenth century, the combination of English hostility at sea and French aggression on land reduced the republic to a second-rate power and eclipsed the commercial supremacy of Amsterdam.

Architecture, Art, and Learning.

The rich style of late mannerism began to have a noticeable effect on Amsterdam architecture around 1600 through the work of Hendrick de Keyser (1565–1621). He was Amsterdam's leading architect and sculptor of the period, and his most famous works were the Zuiderkerk (South Church; 1606) and the Westerkerk (West Church; 1620). De Keyser also marked the transition from late mannerism to a more restrained classicist style that became dominant in Amsterdam architecture in the 1620s and 1630s. The stately private residences along the Herengracht best represent this classicist style, of which Philips Vingboons was the most accomplished practitioner in the 1630s.

The form of art for which Amsterdam is most well known during the late Renaissance period is painting. Not only did painters generate an amazing quantity of work for local and foreign patrons, but Amsterdam also became the locus of the international art trade in Europe. After the arrival of Rembrandt van Rijn (1606–1669) in 1631, Amsterdam outstripped Haarlem as the leading center for Dutch baroque painting. Rembrandt and pupils such as Gerrit Dou (1613–1675) and Carel Fabritis (1622–1654) elevated the still life to a distinct artistic category and brought everyday domestic life to canvas.

Amsterdam was one of the most open and tolerant civic societies in the world, despite frequent tension between the theocratic tendencies of Calvinist church leaders and the pluralistic policies of city magistrates. For the most part, the city government was able to preserve freedom of private worship for those outside the Dutch Reformed Church. Although officially proscribed, the Catholic Church actually grew significantly from 1600 to 1650. At midcentury Catholics made up 20 percent of the city's population. The city government also provided a great deal of latitude for writers, publishers, and artists. Indeed, local publishers were prolific; between 1639 and 1650 they produced 1,463 titles. Amsterdam, though, boasted only a few native writers who gained any international attention. The most notable was the poet and playwright Joost van den Vondel (1587–1679). Nevertheless, the openness of Amsterdam's civic culture made it a temporary home for some of the greatest luminaries of the seventeenth century.

See also **Netherlands,** *subentries on* **The Netherlands in the Renaissance** *and* **Art in the Netherlands.**

BIBLIOGRAPHY

Israel, Jonathan. *The Dutch Republic, Its Rise, Greatness, and Fall, 1477–1806.* Oxford, 1995. The most exhaustive recent history of the Low Countries, which covers Amsterdam extremely well.

Mak, Geert. *Een kleine geschiedenis van Amsterdam.* Amsterdam, 1994. A historical treatment of the city from its origins to modern times through the stories of ordinary and extraordinary people.

Rosenberg, Jakob, Seymour Slive, and E. H. ter Kuile. *Dutch Art and Architecture: 1600 to 1800.* London, 1977. Standard treatment of Dutch art and architecture in their historical context.

Wagenaar, Jan. *Amsterdam in zyne opkomst, aanwas geschiedenissen, voor regten, koophandel, gebouwen, kerkenstaat, schoolen, schuttery, gilden en regeeringe.* 4 vols. Amsterdam, 1760–1767. Despite the date, this multivolume work remains the most exhaustive treatment of political developments in Amsterdam to the eighteenth century. Detailed information on buildings.

CHARLES H. PARKER

AMYOT, JACQUES (1513–1593), French translator, ecclesiastic, poet. Jacques Amyot was the son of a leather-dresser in Melun. After studying Latin and Greek at the Collège du Cardinal Lemoine and the Collège des Lecteurs Royaux in Paris, he went to Bourges in 1535, where he directed a small school and where he also became lecturer of Greek and Latin at the University of Bourges (c. 1536–1546). Amyot began translating Greek literature and was able to procure from Francis I a commission to translate Plutarch into French. To support his translation work he was given the Abbey of Bellozanne in Normandy. He traveled to libraries in Venice and Rome between 1547 and 1552. He became tutor of the king's sons, the future Charles IX and Henry III, in 1557. After being appointed grand almoner of France in 1560, Amyot's ecclesiastical career was crowned by his nomination as bishop of Auxerre in 1570, where he supervised the reconstruction of the cathedral and other churches destroyed during the religious wars. Although he participated actively in the defense of the Catholic Church against the Protestants, his close connection to Henry III provoked the enmity of the Catholic League, which, having established itself in Auxerre, campaigned violently against the bishop in the last years of his life. Although Amyot wrote Latin verse, translated Euripides, Longus, Diodorus Siculus, and Heliodorus, and wrote a treatise on eloquence for Henry III, he is best known for his monumental translation of Plutarch's *Parallel Lives* (1559) and the *Moralia* (1572). Both works had an enormous influence on French letters in the sixteenth century, inspiring moral essayists such as

Michel de Montaigne and André Thevet, and dramatists well into the seventeenth century.

BIBLIOGRAPHY

Primary Works

Amyot, Jacques. *Projet d'éloquence royale*. With a preface by Philippe-Joseph Salazar. Paris, 1992.

Amyot, Jacques, trans. *Les oeuvres morales et meslees de Plutarque* (Moralia). 2 vols. 1572. Reprint, with an introduction by Michael Andrew Screech. London, 1971.

Amyot, Jacques, trans. *Plutarque: Les vies des hommes illustres*. 2 vols. Edited by Gérard Walter. Paris, 1951.

Secondary Works

Aulotte, Robert. *Amyot et Plutarque: La tradition des* Moralia *au XVIᵉ siècle*. Geneva, 1965.

Balard, Michel, ed. *Fortunes de Jacques Amyot*. Paris, 1986.

ULLRICH LANGER

ANATOMY. Renaissance anatomy elevated observation as a way of gaining knowledge. Its practitioners saw themselves as being at the forefront of learned, university-based medicine, but they were not revolutionaries. In matters of theory they stayed within the framework laid down by the ancients. Although radical change in medicine would come from elsewhere, anatomy was the success story of Renaissance medicine. Contemporaries applauded its achievements and saw it rise in status. In the Middle Ages anatomy was mainly taught to surgeons, and lecturers in anatomy held a low position in the medical hierarchy. In the twelfth and thirteenth centuries pigs substituted for human bodies in the anatomies carried out in Salerno and Bologna. By the middle of the thirteenth century surgeons were conducting autopsies in towns in France, Germany, and Italy.

The first systematic human dissection for medical education was carried out in 1315/16 by Mondino dei Liuzzi in Bologna, and his *Anatomia* (1316) served to structure the anatomies that were sporadically performed in European universities in the fourteenth and fifteenth centuries. Medieval anatomies were designed to show the parts of the body to the audience and to demonstrate what was mentioned in Mondino's text, and perhaps in Galen, from whom Mondino had drawn some of his descriptions. In the sixteenth century the essentially didactic nature of anatomical teaching began to change into a more critical, research-oriented activity. Yet its practitioners retained and increased the sense emerging at the time of Mondino that anatomy was a medical rather than a surgical discipline. In this way they elevated its status, since medicine, being based on book learning, was then considered more worthy than the manual skill of surgery. The sixteenth-century anat-

omists also emphasized anatomy's theological and philosophical roles, for it demonstrated God's marvellous workmanship in creating the body. Such was the impact of anatomy upon medicine that by the end of the century the students at Padua, the center for sixteenth-century anatomy, were asserting that anatomy and not philosophy was the foundation of medicine.

Initial Changes. The naturalistic, representational movement of Renaissance art helped to bring into anatomy the desire to see the body for oneself rather than through the eyes of past authorities. Leon Battista Alberti and Lorenzo Ghiberti in their treatises on sculpture, *De statua* (On the statue; c. 1435), and *I commentarii* (Commentaries; c. 1447–1448), respectively, urged the necessity of anatomy for the artist. By the early sixteenth century Raphael (1483–1520), Albrecht Dürer (1471–1528), and Michelangelo (1475–1564) were integrating their knowledge of surface and deeper anatomy into their paintings. Leonardo da Vinci (1452–1519) famously sought out cadavers to dissect from the hospital of Santa Maria Nuova in Florence. Although Leonardo drew the traditional five-lobed liver and localized the mental faculties such as the imagination in the ventricles of the brain as Galenic and medieval texts taught him, he depicted with increasing naturalism and detail parts of the body such as the hand, foot, shoulder, head, and internal organs. Leonardo, who wrote that pictures could say more than words, planned an anatomical atlas of the stages of man from fetus to death. Although this was not produced, his attitude was representative of both anatomists and artists: the body had to be drawn from nature, not from books.

The Revival of Classical Anatomy. Artists drew inspiration for their naturalistic studies from the Greek and Roman emphasis on naturalistic representation, especially in sculpture. The anatomists also looked back to the ancients. The humanist revival of Greek medicine brought into view Galen's physiological treatises: *On the Natural Faculties* (1523, in a translation by Thomas Linacre) and *On the Use of the Parts of the Body,* the full text of which became widely available with the advent of printing (it had been too long to be frequently copied in the Middle Ages). Galen's anatomical treatise, *On Anatomical Procedures,* was discovered, though incomplete, and was translated in 1531 by Johann Guinther von Andernach. These works provided a wealth of information about the functioning of the body and also exemplified Galen's attitude to anatomical re-

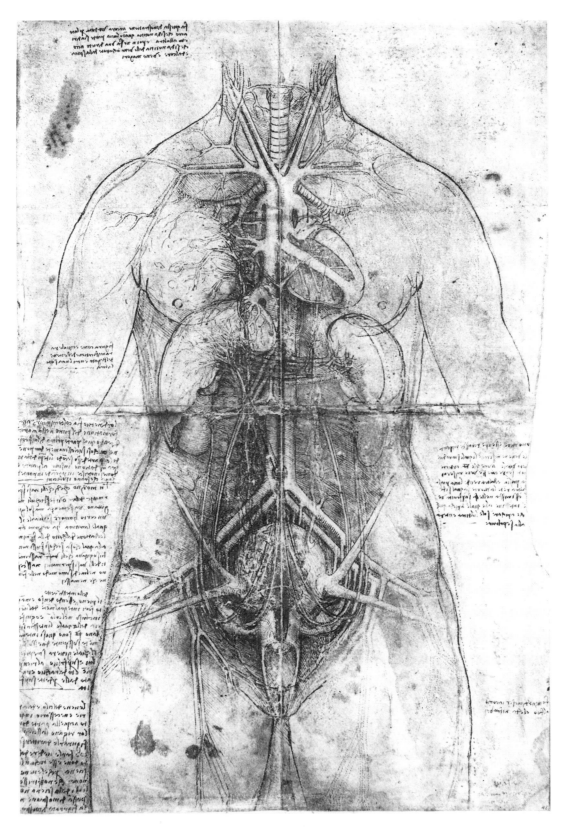

Leonardo da Vinci. *Anatomical Study.* ANDERSON/ALINARI/ART RESOURCE

search, which was based on *autopsia,* seeing for oneself.

The first "Greek" anatomy was that of the humanist Alessandro Benedetti (c. 1450–1512); his book *Historia corporis humani: sive anatomice* (Account of the human body: or anatomy; c. 1502) self-consciously replaced "barbarous" Arabic and medieval anatomical terms with Greek words. A renewed emphasis on seeing for oneself was introduced into anatomy by Jacopo Berengario da Carpi (c. 1460–c. 1530), who lectured on anatomy and surgery at Bologna. In his *Commentaria . . . Super Anatomia Mundini* (Commentary on the anatomy of Mondino; 1521) and his *Isagoge breves* (Short introduction to anatomy; 1522), he emphasized his belief that observation could contradict authority, and that the subject matter of his study was *anatomia sensibilis,* the study of observable things. The Venetian physician Niccolò Massa (c. 1485–1569), in his *Liber introductorius anatomiae* (Introductory book of anatomy; 1536), also stated that anatomy had to be based on observation, on *anatomia sensata,* and that one should not rely only on books.

Neither Berengario nor Massa subjected Galen's anatomy to systematic criticism. They did, however, throw doubt on two anatomical structures that were crucial to Galenic physiology. Berengario denied the existence in man of Galen's *rete mirabile,* the "marvellous network" of blood vessels at the base of the brain, in which arterial blood was changed into animal spirits, or superfine blood, conveying sensation and motion through the nerves and brain (the plexus of vessels is found in some animals but not in man). Massa threw doubt on the permeability of the intraventricular septum through which blood flowed, in Galen's teaching, from the right to the left side of the heart by means of invisible pores. Although Massa stated that the septum was solid, he still believed that some blood could seep through it.

Andreas Vesalius. The systematic redrawing of human anatomy was very visibly carried out by Vesalius (1514–1564). Born in Brussels, educated in Louvain and in Paris, where the humanistic study of a purified Galenic medicine was in full swing, Vesalius was appointed in 1537 lecturer in anatomy and surgery at Padua. He brought to the position a scholarly reputation in medicine (he had helped Guinther von Andernach in Paris with translating Galen), and he transformed the post into one relevant to learned physic or medicine. After publishing in 1538 the *Tabulae anatomicae sex,* six anatomical charts designed for students and often plagiarized, he began

to be critical of Galen's anatomy. He realized that Galen had dissected animals, especially apes, rather than humans (Galen was open about the lack of human material available), and that consequently the whole of Galenic anatomy had to be checked with reference to the human body.

The result of his systematic rewriting of Galenic anatomy was the massive yet elegant *De humani corporis fabrica* (On the structure of the human body; 1543), profusely and brilliantly illustrated, most probably by Jan Steven of Calcar (d.c. 1546), a pupil of Titian's. *Fabrica* was both a critique of Galen and a development of Galen's program for anatomy. Vesalius contradicted Galen on a number of observational details: he established that the liver was undifferentiated rather than five-lobed, denied that the vena cava originated in the liver, confirmed the impermeability of the intraventricular septum (in the second edition of *Fabrica,* 1555), and denied the existence of the *rete mirabile* in humans and the localization of mental faculties in particular parts of the ventricles of the brain. However, Vesalius was the first Renaissance anatomist to follow Galen's order of performing a dissection; instead of beginning, as medieval anatomists had, with the internal organs because of the danger that they would putrefy, he began with the bones and proceeded to the muscles, the vascular system, nervous system, abdominal organs, and organs of the thorax, ending with the brain in the seventh book. Despite the vitriolic criticism of Jacobus Sylvius, another of Vesalius's Galenic teachers in Paris, who believed that Galen could not err and that discrepancies between Galen's observations and Renaissance findings could be explained by the body having changed over time, it can be argued that Vesalius was following Galen in creating a true human anatomy based on observation, but now with the human material denied to Galen.

However, though Vesalius and the anatomists who followed him prided themselves on their observational accuracy, they did not challenge Galen's theories of how the body worked. Despite denying the existence of structures like the *rete mirabile* and pores in the septum that were the linchpins of Galenic physiology, their vision of the working of the body remained the same as that of their fellow learned physicians, who had been taught Galen's medical philosophy in the universities of Europe.

Some anatomists, like Gabriele Fallopio (1523–1562) and Caspar Bauhin (1560–1624), sought to surpass Vesalius in creating an even more precise anatomy of the body. Others produced detailed anatomical studies of particular parts of the body, such

Anatomy Lecture. An anatomy lecture from *De re anatomica* (1559) by Realdo Colombo (c. 1510–1559), professor of medicine at the universities of Padua, Pisa, and Rome.

as the descriptions of the kidney, ear, and venous system in *Opuscula anatomica* (Anatomical studies; 1564) by Bartolomeo Eustachio (c. 1500–1574). Most significant was the move from depicting human anatomy to studying many animals including man in order to create an overall picture of particular organs. Although Volcher Coiter (1534–1600?) began the study of comparative anatomy, it was Girolamo Fabrici da Aquapendente (1533–1619), the successor to Fallopio at Padua, who created a coherent research project in comparative anatomy, based on the example of Aristotle's comparative descriptions of animals and his study of embryology and generation. Fabrici's aim was to produce a complete comparative anatomy entitled *The Theater of All the Animal Fabric,* in which the emphasis would be on the action and use of the parts as opposed to the Vesalian focus on structure. This never came to fruition, though parts of it, such as *De visione, voce, auditu*

(On vision, speech, hearing; 1600), were published, as were his *De formatione ovi et pulli* (On the formation of the egg and chick; 1621) and *De formato foetu* (On the formation of the fetus; 1600, but written after his treatise on the egg and chick). These last two treatises were to influence his pupil William Harvey (1578–1657) in his work on generation.

The Circulation of the Blood. The last great achievement of the Paduan school of anatomy was the discovery of the systemic circulation of the blood by Harvey. He built upon the work of others. Vesalius's rival at Padua, Matteo Realdo Colombo (1516?–1559) had shown in his *De re anatomica* (On anatomical matters; 1559) by vivisection on dogs that venous blood went from the pulmonary artery to the lungs and there mixed with air to become arterial blood. It was then conveyed through the pulmonary vein to the heart. This transit of blood through the lungs replaced Galen's movement of blood through the invisible pores of the intraventricular septum. But Colombo held that the blood was replaced as it moved through the body, for he believed in the Galenic theory that blood was made from chyle (a product of digested food) in the liver and was used up by the parts of the body as and when needed. Colombo also prepared the ground for Harvey by showing that the arteries filled with blood after the heart constricted, acting in systole and not in diastole as Galen had thought.

Juan Valverde, Colombo's student, publicized the pulmonary transit in his *De la composicion del cuerpo humano* (On the composition of the human body; 1556) but made it clear that it was his teacher's discovery. Michael Servetus (1511–1553), an anatomist and a theologian who denied the Trinity, also posited a pulmonary transit. In his *Christianismi restitutio* (The restitution of Christianity; 1553) he argued that God breathed the divine spirit or soul into the blood, and the best place for this to happen was in the lungs, as its area was larger than the left ventricle of the heart, the Galenic locus for the production of arterial blood. Servetus used his anatomical experience—he had been a pupil of Guinther von Andernach in Paris—to develop his argument, which relied also on the impermeability of the septum (though he conceded that a little blood might "sweat" across it). Servetus was burned as a heretic in 1553 in Calvin's Geneva together with most of the copies of the *Restitutio,* and his work had no influence upon Harvey, but it illustrates an increasing consensus among anatomists that there was a pulmonary transit, as well as showing how religion could penetrate even the most technical aspects of medicine.

Harvey's notes for the anatomy lectures that he gave to the College of Physicians in London indicate that by 1616 he agreed with Colombo on the pulmonary transit and the action of the heart, and they contain a brief allusion to the general circulation, added perhaps around 1627. Harvey announced his discovery of the circulation in a small treatise, *Exercitatio anatomica de motu cordis et sanguinis in animalibus* (An anatomical exercise concerning the movement of the heart and blood in animals; 1628). The first half discussed the pulmonary transit and established that the heart acts like a muscle by its contraction in systole; contradictions in the Galenic cardiovascular system were also pointed out, such as the two-way flow of air and sooty vapors in the pulmonary vein, the latter being the by-product of the concoction of vital arterial blood in the left ven-

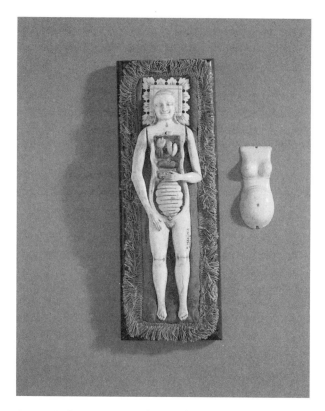

Anatomical Figure. Ivory figure of a pregnant woman with some removable internal organs; the abdomen is open with the cover next to the right. Italian; late sixteenth century. SCIENCE AND SOCIETY PICTURE LIBRARY, SCIENCE MUSEUM, LONDON

tricle. Harvey, who was an Aristotelian like his teacher Fabrici, argued that comparative anatomy had to be employed to produce a complete picture of the action of the heart.

In the second half of *De motu cordis,* from chapter eight onward, Harvey set out his novel discovery. He stated that the blood was not continually produced and used up, but that the same blood circulated around the body. He calculated the amount of blood that was ejected from the heart in a given time and concluded that it was so much that it must move in a circle, otherwise the body would burst. Using Fabrici's discovery of the valves of the veins (*De venarum ostiolis* [On the little doors of the veins; 1603]), which Fabrici had thought were designed to prevent the extremities of the body from being flooded with blood, Harvey showed that the valves in the veins led the blood back from the extremities to the heart. Although he could not show how the arteries were joined to the veins (the capillaries were discovered by Marcello Malpighi in 1661 using a microscope; Harvey relied on a simple magnifying glass), he was able to infer that there was a connection using a tight ligature that he loosened to medium tight (when tight, the ligature prevented blood from going down through the artery; when it was medium tight, it allowed blood to travel down the artery and then up along the vein until it was stopped below the ligature).

Despite his quantitative techniques, which seemed to anticipate the "new science" of Galileo, Descartes, and Newton, Harvey, like many anatomists, was a conservative when it came to theory. He argued for the centrality of the heart on Aristotelian lines and saw it as the source of the body's vitality, which it communicated to the blood and thence to the body (the heart reenergized the exhausted venous blood when it returned to the heart). He did not agree with the new mechanical views of the world and the body which René Descartes (1596–1650) and others were putting forward. Harvey saw the circulation of the blood as an observational discovery, and he did not accept that it undermined the whole of Galenic physiology. In his later work on the generation of animals, *De generatione* (1651), he reiterated his view of a purposive nature, in which life consisted of vitalistic formative powers. Such sentiments were anathema to the philosophy of the new science, which sought to exclude consideration of teleology or purpose from philosophical explanations, and which denied the existence of vital powers, reducing living processes, instead, to mechanical and chemical processes.

See also **Galen**; **Medicine**; *and biographies of figures mentioned in this entry.*

BIBLIOGRAPHY

Primary Works
Berengario Da Carpi, Jacopo. *A Short Introduction to Anatomy.* Translated by L. R. Lind. 1959. Reprint, New York, 1969. Translation of *Isagoge breves . . . in anatomiam humani corporis* (1522).
Harvey, William. *The Circulation of the Blood and Other Writings.* Translated by Kenneth J. Franklin. London, 1993. Translation of *De motu cordis* and other writings on circulation.
Vesalius, Andreas. *The Epitome of Andreas Vesalius.* Translated by L. R. Lind. New York, 1949.

Secondary Works
Bylebyl, Jerome J. "The School of Padua: Humanistic Medicine in the Sixteenth Century." In *Health, Medicine, and Mortality in the Sixteenth Century.* Edited by Charles Webster. Cambridge, U.K., 1979. Pages 335–370.
Choulant, Ludwig. *History and Bibliography of Anatomic Illustration.* Translated by Mortimer Frank and Edward C. Streeter. Rev. ed., New York, 1945.
Cunningham, Andrew. *The Anatomical Renaissance.* Aldershot, U.K., 1997. A brilliant book, but highly controversial in those parts dealing with the relationship between anatomy and religion.
Herrlinger, Robert. *History of Medical Illustration from Antiquity to A.D. 1600.* Translated by Graham Fulton-Smith. London, 1970.
Kemp, Martin. *Leonardo da Vinci, The Marvellous Works of Nature and Man.* London, 1981.
Lind, L. R. *Studies in Pre-Vesalian Anatomy.* Philadelphia, 1975. Has translations of late fifteenth- and early sixteenth-century anatomical texts.
O'Malley, Charles Donald. *Andreas Vesalius of Brussels, 1514–1564.* Berkeley and Los Angeles, 1964. The standard study of Vesalius.
Schulz, Bernard. *Art and Anatomy in Renaissance Italy.* Ann Arbor, Mich., 1985.

ANDREW WEAR

ANCIENT WORLD. *See* **Classical Antiquity.**

ANDREA DEL SARTO. *See* **Florence,** *subentry* on **Art of the Sixteenth Century.**

ANDREINI, ISABELLA (1562–1604), Venetian actress and writer. Born in Padua in 1562 to a Venetian family named Canali, Isabella Andreini joined an acting company at the age of sixteen and soon became the foremost actress of her time. Renowned for her virtue and intellect as well as for her acting skill, she elevated the status of women in her profession and contributed to commedia dell'arte the mask (or role) she played under her own name, "Isabella." Her erudition won her admission to the Academy of the Intenti at Pavia by the name of "Accesa." Her first written work, a verse pastoral entitled *Mirtilla* and published in Verona in 1588, reveals a feminist sensibility; the drama was reissued many times. Her *Rime,* a collection of more than three hundred poems, was published in 1601 and in Paris in 1603, the year Andreini and her troupe traveled to France for performances at the court of Henry IV, where Marie de Médici praised her acting. On the return trip to Italy in 1604, near Lyon, the celebrated actress died at the age of forty-two, miscarrying her eighth child.

Torquato Tasso and Giambattista Marini praised her in verse, as did her son, the actor and writer Giambattista Andreini, who dedicated a volume of poems to her in 1606. Three years after her death, her husband and acting partner, Francesco Andreini, published her *Lettere* (letters). In 1616 he and Flaminio Scala, head of Andreini's acting troupe, the Gelosi, published thirty-one dialogues Isabella had composed during her career. *Frammenti d'alcune scritture* (Fragments of writing) includes bits of dialogue that appear also in scripted Renaissance comedy, most famously in Shakespeare's *Much Ado about Nothing*.

On stage, Andreini played a *prima donna innamorata* (romantic first lady) in a series of plays: *La fortunata Isabella* (Lucky Isabella), *Le burle di Isabella* (Isabella's pranks), *La gelosa Isabella* (Jealous Isabella), and *Isabella astrologa* (Isabella the astrologer). Her signature role was in *La pazzia di Isabella* (Isabella's madness), which she performed in Florence in 1589 for festivities celebrating the wedding of the grand duke Ferdinand de' Medici to Christine of Lorraine. A journal account of her performance describes how Isabella lapses into madness after being tricked into marrying the wrong man. Unlike actresses who represented madness by tearing melodramatically at their clothes and baring their breasts, Andreini invented a scene based on her knowledge of several languages. She began by speaking to passersby in Spanish, Greek, Italian, and French, and singing French songs for the bride; she then imitated the dialects of her companion comic masks: Pantalone, Graziano, Zanni, Pedrolino, Francatrippa, Burattino, Capitano, Cardone, and Franceschina. Andreini used her fluency in the languages of the stage as well as the world of her public to fashion an image of madness that also suggested her inability to claim a personal identity in a society that denied women their choice of a marriage partner and denied women the freedom to speak in public.

The ill-fated love that drove Isabella to madness on stage is thematized in Andreini's poetry, in which love in the Petrarchan tradition overwhelms "senses, reason, and soul." In an original introductory poem she likens her lyrics to the joys and sorrows she pretended on stage, urging real lovers to be sincere. Thirty-four musical settings of her poems by twenty composers, all dated after her death, are part of her legacy.

BIBLIOGRAPHY

Clubb, Louise George. *Italian Drama in Shakespeare's Time.* New Haven, Conn., 1989.

Stortoni, Laura Anna, "Isabella Andreini." In *Women Poets of the Italian Renaissance.* Edited by Laura Anna Stortoni. Translated by Laura Anna Stortoni and Mary Prentice Lillie. New York, 1997. Pages 221–249. Includes an introduction and some texts with English translations.

NANCY DERSOFI

ANDREWES, LANCELOT. *See* **Bible**, *subentry on* **The English Bible.**

ANGELICO, FRA (Guido di Pietro; c. 1400–1455), Florentine painter. Fra Angelico was born near Florence, where he and his brother Benedetto were trained in the manuscript industry, Fra Angelico as an illuminator and Benedetto as a scribe. Precisely when they began their apprenticeships is not known; but Fra Angelico was receiving commissions by 1417, and by 1425 both brothers had entered the Order of Preachers (Dominicans) at the convent of San Domenico in Fiesole. On entering the Dominicans, Guido changed his name to Fra Giovanni; but within fifteen years of his death the Dominicans had already begun to call him Fra Angelico, the angelic friar.

From the early 1420s until Fra Benedetto's death in 1448, the two brothers operated a large and prosperous scriptorium and painter's workshop in Fiesole. The majority of their commissions were for Dominican houses in Tuscany. However, by the early 1430s Fra Angelico had attracted the attention of the most ambitious patrons in Florence. By the late 1440s he was working in Rome for Pope Eugenius IV and then Pope Nicholas V. While there, Fra Angelico lived in the Dominican community at Santa Maria sopra Minerva, where he died and was buried.

Fra Angelico is difficult to fit among his contemporaries. He was not forward-looking like Masaccio (1401–1428); he never aligned himself with the refined, slightly classicizing taste of the Florentine upper classes, as did Fra Filippo Lippi (c. 1406–1469); nor was he willing to surrender pictorial beauty and fidelity to nature, as were Paolo Uccello (1397–1475) and Andrea del Castagno (c. 1421–1457), for the sake of endowing figures with the sculpturesque relief of chiaroscuro (the arrangement or treatment of light and dark parts) or of excavating dramatic spatial recessions with vanishing-point perspective. Although paintings such as *Coronation of the Virgin* (Paris, Louvre), which Fra Angelico made for San Domenico in Fiesole around 1430, make it obvious that he was thoroughly familiar with these new techniques, in that work he retained the old-fashioned allegiance to gilding, punchwork (a small repetitive pattern made with a steel punch), and brilliant pigments codified in the tradition of sacred art begun by Duccio di Buoninsegna (1255?–1318), Simone Martini (c. 1284–1344), and other painters of the early fourteenth century. Similarly, both the iconography and the radiance of Fra Angelico's *Annunciation* for San Domenico in Cortona (Cortona, Museo Diocesano) are rooted in the traditions of fourteenth-century Tuscan painting.

Fra Angelico. *Madonna and Child with Saints.* Fresco in the Convent of San Marco, Florence. MUSEO DI SAN MARCO, FLORENCE/ALINARI/ART RESOURCE

Even so, by the mid-1430s Fra Angelico was operating the largest painter's workshop in Florence. When his workload demanded it, he seems to have employed fully trained but temporary assistants. It could be argued that some paintings from this period, such as the Linaiuoli Tabernacle and *Descent from the Cross* (Florence, Museo di San Marco), include the collaboration of younger artists, such as Domenico Veneziano (d. 1461) and Piero della Francesca (c. 1420–1492), who later enjoyed great independent success.

Like every other ambitious Tuscan painter of the fifteenth century, however, Fra Angelico reached the pinnacle of his career working as a muralist. His largest fresco project is at the Dominican convent of San Marco in Florence, a commission from Cosimo de' Medici that occupied him intermittently from about 1440 until about 1450. Among other frescoes on the ground floor are *Crucifixion with Saints* in the Chapter Room and a life-size representation of St. Domi-

nic kneeling and embracing the crucifix, on which the equally life-size figure of Jesus is still alive. This theme of an intimate colloquy between Christ and St. Dominic (and, by extension, every Dominican friar) underlies the more numerous frescoes in the second-floor dormitory. There, Fra Angelico and his shop made a fresco in each of the forty-eight cells as well as on three walls of the corridors. Some of these are among the greatest achievements of fifteenth-century painting, particularly *Annunciation* in the north corridor and *Transfiguration* in cell 6. In them Fra Angelico fused the profoundly Christ-centered mysticism of the Order of Preachers with pictorial inventions of such originality that they remained largely unexplored by other painters for better than a generation.

The cells of Dominican convents were generally inaccessible to the lay public; thus Fra Angelico's professional admirers may not have seen some of his work at San Marco. In Rome, however, he worked

Fra Angelico. *Annunciation.* Diptych in the church of Santa Maria delle Grazie in the village of San Giovanni Valdarno, Italy. S. MARIA DELLE GRAZIE, VALDARNO, ITALY/SCALA/ART RESOURCE

on the monumental scale in more public spaces such as Saint Peter's, the Vatican Palace, and the cloister of Santa Maria sopra Minerva. The paintings in Saint Peter's and the Minerva cloister have disappeared. All that survives of Fra Angelico's work as a fresco painter outside Florence are some figures in the vaults of the San Brizio Chapel in Orvieto Cathedral (1447) and a cycle of the lives of St. Stephen and St. Lawrence in the private chapel of Pope Nicholas V

in the Vatican Palace (1448–1449). The pope shared his fellow humanists' keen interest in Christian, not just classical, antiquity. Thus the choice of the lives of St. Stephen and St. Lawrence bespeaks the pope's interest in the earliest period of Christian history, focused through the lives of two deacon martyrs. When Fra Angelico was working in the pope's chapel, moreover, the humanist architect Leon Battista Alberti was also resident at the pontifical court.

Alberti may have influenced the highly classicizing design of the background architecture in Fra Angelico's scenes.

The late work of Benozzo Gozzoli (1420–1497), Fra Angelico's major assistant, gives some idea of where his thinking was leading him at the time of his death; in Benozzo's *Procession of the Magi* in San Marco, Florence, for example, one detects the impress of Fra Angelico's having studied the relief sculpture of Roman antiquity. Roman artists of a younger generation, such as Antoniazzo Romano (1452–1508), likewise furthered the friar painter's late researches. However, in the great papal building campaigns of the sixteenth and seventeenth centuries, so much early Renaissance art was destroyed that most of Fra Angelico's Roman legacy has been lost. Had it survived, one might have a very different understanding of the major fresco projects of later generations, including those of Filippino Lippi (c. 1457–1504) and perhaps even of Raphael (1483–1520) and Michelangelo (1475–1564).

[*Adoration of the Magi* by Fra Angelico and Fra Filippo appears in the color plates in this volume.]

See also **Florence**, *subentry on* **Art of the Fifteenth Century.**

BIBLIOGRAPHY

Didi-Huberman, Georges. *Fra Angelico: Dissemblance and Figuration.* Translated by Jane Marie Todd. Chicago, 1995. A brilliant interpretation of Fra Angelico's work based on a postmodern rethinking of medieval philosophical precepts.
Hood, William. *Fra Angelico at San Marco.* New Haven, Conn., 1993. The most extended study of the frescoes at San Marco, and related paintings, from the viewpoint of Dominican customs, rules, and practice.
Pope-Hennessy, John. *Fra Angelico.* 2d ed. Ithaca, N.Y., 1974. The classic English-language essay with a complete list of Fra Angelico's works, including comprehensive bibliography.
Spike, John T. *Fra Angelico.* New York, 1996. New catalog, up-to-date bibliography, richly illustrated.

WILLIAM HOOD

ANGELS IN RENAISSANCE ART. *See* Religious Themes in Renaissance Art.

ANGUISSOLA, SOFONISBA (Anguisciola, Angussola; c. 1532–1625), Italian painter. Sofonisba Anguissola was the second internationally known female artist (after Levina Teerlinc), and the first woman to establish an artistic identity in a substantial body of work. Her portraits with narrative overtones proved to be ahead of their time when "truth to nature" and genre themes became ascendant interests in Italian art at the end of the sixteenth century.

Born in Cremona, Sofonisba was the eldest child in a family of six daughters and a son. The daughters received a humanist education. Four became artists (Sofonisba, Lucia, Europa, Anna Maria); another (Minerva) was noted for literary studies. Sofonisba's artistic emergence in a humanist context was unusual in a period when women were typically trained by artist-fathers. Her model inspired other noblewomen to take up painting, for example, Irene di Spilimbergo (1541–1559) and Bolognese artist Lavinia Fontana (1552–1614).

Sofonisba studied painting with local artists, and she taught her younger sisters, of whom Lucia was the most active. Sofonisba's specialization in portraits and self-portraits was shaped by gender restraints, since women artists were not allowed to study anatomy or male models and thus lacked access to large-scale history painting. Her depiction of animated faces, firmly drawn, within a delicate atmospheric film is distinctive. Her earliest known works are the *Portrait of a Nun* (1551; Southhampton) and *Self-Portrait* of 1554 (Vienna, Kunsthistorisches Museum). Other early portraits include the artist *Giulio Clovio* (Collection F. Zeri) and the young *Massimiliano Stampa* (Baltimore, Walters Art Gallery).

Anguissola's paintings were admired by contemporaries such as the Roman nobleman Tommaso Cavalieri, who excepted her from the Renaissance precept that linked artistic creativity exclusively with masculinity. She was encouraged by Michelangelo, who said of her drawing of a smiling girl teaching her nurse to read (Florence, Uffizi) that a weeping boy would have been more difficult to draw—which prompted her to make a drawing of a boy bitten by a crayfish (her brother Asdrubale; Naples, Capodimonte). This drawing was probably the model for Caravaggio's painting *Boy Bitten by Lizard* (c. 1596), an instance of Sofonisba's role in the development of early baroque naturalism and genre painting.

Working against the constraints of a disparaged genre, Anguissola used portraiture for metaphoric expressions of artistic achievement. In *The Chess Game* (1555; Poznan), Anguissola depicted her sisters Lucia, Europa, and Minerva at the chess board, affirming female proficiency at an intellectual game and alluding to the sisters' shared history as aspiring artists who competed with and learned from one another. In works of the late 1550s, such as *Bernardino Campi Painting Sofonisba Anguissola* (Siena), and

Sofonisba Anguissola. *A Game of Chess.* The painting shows the painter's three sisters and a servant. Oil on canvas; 1555; 72 × 97 cm (28 × 38 in.). MUSEUM NARODOVE, POZNAŃ, POLAND/ERICH LESSING/ART RESOURCE, NY

The Family Group (Nivaa), the expression of pride in female achievement is inverted to become a wry commentary on patriarchal norms and values.

Sofonisba Anguissola spent the years 1559 to 1573 in Madrid as court painter and lady-in-waiting to Queen Isabella of Valois, whom she taught to paint. Anguissola's Spanish paintings are not well documented and have been confused with works by Sánchez Coello and Juan Pantoja de la Cruz. Among the few certain portraits are *Philip II* and *Isabella of Valois* (both Madrid, Prado; c. 1565). Sofonisba's marriage in 1573 to a Sicilian nobleman, Don Fabrizio de Moncada, ended with her husband's untimely death in 1578/79. Her marriage in 1580 to the Genoese nobleman Orazio Lomellini took her to Genoa for the next four decades, where she found her way to the new baroque style. Her last years were spent in Palermo. There the nonagenarian Anguissola was visited in 1624 by the Flemish artist Anthony Van Dyck. He sketched her in his Italian notebooks and painted her portrait, noting her clear memory, good stories, and advice on handling light. Her greatest sorrow, she told Van Dyck, was that her failing eyesight kept her from painting.

BIBLIOGRAPHY

Ferino-Pagden, Sylvia, and Maria Kusche. *Sofonisba Anguissola, a Renaissance Woman*. Washington, D.C. 1995. Short, informal catalog of exhibition at the National Museum of Women in the Arts, an abbreviated version of a major exhibition in Cremona, Italy (1994).

Garrard, Mary D. "Here's Looking at Me: Sofonisba Anguissola and the Problem of the Woman Artist." *Renaissance Quarterly* 47 (1994): 556–622.

Jacobs, Fredrika H. "Woman's Capacity to Create: The Unusual Case of Sofonisba Anguissola." *Renaissance Quarterly* 47 (1994): 74–101.

Perlingieri, Ilya Sandra. *Sofonisba Anguissola: The First Great Woman Artist of the Renaissance*. New York, 1992. First book on the artist in English.

MARY D. GARRARD

ANJOU, FRANÇOIS DE VALOIS, DUC D'ALENÇON ET D' (1555–1584), duke of Alençon (1566–1584), duke of Anjou (1576–1584). François de Valois was the fourth and youngest son of Henry II (1547–1559) and Catherine de Médicis. Unlike his three elder brothers, Anjou never became king of France, though after 1574 when his childless brother, Henry III, ascended the French throne, Anjou was the heir presumptive. As such he was a powerful figure in France. While he was courting the English queen Elizabeth (ruled 1558–1603) from 1579 to 1582, as well as accepting the sovereignty of the Dutch provinces in revolt against Philip II of Spain (ruled 1556–1598), he appeared to be on the way to wearing three different crowns. None of these

crowns ever materialized, since he died before his brother, was dropped as a suitor by Elizabeth, and was never warmly accepted in the Netherlands.

Anjou's potential for power nevertheless attracted a number of intellectuals to his household and many others sought to become his clients. Jean Bodin, Guy Le Fèvre de La Boderie, Guillaume Postel, Pierre de Ronsard, and Christophe Plantin were only the most notable of those intellectuals who either worked for Anjou, dedicated books to him, or otherwise sought his patronage. Anjou was neither a soldier nor an intellectual himself. His greatest shortcoming was failing to seize an opportunity to serve as an intermediary between militant French Catholics and Protestants. He died of tuberculosis in 1584 at age twenty-nine.

BIBLIOGRAPHY

Holt, Mack P. *The Duke of Anjou and the Politique Struggle during the Wars of Religion.* Cambridge, U.K., 1986.

Yates, Frances A. *The Valois Tapestries.* 2d ed. London, 1975.

MACK P. HOLT

ANNA OF SAXONY (Anna of Oldenburg, Anna of Denmark; 1532–1585), Danish princess, wife of Elector Augustus of Saxony. Anna was the daughter of the Lutheran king Christian III of Denmark and Norway. Little is known about her early years until 1548, when she married Augustus, duke, and later elector, of Saxony. Anna's influence on her husband was substantial, and she left her mark on the economic and religious policies of the electoral court. She was particularly active in developing the textile industry in Saxony and was entirely responsible for the court's efforts to further horticulture (particularly wine- and fruit-growing) in the region. In religious matters, Anna's strident Lutheranism checked the influence of the more ecumenical Philippists (moderate Lutherans following Philipp Melanchthon) at court. She served as both adviser to and collaborator with Augustus throughout his reign. Later generations in Saxony remembered them as "Father Augustus" and "Mother Anna."

Like many nobles of this period, Anna took an interest in the study of nature and medicine. Her Dresden botanical garden, in which she cultivated and studied medicinal herbs, was well known to contemporaries. She used these herbs in her own medical recipes, which she shared in letters filled with medical advice to her family in Denmark and other princely courts in the Holy Roman Empire. Anna offered her medical knowledge to her own Dresden court as well, in 1581 founding the Dresden

Hofapotheke, a court apothecary, which remained in existence until the nineteenth century.

Anna eventually set down her medical expertise in her *Ertzneibüchlein* (medical book), a collection of hundreds of recipes gathered from a variety of sources, including Paul Luther (Martin Luther's physician son), shepherds, empirics, executioners, and other women practitioners. She thanked the executioner of Torgau, for example, for a salve of human fat and ram suet and learned of a recipe for "a good remedy for growing taller" from a shepherdess in Bischofswerda.

From 1572 to 1575 Anna and her husband built a palace in Lochauer Heide, a hunting area north of Torgau. Augustus named it Annaburg, after his wife. Anna no doubt continued her investigations of nature there, as the palace soon developed a reputation as an alchemical laboratory. Anna died in 1585, only a year before her husband.

BIBLIOGRAPHY

Kretzschmar, Hellmut. "Staatswirtschaft, konfessionelle Landespolitik und materieller Aufschwung im ausgehenden 16. Jahrhundert." Part 17: *Sächsische Geschichte.* Edited by Rudolf Kötzschke and Hellmut Kretzschmar. Frankfurt, Germany, 1965. Pages 219–235.

Wiesner, Merry E. *Working Women in Renaissance Germany.* New Brunswick, N.J., 1986.

TARA E. NUMMEDAL

ANNE DE BEAUJEU (1461–1522), regent of France (1483–1491) during the first half of her brother Charles VIII's reign. Anne was the firstborn daughter of Louis XI and his second wife, Charlotte of Savoy. In 1474 Anne was married to Pierre de Beaujeu, the younger brother of Jean, duc de Bourbon. In 1488, with the death of his brother, Pierre de Beaujeu inherited the Bourbon title and Anne was henceforth known as the duchess of Bourbon.

At the time of Louis XI's death in August 1483, Anne and Pierre de Beaujeu were designated coregents during the minority of Charles VIII, but their authority was disputed by several powerful nobles, including Louis d'Orléans, the future Louis XII. The factional struggle forced Anne to summon the Estates General, which met at Tours in early 1484. After a lively debate between supporters of the Beaujeu and of Orléans, the Estates General endorsed the regency of Anne and Pierre. The outcome did not satisfy the opposing factions, and in December 1486 the tensions burst into open conflict. The so-called *Guerre Folle* (Silly war), a pale replay of the War of the Public Weal that had troubled the first decade of Louis XI's reign, was put down with relative ease. The rebels were defeated at Saint-Aubin-de-Cormier in July 1488, and their leader, Louis d'Orléans, was placed under arrest and incarcerated for close to three years.

Anne was also instrumental in the successful integration of Brittany into France. After the death in 1488 of Francis II of Brittany, who had for so long zealously defended his duchy's autonomy, Anne seized the opportunity to incorporate Brittany into France through a strategic marriage between Charles VIII and the Breton heiress, Anne (who was forced to repudiate a previous unconsummated union with Maximilian of Austria). The public reconciliation in 1491 between Orléans and Charles VIII and the king's marriage to Anne of Brittany marked the end of Anne de Beaujeu's governmental involvement. She retired to the Bourbonnais capital of Moulins, whence she worked to protect the Bourbon fiefs and to secure the marriage of her only daughter, Suzanne, to Charles de Montpensier.

From all accounts, Anne was considered an able regent. The memorialist Pierre de Brantôme goes so far as to declare that it was on account of her shrewd administration that Charles VIII was later considered one of the greatest kings of France. Anne's father, Louis XI, was said to have characterized her as the least stupid woman in France. Along with her reputation for political sagacity, however, Anne was also considered willful, deceitful, cunning, and vindictive—in short, a feminine version of her father. Later polemicists would often cite Anne de Beaujeu's regency as a prime example of the horrors that could accompany female rule in France.

BIBLIOGRAPHY

Chombart de Lauwe, Marc. *Anne de Beaujeu.* Paris, 1980.

Pélicier, Paul. *Essai sur le gouvernement de la dame de Beaujeu.* Chartres, France, 1882. Reprint, Marseille, France, 1983.

Polignac, Hedwige Chabannes de. *Anne de Beaujeu.* Paris, 1955.

ADRIANNA E. BAKOS

ANNE OF BRITTANY (1477–1514), sovereign head of the duchy of Brittany and wife of consecutive French kings, Charles VIII and Louis XII. Anne held a politically and culturally pivotal role during the early French Renaissance. As the inheritor of the strategically placed province of Brittany, Anne was, at the close of the fifteenth century, one of the most sought-after mates for European monarchs. With Anne's marriage to Charles VIII in 1491, France acquired future annexation rights to Brittany and continued the consolidation of French territory, begun

Anne of Brittany. A statue of Anne marks her tomb by Jean Juste (1531) at the basilica of Saint-Denis, France. PHOTO CICCIONE-BULLOZ

by Louis XI. Anne had no surviving children with Charles and two surviving daughters with Louis XII, whom she married in 1499. Daughter Claude (1499–1524) would become the wife of Francis I (1494–1547) and mother to the future Henry II (1519–1559).

Anne initiated the modern royal court, particularly during her second reign, by surrounding the king and herself with not only astute advisers and members of the highest nobility but also poets, translators, painters, and decorators. These artists were to lend luster and prestige to the image of the sovereign. Anne was an active patron: the *grand rhétoriqueur* poet Jean Marot, father of Clément, was her secretary, while her support of the illuminator Jean Bourdichon resulted in the famous 1508 illustrated prayer book, *Les heures d'Anne de Bretagne.* Never fully reconciled to the dissolution of Brittany's status as an independent duchy as brokered by her father, Anne always considered herself first a Breton and requested that upon her death her heart be interred in Nantes, the ducal capital.

BIBLIOGRAPHY

Baumgartner, Frederic J. *Louis XII*. New York, 1994.

Stone, Donald. *France in the Sixteenth Century: A Medieval Society Transformed*. Englewood Cliffs, N.J., 1969.

MARGARET HARP

ANTIQUARIANISM. The urge to study ancient monuments, records, and relics exemplifies the Renaissance impulse to seek truth in historical sources. In Italy, Flavio Biondo's *Italia illustra* (1474), a survey of all Italian antiquities, anticipated scholarship throughout Europe during the next two centuries. Sections of Pausanias's massive survey of Greek antiquities saw print as early as 1500, providing a classical model for this kind of work. Painstaking research into ancient origins led to profound changes in nearly every area of culture and learning, from architecture to law to religion. The availability of Vitruvius's treatise on architecture, from 1484, led to a century or more of innovation in building design and theater construction supported by investigation of actual ancient ruins. In such circumstances antiquarian undertakings were inseparable from the defining activities of the Renaissance as a whole. Not all antiquarians were merely, as Friedrich Nietzsche described them in the nineteenth century, beetles crawling on the face of the pyramids. John Leland, commissioned by Henry VIII to survey and inventory English antiquities, typified his successors in delving into the past both for mere knowledge and for practical ends (to support Henry's claims to head the church). While his contemporary John Bale was compiling a biographical dictionary of English authors beginning with Adam, Leland used his research in an effort to prove Arthur a Protestant king.

Legendary Britain. A whole field of English antiquarianism concerned itself with Arthur and the other legendary rulers chronicled in Geoffrey of Monmouth's twelfth-century *Historia regum Britanniae* (History of the Kings of Britain). Throughout the 1500s Geoffrey's historical validity was alternately questioned (by Henry VII's historian Polydore Vergil and by his granddaughter Elizabeth's chronicler William Camden) and affirmed (by Edmund Spenser, Michael Drayton, and countless other poets and mythologizers). Geoffrey's history found its way into Raphael Holinshed's *Chronicles of England, Scotlande, and Irelande* (1577), thence into Shakespeare's *King Lear* and *Cymbeline*. English patriots looked to Geoffrey for evidence of a British history almost as old and, in earlier ages, just as cultivated as that of Rome. Legal historians used him to argue

the antiquity of the so-called Molmutine laws, simple statements of rights and social practices, supposedly codified by King Dunwallo Mulmutius centuries before Roman civil law came into existence. A decade after Elizabeth, younger antiquaries like Henry Spelman would begin undoing this legal myth, as it became evident that English law, far from being a native product, originated in European feudal law.

Law and Politics. Legal antiquarian research flourished during Elizabeth's reign (1558–1603), especially in the Inns of Court, the four London schools of common law (Gray's Inn, Lincoln's Inn, and the Inner Temple and Middle Temple—two schools so called because they adjoined the ancient Knights Templars' church, the Temple). William Lambarde published his treatise on Saxon law and customs a year after becoming a Lincoln's Inn barrister in 1567. John Ferne, Henry Ferrers, and Francis Tate all entered the Middle Temple in the 1570s, leaving more antiquarian studies in manuscript than in print (Tate on lawful combat, the privileges of cities, and the antiquity of parliaments), while their fellow student Richard Carew undertook his *Survey of Cornwall* in the next decade. Such regional "surveys" or descriptions characterize many antiquarian efforts, not a few of them by members of the Inns of Court (Lambarde on Kent, Simon Archer on Warwickshire, John Doddridge on Wales, Cornwall, and Chester). This tradition of lawyer-scholars culminated with the Inner Temple member John Selden, who investigated the origins of dueling, titles of honor, and, to the great consternation of clergymen, the practice of tithing. His scholarship also fed the controversies developing between the prerogatives of crown and parliament. Selden's *Jani Anglorum facies altera* (The reverse face of the English Janus; 1610), says Graham Parry, "portrays the Conquest as an overlaying of Norman authority upon surviving Saxon traditions of custom and law" (*Trophies of Time*). Other writings show how far Selden transcended his national boundaries: *De dis Syris syntagmata* (On the Syrian gods; 1617), a pioneering study in comparative religion, provided Milton with the names of the devils in hell; *De jure naturali et gentium juxta disciplinam Ebraeorum* (Natural and civil law according to the Hebrews; 1640) sought to locate the origins of society itself in Hebrew thought on natural law.

Camden and the Society of Antiquaries. It is thus no coincidence that three of the most important members of the Society of Antiquaries, Selden, Robert Cotton, and Henry Spelman, first met at the Inns of Court. The society was formed about 1586, following on the heels of a similar, short-lived group begun by Archbishop Parker in 1572. Its king-pin, William Camden, published his esteemed *Britannia* (1586), an encyclopedic, detailed Latin survey of Britain's geography and history. Camden mentored the younger Cotton, a Middle Temple student who soon accumulated a great library, part of the modern British Library's core collection, with many books and manuscripts in British antiquity. (It includes the sole manuscript of the Anglo-Saxon *Beowulf*.) For twenty years the society met to hear papers on law, religion, heraldry, topography, and customs. Despite Cotton's friendship with James I, the king ordered the society to cease in 1607, concerned that it was meddling with the royal prerogative. Monarchal ire also induced Charles I to throw Cotton himself in prison, then forbid him to use his library. With some justification both kings feared that antiquarianism had become a tool of their political enemies. Many papers of the society survive in Thomas Hearne's *Collection of Curious Discourses* (1720).

Other Antiquarian Concerns. In addition to legal studies, genealogy and heraldry occupied many researchers: John Ferne's *Blazon of Gentrie* (1586) chronicles the Lacy family; Ferrers's manuscript studies of Warwickshire families survived in William Dugdale's *Antiquities of Warwickshire* (1656); William Burton's *Description of Leicestershire* (begun 1597, published 1622) displays the arms and descent of important families in his region. Early Anglo-Saxon language study by Elizabethans like Richard Verstegan led, by the 1650s, to a full dictionary of that language by the Kentish William Somner. Finally, the search for the ancient origins of the English church begot an ecclesiastical antiquarianism that found its principal scholar in James Ussher, who at Camden's and Cotton's urging wrote extensively on the history of Irish and English Christianity. In his *Annales* (1650) Bishop Ussher would earn his later fame computing the date of creation as 23 October 4004 B.C.

In England, as elsewhere, antiquarian scholars and societies developed in response to the era's newly found historical sense. Antiquarianism found expression sometimes as political self-celebratory mythmaking, sometimes as critical, demythologizing history. In the latter mode, usually, the legal antiquarians provided the most significant legacy of the movement, working toward a new understanding of the origins of the constitution and government of England.

BIBLIOGRAPHY

Evans, Joan. *A History of the Society of Antiquaries.* Oxford, 1956.
Hunter, Michael. *John Aubrey and the Realm of Learning.* London, 1975.
Kendrick, T. D. *British Antiquity.* London, 1950. The history of how Geoffrey of Monmouth's work was used and interpreted through the centuries.
Parry, Graham. *The Trophies of Time: English Antiquarians of the Seventeenth Century.* Oxford, 1995.

RICHARD F. HARDIN

ANTI-SEMITISM. Anti-Semitism, a formal term born of late nineteenth-century central European politics, is nonetheless used regularly to describe negative attitudes to Jews in earlier times as well. Some scholars argue for a sharp division between anti-Semitism and anti-Judaism, the latter applying to attitudes derived strictly from Christian theology and referring principally to premodern times. This is a potentially artificial division, implying, incorrectly, the absence of overlap. Indeed, the very resort to such terms as anti-Semitism or anti-Judaism tends to oversimplify, allowing facile generalization to replace articulate historical explanations, and separating postures toward Jews from a wider historical context.

Medieval Background. Renaissance attitudes toward Jews grew out of those of the medieval past and elaborated on them, particularly in the realms of economics and humanism, but also with respect to Jewish everyday culture and especially to the mythical Jewish image. The Jew whom people felt estranged from was often a chimera, such as the Jew of the blood libel, who killed Christian boys to use their blood for magical ritual, or the Jew who stood for the economic perversity, most importantly reputed to by money lending. Moreover, such views did not require a physical Jewish presence. Both Chaucer's Wife of Bath, whether she may be judged as skeptical of popular ideas or as their exponent, and Shakespeare's very human Shylock, for example, are the products of a time, between 1290 and about 1655, when Jews were not (legally) to be found in England.

Spanish attitudes focused not on Jews per se, especially after the riots of 1391 that destroyed most Spanish Jewish communities through massacre and forced conversion, but on the "Jewishness" that was considered irradicable from the New Christians, the conversos, also called Marranos (pigs). This phobia produced the Spanish and then the Portuguese national Inquisitions (all Portuguese Jews were forcibly

The Blood Libel. Woodcut of Jews taking blood from Simon of Trent. From Hartmann Schedel and Anton Koberger, *Liber chronicarum* (The Nürnberg Chronicle; 1493).

converted in 1497) and the laws of purity of blood (*limpieza de sangre*) aimed at converts' descendants. German attitudes expressed themselves foremost in riots and blood libels. Jews were regularly identified with forces working to obstruct civic autonomy and unity, and because this unity was considered to personify the Corpus Christi, the unsullied body of Christ, the reactions against the Jews were violent.

Blood Libels and Catholic Humanists. It is uncertain whether this overall portrait applies to the Italian blood libels, that of Trent in particular, where the accusation that Jews had murdered a Christian boy led to the destruction of the entire Jewish community in 1475. After the fact, Observant Franciscan preachers linked the blood libel to their preaching about Jewish lending. Bernardino da Feltre (1439–1494) likened money to the blood flowing in the veins and Jews to a gangrene poisoning the body that had to be cut out. Motifs of lending were also linked directly to the host libel, as in the painting (1468) by Paolo Uccello depicting a tale told in Paris in 1290. A Christian woman was pressed to steal a host, which she gave to a Jew in lieu of repaying her

debts, so that this Jew could torture Christ—the host—anew. The host libel was preceded by the blood libel, which restructured the twelfth-century crucifixion libel accusing Jews of killing Christian children. The blood libel asserts that the blood is used in circumcisions and in the baking of Passover matzos or unleavened bread. At times it is also linked to the cult of the Virgin, who miraculously appears to save the mutilated child's soul.

Striking in the case of Trent is that the fomentors were all humanists, steeped in classical learning, perhaps deriving their libels from ancient motifs in Tacitus, whom they were reading for the first time. These humanists were also linked to Paduan legists who advocated canons of separation aimed at preventing what was called the pollution of Christians and Christianity through any form of contact with Jews. By contrast, some of the the greatest medieval and Renaissance jurists, associated with the University of Perugia, supported a moderate equilibrium balancing Jewish *tolerantiae* (privileges) with *gravamina* (restrictions).

The meaning of Jewish privileges was undermined by the Franciscan Bernardino da Busti (1450–1513/15), who inverted the venerable principle of

Roman law that posits that Jews living peacefully are to be privileged, instead arguing that Jews violating privileges are to be expelled. A corollary of this position was that Jewish children were to be "saved" at any price, including forcibly baptizing them despite parental refusal—an argument that rejected the specific prohibition of this practice voiced by Thomas Aquinas two hundred years earlier.

Social Aspects of Catholic Approaches.

This notion of pollution used against Jews took a very modern turn, a change from a spiritual to a physical notion of pollution. Whereas Franciscans like Bernardino da Busti, Bernardino da Feltre, or Giovanni da Capistrano—all advocates of separation and the destruction of what they called pernicious rabbinic literature—had thought of pollution as spiritual, as an attack on Christian beliefs or the Christian body joined through baptism to Christ, humanists like the chronicler Sigismondo de' Conte da Foligno (d. 1512) spoke of direct physical infection, specifically through the importation by "Marranos" (a conflation, in this case, of real Jews and conversos) of the new and then virulent disease syphilis. It remains to be investigated whether there is a link between Sigismondo de' Conte's claim and medieval clerical condemnations of the Jewish view that sexuality was a potential vehicle for sanctity rather than being, as the church taught, a perennial vehicle for sin. There was surely some link between this theory of infection and the Spanish concept of purity of blood that sought to prevent New Christians—even in the tenth generation—from contaminating the old.

The humanists who espouse this position gravitated to the papal Curia, but the popes resisted calls for separation and unflagging restriction, maintaining traditional legal formats, until the mid-sixteenth century, when they began to espouse conversionary programs and decreed the physical separation of Jews from society in the ghetto. Because the ghetto wall was a cultural and social as much as a religious barrier, religious conversion to escape the ghetto also meant relinquishing Jewish cultural and social identity. This demand—always implied, never explicit—anticipated the perception of modern (political) anti-Semites that Jews were socially and culturally—far more than religiously—unassimilable. It is no coincidence that papal challenges to Jewish social integrity were matched by attitudes like the one expressed in 1556 by patricians from Udine, in northern Italy, who viewed a threat to Jewish safety during a plague as an "*occasione scacciare gli ebrei*" (an opportunity to be rid of the Jews).

Protestant Attitudes.

Catholic attitudes were matched by Lutheran ones. Traditionally, Luther is said to have sought Jewish conversion; when that quest failed he is said to have attacked Jews in anger. In fact, Luther's original intention was not so much to convert Jews as to deride Catholic doctrine, which he deemed so perverse that Jews were bound not to understand. Likewise, his *Von den Jüden und jren Lügen* (The Jews and their lies; 1543) is ultimately a typical example of anti-Jewish literature (in the strict sense that its aim was to denigrate), not a reflection of his failure to achieve mass Jewish conversion. Luther's real stance toward the Jews appears in his tract on the Sabbatarians. Harking back to patristic literature, as well as to Paul in Galatians (4–5), Luther condemned the so-called Judaizing of the Sabbatarians, whom he accused of drawing inspiration for their observance of the Sabbath from contemporary Jews. Although Paul was not attacking Jews in Galatians, Luther was. Consequently, he was propelling toward modernity the anti-Jewish militance and violence that marked German actions in the later Middle Ages and the early modern period, both justified under the guise of sustaining pristine Pauline truths.

See also **Ghetto**; **Jews**, *subentry on* **Jews and the Catholic Church**.

BIBLIOGRAPHY

Baer, Yitzhak F. *A History of the Jews in Christian Spain*. Translated by Louis Schoffman. Vol. 2. Philadelphia, 1966. Pages 324–423.

Cohen, Jeremy, ed. *From Witness to Witchcraft: Jews and Judaism in Medieval Christian Thought*. Weisbaden, Germany, 1996.

Foa, Anna. "The New and the Old: The Spread of Syphilis (1494–1530)." In *Sex and Gender in Historical Perspective*. Edited by Edward Muir and Guido Ruggiero. Baltimore, 1990. Pages 26–45.

Hsia, R. Po-Chia. *Trent 1475: Stories of a Ritual Murder Trial*. New Haven, Conn., 1992.

Langmuir, Gavin I. *History, Religion, and Antisemitism*. Berkeley, Calif., 1990.

Langmuir, Gavin I. *Toward a Definition of Antisemitism*. Berkeley, Calif., 1990.

Oberman, Heiko A. *The Roots of Antisemitism in the Age of Renaissance and Reformation*. Translated by J. I. Porter. Philadelphia, 1984.

Stow, Kenneth R. *Alienated Minority: The Jews of Medieval Latin Europe*. Cambridge, Mass., 1992. See chapter 11, part 1.

Wood, Diana, ed. *Christianity and Judaism*. Cambridge, Mass., 1992.

Yerushalmi, Yosef Hayim. *Assimilation and Racial Antisemitism*. New York, 1982.

KENNETH STOW

ANTONINUS (Antonio Pierozzi; 1389–1459), saint, observant Dominican, prior of San Marco (1436–1444), archbishop of Florence (1446–1459), church reformer, moralist, canonist, historian. Antoninus's legal acumen, administrative ability, and political skill enabled him to rise rapidly in the new reforming wing of the Dominican order, the Observants, to become one of Italy's most successful prelates and widely published moralists. Born during the papal schism to a Florentine notary, Antonio "Antonino" Pierozzi made his profession as a Dominican friar to Giovanni Dominici (c. 1357–1419) in 1405. He helped establish the first Florentine house of the Observance at San Domenico in Fiesole in 1406, then fled in 1409 to Foligno and then Cortona with his mentor (now a cardinal of the Roman pope Gregory XII [1406–1415]), rather than accept Pope Alexander V's (1409–1410) election by the Council of Pisa. Ordained at Cortona in 1413 and prior there from 1418 to 1421, Antoninus alternated between priorates at San Domenico and San Pier Martire in Naples between 1421 and 1430. As prior of Santa Maria sopra Minerva in Rome (1430–1432) he hosted the conclave that elected Pope Eugenius IV (1431–1447), who appointed him auditor general of the Rota (1431–1446) and vicar general of the Observant Dominicans in Italy (1432/37–c. 1446), and who himself fled to Florence in 1434. Antoninus had returned to San Domenico in 1432, where he oversaw the Observants' acquisition of San Marco in Florence with the patronage of Cosimo de' Medici (1389–1464) in 1435–1436, and assumed the joint priorate of the two houses (1439–1444). He witnessed the Council of Florence in 1439, mediated between the Observants and Bologna in 1441, and in 1442 founded the *Buonuomini di San Martino* (Saint Martin's good men), a confraternity that distributed alms to the *poveri vergognosi* (poor too proud to beg). In early 1446 Eugenius chose him to be Florence's new archbishop.

As an episcopal reformer, Antoninus utilized confrontation and negotiation to rebalance the relations between the Florentine state and the church in its territory, to reimpose hierarchical authority on the clergy, and to reassert ecclesiastical leadership of lay religious life. He halted the onerous taxes that Florence had regularly imposed on its clergy, checked fraudulent transfers of lay property to ecclesiastical tax havens, got the city to rescind its laws regulating benefices and confraternities, and likely abetted the passage of new sumptuary legislation and anti-Jewish measures. To reform the clergy, Antoninus convoked regular episcopal synods, issued updated constitutions, and in his visitations reorganized defunct parishes, disciplined priests, and carried Eugenius's reform of Florentine monasteries to all dioceses of the Florentine territory. Turning to the laity, he condemned the *fraticello* (little brother) Giovanni Cani for heresy in 1450, curbed the pageantry of civic religious festivals, revised the constitutions of lay confraternities, and continued Eugenius's support of youth confraternities. His initiatives in disaster and poor relief earned him public favor, and his defense of women and the poor popularized the episcopal court. Eugenius brought him to Rome for the "Concordat of Princes" in 1447, and in 1455–1456 Pope Calixtus III (1455–1458) made him a collector of revenue for his crusade against the Turks. Florence appointed him to lead embassies to greet the visiting emperor Frederick III (1440–1493) in 1452 and to congratulate Popes Calixtus III (1455–1458) and Pius II (1458–1464) on their elections. Although connected to the Medici through San Marco, Antoninus confirmed his reputation for political independence in 1458 by publicly condemning Medicean efforts to subvert voting procedures in the republic's councils.

Renowned as an expert on moral, economic, social, and legal issues, Antoninus was one of the most widely published authors of the fifteenth and sixteenth centuries. He wrote a popular manual on confession for a Neapolitan nobleman in 1429 (*Confessionale,* first published in Florence, 1457), which he revised before 1440 into condensed and expanded versions for priests. He then composed several devotional manuals for Florentine patrician ladies; these works are noted for their social practicality and clerical discretion. His cycle of Lenten sermons, preached in Florence in 1427 or 1432, never brought Antoninus the acclaim of Dominici or Bernardino of Siena (1380–1444). But they established the framework of his four-volume *Summa theologica* (or *Summa moralis,* first published in Venice, 1477–1480), which incorporated many of his treatises on contemporary issues, and his three-volume *Chronica* (first published in Nürnberg, 1484), both written from 1440–c. 1454. Although Antoninus deferred to the authority of Thomas Aquinas on many points, he was neither a Thomistic clone nor a humanist-baiter like Dominici. Eschewing the scholastic model of disputation, he distilled theology and incorporated recent jurisprudence into a synthesis that met the humanists' demands for a turn from speculative theology to practical Christian ethics, and the needs of preachers and educated laity for a canonistic and doctrinal guide to contemporary issues. Papalist in his view of church government, he was a republican in Florentine politics. He defended both merchants' rights to legitimate profits, and workers' and womens' rights to living wages. His *Chronica,* framed as a Christian history of the world in six ages, was organized to provide practical examples and contains much original material for his own age. Together, *Summa* and *Chronica* put much of the latest canonistic scholarship and the riches of San Marco's library at the fingertips of pastors, preachers, and laymen in simple, readable Latin.

Savonarola lauded Antoninus as a forebear, and the Medici sponsored his canonization by Pope Adrian VI in 1523 (feast day 10 May). Although the revival of Thomistic theology and stricter pastoral discipline after the Council of Trent contributed to the eclipse of Antoninus's writings, his episcopate was itself a model for many Tridentine reforms. He was made a doctor of the church in 1960.

BIBLIOGRAPHY

Primary Works

Antoninus. *Opera a ben vivere* (The art of living well). Edited by Francesco Palermo. Florence, 1858. A devotional manual for Florentine women.

Antoninus. *Summa theologica* (Theological summary). 4 vols. Verona, Italy, 1740. Reprint, Graz, Austria, 1959. The most accurate and accessible edition, it incorporates many of Antoninus's shorter treatises. There are no preferred or modern critical editions of the *Chronica* and *Confessionale.*

Secondary Works

Howard, Peter Francis. *Beyond the Written Word: Preaching and Theology in the Florence of Archbishop Antoninus, 1427–1459.* Florence, 1995. The best recent study, with a full bibliography.

Morçay, Raoul. *Saint Antonin, archevêque de Florence (1389–1459).* Paris, 1914. Still the fundamental biography of Antoninus.

Orlandi, P. Stefano, O.P. *Bibliografia Antoniniana. Descrizione dei manoscritti della vita e delle opere di S. Antonino O.P. arcivescovo di Firenze e degli studi stampati che lo riguardano.* Vatican City, 1962.

DAVID S. PETERSON

ANTWERP. From the late fifteenth century onward, the city of Antwerp experienced an almost unparalleled demographic and economic expansion. Because of the influx of Portuguese spices, south German copper and silver, and English cloth, Antwerp became the central market of Europe. At the same time, commercial expansion stimulated existing industries and attracted several new ones. The population exploded from 40,000 at the end of the fifteenth century to 100,000 in the 1560s. The economic and demographic growth profoundly affected

the city's social fabric. Social relations were severely strained in a metropolis where a small number of big merchants and entrepreneurs accumulated enormous wealth. Yet a place remained for a broad middle class of modest merchants, master craftsmen, and skilled artisans who benefited from the economic expansion.

The social tensions generated by the capitalist economy did not escalate into an overthrow of Antwerp's political regime that was dominated by a noble rentier, or property-owning class. Until the political and religious turmoil of the Wonderyear (1566) the city councillors succeeded in maintaining Antwerp's privileges and autonomy, effectively resisting central government measures that threatened the city's commercial welfare. Beginning in the early 1520s the monopoly of the Catholic church was challenged by the evangelical movement. After the first stirrings of Lutheranism, Anabaptism and, to an even greater extent, Calvinism gained force in Antwerp. Between 1579 and 1585 the Calvinists successfully seized power in the city. When the city surrendered to the besieging Spanish troops in 1585, thousands of Protestants fled to the Dutch Republic, and Antwerp became a bulwark of the Counter-Reformation.

Education and Printing. Antwerp's economic expansion profoundly affected its cultural life. Commercial activities demanded specific requirements in training and education, and the rich upper class and broad middle classes created enormous opportunities for consumption. Around the middle of the sixteenth century Antwerp had a well-organized and laicized educational system. In theory, advanced Latin teaching was reserved to the five parish schools, but they faced growing competition from private schools. Private schoolmasters not only taught the Dutch mother tongue and arithmetic, but a growing number also taught bookkeeping and other languages, such as French, Spanish, and Italian; some taught Latin. An unusual feature of Antwerp schools was the high number of schoolmistresses. In 1576 records show eighty-eight officially registered schoolmasters and seventy schoolmistresses. After 1585 education was closely interwoven with the policy of the Counter-Reformation church. Latin education, provided by the parish schools and a few regular orders such as the Jesuits, focused on the formation of a wordly and ecclesiastical elite, while popular education tried to catechize the masses.

Three Antwerp chambers of rhetoric, founded at the turn of the fifteenth and sixteenth centuries, had

View of Antwerp, 1515. MUSEUM PLANTIN-MORETUS/STEDELIJK PRENTENKABINET, ANTWERP, BELGIUM

a prominent place in literary life. These lay associations concentrated on poetry readings and theatricals in the vernacular and reflected the emancipated middle-class culture. Renaissance influence did not appear before the middle of the sixteenth century. Cornelis van Ghistele (c. 1510–1573), the artistic mind behind one of the Antwerp chambers of rhetoric, introduced ancient culture in his translations of Ovid, Virgil, Terence, and Horace, but his plays remained traditional in form. The poet Jan van der Noot (c. 1539–c. 1595) is considered the first real Renaissance representative within these groups. He was probably influenced by literary "academies" that flourished in Italian merchant circles in Antwerp.

At the same time, Antwerp's abundant distribution channels, skilled labor, and a large reading public made it an international center of book production and book trade. That at least 50 percent of all books printed in sixteenth-century Antwerp were published in Latin confirms the city's international orientation. Of the works produced by the famous printer Christophe Plantin (c. 1520–1589), 20 percent were humanist works, and the sciences, geography, history, grammars, and dictionaries represented 26 percent.

Humanism and the Arts. The presence of a well-organized educational system and scholarly books and printers created a fertile soil for humanist activities. In a first phase (1470–1555) humanism found adherents in the Latin parish schools, the chapter of Our Lady church, and the city administration. The city clerk Peter Gillis (1486–1533) and the secretary Cornelius Grapheus (d. 1558) are the best known representatives of the Erasmian humanism. The second phase (1555–1585) was marked by the stimulating role of Christophe Plantin, whose *officina* became an international meeting place for humanist authors and scholars. Among them were the philosopher Justus Lipsius, the cartographer Abra-

ham Ortelius, the orientalist Franciscus Raphelengius, and many others. The humanists paid special attention to the study of the "national" mother tongue, the Dutch vernacular. After 1585 humanism became less international and imbued with the spirit of the Catholic Reformation, a trend that was clearest in the Latin schools of the Jesuits. In general, interest shifted from literary toward antiquarian matters.

Artistic life flourished simultaneously with economic expansion. Antwerp became an international export center of artistic and luxury products. At the same time, the urban middle classes demanded more and more luxury products. As a result, artistic output was increasingly industrialized and commercialized. Artists tried to follow new trends, incorporating, for example, Renaissance elements. In painting, the first Renaissance influences appeared shortly after 1500 with Quinten Metsijs (c. 1465–1530). The growing interest in landscapes and nature in general also points to Renaissance influence. A genuinely new style, inspired on the grand manner of the Italian sixteenth century, was not introduced until the middle of the sixteenth century by the painter Frans Floris De Vriendt (c. 1519–1570). In sculpture, Cornelis II Floris De Vriendt, brother of Frans, in particular realized a Renaissance breakthrough. In architecture, Italian influences appeared around 1540. The new city hall, built in 1561–1565 and designed by the same Cornelis II Floris De Vriendt, strikingly displays the Italian architectural concepts. This city hall at the Great Market, once a symbol of the city's wealth and autonomy, is one of the best examples of Renaissance architecture in Antwerp. The unique *Officina Plantiniana* at the Vrijdagmarkt is also noteworthy.

See also **Plantin, Christophe.**

BIBLIOGRAPHY

Antwerpen in de XVIde eeuw. Antwerp, Belgium, 1975. Collection of articles covering most aspects of history and art history.

Antwerpen in de XVIIde eeuw. Antwerp, Belgium, 1989. Collection of articles on art and art history in the seventeenth century.

Burke, Peter. *Antwerp, a Metropolis in Comparative Perspective.* Antwerp, Belgium, 1993. Comparison of centers of painting, performance, and printing.

Honig, Elizabeth Alice. *Painting and the Market in Early Modern Antwerp.* New Haven, Conn., 1998. Explores the way in which Flemish painting between 1550 and 1650 represented and reflected the burgeoning capitalism of the Antwerp market.

Marnef, Guido. *Antwerp in the Age of Reformation: Underground Protestantism in a Commercial Metropolis, 1550–1577.* Translated by J. C. Grayson. Baltimore and London, 1996. Includes lengthy introduction on urban society in sixteenth-century Antwerp.

Van der Stock, Jan, ed. *Antwerp: Story of a Metropolis, 16th–17th Century.* Antwerp and Ghent, 1993. Collection of articles on Antwerp's Golden Age written by leading scholars.

Voet, Leon. *Antwerp, the Golden Age: The Rise and Glory of the Metropolis in the Sixteenth Century.* Antwerp, Belgium, 1973.

Voet, Leon. *The Golden Compasses: A History and Evaluation of the Printing and Publishing Activities of the Officina Plantiniana at Antwerp.* 2 vols. Amsterdam and New York, 1969–1972.

GUIDO MARNEF

ARABIC LITERATURE AND LANGUAGE.

The Islamic world experienced a renaissance of culture in the fourteenth, fifteenth, and sixteenth centuries. Largely due to political circumstances, Arabic literature shared in this renaissance only to a limited extent.

Historical Context.

In the classical first four centuries of Islamic civilization, Arabic *adab,* urbane learning, contrasted with *'ilm,* religious learning. By the ninth century C.E., *adab* can be labeled *humanitas:* the knowledge of poetry, metrics, lexicography, Arab lore and belles lettres, and areas of the culture of pre-Islamic civilizations—Persian, Greek, and Indian—with which the Arab Muslim world was familiar. The cultivated man might know a considerable amount about Greek science, medicine, and philosophy, but nothing of Greek literature. History was originally a part of *'ilm,* but with time it was seen also to adorn literary culture. Until the tenth century C.E., learning was conducted entirely in Arabic, even by Persian Muslims. Only under the patronage of east Persian princes in the latter half of the tenth century did a Persian *adab,* now written with the Arabic alphabet, emerge. Islam necessarily cultivates Arabic for understanding the Qur'an, the sayings of the Prophet, and for insight into the Law (*fiqh*); it "thinks in Arabic." Philosophers and scientists also continued to write in Arabic, with its rich vocabulary, and humane culture required correct knowledge of it.

The Mongol invasions of the thirteenth century changed all this. Great cities, academies, and libraries in many cases were destroyed, and the invaders preferred Persian, which was much easier for them to learn than Arabic. Very quickly correct knowledge of Arabic began to vanish even in Iraq, long the leading province of Arab learning. By 1327, in the renaissance of Islamic culture that came after the disasters of the thirteenth century, the Moroccan traveler Ibn Battuta could lament that in all Basra, once the city of the Arab grammarians, no scholar remained who could give a sermon or public address accurately in Arabic.

Arabic *adab* thus could be found only in Syria, Egypt, and the lands west. However, Arabic literary culture had depended heavily on the patronage of princes who cared about it and could appreciate it. The Mamluk military elite who ruled Egypt and Syria spoke Arabic poorly, if at all, and used a barracks dialect of Turkish among themselves. Their bureaucrats and the religious scholars of *'ilm,* the *'ulama,* were predominantly natives of their realms who spoke Arabic and thus could act to some extent as patrons. However, Arabic was cultivated mainly in the many academies that the ruling class endowed, primarily for the education of those who studied *'ilm.* Even chancery documents, in which professional bureaucrats sought for elaborate and felicitous expression, declined in this period.

These developments meant that the establishments of *'ilm* proliferated, but literature was chiefly valued for what it could contribute to religious learning. Thus pre-Islamic Arab poetry was carefully studied and commented upon because lexicography, necessary for properly understanding the Qur'an and the sayings of the Prophet and his Companions, depended upon it. Early histories of Islam and collections of court poetry were also cultivated for the information on the religious community that they contained. The result was the development of a distinctive sort of literary scholarship, one that is very valuable to scholars even today, but one that generally sought preservation rather than originality. In Arabic literature it is the age of retrospection, collection, commentary, and systematization.

Authors and Works.

Voluminous biographical dictionaries were compiled, chiefly to evaluate those who transmitted hadiths, sayings of the Prophet, since validation of each saying depends on a chain of transmitters, each of whom must be found of good character and dependable. A leader in this sort of compilation was Shams al-Din al-Dhahabi of

Damascus (1274–1348), who studied in the academies of Damascus and Cairo and taught hadith and Islamic law in his native city. His major work, *History of Islam,* comprises a general narrative for the events of each century and biographical notices for all notable people who died in each of seventy decades (called *tabaqat,* classes) up to the year A.H.700/1300 C.E. This great compendium of many volumes included references to the authorities he consulted and attempted to record the development of the entire Islamic community, including Persia and western Islam (North Africa and Spain). He himself abridged it and derived from it also works dealing with the Companions of the Prophet, reciters of the Qur'an, famous *'ulama,* and Islamic notables.

Al-Dhahabi's teacher, Yusuf al-Mizzi (1256–1341), had been an exhaustive Damascene collector of biographical notices of transmitters of hadiths from the "six books," the Sunni canonical collections of hadiths, and more. Al-Dhahabi's contemporary and friend Khalil ibn Aybak al-Safadi (1297–1363) was a humanist who wrote not only an alphabetically arranged dictionary of biographies but also extensive poetry as well as prose essays, epigrams, and literary criticism. Ibn Hajar al-'Asqalani (1372–1449), from a wealthy mercantile family of Cairo, educated in Egypt, Palestine, and Syria and chief judge of Egypt at various times for a total of twenty-one years, was widely regarded as the greatest exemplar of religious scholarship in his age. He was a commentator on hadiths and their transmitters, with many works. One of these was an annal of events from his birth in 1372 to 1446, the *Inba' al-ghumr* (Instruction of the ignorant). He wrote a history of the Islamic eighth century, *al-Durar al-kamina* (The hidden pearls). While often mechanical collections, his books are indispensable reference works. The *Subh al-a'sha* (Morning for the night-blind) of al-Qalqashandi (1355–1418), an encyclopedic manual for secretaries, gives information on pens, paper, ink, margins, formulas, communication routes, geography of Muslim and non-Muslim lands, examples of correspondence with foreign rulers, protocol, and how to file and to write a precis. It is a fund of information on the officialdom of the day.

The Mamluk historians were conscientious and thorough but rarely original. Al-Maqrizi of Cairo (1364–1442), after a distinguished public career in Egypt and Syria, decided to give himself fully to historiography, probably after contact with Ibn Khaldun. He wrote many works, lived for some years in Mecca, and returned to Cairo, where he died. His topography of the Muslim monuments of Cairo, *al-*

Khitat, is indispensable. *Itti'az al-hunafa'* (Admonition for sincere Muslims), and *al-Suluk,* his long history of the Ayyubids and Mamluks who succeeded them, are of great importance. His contemporary, critic, and continuator, the court-based annalist Abu al-Mahasin ibn Taghribirdi (1409–1470), also left a number of valuable works on the history of Muslim Egypt.

For original historians in Arabic, one must look abroad. In Persia, the chief minister Rashid al-Din (1247–1318), to bring his Mongol overlords into Islamic civilization, wrote in both Persian and Arabic a universal history, which seeks to situate Islam in larger world history. The brilliant 'Abd al-Rahman Ibn Khaldun of Tunis (1332–1406), a solitary genius who nonetheless was a great academic and even a statesman, an Islamic "Renaissance man," wrote a universal history (*al-'Ibar*) that is flawed but especially valuable for the history of the Muslim West and of the Berbers. His *Muqaddima,* or introduction to his history, is a philosophical and sociopsychological work that compels the admiration of all who study it, though in his own day not many did. One of the greatest polygraphs of Arabic, Jalal al-Din al-Suyuti (1445–1505), worked in Egypt, with 561 titles to his credit. Inevitably, some of his books are derivative, but he is an authoritative epitomizer of the tradition.

While court literature languished in Cairo, popular and oral literature, meant to be recited in the coffeehouse or at gatherings, flourished. The definitive form of the *Thousand and One Nights,* best known of all Arabic literature in the West, was collected from these tales; also notable are the *Sirat 'Antar,* the epic of 'Antar, black poet-hero of the desert, and the *Sirat bani hilal,* the epic tale of bedouin tribes who invaded North Africa from Egypt in the eleventh century. The shadow plays (plays performed with shadow puppets) of Ibn Daniyal are also important.

A wonderful picture of the fourteenth-century Islamic world has been left by Ibn Battuta of Tangier (1304–1377), a Maliki legal scholar who traveled through all the lands of Islam, even to the Muslim colonies in Indonesia and China as well as in black Africa, and described his adventurous life in anecdotal detail on his return. In Muslim Spain, the cultivated Ibn al-Khatib of Granada (1313–1375), vizier and historian, had a stormy career in Spain and North Africa but in periods of exile wrote history and poetry as well as works on poetry, *adab,* medicine, and mystical philosophy. He was executed for "un-Islamic opinions" through the intrigues of his rival and former protégé, the vizier Ibn Zamrak (1333–1394?), himself an accomplished poet. Except among the émigrés from Muslim Spain, Arabic literature in North Africa generally did not prosper in this time. The rulers were Berbers and sometimes only semi-lettered. Al-Makkari of Tlemcen (c. 1577–1632 in Cairo), a major compiler of information on Muslim Spain and North Africa, was an exception.

The conquest of the Mamluk empire, Tunisia, and Algeria by the Turkish Ottoman empire was in general damaging to the cultivation of Arabic literature.

See also **Islam.**

BIBLIOGRAPHY

Primary Work

Ibn Battuta. *Ibn Battuta: Travels in Asia and Africa, 1325–1354.* Translated by H. A. R. Gibb. London, 1953.

Secondary Works

Brockelmann, Carl. *Geschichte der arabischen Litteratur.* Leipzig, 1903.

Gibb, H. A. R. *Arabic Literature.* Oxford, 1963.

Gibb, H. A. R., J. H. Kramers, E. Lévi-Provençal, and J. Schacht, eds. *The Encyclopaedia of Islam.* Rev. ed. 9 vols. Leiden, Netherlands, and London, 1960–. See entries on Ibn Battuta, Ibn Daniyal, Ibn Hadjar al-Askalani, Ibn Khaldun, Ibn al-Khatib, Ibn Zamrak, al-Dhahabi, al-Kalkashandi, al-Makkari, al-Makrizi, and al-Safadi.

Nicholson, Reynold A. *Literary History of the Arabs.* 2d ed. Cambridge, U.K., 1963.

JOHN ALDEN WILLIAMS

ARAGONA, TULLIA D' (c. 1510–1556), Italian courtesan and writer. Celebrated for her wit and for her musical and literary accomplishments, Tullia d'Aragona began her profession at an early age in Rome, during the turbulent but still tolerant pontificate of Clement VII (1523–1534). After the sack of the city in 1527, she moved her residence successively to Venice, Ferrara, Siena, and Florence. In each new location she maintained a salon where some of the best-known men of letters, politicians, and prelates of the day debated literary and intellectual issues. In 1547 she returned to Rome; there she died and was buried in the church of Sant'Agostino.

Aragona authored a collection of poetry, *Rime* (Rhymes), and a prose work, *Dialogo della infinità d'amore* (Dialogue on the infinity of love), both published in 1547 in Venice by the celebrated firm of Gabriel Giolito de' Ferrari. Most of her poems are sonnets of direct address. Some celebrate Cosimo I de' Medici, duke of Florence, his wife, and members of the court; other sonnets, addressed to friends, meditate on the vicissitudes of life and debate points of literary fame. Benedetto Varchi, then the literary arbiter of Florence, is addressed in a verse sequence that appropriates pastoral-Platonic situations and im-

agery. In the rest of her collection, Aragona either expresses her grateful affection for Girolamo Muzio, a courtier, writer, and former lover of the author, or, in a direct but still elegant manner, she declares her passion for a man much younger than herself. In two sonnets, remarkable in their original treatment of mythological images and narratives, Aragona declares her regained, though short-lived, emotional independence.

Her *Dialogo della infinità d'amore* describes a conversation on the nature of human love taking place in Aragona's Florentine quarters. Many publications at the time popularized fashionable Platonic theories, either in treatise or in dialogue form. They briefly considered various categories of love and often gave their consent exclusively to the spiritual elements in human relationships, concluding with a paean to Platonic love as the only kind appropriate to mature Christian men. Aragona's dialogue instead proposed a definition of love that differed substantially from both the Christian and the Platonic views. Strategically employing concepts and methods drawn from current philosophical discourse, Aragona maintained that the only moral and lasting bond possible between woman and man is one founded on the true nature of humankind, which is both spiritual and sensual, and must therefore satisfy both drives in each partner. Her discussion of love and sexuality becomes further radicalized by being linked throughout the dialogue to the ongoing debate on women and contemporary gender issues. Aragona's arguments implicitly expose the basic misogynistic nature of Platonic love in both the popular heterosexual variation and the classical homosexual form. By positing an attachment based on the intellectual and sensual parity of the sexes, Aragona's theory removes women from the position of physicality and sin to which traditional ethics had relegated them, and Aragona thereby establishes a new meaning of womanhood and an innovative morality of love.

Traditionally assimilated into the literary output of writers influenced by Platonic ideas, and often dismissed as a courtesan's attempt to gloss over a disreputable life, Aragona's writings have been recently reassessed as the work of a woman intent on constructing her chosen literary image and on modifying contemporary concepts of love and sexuality.

BIBLIOGRAPHY

Primary Work

Aragona, Tullia d'. *Dialogue on the Infinity of Love.* Edited and translated by Rinaldina Russell and Bruce Merry. Introduction and notes by Rinaldina Russell. Chicago, 1997. Translation of *Dialogo della infinità d'amore* (1547).

Secondary Works

Jones, Ann Rosalind. *The Currency of Eros: Women's Love Lyric in Europe, 1540–1620*. Bloomington, Ind., 1990.

Russell, Rinaldina. "Tullia d'Aragona." In *Italian Women Writers*. Edited by Rinaldina Russell. Westport, Conn., 1994. Pages 26–34.

RINALDINA RUSSELL

ARCHAEOLOGY. *See* Classical Antiquity, Discovery of.

ARCHITECTURE. [This entry includes two subentries, Architecture in the Renaissance and Architectural Treatises.]

Architecture in the Renaissance

The formulation of a formal architectural vocabulary indebted to antiquity in the period 1400–1600 marks the high point of Western civilization's fascination with classicism. This formulation was part of a larger, pan-European phenomenon, yet its cradle was Italy, where these forms were first and most self-consciously crafted, employed, theorized, and promoted. In the North the Gothic manner was never altogether abandoned and survived in modified forms well into the seventeenth century. Conversely, in Italy the rejection of an alien, northern style of building united architects in an unprecedented collective enterprise of recuperation and assimilation of ancient practices. Petrarch's definition of the Middle Ages as "a thousand years of darkness" captures their attitude toward the more immediate past just as much as that of their humanist and artist colleagues.

Already in the fifteenth century Renaissance texts such as Leon Battista Alberti's *De pictura* (On painting; 1435) and Filarete's *Trattato d'architettura* (Treatise on Architecture; c. 1460–1464) voiced this view and located the first stirring of the Renaissance in Florence, particularly in the work of Filippo Brunelleschi. That the architects felt themselves to be participating in a larger, cross-cultural phenomenon is most eloquently illustrated by Filarete, who enjoined his patron, Francesco Sforza, the duke of Milan,

> to abandon modern [late medieval] usage. . . . I think only barbaric people could have brought it into Italy. . . . I will give you an example. There is the same comparison between ancient and modern architecture as there is in literature. That is, there is the same difference between the speech of Cicero or Virgil and that used thirty or forty years ago. Today it has been brought back

to better usage than had prevailed in past times—during at least seven hundred years—for today one speaks in prose with ornate language.

This rejection of the Middle Ages and exaltation of antiquity informed the writings of architectural theorists and architects such as Francesco di Giorgio Martini, Sebastiano Serlio, and Andrea Palladio throughout the Renaissance. But it was consecrated into the mainstream of art criticism by Giorgio Vasari in *Vite de' più eccelenti architetti, pittori, ed scultori italiani* (Lives of the most excellent Italian architects, painters, and sculptors; 1550 and 1568). For him Renaissance architecture existed in confrontation with the "barbarous style" of the Gothic, which was monstrous and lacked order, proportion, and beauty. According to him, good architecture had been first adumbrated by Brunelleschi, led to self-assured maturity by Donato Bramante in his Roman works, performed successfully in his wake by Antonio da Sangallo the Younger, Raphael, Baldassare Peruzzi, Giulio Romano, and Jacopo Sansovino and had reached perfection with Michelangelo. If not all his principal protagonists were Tuscan, at least all had reached stylistic accomplishment through the obligatory encounter with the antiquities and culture of Rome.

Such a theoretical model focused on the Florence-Rome axis, which was fashioned and endorsed in large measure by a succession of Florentines (and buttressed by the cultural imperialism of a succession of Tuscan grand dukes), did not accurately describe the situation on the edges of the peninsula. In Venice, Lombardy, Naples, and Sicily local traditions and outside influences (Western and Eastern) led to the creation of idiosyncratic architectural vocabularies. Brunelleschi's Florentine church of Santo Spirito (1444) and Alberti's Sant'Andrea in Mantua (1471) are distinctly different from Giovanni Antonio Amadeo's Certosa at Pavia (second half of the fifteenth century) and his Colleoni Chapel in Bergamo (1470–1474) or Mauro Codussi's San Zaccaria (1458–1515) in Venice. Although the archaeologically informed Roman manner spread to these provinces in the aftermath of the artists' diaspora caused by the Sack of Rome (1527), regionalist features were retained. Thus in the work of architects like Galeazzo Alessi, Andrea Sansovino, and Pellegrino Tebaldi, the highly plastic and textured surfaces typical of northern Italian architecture were blended into the rational geometrical and tectonic systems bequeathed by Bramante.

The Vasarian model also did not account for the many venerated Gothic buildings throughout Italy

French Architecture. Facade of the Cour Carrée of the Louvre, Paris, by Pierre Lescot (c. 1515–1578). In the center is the Le Mercier clock pavilion. The pyramid constructed by I. M. Pei from 1984 to 1988 is visible through the center archway. ERICH LESSING/ART RESOURCE

(Bologna, Milan, Venice, Orvieto, Florence). Left unfinished (San Petronio, Bologna) or damaged as a result of deterioration or conflagrations (Doge's Palace, Venice), they required rebuilding and commanded many distinguished proposals to complete them in the style in which they had been originally conceived. The architectural competitions and construction sites that resulted provided opportunities for an appreciation of the Gothic style and its engineering subtleties that carried over into the baroque and affected the work of Francesco Borromini, Guarino Guarini, and others.

The definition of the Renaissance from an Italian perspective, endorsed and perpetuated by nineteenth- and twentieth-century historians and critics (Jakob Burckhardt, Heinrich Wölfflin) who laid the foundations of art history as a discipline, causes problems when applied to French, Spanish, Portuguese, Flemish, and German architecture. Here local traditions and Gothic forms were constantly blended

with the learned classical idiom imported from Italy into new assemblages of great originality, such as the Hospital of Santa Cruz (1520–1524) in Toledo by Enrique Egas and Alonso de Covarrubias. Indeed, it took more than a century (and in some cases until the seventeenth century) for a deliberately classicizing style to take hold in France, the Iberian Peninsula, and the North, and it is only with buildings such as Juan de Herrera's Escorial in Madrid (1563–1584), Cornelis Floris's town hall in Antwerp (1561–1565), and Pierre Lescot's Louvre in Paris (from 1546) that we can speak of anything approaching an international classical style. Yet even then classicism was inflected by local planning traditions, building materials and their use, by climate and local topography, ornamental preferences, and social practices, and the ensuing forms carried the full flavor of geographic individualism. The fondness for a form of architectural *plateria* (goldsmithing) in Spain, for mansarded roofs, fortified chateaux, verticality, and anthropomorphic ornament in France, and for Gothic tracery in the North left indelible marks on the imported italianizing style.

The Appropriation of Antiquity and the Rise of Theory.

No matter how close or distant the echo of antiquity, it nevertheless shaped European culture and its architecture. But no matter how sanguine Alberti, Filarete, and their successors may have been about the need to imitate and emulate the ancients, the recuperation of ancient forms was an arduous task, particularly for architecture. Much of the Roman heritage had disappeared, been badly damaged, or been used for subsequent building campaigns, and little of the magnificence of imperial Rome could be teased out of the scattered ruins. For architects outside Italy these fragments held an even more elusive spell, as only a privileged few accessed the sites directly. More commonly, they depended on drawings, sketches, and books handed down from master to student to form any kind of conception of the erstwhile splendors of Rome.

The "rediscovery" of Vitruvius's *De architectura* (On architecture; c. 27 B.C.) in 1416 offered much insight into the theory and practice of the ancients and mitigated some of these losses. Yet the text had been written in the age of Augustus (ruled 30 B.C.–A.D. 14) and offered no guidance to understanding architectural developments in the subsequent imperial period. Much that could be seen was at odds with what was written and left architects grappling for the true principles of architecture. Indeed, the acrimonious debates in the sixteenth century over the correct use of the orders can be traced back to this fundamental discrepancy. As a result, the recovery process required a significant leap of the imagination, and although this hindered reconstruction to a degree, it also fueled much of the enthusiasm attending it. In Raphael's letter to Pope Leo X (c. 1518) laying out what amounted to the inaugural program for archaeological recovery and recording technique, this creative and imaginative impulse can be sensed behind his lucidly analytical strategy:

> Holy Father, there are many who, measuring with their small judgment the great things that are written of the Romans' arms and of the city of Rome regarding its marvelous artifice, richness, and ornaments, sooner estimate these to be fabulous rather than true, however to me it seems otherwise, because, judging the divinity of those ancient spirits from the relics that can still be seen among the ruins of Rome, I do not think it beyond reason to believe that many of those things that to us seem impossible to them seemed extremely easy.

If the absence of consistent archaeological data led architects to oscillate between fanciful invention and accurate reconstruction, the same may be said of their engagement with theory. Although Vitruvius offered a sizable body of prescriptions, he left many questions unanswered; this gap set off probably the most intense textual activity in the history of architectural discourse. Not only was his *De architectura* text printed (1486), illustrated (1511), translated, and commented on (starting in 1521), but a great many new treatises were published. Alberti's *De re aedificatoria* (written c. 1450, printed 1486) led the way, but it was closely followed by Sebastiano Serlio's multivolume treatise (on the orders, antiquities, domestic architecture, perspective and geometry, gates, and so on from 1537 onward), Giacomo Barozzi da Vignola's *Regola delli cinque ordini d'architettura* (Rules of the five architectural orders; 1562), Andrea Palladio's *Quattro libri dell'architettura* (Four books on architecture; 1570), and Vincenzo Scamozzi's *L'idea dell'architettura universale* (The idea of universal architecture; 1615). Many more were written but were never published and in some cases were lost (Filarete, Francesco di Giorgio, Martini, Baldassare Peruzzi, Antonio da Sangallo [the Younger], Francesco Fortuna, and so on).

What preoccupied architects most in these literary contexts was to identify the governing paradigm for architecture. Part of a visual culture oriented toward the imitation of nature, they sought points of reference in the world of natural phenomena for their own art. Ideal geometries, commensuration, the human body were the answers the ancients provided. Such a focus tied architecture into the larger cultural fabric of its time, for it demonstrated shared aspirations with the figural arts; it also drew architecture closer to the literary arts, the traditional purveyors of theory on imitation. Because most architects (Francesco di Giorgio, Raphael, Peruzzi, Giulio Romano, Michelangelo) were active and successful in two if not all three of the visual arts, crossovers between them were inevitable. Moreover, like their artist peers, architects tried to elevate their art above the mechanical and manual. And the learned treatise displaying knowledge of rhetoric, history, mathematics, music, optics, philosophy, and letters went a long way toward achieving this goal, as did the formation of academies of design, modeled on the literary academies that proliferated throughout Italy in the sixteenth century. Inaugurated in Florence in 1563 and set up through the agency of Vasari, the Accademia del Disegno united all artists and provided them with a professional identity and a forum for discussion and teaching. *Disegno* was identified as the common root for all the arts. Such an emphasis tended to suggest that architecture was subordinated to painting, and this was nowhere more explicitly stated than in Federico Zuccaro's discourses while *principe* of the Roman Accademia di San Luca (1593–1594). However, it also gradually led architects to spell out the unique nature of their art and to emphasize its close links to science (especially mechanics) and to natural philosophy.

If the treatises offered architects the opportunity to reflect on their art, they also acted as agents of dissemination that allowed the discourse on architecture that had been building up for nearly a century in Italy to reach the rest of Europe. Indeed, the remarkable speed with which most of these treatises were translated into French, Spanish, Dutch, and German testifies to an eager market of architects, craftsmen, and patrons who needed images and explication. Soon architects and theoreticians like Jean Martin, Guillaume Philandrier, Philibert Delorme, Jean Bullant, and Androuet Du Cerceau in France, John Shute in England, Diego de Sagredo in Spain, and Vredeman de Vries in Holland emulated their Italian counterparts and entered the literary arena. However, in these works the Italians' intricately worded passages on aesthetics gave way to practical information and increasingly accomplished illustrations of buildings and ornaments intended to guide selection and design of forms *all'antica* (in the antique style). Yet despite the fascination with antiquity, whose display became a sign that client and architect belonged to an international intellectual elite, regional features persisted. Delorme's addition of a French columnar order (*ordre françois*) to the Vitruvian canon in 1567 spoke as much of a resistance to classicism's imperialism on nationalistic grounds as of a persistent fondness for the organic forms of a surviving Gothic.

Building Formats. Although regional diversity marked the output of the Renaissance, common features testify to shared principles, interests, and practices. This is particularly true of building types such as churches, where similar liturgical needs and symbolic references to Rome as the seat of Western Christianity privileged certain plan and elevation formats over others. However, clear patterns did not become established for some time. Palace and villa architecture was marked by greater variety and local independence than church architecture. Tied to specific social and cultural rituals, it reflected their variety.

Religious buildings. Nowhere is the fluctuation between the traditional basilican plan with a longitudinal nave and the ideal geometries of the central plan (circular or Greek cross) more evident than in the building history of the basilica of Saint Peter's in Rome. Initiated by Bramante and continued by Raphael, Peruzzi, Antonio da Sangallo the Younger, Michelangelo, Giacomo della Porta, and Carlo Maderno, its plan underwent a dizzying number of changes before construction finally ended at the beginning of the seventeenth century. The central plan (based on the square and circle) recommended itself with its references to the heavenly sphere and to perfect geometrical figures. The connection between macrocosm (the universe) and microcosm (the human body) by way of number and form constituted another attraction. This reciprocal relationship discussed by Vitruvius and other classical sources had received additional reinforcement in medieval theological texts and thus had led to a fascination with the symbolic potential of central plans for religious buildings (see Bramante's Tempietto, San Pietro in Montorio, Rome [1502]; Cola da Caprarola's Santa Maria della Consolazione in Todi [1508]; Antonio da Sangallo the Elder's Santa Maria di San Biagio in Montepulciano [1518]).

However, liturgically such plans posed problems, for their short, truncated naves, indistinguishable from apse and transept arms, did not allow for a clear relationship between congregation and celebrant, nor did they provide for a large enough audience. For this reason, after the conclusion of the Council of Trent in 1563 Catholic Rome promoted a return to the simple formats of early church tradition as part of its Counter-Reformation policies (see St. Carlo Borromeo, *Instructiones fabricae et supellectilis ecclesiasticae* [1577]). Thus in Il Gesù (from 1568; Rome), the aisle-less and barrel-vaulted mother church of the newly created Society of Jesus, Giacomo Barozzi da Vignola and Giacomo della Porta returned to a formula proposed more than a century earlier by Alberti (Sant'Andrea, Mantua). Like the Jesuits, the Oratorians, Theatines, and other orders initiated many building campaigns in this period, though most were not completed until well into the seventeenth century. Thus, it is the Gesù type of church that the Jesuit missionaries spread to the four corners of the world as part of their propaganda activities.

Elsewhere in Europe, the wars of religion discouraged the building of large religious complexes. In France architects tended to retain the Gothic patterns and only superficially applied classical orna-

Religious Architecture. An aerial view of St. Peter's Basilica, Rome—showing the dome, the longitudinal nave, and the facade—reflects the change from a central plan to a longitudinal plan. ALINARI/ART RESOURCE

ment (for example, Saint Eustache, Paris); instead, most of the imported vocabulary was used for interior structures (organs, rood screens, and so on). In Spain, until the reign of Philip II, few large new churches were commissioned in the classical manner, and what innovation there was tended to be attached to Gothic buildings in need of completion (Diego de Siloé, Cathedral of Granada). Philip II, however, promoted an ascetic classicism (San Lorenzo in the Escorial complex) that ultimately moved Spanish Counter-Reformation architecture in a direction diametrically opposed to the exuberance of the Italian baroque. In the Protestant North, where the emphasis was on preaching and texts rather than on processions and the Eucharist, the longitudinal nave was gradually supplanted by a more functional auditorium type of seating; however, even here the new formats took time to evolve.

Domestic architecture. In Italy the fourteenth-century palace seemingly carved out of one rough block of stone was modified gradually to approximate the ancient Roman *domus* described by Vitruvius. In palaces such as the Farnese in Rome (1525–1589), elegant sequences of frescoed rooms, colonnaded courtyards, and a profusion of ornament in-

side and out allowed wealthy patrons to imagine themselves living *all'antica*. But dwelling in the city also meant respecting its codes and hierarchies, and the same classical sources led architects and patrons to devise a finely tuned theory of magnificence and civic decorum that established clear connections between socioeconomic status and decoration.

Freedom from rules and the ideal of re-creating the lifestyle of the ancients were nowhere more successfully formulated than in the country villa. Influenced by descriptions of pleasure retreats such as those of Pliny the Younger and surviving ancient examples, such as Hadrian's villa, patrons and architects gave their imaginations free rein. Gardens and grottoes, sculpture courtyards, and amphitheaters for performances, trompe l'oeil effects, and complex iconographic programs intended to entertain and bemuse visitors were the principal features of these leisure buildings.

If the Villa Madama by Raphael (designed 1518; Rome) or the Palazzo del Tè by Giulio Romano (1525–1534; Mantua) arose mainly from such considerations, the same cannot be said of the villas on the Venetian mainland. Here, economic reversals had shifted the aristocracy's attention from com-

Domestic Architecture. The Loggia di Davide (or Loggia d'Honore) of the Palazzo del Tè, Mantua, designed by Giulio Romano. In the distance is the Exedra, whose design (c. 1651) is attributed to Nicolo Sebregondi. THE BRIDGEMAN ART LIBRARY

merce to agriculture and had led to the development of a hybrid genre: part Roman leisure villa, part working farm, these buildings proclaimed landownership while simultaneously providing the refined living environment expected by humanist patrons. The restrained architectural vocabulary of plain stuccoed walls and monumental porticoed entrances that architects like Palladio devised for these working Elysia, or places of delight, set up a type that resisted fashion and geographic boundaries and was copied well into the twentieth century. [See the photograph of Palladio's La Rotunda in the color plates in volume 4.]

In France the Vitruvian Roman house met with little favor, as did small country villas. Instead, the tradition of the medieval fortified château survived, although it was modified by the italianate plans and elevation systems popularized by Serlio. The large complexes made up of courtyards, wings, and articulated corner pavilions at Ancy-le-Franc, Delorme's Château d'Anet, or Bullant's Château d' Écouen mark the stages in the formation of a distinct French type. The combination of brick and stone that gained popularity toward the later sixteenth century constituted another characteristic feature and played an important part in the successful insertion of large new complexes into existing urban fabrics (Place Dauphine and Place des Vosges in Paris).

Town Planning. The design of the city galvanized as much discussion as did the use and transformation of classical ornament. The remnants of ancient forums, triumphal arches, temple complexes, and gates suggested something of the splendor of Rome as an ensemble, yet, compromised by centuries of neglect, the design of the ancient city remained opaque. As a result, many of the theories associated with ideal city layouts were developed from a few textual sources, architectural and military, such as Vitruvius and Polybius (c. 200–c. 118 B.C.), rather than from firsthand experience. This relative absence of sources left much to the imagination and invited architects to propose new solutions.

Perhaps these are nowhere better displayed than in two examples that bracket the Renaissance: the cities of Pienza (c. 1460; see the entry on Art, subentry on Renaissance Art in this volume) and Palmanova (c. 1590; see the entry on Fortifications in volume 2). In both cases the emphasis is on simple geometry and central plans (trapezoidal and star-shaped), on order and perspectival effects that establish a hierarchy among buildings. The same principles informed interventions in existing cities, though the opportunities for grand designs were limited. As a result, most attention was lavished on the layout of squares and streets, with the object of facilitating movement and featuring major buildings along these routes (Ferrara, Florence, Venice). The large-scale urban renewal of Rome during the pontificate of Sixtus V (1585–1590; see the entry on Sixtus in volume 6) constituted the climax of this trend, transforming the city into a network of axes and squares, the better to process vast numbers of pilgrims and assert the power of the papacy. As such it set a powerful example for the politicized transformation of the city and landscape that had important consequences in the centuries to come.

Another branch of city design was influenced by the problems resulting from the uncertain political climate, the growth of seafaring routes, and the changing face of warfare (due to the increased efficiency and deadliness of firearms). As a result, many discussions (Filarete, Serlio, Pietro Cataneo, Francesco de Marchi, Jacques Perret) centered on the design of fortified cities, port cities, and garrison towns. Here, too, the emphasis was on central plans and geometrical rationalization, though not for aesthetic reasons. Both types of plans were intended to facilitate army deployment and bullet and cannon trajectories and thus to help turn the city into as well tuned an instrument as that against which it sought to defend itself.

See also **Palaces and Townhouses; Urbanism; Villas.**

BIBLIOGRAPHY

Ackerman, James. *The Villa: Form and Ideology of Country Houses.* Princeton, N.J., 1990.

Ballon, Hilary. *The Paris of Henry IV: Architecture and Urbanism.* Cambridge, Mass., 1991.

Guillaume, Jean, ed. *L'emploi des ordres à la Renaissance.* Paris, 1992.

Guillaume, Jean, ed. *Les traités d'architecture de la Renaissance.* Paris, 1988.

Heydenreich, Ludwig H., and Wolfgang Lotz. *Architecture in Italy, 1400–1600.* Translated by Mary Hottinger. Harmondsworth, U.K., 1974.

Hitchcock, Henry Russell. *German Renaissance Architecture.* Princeton, N.J., 1981.

Lazzaro, Claudia. *The Italian Renaissance Garden.* New Haven, Conn., 1990.

Millon, Henry, and Vittorio Lampugnani. *The Renaissance from Brunelleschi to Michelangelo: The Representation of Architecture.* Milan, 1994.

Payne, Alina. *The Architectural Treatise in the Italian Renaissance.* Cambridge, U.K., and New York, 1999.

Wilkinson-Zerner, Catherine. *Juan de Herrera: Architect to Philip II of Spain.* New Haven, Conn., 1993.

Wittkower, Rudolf. *Gothic vs. Classic: Architectural Projects in Seventeenth-Century Italy.* New York, 1974.

ALINA A. PAYNE

Architectural Treatises

The appearance of the first manuscripts on architecture in the middle of the fifteenth century, together with the first printed treatises after 1486, closely followed the renewed use in Italy of the five "styles" of building, as the antique columns were called. Renaissance architecture was accompanied by its own literature almost from the start. Early writers on architecture sought to emulate the Roman author Vitruvius (fl. late first century B.C.), whose *De architectura* (*On Architecture*) was the only comprehensive treatise solely on the theory of architecture to survive from antiquity.

Vitruvius. An architect and engineer in the time of the emperor Augustus (to whom Vitruvius's treatise is dedicated), Vitruvius set out to record the foundation rituals that inaugurated ancient cities, the arrangement of forums, basilicas, temples, theaters, and more exotic structures such as the Greek tower of the winds.

Vitruvius also recorded the origins and characteristics of the antique columns, describing two models that were imitated by the orders—as the columns would be termed by Raphael (1483–1520)—in the form of the hut supposedly built by primitive man and the proportions and features of the human body. In particular, he recorded that the body had dictated the proportions and gender of the Greek columns, which ranged from the "masculine" Doric and "matronly" Ionic to the "maidenly" Corinthian. In describing the principle of decorum, Vitruvius linked these types to temples dedicated to particular gods: Doric for Minerva, Mars, and Hercules; Ionic for Juno, Diana, and Bacchus; and Corinthian for Venus and Flora.

Moreover, in outlining the planning of temple architecture, Vitruvius famously observed that the extremities of a man with outstretched limbs conformed to the geometry of a circle (centered on the navel) and a square (with an unspecified center). Vitruvius described the human body as the ultimate source of Platonic "perfect" numbers—particularly six and ten—and of units of measurement (the "finger" or inch, "palm," "foot," and "cubit" or forearm from elbow to fingertips). Following the celebrated drawing of this so-called "Vitruvian man" by Leonardo da Vinci (c. 1490), the Roman's description was to become one of those most frequently illustrated in Renaissance editions of his treatise, while these treatises inevitably extended the body-temple analogy to the planning of secular building types.

In codifying the rules for the correct carving of the orders, early Renaissance authors surveyed the (often conflicting) use of the column on ancient Roman remains and also studied the writings of Pliny on specific monuments such as the Pantheon, of Polybius on Roman camps, and of Julius Frontinus on aqueducts. But it was Vitruvius's treatise that provided Renaissance theorists with the principal antique precedent for a treatise on architecture, and as such largely determined the content of Renaissance architectural books. Indeed, without the chance survival of Vitruvius's manuscript, Renaissance architectural literature would not have been able to explain with such certainty the relationship, for example, between architectural and human proportion or between the timber hut and the origins of ornament. Moreover, without the Vitruvian models of hut and body, Renaissance architecture would itself surely have looked very different.

Alberti. The principles of Gothic architecture had been transmitted orally, within secretive guilds and craft lodges, and, as an *ars mechanica* (mechanical art), architecture occupied a relatively low status in the medieval hierarchy of knowledge. As a consequence, literary evidence on Gothic building procedures is scarce. Surviving works (with a didactic purpose) on Gothic architecture are limited to Villard de Honnecourt's "lodge-book" (c. 1225–1250), which was an illustrated sketchbook rather than a publication; and two books published in the German lands where printing began, Mathes Roriczer's *Das Büchlein von der Fialen Gerechtigkeit* (Booklet on pinnacle correctitude), published in Regensburg in 1486, and Hans Schmuttermayer's "Fialenbüchlein" (Pinnacle booklet), published without title or date in Nürnberg in the 1480s. Honnecourt's sketchbook dealt mostly with geometric procedures, the two German books more specifically with the application of the geometric setting-out procedure known as *ad quadratum,* but it is impossible to say to what extent they reflected the mason's legendary craft "secret."

The first treatise on the Vitruvian model was *De re aedificatoria* (On the art of building) by Leon Battista Alberti (1404–1472), written in Latin and presented in manuscript form to Pope Nicholas V in 1452 and eventually published in Florence in 1486. It offered a coherent account of the principles of antique architecture, addressed in the main to patrons rather than to architects. Although Alberti clearly sought to emulate the Roman author in producing a treatise on architecture in ten books, it was perhaps Alberti's training in canon law that lay behind his decision to record "laws" for the art of building in explaining problems of ornament, form, and proportion.

Following Vitruvius's example, the simile of the architectural "body" frequently recurred in Renaissance literature and represented an important departure from Gothic practices in which the human body was not, as far as the evidence suggests, a principal model (although geometrical studies of the face are featured in Honnecourt's sketchbook). The body analogy plays an important part in Alberti's treatise, which famously redefined architectural beauty with reference to the "reasoned harmony of all the parts within a body, so that nothing may be added, taken away, or altered, but for the worse" (book 6, chapter 2).

Alberti's aims differed substantially from those of his Roman counterpart. For whereas Vitruvius sought to codify the practice of Hellenistic architects from the preceding four centuries, Alberti attempted to prescribe how the structures of the future should be built. Hence Alberti's reference to the past was largely literary, in that the famous ancient buildings he gives as examples were either ruined or buried; the few exceptions, such as the Roman Pantheon or the Tomb of Theodoric in Ravenna, resulted from a building industry unrelated to practice current in his time.

Filarete. The nobility of the art of architecture and its basis in the proportions of the human body, notions fundamental to Vitruvius and elaborated by Alberti, were subsequently defended in the illustrated manuscript *Trattato d'architettura* (On architecture) by Antonio Averlino (c. 1400–c. 1469), called Filarete (from the Greek *philaretos,* meaning "lover of virtue"), which was written in Italian in the early 1460s. Two autograph versions of the treatise survive in Italian, one written for Francesco Sforza, duke of Milan, the second (revised) with a new dedication to Piero de' Medici (written, according to Vasari, in 1464): of this second version, the Codex Magliabechiano (Florence, Biblioteca Nazionale, 2. 1. 140) contains the author's final revision of the text and is the most complete as regards the illustrations.

The text is composed as a dialogue between Filarete and a lord (or, on occasion, his son) and outlines the circumstances that lead this lord (a thinly disguised Sforza) to employ Filarete to build a new city, Sforzinda, to reflect the architect's anthropomorphic theory. Filarete's fortified city, with its central square, ducal palace, and cathedral, is the first thoroughly planned ideal city of the Renaissance, albeit reflecting the particular structure of Milan.

Unlike Alberti's text, with its abstract (unillustrated) consideration of Vitruvian concepts, Filarete sought to apply these principles, and that of decorum in particular, through a series of illustrations of building types designed to be expressive of the social order of fifteenth-century Italy. Here Vitruvius's characterization of the columns was developed to form a "language of use," in which particular orders were matched with particular modern building types with regard to dedication, function, or character and status of owner. Hence, according to Filarete, the Doric column was suited to the residence of a gentleman, the Corinthian to that of a merchant, and the Ionic to that of a craftsman.

Filarete covered topics ranging from the orders (book 8), decoration (books 9, 11, and 24 on mosaic; 12 and 16 on frescoes), and drawing (books 22–24), to contemporary architectural commissions of the Medici (book 25). Concerning churches, Filarete indicates the symbolic reasons for the cross plan, affirming that "the reason why churches are made in the shape of a cross is because with the coming of Christ, the shape became used out of reverence for Him, in that He was put on a cross" (book 7, 186).

Francesco di Giorgio. Following Filarete's example, the next set of illustrated manuscripts on architecture, written in Italian in the 1470s and 1490s by Francesco di Giorgio (1439–1501), included an illustration of a plan for a citadel laid out as a human body, thereby interpreting the anthropomorphic basis to *all'antica* architecture (building in the antique manner) more literally still. Di Giorgio interpreted Vitruvius's body-column analogy by drawing the body inside columns, and the face inside entablatures (to represent the idea of dentils as a row of toothlike blocks) and inside capitals (to show their proportion). The early manuscript treatises thus introduced Vitruvian architecture as the "embodiment" of civic harmony, necessarily modeled on the image of bodily harmony.

Of di Giorgio's *Trattati di architettura, ingegneria e arte militare* (Treatise on architecture, engineering, and military matters), two principal versions remain. The first version is represented by the parchment codices L (Florence, Biblioteca Mediceo-Laurenziana, Ashburnham 361) and T (Turin, Biblioteca Reale, Saluzziano 148), and the second version is preserved in the paper codices S (Siena, Biblioteca Comunale, s. 4.4) and M (Florence, Biblioteca Nazionale, Magliabechiano 2.1.141). The date of the first version should be placed after the long preparation period begun in Siena and continued in Urbino, in other words between the very end of the 1480s and the beginning of the 1490s. The second version is there-

fore to be dated between 1496 and di Giorgio's death.

In the first version of the *Trattati* as represented by L and T (but citing the fuller version in T) the subjects treated include fortresses and cities; hydraulic works and temples; theaters and columns; ancient and modern architecture and building practices; geometry and methods for measuring distances, heights, and depths; levers for wheels and mills; springs and how to raise and channel water; metals; water pipes, reservoirs, winches, and cranes; the military arts and war machines; convents; machines and various pieces of practical advice; bell towers and gardens; extracts from the "Book of Fires" by Marco Greco; and ancient monuments. In his discussion of these practically oriented topics, di Giorgio applied his wide experience as an architect. He gained direct experience of contemporary geometric fortress design during his years of service as architect to Federico da Montefeltro, one of the greatest condottieri (professional soldiers) of the period.

The second version of the *Trattati* is not a simple rewriting entrusted to humanist friends but a complete rethinking and critical reordering of the whole. While in S the treatise on fortresses is placed fourth in order, M has the following parts: preamble; necessary and common principles and norms; parts of houses, methods for finding water; castles and cities; temples; forms of mountain strongholds and fortresses; parts and forms of ports; machines for moving weights and drawing water, presses, and mills; and conclusion. This second version, with its seven parts, is thus more clearly organized than the first.

Serlio. Vitruvius's text was not clearly organized from a didactic point of view, and Alberti had ordered his Latin text around philosophical concepts rather than, say, the orders or distinct building types. In short none of the earlier writers, with their various philological, utopian, and anthropomorphic priorities, answered the practical needs of a practicing architect. This need was addressed by Sebastiano Serlio (1475–1554) through unprecedented design patterns, or *invenzioni,* that matched an easily understood Italian text with woodcuts. Serlio's pioneering conception of a clear program of instruction for the would-be architect, which he outlined in his first published book of 1537 (but entitled "book 4"), was to be realized through a series of separately published books designed to form a complete treatise.

Serlio's didactic *Tutte l'opere d'architettura et prospetiva* (Complete works on architecture and perspective; 1537–1575) commences with a fully illustrated instruction in the traditional craft, and painterly rules of geometry and perspective (books 1 and 2, respectively, published in one volume in Paris in 1545); moves on to a study of Roman building types (book 3, published in Venice in 1540) and the rules for the carving and use of the five orders, arranged sequentially from Tuscan to Composite (book 4, published in Venice in 1537); then descends through sacred and secular architectural projects (books 5 and 6, respectively, the former published in Paris in 1547 and the latter unpublished [Avery Library, New York, aa.520.se.619.f; Staatsbibliothek, Munich, Codex Icon. 189]) to conclude with practical problems that an architect might encounter, such as building on irregular or sloping sites (book 7, published posthumously in Frankfurt in 1575). Serlio's conception of a didactic program in seven books reflected contemporary rhetorical-mnemonic theory as outlined by the Neoplatonist Giulio Camillo (as well as di Giorgio's revised manuscript, reduced from ten to seven books), rather than Vitruvius's classical ten-book organization as revived by Alberti. In addition, Serlio published in 1551 an (unnumbered) book on gate designs, and prepared a manuscript on Roman fortification (Staatsbibliothek, Munich, Codex Icon. 190).

Serlio's books largely defined the categories of subsequent Vitruvian literature, not least the ever-popular idea of a separate book on the orders (as published by Hans Blum in 1550, Giacomo Barozzi da Vignola in 1562, and John Shute in 1563). Serlio's treatise offered the most complete development to date of the Vitruvian principle of decorum based on human types, according to which the Tuscan was matched to fortresses, the Doric to buildings for men of arms, Ionic to those for men of letters, and Corinthian to convents.

Palladio. Despite the spread of mannerist architecture in northern Europe after 1550, the *all'antica* style was destined to enjoy a continued vitality through the enormous popularity of Andrea Palladio's design models as illustrated in his *I quattro libri dell' architettura* (trans. *The Four Books on Architecture;* 1570). Palladio also produced illustrations for Daniele Barbaro's 1556 translation of Vitruvius, which itself breathed new life into Vitruvian debate by correcting the misinterpretations of the earlier editions of the Roman treatise published by Fra Giocondo (Venice, 1511) and Cesare Cesariano (Como, 1521). While Serlio had illustrated the application of the orders to such modern elements as house facades, fireplaces, and even church domes

(Donato Bramante's dome for Saint Peter's Basilica is illustrated in book 3), this spirit of Vitruvian invention reached its full expression in Palladio's woodcuts. Most notably, in the absence of any surviving antique houses other than in ruined form, Palladio illustrated a series of *all'antica* villas and palazzos that, unlike Serlio's and the French theorist Philibert de l'Orme's (1514–1570) northern European prototypes, were now independent of Gothic forms and fully adapted to suit modern needs of comfort and convenience.

Palladio's book 1 outlines the preparations necessary before building can commence, describes the orders, and gives an account of different room types and the main parts of a building. Book 2 deals with dwellings, starting with the Greek and Roman house, and moves on to illustrate how the author's own designs for palazzi and villas have been adapted from these precedents. Book 3 deals with public works (public spaces, roads, bridges, and basilicas). Book 4 covers ancient temples but includes a description of Bramante's early-sixteenth-century Tempietto at Montorio, Rome (after 1502), as an example of the best of modern architectural design.

Palladio, more than any other treatise writer, shifted the content of architectural books from the lengthy theoretical interpretations of Vitruvius initiated by Alberti toward the architect-oriented practical designs found in the later pattern books. Although the treatises of Serlio, Vignola, and Palladio could not replace Vitruvius's text, from which they had evolved, in the second half of the sixteenth century they now held equal rank alongside it. Moreover, Palladio's many woodcuts of his own domestic architecture underlined the growing bond between "paper palaces" and actual ones. The woodcuts illustrate the fact that the content of architectural treatises was increasingly determined not by philological concerns but by active areas of contemporary patronage, chief among which was domestic architecture.

At the outset of book 2 Palladio directly compared the proportions of the human body with the planning of private dwellings (but not with the layout of churches, which are not discussed in the treatise). Palladio's woodcut views inside the "body" of his buildings have been compared to Andreas Vesalius's early dissection drawings, published in 1543; Vesalius pictures the parts of the human body as the object of anatomical investigation, cut open, rather than based on a divine pattern established by external qualities of proportion and profile as illustrated by the "Vitruvian man." Indeed Palladio's drawing of the Vitruvian figure, published in the 1567 Daniele

Barbaro edition of Vitruvius, takes a step in this practical direction in illustrating the human figure as a study of measured relationships between parts; that is, the figure is no longer encompassed by the Vitruvian geometric outline so resonant of divine ideals to earlier commentators.

The effectiveness of the Vitruvian system lay in its ability to embody the Renaissance view of an animistic, interconnected natural world in which man was at the center and the ultimate pattern. Indeed, in seeking to explain this architecture, the early treatises naturally aspired toward a poetic or metaphoric imitation of nature rather than one of scientific exactitude. Absolute values of proportion and measure were always to be modified with respect to human optical perceptions: the tendency was to offer inspirational patterns rather than prescriptions. The architecture of Palladio and his pupil Vincenzo Scamozzi marks the fulfillment of this project to make *all'antica* architecture relevant, adapting it to suit modern needs so that, following the title of Scamozzi's treatise *L'idea della architettura universale* (The idea of universal architecture; 1615), it might become a truly universal design language. Indeed, their treatises were largely responsible for the exportation of what we now call Palladianism to the New World.

Beyond the Treatise. It follows, however, that the gradual replacement of the Renaissance view of nature by instrumental, mathematical concepts during the seventeenth century would be paralleled by, and would help stimulate, the substitution of an architecture regulated by antiquity with one of mannerist forms no longer dependent on models offered by either the human body or the past. In fact, the published treatises had themselves participated in this process, since the particular desire from the early sixteenth century onward to codify the Vitruvian column "types" assisted the rise of rational modes of thought that, ironically enough, rendered obsolete the body-centered analogies that had underpinned the very meaning of the antique orders. Serlio's variant woodcut designs had introduced the concept of the architect-as-selector, as opposed to an inspired designer of unique buildings in the tradition of Alberti, and initiated the process whereby the architectural treatise became replaced by the modern manual or pattern book.

See also **Alberti, Leon Battista; Filarete (Antonio Averlino); Francesco di Giorgio; Palladio, Andrea; Serlio, Sebastiano; Space and Perspective.**

BIBLIOGRAPHY

Primary Works

Alberti, Leon Battista. *On the Art of Building in Ten Books.* Translated by Joseph Rykwert, Neil Leach, and Robert Tavernor. Cambridge, Mass., 1988. Translation of *De re aedificatoria* (Florence, 1486).

De Honnecourt, Villard. *The Sketchbook of Villard de Honnecourt.* Edited by Theodore Bowie. Bloomington, Ind., 1959.

Di Giorgio Martini, Francesco. *Trattati di architettura, ingegneria e arte militare* (Treatise on architecture, engineering, and military matters). Edited by Corrado Maltese. 2 vols. Milan, 1967.

Filarete. *Trattato di architettura.* Edited by Anna Maria Finoli and Liliana Grassi. 2 vols. Milan, 1972. An unreliable English translation by John Spencer is *Treatise on Architecture.* London and New Haven, Conn., 1965.

Palladio, Andrea. *The Four Books on Architecture.* Translated by Robert Tavernor and Richard Schofield. Cambridge, Mass., and London, 1997. Translation of *I quattro libri dell' architettura* (1570).

Perrault, Claude. *Ordonnance for the Five Kinds of Columns after the Method of the Ancients.* Translated by Indra Kagis McEwen. Santa Monica, Calif., 1993. Translation of *Ordonnance des cinq espèces de colonnes selon la méthode des anciens* (1683).

Scamozzi, Vincenzo. *L'idea della architettura universale* (The idea of universal architecture). Venice, 1615. Reprint, 2 vols., Ringwood, N.J., 1964.

Serlio, Sebastiano. *Architettura civile. Libri sesto, settimo e ottavo nei manoscritti di Monaco e Vienna.* Transcription and notes of books 6–8 by Francesco Paolo Fiore and Tancredi Carunchio. Milan, 1994.

Serlio, Sebastiano. *Sebastiano Serlio on Architecture.* Vols. 1 and 2. Translated by Vaughan Hart and Peter Hicks. New Haven, Conn., 1996. Translation of books 1–5 and 6–8 of *Tutte l'opere d'architettura et prospetiva* (1537–1575).

Serlio, Sebastiano. *Sebastiano Serlio on Domestic Architecture.* Edited by Myra Nan Rosenfeld. New York, 1978. Facsimile of the Avery manuscript of Serlio's book 6; republished without Serlio's Italian text, New York, 1996.

Vitruvius. *On Architecture.* Translated by Frank Granger. London and Cambridge, Mass., 1931. Translation of the *De architectura.*

Vitruvius. *On Architecture.* Translation by Ingrid D. Rowland. New York, forthcoming.

Secondary Works

Choay, Françoise. *The Rule and the Model.* Edited by Denise Bratton. Cambridge, Mass., 1997.

The Fowler Architectural Collection of the Johns Hopkins University. Compiled by Lawrence Hall Fowler and Elizabeth Baer. Baltimore, 1961.

Guillaume, Jean, ed. *Les traités d'architecture de la Renaissance.* Paris, 1988. See especially John Bury, "Renaissance Architectural Treatises and Architectural Books: A Bibliography." Pages 485–503.

Hart, Vaughan, and Nicola Thwaite. *Paper Palaces: Architectural Works from the Collections of Cambridge University Library.* Cambridge, U.K., 1997.

Hart, Vaughan, and Peter Hicks, eds. *Paper Palaces: The Rise of the Renaissance Architectural Treatise.* New Haven, Conn., and London, 1998.

Kruft, Hanno-Walter. *A History of Architectural Theory from Vitruvius to the Present.* Translated by Ronald Taylor, Elsie Callander, and Antony Wood. New York and London, 1994.

Middleton, Robin, and Nicholas Savage, eds. *The Mark J. Millard Architectural Collection.* Vol. 2. *British Books.* Washington, D.C., 1998.

Onians, John. *Bearers of Meaning: The Classical Orders in Antiquity, the Middle Ages, and the Renaissance.* Princeton, N.J., 1988.

Payne, Alina. *The Architectural Treatise in the Italian Renaissance.* New York, 1999.

Rykwert, Joseph. *The Dancing Column: On Order in Architecture.* Cambridge, Mass., 1996.

Wiebenson, Dora, ed. *Architectural Theory and Practice from Alberti to Ledoux.* Chicago, 1982.

Wiebenson, Dora, and Claire Baines, eds. *The Mark J. Millard Architectural Collection.* Vol. 1. *French Books.* Washington, D.C., 1993.

VAUGHAN HART

ARETINO, PIETRO (1492–1556), Italian vernacular writer. Born in Arezzo, from whence he took his surname, Pietro Aretino was the son of a cobbler, Luca. By his late teens Aretino was in Perugia, publishing a volume of poetry and describing himself as a painter. This combination of interests, in literature

Pietro Aretino. Portrait by Titian, 1545. GALLERIA PALATINA, PALAZZO PITTI, FLORENCE/ALINARI/ART RESOURCE, NY

and in art, would prove to be his destiny. By 1517 he was living in Rome and had established himself in the household of Agostino Chigi, an influential banker and arts patron. Here he associated with prominent artists, including Raphael (Rafaello Sanzio), while launching himself as a court poet. Aretino first achieved notoriety for his *pasquinades* (a kind of satire) during the papal election of 1521; his fame intensified in 1524 when he wrote sonnets giving voice to a series of sixteen erotic engravings that Clement VII had banned. After he was wounded in a 1525 assassination attempt, Aretino left Rome for good. Following an interlude in Mantua at the Gonzaga court, he found his home in Venice.

Inspired by the republic's atmosphere of freedom and energized by its famous printing industry, Aretino thrived. He formed a close friendship with Titian, staunchly promoting his work; in turn Titian painted portraits of Aretino. Together with Jacopo Sansovino they constituted an artistic triumvirate. Rome had given Aretino basic training in the tactics of epideictic verse (verses for special occasions), praise, and blame. Writing for the popular press in Venice, he shifted from poetry to prose and identified himself increasingly as a satirist, with Petrarchism, Neoplatonism, Rome, courts, and sexual hypocrisy as favorite targets. Although he produced a remarkable variety of work, including sonnets, an epic, six plays, satiric prognostications, dialogues, biblical paraphrases, and hagiography, undoubtedly his greatest success came from his letters (six volumes, 1538–1557). The first vernacular writer to publish his correspondence, Aretino created an enormous vogue for books of letters. His letters were a medium of self-expression that anticipated Montaigne's essays, and their range is extraordinary; the volumes contain advice to princes; maledictions upon enemies; social correspondence to friends and patrons; literary and artistic criticism; and narratives of everyday life. "Follow nature" was Aretino's proclaimed aesthetic; he insisted that his writing was spontaneous and unstudied. In fact, his writing exemplifies Castiglione's principle of *sprezzatura,* the art of seeming artless. Aretino's parodies of literary conventions reveal a satirist's deftness in hitting targets that he pretends not to notice. In descriptive and narrative prose Aretino often attempted a written equivalent of an artist's style, most notably Titian's.

Above all, Aretino was a master of self-projection. The first modern celebrity, famous for being famous, he accurately boasted that his was a household name and that his face was reproduced everywhere. Aside from painted portraits and sculptures, he exploited the new resources of mechanical reproduction—including engravings, medals, and woodcut portraits in his books. He cultivated epithets and mottoes, the most celebrated being Ariosto's "the divine Pietro Aretino, scourge of princes" (*Orlando furioso,* canto 46). In most English-language criticism, Aretino's reputation as pornographer and blackmailer has detracted from his considerable accomplishments. "But," as Jakob Burckhardt, noted scholar of the Renaissance, said, "historical criticism will always find in Aretino an important study" (Middlemore trans., *The Civilization of the Renaissance in Italy*).

BIBLIOGRAPHY

Primary Works

Aretino, Pietro. *Aretino's Dialogues.* Translated by Raymond Rosenthal. New York, 1971. Translation of the *Ragionamenti* (1534 and 1536), dialogues about prostitution.

Aretino, Pietro. *Edizione nazionale delle opere di Pietro Aretino.* Edited by Giovanni Aquilecchia and Angelo Romano. Rome, 1992–. The definitive, complete scholarly edition; three volumes published to date.

Aretino, Pietro. *Lettere sull' arte di Pietro Aretino.* Edited by Fidenzio Pertile and Ettore Camesasca. 3 vols. Milan, 1957–1960. Invaluable source for Aretino's relations with artists.

Aretino, Pietro. *The Letters of Pietro Aretino.* Translated by Thomas Caldecot Chubb. Hamden, Conn., 1967. A selection from all six volumes.

Aretino, Pietro. *The Marescalco.* Translated by Leonard G. Sbrocchi and J. Douglas Campbell. Ottawa, Canada, 1986. Annotated translation of *Il Marescalco* (1533), Aretino's best-known comedy.

Aretino, Pietro. *I Modi. The Sixteen Pleasures: An Erotic Album of the Italian Renaissance.* Edited and translated by Lynne Lawner. Evanston, Ill., 1988. Includes translations of Aretino's *Sonetti lussuriosi.*

Secondary Works

Cairns, Christopher. *Pietro Aretino and the Republic of Venice: Researches on Aretino and His Circle in Venice, 1527–1556.* Florence, 1985.

Freedman, Luba. *Titian's Portraits through Aretino's Lens.* University Park, Pa., 1995.

Waddington, Raymond B. "A Satirist's Impresa: The Medals of Pietro Aretino." *Renaissance Quarterly* 42 (1989): 655–681.

RAYMOND B. WADDINGTON

ARIOSTO, LUDOVICO (1474–1533), Italian poet. Born in Reggio Emilia, Ariosto grew up in neighboring Ferrar, where his father, Count Niccolò Ariosto, was a captain in the service of the ruling Este family. His mother, Daria, was the daughter of a scholar and poet, Gabriele Malaguzzi.

Education and Career. Young Ludovico was probably given lessons in grammar and rhetoric by Luca Ripa, a humanist who attended the famous local school run by the descendants of Guarino da Verona. This private instruction prepared him well for the study of Latin literature and philosophy at the University of Ferrara. But his father, envisioning for him a career as a civil servant, forced him to study law, which he did with great reluctance.

Gregorio da Spoelto, a private humanities teacher with whom Ariosto studied from 1492 to 1497, is most responsible for transforming the young man into one of the great vernacular humanists of the Renaissance. In 1495, at the age of twenty-one, Ariosto delivered the inaugural oration for the academic year at the university, choosing as his theme the praise of philosophy ("De laudibus philosophiae"). His earliest surviving letter (1498) documents his desire to participate in the humanistic culture fostered by his teachers: he places an order with the Venetian publisher Aldo Manuzio for books of Platonic and Neoplatonic philosophy.

Ariosto's studies were cut short by the death of his father in 1500, which obliged him to assume the responsibility of head of his extended family. Unaccustomed duties such as amassing dowries for his sisters created financial burdens that Ariosto and his younger siblings had to deal with for many years. To earn a living he began to serve Cardinal Ippolito d'Este in various capacities, mainly diplomatic and administrative. Frequently sent on diplomatic missions to governments in north and central Italy during the first two decades of the 1500s, he would later refer to having been "oppressed by the yoke of the Este Cardinal."

After a break with Ippolito for refusing to follow him to Hungary in 1517, Ariosto was welcomed as a courtier by the cardinal's older brother, Alfonso I, who had assumed the leadership of Ferrara at the death of Ercole I in 1505. As he had done with Ippolito, Ariosto maintained a degree of independence from Duke Alfonso, though he always seemed to be on friendly terms with their sister, Isabella d'Este, who had become the marchioness of Mantua through her marriage to Francesco Gonzaga. He kept Isabella apprised of the progress of his big work, *Orlando furioso* (Mad Roland), even reading excerpts to her. He published the poem in 1516, then revised it in 1521, to bring it into line with the linguistic strictures of Pietro Bembo. Shortly thereafter Alfonso appointed him the local Estense official in the mountainous province of the Garfagnana on the borders between Tuscany and Romagna, a post he held until 1525. Despite his dissatisfaction with the position, made difficult by the complicated political relations between Ferrera and Florence, Ariosto was an effective commissioner. Upon returning from the

Garfagnana, he supervised the construction and operation of the ducal theater, which enabled him to collaborate with Dosso Dossi and other painters who designed sets for several of his plays.

He dedicated his final years to literary projects in the company of Alessandra Benucci (whom he wed secretly in 1528 so as not to lose his ecclesiastical benefices). Together they enjoyed Ariosto's new house built on one of the straight streets of the "Herculean Addition," the masterpiece of urban planning that doubled the size of medieval Ferrara to create what Jakob Burckhardt referred to as Europe's first modern city. The aging poet had inscribed over the door of his home an elegant Latin couplet: "It may be small but it suits me; it's not offensive or ugly; and I paid for it with my own money." The third and definitive edition of the *Furioso* came out in 1532 with four new episodes that increased the poem's length from forty to forty-six cantos. Ariosto died the following year in Ferrara.

Humanism in Ferrara. Ariosto's work is marked by his responses, positive and negative, to humanism. Therefore we need to consider Guarino's school, the institution most responsible for promoting the reassessment of the past in early modern Ferrar, before we look at Ariosto's specific writings. In 1429 Niccolò III of Este invited Guarino da Verona (1374–1460) to establish a school in Ferrar for the young prince, Leonello. Guarino's school rapidly gained prestige throughout Europe as one of the best places to study ancient Latin and Greek literature. Guarino personally directed the school until his death in 1460, when his son Battista (followed in turn by his son Alessandro) assumed its direction. The ideology espoused publicly by the school—that the learned citizen is a better citizen—became a commonplace in Renaissance discourse.

Guarino's school and its Estense patrons attracted numerous humanists to Ferrara from abroad. Writers like Ariosto who did not attend the school benefited from its presence in Ferrara nevertheless. Growing up in Ferrara during these decades, one could see, read, and hear works inspired by humanism's reassessment of the classical past. Readers in Ferrara were able to use the manuscripts and printed editions that were lodged in the school and the ducal library (or copies of those books in circulation). Guarino's legacy guaranteed Ariosto the linguistic and material means to read Latin texts in the original and Greek works in Latin translation.

The Limits of a Humanistic Education. Ariosto does not comment on his upbringing or edu-

cation in his correspondence, nor are there any descriptive contemporary reports on the early years of his life. For our information, we must rely on excerpts from his autobiographical *Satires* and on what we can gather from biographies written later in the sixteenth century. In the sixth satire, composed for Pietro Bembo sometime between 1524 and 1525, Ariosto refers directly to his engagement with classical literary culture. The occasion for the poem is the author's request that his friend help him locate a tutor of Greek for Virginio, his son, who was around fifteen at the time. Although Virginio was an illegitimate child, the father was very solicitous of his well-being. Ariosto explains that he has taught the boy something of the Latin tradition:

> Through me he's already learned what Virgil's text is like, and how Terence, Ovid and Horace write theirs, and he has seen Plautus staged. (6.142–44)

But he confesses that he does not know Greek well enough to teach it to his son because his priorities have always been with the language of Rome:

> I don't believe that knowing the language of the Achaeans will bring me honor, unless I first understand the way my Latins speak. (6.178–80)

The author then recounts in some detail the autobiographical circumstances that fostered, then eventually hindered, his education. The remembrance of things past yields to what seems at first glance a conventional humanistic encomium of classical culture, concluding with a plea that Bembo help the boy scale the top of Mount Parnassus. But the satire, in keeping with its generic conventions, allows the author a certain liberty of expression, which he uses to register an implicit critique of humanism. The autograph copy shows that he rewrote the verse to highlight the noun "umanista," but any positive value associated with this relatively new word in the Italian language is undermined by its context: "Few humanists are without that vice that forced God (it didn't take much persuading) to render Gomorrah and her neighbors woeful!" (6.25–27). By impugning humanists as potential sodomites, Ariosto suggests that the typical humanistic education is deficient and sterile. This criticism is borne out in the person of Ruggiero in the *Furioso,* the character who appears impervious to didactic instruction in much of the first part of the poem, notwithstanding the fact that he is destined to be the founder of the Ferrarese house of Este and progenitor of Ariosto's (sometime) patrons.

By the mid-1520s, when Ariosto sounded these ambiguous notes about humanistic learning in the sixth satire, he had moved beyond his youthful enthusiasm for classical knowledge for its own sake. Several years later he carried the criticism of humanism further in his *Erbolato,* a prose parody of the work of Giovanni Pico della Mirandola and other Neoplatonists. The *Erbolato* is composed in the form of a speech delivered by Master Antonio Faventino. Faventino, an amalgam of several identifiable contemporaries of Ariosto, is portrayed hawking a miraculous medicinal potion in the town square. In the venerable tradition of the charlatan or quack doctor, he claims that his herbal medicine—the "erbolato" that gives the work its title—is a universal remedy for any illness. His pseudophilosophical description of the importance of medicine for humankind, in part based on the proem to book 7 of Pliny's *Natural History,* eventually becomes a theatrical sales pitch for his elixir, recalling one of Ariosto's dramatic works, *Il negromante* (The necromancer; 1520). As the rhetoric modulates from a pastiche of Pliny and Neoplatonic oratory to the verbal playfulness of street theater, we witness Ariosto's searing criticism of the academy and its relation to the marketplace. That vague sociological construct, the marketplace of ideas, gives way to the actual market stall from which Faventino tries to sell his brainchild. This short work provides a good example of how Ariosto employed the classics in an ironic critique of his own contemporary culture. Despite his Horatian disdain for all the hoopla of courtly life, Ariosto was very aware of his surroundings, and he disapproved of much of what he saw.

Lyric Poetry. Ariosto wrote lyric verse in Italian and Latin. Although there is no indication that Ariosto intended his Latin poems to be published as a volume, Giovanbattista Pigna assembled them into a collection that he brought to light in 1553. The poems reveal a keen awareness of the Latin lyric tradition with imitations of Horace, Catullus, Tibullus, and Ovid, and even some knowledge of poets from the Greek Anthology, whom Ariosto knew in Latin translation. His polished latinity won him praise from the sternest critic, Pietro Bembo. The most interesting aspect of the collected Latin lyrics is arguably the collocation of subsequent versions of a given poem. We can observe the author's attempt at perfecting the latinity of "Ad Philiroë" (poem 2) and numerous epitaphs (14, 61), including his own (58). He experiments with classical meters, diction, and style, aspects of which reappear in his Italian *Rime* and in his narrative poetry. Published posthumously in

Ludovico Ariosto. Portrait by Palma Vecchio. Painted 1520–1525. © NATIONAL GALLERY, LONDON

1546, his Italian lyric poems, for their part, bear the imprint of the day's reigning fad, Petrarchism.

Theater. The revival of Terence and Plautus in northern Italy in the late fifteenth century is the most important influence on Ariosto's drama. The restoration of Latin comedy in Ferrara began in the 1470s and 1480s under the impetus of Ercole I, who was an avid reader of classics in translation. Ercole sponsored events that frequently included recreations of Roman comedies, and Ariosto himself may have performed in Plautus's *Menaechmi* at the wedding festivities of Ludovico Sforza and Beatrice d'Este, another of Ercole's children, in 1491. At the end of the first decade of the sixteenth century, while still employed by Ippolito, Ariosto produced two plays, *La cassaria* (The coffer comedy) and *I suppositi* (The pretenders). These works were in the vein of the new humanistic *commedia erudita,* that is, comedy based on Roman models but adapted to contemporary Italian life. He revived these plays in the late 1520s, when he brought out what most critics consider his best theatrical work, *La Lena* (Lena).

99

At the beginning of *I suppositi,* Ariosto accounts for some of his artistic choices in an explanatory prologue, noting that he treats his Latin models, Plautus and Terence, as the Roman authors treated their Greek models:

> In this play, among other things, the servant is substituted for the master and the master for the servant. The author confesses that in this he has followed both Plautus and Terence. . . . He has done so because he wants to imitate the celebrated classical poets as much as possible, not only in the form of their plays, but also in the content. And just as they in their Latin plays followed Menander, Apollodorus, and other Greek writers so he, too, in his vernacular plays is not averse to imitating the method and procedure of the Latin writers.

Ariosto's remarks recall a passage from the opening of Terence's *Andria,* familiar to readers and audiences of his day, in which the Roman playwright explains that he has combined two comedies of Menander into his own. Terence's image for this combination of sources is *contaminatio,* the mixing of multiple models through imitation. Ariosto, for his part, does his Roman model one better by combining two plays of two different authors. But he assures the audience at the end of the prologue that his Roman models "would not be offended and would call it poetic imitation rather than plagiarism." This bold mixing of sources is characteristic of Ariosto's artistry in general and it is most noticeable in his major work, *Orlando furioso.*

Orlando Furioso.

Ariosto's fame deservedly rests on his narrative poem in octave stanzas, *Orlando furioso* (Mad Roland; 1516, 1521, 1532). In the poem he uses Charlemagne's war against the Saracens as a backdrop to explore typical Renaissance themes such as love, madness, and fidelity, with an elaborate subplot that dramatizes how these themes affect the dynastic fortunes of the house of Este. The fiction is that the poet as minstrel or *cantastorie* recites the poem before his patron, Ippolito, a guise maintained after Ippolito dismissed Ariosto in 1517 and even after his former patron died in 1520. The minstrel's voice lends the narrative the air of a medieval romance, while the backdrop of war provides the poem with an epic setting.

The poet registers the *Furioso*'s epic pretensions by paraphrasing the beginning and ending verses of the *Aeneid* at his poem's start and finish—but the reader who expects to find the poem full of the stuff of epic will be disappointed. The poem's titular hero, Orlando, who carries much of its epic burden, goes mad at the narrative's middle and therefore cannot

Ariosto's *Orlando furioso.* Title page of the edition by Francesco Rosso, Ferrara, 1532. This is considered the definitive edition of the poem published in the author's lifetime.

move inexorably toward the completion of his appointed task in the manner of an epic hero. The protagonist's course is characteristic of chivalric romance, for he wanders off his literal track, eventually falling into madness. The narrative characteristics of chivalric romance defy the straightforward teleology of epic: deviation, diversion, and digression are typical of its design. And there is at least one notable romance precedent for Orlando's madness: Chrétien de Troyes's Yvain also deviates from the typical behavior of a proper knight. Orlando, however, exists in a netherworld somewhere between the two generic possibilities offered by epic and romance. He sets out on a quest for Angelica like a good knight of medieval romance (9.7.6), zigzagging inevitably along the way. But despite occasional deviations like the episode of Olimpia (9–11) or Atlante's castle (12), his application to the quest has an epic seriousness about it. The narrator draws our attention to the heroic expansiveness of Orlando's search with an unusual classical allusion that likens his quest for Angelica to Demeter's for Persephone (12.1–4). And just before he comes upon the site of Angelica's betrayal (as he sees it), a simile of Homeric inspiration describes Orlando in heroic terms (23.83). When Orlando finds himself in the pastoral romance setting at the end of canto 23, whereas the romance knight in him should defer the quest and indulge momentarily in this place of pleasure, the epic misfit goes berserk.

Ariosto's treatment of Orlando as a creature who moves between two genres, two traditions, two kinds of narrative, depends on his immediate predecessor at the Estense court, Matteo Maria Boiardo (1441–1494). Orlando, a traditional figure in medieval Franco-Italian literature, is associated with the *chanson de geste,* the heroic war poetry of medieval France. In that literary tradition he fights and dies nobly as befits Charlemagne's most heroic knight. For later Italian writers, however, Boiardo's treatment of Orlando is the prism through which prior literary representations of his heroism are refracted. And Boiardo blends the Carolingian stories of war with Arthurian legends full of love and magic to create a paradoxical Orlando who falls madly in love, as caught in his poem's title, *Orlando innamorato* (Roland in love; 1483, 1495). In such condition he is hardly the stuff of literary heroism. Add to this mix the resurgent classical humanism that was coming into its own in Ferrara and one can see that Ariosto had his hands full (not to say tied) when he began to sketch his own picture of Orlando. His version recalls the figure of medieval legend and bears some resemblance to Boiardo's courtly lover, but at the same time there is much to suggest that his Orlando is a creature of the new classicism. Perhaps, as has been suggested, Ariosto's Orlando plays the part of a "burly male Dido," Aeneas's abandoned love, if not exactly that of a new Aeneas. In other words, the reception of the classical tradition is affected by the other traditions that Ariosto's chronological position requires him to hold in the balance. The intervention of medieval romance turns Ariosto's would-be Aeneas into an imitation of Dido in a compromise of the Virgilian epic model. In other episodes of the poem similar confrontations occur between romance and epic, often brought about through the imitation of somewhat more marginal classical models like Lucan and Lucian. This dynamic is also shaped by the way that counterclassical epic narratives from antiquity, especially Ovid's *Metamorphoses,* which bears some resemblance to medieval romance, complicate Ariosto's reception of the Virgilian narrative ideal.

Under the influence of Benedetto Croce, many critics, from approximately the 1920s until the 1980s, read the *Furioso* as an ahistorical and timeless text of cosmic harmony, a perfect example of Renaissance classicism. But critics now make the case for a different interpretation of the poem, drawing attention to its narrative structure, its threatened thematic coherency, its linguistic polish and lack thereof. Moreover, Ariosto's engagement with current events doesn't support the romanticized image of the aloof poet. His poem contains numerous passages, often in the proems to cantos, where he expresses, among many other views, his concern about political and military alliances of the day; his fascination with the increasing knowledge about geography; his abhorrence for the application of new technology to war machines; and his position on the place of women in Renaissance society. The *Furioso* is a fantastic poem very much rooted in the real world. This is also true of a substantial fragment in octave stanzas, which Ariosto perhaps meant to add to the *Furioso, Cinque canti* (Five cantos), begun in 1519 or so and worked on sporadically during the 1520s.

Influence of *Orlando Furioso*. Ariosto's *Furioso* had become wildly successful by the time he died in 1533. Print records document that the poem was a best-seller, its popularity lasting well into the next century. The third edition of the *Furioso,* published under Ariosto's watchful eye over the summer of 1532, came out in an unusually large run of some three thousand copies. By 1600 well over one hundred editions had been published. Often produced to look like classical texts with commentaries and other accompanying paratexts (e.g., the life of the poet, lists of classical allusions, historical notes), these editions helped the poem become an important touchstone in debates over narrative poetry, with readers arguing that *Orlando furioso* was equal or even superior to classical epics. This process of the poem's canonization as an authoritative text would eventually earn it the status of a new kind of classical work, a vernacular classic that granted Italian instant linguistic nobility.

The debate between neo-Aristotelians and everyone else over the *Furioso*'s status as a classicizing poem focused on the degree to which it abided by rules governing the epic genre, which were deduced from Aristotle's *Poetics* and Horace's *Ars poetica.* One strategy to make the poem legitimate was to claim that it resembled a canonical epic of antiquity, a position that could lead a critic like Giovanbattista Pigna to interpret Ariosto's poem (not to mention his life) as Virgilian. Another tactic directly in response to Aristotelian criticism of the *Furioso* was to turn the argument around and claim that the poem was a new kind of long narrative, not an epic but a romance, a theory propounded most vigorously by Giovanni Battista Giraldi Cinzio in the middle of the sixteenth century. Proponents of this argument pointed to classical models of romancelike narratives such as Ovid's *Metamorphoses* as precedents for the *Furioso*'s interlaced narrative. This line of argument could lead no less a critic than Lionardo Salviati, the guiding force behind the foundation of the Accademia della Crusca, to revise his interpretations of the classical poems themselves in the 1580s. In a curious role of reversed influence, interpretations and translations of certain classical poems began to be influenced by the *Furioso*.

The *Furioso* was a source of inspiration for European illustrators and painters from the sixteenth to the nineteenth centuries, including Annibale Carracci, Guido Reni, Peter Paul Rubens, Nicolas Poussin, and Giovanni Battista Tiepolo. This may be in part because the poem itself highlights Ariosto's interest in art: it contains many ecphrases (descriptions of works of art; e.g., in cantos 3, 33, 42, 46), and it includes a detailed description of a woman (7.11–15) that became a prominent example in subsequent theoretical discussions of descriptive poetry (Ludovico Dolce's *Dialogo della pittura* [Dialogue on painting; 1557] and Gotthold Ephraim Lessing's *Laokoon* [1766]); the poem praises nine contemporary artists at 33.2; and, according to some readings, the poem exhibits a classical harmony like that which dominated art in Italy during Ariosto's lifetime. The definitive third edition of the poem is decorated with a woodcut portrait of Ariosto supposedly based on a drawing by Titian. The illustrations in the editions of Gabriel Giolito (Venice, 1542) and Francesco dei Franceschi (Venice, 1584) are especially handsome. In the 1780s Jean-Honoré Fragonard prepared over 150 drawings for a volume that was never published. A noteworthy later edition contains over five hundred drawings by Gustave Doré (Paris, 1879). Anonymous artisans have used the poem for decorating everything from ceramics and weavings of the late Renaissance to the carts and marionettes of nineteenth- and twentieth-century Sicilian folk art.

The *Furioso* was also a source of material for musicians, playwrights, nondramatic authors, and at least one landscape designer, from the sixteenth to the eighteenth centuries. As early as 1517, Bartolomeo Tromboncino set to music Orlando's lament from the scene at the center of the poem where the protagonist goes mad (23.126). Subsequent composers, including Claudio Monteverdi (1567–1643), adapted the poem's more popular passages, its idyllic scene and lovers' laments, for madrigal settings. Many European authors rewrote, alluded to, or parodied *Furioso*, elaborating on the poem's character and multiple plots, perhaps challenged by the poet himself, who invites later and "better" writers to resume the story of Angelica and Medoro (30.16). Lope de Vega, for example, accepts the challenge with *La hermosura de Angélica* (The beauty of Angelica; 1602). Notable operatic works that take their inspiration from the *Furioso* include Vivaldi's *Orlando furioso* (1727) and Handel's *Orlando* (1733) and *Alcina* (1735). The garden at the Villa Orsini in Bomarzo, near Viterbo, may have been designed to recreate in three dimensions the experience of reading the *Furioso*'s narrative.

BIBLIOGRAPHY

Primary Works

Ariosto, Ludovico. *Cinque Canto. Five Cantos.* Translated by Alexander Sheers and David Quint. Berkeley, Calif., 1996.

Ariosto, Ludovico. *The Comedies of Ariosto.* Translated and edited by Edmond M. Beame and Leonard G. Sbrocchi. Chicago, 1975.

Ariosto, Ludovico. *Lirica.* Edited by Giuseppe Fatini. Bari, Italy, 1924.

Ariosto, Ludovico. *Orlando Furioso.* 2 vols. Edited by Emilio Bigi. Milan, 1982.

Ariosto, Ludovico. *Orlando Furioso.* Translated by Guido Waldman. New York, 1974.

Ariosto, Ludovico. *The Satires of Ludovico Ariosto.* Translated by Peter DeSa Wiggins. Athens, Ohio, 1976.

Ariosto, Ludovico. *Satire.* Edited by Cesare Segre. *Erbolato* (The charlatan). Edited by Gabriella Ronchi. *Lettere.* Edited by Angelo Stella. Milan, 1984.

Secondary Works

Ascoli, Albert Russell. *Ariosto's Bitter Harmony.* Princeton, N.J., 1987.

Carducci, Giosuè. *La gioventù di Ludovico Ariosto e la poesia latina in Ferrara.* In *Opere*, vol. 13. Bologna, Italy, 1939. Pages 115–374.

Catalano, Michele. *Vita di Lodovico Ariosto.* 2 vols. Florence, 1930–1931.

Clubb, Louise George. *Italian Drama in Shakespeare's Time.* New Haven, Conn., 1989.

Fahy, Conor. *L'Orlando Furioso del 1532: Profilo di una edizione.* Milan, 1989.

Gardner, Edmund G. *The King of Court Poets: A Study of the Work, Life, and Times of Lodovico Ariosto.* 1906. Reprint, New York, 1968.

Gnudi, Cesare. "L'Ariosto e le arti figurative." *Congresso Internazionale Ludovico Ariosto.* 1975. Pages 331–401.

Javitch, Daniel. *Proclaiming a Classic: The Canonization of* Orlando Furioso. Princeton, N.J., 1991.

Looney, Dennis. *Compromising the Classics: Romance Epic Narrative in the Italian Renaissance.* Detroit, 1996.

Marinelli, Peter V. *Ariosto and Boiardo: The Origins of* Orlando Furioso. Columbia, Mo., 1987.

Mori, Barbara. "Le vite ariostesche del Fornari, Pigna e Garofalo." *Schifanoia* 17/18 (1997): 135–78.

Parker, Patricia A. *Inescapable Romance: Studies in the Poetics of a Mode.* Princeton, N.J., 1979.

Quint, David. *Epic and Empire: Politics and Generic Form from Virgil to Milton.* Princeton, N.J., 1993.

Sabbadini, Remigio. *Guariniana.* Edited by Mario Sancipriano. Turin, Italy, 1964.

Sapegno, Natalino. "Ludovico Ariosto." In *Dizionario biografico degli Italiani.* Vol. 4. Rome, 1960–. Pages 172–188.

Weil, Marc. "Il Sacro Bosco di Bomarzo." *Journal of Garden History* 4 (1984): 1–94.

Wiggins, Peter DeSa. *Figures in Ariosto's Tapestry: Character and Design in the* Orlando Furioso. Baltimore, 1986.

DENNIS LOONEY

ARISTOCRACY. Renaissance men and women had a complicated set of traditions and preconceptions for understanding the concept of aristocracy, some of them mutually reinforcing, some of them contradictory.

Background. Greek philosophy stressed the term's political dimensions: the word denoted a polity in which the best men ruled, and eventually extended to cover the group capable of holding ruling positions. In the nature of things, these were likely to be the rich, for acquiring the ability to govern typically presupposed wealth, but the overlap was not complete; the poor and their children (mainly their sons) could also figure among "the best." However, both the ancient world and the barbarian kingdoms that succeeded it made use of a second set of ideas, attaching the idea of aristocracy to birth. Greatness, this set of ideas taught, had biological foundations; the great descended from great ancestors, who in some instances included divinities, and benefited from the qualities they inherited. A third notion had developed in the eleventh and twelfth centuries and pointed to a different set of functions. On this view, the nobleman was a man who fought, contributing to society alongside those who prayed, the clergy, and those who worked, the commoners who would come to be known as the Third Estate.

These diverse traditions agreed in presenting social inequalities as natural and constructive, part of what made for a good society; they agreed also in their focus on what were seen as male social roles, governing and fighting. But in other ways they pointed to very different ideas of social life. Both the political and the military vision of aristocracy, for instance, accorded a significant place to social mobility. It made sense within these traditions that able individuals might rise to high positions, whereas the biological vision had little room for such advancement. On the other hand, the biological and the military visions allowed a substantial place to poorer men, described usually not as aristocrats but as nobles, esquires, or gentlemen. These traditions implied that there was no essential difference between a great leader and his warrior comrades, who shared his social functions and like him claimed to descend from honorable families.

Renaissance Definitions of Aristocracy. All three traditions remained powerful between the fifteenth and the seventeenth centuries, despite their contradictory implications. Europeans admired those who combined these ideals, serving as warriors and governors and representing ancient families. Such men were rare, however, and as a result a basic instability marked ideas about aristocracy. The concept could be used in diverse ways, depending on the social or political concerns of the moment, and its contradictions left significant openings for social critics. Criticism of the aristocracy was already heard in the fourteenth century, and it reemerged with every social and political crisis thereafter. Partly in response, changes in the relative importance of the traditions surrounding aristocracy form an important theme of Renaissance cultural and social history. The ideal of the governor tended to rise in importance, while the biological underpinnings of aristocracy came to seem somewhat less important and violence somewhat less glorious.

Renaissance humanism played a significant role in this process. Desiderius Erasmus and Thomas More repeatedly made fun of the ignorant nobleman, who had nothing to recommend him but his habits of violence, and their followers encouraged all would-be social leaders to educate themselves if they hoped to play a distinguished social role. Aristocrats across Europe responded to the humanists' educational message. Some medieval aristocrats had been literate, and some had even attended universities. In the sixteenth century, though, good educations became the norm. Aristocrats attended universities in large numbers, with the clear understanding that staying away would exclude them from many high governmental positions. The development of salons and learned societies in the early seventeenth century represented further steps in this process. This shift in values favored the position of women within the aristocracy by diminishing the importance of violence and placing new emphasis on areas in which women could interact as relative equals with men. Though they could not attend universities or participate easily in the Latin-based culture dispensed there, they could involve themselves deeply in vernacular culture, in some cases writing their own works, more often reading and discussing those of others.

Regional Variations. Experience of aristocracy and nobility varied enormously across Europe. An important contrast distinguished Europe's borderlands from its central core. In Poland and Hungary, in the east, mainly German wars of conquest and colonization against Slavic inhabitants created numerous places for a warrior nobility; as a result, nobles counted for about 10 percent of the population in these regions. The vast majority of these were poor, but the unsettled military situation also allowed great families to accumulate enormous estates. A comparable situation prevailed in late medieval Spain, another frontier region, whose history was dominated by the expansion of Christian against Muslim states. There too, military conditions favored the nobility's expansion, while glorifying the warrior's role by emphasizing its religious dimensions. As a result, Spain was another region where nobles counted for roughly one-tenth of the total population, and Spanish society expressed particular admiration for the figure of the warrior nobleman. In contrast, the longer-settled core regions of Europe had relatively few nobles and great estates. In France, central Germany, and Bohemia, nobles probably numbered about 2 percent of population in 1500 and perhaps closer to 1 percent in 1650. Nor were great estates so large in these regions as in the frontier east.

A second contrast separated the Mediterranean world, and especially northern Italy, from the north. In Italy, aristocrats had long had close connections with urban life. The development of the Italian city-states in some instances led to the aristocrats' forced urbanization: urban governments wanted the aristocrats in their regions to live in the cities, where they could be kept under control and their tendencies to violence diminished, or at least channeled to the city-states' benefit. Florence employed a different strategy, initially banning aristocratic families from the city altogether. The wealth of the Italian cities also affected views of aristocracy. Italy could not take seriously the idea that military valor represented the highest form of social life, when bankers and

merchants so clearly outstripped the warrior aristocracy in wealth, power, and cultural sophistication. With these examples before them, many Italian aristocrats eagerly involved themselves in trade. In northern Europe, few aristocrats spent much time in the cities or had much sympathy for urban values. In the fifteenth and early sixteenth centuries, a few great French aristocrats had houses in Paris, but they were more comfortable on their estates in the countryside. The idea of aristocratic involvement in commerce seemed alien, at odds with the very purposes for which aristocracy existed.

Elements of this diversity persisted throughout the Renaissance, but diversity tended to diminish sharply after about 1500, as a by-product of fundamental political and social changes. Aristocrats had always traveled throughout Europe, but the frequency of encounter rose considerably in the later Renaissance. In 1494 the French invasion of Italy opened a long period in which aristocratic warriors from the north encountered Italian urban culture. The eventual Spanish victory in the struggle to control most of Italy meant that aristocratic values acquired new prominence there; the Spaniards' success even inspired enthusiasm for their fashions in France itself. Italy's glamour as a center of art and literary culture brought many more pacific travelers as well. Changes in Italian society also made it more receptive to northern values. In the fifteenth century, Italian urban elites began buying land and building country houses, to some extent as protection against troubled economic times, to some extent because they found aristocratic values more appealing. With a considerable lag, northerners were also coming to find city life more attractive. By about 1600, leading aristocrats in both England and France expected to spend considerable time in the city, and a wave of elegant new urban neighborhoods were being built to meet their needs.

The fourteenth and fifteenth centuries were a time of severe troubles for nearly all the European aristocracies. The French suffered a series of humiliating and bloody losses in the Hundred Years' War with England (1337–1453). This was also a time of recurrent civil war, usually involving conflicts among the greatest aristocratic families. The Wars of the Roses in England (1455–1485) were matched by comparable dynastic struggles in France and Castile. Justifiably nervous about conspiracies against them, kings tended to act quickly against families whose loyalty they doubted, leading to more deaths and the complete disappearance of some great families. Nearly half of English dukes in the fourteenth and fifteenth centuries died violent deaths. These were also years of lower-class discontent about aristocratic privilege and power. France and England experienced major rural rebellions in the fourteenth century, Catalonia in 1484–1485. The French chronicler Jean Froissart (c. 1337–after 1404) believed that the French peasants rose against their lords because of their military failures. The peasants no longer believed that aristocrats performed useful social functions. In the late fifteenth century a series of rural revolts began in western Germany, again specifically questioning the aristocracy's suitability to dominate society. The wave of discontent culminated in the great Peasants' War of 1525, which involved hundreds of thousands of villagers and included extended published criticisms of aristocratic misbehavior. Social criticism of this sort was especially serious because these were also years of aristocratic economic troubles. The Black Death of 1348 reduced population throughout Europe; war and disease brought further declines over the next 150 years. These disasters meant economic trouble for almost all aristocracies because their wealth rested heavily on landownership. Agricultural prices dropped, labor became more expensive, and tenant farmers could be attracted only with advantageous conditions. Aristocratic incomes diminished substantially—one reason, it has been suggested, that so many aristocrats engaged in political conspiracies.

Economic Changes. After 1500, though, some of these trends began to reverse. Population again grew and the losses of the previous two centuries were soon made good. For landowners, this meant higher prices for what they produced and lower production costs, since an abundance of laborers now competed for jobs. The exploitation of the New World added further buoyancy to the European economy, and even political change contributed: though violence remained common throughout western Europe in the sixteenth century, it was far less frequent and less destructive than in the fourteenth and fifteenth centuries. Controlling large stretches of land and forest, the aristocracies were well positioned to benefit from these economic changes, but only if they revised some of their ways of doing business. In the late Middle Ages, aristocrats continued to depend heavily on seigniorial forms of income: typically, that is, on rents that were permanently fixed and on the exercise of public powers of justice and police. This complex of rights and powers was seriously damaged by the tumults of the late Middle Ages and the sixteenth century, though in

most places its structures remained in place (and continued to supply some share of aristocrats' incomes) until the French Revolution of 1789. Inflation reduced the value of customary rents, which had been set to the conditions of previous centuries, and villagers were less willing to follow the rules of lordship after the rebellions of the fourteenth and fifteenth centuries. Lords who hoped to prosper from the economic buoyancy of the sixteenth century had to take direct control of lands and forests, so that they would draw the benefits of rising prices and wider markets. This process, which the French historian Marc Bloch called "the reconstitution of the domain," took place throughout Europe. Through both purchases and political manipulations, by the early seventeenth century aristocrats took direct control of the land.

How they administered this land varied considerably from place to place and determined some of the important qualities of aristocrats' place within their societies. A few lesser nobles might manage their farms directly, but in most countries this procedure clashed with ideas about the nobles' functions; they were to concern themselves with public life and war, and this was especially true of the leading aristocrats. In northwestern Europe, the favored solution was tenant farming. Aristocrats rented their land for long terms to substantial farmers, who paid cash rents and took full responsibility for the properties. Especially in England, where leases might run for thirty years or more, farmers had a considerable interest in improving the land. In Italy and southern France, forms of sharecropping prevailed, in which the landowner supplied most of the capital needed for running the farm and took at least half the year's harvest. Such arrangements gave landowners far more power than they enjoyed in the north, since they controlled most of the means of production; the sharecroppers tended to be poor, insecure, and subservient to landowners' interests. Eastern European aristocrats established still greater control over local peasants, especially after 1600. The relatively weak governments of the region accorded estate owners extensive rights to demand labor services from the villagers around them. In these regions, the aristocracies in effect reinvented lordship so as to take advantage of new economic possibilities; like their western counterparts, they now depended on selling the produce of their domains, but they made use of unfree labor to farm them. Villagers had some weapons of their own to resist these impositions, but the system accorded local powers to the aristocrats that existed nowhere else in Europe.

Aristocracy and the State. Alongside these economic changes, the greatest influence on the aristocracies' situations after 1500 was the growing power of western European governments. Everywhere states had more officials, larger armies, and more resources. The state's powers touched the aristocrats in very direct ways, most dramatically by playing a larger role in defining what aristocracy itself consisted of. Through the fifteenth century in most countries, decisions about social status rested on informal local consensus. In the sixteenth century, governments paid more attention to these processes, and by 1600 they had taken them over altogether. Formal letters of ennoblement now defined nobility and aristocracy, and governments punished those who sought to do without them. Governments also developed increasingly elaborate systems of rankings within the high aristocracy. Charles V, in his capacity of king of Spain, in 1520 instituted the new rank of grandees; where previously there had been only a vague understanding that some families represented the highest level of the aristocracy, now both the families and their rankings were clearly marked out. The French monarchy took similar steps in the late sixteenth century. Having created these rankings, governments tended also to fill them with new members, especially after 1600. "Inflation of honors" characterized most of Europe in around 1600, as governments created more titles of high nobility and in some cases sold them to status-hungry families.

Governments had succeeded in controlling social status itself, determining who was noble and setting even the greatest individual aristocrats within a universally acknowledged hierarchy of rank. This was only one of several ways in which the aristocrats' situation tended to become less autonomous during the Renaissance. Private warfare between aristocratic families had been an accepted practice in the fourteenth and fifteenth centuries. Governments ended it in the sixteenth century, though much feuding between individuals remained. Governments also encouraged aristocrats to spend more time near their princes, at court, where they could be watched and controlled. Courts had long existed, since princes had always wanted advisers and companions, and aristocrats had always seen themselves as suited to these roles, but in the Renaissance they acquired a new importance. Smaller states led the way in this fashion, advertising their claims to great power status by means of a luxurious and elegant court life. In the fifteenth century, Europe's best-known court was that of the dukes of Burgundy, who were attempting

to establish full independence from their cousins the kings of France. After 1500, the larger states too made life at their courts more attractive, building more elaborate palaces and staging more entertainments, and by the early seventeenth century it became the norm for aristocrats to spend as much time there as possible.

Such changes form part of a familiar theme in European political history, the rise of stronger governments, governments that concerned themselves less with the opinions of even their leading subjects. But the rise of absolutism (as the process has traditionally been described) probably brought more benefits than losses to the aristocracies. In several countries, such as France, Spain, and much of Germany, the benefits included freedom from most taxation—an increasingly valuable right, because royal taxation rose quickly in the sixteenth and seventeenth centuries. More importantly, everywhere aristocrats received a disproportionate share of the tax money that was raised, in the form of salaries for governmental positions and direct gifts from the prince. This was one reason that leading aristocrats attended court so regularly, since only thus could they assure themselves a full share of what the king had to offer: above all, well-paid and prestigious military positions.

The advent of gunpowder in the fifteenth century changed many of the rules of military life, but in no way did it render obsolete the aristocratic warrior. On the contrary, the new technology demanded a higher degree of professionalization from warriors, and eventually it encouraged the development of much larger armies. By 1600 there were many more military positions than there had been a century earlier, and members of military families had the first claim to them.

This did not mean that the aristocracies' relations with the state lacked anxieties or tensions, for the state's growth favored other groups as well. At least in western Europe, states had many more administrators than in the past, some of them drawn from the lesser nobility, some of them commoners, all of them accumulating power and wealth. The aristocracies were encountering new social competition, even as they enjoyed new degrees of wealth and power. But they had successfully navigated a period of difficult changes. At the end of the Renaissance they remained central to European society and indeed to Europe's self-image. More than their medieval predecessors, seventeenth-century writers and artists presented them as especially revealing examples of the human condition, worth close attention from men and women of all social ranks.

See also **Chivalry; Civility; Social Status.**

BIBLIOGRAPHY

Primary Works

Castiglione, Baldassare. *The Book of the Courtier.* Translated by
    Charles Singleton. Garden City, N.Y., 1959. Translation of *Il
    cortegiano* (1528).
Froissart, Jean. *Chronicles.* Translated and edited by Geoffrey
    Brereton. 1968. Reprint, New York and Harmondsworth,
    U.K., 1978.

Secondary Works

Bloch, Marc. *French Rural History: An Essay on Its Basic Char-
    acteristics.* Translated by Janet Sondheimer. Berkeley, Calif.,
    1966.
Bois, Guy. *The Crisis of Feudalism: Economy and Society in
    Eastern Normandy, c. 1300–1550.* Cambridge, U.K., 1984.
Dewald, Jonathan. *Aristocratic Experience and the Origins of
    Modern Culture: France, 1570–1715.* Berkeley, Calif., 1993.
Dewald, Jonathan. *The European Nobility, 1400–1800.* New
    York, 1996.
Elliott, J. H. *Spain and Its World, 1500–1700: Selected Essays.*
    New Haven, Conn., 1989.
Huppert, George. *Les Bourgeois Gentilshommes: An Essay on the
    Definition of Elites in Early Renaissance France.* Chicago,
    1977.
Nader, Helen. *The Mendoza Family in the Spanish Renaissance,
    1350 to 1550.* New Brunswick, N.J., 1979.
Stone, Lawrence. *The Crisis of the Aristocracy, 1558–1642.*
    Oxford, 1965.

                                        JONATHAN DEWALD

ARISTOTLE AND ARISTOTELIANISM.

The Greek philosopher Aristotle (384–322 B.C.) and his system of thought. Born in Stagira, Greece, and hence known as the Stagirite, Aristotle spent his life in Greece, Macedonia, and Asia Minor and died in Chalcis, Greece. A student of Plato (c. 428–348/47 B.C.), whose Academy he attended for twenty years, Aristotle then founded his own school of philosophy, the Lyceum, whose members were known as Peripatetics. Both philosophers have been extremely influential in the Western world. Plato was favored in early Christian thought because of his teaching on the soul and creation, but Aristotle surpassed him in the twelfth and thirteenth centuries when the broad range of his teachings on arts and sciences, lost for centuries, became available in the Latin West. The Renaissance saw a resurgence of interest in Plato as his writings, also long lost, were being recovered at that time. Early historians of the Renaissance tended to regard Plato as the dominant philosopher of their period, but recent studies have reversed that judgment, seeing Aristotle as outstripping his teacher in interest and influence.

Aristotle's Works and Teachings.

In later antiquity Aristotle's writings filled several hundred rolls and were divided into three classes: hypom-

nematic, exoteric, and acroamatic. The first were notes to aid the memory and prepare for further work, and all of these have been lost. The second were written for the general reading public, in dialogue or other accessible form, and included titles such as *On Philosophy, Protrepticus, Eudemus, On Justice,* and *On Ideas.* Only fragments of these survive, though some idea of their contents can be gained from comments made by later Greek and Roman scholars. The third class consisted of treatises written in a terse style and meant for school use, and to this class belong the surviving works of Aristotle. These were open to additions and changes in arrangement throughout Aristotle's teaching career, making the dating of individual works difficult, if not impossible. As yet there is no satisfactory account of their order of development or their precise relation to Plato's teachings, although several theories have been proposed.

Philosophy for Aristotle had a much wider scope than it has now. It covered traditional subjects such as logic, natural philosophy, metaphysics, and ethics, but also included rhetoric, poetics, mathematics, and both natural and political science. Aristotle was a pioneer in the systematic classification of all fields of knowledge. His ideal was science (Greek *epistēmē,* Latin *scientia*), which he defined as universal and necessary knowledge through causes, and which he classified on the basis of its starting point and purpose. One type started with things known and aimed at knowledge alone. As a speculative insight into things (*theoria*), he called it theoretical science and gave it three divisions: natural, mathematical, and divine. The opposed type started with the knower and aimed at something over and above knowledge, either action or production. If the starting point was free choice, the aim was confined to human conduct (*praxis*) and he called the science practical. If it was a conception of something to be made (*poēsis*), the aim was a product different from the action itself and he called it productive.

Logic. Although Aristotle referred to logic as a science, he did not classify it with the above disciplines but saw it as a preparation or instrument (*organon*) for science proper. Its basic function for him was "analytics," an unraveling of the complicated processes of human thought. This regarded sensible things, in which cognition originates, as knowable under universal aspects through a process Aristotle called induction (*epagōgē*). Manipulating such "universals" in the mind without error was for him the work of logic, and for it he invented such constructs

Aristotle. One of the series of twenty-eight illustrious figures painted by Justus (Joos) van Gent (1435?–1480?) for the studiolo of Federico da Montefeltro, lord of Urbino. Painting on wood; c. 1475; 104 × 68 cm (41 × 27 in.). MUSÉE DU LOUVRE, PARIS/ERICH LESSING/ART RESOURCE

as the category, the proposition, the syllogism, and the particular type of syllogism generative of science, which he called demonstration (*apodeixis*).

Theoretical sciences. The first theoretical science, for Aristotle, is natural philosophy, which is concerned with nature, things that are sensible or changeable and so composed of matter and form. Matter and form are two of their causes; the other two are agent and end, or purpose. On the basis of these causes Aristotle investigated topics such as chance, motion, the infinite, place, the void, time, chains of movers and moveds, and the First Unmoved Mover. For living things he also studied the soul and its powers, including the human soul, which is in a certain way all things and a part of which is immortal and eternal.

Mathematics, for Aristotle, is the second theoretical science. It is concerned with objects such as num-

bers, lines, surfaces, and solids, which exist in sensible things, but, through a process of abstraction, can be considered as existent in intelligible matter. Allied to these are "mixed sciences" such as optics, harmonics, astronomy, and mechanics, which apply mathematics to the study of natural things.

The third theoretical science is then metaphysics, which considers being completely separated from matter, and which Aristotle regarded as divine science. The substance it studies is real form without matter, real actuality without potency. In its ultimate instantiation it is thinking that has itself as its object, or Thought Thinking Itself.

Practical sciences. These sciences, ethics, and politics make up moral philosophy for Aristotle. Their subject matter is human conduct, and their aim is to achieve the good. This good, continually fluctuating, consists in an ever-changing mean between the extremes of excess and defect, ascertainable by the judgment of the prudent person. Such a mean can serve as a universal that makes possible the reasoning involved in a practical science. To be prudent, a person needs the moral virtues, of which the three basic are moderation, courage, and justice.

Such virtues, in Aristotle's view, have to be inculcated together by correct education from earliest youth. Good laws and customs are all-important for this process. If accompanied over a lifetime by bodily welfare, good fortune, sufficient riches, and friends, such virtues make possible a life of contemplation. This, for Aristotle, is the highest human activity; it alone produces happiness (*eudaimonia*). True forms of government aim at the common good, not that of a particular class, and provide conditions in which happiness can be achieved.

Productive sciences. Aristotle developed productive sciences in his treatises on poetics and rhetoric. In his *Poetics* he makes "re-presenting" (*mimesis*) the basis of fine art, and focuses on tragedy to explain its function of catharsis. In his *Rhetoric* he investigates persuasive arguments through logical, emotional, and ethical appeals, and then their use through proper delivery, style, and composition.

Renaissance Aristotelianism. The Aristotle who was studied in the Renaissance was inevitably different from the Aristotle of late antiquity. His Greek writings had been preserved and commented on in that language, notably by Alexander of Aphrodisias (fl. c. 200 A.D.), who interpreted him in a naturalistic and anti-Platonic way, and then by a succession of Neoplatonists to the sixth century, including Themistius (c. 317–c. 388), John Philoponus (fl. 6th century), and Simplicius of Cilicia (fl. c. 530), who were committed to synthesizing his thought with Plato's. In that century portions of his logical treatises were translated into Latin by Boethius (c. 480–524). Then, from the mid-eleventh century to the thirteenth, a nearly complete Aristotelian corpus also was put into Latin. This was accompanied by a few Latin versions of Greek, and a larger body of Arabic, commentaries, including those of Avicenna (Ibn Sīnā; 980–1037) and Averroes (Ibn Rushd; 1126–1198).

Following the fall of Constantinople in 1453, Greek scholars with their textual knowledge moved to the West, where they worked with Latin humanists to expand the bases of studies of both Plato and Aristotle. Their translation efforts gave distinctive shape to the Aristotelianism and Platonism of the Renaissance and the interactions between the two. Improved knowledge of the respective Greek texts and commentaries led to retranslations and new interpretations of Aristotle's thought. These resulted, among other things, in serious questioning of the scholastic Aristotelianism that had been inherited from the Middle Ages.

An overall view of the textual bases for Renaissance Aristotelianism is provided in table 1, which lists the contents of various *Opera* (Complete works) of Aristotle published between 1483 and 1563 in either Latin or Greek, along with the two bilingual editions of 1590 and 1619. Titles of the works contained in each edition are given in English translation and in their usual order within the editions. A quick perusal will reveal that some works added in editions after the first are authentic, but a much greater number are now attributed to Pseudo-Aristotle.

Some general features of Renaissance Aristotelianism to be noted are the following: it was an international movement, with an internal development of its own, though influenced by external factors; the movement was never a blind continuation of its medieval counterpart; some of its proponents were progressive thinkers who laid foundations for seventeenth-century developments; and there was a great diversity of attitudes, methods, and translated materials among its proponents. Thus it is preferable to refer to Renaissance Aristotelianisms in the plural rather than to a single system of thought. Recent historians have characterized these systems in two ways, Charles Schmitt (1983) as eclectic Aristotelianisms, focusing on the positive choices and preferences of the proponents, and Dominick Iorio (1991) as exclusivist Aristotelianisms, focusing more on the materials they tended to reject.

Plural Aristotelianisms. The need for diverse typologies within the movement can be seen by contrasting two Aristotelians who taught successively at Padua, Jacopo Zabarella (1533–1589) and Cesare Cremonini (1550–1631). The first used observation to determine the truth about nature, while the second was content to find truth in the text of Aristotle alone. There were also strong Aristotelian elements in the works of Leonardo Bruni (c. 1370–1444), Pietro Pomponazzi (1462–1525), Philipp Melanchthon (1497–1560), Francisco Suárez (1548–1617), William Harvey (1578–1657), and Galileo Galilei (1564–1642), but in very different ways. Bruni was a translator, Pomponazzi an Alexandrist and anti-Averroist, Melanchthon and Suarez were theologians, and Harvey and Galileo natural scientists.

Many fifteenth-century humanists, such as Bruni, Ermolao Barbaro (1454–1493), and Angelo Poliziano (1454–1494), promoted Aristotelian studies, but their interests in textual accuracy and philology set them off sharply from scholastic thinkers such as Paul of Venice (c. 1370–1428/29), Gaetano da Thiene (1387–1465), and Pomponazzi. Similarly, sixteenth-century humanist interpreters and translators such as Joachim Périon (1498/99–1559), Johann Sturm (1507–1589), and Pietro Vettori (1499–1585) had styles and methods markedly different from university professors such as Jakob Schegk (1511–1587), John Case (c. 1540–1600), and Antonio Montecatini (1537–1599). The first focused on *adnotationes* (annotations) and on grammatical, historical, and cultural allusions, whereas the second aimed at philosophical understanding and formulated replies to difficult *quaestiones* (questions).

Early historians of the Renaissance portrayed humanism as a philosophy that displaced Aristotelianism in the fifteenth and sixteenth centuries. The recent view sees humanism's mainstays to be Greek and Latin grammar, history, rhetoric, and literature, with no particular philosophy characterizing its work. Some humanists were Platonists, others Aristotelians, yet others Stoics, Epicureans, and even Skeptics. Bruni's view was that philosophy is conditioned historically by time, place, and culture, factors that surely impact its practical and productive branches. But for its logical and theoretical branches, the Renaissance Aristotle could not be far different from the ancient and medieval Aristotle, whose works still made up the core of university teaching. There the Aristotelianisms remained scholastic, as can be seen in the writings of the Anglican Case, the Catholic Franciscus Toletus (1532–1596), the Lutheran Johannes Magirus (c. 1560–1596), and the

TABLE 1. Editions of "Complete Works" of Aristotle in the Renaissance

Title[1]	1483[2] Latin	1495–1498[3] Greek	1549[4] Latin	1550–1552[5] Latin	1563[6] Latin	1590[7] Latin-Greek	1619[8] Latin-Greek
Organon							
Categories	A	A	A	A	A	A	A
On Interpretation	A	A	A	A	A	A	A
Prior Analytics	A	A	A	A	A	A	A
Topics	A	A	A	A	A	A	A
Sophistical Refutations	A	A	A	A	A	A	A
Physics	A	A	A	A	A	A	A
On the Heavens	A	A	A	A	A	A	A
On Generation and Corruption	A	A	A	A	A	A	A
Meteorology	A	A	A	A	A	A	A
On the Earth	–	Ps	Ps	Ps	Ps	Ps	Ps
On the Soul	A	A	A	A	A	A	A
Short Natural Treatises							
On Sense	A	A	A	A	A	A	A
On Memory and Recollection	A	A	A	A	A	A	A
On Sleep and Wakefulness	A	A	A	A	A	A	A
On Sleeplessness	A	A	A	A	A	A	A
On Prophesy in Sleep	A	A	A	A	A	A	A
On Length and Brevity of Life	A	A	A	A	A	A	A
On Youth and Old Age	–	A	A	A	A	A	A
On Life and Death	–	A	A	A	A	A	A
On Breath	–	A	A	A	A	A	A
On Spirit	–	Ps	Ps	Ps	Ps	Ps	Ps
On the Motion of Animals	–	A	A	A	A	A	A
On the Progression of Animals	–	A	A	A	A	A	A
On the History of Animals	–	A	A	A	A	A	A
On the Parts of Animals	–	A	A	A	A	A	A
On the Generation of Animals	–	A	A	A	A	A	A
On Marvelous Things Heard	–	Ps	Ps	Ps	Ps	Ps	Ps
Physiognomics	–	Ps	Ps	Ps	Ps	Ps	Ps
Mechanical Questions	–	Ps	Ps	Ps	Ps	Ps	Ps
On Colors	–	Ps	Ps	Ps	Ps	Ps	Ps
On Indivisible Lines	–	Ps	Ps	Ps	Ps	Ps	Ps
On Xenocrates, On Zeno, On Gorgias	–	Ps	Ps	Ps	Ps	Ps	Ps
Nicomachean Ethics	A	A	A	A	A	A	A
Great Moral Treatises	–	A	A	A	A	A	A
Eudemian Ethics	–	A	A	A	A	A	A
On Virtues	–	Ps	Ps	Ps	Ps	Ps	Ps
Politics	A	A	A	A	A	A	A
Economics	Ps	Ps	Ps	Ps	Ps	Ps	Ps
Rhetoric to Theodecten	–	–	A	A	A	A	A
Rhetoric to Alexander	–	–	Ps	Ps	Ps	Ps	Ps
Poetics	–	–	A	A	A	A	A
Problems	–	Ps	Ps	Ps	Ps	Ps	Ps
Metaphysics	A	A	A	A	A	A	A
On Plants	–	Ps	Ps	Ps	Ps	Ps	Ps
On Things Heard	–	–	–	–	–	Ps	Ps
The Situations and Names of Winds	–	–	–	–	–	Ps	Ps
On the Flooding of the Nile	–	–	–	–	Ps	–	–
On the Causes of the Properties of the Elements	–	–	–	Ps	–	–	–
The Book of Causes	–	–	–	Ps	–	–	–
Theology	–	–	–	–	–	–	Ps

NOTES: 1. A dash in the list indicates that the treatise is omitted from the edition, an "A" that the work is now generally thought to be Aristotle's, and a "Ps" that it is not but is now attributed to him as Pseudo-Aristotle's. 2. *Opera,* in Latin (Venice: And. Torresanus and Bart. de Blavis, 1483). 3. *Opera,* in Greek (Venice; Aldus Manutius, 1495–1498). 4. *Opera,* in Latin (Lyon; Ioannes Frellonius, 1549). 5. *Opera,* in Latin (Venice; Giunti Press, 1550–1552). 6. *Opera,* in Latin (Basel; Ioannes Hervagius, 1563). 7. *Opera,* in Greek and Latin (Lyon; Gulielmus Lemarius, 1590). 8. *Opera,* in Greek and Latin (Paris; Typis Regiis, 1619).

Adapted from Charles B. Schmitt, *Aristotle and the Renaissance,* pp. 149–151

Calvinist Clemens Timpler (1567/68–1624). Some medieval interests became obsolete, such as logical subtleties and sophisms, but the new logic of the *Analytics* underwent development and received more attention than in earlier centuries.

Another factor inducing diversity was the reawakening of interest in Averroism, which actually coincided with the rise of humanism, along with other medieval systems such as Thomism, Scotism, and Ockhamism. Averroism was particularly strong at Padua, where Nicoletto Vernia (c. 1420–1499), Agostino Nifo (c. 1470–1538), and Marcantonio Zimara (c. 1475–1532) were among its supporters. So highly regarded was Averroes as a commentator that the Giunti Press *Opera* edition of 1550–1552 (see table 1) was actually an Aristotle-Averroes edition, presenting Ibn Rushd's commentaries along with the Aristotelian text. Like the followers of Alexander of Aphrodisias, those of Averroes denied that the soul's immortality could be proved in philosophy, a topic that sparked intense debate in Renaissance universities, first among Alexandrists and Averroists, then among Averroists and followers of other medieval schools.

Scholastic efforts to reconcile Aristotle's teachings with Catholic faith on this and related subjects were many. Among notable Thomist commentators are Dominic of Flanders (c. 1425–1479), Thomas de Vio Cajetan (1469–1534), Giovanni Crisostomo Javelli (c. 1470–c. 1538), and Francesco Silvestri (Ferrariensis; c. 1474–1528). Scotist commentators include Antonio Trombeta (1436–1517) and Francesco Licheto (d. 1520); Ockhamists included Alessandro Achillini (1463–1512) and John Major (1469–1550).

Translations. Although written in Greek, Aristotle's works were studied mainly in Latin throughout the Renaissance. Translations to that language occurred in three stages: a few works, mainly logical, by Boethius from Greek in the sixth century; most of the known works between 1130 and 1280 from Greek and Arabic; and comprehensively from fuller Greek sources between 1400 and 1600, the focus in what follows. The motivation for new translations came from the advent of printing, from the discovery of new texts, from a public becoming more literate and with humanist tastes, from the availability of Greek scholars and patrons to support them, and from changing attitudes toward history and cultural interpretation. In the resulting atmosphere the earlier practice of word for word (*verbum a verbo*) rendering was found insufficient. In place of simple transliteration Bruni proposed to replace Greek grammar with constructions proper to the Latin language and to develop a new philosophical vocabulary. His translations were mainly the books of moral philosophy, but it was he, along with Jacques Lefèvre d'Étaples (c. 1455–1536), who inaugurated the celebrated polemic against the "barbarity" of medieval translations.

In the fifteenth century an early translator of numerous works was the Greek émigré to Italy, George of Trebizond (1395–1496). Perhaps the most prolific was the Byzantine Johannes Argyropoulos (1415–1487), who translated much of the entire Aristotelian corpus. His translations were free, bordering on paraphrase, but they became very popular in the early sixteenth century. Later in that century the urge to "humanize" Aristotle reached its climax in the work of Joachim Périon (c. 1499–1559), a French Benedictine, who translated most of the *Opera* (1563, see table 1) while attempting to force Aristotle's Greek into Cicero's Latin. His Latinity was much praised, but he was also criticized for putting words over meaning and creating a misleading philosophical terminology. One of his critics, Nicolas de Grouchy (1509–1572), systematically revised Périon's renderings, but they never came to be incorporated in the received *Opera*.

Giovanni Pico della Mirandola (1463–1494), though a humanist himself, objected to the charge that technical Latin was barbaric; for him, truth was more important than style. A translator who appreciated this was Francesco Vicomercato (c. 1512–c. 1571), who sought to imitate Aristotle's brief and concise style to the extent that this could be done in Latin. Among later translators who were similarly motivated, most notable is Giulio Pace (1550–1635), who reedited the *Opera* of Isaac Casaubon (1559–1614) in 1597. After this, translation activity dropped off considerably, mainly because of the decline of Latin as the cultural language for science and philosophy.

Aristotelian literature. The diversity of Aristotelianisms is reflected in the types of literature that were used in their study. The central core, of course, was the text of Aristotle, which was read aloud in the three stages of *lectio, repetitio,* and *disputatio* (reading or lecture, repetition, and disputation). With the availability of printing, books containing the text could be made available for professors, then working copies for students, and finally teaching aids of various types. These included tables and indexes, summaries, divisions of text and chapter headings, and marginal notes. First came the printing

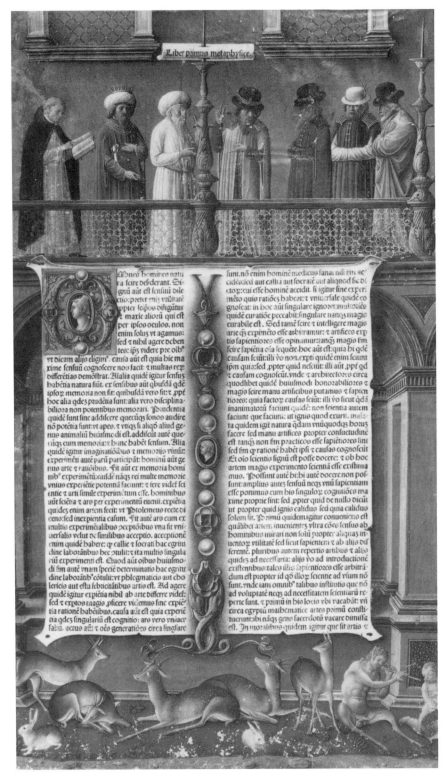

An Early Edition of Aristotle. A page illuminated by hand from an early printed edition of the Latin translation of Aristotle's works (Venice: Torresanus and Blavis, 1483). PIERPONT MORGAN LIBRARY/ART RESOURCE

of individual works, such as those of the *Organon,* then collections of two or more works, and finally the *Opera* (Complete works). The first serious study was in Latin, the next—the Aldine edition of 1495–1498—was in Greek (see table 1).

The traditional method of studying Aristotle's text was through the use of philosophical commentaries, and medieval commentaries such as those of Aquinas were frequently reproduced throughout the sixteenth century. Along with these came the new humanist translations, which were a source of confusion when matching the commentary with the text being commented on. One of the most successful attempts at combining the new with the old was the Giunti Press Aristotle-Averroes edition (1550–1552, see table 1), which incorporated the best results of humanistic method while presenting an author universally scorned by humanists. Then, along with the Greek text, came the assimilation of the Greek commentators Alexander of Aphrodisias, Themistius, Simplicius of Cilicia, and John Philoponus, especially in their teachings on the soul. Not infrequently Aristotle's text was printed along with that of his commentators.

Bilingual editions of various works began to appear around 1590, those of Pacius on the *Organon* and of the Coimbra Jesuits on the *Physics* being of exceptional quality, the first for its philological and historical explanations, the second for its introductions, summaries, and materials from commentators. Compendia were also printed in greater numbers; noteworthy are those of Alessandro Piccolomini (1508–1578), Johannes Magirus, and Benito Pereira (c. 1535–1610), foreshadowing the modern textbook. Other teaching aids included the *Tabula* and *Theoremata* of Zimara, and the indexes of the Italian jurist Giambattista Bernardi (fl. 1570/85). Tables in fact were a common feature of Aristotelian textbooks before they were popularized by Petrus Ramus (1515–1572). Finally, there were also books of instruction for younger students, such as Case's *AB-Cedarium philosophiae moralis* (1596) and his *Ancilla philosophiae* (1599), and books for unlettered readers—collections of quotations and snippets from Aristotle, such as the *Sayings of the Wise* of William Baldwin (c. 1515–1563).

In many ways Aristotelianism had reached the peak of its development and influence by the end of the sixteenth century. In important fields of investigation it provided the seedbed from which modern science and modern philosophy would emerge in the seventeenth century. But the system of thought it provided was complex, elitist, and overburdened, and eventually it collapsed from its own weight. Aristotelianism declined steadily throughout the seventeenth and eighteenth centuries. It began to revive in the nineteenth century through scholarly interest in England, France, Italy, and especially Germany. There the Berlin Academy sponsored a definitive edition of the *Corpus Aristotelicum* (1831) under the supervision of J. Bekker, which was to become the major source for the study of Aristotle in the twentieth century.

See also **Aristotle and Cinquecento Poetics; Logic; Matter, Structure of; Philosophy; Scholasticism; Science;** *and biographies of other figures mentioned in this article.*

BIBLIOGRAPHY

Primary Works
Aristotle. *The Complete Works of Aristotle.* Edited by Jonathan Barnes. 2 vols. Princeton, N.J., 1984.
Cranz, F. Edward. *A Bibliography of Aristotle Editions, 1501–1600.* 2d ed., with addenda and revisions by Charles B. Schmitt. Baden-Baden, Germany, 1984.
Lohr, Charles H. *Latin Aristotle Commentaries.* Vol. 2, *Renaissance Authors.* Florence, 1988.

Secondary Works
Barnes, Jonathan, ed. *The Cambridge Companion to Aristotle.* Cambridge, U.K.; New York; and Melbourne, 1995. Excellent overview, with recent bibliographies.
Iorio, Dominick A. *The Aristotelians of Renaissance Italy: A Philosophical Exposition.* Lewiston, N.Y., 1991.
Kristeller, Paul Oskar. *Medieval Aspects of Renaissance Learning.* Edited and translated by Edward P. Mahoney. Durham, N.C., 1974.
Kristeller, Paul Oskar. *Renaissance Thought and Its Sources.* Edited by Michael Mooney. New York, 1979.
Schmitt, Charles B. *Aristotle and the Renaissance.* Cambridge, Mass., and London, 1983.
Schmitt, Charles B. *The Aristotelian Tradition and Renaissance Universities.* London, 1984.
Schmitt, Charles B. *Reappraisals in Renaissance Thought.* Edited by Charles Webster. London, 1989.
Schmitt, Charles B. *Studies in Renaissance Philosophy and Science.* London, 1981.
Wallace, William A. "Aristotle in the Middle Ages." In *Dictionary of the Middle Ages.* Edited by Joseph R. Strayer. Vol. 1. New York, 1982. Pages 456–469.

WILLIAM A. WALLACE

ARISTOTLE AND CINQUECENTO POETICS.

Aristotle's *Poetics,* one of the most important documents in the history of literary criticism, was known to few people at the end of the fifteenth century, and those familiar with it had only a corrupt medieval version that had distorted Aristotle's system almost beyond recognition. A hundred years later the *Poetics* had become the common intellectual property of scholars throughout Europe; the text they were working with was comparable to that available in the twentieth century.

The *Poetics* and Medieval Culture. The *Poetics* exercised little direct influence in antiquity. However, manuscripts were taken east, where the Greek text was translated into Syriac, then Arabic. Aristotle was studied a good deal in the Arabic world from the tenth to the twelfth century, and there the Muslim philosopher al-Fārābī approached the *Poetics* as part not of the productive arts but of the organon, the instrumental techniques or faculties that have no content, such as logic. The *Poetics* was studied in detail from this perspective by the Islamic philosopher Averroes (Ibn Rushd; 1126–1198), whose work was translated into Latin in 1256 by Hermannus Alemannus, a monk working in Toledo. Two key principles drive this translation. The first, which conflates poetry with epideictic rhetoric (that is, a mode of speech intended for public occasions), asserts that all poetry is either praise of good characters or condemnation of bad ones, which makes tragedy the *ars laudandi* (art of praising) and comedy the *ars vituperandi* (art of condemning). The second principle, which is required by the placement of the *Poetics* in the organon, is that poetry is based on "image making" or "likening," a technique that relies on "imaginative syllogism." This idea is far removed from Aristotle but not incomprehensible, since the scholars who devised this scheme had little if any knowledge of Greek literature and its forms.

The *Poetics* in the Renaissance. In 1481 Hermannus Alemannus's Latin translation of Averroes's version of the *Poetics* was published in Venice. This form of Aristotle's *Poetics* entered the Renaissance and continued to surface throughout the following century. In 1579, for example, Antonio Riccoboni published a prefatory notice to his translation titled "Quomodo ars poetica sit pars logicae" (How the art of poetry is part of logic) that relies on the basic Averroistic principles to refine the arguments of Bartolomeo Lombardi and Jacopo Zabarella, who had also studied the relationship of poetry to logic. However, during the sixteenth century dozens of Italian scholars gradually sifted through Averroes's alien accretions in search of a more accurate Aristotelian literary theory. As Bernard Weinberg has shown, this process had five phases.

An accurate text. The first phase involved publishing a more or less accurate text and a basic exegesis. Aristotle's *Poetics* can best be described as revised lecture notes that presented serious challenges to textual and literary critics of the Renaissance. Efforts to recover a non-Averroistic *Poetics* began with the Latin translation published by Giorgio Valla in Venice in 1498. Latin was the language of all serious scholarship in the Renaissance, and Valla did a real service by making the *Poetics* available in a reasonably accurate translation that any educated person of his day could read. The first edition of the Greek text was published ten years later by the editor and publisher Aldo Manuzio in a collection of rhetorical texts, a placement undoubtedly suggested by Averroes's blending poetics with the rhetoric of praise and blame. In 1536 Alessandro de' Pazzi published a revised Greek text and an improved Latin translation.

The new version attracted little sustained interest at first, and during this initial phase scholars had difficulty grasping what was distinctively Aristotelian in it. In 1541 Bartolomeo Lombardi began his public lectures on the *Poetics* at Padua, and after his death his collaborator Vincenzo Maggi continued the lectures and published *In Aristotelis librum de poetica communes explanationes* (Public commentary on Aristotle's book on the art of poetry; 1550). Maggi attempted to introduce the *Poetics* into the critical canon by comparing it to a familiar work on the same topic, Horace's *Ars poetica* (Art of poetry). This approach had certain advantages, but when Maggi gives utility as the primary end of poetry and distinguishes character types through decorum, he confuses Aristotle with Horace. The major commentary of this period, Francesco Robortello's *In librum Aristotelis de arte poetica explicationes* (Commentary on Aristotle's book concerning the art of poetry; 1548), shows some of the same tendencies: describing the effect of a literary work as moral betterment accompanied by pleasurable sensation is Horatian, not Aristotelian, and Aristotle's plot, character, and expressive form ultimately end up being analyzed in relation to rhetorical persuasion. In 1549 Bernardo Segni published an Italian translation, along with a brief commentary indebted to Robortello, which significantly expanded the potential reading public of the new work. However, the next year Jacob Mantino published a new translation of the Averroes translation, showing that progress during this initial phase was by no means consistent.

Speculations on poetry. During phase two in the sixteenth-century reception of the *Poetics*, critics still searched for parallels between Aristotle and Horace, but an increasing theoretical sophistication also led to original works on the art of poetry and innovative speculations on genre based on the *Poetics*. Benedetto Varchi's lectures given in 1553 and 1554, *Lezzioni della poetica* (Lectures on the art of poetry; 1590), is one such work with an Aristotelian foundation, though Horace appears in its pages as well. Appearing at about the same time, Giambattista Cinzio Giraldi's *Discorso intorno al comporre dei romanzi* (Discourse on the composition of romances) begins with an Aristotelian definition of epic to differentiate it from the romance; Giovan Battista Pigna's *I romanzi* (The romances; 1554) in turn seeks to clarify the nature of the romance by looking for points of contact with different genres as they were treated in the *Poetics*.

Pietro Vettori's *Commentarii in primum librum Aristotelis de arte poetarum* (Commentary on the first book of Aristotle concerning the art of poetry; 1560), however, is the most significant treatise of this period. This commentary marks some critical advances: Vettori, for example, was the first to distribute Aristotle's six parts of tragedy correctly among the categories of means, object, and manner. Yet Vettori, too, proved unable to escape the weight of tradition, for when he writes that the poet must please his audience or that poetry must be written in verse, he is drawing on Horace, not Aristotle.

Vernacular commentaries and translations.
The years 1562–1575 mark the third phase of the sixteenth-century reception of the *Poetics*. During this period great vernacular commentaries and translations were produced, including Lodovico Castelvetro's *Poetica d'Aristotele vulgarizzata et sposta* (The poetics of Aristotle translated and explained; 1570), in which the author analyzes the *Poetics* while developing his own rhetorically based theory of poetry that emphasizes the audience over the poem. For Castelvetro, the end of poetry is pleasure, although catharsis also provides a secondary utilitarian end. Poetic pleasure arises from the credible, the joining of probable actions to historical fact. The credible is determined by what the audience will accept and makes the unities necessary, leading Castelvetro to tighten the constraints on place, time, and action beyond what the text of the *Poetics* actually allows.

Alessandro Piccolomini's translation (1572), following on those of Segni and Castelvetro, continued the process of making the text more accessible. The titles of some minor treatises from this period confirm that critics were coming to a better understanding of such basic Aristotelian concepts as the primacy of plot—Baccio Neroni's *Che la favola è di*

maggiore importanza nella poesia che i costumi (That the story is of greater importance in poetry than character; c. 1571)—and the imitation of action, such as in Giulio Del Bene's *Che egli è necessario à l'esser poeta imitare actioni* (That imitating action is necessary for one to be a poet; 1574). The second great vernacular commentary, Alessandro Piccolomini's *Annotationi nel libro della Poetica d'Aristotele* (Annotations on Aristotle's book concerning the art of poetry; 1575), resembles Castelvetro's work in explicating Aristotle while also developing the author's own theory of literature, but Piccolomini's theory is more utilitarian. Unlike Castelvetro, Piccolomini sees (correctly) in Aristotle a clear distinction between nature and the art that imitates it. Similar to many other treatises of this period, Piccolomini's marks a turn from the Latin scholarly tradition to a more amateurish literary criticism driven, ultimately, by an interest in Italian literature.

Literary quarrels.
During the fourth phase of the Italian reception of the *Poetics* (1575–1586), commentaries similar to those of the preceding decade continued to appear: for example, Antonio Riccoboni's *Poetica Antonii Riccoboni poeticam Aristotelis per paraphrasim explicans* (The art of poetry by Antonio Riccoboni, explicating by paraphrase Aristotle's art of poetry; 1585) and Lionardo Salviati's *Poetica d'Aristotile parafrasata e comentata* (Aristotle's art of poetry, paraphrased and explicated; 1586). The more interesting treatises of this period, however, engage in the great literary quarrels of the day. These quarrels centered on several key works of vernacular literature—Dante's *Divine Comedy,* Sperone Speroni's *Canace e Macareo,* Ludovico Ariosto's *Orlando furioso,* Torquato Tasso's *Gerusalemme liberata* (Jerusalem delivered), Giovanni and Battista Guarini's *Il pastor fido* (trans. *The Faithful Shepherd*)—each of which raised the same basic question: Do the rules governing generic composition derive from the authority of the ancients or the practice of modern writers?

Critics who looked to the past generally measured literary achievement against the rules they deduced from Aristotle, while those who championed the practice of the moderns argued (at least initially) that standards evolve as experimental geniuses create genres that were unknown in antiquity. Nuanced positions, however, were possible. Such critics as Filippo Sassetti, in his *Discorso contro l'Ariosto* (Discourse against Ariosto; 1575–1576), launched predictable attacks on Ariosto by analyzing the romance as if it were simply bad epic. Others, such as

Orazio Ariosto, in his *Difese dell'Orlando furioso dell'Ariosto* (In defense of Ariosto's *Orlando furioso*; 1585), and Lionardo Salviati, in his *Degli Accademici della Crusca difesa dell'Orlando furioso* (In defense of *Orlando furioso* by the members of the Accademia della Crusca; 1585), defend the romance by arguing that Aristotelian principles can be extended to allow modern adaptations of ancient genres. In each of the major literary quarrels, discussion centered on topics that clearly derived from an increasingly sophisticated understanding of the *Poetics*: unity of plot and the relation of episodes to that plot; the genre to which a particular poem belonged and the relation of plot to generic assignment; and the role of history, verisimilitude, and the marvelous in plot construction.

Aristotle and genre. The final phase in the sixteenth-century reception of the *Poetics*, which lasted through the end of the century, is characterized by further expansion of the literary quarrels into discussions of Aristotle and by a continued preoccupation with genre. The dominant figure of the period is Riccoboni, who published several works reiterating and expanding his previous positions: *Poetica Aristotelis ab Antonio Riccobono Latina conversa* (Aristotle's *Poetics* translated into Latin by Antonio Riccoboni; 1587), *Compendium artis poeticae Aristotelis ad usum conficiendorum poematum* (Summary of Aristotle's art of poetry to be used for making poems; 1591), *De poetica Aristoteles cum Horatio collatus* (On Aristotle's art of poetry compared with Horace; 1599), and others.

Jacopo Mazzoni's *Della difesa della Comedia di Dante* (On the defense of Dante's *Divine Comedy*; 1587), however, is also noteworthy for building a defense of the *Divine Comedy* on Aristotle's four causes (material, formal, efficient, and final), while Francesco Buonamici's *Discorsi poetici nella Accademia fiorentina in difesa d'Aristotile* (Poetic discourses in the Florentine Academy in defense of Aristotle; 1597) offers an unusually clear understanding of poetry as a productive art within the Aristotelian schema of knowledge. Here, as before, Aristotle's authority was sometimes challenged, but for many critics the *Poetics* continued to structure debate, and in the end Aristotle was made to serve both sides of the literary quarrels of the Renaissance.

The Diffusion of Italian Criticism on the *Poetics*.

In literary criticism, as in other areas, Italian books were exported throughout Europe, and the increasingly accurate, non-Averroistic interpretations of Aristotle guided the development of literary criticism throughout Renaissance Europe. Julius Caesar Scaliger's *Poetice* (Poetics; 1561), for example, served as a bridge between Italian work on Aristotle and French criticism, as did Jean Vauquelin de Le Fresnaye's *Art poétique* (Art of poetry; 1605), while the various discussions of the dramatic unities as interpreted by Aristotle's later readers influenced the drama of Pierre Corneille and his age.

Aristotelian ideas, mediated by the critic Antonio Sebastiano Minturno, among others, made a decisive entrance into English criticism with Sir Philip Sidney's *Defense of Poesie* (1595), while the preface to John Milton's *Samson Agonistes* (1671) anchors tragic purgation firmly in the tradition of sixteenth-century Aristotelian theory. By now Averroes has receded into the background, and the main line of the interpretive tradition leads directly to the efforts of Augusto Rostagni, Alfred Gudeman, S. H. Butcher, Ingram Bywater, Leon Golden, O. B. Hardison Jr., and Gerald F. Else, the scholars who have contributed to a modern understanding of the *Poetics*.

See also **Horace**; **Poetics**.

BIBLIOGRAPHY

Primary Works

Aristotle. *Poetics: A Translation and Commentary for Students of Literature*. Translated by Leon Golden. Englewood Cliffs, N.J., 1968. Commentary by O. B. Hardison Jr.

Gilbert, Allan H., ed. *Literary Criticism: Plato to Dryden*. Detroit, Mich., 1962. Contains a selection of important Renaissance treatises in English translation.

Weinberg, Bernard, comp. *Trattati di poetica e retorica del Cinquecento*. 4 vols. Bari, Italy, 1968–1974. The major treatises of sixteenth-century criticism, in the original Latin and Italian.

Secondary Works

Aguzzi-Barbagli, Danilo. "Humanism and Poetics." In *Renaissance Humanism: Foundations, Forms, and Legacy*. Vol. 3: *Humanism and the Disciplines*. Edited by Albert Rabil Jr. Philadelphia, 1988. Pages 85–169.

Greenfield, Concetta Carestia. *Humanist and Scholastic Poetics, 1250–1500*. Lewisburg, Pa., 1981.

Hardison, O. B., Jr. "The Place of Averroes' Commentary on the *Poetics* in the History of Medieval Criticism." In *Medieval and Renaissance Studies*. Vol. 4. Edited by John L. Lievsay. Durham, N.C., 1970. Pages 57–81.

Hathaway, Baxter. *The Age of Criticism: The Late Renaissance in Italy*. Ithaca, N.Y., 1962.

Hathaway, Baxter. *Marvels and Commonplaces: Renaissance Literary Criticism*. New York, 1968.

Herrick, Marvin Theodore. *The Fusion of Horatian and Aristotelian Literary Criticism, 1531–1555*. Urbana, Ill., 1946.

Herrick, Marvin Theodore. *Italian Comedy in the Renaissance*. Urbana, Ill., 1960.

Herrick, Marvin Theodore. *Italian Tragedy in the Renaissance*. Urbana, Ill., 1965.

Schmitt, Charles B. *Aristotle and the Renaissance*. Cambridge, Mass., 1983.

Tigerstedt, E. N. "Observations on the Reception of the Aristotelian *Poetics* in the Latin West." *Studies in the Renaissance* 15 (1968): 7–24.

Weinberg, Bernard. *A History of Literary Criticism in the Italian Renaissance.* 2 vols. Chicago, 1961. The standard survey of this material.

CRAIG KALLENDORF

ARMADA, SPANISH. An invasion fleet that was popularly dubbed "the Invincible," the Spanish Armada was launched in 1588 by Philip II of Spain against England. Its defeat carried global implications in an age of budding empire, when Europeans began to realize the importance of sea power.

From 1580 to 1583, Philip II of Spain annexed Portugal and its overseas empire, with his naval forces playing a crucial role. England and France opposed him, England mostly with words, France with ships and men in support of Portuguese pretender Dom António. Don Álvaro de Bazán, marquis of Santa Cruz and veteran of the Battle of Lepanto (1571), smashed a Franco-Portuguese fleet at the Battle of San Miguel (1582) and after completing the conquest of the Azores, proposed to Philip that Spain's victorious ships and men might settle matters with England too.

War Plans. England had edged into hostility against Philip chiefly over the Revolt of the Netherlands, where the religious issue was central. Protestant Queen Elizabeth I, fearing that Philip's Army of Flanders would turn against England once the revolt was crushed, gave aid and comfort to the rebels. Her excommunication by Pope Pius V in 1570 legitimized Catholic unrest in England and whetted the ambitions of Catholic princes. Elizabeth allowed subjects such as Francis Drake to engage in piratical activities against Philip's empire. Preoccupied with the Netherlands revolt and war with the Ottoman Turks, Philip connived in Catholic plots against her.

Contrary to the advice of many, Philip in 1583 disbanded most of Santa Cruz's armada. He preferred to strengthen his Army of Flanders and stick with plots against Elizabeth. He did restore the Portuguese galleon fleet, and launched eight light galleons in 1584 to escort Spain's treasure fleets. He continued to maintain substantial forces in the Mediterranean, although after 1578 he enjoyed a truce with the Turks. Philip's war fleets consisted of two types of vessels that were not interchangeable: the Atlantic galleon and the oared Mediterranean galley. His Atlantic commanders employed galleys chiefly for harbor defense and amphibious operations.

By August 1585 Philip's Army of Flanders seemed close to subduing the Netherlands revolt, which drove Elizabeth to ally openly with the Dutch rebels. Drake raided the Spanish coast and the Caribbean. Philip then ordered Santa Cruz to reassemble his armada "to punish Drake" and asked him for a plan of attack against Elizabeth. Santa Cruz proposed an armada of over five hundred vessels: some one hundred combat ships; forty galleys; scores of hulks to transport troops, animals, and artillery; and over two hundred small craft for landing operations. The armada would land 55,000 men and their equipment in unruly Ireland, and if Elizabeth did not abandon the Dutch, they would cross to England.

Philip also sought a plan from the governor-general of the rebellious Netherlands, Alexander Farnese, duke of Parma. Parma proposed to assemble armed ships and two hundred sailing barges on the Flemish coast, purportedly to reconquer Zeeland, and with an east wind ferry thirty thousand men of his Army of Flanders by night across the narrows to surprise England. While the use of Parma's veterans made sense, Madrid feared that Parma's plan entailed too many uncertainties and preferred to employ Santa Cruz's armada to reinforce Parma's army and cover its crossing to England. While Madrid's plan seemed the most effective use of available resources, it would demand a level of coordination and communication that would require a miracle to achieve. But the age believed in miracles and Philip appeared certain of God's favor.

At Lisbon, Cádiz, and La Coruña, Santa Cruz assembled nine Portuguese galleons, another that belonged to the grand duke of Tuscany, some twenty stout Basque ships, a dozen ships commandeered from the Indies fleets, ten big Mediterranean ships, and two dozen German hulks, hardly the numbers he wanted. While Santa Cruz rounded up dozens of smaller vessels, he got only four galleys. He did get four Neapolitan galleasses, big-oared vessels with guns in broadsides.

All admitted that Elizabeth had Europe's finest navy. Her two dozen royal galleons were better armed and of an improved design that made them far handier than Santa Cruz's best-gunned ships. Close to one hundred armed merchantmen and swarms of small craft would support them. But with her best troops in Ireland, Elizabeth lacked veterans for the defense of England and depended on county militias. If the Army of Flanders landed in England and found support among English Catholics, her regime might be overthrown. Her navy was her prime defense.

English Ships and the Spanish Armada. Anonymous painting. Sixteenth century.
NATIONAL MARITIME MUSEUM, LONDON

Drake wanted to attack first and in early 1587 got his way. His raid on Cádiz destroyed two dozen vessels and set back Spanish preparations. Santa Cruz wasted the summer chasing Drake to the Azores and covering the return of the treasure fleets. When he returned, storm-tossed, to Lisbon, he received Philip's latest plan: he must sail at once for the Strait of Dover, to cover Parma's crossing and provide a reinforcement of six thousand men. Bad weather, the need to repair damages, and likely disgust with the new plan kept him at Lisbon, where he died at the beginning of February 1588.

Philip replaced him not with one of the Armada's contentious squadron commanders, but with the prestigious and affable duke of Medina Sidonia, a competent naval administrator but not a seaman. Philip also enlarged the Armada with ten more handy but lightly gunned galleons of the Indies squadron. Broadsheets published in Lisbon ballyhooed the "Felicíssima" (most happy) Armada's strength. At the beginning of May the Armada sailed from Lisbon, only to be driven by storms into La Coruña and nearby ports. Six weeks' repairs strengthened the Armada, and in late July its 125 ships and 28,000 men sailed for the Channel. Rough seas forced the galleys to quit.

The Battle. English lord admiral Charles Howard, on the urging of Drake, his vice admiral, concentrated over sixty galleons and great ships at Plymouth, while leaving a strong squadron to screen the Flemish coast, a task the Dutch also undertook. Medina Sidonia hewed to Philip's instructions and overruled those who would attack Plymouth. In battle formation the Armada inched toward its rendezvous with Parma. The English slipped out of Plymouth at night, worked their way to the Armada's rear, and gained advantage of the wind. The first fight on 31 July was a sparring match, but afterwards the Armada lost two big ships to accidents. One blew up, the other damaged its rigging in a collision. Medina Sidonia abandoned it to capture, which most later agreed was a crucial mistake; the blame fell on his chief nautical adviser, who recommended the ship's abandonment.

On each side some thirty ships, mostly royal, bore the brunt of the fighting throughout the campaign. The English fleet probed the disciplined Armada's defenses and on 2 August the Armada lashed back. The Spaniards admitted the superiority of English gunnery, which recent scholarship has reaffirmed, and knew that they had to force a melee, then grapple and board, so that their superior soldiery could triumph. The English harbored no doubts about Spanish intentions and kept their distance. Spanish hopes that the galleasses might force a melee foundered on tidal races off Portland Bill. On 4 August the English thwarted Spanish efforts to gain an anchorage in the lee of the Isle of Wight, where the Armada might await news of Parma's preparations. Without a haven, the Armada proceeded to the open roads of Calais, the English fleet dogging it.

Parma had barely received news of the Armada's approach and at Calais, Medina Sidonia learned that Parma needed several more days to embark his seventeen thousand soldiers. The English did not wait. Using eight fireships on the night of 7–8 August, they forced the Armada to flee its anchorage. One galleass grounded and was lost. The Armada, its formation broken, suffered close-range attacks. One ship sank and two galleons beached, to be captured by the Dutch. Regrouped, the Armada escaped grounding on the Flemish banks into the North Sea, where its divided commanders opted to return to Spain around Scotland and Ireland. In the storm-plagued voyage that followed, over two dozen ships wrecked on the Irish coast and barely half returned to Spain. Of the people, not half survived the voyage and its aftermath, despite the efforts of hastily established Spanish hospitals. Disease was the big killer, though as many as four thousand died from combat or drowning, and hundreds more were killed by the English in Ireland.

The English, low on ammunition and facing the spread of disease, shadowed the Armada as far as Edinburgh, then returned to port. Hundreds of seamen succumbed to sickness, neglected by a niggardly government, while Drake and squadron commander Martin Frobisher squabbled over credit, spoils, and blame.

The Aftermath. The defeat of the Armada led to exultation in England and the Dutch Republic. Sermons, processions, and bombastic broadsheets extolled the victory. Lord Admiral Howard commissioned a set of tapestries of the campaign that survive in engravings. Engravers illustrated the actions for popular histories. Dutch artists produced canvases of the triumph. In Spain, king and subjects did penance for their sins and resolved to continue the fight. The defeat of the Armada did not end the war, which raged with successes and failures on both sides until 1604, when James I of England and Philip III of Spain made peace by the Treaty of London.

In their national myths, Englishmen began to view the Elizabethan era as the heroic dawn of Britain's

age of empire, though they ignored their bigger guns and handier ships and made it a case of David against Goliath, cockleshells against behemoths. In Spain the "Invincible's" defeat came to be viewed as the harbinger of a long decline and the loss of empire.

See also biographies of Francis Drake, Elizabeth I, and Philip II.

BIBLIOGRAPHY

Calvar Gross, Jorge, et al. *La Batalla del Mar Océano: Corpus Documental de las hostilidas entre España e Inglaterre (1568–1604).* A splendid collection of primary source material. 3 vols. Madrid, 1988–1993.

Kelsey, Harry. *Sir Francis Drake: The Queen's Pirate.* New Haven, Conn., and London, 1998.

Martin, Colin, and Geoffrey Parker. *The Spanish Armada.* Rev. ed. Manchester, U.K., 1999. An update of the best study, it takes advantage of fresh documentation and Martin's underwater archaeological work.

Mattingly, Garrett. *The Armada.* Boston, 1959. Brilliantly written and superb on diplomacy and the times, outdated in its treatment of the campaign.

Pierson, Peter. *Commander of the Armada: The Seventh Duke of Medina Sidonia.* New Haven, Conn., and London, 1989.

Rodríguez-Salgado, M. J., ed. *Armada 1588–1988: An International Exhibition to Commemorate the Spanish Armada.* London, 1988. The spectacular catalog of the exhibition at the National Maritime Museum in Greenwich, England.

Rodríguez-Salgado, M. J., and Simon Adams, eds. *England, Spain, and the Gran Armada: Essays from the Anglo-Spanish Conferences, London and Madrid, 1988.* Savage, Md., and Edinburgh, 1991.

PETER PIERSON

ARMS AND ARMOR. Arms and armor, in addition to their fundamentally military nature, had very important social and artistic aspects throughout the Renaissance. The terms encompass the purely functional equipment intended for the field of battle, the highly specialized armor and accoutrements required in tournaments, and the often ornately decorated armor and weapons sometimes worn by the nobility, especially at court and on ceremonial occasions. The development of arms and armor was a fluid and ongoing process, driven by constant changes in military tactics and techniques as well as by the ever-evolving dictates of fashion.

The Development of Armor. During the Middle Ages the predominate and most effective form of body armor was mail—a supple yet strong mesh composed of interlocked iron rings. The primary shortcoming of mail was its lack of rigidity. By the early thirteenth-century armorers began to reinforce mail with solid plates, utilizing a variety of materials such as whalebone, *cuir bouilli* (hardened leather), and, with increasing frequency, steel. First the lower legs and knees—a horseman's most exposed area when attacking infantry—then the arms were encased in ever more refined and functional plates. Throughout the fourteenth century the torso was defended by variations on the coat-of-plates, a type of sleeveless jacket reinforced by metal plates riveted to a fabric base. The first full suits of armor, covering the wearer from head to toe in an articulated sheathing of steel, were accomplished by the armorers of Milan by about 1420. The peak use of full plate armor and its dominance of the battlefield occurred over the ensuing one hundred years.

In a full suit of armor each plate was carefully constructed so as to overlap or interlock with the plates adjacent to it. The articulation, or flexibility, of the plates was achieved through the use of rivets and leather straps, both internal and external. A complete armor for battle, referred to simply as a field armor, weighed on average between forty-five and sixty pounds. The weight was distributed over the entire body, allowing the man who was accustomed to wearing armor to move about with relative ease. He was able, for instance, to mount and dismount a horse, or lie down and get up unaided. Field armor was worn by both cavalry and infantry in varying amounts. Infantry tended to be more lightly armed, with equipment generally consisting of an open-faced helmet, breast and back plates, a shirt of mail or other light arms defenses, and armor reaching to the thighs or knees. Armor was also worn by horses.

The proliferation of hand-held firearms on the battlefields of Europe from the late fifteenth century onward had a significant effect on tactics and on the wearing of armor. In response to the use of firearms, armorers experimented with various ways of making armor shot-proof, that is, able to withstand the impact of a projectile fired from a pistol or musket. By the mid-fifteenth century armor made in northern Italy and in southern Germany and Austria was famous for the hardness of its steel, which made it nearly impervious to penetration by weapons such as swords, axes, maces, daggers, and, depending on the range, arrows. Within fifty years, however, it became apparent to some armorers that this same hardness was a liability in the face of firearms because the armor tended to break or splinter under the impact of bullets. Consequently, the armorers of northern Italy appear to have rapidly changed their techniques to make armor that was more ductile than it was hard, in order to produce a steel that would be more inclined to dent than break when struck by a bullet. Armorers north of the Alps appear to have

Armor for Horse and Man. The suit of armor bears the mark of Kunz Lochner, a Nürnberg armorer; c. 1550. THE METROPOLITAN MUSEUM OF ART, GIFT OF MRS. BASHFORD DEAN, 1929. BASHFORD DEAN MEMORIAL COLLECTION.

approached the problem by trying to increase the hardness of their products, but in the end both methods failed to overcome the challenge of firearms. The most reliable method of making armor shot-proof was to increase its thickness, and therefore its weight, making full armor too burdensome to wear. The most common alternative was to make only vital areas shot-proof, such as the helmet or breastplate.

For these reasons and due to changes in tactics that emphasized more lightly armed cavalry over the traditional heavy cavalry, the amount of armor worn was generally reduced between 1550 and 1600. By the early to middle seventeenth century, three-quarter armor (reaching from head to knee, also known as cuirassier armor), was still worn, but its use was on the wane. Most heavy cavalry wore only an open-faced helmet, a shot-proof breastplate, a backplate, and sometimes a bridle gauntlet, which covered the left arm up to the elbow. This type of armor remained in use as late as 1700 when armor virtually ceased to be worn in battle until its revival in modern times.

Tournament armor. Medieval tournaments were treated as a training ground for actual battle and, as a consequence, were often bloody affairs only marginally separated from open warfare. By the Renaissance, however, the emphasis in tournaments had shifted to more sporting, social, and festive concerns. Tournaments involved a wide variety of well-regulated forms of combat, each of which generally required a different type of specialized armor suitable only for tournament use. Tournament armor was often heavier than field armor in order to maximize protection. This increase in weight was possible because the armor was used under controlled circumstances and was worn only for short periods of time. The basic forms of tournament combat involved contests on horseback fought with lances or with lances and swords and contests fought on foot with swords, poleaxes, and other weapons. Mounted courses with lances were frequently run with a lengthwise barrier, known as a tilt, separating the riders. By the late sixteenth century, foot combats were also frequently fought over a waist-high barrier.

The decoration of armor. Nearly all armor, even the most battle worthy, was embellished with some type of decoration. At its most simple and subtle the embellishment might take the form of narrow recessed bands and roped borders framing the edges of a plate, set off by gilt rivet heads and buckles. As a general rule it seems that those who could afford to do so had their armor and weapons made as decorative as their purse and the intended function of the equipment would allow. Many forms of decoration did not impede the function of armor and therefore were used liberally. Chief among these was etching, a process made more familiar today through its use in printmaking, but one that was originally developed as a method for decorating armor. The least elaborate etched decoration was confined to the borders of an armor and usually consisted of stylized floral motifs. At its most elaborate, the etching covered large parts of an armor's surface with various combinations of secular, religious, and ornamental motifs, including saints, biblical quotations, and classical heroes.

These various etched designs were sometimes highlighted against a gilt ground by the technique known as fire or mercury gilding. Bluing was also used in conjunction with etching and gilding to produce a rich, colorful effect. Further decorative details could be added by inlaying in silver and gold. Some armor and weapons were designed primarily as luxury items, symbols of status and connoisseurship that rank among the greatest triumphs in the field of Renaissance decorative arts. The most dramatic effects were achieved by embossing, or repoussé, a technique by which the surface of an armor was treated as a sculpture executed in high and low relief. The foremost masters of this art were the Negroli, a Milanese family, praised by their contemporaries as consummate artists, who flourished under imperial, royal, and noble patronage from the 1530s to the 1550s.

Notable armorers and armor-making centers. Like the Negroli, other leading armorers in the fifteenth and sixteenth centuries also maintained an international clientele and a renown that sometimes extended through successive generations in the same family of craftsmen. The Helmschmid family of Augsburg is a prime example of this. Beginning with Lorenz Helmschmid in the last quarter of the fifteenth century and continuing with his son Kolman and grandson Desiderius, the Helmschmids provided armor to the Holy Roman emperors and their courtiers for more than seventy-five years. Another of the most highly regarded armorers of the early sixteenth century was Conrad Seusenhofer, court armorer to Emperor Maximilian I. Seusenhofer and Lorenz and Kolman Helmschmid, along with Filippo Negroli, are considered the greatest artist-armorers of the period. Their work is distinguished by a combination of inventiveness, artistic sensibility, and technical excellence.

The major armor-making centers of the Renaissance were found in Milan, Brescia, Augsburg, Nürnberg, and Landshut. The Missaglia family of Milan was for generations one of Europe's leading suppliers both of munitions armors, which were ordered in bulk to outfit the rank and file, and of individually commissioned armors for noble patrons. Nürnberg was also a principal supplier of munitions armors, as was Flanders. In 1504 Maximilian I founded a court workshop in Innsbruck, drawing many armorers from the nearby and well-established armor-making town of Mühlau. He was emulated by Henry VIII, who founded his own royal workshop in the vicinity of London in 1515 and staffed it with armorers imported from Flanders, Italy, and Germany.

Weapons. The wide variety of weapons that were used in the Renaissance can be divided into three broad categories: edged weapons, staff weapons, and projectile weapons. The term edged weapons generally refers to swords and daggers, although many staff weapons can be placed in this category.

Shield of Charles IX of France. Gold plate and enamel on repoussé iron; c. 1572; 68 × 49 cm (27 × 19 in.). MUSÉE DU LOUVRE, PARIS/SCALA/ART RESOURCE

Staff weapons, also known as polearms or shafted weapons, refers to the many types of arms that consist of a pole or shaft fitted with a cutting, thrusting, or percussive head. The term projectile weapons refers here only to handheld weapons powered by human energy rather than by explosive propellant such as gunpowder. Projectile weapons include slings, bows, crossbows, and light spears or javelins. Firearms, missile-hurling siege engines, and artillery are discussed elsewhere.

Edged weapons. The sword was for centuries the preeminent weapon in hand-to-hand combat. The Bronze Age sword is considered the first

weapon specifically invented for fighting, rather than one adapted from a tool or an agricultural implement. The medieval sword was designed more for cutting than thrusting. The increased use of plate armor in the Renaissance, however, necessitated a thrusting sword with a narrower, stiffer blade that could pierce the gaps between the plates of a field armor. Most swords were straight-bladed and double-edged, although different types of single-edged, slightly curved swords were also widely used. Various hand-and-a-half and two-hand swords were used throughout the Middle Ages and the Renaissance. In the Renaissance, however, the two-hand sword for use on foot developed into a specialized weapon, particularly favored among the infantry of Germany and Switzerland. Rapiers were swords with relatively long and thin blades, designed predominantly for thrusting and intended to be worn in civilian settings rather than in battle. Rapiers are characterized by complex hilt forms built up of slender bars that wrap around and protect the sword hand.

Daggers were carried by all ranks of society both as weapons and as utensils. Military daggers were intended for close combat. The parrying dagger was widely known and made to be held in the left hand and used in tandem with a rapier.

Staff weapons. The lance, a steel-tipped tapering wooden shaft from ten to twelve feet or more, was the premier weapon of the heavy cavalry until about the mid-sixteenth century. Couched under the right arm and leveled at the charge, the lance combined the speed, weight, and strength of horse and rider in a powerful blow, the force of which was concentrated in its steel tip.

The halberd is the most well-known of the many types of staff weapons used on foot. It consisted of a five- to seven-foot shaft fitted with a head that combines the features of an ax and a short sword to make a lethal cutting and thrusting weapon. It achieved notoriety as the characteristic weapon of the Swiss infantry. Other staff weapons such as maces, axes, and war hammers were used both on foot and on horseback throughout the period.

Projectile weapons. Often overlooked because of its primitive simplicity, the sling, capable of hurling a stone or lead pellet at great velocity, was an effective and much used weapon well into the fifteenth century. The longbow and crossbow played major roles in European warfare, culminating in the dominance of the English longbow on the battlefields of France in the fourteenth and fifteenth centuries during the Hundred Years' War. Both weapons were able to penetrate armor at certain ranges and therefore effectively countered the massed cavalry charge, which previously had been the dominant military tactic in feudal Europe. During the course of the sixteenth century, however, the longbow and the crossbow were gradually supplanted by firearms.

The Role of Arms and Armor in Renaissance Society.
As military equipment, armor and weapons were a ubiquitous sight in Renaissance Europe due to the constant movement of armies and the incessant conflicts, large and small, that occurred throughout the period. Beyond this arms and armor had an ever present significance as clearly recog-

nized symbols of rank and authority, both noble and civic. As luxury items and objects of connoisseurship, finely made armor and weapons regularly served as diplomatic gifts and often figured among a nobleman's most prized possessions.

See also **Tournaments; Warfare.**

BIBLIOGRAPHY

Barber, Richard, and Juliet Barker. *Tournaments: Jousts, Chivalry, and Pageants in the Middle Ages.* Woodbridge, U.K., 1989.

Blair, Claude. *European Armour, circa 1066 to circa 1700.* London, 1958. Reprint, 1972. Remains the most comprehensive and scholarly one-volume treatment of the subject in English.

Boccia, Lionello G., and Eduardo T. Coelho. *Armi Bianche Italiane.* Milan, 1975. A detailed survey of Italian edged weapons, including staff weapons, with emphasis on the fifteenth, sixteenth, and seventeenth centuries.

Boccia, Lionello G., and Eduardo T. Coelho. *L'Arte dell'armatura in Italia.* Milan, 1967. The most authoritative study of armor in Renaissance Italy.

Coe, Michael D., et al. *Swords and Hilt Weapons.* London, 1989. Useful survey of edged weapons from prehistory to the twentieth century, with chapters devoted to the Renaissance period.

De Reuck, Anthony. "The Armourer's Dilemma: Hard or Tough." In *The Royal Armouries Yearbook, 1997.* Leeds, U.K., 1998. Pages 72–80.

Journal of the Arms and Armour Society. London, 1953–. Foremost English-language journal devoted to the study of historical arms and armor, with many articles discussing Renaissance arms and armor.

Norman, A. V. B. *The Rapier and Small-Sword, 1460–1820.* London and New York, 1980. Extremely detailed typological and developmental study of sword hilts.

Stone, George Cameron. *A Glossary of the Construction, Decoration, and Use of Arms and Armor in All Countries and in All Times, together with Some Closely Related Subjects.* Portland, Me., 1934. Reprint, New York, 1961. Although in some respects dated, this book comes very close to living up to its ambitious title and contains material not readily available elsewhere.

Zeitschrift für historische Waffenkunde. Journal of the Verein für historische Waffenkunde, 17 vols., Dresden and Berlin, 1897–1944. Resumed from 1955 to 1959 as *Mitteilungen der Gesellschaft für historische Kostüm- und Waffenkunde,* Berlin; and from 1960 to present as *Waffen- und Kostümkunde.* A treasure trove of scholarly articles, including many fundamental studies of Renaissance arms and armor.

DONALD J. LaRocca

ART. [This article, a general overview of Renaissance art, includes three subentries:

Renaissance Art
Education and Training
Women Artists

See also Architecture; Painting; Performing Arts; Practical Arts; Sculpture. Regional and national art schools and traditions are treated in subentries within the entry on the region or nation; for example, for discussion of art in France, see France, subentry on Art in France.]

Renaissance Art

Art and artists, as we now understand them, arguably developed in the Renaissance, a period in which the communal values that governed the creative lives of medieval guild members gradually gave way to the entrepreneurship of individuals who produced works of art as independent aesthetic objects. This transition culminated in figures like the voluble, socially mobile Raphael, the tormented genius Michelangelo, the outrageous writer, sculptor, and jeweler Benvenuto Cellini, and the urbane, learned Peter Paul Rubens, who not only painted on an industrial scale for the absolute monarchs of Europe, but also served them as a diplomat. Social and economic forces worked together to transform Renaissance art from a practical craft into an overtly aesthetic endeavor, and artists into autonomous creators rather than community-minded guildsmen. Yet it would be excessively simplistic to attribute the creative explosion of Renaissance artistry solely to an increasingly wealthy society's taste for luxury goods. Like a very different form of expression, classical Greek tragedy, Renaissance art achieved so much because, on an imaginative level, it was so engaged with the awareness of a heroic past, and, on a spiritual level, so infused with a religious conception of the world and humanity's place in it.

Patrons. Renaissance art was commissioned by heads of state, from grand monarchs and popes to small-town condottieri (mercenary captains), by city councils, by monastic orders, by churches, by individual prelates, but also, significantly, by private citizens, ranging from middle-class burghers who bought cheap prints or devotional images, to international bankers like the Fugger family in Augsburg and Agostino Chigi in Rome, who acted as virtual statesmen in their own right and endowed artistic and architectural projects with suitable generosity. Not surprisingly, this plethora of individual patrons made portraiture one of the distinctive genres of Renaissance artistic production.

Sources. The history of Renaissance art is irrevocably biased toward Italy, not only because the Italians took such a self-consciously literary attitude to their artistic tradition, but also because Italy produced a greater volume of art in the Renaissance than did any other place. The first self-conscious histories of Renaissance art were written in the fifteenth and sixteenth centuries by Italian writers who mod-

eled their work on that of ancient authors like Pliny the Elder and Plutarch. In marked contrast to their antique forerunners, however, most of these early writers about art were themselves practicing artists. Disparate works like Leon Battista Alberti's *On Painting* (1435), *On the Statue* (1464?), and *On Architecture* (1452), Lorenzo Ghiberti's *Commentaries* (1447–1455), Raphael's *Letter to Pope Leo X* (final draft c. 1519), and Benvenuto Cellini's *Autobiography* (1562) all touched on the history of art in the course of writing about contemporary artistic practice (their own included). Most influentially, Giorgio Vasari's massive compendium, *The Lives of the Artists* (1550; rev. 1568), inspired a whole genre of artistic biography. Although Vasari is often wrong about his facts, his claim to close acquaintance with many of his informants, together with a winning combination of lively prose, choice anecdotes, and pungent opinions, lent his biographies an immediate and perennial authority.

Nonetheless, the factors that created Italian Renaissance art—merchant capitalism, the humanist movement, and a classically based aesthetic system—quickly spread beyond the borders of Italy to flourish on both sides of the Alps. Hence Albrecht Dürer of Nürnberg, deeply inspired by Italian models, wrote manuals on measurement (1525) and proportion (1528) to address the art lovers of northern Europe, and many of his contemporaries followed suit.

Because Renaissance writers on art chose to concentrate mostly on painting, sculpture, and architecture, our own definition of art in the Renaissance has tended to employ their same categories. In fact, the reality of fifteenth- and sixteenth-century artistic practice was a good deal broader. Contracts and surviving artifacts reveal, for example, that patrons regarded metalwork on a small scale, for reliquaries, candlesticks, chalices, table services, and tabletop decorations as a major, not a minor art; Benvenuto Cellini's international career provides further confirmation. Chapel commissions often included textiles: not only priestly vestments, altar cloths, and banners, but also temporary festival wrappings for architectural elements, not to mention tapestries, which were effectively an industry unto themselves. Because textiles received heavy use, they have tended not to survive in great numbers, yet, like the other decorative arts, they represented huge investments of time, skill, and money.

To a certain extent, moreover, a broader redefinition of Renaissance art would immediately adjust the number and status of women artists in the period. The dormitory atmosphere of workshop prac-

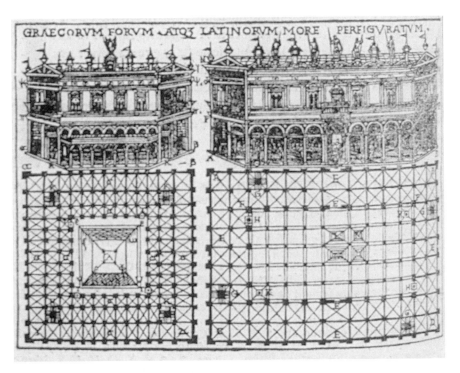

Cesariano's Edition of Vitruvius. Plan of a Greek forum, from Cesare Cesariano's translation of Vitruvius, *De Lucio Vitruvio Pollione de architectura libri dece* (Cano, 1521). COURTESY ART INSTITUTE OF CHICAGO, RYERSON AND BURNHAM LIBRARIES

tice militated against young girls joining a team of painters, sculptors, or architects as apprentices—the rape of the painter Artemisia Gentileschi by her painter father's associate Agostino Tassi tragically illustrates why—but women regularly participated in such arts as manuscript illumination and textiles, and were not necessarily ill paid for their efforts.

Origins. Writing in the mid-sixteenth century, the Tuscan writer, painter, and architect Giorgio Vasari identified the beginnings of "modern" art with the Florentine painter Giotto di Bondone (1266–1337), calling explicit attention to his innovative style, inspired, in Vasari's view, by nature alone. Yet Vasari's biography also shows in the telling that Giotto carefully marketed his exceptional skill in painting to attract a large and diverse group of patrons, including the pope in Rome, the Angevin king of Naples, the Franciscan friars of Florence and Assisi, and private patrons like the wealthy Paduan merchant Enrico Scrovegni. With confidence and panache, Giotto created and promoted a distinctive artistic personality, as when he sent Pope Boniface VIII a painted circle rather than a sketch, claiming that its perfect roundness was sufficient proof of his superior skill. Although Vasari does not mention antiquity as an explicit influence on Giotto (for reasons to be

discussed below), the enterprising Florentine's artistic persona evidently included the careful study of ancient painting, sculpture, and architecture alongside the "imitation of nature," as if living masters, like his irascible teacher Cimabue (c. 1240–c. 1302), were ultimately inadequate to the task of teaching him to create truly successful art.

Giotto's powerful figures and his ability to give spatial depth to his compositions, visible today in works like the Scrovegni Chapel in Padua's ancient Roman arena (1302–1305) made his paintings uncannily lifelike in the eyes of his contemporaries, and he infused these statuesque characters with a fierce intensity of emotion. For his most successful predecessors' ornate patterns, exotic materials, and vivid colors, he substituted his figures' majestic presence and his own skill at rendering them in the crisp media of tempera and fresco; once achieved, the combination proved irresistible. The Scrovegni Chapel's parallel lives of Christ and the Virgin Mary reveal that this great stager of individual scenes (Giotto also produced Passion plays) was equally effective at telling a longer story through dramatically chosen episodes.

As a taste for Giotto's style spread throughout Italy, northern European painters developed their own quite different version of innovative style. Working mostly in oils, they sought after and obtained paintings whose shimmering surfaces effect a mastery of light, shadow, and color, and seemed no less lifelike to their beholders than Giotto's stately compositions. The textures of the physical world, whether the velvets of a burgher's sleeve, a diaphanous veil, a golden halo, or the wounds of a crucified Christ, took on an unprecedented immediacy, imbued with saturated colors applied with the finest of brushes. Panel paintings and illuminated manuscripts of exquisite delicacy were peopled with insects, flowers, fruits, and dewdrops whose three-dimensional effect could only be dispelled by a touch. A lively trade in portable paintings and manuscripts ensured that patrons and customers on both sides of the Alps came to appreciate both kinds of artistry: Italian gravitas (substance) and northern finish.

For architecture, a comparable break from medieval practice occurred later, in part because both Romanesque and Gothic buildings continued to incorporate so many of the basic principles of classical form. Thus fifteenth-century Florentines regarded their Romanesque baptistery as a fully antique building, and the sixteenth-century Milanese architect Cesare Cesariano used Milan's Gothic cathedral to illustrate the qualities of good classical architecture in his 1521 edition of the ancient Roman author Vitruvius; the design for a Greek forum in the same book combines Renaissance rounded arches with Gothic spires. Still, when the Florentine goldsmith Filippo Brunelleschi (1377–1446) turned his versatile hand to designing a new Ospedale (home for foundlings) for the Florentine silkworkers' guild in 1419, his fellow citizens immediately recognized the result as something subtly new. By imposing a simple system of proportions on every aspect of the Ospedale's construction, from the dimensions of its facade and its graceful arcades to the ground measurements of the floor plan, Brunelleschi thereby achieved a sense of composure and harmony that more freely designed medieval buildings had lacked. Like Giotto, Brunelleschi drew inspiration for his carefully proportioned designs from the ancients—though, ironically, the repertory of ancient buildings on which he drew included the Florentine Baptistery as well as genuinely ancient Roman constructions, which he had studied in Rome in the company of his friend, the sculptor Donatello (1386?–1466).

One of those ancient Roman constructions was the Pantheon, whose massive concrete dome inspired Brunelleschi to erect a comparable structure atop the cavernous crossing of Florence Cathedral. Although he borrowed aspects of the Pantheon's construction system, like the scheme of nesting an interior vault within an exterior shell, he gave his dome—and the Florentine skyline—a distinctively non-Roman shape, tall and angular rather than low and rounded. It has marked the Florentine skyline ever since.

A man of seemingly endless ingenuity, Brunelleschi also invented a clever peep show that portrayed two Florentine landmarks in perspective in 1425 or so: when spectators who stood in front of the Florentine Baptistery peered through the small hole at the front of the apparatus, they saw a perspectival drawing of the building so convincing that they seemed to be seeing the real thing. Leon Battista Alberti's essay *On Painting* provided instructions for setting up similar perspective systems based on a single vanishing point. Painting, relief sculpture, and architecture in Italy all registered perspective's effect in short order.

Like Giotto's paintings, the sculptures of Donatello marked a definite change in style, sacrificing a certain degree of medieval grace for classical ponderance and spatial profundity. Donatello's friend Lorenzo Ghiberti, maker of two sets of bronze doors for the Florentine baptistery, struck a lovely medium between Gothic line and classical vigor, but eventually it was Donatello's powerful angularity and overt classicism that determined contemporary tastes. Medieval Italian sculptors, like Lorenzo Maitani in Orvieto and Andrea Pisano in Florence and Pisa, had already worked with an acute consciousness of classical antiquity, for many ancient bronzes and marbles remained on display throughout the Middle Ages. But the optimistic merchant community that was early fifteenth-century Florence proved uniquely hospitable to the idea of a full-fledged revival of ancient excellence in the arts; in 1427, the city council revised its statutes so that the language in which the Florentine republic expressed its official proceedings would recall the stately cadences, as well as the republican values, of Cicero. By that time the Florentines' visual surroundings had already begun their own process of transformation by looking back at the antique past and forward to a prosperous future.

The Role of Capitalism. As the example of the Florentine city council suggests, the characteristics that distinguished Renaissance artists and their art—both the intense interest in the ancient world

Brunelleschi. Foundling Home. Loggia of the Ospedale degli Innocenti, Florence, built between 1419 and 1426. ANDERSON/ALINARI/ART RESOURCE

and the drive to achieve individual distinction—reflected a set of larger social, political, and economic conditions. Already by the twelfth century, if not earlier, merchant capitalism had created a social class whose chief ties bound citizens to their families and their communes, city-states that might owe vague feudal loyalty to the pope or the Holy Roman Emperor, but to all practical purposes governed their own affairs as autonomous political units. A similar development was occurring in the trading emporiums of northern Europe. Well educated in the writing of contracts and the arithmetic of exchange, townspeople from Antwerp to Amalfi tended to be avid readers and acute judges of fine goods, including works of art. They found a rich source of inspiration for their governmental systems in the ancient Roman Republic, especially as its structure and civic responsibilities were laid out in the works of Cicero. In Italy, merchant communes also felt a strong physical bond with the ancient Roman past: for the residents of Tuscany, Etruscan antiquity provided an additional, purely local, stimulus; for Venice, the annexation of Crete and trade with Constantinople fostered an intense awareness of Greece.

Both Greek and Etruscan civilizations had strong republican traditions that sat well with communal values, but antiquity, in the guise of imperial Rome, had its own appeal for cities with more autocratic governments. Naples, ruled by a Spanish noble family, looked to its Greek past but also boasted the tomb of the Augustan court poet Virgil. Papal Rome, since time immemorial, had consciously appropriated the trappings of the Roman Empire, and the Eternal City's successive layers of history were uniquely impressive to residents and visitors alike. Throughout Europe, but especially in Italy, collections of local antiquities grew up hand in hand with increased appreciation for the style as well as the substance of Cicero and other ancient Latin writers, and it may be no surprise that the same appreciation of ancient aesthetic standards conditioned the demands made on contemporary artists. Renaissance art, from the outset, was a learned art for learned people. It is no accident that these aggressive, attentive individuals fostered a new interest in portraiture as an art form. Artists and patrons looked closely at ancient monuments and at nature, but they also read intensively and subjected artistic practice to endless historical analyses and successive sets of theoretical guidelines.

Generic Composition and the Rhetorical Tradition.

What the ancient aesthetic system offered to the Renaissance was a combination of versatility and consistency. Its criteria for quality and its terminology derived from the same source: rhetoric, the standard curriculum by which young men, first in ancient Greece and then in imperial Rome, had been trained for a life of public service. Balance, harmony, and persuasive power set the standards for effective speechmaking, as laid out in Aristotle's *Rhetoric,* in the works of Cicero, Quintilian, and the anonymous *Rhetorica ad Herennium* ascribed to Cicero. Standards for writing and the visual arts followed suit. A line from Horace's *Ars poetica,* "ut pictura poesis" (poetry is like painting), swiftly became a cliché, but an informative one.

No less influentially, the *Ten Books on Architecture* penned by Horace's contemporary Vitruvius set building within a carefully detailed program of liberal arts in which a rigorously systematic approach to composition, thoroughgoing attention to proportion, insistence on human scale, and meticulous attention to details applied to every aspect of creative endeavor. Vitruvius scaled the length of his treatise to the human attention span, just as he insisted that columns be scaled to the human body. Architectural elements, he declared, should be plausibly robust; so should formal prose—both should exhibit gravitas (substance), and for both the ultimate goal was *auctoritas* (persuasive authority).

Both Cicero and Vitruvius, among many other ancient authors, insisted that the arts adhere to carefully drawn classifications of what they termed genus, a broad term that encompassed a generous range of categories. High, low, and narrative rhetorical style were genera, as were the different musical tunings ("modes"), the varieties of classical column (Doric, Ionic, Corinthian), and the genres of Latin verse (epic, elegiac, lyric). With the invention of the genus, Cicero claimed in *De oratore,* the line was drawn between barbarism and civilization.

Renaissance theorists like Leon Battista Alberti, Pietro Bembo (1470–1547), and Giorgio Vasari applied this ancient compositional system to contemporary creative life with a convert's zeal and the moral certainty granted them by their Christian faith. And although they insisted that they were restoring the incomparable beauties of the ancients, they recognized, at least on some level, that they were trying to create something new.

Imitation.

Inspired perhaps by the thoroughgoing practicality of the rhetorical curriculum, ancient authors agreed with near unanimity that the purpose of art was to imitate nature. Renaissance artists, patrons, and writers on art accepted the same axiom. Imitation, however, meant more than simple copying, for art and nature, as they well realized, were utterly distinct from one another; this is what lent the idea of imitating nature its quixotic thrill. Rather, imitation meant creating a plausible illusion; hence it was an operation that required unfailing presence of mind. Perspective, for example, that defining achievement of Renaissance art, strove not to reproduce real space, but to construct the illusion of real space by limiting the eyes' sweep to a single vantage and building up a compositional structure within those deliberately prescribed limits.

The doctrine of imitation had once supplied ancient Greeks and Romans with credible grounds for making aesthetic decisions amid the cosmopolitan chaos of the ancient Mediterranean world. Imitation provided the same reassurance to the citizens of the greatly expanded world that made up the domain of the Renaissance. The limits of admissible imitation provoked endless debate in antiquity, as when Vitruvius and Horace inveighed in unison against paintings of imaginary monsters or improbably slender columns. Such fantasies, they contended, could be made to seem real, but they depicted what was not real and were therefore morally corrupting as well as aesthetically suspect. In the early sixteenth century, these same authors and their same arguments were brought to bear on the fanciful style of painting known as grotesque, and with equal futility: in sixteenth-century Europe as in ancient Rome, the sheer delight of the paintings themselves vanquished every philosophical stricture. The case of the grotesques reflected a larger trend in the Renaissance practice of literate art: when early sixteenth-century artists like Donato Bramante, Raphael, and Michelangelo finally grasped the finest nuances of ancient compositional methods, they and their successors immediately pushed beyond the attainment of archaeological accuracy to create the fanciful play of forms sometimes identified as mannerism.

The Magic of Images.

Together with its repertory of forms and theories, the ancient world also bequeathed to its Renaissance descendants something of its own belief in the magic power of images. Despite the Hebrew Bible's prohibition of idolatry and graven likenesses, Christian icons, remnants of Greco-Roman cult images, retained all their ancient force. Medieval painted crucifixes famously spoke to St. Francis of Assisi (in Assisi) and St. Thomas Aquinas (in Naples). The environs of Rome in the late fifteenth and early sixteenth centuries witnessed a sudden spate of painted Madonnas appearing in trees, like Santa Maria della Quercia (Our Lady of the Oak) outside Viterbo, and the Madonna della Sughera (Our Lady of the Cork Oak) in Tolfa.

Statues wielded, if anything, still greater power. The Madonna that Jacopo Sansovino carved in 1505 for Sant'Agostino in Rome had the capacity to cure plague and to confer fertility, just like the ancient Kourotrophos (nurturing mother) figures from which she is ultimately derived. Lorenzo Ghiberti reported that the statue of a nude Venus discovered in Siena had stood proudly in the city's central piazza, the Campo, until 1357 when, certain that the pagan deity had attracted calamity, the Sienese chopped the statue to bits ("lacerated" is Ghiberti's term), carried it just across the Florentine border, and buried it there in a typical show of Tuscan neighborliness.

Images took on a sharpened religious and philosophical meaning when the fifteenth century's intensified interest in Platonic philosophy reactivated an enduring Platonic current in Christian thought (inspired by such texts as the Gospel of John, the Pauline letters, and the writings of St. Augustine). Pictures and statues, both religious and secular, served as reminders that the material world was itself only a representation of divine reality. By the same token, however, art, in all its unreality, acted as a valuable aid to contemplation.

Mental images, in turn, played a central, and indeed a magical role in one of the most important components of ancient rhetorical instruction: training the memory to learn long speeches by heart. The standard ancient mnemonic technique, whose use continued uninterrupted well into the Renaissance and beyond, was called the "artificial memory"; it coupled words, phrases, or sections of a speech to be memorized with striking mental images set in careful sequence within an imaginary structure, a "theater" or "palace" of memory. By recalling these figures in order, one by one, the speaker could retrieve the memorized speech.

Although it sounds cumbersome (and Cicero for one thought it overrated), the artificial memory's combination of verbal and visual stimuli could produce dramatic successes, and its popularity continued for millennia. (The capsule headings of some sixteenth-century printed books are explicitly touted as units ready for storage in the reader's memory system!) The dramatic poses, prominent attributes,

and eloquent gestures of Renaissance figures probably owe a good deal to this long-lost aspect of contemporary mental life. In a larger social context, therefore, images and the details of their placement could command a broad range of meanings. Some were plain, like the significance of the crucifix, or the Florentine guilds' statues of their respective patron saints ranged around the outdoor niches of the granary-chapel known as Orsanmichele. Some, building on their viewers' complex mental apparatuses, were forbiddingly allusive, like Botticelli's (1445–1510) opaque allegories for the Medici.

Nature and Antiquity. For Giorgio Vasari, Giotto's achievement as an artist had been to imitate nature better than any of his contemporaries. Ancient writers on art ascribed this same superior skill at imitating nature to the greatest artists of their own time: Zeuxis, who painted grapes so juicy-looking that the birds pecked them; Praxiteles, whose voluptuous statue of Aphrodite for the city of Knidos drove men to fling themselves upon her marble flesh. To ancient critics and their Renaissance readers, successful imitation involved careful analysis rather than simple copying. Apelles, when called upon to paint Helen of Troy, used five beautiful women as his models, extracting the most attractive features from each for his final representation. In a sense, therefore, for Renaissance artists, imitating antiquity meant adopting a proven method for imitating nature. Artists' eyes, in any case, tended to scan the world with wide-ranging curiosity, focusing with equal concentration on live models, antique statues, clouds, still life, and landscapes. The same voracious attention greeted ancient treatises and the reports of modern travelers. For today's readers, Renaissance judgments on art often seem to revert to the same millennial cliché: a successful work is so lifelike that it seems to breathe. Repeated ad infinitum about every possible variety of artwork, it tells us as little— and also as much—as that well-thrashed line of Horace, "ut pictura poesis."

Thus Leonardo da Vinci (1452–1519), whose intense preoccupation with nature and its laws is documented by his notebooks, and Michelangelo, whose obsession with the human form just as evidently encompasses both live models and antique statues, recognizably inhabit the same artistic world. At the very end of the Renaissance (in 1593), Michelangelo Merisi da Caravaggio (1573–1610), a Lombard painter trained in Leonardo's tradition of close observation and evocative use of shading, made his way to Rome, where he established a rep-

Caravaggio. *Deposition.* Completed in 1604 for the Oratorian church S. Maria in Vallicella (Chiesa Nuova), Rome. VATICAN MUSEUMS AND GALLERIES, VATICAN CITY/ALINARI/ART RESOURCE

utation based on his ability to create strikingly immediate images. Caravaggio's skill at rendering still life, his use of live models, and his dramatic effects of light and dark were all evident legacies of his north Italian apprenticeship, yet a painting like his *Deposition* (now in the Vatican Picture Gallery), for all its surface color, variegated flesh tones, gnarled hands, wrinkled brows, and dirty feet, clearly borrows its poses from a Roman sarcophagus depicting the death of Meleager. And because Meleager, the Greek hero who died too young, was seen by contemporary theologians as a forerunner of Christ, Caravaggio's lifelike altarpiece, far from presenting a meditation on a simple, popular Christianity, carries a message of profound theological erudition. But perhaps it took northern visitors to Rome, travelers from beyond the Alps like the Dutchman Maerten van Heemskerck (1498–1574) or the Flemish painter Peter Paul Rubens (1577–1640), with their first look at the weed-grown ruins and the silent throngs of broken statues, to make the obvious connection: sooner or later, antiquity simply reverted to nature.

Chivalry. Nourished on ever-popular medieval romances, Renaissance imaginations inevitably saw the heroic stories of Greece, Rome, and the Holy Land through the lens of chivalry. Virgil's *Aeneid* already came with its compelling love story; in medieval and humanistic retellings of tales from antiquity, like those compiled in Ovid's *Metamorphoses,* gods, heroes, and heroines tended to look and behave like knights and ladies, as in the fifteenth-century panel paintings of the Venetian, Carlo Crivelli; the Ferrarese, Cosmè Tura; or the Florentine, Botticelli; and in the hopeful scenes painted on the sides of wedding chests by a host of more modest artists. Antonio Pisanello's (c. 1395–1455) frescoes of the Arthurian legend, executed for the ducal palace at Mantua, reflected the enduring appeal of chivalric stories, and it was no accident that the most popular Renaissance epics, Torquato Tasso's *Gerusalemme liberata* (1581) and Ludovico Ariosto's *Orlando furioso* (1516, 1532), focused on medieval chivalric themes, the crusades, and the *Chanson de Roland.*

One important group of fifteenth-century patrons took chivalric ideals especially to heart: the mercenary captains, or condottieri, who made their living by fighting and sustained their reputations by sponsorship of the arts. Art executed for the Visconti of Milan, the Gonzaga of Mantua, and the Este of Ferrara always retained a certain chivalric flavor and reflected the continuing influence of France, where the Limburg brothers' *Très riches heures* for the duc de Berry show the chivalric aesthetic at its finest, and at its latest. The northern Italian city-states, ruled by warlords, maintained a courtly culture quite distinct from that of merchant communes like Venice, Nürnberg, Antwerp, or Siena. As the Medici grew more autocratic in Florence, they, too, began to emulate courtly style, despite their dynasty's origins as a banking house in a free republic. They staged jousts like that for which the diehard humanist Angelo Poliziano (1454–1494) wrote his surprisingly compelling *Stanze per la giostra* (Verses for the joust) in honor of Lorenzo il Magnifico's brother Giuliano de' Medici.

In central Italy, warriors like Sigismondo Malatesta (1417–1468) of Rimini and his archrival Federico da Montefeltro (1422–1482) of Urbino comported themselves as knights while also modeling themselves on ancient Romans. Their elaborate dress armor partook of the chivalric imagination more than it did the armor from ancient Roman statues. Though it was made as late as 1543, Filippo Negroli's stunning batwing armor for Guidobaldo della Rovere II of Urbino still comes straight out of a dragon's lair, more appropriate for Sir Lancelot or Saint George than the no-nonsense warriors of Roman historical reliefs or battle sarcophagi.

Glamorous the Roman legions may not have been by comparison with the heroes of Troy or Roncesvalles, but they got their job done better than any epic hero, paving the way for Roman colonization, citizenship, city planning, architecture, amenities, and education. Sigismondo Malatesta, himself a gifted military architect, held court in the old Roman colony of Rimini. There, in 1446, he summoned Leon Battista Alberti to transform the city's Franciscan church into his own Roman-style mausoleum, ever after to be called the Tempio Malatestiano, the "Malatesta Temple." What modern technology could not yet do for the Tempio, like cutting the hard colored granites known as serpentine and porphyry, could be resolved by a bit of judicious looting from the late-antique churches of nearby Ravenna. By contrast, his rival Federico da Montefeltro's ducal palace in nearby Urbino, designed by the Dalmatian expatriate Francesco Laurana (c. 1425–c. 1502) has a more chivalric, French air to it with its pair of circular towers and its elevated walkway. At the same time, however, the books from Federico's magnificent library and the palace's sculpted decorations are all rigorous attempts to imitate ancient Roman detail work—even when they depict modern innovations like the hand grenade!

Renaissance Armor. Batwing armor made for Guidobaldo della Rovere II, duke of Urbino, by Filippo Negroli; c. 1434–1543. THE STATE HERMITAGE MUSEUM, ST. PETERSBURG, RUSSIA

The Fifteenth Century—Experimentation.
The fifteenth century, for Renaissance artists and their patrons, was a time of experimentation, as they explored the possibilities afforded by their conscious attention to imitating nature and their simultaneous attempts to revive the elegant standards of antiquity. Because their factual knowledge of ancient art and culture was still relatively restricted and their enthusiasm great, they worked with a generous degree of freedom, creating charming anachronisms and brand-new inventions; some works, like Brunelleschi's Florentine dome or Alberti's Tempio Malatestiano, or indeed the technique of one-point perspective, were touted as old when they were almost entirely new. Artists and patrons alike experimented with style, with medium, with content: Italians marveled at the delicate perfection of Burgundian oil paintings and French enamels, while northern artists hailed the Italians' incomparably deep understanding of antiquity.

A setting like the cathedral square of Pienza succinctly expresses all the contradictory impulses of the fifteenth-century Renaissance: the humanist engagement with antiquity, the rhetorical curriculum's emphasis on harmonious order (with an added Christian mission), and the era's irrepressible spirit of experimentation, sparked significantly by international contacts. Created for a humanist pope, Pius II (1458–1464), who spent a crucial period of his career in Germany, the church, designed by Bernardo Rossellino, combines a German design (the *Hallenkirche*) distinguished by an open floor plan and Gothic arches, with a consciously Roman treatment of the travertine facade, as if to suggest various facets of the pontiff's complex personality. Yet the facade's apparently classical columns do not conform at all to any of the Vitruvian types—most fifteenth-century columns, in fact, do not—they are entirely made up. By comparison with ancient Roman buildings, moreover, the facade is flat, its slender columns little more than a decorative veneer, the central arch too broad to serve as a plausible bulwark against the forces of gravity. Bernardo Rossellino clearly studied Roman architecture with careful attention, but he had not yet discerned the rigorous interior logic that governed Roman architects' choice, and careful weighting, of forms. In essence, then, the looser rules of Gothic composition dominate the whole of Rossellino's Renaissance church built for a humanist pope.

To either side of this Roman-faced Germanic church stand Florentine-style palaces erected by the pope himself and by the most prominent cardinals of the papal court, all executed in the warm brown local building stone; these stately residences pay homage to a third facet of the pontiff's persona, his Tuscan origins—he was born in Pienza. Across the square, the little city hall stands on a sturdy travertine arcade, whose piers, like the columns of the church facade, are classical in inspiration but have little to do with Vitruvius. In miniature, therefore, Pienza is an ideal city that appreciatively evokes the grandeur of the past without any attempt to reproduce it exactly. It belongs to the same visionary impulse as the stately piazzas in which many of the fifteenth century's painted dramas are staged: Botticelli's *Scenes from the Life of St. Zenobius* (1480s), Perugino's *Transfer of the Keys* (1481–1482) from the Sistine Chapel walls, and the enigmatic anonymous paintings of cityscapes (National Gallery of the Marches, Urbino; and Walters Art Gallery, Baltimore) that may actually attempt to reconstruct ancient stage sets. But Pienza, unlike a painting, also needed to leave room for real life, that variegated mix of high, low, middling, and motley; accordingly the last building on the cathedral square is a modest brick tavern that served as the local sports bar in the late 1990s. The Renaissance, true to its communal origins, was a resolutely urban phenomenon. Even as independent communes gave way to nation states, this urban focus for Renaissance culture did not change.

Transition: Bramante and Michelangelo in Rome.

As the fifteenth century turned into the sixteenth and Pope Alexander VI Borgia (reigned 1492–1503) declared a Jubilee, the crucible of Renaissance art shifted from mercantile Florence to papal Rome. As the Romans themselves were more than willing to insist, only direct experience of the city's antiquities could give artists a proper grounding in the ancient style. Thus in 1500, Michelangelo Buonarroti of Florence and Donato Bramante of Urbino and Milan were both to be found seeking their fortunes in the Eternal City, with lasting implications for the subsequent course of Renaissance art.

In 1500, Michelangelo was intent on equaling the ancients as a sculptor; he had tried without success to foist a cocky *Bacchus* on Cardinal Raffaele Riario, and now, rejected, he was at work for a more modest cardinal, the Frenchman Jean de Villiers, on his *Pietà*. The latter statue's silken finish and quiet mood of tragic resignation have now spoken with simple directness for five centuries. Raffaele Riario was a sharp judge of quality, and Michelangelo was a quick learner; the difference between the superficial virtuosity of the sculptor's rejected *Bacchus* and the concentrated force of his *David* (carved in Florence in 1504) shows a trenchant process of self-criticism. *David* was commissioned to celebrate the restoration of the Florentine republic after the temporary expulsion of the Medici. The young David's body, standing as it does for the Florentine body politic, is not that of a classical hero—it is the taut, wiry frame of a contemporary Florentine, with a short man's compact limbs and the gimlet stare of a ruler. Body and soul have been thought through from core to surface, and have communicated their message of human grandeur as unfailingly as the *Pietà* conveys the sorrows of God and humanity.

What Michelangelo's stay in Rome accomplished for sculpture, Bramante's achieved for architecture. By studying a few buildings with unrelenting intensity, this many-talented man—singer, musician, painter, and poet as well as architect—set himself to find out exactly how classical architecture worked. Bramante's own work in Rome shows that he gradually began to notice how ancient builders scaled the individual components of columns, walls, moldings, and doorframes to make each kind of component differ perceptibly from the others. He saw that elements like column capitals, friezes, and columns themselves all had definite tops and bottoms, and that ancient architects had used varying degrees of projection to create patterns of light and shadow on blank walls and to give nonstructural appliqués like pilasters and engaged columns the illusion of structural weight. He also began to see what these subtleties of design lent to the aesthetic impact of ancient buildings, absorbing the sense behind the restricted repertory of formal systems that Vitruvius called *genera* and that he may have begun instead to call "orders."

When the conclave of 1503 elected fierce, driven Cardinal Giuliano della Rovere as Pope Julius II, both Bramante and Michelangelo suddenly found that Rome, with its layered history, its Christian charge, and its growing prosperity, was theirs to transform, and transform it they did under the Pope's watchful, impatient eye. A new Saint Peter's basilica was meant to be so beautiful that doubters would convert on the spot; meanwhile, the Sistine Chapel ceiling set their magnificent vision of Rome within a sweeping panorama of church history that began with the very creation of the universe.

Despite the literary emphasis of their art, Michelangelo, Bramante, and, by his disingenuous admission, Pope Julius all qualified as "unlettered men"—they were not Latin scholars (Julius was certainly guilty of rhetorical exaggeration—he routinely gave orations in Latin and corrected the texts of his own Latin books). In a sense it no longer mattered; they understood classical form, just as another "unlettered" contemporary, Leonardo da Vinci, understood nature: with a humanist's sensitivity to nuance, with utter empathy.

Codification: The Early Sixteenth Century.

The artist who finally penetrated the compositional logic of ancient painting was Raphael, who arrived in Rome in 1508 to help fresco the papal apartments and ended up with the entire commission, now known as the Stanze Vaticane. A young relative of Bramante, he evidently absorbed the latter's systematic understanding of classical architecture and applied similar insights to painting. His sweet, appealing painterly style initially seemed to mask a superb analytical mind, but soon the swift transformation of his art reflected his receptivity to the talents of artistic companions like Bramante, Le-

Cathedral Square at Pienza. Pope Pius II rebuilt his native village, Corsignano, south-east of Siena; it was later named Pienza in his honor. The square in front of the cathedral is named Piazza Pio II. The building to the right is the Palazzo Piccolomini. ERICH LESSING/ART RESOURCE

onardo, and the scholar-architect Fra Giocondo (c. 1433–1515), but also of humanists like Baldassare Castiglione (1478–1529), Angelo Colocci (1474–1549), and Pietro Bembo. He reached his maturity as a painter under Julius II; under that pope's successor, Leo X (1513–1521), he turned increasingly to broad explorations of design in general, from decorative arts to engraving, sculpture, and architecture. The pope asked him to reconstruct ancient Rome in drawings, appointed him an architect of St. Peter's, and set him to designing tapestries for the Sistine Chapel, all as he continued to fresco the papal suite. Raphael responded to these demands by devising a comprehensive philosophy of art, and as one of the first steps in developing that philosophy, he ordered a vernacular translation of Vitruvius to ensure that he would understand the text completely.

Raphael's gleanings from his studies were mostly made manifest in practice, in his workshop's systematic approach to commissions, and in the unprecedented understanding with which he employed the forms of classical art. Occasionally, however, he also made theoretical pronouncements, most notably in the letter he wrote to Pope Leo as a preface to the portfolio of drawings in which he reconstructed an-

cient Rome at the time of the emperors. Writing with the help of the seasoned literati Baldassare Castiglione and Angelo Colocci, he began his address to the pontiff with a brief history of art. Here he called attention to the developments of period style in imperial, late antique, medieval, and contemporary Rome, subjecting the work of each epoch to analysis according to the same criteria of quality that had characterized Renaissance art from the outset (imitation of nature, and what he called *buona maniera,* or good style).

Central to Raphael's idea of *buona maniera* was an idea of design as an orderly sequence. At the very end of his letter to the pope, at least in its latest preserved draft (Munich, Staatsbibliothek, MS It. 37b, fol. 87), he declared that the basis of all architectural composition lay in what he called the "orders," by which he meant the Vitruvian genera (categories) of column: Doric, Ionic, Corinthian, and Tuscan. Together with the idea of order itself, these "orders" of design constituted the backbone of the classical aesthetic system as he saw it. But unlike Vitruvius, who felt that the number of possible architectural genera was as infinite as human ingenuity, Raphael counted only five orders, drawing four of them (Doric, Ionic,

Corinthian, and Tuscan) from the ancient Roman text and adding a fifth (which he called Attic) so that he could give a properly classical name to the square piers that sustained every arcade in ancient Rome, from aqueducts to the Colosseum.

Raphael's classical system followed the same formal and philosophical logic as the ancient rhetorical curriculum. His profound knowledge of Rome's ancient monuments and his sense of period style enabled him, like Lorenzo Valla (1407–1457) with Latin prose, to judge what was plausibly antique in art and what was not. Raphael's own powers of invention ensured that he himself would always transcend his own strivings after archaeological accuracy in his own designs. If his pilasters for the Chigi chapel in Santa Maria del Popolo (designed 1512–1519) were copied directly from the Pantheon, they also featured an anomalous dropped frieze between their capitals, and were set in sober order alongside outrageous red marble pyramids. As profoundly as he understood antiquity's compositional rules, he routinely broke them to make an expressive point. Less imaginative contemporaries simply saw the rules for the orders, and grasped them with relief. Hence, in the work of less gifted artists, this early sixteenth-century codification of the orders and of classical aesthetics in general narrowed the range of experimentation in the visual arts. The sixteenth century increasingly became an era of theories and treatises. Dead in 1520 on his thirty-seventh birthday, Raphael had only begun to mount his own rebellion against the rules he had so recently discerned. That task was left to artists like his old rival Michelangelo.

Maniera. By the time he died, Raphael's reputation had spread throughout Europe. He left behind him unfilled commissions for patrons like the king of France and the duke of Ferrara. In Nürnberg, Albrecht Dürer sought out Raphael engravings and based his own treatises on measurement and proportion on Italian precedents. If Raphael and his associate Marcantonio Raimondi (c. 1480–c. 1534) transformed engraving into a vehicle for the mass dissemination of his images, and thereby his aesthetic philosophy, Dürer raised this same medium, together with the related techniques of woodcuts and etching, into the realm of high art. An immense paper arch for the emperor Maximilian I (dated 1515; executed 1512–1518), although it was made to be assembled from engravings, effectively obtained the status of a unique object; likewise, Dürer's incomparably intricate prints, for the sheer density of their detail, each came close to being one of a kind.

A third artist of the early sixteenth century, like Raphael and Dürer, also learned early to work on an international scale: Titian (1490–1576), the undisputed master of Venetian painting. With his large workshop, his charming manner, his ability to deliver on time, and his unswerving insistence on quality, Titian supplied the crowned heads of Europe, as well as a host of aristocrats and merchants, with voluptuous oils. He was not a theorist; he probed the potential of paint by using it, producing devotional paintings, portraits, and poesie, the word he applied to his mythological scenes. In effect, however, by calling his mythologies "poems" he argued that he was no less of a literary figure than his scurrilous friend, the vernacular writer Pietro Aretino (1492–1556).

Titian's Venetian painterly tradition made relatively little use of preparatory drawings, in marked contrast to central Italian (and also northern) practice. Consequently, he explored the potential of oil paint as a medium with remarkable freedom, using broad impressionistic strokes to suggest outlines and textures, and also to create the illusion of space within his compositions. His huge altarpiece of the *Assumption of the Virgin* for Santa Maria Gloriosa dei Frari in Venice (1518), with its ecstatic Virgin Mary reaching up to embrace the opening heavens, gave a spectacular early glimpse of the artistic innovations that shaped his long career. Younger Venetians like Paolo Veronese (1528–1588) and Jacopo Tintoretto (c. 1518–1594) drew on his techniques, as did foreign artists like El Greco (1541–1614), whose Byzantine training brought a metallic radiance to his color and lent his elongate figures a boldly stylized elegance, but whose freedom of brushwork owed its chief debt to Venice. For Rubens, too, experience of the Venetian masters proved more crucial to his handling of paint than the meticulously polished surfaces of his Flemish predecessors.

Theirs was one version of what sixteenth-century artists and critics had begun to call *maniera,* "manner" or "style," a word that implied both visual distinctiveness and social grace. In English, this development is often termed "mannerism." In Rome and Florence, another version of *maniera* prevailed in painting, sculpture, and architecture, based on drawing, the study of antiquity, and close attention to theoretical principles. When this central Italian *maniera* was imported to France by artists like Cellini, Francesco Primaticcio (1504–1570), and Rosso Fiorentino (1494–1540), it largely supplanted the prevailing local traditions.

The phantasmagoric visions of Matthias Grüne-wald (d. 1528), with their elongate figures and shimmering colors, might be seen as constituting a German version of *maniera*, especially when compared with the Italianate classicism of Dürer's paintings and the careful, restrained, distinctly northern portraits of a Holbein (Hans the Elder, 1465?–1524; Hans the Younger, 1497?–1543).

Maniera in Italy began from deep understanding of classical art, but pushed beyond the classical sense of proportion and harmony to create images that might be playful, like the grotesques; disturbing, like Agnolo Bronzino's (1503–1572) famously perverse *Allegory;* or deeply affecting, like Jacopo Pontormo's (1494–1557) tearful *Deposition* in Santa Felicita, Florence. The strange colors that Michelangelo had applied to the Sistine Chapel ceiling—purples, oranges, sea greens, teal blues, and purples—changed the palette of Renaissance painting and also of manuscript illumination, nowhere more impressively than in Giulio Clovio's (1498–1578) lavish *Farnese Hours* (Pierpont Morgan Library). The elaborately stylish sculptures of Cellini, Giambologna (Jean Boulogne; 1529–1608), and Bartolommeo Ammannati (1511–1592) exulted in the same deliberate artfulness of pose as contemporary paintings, and for shocking color effects substituted silken patinas. Moving away from the unadorned whiteness they mistakenly took as the norm for antique sculpture (the paint had simply worn off over the ages), sculptors working in the *maniera* also explored the use of colored marbles and the challenging stones known in Italy as *pietre dure* (hardstones); the latter especially represented a triumph of technology as well as artistry.

Architects of the *maniera,* like Giulio Romano (c. 1492–1546) at the Palazzo del Tè in Mantua, Giorgio Vasari and Bartolommeo Ammannati at the Uffizi in Florence, or Michelangelo at the Laurentian Library in Florence and St. Peter's in Rome, took the rules of the orders and upended them: Giulio Romano's famous dropped keystones in Mantua, Michelangelo's odd manipulations of scale for the vestibule of the Laurentian Library, and Ammannati's split pediment at the Uffizi forcefully flout the conventions of classical harmony to bring surprising freshness to an aesthetic system that proves more than flexible enough to sustain this kind of challenge.

Aside from the critics and theorists' areas of concern—painting, sculpture, and architecture—other arts emerged as the focus of acute attention in this period of the Renaissance, not perhaps as subjects of the traditional formal debate known as the paragone or "comparison" of the arts, but as important components of real life. The technological sophistication of metallurgy, in Germany especially, meant that guns and armor came to count as works of art in their own right, as did jewelry, medals, and small but exquisite objects for table and altar. Tapestries, especially in Flanders, continued as an international industry, with designs as susceptible to the vagaries of style and taste as any of the other arts.

The deliberate artificiality of *maniera* did not please every taste. Pieter Brueghel's (the Elder; c. 1525/1530–1569) sharply observant depictions of peasants and work and play provided a bracing, and highly popular, contrast to the antics of gods and allegorical personifications on one hand and the high seriousness of religious figures on the other. And when Michelangelo Merisi da Caravaggio arrived in Rome in 1592, trained in Leonardo's Lombard tradition to venerate nature, his dramatic oils delivered something of the lifelike shock that Giotto's paintings had imparted some three hundred years before.

In many ways, the three centuries of artistic exploration that separate Giotto from Caravaggio represented a period of single-minded devotion to the same goals: truth to nature, revival of—and rivalry with—antiquity, exaltation of individuality, and, perhaps most significantly, persuasion, beguiling the sense, bringing souls to God, lending glory to patrons. For no matter how insistently Renaissance viewers might swear that the work of art was as real as life itself, they knew better; for them, art's glory lay in its sheer artifice, and as a result art attained an extraordinary level of finish, sophistication, and raw expressive power.

See also **Mannerism** *and biographies of individuals mentioned in this entry.*

BIBLIOGRAPHY

Primary Work

Vasari, Giorgio. *Lives of the Artists.* Edited by Julia Conaway Bondanella and Peter E. Bondanella. Oxford and New York, 1998.

Secondary Works

Hall, Marcia. *After Raphael.* Cambridge, U.K., 1999.
Hartt, Frederick. *History of Italian Renaissance Art.* 4th ed. Revised by David G. Wilkins. New York, 1994.
Holmes, George. *Renaissance.* London, 1996.
Levey, Michael. *Early Renaissance.* Harmondsworth, U.K., 1967.
Murray, Linda. *High Renaissance and Mannerism: Italy, the North, and Spain, 1500–1600.* London, 1977.
Panofsky, Erwin. *Renaissance and Renascences in Western Art.* Reprint. Stockholm, 1965. A classic study.
Rowland, Ingrid D. *The Culture of the High Renaissance: Ancients and Moderns in Sixteenth-Century Rome.* Cam-

bridge, U.K., 1998. An interpretation of imitation, composition, and the orders.

Shearman, John. *Mannerism*. Harmondsworth, U.K., 1967. Another classic.

INGRID D. ROWLAND

Education and Training

In book 35 of his *Natural History,* the Roman encyclopedist Pliny the Elder tells of the ancient Greek artist Pamphilos, who was "the first painter highly educated in all branches of learning, especially arithmetic and geometry, without the aid of which he maintained art could not attain perfection." Pamphilos, who trained the most famous painter of Greek antiquity, Apelles, put his pupils through what was effectively a twelve-year course of study, and by his influence the art of painting was elevated to the level of a liberal art. Pliny's account provided a powerful model for Renaissance artists, who, between 1400 and 1600, sought to elevate the status of their profession and to enrich the curriculum of artistic training with liberal studies. At the beginning of this period painters and sculptors, like most medieval artisans, underwent an apprenticeship with a master; by its end, both private and state-sponsored artistic academies had been founded in which students' practical instruction was enriched by exposure to art theory, mathematics, and anatomy.

Apprenticeship. Throughout the Renaissance period (and continuing even after the foundation of formal academies), the primary means by which a young artist learned his craft was by apprenticing with a master. Something of the nature of these apprenticeships can be gleaned from guild or municipal regulations, contracts between individual masters and pupils, handbooks or treatises (largely Italian) written by practicing artists, and surviving drawings and prints.

Local guilds regulated apprenticeships to varying degrees to maintain equitable practices among the various workshops and to ensure a consistent level of quality in their products. Hence, guild statutes might specify how many apprentices a master can take into his shop at a time, how long an apprenticeship should last (different cities stipulated anywhere from two to seven years), that a pupil should not leave one master for another during his apprenticeship, or that a pupil may not sell works independently.

Specific terms were also set out in contracts drawn up between the master and the father or guardian of the potential pupil (typically a male between twelve and fourteen years old). Some contracts specify that

in addition to receiving food, lodging, and clothing, the apprentice will also be paid a salary, while others stipulate that the master is to be paid a yearly fee, which may be reduced as the training progresses (and as the youth presumably grows more useful to the shop). While the type of contract that required payment of the master was apparently the norm in northern Europe, Italian apprenticeship agreements might be of either type, suggesting that, at least in Italy, the profession did not draw exclusively from one economic class. The widely varying lengths of time mentioned in these contracts (anywhere from one to eight years, sometimes ignoring guild statutes) would seem to indicate either that not all pupils entered their apprenticeships with the same initial level of skill, or that not all entered with the same goal of becoming a master craftsman. If the apprentice did follow the full course of training and could afford to pay dues to the guild (which were usually substantially lower for children of practicing masters), he could open his own workshop and take on apprentices himself. In some cases (mostly northern European), this process of guild certification also involved submitting a piece of work to demonstrate mastery (that is, a masterpiece). If the fully trained artist could not muster the funds to pay guild dues and start up a workshop, he often hired himself out as a journeyman or assistant until his financial position improved.

The actual program of artistic training that the apprentice followed is not addressed in guild statutes and is usually only hinted at in contracts. Fourteenth-century Italian contracts, for instance, often simply state that the master will teach the principles and practice of his art; in the mid-fifteenth century (in a somewhat atypically explicit example), the Paduan artist Francesco Squarcione promised to teach perspective, proportion, and foreshortening, and to share his study collection of drawings with his young pupils.

A more complete picture of Italian training is found in the painter Cennino Cennini's *Craftsman's Handbook* (*Il libro dell'arte*), written about 1400. Cennini apprenticed in the late fourteenth century under the Florentine painter Agnolo Gaddi (son of Giotto's pupil Taddeo Gaddi), and although his book was apparently composed while he was at the Paduan court, the training it describes probably mirrors, in idealized form, a typical Tuscan apprenticeship. Cennini (who claims to have spent twelve years of study under Agnolo) describes what is in essence a thirteen-year training period. The first year is to be spent copying artistic models with a stylus on a small

Training Artists. Engraving of the academy of the sculptor Bartolommeo (Baccio) Bondinelli (1493–1560) at Rome, 1531. THE METROPOLITAN MUSEUM OF ART, THE ELISHA WHITTELSEY COLLECTION, THE ELISHA WHITTELSEY FUND, 1949 (49.97.144)

wooden panel, the next six are spent working in "all the branches that pertain to our profession" (working up pigments, preparing panels to be painted, etc.), and the final six years are to be spent mastering the techniques of painting on panel and wall.

Cennini tells the artist that throughout this time he should also draw every day, and it is not an exaggeration to say that drawing (*disegno*), to which he devotes some thirty chapters of the book, was at the heart of an Italian artistic education. It is, for instance, through the exercise of drawing—initially copying (and even tracing) drawings, paintings, and frescoes—that the artist trains both his hand and his judgment, thereby developing his own style. Cennini's discussion of imitation—through which the artist finds his own stylistic "voice" by internalizing the tradition that lies behind him—is one of the more sophisticated parts of the book, and may even draw on humanist ideas of literary imitation.

At the end of the fifteenth century, the Tuscan artist Leonardo da Vinci (1452–1519) began to make notes toward a treatise on painting, part of which was to lay out an ideal course of apprenticeship. Although Leonardo's notes reflect changing artistic practice in their advice that the apprentice begin by studying perspective and proportion, it is drawing—copying first two-dimensional, then three-dimensional artistic examples, and finally moving on to living nature—that once again emerges as the central feature of artistic training. Leonardo's treatment of artistic education goes beyond Cennini's in the attention given to those cognitive processes—chiefly memory—by which the apprentice internalizes the principles of good design.

The imitative practices that both Cennini and Leonardo describe are reflected in numerous drawings, from Michelangelo's early sixteenth-century copies after the Florentine frescoes of Giotto and Masaccio to the Flemish master Peter Paul Rubens's early seventeenth-century copies after the figures on Michelangelo's Sistine Chapel ceiling. At the lower corner of the ideal studio represented in Johannes Stradanus's late sixteenth-century *Invention of Oil Painting* (engraved by Theodor Galle), one sees a young boy copying a model eye drawn by the master; just such a sheet, covered with drawings of eyes, was produced in Michelangelo's studio in the 1530s (Oxford, Ashmolean Museum, coll. Parker 323v).

Art Literature in Artistic Training. If both Cennini and Leonardo provide a glimpse into the training program followed by artists, they also represent a new phenomenon that begins in the fifteenth century: artists writing texts that could be used in some manner as part of an artistic education. Although manuscripts certainly had a place in the artist's studio throughout the Middle Ages, these were generally collections of instructions for the preparation of pigments (indeed, much of Cennini's *Libro* is devoted to just such "recipes"). The growth of this new art literature demonstrates the heightened status of the artist (not merely literate, but now a man of letters) and of the arts themselves (not merely matters of practice, but also of doctrine). Yet it may also suggest that there was an audience for such information beyond the workshop proper—a body of interested amateurs, who might wish to acquire artistic skills. If Aristotle's recommendation in *Politics* that drawing instruction be part of a liberal education was noted but not followed in the early fifteenth century, by the early sixteenth century the Italian writer Baldassare Castiglione could claim in *The Book of the Courtier* that an educated person should know not only drawing but also painting. This change may reflect the growth of pedagogical literature on the arts in the intervening century.

The first such book to appear in the wake of Cennini is the Italian humanist, architect, and amateur artist Leon Battista Alberti's *On Painting* (Latin edition 1435; Italian translation, dedicated to Filippo Brunelleschi, 1436). Alberti's text consists of three parts: book one on the foundation of the art of painting in optics (along with a technical account of one-point linear perspective), book two on the composition of a painting, and book three on the qualities and formation of the ideal painter. The purpose of, and audience for, Alberti's treatise has been debated. The initial Latin version was certainly directed to humanistically trained readers (either to guide their experience of paintings or to encourage—following the model of Alberti himself—the nonprofessional

practice of the art). Alberti's vernacular version, however, was more accessible to practicing artists (who were at this time generally literate, but did not necessarily read Latin) and may have been intended for use in professional training. The novelty of Alberti's text is certainly its grounding of painting in geometry and optics, formulating a humanist model that is close to Pamphilos (although also—in its avoidance of any discussion of personal style—distant from the poetic model articulated by Cennini). Alberti's discussion of perspective gave rise to further vernacular writings by fifteenth-century Italian artists, the most notable being *On Perspective in Painting* (*De prospectiva pingendi*) by the painter Piero della Francesca (c. 1415–1492) and the Florentine sculptor Lorenzo Ghiberti's *Commentaries* (*Comentarii;* c. 1447–1455), the third book of which addresses optics, anatomy, and proportion.

By the beginning of the sixteenth century, this interest in art "textbooks" spread north of the Alps in the perspective treatise of Jean Pélerin Viateur (*De artificiali perspectiva;* Toul, 1505) and in the writings of the German painter and printmaker Albrecht Dürer. Dürer began making notes toward an extensive treatise on painting after returning from a sojourn in north Italy in 1507, seemingly in an attempt to elevate the art on an Italian model. He originally intended the work to consist of three parts, the first of which would address the education of the young artist (including the recommendation that he learn Latin). Although he never completed the treatise in the form originally planned, parts were finished and published as separate texts, including Dürer's *Manual on Measurement* (Nürnberg, 1525) and *Four Books on Human Proportion* (Nürnberg, 1528).

The mid-sixteenth to the early seventeenth century saw a flood of art literature in which practical precepts were mixed with increasingly more abstruse art theory, much of which revolved around the complex idea of *disegno* (drawing, but also design). Worthy of note among this literature are the chapters explaining artistic techniques prefacing Giorgio Vasari's *Le vite de' più eccellenti pittori, scultori, e architettori* (Lives of the most excellent painters, sculptors, and architects; Florence, 1550 and 1568), G. B. Armenini's *De' veri precetti della pittura* (On the true precepts of the art of painting; Ravenna, 1587), and, finally, Federico Zuccaro's *L'idea de' scultori, pittori, e architetti* (The idea of sculptors, painters, and architects; Turin, 1607). If Zuccaro's text is far more theoretical than practical (it is largely devoted to *disegno interno*—the inner design or idea, formed in the artist's mind), it is nonetheless the one book from this list that can be directly tied to artistic education, for the author had presented the material in Rome at one of the institutions that characterize the direction of artistic training in the later Renaissance: the artistic academy.

Informal and Formal Academies.

The term "academy" was first associated with the arts on a series of early sixteenth-century engravings of knot patterns that bear the motto "ACADEMIA LEONARDI VINCI." Although this surely did not refer to any kind of formalized art school, the presence of the term "Academia" on Agostino Veneziano's 1531 engraving of artists drawing statuettes by candlelight in the studio of the Italian sculptor Baccio Bandinelli suggests that in early sixteenth-century workshop usage, "academy" may refer to "after-hours" group drawing sessions. Both Cennini and Leonardo discuss the practice of apprentices drawing in groups, and while Leonardo noted that this had the potential to distract the pupil, he also acknowledged that such company could stimulate a healthy competition between young artists.

A later engraving by Enea Vico after Bandinelli (c. 1550) shows artists drawing by lamplight once again, though the repertoire of studio props now includes skeletons, perhaps suggesting that by mid-century the practice of artistic imitation at these gatherings was being supplemented by anatomical study. The term "academy" was used similarly in Northern Europe: in the anonymous biography appended to the 1618 edition of his *Schilderboek* (Painter's book), the Netherlandish artist and art theorist Karel Van Mander (1548–1606) is said to have formed an academy for drawing after the model with several other artists in Haarlem during the 1580s. Van Mander had visited Florence and Rome in the mid-1570s, and it is likely that he imported this practice from Italy.

In fact by the time van Mander passed through Florence, a formal artistic academy, incorporating but also expanding on some of the practices of the unofficial academies, had been founded by the Tuscan artist and artistic biographer Giorgio Vasari (1511–1574). The Compagnia e Accademia del Disegno (incorporated 1563) developed out of the Company of St. Luke, augmenting the traditional social function of that artists' confraternity with an educational program. (The academy also subsumed many of the functions of the painters' and sculptors' guilds, to which, after 1571, the academic artists were no longer required to belong.) Vasari ensured the support of the Florentine ruler Cosimo I de' Medici from the academy's beginnings, and the Accade-

mia del Disegno became a sort of sister institution to the Accademia Fiorentina—the state-sponsored literary academy promoting the use of the Tuscan language.

If the academy was founded in part as "a university [*sapienza*] and study [*studio*] for youths and their instruction" (as Vasari reported to Michelangelo—one of the honorary heads [*capi*] of the group—in a letter of 1563), this educational mission was to be carried out by various means: the organizational statutes provided (among other things) for the creation of a study collection containing drawings, sculptural models, and architectural plans; practical artistic instruction was to be provided by members; and there were to be annual dissections and anatomy lessons, as well as lectures in mathematics. The degree to which this ideal program was actually carried out in the early years of the academy is a matter of some debate (Barzman, "The Florentine Accademia del Disegno," in *Academies of Art*, pp. 14–32, and Dempsey, pp. 555–557, present a positive picture; Goldstein, pp. 20–22, challenges the seriousness of the educational endeavor). What seems beyond question is that one of the organization's chief aims was to produce artists who were both learned and skilled.

The ideals and instructional program of the Florentine Accademia del Disegno became the model for numerous later institutions. Among its progeny were Perugia's Accademia del Disegno, founded in 1573; Rome's Accademia di San Luca, founded in 1577 (though reorganized in 1593 by Federico Zuccaro, who presented his lectures on the idea there); the private academy organized in Bologna by the Carracci family of artists around 1582; and the Ambrosian Accademia del Disegno, founded in Milan in 1620. In 1648 in Paris, the last chapter in the early modern history of artistic education was begun with the founding of the state-sponsored Académie Royale de Peinture et de Sculpture; various national academies followed in Vienna, Madrid, St. Petersburg, and other European capitals over the next century.

See **Alberti, Leon Battista; Leonardo da Vinci.**

BIBLIOGRAPHY

Primary Works

Alberti, Leon Battista. *On Painting.* Translated by Cecil Grayson. Edited by Martin Kemp. New York, 1991. Translation of *De pictura* (1435).

Cennini, Cennino. *The Craftsman's Handbook: Il libro dell' Arte.* Edited and translated by Daniel V. Thompson Jr. New York, 1960.

Leonardo da Vinci. *Leonardo on Painting.* Edited and translated by Martin Kemp and Margaret Walker. New Haven, Conn.,

1989. Anthology of selections from Leonardo's copious writings on art; his ideas on artistic training are in "Part V: The Painter's Practice."

Secondary Works

Bolland, Andrea. "Art and Humanism in Early Renaissance Padua: Cennini, Vergerio and Petrarch on Imitation." *Renaissance Quarterly* 49 (1996): 469–487.

Boschloo, Anton W. A., et al., eds. *Academies of Art between Renaissance and Romanticism.* Leids Kunsthistorisch Jaarboek 5–6 (1986–1987). Collection of essays that updates and corrects Pevsner's classic study; especially useful for the Renaissance period are Karen-Edis Barzman on the Florentine Accademia del Disegno and Charles Dempsey on the Carracci Academy in Bologna.

Campbell, Lorne. "The Early Netherlandish Painters and Their Workshops." In *Le dessin sous-jacent dans la peinture, colloque III, 6–7–8 Septembre 1979: Le problème Maître de Flémalle–van der Weyden.* Louvain, Belgium, 1981.

Children of Mercury: The Education of the Artist in the Sixteenth and Seventeenth Centuries. Providence, R.I., 1984. Companion volume to an exhibition held at Brown University, with useful essays on workshop training and a comprehensive bibliography.

Dempsey, Charles. "Some Observations on the Education of Artists in Florence and Bologna During the Later Sixteenth Century." *Art Bulletin* 62 (1980): 552–569.

Goldstein, Carl. *Teaching Art: Academies and Schools from Vasari to Albers.* Cambridge, U.K., 1996.

Jack, Mary Ann. "The Accademia del Disegno in Late Renaissance Florence." *Sixteenth Century Journal* 7, no. 2 (1976): 3–20.

Pevsner, Nikolaus. *Academies of Art Past and Present.* Cambridge, U.K., 1940.

Wright, D. R. Edward. "Alberti's *De Pictura*: Its Literary Structure and Purpose." *Journal of the Warburg and Courtauld Institutes* 47 (1984): 52–71. Discusses Alberti's text as a "primer of pictorial representation."

ANDREA BOLLAND

Women Artists

Throughout the fifteenth and sixteenth centuries, European women artists worked in virtually every medium. They carved stone, modeled terra-cotta, illuminated manuscripts, painted on canvas and panel, and cut woodblocks and engraved copper plates for prints. Architecture appears to be the only discipline of the visual arts in which women were not represented, although Teodora Danti of Perugia (1498–1573), the daughter of an architect, was described as a "draftswoman" (*disegnatrice*). Despite critical prejudice concerning the female ability to conceive and execute large-scale works, some women artists produced monumental altarpieces for major churches. Lavinia Fontana's (1552–1614) altarpiece of Saint Stephen's martyrdom for Saint Paul Outside the Walls, Rome (destroyed by fire in 1823), is among the most notable examples. Typically, however, women worked on a smaller and more intimate scale. Illuminators of missals, breviaries, books of hours, and other religious texts far outnumber painters. Sculptors are rarer still; although some modeled clay, only one, Properzia de' Rossi (c. 1491–1530), carved stone. Her work can still be seen in and on the facade of San Petronio, Bologna.

Women artists of the Renaissance fall into three distinct but not unrelated categories: nuns, daughters or wives of artists, and laywomen of the lesser nobility. Artists in the first of these categories were probably the most numerous. Unfortunately, their identities were of less consequence than the objects and images they made to honor God's glory. Consequently, references to "schools" of cloistered sisters or unnamed "disciples" of a named abbess, such as Plautilla Nelli (1523–1588), only hint at what was an industry. Early church histories, art histories, inventories, and signed images suggest that in essence convents were workshops.

Cloistered life necessarily effected how nun artists learned their craft with limited outside instruction. Marguerite (or Grietkin) Scheppers, a professional limner, is documented as gratuitously teaching her art to Sister Cornelie van Wulfskerke, a Carmelite nun of Notre Dame de Sion, in modern Switzerland. Sister Cornelie, in turn, taught and collaborated with Sister Marguerite van Rye in illuminating missals and small books of music. Like Sister Cornelie, Plautilla Nelli presided over "disciples" in the Dominican convent of Saint Catherine of Siena, Florence. Although some of the names of Plautilla's charges are known—Prudenza Cambi, Agata Trabelesi, and Maria Ruggieri—their works are not. Other nun artists, such as Maria Ormani and Andriola de Baracchis, signed and dated their works.

Perhaps because of their more famous fathers, daughters of artists are less obscure. Typically, daughters of artists, like sons and, on occasion, wives, worked in the family workshop after having learned their craft and honed their skills under paternal guidance. Marietta Robusti (c. 1552–1590), Jacopo Tintoretto's daughter; Diana Mantuana (c. 1547–1612), the daughter of Giovanni Battista Mantuana; and Lavinia Fontana, the daughter of Prospero Fontana, are among the better known Italian painters in this group of artists. Robusti's career was terminated by her father as soon as she reached the age of maturity. Mantuana, who learned engraving by copying her father's drawings, used her graphic skills to promote her husband's architectural career. In 1575 she received a papal privilege for the making and marketing of prints. Among other works she issued prints of architectural design and deco-

Woman Artist. Self-portrait by Sofonisba Anguissola.
GALLERIA DEGLI UFFIZI, FLORENCE/ALINARI/ART RESOURCE

rative elements devised by her husband, Francesco da Volterra. Fontana came closest to achieving a professional status equal to that of male artists. Despite criticism stating that Fontana, as a woman, should restrict herself to portraiture, she painted biblical stories and mythological figures.

Women working in northern Europe, specifically Flanders, were accorded greater professional status. Women appear on the membership rolls of artist's guilds, studio records, and legal documents. Elizabeth Scepens is named in 1476 as a student of the illuminator Guillaume Vrelant. Levina Teerlinc (c. 1520–1576) learned her art from her father, and accompanied by her husband she joined England's court. Account books of 1546 identify her as the "King's [Henry VIII] paintrix."

The third category of women artists, members of the lesser nobility, is the smallest. Despite attitudinal shifts to the contrary, sixteenth-century perceptions persisted in seeing artists as artisans and the visual arts as mechanical labors. Members of the nobility were discouraged, and in some cases legally barred, from artistic pursuits. Sofonisba Anguissola (c. 1535–1625) is a striking exception. The eldest of six children (five of whom were girls), Sofonisba was sent to study painting first with Bernardino Campi and then with Bernardino Gatti. Promoted by her father, who solicited and received drawings from Michelangelo so that she could study the master's hand, Sofonisba gained notoriety. In 1561 she became a lady-in-waiting to Queen Isabella of Spain. In addition to producing portraits of the royal family and members of the court, she instructed the queen in the art of painting.

See also Women, *subentry on* Women in the Renaissance.

BIBLIOGRAPHY

Chadwick, Whitney. *Women, Art, and Society.* London and New York, 1990.
Fortunati Pietrantonio, Vera. *Lavinia Fontana of Bologna, 1552–1614.* Milan, 1998.
Gaze, Delia, ed. *Dictionary of Women Artists.* 2 vols. London and Chicago, 1997.
Hamburger, Jeffrey F. *Nuns as Artists: The Visual Culture of a Medieval Convent.* Berkeley, Los Angeles, and London, 1997.
Jacobs, Fredrika H. *Defining the Renaissance Virtuosa: Women Artists and the Language of Art History and Criticism.* Cambridge, U.K., and New York, 1997.
Lincoln, Evelyn. "Making a Good Impression: Diana Mantuana's Printmaking Career." *Renaissance Quarterly* 50 (1997): 1101–1147.

FREDRIKA H. JACOBS

ARTHURIAN LEGENDS IN RENAISSANCE ART. *See* **Chivalry,** *subentries on* **Chivalry in Renaissance Art, Romance of Chivalry,** *and* **English Arthurian Romance.**

ARTILLERY. The exact date of the introduction, or invention, of artillery in Europe is unknown, although it is likely to have occurred in the early years of the fourteenth century. The first evidence for the use of artillery, also known as ordnance, in Europe takes the form of two images found in two illuminated manuscripts written around 1326 by Walter de Milemete, who was chaplain to the English king, Edward III. The illustrations appear among the marginalia in *De secretis secretorum* (British Museum Add. MS. 47680) and *De nobilitatibus, sapientiis, et prudentiis regum* (Christ Church, Oxford MS. 92). Each depicts a large cannon, in the shape of a vase or bottle, with a projectile in the form of a large arrow visible at the muzzle. In each illustration the cannon is being fired by means of a match or wick fixed to the end of a staff, which is held by a mail-clad knight. Documented references to cannon proliferate from the middle of the fourteenth century onward.

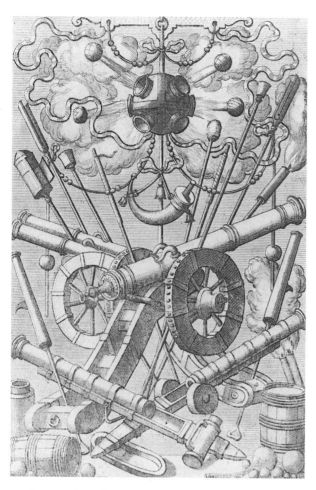

Artillery. Etching from *Panoplia* of Vredeman de Vries (1604–1623). THE METROPOLITAN MUSEUM OF ART, HARRIS BRISBANE DICK FUND, 1924

The majority of cannon were cast in a copper alloy, brass or bronze. Gun founders in the fourteenth century were frequently bell makers, who adapted the techniques established for the casting of large bells to the production of cannon. Wrought-iron cannon were produced by at least as early as the mid-fifteenth century using a hoop and stave construction. The barrel was made of long, flat iron bars, or staves. The staves were held in place by ring-like iron bands—the hoops—which encircled the staves and joined them firmly together. Some cast-iron cannon were made in the fifteenth century, but bronze- and wrought-iron cannon remained the most common materials for artillery throughout the Renaissance.

During the course of the fourteenth and fifteenth centuries, cannon slowly replaced non-gunpowder weapons, such as catapults, trebuchets, and mangonels (siege engines designed to hurl projectiles,

such as large stones, or, in the case of some forms of mangonels, large javelin-like arrows), as the primary heavy projectile weapons in siege warfare. Some siege cannon were very large and immensely powerful. Perhaps the most famous of these is the iron gun (made by the hoop and stave method) known as Mons Meg. Still extant, it measures 404 cm (about 13.5 feet) in length, has an opening of 50 cm (just over 19.5 inches) at the muzzle, weighs 6,040 kg (about 13,300 pounds), and could reputedly fire a stone ball weighing over 150 kg (330 pounds) for a distance of up to two miles. It was made in Mons (in present-day Belgium) in 1449 for Philip the Good, duke of Burgundy, who gave it to his in-law and ally, King James II of Scotland, in 1457. It may have been used militarily, discounting ceremonial firings, as late as 1571, and is still displayed at Edinburgh Castle.

Guns such as Mons Meg represented the greatest firepower known in the world at the time. They were generally intended to be transported by wagon trains to the sites of entrenched sieges and were fired from reinforced earthen platforms. Their purpose was to reduce fortifications to rubble. Because of the efficacy of heavy siege cannon, the traditional medieval castle, both a home and a fortification, was gradually replaced by forts built strictly as military strongholds and designed to both deliver and withstand the maximum amount of artillery fire.

In addition to heavy siege guns, many other types and sizes of cannon were developed, and saw wide use, both on land and at sea. They were known by a great variety of names and were generally classified by weight, length, caliber (the diameter of the muzzle opening), and the size or weight of the shot that a given cannon fired. There was, however, no uniformity in the way the terms were applied. Therefore, guns called by the same name often varied considerably in their proportions and capabilities. The names of some of the more frequently encountered types of artillery, from largest to smallest, included: bombard, basilisk, cannon, demi-cannon, culverin, demi-culverin, saker, minion, falcon, falconet, serpentine, and robinet. Typical weights might range from 8,000 to 200 pounds, length from 12 to 5 feet, caliber from 8.5 to 2.25 inches. The largest guns, bombards, might fire a cannonball weighing over 250 pounds. The majority fired shot (of stone or iron) weighing from 70 pounds to less than one pound. The smaller types were used on ships, as wall guns in fortified positions, and in the field. Field artillery, meaning cannon mounted on wheeled carriages on which they could be fired as well as transported, developed rapidly from the late fifteenth century onward.

The apparatus necessary for firing artillery varied with time and place, but basic equipment generally included a long swab or mop to clean out the barrel and extinguish any hot ashes that could ignite a charge prematurely; a long-handled ladle to place the powder into the barrel; a rammer to pack the powder tightly into the breech of the cannon; and ammunition. In addition, an instrument known as a gunner's quadrant was used to take a sighting of a target in order to determine the proper elevation of the cannon barrel. In Italy gunners also carried a type of dagger known as a gunner's stiletto, the blade of which was marked with a scale for converting the measurement of the caliber of a gun into the proper weight of shot made of stone, iron, or lead. To fire his cannon a gunner was often equipped with a linstock, a long staff on the end of which there were usually two clamps for holding a slow-burning cord known as the match or fuse. The match was placed on the touchhole, also called the vent, which ignited the charge in the breech. Although most artillery in the Renaissance was muzzle loading, breech-loading cannon of various sizes were in regular use from the mid-fifteenth into the sixteenth century.

Sixteenth-century cast-bronze cannon often incorporated sculptural ornament, ranging from architectural moldings to three-dimensional figures. The rulers who commissioned artillery also frequently had their coats of arms, *imprese* (insignia or symbolic devices), mottoes, or other insignia included in the design. Many treatises were devoted to artillery, among the best known of which were Vannuccio Biringucci's *Pirotechnia* (1540) and Niccolò Tartaglia's *Quesiti et inuentioni diuerse* (1546), which was dedicated to Henry VIII, king of England.

See also **Firearms**; **Warfare**.

BIBLIOGRAPHY

Blackmore, Howard L. *The Armouries of the Tower of London: The Ordnance*. London, 1976.

Journal of the Ordnance Society. Ordnance Society, Hampshire, England, 1989 to present.

Kennard, Arthur Norris. *Gunfounding and Gunfounders: A Directory of Cannon Founders from Earliest Times to 1850*. London and New York, 1986.

Smith, Robert D., and Ruth Rhynas Brown. *Bombards: Mons Meg and Her Sisters*. London, 1989.

DONALD J. LAROCCA

ARTISANS. Historians generally use the word "artisan" first when discussing urban developments in Europe in the high Middle Ages. With reinvigoration of long-distance trade during this period, cities became centers of production; the wealth of the merchants encouraged the production of luxury goods such as fine cloth and jewelry, and the growing populations attracted food and clothing producers. These producers recognized the benefits of banding together, and in many parts of Europe the twelfth century witnessed the birth of craft guilds that regulated most aspects of production. A craft guild was an organization of all the producers of one particular item in any town, such as shoemakers or blacksmiths. Each guild set standards of quality for its products and regulated the conduct of its members. The number of assistants, hours of operation, and amount of raw materials available to each master were all limited, thus preventing any one master from dominating the market and assuring every master that his household-workshop would be able to support itself. In most cities individual guilds achieved a monopoly in the production of their product, forbidding nonmembers to work at their trade. In some towns each craft formed its own guild, so that by the thirteenth and fourteenth centuries more than one hundred separate craft guilds had been formed in many cities throughout Europe. In other towns related crafts were combined within larger guilds. The members of these craft guilds are the first workers in Europe who are usually termed "artisans."

Guilds. Each guild set the pattern by which its members were trained. To become a shoemaker, for instance, it was necessary to spend about seven years as an apprentice and then at least that long as a journeyman working in the shop of a master shoemaker. Apprentices or their parents normally paid the master for their training, and they remained with one master the entire period. Journeymen received room and board and sometimes a small wage, and often traveled from master to master gaining skill and experience until ready to make their masterpiece. If the masterpiece was approved by the other master shoemakers, and if they thought the market for shoes large enough in their town to accommodate another shoemaker, the journeyman became a master and opened his own shop. Although the time required to be an apprentice and journeyman varied slightly from craft to craft, all guilds followed this same three-stage process.

Apprentices and journeymen usually lived with the master and his family and were often forbidden to marry. Conversely, most guilds required that masters be married, as they believed a wife was abso-

nities separate from the guild itself for devotional purposes. Guild members marched together in city parades, reinforcing their feelings of solidarity by special ceremonies and distinctive dress. Guild workshops provided an important means of socialization and education for young men and really created an identifiable artisan culture, proud of the traditions of the workshop and often hostile to outsiders. At times these outsiders included women, as formal membership in craft guilds was limited to men. Masters' daughters and wives worked in guild shops alongside the apprentices and journeymen, and a master's widow could generally keep operating a shop, but women could never vote or hold office in craft guilds, except for a few all-female guilds in a handful of European cities. Craft guilds thus reinforced links among men, and, though women worked in many craft shops, the preindustrial artisan was depicted and conceptualized as male.

Changes in the Market. Beginning in the fourteenth century in a few areas of Europe such as Florence and Flanders, and in the sixteenth century in many more, conditions for artisans in Europe began to change, as individuals who had made money in trade and banking invested in production. To make products on a larger scale than guilds would allow they hired many households, with each performing only one step of the process, an organization of labor often termed the "putting-out system" or "proto-industrial capitalism." Where craft guilds were weak, products made through the putting-out system came to dominate the market because they were cheaper; more enterprising or wealthier masters recognized the benefits of the putting-out system and began to hire other households to work for them. This promoted a greater division within the guild between wealthier masters and the poorer masters and journeymen they hired. Some masters became so wealthy that they no longer had to work in a shop themselves, nor did their wives and family members. Instead of being artisans, they became capitalist investors, although they still generally belonged to the craft guild.

While proto-industrial capitalism provided opportunities for some artisans to become investors and entrepreneurs, for many it led to a decrease in income and status. Guilds often responded to competition by limiting membership to existing guild families, which meant that journeymen who were not master's sons or who could not find a master's widow or daughter to marry could never become

Artisans at Work. *Workshop of St. Eligius* by Niklaus Manuel Deutsch (1484–1530). St. Eligius is the patron of goldsmiths. Painted 1515. KUNSTMUSEUM, BERN/FOTO MARBURG/ART RESOURCE

lutely essential to the running of the shop and household. Artisans in medieval cities were thus set off from unskilled laborers and the poor not only by their skill and training, but also by the fact that they were often homeowners and the heads of rather large households. As guilds grew in economic power, they began to demand a share of the political power in their city and came into conflict with the city councils, which were often dominated by merchants. In some cities, the guilds were unsuccessful, and artisans were excluded from political power, while in others they became members of governing bodies.

Craft guilds were not simply economic organizations, but also systems of social support for artisans. They supported elderly masters, widows, and orphans, maintained an altar at a city church, paid for the funerals of their members and the baptisms of their children, and often set up religious confrater-

masters themselves. They remained journeymen their entire lives, losing their sense of solidarity with the masters of their craft and in some cities forming separate journeymen's guilds. These guilds developed elaborate rituals and oaths of initiation and tried to prevent anyone who was not a member of the guild from working in any craft shop, enforcing their aims with boycotts. This worked against women being artisans, for women were very rarely accepted into journeymen's guilds. As their actual status and economic prospects declined, journeymen and poorer masters emphasized skill and honor as the qualities that set them apart from the less skilled workers hired by capitalist investors. They thus continued to regard themselves as artisans, no longer viewing ownership of the means of production as important in achieving this status.

See also Cities and Urban Life; Guilds; Industry.

BIBLIOGRAPHY

Farr, James R. *Hands of Honor: Artisans and Their World in Dijon, 1550–1650.* Ithaca, N.Y., 1988. Discusses economic and ideological factors in artisans' lives in one of France's leading cities.

Leeson, R. A. *Travelling Brothers: The Six Centuries' Road from Craft Fellowship to Trade Unionism.* London, 1979. Explores guilds and other trade organizations in England from the thirteenth to the nineteenth century.

Mackenney, Richard. *Tradesmen and Traders: The World of the Guilds in Venice and Europe, c. 1250–c. 1650.* Totowa, N.J., 1987. Traces developments within artisans' organizations in Venice and compares these with the rest of Europe.

Wiesner, Merry E. "Guilds, Male Bonding, and Women's Work in Early Modern Germany," and "*Wandervögel* and Women: Journeymen's Concepts of Masculinity in Early Modern Germany." In *Gender, Church, and State in Early Modern Germany: Essays by Merry E. Wiesner.* London, 1998. Pages 163–177, 178–196.

MERRY E. WIESNER

ASCHAM, ROGER (1515/1516–1568), English humanist, educator. Born in Yorkshire, Ascham matriculated in 1530 at Cambridge University, where he joined a circle of distinguished humanists devoted to Greek studies and to Ciceronian ideals for the union of "good matter and good utterance." There he came to esteem John Cheke, St. John's College's influential advocate for scriptural religion and classical learning, and from there he launched his notable correspondence with Johann Sturm, Strasbourg's leading Protestant educator.

During his eighteen years at Cambridge, Ascham's enthusiasm for the lifelong pursuit of teaching and learning took deep root, though he also struggled to find patrons to sustain that pursuit. His signal success occurred in 1545, when at the palace in Greenwich he presented his learned, patriotic book on shooting, *Toxophilus* (Lover of the bow), to King Henry VIII. In 1548 the door to royal preferment opened wider when Ascham was called to court to tutor Princess Elizabeth.

Within two years, however, for reasons still unclear, he lost that position, and was forced to "shape [him]self to be a courtier," in "the manner of wayfaring men," as he puts it. Upon her accession Queen Elizabeth continued him as Latin secretary, a treasured post that on occasion allowed him to read Latin and Greek with his former pupil. His *Scholemaster* (slightly incomplete, and published posthumously in 1570), a wide-ranging treatise on "the bringing up of youth" (book 1) and "the ready way to the Latin tongue" (book 2), constitutes the most comprehensive picture we have of mid-Tudor English humanism.

BIBLIOGRAPHY

Primary Works

Ascham, Roger. *Letters of Roger Ascham.* Edited by Maurice Hatch and Alvin Vos. New York, 1989.

Ascham, Roger. *The Whole Works of Roger Ascham.* Edited by J. A. Giles. 3 vols. London, 1864–1865.

Secondary Work

Ryan, Lawrence V. *Roger Ascham.* Stanford, Calif., and London, 1963.

ALVIN VOS

ASIA, EAST. European merchants and missionaries occasionally visited East Asia in the thirteenth and fourteenth centuries. The Ming, who overthrew the Mongol dynasty in 1368, ended this contact with the West. European contact with East Asia did not resume until the early sixteenth century, when Portuguese traders made their way from India to China by way of Malacca, a port city in Malaysia.

Malacca. Ten years after they arrived in India, the Portuguese turned their attention to East Asia. In 1511 a fleet commanded by Diogo Lopes de Siquiera anchored off Malacca and sought permission from the local sultan to engage in trade. Muslim traders, however, saw the arrival of the Portuguese as an intrusion upon their monopoly over trade from the Indian Ocean to the Strait of Malacca and the Indonesian Archipelago. The Muslims of India formed the vanguard of opposition and gained the support of the *bendahara* (a Malay chief justice) for a plan to destroy the Portuguese expedition.

On 20 April 1511, Afonso de Albuquerque sailed from India to Malacca and landed his forces there on

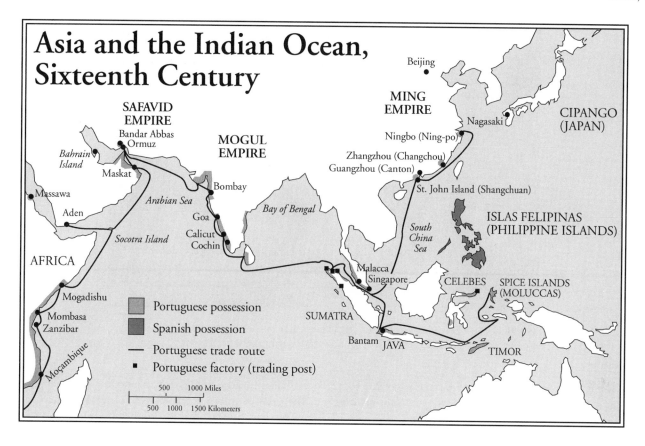

Asia and the Indian Ocean, Sixteenth Century

MING EMPIRE

Beijing

CIPANGO (JAPAN)

SAFAVID EMPIRE

Bandar Abbas
Ormuz

MOGUL EMPIRE

Nagasaki

Bahrain Island

Ningbo (Ning-po)

Maskat

Zhangzhou (Changchou)
Guangzhou (Canton)

Massawa

Arabian Sea

Bombay

St. John Island (Shangchuan)

Aden

Bay of Bengal

South China Sea

ISLAS FELIPINAS (PHILIPPINE ISLANDS)

Socotra Island

Goa
Calicut
Cochin

AFRICA

Mogadishu

Malacca
Singapore

CELEBES

SPICE ISLANDS (MOLUCCAS)

Mombasa
Zanzibar

SUMATRA

Portuguese possession

Spanish possession

Portuguese trade route

Portuguese factory (trading post)

Bantam JAVA

TIMOR

Moçambique

500   1000 Miles

500   1000   1500 Kilometers

---

1 July 1511. A ten-day battle ensued, but in the end Portuguese discipline prevailed and, on 24 August, the sultan fled to Johore, leaving the city's trade to fall under the control of representatives of King Manuel I. Unfair Portuguese trade practices led Asian traders to seek other ports, particularly in northern Sumatra, and the ousted Achinese rulers continued to send their armadas against the Portuguese fortress in Malacca throughout the sixteenth century. The fortress finally fell in 1641 to Dutch-Achinese allied forces and the colony passed to the Dutch East India Trading Company.

China. Portuguese merchant-adventurers made first contact with China between 1512 and 1515, followed in 1517 by a royal squadron carrying Tomé Pires, Portugal's first ambassador to China. Pires established good relations with the Cantonese Chinese, but the arrival of a second squadron led to the arrest of the ambassador and the execution of several members of his company. Pires himself died later of hardship. In 1521 Portuguese ships attempting to renew trade relations were expelled and all dealings with the "barbarian devils" were banned by imperial decree.

For the next thirty years the Portuguese carried on their commerce with China clandestinely. The precarious nature of these contacts and the rapid development of trade with Japan led the Portuguese to seek a firm base on the South China coast within reach of Canton, where the annual fairs were held. In 1554 Captain Major Leonel de Sousa concluded a verbal agreement with the Chinese granting the Portuguese permission to establish a base, which was first located on Saint John's Island, where Francis Xavier had died in 1552. In 1557 they transferred the settlement to Macao, which remained a Portuguese colony until December 1999.

Japan. In 1543 a group of Portuguese traders, blown off course, landed on Tanegashima Island, where they began to engage in trade with the Japanese, initiating a half century of mutual fascination and cross-cultural contact. From the Portuguese, the Japanese quickly learned how to manufacture their own muskets. Within a generation Jesuit missionaries, beginning with Francis Xavier, who arrived in Kagoshima in 1549, converted some 150,000 Japanese. (By contrast, the Jesuits' efforts in China led to just a handful of conversions.) Western decorative

147

Asia Meets Europe. Japanese screen depicting Jesuit missionaries and Portuguese merchants arriving in Cipango (Japan). THE NAMBAN BUNKA KAN, OSAKA

motifs were incorporated into Japanese goods, such as sword hilts, and a few Japanese samurai and Christian converts traveled to Europe. After 1596, however, competition between the Portuguese and Spanish for Japan's lucrative trade (made especially attractive by differing silver-to-gold ratios between China and Japan) and the rise of the new shogun, Ieyasu Tokugawa, led to the souring of East-West relations. In the minds of the rulers of Japan, the Christian faith increasingly began to seem not only subversive of traditional culture and values but also to be linked with potential foreign aggression. In 1637 a rebellion among the mainly Christian inhabitants of the island of Amakusa led to the expulsion of all Japanese Christians from Japan, followed in 1639 by the expulsion of the remaining few Portuguese. An exception was made for the Dutch, who nonetheless were limited to trading from one designated port on the island of Deshima.

The Spice Islands and the Philippines.
The spice trade was far too profitable for other western powers to allow the Portuguese a complete monopoly. First the Spanish, and later the Dutch and English, were drawn to the Spice Islands or Moluccas. Thanks to the Treaty of Tordesillas (1494), the division of the world between the Portuguese and Spanish along 48° west longitude and 134° east longitude meant that the Spanish had a sliver of a claim to the Molucca Islands in the western Pacific. Ferdinand Magellan, who had participated in the Por-

tuguese capture of Malacca, proposed to the Spanish the establishment of contact with the Moluccas by a westward route through the Pacific. Despite great hardship, and the death of Magellan himself on a beach on Mactan (the Philippines) in April 1521, the Spanish expedition successfully arrived in the Moluccas in November 1521, and one ship returned to Spain in September 1522. In 1529 Charles V sold his claims to the Moluccas to the Portuguese for 350,000 gold dobras, but in 1565 the Spanish returned to the Far East to claim the Philippines and Fermosa (Taiwan). Establishing their capital in Manila and fortresses on Fermosa, the Spanish attempted to break the Portuguese monopoly over the Japanese trade, with the disastrous results noted above, and maintained a regular trade route between Manila and Alcapulco (Mexico). From there, goods were transhipped to Spain, although much of the silk and mother-of-pearl remained in the Philippines.

By the close of the Renaissance period, European contact with East Asia had yielded uneven results. In Malaysia, Indonesia, and the Philippines, the Portuguese and Spanish were able to maintain small entrepots in a culturally diverse, politically chaotic, and often hostile environment. Portuguese and Spanish attempts to establish full relations with China and Japan, however, ultimately met with failure, although Europeans' geographic and cultural knowledge of these civilizations was far advanced thanks to accounts published by various travelers and missionaries.

See also Exploration, *and biographies of Afonso de Albuquerque, Francis Xavier, and Ferdinand Magellan.*

BIBLIOGRAPHY

Primary Works

Boxer, Charles R., ed. *South China in the Sixteenth Century: Being the Narratives of Galeote Pereira, Fr. Gaspar da Cruz, O.P., Fr. Martín de Rada, O.E.S.A. (1550–1575).* London, 1953.

Cooper, Michael, S. J., ed. *They Came to Japan: An Anthology of European Reports on Japan, 1543–1640.* London and Berkeley, Calif., 1965.

Earle, T. F., and John Villiers, eds. and trans. *Albuquerque: Caesar of the East, Selected Texts.* Warminster, U.K., 1990.

Galvão, António. *A Treatise on the Moluccas (c. 1544).* Edited by Hubert T. T. M. Jacobs. Rome and St. Louis, Mo., 1971.

González de Mendoza, Juan. *The History of the Great and Mighty Kingdom of China and the Situation Thereof.* Translated by R. Parke. Edited by George T. Staunton. 2 vols. New York, 1970.

Morga, Antonio de. *The Philippine Islands, Moluccas, Siam, Cambodia, Japan, and China, at the Close of the Sixteenth Century.* Translated by Henry E. J. Stanley. New York, 1970.

Pinto, Fernã Mendes. *The Travels of Mendes Pinto.* Edited and translated by Rebecca S. Catz. Chicago, 1989.

Pires, Tomé. *The Suma Oriental of Tomé Pires . . . and the Book of Francisco Rodrigues.* Translated and edited by Armando Cortesão. 2 vols. London, 1944.

Secondary Works

Boxer, Charles R. *Portuguese Merchants and Missionaries in Feudal Japan, 1543–1640.* London, 1986.

Moran, J. F. *The Japanese and the Jesuits: Alessandro Valignano in Sixteenth-Century Japan.* London and New York, 1993.

Ross, Andrew. *A Vision Betrayed: The Jesuits in Japan and China, 1542–1742.* Edinburgh, 1994.

Subrahmanyam, Sanjay. *The Portuguese Empire in Asia, 1500–1700: A Political and Economic History.* New York, 1993.

REBECCA S. CATZ

ASTROLOGY. *See* Magic and Astrology.

ASTRONOMY.
Astronomy in the Renaissance must first be distinguished from cosmology and astrology, although the three were intimately linked from antiquity. Astronomy is the study of the number, size, and motions of the celestial bodies. Astrology is the "science" of the influences of the heavenly bodies on earthly matters, including, for some, the lives and fortunes of men. Finally, cosmology is a study of the nature of the universe as an ordered structure and is closely allied with philosophy and theology. Some of the most famous ideas associated with Renaissance views of the universe, such as infinity and the plurality of worlds, were developed not by astronomers but by philosophers and theologians and were then incorporated into astronomy.

The Revival of the Greek Ptolemy and the Vienna School.
In line with the classicism of the Renaissance, scholars attempted to return to the pure font of Ptolemaic astronomy by translating Ptolemy's great work, *Almagest,* directly from the Greek and issuing commentaries and other texts based upon it. Involved in this movement were the two most famous fifteenth-century astronomers, Georg Peurbach (1423–1461) and Johann Müller, known as Regiomontanus (1436–1476).

Peurbach taught classics and astronomy at the University of Vienna; Regiomontanus was his favorite pupil and later his colleague. In 1460 the Greek-born Cardinal Bessarion came to Vienna and persuaded Peurbach to write a new summary of *Almagest,* which had been translated from the Greek by George of Trebizond in 1451. Peurbach, who knew no Greek, relied on the medieval translation from the Arabic. He died before completing the work. Regiomontanus finished it around 1463, although it was not printed until 1496. This *Epitome in Almagestum Ptalemaei* (Epitome of the Almagest) remained the best commentary on Ptolemy into modern times.

Peurbach's most important work was his *Theoricae novae planetarum* (New theory of the planets), a new version of the medieval text. He completed the work in 1454, but it was first printed by Regiomontanus in 1474, and it went through numerous editions. Peurbach also completed *Tabulae eclipsium* (Tables of eclipses) in the 1450s, although the first printed edition did not appear until 1514.

Regiomontanus, who did know Greek, traveled to Rome, Padua, Hungary, and finally Nürnberg. He established himself there as an astronomer and printer of astronomical texts. During his lifetime, Regiomontanus brought out Peurbach's *Theoricae novae* and produced his own *Tabulae directionum* (Tables of directions; 1467; first printed in 1490) and his planetary *Ephemerides* (Almanac; 1474) for 1475–1506, works crucial not only for astronomy but also for astrology. He died in Rome in 1476, and Bernhard Walther continued Regiomontanus's regular plan of systematic observations for 1475–1504. Walther's observations were published in 1544, but already some had been used by the great Copernicus.

Nicolaus Copernicus and the Copernican Revolution.
Nicolaus Copernicus (1473–1543), the Polish cathedral canon, was the greatest astronomer of the first half of the sixteenth century and initiated a revolution in astronomy. Combining a study of classical, medieval, and Renaissance astro-

ASTRONOMY

nomical works with the practice of systematic observation, Copernicus set out to produce a new vision of the universe along the lines set by the Greek
astronomers. Copernicus first announced his ideas
in the *Commentariolus* (Little commentary), circulated in manuscript form in the early sixteenth century, and fully developed them in his masterpiece,
De revolutionibus orbium coelestium (On the revolutions of the heavenly spheres; 1543). The first
printed announcement of the new Copernican system appeared in the *Narratio prima* (First report;
1540, 1541) of Copernicus's only student, the Lutheran astronomer and astrologer Georg Joachim
Rheticus (1514–1574).

Copernicus was the first astronomer since antiquity to argue for a heliocentric universe in which a
moving Earth was one of the planets circling the central sun. Copernicus believed that this tremendous
innovation was a physical fact, not only a calculating
device.

Copernicus's work was divided into six books, organized on the model of Ptolemy's *Almagest*. Copernicus tackled the astronomical problems handled
by Ptolemy, with some important changes. In the
first book, the most general and cosmological of the
six, he outlined the features of the new heliocentric,
geokinetic universe with the sun at the center and
Earth in motion. He asserted the physical reality of
the new universe, in which the sun was the center
and Earth had two main motions, one the annual
revolution around the sun and the second a daily
rotation on its axis. He thus made Earth a planet.
Motivated by his belief in the physical truth of his
system, Copernicus tried to refute some of the traditional arguments against the motion of Earth.

For example, he asserted that it made more sense
for the small Earth to move diurnally on its axis than
to postulate that the entire heavens rotated once a
day on their axis. He also attempted to refute the
arguments that bodies at or near Earth's surface
would not be able to keep up with Earth as it hurtled
through the heavens while rotating on its axis. He
contended too that it was more fitting for the sun,
which gives light and heat to the world, to be in the
center of the cosmos.

The remainder of Copernicus's masterwork was a
highly technical mathematical treatment of all the
problems concerning heavenly motions based on
the principles of Greek astronomy. Using a point
near the sun as the mathematical center of the heavenly orbits, Copernicus utilized the devices of eccen-
trics, deferent circles, and epicycles to explain planetary and lunar motions. However, Copernicus

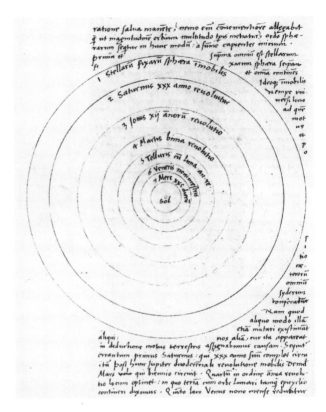

Astronomical Revolution. Drawing of the Copernican
model of the solar system showing the sun at the center
and the planets (among them Telluris, Earth) revolving in
orbit around it. The outermost circle is the sphere of fixed
stars. HULTON GETTY/LIAISON

rejected the equant point invented by Ptolemy. This
point, which was neither the physical center of an
orbit nor the mathematical center of that orbit, was
used to measure the speed of an orbiting body so
that it would remain uniform. Copernicus considered the equant a violation of the Greek rule that all
heavenly motions had to be understood in terms of
uniform circular motions, and he tried to create a
new astronomy without it. In this sense, he was even
more wedded to the principles of Greek astronomy
than the great Ptolemy.

**Astronomy in the Second Half of the Six-
teenth Century.** Most of the professional astronomers during the second half of the sixteenth
century held Copernicus in high regard, but nevertheless rejected the novel aspects of his system. Erasmus Reinhold (1511–1553) issued the *Prutenic Tables* (1551), based on Copernican calculations, to
replace the old *Alfonsine Tables* (astronomical tables
named after King Alfonso of Castile in the thirteenth
century) but did not accept heliocentrism. This move

to greater accuracy in terms of charting planetary and stellar positions and motions, while rejecting Copernicanism, can also be seen in the works of Christopher Clavius (1537–1612) and Tycho Brahe (1546–1601).

Clavius, a member of the scientifically learned Society of Jesus, was the leading Catholic astronomer in the later sixteenth century and was involved in the papally sponsored Gregorian reform of the calendar (1582). In his editions of the medieval *Sphere of Sacrobosco,* Clavius spoke respectfully of Copernicus and utilized his observations and calculations. Nevertheless, he could not accept Copernicanism because of his devotion to Aristotelian physics and the Bible.

Brahe was the greatest pre-telescope astronomer in the history of Western civilization. Danish by birth, he had many distinguished patrons, notably Frederick II of Denmark and the Holy Roman Emperor Rudolf II. Given the island of Ven (or Hven) by Frederick II in 1576, Brahe set up a scientific research institute with major observatories such as Uraniborg (Castle of the heavens) and Stjerneborg (Castle of the stars). He had built the largest and most finely calibrated astronomical instruments ever designed. His observational skills led Brahe to make a number of important astronomical discoveries.

In 1572 a new star appeared, and in 1573 Brahe issued a work demonstrating that this star "above" the moon was more distant. He argued that this proved false the Aristotelian principle of the immutability of the heavens. In 1577 a comet appeared in the heavens, and he issued a German work proving that it also was farther away than the moon. Brahe again took up this topic in his Latin *De mundi aetherei recentioribus phaenomenis* (Concerning recent phenomena of the ethereal world; 1588). His work about the comet demonstrated again that heavenly immutability was untenable, and his analysis of the path of the comet disproved the idea of hard celestial spheres. Brahe's work of 1588 was also important because in it he first announced his own cosmological system, followed by a more detailed treatment in *Astronomiae instauratae progymnasmata* (Preliminary exercises for the restoration of astronomy; 1602).

Brahe's system has come to be known as the geoheliocentric system because he argued that all the planets orbited the sun, and it orbited a stationary central Earth. Adopting this system, Brahe intended to take advantage of the accomplishments of Copernicus without violating some of the basics of Aristotelian physics or certain biblical passages that seemed to uphold an immobile Earth and a mobile sun. The geoheliocentric system was popular in the seventeenth century, especially among Jesuit astronomers, and was the major rival to Copernicanism.

Copernicanism Reformed: Kepler and Galileo. Johannes Kepler (1571–1630) and Galileo Galilei (1564–1642) were the two greatest astronomers of the first half of the seventeenth century. Both transformed the Copernican system.

Educated at the University of Tübingen and trained by the astronomer Michael Mästlin, Kepler became an assistant of Brahe in Prague and inherited his documentation concerning planetary and stellar observations. Kepler brought out the *Tabulae rudolphinae* (Rudolfine tables; 1627) to honor their mutual patron, Emperor Rudolf II, and to honor his own deceased teacher Brahe. Kepler, however, had been since early adulthood a devout Copernican. Convinced of the truth of this system Kepler wrestled with the task of uncovering both the mathematical patterns used by God to frame the universe and the physical causes of planetary motions. His concern with physical causation may qualify him for the title of the first modern astronomer.

Through numerous works, beginning with his earliest, *Mysterium cosmographicum* (The cosmographic mystery; 1596), and including his masterpieces, *Astronomia nova* (New astronomy; 1609), *Harmonices mundi* (Harmonics of the universe; 1619), and *Epitome astronomiae copernicanae* (Epitome of Copernican astronomy; 1618–1621), Kepler worked out a dual program. He announced to the world the three laws of planetary motion. The first is that the planets move in elliptical orbits around the sun, which is at one focus of the ellipse; the second that the radius vector from the sun to a planet sweeps out equal areas in equal times; and the third that the squares of the times of revolution of any two planets around the sun are proportional to the cubes of their mean distances from the sun.

This mathematical brillance was matched by daring physical speculations. Influenced by William Gilbert's work on magnetism, Kepler argued for a solar force that moved the planets and that Earth radiated an offshoot of this force to move the moon. Kepler also profoundly modified the common notion of gravity as heaviness by asserting in *Astronomia nova* that gravity was really the mutual attraction between kindred bodies. Indeed, in his posthumously published *Somnium* (Dream; 1634), Kepler went beyond this redefinition of gravity to characterize it as a force of mutual attraction among all bodies in the universe.

Kepler's mathematical genius and physical speculations were matched by Galileo's excellence as an observational astronomer. As a young man, Galileo attended the University of Pisa, becoming a mathematics professor there and later at the University of Padua. His early astronomical discoveries would lead to his appointment as court mathematician to the grand duke of Tuscany.

While at Padua, Galileo heard of the invention of a telescope in the Netherlands and created his own, which he trained on the heavens. What Galileo discovered and what he did with his discoveries began to remake astronomy. In his first astronomical treatise, *Sidereus nuncius* (The starry messenger or message; 1610), Galileo announced that he had discovered lunar mountains and valleys, four moons of Jupiter, and the true nature of the Milky Way as a myriad of previously unobserved pointed stars. He used the mountains and valleys on the moon to assault the Aristotelian doctrine of the perfection of the heavens and to assert the homogeneity of the universe. He also used the newly discovered nature of the Milky Way to attack the idea that the Aristotelian picture of the universe was correct. Finally, Galileo used the moons of Jupiter not only to enlarge the storehouse of astronomical knowledge but also to bolster the Copernican cause by arguing that they showed that Earth was not the only body moving through space carrying a moon with it. In either the Ptolemaic or the Copernican system, Jupiter would have to be moving around a central body while carrying four moons.

Quickly following these discoveries Galileo reported on the rings of Saturn, the phases of Venus, and, in his *Istoria e dimonstrazioni intorno alle macchie solari* (Letters on sunspots; 1613), sunspots and the axial rotation of the sun. The phases of Venus were crucial because they could not be explained in either the Aristotelian or Ptolemaic geocentric systems. They did fit with the Copernican heliocentric system, and Galileo used them as proof of that system. However, they would also fit with the system of Brahe, an issue that Galileo never fully confronted. He used sunspots and the axial rotation of the sun to argue once again against the perfection of the heavens and also as proof that Earth was not the only body that had an axial rotation. These arguments, along with physical evidence countering objections to a moving Earth, reappeared in Galileo's astronomical tour de force, *Dialogo sopra i due massimi sistemi del mondo* (Dialogue concerning the two chief world systems; 1632). The publication of this work caused Galileo's famous trial in Rome in 1633 for violating an order supposedly given him in 1616 not to hold, teach, or defend the Copernican system. He was sentenced to house arrest for life, and the *Dialogo* was placed on the Roman Index of Prohibited Books.

Infinity and the Plurality of Worlds: Cusanus and Bruno. The two most famous Renaissance exponents of the infinite universe and the plurality of worlds were theologians, not astronomers: Cardinal Nicholas Cusanus (1401–1464) and Giordano Bruno (1548–1600), a former Dominican burned at the stake in Rome. Cusanus argued for a universe that was boundless, had no single center, and contained a multiplicity of inhabited worlds. Bruno took up similar ideas and grafted them onto his own particular version of Copernicanism. He asserted the infinity of the universe and the plurality of inhabited heavenly bodies. In a prescient manner, Bruno also was the first to pronounce that the sun was a star and the stars were suns.

By the end of the seventeenth century, the idea of an infinite universe with a plurality of earths and solar systems merged with the accomplishments of Renaissance astronomers to help produce the Newtonian picture of the cosmos.

See also biographies of figures mentioned in this entry.

BIBLIOGRAPHY

Primary Works

Copernicus, Nicholas. *On the Revolutions.* Edited by J. Dobrzycki and translated by Edward Rosen. Baltimore, 1992. Translation of and commentary on the Latin *De revolutionibus orbium coelestium.*

Galilei, Galileo. *Dialogue Concerning the Two Chief World Systems.* Translated by Stillman Drake. 2d ed. Berkeley, Calif., 1967. Translation of the Italian *Dialogo . . . sopra i due massimi sistemi del mondo.*

Galilei, Galileo. *Discoveries and Opinions of Galileo.* Translated by Stillman Drake. Garden City, N.Y., 1957. Contains, among other works, translations of the Latin *Sidereus nuncius* (Starry messenger) and the Italian *Istoria e dimonstrazioni intorno alle macchie solari e loro accidenti* (Letters on sunspots).

Kepler, Johannes. *New Astronomy.* Translated by William H. Donahue. Cambridge, U.K., and New York, 1992. Translation of the Latin *Astronomia nova.*

Kepler, Johannes. *The Secret of the Universe.* Translated by A. M. Duncan, with commentary by E. J. Aiton. New York, 1981. Translation of the Latin *Mysterium cosmographicum.*

Kepler, Johannes. *Somnium, The Dream.* Translated by Edward Rosen. Madison, Wis., 1967. Translation of the Latin *Somnium.*

Rosen, Edward, ed. and trans., *Three Copernican Treatises.* New York, 1971. Translations of the Latin *Commentariolus* (Little commentary) and the *Narratio Prima* (First report).

Secondary Works

Dick, Steven. *Plurality of Worlds.* Cambridge, U.K., and New York, 1984.

Drake, Stillman. *Galileo at Work.* Chicago, 1978.

North, John. *The Fontana History of Astronomy and Cosmology.* London, 1994.

Rosen, Edward. *Copernicus and His Successors.* London, 1995.

Rosen, Edward. *Copernicus and the Scientific Revolution.* Malabar, Fla., 1984.

IRVING A. KELTER

ASYLUMS.   *See* **Hospitals and Asylums.**

AUBIGNÉ, THÉODORE-AGRIPPA D'   (1552–1630), French poet and historian. The son of a committed Protestant, Théodore-Agrippa d'Aubigné was brought up to fight for what he believed in. As an eight-year-old boy, he was asked by his father to take an oath to avenge the Protestants hung in front of the castle of Amboise after they were found guilty of treason. He was as courageous a warrior with the sword as with the pen; he took an active part in the Wars of Religion and the Protestant-Catholic skirmishes under Henry IV and during the regency of the young Louis XIII.

As evidenced by the remarkable diversity of his works, d'Aubigné was a man of many talents. These include poetry, a history, and a novel, as well as political treatises, pamphlets, and meditations on the Psalms. An avid correspondent, he also wrote letters on a variety of subjects, from the education of women to military science to witchcraft and the occult. His first poetical work, *Le printemps* (Spring), composed in 1570 but published only in 1874, is dedicated to his youthful love, Diane Salviati, niece of Pierre de Ronsard's Cassandra. Today, d'Aubigné is best known for his epic, *Les tragiques.* This 9,302-line poem (with a preface of 414 lines) was written between 1577 and 1600 and first published in 1616 under d'Aubigné's pen name, L. B. D. D. (Le Bouc du Désert; The goat of the desert). Composed as a defense of the Huguenot cause, it narrates, in an epic mode and from a divine perspective, the memorable deeds of the faithful and appeals to the reader's emotions. *Les tragiques* has received much critical attention for its style, viewed as highly representative of the baroque style, and rhetorical devices, such as antithesis, enumeration, repetition, wordplay, personification, allegory, and symbolism.

The grandiosely titled *Histoire universelle* (1618), d'Aubigné's chief prose work, aims at a more objective account of Calvinist history. In 1620 the work was condemned to be burned at the Sorbonne and both the author and his printer (Jean Moussat) were summoned to defend themselves at the Châtelet. Shortly thereafter, d'Aubigné wrote, as a companion to the *Histoire universelle, Sa vie à ses enfants* (His life to his children), a story of his life intended for his surviving children. His novel, *Les avantures du baron de Faeneste* (The adventures of the baron Faeneste), dealing with the confrontation after Condé's disgrace in September 1616 between the Rochelois and the duke of Épernon, was published in several installments between 1617 and 1630. Echoing contemporary pamphlets, the main themes of the satire, introduced under the opposition of "paraître" (to appear) and "être" (to be), concern the customs of the court: its materialism, false sense of honor, and attitudes toward war, women, magic, and religion.

The author's talent for observation has not gone unnoticed. Critics have also commented on the truthful portrayal of character; the extensive use d'Aubigné makes of dialogue (especially in the first two books), a technique that gives the novel its dynamism and its dramatic quality; and various humorous devices (caricature, parody, the use of puns and patois, *fantaisie verbale,* dissonance) reminiscent of Rabelais. D'Aubigné is also the author of several pamphlets. The *Confession catholique du sieur de Sancy* (The Catholic confession of the lord of Sancy), first published in 1660 and republished several times during the seventeenth and eighteenth centuries, is a parody of a confession of a convert to Roman Catholicism. *Le caducée* (The caduceus) was composed in the aftermath of the assembly of the Reformed church held at Saumur from 27 May to 12 September 1611, in an attempt to reconcile the factions that emerged during that meeting. Its interest lies in d'Aubigné's skillful use of dialogue as well as his colorful humor and mordant irony.

BIBLIOGRAPHY

Primary Works

Aubigné, Agrippa d'. *Histoire universelle.* Edited by Alphonse de Ruble. 10 vols. Paris, 1886–1909.

Aubigné, Agrippa d'. *Histoire universelle.* Edited by André Thierry. 6 vols. Geneva, 1981.

Aubigné, Agrippa d'. *Oeuvres.* Edited by Henri Weber, Jacques Bailbé, and Marguerite Soulié. Paris, 1969.

Aubigné, Agrippa d'. *Oeuvres complètes de Théodore Agrippa d'Aubigné.* Edited by E. Réaume and F. de Caussade. 6 vols. Paris, 1873–1892.

Aubigné, Agrippa d'. *Sa vie à ses enfants.* Edited by Gilbert Schrenck. Paris, 1986.

Secondary Works

Buffum, Imbrie. *Agrippa d'Aubigné's* Les tragiques: *A Study of the Baroque Style in Poetry.* New Haven, Conn., 1951.

Duval, Edwin. "The Place of the Present: Ronsard, d'Aubigné, and the 'Misères du temps'." *Yale French Studies* 80 (1991): 13–29.

Randall Coats, Catharine. *Subverting the System: D'Aubigné and Calvinism*. Kirksville, Mo., 1990.

Regosin, Richard. *The Poetry of Inspiration: Agrippa d'Aubigné's Les Tragiques*. Chapel Hill, N.C., 1970.

COLETTE H. WINN

AUGSBURG. One of the most important cities of early modern Germany, Augsburg was a flourishing cultural center from the fifteenth to seventeenth centuries. Renaissance influences passed swiftly along the trade route from Italy to Augsburg, but the development of painting, sculpture, architecture, and scholarship there demonstrated a blending of Italian inspiration with local needs and other styles.

Historical Background. Augsburg was one of the most populous cities in the region, with a population of around thirty thousand in 1520. By 1618 this had risen to over forty thousand, but it declined during the Thirty Years' War to no more than seventeen thousand in the 1630s. From 1450 to 1650, the prosperity of the city stimulated patronage of the arts and the construction of new buildings. This wealth was based on textile production and on investment by merchants in banking and mining. The most important merchants were the Fuggers, Welsers, and Höchstetters. Jakob Fugger (1459–1525) amassed a fortune based on loans to the Habsburgs, which were secured against mining and trading privileges. By the late sixteenth century, several banking firms suffered decline, but the textile and craft industries continued to flourish.

Support for the Reformation grew rapidly after 1518, and by the 1520s Zwinglian teachings had become popular. The council was wary of religious reform but did not obstruct the introduction of changes. In 1537 the city officially adopted Zwinglianism.

An armed confrontation (Schmalkald War, 1546–1547) with the Catholic League brought a setback, however. In 1548 Charles V (1500–1558) reformed the civic constitution in retaliation for Augsburg's support of the Protestant Reformation. Guilds were abolished and political power was vested in the patriciate. Catholicism was restored, but after the Peace of Augsburg (1555) both Lutheranism and Catholicism were officially tolerated. The restoration of Catholic worship stimulated the demand for religious art to replace items lost during the Reformation.

Humanism. Humanist ideals were influential beginning in the 1450s, when the first humanist

Fugger Chapel, Augsburg. Design by Sebastian Loscher for the Fugger family chapel in the church of St. Anna; 1509–1510. STÄDTISCHE KUNSTSAMMLUNGEN AUGSBURG

group was formed. Humanist studies were stimulated by the civic secretary Conrad Peutinger (1465–1547), who accumulated a large library and a collection of classical artifacts and who corresponded with many prominent humanists. Peutinger used humanist scholarship in the service of the city, for example, in his defense of monopoly trading, presented to the Diet of Nürnberg in 1524. There was no university, but in 1531 the council established a Protestant school, the Gymnasium bei St. Anna, which gained a strong reputation, especially under Sixtus Birck (rector, 1536–1554). In 1582 the Jesuit College of St. Salvator was established; it became a focal point of the Counter-Reformation in Augsburg. The council created a civic library in 1531 founded on the contents of former monastic libraries. In 1546 a special building was constructed for the collection.

Patrons of Art and Learning. Artists and scholars benefited from the patronage of Maximilian who, for example, commissioned illustrations for his epic story *Theuerdank* from Hans Burgkmair and Jörg Preu, and had the work printed by Hans Schönsperger. Maximilian contributed to the rebuilding of churches and commissioned monuments to himself in Saint Ulrich and the Dominican church. The most important patrons in Augsburg were the Fuggers, whose most significant commission was the funerary chapel in the Carmelite church of Saint Anna. Built at an estimated cost of 23,000 *florins,* and consecrated in 1518, this was the first structure in Germany designed, constructed, and decorated in the style of the Renaissance. Built on a massive scale, it involved extending the nave to accommodate the choir stalls and the organ. It contains carved marble reliefs from a design by Albrecht Dürer (1471–1528). Its main feature is the sculpture over the altar, depicting the Lamentation, which consists of three free-standing figures supporting the corpse of Christ. These figures show both Italian and German influences and represent an important transitional phase in which the impact of the Renaissance on German sculpture is evident.

Other patrons included Markus Welser (1558–1614) who, among other things, financed a press in order to publish works in Greek and Latin. In the early seventeenth century, the patrician Philipp Hainhofer (1578–1647), a famous connoisseur and collector, also acted as an agent, procuring items for rulers and other collectors. The town council was an important institutional patron, and its most significant commission was for three baroque fountains: the Augustusbrunnen, sculpted in 1594 by Hubert Gerhard, and the Merkurbrunnen (Mercury fountain) and the Herkulesbrunnen (Hercules fountain), which were sculpted by Adriaen de Vries between 1599 and 1602.

Artists and Craftsmen. Augsburg supported many artists and sculptors. In 1529, for example, there were 34 masters in the painters' guild. The most important local artists were Hans Burgkmair the Elder (1473–1531), Hans Holbein the Elder (c. 1460–1524), Jörg Preu the Elder (1475–1537), and Christoph Amberger (c. 1500–1562). The most important sculptors were Gregor Erhart (c. 1470–1540), Adolf Daucher (c. 1460–c. 1523), and Hans Daucher. Augsburg produced an outstanding architect, Elias Holl (1573–1646), who was responsible for designing and building many important civic buildings in the early seventeenth century. These in-

cluded civic fortifications, the arsenal, the Perlach tower, the slaughterhouse, and the massive, imposing town hall, completed in 1624 at a cost of 85,000 to 100,000 *gulden*. This building shows a conscious use of Renaissance forms within a distinct local idiom, as seen in the prominent gable and the twin domed towers. The result is a striking statement of civic identity, at once cosmopolitan, yet strongly individual. Artistic creativity was apparent in the work of local craftsmen. Augsburg was the most important center for gold working in Germany, and in 1615 there were 185 master goldsmiths. Production of luxury items grew in the seventeenth century and created work for cabinetmakers, jewel cutters, and clock makers.

Many Renaissance buildings and works of art have survived, including the Augustusbrunnen, Merkurbrunnen, and Herkulesbrunnen, the Fugger chapel in Saint Anna, the town hall, and many other buildings by Holl. Although much damage was suffered in World War II, extensive restoration has been carried out. Paintings by Hans Holbein the Elder can be seen in the cathedral, and paintings by Cranach are in Saint Anna. Work by local artists and craftsmen can be found in the collection housed in the Schaezlerpalais and the Maximilian Museum.

See also **Fugger Family; Germany, Art in.**

BIBLIOGRAPHY

Baxandall, Michael. *The Limewood Sculptors of Renaissance Germany, 1475–1525.* New Haven, Conn., and London, 1980. Authoritative study on sculpture, especially useful for the debate concerning the construction of the Fugger funerary chapel in Saint Anna.

Gottlieb, Günther, et al., eds. *Geschichte der Stadt Augsburg von der Römerzeit bis zur Gegenwart.* Stuttgart, Germany, 1984. Includes several useful articles on Renaissance Augsburg.

Roeck, Bernd. *Eine Stadt in Krieg und Frieden: Studien zur Geschichte der Reichsstadt Augsburg zwischen Kalenderstreit und Parität.* 2 vols. Göttingen, Germany, 1989.

Roeck, Bernd. *Elias Holl: Architekt eine europäischen Stadt.* Regensburg, Germany, 1985. Valuable account of the work and significance of Holl.

P. J. BROADHEAD

AUGUSTINE OF HIPPO (354–430), church father, bishop of Hippo (396–430). Born at Thagaste in North Africa, Augustine taught rhetoric in Rome and Milan. While in Italy, he gave up Manicheanism for Neoplatonism and then converted to Christianity. After returning home, he became bishop of Hippo on the North African coast. His religious writings made him an enormously influential Latin church father from his own day forward.

During the Renaissance Italian humanists embarked on the recovery of the patristic heritage, finding, editing, and translating texts of the Greek and Latin church fathers unknown or little studied in the Latin Middle Ages. By 1650, the humanists had made available most of the patristic texts we know today. But St. Augustine hardly needed to be discovered. His encyclopedic *City of God* as well as his theological and philosophical writings had found a large audience in the Middle Ages. Nonetheless, the first great Renaissance humanist, Petrarch (Francesco Petrarca; 1304–1374), discovered a "new" Augustine.

When twenty years old, Petrarch purchased the *City of God* and by the next year spoke of the church father as "our Augustine." Eventually Petrarch possessed a great range of Augustinian works, but the decisive text was Augustine's *Confessions*. In his "Letters of Old Age" (*Seniles* 8:6), Petrarch wrote, "that book so changed me . . . that from then on I did not scorn or hate sacred letters." Petrarch's enthusiasm marked the start of the growing popularity of the *Confessions* in the Renaissance. Petrarch loved Augustine's psychological introspection. In his own profoundly personal dialogue, *Secretum meum* (My secret), Petrarch portrayed the chief interlocutor, Augustine, as a voluntarist, urging an act of will to cure Petrarch's attachment to the things of this world. Grace and original sin play no significant role in the dialogue. Petrarch promoted Augustine the psychologist and ignored Augustine the metaphysician and theologian.

Petrarch's selective Augustinianism was not peculiar. Most of the 187 editions of Augustine available before the year 1501 offered pseudonymous works. Augustine was the most printed patristic author of the early Renaissance, but the printed Augustine was not always the historical Augustine; at times he was the Augustine posterity created to serve its own interests.

After Petrarch, the humanist most devoted to Augustine was the papal bureaucrat Maffeo Vegio (1407–1458). Vegio underwent a conversion upon reading the *Confessions*. He frequently cited Augustine in his influential *De educatione liberorum* (On the education of children) and wrote an office for the feasts of St. Augustine and St. Monica, Augustine's mother, to whom Vegio was especially devoted. However, Augustine exercised little influence on Italian humanist thought as a whole. There was no Italian humanist "Augustinianism." Indeed, Lorenzo Valla (1407–1457), the most original thinker of the fifteenth-century humanists, sharply criticized Augustine concerning the Trinity, the interpretation of scripture, original sin, moral philosophy, and for believing in the pseudonymous correspondence between St. Paul and Seneca.

The philosopher Marsilio Ficino (1433–1499) esteemed Augustine and derived from him key doctrines such as the desire for God as a natural appetite of the soul and the notion of the divine illumination of the human mind. In the later Renaissance, another philosopher, the Dominican friar Tommaso Campanella (1568–1639), found inspiration in Augustine for some of his central doctrines, such as his answer to skepticism based on self-consciousness, and his argument for the innate knowledge of God.

Outside Italy, humanist interest in Augustine focused on the *City of God*. Around 1501, young Thomas More lectured on it in London. The most important humanist study of the *City of God* was the edition and commentary published by the Spanish humanist Juan Luis Vives (1492–1540) in 1522. Vives was primarily interested in the work's historical lore and classical literary fragments. In his later pedagogical treatise *De tradendis disciplinis* (On teaching the disciplines) he criticized Augustine's style and recommended only the *City of God* for reading.

Erasmus (c. 1466–1536) was the most important Christian humanist of the sixteenth century. He published Augustine's complete works in 1528–1529 as part of a larger program of editing the works of the church fathers. But Erasmus unequivocally expressed a preference for St. Jerome over Augustine. As an expert in patristic literature, Erasmus could not ignore Augustine's anti-Pelagian writings, which ran counter to his own voluntaristic moral theology. Erasmus cited Augustine primarily as a historical source and as a useful shield against theological critics. The same is true of the Protestant humanist Philipp Melanchthon (1497–1560).

Augustine's manual for the Christian preacher, *De doctrina christiana* (On Christian teaching), had an impact on Renaissance rhetoric, but in general Augustine exercised far greater influence among theologians and philosophers than among humanists. While Catholic theologians such as Girolamo Seripando, Michael Baius, and Cornelius Jansen claimed Augustine's authority in debates with fellow Catholics concerning grace and predestination, Augustine's stress on the church of Rome, his objective notion of the sacraments *ex opere operato* (from the work being done), and his belief in the real presence in the Eucharist were stumbling blocks to Protestants. However much they cited Augustine, Martin Luther, Ulrich Zwingli, and John Calvin did not draw their original inspiration from him.

BIBLIOGRAPHY

Bonansea, Bernardino. *Tommaso Campanella: Renaissance Pioneer of Modern Thought*. Washington, D.C., 1969.

Chomarat, Jacques. *Grammaire et rhétorique chez Erasmus*. 2 vols. Paris, 1981. See vol. 1, pp. 167–179, 424–425, 542–543, 566–567.

Fraenkel, Pierre. *Testimonia Patrum: The Function of the Patristic Argument in the Theology of Philip Melanchthon*. Geneva, 1961.

Gerosa, P. P. *Umanesimo cristiano del Petrarca: Influenza agostiniana, attinenze medievali*. Turin, Italy, 1966.

Kristeller, Paul Oskar. "Augustine and the Early Renaissance." In his *Studies in Renaissance Thought and Letters*. Rome, 1956. Pages 355–372.

Monfasani, John. "The *De doctrina christiana* and Renaissance Rhetoric." In *Reading and Wisdom: The* De Doctrina Christiana *of Augustine in the Middle Ages*. Edited by Edward D. English. Notre Dame, Ind., 1995. Pages 172–188.

Trinkaus, Charles. *In Our Image and Likeness: Humanity and Divinity in Italian Humanist Thought*. 2 vols. Chicago, 1970.

JOHN MONFASANI

AUSTRIA. [This entry includes two subentries, one on the history of Austria in the Renaissance and the other on artists active in Austria.]

Austria in the Renaissance

Österreich, or Austria, appeared on the map of Europe as a sovereign entity only after World War I. The geographical application of the name and its derivatives have shifted considerably throughout the course of history. At the outset of the sixteenth century, Lower Austria (Niederösterreich) included the modern province of that name, along with what are present-day Upper Austria, Styria, Carinthia, and Carniola. (The last is largely part of present-day Slovenia.) "Upper Austria" was the Tyrol, Anterior Austria (Vorderösterreich), and the scattered holdings of the Habsburg dynasty in southwestern Germany, along with present-day Vorarlberg. Following the division of the Austrian territories among the three sons of Ferdinand I (1503–1564), the term Inner Austria was used to designate Styria, Carinthia, and Carniola. These were governed by Archduke Charles, the youngest son of the late emperor. Together, these lands belonged to the patrimony of the house of Habsburg, or, as it called itself from the fifteenth century, the house of Austria, an affiliation that linked both the central European and Spanish branches of the dynasty.

Habsburg Austria and Habsburg Central Europe.

The Habsburgs had come into possession of these lands in the thirteenth and fourteenth centuries. Male primogeniture was not observed in the house until the reign of Emperor Ferdinand II

Austrian Rulers

Maximilian I (Holy Roman Emperor 1493–1519)
Charles V (Holy Roman Emperor 1519–1556)
Ferdinand I (Holy Roman Emperor 1558–1564)
Maximilian II (Holy Roman Emperor 1564–1576)
Ferdinand II of the Tyrol (1564–1595)
Charles II (archduke of Inner Austria 1564–1590)
Rudolf II (Holy Roman Emperor 1576–1612)
Matthias (Holy Roman Emperor 1612–1619)
Ferdinand II (Holy Roman Emperor 1619–1637)

(ruled 1619–1637), and even then with some qualifications. Before that, the Habsburgs routinely divided their lands among their sons. During this period, only Emperors Maximilian I (ruled 1493–1519), Ferdinand I (ruled 1558–1564), and Ferdinand II (ruled 1619–1637) held the lands as a totality. However, the Austrian provinces were not their exclusive interest. The first of the Habsburgs to come to the territory, Rudolf I (ruled 1273–1291), had been German king and emperor. Several of his successors in the fourteenth and fifteenth centuries had either held these offices or had actively sought them. With Frederick III (ruled 1442–1493), the German emperorship came to Habsburg hands, leaving briefly only once, during the eighteenth century, before the title and institution of "Holy Roman Emperor" disappeared entirely in 1806.

Habsburg Austria was subject to the political currents found in most European polities from the fifteenth to the seventeenth centuries. Tensions between the centralizing ambitions of princes and the regional and corporate loyalties of their estates were as common in the Austrian lands as they were on the Iberian Peninsula or in France. As in all of Germany, the Protestant Reformation radically altered the confessional profile of the Austrian territories. Except for the Tyrol, the entire region was divided along doctrinal lines, which complicated the tasks of government in new and unwelcome ways. The expenses of ruling far outran available resources, making the search for cash and credit the driving administrative issue of the day.

The Renaissance in Austria. Despite the universality of the challenges faced by the Habsburgs, their experience differed significantly from other European kingdoms. These, in turn, shaped the impact that the thought and culture of the Renaissance had in Austria, as well as the form of its expression there. As Holy Roman Emperors, the

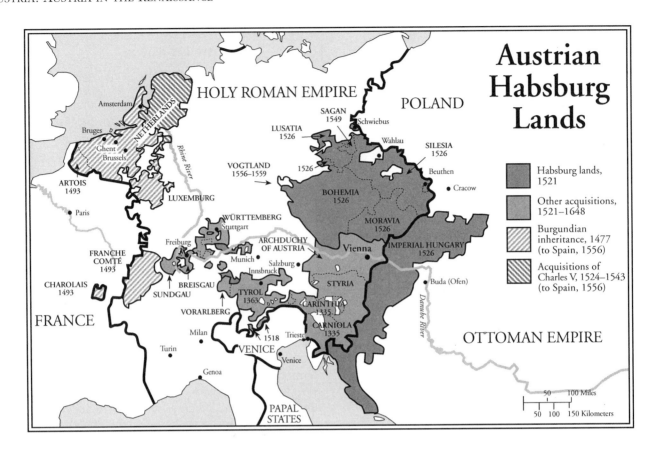

Habsburgs were constitutionally tied to all of Germany, including patches of northern Italy that had been imperial fiefs since medieval times. The duchy of Milan was perhaps the most important of these, but others of more recent creation were significant too. It was only in 1537, during the reign of Charles V (ruled 1519–1558), that the Medici became dukes of Florence, a title conferred by the emperor.

Thus scholars have found it difficult to fix a meaningful dividing line between Austria and Germany during the early modern era, in political as well as linguistic and cultural matters. Important Austrian scholars and artists lived and worked in Germany. Paul Rebhuhn (b. 1505), for example, a Lutheran from Waidhofen on the Ybbs in Lower Austria, introduced the five-foot iamb and the four-foot troche into German poetry, but found it more congenial to reside in Protestant Germany. Germans, in turn, were drawn to the court of Austrian princes and found patronage there. Themselves German princes, the Habsburgs drew heavily upon German talent for administrators, artists, and scholars to serve them. Thus, their habits of patronage and their tastes had a profound impact on their native Austria but largely through its presence in a larger Germany.

The career of Conrad Celtis (1459–1508) is instructive. Born in Franconia, now part of Bavaria, the humanist made his way to Vienna in 1490. The university was not altogether innocent of new learning. It was particularly accomplished in the sciences and mathematics. The Franconian humanist Regiomontanus (1436–1476) had edited Ptolemy's *Almagest* there. But, when Celtis settled in Vienna at the invitation of Maximilian I in 1497, he broadened the institution's intellectual reach considerably. Maximilian created a chair of rhetoric an poetry expressly for him. At the scholar's prompting, Maximilian also established a Collegium Poetarum et Mathematicarum (College of poetry and mathematics) independent of the university, which fostered both the scientific as well as the literary side of the humanist enterprise. Working under these auspices, Celtis edited and published texts crucial to the understanding of German history and culture. These included a Latin edition of Tacitus's *Germania* and an edition of the Latin plays of the tenth-century German nun Hrosvitha von Gandersheim.

One of Celtis's successors, Joachim von Watt, or Vadianus (1484–1551), gave the first university lecture on German literature during the winter semester of 1512–1513. It was published five years later. In preparation for writing a vast history of Austria based on a variety of documentary sources, Wolfgang Lazius (1514–1565), a physician and privy counselor to Ferdinand I, edited works of early German poetry and prose that he himself had discovered, including the medieval *Niebelungenlied*.

Patronage of Art. Distinguishing the Austrian from the German is even more difficult when one looks at Habsburg patronage of art. In general, Maximilian I drew heavily upon the entire southern German area for painters and graphic artists. Albrecht Dürer from Nürnberg (1471–1528), Hans Burgkmair from Augsburg (1473–1531), and Albrecht Altdorfer from Regensburg (c. 1480–1538) all received commissions from him. The traffic moved the other way as well. Jakob Seisenegger (1505–1567), Ferdinand I's court painter, was probably from Lower Austria. Nevertheless, he generally worked throughout southern Germany.

Nor did the central European Habsburgs confine themselves to rule as archdukes of Austria and Holy Roman Emperors. Following the death of King Louis of Hungary and Bohemia and his defeat by the Turks in 1526, Ferdinand I became ruler of both kingdoms. Inevitably the Habsburgs shifted part of their patronage eastward. Thus some of the most striking architectural monuments of the Renaissance in central and east central Europe are outside German-speaking lands altogether. Ferdinand I's delicately colonnaded Belvedere, an exquisite example of Italianate architecture constructed between 1534 and 1563, is in Prague, not Vienna or Innsbruck. Emperor Rudolf II (ruled 1576–1612), an avid collector whose holdings became the core of the Kunsthistorisches Museum, lived in the Bohemian capital exclusively after 1583.

At the very least, the internationality of the Habsburgs often forces one to distinguish between the notion of a Renaissance in Austria and a uniquely Austrian Renaissance. The dynasty ranged far and wide for the artists, architects, humanists, and painters who served them in the Austrian lands and elsewhere in their burgeoning polyglot empire. The most notable humanist to serve the Habsburgs was probably Enea Silvio Piccolomini (1405–1464), who in 1458 became Pius II. He was made imperial poet laureate in 1442 by Emperor Frederick III, then imperial chancellory secretary.

There was relatively little monumental building, either secular or sacral, during the fifteenth and sixteenth centuries in the Austrian provinces; the Turks were too close for comfort and local financial resources all too limited. Construction came often in the way of add-ons to existing buildings, rather than wholly original work. But when the ruling house looked for architects, as did Maximilian II (ruled 1564–1576) for his never-finished Neugebäude, a vast gardened structure on the outskirts of Vienna in which nature, art, and sculpture were combined so that each complemented the other, he looked to Lombardy, Venice, the Netherlands, and perhaps even France for architectural and decorative advice. The results, at least on paper, were quite original, with galleries replacing fortified walls. But they were not the product of Austrian design.

The same can be said of the medieval Ambras Castle, south of Innsbruck, renovated also in part for collection display by Maximilian's brother, Archduke Ferdinand II of the Tyrol. While not directly the product of foreign models—if anything, its setting recalls Ferdinand I's Belvedere—it was the handiwork of Italian and Netherlandish architects and decorative artists. Individual features of several noble castles bespeak a strong Italian influence, for example, the striking terra-cotta accents of the central courtyard of Schallaburg in Lower Austria, the arcaded tournament ground of Rosenburg castle, also in Lower Austria, the brilliant stucco chapel in the Styrian castle of Strechau in Styria.

Effects of Internationalism. But internationality was one of the hallmarks of the Renaissance. Artists and scholars were on the lookout for patrons and employers wherever they were to be had, and from this standpoint Renaissance Austria differed little from England, France, or Jagiellonian Poland. In order to develop a conception of the Renaissance in the Habsburg Austrian lands, one must take into consideration the accomplishments of foreign artists and scholars in Austria. This in turn sheds light on the ways in which Renaissance learning and art significantly shaped what would become distinctively Austrian cultural preoccupations.

At the very least, foreign humanists told Austrians something about themselves. Enea Silvio Piccolomini's description of Vienna in his *Historia Australis* (completed c. 1458, published 1685) ranks among the best literary depictions of a city ever written. But it is in music and literature that we see the best examples of the close intertwining of Renaissance art and learning with Austrian culture. Habsburg patronage of music was early and intense. Maximilian I employed German composers such as Paul Hofhaimer (1459–1537) of Salzburg, then still an inde-

Division of the Austrian Lands. The emperor Rudolf I (ruled 1273–1291) divides his lands between his two sons, Albert and Rudolf, in 1282. Albert became king of the Germans in 1298. BILDARCHIV, ÖSTERREICHISCHE NATIONAL BIBLIOTHEK, VIENNA

pendent prince-bishopric, Ludwig Senfl (c. 1486–1542) born in Basel, and the Netherlander Heinrich Isaac (c. 1450–1517). It was under Ferdinand I, however, that the influence of Netherlanders became predominant.

In general, advances in music during the Renaissance were marked by the development of symbolic associations with musical forms, the birth of opera, and the increase in orchestral music independent of the voice. Composers strove to equalize all instruments, both vocal and constructed, in an effort to develop a pleasing whole. Chromaticism and dissonance were deliberately employed to raise the expressive effect of the composition. The Netherlanders were leaders in this movement; their impact was especially heavy in Vienna, due to the work of Jakob Vaet (d. 1567), the director of the court chapel from 1564 to 1567, and Philipp de Monte (1521–1603), who served as director from 1568 to 1603. Vaet's compositions in particular represent a transition between Josquin des Prez (c. 1440–1521) and Pale-

strina (c. 1525–1594). Austria's tradition as a musical center, both creatively and in performance, had taken root. It should be noted as well that these conditions were not limited to Vienna. Netherlanders, along with Italians, were also prominent in musical life at the late-sixteenth-century Habsburg court of Inner Austria in Graz.

In a more complex way, Renaissance learning played an equally important role in what would become another distinctive feature of Austrian culture, the theater. Conrad Celtis's students put on Latin comedies of Terence and Plautus as well as comic plays written by Celtis himself. Stage performances would become integral parts of the Protestant and Catholic pedagogical agenda in the sixteenth century. Many of these presentations, both Protestant and Catholic, were done in costume with stage effects and musical accompaniment. In 1555, the Jesuits, recently arrived in Vienna, put on their first performance of one of Terence's comedies in a local Carmelite cloister. Intended as much for entertainment as instruction, some of their subsequent offerings drew audiences in the thousands, despite the preference the order gave to Latin over German in their presentations. They did, however, continue to use scenery, music, and ever more elaborate costuming for their actors.

See also **Habsburg Dynasty; Holy Roman Empire.**

BIBLIOGRAPHY

Evans, Robert John Weston. *Rudolf II and His World: A Study in Intellectual History, 1576–1612.* Oxford, 1973. A subtle analysis of late Renaissance thought and culture.

Feuchtmüller, Rupert. *Kunst in Österreich. Vom frühen Mittelalter bis zum Gegenwart.* Vol. 1. Vienna; Hannover, Germany; and Basel, Switzerland; 1972. Pages 187–264. Synthetic, insightful, and detailed. Illustrations very well chosen.

Feuchtmüller, Rupert, ed. *Renaissance in Österreich: Geschichte-Wissenschaft-Kunst.* Horn, Austria, 1974. A wide-ranging and comprehensive collection of essays that grew out of an exhibition in the Schallaburg castle. While some of the articles are little more than recitations of names and works, many contributions merit close attention.

Kaufmann, Thomas DaCosta. *The Mastery of Nature: Aspects of Art, Science, and Humanism.* Princeton, N.J., 1993. Central European focus.

Kaufmann, Thomas DaCosta. *Variations on the Imperial Theme: Studies in Ceremonial Art and Collecting in the Age of Maximilian II and Rudolph II.* New York and London, 1978.

Lhotsky, Alphons. *Festschrift des kunsthistorischen Museums zur Feier des fünfzigjährigen Bestandes.* 2 vols. in 3. Horn, Austria, 1941–1945. Still an authoritative history of the collections.

Lietzmann, Hilda. *Das Neugebäude in Wien: Sultan Suleymans Zelt-Kaiser Maximilians Lustschloss, Ein Beitrag zur Kunst und Kulturgeschichte des sechzehnten Jahrhunderts.* Munich and Berlin, 1987. An exemplary study, richly illustrated.

Scheicher, Elisabeth, et al. *Die Kunst und Wunderkammer der Habsburger.* Vienna, Munich, and Zurich, Switzerland, 1979.

Wiesflecker, Hermann. *Kaiser Maximilian I.* 5 vols. Vienna, 1971–1986. The authoritative work on a crucial figure. Vol. 5 especially useful on cultural affairs.

PAULA SUTTER FICHTNER

Art in Austria

By far the most important artistic programs of the Austrian Renaissance were devised by the members of the Habsburg dynasty, which, following the ascension of Charles I (later Emperor Charles V, 1530–1556) to the throne of Spain in 1516, was split into an Austrian and a Spanish branch. Even though the Habsburgs ruled a considerable area in central Europe, only present-day Austria is considered here.

Habsburg Patronage. Emperor Maximilian I (ruled 1493–1519) was the first Habsburg ruler to commission works from some of the major artists of the northern European Renaissance. Most of the emperor's projects were of autobiographical character

and revealed a deep fascination with the historical role of his own dynasty. Among his principal commissions were two colossal woodcut assemblages, the *Triumphal Arch* (1517–1518), which imitates Roman structures and aggrandizes Maximilian through a family tree, and the *Triumphal Procession* (1516–1518), representing a cortège of the Habsburg family, past and present. The contributing artists included Jörg Kölderer, Hans Springinklee, Albrecht Dürer, and Hans Burgkmair the Elder, with the court historiographer Johannes Stabius and the emperor's secretary Marx Treitzsauerwein serving as principal iconographical advisers. Maximilian also used the still relatively new medium of print to illustrate his own literary works, including the *Weisskunig* (begun 1505), an allegorical novel devised with the help of the humanist Conrad Celtis, and featuring woodcuts by Burgkmair, Springinklee, and Leonard Beck. Maximilian's efforts to immortalize himself and ensure the lasting fame of the house of Austria culminated in the plans for his own funerary monument in the Innsbruck Hofkirche. Albrecht Dürer, Veit Stoss, Hans Leinberger, and Conrat Meit were among those to produce the initial designs for the colossal bronze figures, which were then cast by Gilg Sesselschreiber, Stefan Godl, and the Vischer workshop in Nürnberg. Work began in 1502 and continued, with interruptions due to the lack of funds, until 1585. Still, the memorial remains incomplete. At the center of the present monument stands Maximilian's cenotaph, executed after 1561 by Florian Abel and Alexander Colin, and featuring a bronze figure of the kneeling emperor, as well as twenty-four marble reliefs with scenes from his life. Of the almost two hundred bronze statues that were originally intended to accompany him, only a fraction were ever executed. These are larger-than-life figures of the emperor's Habsburg forerunners and of historical and mythical personages considered to embody the virtues of kingship, including King Arthur and Clovis of France.

The architectural setting of the tomb was built between 1553 and 1563 by Andrea Crivelli, Niclas Türing the Younger, and Marx della Bolla, at the incentive of Emperor Ferdinand I (ruled 1526–1564), grandson of Maximilian I, and ranks among the most important ecclesiastical buildings in sixteenth-century Austria. A three-aisled hall church with a projecting 5/8 choir (a choir derived from five sides of an octagon), the Hofkirche originally featured pointed windows and a complex net vault, with the use of Renaissance motifs relegated to the portal and vestibule areas. This style, which has been labeled post-

Austrian *Kunststuckh.* South Tyrolean writing set in the form of a central-plan building, late sixteenth century. KUNSTHISTORISCHES MUSEUM, VIENNA, SAMMLUNGEN SCHLOSS AMBRAS, INV. NO. PA 779

Gothic (*Nachgotik*) represented an attempt to create a new, even progressive, manner of building. A markedly ecclesiastical style, *Nachgotik* was the result of an essentially positive evaluation of medieval architecture, which was regarded as the forerunner of the contemporary building style. Though used by both denominations, the post-Gothic style and detail are mostly associated with the patronage of post-Tridentine Catholicism, and were often used to accentuate liturgical furnishings particular to the Catholic faith (for instance, the eucharistic tabernacle of Götzis, Vorarlberg, made by Esaias Gruber in 1597).

Significant secular buildings patronized by the Habsburgs included the Hofburg in Vienna, converted from a medieval castle (1533–1568) and bearing witness to the influence of Italian architectural treatises, in particular to Sebastiano Serlio (Schweizertor, 1552–1553); the Schloss Neugebäude, a villa erected for Emperor Maximilian II (ruled 1564–1576) outside the gates of Vienna, and indebted to the pal-

aces of Andrea Palladio and Giulio Romano (for instance, the Palazzo del Tè in Mantua); and Schloss Ambras, Innsbruck, extensively rebuilt by Ferdinand of Tyrol, archduke of Austria (1529–1595). The latter edifice is especially well known for its Spanischer Saal (Spanish Hall; 1570–1572) with its rich, coffered ceiling by Johann Gottlieb and wall paintings depicting the princes of the Tyrol. The so-called Unterschloss (Lower Schloss; c. 1572–1580) included an armory, an antiquarium (a room with eighty-five niches used for the display of antique or pseudo-antique statues), and the Kunstkammer (literally meaning "art chamber"). Like other examples of its kind, the Ambras Kunstkammer was used to show *artefacta* (items produced by humans, such as metalwork objects, automata, glassware) side by side with *naturalia* (things brought forth by nature, such as minerals, rare animals, and other curiosities). The collection in many ways represented a kind of abbreviation of the known universe. Often natural and artificial objects were also combined to form hybrids, such as display vessels made from coconuts or ostrich eggs and encased in silver or gold ornament. Other artifacts were produced by wood-turning or ivory-turning, with the material frequently worked to its utmost limits. One example of such a *Kunststuckh,* or virtuoso piece, is a writing set in the form of a centralized building, produced in the second half of the sixteenth century, most probably by a Tyrolean artist (Kunsthistorisches Museum, Sammlungen Schloss Ambras, Inv. No. PA 779). Kunstkammern have their origins in late fourteenth-century France and during the Renaissance became popular throughout Europe, but they are particularly associated with Habsburg patronage. Later Habsburg rulers to continue this tradition included Emperor Rudolf II (ruled 1576–1612), who at his residence in Prague combined the idea of a Kunstkammer with an extensive art collection.

Noble Patronage. Competing with the artistic self-representation of the Habsburgs, some members of the predominantly Protestant aristocracy also established themselves as important patrons of the arts. Like other families of the Austrian nobility, the Khevenhüller of Carinthia developed a marked genealogical interest, which they sought to pictorialize in a number of ways. About 1550, for example, Christoph Khevenhüller ordered a series of portraits of himself, his family, and predecessors from a number of unknown local artists; some of these still survive in their family residence Schloss Hochosterwitz. The same family also commissioned the so-called

Khevenhüller-Chronik, a picture chronicle produced by Georg Moshammer that shows ancestors, their estates, and castles (1623–1625).

Among the most important architectural manifestations of aristocratic patronage are a number of stately Renaissance palaces, including Schloss Porcia in Spittal an der Drau, Carinthia (1533–1590s), begun by Gabriel of Salamanca, treasurer and secretary of Emperor Ferdinand I. Modeled on buildings in Tuscany and Lombardy, and erected over a square ground plan with two round towers marking one diagonal axis, the edifice is especially outstanding for its three-storied courtyard, with its voluted and composite columns, and sculptures depicting virtues, emperors, and scenes from classical mythology, including the popular motif of Hercules at the Crossroads. Schloss Schallaburg in Lower Austria, originally a medieval fortification remodeled between 1572 and 1600 by Hans Wilhelm von Losenstein, is characterized by a similar courtyard, here of two tiers, which is accentuated by rich classical-style terra-cotta ornaments; these include masks, grotesques, personifications of virtues, and narrative illustrations of parables and mythological subjects, including a selection from the Twelve Labors of Hercules, based on a cycle of engravings by Heinrich Aldegrever.

BIBLIOGRAPHY

Kaufmann, Thomas DaCosta. *Court, Cloister, and City: The Art and Culture of Central Europe, 1450–1800.* London, 1995.
Renaissance in Österreich. Exhibition catalog, Schloss Schallaburg. Vienna, 1974.
Ruhm und Sinnlichkeit: Innsbrucker Bronzeguss 1500–1650, von Kaiser Maximilian I. bis Erzherzog Ferdinand Karl. Exhibition catalog, Tiroler Landesmuseum Ferdinandeum. Innsbruck, Austria, 1996.

ACHIM TIMMERMANN

AUTOBIOGRAPHY. *See* **Biography and Autobiography.**

AVIS DYNASTY. *See* **Portugal.**

BACON, FRANCIS (1561–1626), Renaissance polymath, lord chancellor of England, one of the founding figures of the scientific revolution. Born on 22 January 1561 at York House, London, Francis Bacon was the second son of Elizabeth I's lord keeper, Sir Nicholas Bacon, and his second wife, Anne Cooke, sister-in-law to Sir William Cecil, later Lord Burghley. He matriculated at Trinity College, Cambridge, with his elder brother Anthony in 1573. He left without taking a degree in 1575, and in 1576 accompanied the embassy of Sir Amias Paulet to France. It was Bacon's only trip abroad. He returned at the death of his father in 1579, and finding himself in difficult financial circumstances, enrolled at Gray's Inn in 1580, becoming a barrister in 1582. In 1581 he was elected MP for the Cornish borough of Bossiney, and he served in every parliament thereafter until 1621.

Bacon's talents were displayed early, but apart from a reversion to the lucrative clerkship of the Star Chamber, granted him in 1589, he had no preferment under Elizabeth. Bacon's quest for office was frustrated by his patron, Burghley, who saw him as a rival to his own son, Sir Robert Cecil. When Cecil succeeded his father as James I's chief minister in 1603, he continued to impede Bacon's progress. To offset this, Bacon attached himself to the earl of Essex in 1591, but Essex was unable to obtain for him either the vacant attorney generalship he sought in 1593 or even the lesser post of solicitor. When Essex was tried for treason in 1601 after a failed revolt Bacon was assigned the distasteful task of prosecuting him. The episode continued to haunt him, and he

felt compelled to defend his conduct in an *Apology* (1604).

Bacon was knighted at James's accession, a faint acknowledgment, but after his appointment in 1607 as solicitor his rise was rapid: treasurer of Gray's Inn (where he maintained lodgings to the end of his life) in 1608; attorney general at last in 1613; lord keeper, his father's old position, in 1617; and lord chancellor, the highest appointive post in the kingdom, in 1618. Ennoblement followed, as Baron Verulam in 1618 and Viscount St. Albans in 1621.

Bacon's fortunes were now at their apex, and, to crown them, his chief rival, Sir Edward Coke, was dismissed (with Bacon's active connivance) as chief justice of the King's Bench in 1616. Certainly no other contemporary European sovereign was served by a man of Bacon's abilities. But Bacon again found himself in the shadow of a royal favorite, George Villiers, created marquis and subsequently duke of Buckingham by James I. Buckingham's grasping family had exacerbated the problem of royal monopolies, an indirect but much-resented form of taxation, and his parvenu status profoundly alienated the nobility. When the fallen Coke, elected MP in the Parliament of 1621, led an attack on monopolies that threatened Buckingham's position, James reluctantly permitted Bacon to be sacrificed in Buckingham's stead on grounds of bribery and corruption. These charges were essentially unjustified; Bacon had done no more than accept the usual fees of office, and no one could demonstrate that his judgment had ever been swayed by them. His fall was dictated by politics. He was compelled to resign, imprisoned at plea-

Francis Bacon. Woodcut, 1640. CORBIS-BETTMANN

sure, fined forty thousand marks, forbidden access to the royal court, and disabled from sitting in parliament. James remitted all but the last of these penalties, but Bacon never again served the state.

Bacon's last years were embittered, but characteristically productive. He attempted to win royal favor again with his *History of the Reign of King Henry VII* (1622), now regarded as a classic of Renaissance historiography, but was rebuffed even in his petition for minor office. In 1606 he had married the fourteen-year-old Alice Barnham, the heiress of a London alderman. The marriage was childless. In his last months Bacon discovered Alice in an adulterous affair, and excluded her from all but her legal portion in his will. He died at Gray's Inn on 9 April 1626.

Writings and Intellectual Legacy. "I have taken all knowledge for my province," Bacon wrote in 1592, and he made good his word. The first ten of the *Essays*, brilliant literary performances modeled on the French essayist Michel de Montaigne, were published in 1597; their number had grown to fifty-eight by the third edition of 1625. Bacon's major works in science and logic, *The Advancement of Learning* (1605; expanded as *De augmentis scien-*

tarium, 1623) and the *Novum organum* (New instrument; 1620), were the products of his busiest years, as were the *New Atlantis* (published 1627), *De sapientia veterum* (On ancient wisdom; 1609), *The Beginning of the History of Great Britain* (1610), important legal treatises, and miscellaneous literary, ecclesiological, and scientific works.

The scope of his ambition can be read in some of their titles: *Descriptio globi intellectualis* (Description of the world of thought; 1612), *Thema coeli* (Thesis on the heavens; 1612). Only a twenty-page précis of his grand project for a new natural philosophy based on the empirical method, *Instauratio magna* or *Great Instauration,* appeared as a pendant to the *Novum organum,* but all his work is in a sense a commentary on it.

The essence of Bacon's intellectual project was to refine and consolidate the Renaissance critique of Aristotelian reason, and to produce a critical method for achieving knowledge. Bacon divided human reasoning into two distinct processes or "moments," invention and judgment. The former involved determining the fundamental axioms and procedures of each art or science and their relation to the first principles of knowledge in general; the latter, the application of such axioms to specific questions. The crux of all rational inquiry was thus the proper determination of the axioms appropriate to each discipline. At the same time, Bacon regarded two realms of understanding as beyond the scope of reason, although not of rational articulation: divine revelation, which presented itself to the mind from a point above it, and social or political precept, which involved an irreducible element of moral choice or preference. Each realm of understanding involved its own method of apprehension and its own mode of expression; each, too, involved the overcoming of its specific "idols," or predilections for error.

In retirement, Bacon produced, in addition to *Henry VII* and expanded editions of the *Essays* and *The Advancement of Learning,* a *Historia naturalis et experimentalis* (Natural and experimental history; 1622), a collection of *Apothegms New and Old* (1624), a translation of the Psalms, and a utopian fable, *The New Atlantis* (1627). Perhaps posterity's greatest compliment is the persistent tradition that attributes to him the plays of Shakespeare as well.

Bacon's importance was well recognized by his contemporaries, and has been saluted in each generation since by such figures as John Dryden, Alexander Pope, Giambattista Vico, Alexander Hume, Immanuel Kant (who dedicated his *Critique of Pure Reason* to him in 1781), John Stuart Mill, and Karl

Popper. His significance to the development of modern science lies not so much in the specific empirical method he championed as in his demolition of the vestiges of scholastic thought that he called the "idols of the mind"—the belief in native reason, dialectical logic, and natural correspondences as an adequate basis for understanding. Instead he insisted on a step-by-step accretion beginning not with first principles but first perceptions, and proceeding by progressive stages of observation and experiment toward certainty. Like his contemporary René Descartes, although by an opposed path, his project was to refound and ultimately to reunify all human knowledge by a Socratic confession of ignorance.

BIBLIOGRAPHY

Primary Works

Bacon, Francis. *The Works of Francis Bacon.* Edited by James Spedding, Robert L. Ellis, and Douglas Heath. 14 vols. London, 1857–1874.

Secondary Works

Jardine, Lisa. *Francis Bacon: Discovery and the Art of Discourse.* Cambridge, U.K., 1974.
Martin, Julian. *Francis Bacon, the State, and the Reform of Natural Philosophy.* Cambridge, U.K., and New York, 1992.
Mathews, Nieves. *Francis Bacon: The History of a Character Assassination.* New Haven, Conn., 1996.
Zagorin, Perez. *Francis Bacon.* Princeton, N.J., 1998.

ROBERT ZALLER

BAÏF, LAZARE DE

(c. 1496–1547), French diplomat and humanist scholar. Born in Anjou, Lazare de Baïf became an important diplomat in the service of Francis I and a noted humanist. He learned Greek in Rome, where he remained for five years (1514–1519), under the tutelage of the famous Hellenist teachers John Lascaris and Marc Musurus. A fervent Hellenist, he devoted his life to founding Greek studies in France. His scholarly publications include archaeological works on ancient clothes (*De re vestiaria* [On clothes; Basel, 1526]), on Greek vases (*De vasculus* [On vases; 1531]), and on ancient naval practices (*De re navali* [On naval matters; 1536]). He translated Plutarch's first four *Lives* (Theseus, Romulus, Lycurgus, and Numa) and published French alexandrine verse translations of Sophocles's *Electra* (1537) and Euripides's *Hecuba* (1550). In June 1529 he became ambassador to Venice and frequented renowned Italian humanists such as Pietro Bembo and Jacopo Sadoleto. His son Jean-Antoine de Baïf was born in Venice in 1532. Upon returning to France in 1534, he became a magistrate at the Parlement of Paris and, in 1538, *maître des requêtes* (master of requests) of the king's household. As a secretary to German princes in 1540, he took along with him the young Pierre de Ronsard.

BIBLIOGRAPHY

Chamard, Henri. *Histoire de la Pléiade.* Vol. 1. Paris, 1961. Chapter 1 provides a good introduction.
Hauréau, B. *Histoire littéraire du Maine.* Vol. 1. Paris, 1871. Pages 227–245.
Pinvert, Lucien. *Lazare de Baïf.* Paris, 1900. The standard work.

ANNE R. LARSEN

BALASSI, BÁLINT

(1554–1594), Hungarian aristocrat, poet, dramatist. Count Balassi lived a life of adventure and turmoil. He was born in the fortress of Zólyom (today Zvolen, Slovakia), home tutored by Péter Bornemisza, a Protestant humanist and minister, studied in Nürnberg, and spoke several languages. He stood in the service of the prince of Transylvania from 1575 to 1577 and became the lieutenant of fifty horsemen at the famous stronghold at Eger. He wrote several poems inspired by his military experiences and love poems dedicated to his first beloved, Anna Losonczy. In 1586 he converted from Lutheranism to Roman Catholicism. In 1588 and 1589 he collected his poems under the title *Maga kezével írott könyv* (A manuscript book of verse) and wrote an amorous court drama, *Szép magyar komédia* (A fine comedy in Hungarian). From 1589 to 1591 he stayed in Poland, where he found another worthy aristocratic woman to be loved, the addressee of his *Coelia Poems.* In 1591 he returned to Hungary, took part in the military operations against the Turks, and was mortally wounded by a cannonball at the siege of Esztergom. In his last years he began to translate a theological treatise (*Decem rationes*) written by the Jesuit Edmund Campion. Balassi's confessor, Sándor Dobokay, finished his translation.

His early religious and amorous writing teems with yearnings and ideas of chivalry. He was influenced by Hungarian, Croatian, and Turkish folk poetry; Italian love lyric imitating Petrarch's style, and an anthology of Neo-Latin poetry entitled *Poetae tres elegantissimi* (Three very elegant poets). He employed the same mythological characters, but as his poems were to be sung, he also indicated the source of the melodies (*ad notam*). He collected his poems into two cycles of verse, each containing thirty-three pieces, and supplemented them with a narrative framework. He consciously structured his three hymns of the Trinity in ninety-nine lines. His *istenes* poetry is basically Protestant in inspiration and expresses a restless search for God. He also paraphrased five psalms written by George Buchanan and Théodore de Bèze. In the *Coelia Poems,* he used intricate metaphors and elaborate rhetorical composition and omitted the melodies. His effort to improve the rhyme schemes of his poetry resulted in the invention of the Balassi stanza.

Balassi established amorous courtly drama in Hungary as a new genre by revising and "Hungarianizing" Cristoforo Castelletti's pastoral play, *Amarilli,* and making it rich in autobiographical details. Balassi was the founder of Hungarian amorous, religious, and philosophical poetry, and of courtly drama in the Renaissance. He inherited and transformed the poetics and poetic techniques of the troubadours by way of Petrarchist writing. Poets in the seventeenth century frequently copied and imitated him, but only his religious poems could find their way to the press in his lifetime.

See also **Hungary**.

BIBLIOGRAPHY

Primary Works

Balassi, Bálint. *Összes müvei.* Edited by Sándor Eckhardt. Budapest, 1951–1955. A critical edition of Bálint Balassi's works.

Hungarian Helicon. Edited and translated by Watson Kirkconnell. Calgary, Canada, 1985.

Old Hungarian Literary Reader. Eleventh–Eighteenth Centuries. Edited by Tibor Klaniczay. Budapest, 1985.

Secondary Works

Nagy, Moses M. "Bálint Balassi: The Poet of the Hungarian Renaissance." In *A Journey into History: Essays on Hungarian Literature.* New York, 1990. Pages 51–66.

Pirnát, Antal. *Balassi Bálint poétikája.* Budapest, 1996.

Szőnyi, György E. "Courtly Literature in Renaissance Hungary and England: Bálint Balassi and Philip Sidney." *Hungarian Studies* (Budapest) 10 (1995): 253–278.

Szőnyi, György E. "Self-Representation in Petrarchism: Varieties in England [Sidney] and Hungary [Balassi]." *New Comparison* 9 (spring 1990): 60–72.

ISTVÁN BITSKEY

BALDUNG GRIEN, HANS (Hans Baldung; Hans Grien; c. 1484–1545), German painter, printmaker, and illustrator whose religious, mythological, and demonic images achieved unusual emotional and coloristic intensity. Born probably in Schwäbisch-Gmünd and raised in Strasbourg, Hans Baldung Grien was the only major German artist of his time to come from a family of professional elites. His father was an attorney and episcopal officer; his uncle served as the Holy Roman Emperor Maximilian I's honorary physician; and his university-trained brother was the city advocate of Strasbourg and a member of the imperial chamber court. These connections aided Baldung's career and illuminate the mandarin complexity of his art.

Hans Baldung Grien. *Vanity.* As the young woman admires her image in a hand mirror, the hourglass in the right hand of the cadaver signals that her time is running out. KUNSTHISTORISCHES MUSEUM, VIENNA/BILDARCHIV FOTO MARBURG/ART RESOURCE

In 1503, after early training probably in Schwabia, Baldung entered the shop of Albrecht Dürer in Nürnberg. Working with Dürer was a formative experience for Baldung. From this hugely innovative artist Baldung derived his figure style, calligraphic manner, subject repetoire, and career pattern as a painter and printmaker. Dürer's greatest epigone, Baldung playfully travestied his master's products, as in the early drawing *Death and the Landsknecht* (1503) based on Dürer's idealized nudes.

After executing two altarpieces in Halle, Baldung settled in Strasbourg in 1509, where he married in 1510 and remained intermittently until his death. Early on, Baldung developed the twin themes that garnered him fame: witchcraft, represented by a chiaroscuro woodcut *Witches' Sabbath* (1510), a panel painting titled *Two Weather Witches* (1523), and several obscene drawings on colored ground; and

death, explored especially in panels of a nude woman assaulted by a cadaver. Baldung intended these pictures to arouse and repel the viewer, and he linked that affective confusion allusively to the fall, which he portrayed erotically in paintings and prints.

Baldung lived in Freiburg from 1512 to 1516 while executing the altarpiece for the cathedral choir. With its violent color contrasts (influenced perhaps by the artist Matthias Grünewald), this masterpiece is of such exaggerated and ambivalent emotion that some scholars discern irony in it. With revenues from this commission, Baldung bought land in Strasbourg and rose in local politics to become a city senator. This position allowed him to weather Strasbourg's iconoclasm, which left other artists unemployed. Baldung continued to paint Madonnas, allegories, and portraits for noble clients; and he produced a great series of *Apostles* woodcuts (1519). The demonic sensuality, coy self-reference, and semantic indeterminacy of Baldung's art stand condensed in his late *Wild Horses* woodcuts (1534).

Self-consciousness, eccentricity, and a subversive relation to Dürerian classicism associate Baldung with mannerist art. His work should also be understood in the context of the German Renaissance's heightened uncertainty concerning the nature of art and of interpretation.

BIBLIOGRAPHY

Koch, Carl. *Die Zeichnungen Hans Baldung Griens.* Berlin, 1941.

Koerner, Joseph Leo. *The Moment of Self-Portraiture in German Renaissance Art.* Chicago, 1993.

Marrow, James H., and Alan Shestack, eds. *Hans Baldung Grien: Prints and Drawings.* Exhibition catalog, Yale University Art Gallery. New Haven, Conn., 1981.

Mende, Matthias. *Hans Baldung Grien: Das graphische Werk.* Unterschneidheim, Germany, 1978.

Osten, Gert von der. *Hans Baldung Grien: Gemälde und Dokumente.* Berlin, 1983.

JOSEPH LEO KOERNER

BALTIC STATES. Three major influences reinforced one another to ensure that urban centers in the Baltic world shared widely in the northern Renaissance. First, merchants and burghers in Hanseatic cities (Reval, Riga, Königsberg, Danzig, Elbing, Culm, and Thorn) emulated their peers in Lübeck, Hamburg, and Bremen in civic architecture, brick Gothic homes, and sending their sons away for a university education. Second, the Teutonic Knights sought to maintain their traditional role in cultural leadership and administrative efficiency by sending young men to Italy to be educated; young knights

The Arsenal of Gdańsk. Built by Anthonius van Opbergen, 1602–1605. OFFICE OF THE DOCUMENTATION OF MONUMENTS, GDAŃSK, POLAND

brought from Germany the latest fads in art and letters; and members of the Teutonic Order on diplomatic business were regular visitors to Rome and the imperial court. Third, Germans and Poles living in West Prussia under Polish rule gravitated toward Cracow, then a famous center of Renaissance thought, art, and architecture—and site of the Jagiellonian University.

Prussia. These three influences joined most prominently in Prussia, where Renaissance thought spread widely across the upper and middle classes. Between 1450 and 1540 several scholars of importance were either born or worked in Prussia, and one man of world significance—Nicolaus Copernicus—was born, reared, and employed throughout his life there. East and West Prussia were not rich lands, but effective government at the local and regional levels made the most of the opportunities provided by nature. This attitude carried over into those aspects of high culture that were representative of the Renaissance.

Education. It was no accident that the most prominent university of northeastern Europe was founded in Königsberg by Duke Albert, the former grand master of the Teutonic Order, and that this university was later associated with Johann Gottfried von Herder and Immanuel Kant. Many leaders of Prussian society were educated, most were well traveled, and all wanted to be respected for their sophistication and taste. Most importantly, all believed that education could be applied in practical ways. This belief gave Prussian humanism its distinctly regional flavor.

Knowledge of Latin was the prerequisite for advancement in the church, for the appreciation of literature, and for participation in contemporary scholarship. Prussian bishops had established schools for the education of local youths (including native Prussians) in the fourteenth century, and towns had created schools for the sons of burghers and gentry. In the fifteenth century students were studying in Italy on scholarships and finding ready employment in the small bureaucracies of government and cathedral chapters; by the sixteenth century educated men

were common. Copernicus, the first Prussian or Pole to study Greek, did so in order to argue that there were competing theories about the movements of the sun and the earth.

Art. Prussian art and architecture reflected German models, sometimes the Rhenish homeland of bishops and canons or officers of the Teutonic Order, sometimes the Hanseatic ties of politics, family, trade, and the Low German language. One can see this still in the restored or surviving old town centers of Gdańsk (Danzig), Chelmno (Culm), and Toruń (Thorn), and in the grand master's castle at Malbork (Marienburg), all in Poland.

Prussian cities. Without question Gdańsk is the crown jewel among the surviving Renaissance cities

in the north. Notable for their architectural quality are the town hall, with a fifteenth-century clock tower; the Golden Gate and the Artus Hall, built in the early seventeenth century; and the stately patrician homes along the Long Market Square. Arguably, the best-preserved art is in Frombork (Frauenburg), where the destructive aspects of the Reformation were less extensive than elsewhere. Portraiture was widespread (even Copernicus tried his hand as a painter) though not distinguished.

Livonia. This more northerly territory had a much smaller and more complex population base scattered over a much wider area. Therefore, the clerics, the nobles, the burghers, and the officers of the Livonian order (a semiautonomous branch of the Teutonic Knights) lacked the means for supporting more than an occasional artist or humanist, and they could support only modest building projects. Secular nobles and burghers, unwilling or unable to pay more taxes, showed little enthusiasm for efforts to make the Order's government more centralized and efficient, or to surrender authority to the bishops. Perhaps as important, Livonian nobles lacked models such as Poles and Germans provided for Prussians. Because extensive travel was difficult and costly, and because there was no incentive for visitors to come to them, the nobles concentrated on hunting and drinking. The Low German language market was too small to support much literature until the outbreak of the Livonian War in 1557 provided a subject of sufficient importance to attract both authors and readers. The Reformation similarly provided grounds for religiously oriented scholarship and the construction of more churches, but it narrowed significantly the possibilities for travel and study. Thus, education became more book centered and ingrown. At the same time, the decline of Latin as an international language reduced the potential access to the wider world of arts and letters.

Livonian art and architecture. Two fifteenth-century works by Bernt Notke are the stellar attractions of Tallinn (Reval; in present-day Estonia): the Dance of Death in St. Nicholas and the folding altar in the Holy Ghost Church. The city hall and several of the buildings in the surrounding square retain unchanged their original Hanseatic forms. Riga, Latvia, which was later sufficiently prosperous to replace much of its old city center, is restoring the historic district.

Summary. The importance of the Renaissance era is as obvious to the Baltic peoples today as it is invisible to outsiders. The German burghers, gentry, knights, and clerics have departed, but the Estonian and Latvian peoples take rightful pride in the accomplishments of the past, accomplishments that everyone, rich or poor, contributed to in various ways. Estonia and Latvia are today a part of the West thanks to traditions firmly rooted in the Renaissance. Prussia was even more prominent as a regional center for scholarship and the arts.

See also **Poland.**

BIBLIOGRAPHY

Primary Works
Renner, Johannes. *Johannes Renner's Livonian History, 1551–1561.* Translated by Jerry C. Smith and William Urban. Lewiston, N.Y., 1997.
Smith, Jerry C., and William Urban, trans. *The Chronicle of Balthasar Russow.* Madison, Wis., 1988.

Secondary Works
Kirby, David. *Northern Europe in the Early Modern Period: The Baltic World, 1492–1772.* London and New York, 1990.
Rusinek, Michał. *Land of Nicholas Copernicus.* Translated by A. T. Jordan. New York, 1973.
Segel, Harold B. *Renaissance Culture in Poland: The Rise of Humanism, 1470–1543.* Ithaca, N.Y., 1989.
Urban, William, with Paul Knoll. "Renaissance Humanism in Prussia." *Journal of Baltic Studies* 22 (1991): 5–72, 95–122, 195–232.

WILLIAM L. URBAN

BANDELLO, MATTEO (1485–1561), Italian short story writer, Dominican friar, bishop of Agen. Born in Castelnuovo Scrivia, a Piedmont village now part of Lombardy, Matteo Bandello belonged to a family with connections to powerful Milanese nobles. Dynastic wars in Milan brought him, in 1497, under the protection of his father and mentor, Francesco Bandello, prior of a Dominican convent in that city. Bandello studied at the University of Pavia, although there is no evidence that he ever earned a degree. For more than forty years he served as secretary and emissary to several Italian noble families, among them the Bentivoglio of Bologna and the Gonzaga of Mantua. From 1528 to 1541 he was in the service of Cesare Fregoso and, later, Cesare's spouse and family in their retirement. It was during these years of service that Bandello produced many of his novelle. In 1550 he was appointed bishop of Agen, a position he held until 1555.

Bandello wrote 214 prose narratives whose historical, geographical, and novelistic richness surpassed that of any predecessor in the genre. Instead of employing the frame-tale structure in the Boccaccian tradition, Bandello introduces each novella with a dedicatory letter in which he records, in great detail, the circumstances under which the story was related. The historical accuracy of the letters remains a matter of debate since many were written after the fact, during the years in which he enlarged the collection for publication. The dedicatory letter also functioned, conveniently, as a pulpit from which to blunt ecclesiastic censure for the inclusion of licentious or scabrous material. The first three parts of the collection were printed in 1554 at Lucca. A fourth part was published posthumously in 1573, in Lyon, France.

Despite his prolific literary production and wide acclaim, Bandello is considered a minor *novelliere*. His preoccupation with contemporary political and social events and his belief in their appropriateness for fiction led Bandello to favor historical detail over artistic creativity. Nevertheless, in the trajectory of the novella, Bandello's compilation is the most outstanding sixteenth-century manifestation of the genre, second only to the fourteenth-century example of Boccaccio. Bandello's merit lies in his passion for verisimilitude, his capacity for psychological penetration, and his frequent use of dramatic encounter or direct speech. Within a decade of the publication of the first three parts, portions of the collection were translated into French (1559) and, shortly thereafter, into English (1567). A Spanish translation, drawn from the French, appeared in 1589. The novella's inherent tripartite structure (exposition and introduction of principal characters; complication of the plot; and resolution) also attracted dramatists to the Bandellian opus. It provided the plots for, among others, Shakespeare's *Romeo and Juliet* (1595), John Webster's *Duchess of Malfi* (1612/13), and fourteen plays by Spain's most popular golden age dramatist, Lope de Vega.

BIBLIOGRAPHY

Primary Works

Bandello, Matteo. *Tutte le opere*. 4th ed. 2 vols. Edited by Francesco Flora. Milan, 1966. Complete collection of Bandello's tales with a scholarly introduction by the editor.

Secondary Works

D'Antuono, Nancy L. "The Italian Novella and Lope de Vega's Comedies." Ph.D. diss., University of Michigan, 1975. Examines eight plays taken from Boccacio's *Decameron* (two in detail) and fourteen from Bandello (two in detail); extensive bibliography.

Griffith, T. Gwynor. *Bandello's Fiction: An Examination of the Novelle*. Oxford, 1955. An analysis of Bandello's talents as a writer of short stories and chronicler of the events of his time.

Porcelli, Bruno. *Novelieri italiani. Dal Sacchetti al Basile*. Ravenna, Italy, 1969. Porcelli devotes some sixty pages to an analysis of the structure and content of Bandello's fiction as

well as its importance as a reflection of sixteenth-century Italian cultural reality.

NANCY L. D'ANTUONO

BANDINELLI, BACCIO. *See* **Florence,** *subentry* on **Art of the Sixteenth Century.**

BANKING AND MONEY. Renaissance Europe witnessed the development of techniques and institutions that formed the basis of modern banking. The advances derived largely from medieval innovations, particularly those of Italian merchants, who led in all aspects of the profession. Italian dominance gave way to that of more northerly states in the sixteenth and seventeenth centuries.

Types of Banks. Renaissance banks came in three basic varieties: pawnbroking establishments, merchant or international banks, and local deposit banks. The categories were not exclusive. Merchant bankers occasionally established local deposit banks, while deposit bankers at times dealt in long-distance commerce (like merchant banks) and extended small consumption loans in return for collateral (like pawnbroking shops).

Pawnbrokers. Pawnbrokers occupied the lowest rung of the profession. They serviced the common man, lending money on pledges of personal property, usually at high rates of interest. The practice violated the basic teachings of the church, which held that charging "anything beyond the principal" constituted the sin of usury. States nevertheless needed the services of pawnbrokers and extended to them, albeit grudgingly, the right to do business. In fourteenth- and fifteenth-century Bruges, pawnbrokers charged 43⅓ percent interest on pawns; elsewhere the rate passed as high as 60 percent. Throughout northern Europe, pawnbrokers were often called "Lombards," because many came from northern Italy, particularly in the early days. The term was used derisively, as a synonym for usurer. The profession was dominated by Christians; despite the later stereotype, Jews remained a small minority, although they became increasingly active in the fourteenth and fifteenth centuries. This was particularly true in Italy, where cities, hard hit by the financial dislocations caused by successive plagues, famines, and wars, sought the services of Jewish moneylenders, whom they in turn taxed. The greater reliance on Jews brought them widespread condemnation, especially from observant Franciscans, who accused them of gouging the poor. Such suspicions led, first in Italy and then elsewhere, to the establishment of

Medici Bank. Facade of the Milan branch of the Medici bank. SOPRINTENDENZA PER I BENI ARTISTICI E STORICI DI FIRENZE/ BIBLIOTECA NAZIONALE CENTRALE, FLORENCE, CODICE MAGLIABECHIANO II.I.140 GIA MAGL. XVII.30

monti di pietà, nonprofit Christian pawn banks operated under clerical or monastic auspices. *Monti di pietà* reduced interest rates, often charging 5 percent. They eventually mutated into a species of public banks, which, in Florence, became manipulated by the local leaders to bestow patronage and political favors on friends.

Merchant or international banks. International or merchant banks mobilized capital and extended credit across national borders, facilitating long-distance trade throughout Europe, with networks of correspondents and branches in various cities. The early banking industry leaders were the major trading centers of northern Italy, particularly Siena, Lucca, and Florence. In the thirteenth century, these towns had already possessed companies with sophisticated and substantial organizations, characterized by wide-scale participation of family members, both from the immediate and larger clan. The success of the Italian banks derived in great measure from their tight connections with the pope, whose accounts—or portions thereof—they handled. The papal Curia remained a prime source of profits for Italian bankers through the sixteenth century.

The most spectacular of the early merchant banks were the fourteenth-century concerns operated by the Florentine families Bardi, Peruzzi, and Acciaiuoli. One contemporary labeled them the "pillars of Christian trade"; modern scholars have applied the term "super companies." The Peruzzi, the second-largest of the three, retained some ninety employees or "factors," had fifteen branches spread across Europe, northern Africa, and the Levant, and possessed an operating capital of ninety thousand *florins*. A board consisting of all the partners owned and supervised the company, and shared in the profits, while salaried employees managed the branches abroad.

All three "super companies" collapsed by 1345, which shook the banking world and the European economy in general. The failure was due to a combination of unwise fiscal practices (for example, loans to monarchs), market fluctuations and organizational weaknesses. The unlimited liability of the board of partners caused the branches of the Peruzzi bank to fall like dominoes.

Despite the collapse, Italians maintained their dominance in international banking. The Bardi, Peruzzi, and Acciaiuoli were followed by a new generation of Florentine banking houses, the best known of which was the Medici. The Medici bank never quite reached the size of its predecessors. At the peak of its prosperity in the mid-fifteenth century, the bank had an operating capital of 72,000 florins, with nine branches: five in Italy (Milan, Naples, Pisa, Rome, and Venice) and four beyond the Alps (Avignon, Bruges, Geneva—which moved to Lyons after 1466—and London). Half of the company's profits came from the Rome branch, which serviced the papal court. The Medici owed their success at court to their consistent ability to procure the office of depositary general, the highest position that a lay banker could achieve in the papal financial hierarchy.

The internal organization of the Medici bank differed from the earlier generation of banks, in that each branch was a separate partnership, with its own capital and its own books, directed by a managing partner, who shared in the profits. The senior partners retained control by owning at least 50 percent of the capital of the branches. The advantage of the

Medici style of organization was that it rendered sudden collapse unlikely. Each branch was a distinct legal entity; thus the failure of one did not necessarily lead to the failure of the others. The structure became widespread among banks after 1345.

The Medici and their counterparts engaged in diverse banking activities, including trade and commercial enterprises, tax farming (involving the sale of taxation rights by a local government to a private individual), maritime insurance, speculation in the money market, and foreign exchange. Few, however, focused on all at once. The Borromei bank of Milan, for example, concentrated mostly on trade; the Medici made considerable profit in foreign exchange. Profit in foreign exchange was effected primarily through means of the bill of exchange, one of the great innovations of medieval and Renaissance bankers. The bill derived from the so-called *instrumentum ex causa cambii,* a notarial document in which a debtor promised repayment in an equivalent sum in another place. These were commonly used at the international trading fairs at Champaigne in the thirteenth century.

The bill of exchange was a more sophisticated instrument. It usually involved four parties: a deliverer and taker in one place, and a payer and a payee in another place. The deliverer lent money to the taker, who gave a bill of exchange back in return. The bill was then payable in another location in another currency after a certain period of time (usance). Generally, the deliverer and the payee were affiliated with each other (banking house and correspondent), as were the taker and payer (banking house and correspondent). The profit from bills of exchange came from hiding interest rates in the exchange rates, which allowed the deliverer to receive more money than he originally paid out. This elaborate scheme was used to avoid the church ban on usury.

Bills of exchange also helped in the transfer of credit balances over long distances without the risk and cost of transporting money in coins. Popes and their bankers made use of bills to transmit money from far-off places back to the papal court. In places where lending at interest was not as restricted, such as the Netherlands in the sixteenth century and England in the seventeenth century, the bill of exchange functioned primarily as a means of effecting credit transfers. The practice of endorsing bills of exchange, that is, making them negotiable, was not widespread before the sixteenth century.

Local deposit banks. Venice led the way in local deposit banking. Local deposit banking was well suited to the city, which had always functioned as a clearinghouse for international merchants. The banks were located along the Rialto bridge and were known locally as *banche di scritta* or *banche di giro.* They performed manual exchange of coins, both local and foreign, accepted deposits, and made payments via transfer. Deposits typically came in two forms: noninterest-bearing current accounts, used primarily by merchants to settle balances on demand, and interest-bearing time deposits, representing more long-term deposits.

Although the Venetians were by the fifteenth century the industry leader, the earliest evidence for local deposit banking comes from Venice's great rival, Genoa. Documents from the twelfth century indicate the existence of moneychangers and the acceptance of deposits. In subsequent years, Genoese banks added more functions. By the fourteenth and early fifteenth century, deposit banks were common throughout Europe in major trading centers. Local deposit banks are the most direct ancestors of modern banks. The practice of payment through book transfer rather than coin encouraged bankers to leave only a portion of their deposits on reserve. This then freed the banker to invest the rest in commercial ventures or in loans to third parties. The effect was to create "bank money," a hallmark of the modern banking system. In the fourteenth century, Venetian bankers already operated on a fractional reserve system, and by the fifteenth century sources speak openly of *monete di banco* (bank money).

One of the peculiarities of deposit banks was that they required merchants to transact business in person. Thus merchant A gave the banker verbal instructions to transfer from his account the amount owed to the account of merchant B. These verbal instructions were legally binding. The fourteenth century offers evidence that written orders or checks were used to enact transfers in Italy (where they were called *polizze*). This became more common in the sixteenth century, particularly after 1570. The first checks issued in England date from the 1660s. The Venetians, however, remained steadfast in requiring the physical presence of merchants to enact transfers.

The reliance on fractional reserve and the creation of bank money proved risky business. While it had the salutary effect of increasing the amount of money in circulation without increasing stocks of coins and precious metals, it rendered the banks themselves precarious. In this era of high-risk investments, the mortality rate of deposit banks was frighteningly high. The Venetians experienced frequent failures;

the "panic" of 1498–1499 saw the collapse of three out of every four Venetian banks. The dukes of Burgundy forbade local banks to accept deposits and make payments in transfer in an attempt to forestall the same occurrence in their realm. Meanwhile, in the Low Countries, deposit banks all but disappeared in the fifteenth century.

Public banks. The failure of local deposit banks led to the widespread creation of public banks. These were government institutions, monitored and controlled by public officials. The earliest was the so-called Taula de Canvi (exchange bank), founded in Barcelona in 1401. It received surplus taxes, extended credit to the city at a rate of 5 percent, and administered and received the savings of citizens. This bank was expressly forbidden, however, to lend money to private citizens or, after 1437, to hold the accounts of private banks, measures intended to limit speculation. The bank lasted until 1853, when it was absorbed by the Bank of Spain. Valencia and Genoa followed Barcelona's lead in 1408.

Public banks became more common in the sixteenth century. Palermo and Naples, cities where Aragonese influence was strong, founded public banks in the middle of the century. In 1586 the Genoese created the Cartulario d'Oro, a public bank that handled much of the gold from the Spanish colonies in the Americas, for which the Genoese served as middlemen. The bank was so successful that in 1606 Genoa established a second one, the Cartulario d'Argento, to handle Spanish silver. The Venetians followed suit, opening the Banco della Piazza di Rialto in 1587. The Milanese, in turn, founded the Banco di San Ambrogio in 1593, and then the Romans started the Banco di San Spirito in 1605. In northern Europe, the Wisselbank (exchange bank) of Amsterdam opened in 1609, followed by the Bank of Hamburg in 1619. Public banks were also founded in Nürnberg (1621), Delft (1621), Rotterdam (1635), and Stockholm (1656). By the end of the seventeenth century, some twenty-five public banks were operating in Europe.

With the rise of public banks came shifts in the pattern of international banking. The Florentines, the bellwethers of the profession, declined in importance in the late fifteenth and sixteenth century, with merchant banks declining from eighty in 1338 to eight by 1516. The Medici bank closed its doors forever in the last decade of the fifteenth century, as did several other Florentine firms. The reasons for the eclipse of the Florentines are not entirely clear. Scholars originally blamed the Medici's problems on poor management by Lorenzo de' Medici (the Magnificent), who was accused of being more concerned with the arts than with business. Scholars today look to more general causes for what was in fact a much broader phenomenon. Some cite difficulties in Rome, Florence's traditional source of ready cash, while others speak of slowness in recognizing such new and growing markets as Antwerp, as well as reluctance to abandon traditional and then declining markets such as Bruges and Lyon.

Italians nevertheless remained active in international banking, particularly the Genoese. In general, however, the locus of activity moved north, to southern Germany. The decline of the Medici coincided neatly with the rise of Jacob Fugger, the great merchant from Augsburg. In addition to the Fuggers were numerous other firms, including the Welsers, Hochstetters, and Meuting of Nürnberg. In France, the era also saw the spectacular rise of the banking enterprises of Jacques Couer.

The success of the German firms was aided by the discovery and exploitation of silver and copper mines in Saxony, Moravia, Silesia, and Tyrol. The Fugger monopolized the lucrative silver mines of Tyrol, from which it derived huge profits. Southern German towns also enjoyed the advantage of agricultural surplus and general prosperity. Unlike their Italian counterparts, German firms were quick to realize the potential of Antwerp and had already established themselves there in significant numbers by the late fifteenth century.

The structure and organization of the German firms resembled that of their Italian forebears. German companies drew up similar articles of association, relied heavily on family members to staff key positions, and made use of bills of exchange. Substantial differences remained, however. German banks were more highly centralized and more inclined to form monopolies. Although they were aware of the technique, they did not keep their account books in double entry, as contemporary Italian firms did.

Nevertheless, it was the public bank, not the international one, that constituted Europe's most common form of banking from the sixteenth to the eighteenth century. The profession's center of gravity shifted progressively north, to the new commercial leaders, the Dutch and the English. The bulk of the later innovations occurred in these countries.

Money. Banks played an important role in the money supply. Bankers, money changers, and merchants brought metal to the mint. The mint then struck money, deducting operating costs and seigniorage, a tax imposed by the state. Although sovereign authorities monitored the minting of coins, the marketplace determined the quantity of coins struck. The amount of money produced is often expressed by economic historians by the equation $M = P + (C + S)$, where M represents the total amount of money coined from the metal handed over to the mint, P equals the amount of money received in return by the merchant who brought the metal to the mint, C is the amount kept by the mint to cover operating costs, and S represents the money forwarded to the government in taxes (seigniorage).

While contemporary China already used paper money, Renaissance Europe relied on metal, with three basic types of coins: gold, silver, and billon. The value of coins was determined by weight and fineness. Billon coins were the least valuable, consisting of minimal amounts of silver, heavily alloyed with other less valuable metals (notably copper). Coins were the medium of exchange of the common man, used in the marketplace and for petty transactions. Gold coins, the most valuable, were used primarily for large transactions, such as those conducted by international merchants and industrialists, while higher-quality silver coins were standard for many other transactions, including rents and substantial domestic purchases. The lines of distinction were, however, not always clear-cut.

Gold coins came back into widespread use in western Europe in the thirteenth century. The trading centers of Genoa (1252), Florence (1252), and Venice (1284) led the way. The Florentine *florin,* consisting of 3.5 grams of gold of 24-karat purity, quickly became a favorite means of exchange on the international market and was widely imitated. Derivatives were struck in France, the Holy Roman Empire, the Netherlands, and the Baltic region. The Venetian *ducat,* a coin of 24-karat purity that weighed 3.56 grams, became standard in trade between western Europe and the Levant. By the fourteenth and fifteenth century, gold coins were widely used throughout Europe (table 1).

Europe's silver coinage generally consisted of large silver pieces and various smaller ones. At the beginning of the thirteenth century, Italian states introduced *grossi* (literally, "big ones"), coins of almost pure silver that weighed approximately two grams. The English followed suit with the groat; the French with the *gros tournois;* the Low Countries with the *groten;* and the Holy Roman Empire with the *groschen.* Like gold coins, silver coins were of varying size and weight. The French *gros tournois,* for ex-

TABLE 1. Gold Coins in Use in Europe in the Fourteenth and Fifteenth Centuries

Place	Coin/Date	Weight in grams	Fineness in karats
Florence	florin (1252)	3.52	24
Genoa	genovino (1252)	3.56	24
Venice	ducat (1284)	3.56	24
France	ecu (1358)	4.08	24
	salut (1423)	3.5	24
England	noble (1351–1412)	7.78	24
	noble (1412–1463)	7.0	24
Aragon	florin (1369–1475)	3.48	18
	ducado (1475/76)	3.5	24
Castile	excelente (1477)	3.74	23¾
Portugal	cruzado (1457)	3.74	23¾
Hungary	florin/ducat (1328)	3.54	24
Brittany	rider (1420)	3.05	24
Burgundian Netherlands	philippus/rider/ cavalier (1433–1447)	3.63	23¹³⁄₁₆

Source: Carlo M. Cipolla, *Before the Industrial Revolution,* pp. 176–177; Peter Spufford, *Money and Its Use in Medieval Europe,* p. 322.

ample, was approximately twice as big as its Italian counterpart. In the fifteenth century, the discovery of rich deposits of silver at Tyrol and Saxony greatly increased silver stocks, as did the opening up of the Americas in the next century. As a result, states began introducing still larger silver pieces. In the late fifteenth century, the Milanese introduced the *testerone* (big head), weighing 9.79 grams; the Tyrolese produced the silver *guldiner,* which weighed 31.6 grams. In the sixteenth century, the Spanish, capitalizing on the influx of silver, coined the famous piece of eight, weighing 30 grams.

The smallest denomination of the silver coinage in all these countries was the silver penny. As with other coins, its name varied (*denaro, denier, denar, pfennig*). The coin usually contained a minimum amount of silver and was frequently debased (reduced to billon). Debased pennies often darkened (from the alloy with copper) and thus became known as "black money." The Venetian penny became so flimsy and thin that it might crumble if grasped too tightly. The English, however, were among the few who managed to maintain the quality of their silver penny. Since mints profited little from the coining of these dark and dirty disks, they produced relatively few. This created a general scarcity throughout Europe.

Europe's coinage was continually changing. New coins were introduced as old ones were eliminated.

Many Italian cities, for instance, produced the *quattrino,* worth four pennies. Conversely, the English produced a coin worth a fourth of a penny. Debasement remained a constant problem, particularly in Italy and France. The French *ecu* dropped from 24-karat fineness and a weight of 4.08 grams in 1388 to a fineness of 18 karats and a weight of 3.5 grams in 1429.

The return in goods and services of the various coins depended on local market conditions. In Antwerp in 1433 a gold *cavalier* bought nine days' worth of work from a master builder, while three silver *grossi* (worth about one-fifth of the gold *florin*) in Florence at the same time bought a single day's work of a master builder. In France, a silver *blanc* (which replaced the *gros tournois* in the middle of the fourteenth century) paid for a half-hour session with a prostitute in Dijon.

One of the peculiarities of the premodern European monetary system was the use of moneys of account—what Carlo M. Cipolla called "ghost monies." These were common from the Middle Ages even into the eighteenth and early nineteenth centuries. Moneys of account were used for accounting purposes in budgets and business ledgers. They represented a measure of value rather than, as with actual coins, a medium of exchange and store of wealth. Throughout Italy, for example, books were kept in *lire, soldi,* and *denari.* Only the last unit *(denari)* corresponded to an actual coin; the others represented imaginary units, figured at 20 *soldi* or 240 *denari* per *lira* (12 *denari* = 1 *soldo*), with their values dating from the time of Charlemagne.

An exchange rate existed between the physical coin and the money of account, which fluctuated over the years. The introduction of new coins complicated the system further. The coining of the silver *matapan* in Venice in the thirteenth century led to the use of two moneys of account, one based on the old *denaro* and another on the new coin. This also occurred in Florence when that city introduced its own large silver piece. The Florentine exchange figures cited above in *soldi a piccioli* refer to the money of account pegged to the silver *denaro.* In subsequent years the system would mutate still further. By the High Renaissance scores of moneys of account were in use throughout Renaissance Europe, creating a maze that scholars have shown reluctance to follow through all its twists.

[For an image of a moneylender at work, see the painting by Quentin Massys in the color plates in this volume.]

See also **Coins, Medals, and Plaquettes; Datini, Francesco; Fugger Family.**

BIBLIOGRAPHY

Cipolla, Carlo M. *Before the Industrial Revolution.* Reprint. New York, 1992.

Cipolla, Carlo M. *The Monetary Policy of Fourteenth-Century Florence.* Berkeley, Calif., 1982.

The Dawn of Modern Banking. New Haven, Conn., and London, 1979. A collection of still useful essays.

De Roover, Raymond. *Money, Banking, and Credit in Medieval Bruges.* Cambridge, Mass., 1948.

De Roover, Raymond. "New Interpretations of the History of Banking." In *Business, Banking, and Economic Thought in Late Medieval and Early Modern Europe.* Edited by Julius Kirshner. Chicago, 1974. Pages 200–238. Still the best introduction to the subject.

De Roover, Raymond. *The Rise and Decline of the Medici Bank.* New York, 1966.

Dillen, J. G. van, ed. *History of the Principal Public Banks.* Reprint. London, 1964.

Ehrenberg, Richard. *Capital and Finance in the Age of the Renaissance.* 1928. Reprint. New York, 1963. An abbreviated version of the original German version.

Goldthwaite, Richard A. "Local Banking in Renaissance Florence." *The Journal of European Economic History* 14 (1985): 5–53.

Goldthwaite, Richard A. "The Medici Bank and the World of Florentine Capitalism." *Past and Present* 14 (1987): 3–31. An important reconsideration of the Medici and the Florentine banking world in general.

Lane, Frederic C., and Reinhold Mueller. *Money and Banking in Medieval and Renaissance Venice: Coins and Moneys of Account.* Baltimore, 1985.

Mueller, Reinhold. *The Venetian Money Market: Banks, Panics and the Public Debt, 1200–1500.* Baltimore, 1997.

Munro, John H. *Bullion Flows and Monetary Policies in England and the Low Countries, 1350–1500.* Brookfield, Vt., 1992.

Spufford, Peter. *Handbook on Medieval Exchange.* London, 1986.

Spufford, Peter. *Money and Its Use in Medieval Europe.* Cambridge, U.K., 1989.

Usher, A. P. *The Early History of Deposit Banking in Mediterranean Europe.* Cambridge, Mass., 1943.

WILLIAM CAFERRO

BARBARO, FRANCESCO (1390–1454), Venetian statesman, intellectual. Franesco Barbaro was born to the highest nobility of the merchant empire of Venice. He received a private education just as the first generation of humanist pedagogues—which included his teachers Giovanni Conversino da Ravenna, Gasparino Barzizza, and Guarino Veronese—was systematizing the teaching of classical literature and defining its relation to the formation of character. Patrician mentors also influenced Barbaro's intellectual development, as did his stay at the University of Padua, where he received a doctorate in arts in 1412. Barbaro became one of the first patrician humanists, an amateur of consummate skill, a type that prevailed in the fifteenth century in Italy and that characterized humanism in Venice.

Barbaro's humanist culture reached early expression in a work that had huge success throughout the Renaissance. *De re uxoria* (On marriage) was widely read in manuscript in its original Latin form, as well as later in print in Latin and all the major vernaculars. When he was twenty-five, Barbaro dedicated the work to his Florentine friend Lorenzo de' Medici as a gift on the occasion of the latter's marriage in 1416. The book, the gift, and the personalities involved make this exchange a perfect Renaissance moment. In an environment where the high nobility had adopted humanism as a mark of superior status, the gift of a book in classicizing Latin from one young patrician to another constituted an exquisite act of courtesy. That the book celebrated marriage as the central institution by which an aristocracy secured its continuity made the act also a substantial statement of patrician ideology.

The two sections of *De re uxoria* speak respectively of choosing a wife and of a wife's duties. A wife should be chosen, argues Barbaro, neither for her beauty nor her wealth but for her nobility and virtue. As a mother, she will transmit her character attributes to her offspring. Only such a woman can ensure that a nobleman's children will be worthy of their ancestors and thus continue to merit their status as leaders of the state. Beyond childbirth, child rearing, and the management of household and servants, a wife is required above all to achieve "unanimity" with her spouse—she must obey, comfort, and understand him, while preserving decorum in private and displaying, by her dress and adornment, the signs of his status in public. In sum, the work is a recipe for aristocratic marriage in an age when marriage alliances undergirded aristocratic preeminence.

Barbaro's other literary activity was letter writing, evidenced in the enormous correspondence that survives. Models of humanist epistolary style, Barbaro's letters track the political career of Venice during its mainland expansion, as well as the personal relations among patrician leaders, humanist friends, and family members. Of special interest are the letters recording Barbaro's heroic role as military governor of the city of Brescia during its siege (1437–1440) by Milanese forces.

Barbaro also served as governor of mainland cities and as foreign ambassador, on the Venetian Council of Ten, as a ducal adviser (*savio grande*) repeatedly from 1442 to 1452, and, beginning in 1452, as procurator of St. Mark, the highest political position (with life tenure) available in Venice short of the dogeship. Barbaro achieved what the Renais-

sance much admired: a combination of conspicuous cultural and political excellence.

BIBLIOGRAPHY

Primary Works

Barbaro, Francesco. *De re uxoria liber* (On marriage). Edited by Attilio Gnesotto. *Atti e memorie della Regia Accademia di Scienze, Lettere ed Arti in Padova* n.s., 32 (1916): 6–105. Translated by Percy Gothein in *Das Buch von der Ehe* (The book on marriage). Berlin, 1933. Preface and second part translated by B. G. Kohl in B. G. Kohl and Ronald Witt, eds. *The Earthly Republic: Italian Humanists on Government and Society.* Philadelphia, 1978. Pages 177–228.

Barbaro, Francesco. *Epistolario* (Correspondence). Edited by Claudio Griggio. Vol. 1 of *La tradizione manoscritta e a stampa* (The manuscript and printed book tradition). Florence, 1991–.

Secondary Works

King, Margaret L. "Caldiera and the Barbaros on Marriage and the Family: Humanist Reflections on Venetian Realities." *Journal of Medieval and Renaissance Studies* 6 (1976): 19–50.

King, Margaret L. *Venetian Humanism in an Age of Patrician Dominance.* Princeton, N.J., 1986. Pages 323–325 and *passim.*

MARGARET L. KING

BAROCCI, FEDERICO (c. 1535–1612), Italian painter. Barocci helped initiate the reform of painting begun in the late sixteenth century that heralded the creation of early baroque style. His naturalistic approach to color and the representation of emotions departed strongly from the prevailing late mannerist styles of the time, which emphasized stereotyped formulas and stylish artifice. He contributed heartfelt and unforgettable images of penance, saintly ecstasy, and transcendent joy to the iconography of the Catholic Reformation

Training and Early Career. Barocci learned painting from Battista Franco in Urbino, his hometown. He also encountered Venetian colorism from examples of Titian's work in the ducal collections in Pesaro. Trips to Rome in the 1550s and 1560s gave him access to the high Renaissance style of Raphael. From 1561 to 1563, he collaborated with Federico Zuccaro on several fresco cycles, the decoration of the Casino of Pius IV, and the Belvedere in the Vatican. He was supposedly poisoned in Rome, a mishap that sent him back to Urbino and virtually halted his painting work until 1567. When he took up his brush again, he had remade his own style on the model of Correggio's vibrant colorism and fervid emotionalism. This mature style, strongly grounded in exhaustive drawings from life, led the way to a dramatic stylistic change for many artists, away from stock late mannerist conventions and toward the expressive naturalism of the early baroque.

Paintings. First among Barocci's major works in his new eloquent style is his *Deposition* done for Perugia Cathedral (1567–1569). The painting unites two dramatic actions, the taking down of Christ's body from the cross and the compassionate swoon of the Virgin, which elicits a flurry of concern in a sudden rush of movement from the three Marys. The emotional intensity of the expressions and actions is matched by a fierce wind that whips the hair and draperies of the figures attendant on Christ. His pale motionless form creates an icy coloristic core around which even the most vivid yellows and reds of draperies are tempered and cooled.

Another of Barocci's early masterpieces that won him considerable acclaim outside his native Urbino was the *Madonna del Popolo* (now in the Uffizi, Florence) made for the confraternity of S. Maria della Misericordia of Arezzo between 1575 and 1579. The sweetness and freshness of the faces of infants and women earned Barocci much praise. The swirling compositional core of the work uniting heaven and earth anticipates the dynamic structures of baroque altarpieces to come. The frank piety of the worshipers drawn from all levels of society proclaims in visual form the emphasis on an individual's direct connection with God, part of a popular reform movement arising from lay practice initiated by Filippo Neri that was taking shape in Rome around the same time.

For the Chiesa Nuova, Filippo Neri's "New Church" of the Oratorians (a congregation of secular priests and clerics) in Rome, Barocci painted several altarpieces, the *Visitation* (1582–1586) and the *Presentation of the Virgin* (1593–1594). The *Visitation* presents a down-to-earth and homey interpretation of the greeting handclasp exchanged between the cousins Elizabeth and the Virgin Mary. The prosaic solidity of Barocci's figures grounds his work firmly in observed reality and achieves the simplicity and clarity in sacred subjects called for by many Catholic Reformation writers. The work was a favorite of Neri's, who often stood rapt in ecstasy before it. The Oratorians had a long wait for the *Presentation,* since it was not installed until 1603, a full decade after it was begun. Barocci routinely worked slowly and painstakingly, to the exasperation of some of his patrons.

Excellent examples of Barocci's lyric colorism are found in his smaller works. The touching encounter between the awestruck Magdalen and Christ newly

Federico Barocci. *Madonna del Popolo.* Painted between 1575 and 1579 for the confraternity of S. Maria della Misericordia, Arezzo, Italy. GALLERIA DEGLI UFFIZI, FLORENCE/ALINARI/ART RESOURCE

raised from the dead in the Correggesque *Noli me tangere* (Uffizi, Florence) is heightened by the misty luminosity of a golden dawn glimpsed through an open arch behind the Magdalen. In the splendid night *Nativity* (Madrid), the supernatural light emanating from the Christ child sets the luminous pinks and yellows of Mary's robes softly aglow. In the *Rest on the Flight into Egypt* (1573; Vatican) the full red of the ripe cherries handed from Joseph to the youthful Christ accents the changing reds and pinks that play across the faceted folds of the Madonna's dress.

A skilled portraitist, Barocci captured subtle nuances of expression in his subjects. His portrait of *Duke Francesco Maria II Delle Rovere* (1572; Florence, Uffizi), his chief patron, is characteristic of his approach. The soldier's fingers delicately touch the gleaming helmet, and a soft blush is given to the warrior's cheek. Barocci's *Self-Portrait* at around age sixty (Florence, Uffizi) is a thoughtful, melancholy work that reveals the somewhat ascetic soul of the solitary master.

Barocci typically created dozens of drawings in preparation for each of his painted works, from quick first ideas in pen and ink, through detailed individual figure studies, studies of light and shade, to complete compositional drawings. At times he worked on blue paper, a medium also favored by Venetian draftsmen. In addition, Barocci employed pastels and colored chalks, which he often used for graceful studies of heads. His few prints, such as the *Madonna and Child on the Clouds,* display sweetly pious subjects graced with subtly etched atmospheric effects.

Influence. Barocci's example inspired many younger artists of the generation after his own. Lodovico, Annibale, and Agostino Carracci from Bologna; Antonio Viviani of the Marches; Bernardino Poccetti, Cigoli (Lodovico Cardi), and Gregorio Pagani in Florence; and Francesco Vanni and Ventura Salimbeni in Siena were among the Italian painters most strongly influenced by Barocci's paintings and drawings. In the 1580s Cigoli traveled with Pagani to Arezzo and Domenico Passignano to Perugia to study Barocci's *Deposition* and *Madonna del Popolo.* Barocci led the way for many of these young reformers, pointing them back to a study of the art of Correggio and the Venetians, thus accelerating the revivification of color in Tuscan and Roman painting of the late sixteenth century.

BIBLIOGRAPHY

Bellori, Giovanni Pietro. *Le vite de' pittori, scultori ed architetti moderni.* (Lives of the modern painters, sculptors and architects, 1672). Edited by Evelina Borea. Rome, 1976. Life of Barocci, in Italian.

Emiliani, Andrea. *Federico Barocci: Urbino, 1535–1612.* 2 vols. Bologna, 1985. Major, modern evaluation of Barocci as painter and draftsman, in Italian. Well-illustrated, with some color.

Olsen, Harald. *Federico Barocci.* 2d rev. ed. Copenhagen, 1962. Useful early study in English with catalog of works.

Pillsbury, Edmund. "Barocci, Federico." In *Dictionary of Art.* Edited by Jane Turner. Vol. 3. New York, 1996. Pages 252–258. Useful short summary of life and works.

Pillsbury, Edmund, and Louise Richards. *The Graphic Art of Federico Barocci: Selected Drawings and Prints.* Exhibition catalog. Cleveland, Ohio, and New Haven, Conn., 1978. Includes an English translation from Bellori's *Vite,* pp. 11–24.

SUSAN E. WEGNER

BARON, HANS. *See* **Renaissance, Interpretations of the,** *subentry on* **Hans Baron.**

BARONIO, CESARE (1538–1607), Counter-Reformation historian. Baronio (latinized as Caesar Baronius) was born in the ancient Roman city of Sora in the Kingdom of Naples into a family of limited means but respectable lineage. He received an early formal education in the small town of Veroli, after which he was sent to Naples to start his training as a lawyer at the university. Perhaps for fear of an impending French invasion of Naples, young Baronio left for Rome in 1556, at the age of eighteen. In Rome, Baronio soon fell under the influence of Philip Neri, whose charisma, simple piety, and eccentricities attracted young students, established humanists, and churchmen into his orbit. Neri frequently held informal evening gatherings either to pray, to discuss literature or church reform, or to enjoy musical performances. These gatherings were gradually formalized into the Congregation of the Oratory in 1575, with Baronio as one of its founding members. The career plan of the young man from Sora thus changed from a life in the law courts to a life in the church. By receiving a doctorate in law in 1561, he fulfilled a promise to his father, but by being ordained a priest in 1564 he fulfilled the wish of his spiritual mentor Neri.

Cesare Baronio.

Works. Baronio made many contributions in his career as a churchman. The most important was his compilation of the *Annales Ecclesiastici* (Ecclesiastical annals; 1588–1607), a twelve-volume history of the church to the year 1198, using original documents. Initiated by Neri in 1558 as a series of lectures at the Oratory, the *Annales* eventually became a most influential work. It also served as a refutation of the *Centuriae Magdeburgenses* (Magdeburg centuries; 1579), the Lutheran work that attempted to prove historically that the Catholic hierarchy was an aberration of the apostolic tradition. In the hands of Counter-Reformation church leaders and preachers, the *Annales* became a powerful tool against Protestantism, and its impact was considerable, on Eastern Orthodoxy as well as Western Christendom. Among the many other religious or liturgical works that Baronio either authored or contributed to were the very popular *Martyrologium Romanum* (Roman martyrology; 1584), commissioned by Pope Gregory XIII, a biography of St. Ambrose, the *Roman Breviary* (1602), the *Roman Missal* (1604), and the *Roman Ritual* (1614).

The phenomenal success of the *Annales* and the popularity of the *Martyrology* made Baronio one of the most respected churchmen in Rome. Monarchs, prelates, and popes sought his counsel and company. Pope Clement VIII chose him to be his confessor and personal counselor. He was also elevated to the high dignity of the cardinalate on 4 June 1596. Pope Leo XI and Pope Paul V (who succeeded Clement VIII in 1605) also sought his counsel on major issues. Thus Baronio was a key player in the center of papal policies and European politics for over a decade spanning evenly between the sixteenth and seventeenth centuries. Among the major policy issues on which Baronio had significant influence were the absolution of the French king Henry IV from apostasy and his reacceptance into Catholic communion (1595), the reinstitution of Ferrara as a papal state (1597), the reimposition of direct papal administration over the church in the Kingdom of the Two Sicilies (1605), and the imposition of a papal interdict on the Republic of Venice (1606–1607).

Baronio's active role in these and other major events involving several European rulers evoked extreme responses to him personally, both favorable and unfavorable. The Spanish monarchs Philip II and Philip III thought of him as an adversary, even though he was technically a Spanish subject, coming from the Kingdom of the Two Sicilies, then under Spanish rule. He opposed Spanish claims to Sicily, supporting papal claims against Spain instead. This was the reason Philip III vetoed Baronio's election to the papacy in the conclaves that were held upon the deaths of Clement VIII and Leo XI, both in 1605. The "jus exclusivum," a right exercised by major European monarchs to exclude candidates for papacy who were odious to them, was invoked in these instances.

Years of hard work, austere living, and the neglect of his physical well-being caused Baronio's health to deteriorate. A painful ulcer finally claimed his life on 30 June 1607. His supporters soon rallied to canonize him as a saint. As in the case of the conclaves, his political enemies had greater influence and the canonization procedure did not progress very far. His fame and importance rest primarily on his pioneering historical work, the *Annales Ecclesiastici*.

See also **Historiography**, *subentry on* **Italian Historiography**; *biographies of figures mentioned in this entry.*

BIBLIOGRAPHY

A Cesare Baronio: Scritti Vari. Sora, Italy, 1963. A complete bibliography of Baronio scholarship.
De Maio, Romeo, et al., eds. *Baronio e l'arte: Atti del Convegno Internazionale di Studi, Sora, 1984.* Sora, Italy, 1985.
De Maio, Romeo, Luigi Gulia, and Aldo Mazzacane, eds. *Baronio Storico e la Controriforma: Atti del Convegno Internazionale di Studi, Sora, 1979.* Sora, Italy, 1982.
Pullapilly, Cyriac K. *Caesar Baronius: Counter-Reformation Historian.* Notre Dame, Ind., and London, 1975.

CYRIAC K. PULLAPILLY

BAROQUE, CONCEPT OF THE. The concept "baroque" is generally used to describe the music, art, literature, and philosophy of the seventeenth century and to specify the philosophical assumptions that unite them. It is also used more discriminately to describe a stylistic trend characterizing only certain work of that century.

The first sense of the baroque is popular because it conveniently underscores the importance and unity of a century that encompassed the Protestant Reformation, the Counter-Reformation, the development of Renaissance preoccupations, anticipations of the Enlightenment, and rapid change. But this first sense presumes that diverse cultural products deserve the same designation despite conspicuous differences. The seventeenth-century painters Pietro da Cortona (Italian), Nicolas Poussin (French), Peter Paul Rubens (Flemish), and Jan Vermeer (Dutch) may well share a "naturalistic vision" (Martin, *Baroque*, p. 13), yet they expressed it in very distinctive ways.

Baroque Art. Ceiling of the nave of the church of the Gesù, Rome. The central fresco is *The Triumph of the Name of Jesus* (1672–1685) by G. B. G. Baciccia (1639–1709). ALINARI/ART RESOURCE

The second sense of the baroque identifies the predominant style of the century, and holds it up as a standard by which artists are included or excluded. The baroque style is exuberant, sensuous, expressive, and dynamic, and these characteristics distinguish it from the more restrained and disciplined classical style typical of the Renaissance. In this more exclusive use of the term, Rubens and Pietro da Cortona are baroque artists, but not Vermeer and Poussin. This sense of the "baroque" does not take into account the relationships and exchanges among artists who, after all, were not aware that they worked in a baroque or a classical style. Such terms were not part of seventeenth-century artistic discourse.

The two definitions described here evolved from a nineteenth-century conception of the baroque, which developed in reaction against the prior, purely pejorative use of "baroque" as a synonym for all in the seventeenth century that offended eighteenth-century sensibilities. For advocates of neoclassicism, the era following the Renaissance was an age of decadence; its manners, morals, and arts—architecture above all—were absurd, grotesque, corrupt, and contrary to good (that is, classical) principles. Whether the word "baroque" derived from the Portuguese *barroco* and Spanish *barrueco,* a misshapen pearl, or from *baroco,* a nonsensical word created by medieval logicians as a memory aid for a convoluted argument in syllogism, the eighteenth century carried on its negative connotations to condemn the baroque for not being the Renaissance.

In the nineteenth century, Heinrich Wölfflin (*Renaissance and Baroque,* 1888) influentially reassessed baroque architecture in appreciative terms. In his view, the baroque was not a decadent and derelict, but a different historical style, with aims, motives, and formal qualities distinct from those of the Renaissance. In *Principles of Art History* (1915), Wölfflin explored the baroque style further, expanding his discussion to include painting and sculpture. He presented the classical (Renaissance) and baroque styles as two antithetical ways of seeing and composing, which he categorized in strictly formal terms: linear and painterly, closed and open form, plane and recession, multiplicity and unity, and absolute and relative clarity. The implication of Wölfflin's *Principles* was that, while these opposing modes of perception typified the Renaissance and baroque eras, they were not necessarily temporally fixed, but might be valid for other ages.

In the decades following Wölfflin and always in response to him, scholars debated the identity of "baroque": is it recurrent or the product of the spirit of its age? Benedetto Croce tried to return the term to its original, derogatory meaning, arguing that baroque was a morally-suspect aesthetic not bound by time or place. But Werner Weisbach, Nikolaus Pevsner, and Giulio Briganti, among others, defined baroque as a historical style, and for them, the challenge was to discover the historical, political, and religious conditions from which it emerged. As a result of their various discoveries, we now celebrate several birthdays of the baroque: in the later sixteenth century, in the 1620s, and in 1630.

Scholars still struggle with the Wölfflinian legacy of the classical-baroque synthesis, of an abstracted history of style. But calls for new words that would accommodate scholars' interests in the particular, their searches for authentic "period" discourses, and their applications of new approaches to the past have not yielded any satisfactory substitutes. Until they do coin a replacement that commends itself to all, perhaps the best counsel is to admit the ambiguity and to define one's terms: "by 'baroque', I mean. . . ."

See also **Rubens, Peter Paul**.

BIBLIOGRAPHY

Briganti, Giulio. *Pietro da Cortona; o, della pittura barocca* (Pietro da Cortona; or, about baroque painting). Florence, 1962.

Croce, Benedetto. *La storia dell'età barocca in Italia* (The history of the baroque age in Italy). Bari, Italy, 1929. 5th ed. 1967

Kurz, Otto. "Barocco, storia di una parola." *Lettere italiane* 12 (1960): 414–444.

Martin, John R. *Baroque.* New York, 1977.

Pevsner, Nikolaus. *Studies in Art, Architecture, and Design.* London, 1968.

Weisbach, Werner. *Der Barock als Kunst der Gegenreformation.* Berlin, 1921.

Wölfflin, Heinrich. *Principles of Art History.* Translated by M. D. Hottinger. Reprint. New York, 1950. Translation of *Kunstgeschichtliche Grundbegriffe* (1915).

Wölfflin, Heinrich. *Renaissance and Baroque.* Translated by K. Simon. Reprint. Ithaca, N.Y., 1964. Translation of *Renaissance und Barock* (1888).

CAROLYN H. WOOD

BARTOLOMMEO, FRA. *See* **Florence,** *subentry on* **Art of the Sixteenth Century.**

BARTOLOMMEO DELLA PORTA, FRA (Baccio della Porta; 1472–1517), Florentine painter. Baccio, a muleteer's son, is recorded in the workshop of Cosimo Rosselli in 1485. There he was influenced by the work of Rosselli's assistant Piero di Cosimo and befriended the painter Mariotto Albertinelli. Baccio left Rosselli's *bottega* at an unknown date and set up

Bartolommeo della Porta. *Madonna Enthroned with Saints.* Fra Bartolommeo is the second figure from the left, looking at the viewer. CONVENTO E MUSEO DI SAN MARCO, FLORENCE/ALINARI/ART RESOURCE

a workshop with Albertinelli in Florence. Few of the paintings executed in the 1490s by Baccio alone or in collaboration with Albertinelli have come to light. The *Last Judgment* fresco (Florence, Museo di San Marco) for the Hospital of Santa Maria Nuova, begun in 1499 and completed by Albertinelli in 1501, is unfortunately gravely damaged. However, its tonal unity and harmonious symmetrical organization, which owe much to the example of Leonardo da Vinci and inspired Raphael's fresco of the *Disputation on the Trinity* at the Vatican, can still be recognized.

Baccio came under the spell of the Dominican preacher Girolamo Savonarola about 1493 and joined the convent of San Domenico in Prato outside Florence on 26 July 1500. He apparently abandoned painting, left his drawings to Albertinelli, took the vows of the Dominican order, and adopted the name

Fra Bartolommeo. However, on 18 November 1504 he signed the contract for the *Vision of St. Bernard* (Florence, Uffizi), which places him at the convent of San Marco in Florence. Perhaps the new prior of San Marco, Sante Pagnini, urged Bartolommeo to resume painting. The *Vision,* which was completed by June 1507 for a new chapel in the Badia of Florence, is organized in a relief-like fashion, with the figures arranged almost parallel to the plane before a distant, blurred landscape. Although Bartolommeo contemplated Filippino Lippi's picture of the same subject (Florence, Badia), his painting—minus its surge of divine motion—is influenced by Perugino's refined figure style.

Bartolommeo traveled to Venice in the spring of 1508 and, upon his return, filled the void left by the departure of Michelangelo, Leonardo, and Raphael. He revived his partnership with Albertinelli after November 1508 (under the authority of the convent of San Marco) and dissolved it in 1513. In November 1510 Bartolommeo was awarded the prestigious commission for the altarpiece of *St. Anne, the Virgin and Child, with Saints* (Florence, Museo di San Marco) for the Hall of Great Council of the Palazzo della Signoria, Florence. However, he executed only the monochrome underpainting, which reveals his close examination of Leonardo's unfinished pictures. This tonal underpainting was to be overlaid by the warm, atmospheric coloring Bartolommeo had observed in Venice. In March 1512 the Republican government offered Bartolommeo's *Sacra Conversazione with the Mystic Marriage of St. Catherine of Siena* (Paris, Louvre), painted for the church of San Marco, to the departing French ambassador to Florence—a gesture that says much about his status. The lively figures' symmetrical arrangement is reinforced in both altarpieces by colossal half-circular niches flanked by half columns, which serve as foils. The geometric clarity of these paintings' designs is inspired by Giovanni Bellini's altarpieces for San Giobbe and San Zaccaria in Venice and Raphael's unfinished *Virgin and Child Enthroned with Saints* in Florence (Palazzo Pitti). The increased monumentality of the atmospherically rendered forms results from exposure to works by Bellini, Raphael, Leonardo, and Michelangelo.

Bartolommeo traveled to Rome in 1513, where he saw Michelangelo's Sistine ceiling and Raphael's ongoing work on the frescoes in the papal apartments at the Vatican. The urgency, complex counterpoise, and amplitude of form of the oddly proportioned figures in the *Salvator Mundi* triptych (Florence, Palazzo Pitti), which was completed in 1516 for a chapel in the SS. Annunziata, reveal his debt to Michelangelo's and Raphael's recent achievements.

On his visit to Ferrara in March 1516, Bartolommeo promised to paint a *Feast of Venus* for Duke Alfonso d'Este's study, the Camerino d'Alabastro. His death prevented him from carrying out this commission, which was passed on to Titian, whose picture the *Worship of Venus* (Madrid, Prado) is based on Bartolommeo's preparatory drawing (Florence, Uffizi).

Fra Bartolommeo was a formidable draftsman whose many studies were almost always preparatory for painting. Thus, it is often possible to reconstruct the design process of major paintings and to form an idea about pictures now lost or never completed. The visual excitement arrived at by the atmospheric overlaying of successive layers of (usually black) chalk upon a sheet, while searching for the final design (in emulation of Leonardo), is markedly tempered in the less spontaneous, definitive paintings. Bartolommeo's influence on Raphael and Andrea del Sarto (which was in both cases reciprocal), Albertinelli and Fra Paolino (his assistant), and the young prodigies Jacopo da Pontormo, Rosso Fiorentino, and even Titian was considerable.

See also biographies of figures mentioned in this entry.

BIBLIOGRAPHY

Borgo, Ludovico, and Margot Borgo. "Bartolommeo, Fra." In *The Dictionary of Art*. Edited by Jane Turner. Vol. 3. New York, 1996. Pages 302–307.

Fischer, Chris. *Fra Bartolommeo, Master Draughtsman of the High Renaissance: A Selection from the Rotterdam Albums and Landscape Drawings from Various Collections.* Rotterdam, Netherlands, 1990. Exhibition catalog.

Padovani, Serena, et al. *L'età di Savonarola: Fra Bartolomeo e la scuola di San Marco.* Venice and Florence, 1996. Exhibition catalog, Florence, Palazzo Pitti, and Museo di San Marco, 25 April–28 July 1996.

MICHAËL J. AMY

BASEL. Celts first settled where the Rhine becomes navigable and then begins its northward course toward the sea. Romans established an outpost there, followed by Christians settlers. By 1032, the city lay within the jurisdiction of the Holy Roman Empire. An episcopal see from its earliest beginnings as a city, Basel also fell under the jurisdiction of a bishop whose power waxed and waned according to the individual, and which the town council repudiated in 1521. In 1501, after contentious debate, the town council of Basel, signing on behalf of a "free city" of Basel, formally joined the Swiss Confederation, setting for it a course that would make of it a "Swiss" city with the Peace of Westphalia in 1648. In the years following, the town council made explicit the nature of the jurisdiction it claimed over the political life of the town. The town council refered to the city as an Imperial Free City, thereby expressly placing it under the patronage of the emperor, who—as they found in the 1520s—was actively and powerfully opposed to the independent reform of the religious life of his cities. It sought, and ultimately failed, to adjudicate reform within the city, the pace and extent of which the people finally determined in 1529.

In 1501 Basel brought to the Confederation not only one of its largest cities, with a population of roughly ten thousand, but more importantly, the place Erasmus would later choose as the most urbane and learned center north of Italy. An ambivalent component in that cosmopolitanism was the university, one of the oldest in Switzerland. It had been reformed in the 1490s; new statutes were published in 1500, but intellectually it remained conservative and closed during the Reformation in 1529 (reopening as a Protestant institution in 1532). Its student body remained more provincial than those of Paris, Oxford, or Bologna. Basel drew the ambitious and talented, but not to its university so much as to its informal circles of humanists and biblical scholars.

Humanist Scholarship and Book Production. Erasmus made of Basel the humanist capital of northern Europe, and he came there to work more closely with his publisher. Publishing and humanist scholarship were closely intertwined in Basel. Johann Amerbach, Adam Petri, and Anton Koberger were the earliest publishers to draw scholars to Basel to work with their publishing houses. Johann Froben, who took over Amerbach's publishing house in 1513, was equalled only by Aldo Manuzio in Venice in the quality of his typefonts and meticulousness of production. Erasmus moved to Basel to oversee the production of his works through Froben's house, and for many years served as Froben's editor. He published his edition of the Greek New Testament in 1516 with Froben. Johann Oecolampadius published editions of the Greek church fathers. Basel became the center of patristic publication in the north, a center for the publication of Bibles whose quality scholars could trust, and for the publication of exegeses, commentaries, and other forms of biblical scholarship. Other humanists worked for the presses; Beatus Rhenanus, for example, served as proofreader and editor for a number of the presses. The satirist and dramatist Pamphilius Gengenbach

Basel. Woodcut (detail). From Hartmann Schedel and Anton Koberger, *Liber chronicarum* (The Nürnberg Chronicle; 1493). BIBLIOTHÈQUE NATIONALE, PARIS

set up his own press, where he published his and others' works in German. Basel's publishers produced the full range of sixteenth-century books—histories, satires, poetry, exegeses, textual editions—in Latin, Greek, and German. The production of those books was overseen by Greek and Latin scholars, whose circles then received the books for discussion, criticism, and further dissemination.

Book production in Basel rested upon a complex economy of cultural production. Skilled artisans in Basel produced two- and three-dimensional images for the adornment of homes, prayer, books, illustration, liturgy, devout contemplation, and worship. Basel boasted a significant population of image carvers, stone sculptors, glass painters, carpenters, calligraphers, and designers of playing cards and devotional images. The names of some remain famous to this day. Hans Holbein the Younger became a citizen of Basel in 1520. There he found not only rich com-

missions for his paintings, but a market for his engravings and designs for woodcuts in books, and a circle of humanists with whom he sought to affiliate. Urs Graf, native of Solothurn, became a citizen of Basel in 1512, working first as a goldsmith and glass painter, then producing paintings, engravings, and woodcuts for books. Others who made Basel their home, such as the goldsmiths Jörg Schweiger and Ulrich Bissinger from Nürnberg and Nachbur and Kopf from Ulm, were renowned at the time but have slipped into relative oblivion.

In Basel, not only goldsmiths and jewelers, but papermakers, printers, bookbinders, booksellers, calligraphers, cartographers, painters of coats of arms, and preparers of parchment belonged to the prestigious and powerful Safran guild. Between 1501 and 1550, twenty-seven printers joined the Safran guild; seven joined the less powerful Gardeners' guild. Book production was a major industry in the town, requiring skilled laborers not only in the production of books, but in books' dependent industries: paper manufacture and leather preparation. Other industries in the town included wine production, fishing, and weaving, as well as the universally necessary trades of the miller, baker, butcher, copper and iron smiths, cooper, carpenter, glazier, painter, and tailor.

Reformation. The year 1529 marked a watershed in the history of Basel. On 9 February some two hundred citizens of Basel stormed first the cathedral, then parish churches, smashing altarpieces, panel paintings, sculpted figures, patens, chalices, crucifixes, choir screens, reliquaries, and monstrances. Within four hours, the accumulated material culture of medieval Christianity was destroyed. Shortly thereafter, the conservative members of the town council fled the city, and a rump council legislated formal Reformation of the practice of Christianity in the town. In the wake of the violence Erasmus, most of the university faculty and students, and a number of other prominent residents of the town departed. Over the rest of the century, Basel vacillated between Lutheran and Reformed (Calvinist) paths, definitively choosing Reformed by the end of the century. Erasmus returned to die peacefully in the city on the Rhine, but the Reformation had altered permanently the character of its urban culture.

The Reformation stilled the production of painted and sculpted images in Basel, a capital of late medieval artistic production. Iconoclasm may have also had a less explicit effect: no major public buildings were constructed during the period that architecturally is known as the Renaissance in northern Europe. Among the public buildings, only the Wine Merchants' Guild Hall was built in the Renaissance style. The great public buildings in Basel, the Münster, a late-fourteenth-century cathedral, and the Town Hall (1504–1521), were built before the Reformation, in the late Burgundian Gothic style, with its elaborate stonework and graceful proportions. The murals on the courtyard walls of the Town Hall were not painted until long after, from 1608 to 1611, by Hans Bock. Not until the nineteenth century would Basel emerge again as a center of artistic and architectural innovation and creativity.

BIBLIOGRAPHY

Primary Work

Basler Chroniken. Vol. 1. Edited by Wilhelm Vischer and Alfred Stern. Leipzig, Germany, 1872. Vol. 6. Edited by August Bernoulli. Leipzig, Germany, 1902.

Secondary Works

Bietenholz, Peter G. *Basle and France in the Sixteenth Century: The Basle Humanists and Printers in Their Contacts with Francophone Culture.* Geneva and Toronto, 1971.

Füglister, Hans. *Handwerksregiment. Untersuchungen und Materialien zur sozialen und politischen Struktur der Stadt Basel in der ersten Hälfte des 16. Jahrhunderts.* Basel, Switzerland, and Frankfurt am Main, Germany, 1981.

Guggisberg, Hans R. *Basel in the Sixteenth Century: Aspects of the City Republic before, during, and after the Reformation.* St. Louis, Mo., 1982.

Wackernagel, Rudolf. *Geschichte der Stadt Basel.* 3 vols. Basel, Switzerland, 1907–1924.

LEE PALMER WANDEL

BASEL, COUNCIL OF (1431–1449). The longest council in church history, the Council of Basel was initially convoked by Pope Martin V following the decree *Frequens* (1417), which had fixed the periodicity of general councils. Presided over by Cardinal Giuliano Cesarini, its main purposes were church reform, universal peace, extirpation of heresies, and church unity. Eugenius IV's quick attempt to adjourn the council failed. The synod grew in size with ecclesiastical and princely delegations totaling about 3,500 incorporates, mostly middle-class and university clergy. The council negotiated a treaty with the Bohemian Hussites, published valuable reform decrees (concerning papal provisions, canonical elections, provincial synods, morality of clergy, and so forth), and discussed various problems of a constitutional nature (supreme power in the church) and of theology (Immaculate Conception of the Virgin). A final rupture resulted from a quarrel concerning the location of a union council with the Orthodox Greeks in 1437. The pope suggested an Italian city, which the Greeks preferred. Eugenius IV transferred the council to Italy. A minority of the council moved to Ferrara and then Florence, where in fact the bull of union, *Laetentur Coeli,* was signed (1439); however, the majority remained in the upper-Rhine town of Basel, deposed Eugenius, and elected the duke of Savoy, Amadeus VIII, as pope Felix V (1439–1449). The coexistence of two councils and two papal curias polarized church and princes. Rapidly losing support after 1443, the Basel rump-synod dissolved itself at Lausanne in 1449.

The organization given to Basel ensured a maximum of equality of votes and participation (down to simple priests)—unique in conciliar history. Conciliarists played an important role in the development of political theory (constitutionalism versus monarchism). Like the Council of Constance (1414–1418), Basel functioned secondarily as a European congress, as a stage or forum for intellectuals, and as a market for manuscripts. Its conflicts led to increasing diplomatic activities, and produced an enormous number of letters, decrees, orations, and controversial tracts. The council also marked an important stage in the history of communication. Basel became attractive for bankers, artists, and musicians. A branch of the Florentine Medici bank was opened in 1433, and continued to operate until 1444. The painter Konrad Witz went to Basel; his *St. Peter's Draft of Fish* represents one of the first true-to-life landscapes in European painting. The composers Guillaume Dufay and Johannes Brassart stayed temporarily in Basel, too.

There was no explicit affinity of humanism to conciliarism, although many humanists were employed with the Roman curia. But Basel automatically attracted humanists as bishops, diplomats, or secretaries. In this upper-Rhine city they cultivated their literary connections and used the opportunity for book hunting, as Poggio Bracciolini had done in Constance. An important figure, with multiple connections, was Francesco Pizolpasso, bishop of Pavia and archbishop of Milan, who stayed at Basel from 1432 to 1439. Giovanni Aurispa served the synod as interpreter of Greek. He found manuscripts of the unknown Donatus commentary on Terence, the *Physica Plinii,* and probably the *Phoenix* of Pseudo-Lactancius; Tommaso Parentucelli (in 1447 elected Pope Nicholas V) unearthed the works of Tertullian; Pietro Donato, bishop of Padua, found a commentary to Donatus; Gregorio Corraro the 'de providentia' of Salvian. Nicholas of Cusa, not a humanist in the strict sense but a famous discoverer of manuscripts, published his "De concordantia catholica" in 1433 at Basel. The Council of Ferrara-Florence, through its reception of Platonism and Greek literature, was of profound importance to the western Renaissance.

The direct influence of humanism on northern Europe caused by Basel is difficult to determine. Some disparate traces of humanist script can be found. After all, the first presentations of the new "Ciceronian" oratory in the north were given in the conciliar aula of Basel: by Gerardo Landriani, bishop of Lodi; by Ambrogio Traversari, general of the Camaldolese order; by Corraro, Ugolino Pisani, and Lodovico da Pirano; and above all by Enea Silvio Piccolomini (1405–1464; Pope Pius II, 1458–1464). Piccolomini, who became secretary to Felix V, assembled a circle of humanist friends (Petrus de Noxeto, Giulio Romano), and in 1442, after his coronation by the em-

peror as "poeta laureate," gathered another group at the imperial chancery of Frederick III. In this regard he acted as an "apostle of humanism" (Georg Voigt), becoming the most precious legacy of Basel for the spread of humanism in central Europe.

See also Conciliarism.

BIBLIOGRAPHY

Primary Works

Acta Cusana: Quellen zur Lebensgeschichte. Edited by Erich Meuthen and Hermann Hallauer. Hamburg, Germany, 1976–1984.

Concilium Basiliense. 8 vols. Edited by Johannes Haller, Gustav Beckmann, and Hermann Herre. Basel, Switzerland, 1896–1936. Reprint, Liechtenstein, 1976.

Monumenta conciliorum generalium seculi decimi quinti. 4 vols. Edited by Frantisek Palacký and Ernst Ritter von Birk. Vienna and Basel, Switzerland, 1857–1935. Reprint, Vienna, 1977.

Piccolominus, Aeneas Sylvius (Pius II). *De gestis concilii Basiliensis commentariorum, libri duo* (Two books commenting on the acts of the Council of Basel). Edited and translated by Denys Hay and W. K. Smith. Oxford, 1992.

Secondary Works

Black, Antony. *Council and Commune.* London, 1979.

Helmrath, Johannes. *Das Basler Konzil 1431–1449: Forschungsstand und Probleme.* Cologne and Vienna, 1987. Includes bibliography. For humanists at Basel, see pp. 166–176.

Müller, Heribert. *Die Franzosen, Frankreich, und das Basler Konzil.* 2 vols. Paderborn, Germany, 1990.

Stieber, Joachim W. *Pope Eugenius IV, the Council of Basel, and the Secular and Ecclesiastical Authorities in the Empire.* Leiden, Netherlands, 1978.

Tanner, Norman P., ed. *Decrees of the Ecumenical Councils.* Vol. 1: *Nicaea to Lateran V.* London and Washington, D.C., 1990. Original text established by Giuseppe Alberigo et al. Texts of the conciliar decisions in the original languages with English translation.

JOHANNES HELMRATH

BASILE, GIAMBATTISTA (c. 1575–1632), Neapolitan litterateur. Giambattista Basile was born outside of Naples to a middle-class family that included a number of courtiers and artists. He spent his life in military and intellectual service at courts in Italy and abroad, was active in several academies, and held administrative positions in the government of the Neapolitan provinces. During his lifetime he was fairly well known for his poetic works in Italian, though today he is remembered principally for his masterpiece in the Neapolitan dialect: *Lo cunto de li cunti* (The tale of tales; 1634–1636), often called the *Pentamerone.*

Basile initiated his literary career with the sacred poem *Il pianto della Vergine* (The lament of the virgin; 1608). Subsequent works included several editions of his *Madriali et ode* (Madrigals and odes; first published in 1609); the marine pastoral *Le avventurose disavventure* (The adventurous misadventures; 1611); and a version of Heliodorus's *Aethiopica,* entitled *Del teagene,* published posthumously in 1637. Besides *Lo cunto,* Basile's literary corpus in Neapolitan consists of *Le Muse napolitane* (The Neapolitan muses; 1635), satiric eclogues depicting popular culture in Naples; and a series of jocose *Lettere* (Letters; 1612).

Lo cunto de li cunti is composed of forty-nine fairy tales framed by a fiftieth, and is the first such framed collection of fairy tales in Western literature. In many ways the structure of Basile's work mirrors, often in parodic fashion, that of Boccaccio's *Decameron*: there are five days of telling that contain ten tales each; the tales are told by ten grotesque lower-class women; the tale-telling activity of each day is preceded by a banquet, games, and other entertainment; and verse eclogues that satirize the social ills of Basile's time follow each day's tales. *Lo cunto* contains some of the best-known fairy-tale types (Sleeping Beauty, Puss in Boots, Cinderella, and many others), and has been a central point of reference for subsequent fairy-tale writers in Europe as well as a treasure chest for folklorists.

Lo cunto constituted a culmination of Renaissance interest in popular culture and folk traditions and was one of the most significant expressions of the baroque "poetics of the marvelous," known for its thirst for discovering new worlds, new inspirations, and new forms of poetic expression. Structurally, Basile's tales are close to the popular tales of the oral tradition from which he draws. But through his choice of Neapolitan as a literary language, his use of extravagant metaphor, and the representation of the rituals of daily life that permeate *Lo cunto,* his tales become a laboratory of rhetorical experimentation as well as an encyclopedia of Neapolitan popular culture. In his work Basile also engages in a critical and often carnivalesque dialogue with contemporary society—especially courtly culture—and the canonical literary tradition. His dynamic form of telling thus transgresses both thematic and formal conventions, and conflates high and low genres into an original genre, the literary fairy tale.

Lo cunto is one of the founding texts of the European fairy-tale tradition. Besides being one of the richest and most suggestive creations of the Italian baroque, Basile's work exerted a notable influence on later fairy-tale writers such as Charles Perrault, the Brothers Grimm, and Carlo Gozzi.

BIBLIOGRAPHY

Primary Works

Basile, Giambattista. *Lo cunto de li cunti*. Edited and translated by Michele Rak. Milan, 1986. Bilingual Neapolitan-Italian edition with extensive notes, indices, and introductory material.

Basile, Giambattista. *The "Pentamerone" of Giambattista Basile*. Edited and translated by Norman Penzer. 2 vols. London, 1932. English translation from B. Croce's Italian; includes extensive introductory material.

Secondary Works

Canepa, Nancy L. *From Court to Forest: Giambattista Basile's "Lo cunto de li cunti" and the Birth of the Literary Fairy Tale*. Detroit, Mich., 1999. First book-length critical study of Basile in English.

Croce, Benedetto. *Saggi sulla letteratura italiana del seicento*. Bari, Italy, 1911. See "Giambattista Basile e il 'Cunto de li cunti,'" pp. 3–118. Seminal essay on Basile's *Cunto* and its place in baroque culture.

NANCY L. CANEPA

BASSANO, JACOPO DA PONTE. *See* **Venice,** *subentry on* **Art in Venice.**

BAVARIA. The duchy of Bavaria from the 1400s through the 1600s was a large, geographically consolidated territory in the southeastern part of the Holy Roman Empire. Bordered in the south and east by Habsburg territories and the archbishopric of Salzburg, it stretched in the north to beyond the Danube and in the west to the Lech River.

Origins to the Fifteenth Century. Bavaria was one of the duchies into which the Holy Roman Empire was divided in the tenth and eleventh centuries. In 1180 Holy Roman Emperor Frederick I (ruled 1152–1190) consigned the duchy to his Bavarian ally Otto of Wittelsbach, whose descendants reigned in Bavaria until 1918. By the early 1400s the duchy was divided into Bavaria-Ingolstadt, Bavaria-Landshut, Bavaria-Munich, and Bavaria-Straubing.

Disputes and wars among Wittelsbach brothers and cousins plagued Bavaria during the fifteenth century. In 1445 the duchy of Bavaria-Ingolstadt was taken over by Duke Heinrich of Bavaria-Landshut. When in 1503 Heinrich's grandson, George the Rich, died without male heirs, he sought to leave his duchy to his son-in-law, Rupert of the Palatinate. This was opposed by Albrecht IV of Bavaria-Munich (ruled 1467–1508), who claimed the duchy as the next direct male heir. Following Albrecht's victory in the Landshut succession war (1504), the Upper Pa-

---

Bavarian Rulers, Fifteenth through Seventeenth Centuries

Dukes of Bavaria-Straubing
Albrecht I (ruled 1349–1404)
Wilhelm II (ruled 1404–1417)
Johann (ruled 1417–1425)
(*This particular line of the family expired in 1425; its territories were divided among the three remaining duchies.*)

Dukes of Bavaria-Ingolstadt
Stephen III (ruled 1375–1413)
Ludwig VII, the Bearded (ruled 1413–1443; d. 1447)
(*In 1445 territories were taken over by dukes of Bavaria-Landshut.*)

Dukes of Bavaria-Landshut
Heinrich IV, the Rich (ruled 1393–1450)
Ludwig IX, the Rich (ruled 1450–1479)
George the Rich (ruled 1479–1503)
(*In 1503 George died without any male heirs; territories were successfully claimed by Duke Albrecht IV of Bavaria-Munich.*)

Dukes of Bavaria-Munich (Upper Bavaria)
Ernst (ruled 1397–1438) and Wilhelm III (ruled 1397–1435) [corulers]
Albrecht III, the Pious (ruled 1438–1460)
Albrecht IV, the Wise (ruled 1467–1508)

Dukes of Bavaria
Albrecht IV, the Wise (ruled 1467–1508)
Wilhelm IV (ruled 1508–1550)
Albrecht V (ruled 1550–1579)
Wilhelm V (ruled 1579–1597, d. 1626)
Maximilian I (ruled 1597–1651) [elector of Bavaria, 1623–1651]

---

latinate was conceded to Rupert, but the rest of Bavaria came under the control of Albrecht. Bavaria once more was a united duchy. In order to prevent future partitions, in 1506 Albrecht established by decree the principle of primogeniture.

Throughout this period Bavaria's economy remained firmly rooted in agriculture, with more than 80 percent of its population composed of peasants who lived in small villages and produced for their own needs or local markets. Land ownership was divided among the Wittelsbach dukes, the church, and the numerous Bavarian nobility. The two largest cities were Munich, with a population around 1500 of approximately twelve thousand, and Straubing, with a population of approximately four thousand. Munich supported a modest textile industry and was a minor trade center linking Italy and the Tyrol to

southeastern Germany, Austria, and parts of Switzerland. In the second half of the sixteenth century, high taxation and the expulsion of Protestant artisans and merchants from many towns hampered economic growth.

The Sixteenth Century. The sixteenth century witnessed a striking increase in the power of the dukes. This meant a decline in the Bavarian Estates, composed of high churchmen, nobles, and burghers, whose role in government had expanded during the 1400s. Following policies laid down by Wilhelm IV's chancellor, Leonhard von Eck (1480–1550), sixteenth-century dukes introduced Roman law, assumed greater judicial powers, extended their authority over the church, and established a centralized administration made up of a privy council, council of war, spiritual council (to oversee the church), and *Hofkammer* (treasury department). By the 1600s Maximilian I (ruled 1597–1651) made new laws, raised taxes, and decided foreign policy issues without consulting the estates, making Bavaria an early prototype of an absolutist state.

Protestantism was slow to gain support in Bavaria, but in the 1550s pro-Lutheran nobles and burghers in the estates petitioned Albrecht V to permit communion in both kinds (whereby the consecrated bread and wine were given to the laity, as opposed to the wine being drunk only by the priest), clerical marriage, and the freedom to eat meat during Lent. Although staunchly Catholic himself, Albrecht at first made concessions to such demands in return for the estate's financial support. But by the 1560s, after he discovered (but never proved) a pro-Lutheran conspiracy among the nobility, Albrecht's attitude toward Protestantism hardened. He encouraged the activities of the Capuchins and Jesuits, established strict censorship, promoted the decrees of the Council of Trent, and established the spiritual council, made up of lay councilors, to oversee church affairs. By the 1580s, Lutheranism had virtually disappeared, and Bavaria became a bastion of Catholic orthodoxy and the political leader of resurgent German Catholicism.

During the late sixteenth century Wittelsbachs were elevated to episcopal sees in Freising, Regensburg, Passau, Eichstadt, and, most important, to that of the archbishopric of Cologne in 1583. In 1609 Duke Maximilian I was instrumental in the formation of the alliance of Catholic princes known as the Catholic League, and he became its first political and military director. When the Thirty Years' War began in 1618, Maximilian allied himself with his cousin and

Habsburg emperor Ferdinand II (ruled 1619–1637), and his army of thirty thousand men played a decisive role in early imperial victories. In 1623 he was elevated to the status of an imperial elector and received the Upper Palatinate. From 1632 to the close of the war in 1648, Bavaria suffered invasion and devastation by Swedish and French armies. At the Treaty of Westphalia (1648), however, the Bavarian Wittelsbachs retained the Upper Palatinate and the position as elector.

Cultural and Intellectual Life. Bavaria's political importance in the 1500s and 1600s was matched by its cultural and intellectual prominence. The University of Ingolstadt (founded 1472) was an early center of humanism in southern Germany beginning in the 1490s. The poet Conrad Celtis (1459–1508) taught there in the 1490s, and the Hebraist Johann Reuchlin (1455–1522) was a faculty member (1519–1521), as was Johann Eck, Luther's opponent at the Leipzig debates, who lent distinction to the philosophy and theology faculties (1510–1543). Beginning in the 1550s Jesuits increased their role in the Faculty of Theology and gradually extended their influence throughout the whole institution.

Bavaria's many churches, monasteries, and religious foundations provided commissions for numerous painters and sculptors in the 1400s and early 1500s, including such prominent figures as Hans Burgkmair (1473–c. 1531) and Albrecht Altdorfer (c. 1480–1538). Only after the political consolidation of the duchy in the sixteenth century, however, did the Italian-inspired tastes and lavish patronage of the dukes make the region a center of artistic innovation in Germany. Albrecht V (ruled 1550–1579) initiated several new building projects at the Munich Residenz, including a court museum for his collection of paintings and the Antiquarium for his collection of ancient sculptures. Under Wilhelm V (ruled 1579–1597), Friedrich Sustris (1540–1599), a Dutch artist trained in Italy, oversaw several impressive projects, including the Italian-inspired frescoes for the Antiquarium and the building of Michaelkirche in Munich, the first great Jesuit church built in northern Europe.

In the 1580s and 1590s work on the Residenz and Michaelkirche attracted to Munich large numbers of Italian and Italian-trained sculptors and painters, most notably the Dutch sculptor Hubert Gerhard (c. 1540–1621) and the Flemish successor to Sustris, Pieter Candid (c. 1548–1628). Maximilian I continued work on the Munich Residenz and funded the construction of another Jesuit church, Sankt Maria

Himmelfahrtskirche in Cologne, between 1618 and 1629. Only with the outbreak of the Thirty Years' War and the Swedish occupation of Munich after 1632 did this rich period in Bavaria's artistic history come to an end.

See also **Germany, Art in; Habsburg Dynasty; Holy Roman Empire.**

BIBLIOGRAPHY

Bauerreiss, Romuald. *Kirchengeschichte Bayerns*. Vols. 5–7. St. Ottilien, Germany, 1949–1955.

Carsten, Francis L. *Princes and Parliaments in Germany*. Oxford, 1959. See pp. 348–422.

Doeberl, Michael. *Entwickelungsgeschichte Bayerns*. Vol. 1. Munich, 1908.

Riezler, Sigmund. *Geschichte Baierns*. Vols. 3–5. Gotha, Germany, 1878.

Spindler, Max, ed. *Handbuch der bayerischen Geschichte*. 3 vols. Munich, 1967–1995. See vol. 2.

JAMES H. OVERFIELD

BAWDY, ELIZABETHAN. Elizabethan bawdy takes many forms and has popular origins (bawdy of the popular stage, jokes—sometimes bordering on or even including the scatological—in jest books) as well as learned and foreign ones. Attempts at a strict definition of bawdy have been made but it seems to have proved somewhat elusive. Roger Thompson saw it as an intent to provoke amusement about sex, distinguishing it from the pornographic (writing or representation to arouse lust or feed autoerotic fantasies), from the obscene (intended to shock or disgust, particularly through use of taboo words), and from the erotic (which places sex within the context of mutual love and affection). But since the most concise modern definition of the adjective "bawdy" is "humorously indecent," it is understandable that critics will disagree about what is humorous intent or how far indecency must be pursued to be pornographic or even obscene.

In addition, standards of what is indecent and what is humorous have changed. To write about Elizabethan bawdy often requires considerable historicizing: there was humor about the mentally ill (even medical works do not hesitate to tell "the most laughable" story of a "melancholic" who ceased to urinate because he feared he would drown the world and the clever stratagem of the physician who, after pretending that a neighboring village was on fire, called on the retentive's powers to extinguish it); humor about and at the expense of the uneducated, such as Touchstone's ridiculing of Audrey in Shakespeare's *As You Like It* (for instance when Touchstone makes a disquisition on "horned beasts" [3,3], which the shepherdess does not understand); and humor at the expense of women and their sexuality (some tied to notions of Galenic physiology, as, for instance, that only women can be "hysterical").

On the Elizabethan stage there was the bawdy jest, easily recognized and sometimes not so easily appreciated; the bawdy pun, sometimes indicated by contextual or verbal markers like the phrase "thereby hangs a tale/tail"; and the bawdy gesture. Naturally gestures are much harder to demonstrate, partly because of the paucity of stage directions in the period and because rules of decorum forbade explicit sexual reference, but mainly because it was the actor's role to play to the particular audience at hand. Thus it was up to the person playing Audrey in *As You Like It* to find a posture or gesture to elicit Touchstone's rebuke, "Bear your body more seeming, Audrey" (5.4.68–69). In the same play, "melancholy" Jaques ecstatically "did laugh sans intermission" (2.7.32) after seeing the jester Touchstone in the forest drawing "a dial from his poke" (20), looking at it and reading the time "It is ten a' clock" (22). After a few bawdy puns, which Helge Kökeritz first identified, Jaques concludes, "And thereby hangs a tale" (28). Would Jaques, by a risqué gesture, have led the spectators to understand the "dial from his poke" as the male member? In the Globe he could have, although for some audiences such a gesture would have been in the folk-etymological sense "obscene," that is, not appropriate for the scene or stage. Similarly when Maria says to Sir Andrew, who has offered her his hand: "I pray you bring your hand to th' butt'ry-bar, and let it drink" (*Twelfth Night* 1, 3, 70), several obscene meanings and gestures can be imagined and indicated by the person playing Maria: taking his hand and placing it on one of her breasts might have been the least bawdy. In light of the references that follow, it is impossible not to consider the script as an invitation to come up with some bawdy gesture.

Besides the popular traditions of bawdy (including fabliaux, which often pivot on some unlearned person's failure to understand a bawdy pun, and jests, some of which were recorded in Elizabethan jest books), at least four imported traditions were current. First, Ovidian poetry and the *Priapeia*, a collection of poems to the ithyphallic god of fertility, were taken or allegedly taken from ancient inscriptions and represented many varieties of sexuality and sensuality. Various editions of these poems appeared in the Renaissance, including one in 1606 (probably published by Gaspar Schoppe) with an elaborate scholarly apparatus decoding the language

(giving, for instance, the many Latin and Greek synonyms for the male member). In what is possibly the most pornographic and perhaps also the most bawdy Elizabethan poem, Thomas Nashe's (1567–c. 1601) "Choice of Valentines," the author refers to Ovid and to Priapus. Second, coded poetry came from mid-sixteenth-century Italy, sometimes connected with literary academies such as Francesco Berni's (1497/98–1535) Accademia dei Vignaiuoli. One teasingly lighthearted but coded poem by a young cleric, later a bishop, became known in the Protestant north as "The Praise of Sodomy" by Giovanni della Casa (1503–1556). Under attack, the author later "defended" himself by arguing that the coding had been misread, that the poem was not about same-sex love but unconventional heterosexual intercourse. The third tradition was the poetry of Pietro Aretino (1492–1556), best known in England for the *sonnetti caudati* or sonnets with tails—two extra lines, playing on the pun tail/*cauda*—accompanying and wittily explicating the sixteen "modi" or sexual positions drawn by the painter Giulio Romano (mentioned by Shakespeare in *The Winter's Tale*). Finally there was the *Amadis de Gaule,* a series of chivalric romances of Spanish origin, which was often decried from the pulpit. It is a work of over twenty volumes by several authors that, in its French translation, seems to have functioned for educated Elizabethans as something of a sexual primer. For literature of the time it is important not only because Sir Philip Sidney (1554–1586) borrowed elements of its amorous relationships for the plot of his pastoral romance *Arcadia,* but also because incidents when protagonists retreated from their erotic experience to mull about it in poetry inspired John Donne's (1572–1631) "Extasie."

Among examples of Elizabethan bawdy, Nashe's "Choice of Valentines," which recounts a visit to a house of prostitution, and passages from his *Unfortunate Traveller* (the rape of Heraclide, told by a voyeuristic narrator) deserve first notice. Aretino appears as a character in the latter work, which contains a praise, several pages long, of the master of Italian bawdy. John Marston's (1576–1634) poem *The Metamorphosis of Pigmalion's Image,* very much in the Ovidian vein, reminds us that in Renaissance hand- or commonplace books (encyclopedias arranged by subject, such as the *Theatrum vitae humanae* [1565] by Theodor Zwinger) intercourse with statues is as much an "unmentionable" sexual transgression as incest, bestiality, and same-sex intercourse. In his *Hero and Leander,* Christopher Marlowe (1564–1593) has Neptune fondling Leander as Leander is trying to swim across the Hellespont.

Other than his Ovidian "Venus and Adonis," Shakespeare's playfully obscene but complimentary sonnet 20 may be his most daring poem: possibly harking back to Aretino's "tailed" sonnets, it makes reference to a penis when the speaker regrets, at least ostensibly, that nature "pricked . . . out" his admired friend with a male member. By contrast, with the exception of the poem "Sapho to Philaenis," John Donne's bawdy is unambiguously "hetero" in his elegy 19, "Going to Bed," where he describes the undressing of his beloved in terms of geographical discovery leading him to exclaim, "O, my America! my new-found-land." In his *New Discourse of a Stale Subject, called The Metamophosis of Ajax,* John Harington (1561–1612), inventor of the flush toilet, perfected scatological bawdy, possibly the only subcategory of bawdy in which the Elizabethans surpassed the Italians.

See also **Aretino, Pietro; Della Casa, Giovanni; Humor; Pornography.**

BIBLIOGRAPHY

Frantz, David O. *"Festum Voluptatis": A Study of Renaissance Erotica.* Columbus, Ohio, 1989.

Kökeritz, Helge. *Shakespeare's Pronunciation.* New Haven, Conn., 1953.

Moulton, Ian. "Transmuted into a Woman or Worse: Masculine Gender Identity and Thomas Nashe's 'Choice of Valentines.' " *English Literary Renaissance* 27 (1997): 57–88.

Partridge, Eric. *Shakespeare's Bawdy.* Rev. ed. London, 1968.

Romano, Giulio, Marcantonio Raimondi, Pietro Aretino, and Count Jean-Frederic-Maximilien de Waldeck. *I modi, The Sixteen Pleasures: An Erotic Album of the Renaissance.* Edited and translated by Lynn Lawner. Evanston, Ill., 1988.

Rubinstein, Frankie. *A Dictionary of Shakespeare's Puns and Their Significance.* 2d ed. New York, 1995.

Schleiner, Winfried. " 'That Matter Which Ought Not to Be Heard Of': Homophobic Slurs in Renaissance Cultural Politics." *Journal of Homosexuality* 26 (1994): 41–75.

Thompson, Roger. *Unfit for Modest Ears.* London, 1979.

WINFRIED SCHLEINER

BEATUS RHENANUS (1485–1547), German humanist. Beatus Rhenanus was the latinized name of Beatus Rhinower (original surname, Bild), a preeminent humanist in the personal circle of Erasmus (c. 1466–1536) and the humanist coteries of Basel and Alsace. Renowned as perhaps the most astute German textual critic of his era, he refined his critical techniques by editing ancient texts and writing insightful commentaries on them; he also produced unbiased historical writings.

Beatus received his early education at a distinguished humanistic school in his hometown of Sélestat in Alsace. From 1503 to 1507 he studied and collaborated with outstanding humanists in Paris, earning the high respect of Jacques Lefèvre d'Étaples (c. 1453–1536). He combined study with scholarly travel until 1511, when he settled in Basel for sixteen years as editor and corrector for the Froben press. His most significant works were editions of ancient pagan and early Christian writings, notably the works of the Roman historian Velleius Paterculus (1520) and the controversial Christian theologian Tertullian (1521), the early Christian histories *Autores historiae ecclesiasticae* (1523), and his own *Annotationes* for Pliny's *Naturalis historia* (1526). In this last work Beatus articulated his norms for editing texts.

From 1514, Beatus enjoyed a close personal friendship with Erasmus, who had the highest regard for Beatus's work and character. Erasmus occasionally left Beatus in charge of his personal and scholarly affairs. Beatus for his part considered Erasmus his "father and teacher." They grew somewhat apart as Beatus established his own reputation in the mid-1520s. Yet Erasmus continued to consider him among his most trusted friends. Beatus oversaw the posthumous edition of Erasmus's complete works (1540), which he furnished with an official biography of Erasmus, dedicated to the emperor Charles V.

At first Beatus considered Martin Luther (1483–1546) congruent with Erasmus's ideals, and he probably collaborated on an early collection of Luther's works. His support diminished after 1523 as he saw political divisions and peasant revolts, which he considered to be inspired by Luther. To avoid involvement in the religious upheavals at Basel, and to free himself from working for Froben, he withdrew in 1527 to Sélestat, where he devoted his remaining twenty years to historical research. His masterpiece, *Rerum Germanicarum libri tres* (Three books on German matters; 1531), offered a careful account of early German history. He did not glorify German antiquity as earlier German humanist writers had done, but advanced the use of straightforward historical analysis, including the use of coins, ruins, and other nontextual materials. Subsequent historians respected his high level of scholarship. He also brought out editions of the Roman historians Tacitus (1533) and Livy (1535).

Revisions in later editions of Tertullian (1528, 1539) show that Beatus became more conservative, or at any rate more cautious, in his doctrinal views. From 1539, he diminished his support for Protestant reformers and admitted the papacy's capacity to bring about a religious settlement. Yet he seems to have remained quietly Protestant in the Catholic Sélestat, and was attended by Protestant clergy at his death in 1547 during a journey through Strasbourg. In a biography of Beatus in 1551, the great Protestant humanist educator Johann Sturm praised Beatus's scholarship but subtly rebuked his lack of engagement in civic and religious affairs.

BIBLIOGRAPHY

D'Amico, John F. *Theory and Practice in Renaissance Textual Criticism: Beatus Rhenanus between Conjecture and History*. Berkeley, Los Angeles, and London, 1988. The best available study of Beatus's life and work.

Scarpatetti, Beat von. "Beatus Rhenanus." In *Contemporaries of Erasmus: A Biographical Register of the Renaissance and Reformation*. Edited by Peter G. Bietenholz and Thomas B. Deutscher. Vol. 1. Toronto, 1985. Pages 104–109 provide a detailed introduction.

JAMES MICHAEL WEISS

BEAUFORT, MARGARET (1443–1509), mother of King Henry VII of England, founder of Christ's and Saint John's Colleges, Cambridge. The mother of Henry VII, the first of the Tudor rulers of England, Lady Margaret Beaufort was the daughter of John Beaufort, duke of Somerset, and thus a descendant of Edward III and John of Gaunt. Her father having died when she was two years old, she was brought up by her mother until she was nine, when she became a ward of the duke of Suffolk and was brought to the court. It appears to have been Henry VI who conceived the idea of her marriage to his half-brother Edmund Tudor, earl of Richmond. The union was solemnized in 1455.

Edmund died within a year of the marriage; his son, later to be Henry VII, was born in January 1457 after his father's death. Margaret then married Henry Stafford, son of the duke of Buckingham. As Lancastrians Margaret and her husband were in some danger following the outbreak of the Wars of the Roses and the triumph of the Yorkists. Margaret remained in retirement and took as her third husband Lord Stanley, a favorite of the Yorkist king Edward IV.

After the accession of Richard III in 1483, Margaret's son Henry was acclaimed as the Lancastrian heir to the throne and began planning to claim it. He invaded England in 1485 and gained the crown at the Battle of Bosworth Field, in which Richard was slain. The defection of Lord Stanley to his stepson's camp during the battle may have aided the Tudor victory.

Although Margaret seldom appeared at court during Henry VII's reign, preferring to reside at her manors of Woking in Surrey and Collyweston in Northamptonshire, she took a keen interest in politics and made her opinions known. She was greatly influenced by John Fisher, bishop of Rochester, who became her friend and spiritual adviser. Encouraged by him to become a patron of learning, she endowed the Lady Margaret Professorships in Divinity at both Oxford and Cambridge, and Fisher became the first holder of the Cambridge chair. In 1503 she founded a preachership at Cambridge University; this position still exists, and the annual incumbent preaches at the university's Commemoration of Benefactors.

Margaret Beaufort. Effigy by Pietro Torrigiano in Westminster Abbey, London. COPYRIGHT DEAN AND CHAPTER OF WESTMINSTER, WESTMINSTER ABBEY, LONDON

Shortly before her death Margaret was inclined to bequeath her substantial estates to Westminster Abbey, but Fisher persuaded her to support educational institutions at Cambridge instead. She took over God's House, which had been founded by Henry VI, and turned it into Christ's College, which opened in 1505. Next she refounded a monastic house as Saint John's College. It was to become one of the largest and wealthiest colleges in either of the universities. At the time of his succession in 1509, Henry VIII and his advisers sought to overturn Margaret's will, so that her property would come to the crown rather than the college, but Fisher secured a papal bull supporting the educational institution, and the king finally acquiesced in the foundation of Saint John's, which was completed in 1511. During the later years of her life Margaret spent considerable time at Cambridge, residing in the chambers she had designed and set aside for herself at Christ's, and she dominated the development of the university as few outsiders have ever done. She is also credited with adjudicating bitter disagreements between town and gown. In addition Margaret was a patron of England's earliest printers, William Caxton and Wynkyn de Worde, and established a school and chantry at Wimborne Minster, where her parents were buried.

Preaching her funeral sermon, Bishop Fisher extolled Margaret's devoutness and deeds of charity. All England, he said, wept at her death. Her benefactions to Cambridge University aided the rise of humanism there.

BIBLIOGRAPHY

Jones, Michael K., and Malcolm G. Underwood. *The King's Mother: Lady Margaret Beaufort, Countess of Richmond and Derby*. Cambridge, U.K., 1992.

Simon, Linda. *Of Virtue Rare: Margaret Beaufort, Matriarch of the House of Tudor*. Boston, 1982.

STANFORD E. LEHMBERG

BEAUMONT AND FLETCHER. *See* **Drama, English,** *subentry on* **Jacobean Drama.**

BECCADELLI, ANTONIO, IL PANORMITA. *See* **Pornography.**

BECCAFUMI, DOMENICO. *See* **Siena,** *subentry on* **Art in Siena.**

BEHN, APHRA (1640–1689), English Restoration playwright, novelist, poet. Aphra Behn was the most prolific among late seventeenth-century women writers, and she was the first Englishwoman to survive from the proceeds of her pen. She lived an adventurous life, traveling to Surinam as a young woman with her family and later being a royal spy during the early days of Charles II's Restoration. Behn's reputation emerged from her sixteen plays produced on the London stage in the 1670s and 1680s. She was also an accomplished poet and wrote some of the earliest English novels. Behn translated Bernard Le Bovier de Fontenelle's *Entretiens sur la pluralité des mondes* (1686; trans. *A Discovery of New Worlds*) from the French in 1688, highlighting its encouragement of a young woman's ability to pursue philosophic and scientific knowledge but criticizing its unrealistic and often demeaning treat-

ment of women's intellectual potential. In Behn's words: "He makes her say a great many very sill things, tho' sometimes she makes observations so learned, that the greatest Philosophers in Europe make no better."

She was the first woman to write for the Restoration stage, and gained assistance in doing so from her friends Thomas Killigrew and John Dryden; her first play *The Forc'd Marriage, or the Jealous Bridegroom* (1671) was performed at the Duke's Theater. The prologue draws attention to this momentous occasion by claiming that "Women, those charming victors" who had relied on beauty now "like Wise and Politick states, / Court a new power . . . / Thel'le joyn the Force of Wit to Beauty now." The play was a tragicomedy that included passages on Charles I and the restored Charles II in a romance castigating the planned marriage of the heroine Ermina, who resisted its consummation. The play foreshadowed Behn's later, better-known works and their subversion of controls over romance and marriage and the lesser power afforded women in such situations, while making space for a royalist perspective in the narrative.

Her plays adopt a Tory point of view tied to an identification with England's "best people," embodied especially in the young Cavalier heroes who so dominate her drama. She ridiculed moralistic Dissenters (Protestants outside the Church of England) mercilessly and created sharp satires against social parvenus among Whiggish merchants and politicians (or those who had made large fortunes through trade and financial manipulation rather than from land and who supported policies that enriched themselves and enhanced London at the expense of landowning families) who would corrupt standards of royal and social honor. Her plays fit easily within the risqué language and sexual encounters that characterized Restoration comedy, and she differed little in her perspective from male contemporary playwrights. Yet feminist scholars have noted a stronger awareness of and identification with the greater risks experienced by her female characters' sexuality than that revealed in the plays of her male contemporaries. Even so, she most admired her Cavalier heroes, who represented the values of independence, honor, and cultural sophistication that most mattered to her.

In her later years, after being imprisoned for criticism of Monmouth's Rebellion (an uprising led by Charles II's illegitimate son), she became more disillusioned with the royalist cause, and her later drama is more pessimistic than her earlier plays. Her most prominent dramas are *Sir Patient Fancy* (1678), *The Feign'd Courtizans* (1679), *The Roundheads* (1682), *The Rover* (part 1, 1677; part 2, 1681), and *The City Heiress* (1682). These plays emphasize the elaborate struggles between men and women to establish viable romantic attachments; the competition for domination in English society between Whiggish financial interests and the older (and purer) interests of land, crown, and church; and the clashes between pedestrian personalities and those that exemplify the best of England's past, and ideally its future as well. While John Dryden and Behn shared Tory values, they were not personally close until Dryden asked her to collaborate in his translation of Ovid's *Heroides,* even though she lacked Latin. He praised the poetic quality of her version (based on someone else's translating Ovid's language), but by the mid-1680s he was praising the piety of Ann Killigrew's poetry and looking askance at the more vulgar work of other women, clearly implying Behn.

Behn's novel *Oroonoko; or, The Royal Slave* (1688) describes a slave revolt that she claims to have witnessed as a young woman in Surinam. In her narrative of this revolt, and especially in the portrayal of Oroonoko, an educated African prince made slave, she incorporates all of her cherished values: the noble hero who gives up all (killing his wife, child, and self) for honor, and the evils of property in the form of slavery. Her last play, on Bacon's unsuccessful revolt in the Virginia colony, reflects a growing disillusion with monarchy in the person of James II. She died after refusing an opportunity to compose a poem to honor the incoming royal pair, William and Mary. Behn symbolized her loyalty to the Stuart cause by dying at the time William and Mary came to the throne, and she was buried at Westminster Abbey under a marble slab that gave no information about her family. On it was inscribed, "Here lies a Proof that Wit can never be / Defence enough against Mortality."

BIBLIOGRAPHY

Primary Work

Behn, Aphra. *The Works of Aphra Behn.* Edited by Janet Todd. Columbus, Ohio, 1992.

Secondary Works

Todd, Janet, ed. *Aphra Behn Studies.* Cambridge, U.K., 1996.
Todd, Janet. *The Secret Life of Aphra Behn.* New Brunswick, N.J., 1977.
Zook, Melinda. "Contextualizing Aphra Behn: Plays, Politics, and Party, 1679–1689." In *Women Writers and the Early Modern British Political Tradition.* Edited by Hilda L. Smith. Cambridge, U.K., 1998. Pages 75–93.

HILDA SMITH

BELLARMINE, ROBERT (Roberto Francesco Romolo Bellarmino; 1542–1621), Italian prelate, theologian, and opponent of Protestant doctrines. Robert Bellarmine was born at Montepulciano, Italy, where he attended the Jesuit college before entering the Jesuit novitiate at Rome in 1560. His Jesuit training was fairly standard: he studied philosophy at Rome, briefly taught classical languages at Florence and Mondovì, then studied theology at Padua and Louvain, where he was ordained in 1570. From 1570 to 1576 Bellarmine taught theology at Louvain, devoting his study lectures largely to refuting Protestant theologians. This led to his appointment to the new chair in controversial theology at the Collegio Romano, the premier Jesuit theological center. His Roman lectures, *Disputationes de controversiis Christianae fidei huius temporis haereticos* (Lectures concerning the controversies of the Christian faith against the heretics of this time; generally known as the *Controversies*), were published in three volumes (1586, 1588, 1593) and have long been regarded as the leading Catholic answer to early Protestant theology. Medieval scholastic theologians, above all St. Thomas Aquinas, strongly influenced Bellarmine, but his approach to theology depends more on history and less on philosophy than did that of the medieval theologians or the Spanish Counter-Reformation theologians of his day.

Bellarmine was drawn into many theological disputes. He defended his fellow Jesuit Leonard Lessius, (1554–1623), whose teachings on grace and predestination were condemned at the University of Louvain, where Augustinian views dominated. In the controversy on nature, grace, and predestination between the Jesuits and the Dominicans, Bellarmine stressed God's primacy more than did his fellow Jesuit Luis de Molina (1535–1600). Bellarmine played a key role in preparing the Sixto-Clementine Vulgate (1592), which served as the official Catholic Bible for centuries. His most popular book, *Dottrina cristiana breve,* a short catechism for children that eventually ran through hundreds of editions in many languages, appeared in 1597; a long catechism for adults followed in 1598.

Bellarmine was also involved in controversies over church-state relations. He wrote against Henry of Navarre's claims to be king of France and produced several pamphlets supporting Paul V when that pope imposed an interdict on Venice in 1606 and saw it fail to achieve the intended result. Bellarmine quarreled with King James I of England (1603–1625) and Bishop Lancelot Andrewes (1555–1626) over papal authority and the rights of English Catholics. Bellarmine and two British Catholics, Thomas Preston and William Barclay, bitterly contested the relative authority of church and state. Although Bellarmine was a strong supporter of the papacy, he denied direct papal authority in civil matters, much to the annoyance of Sixtus V (1585–1590).

Jesuit generals and the popes employed Bellarmine in many tasks. Thus in 1590 Bellarmine served as theological adviser of the cardinal legate at Paris when Henry of Navarre besieged the city. After returning to Rome, Bellarmine was spiritual director and rector at the Collegio Romano. He also served as provincial superior of the Jesuit Province of Naples from 1594 to 1597. Clement VIII (1592–1605) made Bellarmine a cardinal in 1599 and appointed him archbishop of Capua in 1602. He immediately resigned his many curial offices and took up residence in that small city, where he spent three years in preaching, visiting parishes, helping the poor, and fostering reform. When Clement died in 1605 Bellarmine returned to Rome for the conclave that elected Paul V (1605–1621). The new pope respected Bellarmine and commanded him to resume work at the papal curia. Bellarmine quickly resigned the metropolitan see of Capua.

Bellarmine spent his last sixteen years working on various papal commissions, especially in the Holy Office or Inquisition, where his skill as a theologian was needed. In 1616 Bellarmine forbade Galileo in the name of the Holy Office to teach that the earth circles the sun. Administrative paperwork left little time for scholarship. Still, Bellarmine was able to devote some time to spiritual writings. In 1611 he published a long, pious commentary on the Psalms. Each year from 1614 to 1619 he remade the Spiritual Exercises of Ignatius of Loyola for thirty days. He regarded this as his vacation, but during each of these retreats he wrote a short devotional book: the subject in 1614 was the ascent of the mind to God, in 1615 the happiness of the saints, in 1616 the miseries of this life, in 1617 Christ's seven last words on the cross, in 1618 the duties of a Christian prince, and in 1619 the art of dying well. Except for that on a Christian prince, all these books sold widely. The first and the last in the series have been widely translated and have gone through more than fifty editions.

The popularity of Bellarmine's writings was largely due to his clear Latin style and careful organization. His controversial works reveal vast erudition. Bellarmine was canonized by Pius XI in 1930.

BIBLIOGRAPHY

Primary Work

Bellarmine, Robert. *Spiritual Writings.* Edited by John Patrick Donnelly and Roland J. Teske, eds. and trans. New York and Mahwah, N.J., 1989.

Secondary Works

Blackwell, Richard. *Galileo, Bellarmine, and the Bible.* Notre Dame, Ind., 1991.

Brodrick, James. *Robert Bellarmine: Saint and Scholar.* London, 1966.

JOHN PATRICK DONNELLY, S.J.

BELLIÈVRE, POMPONNE DE (1529–1607), French royal minister, chancellor of France. Born into an eminent Lyonnais family, Pomponne de Bellièvre received a humanist education before studying law at Toulouse and Padua. Upon his return to Lyon he acquired local offices and clerical benefices, then in 1560 began almost forty years of royal service. Successful diplomatic missions to the Swiss Confederation were rewarded with the post of *conseiller d'état* (counselor of state) in 1570. During the reign of Henry III (1574–1589), Bellièvre was the principal emissary of Catherine de Médicis and the king to the duke of Anjou, the Huguenots, and the Catholic League rebels, and was a major figure in the direction of the crown's finances. In September 1588, Henry III dismissed Bellièvre and his other ministers. Bellièvre retired to his estate and tried to promote a reconciliation between royalist followers of the Huguenot Henry IV and the rebel Catholic Leaguers.

Recalled to power by Henry IV in April 1593, Bellièvre spent the next five years aiding the king's pacification of his realm. His last diplomatic mission was negotiating the Peace of Vervins with Spain (1598). In August 1599, Bellièvre secured France's highest office, that of chancellor. Bellièvre and Henry IV clashed over the king's interference in judicial decisions and Bellièvre's opposition to the king's and the duke of Sully's plans to make many royal offices venal and hereditary. Piqued at Bellièvre's principled opposition, Henry created in December 1604 a keeper of the seals (Nicolas Brûlart de Sillery). Stripped of the seals of his office nine months later, Bellièvre languished in semidisgrace until his death.

BIBLIOGRAPHY

Dickerman, Edmund H. *Bellièvre and Villeroy: Power in France under Henry III and Henry IV.* Providence, R.I., 1971.

Kierstead, Raymond F. *Pomponne de Bellièvre: A Study of the King's Men in the Age of Henry IV.* Evanston, Ill., 1968.

EDMUND H. DICKERMAN

BELLINI FAMILY, Venetian family of painters. The Bellini family is distinguished for its exceptional contribution to Renaissance painting in Venice. The careers of Jacopo Bellini and two of his sons, Gentile and Giovanni, represent the strength of the traditional Venetian family workshop of painters during the Renaissance. Presumably trained under Jacopo, the brothers were practicing as independent masters by the 1460s but continued to assist their father on various projects and may have shared workspace around this time. The birth dates of the brothers are unknown and subject to wide speculation. In 1453, Nicolosia Bellini, Jacopo's daughter, married the Paduan artist Andrea Mantegna. Jacopo's nephew and student, Leonardo Bellini (active c. 1443–1490), was a successful manuscript painter.

Jacopo Bellini, (c. 1400–1470).

Son of a Venetian pewterer, Nicoletto Bellini, and his wife, Franceschina, Jacopo Bellini was the pupil of the renowned painter from the Marches in central Italy, Gentile da Fabriano, who was active in Venice from 1408 to 1413 and whom Jacopo is likely to have served as apprentice c.1414–1419 in Brescia; a document possibly citing Jacopo as Gentile's assistant in Florence in 1423 has been questioned. Although no longer extant, several significant projects are recorded for Jacopo's mature years and attest to his considerable reputation. They include a large multifigured *Crucifixion* fresco for the Cathedral of Verona (1436); a portrait of Leonello d'Este, marquess of Ferrara (with which Jacopo defeated the distinguished Veronese artist Antonio Pisanello in a contest in 1441); an altarpiece for the Gattamelata funerary chapel (1459/60; Santo, Padua); and narrative canvases for two of the four major confraternities in Venice, the Scuola Grande di San Giovanni Evangelista and the Scuola Grande di San Marco (1460s).

Paintings. Although few, Jacopo's preserved paintings permit assessment of him as the most advanced Venetian painter of his generation. They reflect understanding of Gentile da Fabriano's experimentation in rendering the effects of light as well as the Florentine artist Leon Battista Alberti's theory of one-point perspective. Jacopo may have had direct contact with Alberti in Venice in 1437 or later in Ferrara. A *Madonna and Child* of c.1440 (Paris, Louvre) incorporates a diminutive kneeling figure of a donor and is allied in the drapery patterns and use of gold with the International Gothic style as embraced by Gentile da Fabriano. This panel reveals Jacopo's skill in portraiture and luminous treatment of firmly modeled flesh. It is most noteworthy for the innovative observation of the sky at dawn and the extraordinary breadth of vision in the light-bathed panoramic landscape.

An *Annunciation* altarpiece (documented 1444, but probably executed earlier; Brescia, Sant'Alessandro) ascribed to Jacopo shows Gentile's influence in the opulent gilt-brocade drapery. The weighty figures are set in a coherent architectural space; Albertian perspective is also applied in the narrative scenes of the predella (altarpiece base). Several half-length Madonnas document Jacopo's increasing focus on volumetric form and simplification of detail. Only one, depicting the image as a painting within an illusionistic frame, is dated (1448; Milan, Brera). Around this time, Jacopo most likely contributed the cartoon for the *Visitation* mosaic in the Cappella Nova (New Chapel; also called Mascoli Chapel) in St. Mark's Basilica in Venice. A *Sts. Anthony Abbot and Bernardino of Siena* (Washington, National Gallery) probably originally constituted the left lateral panel of the Gattamelata altarpiece, thereby documenting Jacopo's collaboration with his sons Gentile and Giovanni, who are recorded (1590) as having been named in the inscription.

Books of drawings. Among the outstanding indexes of a Renaissance artist's inventive process are the two bound volumes of Jacopo's nearly three hundred metalpoint drawings that were highly prized in the period and are now in the Louvre, Paris (parchment folios), and British Museum, London (paper folios). These include records and fantasies of classical artifacts, some studies of nature and everyday life, and mostly religious compositions conceived as self-sufficient works of art. The Paris drawings are believed to range in date from the mid-1430s to the mid-1450s, the London drawings from the mid-1450s to the mid-1460s. Many are remarkable as scenographic inventions realistically subordinating figural action to grand-scale architecture; these employ dramatic perspectival effects and combine elements of the Venetian cityscape with imaginative structures. Others are distinctive as personal reinterpretations of antique themes. Anna Rinversi, Jacopo's widow, bequeathed the albums to Gentile (will of 1471), who probably took one to Turkey and who bequeathed the other to Giovanni (will of 1507).

Influence. The pioneer of the Renaissance style in Venetian painting, Jacopo shared his interests in

Gentile Bellini. *St. Mark Preaching in Alexandria.* The work, begun in 1505, was finished by Giovanni Bellini. PINA-COTECA DI BRERA, MILAN/ALINARI/ART RESOURCE

perspective and in classical form with his son-in-law Mantegna and the Florentine sculptor Donatello, resident in Padua from 1443 to 1453; reciprocal influence is assumed. Jacopo strongly influenced the next generation of Venetian painters, including Carlo Crivelli (1430?–?1494) and Cima da Conegliano (c. 1459–1517/18). His considerable legacy to his sons is manifest in distinct ways: Gentile was to practice the scenographic mode of narrative painting indicated by Jacopo's drawings, Giovanni to carry forward his father's experimentation with landscape and the atmospheric effects of light.

Gentile Bellini (b. c. 1429–1435(?); d. 1507). Gentile collaborated with Jacopo and Giovanni Bellini on the Gattamelata altarpiece; the execution of the extant panel in Washington has been attributed by some scholars to him. A portrait of the Venetian patriarch St. Lorenzo Giustinian is signed and dated 1465 (Venice, Accademia); around this time, Gentile painted organ shutters for St. Mark's Basilica. The precise linearism of these works reflects Paduan influence and remained characteristic of Gentile's style. In 1466, he was at work with Jacopo and Giovanni at the Scuola di San Marco. The esteem Gentile commanded among his contemporaries is indicated by the knighthood granted him by the Holy Roman Emperor Frederick III while in Venice in 1469 and by the award of the commission in 1474 for the redecoration of the Sala del Maggior Consiglio (Chamber of the Great Council) of the Doge's Palace in Venice. The signal project of Gen-

tile's career, this assignment was to replace on canvas the deteriorating fresco cycle of legendary Venetian history paintings and to paint the portrait of each new doge. Although the new cycle and portraits were destroyed by fire in 1577, a drawing of Gentile's *Doge Receiving a Sword* (London, British Museum) and copies of three ducal profile portraits suggest their character.

In 1479, the Venetian government sent Gentile on a diplomatic mission to Constantinople, where he painted a portrait of Sultan Mehmed II (copies and a medal are known). The artist is best known today for the large, detailed narrative canvases executed after his return to Venice c. 1481: the *Procession of the True Cross in the Piazza San Marco* and *Miracle of the True Cross at the Bridge of San Lorenzo* (1496, 1500; Venice, Accademia). These "eye-witness" scenes include numerous portraits and exact depiction of contemporary buildings, costume, and ritual. *St. Mark Preaching in Alexandria* (Milan, Brera), incorporates orientalizing motifs. Begun by Gentile in 1504, it was completed after his death by Giovanni c. 1510.

Giovanni Bellini (b. c. 1431–1438?; d. 1516). Among the great innovative masters of the fifteenth century and one of the greatest of all Venetian painters, Giovanni Bellini revolutionized painting in Venice through his embrace of the Netherlandish oil technique, setting the stage for the accomplishments of Giorgione, Titian, and other Venetian artists in the century following. Giovanni achieved a monumental figural conception and his chiefly religious works are characterized by a profound sense of human dignity, therein comparable to the attainments of the early Renaissance Florentine masters Masaccio and Donatello. Revealing acute observation of the natural world, Giovanni Bellini portrayed landscape and changing atmospheric effects with an outstanding sense of immediacy. Well before the end of his long and productive lifetime, his works were highly prized by collectors and he was eulogized as the greatest painter in the world. The German painter Albrecht Dürer and the Tuscan artist and historian Giorgio Vasari recorded Bellini's courtesy and kindness as well as his stature in the arts.

Life and works. Giovanni is first recorded in a document of 1459; a *Crucifixion* (Venice, Museo Correr) has been thought by some scholars to come from the Gattamelata altarpiece and to reflect his participation. Four triptychs for the church of Santa Maria della Carità (1461–1464; Venice, Accademia) were probably commissioned from Jacopo's shop and may have been executed largely by Giovanni. Documents for his early career are sparse, but relative chronology of his numerous deeply moving devotional paintings—including many interpretations of the Madonna and Child and the Dead Christ—is established. A portrait of the Augsburger Jörg Fugger (Pasadena, Norton Simon Foundation) is datable to 1474, and documentation from 1476 suggests that Bellini's *Coronation of the Virgin* (Pesaro, Museo Civico) had been completed.

In the *Coronation,* a high altarpiece for the church of San Francesco in Pesaro, Bellini employs an aggrandized, highly plastic figural form as well as a newly rationalized and harmonious spatial system. In addition to tempera, he uses oil as a binding medium for pigment (as also in the Fugger portrait). This permits a greater fluidity of technique, promoting his experimentation with the unification of light and space. Apparently, Giovanni seldom left Venice, but he may have traveled to Pesaro at the time of this commission and been influenced by the Tuscan painter Piero della Francesca (c. 1420–1492)—resident in nearby Urbino—in taking these new steps. Bellini's sensitivity to the site intended for the altarpiece and to specific contemporary Franciscan devotional concerns are evident in his composition and imagery. Scenes in the predella employ motifs found in Jacopo's drawings. Bellini's great altarpieces designed for aisle locations in Venetian churches, notably that for San Giobbe (1470s/c. 1480?; Venice,

Accademia) and that of 1505 (Venice, San Zaccaria), utilize a perspective system that defines the space as a chapel-like extension of the actual space to accommodate his figures: the Madonna seated on a high throne with saints assembled below. To enhance the illusionism of these scenes, Bellini repeats the architectural ornamentation of the frame in the painted architecture.

Also apparent in the Pesaro altarpiece is Bellini's experimentation with conveying recession into space in landscape using superposed planes, an innovation to be fully developed by about 1500–1502 in his *Baptism of Christ* (Vicenza, Santa Corona). Bellini's explorations and mastery of landscape are further well exemplified by his *Saint Francis in Ecstasy* (1470s; New York, Frick Collection) and *Transfiguration* (1480s; Naples, Museo di Capodimonte). Excelling in every category of painting, Giovanni joined Gentile in 1479 in the commission for historical narratives at the Doge's Palace. Among Giovanni's many superb portraits is the lifelike *Doge Leonardo Loredan* (c. 1501; London, National Gallery). Subsequent works bespeak an extraordinary flexibility and receptivity to new artistic currents: *The Feast of the Gods* (1514; Washington, National Gallery of Art); *The Drunkenness of Noah* (c. 1514; Besançon, Musée des Beaux-Arts); *Nude Woman Holding a Mirror* (1515; Vienna, Kunsthistorisches Museum).

Workshop and influence. Bellini most likely expanded his workshop c. 1479, and by around 1490, when demand for his devotional paintings had become enormous, as it remained well into sixteenth century, he maintained one of the largest and best organized workshops of the Renaissance. Drawings on paper (cartoons), with contour lines pricked and sprinkled with charcoal to transfer the design (pouncing), were sometimes used for replication. Bellini trained or directed numerous painters of the next generation. Many, now referred to as "the *belliniani,*" practiced his style; others—Giorgione, Titian, Sebastiano del Piombo, Lorenzo Lotto—developed distinctly personal styles and include the great pioneers of sixteenth-century art, further realizing the potential of oil painting and enhancing the international reputation of Venetian art Giovanni Bellini had established.

See also **Venice**, *subentry on* **Art in Venice**; *and biographies of figures mentioned in this essay.*

BIBLIOGRAPHY

Jacopo Bellini
Degenhart, Bernhard, and Annegrit Schmitt. *Corpus der italienischen Zeichnungen, 1300–1450.* Part 2, *Venedig: Jacopo*

Bellini. Vols. 5–8. Berlin, 1990. Essential for sequence and revised dating of drawings.

Eisler, Colin. *The Genius of Jacopo Bellini.* New York and Cologne, 1989. Important especially for discussion, illustration, and revised chronology of paintings; discussion of historical context and themes.

Paris, Jean. *L'atelier Bellini.* Paris, 1995. See for Bellini family; outstanding plates.

Gentile Bellini

Brown, Patricia Fortini. *Venetian Narrative Painting in the Age of Carpaccio.* New Haven, Conn., 1988. Establishes historical context and important social function of the major narrative cycles commissioned by Venetian confraternities.

Meyer zur Capellen, Jürg. *Gentile Bellini.* Stuttgart, Germany, 1985.

Giovanni Bellini

Goffen, Rona. *Giovanni Bellini.* New Haven, Conn., and London, 1989.

Heinemann, Fritz. *Giovanni Bellini e i Belliniani.* 3 vols. Venice, 1991. Important for illustration of vast corpus of works deriving from Bellini's inventions.

Humfrey, Peter. *The Altarpiece in Renaissance Venice.* New Haven, Conn., and London, 1993. See for Bellini family altarpiece, Giovanni Bellini's altarpieces, and further references.

Humfrey, Peter, ed. *The Cambridge Companion to Giovanni Bellini.* Cambridge and New York, forthcoming.

CAROLYN C. WILSON

BEMBO, PIETRO (1470–1547), Italian philologist, literary theorist, poet, historian, cardinal. Born in Venice to patrician parents (Elena Marcello and Bernardo, an important trader and politician for the republic), Bembo received a first-class humanist education at home and in Florence (1478–1480), Rome (1487–1488), and Bergamo (1489–1490). At the age of twenty he was already recognized for his Latin poetry. He studied with the Hellenist Constantine Lascaris in Messina (1492–1494), where he met his lifelong companion and secretary, Cola Bruno. Bembo's first work, *De Aetna,* a dialogue with his father about climbing Mt. Aetna, was published in 1496. His early literary successes, his unsuitability for the political career for which he was being prepared—repeated failures plagued his early attempts to secure political appointment—and his meeting with Angelo Poliziano in 1491 helped him decide to dedicate himself to literary pursuits.

After attending courses in philosophy at the University of Padua (1494/95) and while continuing his studies at the school of Niccolò Leoniceno in Ferrara (1497), he began writing *Gli Asolani,* vernacular dialogues in prose and poetry on the theme of love. These dialogues, soon to be inspired by his love for Maria Savorgnan (1500), sought to reconcile Platonic, Aristotelian, and Christian spirituality, and in

Pietro Bembo. Monument to Cardinal Bembo by Michele Sammicheli (1484–1559), Basilica of S. Antonio, Padua, Italy. ALINARI/ART RESOURCE

the process advocated the dignity of women. In 1501–1502 he began composing *Prose della volgar lingua* (Prose writings about the vernacular language), which he was to work on for many years, and prepared critical editions of Petrarch's *Rime* (Rhymes; 1501) and Dante's *Commedia* (Divine comedy, which Bembo called *Terze Rime;* 1502) for Aldo Manuzio's prestigious series of classical authors, thus giving birth to vernacular philology and humanism. Before leaving Ferrara in 1504 to attend to family duties in Venice, Bembo carried on yet another love affair, this time with Lucrezia Borgia, to whom he dedicated his *Asolani,* published by Manuzio in 1505. At the same time his ambition, if not his natural disposition, prompted him to seek opportunities for an ecclesiastical career, beginning with a visit to Rome to make himself known at the papal court of Julius II. In 1506 he abandoned his homeland, Venice, for the court of Urbino, where he pursued his literary interests, both Latin and vernacular, especially the writing of the *Prose.*

In 1512 he moved to Rome to the house of the arts patron Federico Fregoso, archbishop of Salerno, where he lived with his friend and fellow humanist Jacopo Sadoleto. The following year Bembo wrote

De imitatione, his manifesto of Latin Ciceronian humanism, in answer to Gianfrancesco Pico della Mirandola's epistle on the theory of imitation. Bembo's successful thesis upheld unity of style—imitation and emulation of one model as exemplum, Cicero for Latin prose and Virgil for poetry—versus Poliziano's and Pico's eclecticism. Thus Bembo was confirmed in his role as arbiter of humanism, and the way was paved for the future success of vernacular humanism as he was defining it in the *Prose.* The following year, in recognition of this success, the newly elected pope Leo X named Bembo, along with Sadoleto, as secretary of papal briefs in Latin, an office that caused him for a time to neglect his vernacular literary pursuits in the interest of his political ambitions. Probably due to the failure of his mission as papal ambassador to Venice in 1514 and to the loss of his greatest friend and supporter at the Medici court, the playwright and cardinal Bernardo Dovizi da Bibbiena, these ambitions did not come to fruition except for the acquisition of some minor ecclesiastical benefices. In 1519 Bembo was forced both for these and for health reasons to retire to his villa in Padua, accompanied by Faustina Morosina della Torre, whom he had met in 1513 when she was sixteen. Morosina bore Bembo three children and remained with him until her death in 1535 despite the fact that, in order to maintain his ecclesiastical benefits, he took a vow of chastity in 1522 when he became a member of the Order of St. John of Jerusalem (today commonly known as the Knights of Malta).

Bembo spent the years from 1521 to 1539 mostly in Padua and Venice attending to the expansion, revision, and publication—or republication—of his vernacular works. The *Prose,* completed in 1524 after years of fine tuning and published in Venice in 1525, consists of dialogues on the "questione della lingua," the dispute over which was the best language to use for literature, Latin or the vernacular, and whether the latter should be Florentine, general Italian, or the Italian of the court. Bembo's conclusions met with immediate approval among many Italian writers who were profoundly influenced by his theory of imitation and emulation of fourteenth-century vernacular literature, modeled on the exempla of Petrarch for poetry and Boccaccio for prose. Among the writers who acknowledged Bembo's literary leadership in the construction of the new and improved Italian literature were Bernardo Tasso, Benedetto Varchi, Giovanni della Casa, and Ludovico Ariosto, who corrected his *Orlando furioso* to accord with Bembo's precepts of "varietà" (differentiation), "gravità" (dignity), "purezza" (correct-

ness), "dolcezza" (spontaneity and pleasure to the ear), and "piacevolezza" (pleasure to the intellect). With the publication of his *Rime* in 1530, Bembo provided his followers with an authoritative exemplum that, along with others published around the same date (those of Jacopo Sannazaro, Bernardo Tasso, and Luigi Alamanni), marked the birth of lyric Petrarchism, a movement that soon spread throughout Europe.

In 1529 Bembo was named historian and librarian of the Venetian Republic with the responsibility of continuing Sabellico's history—Bembo's *Historia Veneta, 1487–1513,* was published posthumously both in Latin and in his own Italian translation—and administering the Biblioteca Nicena (now Marciana). In 1539 under Pope Paul III Bembo became a cardinal and was ordained a priest. He had finally realized his greatest ambition through the help of his many friends (especially Vittoria Colonna and Carlo Gualteruzzi) and despite his many enemies. He spent the last eight years of his life either in Rome, where he participated actively in the Curia, mediating between the factions warring over church reforms, or in his bishoprics, first Gubbio, then Bergamo. During these final years, true to the spirit of the age that he represented, Bembo continued to add to his outstanding collection of books and art objects and to work on the preparation of the complete edition of his writings, both Latin and Italian, to be published after his death—his gifts to posterity.

BIBLIOGRAPHY

Primary Works
Bembo, Pietro. *Opere.* Venice, 1729. Reprint, Ridgewood, N.J., 1965.
Bembo, Pietro. *Gli Asolani.* Translated by Rudolf B. Gottfried. Bloomington, Ind., 1954.
Kilpatrick, Ross. "The *De Aetna* of Pietro Bembo: A Translation." *Studies in Philology* 83 (1986): 330–358.
Salemi, Joseph S. "The Faunus Poems of Pietro Bembo." *Allegorica* 7, no. 2 (1982): 31–57. Translation of selected early Latin poems.

Secondary Works
Dionisotti, Carlo. "Bembo, Pietro." In *Dizionario biografico degli italiani.* Vol. 8. Rome, 1966. Pages 133–151. Excellent biography and bibliography by Bembo's best critic.
McLaughlin, Martin L. "The Dispute between Giovan Francesco Pico and Bembo." In *Literary Imitation in the Italian Renaissance.* Oxford, 1995. Pages 249–274.
Santangelo, Giorgio. "Bembo, Pietro." In *Dizionario critico della letteratura italiana* 2d ed. Vol. 1. Edited by Vittore Branca. Torino, Italy 1986. Pages 255–269. Especially for the question of imitation.

DENNIS JAMES MCAULIFFE

BENEDETTI, GIOVANNI BATTISTA (1530–1590), Italian mathematician and philosopher. Benedetti was a patrician of Venice, a mathematician, and a natural philosopher whose criticisms of Aristotle's laws of motion prepared the way for Galileo's work in mechanics. Born in Venice, Benedetti was educated mainly by his father but studied Euclid under Niccolò Tartaglia (1499–1557). He entered the employ of the duke of Parma as a mathematician in 1558, then in 1567 moved to the court of the duke of Savoy, where he held the same position until his death.

Benedetti's most significant works include his *Resolutio omnium Euclidis problematum* (A solution of all Euclid's problems; Venice, 1553); his *Demonstratio proportionum motuum localium* (A demonstration of the ratios of local motions; two editions, both Venice, 1554); his *De gnomonum usu* (On the use of sundials; Turin, 1573); his *De temporum emendatione* (On the renovation of the calendar; Turin, 1578, intended for Pope Gregory XIII); and his *Speculationum liber* (Book of speculations; Turin, 1585; Venice, 1586, 1599), which contains essays on mathematics, mechanics, and music. In a preface to his *Resolutio,* Benedetti sketched the elements of his teaching on falling bodies, then took it up again in his *Demonstratio.* The first edition of this was plagiarized by Jean Taisnier (1509–c. 1562) and published in a collection of Taisnier's essays (Cologne, 1562, 1583), which received a wider diffusion than the original and was translated into English around 1578.

Benedetti's demonstration, directed "against Aristotle and all philosophers," was based on the buoyancy principle of Archimedes and argued that a body's speed of fall in a medium depends not on its absolute weight but on its weight in the medium. From this he concluded that unequal bodies of the same material will fall through the same medium at equal speed. He also held, in the second edition of his *Demonstratio,* that the resistance the body encounters in its fall will depend on the surface of the body, not its volume. In his *Speculationum liber* he then reasoned that bodies of the same material but different weight will fall with the same speed only in a vacuum, where buoyancy and resistive effects can be neglected.

Benedetti saw his philosophy as differing from Aristotle's mainly in its use of mathematical demonstrations to determine the true causes (*verae causae*) of natural phenomena. This required Benedetti to make extensive use of suppositions and thought experiments. On the supposition that two bodies of equal weight are connected by a string of negligible weight, he reasoned that they will fall in a vacuum at the same speed as one body with their combined weight; thus, contrary to Aristotle, a body's weight does not determine its speed of fall. For Benedetti, circular motion may be the only truly natural motion, but there is no noteworthy difference between a perfect sphere and a plane surface of small extent. Thus, if all impediment is removed, a sphere can be moved along a horizontal surface by "a force no matter how small" (*quamlibet minimam vim*). For him, again, the natural tendency of a body when released from a sling will be to move in a straight line. Impetus he regarded as a force impressed on a body from without but that moves it from within. He saw trajectories as resulting from a composition of motions, partly natural and partly forced, here advancing beyond the teaching of his teacher Tartaglia.

Galileo nowhere mentions Benedetti in his writings, and so the latter's influence on Galileo is controverted, Alexandre Koyré favoring, Stillman Drake against. The many similarities in their thought and expression suggest that Benedetti's advances were known to Galileo, most probably by way of Jacopo Mazzoni (c. 1548–1598), with whom Galileo studied in 1590.

See also **Mechanics.**

BIBLIOGRAPHY

Primary Work

Drake, Stillman, and I. E. Drabkin, eds. *Mechanics in Sixteenth-Century Italy.* Madison, Wis., and London, 1969. Selections from Tartaglia, Benedetti, Guido Ubaldo, and Galileo, translated and annotated.

Secondary Works

Convegno Internazionale di Studio "Giovan Battista Benedetti e il suo Tempo." *Cultura, scienze, e tecniche nella Venezia del cinquecento.* Venice, 1987.

Drake, Stillman. "Benedetti, Giovanni Battista." In *Dictionary of Scientific Biography.* Vol. 1. New York, 1970. Pages 604–609.

Koyré, Alexandre. *Galileo Studies.* Translated by John Mepham. Atlantic Highlands, N.J., 1978.

WILLIAM A. WALLACE

BENI, PAOLO (c. 1552–1625), Italian man of letters, theologian, philosopher, educator, literary and language critic. Paolo Beni studied at the University of Padua, where he received his doctorate in philosophy and theology in 1576. There he met Torquato Tasso, whom he later celebrated and defended from his detractors. In 1581 Beni entered the Jesuit novitiate in Rome; he completed his studies in 1584 and after a short time left the order. Subsequently he taught in Rome, Perugia, and elsewhere. In 1600 he was called back to the University of Padua to fill the

chair of humanities, thereby becoming a colleague of Galileo Galilei. During the next ten years Beni witnessed and helped to disseminate the astronomical discoveries of Galileo.

Beni was the author of several works in Latin and in Italian. His major Latin writings deal with poetics and history. According to Beni, while history should only narrate the true happenings of human events, poetry is a fabulous invention, although it should have the semblance of truth, or verisimilitude. In Beni's estimation, the more rigorous the linguistic and stylistic observance, the greater the inventive poet will be. In this sense, Beni's exemplary poet was Torquato Tasso.

Beni's works on Tasso are written in Italian and parallel his linguistic polemics with the Accademia della Crusca on matters of diction and style. In *L'Anticrusca* (The Anticrusca) of 1612, Beni's main criticism was that the Accademia's newly published *Vocabolario* could not constitute an authority because it was based only on Florentine writers of the thirteenth and fourteenth centuries. He claimed that the ancient authors, such as Dante, Giovanni Boccaccio, and Franco Sacchetti, had been surpassed by the purity of diction and regulated style of modern writers, such as Tasso, Pietro Bembo, and Ludovico Ariosto. Thus Beni is seen as partaking fully in the Renaissance ancients-versus-moderns controversy.

BIBLIOGRAPHY

Primary Work

L'Anticrusca: Parte 2, 3, 4. Edited by G. Casagrande. Florence, 1982.

Secondary Work

Diffley, P. B. *Paolo Beni: A Biographical and Critical Study.* Oxford, 1988. A valuable monograph, with an exhaustive bibliography of Beni's published and unpublished works, as well as a good bibliography of secondary sources.

GINO CASAGRANDE

BERENSON, BERNARD. *See* **Renaissance, Interpretations of the,** *subentry on* **Bernard Berenson;** *see also* **Villa I Tatti.**

BERNARDINO OF SIENA (1380–1444), preacher, peacemaker. Bernardino of Siena, was born in Massa Marittima, the son of a Sienese nobleman, Tollo degli Albizzeschi, and a local woman, Nera degli Avveduti. Orphaned as a young child, Bernardino was educated in Siena, where his religious vocation came early after he spent four months in the city's hospital nursing the sick and dying during the plague year of 1400. Bernardino joined the

Bernardino of Siena. Bernardino preaching in the Piazza del Campo, Siena, 15 August 1427. Painting by Sano di Pietro (1406–1481). DUOMO, SIENA, ITALY/SCALA/ART RESOURCE

Franciscan order in 1402 and trained as a novice at Il Columbaio, a convent of the strict Observants on Mt. Amiata. His early years as a Franciscan were busy ones, with the foundation of La Capriola, an Observant monastery near Siena, and preaching forays both locally and elsewhere in northern Italy. However, real fame awaited him when he began an extended preaching tour of the north in 1417.

Listeners in the thousands gathered to hear him. Through rhetoric and ritual, Bernardino mastered the crowds. His sermons covered a vast range of topics, from witchcraft and heresy to sexuality and the smallest details of domestic life. Each topic was enlivened by flexible variations in tone, including earthy humor, furious tirades against partisans, and tenderness when he described flowers blooming in springtime. His preaching attracted a wide variety of listeners, but women formed the majority of his audience and he often addressed them directly. Bernardino's powerful and often colloquial language has been preserved in several collections of vernacular sermons, which were recorded by devout listeners as he spoke. The most accurate are the 1427 Siena sermons, which note sudden interruptions and the preacher's frequent exasperation at restless listeners.

Even more effective than Bernardino's vibrant language was his adept manipulation of ritual. He often preached in public squares, interweaving his sermons with a virtuoso domination of public space. His preaching visits culminated in spectacular public rituals, especially bonfires of vanities and mass peacemakings. A favorite device was the "YHS," an emblem that he designed signifying the Holy Name of Jesus. As a peacemaker, Bernardino urged partisans to replace their divisive emblems and banners with this sign of Christian unity. At other times he dramatically displayed the YHS at the end of important sermons, inciting weeping and even exorcisms among his listeners. The great popularity of the YHS caused uneasiness among clerical rivals, who claimed that it was idolatrous, and Bernardino was accused of heresy in 1426, 1431, and 1438. However, his firm orthodoxy convinced his judges to exonerate him each time. In 1438 he became vicar general of the Franciscan Observants in Italy, won numerous recruits to its reforms, and attended the Council of Florence in 1439.

Bernardino remained an active preacher to the end of his life and died during a mission, at L'Aquila in the Abruzzi. His relics immediately attracted devotees and produced healing miracles. He was canonized by Pope Nicholas V in 1450. The deceased holy man soon became a popular subject in altarpieces, readily identifiable by his emaciated features and often holding his signature YHS.

See also **Preaching and Sermons,** *subentry on* **Christian Preaching and Sermons.**

BIBLIOGRAPHY

Primary Works

Bernardino da Siena. *Le prediche volgari.* 7 vols. Edited by Ciro Cannarozzi. Florence, 1934. Reprint, 1940, 1958.

Bernardino da Siena. *Prediche volgari sul campo di Siena, 1427.* Edited by Carlo Delcorno. Milan, 1989.

Secondary Works

Bernardino predicatore nella società del suo tempo. Centro di studi sulla spiritualità. Todi, Italy, 1976. Collection of articles on various aspects of Bernardino's mission.

Mormando, Franco. *The Preacher's Demons: Bernardino of Siena and the Social Underworld of Early Renaissance Italy.* Chicago, 1999.

Origo, Iris. *The World of San Bernardino.* New York, 1962.

CYNTHIA L. POLECRITTI

BERNI, FRANCESCO (1497 or 1498–1535), Italian burlesque and satiric poet. Francesco Berni was born in Lamporecchio, Tuscany, and educated in the humanist circles of the Medici in Florence. An early work, *La Catrina* (1516?), a rustic drama, was written in imitation of the *Nencia da Barberino,* attributed to Lorenzo de' Medici, and reveals Berni's interest in using popular language in his verse. Berni left Florence for Rome in 1517 to enter the household of Cardinal Bernardo Dovizi da Bibbiena. His Roman period is marked by a vital interest in the political and social life of the city and by a number of friendships with important contemporaries; it is also the period of his earliest poetic compositions known as *capitoli,* poems of varying length in terza rima that are comic and/or polemical. While in Rome, he began the rewriting, or *rifacimento,* of Matteo Maria Boiardo's *Orlando innamorato* (Roland in love; 1487) in an attempt to purify it of linguistic regionalisms in favor of a standard—that is, Tuscan—poetic language. His revision of Boiardo's chivalric romance, important for the history of the "questione della lingua" (question of the language), was completed around 1531 and published posthumously in 1541.

Berni is known primarily as a nonconformist poet whose *capitoli,* sonnets, and *sonetti caudati* (tailed sonnets) are explicit polemics against the Renaissance tradition of imitation—especially of Petrarch—and enlivened by a poetic language that ranges from biting satire to clever plays on words, often about mundane subjects such as syphilis and food. In *Dialogo contro i poeti* (Dialogue against poets; 1526) he takes issue with the humanist concept of the vatic, or prophetic, nature of poetry and with the importance given to the imitation of poetic models (especially as espoused by Pietro Bembo) and proclaims that poetry is essentially no more than a literary diversion.

Berni's comic style, which has come to be known as *stile bernesco,* consists of lexical virtuosity, with plays on words, puns, and all the elements that characterize the spoken language of his contemporaries. In the same vein, his subjects range from the vulgar, as seen, for example, in *Capitolo dell'orinale* (Capitolo in praise of the urinal; 1522), to the banal, with poems in praise of sausages and eels. Frequently, such poems are obscene in their allusions and become part of a linguistic code for sexual acts and bodily functions. On the other hand, Berni's comic poetry often betrays serious moral concerns: it emphasizes a life of modesty and moderation and considers the inconstancy of human nature and humankind's general selfishness.

The Italian Renaissance is often equated with the refinements of artists such as Petrarch, Poliziano (Angelo Ambrogini), and Baldassare Castiglione or the serious tracts of writers such as Leon Battista Alberti and Machiavelli. However, from the Middle Ages on there was a lively tradition of comic poetry that was often a polemic against humanist values and parodied the aesthetic sensibilities of the period. Poets such as Antonio Cammelli (called Il Pistoia) and Domenico di Giovanni (Burchiello) were important predecessors of Berni, and an entire tradition of Florentine nonconformist poets flourished in the wake of Berni's poetic production, including Benvenuto Cellini and Anton Francesco Grazzini.

BIBLIOGRAPHY

Primary Work
Berni, Francesco. *Rime.* Edited by Giorgio Bàrberi Squarotti. Turin, Italy, 1969.

Secondary Works
Reynolds, Anne. "Francesco Berni: Satire and Criticism in the Italian Sixteenth Century." In *Comic Relations: Studies in the Comic, Satire, and Parody.* Edited by Pavel Petr, David Roberts, and Philip Thomson. Frankfurt, Germany, 1985. Pages 129–138.
Reynolds, Anne. "The Poet in Society: Francesco Berni and Court Life in Cinquecento Rome." *Spunti e ricerche: Rivista d'italianistica* 4–5 (1988–1989): 51–62.
Reynolds, Anne. *Renaissance Humanism at the Court of Clement VII: Francesco Berni's "Dialogue against Poets" in Context.* New York, 1997. Includes an English translation of *Dialogo contro i poeti.*
Weaver, Elissa. "Erotic Language and Imagery in Francesco Berni's Rifacimento." *MLN* 99, no. 1 (1984): 80–100.

ROBERT J. RODINI

BÉROALDE DE VERVILLE, FRANÇOIS (1556–1626), French writer.

Born in Paris, educated in Geneva, and converted to Catholicism in the 1580s, Béroalde is best known for his authorship of *Le moyen de parvenir* (The way to attain; c. 1612). Critics have been challenged by the complex organization of *Le moyen de parvenir,* which includes a long opening paragraph dating its composition to the time of the introduction of soft balls in tennis; chapter headings that suggest many varieties of written forms (gloss, conclusion, genealogy, article, and summary); and a banquet frame with four hundred eminent characters from antiquity to Rabelais and Erasmus.

The ribald—some would say pornographic—nature of *Le moyen de parvenir* has made it difficult for scholars to understand how the erudition of Béroalde's earlier encyclopedic and philosophical texts—prose treatises and long poems—fit within the daring context of that work. It is possible to reconstruct a progression from the early *Apprehensions spirituelles* (Spiritual understanding; Paris, 1583), a collection that includes prose works on ethics and alchemy, extended philosophical poems, and dialogues. Béroalde subsequently tried out a series of prose romance narratives that show a looser and less structured style already tending toward the miscellany: *Les avantures de Floride* (The adventures of Florida; Tours, 1592–1596) and *Voyage des princes fortunez* (Journey of fortunate princes; 1610). Having passed a brief period at the end of the sixteenth century writing quasi-historical works, *Le restablissement de Troye* (The reestablishment of Troy; Tours, 1597) and *La pucelle d'Orléans* (The maid of Orléans; Paris, 1599), Béroalde turned to a loosely structured Menippean satire, *Le cabinet de Minerve* (Minerva's room; Paris, 1596), and the work that is most closely linked to *Le moyen de parvenir,* *Le palais des curieux* (The palace of the curious; Paris, 1612), where paradox, questions, and extraordinary marvels are juxtaposed in the hybrid characteristic of miscellany or *bigarrure.*

The apparent contradictions in the biographical details surrounding Béroalde—a medical doctor, a Calvinist turned Catholic, an erudite scholar with a keen interest in alchemy, and the canon of St. Gatien's in Tours—in addition to the progression of his works, from the vast encyclopedic scope of *Les apprehensions spirituelles* to the ribald and irreverent treatment of humanist endeavors in *Le moyen de parvenir,* make it perhaps easier to understand that, like Rabelais, Béroalde was a man with a vast enthusiasm for knowledge and a gift for exploring all the potential of language, but who grew increasingly skeptical of the boundaries of science and its potential for solving the problems of daily life. The title of his most famous work, along with the tongue-in-cheek promise near the outset, "ce livre est le centre de tous les livres" (this book is the center of all books [chapter 12]), points to the folly of ever trying to conclude that the philosopher's stone is within our grasp.

BIBLIOGRAPHY

Primary Works

Béroalde de Verville, François. *Anthologie poétique de Béroalde de Verville*. Edited by V.-L. Saulnier. Paris, 1945.

Béroalde de Verville, François. *Fantastic Tales; or, The Way to Attain—A Book Full of Pantagruelism*. Translated by Arthur Machen. London, 1923.

Béroalde de Verville, François. *Le moyen de parvenir*. 2 vols. Edited by Hélène Moreau and André Tournon. Aix-en-Provence, France, 1984.

Secondary Works

Bowen, Barbara C. "Béroalde de Verville and the Self-Destructing Book." In *Essays in Early French Literature: Presented to Barbara M. Craig*. Edited by Norris J. Lacy and Jerry C. Nash. York, S.C., 1982.

Bowen, Barbara C. *Words and the Man in French Renaissance Literature*. Lexington, Ky., 1983.

Kenny, Neil. *The Palace of Secrets: Béroalde de Verville and Renaissance Conceptions of Knowledge*. Oxford, 1991.

Pallister, Janis L. *The World View of Béroalde de Verville, Expressed through Satirical Baroque Style in* Le Moyen de Parvenir. Paris, 1971.

Zinger, Ilana. *Structures narratives du* Moyen de parvenir *de Béroalde de Verville*. Paris, 1979.

DEBORAH N. LOSSE

BESSARION (1403 or 1408–1472), cardinal, Greek religious leader and humanist, founder of the Biblioteca Marciana. Little is known of Bessarion's early life. Christened Basil, he took the name Bessarion when he became a Basilian monk. He was born in Trebizond and entrusted by his parents to the care of Dositheus, the metropolitan of Trebizond, who brought him to Constantinople around 1417. He received monastic tonsure in 1423 and was ordained a priest in 1430. Viewed as something of a prodigy at Constantinople, he transferred to a monastery at Mistra in the Peloponnesus in the 1430s. At Mistra he studied with the Platonist philosopher George Gemistus Pletho (1355–1452 or 1454). In 1436, when the Greeks were preparing for the Roman Catholic council of union in Italy and were anxious to have their most learned men speak for them, he was called back to Constantinople and consecrated bishop of Nicaea ("Nicenus" became his sobriquet for the rest of his life).

Bessarion played a leading role in the council from its start in Ferrara in 1438 to the achievement of union in Florence in July 1439. During the council he became a strong proponent of union, and afterward, in December 1439, when he was on his way back to Constantinople, Pope Eugenius IV named him a cardinal so that he could act as a mediator between the Greek and Latin churches. He left Greece for the papal court in 1440, never to return.

Bessarion. Cardinal Bessarion with two fathers of the Scuola della Carità by Gentile Bellini (1429–1507). Oil on poplar wood; 1472; 102.5 × 37 cm (40.4 × 14.6 in.). KUNSTHISTORISCHES MUSEUM, GEMÄLDEGALERIE, VIENNA/ERICH LESSING/ART RESOURCE

The union quickly failed, but the speeches Bessarion gave at the council and the treatises and public letters he wrote in justification of the union constitute a major body of theological work.

After the fall of Constantinople in 1453, Bessarion campaigned continually for a crusade to recover the city, but he was never able to garner the necessary support. He did come very close to mounting the chair of Saint Peter in the conclave of 1455. Subsequently, he could only act as a senior cardinal and depend on the support of the reigning pope. The most enduring tribute to Bessarion's Greek patriotism is the Biblioteca Marciana. Determined to salvage all he could of the Greek heritage, Bessarion assembled the greatest Greek library of the time. Among its treasures are some of the most important Greek manuscripts extant today. He also formed a very large and important Latin library. In 1468 he bequeathed the collection to Venice, the city Bessarion viewed as "a second Byzantium." In 1537 Venice commissioned Jacopo Sansovino (1486–1570) to build the beautiful *Libreria* to house Bessarion's collection. As the Biblioteca Marciana, it became one of the great public libraries of the Renaissance.

As a cardinal, Bessarion made his household a significant center of intellectual activity. He brought into his circle of friends and clients a wide group of scholars, whose work and careers he encouraged. These scholars included Greeks such as George of Trebizond (1395–1472/73) and Theodore Gaza (1400–c. 1476), Latin humanists such as Lorenzo Valla (1407–1457) and Niccolò Perotti (1429–1480), Latin Scholastics such as Francesco Della Rovere (1414–1484), and scientists such as the Germans Georg von Peuerbach (1423–1461) and Johann Müller (Regiomontanus; 1436–1476).

Bessarion never ceased to be a scholar. Apart from his theological writings, he translated into Latin Aristotle's *Metaphysics*, Xenophon's *Memorabilia*, and some orations of Demosthenes and Saint Basil the Great. He also was much engaged in the Plato-Aristotle controversy. Following Neoplatonic tradition, he saw Plato and Aristotle as basically in agreement. Therefore, in the 1450s he questioned the attempt of his mentor, the Platonic philosopher George Gemistus Pletho, to set the two in opposition. When the controversy broke out among Greeks, he wrote several Greek opuscules reconciling the two philosophers. But the decisive event for him was George of Trebizond's publication in Latin at the end of 1457 of his *Comparison of Plato and Aristotle* praising Aristotle and condemning Plato

and Pletho. Bessarion wrote his initial response in Greek, but since the audience was now Latin, he translated it into Latin. He published the work, now called *Against the Calumniator of Plato (In Calumniatorem Platonis),* only in 1469, after he had considerably expanded the original version and after his client Niccolò Perotti had brought the Latin up to humanist standards. Writing in Rome in the years immediately before the great diffusion of Florentine Platonism, Bessarion set out to expound the "true" doctrine of Plato and its compatibility with Christianity (Bessarion's Plato was essentially Neoplatonic). He also refuted George of Trebizond point by point on Aristotle, while remaining completely silent concerning George's attacks on Pletho as a neopagan. As several subsequent printings by the Aldine Press in Venice show, Bessarion's work remained an important source of Platonic doctrine for Renaissance readers, even into the first decades of the sixteenth century.

BIBLIOGRAPHY

Bessarione e l'Umanesimo: Catalogo della mostra. Edited by G. Fiaccadori et al. Naples, Italy, 1994.

Labowsky, Lotte. "Bessarione." In *Dizionario biografico degli italiani.* Vol. 9. Rome, 1967. Pages 686–696.

Labowsky, Lotte. *Bessarion's Library and the Biblioteca Marciana: Six Early Inventories.* Rome, 1979.

Mohler, Ludwig. *Kardinal Bessarion.* 3 vols. Paderborn, Germany, 1923–1942. Reprinted Aalen-Paderborn, Germany, 1967. Also contains Bessarion's *In Calumniatorem Platonis* (in vol. 2) and *Opuscules* (in vol. 3).

Monfasani, John. *Byzantine Scholars in Renaissance Italy: Cardinal Bessarion and Other Emigrés.* Aldershot, U.K., and Brookfield, Vt., 1995.

JOHN MONFASANI

BESTIARIES. *See* **Zoology.**

BÈZE, THÉODORE DE (known as Beza; 1519–1605), French humanist scholar and Reformed theologian. Though better known for his influential role during the formative years of the Calvinist Reformation at Geneva and in France, Beza made important contributions to the development of Renaissance humanism.

Born at Vézelay on 24 June 1519, he was christened Dieudonné de Bèze, which he later hellenized to Théodore de Bèze. His family was from the petty nobility and he spent his early years at Paris with an uncle who was a royal judge. Then, at the age of nine, Beza went to Orléans for schooling. Under the tutelage of the humanist Melchior Wolmar, he acquired a strong command of elegant Latin and Greek. Wolmar also introduced the young Beza to the new Protestant religious ideas that were circulating in France. By 1535 Beza settled unenthusiastically on the study of law and, with the completion of his training four years later, returned to Paris.

Beza possessed considerable poetic talent and in 1548 published his first book, the *Poemata,* known as the *Juvenilia* in subsequent editions. This collection of amorous verses quickly established his reputation as a Latinist. Yet Beza's Protestant views forced him to flee France in the autumn of 1548, following a conversion experience. He went first to Geneva and then Lausanne, becoming professor of Greek and later rector of the academy there. It was during his stay at Lausanne that Beza wrote the tragic drama *Abraham sacrifiant* (1550). The biblical story of Abraham became a powerful propaganda vehicle for the Reformed faith and its insistence upon obedience to the divine will. Beza left Lausanne in 1558 after a heated dispute over predestination. The next year, John Calvin appointed him first rector of the newly created Academy of Geneva, an institution that soon became famous for promoting Calvinist doctrine and training pastors. Beza remained closely associated with the academy until retirement from his professorship of theology in 1599.

Several other humanist endeavors, which Beza had begun at Lausanne, came to fruition at Geneva. Among them was the translation of numerous Psalms. Beza's work complemented the Huguenot Psalter prepared earlier by the poet Clément Marot. It meant putting the Psalms into metrical French and incorporating them into the Reformed liturgy. Beza also made significant contributions to biblical scholarship through his annotations, Latin translations, and Greek editions of the New Testament. The English Geneva Bible of 1560 benefited enormously from his scriptural scholarship, and Beza's Greek New Testament of 1565 was undoubtedly the best edition available at the time. In addition, he and Corneille Bertram directed publication of the French Geneva Bible of 1588.

Beza was a pastor and Calvin's chief assistant at Geneva. As the Reformation gathered strength, he frequently visited his native France to advise and assist in the establishment of Reformed churches. Upon Calvin's death in 1564, Beza succeeded as moderator of the Venerable Company of Pastors, a post which he held until 1580. In 1574 he published anonymously *Du droit des magistrats* (On the right of magistrates), one of the most powerful justifications of Huguenot resistance. Beza remained actively involved in intellectual and religious affairs, skillfully blending his humanist ability and Protestant com-mitment, until his death in Geneva on 13 October 1605 at the age of eighty-six.

BIBLIOGRAPHY

Primary Works
Bèze, Théodore de. *Abraham sacrifiant.* Edited by Keith Cameron, Kathleen M. Hall, and Francis Higman. Geneva, 1967.
Bèze, Théodore de. *Correspondance.* Edited by Alain Dufour et al. Geneva, 1960.
Bèze, Théodore de. *Du droit des magistrats.* Edited by Robert M. Kingdon. Geneva, 1970.
Bèze, Théodore de. *Psaumes mis en vers français (1551–1562).* Edited by Pierre Pidoux. Geneva, 1984.

Secondary Works
Gardy, Frédéric. *Bibliographie des oeuvres théologiques, littéraires, historiques et juridiques de Théodore de Bèze.* Geneva, 1960.
Geisendorf, Paul-F. *Théodore de Bèze.* Geneva, 1967.

RAYMOND A. MENTZER

BIBBIENA, IL.   *See* Dovizi, Bernardo.

BIBLE.   [This entry includes six subentries:

Texts and Textual Criticism
Christian Interpretation of the Bible
Jewish Interpretation of the Bible
Printed Bibles
German Translations
The English Bible]

Texts and Textual Criticism

Clerics and scholars of the Middle Ages possessed a thorough, detailed knowledge of the Bible, even though that knowledge was based mostly on the Latin translation called the Vulgate. In the Renaissance the Vulgate was widely regarded as the work of Jerome (c. 347–419/20), who was expert in the three languages then considered sacred: Hebrew, Greek, and Latin. Modern scholars credit him only with a revision of the texts then in circulation. Giants of Western thought such as Augustine (354–430) and Thomas Aquinas (1224/25–1274) did not know Greek. And Christendom's understanding of Hebrew was limited to converted Jews, with a few exceptions, like André de Saint-Victor (d. 1175) and Nicolas of Lyra (c. 1270–1349). Hence the biblical humanism of the Renaissance consisted primarily of returning to the original texts, studying the manuscripts, and preparing a better version of the Vulgate.

The Precursors.   The revival of interest in Greek was born in the renewal of theological negotiations with the Eastern Church of Byzantium in 1274 at the Second Council of Lyon and again between 1438 and 1445 at the councils of Basel and Florence. John Stojkovic (c. 1390–1443), known as John of Ragusa (modern Dubrovnik), ambassador from the Council of Basel to Constantinople, brought back numerous manuscripts, which he passed on to the Dominicans at Basel. Desiderius Erasmus later used them. Pope Eugenius IV (reigned 1431–1447) charged Ciriaco d'Ancona (1391–c. 1452) with collecting manuscripts in the East. The arrival of the Turks in Constantinople in 1453 drove numerous erudite Greeks to the West, where they taught their language, which educated people soon valued highly.

Philological interest in the New Testament began with Lorenzo Valla (1407–1457). In his *Collatio Novi Testamenti* (c. 1444) he uncovered errors in the Vulgate by making a comparison (*collatio*) with a Greek text. Erasmus in 1505 published the second version (c. 1455) of Valla's *Collatio* under the title *Adnotationes*. This study of the "veritas graeca" (Greek truth) was intended to improve the accuracy and elegance of the Latin language, previously defended by Valla in *De Elegantiae linguae latinae* (1471). In the *Collatio* Valla discussed variants found in the manuscripts, but he did not choose between them. Nevertheless, Valla was a precursor, opening the way for criticism.

Valla's contemporary, the Florentine Giannozzo Manetti (1396–1459), went further to propose, at the suggestion of Pope Nicholas V, new translations of the New Testament and the Psalms. Manetti undertook to translate the Psalms himself after learning Hebrew from a converted Jew. With this knowledge he could rely on rabbinical commentaries. He presented his translation of the New Testament synoptically (that is, with the first three gospels alongside each other), with the Vulgate and the Itala (or pre-Vulgate Old Latin version). This was a return to the comparative method, used for the first time with the goal of clarifying theology. Manetti justified his enterprise by affirming his desire to strengthen the authority of the scriptures through a study of the history of the text and examination of its variants. One could then respond to objections made by Jews and Gentiles to the Christian truth.

The Renewal of Interpretation. The publication of a critical edition of a text necessarily involves interpreting it. As the humanists in the early sixteenth century produced such editions, they provided the basis for all subsequent biblical research of the Renaissance.

Jacques Lefèvre d'Étaples (c. 1460–1536) developed the technique of presenting texts alongside each other. In 1509 and 1513 he published a Psalter using this method. In his *Quincuplex Psalterium,* along with four traditional versions, Lefèvre presented a composite and personal (*conciliatum*) text in which he favored the "versio hebraica" of Jerome and relied on the commentary of Jaime Perez de Valencia (1408–1490). Martin Luther and Huldrych Zwingli later studied and annotated Lefèvre's work. Lefèvre provided an original Latin translation for the Pauline Epistles (1512), the Gospels (1522), and the Catholic Epistles (seven New Testament letters addressed to the Christian church at large; text edited in 1524 and published in 1527). Throughout Lefèvre used the pedagogical method of his Aristotelian commentaries, explaining each word of the text, then each verse, and finally dealing with the main difficulties. However, Lefèvre's Hebrew was poor and his Greek imperfect.

In order to offer a French translation of the Bible and because he wished to place the scriptures in the hands of those lacking Latin, both clergy and laity, Lefèvre based his work on the Vulgate. He published his French translation piece by piece, beginning with the Gospels in 1523. The complete work was published in Antwerp in 1530. It served as part of the French translation of Pierre Robert (Olivétan), which John Calvin revised.

In his interpretation of scripture Lefèvre departed from the medieval fourfold method of exegesis (literal, allegorical, moral, anagogical), as he attempted to find the method that intimately united the letter and the spirit. At the center of his approach was the search for harmony, concord, and a conciliation among texts, to be obtained by assembling them all together. Despite his willingness to return to the sources and to read scripture by itself, Lefèvre always favored the interpretion that he judged most pious and respectful of the Christian mystery. For example, in his 1517 dispute with Erasmus over Psalm 8:6, which is cited in Hebrews 2:6–9, he preferred an interpretation befitting a theology he believed to be more respectful of the divine nature of Christ.

Erasmus's biblical scholarship was less systematic than Lefèvre's, but more rooted in the study of the church fathers, especially Origen and Augustine, and it proved to be more durable. Erasmus began by publishing the Greek text of the New Testament in his *Novum instrumentum* (1516), which he based solely on four manuscripts available to him in Basel, none older than four centuries. To this he joined a Latin version of the New Testament, in which he introduced a number of stylistic improvements. The second edition of 1519, which returned to the traditional title *Novum Testamentum,* and subsequent editions (1522, 1527, 1535) contained additional corrections and revisions based on better manuscripts, some of which affected the meaning and caused an outcry among conservative theologians. Luther used the second edition for his German translation of the Bible.

In 1516 Erasmus had already composed *Annotations,* which accompanied his edition. These comprised a philological commentary in which he tackled questions of dogmatic and moral theology that interested him or were the subject of contemporary debates. He continued to revise and expand these *Annotations* through 1535. Starting in 1517 he began issuing his *Paraphrases,* which provided a more narrative explication of the text of the New Testament. An excellent Greek scholar, Erasmus was not a good Hebraist, which helps to explain why he did not write commentaries on the Old Testament, except for a few Psalms.

In his interpretations, Erasmus, like Origen, employed allegory, which he called "the way of Christ"; he used it with surprising freedom, independence, and common sense. "The way of Christ" was close to Erasmus's "philosophy of Christ," which he articulated in his prefaces to the New Testament and throughout his works. Erasmus favored moral action and right conduct of the Christian life; reasoning and clear ideas were less important than the internal transformation of the disciple of Christ.

The examples of Lefèvre d'Étaples and Erasmus show the intimate relationship between work on the text itself and commentary. This relationship was also important for the majority of biblical scholars, Catholic and Protestant alike. For example, Cardinal Tommaso de Vio (Cajetan; 1469–1534) consulted Jewish scholars in order to comment on nearly all the books of the Bible. The Protestant Martin Bucer (1491–1551) was surrounded by a circle of scholars in Strasbourg in the mid-1520s, and Martin Luther and Philipp Melanchthon led a Wittenberg circle, which included Hebraists like Caspar Cruciger (1504–1548), and Matthäus Aurogallus (c. 1490–1543). While Jewish exegesis developed without breaking with medieval traditions, sixteenth-century Christian interpreters of the Bible broke with their medieval predecessors. Coming from humanism, Renaissance biblical scholarship aimed at the establishment of more authoritative texts of the scriptures. This suggests that humanism played an important role in laying the foundations for both the Protestant and Catholic Reformations.

Improving the Texts. Teams of scholars carried out the great tasks of establishing the text of the Bible.

The Complutensian Polyglot Bible edition (the name came from the Latin name of the University of Alcalá de Henares) was the first of these enterprises. Cardinal Francisco Jiménez de Cisneros (1436–1517), who also founded the university, bought or borrowed the necessary manuscripts, gathered a team of scholars, and hired the talented printer Arnao Guillén de Brócar. The scholars included the converso Hebraist Alfonso de Zamora (c. 1474–1545) and the Hellenist Elio Antonio de Nebrija (1441–1522), who was later replaced by Demetrios Doukas of Crete. The edition was based mainly on a collation of manuscripts of the same language, with the different linguistic versions printed side by side. Changes in the various versions were allowed only in those cases justified by the wording of the more ancient texts.

Because of a series of delays, including that caused by the death of Cardinal Jiménez, the six volumes of the Complutensian Polyglot Bible did not appear until 1521. For the Old Testament, the Latin Vulgate was surrounded by the Hebrew text and the Septuagint (the Greek version of the Old Testament). Another Latin translation appeared between the lines. For the Pentateuch (the first five books of the Old Testament), the Targums of Onkelos (the free translation from Hebrew into Aramaic attributed to the Babylonian Jew Onkelos) was added, accompanied by a Latin interpretation. The original Greek and the Latin Vulgate were used for the New Testament. The edition had only a few annotations.

In 1572 Christophe Plantin of Antwerp finished printing the eight-volume *Biblia sacra, Hebraice, Chaldaice, Graece, et Latine.* The Antwerp Polyglot was a remarkable achievement that benefited from earlier partial editions, especially those of Robert Estienne. It also benefited from the purchase of Hebrew characters, which permitted the printing of accents and signs. It was based on a large collection of manuscripts, which Benito Arias Montano (1527–1598), the leader of a large group of scholars, put to good use. The first four volumes contained the Old Testament. The fifth volume comprised the New Testament, including the Syriac version, the Peshitta, accompanied by a Latin translation and a Hebrew transcription. A sixth volume included the famous

Latin translation of the Old Testament by the Italian Dominican Sante Pagnini (1470–1536). His translation had first appeared in 1528 and was reprinted by Miguel Servetus in 1542. A seventh volume included lexicons and grammars, and an eighth held various treatises, the majority written by Arias Montano.

There were many printed editions of the Bible, which often borrowed from each other, in the sixteenth century. A few were sufficiently authoritative to become standard texts at the time.

For the Hebrew Bible, the 1524–1525 edition printed by Daniel Bomberg, a Flemish Catholic living in Venice, was the standard. It was based on a 1516–1517 edition done by Felice da Prato (d. 1558), the son of a rabbi, who became a Christian. It used the Masoretic text of the Old Testament (the received Hebrew text set by rabbis in the sixth century A.D. that added vowel signs to the consonants and notations in the margins) prepared by another Jewish convert to Christianity, Jacob ben Hayyim ibn Adoniya, and corrected by Elijah Levita (1469–1549). The Protestant Sebastian Münster (1489–1552) relied on the version of Felice da Prato for his own Hebrew Bible published in Basel in 1534.

The folio volume of the Greek text of the New Testament published by Robert Estienne in Paris (1550) was soon considered the *textus receptus* (received text). This *editio regia* (royal edition) benefited from Greek characters made in 1546 and modeled on the handwriting of a calligrapher at the French court. The preparation of this text took into account the Complutensian Polyglot Bible but relied primarily on fifteen manuscripts, including the fifth-century manuscript known as the Codex Bezae.

An edition of the Septuagint, proposed by some bishops at the Council of Trent, was prepared by a commission created by Cardinal Felice Peretti da Montalto (later Pope Sixtus V) and directed by Cardinal Antonio Carafa. It was published in 1587. A second volume containing the literal Latin version appeared in 1588.

The Council of Trent declared the Latin Vulgate to be "authentic," meaning only that the Roman Catholic Church held it to be sufficiently accurate for teaching, controversy, and debate. But preparing a critical edition based on the best manuscripts proved difficult. Pope Sixtus V (reigned 1585–1590) named a commission to do the revision but decided to do some of the editing himself, even though he lacked the necessary expertise. The "Sistine" edition was completed and printed in May 1590. It received numerous, if respectfully formulated, criticisms, especially of Sixtus's own emendations. It was then tactfully withdrawn after the pope's death. Pope Clement VIII (reigned 1592–1605) ordered a thorough revision of the text, and this version was published on 9 November 1592. This "Sisto-Clementine" version remained the main text for the Roman Catholic Church until it was replaced by a critical edition produced in the early twentieth century.

The Bible, the sacred text of the West and the first book to be printed, was explicitly or implicitly at the center of Renaissance culture. The development in biblical studies in the fifteenth century resulted in a critical approach to the text. This in turn required a reformulation of traditional hermeneutics on a new basis, which would have been impossible without the vast textual work of the Renaissance scholars.

See also **Complutensian Polyglot.**

BIBLIOGRAPHY

Backus, Irena, Guy Bedouelle, and R. Gerald Hobbs. "Bible." In *The Oxford Encyclopedia of the Reformation.* Edited by Hans J. Hildebrand. Vol. 1. New York and Oxford, 1996. Pages 152–171.

Barthélemy, Dominique, ed. *Critique textuelle de l'Ancien Testament.* Fribourg, Switzerland, 1986.

Bedouelle, Guy, and Bernard Roussel, eds. *Le temps des Réformes et la Bible.* Paris, 1989.

Bentley, Jerry H. *Humanists and Holy Writ: New Testament Scholarship in the Renaissance.* Princeton, N.J., 1983.

Centi, T. M. "L'attività letteraria di Santi Pagnini nel campo delle scienze bibliche." *Archivum Fratrum Praedicatorum* 15 (1945): 5–51.

Garofalo, Salvatore. "Gli umanisti italiani del secolo quindici e la Bibbia." *Biblica* 27 (1946): 338–375.

Greenslade, S. L., ed. *The West from the Reformation to the Present Day.* Vol. 3 of *The Cambridge History of the Bible.* Cambridge, U.K., 1963–1970.

Hall, Basil. "The Trilingual College of San Ildefonso and the Making of the Complutensian Polyglot Bible." In *Studies in Church History.* Vol. 5: *The Church and Academic Learning.* Edited by G. J. Cumming. Leiden, Netherlands, 1969. Pages 114–146.

Lampe, G. W. H. ed. *The West from the Fathers to the Reformation.* Vol. 2 of *The Cambridge History of the Bible.* Cambridge, U.K., 1963–1970.

Pani, Giancarlo. "Un centenaire à rappeler: l'édition sixtine de la Septante." In *Théorie et pratique de l'exégèse.* Edited by Irena Backus and Francis Higman. Geneva, 1990. Pages 413–428.

Pelikan, Jaroslav. *The Reformation of the Bible, The Bible of the Reformation.* Catalog of exhibition by Valerie R. Hotchkiss and David Price. New Haven, Conn., and Dallas, Tex., 1996.

Steinmetz, David C., ed. *The Bible in the Sixteenth Century.* Durham, N.C., 1990.

Vernet, A. "Les manuscrits grecs de Jean de Raguse." *Basler Zeitschrift* 61 (1961): 75–108.

Plate 1. Fra Angelico. *Adoration of the Magi.* The work is by Fra Angelico (Guido di Pietro, c. 1400–1455) and Fra Filippo Lippi (c. 1406–1469). Wood; c. 1445; 137.2 cm (54 in.) diameter. [See the entry on Fra Angelico in this volume.] NATIONAL GALLERY OF ART, WASHINGTON, D.C./THE BRIDGEMAN ART LIBRARY

Plate 2. Banking and Money. *The Moneylender and His Wife* by Quentin Massys (c. 1466–1530), 70.5 x 67 cm (27.8 x 26.4 in.). [See the entry on Banking and Money in this volume.] MUSÉE DU LOUVRE, PARIS/ERICH LESSING/ART RESOURCE

Plate 3. Giovanni Bellini. *Madonna and Child.* Oil on wood; 1480s; 88.9 x 71.1 cm (35 x 28 in.). [See the article on the Bellini family in this volume.] METROPOLITAN MUSEUM OF ART, ROGERS FUND, 1908, 08.183.1

Plate 4. Hieronymus Bosch. *The Garden of Earthly Delights.* The left panel shows the Garden of Eden; the center, the World before the Flood; the right, Hell. Triptych; c. 1505–1510; side panels 218.5 x 91.5 cm (86 x 36 in.); center panel 218.5 x 195 cm. (86 x 76 in.). [See the entry on Hieronymus Bosch in this volume.] MUSEO DEL PRADO, MADRID/GIRAUDON, PARIS/SUPERSTOCK

Plate 5. Sandro Botticelli. *Primavera* (Spring). The painting is also called *The Realm of Venus*. To the right, Zephyr embraces the Nymph Cloris, who is transformed into Flora; Venus stands in the center with Cupid above her, while to the left the three Graces dance and Mercury disperses clouds with his wand. Panel; c. 1478; 203 x 315 cm (80 x 124 in.). [See the entry on Botticelli in this volume.] GALLERIA DEGLI UFFIZI, FLORENCE/CANALI PHOTOBANK, MILAN/SUPERSTOCK

Plate 6. Sandro Botticelli. *Adoration of the Magi.* Botticelli painted *The Adoration of the Magi* for the church of Santa Maria Novella, Florence. In it he depicted Cosimo, Lorenzo, and Giuliano de' Medici as the three Magi; among the spectators are Giovanni Pico della Mirandola and Poliziano. At the far right, Botticelli himself turns to look at the viewer. Tempera on wood; 1476–1477; 111 x 134 cm (43.7 x 52.8 in.) [See the entry on Botticelli in this volume; see the entries on the Medici in volume 4.] GALLERIA DEGLI UFFIZI, FLORENCE/ERICH LESSING/ART RESOURCE

Plate 11. Carnival. *The Battle between Carnival and Lent,* by Pieter Brueghel the Elder (c. 1525 or 1530–1569). Oil on oakwood; 1559; 118 x 164.5 cm (46.5 x 65 in.). [See the entries on Brueghel and Carnival in this volume.] Kunsthistorisches Museum, Gemäldgalerie, Vienna/Erich Lessing/Art Resource

Plate 12. Baldassare Castiglione. Portrait of Baldassare Castiglione (1478–1529), author of *The Courtier,* by Raphael (Raffaelo Sanzio, 1483–1520). Oil on canvas; c. 1514 and 1515; 82 x 67 cm (32.25 x 26.5 in.). [See the entry on Castiglione in this volume and the entry on Raphael in volume 5.] Musée du Louvre, Paris/Erich Lessing/Art Resource

Plate 13. The Catholic Reformation. El Greco's *Burial of the Count of Orgaz* in the church of Santo Tomé, Toledo, commemorates a miracle that occurred, according to local legend, at the funeral of Gonzalo de Ruiz, lord of Orgaz, in 1323. Ruiz had been noted for his charitable works and benefactions to religious institutions in Toledo; St. Stephen and St. Augustine appeared and lowered his body into the tomb. In the upper part of the painting an angel introduces the soul of the count into heaven. The painting depicts many of the themes of the Catholic Reformation: the importance of charity and works, the intercession of the saints, the communion of living and dead, the mediation of the clergy, and the liturgy. 480 x 360 cm (189 x 142 in.) [See the entry on the Catholic Reformation and Counter-Reformation in this volume and the entry on El Greco in volume 2.] IGLESIA SANTO TOMÉ, TOLEDO, SPAIN/SUPERSTOCK

Plate 14. Ceramics "Aeneas at the Tomb of Polydorous," by Francesco Xanto Avelli of Rovigo (Urbino, Italy). The scene depicted is from Virgil's *Aeneid,* book 3. Maiolica plate; 1532; 29 cm (11.5 in.). [See the entry on Ceramics in this volume.] METROPOLITAN MUSEUM OF ART

Plate 15. Charles V. Titian (Tiziano Vecellio, c. 1488 or 1490–1576) painted the Holy Roman Emperor Charles V in Augsburg after his victory over German Protestant princes at the Battle of Mühlberg (1547). Oil on canvas; 1548; 332 x 279 cm (130.75 x 109.75 in.). [See the entry on Charles V in this volume and the entry on Titian in volume 6.] MUSEO DEL PRADO, MADRID/ERICH LESSING/ART RESOURCE

Wagenast, Klaus. "Bibel IV: Reformationszeit" In *Theologische Realenzyklopädie*. Edited by Gerhard Krause and Gerhard Muller. Vol. 6. Berlin and New York, 1977–. Pages 70–77.

GUY BEDOULLE, O.P.

Translated from French by Sylvia J. Cannizzaro

Christian Interpretation of the Bible

Renaissance humanistic textual criticism and Reformation polemics came together to make the years from 1450 to 1650 a very fruitful period in the history of Christian interpretation of the Bible. This vigorous interpretative activity was due to several factors: renewal of interest in Greek and Hebrew, leading to revision of the Vulgate; renewal of interest in classical rhetoric and its applications to the sacred text; humanist interest in the Bible as a textbook of Christian morals; the Reformation with its insistence on the Bible as the unique source of salvation; and the resulting interconfessional polemics and the need in both camps to educate the faithful by applying the Bible to contemporary problems via vernacular sermons. Theology, philology, history, and rhetoric were all put to the service of Bible interpretation.

Tools and Methods. The principal Renaissance achievements were correction of the Vulgate and mass production of Bibles in original languages. Commentators consequently became more interested in the text of the Bible, without ever really becoming textual critics in the modern sense of the term. At the same time a new emphasis on the relationship between the Old and the New Testaments emerged, which saw Old Testament characters and events as foreshadowing the Gospels. This view (known formally as "typology") gradually prevailed over, though it did not entirely displace, allegorical interpretations. Furthermore, the availability from the early 1500s onward of the commentaries of church fathers such as Jerome, Chrysostom, Augustine, Hilary, and Origen provided a yardstick for biblical interpretation, although these commentaries were never slavishly followed. Sixteenth-century Protestant commentaries on the Apocalypse (Revelation) are an excellent example of the need of the commentators to situate themselves within the patristic tradition.

Humanist Biblical Interpretation. The first Renaissance philological commentary on the New Testament was from Lorenzo Valla (1406–1457). His *Collatio Novi Testamenti* (Collation of the New Testament; 1442–1443) was a series of annotations resulting from a comparison of the New Testament text of the Latin Vulgate (which Valla did not consider to be the work of Jerome) with the Greek version. Criticized for interfering with the sacred text, Valla after 1453 produced the more moderate *Adnotationes in Novum Testamentum* (Annotations on the New Testament), which were published in 1505 by Erasmus, whose own work they influenced. Indeed, it has been argued that Erasmus's own Greek and Latin New Testament of 1516 was primarily an attempt to correct the Vulgate, with the Greek text serving as a visual aid. Erasmus's *Annotations*, initially intended as glosses on both the text and the translation, expanded between 1516 and 1536 into a commentary on issues as diverse as the Trinity, the deficiencies of Scholastic theology, and pacifism. They retained, however, their philological slant and, unlike Erasmus's *Paraphrases on the New Testament* (1517–1536), were intended as a commentary for the learned. The *Paraphrases,* loosely modeled on paraphrases of Aristotle by the pagan rhetorician Themistius (c. 317–388), were meant to make the New Testament comprehensible to the uninitiated by rewriting it in simpler terms and at greater length. Paraphrasing of biblical passages was to become an intrinsic part of many commentaries.

The exegetical work of Erasmus and his followers must be viewed not only in the light of Valla's efforts, but also in the light of the work of the English humanist John Colet (1467–1519) and of the French scholar Jacques Lefèvre d'Étaples (1455–1536). Although neither had Erasmus's linguistic skills, both influenced his method of interpreting the Bible. Colet, whom Erasmus met in England in 1499 or 1500, wrote commentaries on Romans and Corinthians (unpublished in his lifetime) that took the Bible as the normative ethical text. He also applied Augustine's principle of interpreting the scripture by the scripture (for example, clarifying obscure passages of the Bible by comparing them with those whose meanings are more transparent). This practice also marked much of Erasmus's exegetical endeavor. Lefèvre d'Étaples made his greatest exegetical impact with his *Quincuplex Psalterium* (The five-fold Psalter, 1509) made up of Old Latin, Gallican, Roman, and Hebrew Psalters accompanied by his own *Psalterium conciliatum* (Unified Psalter) with his own commentary. The latter feature of the work constituted an innovation: Lefèvre sought by scriptural exegesis to achieve a unity between the two testaments, between the two natures of Christ, and between philology and theology.

The Reformation. The reforms initiated by Martin Luther (1483–1546) in 1517 spurred biblical exegesis because the Wittenberg reformer, although no humanist, considered the Bible as the sole source of salvation at the expense of existing ecclesiastical traditions and structures. Furthermore, in 1506, the publication by the German lawyer and scholar Johannes Reuchlin (1455–1522) of *De rudimentis linguae hebraicae* (The Principles of the Hebrew Language) enabled Christians to gain access to the Hebrew text of the Bible, the first Christian edition of which appeared in Venice in 1517, practically at the same time as Luther's break with Rome. The stage was set for development of Old Testament exegesis.

In Luther's first pre-Reformation commentary on the Psalms of 1513–1515, *Dictata* (Lectures), Luther had followed Lefèvre in identifying one literal, christological meaning. In his *Operationes in Psalmos* (Works on the Psalms) of 1519–1521, he discovered an independent edifying meaning in the Hebrew text by analyzing it from a theological standpoint in its historical context. Christological interpretation, however, did not disappear and is present notably in his comments on Psalm 3. Linguistic, historical, and christological elements were also combined in his commentaries on the prophets, for example, the Isaiah lectures of 1534. While the Old Testament as such had much to teach Christians, its chief value lay in helping them comprehend the meaning of Christ.

Luther's humanist colleague Philipp Melanchthon (1497–1560) made an effort to spread the Reformation message through New Testament commentaries (Romans, 1 and 2 Corinthians, Matthew, John). His commentaries are characterized by the *loci communes* (commonplaces) method. This was a device taken over from pagan rhetoric that consisted of dividing the given biblical text into a set number of themes (for example, justification, grace, and sin), which were then expounded.

The exegetical writings (1525–1531) of the Zurich reformer Ulrich Zwingli (1484–1531), many of which are in the form of lecture notes, for the years 1525 to 1531, show the reformer's humanist training by their emphasis on linguistic questions and by their reliance on patristic exegesis. According to Zwingli, it was only when correctly understood with the aid of grammar, rhetoric, and the church fathers, that the Bible could be used to solve the church's problems, edify the faithful, and train the clergy. This was also the aim of the *Prophezei* (Forth-telling) meetings started in 1525, at which the scripture was read in Greek or Hebrew with Zwingli or his colleague, Leo Jud (1482–1542), giving the Latin translation.

The training of the clergy was also the chief aim of the Strasbourg-Basel school of exegesis typified by the commentaries of Martin Bucer (1491–1551). Increasingly eschewing the commonplaces approach, Bucer preferred to divide the text into sections or *pericopes* on which he commented in different ways. Each section was paraphrased and annotated, and the corresponding patristic interpretations were analyzed. There followed "observations," remarks on doctrinal issues; and "reconciliations" and "questions" for use in theological disputes. As well as Romans, Bucer commented notably on the Gospels and the Psalms.

The commentaries of the Genevan reformer John Calvin (1509–1564) showed a similar concern by staying close to the text while seeking to instruct the clergy in the doctrines of the Reformation. Calvin commented most on the Old Testament, excluding the Apocrypha and the Song of Songs, and on much of the New Testament, concentrating on the Pauline Epistles but omitting the Apocalypse. Like most other reformers, he also preached in the *lectio continua* format (a running commentary on a particular biblical book) and several of his sermons survive to this day. Issues that receive philological or abstract treatment in Calvin's commentaries (for example, the role of Eve in the original sin) are discussed much more impulsively in the sermons where he allows himself some rash judgments (such as on Eve and women in general). In 1565 Théodore de Bèze (Beza; 1519–1605), Calvin's successor, produced his own annotated Greek and Latin New Testament with the express aim of improving upon Erasmus, both philologically and doctrinally. Beza's translation went through nine editions in his lifetime.

Roman Catholic Biblical Interpretation. Roman Catholic commentators did not remain impervious to new tools and methods. In 1524 the Roman theologian Agazio Guidacerio (1477–1540) wanted to improve upon Origen's commentary on the Song of Songs. Guidacerio published the text in Hebrew, collated it with Greek and Latin versions, and gave it an anti-Lutheran commentary. The Louvain Franciscan François Titelmans (1502–1537), although a severe critic of Erasmus, was also much indebted to him. More successful than his New Testament exegesis, his commentary on the Psalms went through twenty-six editions between 1531 and 1573. He summarizes (*argumentum*) each Psalm so as to show how it refers exclusively to Christ. A Latin paraphrase of the text is followed by annotations that contain philological comments and bring out the allegorical significance of the text. At the very end of the commentary he gives notes on differences among Hebrew, Greek, and Latin versions.

Naturally, after Luther posted his ninety-five theses in 1517, all commentaries, whatever their confessional provenance, contained a good dose of polemic. Thus, the interpretation of the sixth verse of John became a battleground in the eucharistic dispute between Zwinglians and Lutherans (1525–1536), while all commentaries on Romans took a stand on the question of justification by faith or works. The polemic hardened in the period after the Council of Trent (1545–1563). Thus the Spanish Jesuit Juan Maldonado (1533–1583), who taught in France, devoted most of his exegetical effort to doctrinal issues, notably predestination, and to showing that the Bible, contrary to Protestant claims, was not clear. In Maldonado's view, the final arbiter of biblical interpretation was the church, which could not be reformed by scripture alone. Maldonado's New Testament commentaries were embraced by Roman theologians. The real standard for post-Tridentine Roman Catholic exegesis, however, was set by the Flemish Jesuit Cornelius à Lapide (1567–1637), who drew heavily on patristic tradition in his defense of Roman doctrines and frequently had recourse to allegory in his commentary on all the canonical books of the Bible excepting Job and Psalms.

See also **Catholic Reformation and Counter-Reformation; Christian Theology; Froben Press; Protestant Reformation;** *and biographies of many of the figures mentioned in this entry.*

BIBLIOGRAPHY

Backus, Irena. "Biblical Hermeneutics and Exegesis." In *The Oxford Encyclopedia of the Reformation.* Edited by Hans J. Hillerbrand. Oxford and New York, 1996. Vol. 1. Pages 152–158.

Backus, Irena. *Les sept visions et la fin des temps. Les commentaires genevois de "l'Apocalypse" entre 1539 et 1584. Cahiers de la Revue de théologie et de philosophie.* Vol. 19. Geneva, Lausanne, and Neuchâtel, Switzerland, 1997. Studies both the dependence of the biblical commentators on patristic tradition and their efforts to apply the meaning of the text to their own situation.

Backus, Irena, ed. *Reception of the Church Fathers in the West: From the Carolingians to the Maurists.* Leiden, Netherlands, 1997. Chapters on the Renaissance and Reformation also give information on the availability of patristic commentaries and their influence.

Bedouelle, Guy, and Bernard Roussel, eds. *Bible de tous les temps.* Vol. 5: *Le temps des Réformes et la Bible.* Paris, 1989. Deals with translation as well as interpretation of the Bible. Very comprehensive treatment and a full bibliography.

Fatio, Olivier, and Pierre Fraenkel, eds. *Histoire de l'exégèse au seizième siècle: Textes du colloque international tenu à Genève en 1976.* Geneva, 1978. Papers on major biblical commentators of the period, in English, French, and German.

Parker, T. H. L. *Calvin's New Testament Commentaries.* 2d rev. ed. Louisville, Ky., 1993. Emphasizes Calvin's skills in Greek and Hebrew and his humanism.

Parker, T. H. L. *Calvin's Old Testament Commentaries.* Edinburgh, 1986. Reprint, Louisville, Ky., 1993.

Rummel, Erika. *Erasmus' Annotations on the New Testament: From Philologist to Theologian.* Toronto, 1986. A thorough analysis of the main theological issues discussed in the *Annotations.*

Steinmetz, David. "Hermeneutic and Old Testament Interpretation in Staupitz and the Young Martin Luther." *Archiv für Reformationsgeschichte* 70 (1979), 24–58.

Steinmetz, David, ed. *The Bible in the Sixteenth Century. Proceedings of the Second International Colloquium on the History of Biblical Exegesis, Durham, N.C., 1982.* Durham, N.C., 1990.

IRENA BACKUS

Jewish Interpretation of the Bible

To meet the needs and expectations of the communities they served, medieval Jewish scholars were obliged to master the Bible. Their mastery presupposed foundational expertise in two sorts of knowledge, philological and traditional. The philological included the vocabulary, grammar, and rhetoric of biblical Hebrew. The traditional included the entire legacy of classical talmudic literature, both legal (halakah) and homiletic-theological (Haggadah). Resting upon these foundations were the claims of secular philosophy, in all of its Platonic and Aristotelian varieties, and mysticism (Kabbalah), in all of its major trends. Some scholars specialized, becoming biblicists if they favored philology over the other branches of medieval lore, Talmudists if they advocated the superiority and autonomy of traditional rabbinic learning, philosophers if they were inclined to humanistic and universal rationalism, or Kabbalists if they were attracted to myth and mysteries. Partisan controversy was lively. Most scholars, however, were eclectic. Teaching in classrooms, preaching in synagogues, adjudicating in courtrooms, composing topical treatises or exegetical commentaries, they anthologized and harmonized various combinations of philology, rabbinic tradition, secular philosophy, and mysticism. Collectively, their guiding principle was not *sola scriptura,* scripture alone.

No geographical settlement of Jews lacked biblical experts, but none surpassed the achievements of Jews native to Islamic or Christian Spain. Among Jewish Iberia's most illustrious commentators were Abraham ibn Ezra (1092–1167), Nahmanides (Moses ben Nahman, c. 1194–1270), Bahya ben Asher (died 1340), and Isaac Abravanel (1437–1508); among its great preachers were Joshua ibn Shueib (first half of the fourteenth century) and Isaac Arama (c. 1420–1494). Spanish Jewry produced Moses Maimonides and *The Guide of the Perplexed,* Abraham Abulafia and the ecstatic Kabbalah, Moses De Leon and the *Zohar.* They were profound stimulants for intense biblical study. No wonder that Judah ben Asher, a talmudic scholar trained in Germany who became the chief rabbi of Toledo in the middle of the fourteenth century, counseled his son to adopt the distinctive practice of Spanish Jewry by "establishing a regular routine for the study of Scripture based on grammar and commentaries."

Jewish life in Spain ended abruptly and traumatically with the royal edict of expulsion in 1492. Many of the exiles made their way to Portugal, where they were all forcibly converted to Christianity in 1497. Other exiles headed for nearby Islamic North Africa, either remaining there or joining the mass of refugees who eventually found havens farther east in Italy or the Ottoman Empire. Isaac Abravanel, for example, reestablished his diplomatic and scholarly career in Naples and Venice, where he composed the bulk of his biblical commentaries. Isaac Arama died at Naples. Rabbi Isaac Karo (1440–1518), a philosophizing preacher active in the Ottoman Empire, left his native Toledo several years before the expulsion. He settled in Portugal only to escape to Constantinople in 1497. In Salonika, Rabbi Joseph Taitazak, a Spanish native, impressed his disciples with an innovative method for close readings of scripture. He combined talmudic dialectics with logic and rhetoric derived from Jewish and gentile sources, both classical and medieval. His influential and prolific disciple, Rabbi Moses Alsheikh (c. 1508–1600), migrated to the remarkably creative community of saints and scholars living in sixteenth-century Safed in the Galilee. Gifted with shrewd psychological insight and a keen eye for narrative detail, Rabbi Moses taught and preached scripture for four decades. He left indelible marks on the contemporary and subsequent history of traditional biblical interpretation, especially among the Ashkenazic Jews of Slavic eastern Europe. Wherever they went, the Spanish exiles aggressively transplanted their Sephardic culture, adapting it to the realities they currently faced. They gave new life to the old arguments between biblicists, Talmudists, philosophers, and mystics.

Despite divisive ideological preferences, these scholars collectively subscribed to beliefs enunciated by Isaac Karo: "our sacred Torah provides us with perfection in this world, as well as in the world to come. . . . In our cleaving [unto Torah], we cleave unto God. . . . The perfection of our Torah is great and mighty, for contained within it are all the sciences." They understood these beliefs to mean that scripture is vastly complex, that there is nothing adventitious or merely decorative in scriptural rhetoric, and that scripture speaks in allegories or tantalizes its students by demanding vigorous intellectual interrogation. Their commentaries and sermons were therefore designed to articulate explicitly the subtle strata of scripture's allusive references to physics, psychology, politics, ethics, metaphysics, and theology.

This fusion of biblical text with encyclopedic learning was often accomplished by means of a formalistic device partially borrowed from the scholastic practice of listing pros and cons, questions and objections, before resolving them in lengthy expositions. Having raised the theoretical possibility that scripture may have gotten something wrong or phrased something inappropriately, the teacher or preacher would then systematically rationalize, justify, and eliminate the apparent error. For example, Rabbi Moses Alsheikh prefaced his sermon on I Samuel 15 by listing no less than twenty-six objections or queries whose answers finally explain why the prophet Samuel was angry with King Saul's conduct of the war against the Amalekites. Structuring their biblical lessons with lists of uninhibited questions and catalogs of barbed replies, the preachers and commentators displayed a communal preference for the complex and subtle over the simple and straightforward. Together with their audiences, they apparently took delight in discovering hidden affinities between disparate domains and inventing multiple answers to single problems. It pleased them to take a biblical verse, associate it with a traditional talmudic dictum, and explicate the thematic unity linking them. So doing, they reassured themselves that ancient Jewish lore was the true source and authentic repository of the world's wisdom. They were also fulfilling Rabbi Isaac Arama's admonition that Jewish teachers and preachers are obliged to compete with and vanquish gentile scholars by "exalt[ing] the image of our Torah to our own people by regaling them with gems from its narratives and laws."

The tumultuous and inventive sixteenth century transformed Jewish life. Dislocation and the emergence of new centers in Italy, the Ottoman Empire, and eastern Europe spurred creativity. The Sephardic heritage of biblical study made that creativity possible.

See also **Jews,** *subentry on* **Jewish Religious Life.**

BIBLIOGRAPHY

Bland, Kalman P. "Issues in Sixteenth-Century Exegesis." In *The Bible and the Sixteenth Century*. Edited by David Steinmetz. Durham, N.C., 1990. Pages 50–67.

Hacker, Joseph. "The Intellectual Activity of Jews of the Ottoman Empire during the Sixteenth and Seventeenth Centuries." In *Jewish Thought in the Seventeenth Century*. Edited by Isadore Twersky and Bernard Septimus. Cambridge, Mass., 1987. Pages 95–135.

Ruderman, David B., ed. *Preachers of the Italian Ghetto*. Berkeley, Calif., 1992.

Saperstein, Marc. *Jewish Preaching, 1200–1800: An Anthology*. New Haven, Conn., 1989.

KALMAN P. BLAND

Printed Bibles

The late Middle Ages and Renaissance witnessed the distribution of the Bible text on a scale and in a variety of formats unimaginable before the technological breakthrough of printing with movable type. As the agent of what is often called a revolution, the printing press transformed both popular and intellectual culture, in part by supporting widespread circulation of the Bible and fostering scholarly analysis of its texts.

Advances in Printing and Text. Nonetheless, printing did not immediately divorce the Bible from all the elements of its manuscript past. As illustrated by the editio princeps (Mainz: Johann Gutenberg, c. 1454), the earliest printed Bibles do not differ much in appearance or textual substance from manuscript Bibles. The Gutenberg Bible looks like a fifteenth-century manuscript Bible in folio, with its text arranged in two columns per page and its lettering executed in a bold textura style. The page designs left space for the insertion of initials by hand, a common strategy of the early printed Bible that was only gradually superseded by the use of woodcut initials and multicolor printing. Before 1481, when Adolf Rusch of Strasbourg accomplished the feat, printers were not able to imitate the complex pages of those medieval Bibles that provided the text with the Ordinary Gloss (standard medieval commentary in biblical manuscripts) or the commentaries of such significant scholars as Nicholas of Lyra. An equally important technological advance was the gradual miniaturization of fonts, which allowed the printing of folio Bibles in one volume (as in the editio princeps of the German Bible [Strasbourg: Mentelin, 1466]) and of smaller format Bibles. The first quarto Bible appeared in 1475 (Piacenza: Johannes Petrus de Ferratis); Johann Froben was the first to print a Bible in a compact octavo format (Basel, 1491), for which he managed to set a remarkable fifty-six lines of type per small page.

Improvements in the quality of the biblical text were modest in fifteenth-century printing. The Vulgate text (the Latin translation by St. Jerome), in highly interpolated versions, dominated the early period. Of the 127 Bibles printed before 1501, 94 are in Latin (Vulgate version), 3 in Hebrew, 30 in vernaculars, and none in Greek. A small subset of Vulgate imprints called "Fontibus ex graecis" editions purport to emend the text in accord with Greek and Hebrew sources, although these texts do not differ greatly from other Vulgates. Systematic textual improvement of the Vulgate began with the pioneering work of Robert Estienne, whose first critical edition of the Vulgate appeared in 1527–1528 in Paris. His edition of 1538–1540 became, by way of the Louvain Bible of 1547, a basis for the authorized Catholic edition of the Vulgate, the Sixto-Clementine Bible of 1592.

The most important philological advance in the fifteenth century resulted from the printing of Hebrew texts. The earliest attempt to print a book of the Bible in Hebrew was a 1477 edition of Psalms (probably from Bologna), which was unable to align the vowel points with the text. This typographical challenge was overcome in Abraham ben Hayyim's Bologna Pentateuch of 1482, a work that included the Targums (ancient Aramaic paraphrases) for the first time. Abraham ben Hayyim would soon join the Soncino press, initially operated in the small Italian town of Soncino by Joshua Solomon Soncino, where in 1488 the first complete Hebrew Bible was produced. The third and final complete Hebrew Bible of the fifteenth century, produced by the Soncinos in Brescia in 1494, was executed in the convenient octavo format. It was this edition that Luther had in hand when he began his translations from Hebrew scriptures. On the eve of the cataclysmic Jewish expulsions and persecutions, Spain and Portugal produced several partial Bibles in Hebrew, perhaps the most significant of which is the two-volume Pentateuch from Lisbon (1491), which included both the Targums and the medieval commentary of Rashi. One of the greatest moments in Hebrew printing occurred in 1524–1525 with the printing of the second great rabbinic Bible at the press of Daniel Bomberg in Venice. This work, the result of the careful scholarship of Jacob ben Hayyim, presented the Masoretic text in a form that set a standard for over four hundred years.

Illustrated Bibles. In the fifteenth century, Bibles in German and Italian were printed with significant programs of woodcut illustration. The most influential illustrations were the 123 woodcuts of the Cologne Bible (1478/79), most of which were reissued in the Koberger Bible of 1483 (Nürnberg). The most extensive program of illustration in Germany was the Lübeck Bible (Lübeck: Steffen Arndes, 1494) with 152 woodcuts, several of which show the influence of an Italian Renaissance style. The translation by Niccolò Malermi was the editio princeps in Italian (Venice: Wendelin von Speyer, August 1471). Beginning with a reprint of 1490 (Venice: Giovanni Ragazzo for Lucantonio di Giunta), the Malermi Bible was extensively illustrated, with this edition containing 387 woodcuts (some repeated).

Vulgates printed before 1501 only rarely had woodcut illustrations. The earliest known uses were title-page woodcuts: a depiction of St. Peter in a Bible of 1492 (Venice: Hieronymus de Paganinis Brixiensis) and a representation of Jerome translating Genesis (Basel: Johann Froben, 1495). Albrecht Dürer's publication of the Book of Revelation in Latin and German editions (Nürnberg: Anton Koberger for Albrecht Dürer, 1498) would exert tremendous influence on the subsequent history of Bible illustration. A complete Latin Bible was printed in 1498 (Venice: Simon Brevilaqua) with seventy-three woodcuts, apparently taken from the Malermi Bible. After the onset of the Reformation, Hans Holbein the Younger created designs for Latin Bibles that appeared at the press of Melchior and Gaspar Trechsel (Lyon, 1538 and 1544).

Polyglot Bibles. The ultimate challenge to editors and printers was production of synoptic polyglot Bibles. The first example of polyglot printing was probably the Genoa Psalter (Genoa: Porrus, 1516), which gave Psalms in Hebrew, Greek, Arabic, and Aramaic, along with three Latin versions. It was an act of dedication to scholarship and faith when Cardinal Francisco Jiménes de Cisneros, archbishop of Toledo and regent of Castille, began in 1502 the Herculean task of creating a polyglot of the entire Bible. The resulting Complutensian Polyglot, carefully printed by Arnaldo Guillén de Brocar, imperial typographer for Charles V, included the Hebrew text (printed with vowel points but without accents), Vulgate translation, Septuagint version along with an interlinear Latin translation, and for the Pentateuch volume, the Targums with a Latin translation; the New Testament volume provides the Greek text and the Vulgate translation. [For an illustration of a page of the Complutensian Polyglot, see the entry on it in volume 2.] The printing was executed between 1514 and 1517, but distribution was delayed until 1522 while papal permission was sought. Three other extensive polyglots deserve mention: The Antwerp Polyglot in eight volumes (Antwerp: Christophe Plantin, 1569–1572), edited chiefly by Benito Arias Montano and produced with the patronage of Philip II of Spain; the Paris Polyglot, edited by the lawyer Guy-Michel Le Jay and others in ten volumes (Paris: Jacques Vitré 1629–1645); and the London Polyglot of Brian Walton and others in six volumes (London: Thomas Roycroft, 1655–1657), considered the most accurate of the four.

Printers. Several outstanding printers of the Bible were scholars in their own right. Johann Froben of Basel (c. 1460–1527), who was learned in the biblical languages and published his own Hebrew grammar in 1527, encouraged Erasmus to bring out the first edition of the Bible in Greek (1516). All five Froben editions of the Erasmus Bible are strikingly handsome books, elegantly designed and decorated with significant woodcuts, some of which were executed by Urs Graf. The corrected second edition of 1519 was the version Luther used for his first translation of the Bible, the September Testament of 1522. Robert Estienne, who took up printing from his father, Henri Estienne (I), and as of 1539 enjoyed the title of "royal printer," produced the most beautiful and most accurate versions of the Greek New Testament. He became expert in Greek philology and conducted much of the research for his editions, though he was later assisted by his son, Henri Estienne (II).

Estienne printed his first Greek New Testament in 1546, but it was in 1550 that he printed the New Testament that would have ultimate authority as the *Textus Receptus* (received standard text). This imprint, which was known as the Editio Regia (royal edition) and later dubbed the "Protestant Pope" by Richard Bentley, was the first to provide variant readings from manuscripts printed in a critical apparatus, a process aided by Claude Garamond's creation of three sizes for the *grecs du roi* font he had designed for Estienne. Estienne used several excellent manuscripts for the edition, the most important of which was the fifth-century Codex Bezae. His editorial decisions were markedly conservative; he retained, for example, the much debated *Comma Johanneum* (1 John 5:7–8), which Erasmus had restored in his third edition of the Bible in 1522. In 1551 Estienne published an edition of the New Testament in three versions (Greek along with Erasmus's Latin translation and the Vulgate) in sextodecimo format, in which he divided the Bible into verses. With very few excep-

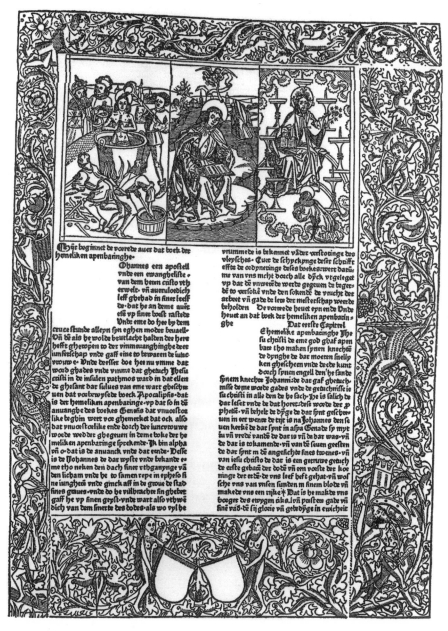

Cologne Bible. Page with scenes from the life of St. John the Evangelist and the book of Revelation from the Cologne Bible, printed by Heinrich Quentell in 1478.

tions, Estienne's verse divisions became standard and are still used in modern editions.

Translations. Martin Luther's translations of the Bible—his first edition of the New Testament appeared in 1522 and first complete translation in 1534—were such huge publishing successes that the Bible became virtually ubiquitous in central European culture. According to Heimo Reinitzer, some 430 editions of the complete or partial Lutheran translations appeared between 1522 and Luther's

death in 1546. Wittenberg would remain an important center for printing the Lutheran Bible, although pirated imprints were issued in even greater numbers from presses in other cities. Typically, the complete Lutheran Bibles were issued in richly illustrated folio, although the partial Bibles, including separate New Testaments, were often in octavo (and occasionally in quarto). The Zurich Bible, the earliest biblical translation in the Reformed tradition, grew initially out of enthusiasm for—and reliance on—Luther's Bible to become an independent and philologically sophisticated version. The Zurich printer Christoph Froschauer was a driving force in the creation of the version.

English translations. The earliest printings of the English Bible were illegal in England, an abiding legacy from the suppression of the Wycliffite Bible (as in the Oxford Constitutions of 1408) and, more important, a response to the fear that the Lutheran movement could sweep across the island. William Tyndale (c. 1494–1536) went to the Continent to translate the Bible from the original languages and to have his translations printed. A first attempt to print the New Testament in 1525 at the press of Peter Quentell in Cologne was stopped by authorities; a single fragment of that effort, which breaks off in the middle of Matthew 22, survives. The first complete edition of Tyndale's New Testament was printed in all likelihood by Peter Schöffer in Worms in 1526. Although the print run was probably 3,000, this book was so thoroughly suppressed by English authorities that only three copies (one of which is seriously defective) are known to have survived. Most of Tyndale's subsequent imprints were probably done in Antwerp, where he resided for many years until his imprisonment in 1535 and execution at Vilvorde in 1536. He did see his Pentateuch (1530) and translation of Jonah (1531?) through press; it is assumed that John Rogers published what survived of Tyndale's further progress on the Old Testament (through 2 Chronicles) in an imprint known as "Matthew's Bible" (1537) after the pseudonym of Thomas Matthew used by the editor. This was probably printed in Antwerp and imported into England by the firm of Richard Grafton and Edward Whitchurch; it was distributed, according to the title page, with the "Kinges most gracyous lyce[n]ce."

The first complete English Bible (1535), not done from the original languages but "out of Douche and Latyn," was the work of Miles Coverdale. It was printed on the Continent and released legally in England and with a new title page and preface printed probably by James Nicholson in Southwark (London). It is this title-page woodcut that shows Henry VIII dispensing scripture to ecclesiastical and secular princes (representing perhaps Archbishop Thomas Cranmer on the left and Chancellor Thomas Cromwell on the right). Soon, under the encouragement of Cromwell and Cranmer, Coverdale was enlisted to produce a new version—grounded in the "Matthew's Bible" and consequently Tyndale's scholarship and artistry—which was to be set up in every church in England: the Great Bible (1539; see the

illustration in the subentry on the English Bible). This grand folio Bible was richly illustrated and went through six subsequent official editions, all of which were produced by Richard Grafton and Edward Whitchurch.

Perhaps the most lavishly designed Bible of the English Renaissance was the "Bishops' Bible," an important revision undertaken by Archbishop Matthew Parker and other bishops. It first appeared in a deluxe folio edition printed by Richard Jugge (London, 1568), with 143 woodcuts, engravings, and maps. Many of the woodcuts are by the German artist Virgil Solis, and two engraved portraits are apparently the work of Franz Hogenberg. The engraved title page features Queen Elizabeth, and two further engraved portraits are of court favorites: Robert Dudley, earl of Leicester, and William Cecil, baron of Burghley. This text went through at least thirty-eight different editions, the last coming in 1633.

The King James Version (London: Robert Barker, 1611)—the definitive revision, for which the Tyndale-derived Bibles, as well as the Geneva Bible and the Douai New Testament, were consulted—was a majestic black-letter folio Bible worthy of its rhetorical and philological grandeur. The imprint features an engraved title page by Cornelis Boel, thirty-four pages of genealogical tables, and a map of biblical lands preceding Genesis. Thereafter the book is without illustration, an austerity that accords with the editors' decision (encouraged by the royal will) to eschew theological or contentious sidenotes, a feature of the Geneva Bible that was deemed a flaw.

The early Catholic Bible in English was also printed abroad. Hostility to Catholicism in England during the reign of Elizabeth I resulted in the formation in 1568 of an English Catholic College at the University of Douai, where the Catholic translations, initiated by Gregory Martin, according to the Vulgate were done. The New Testament appeared in Reims (John Fogny, 1582) and the Old Testament in Douai (Laurence Kellam, 1609 and 1610).

French translations. The first complete translation of the Bible into French was done by Jacques Lefèvre d'Étaples and published in Antwerp by Martin Lempereur in 1530 (preceded by a publication of Lefèvre's New Testament in 1523). This version, though grounded in the Vulgate, continued to enjoy reprintings throughout the first half of the sixteenth century outside of Geneva. The first Protestant translation, and the first to be based on the original languages, was completed by Pierre Robert Olivétan (Neuchâtel: Pierre de Wingle, 1535). This version, equipped with introductions by John Calvin, went through numerous revisions, in the course of which it became the French Geneva version, one of the most influential and popular versions of the Bible in any language.

Calvin's own efforts at revision are first acknowledged in a New Testament of 1543. In 1546 he completed a revision of the entire Bible and directed revisions in 1551 (aided by Théodore de Bèze and Louis Budé), in 1553 (assisted by Robert Estienne), and of the New Testament only in 1560 (assisted by Bèze). The pastors of Geneva undertook a final revision in 1585 that went substantially unchanged for some two centuries. The Geneva Bibles gradually grew in scope by the addition of aids and notes to the readers, most of which were for historical clarification, but many were also harshly polemical. The main center for the publication of French Bibles outside of Geneva was Lyon. Most Lyon editions were based on a non-Calvinist Geneva edition of 1540 until 1565, when Calvinist Geneva versions began to be printed freely.

The first Catholic translation into French, by René Benoist (1566), was profoundly dependent on the Geneva version and was, consequently, condemned by the theological faculty of the University of Paris. Christophe Plantin's revision of Benoist's translation, of which he first printed the New Testament in 1573 and the entire Bible in 1578, became known as the "Louvain Bible" because Plantin prudently secured an endorsement of the version for Catholics from the theological faculty of Louvain.

Other translations. With the influx of religious refugees from all over Europe and the growing distinction of biblical philology at its academy, Geneva became an important center for the creation and printing of Bible versions in English, Italian, and Spanish. It was there that Giovanni Diodati, who would also produce a French translation (Geneva: Pierre Chouet, 1644), completed the first Italian translation for Protestants and did so from the original languages (Jean de Tournes, 1607). English refugees during the reign of Queen Mary also produced the extraordinarily successful Geneva Bible (Rowland Hall, 1560), the first complete English Bible printed in roman type. Its format—a modest sized quarto with double-column page layouts and roman font—is considered the model for the typical modern Bible design in English. At least 144 editions of this Bible appeared between 1560 and 1644, indicating by its longevity that, for a time, it offered the King James Version serious competition. The Ge-

nevan printer Jean Crespin, using the pseudonym of "Juan Philadelpho," printed the second edition of the New Testament in Spanish, which was translated by the expatriate Juan Pérez de Pineda.

Of the major vernacular versions, the Spanish Bible suffered the longest estrangement from its homeland. A Catalan translation by Bonifacio Ferrer was published in Valencia in 1478 but so thoroughly suppressed by the Spanish Inquisition that only a single page of one copy has survived. Thereafter, with the exception of two imprints of liturgical Gospels and one of a Gospel harmony, the Bible in Spanish was not to be printed in Spain until 1790–1793. The editio princeps of the Spanish New Testament (Antwerp: Steven Mierdman, 1543) landed its translator, Francisco de Enzinas, in prison. The first Old Testament printed in Spanish was produced for Jewish expatriates living in Italy (Ferrara, 1553). The first complete translation would also be the most enduring: the version by Cassiodoro de Reina, which is still the basis of Spanish Bibles for Protestants. It first appeared in a print run of 2,600 copies in 1569 at the press of Samuel Apiarius in Basel, although it is likely a collaborative project with the printer Thomas Guarin.

The Renaissance did not create awareness of the need to improve the text of the Bible, nor did it mark the first attempt to disseminate it to a broader public, for those goals had been pursued at various times and places throughout the Middle Ages. But, with the invention of printing, the Renaissance had a workable means to these ends. To be sure, each successive printing of the Bible was not necessarily an improvement. But the publication of textual criticism advanced biblical philology to the point where the text was stabilized, with its variants for the most part well documented and understood. As printing developed, however, the availability of the Bible in so many formats raised anxieties about the authority of the text to a level never previously experienced in the history of Christianity. The first century of printing the Bible had its paradoxical side: scripture was at the same time energetically distributed and vigorously suppressed.

See also **Complutensian Polyglot Bible**; **Printing and Publishing**; *and biographies of figures mentioned in this entry.*

BIBLIOGRAPHY

Die Bibel in der Schweiz. Edited by Die Schweizerische Bibelgesellschaft. Basel, Switzerland, 1997.

Black, M. H. "The Printed Bible." In *The Cambridge History of the Bible.* Edited by S. L. Greenslade. Vol. 3. Cambridge, U.K., 1963. Pages 408–475.

Chambers, Bettye Thomas. *Bibliography of French Bibles.* 2 vols. Geneva, 1983–1994.

Darlow, T. H., and H. F. Moule. *Historical Catalogue of the Printed Editions of Holy Scripture in the Library of the British and Foreign Bible Society.* 4 vols. 1903. Reprint, New York, 1963.

Herbert, A. S. *Historical Catalogue of Printed Editions of the English Bible, 1525–1961.* Revised and expanded from the edition of T. H. Darlow and H. F. Moule, 1903. London, 1968.

Hotchkiss, Valerie R., and Charles C. Ryrie, eds. *Formatting the Word of God.* Dallas, 1998.

Kinder, A. Gordon. *Casiodoro de Reina.* London, 1975.

Pelikan, Jaroslav, with Valerie R. Hotchkiss and David Price. *The Reformation of the Bible/The Bible of the Reformation.* New Haven, Conn., 1996.

Reinitzer, Heimo. *Biblia deutsch: Luthers Bibelübersetzung und ihre Tradition.* Wolfenbüttel, Germany, 1983.

Reinitzer, Heimo. "Bibeldruck." In *Lexikon des gesamten Buchwesens.* Edited by Bernard Bischoff, Severin Corsten, Günther Pflug, and Friedrich Adolf Schmidt-Künsemüller. Vol. 1. Stuttgart, Germany, 1985. Pages 349–353.

Snaith, Norman Henry. "Bible: Printed Editions (Hebrew)." In *Encyclopaedia Judaica.* Vol. 4. Jerusalem, 1971. Pages 836–841.

DAVID PRICE

German Translations

The earliest evidence of the Bible in German is a ninth-century manuscript of Matthew's Gospel. Until the twelfth century, most Bible translations in German appeared in verse rather than prose and were limited to individual books. The earliest complete New Testament is the Augsburg Bible (1350), and the earliest Old Testament the Wenzel Bible (c. 1390).

The first printed Bible in German, indeed in any vernacular, came from the press of Johann Mentelin (Strasbourg, 1466). He based it on a fourteenth-century German translation of the Vulgate, the Latin version of the Bible attributed to St. Jerome. The seventeen Bibles in High and Low German that followed, until Martin Luther's translation of the New Testament in 1522, likewise found their roots in the Latin. The most notable, if slight, revisions of Mentelin came from Günther Zainer (Augsburg, 1475) and Anton Koberger (Nürnberg, 1483).

Luther's German New Testament hit the marketplace in September 1522 and became known as the "September Testament." As a base text, he used the Greek/Latin New Testament of Desiderius Erasmus (1516, revised 1519), and translated all twenty-seven books in a mere eleven weeks. Unbound and unadorned, it cost half a gulden, the week's wage of a journeyman carpenter. The first issue of three thousand sold quickly, as did the revised "December Testament" three months later.

Using the Hebrew Bible printed in Brescia (1492/94), Luther set to work on the Old Testament. But troubled by problems of translation, and occupied on other fronts in the Reformation, he published sections only intermittently. It took him twelve years to finish the whole, the "Wittenberg Bible" of 1534. Before he died in 1546, Europeans purchased about 500,000 partial or complete copies of his translation. It was the most printed book in German. And it drew fire. Critics tendered what they called their own translations (largely Catholic revisions of Luther): Hieronymus Emser (Dresden, 1527), Johann Dietenberger (Mainz, 1534), and Johannes Eck (Ingolstadt and Augsburg, 1537). But no defense could stay the flood of unauthorized Bibles. By comparison, from the entire fourteenth and fifteenth centuries we have only eight hundred manuscripts of (mostly fragmentary) German Bibles.

Nothing during the Renaissance fostered a recovery of purer Testaments in Greek and Hebrew, or helped refine German versions of them, more profoundly than the tools of philology and textual criticism taught by humanists. And nothing marked the variety of vernacular Bibles available more distinctly than contemporary debates about translation: are readers better served by a slavish adherence to preposition-for-preposition literalism or a free rendering of the general sense into native colloquial expressions? The most cogent, if controversial, defense of the vernacular was Luther's 1530 *Sendbrief von Dolmetschen* (On translating: an open letter), about German as a fitting language for scripture.

Luther collaborated with eminent Hellenists and Hebraists. They went to great lengths to find fitting expressions for every Greek and Hebrew phrase, consulting linguists, reading commentaries, and listening to the common people in the street. When Luther came to describe sacrifices in Leviticus, he went to a butcher, who taught him the anatomy of sheep in German. The language chosen for the Luther Bible was not a regional patois but the court parlance of electoral Saxony, elegant and living. And Luther fine-tuned every sentence to make it accessible to as many German speakers as possible.

See also **Translation.**

BIBLIOGRAPHY

Bedouelle, Guy, and Bernard Roussel, eds. *Bible de tous les temps.* Vol. 5: *Le temps des Réformes et la Bible.* Paris, 1989.

Lockwood, W. B. "Vernacular Scriptures in Germany and the Low Countries before 1500." In vol. 2 of *The Cambridge History of the Bible: The West from the Fathers to the Reformation.* Edited by G. W. H. Lampe. Cambridge, U.K., 1969. Pages 415–436.

Vogel, Paul Heinz. *Europäische Bibeldrucke des 15. und 16. Jahrhunderts in den Volkssprachen: Ein Beitrag zur Bibliographie des Bibeldrucks.* Baden-Baden, Germany, 1962.

Volz, Hans. "German Versions." In vol. 3 of *The Cambridge History of the Bible: The West from the Reformation to the Present Day.* Edited by S. L. Greenslade. Cambridge, U.K., 1963. Pages 94–109.

MICHAEL MILWAY

The English Bible

The Old Testament was originally written in Hebrew, a language unique to those writings, and the New Testament in the working Greek of the eastern Mediterranean. Jerome's fourth-century translation into Latin, however, became standard and was later known as the "common version" or Vulgate. Parts of this Vulgate were translated into various dialects of Old English, beginning with the interlinear insertions in the Lindisfarne Gospels of 698. It was translated in its entirety twice into late Middle English under John Wyclif (c. 1330–1389) in the 1380s. As the rediscovery of Greek by Italian humanists such as Giannozzo Manetti (1396–1459), Lorenzo Valla (1407–1457), and Marsilio Ficino (1433–1499) gathered force during the 1400s, discomfort mounted with the increasing errors of the Vulgate. But it was Erasmus (c. 1466–1536) who made the most serious challenge to the Vulgate in 1516, when he revised the New Testament into Latin himself, in his *Novum Instrumentum.* To support the accuracy of his translation, he printed the original Greek alongside. His Latin version had some influence, but his printed Greek New Testament, the first such text to become available, set Europe ablaze. In September 1522, Martin Luther (1483–1546) printed his New Testament in German from Erasmus's Greek: this widely disseminated volume gave to Germany a common language, and to translators throughout Europe a standard.

William Tyndale. In England, William Tyndale, having learned Greek as well as good Latin at Oxford, set out to make an English New Testament. In 1408 English translations had been banned on pain of excommunication, trial for heresy, and being burned alive, because translation was one of the activities associated with John Wyclif, who had been declared a heretic. However, times were changing, and England, as Tyndale correctly saw, was hungry for a vernacular Bible. His plea to the bishop of London was rejected; and in Germany his first attempt, in Cologne in 1525, was defeated. In Worms, however, in 1526, he printed the first English New Testament that was translated directly from the Greek.

Four Versions of a Gospel Passage (Luke 2:18–20)

Tyndale's Revision (1534)
And all that heard it, wondered at those things which were told them of the shepherds. But Mary kept all those sayings, and pondered them in her heart. And the shepherds returned, praising and lauding God for all that they had heard and seen, even as it was told unto them.

The Geneva Bible (1560)
And all that heard it, wondered at those things which were told them of the shepherds. But Mary kept all those sayings, and pondered *them* in her heart. And the shepherds returned glorifying and praising God for all that they had heard and seen, even as it was told unto them.

Douai-Rheims Version (A Roman Catholic translation from the Latin Vulgate; 1582)
And all that heard, did marvel: and concerning those things that were reported to them by the shepherds. But MARY kept all these words, conferring them in her heart. And the shepherds returned, glorifying and praising God in all things that they had heard, and seen, as it was said unto them.

The Authorized (King James) Version (1611)
And all they that heard it, wondered at those things, which were told them by the shepherds. But Mary kept all these things, and pondered them in her heart. And the shepherds returned, glorifying and praising God for all the things that they had heard and seen, even as it was told unto them.

Three thousand (some say, six thousand) copies of this well-made small octavo were smuggled down the Rhine in bales of cloth and were swiftly bought in London and the south and east.

Only two complete copies have survived (one is a treasure of the British Library) of the small book that is the foundation of all later English versions. Tyndale created an English Bible whose language is accurate, direct, and speaks to the heart. It has had incalculable influence. In the Gospels, the Christmas stories are still known largely in Tyndale's words, as are Jesus's parables, and the accounts of the crucifixion. Tyndale echoed Luther in Englishing Paul's Epistle to the Romans: the translation of passages of Paul's writings in modern Bibles is still recognizably Tyndale's.

The Great Bible. Title page showing King Henry VIII presenting copies to Thomas Cranmer *(left)* and Thomas Cromwell *(right),* who distribute them to clergy and people, inspiring a universal cry of "Vivat Rex" (Long live the king). The Great Bible was published in 1539. BY PERMISSION OF THE BRITISH LIBRARY. C18D1

Most copies of Tyndale's New Testament were collected by the English church authorities and, in a ceremony at St. Paul's Cathedral, publicly burned. Tyndale in Germany, undeterred, learned Hebrew, a language almost completely unknown in Britain. In 1535 Tyndale was tricked into arrest in Antwerp; he was convicted of heresy, and strangled and burned on 6 October 1536. Still, his translations of the Pentateuch, and of the Old Testament historical books, along with his 1534 revision of his New Testament, were printed in 1537. The first complete English Bible to obtain Henry VIII's license as not heretical, it was known as Matthew's Bible. The first complete printed Bible in English, however, had been published in 1535 in Antwerp by Miles Coverdale (1488–1569). Coverdale's version, however, was not translated from the original languages. Using Tyndale's work, in 1539 Coverdale went on to prepare the only English Bible to be authorized to be issued by the new Church of England, the Great Bible, a copy of which was to be placed in every church.

The Geneva Bible. Between 1553 and 1558, Queen Mary's persecutions caused many English Bible scholars to flee to Europe. In Geneva, a center of textual research and translation, the first Geneva Bible was published in 1560. A triumph of Renaissance and Reformation learning, the Geneva Bible relied on better Greek and Hebrew texts, and an increased understanding of Hebrew. Even so, it was still dependent on Tyndale. Partly revised in 1576, and again in 1599, these volumes were issued with copious notes, commentaries, summaries, tables, maps, pictures, concordances, indexes, and, later, Prayer Books and metrical psalms. The Geneva Bible was meant for all readers, and it was "the Bible" during Elizabeth's reign: its Calvinism was not objectionable, and it influenced the writers and thinkers of the time, including Shakespeare.

The King James Version. The success of the Geneva Bible provoked a retort, led by bishops who still clung to the Vulgate as the standard Latin Bible. The resulting Bishops' Bible of 1567 was inadequate. A Roman Catholic English translation from Rheims in 1582 was still indebted primarily to Tyndale, but used strange latinate vocabulary. Nearly half a century after the first Geneva Bible, King James was persuaded to inaugurate moves toward a new translation. For his own reasons, he insisted that the basis should be the Bishops' Bible. The result in 1611 was and is known in Britain as the Authorized Version (though it was never authorized) and elsewhere as the King James Version (though that monarch had little to do with it). But it was essentially Tyndale's translation with a latinate coloring, occasionally felicitous but often archaic. Minimal cross-references and a few glosses made it an instrument of authority rather than domestic study. Contrary to the later prevailing view, it was disliked on its first appearance, and only overtook the Geneva Bible for commercial and political reasons. Idolization of the King James Version did not begin until the later eighteenth century. Thus, one of the cores of the English Renaissance experience, a full awareness of the content and form of the whole Bible, owes more to Tyndale and the Geneva Bible than to King James and his version.

The Psalms. There were many English versions of the Psalms in the sixteenth and seventeenth centuries. At first these were for the newly liberated congregational singing, partly Lutheran in origin and partly from Calvinist Geneva, where the long history of metrical psalms (as in the Prayer Book) began. English poets, however, took these scriptural poems as evidence that God approved of poetry, and used them as models. Psalms were translated (frequently from the Hebrew) by, among many others, Sir Philip Sidney, Francis Bacon, John Milton, George Herbert, Richard Crashaw, and Henry Vaughan.

See also **Luther, Martin; Tyndale, William.**

BIBLIOGRAPHY

Primary Works

The Geneva Bible: A Facsimile of the 1560 Edition. With an introduction by Lloyd E. Berry. Madison, Wis., and London, 1969.

The Geneva Bible: The Annotated New Testament, 1602 Edition. Edited by Gerald T. Sheppard. New York, 1989.

Tyndale's New Testament. A modern spelling edition with an introduction by David Daniell. New Haven, Conn., and London, 1995.

Tyndale's Old Testament: Being the Pentateuch of 1530, Joshua to 2 Chronicles of 1537, and Jonah. A modern spelling edition with an introduction by David Daniell. New Haven, Conn., and London, 1992.

Secondary Works

Bruce, Frederick F. *The English Bible: A History of Translations.* London, 1961.

Daniell, David. *William Tyndale: A Biography.* New Haven, Conn., and London, 1994.

Hamilton, Alistair. "Humanists and the Bible." In *The Cambridge Companion to Renaissance Humanism.* Edited by Jill Kraye. Cambridge, U.K., and New York, 1996.

Hammond, Gerald. *The Making of the English Bible.* Manchester, U.K., 1982.

DAVID DANIELL

BIDERMANN, JAKOB (1578–1639), German Jesuit playwright. Jakob Bidermann is considered the greatest Jesuit dramatist and the most important figure in German drama before Andreas Gryphius. Born in 1578 in Ehingen in Swabia, Bidermann was enrolled at age eight at the Jesuit college in Augsburg. In 1594 he entered the Jesuit order and was ordained a priest two years later. After his novitiate, he studied at the University of Ingolstadt and then taught liberal arts at Augsburg from 1600 to 1603. After studying theology at Ingolstadt, Bidermann was transferred in 1606 to the Jesuit college in Munich, where his responsibilities included the production of Latin plays. After nearly ten years at Munich, he was appointed professor of philosophy and theology at the Jesuit-controlled university of Dillingen. Sometime between 1626 and 1628 Bidermann was summoned to Rome to be an official theologian and censor of books. He died there in 1639.

Bidermann was a man of extraordinary literary productivity. His works—all written in Latin, the language of the Catholic Church and of scholarly discourse at the time—include three books of religious epigrams (*Epigrammatum libri tres;* 1620); two collections of epistolary poems (*Heroum epistolae* [Letters of heroes; 1630], *Heroidum epistolae* [Letters of heroines; 1638]); a verse epic on King Herod and the massacre of the innocents (*Herodiados;* 1622); and a novel called *Utopia* (1640).

Bidermann's fame, however, rests on his plays. He was the most prominent exponent of the flourishing theater that the Jesuits had forged into a powerful weapon for propagating Catholic doctrines and countering the effect of the Reformation. Of his nine extant plays published posthumously in 1666 (*Belisarius, Cenodoxus, Cosmarchia, Philemon Martyr, Jacobus Usurarius, Josephus, Macarius, Josophatus,* and *Joannes Calybita*) his *Cenodoxus* is the best known. First performed in 1602, it was translated into German in 1635 by Joachim Meichel. It is still read and occasionally performed.

Cenodoxus is associated with the founding of the Carthusians by St. Bruno in 1082. According to legend, as the funeral rites of Bruno's teacher, a doctor famed for his erudition and virtue, were about to commence, his corpse rose three times, declaring, "I have been accused!"; "I have been judged!"; and "I have been condemned!" Startled by this "miracle," Bruno, along with six companions, withdrew into the wilderness to form a new community of monks. Although in the legend the doctor remains nameless and the sins for which he is condemned are not identified, Bidermann gives the doctor the speaking name Cenodoxus, or "vainglorious," and identifies his sins as pride and hypocrisy.

Bidermann's *Cenodoxus* has often been interpreted as an attack on Renaissance humanism which, because of its pride in human accomplishments and its pursuit of fame as an earthly form of immortality, presented a challenge to the authority of the church. This is only partially true. Bidermann does not denounce scholarship or the pursuit of knowledge as such but rather their perversions in the form of pride, sanctimoniousness, and the neo-Stoic notion that humans can work out their salvation independent from God.

The play's success was also due to its effective theatrics: the vivid visualization of heaven and hell; the use of allegorical figures such as Philautia (self-love), Hypocrisy, and Conscientia, which, though meant to externalize mental processes, assumed lives of their own; the skillful interplay of comic and serious scenes; and the use of Latin with its epigrammatic compactness and witty word plays.

BIBLIOGRAPHY

Primary Work

Bidermann, Jacob. *Cenodoxus.* Edited and translated by D. G. Dyer. Austin, Tex., 1974. Latin text and English translation of *Cenodoxus* (1666), with an excellent introduction.

Secondary Works

Best, Thomas W. *Jacob Bidermann.* New York, 1975. The only full-length study of Bidermann in English.

Best, Thomas W. "Jacob Bidermann." In *Dictionary of Literary Biography.* Vol. 164, *German Baroque Writers, 1580–1660.* Detroit, Mich.; Washington, D.C.; and London; 1996. Pages 45–49.

Valentin, Jean-Marie. "Die Jesuitendichter Bidermann und Avancini." In *Deutsche Dichter des 17. Jahrhunderts.* Edited by Harald Steinhagen and Benno von Wiese. Berlin, 1984. Pages 385–414.

ECKHARD BERNSTEIN

BIOGRAPHY AND AUTOBIOGRAPHY. [This entry includes two subentries, the first on biography and autobiography on the European continent, the second on biography in England.]

Europe

A specific genre called biography—a more inclusive term is "life-writing"—did not exist during the Renaissance. No European language had a word for it before the late seventeenth century. Nevertheless, life-writing flourished in multiple forms and media, often interwoven with other forms of literature, especially history. The humanist stress on example gave the genre a powerful impetus. Yet humanists had no monopoly on life-writing, which despite the recovery of classical models continued along many of the paths followed by medieval writers. Renaissance biographers did not intend to represent lives as lived, but rather as instances of a particular model or a rhetorical object, especially of the rhetoric of praise and blame. Still, many Renaissance biographers insisted on accurate portrayals and sought reliable information on their subjects. Writers such as Paolo Giovio (1486–1552) were careful to distinguish history from encomium. The same dialectic characterized Renaissance portrait painters, who represent one of the most important modes of life-writing. The overlap between plastic and written forms is embodied in the language used to describe the biographer's and the portraitist's object: for both, the goal was a "portrait" (*effigies* in Latin).

Generic Confusion. History could be biography; the line between them was difficult to draw. On the one hand, individual deeds and wider context were inextricably bound in *De dictis et factis Alphonsi regis Aragonum et Neapolis* (On the sayings and deeds of Alfonso, king of the Aragonese and Neapolitans; written 1455) by Antonio Beccadelli (Il Panormita), and even more so in *De rebus gestis ab Alphonso primo Neapolitanorum rege commentariorum libri decem* (Ten books of commentary on the things done by Alphonso I, king of the Neapolitans), the work of his rival, Bartolomeo Fazio (c. 1400–1457). On the other hand, works of history like Leonardo Bruni's (1369–1444) *Historia Florentini populi libri* (Books of the history of the Florentine people; 1476) were studded with capsule lives.

Another post-Renaissance distinction had little meaning, that between biography and autobiography. Biographers often drew on their subjects' own view of themselves, sometimes explicitly at the subject's direction. This was the case, for example, with William Roper's *Life of Sir Thomas More, Knight* (c. 1557) and in the two lives of Reginald Pole, one by Ludovico Beccadelli (c. 1561) and the other by Andras Dudic (printed 1563). Both the latter two biographers had access to Pole's archive (albeit at different times) and also adopted Pole's own image as a saintly martyr.

Ancient Models. Many ancient models influenced Renaissance life-writing, although Renaissance writers felt free to pick and choose, combine and recombine different models at will. Since Hellenic times, the Greeks had written both biography and autobiography. Xenophon was perhaps the most important Greek biographer, composing his

life of Cyrus for educational purposes, adding biographical appendices to his history of the Persian wars, and defending Socrates through a series of biographical vignettes. In the Hellenistic and Roman eras, biography became an industry, its popularity no doubt increased by the blurring of the distinction between biography and fiction. Collected biographies by Roman authors such as Suetonius, Cornelius Nepos, and Plutarch were very popular in the Renaissance. Suetonius's *Lives of the Twelve Caesars*—together with his similar *De viris illustribus* (On famous men), which covered scholars—and Plutarch's *Lives* stood at opposite ends of the spectrum, Suetonius stressing deeds (and physical characteristics), Plutarch placing greater emphasis on character than on action. Both models, singly and then in combination, lent themselves perfectly to humanist imitation.

Ancient Christian biographers, especially Jerome, looked to classical models to solve a new problem, how to represent the holy individual. Medieval authors of sacred biography (or hagiography) adopted this earlier approach, which continued to be very influential throughout the Renaissance. Despite its critical attitude to saints' lives, humanist philology ironically contributed to the survival of the genre in the hands of the Maurists and the Bollandists beginning in the mid-seventeenth century. Outside the mainstream of learned biography, many laymen, especially merchants, began in the fourteenth century to record their lives through diaries. The best known of them are the many Florentine *ricordanze* (literally, remembrances).

Collective Biography. Although greatly indebted to the ancients, humanist biographers invented a new form of life-writing, the exemplary life, beginning with the *Life of Dante* (c. 1348), written by Giovanni Boccaccio (1313–1375), and followed later by Leonardo Bruni's life of Dante (c. 1436). Bruni wrote his biography of Dante to eliminate the fiction in Boccaccio's work. Similarly, Petrarch (1304–1374) initiated in *De viris illustribus* (On famous men) one of the most common forms of Renaissance biography, collected lives, and Boccaccio popularized the mode in his *De casibus virorum illustrium* (On cases of famous men; 1355–1374) and *De claris mulieribus* (On famous women; 1360–1374). Boccaccio's biographies of famous men proved popular outside Italy, particularly in England, where his book was translated in the fifteenth century and provided much of the material for the *Mirror for Magistrates* (1559) in the sixteenth. France showed more interest in the second, which Christine de Pizan (1361–c. 1430) loosely adapted in *Le livre de cité des dames,* which was, however, read mainly in translation as *The Book of the City of Ladies.* Less explicitly exemplary was Aeneas Silvius Piccolomini's *De viris aetate sua claris* (On the famous men of his time; 1440–1450), to which Fazio contributed a sequel, *De viris illustribus* (On famous men; 1456), which was dedicated to Piccolomini as Pope Pius II (reigned 1458–1464). Perhaps the most famous of collective biographies was Giorgio Vasari's (1511–1574) *Le vite de' più eccellenti architetti, pittori, e scultori italiani* (trans. *Lives of the Artists;* 1550), which went beyond its classical models by introducing the modern discipline of art history. Vasari's example was widely imitated until at least the middle of the seventeenth century, especially in the Netherlands by Vasari's informant, Dominic Lampson (1532–1599), who composed a life of his master, Lambert Lombard, and above all in Karel van Mander's *Het Schilder-Boeck* (The painter book; 1604).

Nonhumanist collective biography continued to flourish, perhaps best in Vespasiano da Bisticci's late-fifteenth-century *Vite di uomini illustri* (Lives of famous men), in which the lives are organized according to profession: churchmen, statesmen, writers. Ecclesiastical biography, related to sacred biography but moving in much more critical directions, began with Bartolomeo Platina's *Historia de vitis pontificum Romanarum* (trans. *Lives of the Popes;* 1474), a work known under many different titles, which attests to its popularity, before concluding with Alfonso Chacón's (1540–1599) *Vitae et res gestae pontificum romanorum et S. R. E. cardinalium* (Lives and deeds of the Roman pontiffs and cardinals of the Holy Roman Church; 1601). In a less scholarly form, lives of ecclesiastics intended as examples were broadly popular.

Autobiography. Ancient models were as important in the writing of autobiography as they were in biography. St. Augustine's *Confessions* offered an influential framework for Renaissance autobiography, while Julius Caesar's third-person *Commentaries* offered a more difficult model, although both were only rarely explicitly followed. Augustine's example proved slightly easier to imitate, beginning with Dante's *La vita nuova* (The new life; 1293–1294) and Petrarch's allegorical autobiographical letter "The Ascent of Mount Ventoux" (probably 1352–1353), which climaxes in a meditation on Augustine. Many Protestant writers drew inspiration from Augustine's example, which provided the basis for the widespread phenomenon of spiritual autobiography in the seventeenth century. Caesar influenced Piccolomini's own *Commentaries* (1458), and it proved appealing to others, such as Philippe de Commynes (1447–1511). Autobiography in the form of letter collections, pioneered by Petrarch, proved especially useful to women, notably Cassandra Fedele (c. 1465–1558) and Laura Cereta (1469–1499), while other women, such as Vittoria Colonna (1490–1547), turned to poetry to construct a record of their lives. They were succeeded in the seventeenth century by large numbers of female autobiographers.

Undoubtedly the most famous autobiography was Benvenuto Cellini's (written 1558–1566). By turns goldsmith, soldier, writer, and sculptor, Cellini portrayed himself as a phantasmagorical figure who could do literally anything. Recounted almost at random, the events of his life were loosely linked primarily through astrology and Cellini's agonistic temper. Perhaps the most distinctive form of Renaissance autobiography was Michel de Montaigne's *Essays* (1572–1580 and 1588), in which he claimed to subject his own existence to minute examination while offering highly skeptical opinions on a range of topics.

Pictorial Life-writing. Pictorial life-writing took several forms, usually in open tension with written lives. Formal portraiture served exactly the same end as other Renaissance life-writing: it provided a permanent memorial of an exemplary character. Like the biographer, the portraitist had to balance the typical and the individual in order to meet the demands of sitter and patron. The portraitist made use of the printing press both to construct and to replicate a visual identity. One of the most striking is the image of Martin Luther during the German pamphlet wars of the sixteenth century. Many of the first images were rendered on woodblocks, which produced a less sophisticated image than type. New techniques such as copperplate engraving—perhaps most famously Albrecht Dürer's self-portraits—drypoint, and etching brought image and text closer together. Print also contributed to the development of one of the oddest and certainly most difficult to understand forms of life-writing, emblem books. A typical instance is Achille Bocchi's *Symbolicarum quaestionum* of 1555.

Giovio also had a hand in two final forms of graphic life-writing, collective portraiture both painted and printed. The first came in his plans for Vasari's frescoes in the Sala dei Cento Giorni in the Palazzo della Cancelleria in Rome (1546), which illustrated the wonders of Pope Paul III's (Farnese) pontificate (1534–1549). The Zuccaro brothers (Taddeo and Francesco) created in the early 1560s another similar set of frescoes at the Villa Farnese at Caprarola, where history, painting, and lives were all rolled together into one grand celebration of the Farnese. The illustration of famous deeds of the family on the walls of its villa was by then a well-established mode of life-writing; for example, in Palazzo Vitelli at Città di Castello, like the fourteenth-century illustrations of famous ancients at Ascianio (Siena), graphic life-writing served both as examples and as decoration. Giovio's celebrated museum, eventually installed in his villa outside Como, assembled portraits of all the subjects of his biographies. Giovio's museum quickly became a European phenomenon, with copies of his collection being made for the duke of Florence and Henry, prince of Wales, among others. Similar series are found quite frequently just a bit lower down the social scale, for example at Hardwick Hall or at the Sorbonne in Paris. What had once been strictly private was becoming public. Print made possible the dissemination of both lives and images on a European stage, as evidenced by the wide and rapid diffusion of Giovio's *Elogia* (Praises), written biographies that were first published without plates in 1546 and later replaced by copiously illustrated versions in the 1570s. Giovio's was only one of many similar collections, including Andrea Fulvio's *Illustrium imagines* (1517) and the *Icones* of Théodore de Bèze (1605).

See also **Diaries and Memoirs; Emblem; Hagiography.**

BIBLIOGRAPHY

Anderson, Judith H. *Biographical Truth: The Representation of Historical Persons in Tudor-Stuart Writing.* New Haven, Conn., 1984.

Cochrane, Eric. *Historians and Historiography in the Italian Renaissance.* Chicago, 1981.

Fueter, Eduard. *Geschichte der Neueren Historiographie.* Munich, 1911.

Heffernan, Thomas J. *Sacred Biography: Saints and Their Biographers in the Middle Ages.* New York, 1988.

Lyons, John D. *Exemplum: The Rhetoric of Example in Early Modern France and Italy.* Ithaca, N.Y., 1989.

Mann, Nicholas, and Luke Syson, eds. *The Image of the Individual: Portraits in the Renaissance.* London, 1998.

Mayer, Thomas F., and D. R. Woolf, eds. *The Rhetorics of Life-Writing in Early Modern Europe: Forms of Biography from Cassandra Fedele to Louis XIV.* Ann Arbor, Mich., 1995.

THOMAS F. MAYER

England

The word "biography" itself was not familiar to the English Renaissance. Its first recorded instances belong rather to the Restoration (1660–1688), the period in which the genre began to flourish. Francis Bacon, writing in 1605, could still lament the lack of what he termed "lives," a form that he understands as a part of history:

> For lives, I do find strange that these times have so little esteemed the virtues of the times, as that the writings of lives should be no more frequent. For although there be not many sovereign princes or absolute commanders, and that states are most collected into monarchies, yet there are many worthy personages that deserve better than dispersed report, or barren elogies. (*The Advancement of Learning,* p. 75)

Bacon understood the utility of such "lives" within the framework of a centralized monarchy, and his text, *The Advancement of Learning,* was addressed to the new Stuart monarch, James I. His understanding of the "life" was strongly secular, and he paid no attention to the dominant medieval form of biography, the "life of the saint." The chronicle tradition, moreover, no longer appeared adequate to the needs of an increasingly diffuse state.

Humanist Biography. One can argue, however, that another highly placed counsellor, Sir Thomas More, had anticipated the need for such newer forms of biography with his classically inspired lives of Richard III (c. 1513) and Giovanni Pico della Mirandola (c. 1510), the latter basically a translation of the life written by Pico's nephew Gianfrancesco. The Roman historians Tacitus and Suetonius inform More's humanist version of biography, but his hostile account of Richard III clearly served the interests of the Tudor state as well. More's text remains a compelling narrative of political manipulation, in many respects a counterpart to Machiavelli's *The Prince,* but its interest in the figure of Edward IV's former mistress, Jane Shore ("Shores wife"), also anticipated newer forms of life-narrative. More is aware that "some shal think this woman to sleight a thing, to be written of & set amonge the remembraunces of great matters" (*The History of King Richard III,* p. 56), but this does not prevent him from providing a lively portrait that memorably juxtaposes this "sleight" person with his account of the treachery of Richard. Some of the most enduring elements of this work, such as his account of Jane Shore, owe as much to hagiographic traditions as to classical inspiration.

The same argument can be made for the other notable lives of the Tudor period, George Cavendish's *Life and Death of Cardinal Wolsey* (c. 1558) and William Roper's *Life of Sir Thomas More* (c.

1556). Both works benefit, at least from our perspective, from the personal proximity of the writers to their subjects, producing a level of intimate detail that is as striking as the general adherence of the lives to medieval narrative models (the wheel of fortune, the "life of the saint").

Protestant Influences. At the same time that medieval models continued to exert considerable influence over the shape of the lives of the "great men," a form more specific to the central event of the sixteenth century, the Reformation, was also emerging. This was the sense of a "spiritual accounting," related to the Lutheran concept of "vocation" and the Calvinist notion of "election." The first separately printed prose autobiography in English, in fact, is that of the Protestant Tudor antiquarian John Bale: *The vocacyon of Johan Bale to the Bishoprick of Ossorie in Ireland, his persecucions in the same, and finall delyveraunce* (1553).

The form of spiritual accounting thereafter continuously migrated from the world of public controversy instanced by Bale to the world of private or even "domestic" concern, producing what Donald A. Stauffer terms the "intimate biography" that came to dominate the genre. Sir Thomas Bodley's autobiography (1609) produces a self-justifying narrative of "good works" (the foundation of the Bodleian Library at Oxford). It was also this period—the same period in which Bacon regrets the absence of lives—that witnessed the appearance of edifying lives of London merchants as well as ecclesiastical lives (for which St. Augustine's *Confessions,* first translated into English in 1620, was a popular model) and even lives of English poets.

The Flowering of Biography. Izaak Walton is the first widely known English biographer, and his first life, "The Life and Death of Dr. Donne, Late Deane of St. Pauls London," was, as the title indicates, very much an ecclesiastical biography trying to ignore as much as possible Donne's "profane" poetry. The life of Donne was originally a part of the editorial apparatus of Donne's *LXXX Sermons* (1640). Walton's subsequent lives and their popularity (they were issued together during the Restoration independently of their original status as appended texts) perhaps serve as the best marker of the arrival of biography in the modern sense of the word: an expanded range of potential subjects along with greater attention to the details of "private" life. In this sense, the genre of biography is perhaps best understood as proximate to the novel, another form emerging in the early modern period, and the eigh-

teenth century saw what can be described as a generic competition between the two.

Walton's career as biographer spans the middle years of the seventeenth century, the years in which the genre substantially consolidated itself. Autobiography began to flourish as well. John Donne's *Devotions upon Emergent Occasions* (1624) and Sir Thomas Browne's *Religio Medici* (c. 1634) provided highly sophisticated models of spiritual and intellectual introspection. Conversely, the autobiography of Lord Herbert of Cherbury (c. 1643) largely ignored his philosophical work in favor of the narrative of a dashing courtier, expatiating on the subject of the defense of ladies' honor, exploits of military bravado, and his popularity at court. The civil war spurred new forms of biographical and autobiographical writing, often combining a religious concept of vocation with a newer sense of political mission. Certainly, the Restoration itself, the age of Samuel Pepys and John Aubrey, witnessed the widespread proliferation of biographical forms. Aubrey himself is startling and refreshing for his lack of moral commentary on his subjects. In a very different vein, John Evelyn's *Life of Mrs. Godolphin* (1678), one of the first English biographies of a woman to be published, treats with approval her "retirement" within the very public—and theatricalized—court of Charles II:

> Amidst all this pomp and serious impertinence [of a masque in which she played a leading role], whilst the rest were acting, and that her part was sometymes to goe off, as the scenes required, into the tireing roome, where severall Ladyes her companions were railing with the Gallants trifleingly enough till they were called to reenter, she, under pretence of conning her next part, was retired into a Corner, reading a booke of devotion, without att all concerning herselfe or mingling with the young Company. (pp. 97–98)

Bacon lamented the scarcity of lives of "worthy personages," but such lives became by the end of the seventeenth century an important form for the representation of a new (Protestant) form of subjectivity in English society.

BIBLIOGRAPHY

Primary Works

Bacon, Francis. *The Advancement of Learning and New Atlantis.* Edited by Arthur Johnson. Oxford, 1974.

Herbert, Edward. *The Life of Edward, First Lord Herbert of Cherbury, Written by Himself.* Edited by J. M. Shuttleworth. London, 1976.

More, St. Thomas. *The History of King Richard III.* Edited by Richard S. Sylvester. In *Complete Works of St. Thomas More,* vol. 2. New Haven, Conn., and London, 1963.

Sylvester, Richard S., and Davis P. Harding, eds. *Two Early Tudor Lives.* (*The Life and Death of Cardinal Wolsey* by George Cavendish and *The Life of Sir Thomas More* by William Roper.) New Haven, Conn., and London, 1962.

Walton, Izaak. *The Lives of John Donne, Sir Henry Wotton, Richard Hooker, George Herbert, and Robert Sanderson.* London, 1951.

Secondary Works

Anderson, Judith H. *Biographical Truth: The Representation of Historical Persons in Tudor-Stuart Writing.* New Haven, Conn., and London, 1984.

Bottrall, Margaret. *Every Man a Phoenix: Studies in Seventeenth-Century Autobiography.* London, 1958.

Osborn, James M. *The Beginnings of Autobiography in England.* Los Angeles, 1960.

Pask, Kevin. *The Emergence of the English Author: Scripting the Life of the Poet in Early Modern England.* Cambridge, U.K., 1996.

Stauffer, Donald A. *English Biography before 1700.* Cambridge, Mass., 1930.

Webber, Joan. *The Eloquent "I": Style and Self in Seventeenth-Century Prose.* Madison, Wis., and London, 1968.

KEVIN PASK

BIONDO, FLAVIO (Blondus Flavius; 1392–1463), Italian humanist, pioneering antiquarian, historian. Biondo Flavio was born at Forlì and became a notary and professional civil servant. He also became a humanist, taking part in the rediscovery of ancient literature; his *Italia illustrata* (Italy illustrated; 1474) is the only extant source for several passages from the historian Ammianus Marcellinus. Biondo's own Latin is awkward, but the content of his works makes him a figure of seminal importance in the Italian Renaissance. His status rose in 1432, when he joined the court of Pope Eugenius IV (reigned 1431–1447). The pope and Curia were resident in Florence from 1434 to 1443, and Biondo played an important role in the Council of Ferrara-Florence (1438–c. 1445). He fell from favor under Pope Nicholas V (1447–1455) and in 1449 withdrew from the Curia to seek princely patronage.

His shortest work, *De verbis Romanae locutionis* (On the words of Roman speech), launched a humanist debate in the 1430s. Biondo argued on historical grounds that the Latin language must have been acquired and used naturally by all the Romans, whether they had had schooling or not. Leonardo Bruni, influenced by a priori medieval notions, asserted that the complex grammar of Latin could not have been acquired except through formal learning, and that the common people of ancient Rome must have used a vulgar tongue lacking cases and declensions.

Roma instaurata (Rome restored; 1481) is a topography of the ancient city and its ruins. *Roma triumphans* (Rome triumphant; 1482) attempts to reconstruct Roman religion, public administration, the army, and private institutions, and ends with a vivid description of a Roman triumphal procession, modulating into a comparison between a Roman commander, senators, and army officers in triumph, and the Roman pope, his cardinals, and the princes of Europe (in other words, Christendom united under papal leadership) engaged in a crusade against the Ottoman Empire.

The first part of Biondo's *Historiarum ab inclinatione Romanorum libri* (Books of history from the fall of the Roman Empire; 1483, also known as *Decades*) covers the period from A.D. 410 to 1410 in twenty books. The concept of the decline and fall of Rome, and of a new Italian civilization originating in the Middle Ages, had great influence on later historians. The critical use of sources, the attempt to illuminate periods that were virtually unknown, and the nonprovidential account of medieval history as a series of human deeds were revolutionary developments made possible by the culture of Renaissance humanism. The second part of the *Decades* (consisting of eleven books published in the Renaissance editions, and part of a twelfth by Bartolomeo Nogara) was actually written first and deals with contemporary Italy down to the early 1440s in a typical humanist manner: few hard dates; plenty of dramatized orations; and coverage of interstate wars and diplomacy but not of internal politics. It has the unusual virtue of impartially surveying developments throughout the entire nexus of Italian states.

Italia illustrata is a work of extraordinary richness and originality, although Biondo had the literary topographies of antiquity for a remote model. From them he adopted a division of Italy into regions that did not correspond to the modern territorial states. He added Lombardy, the great northern region that had arisen out of the vicissitudes of medieval history, but failed to use the accurate contemporary maps and coastal charts that would have increased the accuracy of his physical description. His primary purpose was not simply to describe Italy, but rather to link the glorious past of Roman Italy to the glorious present of the Renaissance by gathering information about cities and illustrious men across the whole span of time, a quintessentially humanist endeavor to recover knowledge from obscurity and preserve it in monumental literary form.

In the section on his native Romagna region in *Italia illustrata,* Biondo gives a significant interpretation of the origins of the Italian Renaissance, which he dated to the later fourteenth century. Though Petrarch led the revival of learning, Biondo emphasized how rapidly a school of Romagnol humanists sprang up. At the same time, he said, the condottiere Alberico da Barbiano (active from the 1370s to 1409), by renovating Italian military culture and expelling the foreign mercenary companies, brought glory and an age of less destructive wars to the peninsula. That and the return of the papacy from Avignon, Biondo concluded, led to the present age of wealth and luxury (essential components of the Renaissance for him). Romagna's crowning contribution was Flavio Biondo himself, the writer who had restored integral knowledge of the material culture of ancient Rome and the continuity of Italian history.

BIBLIOGRAPHY

Primary Works

Biondo, Flavio. *Blondi Flauii Forliuiensis De Roma Triumphante libri decem; Romae Instauratae libri III; Italia Illustrata; Historiarum ab Inclinatione Romanorum Libri XXXI.* Basel, 1531 (still the standard edition of Biondo's works; reprinted in 1559 with the pagination unchanged).

Biondo, Flavio. *Scritti inediti e rari di Biondi Flavio.* Edited by Bartolomeo Nogara. Vatican City, 1927. Includes *De verbis Romanae locutionis.*

Secondary Works

Fubini, Riccardo. "Biondo, Flavio." In *Dizionario biografico degli italiani.* Vol. 10. Rome, 1968. Pages 536–559. An article-length entry of fundamental importance.

Clavuot, Ottavio. *Biondos "Italia illustrata." Summa oder Neuschöpfung? Über die Arbeitsmethoden eines Humanisten.* Tübingen, Germany, 1990. An important work with full bibliography down to 1990.

WILLIAM McCUAIG

BIRTH AND INFANCY. Even though birth and infancy were common to all in the Renaissance, very little firsthand information is available because women did not write about the subject and men were seldom witnesses. Previously untapped sources, like church records and burials, have recently yielded some valuable information about the experiences of ordinary people. What is clear is that birth and infancy were fraught with peril, especially for the child.

Childbirth. Women gave birth in the company of many women. It was an occasion for a gathering of relatives and neighbors, not only to give help and comfort but also to make social contact. This custom transcended geography and class. Even medical men were completely excluded, and thus their obstetrical knowledge, as a consequence, was drawn mainly from books rather than observation. The intrusion of an ordinary man in such a setting

was considered something of an abomination. In spite of this, male painters frequently depicted birth scenes, usually as part of cycles on the lives of saints. These paintings cannot be considered accurate but do show the presence of many women.

The most important attendant at birth was the midwife. Typically of a social rank not far removed from that of the mother, she was an older woman who had had several babies herself. Her skills were greatly respected, even by physicians. She was trained by a practicing midwife, who passed along her knowledge much as masters trained apprentices. Midwives were often the target of men's suspicions about secret activities involving women and were sometimes feared as witches, who might consign the souls of the newborn to the devil before they could be baptized.

The basic techniques of midwives seem to have worked well in most births. The woman in labor was encouraged to sit up and bear down to ease the passage through the birth canal, often using a so-called birthing chair. Some problem births were handled effectively. Midwives knew how to turn infants who were incorrectly positioned. Problems that could be dealt with only by using instruments required the intervention of a surgeon. The appearance of a male practitioner, however, was tantamount to an announcement of imminent death. If the birth canal was blocked, a surgeon used hooks and knives to remove the infant in pieces. Cesarean sections were performed only if the mother died and there was a chance of saving the infant.

The first medical treatise on childbirth written since antiquity was a manual for pregnant women and midwives by the German physician Eucharius Rösslin published in 1513. It was published in England three decades later as *The Byrth of Mankynde* and was translated into other languages and republished many times until the end of the seventeenth century. Rösslin's aim was to combine medical lore derived from classical antiquity with what he could find out about midwives' methods in order to improve them, not to supplant the midwives. The emergence of male midwives, or obstetricians, came much later.

Although the danger of death in childbirth was great, most women survived and gave birth many times. Nevertheless, many writers, mostly male, expressed a widespread fear of childbirth. They spoke of illness, pangs, travail, even "pains of Hell" and "snares of Death." The main cause of childbed death was probably infection, usually a consequence of a hand or an instrument being inserted into the birth

Giving Birth. A wetnurse suckles a newborn baby as the child's mother rests in bed. Domenico Ghirlandaio (1449–1494), *Birth of St. John the Baptist,* church of Santa Maria Novella, Florence. ALINARI/ART RESOURCE, NY

canal. For example, a midwife might attempt to remove a placenta that had not been expelled. This probably caused most cases of postpartum illness and death. A seemingly normal delivery would be followed by a prolonged fever, and death would come within a month.

Feeding Infants. The normal food for newborns was human milk. Most mothers breast-fed their babies, particularly in the lower classes. A few lower-class babies could not be nursed by their mothers, who had died or were ill. Some unfortunate infants were fed animals' milk or even thin wheat gruel.

Maternal breast-feeding had the enthusiastic approval of respected authorities. The medical profession recommended it, and the clergy was strongly in favor of it. Saint Bernardino of Siena, among others, preached against women who forsook their duty in order to indulge their vanity and sensuality—a common theme in sermons on the subject. The motif of

the nursing Madonna was exploited in Renaissance painting as never before.

Wet nurses. In spite of the overwhelming approval of maternal nursing, wet-nursing was a thriving business. It may be the best-documented aspect of infancy in the Renaissance. The typical wet nurse was a married peasant woman whose own infant had died. If her own child was not dead she might undertake to suckle it along with the child she was hired to feed, but this was considered highly undesirable. Wet nurses usually stayed in their own homes, so that a newborn might be sent to live in a strange house, more modest than that of his or her parents. A few exceptionally wealthy families kept at least some of their infants at home, most often their sons, thus assuring that the infant would get the nurse's undivided attention and that she would be well rested and well nourished.

Renaissance society expressed ambivalence toward wet-nursing. Writers who recommended that mothers nurse their own babies also offered advice on how to select wet nurses. The reasons for using wet nurses were fairly complex. Christian moralists thought wet nurses could prevent marital infidelity, which was a risk because nursing mothers were not supposed to be sexually active. The prospect of uninterrupted sexual relations was appealing to couples and carried with it the possible benefit that wives might conceive more often. There seems to have been a feeling, rarely expressed directly, that a nursing woman was reduced to subhuman status, and this may have been all right for common women but not for women of gentle birth. Whether these ideas were consciously held by all men and women of the privileged classes we do not know, but it is clear that they routinely avoided having to deal with them. They lived with the ambivalence of seeing images of the Virgin Mary doing what they recoiled from.

There were other sources of ambivalence as well. Milk was thought to transmit character and personality traits, so that a baby was formed as much by milk from the breast as by the environment of the womb. Michelangelo joked that he became a sculptor because his nurse was a stonecutter's wife. A baby could presumably take on undesirable peasant characteristics from its nurse. Giorgio Vasari said that Raphael was nursed by his mother because his father did not want him to be "in the houses of peasants or common people" (*Lives of the Artists*, 1550). Few parents seem to have been deterred by such thoughts, however.

The business of wet-nursing operated in much the same way throughout western Europe. The father chose the nurse and made a contract with her husband, who received regular payments. Some cities had nurses' registries, privately run or under government control. The best known registry was founded in Paris before 1350. Like a careful father, a registry was supposed to check that nurses were of good moral character and had pleasant dispositions. Their milk was tested and judged as to thickness, color, and taste. One function of registries was to provide nurses for foundlings and orphans in the care of religious institutions or municipalities. This aspect of wet-nursing was also the most complicated and bureaucratic, and generated copious records that paint a disheartening, if unrepresentative, picture.

Infant Mortality.   Life was precarious for newborns. The infant death rate remained more or less constant throughout the preindustrial era. Between 20 and 40 percent of all babies died before their first birthday. At that age they still had only a 50 percent chance of surviving past the age of ten. These figures applied to all classes. The main reason for this widespread phenomenon was the susceptibility of immature bodies to disease. In addition, infants' digestive and respiratory systems were less able to withstand environmental hazards like extremes of weather and impure water. Poverty added more dangers, such as malnourished nursing mothers. Poor foundlings were exposed to the greatest dangers of all in the crowded houses of overworked, inattentive wet nurses. Yet the better conditions of the rich hardly negated the stark fact that there was neither prevention nor cure for the diseases of infancy.

There is an ongoing controversy among historians about the effect of high infant mortality on attitudes toward babies. Some historians, like Philippe Ariès, have claimed that people invested little emotion in babies and were relatively indifferent to their deaths. Others make a distinction between babies in general and the individual babies of individual parents, many of whom showered their offspring with love and were grief-stricken at their death. What is usually left out of the discussion is how mothers felt, which is something we admittedly do not know much about. People seem to have been resigned to the inevitability of frequent death and might reuse the name of a dead infant for a later child. Resilience, rather than indifference or despair, seems to have been a common response to the continual loss of babies. The tenderness shown to images of the Infant Jesus could have reflected an attitude to babies in general. There was much concern that a baby be baptized as soon as possible to avoid the risk of its soul remaining in limbo for eternity should it die prematurely.

The Care of Infants.   Soon after birth a baby was wrapped in swaddling clothes, an intricate arrangement of cloth that kept the arms and legs straight and the body warm and easy to handle. The cloths were changed from time to time, but apparently only babies in the care of live-in nurses in well-to-do houses had this done several times a day.

Breast-feeding lasted at least a year, sometimes more than two years. The preferred food for weaning, before the child switched to a regular adult diet, was a pap made of fine white wheat, which the child was fed with a spoon.

The supervision of children was a haphazard affair. Most children, who lived in small houses, were placed in cradles or other receptacles near the fire until they were able to get about by themselves. The mother, a servant, or an older child would keep an eye on the baby while going about other tasks. Swaddled infants were often victims of fatal accidents; they were burned after being placed too near unwatched fires or smothered when sleeping in large beds with adults—poor people practiced this for convenience and warmth, and "overlaying" was a commonly listed cause of death. In large houses there were usually servants to mind children. Nothing suggests that any home, rich or poor, was child-centered. Wealthier children were better fed and safer, but they were also less visible, since they spent most of their time in that world of women that men had little to do with. Once out of swaddling clothes, babies were not encouraged to crawl freely or walk without walkers or leading strings. Poorer children were probably subject to less control. Untended children who could walk might knock over (and be burned by) scalding liquids in their wanderings, fall into ditches, or be attacked by animals. Since Renaissance children—boys, at any rate—did not emerge into the light of historical observation until they were old enough to leave the world of women, what we know most about their earliest years are their misfortunes.

See also **Childhood; Family and Kinship; Motherhood; Pregnancy.**

BIBLIOGRAPHY

Ariès, Philippe. *Centuries of Childhood: A Social History of Family Life.* Translated by Robert Baldick. New York, 1962. Translation of *L'enfant et la vie familiale sous l'ancien régime* (1960). An influential work, which has been criticized on many counts since its publication.

Biraben, Jean-Noël. "La médecine et l'enfant au Moyen Age." *Annales de démographie historique* (1973): 73–75. A very brief, helpful survey from late antiquity to 1600.

De Mause, Lloyd, ed. *The History of Childhood.* New York, 1974. A collection of essays on a variety of topics. The introduction is a provocative statement about the mistreatment of children in the past.

Donnison, Jean. *Midwives and Medical Men: A History of Inter-Professional Rivalries and Women's Rights.* New York, 1977.

Fildes, Valerie A. *Breasts, Bottles, and Babies: A History of Infant Feeding.* Edinburgh, 1986.

Forbes, Thomas Rogers. *Chronicle from Aldgate: Life and Death in Shakespeare's London.* New Haven, Conn., 1971. Based on the records of one parish, starting in 1558.

Gélis, Jacques. *The History of Childbirth: Fertility, Pregnancy, and Birth in Early Modern Europe.* Cambridge, U.K., 1991. Translation of *L'arbre et le fruit.*

Klapisch-Zuber, Christiane. *Women, Family, and Ritual in Renaissance Italy.* Translated by Lydia Cochrane. Chicago, 1985.

Ozment, Steven. *When Fathers Ruled: Family Life in Reformation Europe.* Cambridge, Mass., and London, 1983.

BEATRICE GOTTLIEB

BLACK DEATH. *See* **Plague.**

BOCCACCIO, GIOVANNI (1313–1375), Italian author. Boccaccio's prolific writing career spanned nearly fifty years and two centers of culture: Naples and Florence. An experimental writer, he wrote a large quantity and a wide variety of texts: verse and prose, Latin and Italian, fiction and scholarship. Many of these works were translated into French, Spanish, and English during the Renaissance.

Early Life and Studies. The family hometown was Certaldo, just south of Florence in Tuscany, but Boccaccio's father worked for the Bardi bank in Florence. The identity of Boccaccio's mother is unknown. His father had him legitimized and sought a practical education for him beyond basic literacy, first in banking and then in the study of canon law. But Boccaccio, after pursuing these studies for nearly six years each, disappointed his father by asserting his overwhelming interest in literature and classical learning.

Boccaccio and his father moved to Naples on banking business, probably when Boccaccio was a young teenager. While pursuing his apprenticeship in banking and his more academic study of law, Boccaccio also became acquainted with men of letters at the university and at the court. One of his teachers of law was Cino da Pistoia, a well-known Tuscan poet, who probably encouraged Boccaccio's admiration of Dante and may have introduced Boccaccio to other Tuscan poetry. The theologian Dionigi da Borgo San Sepolcro taught Boccaccio much about Petrarch. Boccaccio was friends with Paolo da Perugia, the royal librarian, who began the encyclopedia of classical mythology that Boccaccio later finished. In this work, the *Genealogia deorum gentilium* (Genealogy of the pagan gods), Boccaccio names some of the cultured men who influenced him, including Dante and Paolo da Perugia; Andalò del Negro, with whom he studied astronomy; Barlaam, a Calabrian monk with a knowledge of Greek; and Petrarch, whom Boccaccio first met in 1350.

Neapolitan Writings. Boccaccio's early writings clearly reveal the mix of models, both ancient and modern, to which he aspired. The "Elegia di Costanza" (Elegy of Costanza), Boccaccio's earliest Latin poem, is based on a classical funereal inscription. His Italian *Caccia di Diana* (Diana's hunt;

Giovanni Boccaccio. Portrait by Andrea del Castagno originally in the Convent of Sant'Apollonia, Florence. Detail. GALLERIA DEGLI UFFIZI, FLORENCE/ALINARI/ART RESOURCE

1333–1334) draws from Dante's *Vita Nuova,* from a description of the hunt by the fourth-century Roman poet Claudianus, from Ovid's *Metamorphoses,* and from medieval encyclopedias and Bible commentaries that offered moral meanings for natural lore.

The stanzaic narrative *Filostrato* (c. 1335) tells the tragic tale of a prince of Troy and his unhappily betrayed love for Criseida, the daughter of a treacherous priest. The poem was the source of Chaucer's *Troilus and Criseyde.* In focusing the poem on Troy and giving the narrator a significant Greek name, Boccaccio shows his early passion for classical culture. Yet the stanzas often read like an outpouring of amorous emotion similar to contemporary Tuscan poetry.

The *Filocolo* (c. 1336), a long, ambitious prose epic in Italian, blends Christian history, pilgrimage, and conversion; Virgilian epic; Ovidian metamorphoses; medieval French debates about love; a popular romance; and classical mythology as a code for contemporary references. Biancifiore, the beloved of Prince Florio, is sold by Florio's father in order to end the prince's love for a seemingly unsuitable partner. Florio finds her at last in a tower of the admiral of Alexandria. They wed privately, only to be caught by the admiral and threatened with death. A fortunate intercession saves the young couple, who, having discovered Biancifiore's Christian background, convert themselves and many others to Christianity. The book was still being read in the sixteenth century when a Florentine nun, Beatrice del Sera, used it as the basis for a convent play. The elaborate periphrastic Italian is aimed at the sophisticated court society of Naples, and the book claims to be written at the request of a daughter of King Robert.

Teseida delle nozze d'Emilia (Thesiad of the marriage of Emilia; 1340–1341?) combines an interest in classical culture and epic with a vernacular romance addressed to a female reader. The twelve-book narrative, taking off from the end of Statius's *Thebaid,* was the first epic in Italian stanzaic verse. Boccaccio's glosses to the text educate the reader about classical names, myths, customs, and allegories. Chaucer based his "Knight's Tale" on this work and used the episode of Arcita's ascent to heaven as an ending for his *Troilus and Criseyde.* He also borrowed the long description of Venus's temple for his "Parliament of Fowls" (Parlement of Foules). While Petrarch attempted to revive classical epic by writing *Africa* in Latin, Boccaccio sought to modernize the genre by writing in Italian. Later Renaissance epic poets such as Ludovico Ariosto, Torquato Tasso, and Edmund Spenser followed Boccaccio rather than Petrarch in the use of the vernacular and a stanzaic form.

Return to Florence. In 1341 the Bardi bank suffered a disastrous crash, which forced Boccaccio's father to return to Florence and placed the family in an economically difficult situation. In his *Comedia delle ninfe fiorentine* (Comedy of Florentine nymphs), sometimes called the *Ameto* (1341–1342), Boccaccio laments the change from the brilliant courtly culture of Naples to austere and commercial Florence. The *Comedia*'s title evokes Dante's masterpiece, and imitates it in many ways. Alternating chapters of prose and terza rima poetry recount the moral and religious allegory of how the seven nymphs or virtues allure their lovers; Ameto, a primitive shepherd who overhears their tales, casts off his animal skins and is baptized, as Venus descends announcing herself to be the triune God. The tensions between the surface and meanings of this work have drawn criticism, but the work effectively reveals Boccaccio's continuing interest in allegory as a means of linking classical gods and genres, in this case the pastoral, with modern literary models and Christian themes.

Another pastoral work is the charming *Ninfale fiesolano* (Nymphs of Fiesole; 1344–1346). This limpid Ovidian verse narrative of unhappy love and the metamorphosis of the lovers into a river of Fiesole provided a model for later Renaissance mythicization of local geographical features, as in Spenser's *Faerie Queene*. It was also a model for the combination of pastoral setting and romantic narrative, which became very popular in the Renaissance. Scholars have argued about whether Boccaccio is to be considered a medieval or Renaissance writer, but the *Ninfale fiesolano* has a thoroughly Renaissance feel.

The *Amorosa Visione* (Amorous vision; 1342–1343, revised 1355–1360) resembles the *Comedia delle ninfe* in its Dantean rather than its pastoral aspect. The fifty cantos of terza rima present an allegorical dream in which the narrator surveys painted frescoes of the triumphs of Wisdom, Glory, Wealth, Love, and Fortune, and then wanders into a garden of love. At the end of the poem he begins to ascend the narrow stair toward which his guide has been urging him throughout. This self-deprecating parody of Dante's guided journey includes passages of praise for Dante and Giotto, and of gratitude and pity for Boccaccio's own father, who is shown scratching vainly at the pile of Wealth. The idea of a series of triumphs had an enormous success in the Renaissance, beginning with its influence on Petrarch's *Trionfi*.

A totally different kind of book, yet similar in its combination of classical and contemporary elements, is *Elegia di madonna Fiammetta* (Elegy of Madam Fiammetta; 1343–1344). Sometimes called the first psychological novel, this prose account of a brief love affair and its disastrous consequences for the unhappy Fiammetta is told in the first person from the woman's point of view. The book portrays contemporary life in Naples and its seaside resorts but often in classical terms. Small incidents set off long internal responses as Fiammetta, increasingly

miserable, guilty, and proud, attempts suicide and finally compares her situation to that of famous classical victims. Women writers of the Renaissance were encouraged by this female narrator: Hélisenne de Crenne's *Les angoysses douleureuses qui procedent d'amours* (The torments of love; 1538) is partially based on this work.

Boccaccio's masterpiece is, of course, the *Decameron* (1348–1351). The framed collection of a hundred tales, told on ten days by ten young men and women during the Black Death, spawned countless imitations all over Renaissance Europe. All but two days have topics assigned for the storytelling: examples of the power of fortune or of human will, love tales that end tragically or happily, clever replies that save the speaker, tricks that women play on men or that men play on each other, and finally examples of magnanimous virtue. Only Dioneo, a witty devil's advocate, is allowed to break the topic, although his tales, the last on each day, often parody earlier stories. The interactions among tales both within a topic and across different days are an important part of the work's effect, as Boccaccio spins variations and reversals of previous material. Thus the book truly forms a whole and is not merely a collection of separate stories. Many of the tales mock the lust, greed, and deceitfulness of the clergy. Other stories show the tensions in Italian society between the new wealthy commercial class and the old noble families. Yet others recount the perils and adventures of traveling merchants; the modern biographer Vittore Branca even called this book a "mercantile epic" in which merchants replace the wandering knights of medieval romance. The *Decameron*'s style (complex Latinate sentences combined with lively speeches and witty wordplay), tight plotting, and psychological insight all contribute to making this book a widely enjoyed masterpiece. Boccaccio's stories are discussed by the gathering in Castiglione's *Il cortegiano* (*The Book of the Courtier*), and they provided the plots for dramas by Shakespeare, Lope de Vega, and others. Famous artists such as Botticelli painted scenes from the tales, while other painters reproduced them on marriage chests and platters. The *Decameron* continues to influence writers and filmmakers to this day.

Corbaccio, Boccaccio's last Italian fiction (1354–1355 or 1365), presents a diatribe against a lustful widow who has mocked the narrating lover; his own folly in pursuing a bestial love is likewise criticized and rejected. This seemingly misogynist tirade has appeared to some to be a dramatic change from Boccaccio's earlier writings on women and love, but

Boccaccio's *Decameron.* *The Banquet,* one of four panels painted by Sandro Botticelli to illustrate scenes from Boccaccio's masterpiece. 1483 or 1487; 82 × 142 cm (32 × 56 in.). MUSEO DEL PRADO, MADRID/GIRAUDON/ART RESOURCE, NY

Boccaccio was always a moral writer, and the misogyny can be read ironically as a reflection on the male lover. Many of Boccaccio's narratives reverse elements in previous narratives; for example, *Corbaccio*'s defamation of the woman to whom it is directed reverses an earlier habit of writing to honor and please the female reader. Its plot is also similar to a story in the *Decameron* that recounts the harsh revenge of a lover mocked by a widow.

Latin Writings. While Boccaccio was writing these Italian fictions, he was also producing Latin texts. Over a period of several decades he wrote a series of eclogues, *Buccolicum carmen* (1341?– 1372), another successful revival of a classical genre. Partway through his writing of these eclogues, Boccaccio discovered that Petrarch was also at work in this genre; eagerly reading Petrarch's poems, Boccaccio absorbed them as further models for his work. Dante's influence remained strong; three of Boccaccio's eclogues depict hell, heaven, and a purgatorial ascent. Others discuss the turbulent political affairs of Naples. The eclogue genre was practiced both in Latin and in the vernaculars during later centuries of the Renaissance. The eclogues of Boccaccio and Petrarch inspired a wide-ranging use of the pastoral mode, for moral, religious, political, and amatory topics.

Boccaccio's meeting with Petrarch in Florence in 1350 began a lifelong friendship and mutually influential relationship. They shared an interest both in classical culture and in the development of literary Italian, but especially in the defense of a life devoted to literature. Petrarch, with his explicit disdain for the popular, probably encouraged Boccaccio in a more scholarly direction, while Boccaccio gave his friend a personally copied manuscript of Dante's *Divine Comedy,* urging Petrarch to acknowledge its greatness. During the 1350s the commune of Florence sent Boccaccio on a number of political missions. He was horrified when Petrarch, turning down an invitation from republican Florence, went to work for the tyrant of Milan, Florence's worst enemy. However, the friendship of these two men survived their political differences; together they may be said to have launched the literary Renaissance.

Boccaccio's *De casibus virorum illustrium* (The fates of illustrious men; 1355–1373) offers historical examples, stretching from Adam and Eve to contemporary Naples, of the power of Fortune over even the most powerful men and women. Often the fall is morally deserved; sometimes it is purely misfortune. Most examples come from ancient histories of Greece, Rome, Persia, and the Middle East; medieval examples include King Arthur and Pope Joan. In a famous digression, Poverty challenges Fortune's power. Boccaccio's aforementioned *Genealogia* similarly includes a chapter in praise of poverty, and his *Buccolicum carmen* ends with Boccaccio's proud declaration of an impoverished independence. This was a renunciation of Boccaccio's earlier desire to return to the court at Naples as an honored man of letters; the brief opportunity to realize this dream had ended in a deeply bitter experience, wrathfully recorded both in his eclogues and in his letters. *De Casibus* was an instant success; it was imitated in Chaucer's "Monk's Tale" and Georges Chastellain's *Le Temple de Bocace* (1465). Boccaccio's moral approach to history well suited the tastes both of medieval readers and of Renaissance humanists.

De mulieribus claris (On famous women; 1361) opens with a criticism of historians who leave women's deeds untold. Like *De casibus* on men, this work offers the first series of biographical portraits devoted to women; the examples are mostly classical, and explicitly exclude Christians. Boccaccio praises women who became learned, wrote, or even waged battle and ruled kingdoms, disparaging those who allowed their lives to be frittered in frivolities. The work was presented to Andrea Acciaiuoli, sister of a Florentine who had risen to become the power behind the throne of Naples. Yet Boccaccio intended his book for men too and tries to shame men who allow these women to outdo them in the pursuit of worthy fame. This book, which provided a basis for Christine de Pizan's *Book of the City of Ladies* (1405), remained an important source for Renaissance writers seeking to list famous women in the debates about whether women should be educated or allowed to rule.

Boccaccio's *Genealogia deorum gentilium* (Genealogy of the pagan gods; 1350–1373), used by painters and men of letters, remained a major reference compendium of pagan mythology well into the Renaissance. Unlike some earlier mythographers who gave the myths Christian meanings, Boccaccio sought to present only meanings that the ancients themselves might have intended: historical, natural or scientific, and moral. The *Genealogia*'s final two books defended the reading of pagan literature, basing their argument on the notion that poets hid philosophical meanings within their apparent fables. This defense of pagan literature—and of literature in general—pointed the way for later defenses of poetry. The defense and praise of literature had occupied Boccaccio in earlier years as well, in his treatises on Dante and on Petrarch; appropriately, *Trattatello in laude di Dante* (Little treatise in praise of Dante; 1351–1355, revised c. 1360) is in Italian, *De vita et moribus domini Francisci Petracchi* (On the life and manners of master Francis Petrarch; 1341) in Latin. Boccaccio led the way in turning the writer into a worthy subject of biography.

One of his last works was a commentary on the poem that had inspired his own writings since the beginning: Dante's *Inferno*. The commune of Florence had invited Boccaccio to present this commentary as a series of public lectures (1373–1374). *Esposizioni sopra la "Comedia" di Dante* (Commentary on Dante's *Comedia*) discusses the poem's literal and allegorical meanings. Interrupting these lectures in canto 17 because of illness, Boccaccio, in four of the lyric poems (*Rime*) that he had been composing throughout his life, explored the issue of whether it was not perhaps inappropriate to try to explain great poetry to uneducated people. His death left the commentary incomplete.

Retrospect. Boccaccio was generally humble and self-deprecating, but as he reviewed his life in *Genealogia,* he boasted of one thing: his establishment of a Greek professor, Leontius Pilatus, at the University of Florence. Boccaccio was the first European in many centuries to learn Greek for the purpose of reading pagan literature. He encouraged Leontius to translate Homer and Euripides into Latin for the first time (1360–1362), allowing Petrarch and other friends, for whom these writers had been merely famous names, to read their works. This contribution to the study of classical Greek had a profound and lasting impact on the Renaissance and, indeed, on the rest of western history.

It is difficult to sum up the work of a man who was so influential in so many different ways. While attempting a scholarly reconstruction of the classical world and a revival of its genres, Boccaccio continued to be involved in contemporary popular culture. While seriously concerned with moral philosophy, he still viewed human behavior with a certain tolerant humor. He was as concerned with the recovery of history as with the invention of good fiction, and he was a devout Christian with an endless fascination for pagan mythology. Boccaccio's breadth and complexity is the very source of his inexhaustible interest for readers ever since.

See also **Italian Literature and Language**.

BIBLIOGRAPHY

Primary Works

Boccaccio, Giovanni. *Tutte le Opere.* 12 vols. Edited by Vittore Branca. Verona, Italy, 1964–. For English translations see bibliographies below.

Bibliographies

Consoli, Joseph P. *Giovanni Boccaccio: An Annotated Bibliography (1939–86).* New York, 1992.

Stych, Franklin Samuel. *Boccaccio in English: A Bibliography of Editions, Adaptations, and Criticism.* Westport, Conn., 1995.

Biography and Criticism

Branca, Vittore. *Boccaccio: The Man and His Works.* Translated by Richard Monges. New York, 1976. Translation of "Profilo biografico" (1967) and *Boccaccio Medievale* (1956). The best biography.

Forni, Pier Massimo. *Adventures in Speech: Rhetoric and Narration in Boccaccio's Decameron.* Philadelphia, 1996.

Hollander, Robert. *Boccaccio's Two Venuses.* New York, 1977. An ironic and Christian reading of the Italian works other than the *Decameron.*

Kirkham, Victoria. *The Sign of Reason in Boccaccio's Fiction.* Florence, 1993. Essays on different aspects of various fictional works.

Marcus, Millicent. *An Allegory of Form: Literary Self-Consciousness in the Decameron.* Stanford French and Italian Studies, 18. Saratoga, Calif., 1979.

Serafini-Sauli, Judith Powers. *Giovanni Boccaccio.* Twayne World Authors Series, 644. Boston, 1982.

Smarr, Janet Levarie. *Boccaccio and Fiammetta: The Narrator as Lover.* Urbana, Ill., 1986. The use of narrators and their relations with their readers, both within and beyond the fictions.

Wallace, David. *Giovanni Boccaccio: Decameron.* Landmarks of World Literature. Cambridge, U.K., 1991.

JANET LEVARIE SMARR

BODIN, JEAN (1529–1596), French philosopher and polymath. Before he became famous for his *Six livres de la république* (Six books of the commonwealth; 1576), Jean Bodin is easily confused in historical references with other contemporaries of the same name, and his biography remains uncertain in parts.

Life and Career. Bodin was born in Angers to a family of modest means. His father was a master tailor and his mother, despite a persistent myth, was neither Marrano nor Jewish. He was educated by the Carmelites, first in Angers, then in Paris (c. 1545–1548), where he was exposed to the humanist trends of the day. He studied law in Toulouse and became a barrister (*avocat*) at the Parlement of Paris, taking the required oath of Catholicity in 1562.

During the early 1570s Bodin gravitated toward the royal court, where Henry III reportedly admired his adorned conversation. But Bodin fell out of favor at the Estates General of 1576, where, as a representative of the third estate, he refused to endorse the king's plan to raise money for further religious wars. Bodin entered the retinue of one of the king's younger brothers, François, duke of Anjou. The duke was at the center of a group of malcontents called the Politiques who supported an end to religious war through negotiated acts of toleration for the Protestant minority. Bodin accompanied François to England in 1581 in a bid for Queen Elizabeth's hand, and in 1582 on a military expedition to Flanders to drive out the Spaniards. Both ventures failed, but during these trips Bodin met other humanists like John Dee and Abraham Ortelius.

His hopes for advancement dashed by François's death in 1584, Bodin became *procureur du roi* (representative of the king's interest in legal affairs) in the northern French town of Laon, where he had married a local woman. Bodin remained in Laon until his death of the plague in 1596; he weathered the difficult years (1589–1594) when Laon was ruled by the Catholic League, in revolt against royal policies that they considered excessively conciliatory toward the Protestants. Bodin was treated with suspicion because of his Politique views; he survived an inquisition of his house in 1590, which resulted in the burning of books from his library. At his death Bodin left no autograph papers or letters. An anonymous manuscript, the *Colloquium heptaplomeres* (Colloquium of the seven), containing a daring critique of the various religions yet calling for their harmonious coexistence, was attributed to him as it circulated clandestinely from the late sixteenth century to its first publication in 1841.

Writings. Most of Bodin's adult life was plagued by the French Wars of Religion (1562–1598), and after beginning in a more traditional humanist vein, Bodin was increasingly concerned to put his learning in service of a resolution to the conflict. Bodin's first work, a Latin translation with commentary of Oppian's poem on the hunt (*Cynegetica*, 1555), was so unexceptional that he was accused of plagiarizing from the work of the contemporary humanist Adrien Turnèbe on the same topic. More original was Bodin's contribution to the late humanist genre of the *ars historica* (art of history). His *Methodus ad facilem historiarum cognitionem* (Method for the easy comprehension of history; 1566) set out a three-fold program for the study of history: human, natural, and divine. ("History" here designates the inquiry into facts in any area.) Bodin advocated keeping a commonplace book to record events worthy of emulation and criticism, paying attention to the quality and biases of the sources used, and developing a comparative history of peoples in all times and places to devise laws of human behavior, notably by correlating human temperament with climate.

Following his own advice, Bodin used a vast collection of examples of human history as evidence for the political arguments that propelled him to national and international fame, in his day and since, in *Six livres de la république*. The French work was translated into Latin by Bodin himself in 1586, with revisions designed for an international audience, and subsequently into a number of other vernaculars. Starting from the authority of the father in the family and moving on to the exercise of power in the state, he argues that sovereignty is necessarily absolute and indivisible. Bodin has been hailed as the founder of modern political philosophy for this definition, which rejects received Aristotelian notions about the possibility of mixed constitutions. But *République* was primarily a response to the immediate problems of the French civil wars; Bodin barred as illegitimate any resistance to the sovereign, however tyrannical his behavior. The sovereign was bound to respect what Bodin called the "law of God and of nature," but God alone held him responsible for violations of it; the subjects were expected to endure his authority in peace. Removing religious arguments from the sphere of politics is one of the ways by which Bodin proposed to end the religious strife.

At the same time, however, Bodin called for a vigorous attack on irreligion, which he feared was gaining ground in war-torn France. In his manual for witch-hunting, *De la démonomanie des sorciers* (On the demon-mania of witches; 1580), which was widely reprinted in many languages, Bodin took a more virulent stand than most French magistrates of his time, calling for the loosening of juridical standards in order to eradicate what he saw as the ever-growing cult of Satan worship by witches and sorcerers. In his last major work, the *Universae naturae theatrum* (Theater of all nature; 1596), Bodin attacked natural philosophers (notably Aristotelians) for providing only naturalistic explanations and neglecting to pay due homage to the divine governance of nature. Bodin hoped, in combating impiety, to restore his country in the favor of God and thus bring the civil wars to an end.

Bodin's shorter works include an outline of universal justice, *Iuris universi distributio* (Outline of universal justice; 1578), a quantitative theory of the causes of monetary inflation in the sixteenth century, *La response aux paradoxes de M. de Malestroit* (Re-

Jean Bodin. JEAN-LOUP CHARMET, PARIS

sponse to the paradoxes of Malestroit; 1568), and a dialogue condemning the Aristotelian definition of virtue as the mean between two vices, *Paradoxon* (Paradox; 1596). Bodin integrated sources of all kinds—ancient, medieval, and contemporary, including Jewish and Islamic authors, and his own experience—in a project of encyclopedic study that he hoped would resolve the various problems of his day. Deeply convinced of the constant governance of God in things human and natural (notably through the action of demons), Bodin was also indifferent to the specific religious disputes of the time. He repeatedly rejected received philosophical opinion in favor of building a state that would be safe and durable and a philosophy that would be reasoned yet pious, in order to foster the highest good—the life of contemplation.

BIBLIOGRAPHY

Primary Works

Bodin, Jean. *Colloquium of the Seven about Secrets of the Sublime*. Edited and translated by Marion Leathers Daniels Kuntz. Princeton, N.J., 1975.

Bodin, Jean. *Method for the Easy Comprehension of History*. Edited and translated by Beatrice Reynolds. New York, 1969.

Bodin, Jean. *On the Demon-Mania of Witches*. Translated by Randy A. Scott, abridged by Jonathan Pearl. Toronto, 1995.

Bodin, Jean. *On Sovereignty: Four Chapters from the Six Books of the Commonwealth*. Edited and translated by Julian H. Franklin. Cambridge, U.K., 1992.

Bodin, Jean. *The Six Bookes of a Commonweale*. Edited by Kenneth D. McRae. Cambridge, Mass., 1962. The best general introduction to Bodin's life and political philosophy.

Jean Bodin: Selected Writings on Philosophy, Religion, and Politics. Edited by Paul L. Rose. Geneva, 1980.

Secondary Works

Blair, Ann. *The Theater of Nature: Jean Bodin and Renaissance Science*. Princeton, N.J., 1997.

Couzinet, Marie-Dominique. *Histoire et méthode à la Renaissance*. Paris, 1996.

Crahay, Roland, et al. *Bibliographie critique des éditions anciennes de Jean Bodin*. Brussels, Belgium, 1992.

Rose, Paul L. *Bodin and the Great God of Nature*. Geneva, 1980.

ANN M. BLAIR

BODLEY, THOMAS. *See* **Libraries.**

BODY IN RENAISSANCE ART. *See* **Human Body in Renaissance Art.**

BOHEMIA. In the fourteenth century the kingdom of Bohemia encompassed Bohemia proper, Moravia, Silesia, and Lusatia. In 1355 King Charles IV (1316–1378) was crowned Holy Roman Emperor. The following year he enshrined the privileged position of his country in the constitution of the empire, the Golden Bull, making Bohemia one of the seven electoral principalities. He made Prague his imperial residence and raised the bishopric to the status of an archbishopric; he founded the University of Prague, the first in central Europe (1348); and he pursued an ambitious building program, transforming the city into a "second Rome." He attracted scholars and artists to Prague and thus brought Bohemia in contact with the Italian Renaissance.

Vladislav II Jagiello. A renewal of cultural relations with Italy and the beginning of the acceptance of humanism came about in Bohemia under Vladislav II Jagiello (ruled 1471–1516), particularly after he also acceded to the Hungarian throne (1490). It was a condition of the election that Vladislav should move to Buda which, under Matthias Corvinus (ruled 1458–1490), had become one of the main centers of humanism outside Italy. But Vladislav's interest in Prague did not decline, rather the reverse. After he left Prague Castle, he had it rebuilt on a grand scale as a Renaissance seat. Thanks to Charles IV (Vladislav's maternal great-grandfather) the Prague throne was regarded as the gateway to the title of Holy Roman Emperor and it is symptomatic that Vladislav concentrated mainly on the radical

rebuilding of Charles's palace in Prague Castle, where he had a magnificent hall built (1493–1502); the hall was designed by Benedict Ried (c. 1454–1534).

The first Bohemian building based entirely on Italian Renaissance models was the new southern wing of Prague Castle (1501–1509). Both were designed by Ried. A monumental altar (now in the Regional Museum in Litoměřice) by the anonymous Master of Litoměřice (active 1500–1510), who introduced contemporary Italian Renaissance painting into Bohemia, was probably intended for the Church of All Saints in Prague Castle. Jagiello had the Saint Wenceslas chapel in the cathedral of Saint Vitus decorated with scenes from the life of Saint Wenceslas (c. 1504). The most ambitious Italian-style cycle north of the Alps, these, too, are by the painter known as the Master of Litoměřice.

Jagiello's orientation toward Renaissance Italy penetrated to burghers' circles as well, as can be seen from the decoration (c. 1496) of the Smíšek Chapel in the cathedral of Saint Barbara in Kutná Hora. It is typical of the important position held by the leading aristocracy in the Bohemian kingdom that the best local sculptor did not work for the royal court, but for Baron Leo of Rožmitál. This artist, a woodcarver known by the monogram I.P. (active 1521–1525), mastered the Renaissance style perfectly. The aristocrats in Moravia were closer to the humanist-oriented royal court in Buda, the most important representative of which was Ladislas Velen of Boskovice, the supreme chamberlain of the kingdom, who had been well educated in Italy, and who formed a humanist court at his mansion in Moravská Třebová, which he had rebuilt in Renaissance style.

Ferdinand I and Maxmilian II. In 1526 Vladislav's son, Louis II, died in the battle of Mohács, and was succeeded on the throne by his Habsburg brother-in-law, Ferdinand I (1503–1564, emperor 1556–1564). Throughout the fourteenth century the Bohemian kings had tried without success to curtail the power of the nobility. Primarily adherents of the utraquist church (Hussites), the nobility resisted both the centralizing tendencies and the religious policy of the Catholic Habsburgs. Their opposition culminated in a revolt during the Schmalkaldic War (1546–1547), and the victory of the Habsburgs was followed by severe reprisals against the rebellious nobles.

Under the Habsburgs, Prague remained an important city, as can be seen from the ambitious building program initiated by Ferdinand I. The influence of Renaissance Italy is apparent in his first project, the royal gardens in Prague begun in 1534. The garden included a wooden orangery for the cultivation of southern plants, one of the first in Europe. (In 1590 the emperor Rudolf II replaced it with a brick-walled building, certainly the first in Europe.) This large garden was dominated by a summer palace, the Belvedere (begun in 1538), at its eastern end. While the overall disposition of the palace directly evokes an ancient Greek temple, the windows and portals were copied from ancient Roman buildings. The relief decoration, inspired by ancient mythology and history, is an extensive central-European cycle of Renaissance figural panels.

Later, the Habsburg tomb was erected in Prague Castle; in Saint Vitus cathedral stands a mausoleum in which lie figures of Ferdinand I, Anna Jagiello, and their son Maxmilian II sculpted by Alexander Colin. The second son of the emperor Ferdinand I, Archduke Ferdinand of Tyrol (1529–1595), administered Bohemia from 1547 to 1567 and built an innovative summer palace in Prague called the Star Castle. The builder's design was carried out by Juan Maria del Pambio, Giovanni Luchese, and others in 1555–1556. The mannerist conception of the building on the ground plan of a six-pointed star was combined in the interior with white stucco ceilings (1556–1560) imitating the stucco work of ancient Rome, which was exceptional even in Italy.

In 1592 Boniface Wohlmut became the Prague court architect, retaining this post until 1570. His personal library proves the interest of the period in mathematics, astronomy, astrology, and philosophy. (Besides the great libraries of the leading aristocratic families, there also existed libraries belonging to burghers and outstanding artists.) Wohlmut adorned Saint Vitus cathedral with an organ loft (1556–1561) in which the system of ancient architectonic orders, although in a mannerist version, was used for the first time in Czech lands. Wohlmut also worked for the son and successor of Ferdinand I, the emperor Maxmilian II (1527–1576), who admired ancient Greek and Roman culture even more than his father. His contribution to Prague architecture was one of the first buildings dedicated to sport, the Great Ball Court in the royal garden of Prague Castle (1567–1569). Wohlmut linked the two stories of the building with Ionic columns on the facade in probably the first use of that colossal order in central Europe. The facade of the Ball Court was covered with graffiti, and graffito decoration of exteriors became extremely popular in the Czech lands in the following decades.

Favorable economic conditions prevailing in the sixteenth century clearly benefited the arts. Bohemian nobles were successful in agricultural production (the breeding of fish in the new fishponds became a south Bohemian specialty), brewing, mining, and metal working. From the second quarter of the sixteenth century the leading Czech lords built Italian-style mansions (a typical feature of which were three-story arcaded courtyards) that were unparalleled in quantity and quality anywhere in Europe north of the Alps. Perhaps one of the most beautiful in central Europe is the mansion in Bučovice, built in 1567–c. 1587, with unique stucco statues in the lunettes in the ground-floor hall. A reevaluation of the relationship between humans and nature could be seen in the popularity of Italian-style villas, the most interesting of which is the Kratochvíle summer palace, built by Baldassare Maggi in 1582–1589 for William of Rožmberk. The interiors of the rooms were decorated according to the Italian model, with murals of dream landscapes.

The humanist idea was accepted most warmly among the Czech and Moravian aristocracy, especially by the powerful Pernštejn family, who attempted to create "the ideal town" in Nové Město nad Metují (1527); in Pardubice the houses were also systematically unified (1538). In the sixteenth century, towns in the Czech lands (especially in the southern regions) were rebuilt in rusticated Renaissance style and enriched with town halls, schools, and other public buildings intended to show off the economic and social advancement of the town.

Rudolf II. The son of Maxmilian II, Rudolf II (1552–1612) acceded to the throne as Holy Roman Emperor and Bohemian king in 1576. In 1583 he made Prague his imperial seat officially, and cultural inspiration flowed from there to surrounding European countries, as it had under the emperor Charles IV.

The humanist character of Rudolfine Prague was created by the emperor himself, who pledged to carry on traditions of ancient Rome. The philosophical framework of the intellectual activity supported by the emperor was pan-Sophism, a universal science examining the world in all its mutually connected aspects. Therefore imperial Prague became the center of late-Renaissance science, and scholars made good use of the well-developed Prague printing industry, which enabled the rapid spread of newly gained knowledge. There were excellent doctors working in the city, as well as chemists, botanists, lawyers, historians, and especially astronomers, who found the technical support they needed in the outstanding Prague workshops specializing in precision mechanics. The Danish astronomer Tycho Brahe (1546–1601), who discovered that the universe develops, lived in Prague from 1599 until his death. The German astronomer Johannes Kepler (1571–1630), who lived in Prague from 1600 to 1612, proved that planets move in an ellipse, a revolutionary discovery throwing doubt on the traditional idea of the circle as the most perfect shape. The maturity of the Prague artistic scene in Rudolf's time is apparent in the Italian chapel in Prague's old town (1590). Built by a congregation of Italians settled in Prague, it is one of the first buildings where the static circular ground plan is replaced by a dynamic ellipse.

The main building activity during Rudolf's reign concentrated on the palace of Prague Castle and was designed to meet new needs. Rudolf made the southern wing his living quarters, joining it by transverse galleries in which he housed his enormous art collection to a north wing occupied by state rooms. A European novelty was the grandiose New Hall designed by the architect G. M. Filippi (1597) with its architectonically divided walls decorated with white stucco statues imitating ancient Roman marble ones. One Rudolfine villa that deserves attention is the summer palace that was built near the imperial mill in Bubeneč (1578–1579). Designed by the architect Ulrico Aostalli, it included an ancient-Roman-style grotto (1594) and housed a swimming pool, a glassworks, and a stone-grinding shop where Ottavio Miseroni (1560–1624) worked. Miseroni's workshop revived the technically exacting ancient art of carving vessels of crystal, agate, jasper, bloodstone, and topaz.

Rudolf's court in Prague became the European center of Renaissance painting and sculpture. The best-known painter of Rudolf's court is Giuseppe Arcimboldo (c. 1527–1593), who created his portraits (which were composed of objects, plants, and animals) earlier for Ferdinand I and Maxmilian II. Arcimboldo also devoted himself to technical inventions and concerned himself with the relationship of colors and music, which he tried to define mathematically. Another remarkable painter working in Prague was Hans von Aachen (c. 1551–1615) with his psychological portraits; but the one to have the greatest influence on contemporary European art was Bartolomeus Spranger (1546–1611), who directly contributed to the development of the late-mannerist style in painting. The sculptural counterpart of the mannerist paintings by Spranger and von

Aachen was the work of Flemish sculptor Giambologna's pupil, the bronze worker Adrian de Vries (c. 1546–1626), who came to Prague in the early 1590s. A painter who thought out the Renaissance reevaluation of the relationship of man to nature in his pictures was Roelant Savery (1576–1639), who settled in Prague in 1603. There he painted the first Renaissance still life (of a flower) and contributed to the developing animal genre, but his greatest legacy was the new style of portraying landscape (often with people), based on sketches made on the spot and not touched up at all.

The flood of foreigners changed Prague, which had been mainly Czech, into a cosmopolitan metropolis, where an important role was played by the flourishing Jewish community, which included a number of scholars. Prague became a much-sought-after cultural center thanks to the presence of rich patrons of the arts. Eloquent testimony to the exceptional atmosphere of Rudolf's Prague is given by the fact that the only English Renaissance poetess celebrated in her day, Elizabeth Weston, known as Westonia (1582–1612), lived and died there.

The religious policy of the Habsburgs continued to cause tension with the Bohemian nobility. They pursued a campaign of re-Catholicization that was modified only by the continued need to rely on the financial support of the Bohemian estates. Under Rudolf, the Counter-Reformation stategy was taken up with renewed vigor on the initiative of Grand Chancellor Wenzel von Lobkowitz, a Catholic. Ferdinand II (ruled 1619–1637) likewise followed a policy of deliberate Catholic restoration. The resulting confessional polarization led to a revolt in 1619. The Bohemian nobles deposed Ferdinand, an action that precipitated the Thirty Years' War. The victorious Ferdinand purged the ranks of his enemies, publicly executing the leaders and rescinding the political privileges of the Czech lands. The Peace of Westphalia (1648) confirmed the political and religious control of the Habsburgs over Bohemia.

See also **East Central Europe, Art in**; **Habsburg Dynasty**; **Holy Roman Empire**; **Prague**; **Thirty Years' War.**

BIBLIOGRAPHY

Bialostocki, Jan. *The Art of the Renaissance in Eastern Europe: Hungary, Bohemia, Poland.* Ithaca, N.Y., 1976.

Evans, Robert John Weston. *Rudolf II and His World: A Study in Intellectual History, 1576–1612.* Oxford, 1973.

Fučíková, Eliška, ed.. *Rudolf II and Prague: The Court and the City.* Prague and London, 1997.

Hořejší, Jiřina, et al. *Renaissance Art in Bohemia.* London; New York; Sydney, Australia; and Toronto, 1979.

Kaufmann, Thomas DaCosta. *Variations on the Imperial Theme in the Age of Maximilian II and Rudolf II.* New York, 1978.

Muchka, Ivan, et al. *Rudolfine Prague: Prague in the Years 1576–1611.* Prague, 1997.

Seibt, Ferdinand, and Bozena Borgesa-Kormundová, eds. *Renaissance in Böhmen: Geschichte, Wissenschaft, Architektur, Plastik, Malerei, Kunsthandwerk.* Munich, 1985.

Stejskal, Karel. *L'empéreur Charles IV: L'art en Europe au XIVe siècle.* Paris, 1980.

JAN BAŽANT

BÖHME, JAKOB (1575–1624), German shoemaker and lay theologian. Born in 1575 near Görlitz in Upper Lusatia to peasants of means, Böhme was apprenticed to a cobbler at a young age. After completing his apprenticeship, he began years of wandering as a journeyman. He returned to Görlitz in 1592, became a master shoemaker in 1594, and married in 1599. By 1612 he had written down a vision he claimed to have had in 1600. Although this work, *Aurora, oder die Morgenröte im Aufgang* (1634; trans. *Aurora: That Is, the Day-Spring or Dawning of the Day,* 1656), was circulated only in manuscript form, it aroused the enmity of Gregor Richter, an orthodox Lutheran pastor in Görlitz. Böhme was subjected to questioning by the city council and was asked to abstain from writing. By 1613 he had given up shoemaking to begin a yarn trade, traveling extensively. Although he complied with the writing prohibition for six years, Böhme completed his next work, *Von den drei Prinzipien des Göttlichen Wesens* (trans. *The Seconde Booke: Concerning the Three Principles of the Divine Essence,* 1648), in 1619. It was followed in the next years by numerous other theological and mystical works. With the exception of *Der Weg zu Christo* (1624; trans. *The Way to Christo Discovered,* 1648), none of his works were published during his lifetime, although his manuscripts continued to be circulated and copied. In 1624 another confrontation with Richter took place, and Böhme was ridiculed by the citizens and the church. He died in the same year.

Rejecting the "Mauer-Kirche" (walled church) or "Steinkirche" (church of stone), that is, organized religion, Böhme embarked on his own idiosyncratic exploration of God's mystery. Since God reveals himself in nature, Böhme argues that a study of nature will allow a person to understand God's greatness as well as the secrets of the universe. God also manifests himself in the creation of humankind, and Böhme interprets humanity as an androgynous being comprising male and female elements. In this sense, the Virgin Mary is viewed as the symbol of this union since she, as a woman, gave birth to God's son, a man. In his philosophy Böhme always searches for a resolution of the contradictions and dualities in life. Even God is understood to include both good and evil.

For many years Böhme was viewed as a poor, uneducated, and lonely visionary. Late-twentieth-century research has shown that he was relatively well off and well read, and that he had a sizable following. Scholars have also illuminated the cultural, religious, and intellectual milieu prevailing in Görlitz at the end of the century, showing that this city was "a breeding ground for heterodox theories and doctrines" (Weeks, *Boehme,* p. 26) on which Böhme could draw and which provided the matrix for independent meditation on religious issues.

The works of the "teutonicus philosophus," as he was called in his own time, had a great impact not only on Böhme's contemporaries but also on posterity. During the baroque period, the poets Daniel Czepko, Johannes Scheffler (Angelus Silesius), and Quirinus Kuhlmann were influenced by Böhme's mysticism. Although he fell into obscurity during most of the eighteenth century, Böhme was rehabilitated by the romantics. Novalis, Ludwig Tieck, and Friedrich Schlegel admired him. The philosopher Friedrich Wilhelm Schelling called him "a miracle in human history." Böhme's influence abroad was equally great. The first edition of his works appeared in Holland; in successive waves Böhme came to England, France, Russia, and the United States, where Ralph Waldo Emerson was fascinated by him.

BIBLIOGRAPHY

Primary Work

Jacob Boehme's The Way to Christ, *in a New Translation.* Translated by John Joseph Stoudt. New York and London, 1947. Translation of *Der Weg zu Christo. In zweyen Büchlein* (1624).

Secondary Works

Classen, Albrecht. "Jakob Böhme." In *Dictionary of Literary Biography.* Vol. 164, *German Baroque Writers, 1580–1660.* Detroit, Mich.; Washington, D.C.; and London; 1996. Pages 64–73. Concise article in English with bibliography, including English translations of his works.

Weeks, Andrew. *Boehme: An Intellectual Biography of the Seventeenth-Century Philosopher and Mystic.* Albany, N.Y., 1991. Excellent analysis of Böhme's writings in the context of his time.

ECKHARD BERNSTEIN

BOIARDO, MATTEO MARIA (1441–1494), Italian humanist poet and author of the romance epic *Orlando innamorato.* Grandson of the humanist Feltrino Boiardo, nephew of the poet Tito Vespasiano Strozzi, and cousin of the philosopher Giovanni Pico della Mirandola, M. M. Boiardo passed the first ten years of his life in Ferrara. His father's death brought him under his grandfather's tutelage in the family castle in Scandiano. Inheriting the title of count in 1460, he frequented the Este court in Ferrara and enjoyed the status of one of Duke Ercole I d'Este's privileged *compagni* (companions). He married Taddea dei Gonzaga di Novellara in 1479; the following year he was appointed by Ercole d'Este as military governor of the tumultuous Modena. In early 1483 he left to defend Scandiano, which was in danger of attack during the Venice-Ferrara War (1482–1484). In 1487 Ercole appointed Boiardo military governor of nearby Reggio Emilia, a post he occupied until his death.

Minor Works. Boiardo's earliest poetry was in Latin: *Carmina de laudibus Estensium* (Songs in praise of the Estes) and *Pastoralia* (1463–1464); and *Epigrammata* (1476). His poetic production in the vernacular consists of the *Pastorale* (1482–1483), ten eclogues—poems in which shepherds converse—on personal and political themes, and *Amorum libri tres* (Three books on love; 1477), a sequence of 180 love poems divided into three books. Petrarchan in inspiration, these books incorporate classical, medieval, and contemporary poetry into an autobiographical account of the illusions and delusions of love. Consonant with his humanist education, Boiardo translated into Italian Cornelius Nepos (*De viris illustribus*), Xenophon (*Cyropaedeia*), the medieval Ferrarese historian Ricobaldo (*Istoria imperialis*), Herodotus (*History*), and Lucius Apuleius (*The Golden Ass*). His translations of the four historical texts contain dedicatory letters addressed to Ercole d'Este underscoring the role of history as a teacher of moral conduct and a manual of good government. His comedy *Il Timone* (1491), a revision of Lucian of Samosata's *Timon,* attests to the interest in classical theater in late-fifteenth-century Ferrara. Boiardo also composed verses with moral symbolism meant to accompany Tarot cards. His extant correspondence (204 letters), written mostly while military governor, ranges from accounts of how he handled cases of rape, murder, and theft to descriptions of the French troops passing through Reggio Emilia in 1494.

Orlando Innamorato (Roland in Love).
This chivalric poem in ottava rima first appeared in two books in 1482 or 1483 (printed in Scandiano, Reggio Emilia, or Modena) and was published in its final form, which included nine cantos of a third book, in 1495 (Scandiano). In the opening canto of book 1, Charlemagne's hitherto dutiful nephew Or-

lando (from the French Roland) falls in love with an enchanting Saracen princess named Angelica and tries to play the role of courtly lover, setting the stage for a fusion of the Carolingian and Arthurian cycles. Boiardo's innovation with regard to sources, however, goes beyond his merging of medieval epic and romance. He incorporates Greek, Latin, French, and Italian material from genres as diverse as tragedy, comedy, history, allegory, the novella, and the lyric. The technique of *entrelacement*—"interlacing" of multiple stories—allows him to juxtapose narratives that invite comparison and to alternate between magic and love adventures and epic battles.

An archetypal romance, it has courtly and civic ideals coming up against the fraud and violence of monsters and giants, the enchantments of seductresses, and the unbridled greed and ambition of tyrants. The epic battles move from the pagan Gradasso's attack on Paris (book 1), to the love war waged over Angelica at Albraca (book 2), to the forces of Africa and Asia converging in a siege of Paris (book 3). The African king Agramante, whose imperialistic designs willfully imitate his ancestor Alexander of Macedonia, is destined to be defeated by the Christians, who include the perfect knight Ruggiero, descendant of Hector of Troy and embodiment of the chivalric ideal of courtesy. The poem, however, remains unfinished. The final stanzas, written shortly before Boiardo's death, refer with alarm to the state of Italy during the French invasion and the resulting silence of his poetic muse.

Influence. Although no autograph manuscript of *Orlando innamorato* exists and no copies remain of the 1482–1483 or 1495 editions, the earliest extant editions are written in an Italian with strong regional (Emilian) tendencies. Indicative of the move toward Tuscanization of Italian in the early sixteenth century, editors printed a linguistically revised version by Ludovico Domenichi. In the middle of the sixteenth century personalities as diverse as Teofilo Folengo, Pietro Aretino, Ludovico Dolce, the cardinal Ippolito de' Medici, and Francesco Berni all set out to write their own Tuscan *rifacimento* (rewriting) of the poem. Only Berni's rendition was completed (1545), and eventually this burlesque-comic Tuscan version became the standard published edition for almost four centuries. Boiardo's "original" poem was not reprinted again until 1830–1831, when Antonio Panizzi, an Italian exile living in London, published it along with Ludovico Ariosto's continuation, *Orlando furioso* (Mad Roland),

and an *Essay on the Romantic Narrative Poetry of the Italians* for his British audience.

In addition to wanting to preserve the poem through translation, various poets set out to complete it. The text had six continuations by four different authors between 1505 and 1532, by far the greatest being that of Ariosto (1474–1533). In fact, due to a number of variables, but especially the increasingly antiquated language and style of *Orlando innamorato,* the debate on the heroic poem that dominated literary studies in the second half of the sixteenth century proclaimed Ariosto as the "champion" of the romance epic genre introduced by Boiardo. Outside Italy, Boiardo's poem was cited by John Milton (*Paradise Lost*) and Miguel de Cervantes (*Don Quixote*), and probably known by William Shakespeare and Edmund Spenser, although Boiardo's possible influence on these latter authors is a matter of debate. A translation into English was begun in the early sixteenth century, but a complete English translation of the poem was not available until Charles S. Ross's 1989 edition.

See also **Ariosto, Ludovico.**

BIBLIOGRAPHY

Primary Works

Boiardo, Matteo Maria. *Amorum Libri: The Lyric Poems of Matteo Maria Boiardo.* Translated by Andrea di Tommaso. Binghamton, N.Y., 1993. Bilingual edition.

Boiardo, Matteo Maria. *Orlando Innamorato.* Translated by Charles S. Ross. Berkeley and Los Angeles, 1989 (bilingual edition). Oxford, 1996 (abridged English edition).

Secondary Works

Cavallo, Jo Ann. *Boiardo's* Orlando Innamorato: *An Ethics of Desire.* Rutherford, N.J., and London, 1993.

Cavallo, Jo Ann, and Charles S. Ross, eds. *Fortune and Romance: Boiardo in America.* Tempe, Ariz., 1998.

Di Tommaso, Andrea. *Structure and Ideology in Boiardo's* Orlando Innamorato. Chapel Hill, N.C., 1972.

Marinelli, Peter. *Ariosto and Boiardo: The Origins of* Orlando Furioso. Columbia, Mo., 1987.

Jo Ann Cavallo

BOLOGNA. Strategically located where a major route across the Apennines meets the fertile Po valley, Bologna's economy, politics, and cultural life were shaped largely by its relations with other centers, chiefly Rome and Milan. Its population average fifty thousand through the fourteenth and fifteenth centuries, and ranged from sixty thousand to seventy thousand by the later sixteenth.

Political History. Part of the papal state from 1278, Bologna through the next century alternated between papal rule (1325–1334, 1360–1376), the signorial rule of the local Pepoli family (1337–1350), and direct or indirect Visconti domination (1350–1360) before restoration of the free commune in 1376. By 1394 the local oligarchy established control over the commune's various councils through an executive body, the Sedici, or Reggimento, but different families still aimed to seize power in concert with the Visconti or the popes. Bologna backed the Council of Pisa, hosted the conclave that elected John XXIII in 1410, and outwitted the efforts of Martin V and Eugenius IV to restore papal authority. Yet local oligarchs did not finally repudiate papal rule, but negotiated a settlement by which the papal legate and the Reggimento ruled jointly. The ambiguously worded Capitulations signed with Pope Nicholas V in 1447 can be considered the city's declaration of semi-independence. While guaranteeing Bologna retention of its own law code, currency, governing bodies, and various privileges and immunities, Bolognese ambassadors rushed to Rome after each papal election for confirmation and possible expansion of its terms.

Through the fifteenth century, efforts to expand Bologna's autonomy were connected to the efforts of the Bentivoglio family to become local rulers. Annibale Bentivoglio led the Bolognese to victory over Milanese and papal forces in 1443 but was assassinated in 1445. He was succeeded by his illegitimate cousin Sante who, under Cosimo de' Medici's mentorship, successfully established peaceful relations with Rome and Milan; on his death in 1463, leadership passed to Annibale's son Giovanni II (1443–1508). Giovanni sought to secure his position through marriages, mercenary contracts, ecclesiastical preferment, and domestic terror. The Malvezzi conspiracy of 1488, the French invasion of 1494, and Cesare Borgia's campaign of 1499–1502 left the family on shaky ground, and it remained only for Pope Julius II to expel them in 1506. He replaced the twenty-one-member Reggimento with the Quaranta Consiglieri, later called the Senato, but local opposition stymied his efforts to suspend the Capitulations of Nicholas V. Expanded to fifty seats by Pope Sixtus V in 1590, the Senate incorporated enough of the ruling group to contain factionalism. By incremental steps, such as the eight Assunterie or administrative committees established from the 1540s, the Senate usurped the powers of other officials and ruling bodies established in the communal period and extended supervision over social, financial, and charitable institutions, as well as over guilds, local government, and territorial administration. Though

Fountain of Neptune, Bologna. By Giambologna.
D. ANDERSON/ALINARI/ART RESOURCE

always subject to papal appointment of its nominees, the Senate faced few challenges to its authority over the second city of the papal state until the end of the ancien régime. Senatorial families further pursued influence and wealth through offices in both the curia and the bureaucracy of the papal state.

Economy. Bologna's prosperity was based on three elements: the university, with its one thousand to two thousand students and their servants and tutors; local agriculture; and the textile industry. Wool and hemp were significant, but silk production and export underwrote the city's prosperity from the fifteenth through the eighteenth centuries. A unique mill allowed Bolognese producers to spin a strong yet soft silk thread with fewer workers. The Silk Guild claimed in 1587 that 24,900 Bolognese were dependent on the industry. Though this figure is certainly exaggerated, modern historians estimate that half the urban population was involved in the textile trade generally, a significant part of it being women engaged in domestic piecework.

Cultural History. Artists such as Jacopo della Quercia, Michelangelo, and Giambologna sojourned briefly in Bologna, but the city fostered few artists of note until the end of the fifteenth century, when the Bentivoglio circle expanded its patronage both of Ferrarese painters such as Francesco Cossa (1436–1478), Ercole de' Roberti (1450–1496), Lorenzo Costa (1460–1535), and of local talent like the sculptor Niccolò dell'Arca (1460–1494), and the goldsmith and painter Francesco Raibolin (called Francia; 1450–1517). Marcantonio Raimondi (1480–1534), Francia's apprentice, and Bartolomeo Passarotti (1529–1592) specialized in prints and drawings. Bologna's sixteenth-century expansion as a center of the baroque grew out of its close ties with Rome.

Senatorial courtier oligarchs began building and adorning palaces and villas, the civic government and charitable institutions put up ambitious public structures, and religious orders and local archbishops such as Gabriele Paleotti saw art and architecture as vehicles for Tridentine reform. Architects like Jacopo Barozzi da Vignola (1507–1573) and Pellegrino Pellegrini (1527–1596) received their earliest training and commissions in Bologna before developing their style elsewhere; Vignola's Portico de Banchi (1568) brought focus, completion, and monumentality to the city's main square. Local patrons and architects preferred building in a restrained classicism, demonstrated by Antonio Morandi's (d. 1568) Archiginasio Palace (1563) for the university and the adjoining Ospedale della Morte (1565), and also by Domenico Tibaldi's (c. 1541–1583) urban palaces and San Francesco hostel (1583). Lodovico Carracci's (1555–1619) academy, the first of its kind, gave painters a formal grounding in classical and Renaissance traditions, anatomical studies, and life drawing. It trained some of the leading artists of the baroque, including Agostino (1557–1602) and Annibale (1560–1609) Carracci, Guido Reni (1575–1642), and Giovanni Il Guercino (Giovanni Barbieri; 1591–1666). Through the Renaissance and into the seventeenth century, Bologna proved particularly hospitable for female artists and patrons. Work by Properzia de' Rossi (c. 1490–1530), the only securely documented female sculptor of the Renaissance, decorated the civic basilica of San Petronio. Lavinia Fontana's (1552–1614) skill in portraits of academics and clerics brought her such fame that by the 1580s she had become the leading society painter, enjoying rich commissions from institutions and individuals, particularly patrician women.

Short prose works like Giovanni Sabadino degli Arienti's *Le Porrettane* (1483) and *Gynevera de le clare donne* (1490) portray Bentivoglio court life according to humanist conventions. Beyond this, intellectual and literary life centered chiefly around the university and professors such as Hellenist Antonio Urceo (1446–1500), philologist Filippo Beroaldo (1453–1505), legal scholar Lodovico Bolognini (1446–1508), and historian Carlo Sigonio (1522/23–1584). Perhaps the leading public intellectual was local naturalist Ulisse Aldrovandi (1522–1605), who directed his research, botanical garden, and polemical energies to improving medical and pharmaceutical services.

BIBLIOGRAPHY

Ady, Cecilia M. *The Bentivoglio of Bologna: A Study in Despotism.* London, 1937. Reprint, London, 1969.

Civic Self-Fashioning in Renaissance Bologna. Special issue of *Renaissance Studies* 13, no. 1 (1999).

De Benedictis, Angela. *Repubblica per contratto, Bologna: Una città europea nello Stato della Chiesa.* Bologna, Italy, 1995.

Miller, Naomi. *Renaissance Bologna: A Study in Architectural Form and Content.* New York, 1989.

Terpstra, Nicholas. *Lay Confraternities and Civic Religion in Renaissance Bologna.* Cambridge, Mass., 1995.

NICHOLAS TERPSTRA

BOLOGNA, UNIVERSITY OF. The University of Bologna was the largest Italian university in the Renaissance and was second only to Padua in intellectual distinction and importance. Teachers and students of law began to gather in Bologna by the end of the eleventh century. The erection of a student organization, support from the city government, and expansion of instruction in both law and medicine created a university by the second half of the twelfth century. Bologna and Paris, which began at about the same time, were the first European universities. All other southern European universities were modeled closely or loosely on Bologna.

Organization. Bologna had more professors and students than any other Italian university during the Renaissance. The university steadily expanded from about sixty professors in 1400 to one hundred in 1450. The figure remained at ninety professors from 1450 to 1550, then declined slightly to between eighty and eighty-five professors from 1551 to 1600. In the fifteenth century Bologna had more law professors (60 percent) than arts and medicine (40 percent), and taught no theology. The number of arts and medicine professors gradually rose to equal, then surpass, the number of law professors, while two or three theologians were added toward the end of the century. The growing importance of arts and medicine was typical of Italian Renaissance universities.

Bologna offered instruction in numerous subjects and specialities. For example, in the 1520s the university's faculty included twenty-four professors of civil law, twenty-one professors of canon law, eighteen professors of medical theory, as well as professors of medical practice, surgery, natural philosophy, metaphysics, logic, mathematics and astronomy, Greek, Hebrew and Aramaic, and rhetoric, poetry, and the humanities. Thanks to an ingenious rotation system in which professors in law, medicine, and natural philosophy taught the required texts in a four-year sequence, students could always hear lectures on the required texts.

Classes met in rented rooms throughout the city until the 1560s. Then in 1561 Pope Pius IV, aware of the need for a building from his own student days at Bologna (he took a degree in civil and canon law in 1525), ordered the erection of a building. The Archiginnasio, as it was called, located in the center of the city, was completed in time for the opening of the academic year in early November 1563. Classes met there until 1803, when it became a library.

Students and Teachers. Although no contemporary enrollment figures exist, it is estimated that Bologna had an annual average enrollment of 1,000 students from 1400 to 1450, rising to about 2,000 by 1550. Enrollment then declined to about 1,500 in the last years of the century. The distribution of law degrees awarded suggests that about 70 percent of the students were Italians and 30 percent non-Italians. France, Germany, Spain, and England sent the largest number of foreign students to Bologna.

Bologna's most famous non-Italian student was Nicolaus Copernicus (1473–1543), who came to study law but concentrated on astronomy during his attendance from 1496 to 1501. The fiery German Protestant Ulrich von Hutten studied law there (1516–1517). Among Italians, five Renaissance popes studied law at Bologna.

The majority of professors were Bolognese men from prominent local families. This parochialism did not diminish the quality of scholarship because Bologna had a strong scholarly tradition. Since most locally born professors taught at Bologna their entire careers, the faculty had great stability. But the government also reserved four prominent positions for outsiders and filled them with "star" professors. Bologna and Padua regularly competed with each other for leading scholars.

Bologna began as a center for the study of law and continued to lead in this field in the Renaissance.

Students at a Lecture. Students listen to a lecture by Giovanni da Legnano (d. 1383), a professor of canon law in the University of Bologna. Detail of Giovanni's tomb sculpted by Jacobello delle Masegne (fl. 1383–1409) and Piero Paolo dalle Masegne (fl. 1383–1403). Museo Civico, Bologna, Italy/Scala/Art Resource, NY

In 1509 Bologna created the first professorship of criminal law anywhere. Many eminent law professors taught at Bologna, which awarded more law than arts and medicine degrees during the Renaissance.

But Bologna offered considerable teaching and scholarship in arts and medicine as well. In the last quarter of the fifteenth century, the university developed a very strong humanistic teaching group that included major humanists who taught there for decades. This tradition continued in the sixteenth century. Carlo Sigonio of Mantua (1522/23–1584), a distinguished humanist and historian, came from the University of Padua to teach at Bologna from 1563 until his death. Alessandro Achillini (c. 1463–1512) was a major scholar in natural philosophy and medicine. Pietro Pomponazzi (1462–1525) came from Padua to the University of Bologna in 1512 and taught there until illness forced him to retire in 1524. He published his most famous work, *De immortalitate animae* (On the immortality of the soul; 1516), while at Bologna. The Bolognese Ulisse Aldrovandi (1522–1605) developed the study of natural history during his long teaching career at Bologna from 1553 to 1600. Gaspare Tagliacozzi of Bologna (1545–1599), who taught anatomy at Bologna from 1570 onward, was a pioneer in plastic surgery.

The university flourished in the midst of political instability. Groups of citizens and members of the princely Bentivoglio family competed, often vio-

lently, for political power in the fifteenth century and first decade of the sixteenth. Because Bologna was part of the papal state, the papacy exerted increasing authority over the city, especially in the sixteenth century. The only issue on which all parties agreed was that the university deserved the strongest possible support. Despite internal conflict and external wars, the university never closed in the fifteenth and sixteenth centuries. A tax on all saleable goods coming into the city provided the basic financial support for the university, while additional money came from minor taxes. A small commission of Bolognese citizens appointed by the city government chose professors, determined stipends, and issued university regulations.

BIBLIOGRAPHY

Dallari, Umberto, ed. *I rotuli dei lettori legisti, e artisit dello Studio Bolognese dal 1384 al 1799.* 4 vols. Bologna, Italy, 1889–1924. The fundamental source because it lists professors and their positions year by year.
Simeoni, Luigi. *L'età moderna (1500–1888).* Vol. 2 of *Storia della Università di Bologna.* Bologna, Italy, 1940. Reprint, Bologna, Italy, 1987.
Sorbelli, Albano. *Il Medioevo (Secoli XI–XV).* Vol. 1 of *Storia della Università di Bologna.* Bologna, Italy, 1940. Reprint, Bologna, Italy, 1987. With Luigi Simeoni's volume, still the best secondary source.
Studi e memorie per la storia dell' Università di Bologna. Vol. 1 (1907) to date; Bologna, Italy, 1907–. A series of volumes issued sporadically, sometimes with gaps of many years, with scholarship on all aspects of the university.

PAUL F. GRENDLER

BOOKKEEPING. *See* **Accounting.**

BOOK OF COMMON PRAYER. *See* **Prayer Book, English.**

BORGIA. [The following three entries deal with the house of Borgia. The first, **Borgia, House of,** provides an overview of the family's history. The following two entries are biographies of Cesare and Lucrezia. See also the biography of Pope Alexander VI.]

BORGIA, HOUSE OF. From modest hidalgo circumstances near Játiva in the province of Valencia in Spain, the Borja (Italianized as Borgia) emerged as perhaps the most notorious family of Renaissance Italy. The unexpected election of the elderly Alfonso de Borja as Pope Calixtus III (1455–1458) made possible the career of his nephew, Rodrigo, who became the second Borgia pontiff, Alexander VI (1492–1503). Alexander's dynastic plans for his numerous children established them and their descendants as important players in the affairs of Italy, Spain, and the church. A total of eleven Borgia became cardinals; Borgia dukes and princes arose in Italy and Spain; and one Borgia, Pope Alexander VI's great-grandson Francisco de Borja (1510–1572), became the third general of the Jesuit order and was canonized a century after his death. Still, it was the controversial policies and actions of Pope Alexander X and his son Cesare that made the greatest mark on Renaissance history.

At the zenith of their power, the pope's vigorous and unscrupulous diplomacy, much of it involving marriage alliances for his children, and his son Cesare's equally belligerent military prowess seemed to have created the foundations for a permanent Borgia state in central Italy. Feared, despised, and maligned by contemporary detractors, the Borgias were vilified in subsequent history and legend as the embodiment of corruption, shamelessly debasing the spiritual authority of the church. While in many respects Alexander VI's dynastic aspirations are representative of more basic trends affecting the Renaissance papacy, his and his son Cesare's exploitation of papal political and fiscal resources for family aggrandizement were unprecedented in their ruthless single-mindedness.

The Early Borja. Alfonso de Borja (1378–1458), the founder of the family fortunes, was trained in canon law in Spain and enjoyed a modest ecclesiastical career until his late thirties, when he attracted the attention of King Alfonso V of Aragon. From 1417 until his elevation as cardinal in 1444, he served this increasingly influential monarch as secretary and chief councilor. As a reward for obtaining the resignation of the Spanish antipope Clement VIII, ending the last holdout of the Great Schism, he received in 1429 the bishopric of Valencia, which was to remain a Borgia sinecure. From 1432 on he spent most of his life in Italy, working for the next decade with King Alfonso in his protracted quest to gain control of the kingdom of Naples. Alfonso de Borja again played a key diplomatic role in negotiating the landmark Treaty of Terracina in 1443, by which Pope Eugenius IV recognized Aragonese claims to Naples and Alfonso in turn abandoned any support for the rival Council of Basel. Borja's becoming cardinal followed in due course the next year, and at age sixty-six he became a resident of the Eternal City. Austere and pious, largely uninvolved in papal affairs, the now elderly cardinal led a modest existence until at the age of seventy-seven he emerged from the conclave of 1455 as Pope Calixtus III. Essentially a com-

Borgia Pope. Portrait of the first Borgia pope, Calixtus III (reigned 1455–1458). His nephew Rodrigo de Borja y Doms became pope as Alexander VI in 1492. CATHEDRAL OF VALENCIA/INSTITUT AMATLLER D'ART HISPÀNIC, BARCELONA

promise candidate, it was hoped that the new pope's Spanish connections would help rally the European powers to a new crusade against the Ottomans, whose conquest of Constantinople in 1453 had shocked the Latin Christian world.

Calixtus's ambitious plans for a naval campaign against the Turks bore little fruit, and to the pope's fury his erstwhile mentor Alfonso, now also king of Naples, refused to cooperate, diverting his promised galleys to a naval attack on Genoa instead. Calixtus's enduring legacy was his dependence on his Catalan entourage to administer the papacy's spiritual and temporal affairs. This included his young nephew, Rodrigo, destined from childhood for an ecclesiastical career. A student of canon law at the University of Bologna, his uncle brought him back to Rome and made him a cardinal in 1456, at the age of twenty-five, dubiously youthful enough to arouse bitter criticism. Calixtus also named Rodrigo vice-chancellor of the church, the key position in the papal Curia, who was responsible for much of the day-to-day administrative operations. For thirty-five years Cardinal Rodrigo held that enormously influential and lucrative post, which provided much of the financial re-

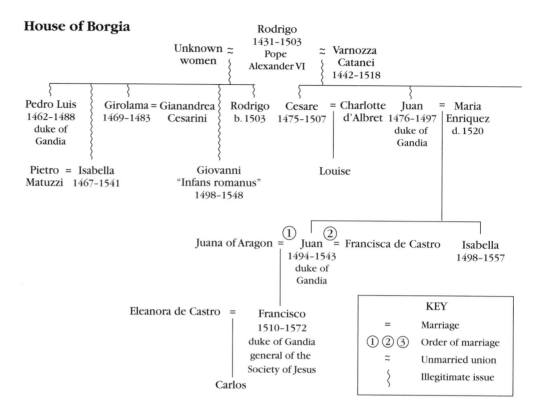

House of Borgia

sources and patronage contacts that eventually made his election as pope possible.

Rodrigo Borgia. As cardinal, Rodrigo Borgia amassed a long list of Italian and Spanish benefices, including the bishopric of Valencia, given him by his uncle. A skilled administrator and an adroit diplomat, he cultivated the personal magnificence increasingly expected of the leading princes of the church. His zest for life's pleasures also made a strong impression on others, including women, for whom he possessed a strong physical attraction. In all he had eight or more likely nine children. The eldest, Pedro Luis (1462–1488), became, through his father's connections with King Ferdinand of Aragon, the first duke of Gandía, a title which at Pedro Luis's death passed on to his younger half-brother Juan and from him to a long line of Borjas, including St. Francis Borgia. Rodrigo's next two offspring, both girls, were married into the Roman nobility while he was a cardinal.

The four most famous of his children were those born to the Roman beauty Vannozza Catanei, who was Rodrigo's mistress for more than a decade. The eldest was Cesare, born in 1475. Then followed Juan in 1476, Lucrezia in 1480, and finally Jofrè, born in 1481. All figured prominently during Alexander's pontificate. By the late 1480s Vannozza was no

longer his mistress; instead, at the time of his election as pope (as Alexander VI), and now sixty, he conducted a highly public affair with the beautiful young Giulia Farnese, member of an important Roman baronial family who at age nineteen had been married to an Orsini, the son of Rodrigo's cousin Adriana de Mila, in the Borgia palace in Rome. Among the first large group of cardinals Alexander promoted in 1493 was Giulia's brother Alessandro Farnese, who eventually became Pope Paul III (1534–1549). As pope, Alexander probably fathered two more sons: first, the somewhat mysterious *Infans Romanus,* Giovanni, born in 1498 and initially recognized as an illegitimate son of Cesare and then of Alexander himself; and second, Rodrigo, born in 1503, who entered the monastic life.

Once elected pope, Alexander was presented with new opportunities to advance the house of Borgia, and in turn his children served as useful negotiating tokens in the kaleidoscopic diplomatic scene that marked Italian politics during the early phase of the Italian Wars. Thus Lucrezia, for whom a Spanish match was planned before the papal election, now helped seal the pope's allegiance to the League of St. Mark with her marriage in 1493 to Giovanni Sforza, the lord of Pesaro. In response, King Ferrante of Naples initiated a new alliance, which included

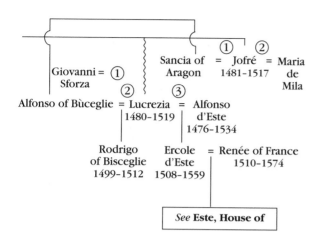

had modest success as a military leader, but made numerous enemies and in 1497 his murdered body was found in the Tiber, the crime never solved. Cesare then emerged as the principal instrument of Borgia dynasticism, and during the last five years of his pontificate Alexander focused his ambitions on creating a permanent Borgia state for Cesare in central Italy.

After Alexander VI. With Alexander's death in 1503 and the rapid eclipse of Cesare's fortunes, the center of Borgia prominence returned to Spain, where as dukes of Gandía the Borja were one of the twenty Spanish grandees. Francisco (1510–1572), the eldest of seventeen legitimate children, was an important figure at the court of Emperor Charles V. A deeply pious upbringing, developing ascetic tendencies, and the death of his wife in 1546 prompted Francisco to join the Jesuits in 1550, rising to become general of the order in 1565. In him the Borgias, notorious as Renaissance princes for their worldly lusts and ambitions, contributed a saint to the great movement of early modern Catholic reform.

BIBLIOGRAPHY

Johnson, Marion. *The Borgias.* London, 1981. Written to accompany a British television production and meant for a general readership, this is a useful overview, especially for its numerous illustrations.

Mallett, Michael. *The Borgias: The Rise and Fall of a Renaissance Dynasty.* New York and London, 1969. The best modern account, by a leading historian of Renaissance Italy, containing an extensive bibliography and genealogical tables.

CHARLES L. STINGER

BORGIA, CESARE (1475–1507), cardinal, duke of Valentinois, captain general of papal army, duke of Romagna. He was the eldest of four children born to Cardinal Rodrigo Borgia and his long-term Roman mistress, Vannozza Catanei. As his father's second son (there was an older half-brother), he was destined for the church. His father's election as Pope Alexander VI in 1492 launched Cesare's career. Immediately appointed archbishop of Valencia in Spain, a Borgia sinecure, a year later he became a cardinal.

The murder in Rome of Cesare's younger brother Juan, his father's favorite, in 1497 fundamentally altered his circumstances. The next year Cesare, now twenty-three, renounced his cardinalate and was sent by his father to France to negotiate an alliance with Louis XII, newly acceded to the French crown. Cesare was armed with a dispensation to permit Louis to divorce his first wife and marry his prede-

the marriage of Jofrè, rescued from ecclesiastical life, to Sancia, illegitimate daughter of Ferrante's son and heir, Alfonso of Calabria. Jofrè became prince of Squillace as well. The Milanese alliance, the motivation behind Lucrezia's marriage, quickly lost political meaning, however, and in 1497 Giovanni, under pressure, agreed to an annulment.

Lucrezia then married again, to Alfonso, duke of Bisceglie, brother of Sancia, and the new couple took up residence in the Vatican. Bad blood between him and Cesare, who by 1500 embodied the most ambitious Borgia dynastic plans, led to Cesare's ordering his notorious henchman, Don Michelotto, to strangle Alfonso. Two years later Lucrezia was married for the third time, to Alfonso d'Este, heir to the duchy of Ferrara. A spectacular proxy wedding ceremony in Rome, coinciding with Carnival festivities, trumpeted Borgia glory, and preceded Lucrezia's equally spectacular month-long progress to Ferrara, where she remained until her death in 1519.

Even more sensational was the fate of Juan, Cesare's younger brother, who had become the second duke of Gandía on the death of Pedro Luis in 1488. Pope Alexander brought Juan, now twenty and his father's favorite, back from Spain to be captain general of the papal forces and to lead the campaign against the long-term Borgia foes, the Orsini. Juan

cessor's widow, together with a cardinalate for the ambitious French prelate, Georges d'Amboise. In turn, Cesare received the French duchy of Valentinois (hence Cesare's Italian nickname, *Il Valentino*), a French princess in marriage, and the promise of a French army to be at his disposal following the seizure of Milan. Milan's rapid fall meant that Cesare could undertake the conquest of the Romagna, nominally part of the Papal States in central Italy, but a refractory region of semiautonomous city-states and feudal principalities. In two rapid campaigns in 1499 and in 1500 to 1501, Cesare conquered the whole of the Romagna and laid the basis for what was intended to be a permanent Borgia state. The further conquests of Camerino and Urbino in 1502 threatened the remaining central Italian princes, and in desperation these condottieri joined in an anti-Borgia conspiracy. In a dramatic action, witnessed by Machiavelli, Cesare drew the conspirators to the siege of the Senigallia, and there had them executed.

By the summer of 1503, as Borgia power reached its zenith, Cesare had gained mastery of large parts of Umbria and threatened Tuscany. But now his fortunes, so meteoric in their ascent, suddenly plummeted. His father's death in August deprived him of crucial resources, and the election of the inveterate Borgia foe Giuliano della Rovere as Pope Julius II left Cesare badly exposed. As his control of the Romagna ebbed away, Cesare became expendable, and King Ferdinand of Spain, anxious to gain the new pope's favor, ordered Cesare's arrest in Naples in 1504 and later that year his imprisonment in Spain. From there Cesare managed to escape in 1506, finding refuge with his brother-in-law, the king of Navarre, only to be killed there in an obscure skirmish the following year.

While in temperament Cesare was arrogant, secretive, and resolute in pursuit of power, the historical image of malevolent depravity was essentially the creation of anti-Borgia and Protestant propaganda. Machiavelli's praise in *The Prince* (chapters 7 and 17) of Cesare's deceptions and "well-used cruelties" as the model for the New Prince only added to the legend of Borgia ruthlessness. His career, while not wholly without precedent, does represent an extreme case of how certain Renaissance popes, especially during the turmoil of the Italian Wars, exploited the political and financial resources of the papacy to serve dynastic ambitions.

See biographies of Alexander VI and Niccolò Machiavelli.

Cesare Borgia. Portrait by an anonymous Lombard painter, sixteenth century, in the Palazzo di Venezia, Rome. ALINARI/ART RESOURCE

BIBLIOGRAPHY

Hillgarth, J. N. "The Image of Alexander VI and Cesare Borgia in the Sixteenth and Seventeenth Centuries." *Journal of the Warburg and Courtauld Institutes* 59 (1996): 119–129.

Mallett, Michael. *The Borgias: The Rise and Fall of a Renaissance Dynasty.* London, 1969. The most judicious modern treatment, with extensive bibliographic references to previous historical scholarship.

Najemy, John M. *Between Friends: Discourses of Power and Desire in the Machiavelli-Vettori Letters of 1513–15.* Princeton, N.J., 1993. A brilliant exposition of Machiavelli's evolving political thought, including his assessments of Cesare Borgia, in the period when Machiavelli was composing *The Prince.*

CHARLES L. STINGER

BORGIA, LUCREZIA (1480–1519), Italian noblewoman. Borgia attained fame because of the ambitions of her male relatives. She was the daughter of Rodrigo Borgia, scion of a noble family of mixed Spanish and Italian ancestry promoted to high church offices through the influence of his uncle, Pope Calixtus III. In 1492, he ascended to the papal throne as Alexander VI. Lucrezia's mother was Alexander's longtime mistress, Vannozza Cattanei, who gave birth to four of Alexander's children. One of Lucrezia's older siblings by Cattanei was Cesare Borgia, a principal and admired figure in the *Prince* of Niccolò Machiavelli. Cesare rose to prominence in the 1490s as his father's lieutenant in the papal territories of Italy and as the architect of his own state.

To further the interests of Alexander and Cesare, Lucrezia was married three times to three men of ascending political importance: first, in 1492, to Giovanni Sforza, lord of the minor state of Pesaro; second, in 1498, to Alfonso, duke of Bisceglie, the illegitimate son of the Aragonese ruler of Naples; third and most splendidly, in 1501, to Alfonso d'Este, who succeeded as duke of Ferrara in 1505. Her first two husbands were eliminated by, respectively, her father (who obtained an annulment in 1497) and (probably) her brother (who arranged an assassination in 1500). She herself was guiltless of the latter crime, and of the incest with both men that was rumored—the work of Borgia political rivals—at the time.

Her third marriage was brilliantly successful. She presided over a cultivated court, patronizing such prominent figures as Ariosto, Pietro Bembo, and Aldus Manutius; engaged in charitable activities that won her the love of the populace; and gave birth to seven children. As a result of the last childbirth, she died.

BIBLIOGRAPHY

Bellonci, Maria. *The Life and Times of Lucrezia Borgia*. Translated by Bernard and Barbara Wall. New York, 1953.

Erlanger, Rachel. *Lucrezia Borgia: A Biography*. New York, 1978.

Grillandi, Massimo. *Lucrezia Borgia*. Milan, 1984. In Italian.

Mallett, Michael E. *The Borgias: The Rise and Fall of a Renaissance Dynasty*. New York, 1969.

MARGARET L. KING

BOSCÁN, JUAN (Joan Boscá y Almugáver; c. 1490–1542), Catalonian poet, translator, humanist. Educated at the court of Ferdinand of Aragon by Lucio Marineo Sículo, Boscán served as tutor to the young Fernando Alvárez de Toledo, future duke of Alba. Boscán's literary career would be inextricably bound with that of his protégé, Garcilaso de la Vega. In 1526 he met the Venetian ambassador, Andrea Navagero, while attending Charles V's wedding to Isabel of Portugal in Granada. Urged by the ambassador to imitate Italian poetry, he in turn pursuaded Garcilaso to do likewise. Boscán was already familiar with the Provençal hendecasyllabic meter used in Catalonian lyric poetry; by adapting into Castilian not only the Petrarchan sonnet, but the tercet and the ottava rima (*octava real*), his new Italianate poetry, together with Garcilaso's, launched Spain's literary renaissance. His letter to the duchess of Soma, which prefaces the Italianate poems in his collection of poetry, became Boscán's poetic manifesto, defending his lyrical innovation as a more precise expression of emotion.

Boscán's poetry was published posthumously by his wife, Ana Girón de Rebolledo, in a book comprising four sections, *Las obras de Boscán y algunas de Garcilasso de la Vega repartidas en quatro libros* (1543). The first section contains his pre-Italianate poetry following the Spanish songbook style. In the second section he introduces his Italianate sonnets and *canciones*. The third section is dedicated to his humanistic work, including the "Epistle to Mendoza" in tercets; an allegory, "Ottava rima" amplifying Pietro Bembo's *Stanze;* and a *Leandro* in free verse based on Musaeus's *Hero and Leander*. The fourth section comprises Garcilaso's poetic production, which soon eclipsed his own.

In retaining the abstract wordplay in the medieval style of the Spanish songbook, Boscán's Petrarchist sonnets lack both the lyricism and the allusive, cod-

Lucrezia Borgia. Portrait medallion. © THE BRITISH MUSEUM, LONDON

ified lexicon of Petrarch's *Canzoniere* (Songbook). Unlike the Tuscan poet, and in contrast to Garcilaso, his most notable poems celebrate domestic tranquillity and the golden mean. Boscán's ten *canciones,* however, not only succeed admirably in acclimating the Petrarchan verse form to Castilian, but effectively reelaborate its thematics of amorous lament. The *canción's* indeterminate length and combined hepta- and hendecasyllabic meters prove more flexible than the sonnet's hendecasyllabic fourteen lines. The form allows the poet ample space in which to develop a paradoxical rhetoric of reticence that continuously expresses his ambivalence on declaring his amorous sentiments to the beloved. True to Boscán's contemplative nature, his last *canción* breaks with the Petrarchan notion of love as moral errancy; in this poem, he compares himself to the biblical figure of Lazarus in proclaiming a Christian redemption from his emotional suffering. The contrast between Boscán and Garcilaso was succinctly remarked on by the latter: in his "Epistola a Boscán," written while on a military expedition in Italy, the Toledan poet and soldier comments nostalgically on his friend's serene life in Barcelona, his poems dedicated to extolling his wife's virtues.

Despite Boscán's Catalonian roots, evinced in his evocation of the medieval Catalonian poet Ausias March and in his choice of residence, Barcelona, where he died, his advocacy of Castilian hegemony is confirmed in his role as tutor to the future duke of Alba; in his friendship with court poets Garcilaso de la Vega and Diego Hurtado de Mendoza; and in his efforts in elevating the Castilian vernacular to the same revered status as Italian. This goal was furthered considerably when, in deference to his mentor's linguistic competence, Garcilaso sent Boscán *Il cortegiano* (The book of the courtier; 1528), Baldassare Castiglione's acclaimed book on the life and spirit of Renaissance court. Boscán's Castilian translation, which became an essential guidebook for all aspiring courtiers to the Habsburg court, is arguably as significant an achievement for the Spanish Renaissance as his poetic endeavor.

See also **Petrarchism** *and biographies of Baldassare Castiglione and Garcilaso de la Vega.*

BIBLIOGRAPHY

Primary Works

Castiglione, Baldassare. *El cortesano.* Translated by Juan Boscán. Madrid, 1942. Preliminary study by Marcelino Menéndez y Pelayo.

Boscán, Juan. *Las obras de Boscán y algunas de Garcilasso de la Vega repartidas en quatro libros.* Edited by Martín de Riquer. Barcelona, 1945.

Boscán, Juan. *Las obras de Juan Boscán repartidas en tres libros.* Edited by William I. Knapp. Madrid, 1875.

Boscán, Juan. *Obras poéticas de Juan Boscán.* Edited by Martín de Riquer, Antonio Comas, and Joaquín Molas. Barcelona, 1957.

Secondary Works

Armisén, Antonio. *Estudios sobre la lengua poética de Boscán.* Saragossa, Spain, 1982. An excellent philological study.

Cruz, Anne J. *Imitación y transformación: El petrarquismo en la poesía de Boscán y Garcilaso de la Vega.* Amsterdam, 1988. Studies the influence of the Italian treatises of imitation in Boscán's imitation of Petrarchist poetics.

Darst, David H. *Juan Boscán.* Boston, 1978.

Morreale, Margherita. *Castiglione y Boscán: El ideal cortesano en el renacimiento español (Estudio léxico-semántico).* Supplement 1 (2 vols.) of the *Boletín de la Real Academia de la Lengua Española.* Madrid, 1959. Compares the lexical values of Castiglione's original to Boscán's translation.

ANNE J. CRUZ

BOSCH, HIERONYMUS (Jheronimus or Jeroen van Aken; 1450–1516), Dutch painter. Born in Hertogenbosch, Hieronymus Bosch was a member of the van Aken (or van Aeken) family of painters, probably from Aachen, that worked in Hertogenbosch from the early fifteenth century.

Life. First mentioned in 1474, Bosch presumably trained with his father, Antonius, but little is known about earlier painting in Hertogenbosch, and Bosch's artistic origins are obscure. His earliest works show affinities with the art of the northern Netherlands, although no evidence exists that he traveled outside Hertogenbosch. An assumed sojourn in Italy c. 1499–1504 is based on a triptych in Venice, often identified as the martyrdom of St. Julia, who was venerated chiefly in northern Italy, but the subject of this triptych is uncertain. Bosch's presumed portrait in the *Recueil d'Arras* is of doubtful authenticity.

Sometime before 1481 Bosch married Aleyt Goyaerts van den Meervenne, who was from a wealthy family. No children are recorded. Tax records place Bosch among the wealthiest citizens in his town. After 1486 Bosch and Aleyt were members of the Brotherhood of Our Lady, whose records indicate that he executed a number of commissions for them, including two altar wings (depicting David and Abigail) for a sculptured altarpiece completed in 1476–1477 by Adriaen van Wesel. Later sources record an *Epiphany* for Saint John, scenes from the stories of Judith and Esther, and *Creation of the World* on two shutters for a carved altarpiece.

Bosch's patrons included leading members of the church and aristocracy. Duke Philip the Fair of Bur-

Hieronymus Bosch. *The Last Judgment.* Triptych; side panels 160 × 60 cm (63 × 24 in.); center panel 164 × 127 cm (64.5 × 50 in.). GEMÄLDEGALERIE DER AKADEMIE DER BILDENDEN KÜNSTE, VIENNA

gundy commissioned a *Last Judgment* in 1504, which is often identified with the Vienna *Last Judgment* or Munich *Last Judgment* fragment. Queen Isabella of Spain owned three of his works by 1505. Bosch's paintings were also owned by Margaret of Austria; Anthony of Burgundy, bishop of Utrecht (a *Stone of Folly* and an unspecified comic subject); and Cardinal Domenico Grimani at Venice (probably Venice *Heaven* and *Hell* panels). Hendrik III of Nassau may have owned the *Garden of Earthly Delights* by 1517.

Works. No surviving work by Bosch is dated or securely documented, nor does his name on a painting or drawing guarantee its authenticity. Attributions and chronology are based on stylistic analysis, complicated by the many existing copies of his paintings. Earlier scholars attributed thirty to fifty paintings and nineteen to twenty-four drawings to Bosch; other scholars, based on scientific examination, have reduced these estimations to about twenty-five paintings and fourteen drawings, plus putative copies of lost works and a few paintings perhaps from Bosch's immediate workshop.

Bosch painted traditional christological scenes (such as the Brussels *Crucifixion*), images of saints,

and highly original moral allegories. Although not without humor, Bosch presents a pessimistic view of sinful humanity. The *Haywain* and probably *Garden of Earthly Delights* (although this is disputed) show the origins of human sin, its progress in the world, and its punishment in hell. Conversely, the lives of Christ and the saints are posited as models for salvation. Often drawing his subjects from traditional Christian writings and imagery, he treated them with remarkable virtuosity, especially the hell scenes.

Bosch's stylistic development is controversial, but it is generally divided into three periods (c. 1470–1490, 1490–1500, and 1500–1516). His early works are fairly homogenous in style, reflecting the art of his Dutch predecessors: *Epiphany* (Philadelphia), *Christ Carrying the Cross* (Vienna), *Ecce Homo* (Frankfurt), and *Tabletop of the Seven Deadly Sins and Four Last Things* (Madrid). Three panels that are probably fragments of a single work, *Death of the Miser* (Washington, D.C.), *Ship of Fools* (Paris), and *Gluttony and Lust* (New Haven), lead to a middle period that shows the earliest manifestations of Bosch's genius, including *Last Judgment* (Vienna) and *Haywain* triptychs (Madrid), the latter an expansive allegory of avarice. The great triptychs of the third phase, *Garden of Earthly Delights* (Madrid), *Temptation of St. Anthony* (Lisbon), and *Epiphany* (Madrid), show brilliant formal innovations and a new compositional clarity. *St. John in the Wilderness* (Madrid) and *Christ Carrying the Cross* (Ghent) are also probably late works.

The chronology and function of Bosch's drawings are unclear. He nourished his visual imagination on a wide range of sources, including prints, late Gothic decoration, and possibly hermetic symbolism. Dutch manuscript illumination perhaps contributed to his "archaizing" tendencies, especially the bright colors and flatly modeled forms. But he was equally an heir to early Netherlandish realism. In this vein, Bosch also created some of the finest landscapes of the period, including *Vagabond* (Rotterdam) and *St. John on Patmos* (Berlin). Underdrawings are fairly elaborate in Bosch's early paintings, but can be summary in his mature pictures, often restricted to the basic compositional elements. Bosch frequently deviated from his later underdrawings, introducing major changes as he painted; this suggests to some scholars that he improvised his imagery as he worked, rather than following a predetermined program, as is frequently assumed.

Influence and Interpretation.

Bosch had assistants, and some works, such as the *Job* triptych, may be workshop productions, but no pupils can be identified. Engravings reflecting his inventions were made in Bosch's lifetime by local designer-architect Alaert du Hameel. After Bosch's death, copies of his paintings and new compositions in his style were produced by many followers, chiefly at Antwerp. Best known are Pieter Huys, Jan Mandyn, and above all Pieter Bruegel the Elder. These followers contributed to Bosch's reputation as a "maker of devils," whose creations were merely "dreams." Bosch's moral seriousness was recognized, however, by Spanish writers Felipe de Guevara (c. 1550) and José de Sigüenza (1605); many of his paintings were acquired by Philip II of Spain. No less controversial today, Bosch's art is interpreted along three basic lines: as an expression of his mental state, amenable to psychoanalysis; as inspired by various medieval heresies, witchcraft, or alchemy and astrology; or as reflecting the religious and social concerns of his time.

BIBLIOGRAPHY

Bosch, Hieronymus. *The Complete Paintings of Bosch.* Introduction by Gregory Martin. Notes and catalog by Mia Cinotti. New York, 1966.

Gibson, Walter S. *Hieronymus Bosch.* London and New York, 1973. Reprint, London and New York, 1988. Useful quick reference.

Gibson, Walter S. *Hieronymus Bosch: An Annotated Bibliography.* Boston, 1983. A nearly complete bibliography of publications on Bosch from the sixteenth century to 1982.

Marijnissen, Roger H., and Peter Ruyffelaere. *Hieronymus Bosch: The Complete Works.* Antwerp, Netherlands, 1987. A detailed study and review of previous literature, with excellent illustrations and a good bibliography.

WALTER S. GIBSON

BOTANY. Botany has a strong claim to be the first of the natural sciences to reflect the Renaissance innovations of humanism, printing, naturalistic art, and encounters with the world beyond Europe. Although humans had been using plants since prehistoric times for food, medicine, textiles, magic, and other practical purposes, there had been—with the exception of Aristotle and Theophrastus in classical antiquity—no systematic study of plants as natural objects. The ability to depict plants accurately, the technology to reproduce words and pictures in multiple identical copies, the intellectual interest in establishing accurate classical texts, and the shock of discovering new plants were all critical to the establishment of botany as a science.

From the late fifteenth century through the mid-sixteenth century, the study of plants—*res herbaria*—was dominated by two concerns: the medical uses of plants and the identification of plants named in Greek and Roman texts. Those medical and humanist preoccupations continued to be reflected in the writing, teaching, and informal interchange of knowledge about plants for another century, although early modern botanists turned their attention increasingly to questions of plant nomenclature, taxonomy, descriptive terminology, and chemical composition.

Late Fifteenth to Mid-Sixteenth Century.

Initially, the interests in medicinal plants and in classical botanical texts were pursued in two quite different circles and published in two different kinds of books: the herbal, and the freshly edited and annotated ancient botanical text.

Herbals constituted the chief genre for disseminating medical information about plants to both learned and popular audiences. Typically arranged as an alphabetical series of entries on individual plants, these works gave the names, brief descriptions, habitats, and general and specific medicinal properties of the plants. The earliest printed herbals either lacked pictures or reproduced the drawings in medieval manuscript herbals. Their generally stylized and schematic woodcut illustrations did not reflect the naturalistic depictions of plants found in an Italian manuscript herbal commissioned by Duke Francesco Novello of Carrara around 1400 or in late fifteenth-century books of hours, tapestries, model books, and panel paintings. The German herbal *Gart der Gesundheit* (Garden of health; published in Mainz in 1485 by Johann Gutenberg's rival Peter Schöffer and ascribed to a Frankfurt physician, Johann Cuba) claimed that its illustrations were drawn from life by an artist hired specifically for the purpose. Many of the woodcuts support this claim; other images, however, bear little resemblance to the plants named.

The humanist endeavor to retrieve the classical texts turned its attention at the end of the fifteenth century to editing key ancient botanical works: Pliny's *Historia naturalis* (Natural history), Galen on simple and compound medicines, Theophrastus's two treatises on plants (first introduced to the Latin West when Giovanni Aurispa brought the Greek manuscripts from Constantinople to Italy in 1405), and, above all, Dioscorides's *De materia medica* (On the materials of medicine). In the 1490s a controversy over Pliny among the humanists Ermolao Barbaro, Pandolfo Collenuccio, and Niccolò Leoniceno drew attention to two startling possibilities: first, that Pliny himself—rather than manuscript copyists—might have committed some of the botanical errors in *Historia naturalis,* and, second, that Pliny and the other ancients might not have known all the plants in the world.

Humanist reforms of medical education, beginning in the 1530s, instituted formal lectures on materia medica, drawn directly from the new humanist editions of Dioscorides and Galen, as well as a new emphasis on direct, hands-on experience. Padua constructed the first public botanical garden in 1545, followed by Pisa, Basel, Montpellier, Leyden, and other medical schools. The professors of newly created chairs of botany and anatomy led students on inspections of pharmacies and botanical field trips. Their summer-term demonstrations of plants in botanical gardens were an innovation that corresponded to their public dissections in anatomical theaters during the winter months. Contemporaries credited Luca Ghini (1490?–1556), who taught botany at Bologna and Pisa, with the invention of a fundamental tool of botanical study: the herbarium—plants pressed, dried, and preserved on sheets of paper.

With Otto Brunfels's herbal, *Herbarum vivae eicones* (Living images of plants; Strasbourg, 1530), the long tradition of illustrated herbals was refashioned into a distinctively Renaissance form. The book's woodcuts brilliantly reproduced the skillful drawings by Albrecht Dürer's student Hans Weiditz (c.1495–c.1537), who had drawn the plants from life, depicting even insect holes and withered leaves found on the individual specimens. Brunfels's Latin text extensively quoted the new editions of classical authors and decried medieval physicians' ignorance of medicinal plants. Brunfels's role in commissioning the illustrations is unclear; the printer, Johann Schott, may have been more responsible for the innovative woodcuts than the author. Brunfels expressed his uneasiness about including local German plants—brought to him by the printer, artist, and herbwomen—that he could not identify in Dioscorides and Pliny.

Other physicians and publishers were quick to capitalize on the success of Brunfels's model. Leonhart Fuchs, professor of medicine at Tübingen and author of many successful medical textbooks, closely supervised the three craftsmen who drew and made the large woodcuts for his *De historia stirpium commentarii insignes* (Notable commentaries on the history of plants; 1542), insisting that they portray the plants in their perfect form, with no cross-hatching or shadows to confuse the viewer. The clarity of the illustrations made them especially easy to reduce to a scale suitable to pocket-sized field manuals, accompanied with a minimum of text. (The pictures were also vulnerable to copying through many plagiarized editions in several vernaculars, which continued to appear in increasingly distorted forms over the next three centuries.) Fuchs also emphasized classical botanical learning but nonetheless included some foreign plants the ancients had not known—notably maize, which he believed had come from Turkey. The unpublished manuscript (now in the Vienna Nationalbibliothek) of his enlarged herbal included many more New World plants.

Complementing the naturalistic illustrations in these herbals was a new interest in description. Fuchs included a glossary of many terms for the parts of plants, most gathered from classical texts, but some newly coined or applied to botany. Arguing that pictures were inherently deceptive, Hieronymus Bock (Tragus) omitted them from his German herbal, *New Kreütter Buch* (New herbal; Strasbourg, 1539), but gave firsthand accounts of plants far more detailed and vivid than anything in ancient sources. The value of Bock's descriptions, however, did not outweigh the market appeal of illustrations, and later editions of his herbal included woodcuts based on both Brunfels and Fuchs. The notes on the watercolors that the polymath naturalist Conrad Gesner prepared for his herbal (left incomplete and unpublished at his death in 1565) reveal his attention to tiny details of plant structure that he would presumably have included in his text.

The Later Sixteenth Century and Early Seventeenth Century.

Students of *res herbaria* in the second half of the sixteenth century took it for granted that herbals would include naturalistic illustrations of plants (often plagiarized from other herbals) and would incorporate the names, descriptions, and medicinal properties from classical authorities while adding new knowledge based on personal experience, correspondence, and exploration. The Italian physician Pier Andrea Mattioli (1500–1577) used his elegantly illustrated commentary on Dioscorides as a springboard for introducing plants that he had discovered himself in Tyrol or that friends in Constantinople and elsewhere had sent him. This was probably the most successful herbal of the century: by the 1580s more than 32,000 copies of various editions in various languages had been sold. Other widely read comprehensive herbals included those by Jacques Dalechamps, Rembert Dodoens, Matthias de L'Obel and Petrus Pena, and Jean Bauhin. The first substantial herbal to appear in English was that of William Turner, in 1568.

Specialized books on local or exotic floras, such as the works on Spanish, Hungarian, Indian, and American plants written or edited by Charles de L'Écluse (Carolus Clusius; 1526–1609), a Flemish scholar who devoted his life to botany, catalogued a growing number of previously unrecorded plants from all parts of Europe and from overseas. L'Écluse's correspondent, Leonhard Rauwolf, a doctor sent to the Levant in 1573 by an Augsburg mercantile firm to study Near Eastern plants and drugs, was representative of a rapidly expanding network of physicians, medical students, pharmacists, garden lovers, merchants, explorers, nobility, diplomats, and missionaries who collected, grew, and exchanged rare plants with the same enthusiasm that marked contemporary collectors of art and curiosities.

By the end of the sixteenth century, the sheer number of known plants—some six thousand, compared to the six hundred in Dioscorides—and proliferation of names for both long-known and newly discovered plants provoked Jean Bauhin's brother, Caspar Bauhin (1560–1624), to introduce some no-

menclatural order before attempting to write his own universal herbal. His *Pinax theatri botanici* (Chart of the botanical theater; Basel, 1623) gave no pictures or medicinal properties but listed Bauhin's preferences of descriptive names, followed by citations of synonyms to be found in over two hundred authorities. Carolus Linnaeus relied heavily on Bauhin's *Pinax* in his own reform of botanical nomenclature (1753), and the book remains an indispensable guide for identifying plants in Renaissance scientific and medical literature.

The confusion of plant names in the Renaissance seriously impeded attempts to classify plants. Although herbals and botanical garden plans often claimed to have arranged various kinds of plants according to their resemblances, their criteria for similarity varied widely. In the unillustrated *De plantis libri XVI* (Sixteen books on plants; Florence, 1583), Andrea Cesalpino appealed to Aristotelian biology in arguing that taxonomy had to be based upon the fundamental operations of the plant soul—growth, nutrition, and especially reproduction; therefore, he emphasized similarities of fruits in his groupings. More typically, Jacques Dalechamps's huge herbal, *Historia generalis plantarum* (General account of plants; Lyon, 1586 and 1587), used whatever category seemed most noteworthy to group a set of plants together, whether that was habitat, growth pattern, morphological features, edibility, domestication, beauty of flowers, exotic origins, or pharmacological effects.

Most sixteenth-century botanists named, pictured, and described plants without ascribing any special significance to the external appearances of the plants. However, the long-standing tradition of the doctrine of signatures held that God had made plants look like human organs or disease symptoms in order to reveal the specific medicinal properties of those herbs. Paracelsan medicine emphasized such internal properties and encouraged the chemical investigation of plant products. The Paris Jardin des Plantes (opened 1640) epitomized the growing alliance between iatrochemistry and botany: its founder, the court physician Guy de la Brosse, insisted medical education needed both botanical gardens and chemical laboratories.

See also Brunfels, Otto; Mattioli, Pier Andrea.

BIBLIOGRAPHY

Primary Work

Meyer, Frederick G., Emily Emmart Trueblood, and John L. Heller. *The Great Herbal of Leonhart Fuchs.* Vol. 1, *De historia stirpium commentarii insignes* (Notable commentaries on the history of plants). 1542. Facsimile, Stanford, Calif., 1999.

Secondary Works

Greene, Edward Lee. *Landmarks of Botanical History.* Edited by Frank N. Egerton, with contributions by Robert P. McIntosh and Rogers McVaugh. 2 vols. Stanford, Calif., 1983. Detailed, idiosyncratic survey of botany from antiquity to the eighteenth century (partially published in 1909), with valuable notes by the editor.

Morton, A. G. *History of Botanical Science: An Account of the Development of Botany from Ancient Times to the Present Day.* London, 1981. Particularly good on technical botanical observations of Renaissance naturalists.

Reeds, Karen Meier. *Botany in Medieval and Renaissance Universities.* New York, 1991. Emphasizes the interplay of humanism, printing, art, and educational reform with botany and medicine.

Riddle, John M. "Dioscorides." In *Catalogus translationum et commentariorum: Mediaeval and Renaissance Latin Translations and Commentaries: Annotated Lists and Guides.* Edited by F. Edward Cranz and Paul Oskar Kristeller. Washington, D. C., 1980. Pages 1–143. Authoritative survey of editions, commentaries, and translations of Dioscorides.

KAREN MEIER REEDS

BOTERO, GIOVANNI

BOTERO, GIOVANNI (1544–1617), Italian writer on statecraft. Born in Piedmont, Botero entered the Jesuit schools. Although the Jesuit superiors valued his talent in Latin verse and drama, they found him discontented and resentful. He taught in Jesuit colleges but was never allowed to become a fully professed Jesuit and in 1580 he was discharged from the order. Botero was rescued by Cardinal Carlo Borromeo, archbishop of Milan, who gave him secretarial, administrative, and diplomatic work. Botero spent the rest of his life as an ecclesiastical courtier and as an educator of princelings—overall, the typical livelihood of a Renaissance intellectual. He served mainly the Borromeo family and the house of Savoy, and his life was itinerant, with periods of residence in Rome and Turin, as well as in France and Spain.

Botero became famous with the publication of *Della ragion di stato* (On reason of state) in 1589. It was frequently republished in augmented editions, together with a shorter companion piece, *Delle cause della grandezza e magnificenza delle città* (On the reasons for the greatness and splendor of cities; 1606). *Della ragion di stato* is important because it reflects an age in which the amoral politics of Machiavelli were denounced with abhorrence while, at the same time, states, dynasties, and Christian confessions (Catholic, Lutheran, and Calvinist) were engaged in a fierce struggle for domination.

Botero is a characteristic "anti-Machiavellian" (that is, he is deeply influenced by Machiavelli). He envisages only one form of polity, the rule of a prince untrammeled by constitutional or traditional restraints, and he insists that only in alliance with Catholic confessionalism will the prince's rule be both moral and effective. Although many of his maxims were trite, Botero's advice that the prince should strongly enforce confessional uniformity by oppressing heterodox groups such as Muslims (in Spain) or Calvinists (in France), while promoting the power and status of the Catholic clergy, is peculiar to the late sixteenth century. *Della ragion di stato* is original in emphasizing demography, economics, and rational administration as factors in state power. The nascent modern state faced a range of new social and military obligations. It could meet them only through careful economic and military planning, direct taxation of the population, and a centralized cadre of professional officeholders. Botero warned that if a prince failed to modernize in these respects he risked losing his state.

The same appreciation of material and quantifiable factors pervades Botero's famous *Relazioni universali* (Global reports; first installment, 1591; first complete edition, 1596), a geographic, ethnic, and political reference guide to the known world, including Asia and America, compiled from secondary sources. It was used for a century as a handbook by European statesmen. Botero was one of the first Italian writers to abandon the national (and often enough, municipal) patriotic focus of the Italian Renaissance, concerning himself with the emerging European state system and the global context of European power.

See also **Machiavelli, Niccolò,** *subentry on* **The Political Theorist.**

BIBLIOGRAPHY

Primary Work

Botero, Giovanni. *The Reason of State,* translated by P. J. Waley and D. P. Waley, and *The Greatness of Cities,* translated by Robert Peterson (1 vol.). London and New Haven, Conn., 1956. Translations of *Della ragion di stato* (1589; from the standard modern edition of Luigi Firpo, 1948) and *Delle cause della grandezza e magnificenza delle città* (1606).

Secondary Works

Baldini, A. Enzo, ed. *Botero e la* Ragion di stato: *Atti del convegno in memoria di Luigi Firpo.* Florence, 1992. The most important modern scholarship on Botero is in Italian, by Federico Chabod and Luigi Firpo. This volume contains a complete bibliography of modern studies on Botero and articles reviewing the portrayal of him by Chabod, Firpo, and other scholars. It also contains original articles on all aspects of Botero's work.

Bireley, Robert. *The Counter-Reformation Prince: Anti-Machiavellianism; or, Catholic Statecraft in Early Modern Europe.* Chapel Hill, N.C., 1990. See chapter 3, "Giovanni Botero:

Founder of the Tradition (1589)," pp. 45–71. A good study in English.

WILLIAM MCCUAIG

BOTTICELLI, SANDRO

BOTTICELLI, SANDRO (Alessandro Filipepi; 1444/45–1510), Florentine painter. Filipepi, nicknamed Botticelli, was the son of a tanner. He perhaps briefly trained as a goldsmith before being apprenticed to the painter Fra Filippo Lippi, whose influence can be discerned in Botticelli's early work. *The Adoration of the Magi* (London, National Gallery) is considered by several critics Botticelli's earliest surviving painting. However, it owes so much to Fra Filippo Lippi that some writers believe it was begun by him. Some critics also emphasize the importance of Andrea del Verrocchio's and even Antonio Pollaiuolo's work on Botticelli's developing style.

Early Career. Botticelli almost certainly became an independent master before 1470, when he was recorded as one among a number of Florentine masters with a workshop. In that year he painted the vigorous, plastically conceived *Fortitude* (Florence, Uffizi), his earliest dated picture. It completes the series *Seven Virtues* commissioned from Piero Pollaiuolo for the hall of the Mercanzia (where the tribunal of six judges governing the Florentine guilds met) on Piazza della Signoria, Florence. The wealthy Medici supporter Tommaso Soderini recommended Botticelli for this task, perhaps at the behest of Lorenzo de' Medici, the Magnificent. In 1472 Botticelli joined the Compagnia di San Luca (the confraternity of Florentine painters), where his late teacher's son, Filippino Lippi, was listed as his pupil. Filippino eventually became the most gifted artist to come out of Botticelli's excellent and prolific workshop.

In January 1474 Botticelli traveled to Pisa to paint frescoes in the Camposanto (monumental graveyard) but instead began a fresco, *The Assumption of the Virgin,* in the cathedral, which was left unfinished and is now lost. In Florence, Botticelli painted decorations (all lost), including Giuliano de' Medici's standard with an allegorical image of Minerva, for the joust won by Giuliano in January 1475 and celebrated in Angelo Poliziano's *Stanze* (Stanzas), which was begun the following year and left unfinished. Five prominent male members of the Medici family and presumably the artist can be recognized among the Magi and their followers in the altarpiece *The Adoration of the Magi* (1475–1476; Florence, Uffizi), commissioned by Gaspare del Lama for his family chapel in Santa Maria Novella, Florence. The fresco *Adoration of the Magi* (now lost) was painted in 1475 at the Palazzo della Signoria, and in 1478 Botticelli painted a fresco (now lost) of the Pazzi conspirators—who were hanged that year for the murder of Giuliano—on the exterior of the same palace.

Mid-Career. In 1480 Botticelli and Domenico Ghirlandaio painted their frescoes *St. Augustine's Vision of the Death of St. Jerome* and *St. Jerome,* respectively, in the choir of Ognissanti, Florence (now transferred to the nave). Botticelli's fresco *The Annunciation* (Florence, Uffizi) was completed in May 1481 for the Hospital of San Martino alla Scala. Several weeks later Pope Sixtus IV ordered Botticelli, Ghirlandaio, and Cosimo Rosselli to join Perugino (Pietro Vannucci) in decorating the walls of the recently erected Cappella Magna (the Sistine Chapel) in Rome. In the chapel's second register Botticelli frescoed the *Temptations of Christ* on the right wall reserved for scenes from *The Life of Christ* and *Moses and the Daughters of Jethro* and the *Punishment of Korah* on the opposite wall showing *The Life of Moses,* which prefigures Jesus's life. In the third register Botticelli and his workshop painted a number of early popes standing inside illusionistic niches, thereby reinforcing the intricate program exalting papal primacy.

Following his return to Florence in 1482 Botticelli was invited on 5 October to join Perugino, Piero Pollaiuolo, and Ghirlandaio in decorating the new Sala Magna (a state anteroom now known as the Sala dei Gigli) of the Palazzo della Signoria; however, only Ghirlandaio seems to have delivered work. In 1485 Botticelli completed his altarpiece *Madonna with SS. John the Baptist and John the Evangelist* (Berlin, Gemäldegalerie) for the Bardi Chapel in Santo Spirito, Florence. In 1489 he received the commission for an *Annunciation* (Florence, Uffizi) for the Guardi Chapel in Cestello (later named Santa Maria Maddalena dei Pazzi), Florence, and in the late 1480s he painted *The Coronation of the Virgin with Four Saints* (Florence, Uffizi) for the goldsmith's chapel dedicated to St. Eligius in San Marco, Florence.

The works Botticelli executed from roughly the time of *Primavera* (c. 1478; Florence, Uffizi) to the *Coronation*—a period of considerable activity that includes *The Birth of Venus* (c. 1484) and the circular *Madonna of the Magnificat* and *Madonna of the Pomegranate* tondi (all Florence, Uffizi)—combine a late-Gothic sinuosity of line and opulence of color with the range of emotions and *contrapposto* (in antithesis) poses derived in large measure from the study of antiquity. This remarkable synthesis was

Botticelli. *The Annunciation.* Tempera and gold on wood; 19.1 × 31.4 cm (7.5 × 12.4 in.). THE METROPOLITAN MUSEUM OF ART, ROBERT LEHMAN COLLECTION, 1975

achieved in the milieu around Lorenzo de' Medici, which included many of Botticelli's most prominent patrons as well as the poet Poliziano and the philosopher Marsilio Ficino, both of whom supplied the subjects, explanations, and underlying values of a number of Botticelli's secular paintings.

Late Career. The frescoes *Youth Presented to the Liberal Arts* and *Young Lady with Venus and the Graces* (both Paris, Louvre), from a cycle in the Villa Tornabuoni (now Villa Lemmi) near Florence, were presumably painted on the occasion of Lorenzo Tornabuoni's second marriage, in 1491. Lorenzo de' Medici's death in April 1492 undoubtedly affected Botticelli, as did Girolamo Savonarola's preaching and the expulsion of the Medici from Florence in November 1494.

In this period Botticelli's precious, courtly style was gradually replaced by a simpler, more direct, and more nervous mode of expression, communicating even greater moral and religious fervor. *The Calumny of Apelles* (Florence, Uffizi) and the *spalliera* panels (installed at shoulder-height above a bench) depicting *The Story of Virginia* (Bergamo, Accademia Carrara) and *The Story of Lucretia* (Bos-

ton, Isabella Stewart Gardner Museum) belong to these years. Among the religious paintings one should mention the four panels of *The Life and Miracles of Saint Zenobius* (London, National Gallery; New York, Metropolitan Museum of Art; Dresden, Gemäldegalerie Alte Meister), *Mystic Crucifixion* (Cambridge, Massachusetts, Fogg Art Museum), and *Mystic Nativity* (London, National Gallery), Botticelli's last dated picture, completed in early 1501. On 15 November 1499 Botticelli matriculated as a painter in the Guild of Doctors and Pharmacists, which had absorbed the painter's guild in the previous century.

Botticelli spent his later years in a state of melancholy, poverty, and religious despair, commenting on Dante and illustrating *The Divine Comedy,* an ambitious project that remained unfinished. The late fifteenth and early sixteenth century was characterized by a shortage of major commissions in Florence, for reasons that have yet to be clarified. When the high Renaissance style became firmly rooted following the return of Leonardo and Michelangelo in 1501, and the arrival of Raphael in 1504, Botticelli's pictorial language presumably struck most potential patrons as a distant echo of the Laurentian Golden Age.

Botticelli was praised during his lifetime by the humanist poet Ugolino Verino, the mathematician Luca Pacioli, and agents to Duke Ludovico Sforza of Milan and Marchioness Isabella d'Este of Mantua. His wit, intelligence, sophistication, and early success were noted by the writer and court artist Giorgio Vasari in 1550, and three of his jokes were recorded in Poliziano's *Detti piacevoli* (Pleasant sayings; 1477–1482) However, he was almost completely forgotten from the time of his death until the reevaluation of his unparalleled achievements in the late nineteenth century.

Mythological paintings. Botticelli's mythological pictures are of fundamental importance to our understanding of the Florentine Renaissance. His paintings of ancient myth offer a pictorial equivalent of the humanist study and imitation of ancient poetry and the development of a highly refined vernacular poetry of love, all of which were successfully promoted and practiced by Lorenzo the Magnificent himself.

The humanist Leon Battista Alberti played a significant part in Lorenzo's thinking about the arts. In his treatise on painting of 1435, *De pictura,* he had recommended poetic invention in painting. Such *inventio* eventually helped raise the painter's status from that of mere craftsman to that of a thinking and highly creative individual whose imagination rivals the divine inspiration or genius of the poet. Botticelli's pictures exemplify in both form and content Horace's dictum *Ut pictura poesis:* "As is painting, so is poetry."

Primavera and *Pallas and the Centaur* (both Florence, Uffizi) were painted for Lorenzo di Pierfrancesco de' Medici (a second cousin of il Magnifico), for they were recorded in 1499 in his Florentine palace, in the room next to his bedroom. Botticelli's mythologies are among the few surviving large secular pictures from fifteenth-century Florence.

The subject of the lush and exquisitely detailed *Primavera* is love [A detail of *Primavera* is the frontispiece to this volume; the complete painting appears in the color plates]. The picture depicts spring in the garden of the Hesperides, with Venus, standing in her dress and cloak, in the center and middle ground of the composition. Above the goddess of love blind Cupid shoots a flaming arrow toward the three Graces dancing in the foreground on the left. Farther left, Mercury disperses ominous clouds with his wand. On the right the wind god Zephyr embraces the nymph Chloris, who, as his bride, is transformed into Flora, scattering flowers on the fertile

Sandro Botticelli. *Portrait of a Young Man with a Medal.* The young man may be the artist's brother or the artist himself; the medal portrays Cosimo de' Medici (1389–1464). Painted c. 1474–1475. GALLERIA DEGLI UFFIZI, FLORENCE/CORBIS-BETTMANN

ground. The allusions to the birth of love and the transformation of a nymph, through wedlock, into the goddess of flowers may characterize this work as a wedding picture.

The rich iconographic program, conceived by Poliziano and so brilliantly interpreted by Botticelli, does not illustrate an episode from ancient myth. Instead, it borrows motifs from the classical poets Lucretius, Ovid, and Horace, as well as the philosopher Seneca and the writer on agriculture Columella, combining their ideas into a highly original, visual poem. The identity of the images and sources influencing this type of Albertian *inventio* remains the subject of scholarly debate, as does the way in which the linked themes should be interpreted and the amount of emphasis that should be placed on the various motifs (ranging from personification to the potential symbolism of fruits and flowers). A number of scholars see a reflection of Ficino's Neoplatonic philosophy of love in this painting. *Primavera,* with its references to classical and Renaissance poetry and ideas, expresses the values of Florence's cultural elite.

The Birth of Venus, painted about half a decade later, is more archaizing. [*The Birth of Venus* appears in the color plates in volume 4.] It shows the goddess freshly risen from the sea, standing on a scallop shell in the center of the composition. She is shown in the nude, perhaps for the first time since antiquity, modestly covering herself with her hair and hands in the guise of a classical *Venus pudica.* Zephyr and Chloris, on the left, blow the goddess toward a shore on the opposite side, where Flora rushes forward to wrap Venus in a cloak. The theme is derived from Poliziano's *Stanze,* and the painting's celebration of the birth of love may make it yet another wedding picture.

Mars and Venus (c. 1485; London, National Gallery), with its languorously reclining deities and mischievous little satyrs, is also probably a wedding picture. *Pallas and the Centaur* (c. 1482–1483)—another allegorical invention—alludes to the Renaissance fascination with the theme of nature overcome by rationality and order through its depiction of luxury (symbolized by the centaur) conquered by chastity.

Religious paintings. In *The Adoration of the Magi* (1475–1476; Florence, Uffizi; see the color plates in this volume), the Virgin is seated at the apex of a wide triangle formed by the gracefully converging men almost occupying the entire width of the altarpiece. This picture was praised by Vasari for the varying poses of the many heads and for the differentiation of the retinues of the three kings. In *The Madonna of the Magnificat* (c. 1480–1481) Botticelli shows his skill in accommodating large figures to the difficult format of a round panel. The Virgin, crowned before a landscape by angels as queen of heaven, dips her pen in an inkwell as she prepares to write once more in the codex in which she has recorded the Magnificat (the canticle praising the Lord in Luke 1:46–55). The magnificent curve of her back and thighs echoes the contour of the panel and is repeated in the pose of her son, seated on her lap and looking up lovingly toward his mother and bride.

Drawings. Botticelli's skill as a draftsman is evident in the quality of his compositions and the linear grace of his paintings. Unfortunately, most of his sheets are lost. Several were used by engravers, including Baccio Baldini, and it is probable that Botticelli provided designs for other artists and artisans as well. However, ninety-three exceptional drawings, executed over a period of years for Dante's *Divine Comedy,* survive (Berlin, Kupferstichkabinett; Rome, Biblioteca Apostolica Vaticana). Most of these crisply executed line drawings are unfinished, and only four are almost completely colored. They are additional testimony to Botticelli's passion for literature and to his unmatched skill in translating words into poignant imagery.

BIBLIOGRAPHY

Dempsey, Charles. "Botticelli, Sandro." In *The Dictionary of Art.* Edited by Jane Turner. Vol. 4. New York, 1996. Pages 493–504.

Dempsey, Charles. *The Portrayal of Love: Botticelli's* Primavera *and Humanist Culture at the Time of Lorenzo the Magnificent.* Princeton, N.J., 1992.

Gombrich, Ernst H. "Botticelli's Mythologies: A Study in the Neoplatonic Symbolism of His Circle." *Journal of the Warburg and Courtauld Institutes* 8 (1945): 7–60. Revised in Gombrich, Ernst H. *Symbolic Images: Studies in the Art of the Renaissance.* London, 1972. Pages 31–81.

Horne, Herbert P. *Alessandro Filipepi, Commonly Called Sandro Botticelli, Painter of Florence.* London, 1908. Reprint, *Botticelli, Painter of Florence.* Princeton, N.J., 1980. An outstanding monograph, with documents and early literary accounts.

Lightbown, Ronald W. "Filipepi, Alessandro (Sandro Botticelli)." In *Dizionario Biografico degli Italiani.* Vol. 47. Rome, 1997. Pages 661–671.

Lightbown, Ronald. *Sandro Botticelli.* Vols. 1–2. London, 1978. Revised as *Sandro Botticelli: Life and Work.* London, 1989. Includes information on paintings restored in the twentieth century.

Mesnil, Jacques. *Botticelli.* Paris, 1938.

Pons, Nicoletta. *Botticelli: Catalogo completo.* Milan, 1989. One of several catalogs in Italian with complete illustrations of Botticelli's works.

Ulmann, Hermann. *Sandro Botticelli.* Munich, 1893.

Warburg, Aby. *Sandro Botticellis* Geburt der Venus *und* Fruhling. Hamburg, Germany, 1893.

Wind, Edgar. *Pagan Mysteries in the Renaissance.* London, 1958. Revised and enlarged edition, New York, 1969. Offers a thorough Neoplatonic interpretation of Botticelli's mythological paintings.

MICHAËL J. AMY

BOURBON FAMILY AND DYNASTY. The Bourbon family was preeminent among the most illustrious princely houses of Renaissance France. Its vast wealth and territorial holdings gave it considerable independence and ambition, both of which occasionally brought it into conflict with the monarchy until by the hazards of royal succession a Bourbon, Henry IV (reigned 1589–1610), came to the throne. The Bourbon dynasty ruled France until the end of the Old Regime in 1792, and again from 1814 to 1848.

265

Bourbon Family and Dynasty

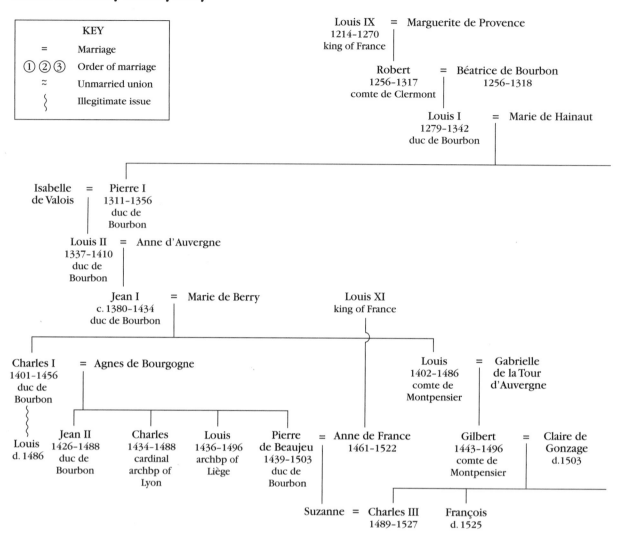

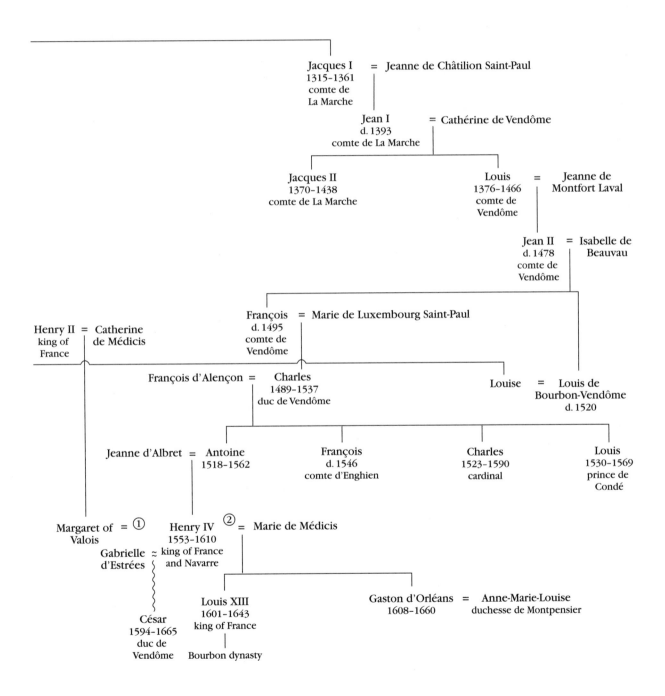

Origins and Early Rise.

The house of Bourbon was a branch of the house of Capet, which constituted the so-called third race of France's kings. Louis IX (reigned 1226–1270), a Capetian of the direct line, was the ancestor of all the Bourbons through his sixth son, Robert, comte de Clermont (1256–1318). Robert's marriage in 1272 to Béatrix of Burgundy brought him title to a vast seigneury that embraced the area of central France known as the Bourbonnais. Under his successor, Louis I (1279–1342), the family's fortunes soared when Charles IV elevated the seigneury of Bourbon to a duchy in 1327. Strategic marriages over the next three generations added considerably to the family's already vast domains, not only on the Bourbon side but also the collateral Vendôme line descended from Louis's second son, Jacques, comte de La Marche and Ponthieu (c. 1315–1361).

Charles I de Bourbon (1401–1456) received through marriage the duchy of Auvergne, while his brother, Louis I (d. 1486), became count of Montpensier. Charles I of Bourbon ably ensconced his four sons and daughter into high positions, such as provincial governor and high episcopal office, and good marriages; even his bastard son, Louis (d. 1486), enjoyed the position of admiral of France. Two other sons became high churchmen: Charles II (1434–1488) served as cardinal archbishop of Lyon, while Louis (1436–1496) became archbishop of Liège. They were the first of a long line of Bourbon scions who held important appointments in the church.

Conflicts with the Crown.

Yet as the power and prestige of the Bourbon increased, so did the likelihood of conflicts between them and the French crown. Jean II, duc de Bourbon (1426–1488), was tried for treason in 1461 after siding with the dukes of Burgundy against Charles VII (reigned 1422–1461). Louis XI (reigned 1461–1483) acquitted him upon his accession and eventually awarded him with the post of constable, making this very powerful and ambitious grandee the supreme military commander of the royal army. Jean II loyally served his king, for he—like many others at the time—feared the wily and ruthless Louis XI. But no sooner had Louis XI died than the dormant ambitions of the Bourbon awakened. Jean II and his brother, Pierre de Beaujeu (1439–1503), who had married Louis XI's daughter, Anne of France (1461–1522), further advanced the family's interests during the Beaujeu regency (1483–1491) during the brief minority of Charles VIII. At the time, the house of Bourbon

rivaled the monarchy itself as a source of patronage and prestige.

The house of Bourbon experienced near catastrophe while headed by Charles III de Bourbon (1489–1527), who through inheritance united the holdings of the Bourbon and Montpensier lines. He also received vast emoluments and important posts, such as constable, from young Francis I (reigned 1515–1547). Trouble began, however, when the king's mother, the rapacious Louise of Savoy (1476–1531), tried to lay hands on the patrimony of his wife, Suzanne de Bourbon, upon her death in 1521. The ensuing clash drove the constable in 1523 to enter into a fateful alliance with the Habsburg emperor Charles V (reigned 1519–1555; d. 1558). Over the next four years, Charles III de Bourbon fought to reclaim his lands and honor and assisted the imperial forces in their victory at Pavia (1525), where they captured the French king. After his release in 1526, Francis I retaliated by occupying all the constable's lands. The constable's violent death the next year during the Sack of Rome set the stage for his posthumous trial as a traitor. The assemblage of territories held by the Bourbon and Bourbon-Montpensier families collapsed as a result of the constable's treason. The duchy of Bourbon was confiscated in 1523, transferred four years later to the king's mother, Louise of Savoy, and then permanently absorbed into the royal domain in 1531. The Bourbons also lost title to the duchy of Auvergne; it remained a private holding of the Valois family until formally absorbed as a royal domain under Louis XIII in the seventeenth century. The constable's sister, Louise de Bourbon, princess of La Roche-sur-Yon, salvaged her title to the inheritance of Forez, Beaujolais, and Dombes. In time, Dombes became part of the holdings of her son, Louis, who was later elevated as duc de Montpensier (d. 1582).

Renewed Fortunes and Ambitions.

The Bourbon, however, survived this disaster due to the steadfast loyalty of Charles, duc de Vendôme (1489–1537), to the king. For this service, Francis I recognized him as first prince of the blood and head of the house of Bourbon. Vendôme's marriage to the king's sister-in-law, Françoise d'Alençon, also strengthened his ties to the ruling family. Affiliation with another royal family came in 1548 when Charles's dashing but dilatory son, Antoine, duc de Bourbon-Vendôme (1518–1562), married Jeanne d'Albret (1528–1572), who became queen of the tiny, truncated kingdom of Navarre, located in the Pyrenees, as well as heiress to the Albret lands of

Henry IV, King of France and Navarre. Anonymous painting. GALLERIA DEGLI UFFIZI, FLORENCE/ALINARI/ART RESOURCE

Béarn, Foix, and Armagnac. From this union was born in 1553 the future Henry IV. With a domain that embraced a significant portion of central and southwestern France, the house of Bourbon again became one of the most powerful families in the kingdom. Antoine and his brother Louis, prince de Condé (1530–1569), advanced the family's interests during the reign of Henry II from 1547 to 1559, with Antoine receiving the appointment of provincial governor of Guyenne. Antoine and Louis also increasingly clashed with the houses of Lorraine and Montmorency for influence at court.

Upon the accidental death of Henry II in 1559, this competition among the princes of the blood and their noble clients quickly degenerated into that series of long civil conflicts known as the Wars of Religion (1562–1598). Several factors exacerbated this agitation among the nobility, which had been endemic for a century. The weak rule of Henry II's three sons, Francis II (reigned 1559–1560), Charles IX (reigned 1560–1574), and Henry III (reigned 1574–1589), encouraged the steady collapse of royal authority. The confessional differences associated with the spread of the Reformation, particularly the Reformed church led by John Calvin, which by the

mid-1550s counted among its converts both the king and queen of Navarre, also widened the scope of these conflicts. Although Antoine eventually returned to Catholicism in the early 1560s, his wife, Jeanne, remained firm in her new faith as well as in her commitment to securing the dynastic ambitions of her young son, Henry of Navarre. She realized this desire, though only posthumously, when Henry married the king's sister, Margaret of Valois (1553–1615), in August 1572 on the eve of the Saint Bartholomew's Day massacre. Four years later, after his enforced captivity and conversion to Catholicism at the royal court, Henry of Navarre reclaimed his role as protector of the Reformed religion and emerged in 1584 as heir presumptive to the French throne according to the Salic law.

The Bourbon Dynasty Begins. In 1589 Henry IV inaugurated the Bourbon dynasty that ruled France, apart from the revolutionary period of 1792–1814, until 1848. His accession was briefly challenged by the rival claim of his uncle Charles, cardinal de Bourbon (1523–1590), whom the Catholic Holy League had put forward as its candidate to the vacated throne. His defeat of the Holy League, attained more by his 1593 conversion to Catholicism than by force of arms, and ensuing accords in 1598 with the Huguenots in the Edict of Nantes and with Spain in the Treaty of Vervins, brought much-needed peace to France.

The house of Bourbon-Vendôme naturally prospered now that its head ruled a mighty kingdom. The first fruit of Henry IV's relationship with Gabrielle d'Estrées (1573–1599), César (1594–1665), received title to the duchy of Vendôme. After the death of Gabrielle d'Estrées, Henry obtained in 1599 an annulment of his marriage to Margaret of Valois that enabled him to wed Marie de Médicis (1573–1642) the next year. In 1601 she bore him a son, the future Louis XIII (reigned 1610–1643), who in collaboration with Cardinal Richelieu promoted the growth of royal absolutism begun by Henry IV. Another son, Gaston d'Orléans (1608–1660), reunited the Montpensier patrimony in 1626 when he wed Anne-Marie-Louise, duchesse de Montespan. Thus, after three centuries, the house of Bourbon succeeded in building its power in France through astute marriages, calculated royal service, and occasional audacious acts of open defiance against the crown that its scions, after 1589, refused to tolerate once they became king.

See also **France** *and biographies of rulers mentioned in this entry.*

BIBLIOGRAPHY

Jouanna, Arlette. *Le devoir de révolte: La noblesse française et la gestation de l'État moderne, 1559–1661.* Paris, 1989. An excellent analysis of the factors animating the endemic conflicts between the monarchy and great families such as the Bourbon.

La Mure, Jean Marie. *Histoire des ducs de Bourbon et des comtes de Forez.* 4 vols. Paris, 1860–1897. An imposing but thorough study of the history of the Bourbon family.

Leguai, André. *Les ducs de Bourbon pendant la crise monarchique au XVe siècle: Contribution à l'étude des apanages.* Paris, 1962. A finely documented study of the Bourbon's involvement in the convulsive struggles of the fifteenth century.

MICHAEL WOLFE

BOURGEOISIE. Each Renaissance urban society was hierarchical in form. Contemporaries recognized two fault lines within these hierarchies: the division between those individuals who had burgher status and those who did not, and the equally important distinction between members of the urban elite and other burghers. The first distinction was established by law. The second was marked by an indefinable sense among elite burghers and other townspeople that the former stood apart from the rest because of their occupations, their wealth, their exercise of political power, and a social unity underwritten by extensive intermarriage. The distinction between burghers and nonburghers as a way of emphasizing their privileged membership in the body politic retained its importance throughout the Renaissance and beyond. Full membership in guilds was reserved for burghers. In Lutheran Germany, the secularization of the urban clergy involved their transformation into burghers, with all the fiscal and military responsibilities that status required. The Amsterdam Burgerweeshuis, an orphanage first opened in the 1520s, was designed exclusively for the children of burghers. In many places, membership in the body politic gave burghers legal protection when traveling beyond a town's jurisdiction. In any external disputes that came to court, it was the town and not the individual burgher that stood there as one of the parties concerned.

Defining Burgher Status. The urban expansion of the sixteenth century both emphasized this distinction between burgher and nonburgher and encouraged further fragmentation within the burgher body. Many of those who swelled the population were subsistence migrants without the skills or resources to aspire to burgher status, and their very numbers came to make of the burghers a minority within urban society. Increases in beggars and

in relatively unskilled workers in those industries such as textiles that experienced the greatest expansion during the century threw into relief the respectability and stability of a burgher body, which could in some ways be called the "middling parts of urban society." Far from a middle class or bourgeoisie in the nineteenth-century sense, these respectable master craftsmen and shopkeepers formed the backbone of urban society in the Renaissance. They provided the membership of urban militias, guilds, and confraternities, and took part in processions, plays, and tableaux. They were in many ways the exponents of an urban popular culture to which others aspired. On the other hand, they did not dominate those societies. Their participation in urban government had been on the decline over a long period of time. The membership rules for governing made it increasingly difficult for all but a very small minority of burghers to aspire to high status, and, although the elite were still technically burghers, it was clear to their contemporaries that they were a group apart.

One reason for the confusion over terminology lies in the term "bourgeois," which was used to refer to wealthy townsmen in France, such as long-distance merchants in Paris or Bordeaux shipowners, and in some ways serves to indicate the ambiguous social position of such men. By appropriating a term derived from urban residence, the bourgeois indicated that they alone now represented the town. On the other hand, by expressing this identification with the town, they also placed themselves below the status of the titled nobility, who delighted in using the name in a pejorative manner. Certainly, as time passed, members of urban elites showed an increasing desire to distance themselves from their fellow townspeople and to aspire to closer relations with the nobility.

Urban Elites. The structure, social composition, and income sources of urban elites varied. Some were closed to outsiders by laws that effectively associated elite membership with the hereditary right to participate in government. Elsewhere, elite membership was more loosely defined in relation to a high status within urban society. Holding political office was only part of this definition, and many elite members either spent only part of their adult life in office or did not do so at all. This elite status was theoretically open to all wealthy outsiders, but all potential members were filtered with great care in order to retain a degree of social cohesion. Two contradictory trends developed during the sixteenth century. In northern and central Italy and in part of southern Germany, the Venetian model of a closed hereditary elite based on membership in the ruling council, which had been established as early as the beginning of the fourteenth century, was taken up by many other cities. Golden books listing the names of all legitimate male members of elite families were widely established. This was more a sign of the aristocratization of the elite and a wish to protect themselves from the threat represented by men with new wealth than an assertion of their social dominance. In many German towns, the dominance exerted by groups of families such as the members of the Lübeck Zirkelkompanie brotherhood was successfully challenged during the sixteenth century. Upheavals during the Reformation combined with a commercial upswing and declines in numbers in the old patrician families to create a more varied elite.

Economic change was a major factor in bringing about change or stagnation in the composition of urban elites. Few master craftsmen were to be found in the elite, and those who retained elite status usually operated on such a scale that they were indistinguishable from wholesale merchants or industrial entrepreneurs. Pedro Gutierrez (fl. c. 1573), a master furrier from Valladolid, and Daniel Wörner (fl. 1621–1699), the Nördlingen textile entrepreneur, operated on a scale well beyond that of their contemporaries. The upswing in the economy favored many merchants. In Newcastle upon Tyne, the rapid growth in coal exports under Elizabeth and James I brought to prominence a number of trading families, such as the Liddells, the Tempests, and the Andersons. Although their monopoly over exports along the Tyne was only confirmed by royal charter in 1600, they had already acquired leading positions on the city council and had created a network of marital and business links with other merchants.

Mercantile wealth was not the only basis for elite membership. Members of the professions, particularly lawyers, came to play an important part in government. Incomes from land, loans, investments, and real estate were also increasingly common as merchants retired from active commerce and sought more secure investments and as their sons devoted themselves to administration and politics. As the power of territorial states over their urban subjects expanded, officeholding came to be an important element in elite membership. Holding offices filled by the territorial ruler conferred even higher status than membership in a city council and offered even greater opportunities of advancement within the ranks of the nobility. Although there were many mar-

ital links between mercantile and officeholding families, the growth of territorial administration effectively created two overlapping elites in provincial centers such as Dijon, Montpellier, and the new princely residential centers in Germany such as Heidelberg and Mannheim. Elsewhere, the experience of economic stagnation, particularly in early seventeenth-century Spain and Italy, reinforced existing social arrangements and perpetuated a situation in which the status and privileges of some elite families were no longer matched by their income levels. Although they were overshadowed by new wealth in economic terms, their social position remained secure.

The Social Hierarchy. Attempts to reinforce social distinctiveness by dress and housing were only partly successful. Generations of medieval sumptuary laws regulating the quality of clothing and its trimmings only testify to the success of elite members of both sexes in setting fashions to be imitated by everyone else with social aspirations and the requisite disposable wealth. Even the sober black gowns worn by members of the Venetian Great Council were imitated by their administrative staff, so that visitors to the city were unable to tell them apart. High-class courtesans imitated Venetian noblewomen in order to distinguish themselves from prostitutes seeking an inferior clientele. Even regulations to limit the scale of celebrations to mark baptisms, betrothals, and weddings must be seen as a reflection of elite cultural influences. It is easier to determine some kind of social zoning in terms of elite housing, particularly in towns where new residential quarters such as Covent Garden in London, the Marais in Paris, and the Antwerp New Town were built to meet the needs of the wealthy. These new quarters offered all kinds of amenities: privacy, space, the latest architectural styles, and the absence of other social groups in close proximity. They were favored less by merchants, who preferred to live close to their business, than by rentiers, administrators, and long-term visitors. Even then, like much speculative building, any original objectives of social zoning were undermined by economic change. In some new ventures, the supply of housing exceeded demand, and the gaps were filled in by smaller houses for the less wealthy. In others, the need for local services away from the center attracted the very shopkeepers and artisans from whom the new residents had fled. Elsewhere, members of the elite renewed their houses where they stood in the middle of the medieval urban fabric. Here social zoning was vertical rather than horizontal.

There were other ways in which the elite were able to impose their social authority, as opposed to the authority of the governmental institutions with which they were identified. The horizontal social links of marriage, common interests, and mutual recognition, which gave most elites their social homogeneity, even when divided into factions on political or religious grounds, were matched by vertical links of deference and patronage. These are more difficult to trace. By their very definition, actions such as covert recommendations on behalf of people seeking employment, gifts of money to help out poorer families with dowries, baptismal or wedding festivities, or even the offer of accommodation to retired servants who had become infirm only emerge from the sources occasionally. On the other hand, the frequency with which members of the elite stood at the font as godfathers of lower-status children or acted as guardians of widows and orphans, executors of wills, and sponsors for applicants for burgher status suggests that the network of patronage and deference was substantial and enduring. Actions such as these were intended to have a long-term importance, something that could be translated into political support, as reflected in the history of the fifteenth-century Florentine Republic.

Relations between members of urban elites and the landed nobility were complicated by the way in which the latter were changing from a feudal to a territorial aristocracy. Well into the sixteenth century, many members of urban elites imitated a noble way of life, not least because they were themselves bound up in feudal relationships with local lords. In Nürnberg some elite families bore coats of arms and hung their livery in churches with which they were connected. The last tournament to be held there was in 1562. These characteristics were even more widespread in Italy and Spain, where it was common for nobles to settle in towns and to join the local elite. The rapprochement was facilitated by the latter's adoption of noble ways of life such as the use of honorific forms of address, the bearing of arms, and conspicuous consumption. In England, as elsewhere, families of the urban elite and rural nobility cemented their relationships by marriage, which eased the arrival among the gentry of townsmen born into the next generation. On the other hand, it would be misleading to suggest that all differences between urban and rural elites disappeared during this period. The process intensified during the seventeenth century, but there was still much that divided them. Suspicion of the social aspirations of townspeople on the part of the nobility was matched by a strong sense of identity with their place of birth on the part of wealthy townspeople, for many of whom the jurisdictional struggles with local feudal lords were more than just a memory. The processes that culminated in the adoption of an aristocratic lifestyle also reinforced the differences between the two elites. As the prestige of a city became increasingly identified with its elite rather than with the burgher community as a whole, it was not surprising that members of the urban elite should wish to identify themselves with their roots.

See also **Cities and Urban Life; Oligarchy.**

BIBLIOGRAPHY

Amelang, James S. *Honored Citizens of Barcelona: Patrician Culture and Class Relations, 1490–1714.* Princeton, N.J., 1987.

Benedict, Philip, ed. *Cities and Social Change in Early Modern France.* London, 1989.

Burke, Peter. *Venice and Amsterdam. A study of Two Seventeenth-Century Elites.* 2d ed. Cambridge, Mass., 1994.

Cowan, Alexander. *Urban Europe 1500–1700.* New York, 1998.

Cowan, Alexander. *The Urban Patriciate: Lübeck and Venice, 1580–1700.* Cologne, Germany, 1986.

Diefendorf, Barbara B. *Paris City Councillors in the Sixteenth Century.* Princeton, N.J., 1983.

Ferraro, Joanne M. *Family and Public Life in Brescia, 1580–1650.* Cambridge, U.K., 1993.

Friedrichs, Christopher R. *The Early Modern City 1450–1750.* New York, 1995.

Hsia, R. Po-Chia. *Society and Religion in Münster 1535–1618.* New Haven, Conn., 1984.

Kent, Francis William. *Household and Lineage in Renaissance Florence: Family Life of the Capponi, Ginori, and Rucellai.* Princeton, N.J., 1977.

Palliser, D. M. *Tudor York.* Oxford, 1979.

Reinhard, Wolfgang, ed. *Power Elites and State Building.* Oxford, 1996.

ALEXANDER COWAN

BOUTS, DIRCK (Dierick, Dirk, Thierry, Theodoricus; c. 1415–1475), Netherlandish painter. Born in Haarlem and presumably trained in his native city, Dirck Bouts married Katharina van der Bruggen from a wealthy Louvain family (c. 1447–1448). By 1457 he settled in Louvain, establishing a large workshop. After Katharina's death in 1472 he married Elizabeth van Voschem, daughter of a former mayor of Louvain. A man of means, Bouts owned two vineyards and inherited four houses.

Bouts was highly praised by later chroniclers, Joannes Molanus and Karel van Mander, for innovations in "depicting the countryside." Many of his pictures include extensive landscapes rendered with

Dirck Bouts. *The Last Supper.* Central panel of polyptych of the Last Supper, church of St.-Pierre, Louvain, Belgium, 1464–1468. GIRAUDON/ART RESOURCE, NY

sensitivity to light effects at different times of the day. He was also a gifted colorist, endowing his paintings with rich hues. Bouts's style was influential in spreading Netherlandish art abroad.

Little is known of Bouts's Haarlem period, and attributions of works painted there are controversial. Major Louvain commissions, however, are well documented. The *Holy Sacrament* altarpiece (1464–1468; Louvain, Saint Peter's) was commissioned by members of the confraternity of the Holy Sacrament for their chapel in Saint Peter's. The preserved contract stipulates subject matter and payment schedule, and that Bouts accept no simultaneous commissions. Two professors of theology were engaged to advise on the iconography. The triptych's central panel de-

picts the moment during the Last Supper when Christ blesses the bread and institutes the Eucharist. The scene is set in a fifteenth-century hall; the four members of the confraternity who signed the contract witness the event, depicted as servants. The Last Supper is framed by its Old Testament prefigurations: the *Meeting of Abraham and Melchizedek* and the *Jewish Passover Feast* on the left wing; the *Gathering of the Manna and Elijah Sleeping in the Desert* on the right.

The high quality and prominence of this altarpiece won Bouts two major commissions from the town council: a triptych of the *Last Judgment* (two wings of which are often identified with those in Lille, Musée des Beaux-Arts on loan from Paris, Louvre; the central panel is lost), and *Examples of Justice* from secular history (Brussels, Musées Royaux des Beaux-Arts) to be displayed as models of just rule in the newly erected town hall of Louvain, where lawsuits were judged. A doctor of theology was appointed to advise Bouts on the *Justice* narratives. In conjunction with these projects Bouts was designated "the city painter," which entitled him to large stipends of wine and clothing and placed him among upper-level civic officials.

Bouts's contract for both ensembles was concluded on 20 May 1468. The *Last Judgment* was finished and installed in the council room in early 1470. The *Justice* panels were probably begun in 1470, and the first of the two paintings illustrating the *Justice of Emperor Otto III* (based on a chronicle by Godfrey of Viterbo, c. 1186), was installed in June 1473. At his death in 1475, Bouts had almost completed the second panel; it was finished by his workshop and delivered by February 1482 (the other panels were never created). The two pictures—the *Execution of the Innocent Count* and the *Ordeal by Fire*—depict a count beheaded on the false accusations of an empress whose advances he rejected; his widow proves his innocence by holding red-hot iron to no harm, and the emperor burns his slanderous wife at the stake. Louvain city council members appear as witnesses to these scenes. The contemporary importance of the *Justice* panels is evidenced by their placement in wooden cases, draped with painted curtains, to protect them from being "ruined by dust."

Several paintings associated with Bouts or his workshop were exported abroad, for Netherlandish art was internationally desired: by the late sixteenth century the *Altarpiece of the Virgin* (Madrid, Prado), the *Altarpiece of the Deposition,* and the *Virgin and Child with Angels* (Granada, Capilla Real) were in Spanish collections. In addition to oil paintings on panel, several tempera paintings on linen are attributed to Bouts: the *Entombment* (London, National Gallery), *Annunciation* (Malibu, Getty Museum), and *Resurrection* (Pasadena, Norton Simon Museum) may have belonged to the same ensemble, probably rendered on cloth for easy export (numerous Flemish canvases appear in Italian fifteenth-century inventories, and the *Entombment* comes from Italy). A *Portrait of a Man* (1462, London, National Gallery) includes a lovely landscape, and several half-length *Virgin and Child* panels (London, National Gallery; New York, Metropolitan Museum of Art) are also ascribed to Bouts. Countless works produced in Bouts's manner complicate the study of his oeuvre.

Bouts's two sons were trained in his workshop; Dierc Bouts the Younger apparently inherited his father's shop; Albert Bouts established his own, also in Louvain.

See also **Netherlands,** *subentry on* **Art in the Netherlands.**

BIBLIOGRAPHY

Châtelet, Albert. *Early Dutch Painting.* Oxford, 1981.
Friedländer, Max J. *Early Netherlandish Painting.* Vol. 3, *Dieric Bouts and Joos van Ghent.* Leiden, Netherlands, and Brussels, Belgium, 1968.
Smeyers, Maurits. *Dirk Bouts: Schilder van de Stilte.* Louvain, Belgium, 1998.
Smeyers, Maurits, ed. *Dirk Bouts (ca. 1410–1475), een Vlaams primitief te Leuven.* Louvain, Belgium, 1998. Exhibition catalog.

MARINA BELOZERSKAYA

BRACCIOLINI, POGGIO (1380–1459), Florentine humanist. Poggio was born in Florentine territory at Terranova in the upper Arno valley. He was never known by the surname Bracciolini in his lifetime: at birth he was Poggio di Guccio; later, as his fame grew, he was commonly known as Poggius Florentinus. He migrated to Florence around the end of the fourteenth century and qualified as a notary there in 1402. The biographer Vespasiano da Bisticci says that he supported himself in his youth by copying manuscripts in *lettera antica;* and he invented, or rather reconstituted from elements of Carolingian script, the new humanist hand of which the modern roman type is a direct descendant. An early customer was Coluccio Salutati, the chancellor of Florence, and with Salutati's assistance Poggio found a place from 1404 onward in the court of Rome, initially as a writer of apostolic letters and later as an apostolic secretary. He was thus a papal bureaucrat, involved in the drafting of pontifical documents; that was his steady occupation, with brief interludes, for fifty years, until he became chancellor of Florence in 1453.

Poggio's post at the Curia was no sinecure, especially in the early years, when there were two or three competing schismatic popes and frequent forced removals when the Romans rebelled against papal government or invasions from external enemies threatened. The Council of Constance (1414–1418) was designed to reunify the Western church, and after much debate it elected Martin V in 1417. Poggio's own master, John XXIII, had been deposed by the Council in 1415, and it is not clear how Poggio supported himself for the next three years. Clearly,

Poggio Bracciolini. Portrait miniature of Bracciolini in initial M, from *De varietate fortunae* (Vatican MS. 224, fol. 2r). © BIBLIOTECA APOSTOLICA VATICANA

however, Poggio took advantage of the international book market created by the advent of a great many learned clergy from all over Europe. From Constance he set out on expeditions in search of classical manuscripts, bringing to light many works that had been hidden to the Middle Ages, notably speeches of Cicero, Lucretius, Ammianus Marcellinus, and the complete Quintilian. Nearly all Latin textual traditions that saw renewed life in the fifteenth century were touched in some way by Poggio.

This activity, as broadcast by Francesco Barbaro in Venice and Niccolò Niccoli in Florence, brought Poggio renown in Italian humanist circles, but his pressing problem was to find employment. When the various papal curias were amalgamated at the end of the council, he was stripped of his secretarial position. He then took up secretarial employment with the bishop of Winchester, Henry Beaufort, the uncle of King Henry V, as he returned to England from the Holy Land. Poggio's stay in England from 1419 onward was gloomy. He did not take to the climate or the people, and the bishop proved a disappointment, being niggardly and unimpressed by learning. The monasteries of England were bare of the classical texts he had hoped to find, and he was obliged to turn to patristic and scholastic authors for reading matter.

After long negotiations from England, Poggio managed to reinsert himself into the Curia and in 1423 returned to Rome, where he was an apostolic secretary under Martin V, Eugenius IV, and Nicholas V. Rome's dealings with England were to a large extent conducted through Poggio, and the post gave him status, a measure of security, and a steady income. Yet, though he acted on the fringes of public life, as a papal apologist or diplomatic negotiator, his real interests lay in the rediscovery and assimilation of the (primarily Latin) classics.

Poggio became an author in his own right from the late 1420s, issuing a series of dialogues and treatises on questions of practical philosophy: the vices of avarice and hypocrisy, the role of Fortune in men's lives, the definition of nobility—fifteenth-century (or older) questions dressed up in classical trimmings and a classicizing style. In 1435, at the age of fifty-five, Poggio married Vaggia Buondelmonti, an eighteen-year-old Florentine of faded aristocratic family, and wrote a dialogue, *An seni sit uxor ducenda* (Should an old man take a wife?), with a predictable answer.

In the years following his marriage Poggio was comfortably off, his duties at the Curia were relaxed, and he could spend ample time bookishly and uxoriously at his homes in Tuscany with his ever-growing family; his last son (of six legitimate offspring) was born when he was seventy. But gradually the world around him changed for the worse as the friends of his youth died off—Niccoli, Ambrogio Traversari, Leonardo Bruni, Cencio de' Rustici, and Antonio Loschi—all within a single decade, and a new sort of professionalism arose in the *studia humanitatis*. He could not compete in the field of Greek with men like Francesco Filelfo, Lorenzo Valla, and Giovanni Tortelli, all of whom became curialists in the 1450s—though late in life he made some very imperfect Latin translations of Diodorus Siculus, Xenophon's *Cyropaedia,* and some of Lucian's *Dialogues*—and he found their technical philology inhumane.

In 1453 Poggio was invited to become the chancellor of Florence, the head of the republic's foreign civil service, following in the tradition of humanist chancellors, and he left the Curia with relief. His initial enthusiasm, however, soon cooled: the letters of his last years are full of complaints about the continuous party strife of Florence and full of nostalgia for his true *patria* in Rome. Old age was also overcast by a feud of epic proportions with Valla, as well as

BRACCIOLINI, POGGIO

by the disaster of the fall of Constantinople in 1453. A profound melancholy emanates from such works as the invective *In fidei violatores* (Violators of good faith; 1456), a protest against infringements on his tax immunities, and in *De miseria humanae conditionis* (On the misery of the human condition; 1455), which contrasts starkly with the treatises on the dignity of man that other humanists of the time were producing.

After his first couple of years as chancellor, Poggio neglected his duties in the conduct of the republic's diplomatic correspondence, and after a movement for reform of the office in 1456 he virtually retired from the post, going to live in his villa outside Florence. Here, and for some time before his retirement, he occupied himself with his last major work, *Historia Florentina* (History of Florence), which continued Bruni's humanist presentation of the external fortunes of the city. It appears unfinished, as was a more ambitious European history, which survives only in fragments, as Poggio died in October 1459. His major work remains the six hundred or so letters, written in a supple and easy Latin, which give unparalleled insight into the daily life of an early humanist. Much the most popular work in his own day and since was the *Facetiae* (1438–1452), a collection of jokes and anecdotes of an often ribald nature.

See also **Classical Scholarship**; **Humanism**, *subentry on* **Italy**; **Manuscripts**.

BIBLIOGRAPHY

Primary Works

Bracciolini, Poggio. *Lettere.* 3 vols. Edited by Helene Harth. Florence, 1984–1987.

Bracciolini, Poggio. *Opera omnia.* 4 vols. Edited by Riccardo Fubini. Turin, Italy, 1964–1969.

Gordan, Phyllis Walter Goodhart, ed. *Two Renaissance Book Hunters: The Letters of Poggius Bracciolini to Nicolaus de Niccolis.* New York, 1974.

Secondary Works

Poggio Bracciolini, 1380–1980: Nel VI centenario della nascita. Edited by Riccardo Fubini and others. Florence, 1982.

Walser, Ernst. *Poggius Florentinus: Leben und Werke.* 1914. Reprint, Hildesheim, Germany, and New York, 1974.

MARTIN DAVIES

BRAHE, TYCHO (Tyge Brahe Ottesen; 1546–1601), Danish aristocrat, alchemist, greatest observational astronomer prior to the invention of the telescope. Tycho was born to Otte Brahe and Beate Bille at the feudal manor of Knudstrup, to which he became hereditary lord. The Brahes and Billes were prominent families in the tightly knit, intermarried high nobility that owned most of Denmark and controlled essentially all Danish political, military, and cultural activity. Very early Tycho began to study literature and philosophy at the University of Copenhagen (1559–1562), becoming an accomplished amateur Latin poet and learning the fundamentals of astronomy, mathematics, and even some medical theory. Under the guidance of his tutor, Tycho continued his studies at various universities in Germany and Switzerland (1562–1570).

Tycho returned to Denmark in 1570 and after his father's death in 1571 relinquished his ancestral estate to his brother and built a laboratory at his uncle's manor, Herrevad, where he turned his attention to his lifelong pursuit of alchemy. Although little record of Tycho's alchemical work survives, there is no indication that he was captivated by the quest for the "philosopher's stone," which reportedly enabled the transmutation of common metals into gold. Instead, Tycho pursued Paracelsian chemistry, seeking medical elixirs and an understanding of the "astral" powers that resided within terrestrial objects and accounted for their special powers. Retiring from the laboratory to the main hall at Herrevad on the evening of 11 November 1572, Tycho noted a bright star in the constellation of Cassiopeia that he had never before observed. Recognizing the significance of a new star in what had been for two thousand years regarded as the "perfect" celestial region, where nothing was created and nothing passed into oblivion, Tycho carefully observed the "new star" (*nova stella* in Latin) as it gradually dimmed and changed colors. The following year he published his observations and speculations about the nature of the *nova*, and although his was but one of several such accounts, *De stella nova* (1573) was more detailed and won him European-wide recognition as an astronomer.

In 1576 King Frederik II offered Tycho the island of Hven, near Copenhagen, and several royal grants to support construction of a feudal manor, where Tycho could establish his own laboratory and observatory, in return for which Tycho was expected to provide the crown astrological advice and carry out several minor administrative duties. Over the course of the next five years, Tycho erected a modest-size but richly embellished and furnished Renaissance villa, which he named Uraniborg, the castle of astronomy. The basement of the house was equipped with sixteen alchemical furnaces, each designed to provide a particular kind of heat for various decoctions, sublimations, and distillations. The lab-

276

oratory rivaled the best in Europe and was a show-piece for visiting dignitaries.

Uraniborg also housed a library and served as an observation platform for various devices that Tycho designed and had built for measuring the fixed angular coordinates of the stars and the ephemeral locations of the sun, moon, and known planets as they moved irregularly through the star field. Tycho had reasoned that the gross errors that were evident in sixteenth-century astronomical predictions, upon which the accuracy of astrology presumably depended, resulted from poor data. Even the relatively new mathematical astronomy of Nicolaus Copernicus was found wanting in this regard. Tycho aimed to reform all astronomy by greatly improving the precision of his instruments, using new methods for computing accurately and elaborating new mathematical theories to explain and predict the motions of the heavenly bodies. Since the precision of sighting instruments depended on their size and stability, Tycho created large quadrants, rules, and sextants that were built from materials chosen for thermal and structural stability. He was a pioneer in calibrating and determining the accuracy of his tools through carefully repeated measurement and analysis of error. To minimize the effect of wind vibrations, Tycho built Stajærneborg (castle of the stars), an auxiliary observatory composed of a series of cylindrical pits, where his largest instruments could be seated on stone foundations and supported below ground level.

Tycho's efforts paid off. It is estimated that his data were fully twice as accurate as that of his forbears, and it was this precision, along with a dependable understanding of the error limits, that permitted Johannes Kepler, several years after Tycho's death, to realize that planets moved about the sun on elliptical paths, with a speed varying according to a well-defined mathematical relationship. Tycho, however, like many of his contemporaries, was convinced by the absence of observable stellar parallax—an annual oscillation of the stellar measurements that would result if the earth were in motion around the sun—that the earth was indeed immobile at the center of the universe, as the ancients had determined and as holy scripture taught, albeit equivocally. For most astronomers, the hypothesis that Copernicus had published in 1543, which put the sun at the center and made the earth another planet, was computationally useful but physically impossible. Tycho's solution was to combine the two in an "inverted Copernican" scheme, where the sun revolves around the stationary, central earth once

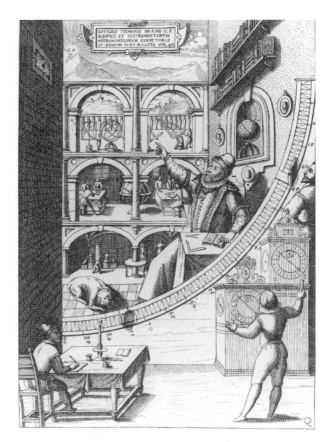

Tycho Brahe. The Danish astronomer in his castle of Uraniborg. Copper engraving from Brahe's *Astronomiae instauratae mechanica* (1602). THE GRANGER COLLECTION

every year, in accordance with the traditional Ptolemaic model, but where the planets then revolve about the sun, in keeping with the Copernican model. The Tychonic system, as it became known, was functionally like the Copernican system but did not require stellar parallax, since the earth did not move. Tycho published an account of his system in 1588, and it enjoyed considerable popularity among Catholic philosophers and astronomers in the seventeenth century, when the Vatican's findings against Galileo discouraged belief in a heliocentric universe.

When Frederik II's son, Christian IV, assumed the throne and gradually stripped Tycho of his royal grants, Tycho packed up his household and moved to Copenhagen and then Germany (1597), seeking to force the king to reconsider or else to win a new royal patron. He found one in Rudolph II, the Holy Roman Emperor, and eventually took up residence at Benátky manor outside Prague. Tycho sent for his instruments and set about rebuilding Uraniborg, including a laboratory. His death in 1601 cut short his planned astronomical reform, but left his assistant, Johannes Kepler, holding his precious observational data.

See also **Alchemy; Astronomy; Kepler, Johannes.**

BIBLIOGRAPHY

Blair, Ann. "Tycho Brahe's Critique of Copernicus and the Copernican System." *Journal of the History of Ideas* 51 (1990): 355–377.

Christianson, John. "Tycho Brahe at the University of Copenhagen, 1559–1562." *Isis* 58 (1967): 198–203.

Moesgaard, Kristian P. "Cosmology in the Wake of Tycho Brahe's Astronomy." In *Cosmology, History, and Theology.* Edited by Wolfgang Yourgrau and Allen D. Breck. New York, 1977. Pages 293–305.

Shackelford, Jole. "Tycho Brahe, Laboratory Design, and the Aim of Science: Reading Plans in Context." *Isis* 84 (1993): 211–230.

Thoren, Victor E. *The Lord of Uraniborg: A Biography of Tycho Brahe.* Cambridge, U.K., 1990.

Zeeberg, Peter. "Science versus Secular Life: A Central Theme in the Latin Poems of Tycho Brahe." In *Acta Conventus Neo-Latini Torontonensis: Proceedings of the Seventh International Congress on Neo-Latin Studies, Toronto 8 August to 13 August 1988.* Edited by Alexander Dalzell, Charles Fantazzi, and Richard J. Schoeck. Binghamton, N.Y., 1991. Pages 831–838.

JOLE SHACKELFORD

BRAMANTE, DONATO (c. 1443/44–1514), Italian architect and painter. Born in Monte Astrualdo (now Fermignano, Marches), Donato Bramante was one of the leading architects of the Renaissance. In Milan, at the end of the fifteenth century, he introduced a style of architecture newly developed in central Italy. Then, after 1500, he went on to develop a new style of his own, distinguished by its monumentality and by its close associations with antiquity, clearly evident both in the construction of his buildings and in his use of the theories of the ancient Roman architect Vitruvius. Bramante's Tempietto in San Pietro in Montorio and his reconstruction of Saint Peter's Basilica epitomize these transformations in architectural design.

Throughout the sixteenth century Bramante was seen as the father of modern architecture. Indeed, the influential Renaissance architect and theorist Sebastiano Serlio described him in 1537 as the "inventor and guiding light of that genuine and excellent architecture which had been buried from antiquity until his own time" ("inventore e luce della vera e buona architettura, che da gli antichi al suo tempo . . . era stata sepolta"). Both Serlio and the Renaissance art historian Giorgio Vasari placed his works alongside those of antiquity as models for a new style of architecture. Sixteenth-century sketchbooks

or treatises on antique architecture included references to Bramante: the Codex Coner (1513/15), Serlio's book on antiquity (1540), and Andrea Palladio's book on ancient temples (1570), in which Palladio promotes Bramante's work, and the Tempietto in particular, as the paradigm of a new architecture.

As was usual in the Renaissance, Bramante was not educated to become an architect. Like many of his contemporary architects, he began his career as a painter. According to Vasari, he was first active in Urbino. He later moved to Lombardy and in 1477 was already working in Bergamo. During this time Bramante apparently specialized in fresco decorations of interiors and facades that joined figures to an architectural structure. (Examples include the Palazzo della Ragione in Bergamo; Casa Fontana in Milan (?); Casa Panigarola in Milan.) In 1481 Bramante produced the design for an engraving of a *veduta* of a ruined temple featuring *all'antica* ornamentation, now known as the Prevedari engraving, after Bernardo Prevedari, who executed Bramante's design.

According to Vasari, Bramante first took an interest in mathematics, the classical foundation of all architecture, turning to architecture itself under the influence of the *cantiere* (stonemason's lodge) for the Milan Cathedral. Despite the strong reservations expressed during the Renaissance for anything having to do with the Middle Ages, the Milanese *cantiere* maintained an extraordinary reputation throughout Europe because it combined the Gothic tradition of building with the theoretical study of *all'antica* architecture. Under commission by the duke of Milan, Bramante evaluated models for the construction of a dome to be erected over the crossing of Milan Cathedral, and suggested finishing the cathedral in Gothic style to preserve its unity of form.

Bramante in Milan. Bramante first appears as an architect in the construction of Santa Maria presso San Satiro, Milan. In 1480 Duke Gian Galeazzo Sforza backed an initiative to rebuild the ninth-century chapel of San Satiro that would include an image of the miracle-working Madonna, declaring that it should belong among the city's most prized jewels.

San Satiro. In 1482 "Donatus de Bramantis de Urbino" appeared as legal witness to the purchase of land needed for the construction. Building records from the next few years refer to him many times as the project's master draftsman (as they also do for the facade plans—an enterprise never completed past the initial stages).

In designing the church, Bramante proved himself a fully competent architect. He confidently employed a vast repertory of styles throughout, venturing highly original solutions for the special circumstances that arose in the development of the plan. The forms are elegant and combine the newest elements of their kind from Urbino (compare the Cathedral of Urbino, begun in 1482 by Francesco di Giorgio) or from Alberti. The richness of the decoration equals that of the Prevedari engraving. The layout contains many noteworthy features, including wide barrel vaulting that spans the windowless nave of the church (like that of Sant'Andrea in Mantua) and the walls of the transept modeled in shallow niches between pilasters. The most impressive feature is the illusionary choir, in which the altar wall runs parallel to the back wall of the transept along an aisle. With the help of a molded and painted stucco surface, Bramante achieved the illusion of a complete choir three bays deep.

Bramante's pupil Cesare Cesariano also attributes to the master the lavish sacristy created at the same time as the church. Noticeably different in style from the rest of the structure, this room rises steeply above an octagonal floor in a design similar to that seen in small, centrally planned buildings from late antiquity. It contains a triforium (window with three openings) positioned above its lower arches and a steep dome. In contrast to the church, this sacristy stands much more in the architectural tradition of Lombardy.

Ludovico il Moro. In the following years Bramante rose to become the architect of Ludovico "il Moro" Sforza, duke of Milan. Although his name often appears in contemporary documents, it is difficult to say with certainty which projects he actually executed. It is certain, however, that Bramante authored the expansion of the Abbey of Sant'Ambrogio in Milan, a work he executed first for the duke and then for the duke's brother, Cardinal Ascanio Sforza. In 1492 Bramante began the Canonica (chapter's residence), but it was only partially completed. After 1492 two cloisters were built, although Bramante may originally have intended to build four. The general arrangement recalls the Ospedale Maggiore in Milan, a building begun by Filarete (Antonio Averlino) for Francesco Sforza. The originality of Bramante's design called for each cloister to be executed in one of the four columnar orders (Doric, Ionic, Corinthian, and Tuscan). However, he saw only the initial phases of construction to completion.

Bramante is recorded by many documents as being involved in the large-scale works commissioned by Ludovico il Moro after 1492 to expand the castle of Vigevano into a residence appropriate for a prince. The work was to include a vast square in front of the castle, framed by columned porticoes. The original design of the square and the painted decoration of the surrounding buildings still remain in good condition. Although the specifications for the structure are similar to those for the Canonica of Sant'Ambrogio (porticoes with an upper story interrupted by high-towered entrances framed by pilasters), the styles of the two buildings differ greatly. Vigevano is more rustic and decorative in design. This does not mean that Bramante did not author both works; rather, it shows that he varied his style to meet demands set by the commission of each building.

Only if we accept his skill in stylistic variation can we credit Bramante with building the choir of Santa Maria delle Grazie in Milan. Documentation is poor because the convent's archive was destroyed, but a number of Milanese chronicles name him as architect. Sometime after 1492 Ludovico il Moro ordered the demolition of the east end of the church, which had just been completed in a Gothic style, in order to construct the new choir as a modern, centrally planned structure. He commissioned the building to contain the tomb for his wife, who died in 1497, and himself. (The cover slab for the burial monument is now in the Certosa di Pavia, the traditional resting place of the rulers of Milan.) Bramante designed the mausoleum as a cubical domed chamber in the style of Filippo Brunelleschi and his Milanese followers (the Portinari Chapel in Sant'Eustorgio), but he combined it with the three-lobed design native to northern Italy and other typically Lombard features.

It is unclear what role Bramante played in Cardinal Ascanio Sforza's planned reconstruction of Pavia Cathedral (1487–1505), whose plan called for a three-aisled nave, a three-aisled transept, each section of which contained a three-story elevation with triforium, and a crossing that extended to an octagon with a high dome. The project unites features characteristic of San Lorenzo in Milan, the most famous ancient building in northern Italy, with elements of Milan Cathedral and of the pilgrimage church of Santa Maria di Loretto (in the Marches, part of the Papal States) then under construction. Here antique and Gothic traditions converge in a new synthesis. This project, in turn, exerted significant influence on plans for the reconstruction of Saint Peter's Basilica.

Bramante also served the duke of Milan as the engineer of ramparts and aqueducts, as painter, and as coordinator of festivals. By 1493 his reputation

Donato **Bramante**. **Tempietto.** The Tempietto is in a courtyard at the church of S. Pietro in Montorio, Rome. Built 1502. ANDERSON/ART RESOURCE

was so secure that, despite having undertaken important commissions in Lombardy, he absconded and Ludovico searched for him in Florence and Rome. At the court in Milan, Bramante encountered humanists and scholars, such as the mathematician Luca Pacioli, as well as fellow artists and poets. Bramante himself dedicated poems to the poet Gaspare Visconti. With Leonardo da Vinci, who had been summoned to the court in 1482, he formed a close friendship and drew inspiration from the architectural style that Leonardo had developed in his manuscript drawings by 1490. The sculptor Gian Cristoforo Romano made his appearance in the court sometime before 1491. Romano's fame rested on his ability to combine practical experience as an artist with a level of schooling in the literary and theoretical writings of antiquity that had not been attained since Leon Battista Alberti. Bramante benefited from his contact with Romano's theoretical studies and generally from theoretical discussions stimulated by the construction of the cathedral of Milan, in the wake of the previous court architect, Filarete, who had prepared the ground for the new Renaissance style of building in his treatise on architecture.

Bramante in Rome. In 1499 the invasion of Louis XII of France dispersed Milan's glittering court.

Bramante traveled to Rome, where the sudden expansion of the papal court signaled a new arena for work. He profited there from his old connections: in 1503 Ascanio Sforza ordered him to adapt the choir of the Church of Santa Maria del Popolo as Sforza's burial place. Pope Alexander VI (Borgia) gave Bramante no notable commissions, but within that pontiff's Spanish or Spanish-influenced circle the famous architect found ready employment.

From 1500 until 1504, under commission to the archbishop of Naples, Cardinal Oliviero Carafa, Bramante built the cloister for Santa Maria della Pace in Rome. The architectural system, including its elements, proportions, and details, had little in common with the cloisters of the Sant'Ambrogio convent that Bramante had begun only shortly before. Now Bramante's work began to reflect his exposure to the Roman tradition of building: thus at Santa Maria della Pace, instead of the usual columnar arcades, he installed ancient-style pilastered arcades like those of Palazzo Venezia. Yet Bramante's design achieves a significantly less volumetric effect than its predecessor; it seems to be more calculated according to theoretical principles.

The Tempietto. For the monarchs of Spain, Ferdinand of Aragon and Isabella of Castile, Bramante created the memorial at the supposed site of Saint Peter's crucifixion at San Pietro in Montorio (foundation stone laid 1502; dome completed after Bramante's death and altered in 1605). The physical specifications for the project were not particularly grand: he was to build a little chapel in the center of a narrow courtyard. However, the symbolic implications of the project were spectacular: according to church doctrine, the site of Peter's crucifixion identified Rome as the New Jerusalem and the foreordained seat of the papacy. The construction of the memorial fit into the context of a new spirit of Spanish patronage, whereby, after unification of Spain, the conquest of Granada, and the discovery of America, the kingdom aimed to set the stage in Rome for status as a superpower.

Although the site at San Pietro in Montorio imposed limitations because existing buildings had to be preserved, Bramante succeeded in creating what in Renaissance terms qualified as an ideal building: the Tempietto. Designed on an ideal pattern, the circle, and a strict, simple system of proportions, the building clearly follows an antique model: the round peripteral temple (a temple completely encircled by columns). Typical of the Renaissance, Bramante's design is guided less by an acquaintance with antique ruins than by Vitruvius's description of the round peripteral temple. For the first time in the Renaissance, Bramante achieved an authentic Doric order of columns as Vitruvius described them.

Around the Tempietto, he had planned a circular courtyard with a columned ambulatory that was to follow the same Doric system as the Tempietto itself (the plan is illustrated in Serlio's book on antiquity). Here architectural theory assumed a real shape, as had never happened before and seldom happened again. Bramante's highly practical architectural skills are evident throughout the design, but particularly in his precise anticipation of the perspectival effect that the building would create within the narrow confines of the proposed courtyard.

Pope Julius II. With the Tempietto, Bramante had so clearly proven his abilities that when Giuliano della Rovere became Pope Julius II in 1503, he appointed the architect to head the papal *cantiere*. With tremendous energy, Pope Julius II took on architectural challenges that had daunted popes before him.

The papal palace, despite various remodelings, was modest in size when compared with the papal palace of Avignon and residences of Italian princes. Earlier, Pope Nicholas V (reigned 1447–1455) had developed the plan for a thorough expansion, but he carried out very little of it. Julius, in his first year as pope, began the enormous extension of the palace. His plan first called for construction of a gigantic courtyard flanked by two lateral corridors, extending from the old living quarters near Saint Peter's Basilica to the Villa Belvedere of Innocent VIII, which contained the papal collection of antique sculpture. Spacious rooms would be attached to the corridors (including a conclave hall and the royal stables, neither of which was ever completed). Some elements in the design of the corridors recall the cloister of Santa Maria della Pace. But there are also distinctly modern features—the rhythmic bays—as well as features directly inspired by antiquity (the steps, the nymphaeum, the interior of the proposed conclave hall). Bramante provided a characteristic accent with the spiral ramp leading up to the Belvedere sculpture court, there demonstrating his theoretical ambitions by superimposing the four classical columnar orders one above the other.

Saint Peter's Basilica, built during the reign of Constantine (306–337) and greatly neglected over time, showed irrevocable signs of deterioration and no longer served the ceremonial demands of an enormously expanded Curia. Neither did the fragile late antique architecture of the basilica adequately serve its purpose as a showpiece of the church; it lacked the soaring vaults that in the course of the fifteenth century became obligatory to ensure high standards of architecture on the model of Gothic architecture as well as that of antiquity. Nicholas V's plans to expand the choir had hardly proceeded beyond the foundation level. In 1505, therefore, Julius II initiated planning for the basilica's renovation, first adopting the design of Nicholas V.

Bramante, however, submitted a model for the complete rebuilding (preserved in Caradosso's foundation medal and the Parchment Plan, Uffizi UA 1): a monumental centrally planned building with a gigantic dome set above the crossing, and posed between four subsidiary domes and four corner towers. Except for some ground measurements, Bramante's design has more in common with Filarete's proposed cathedral of Sforzinda (an ideal building described in his treatise on architecture) than with the actual disposition of old Saint Peter's. To endow his design with the greatest possible majesty, Bramante united the grandest motifs of architecture from all ages: the dome of the ancient Roman Pantheon; the four-armed design of San Lorenzo in Milan; the Byzantine scheme of a church with domes on pendentives in a cross-shaped pattern, with particular reference to Hagia Sophia in Constantinople, a building regarded in northern Italy at the time as the most impressive shrine in Christendom; and, finally, the largest modern church in Italy, Florence Cathedral, the crossing of which extends out to an octagon with domed pillars so massive that each forms an entire side of the crossing.

Thus, in a certain sense, Bramante's vision created an entire museum of renowned architectural motifs that, in their typology, transcend time and place. When Bramante invented ambulatories for the wings of the crossing, he sketched the models of his new idea on the margin of his design (Uffizi UA 8): Milan Cathedral and, once again, San Lorenzo in Milan. Obviously Milan still exerted a powerful impact on his thinking, even when he turned to Roman works like the Pantheon, the Basilica of Maxentius, and the Baths of Diocletian for guidance. In 1506 the foundation stone for the new Saint Peter's was laid, and with great speed the four piers of the crossing were erected. Thereafter, however, the original design was altered in many respects. The changes are often difficult to interpret now from the surviving evidence; at times they seem so incoherent as to suggest intervention by various parties with conflicting concepts of the project. Most notably, the project was adjusted to the site of the Constantinian basilica.

Other Projects in Rome. From 1505 onward, Julius II undertook wide-ranging measures to rehabilitate the urban infrastructures of Rome and to accommodate the population of the rapidly growing city. Once again, Bramante led the planning and execution. Old roads were refurbished, and new ones were laid out, in particular the Via Giulia and, running parallel on the opposite bank of the Tiber, the Via Lungara, connecting the Vatican to Trastevere. These thoroughfares were joined together at the south by the Ponte Sisto (in the north another bridge was planned but never built). A plot of land between the new Via Giulia and the Via Papalis, one of the oldest thoroughfares in Rome, was to be cleared at the point where the two roads came closest together in order to create a wide forecourt for the projected Palazzo dei Tribunali, a building intended to contain all the courts of the papal jurisdiction. Bramante began an imposing rusticated cubical building, to be flanked at each corner by towers (the design is known from contemporary medals). Despite differences in detail, this building compares in typology to the Palazzo Comunale of Bologna, which Bramante rebuilt after Julius II conquered the city in 1506. On the opposite side of the Tiber from Castel Sant'Angelo, he began rebuilding the parish church of Santi Celso e Giuliano after 1509, replacing the medieval basilica with a church with domes arranged in a cross-shaped pattern along the lines that he had envisioned for Saint Peter's, although on a significantly reduced scale. (The design for the church, never completed and entirely rebuilt since, is known from drawings.)

Architectural Theory.

Yet Bramante's fame in his own day was not based exclusively on his spectacular monumental buildings; just as importantly, he counted as the first architect to apply Renaissance architectural theory, in its fully developed form, to actual practice. This is why Serlio refers to Bramante for details of the columnar orders (1537), and why Vasari summarizes Bramante's achievement by claiming that he not only taught how to imitate Roman architecture in new designs, "but also added the greatest beauty and accomplishment to art" ("ma ancora bellezza e difficultà accrebbe grandissima all'arte"). This is why Anton Francesco Doni ascribed a treatise on the columnar orders to him, as well as a treatise on Gothic architecture ("trattato del lavoro tedesco") probably because of his Milanese roots.

In the Renaissance, the columnar orders were regarded as the defining element of architecture; Anton Manetti wrote that only where the columnar orders were found would order itself appear to govern a structure. Strict order counted as architecture's highest principle, and it has been taken so seriously by architects that they often "corrected" even the building plans of antiquity. It was Alberti who first proposed a complete theory for the construction of columns, but this theory was evidently not known until the end of the fifteenth century, and the orders of columns before Bramante were never applied in a correct manner to the practice of building.

Bramante apparently learned of Alberti's theories through his acquaintance with Gian Cristoforo Romano and, on this basis, developed his own columnar system organized according to the strict Renaissance ideas of order, a system in which each successive columnar type was conceived as developed from its predecessor. Bramante did not take over his system completely from antiquity but altered the typical antique prototypes. As the first to apply such a system of columnar orders to actual building, he demonstrated the achievement in such works as the Tempietto and the spiral ramp of the Cortile del Belvedere in the Vatican. He also, however, copied Corinthian elements directly from the Pantheon (as in Saint Peter's and San Biagio), at that time regarded as the epitome of good ancient architecture.

BIBLIOGRAPHY

General
Borsi, Franco. *Bramante.* Milan, 1989.
Bruschi, Arnaldo. *Bramante.* London, 1977. Translated from Italian (1669).
Studi Bramanteschi. Rome, 1974. Papers of an international congress.

Bramante in Milan
Ansperti, Insula. *Il complesso monumentale di S. Satiro.* Milan, 1992.
Patetta, Luciano. *L'architettura del quattrocento a Milano.* Milan, 1987.
Werdehausen, Anna Elisabeth. *Bramante und das Kloster S. Ambrogio in Mailand.* Worms, Germany, 1990.

Bramante in Rome
Ackerman, James S. *The Cortile del Belvedere.* Vatican City, 1954.
Frommel, Christoph L. *Der römische Palastbau der Hochrenaissance.* Tübingen, Germany, 1973.
Frommel, Christoph L. "I tre progetti bramanteschi per il Cortile del Belvedere." In his *Il Cortile delle Statue.* Mainz, Germany, 1998. Pages 17–66.
Günther, Hubertus. "Bramantes Tempietto: Die Memorialanlage der Kreuzigung Petri in S. Pietro in Montorio, Rom." Dissertation. Munich, 1973.

Günther, Hubertus. "Werke Bramantes im Spiegel einer Gruppe von Zeichnungen der Uffizien in Florenz." *Münchner Jahrbuch der bildenden Kunst* 33 (1982): 77–108.

Hubert, Hans. "Bramantes St. Peter-Entwürfe." *Zeitschrift für Kunstgeschichte* 51 (1988): 195–221.

Riegel, Nicole. "Capella Ascanii–Coemiterium Julium." *Römisches Jahrbuch für Kunstgeschichte* 30 (1995): 193–219.

Wolff Metternich, Franz Graf. *Bramante und St. Peter.* Munich, 1975.

Wolff Metternich, Franz Graf, and Christof Thoenes. *Die frühen St.-Peter-Entwürfe: 1505–1514.* Tübingen, Germany, 1987.

Bramante, Architecture, and the Study of the Classics

Denker, Christiane. *Die Säulenordnungen bei Bramante.* Worms, Germany, 1990.

Günther, Hubertus. "Die Anfänge der modernen Dorica." In *L'emploi des ordres dans l'architecture de la Renaissance.* Edited by Jean Guillaume. Paris, 1992. Pages 97–117.

Günther, Hubertus. *Das Studium der antiken Architektur in den Zeichnungen der Hochrenaissance.* Tübingen, Germany, 1988.

HUBERTUS GÜNTHER

Translated from German by Mark Georgiev

BRANDENBURG. The history of early modern Brandenburg began in 1417 when Holy Roman Emperor Sigismund (1368–1437; ruled 1433–1437) gave the electorate and margravate to his loyal lieutenant Frederick of Hohenzollern (1371–1440), burgrave of Nürnberg, whose descendants would rule Brandenburg, and later Prussia and Germany, until 1918. Frederick I was succeeded by his eldest son, Frederick II (1413–1471; ruled 1440–1470), known as "Irontooth" from the rigor of his government. He brought the twin cities Berlin-Cölln under his control (1442–1448), caused all Brandenburg cities to leave the Hanseatic League, and signed a concordat (1447) with Pope Nicholas V (1397–1455; reigned 1447–1455) that gave him extensive rights in the appointment of bishops in the principality's three dioceses (Lebus, Brandenburg, Havelberg). Frederick II's brother and heir, Albert Achilles (1414–1486; ruled 1470–1486) drove back the neighboring Pomeranians who, aided by Matthias Corvinus, king of Hungary (1443–1490; ruled 1458–1490), had taken up arms to challenge the Hohenzollerns' rights of suzerainty over them. Albert's most significant contribution was the establishment of primogeniture with the issuing of the *Dispositio Achillea* (1473). During the elector's lengthy absences, he entrusted the government to John Cicero (1455–1499; ruled 1486–1499), his eldest son and heir, who welcomed Italian scholars to Brandenburg and strove to improve his subjects' education but had to contend with continued attacks from his neighbors and a nobility that, buoyed by its enhanced economic power, was becoming increasingly obstreperous.

Joachim I (1484–1535; ruled 1499–1535) undertook a number of stern measures to impose greater order. In 1506 he founded the University of Frankfurt on the Oder, the Viadrina, the last major medieval university established in northern Germany. Its first rector, the Dominican Konrad Koch, better known as Wimpina (c. 1460–1531), made the Viadrina a citadel of scholasticism. In the winter of 1517–1518 he welcomed John Tetzel (c. 1465–1519), the Dominican indulgence salesman who had provoked Martin Luther's Ninety-five Theses. In spite of its conservatism, the university attracted champions of the new Renaissance learning, among them Ulrich von Hutten (1488–1523), a neo-Latin poet and later supporter of the Reformation. The theological faculty's opposition to Luther's evangelical creed, and the plague that visited Frankfurt repeatedly, contributed to the Viadrina's decline as students increasingly flocked to Wittenberg.

Joachim I's brother was Albert II (1490–1545) archbishop of Magdeburg and Halberstadt (1513–1545), whose acquisition of the archbishopric of Mainz in 1514 led to the famous indulgence controversy that kindled the Reformation. A true Renaissance prince, Albert admired Erasmus, supported Johannes Reuchlin (1455–1522), and patronized leading artists of his age, among them Peter Vischer the Younger (1487–1528), Lucas Cranach the Elder (1472–1553), Matthias Grünewald (d. 1528), and Albrecht Dürer (1471–1528). In 1520 he founded the cathedral church at Halle and furnished it with splendid art works and precious reliquaries. Joachim and Albert both blamed Martin Luther for the outbreak of the Peasants' War in 1524 and, after it had been quashed, joined with the dukes of Brunswick and Saxony in the Anti-Lutheran League of Dessau (1525). While the new evangelical creed was gaining ground in his territories, Joachim continued to oppose it vociferously. Hoping that at least one of his sons would remain loyal to the old faith, he ignored the *Dispositio Achillea,* leaving, in 1535, the New Mark to the younger John of Küstrin (1513–1571) and the Old and Middle Marks, with the electoral title, to the older Joachim.

John of Küstrin publicly embraced Luther's evangelical creed in 1537. His brother, Elector Joachim II (1505–1571; ruled 1535–1571), fearful that such a step might jeopardize his family interests, initially hesitated. With the encouragement of his Erasmian advisers, he hoped instead that a general church council could bridge the widening chasm between the old and new faiths. When such a council did not materialize and as his subjects, especially the landed aristocracy, became more clamorous for reform, Joachim II in 1539 declared himself for the evangelical side. Under the influence of the moderate Prince George III (1507–1553) of Anhalt he issued an ecclesiastical ordinance (1540) that stressed the centrality of the evangelical justification by faith alone but retained much of the old ceremonial (including the elevation of the chalice in the Mass, the preservation of consecrated elements for shut-ins, and exorcism and chrism in baptism). The most Catholic of all German Protestant church orders, Brandenburg's alone gained the seal of approval from both Martin Luther and Charles V (1500–1558; Holy Roman Emperor 1519–1558)—a striking testimonial to Joachim's diplomatic skills and also to the very opaqueness of his reformation. In the Schmalkaldic War (1546–1547) the elector sided with Charles V and, after the war, supported the Augsburg Interim (1548), subordinating, in an at times cynical manner, religion to dynastic concerns. Family interests and the vehement reaction to the Interim, perceived by most Protestants as a thinly veiled attempt to restore the old faith, led Joachim in his final years to move away from the imperial side and further into the Lutheran camp.

Since John of Küstrin had no direct heirs, his lands passed into the hands of John George (1525–1598; ruled 1571–1598), son and heir of Joachim II, thus reuniting the Markish provinces. A severe fiscal crisis forced the new elector to make political concessions that enhanced the influence of the landed aristocracy even further. While retaining the traditional ceremonial of the Joachimian reformation, Elector John George, aided by his superintendent-general Andreas Musculus (1514–1581), cast Brandenburg's church into the rigid mold of Gnesio-Lutheranism, a confessional trend that found its most dramatic expression in the Formula of Concord (1577), which two Brandenburgers—Musculus and Christoph Cornerus (1518–1594)—helped draft. The elector signed and enforced it immediately, thereby strengthening his realm's confessional cohesion but widening the gulf with those groups, notably the Reformed, that it excluded.

The Formula did not gain much of a following at the University of Frankfurt, partly because of the school's humanistic heritage. Philip Melanchthon's son-in-law, George Sabinus (1508–1560), professor of rhetoric there since 1538, had been the leader of a circle of evangelical humanists that included Alexander Alesius (1500–1565), the well-known Scottish Lutheran; Christoph Preuss, a philosopher and physician from Slovakia; and Jodokus Willich (1501–

1552), the Tacitus scholar and founder of the first German collegium musicum. These humanistic tendencies suffered a temporary setback in the 1570s but reemerged at the end of the century when the suppression of Melanchthon's teachings in neighboring Saxony brought many of his disciples to the Oder university; close links between Frankfurt and the University of Leiden, then the center of northern humanist and Calvinist learning, further encouraged these developments.

A significant shift in Brandenburg's confessional orientation began during the reign of Elector Joachim Frederick (1546–1608; ruled 1598–1608). While nominally supportive of the Formula of Concord, he employed foreign Calvinist advisers and, aided by a new privy council (1604), embarked on a more vigorous, often anti-imperial, foreign policy to promote his dynastic interests in Prussia and in the Rhineland. This process was completed by John Sigismund (1572–1619; ruled 1608–1619), who publicly converted to the Reformed creed in 1613, thereby initiating the "Second Reformation" in Brandenburg. Internationally the elector's new creed placed him in the most militant camp of Protestantism, Calvinism, and made Brandenburg, after the demise of the Palatinate in the early years of the Thirty Years' War (1618–1648), the leading Reformed state and proponent of a more active, anti-imperial policy in Germany. Domestically the elector's Calvinism put him into direct opposition to the country's popular Lutheranism, precipitating a constitutional confrontation with the Junker aristocracy that forced him to modify the goals of his reform.

His heir, the hapless George William (1595–1640; ruled 1619–1640), unable to discipline the realm's estates or prevent the incursion of foreign troops, sought to pursue a policy of neutrality, only to surrender political control in his final years to Count Adam zu Schwarzenberg, a Catholic who favored the imperial side yet could not rescue Brandenburg from further devastation. The electorate suffered heavy losses in the Thirty Years' War, but recovered quickly under the able guidance of Frederick William, the Great Elector (1620–1688; ruled 1640–1688), becoming the leading Protestant state, with a military force, by the end of the century, second only to Austria's in the Holy Roman Empire.

See also biographies of figures mentioned in this entry.

BIBLIOGRAPHY

Delius, Hans-Ulrich, Max-Ottoker Kunzendorff, and Friedrich Winter, eds. *"Dem Wort nicht entgegen . . .": Aspekte der Reformation in der Mark Brandenburg.* Berlin, 1988.

Grimm, Heinrich. *Meister der Renaissancemusik an der Viadrina*. Frankfurt an der Oder and Berlin, 1942.

Jürgensmeier, Friedhelm, ed. *Erzbischof Albrecht von Brandenburg 1490–1545: Ein Kirchen- und Reichsfürst der Frühen Neuzeit*. Frankfurt am Main, 1991.

Nischan, Bodo. *Prince, People, and Confession: The Second Reformation in Brandenburg*. Philadelphia, 1994.

Schulze, Johannes. *Die Mark Brandenburg*. 5 vols. Berlin, 1961–1969.

BODO NISCHAN

BRANT, SEBASTIAN (Titio; 1457–1521), German author of legal, historical, and satirical works. Brant is chiefly remembered as the author of *Das Narrenschiff* (The ship of fools, 1494). No other German work before Goethe's *Werther* (1774) was such a success both at home and abroad. Jacob Locher's Latin translation, *Stultifera navis* (1497), was responsible for the European reception of Brant's work. Numerous authorized and pirated editions, translations, and adaptations appeared in quick succession, making it an early European best-seller. *Das Narrenschiff* became the archetype of a major literary genre, the literature of fools, and gave birth to another, minor genre, grobianic literature, literature that ironically praises vulgar, coarse, and selfish behavior in order to teach good manners. Unfortunately, Brant's fame as the author of *Das Narrenschiff* has overshadowed his reputation as an author, poet, historian, editor, and jurist, who wrote in both Latin and the vernacular.

Born in the old imperial city of Strasbourg to the innkeeper Diebolt and his wife, Barbara, Brant enrolled in 1475 at the University of Basel, where he was awarded the baccalaureate degree in 1477, his license to teach and practice law in 1484, and the degree of doctor *utriusque juris* (doctor of civil and canon law) in 1489. In addition to teaching Latin poetry in the arts faculty, he also taught law in the law faculty, publishing numerous legal textbooks for his students. But only in 1496 did he receive a salaried professorship for Roman and canon law. In addition to his obligations at the university he also served as an editor for various printing presses in Basel, aiding the printers in the selection and editing of works as well as in the composition of dedications, prefaces, and colophons. It is estimated that Brant was involved in the editing of about one-third of the books published in Basel in the last quarter of the fifteenth century. In 1498 he published *Varia Sebastiani Brant carmina* (Various poems by Sebastian Brant), a collection of Latin poems, both religious and secular. The majority of the religious poems are devoted to Mary and her worship, and to individual saints.

The secular poems deal with current events like the flood in Basel, hailstorms, and solar eclipses; with literary figures of the past like Hrosvitha von Gandersheim and Petrarch; or were addressed to friends like the Strasbourg preacher Johann Geiler von Kaisersberg, the Basel humanist Johann Heynlin vom Stein, and Emperor Maximilian.

However, the work that secured him a place in European literary history was *Das Narrenschiff*. In 112 chapters, each consisting of a three-line motto, a woodcut, and a text of varying length, Brant presents an almost endless variety of fools ranging from beggars to bishops, from peasants to princes. Amply supported by examples from the Bible and ancient Greek and Roman authors, major vices like greed, usury, adultery, and blasphemy are ridiculed just as forcefully as minor transgressions and foibles. A colorful procession of lax parents, bibliophiles, gluttons, nymphomaniacs, procrastinators, dancers, gamblers, procurers, and knights crowd the ship of fools, although the metaphor of a sea journey to Narragonia is quickly dropped after a few chapters. Intended as a mirror for the fools themselves, the narrative's goal is to lead the fool through self-recognition to wisdom. In this sense it is a prime example of the pedagogical mission of northern humanism and its optimistic belief in the power of education. The simple verse form, the *Knittelvers* (in which four stresses occur with an irregular number of unstressed syllables, the most common meter in the sixteenth century), as well as the superb woodcuts, executed by several artists, including young Albrecht Dürer, contributed to *Das Narrenschiff*'s success.

In 1501 Brant returned to Strasbourg, possibly prompted by Basel's decision to leave the German Empire and join the Swiss Confederation as well as by personal considerations. For the next two decades he served his native city first as legal adviser, then as municipal secretary (Stadtschreiber), the highest administrative position in the city, which involved providing legal opinions, maintaining the official correspondence, and acting as city censor. In addition to these duties he was also appointed imperial councillor by Emperor Maximilian, to whose court he journeyed several times on diplomatic missions. In Strasbourg, Brant continued to engage in such thoroughly humanistic pursuits as editing classical authors (he produced magnificent editions of Virgil and Terence), writing historical chronicles in the vernacular, and taking part in the activities of Strasbourg's literary society, which in 1514 hosted Erasmus of Rotterdam.

Toward the end of his life Brant became increasingly pessimistic. The Reformation, the scope and significance of which he did not and could not comprehend, and the death of Emperor Maximilian, in whom he had placed high hopes for a strong empire, aggravated this pessimism. He died a bitter man in 1521.

BIBLIOGRAPHY

Primary Work

Brant, Sebastian. *The Ship of Fools, by Sebastian Brant. Translated into Rhyming Couplets, with Introduction and Commentary.* Translated by E. H. Zeydel. New York, 1944, 1962. Translation of *Das Narrenschiff* (Basel, 1494).

Secondary Works

Cleve, John van. "Sebastian Brant." In *German Writers of the Renaissance and Reformation 1280–1580.* Dictionary of Literary Biography, vol. 179. Detroit, Mich.; Washington, D.C.; and London; 1997. Pages 14–22. Concise article with good bibliography of primary and secondary literature.
Zeydel, Edwin H. *Sebastian Brant.* New York, 1967. Best biography in English.

ECKHARD BERNSTEIN

BRANTÔME, PIERRE DE BOURDEILLE, SEIGNEUR DE

(1540–1614), French chronicler and memorialist. Brantôme was a member of an ancient noble family. A courtier and soldier, he lived mainly at the royal court or on the battlefield for the first forty years of his life. In 1556, Henry II (ruled 1547–1559), following a royal policy of honoring favorite subjects by giving them exclusive rights to the revenue generated by an abbey or monastery, granted him the abbey of Brantôme (hence his name). Although he was sometimes called the abbot of Brantôme, he was never in religious orders.

In 1582 he quarreled with Henry III (ruled 1574–1589) and left the court. Soon thereafter Brantôme fell from his horse and was seriously injured. He remained an invalid for the rest of his life. He began writing his memoirs, which were composed, eventually, of several books that describe the life and deeds of famous sixteenth-century figures. Portraits of kings and military commanders are set opposite portraits of queens and women who figured prominently at the Valois court (1515–1589). His best-known book is *Les vies des dames galantes* (Lives of gallant ladies), a work the critic Madeleine Lazard has called the sixteenth-century Kinsey Report because it consists of hundreds of anecdotes recounting the amorous adventures of contemporaries.

A vast, sprawling work that is part autobiography, part biography, part chronicle, and part collection of stories remembered from happier days, Brantôme's memoirs depict, in sprightly, vivid language, the values and ethos of the aristocratic class in France in the sixteenth century.

BIBLIOGRAPHY

Primary Work

Brantôme, Pierre de Bourdeille, seigneur de. *Oeuvres complètes de Pierre de Bourdeille.* Edited by Ludovic Lalanne. 11 vols. Paris, 1864–1882.

Secondary Works

Cottrell, Robert D. *Brantôme: The Writer as Portraitist of His Age.* Geneva, 1970.
Lazard, Madeleine. *Pierre de Bourdeille, seigneur de Brantôme.* Paris, 1995.

ROBERT D. COTTRELL

BREUGHEL FAMILY. *See* **Brueghel Family.**

BRITAIN. *See* **England; Ireland; Scotland.**

BRITAIN, ART IN. The commencement of Stuart rule in 1603 with the succession of James VI of Scotland (as James I) marked not only the uniting of the country that we now call Great Britain, but also a period of remarkable cultural achievement. This was reflected in the publication by Francis Bacon of *The Advancement of Learning* (1605), the early works of Ben Jonson (1572–1637), and the late works of William Shakespeare (1564–1616), together with the buildings of the so-called "Vitruvius Britannicus," Inigo Jones (1573–1652), whose unprecedented *all'antica* architecture (building in the antique manner) was heralded so eloquently with the Whitehall Banqueting House of 1619–1622.

The subsequent court of Charles I (1625–1649) was characterized in paintings by Peter Paul Rubens and Anthony Van Dyck, which projected the image of a monarch who ruled by divine right. Having been on the fringe of Renaissance culture since the Reformation, England now became the focus of its development. This development would be relatively short-lived, however, since the civil war that began in 1642 brought a period of iconoclasm during which little art was patronized. Following the eventual restoration of the monarchy in 1660, the growth of continental mannerism provided native artists and architects such as Christopher Wren (1632–1723) with new models that seemed to accord better with the emerging rationalistic attitude to nature.

Tudor Background. Renaissance arts were quickly adapted by court artists to the new sense of nationhood fostered by James's succession. Indeed certain Renaissance—and also mannerist—artistic and aesthetic principles were already well established, having found early expression in Tudor poetry and through the advent of a printed literature on art and architecture under Elizabeth. The Stuart ambassador and author on architecture, Henry Wotton, when advocating the use of the *all'antica* style to his countrymen in 1624, advised that the pointed arch should be "exiled from judicious eyes" and left to "the *Gothes* . . . amongst other *Reliques* of that barbarous *Age*" (*The Elements of Architecture*, p. 51). During the half century prior to Wotton's remarks, the gradual replacement of Gothic forms through the use of the antique orders in court architecture was largely stimulated by the first-ever English architecture books, since the *all'antica* style that they described was increasingly seen as expressing Protestant reforms on equal terms with the continental monuments of the Counter-Reformation.

While a number of these early books prior to Wotton's were by native writers, namely those published by John Shute (1563) and John Dee (1570), English translations of continental treatises on art and architecture were equally influential, notably those of Francesco Colonna (partially translated in 1592), Giovanni Lomazzo (translated in 1598), Hans Blum (in 1601), and Sebastiano Serlio (in 1611). Serlio's woodcuts and more licentious prints by continental designers such as Wendell Dietterlin provided sources for Elizabethan and early Stuart patrons eager to incorporate details that reflected the new *all'antica* style, as with the fireplaces, moldings, and columns in the houses of the surveyor-architect Robert Smythson (c. 1535–1614). The less clearly organized, although more fundamental, Latin architectural treatises by the Roman author Vitruvius (first century B.C.) and the Renaissance architect Leon Battista Alberti (1404–1472) were not translated into English until the eighteenth century, despite their early citation by John Dee. These authors thereby remained inaccessible to the majority of artisans since only a few of them could read a foreign language.

Dee's "Mathematical Preface" to the first English translation of Euclid of 1570 had introduced to artisans commonplace Renaissance principles associated with painting, sculpture, and architecture, explaining the applications of human proportions and perspective. Citing Vitruvius, Alberti, and the Neoplatonist Heinrich Cornelius Agrippa (1486–1535) with reference to the rules of antique architecture, Dee laments that "few (in our dayes) atteyne thereto" (*Elements of Geometrie*, preface). Dee sought to reform medieval arts and crafts (and thereby Elizabethan society) through outlining the

application of Euclidean geometry in particular. By echoing humanists such as Baldassare Castiglione (1478–1529) in redefining fine art as a form of mathematical, rather than mechanical, design (as traditionally defined), Dee challenged the rigid medieval conception of seven liberal arts that had condemned the artisan to a subordinate social status.

Moreover, Elizabethan iconoclasts had associated certain decorative arts with Catholic Rome, especially the unfamiliar *all'antica* architecture of the Italian masters. In this context Renaissance influences were largely restricted to well-established art forms, such as portraiture, following Hans Holbein the Younger's paintings (1526–1528, 1532–1543) for the court of Henry VIII and the early miniatures (1571–1576) by Nicholas Hilliard, and poetry, following the early works of Edmund Spenser, Philip Sidney, and Shakespeare. This prejudice against the decorative arts was addressed by Richard Haydocke in his partial English translation of Giovanni Lomazzo's treatise published as *A Tracte Containing the Artes of Curious Paintinge, Carvinge, and Buildinge* (1598). Haydocke's emblematic title page celebrates the divine origin of the three fine arts, with painting represented as Juno, sculpture as Prometheus, and architecture as Daedalus, while knowledge of these arts was presented in the publications of Thomas Elyot (1490?–1546) and Henry Peacham (1576?–1643?) as essential to those of noble birth.

Stuart Art. The ill-fated Stuart heir, Henry, prince of Wales (1594–1612), was thus to cast himself as a prince in the Renaissance model through the active study and patronage of the arts. Henry introduced Renaissance principles associated with garden design (at Richmond garden designed by the Vitruvian engineer-architects Salomon de Caus and Constantino de Servi, 1611–1612); with architecture (at the prince's lodging at Newmarket by Jones, 1616–1619); and with perspective, as taught to the prince by de Caus. The prince was thus an important catalyst for the introduction of Renaissance art into Britain—the 1611 English translation of Serlio's treatise, with its discussion of geometry, perspective, theater design, and the architectural orders, was dedicated to Henry, as was de Caus's treatise of 1612 on perspective.

The Stuart courtier Thomas Howard, second earl of Arundel (1585–1646), imported a quantity of antique and Renaissance artwork following his much-vaunted trip to Italy between 1613 and 1615; as a consequence court sculptors such as Nicholas Stone (1586–1647) and the Frenchman Hubert Le Sueur (c.

Art in Britain. Equestrian portrait of King Charles I with the sieur de Saint-Antoine by Anthony van Dyck (1599–1641). Oil on canvas; 1633; 368 × 270 cm (145 × 106 in.). THE ROYAL COLLECTION © HER MAJESTY QUEEN ELIZABETH II

1590–1658) and portrait painters such as William Dobson (1610–1646) and the Dutchman Daniel Mytens (Mijtens; c. 1590–c. 1647) were not short of antique models. On arrival in 1618, Mytens famously painted the earl gesturing toward this sculpture displayed in a gallery at Arundel House designed by Jones (c. 1615). Le Sueur was sent to Rome in 1631 to cast copies of antique statues to serve as models, and his subsequent bronze equestrian statue of Charles I at Charing Cross in London (1633) presented the Stuart monarch as a worthy imperial successor to Marcus Aurelius (as sculpted on the Capitol in Rome) and Charles V (as represented by Titian). The parallel portrait of the king on horseback (with M. de St. Antoine) of the same year by Van Dyck (the most famous of the foreign artists to be employed in the British court; 1632–1641), was displayed at the end of the gallery at Saint James's Palace along with pictures of emperors on horseback by Giulio Romano.

Stuart court artists thus worked alongside other propagandists of the royalist cause to fabricate a coherent image of an imperial monarchy whose rule had been sanctioned by divine right and antique precedent. Hence Rubens was commissioned by Charles to present his father as the very embodiment of divine kingship, in ceiling panels painted and installed (c. 1635) in Jones's recently constructed Banqueting House. In one panel James is cast as the British Solomon presiding over the union of Great Britain in a circular *all'antica* temple of a quasi-Tuscan order; in another, James is seen as a Christ-like figure bearing a new golden age and framed by twisting Solomonic columns, after columns in Raphael's cartoon *The Healing of the Lame Man* (1515) purchased by Charles I in 1623; and in the central panel he is ascending heavenward as the apotheosis of divine rule. Nowhere is the Stuart self-image more coherently represented than in these panels set within Jones's column-lined double cube masquing hall.

Rubens's panels immortalized themes that were a commonplace of the court masque, a quintessentially Renaissance theatrical spectacle of which Jones developed a unique form based on the Medici court intermezzi, or performances of theatrical illusion (1589), and Serlio's theatrical woodcuts (published in 1545). The masque united many areas of Renaissance artistry, as initiated in Britain by Dee, from the mathematical arts of perspective (which orchestrated Jones's *all'antica* settings) and of mechanics (which lay behind his scenic illusion) to the reflection in Jones's costume designs of pictorial conventions established by Renaissance emblem books. As such the masque represented perhaps the highest, although least permanent, artistic achievement of the British Renaissance. However, in the absence of a coherent court architectural style under Elizabeth, with little building work undertaken during her reign, Jones's church at Covent Garden (1631–1633), his queen's chapel at Saint James's Palace (1623–1625), Queen's House at Greenwich (1616–1638), Saint Paul's Cathedral refacing (from 1633) and, most notably, the Banqueting House itself (1619–1622), all attempted for the first time to set in stone the Renaissance principles of harmony introduced through his temporary masque stage sets.

In line with Tudor poets and portrait painters, Stuart court artists thus sought to find an appropriate expression for Protestant royalty, a task made ever more urgent with the arrival of the Counter-Reformation mannerist architecture of Rome. This resulted in a uniquely British expression of Renaissance art forms, in which *all'antica* ornament was interwoven with royal heraldry, and where masquers cast as antique heroes danced within Jones's stage realization of the fallen house of British chivalry. For in Stuart Britain, as elsewhere in Europe, the newly established Renaissance art forms were utilized to express regional traditions and national aspirations.

See also Architecture, *subentry on* Architectural Treatises; Drama, English, *subentry on* Jacobean Court Masque; Emblem; Gardens; Mannerism; Royal Iconography, English.

BIBLIOGRAPHY

Gent, Lucy, ed. *Albion's Classicism: The Visual Arts in Britain, 1550–1660.* New Haven, Conn., and London, 1995.

Harris, Eileen, and Nicholas Savage. *British Architectural Books and Writers, 1556–1785.* Cambridge, U.K., 1990.

Hart, Vaughan. *Art and Magic in the Court of the Stuarts.* London and New York, 1994.

Phillips, John. *The Reformation of Images: Destruction of Art in England, 1535–1660.* Berkeley, Calif., 1973.

Summerson, John. *Architecture in Britain, 1530 to 1830.* London and New York, 1991.

Waterhouse, Ellis. *Painting in Britain, 1530 to 1790.* 5th ed. New Haven, Conn., 1994.

Wells-Cole, Anthony. *Art of Decoration in Elizabethan and Jacobean England: The Influence of Continental Prints, 1558–1625.* New Haven, Conn., and London, 1997.

Whinney, Margaret. *Sculpture in Britain, 1530 to 1830.* 2d ed. Revised by John Physick. London, 1988.

VAUGHAN HART

BRITTANY. Few rural areas of western Europe offer so stunning a collection of Renaissance artistic monuments as western Brittany. Throughout the districts of Léon and parts of Cornouaille, the magnificent parish closes, such as Guimiliau (1581) and Saint-Thégonnec (c. 1600) provide us with a vivid reminder of how Renaissance artistic trends spread from Italy even to rural northern Europe. The Renaissance tomb of the bishop of Dol, finished in 1507 by the Juste brothers of Florence, the chapel of the Holy Sacrament at Vannes, modeled on the Farnese Palace of Rome, and the superb tomb of Duke Francis II had a decisive influence on Breton architecture and sculpture. The creators of the parish closes, such as Jean Dauré of Landerneau, mixed elements of Renaissance and late Gothic to illuminate classic Breton themes, such as the dance of death led by Ankou, the Breton Grim Reaper.

Brittany lay at the center of French and European politics and economic development during the Renaissance. The early stages of the Hundred Years' War often focused on the Breton War of Succession (1341–1364), touched off by the death of Duke John III. The pope canonized the husband (Charles of Blois) of one claimant, Joan of Penthièvre, but her opponent, John of Montfort, supported by the king of England, won the war. His son, Duke John IV, founded the dynasty that would rule an independent Brittany until 1491.

Brittany remained closely tied to military events in France throughout the Hundred Years' War and after, but the duchy itself usually remained at peace. The French invasions of 1487–1491, the English descent on Morlaix (1522), and some fierce fighting on the southern borders of the bishopric of Nantes in the Wars of Religion of the 1570s provide the major exceptions. In the 1590s, however, Brittany suffered terribly in the War of the League. Henry IV came to Nantes in April 1598 both to accept the surrender of the duke of Mercoeur, last leader of the League, and to promulgate of the Edict of Nantes, the first western European law of toleration, in a center of staunch Catholicism.

The dukes of Brittany modeled their state institutions after those of the French state, and the Breton noble elite maintained close ties with the French nobility. Two Breton families, the Rohans of the west and central heaths and the barons of Laval, dominated the province. In the fifteenth century both families intermarried with the ducal house and with the French royal family. Culturally, these nobles, as well as the people of eastern Brittany, remained completely French; however, the western peasants adhered to Celtic culture and language until the twentieth century.

The parallel political and cultural development made it much easier for the king of France to integrate Brittany into the kingdom. Charles VIII began that process by allying with several important Breton nobles, chief among them Pierre de Rohan, and by invading the duchy in 1487–1488. The 1488 offensive, led by Louis de La Trémoille, captured Fougères and routed the Bretons and their English and Imperial allies at Saint-Aubin-du-Cormier. Duke Francis II signed a humiliating treaty and died soon afterward, to be succeeded by his eleven-year-old daughter Anne, the last independent ruler of Brittany.

Anne of Brittany remains a towering cultural icon of Breton life: countless hotels, bars, and restaurants today bear her name, which evokes in all Bretons visions of a golden age. She and her advisers sought to maintain an independent Brittany in 1489–1490, but quickly became embroiled in hostilities with France. Breton and French troops pillaged much of the duchy in 1490. Anne sought a powerful protector by becoming engaged to Maximilian of Austria (soon to be Holy Roman Emperor) in 1491; Charles voided the engagement, renounced his own prospective marriage to Marguerite (Maximilian's daughter), and married Anne himself. They had no children. When Charles died in 1498 Anne married his successor, Louis XII. The marriage produced a daughter, Claude, who later married Louis XII's successor-nephew, Francis I. Claude passed the duchy to her sons, Francis (who died young) and then Henry, who as King Henry II (1547–1559) brought Brittany into the royal family demesne.

Anne of Brittany sponsored many artists, in a wide range of media. Her *Great Book of Hours* is a magnificent example of early sixteenth-century book illumination, and her tomb, at Saint-Denis, one of the greatest French sculptures of its time. Anne and Louis allowed Brittany to remain largely independent, although they acted together to limit the independence of Breton towns by confiscating one of their key sources of revenue, the wine sales taxes. Despite its separate institutions, Brittany belonged firmly within the kingdom under both Louis XII and Francis I. Francis levied in Brittany the new taxes created in the 1520s and Bretons contributed large sums to the king's ransom after his capture at Pavia (1525). The Bretons grew sufficiently dissatisfied that the estates of Brittany themselves requested a treaty of union.

Francis, acting as protector of his son, signed a treaty of unification with the estates of Brittany at Plessis-Macé in September 1532. This treaty-edict laid out the fundamental privileges of the province. The Breton courts could preserve Breton customary law, which enshrined the complete equality of female and male heirs (commoners only) and extensive property rights for widows. The Breton estates kept control over taxes until 1789.

Brittany experienced peaceful prosperity for much of the fifteenth, sixteenth, and seventeenth centuries, in contrast with the bloody disasters of the fourteenth and end of the sixteenth centuries. Brittany exported goods all over Europe: salt from the Loire marshes, sent to Holland and the Baltic; Nantais wine, exported mainly to the southern Breton littoral; wheat and rye from Vannes, Cornouaille, Tréguier, and Saint-Brieuc to Nantes, Bordeaux, and Iberia. The interior heaths, so forbidding and seemingly so sterile, in fact supported a diverse pastoral and manufacturing economy, dominated by livestock products and linen cloth. Fishing villages dotted the coastline; Breton legends suggest local fishermen knew about the Grand Banks of Newfoundland long

before Columbus sailed. The Breton merchant marine dominated European coastal trade from the early fifteenth to the mid-sixteenth centuries and continued to play an important role long after that. In the sixteenth century Bretons such as Jacques Cartier of Saint-Malo spearheaded the exploration of Canada. Both as independent duchy and as royal province, Brittany maintained extensive commercial and cultural ties to England, Spain, Aquitaine, and the Low Countries. Ties between rural Léon, the greatest linen manufacturing center of Renaissance Europe, and England were so strong that English merchants sent their children to live in the countryside around Morlaix, so that they could become fluent in Breton.

Breton society strongly resembled that of other areas of France. Brittany had few serfs, but its network of powerful seignorial courts allowed the great nobles to control the province. Although these nobles dominated Breton politics even in the seventeenth century, the economic balance shifted to the towns, above all those involved in textile trade, like Saint-Malo, Morlaix, and Vitré. These towns took great pains to fortify themselves; we can see today the results in the town fortifications of Quimper, Dinan, and Guérande. The great nobles responded in kind, with castles overlooking such towns as Fougères, Vitré, and Pontivy.

Sixteenth-century trade somewhat shifted the axis of Breton development. Much of the cloth and grain went to Iberia, and great Spanish merchants settled in Brittany, above all in Nantes. Trade with Iberia brought in Jewish merchants fleeing persecution; documents of the time call them the "Portuguese." Nominal Catholics, they had to practice Judaism in secret, but they had a thriving community in the Saint-Nicolas suburb of Nantes by the early seventeenth century. Their community illustrates to us the remarkable cosmopolitan life of Renaissance Brittany.

BIBLIOGRAPHY

Collins, James B. *Classes, Estates, and Order in Early-Modern Brittany.* Cambridge, U.K., 1994.
Galliou, Patrick, and Michael Jones. *The Bretons.* Cambridge, Mass., 1991. See chapters 10–13.
Jones, Michael. *Ducal Brittany, 1364–1399.* London, 1970.
The following works contain extensive bibliographies; most titles are in French.
Croix, Alain. *L'âge d'or de la Bretagne: 1532–1675.* Rennes, France, 1993.
Leguay, Jean-Pierre, and Herve Martin. *Fastes et malheurs de la Bretagne ducale, 1213–1532.* Rennes, France, 1982.

Tanguy, Jean, ed. *La Bretagne province, 1532–1789.* Morlaix, France, 1986. See chapter 19 on rural religious art.

JAMES B. COLLINS

BRONZINO. *See* **Florence,** *subentry on* **Art of the Sixteenth Century.**

BROTHERHOODS. *See* **Confraternities.**

BROWNE, THOMAS (1605–1682), English essayist and physician. Favoring a learned, Latinate diction (but often contrasted to vivid Anglo-Saxon phrases), Browne writes a prose at once meditative and witty, conveying the impression of a complex, well-stocked mind speaking its thoughts as they unfold. He has been classified among the "anti-Ciceronian" stylists of the period in his preference for less-balanced sentence structures, for syntax that is frequently oblique and surprising.

Born in London, Thomas Browne was the son of a successful mercer, Thomas Browne, and his wife, Anne Garroway. At age ten, Browne went to Winchester College and in 1623 entered Broadgates Hall, Oxford, as a gentleman commoner. His tutor was Thomas Lushington, a high-church Anglican divine, with whom Browne later shared interests in Neoplatonism. In addition to the usual studies in moral philosophy, theology, Greek, and Hebrew, Browne benefited from newly established chairs in geometry and astronomy and a readership in human anatomy that included an annual dissection. Still, the English universities lagged well behind those on the Continent in medicine, and after taking his B.A. (1626) and M.A. (1629), he began a four-year sojourn abroad, studying first at Montpellier, then for a longer time at Padua, where Vesalius had pioneered anatomy in the previous century and where William Harvey had studied in the late 1590s. Browne completed his studies at Leiden, where he was certified M.D. in 1633. Beyond his medical learning, the experience of these four years also contributed significantly to the breadth of his intellectual interests and to the theological irenicism evident in all his writing.

Returning to England, Browne began a medical apprenticeship in Oxfordshire in 1634 and around the same time composed *Religio Medici* (1642), in which he not only describes the religion of a physician, but examines in witty and eloquent prose the workings of his own mind. "Now for my life," he exclaims, "it is a miracle of thirty years, which to relate, were not a History, but a piece of Poetry, and would sound to common ears like a fable." He refers not to the unremarkable external facts, but to the inner world of self, "the Microcosm of mine own frame that I cast mine eye on." The work circulated in manuscript before it was printed in a pirated edition in 1642, an authorized edition the following year, then six more in his lifetime.

Browne was incorporated M.D. in 1637 and that same year removed to Norwich, where he engaged in a wide medical practice and carried out frequent scientific and medical experiments. In 1641 he married Dorothy Mileham, and the two enjoyed a union as distinguished by its happiness as by its forty-one-year length. They had twelve children, five of whom survived to adulthood; his eldest son, Edward, followed him into medicine and achieved his own distinction in admission to the Royal Society and the Royal College of Physicians.

In 1646 Browne published *Pseudodoxia Epidemica,* an encyclopedic treatment of the common errors that infect human knowledge. Browne divided into seven books this consideration of errors ranging from the natural world to human society and history. The essays *Urne-Buriall* and *The Garden of Cyrus* were published together as companion pieces in 1658. The first uses the discovery of funeral urns near Walsingham as a basis for rumination on burial customs and death, and the second is a discussion, in response to the first essay, of life and growth. His *Letter to a Friend, upon the Occasion of the Death of his Intimate Friend* (1690) was published posthumously, as was the *Christian Morals* (1716), a specifically didactic work.

Browne was knighted by Charles II in 1671. He died on 19 October 1682. An attractive half-length portrait of Browne and his wife, painted shortly after their marriage and attributed to Joan Carlisle, is in the National Portrait Gallery, London.

BIBLIOGRAPHY

Primary Works

Browne, Sir Thomas. *The Major Works.* Edited by C. A. Patrides. Harmondsworth, U.K., 1977. Convenient edition of complete text of five major works with extracts from *Pseudodoxia Epidemica.*

Browne, Sir Thomas. *The Works of Sir Thomas Browne.* Edited by Geoffrey Keynes. 2d ed. 4 vols. London, 1964. Standard edition of Browne.

Secondary Works

Huntley, Frank L. *Sir Thomas Browne: A Biographical and Critical Study.* Ann Arbor, Mich., 1962. Classic critical study of Browne.

Post, Jonathan F. S. *Sir Thomas Browne.* Boston, 1987. Attractive introductory study of Browne, surveying his life and works.

MICHAEL O'CONNELL

BRUEGHEL FAMILY. The Brueghels were a dynasty of Flemish landscape, genre, and still life painters active from the mid-sixteenth to the early eighteenth century, chiefly at Antwerp. The founder and the most famous member was Pieter Bruegel the Elder, but his sons, especially Jan, achieved considerable reputation in their own right. The name is spelled in various ways. Pieter the Elder favored "Bruegel," but his sons used "Brueghel" or "Breughel."

Pieter the Elder (c. 1525–1569). According to his earliest biographer, Karel van Mander (*Het Schilderboeck,* 1604), Bruegel was a pupil of Pieter Coecke van Aelst, the leading Flemish artist of his day, after which he worked (1550–1551) with Pieter Baltens for Claude Dorizi, an artist and art dealer in Malines. Bruegel enrolled in the Antwerp artists' guild in 1550–1551, before departing on an extended trip to southern France (including Lyon), Italy, and the Alps. In Rome about 1553 he collaborated with the manuscript illuminator Giulio Clovio. Bruegel was in Antwerp from about 1555 to 1563, when he moved to Brussels and married Mayken Coecke (called Bessemers), daughter of Pieter Coecke; they had two children, Pieter the Younger and Jan. His association with the print publisher Hieronymus Cock probably introduced him to the mapmaker Abraham Ortelius, the printer Christophe Plantin, and other Flemish humanists.

Remarkably versatile in style and subject matter, Bruegel produced landscapes, religious and allegorical subjects, scenes of peasant festivities, depictions of Flemish proverbs, and compositions in the manner of Hieronymus Bosch. Bruegel's career falls into two major phases. In Antwerp he produced many designs for Cock's printmakers, among them the so-called *Large Landscapes, Vice* and *Virtue* series, satirical subjects (*Elck, The Alchemist*), and two scenes of a peasant kermis, or church festival (*Hoboken Kermis, St. Joris Kermis*). Bruegel made only one print himself, *Landscape with Rabbit Hunters,* etched in 1560. His earliest known paintings were done in Antwerp, *Parable of the Sower* (1557), *Fall of Icarus* (known in two versions), his first multifigured paintings, *Netherlandish Proverbs* (Berlin), and two panels in Vienna, *Children's Games* (1560) and *Carnival and Lent* (1559). All were inspired by Flemish speech and folk life, but with allegorical content, and possibly all three paintings were done in the manner of Bosch.

Once in Brussels, Bruegel continued producing designs for Cock but concentrated on painting. His patrons included Cardinal Antoine Perrenot de Granvelle and two wealthy government officials in Antwerp, Niclaes Jonghelinck and Jean Noirot (the latter's collection was unknown to scholars until 1995). For Jonghelinck, Bruegel painted the *Labors of the Months* (1565), a series of either six or twelve landscapes (the number is disputed), of which five survive, three in Vienna (*Hunters in the Snow, Gloomy Day, Return of the Herd*), and one each in Prague (*Haymaking*) and New York (*Harvesters*). Granvelle owned Bruegel's *Flight to Egypt* (1563) and other pictures, and Noirot possessed five paintings, four of them depicting peasant kermises or weddings (none can be identified with extant works). Bruegel's most important commission according to Van Mander came from the Brussels magistrates shortly before his death. Never executed, it was for a series of paintings, presumably landscapes, commemorating a recently completed canal linking Brussels with Antwerp.

Bruegel's art represents the culmination of the Flemish realistic tradition, often reviving styles and compositions of earlier generations. In his *Procession to Calvary* (1564; Vienna), his largest surviving painting and perhaps owned by Jonghelinck, Bruegel drew upon a traditional composition, possibly invented by Jan van Eyck, and adapted the holy figures from Rogier van der Weyden. His *Death of the Virgin* (1565; Banbury, Upton House) reworks deathbed scenes in earlier books of hours. Bruegel's interest in Bosch appears in some of his earliest print designs (*Big Fish Eat the Little Fish, Vices* series) and in three paintings, *Fall of the Rebel Angels* (1562; Brussels), *Dulle Griet* (Antwerp, Museum Mayer van den Bergh), and especially *Triumph of Death* (Madrid), which is closest to Bosch in its apocalyptic view of human destiny.

His landscapes range from depictions of the Flemish countryside, best seen in *Peasant and Bird Nester* (Vienna) and *Misanthrope* (Naples), to great vistas that infused the traditional Flemish world landscape style of Joachim Patinir and Herri de Bles with a new grandeur inspired by Bruegel's Alpine experience, especially in the *Large Landscapes* prints, *Months,* and *Conversion of Paul* (1567; Vienna). The same vast space and heroic scale distinguish his two paintings of the *Tower of Babel,* one dated 1563 (Vienna), the other (Rotterdam) probably done later. Bruegel's allegorical subjects, often satires of human folly presented with biting wit, share themes and attitudes with the literature and pageantry of the Flemish rhetoricians of his day, suggesting his participation in the *Violieren* chamber of rhetoric

Pieter Brueghel the Elder. *Peasant Wedding.* Painted c. 1566. KUNSTHISTORISCHES MUSEUM, VIENNA/FOTO MARBURG/ART RESOURCE

(which produced allegorical plays, farces, and poetry for various occasions), which was closely associated with the Antwerp artists' guild. A robust good humor pervades Bruegel's peasant scenes; the *Wedding Dance* (1566; Detroit) and two late pictures in Vienna, *Peasant Dance* and *Peasant Wedding,* also contain acute observations of human forms and psychology.

Despite his stay in Italy, Bruegel showed little interest in Italian art until his Brussels period. Many of his works from 1565 on, especially *Christ and the Woman Taken in Adultery* (London, Courtauld), *Land of Cockaigne* (1567; Munich), the Vienna peasant scenes, and two drawings, *Calumny of Apelles* (London, British Museum), and *Summer* (1568; Vienna, Albertina), show more concentrated compositions, larger-scaled, often monumental figures, possibly influenced by a study of Raphael's Vatican cartoons. Some of Bruegel's late paintings, *Massacre of the Innocents* (Vienna) and *Census at Bethlehem* (1566; Brussels), as well as three emblematic pictures

of 1568, *Parable of the Blind* (Naples), *Peasant and Bird Nester* (Vienna), and *Misanthrope* (Vienna), may comment on the troubled times inaugurating the Eighty Years' War (the war of Netherlands independence from Spain, 1568–1648). According to Van Mander, before his death Bruegel destroyed a number of his satirical drawings to save his wife from persecution, and he left her the *Magpie on the Gallows* (1568; Darmstadt), an enigmatic picture evoking an earlier Flemish landscape style. Several lost paintings are perhaps recorded in copies, including a *Crucifixion, Unfaithful Shepherd* (copy attributed to Marten van Cleef in Philadelphia), and *Peasants Fighting over a Card Game.*

Many of Bruegel's paintings were later acquired by Rudolph II, Holy Roman emperor (1576–1612), as well as by two Habsburg governors of the Spanish Netherlands, Archduke Ernst (1594–1595) and Leopold Wilhelm (1647–1656); many of their paintings are part of the great Bruegel collection now in Vienna. Bruegel's paintings and prints were endlessly copied and imitated; his peasant subjects and land-scapes influenced later Netherlandish artists, among them Adriaen Brouwer and Peter Paul Rubens (who owned several Bruegel pictures). Drawings in Bruegel's style, some apparently done as forgeries by Roelant and Jacob Savery, circulated under his name until the 1980s and 1990s. In his lifetime Bruegel was famed as a second Bosch, but Ortelius, who owned his *Death of the Virgin* and had it reproduced in a print for distribution to his friends, warmly praised Bruegel in a 1574 epitaph as a consummate imitator of nature who was the most perfect painter of his century. For Van Mander, Bruegel was chiefly a humorist of peasant origins, an image that persisted until the publication of Ortelius's epitaph in 1931. Pointing to his highly placed patrons and association with Ortelius and his circle, many scholars have seen Bruegel as a painter-philosopher whose art, even his peasant scenes, expresses profound philosophical or moral concepts, often expressed in disguised symbolism. In reaction to this view of an erudite and "hermetic" Bruegel, some critics emphasize both Bruegel's humor and the sources of his subject matter in traditional popular culture, especially its more festive aspects. Since 1970 the number of drawings thought to be by Bruegel has shrunk considerably through reattribution of a number of Alpine scenes and other landscapes, as well a series of peasant figures supposedly done after life, to artists working a generation later, possibly the Savery brothers.

Pieter the Younger ("Hell Brueghel"; 1564–1638).

The elder son and major successor of Pieter the Elder, Pieter the Younger was a pupil of Pieter Goetkindt and possibly Gillis van Coninxloo. He remained all his life in Antwerp, where he entered the artists' guild in 1585. He painted religious subjects and scenes of hell and conflagrations (which gave him his nickname), but specialized in copies or reworked versions of his father's pictures, including the *Massacre of the Innocents, Netherlandish Proverbs, Triumph of Death,* and many pictures of peasant weddings and kermises. He perhaps had access to his father's drawings, and his *Crucifixion,* known in several versions (good examples in Budapest and Hertogenbosch), may reflect a lost composition of Pieter the Elder. In his finest pictures, Pieter the Younger approaches his father in quality, but many inferior pictures attributed to him suggest an active workshop or were done by his son, Pieter III (1589–after 1634), who continued his father's style.

Jan the Elder (Velvet Brueghel; 1568–1625).

The younger son of Pieter the Elder, Jan lived after his father's death with his grandmother, Marie Bessemers, a miniaturist who, according to Van Mander, taught him watercolor; he was also a pupil of Pieter Goetkindt and perhaps the landscape painter Gillis van Coninxloo. After traveling in Germany, Brueghel was in Italy by about 1589. He worked for Cardinal Federigo Borromeo in Rome and Milan, and continued to paint pictures for him after returning to Antwerp in 1596. Jan entered the Antwerp painters' guild in 1597, becoming its dean in 1602. He was a friend of Pieter Paul Rubens, who painted a portrait of Jan and his family (London). Jan was the court painter to the governors of the Spanish Netherlands, Archduke Albert and the Infanta Isabella, for whom he painted a number of pictures. Among his pupils were his son Jan the Younger and Daniel Seghers.

A versatile artist like his father, Jan specialized in landscapes, flower pieces and other still-life subjects, and animals. Often painted on copper, his detailed, delicately executed pictures with their glowing, jewel-like colors earned him the epithet of "Velvet." He often collaborated with other artists, including Hans Rottenhammer (while in Rome), Rubens, and Hendrik van Balen, adding the flora and fauna; a joint effort with Rubens is their *Adam and Eve in Paradise* (1620; The Hague). Jan also painted floral borders around images of the Madonna and Child by other artists.

Jan the Elder was a prolific artist and his paintings can be found in many museums. His earliest landscapes, such as *Harbor* (1599; Munich) and *Battle of Arbela* (1602; Paris), reflect the world landscapes of his father, but he developed his own repertoire of forest and mountain views, as well as rural scenes showing country people at work and play, as in *Landscape with River* (1612; Indianapolis) and *Landscape with Windmills* (Munich). Some of his early landscape drawings were engraved by Aegidius Sadeler. Jan's detailed realism and love of nature also characterize his allegorical paintings, among them *Five Senses* (Madrid) and *Four Elements* (Rome), in collaboration with Rubens and Van Balen respectively. His pictures were very popular and were copied and imitated into the eighteenth century. Two of his sons were also painters; Jan the Younger (1601–1678), who imitated his father's pictures, and Ambrosius (1617–1675). Both artists in turn had sons who followed their fathers' profession.

[Pieter Bruegel the Elder's *The Blind Leading the Blind* appears in the color plates in this volume.]

BIBLIOGRAPHY

Gibson, Walter S. *Bruegel*. London and New York, 1977. Reprint, New York and London, 1988.

Grossmann, F. *Pieter Bruegel: Complete Edition of the Paintings*. 3d ed., rev. London, 1973.

Jong, Jan de, et al., eds. *Pieter Bruegel*. Zwolle, Netherlands, 1997. Collection of nine articles, mostly in English, on various aspects of Bruegel's art, with a nearly complete bibliography of publications on Bruegel.

Larsen, Erik. *Seventeenth Century Flemish Painting*. Freren, Germany, 1985. See pp. 26–27 and 31–37. Short but useful sections on Pieter Brueghel the Younger and Jan "Velvet" Brueghel.

Mielke, Hans. *Pieter Bruegel. Die Zeichnungen*. Turnhout, Belgium, 1996. Most recent catalog, with new attributions for many drawings formerly attributed to Bruegel.

Smolderen, Luc. "Tableaux de Jérôme Bosch, de Pierre Bruegel l'Ancien et de Frans Floris dispersés en vente publique à la monnaie d'Anvers en 1572." *Revue belge d'archéologie et d'histoire de l'art* 65 (1995): 33–41. First publication of an inventory of the important collection of Jean Noirot, including five paintings by Pieter Bruegel the Elder, with an English summary.

WALTER S. GIBSON

BRUGES. The Flemish town of Bruges (Dutch, Brugge), in the fourteenth century northern Europe's commercial capital and numbering forty thousand inhabitants, began a gradual decline in the fifteenth century. As a result of social and political unrest (including insurrections in 1436–1438, 1450, and 1488, causing the town to surrender several privileges each time), foreign merchants transferred their trading activities to other centers, particularly Antwerp, which eclipsed Bruges by 1500. The Reformation era sealed the town's fate. Bruges was given an episcopal see in 1559, but a pro-Calvinist council seized power in 1578 and joined the Union of Utrecht in 1580. In 1584 the town became part of the Spanish Netherlands. With the Flemish north coast remaining in Dutch Protestant hands, Bruges was cut off from the sea and lost its commercial functions.

Culturally, Bruges flowered in the fifteenth century, thanks mainly to the patronage of the dukes of Burgundy, who had acquired Flanders in 1384. From Philip the Good (1396–1467) to Mary of Burgundy (1457–1482), the Prinsenhof at Bruges was their favorite residence. The dukes and their officials especially stimulated the production of books (the Ghent-Bruges school of book illumination flourished c. 1475–1520). An important patron was Lodewijk van Gruuthuse (c. 1420–1492), governor of Holland and Zeeland. The English king Edward IV, who after his deposition in 1470 enjoyed Gruuthuse's hospitality, had several manuscripts copied for his library. The Early Netherlandish school of painting, centered at Bruges, originated when Jan van Eyck entered the service of Philip the Good in 1425; Bruges was his main residence during the last phase of his career (1432–1441). Petrus Christus, probably a student of van Eyck, spent his entire active life at Bruges (from 1444), like Hans Memling (from 1465) and Gerard David (from 1484). Court

Bruges. Map, late fifteenth century.

music played a significant role in the development of the Netherlandish school of music. Jacob Obrecht was cantor of St. Donatian's chapter from 1486 to 1491 and from 1499 to 1500.

Dutch literary life flourished outside the court (the language of which was French), especially in the chambers of rhetoric (literary guilds), present from 1428. Flandres's most important rhetorician, Anthonis de Roovere (c. 1430–1482), was awarded a town's pension from 1466. Printing was introduced by William Caxton, who published the first English book in 1473/74 in Bruges. Intellectual life centered around St. Donatian's chapter school. Important humanist scholars were Juan Luis Vives, who dedicated his *De subventione pauperum* (On the assistance of the poor; 1526) to the town council; Frans van Cranevelt, town pensionary from 1515 to 1522; Marcus Laurinus the Younger (1525–1581), collector of antiquities and patron of the painter and printer Hubert Goltzius (1525/26–1583); the historian Jacob de Meyere (1491–1552); and the jurist Joost de Damhouder (1507–1581). Jan Lernout (Janus Lernutius, 1545–1619) was the town's best Latin poet. After 1584 intellectual and religious life came to be dominated by the Jesuits and other religious orders.

In architecture a late Gothic, heavily ornamental style prevailed until the 1530s and, for private houses, even until the eighteenth century; about 440 mansions from the fifteenth to seventeenth centuries survive, including the fifteenth-century Gruuthuse palace. The first Renaissance building is the Civil Record Office (1534–1537). Painters likewise adapted late to the Italian style. Jan Provoost (c. 1465–1529) and Adriaan Ysenbrandt (or Isenbrandt; d. 1551) are transitional figures; with Lanceloot Blondeel (1498–1561) and Pieter Pourbus (1523/24–1584) mannerism triumphed, but meanwhile Brussels and Antwerp had become much more important artistic centers.

See also **Netherlands**, *subentry on* **Art in the Netherlands.**

BIBLIOGRAPHY

Haan, Corrie de, and Johan Oosterman. *Is Brugge groot?* Amsterdam, 1996. Anthology of Dutch literary and historical texts written at Bruges in the Burgundian era.

Houtte, J. A. van. *De geschiedenis van Brugge.* Tielt, Belgium, 1982. Detailed survey of the town's history.

Martens, Maximiliaan P. J. *Brugge en de Renaissance: Van Memling tot Pourbus.* Bruges, Belgium, 1998.

Wilson, Jean C. *Painting in Bruges at the Close of the Middle Ages: Studies in Society and Visual Culture.* University Park, Pa., 1998.

ISTVÁN BEJCZY

BRÛLART DE SILLERY, NICOLAS (1544–1624), French minister, chancellor of France. Born into an established family of royal officeholders, Sillery received legal training in France and Italy before entering royal service in the Parlement of Paris. In 1587 he was made *conseiller d'état* (counselor of state) and appointed ambassador to the Swiss Confederation by Henry III. Upon the accession of Henry IV (1589), Sillery opted to serve the heretic king and until 1595 kept intact France's vital supply of Swiss mercenaries for Henry's armies.

On his return to France, Sillery became a client of the secretary of state, Nicolas de Villeroy. He assisted Pomponne de Bellièvre's negotiation of the Peace of Vervins with Spain (1598), then undertook two more important missions: the dissolution of Henry's marriage to Margaret of Valois (1599–1600) and the renewal of France's alliance with the Swiss (1601–1602). When he returned to France, Sillery began to assist the aging chancellor Bellièvre at his tasks and, when Bellièvre fell from royal favor, was made keeper of the seals (1605) with succession to the chancellorship. In September 1607 he secured France's highest office.

Always pliable and ingratiating, Sillery, unlike Bellièvre, voiced no objections to royal policies. After Henry's death (1610), Sillery served the regency of Marie de Médicis until his dismissal in 1616. The assassination of Marie's favorite, Concino Concini, brought the chancellor back to power, where he remained until his death. With the outbreak of the Thirty Years' War (1618), Sillery sought to avoid French intervention, a policy reversed when Cardinal Richelieu came to power in 1624.

BIBLIOGRAPHY

Babelon, Jean Pierre. *Henri IV.* Paris, 1982.

Tapié, Victor-L. *France in the Age of Louis XIII and Richelieu.* Translated and edited by D. M. Lockie. New York, 1975.

EDMUND H. DICKERMAN

BRUNELLESCHI, FILIPPO (1377–1446), Italian architect, sculptor, and engineer. Brunelleschi was born in Florence, the second of three sons of an eminent Florentine family. His father, Ser Brunellesco di Lippo Lapi, was a notary in the employ of the republic and traveled throughout Europe. His mother was a member of the wealthy Spini family; part of her dowry was the house in Florence where Brunelleschi lived and died. With only a few exceptions, he did most of his work in his native city, where he also, from time to time, held minor political posts. Such details of his life as exist, apart from archival records, are supplied by the anonymous biography ascribed to his much younger contemporary Antonio di Tuccio Manetti (1423–1497), probably written in the 1480s. This work was the basis of Giorgio Vasari's biography, published long after Brunelleschi's time.

According to Manetti, the architect was a man of great intellect, who had been taught to read, write, and calculate, besides being given some "literary training" (instruction in Latin), in the expectation that he would follow his father's profession. From youth, however, he delighted in drawing and painting. In 1398 he was enrolled in the Silk Guild, the membership of which also included silver- and goldsmiths; in 1404 he became a master goldsmith.

Although Brunelleschi apparently never married, in about 1419, he adopted as his son and heir Andrea di Lazzaro Cavalcanti, Il Buggiano (1412–1462). This sculptor and architect worked with Brunelleschi on several late projects and did a bust of Brunelleschi (1447–1448) now in Florence Cathedral, where the architect is buried.

Earliest Works.   Between 1398 and 1400 Brunelleschi was commissioned to make four (still extant) silver altar figures for the cathedral of Pistoia (near Florence). Other early sculptural works include a life-size wooden statue of Saint Mary Magdalene (destroyed in a fire in 1471) for the basilica of Santo Spirito; and a wooden Crucifix (about 1410–1415), now in the Gondi Chapel of the church of Santa Maria Novella. Attesting to Brunelleschi's rank as a sculptor, he was invited in 1401 to compete with Lorenzo Ghiberti, among others, for the commission to execute the bronze doors of the Baptistery. The assigned theme was the sacrifice of Isaac. Unable to decide between Brunelleschi and Ghiberti, the judges offered the commission jointly, but according to legend, Brunelleschi refused to collaborate with Ghiberti. His bronze panel, a dramatically charged representation of the story, is today housed in the Bargello Museum in Florence.

Thenceforth, the artist turned from sculpture to architecture, and by 1419 was regarded as the leading architect of the day. From about 1402 to 1409 he may have made journeys to Rome with his close friend Donatello, as recounted by Manetti and elaborated upon by Vasari. In Rome they are said to have studied the architecture and sculpture of the ancients, made drawings and measurements (now lost), and performed excavations in order to examine the foundations of ancient Roman buildings.

Brunelleschi's Dome. Cathedral of Santa Maria del Fiore, Florence. ALINARI/ART RESOURCE

As a result of his investigations of classical architecture and his studies with the mathematician Paolo dal Pozzo Toscanelli, Brunelleschi became the first architect to work out a system of structural proportions based on mathematics and the principles of perspective. Indeed, documentary evidence shows that Brunelleschi was regarded by contemporaries as the inventor of linear perspective—which up to that time had been only intuitively understood and applied by artists. Manetti indicates that sometime between 1417 and 1420, Brunelleschi painted two perspective views (now lost) of the Baptistery in Florence, as seen from the door of the Cathedral, and the Palazzo della Signoria (Palazzo Vecchio), viewed from a few yards away. It was left to Leon Battista Alberti, however, to codify these findings in his *Della pittura* (On painting).

Brunelleschi in Florence.   Charged by the Silk Guild to build for them a shelter for foundlings, Brunelleschi designed between 1419 and 1424 the famous portico that became the first component of the piazza in front of the church of Santissima Annunziata. Long considered the first true Renaissance structure, this "wall architecture" (as it has been termed) is now recognized as, rather, a modification of Romanesque and late Gothic styles, reintroducing classical principles of restraint and geometric harmony. It profoundly influenced later Renaissance architecture, with its wide semicircular arches supporting a deep entablature and resting on delicate Corinthian columns. The somewhat austere elegance of the flat planes is relieved by the contrast between the grayish *pietra serena* (a soft sandstone) of the structural elements and the pale plaster walls—a characteristic feature of later Brunelleschian work—and by the roundels set in the spandrels of the arches. These were later filled in by Andrea della Robbia's glazed ceramic tondi of swaddled infants.

San Lorenzo. In 1419 Giovanni di Bicci de' Medici commissioned from the architect a sacristy intended to be a Medici family chapel and part of the projected rebuilding of the basilica of San Lorenzo. This so-called Old Sacristy is located off the left transept, across the church from Michelangelo's New Sacristy, and was constructed between 1421 and 1428, with later interior decoration by Donatello. It is a perfect cube, the center roofed by a hemispherical twelve-ribbed umbrella dome on deep pendentives. Its harmonious effect is achieved by the play of voids and flat surfaces—cubical and spherical forms—and the play of light and shadow.

Brunelleschi has traditionally been associated with the planning of the basilica proper, but since no construction went on from 1428 to about 1442, and Brunelleschi's name does not appear on pertinent documents after 1433, it is now thought that the actual building (with some modification of his plan) was carried on by Michelozzo and others. In any event, the church achieves its effect of visual harmony by mathematical means—proportions being based on a modular unit equivalent to the square of the crossing—and by the contrast between the darker stone of the nave vaults and the plain, lime-washed walls that stretch like white sails beneath them.

The Florence Cathedral dome. In 1417 the Opera del Duomo, the administrative body charged with the upkeep of the Cathedral of Santa Maria del Fiore, called on Brunelleschi to give his opinion on the construction of a dome for the unfinished Gothic edifice. No precedent existed for spanning such a vast octagonal space, 130 feet in diameter, only slightly smaller than the dome of the Pantheon in Rome. A wooden centering for support during construction would not hold, even if sufficient wood could be found to build one.

Applying his knowledge of Roman building methods, and borrowing an idea from the Baptistery dome, Brunelleschi proposed doing away with an armature altogether and erecting a conical dome with an inner and an outer shell, connected by eight principal ribs linked horizontally by rings of stone blocks. The interior ribs are repeated by the eight marble ribs that become a design feature on the tiled exterior of the dome. The vault was constructed of stone below and bricks at the higher levels, set in herringbone courses to spread the weight evenly.

Despite ridicule and opposition, the architect's idea was accepted and work began in 1420, with Ghiberti appointed (according to Manetti) to supervise the somewhat dubious scheme. Within a few years Brunelleschi was left in full authority as *capomaestro* (head architect, or foreman), devising special tools, cranes, hoists, and scaffolding to facilitate the work. His dome, finished and consecrated in 1436, is considered the greatest architectural and engineering feat of the fifteenth century.

Both of Brunelleschi's last designs for the Duomo, the lantern (1439) and the semicircular exedrae around the drum, are important structurally as well as aesthetically. The volutes that terminate the dome ribs on the lantern, and act as buttresses, make their first appearance in Renaissance architecture here; the deeply recessed niches of the exedrae, also functioning as buttresses, were part of Brunelleschi's design repertoire in his later churches.

Palazzo di Parte Guelfa. Brunelleschi's only extant palazzo was the rectangular assembly hall for the Guelph party administration, built over a vaulted lower story. Work may have begun in the mid-1420s but was interrupted by wars with Milan and Lucca and not resumed until 1442. The interior was incomplete at the architect's death.

Pazzi Chapel. Following a fire in 1423, Brunelleschi was commissioned by Andrea de' Pazzi to rebuild the chapter house in the cloisters of the church of Santa Croce as a chapel and family tomb. The structure is almost universally regarded as Brunelleschi's masterpiece. In many ways the Pazzi Chapel is similar to the Old Sacristy, but rectangular rather than cubical. At the center of the small, perfectly proportioned chapel, with deeply curved walls, rises an umbrella dome on pendentives decorated with four polychrome figures of the Evangelists, thought to have been designed by the architect himself. Because of lack of funds, building was only started in 1442 (after the donor's death) and went on after

Filippo Brunelleschi. **Nave and Choir of San Lorenzo, Florence.** Choir and transept begun c. 1425; nave designed 1434?; church built 1442 to 1470s. ALINARI/ART RESOURCE, NY

Brunelleschi's own death. The portico extending across the front, connecting the chapel with the surrounding cloisters, was much altered—for the worse, according to most architectural historians—from his original design.

Santa Maria degli Angeli. This convent oratory develops ideas begun in the San Lorenzo sacristy and the Pazzi Chapel, and is considered to be the first fully centralized Italian Renaissance church. Construction commenced in 1434 but was terminated three years later—another of Brunelleschi's projects left incomplete. Engravings, seemingly based on lost drawings, give an idea of the design, however: it was to be a rotunda, the interior ringed with eight deeply recessed chapels. The dome over the altar in the center of the octagonal interior is supported on piers carved to have a three-dimensional, sculptural quality. It is commonly surmised that the source of Brunelleschi's inspiration was the third-

century A.D. so-called Temple of Minerva Medica (actually a nymphaeum) in Rome. In 1503 a roof was added to the rotunda, and only in 1934 was the structure completed (amid much controversy) by the architect Rodolfo Sabatini.

Santo Spirito. Brunelleschi's last major church design, and the one that Manetti contends gave the architect his greatest satisfaction, was for a basilica on the south side of the Arno River. Begun about 1436 (1444 according to some accounts), Santo Spirito was not finished until 1482, long after Brunelleschi's death. Here he combined a traditional Latin cross ground plan with that for a centralized church, with an umbrella dome and oculus over the crossing. The plans, subsequently altered, called for a series of semicircular family chapels around the interior. Brunelleschi's original proposal was to have the church face north onto a piazza extending to the Arno, thus linking the basilica with city and river life;

but as this meant demolishing intervening residences, the plan was rejected. Nothing now remains of his original facade save the two volutes at the sides.

Engineer and Inventor. Recent research has revealed the extent of Brunelleschi's nonarchitectural work: experimenting with a system to improve the volume of the Duomo organs, designing shallow-draft boats for use on the Arno, designing an aqueduct in Assisi. As cathedral *capomaestro* he was employed also as a military engineer, and between 1423 and 1432 built, for example, fortifications in Pisa and other cities, and a dam to divert the Arno to flood the enemy city of Lucca (1430). Other records chronicle his inventions for stage machinery for the *sacre rappresentazioni* (religious dramas) performed in the churches. His last documented work was essentially sculptural: a wooden model (1443) of a pulpit in Santa Maria Novella. Installed in 1453, the structure has carved reliefs by his protégé Buggiano.

Attributions. Vasari credits Brunelleschi not only with producing a wooden model for the Medici Palace (which Cosimo de' Medici rejected as too sumptuous and likely to arouse envy) but also designing the nucleus of the Pitti Palace. This latter attribution, accepted in most texts, is much contested. The architectural historian Howard Saalman has concluded that the design is not Brunelleschi's; other recent studies confirm his view. Work was not even started for the Pitti family residence until some twelve years after Brunelleschi's death. On the other hand, a number of scholars now accept Vasari's attribution to the architect of the Badia Fiesolana, the monastery in nearby Fiesole rebuilt (1456ff.) under Cosimo de' Medici's sponsorship.

Once regarded as "the father of Renaissance architecture," Brunelleschi is now perceived instead as a transitional figure who reintroduced classical forms that were elaborated on by his high Renaissance successors but who remained in many ways linked to the fourteenth century. Despite the small number of his original, finished works, a marked progression can be traced from the flat, regular planes of his early churches to the more ornate sculptural quality of his later ones. One of the first to assert the professional autonomy of the architect (as in his defense of his scheme for the cathedral dome and his defiance of guild restrictions), Brunelleschi also remains relevant to architects today for his empirical approach and for the rational simplicity of his designs.

BIBLIOGRAPHY

Primary Works

Alberti, Leon Battista. *On Painting.* Translated by John R. Spencer. New Haven, Conn., 1956. Translation of *Della pittura* (1436). Dedicated to Brunelleschi, codifying his discoveries about linear perspective.

Manetti, Antonio di Tuccio. *Vita di Filippo di Ser Brunelleschi/ The Life of Brunelleschi.* English translation by Catherine Enggass. Edited by Howard Saalman. University Park, Pa., 1970. Highly partisan, valuable for descriptions of the state of Brunelleschi's buildings at end of his life, and for detailed account of construction of the cathedral dome.

Vasari, Giorgio. *Lives of the Painters, Sculptors, and Architects,* vol. 1. Revised edition by William Gaunt. London and New York, 1963. Translation of *Le vite de' più eccellenti architetti, pittori, et scultori italiani . . .* (1550). Colorful elaboration of Manetti's *Life,* written a century after the death of an architect Vasari presents as Michelangelo's prototype.

Secondary Works

Battisti, Eugenio. *Filippo Brunelleschi: The Complete Work.* Translated by Robert Erich Wolf. New York, 1981. Essential monograph. Comprehensive text with extensive photographs and diagrams, references to pertinent documents, chronology, and selective bibliography (1568–1980).

Benigni, Paola, ed. *Filippo Brunelleschi, l'uomo e l'artista: ricerche brunelleschiane.* Florence, 1977. Illustrated catalog of 1977 Brunelleschi Congress and exhibition of documents, held in Florence.

Bozzoni, Corrado, and Giovanni Carbonara. *Filippo Brunelleschi: Saggio di bibliografia.* 2 vols. Rome, 1977, 1979. Bibliography listing over 2,000 books and articles on Brunelleschi to end of 1978.

Fabriczy, Cornelius von. *Brunelleschi, Sein Leben und seine Werke.* Stuttgart, Germany, 1892. First comprehensive monograph on the artist, reconciling accounts of Manetti and Vasari with new documentary evidence.

Kemp, Martin. *The Science of Art: Optical Themes in Western Art from Brunelleschi to Seurat.* New Haven, Conn., 1990. Detailed discussion of Brunelleschi as "inventor" of linear perspective, with appendix on his demonstration paintings.

Prager, Frank D., and Gustina Scaglia. *Brunelleschi: Studies of His Technology and Inventions.* Cambridge, Mass., 1970.

Saalman, Howard. *Filippo Brunelleschi: The Cupola of Santa Maria del Fiore.* London, 1980. With companion volume, this work provides detailed analysis of Brunelleschi's architecture, supported by transcripts of extracts from relevant documents.

Saalman, Howard. *Filippo Brunelleschi: The Buildings.* London, 1993.

Zervas, D. Finiello. "Filippo Brunelleschi's Political Career." *Burlington Magazine* 121 (1979): 630–639. Documents activities from 1418 to 1432.

ELEANOR F. WEDGE

BRUNFELS, OTTO (1488–1534), Strasbourg humanist, scholar, teacher, linguist. Brunfels applied his knowledge of Greek and Latin to the Bible and to science. The latter interest and his commitment to Lutheranism kept him outside the inner circle of theologians and scholars in Reformed Strasbourg.

Born in Mainz, a cooper's son, Brunfels studied in Mainz and was influenced by the humanist Nicolas Gerbel. He received his M.A. c. 1510. In 1514 poor health and family and financial difficulties led him to enter the Carthusian monastery in Strasbourg. Despite his monastic seclusion, he renewed his friendship with Gerbel, who had come to Strasbourg; was associated with the Sélestat humanists; and became a friend of Ulrich von Hutten. Brunfels's two treatises published in 1519, *De corrigendis studiis* (On the reform of learning) and *Aphorismi institutionis puerorum* (Aphorisms for teaching boys), contributed to the humanists' efforts to reform education and to replace medieval textbooks with the ancient authors. Because Pythagoras had written that the truth could not be understood without geometry, Brunfels wrote that mathematics and medicine should be included in the school curriculum.

Influenced by Hutten and other followers of Luther, Brunfels converted in 1521. With another monk, Michael Herr, he escaped from the monastery. They were sheltered by Johann Schott, the printer of Hutten's polemic pamphlets, who also became Brunfels's protector and printer. Herr was forced to return to the convent. Brunfels joined Hutten at Ebernburg, Franz von Sickingen's asylum for the persecuted. Brunfels served as a reformed pastor until 1524 when he was called to Strasbourg to take charge of a Latin school organized by the city's reformers.

Settled at the school, Brunfels began his major work. The Strasbourg medical community had divided over the primacy of the Arab or the Greek physicians. Brunfels read the Greek medical texts then being printed in Venice and Paris. Convinced of the superiority of Dioscorides and Galen, he undertook a botany based on their texts. Schott organized a team of apothecaries and herb gatherers to aid Brunfels and Herr, now released from his vows. Johann Weyditz, an artist, was commissioned to draw each plant. The team worked for eleven years to produce *Herbarum vivae icones ad naturae imitationem* (Botany with pictures drawn according to nature; 1530–1536), a novel compilation of ancient and contemporary knowledge. The third and final volume appeared two years after Brunfels's death. Weyditz's illustrations portrayed each plant in bud, in flower, and in seed. Brunfels translated the texts of the Greek botanical writers, adding his own field observations.

A Christian humanist, Brunfels made biblical texts accessible in his *Pandectarum Veteris et Novi Testamenti* (Digest of the Old and New Testaments; 1527; German edition, 1529). *Helden Büchlin* (Book of heroes; 1529) presented popular biographies of biblical men and women. These early popularizations opened the Bible to the laity. Another, more scholarly work discussed forms of biblical discourse: *Pandectarum libri 23. de tropis, figuris et modis loquendi Scriptararum* (Digest of tropes, figures, and methods of scriptural discourse; 1528).

He moved to Basel as professor of medicine in 1532. In 1533 he was appointed city physician in Bern, where he died in 1534.

See also Botany.

BIBLIOGRAPHY

Chrisman, Miriam Usher. *Bibliography of Strasbourg Imprints, 1480–1599.* New Haven, Conn., 1982. Pages 100, 158, and 248.

Chrisman, Miriam Usher. *Lay Culture, Learned Culture: Books and Social Change in Strasbourg, 1480–1599.* New Haven, Conn., 1982. Pages 174–179 and 190–191.

Margolin, Jean-Claude. "Otto Brunfels dans le milieu évangélique rhénan." In *Strasbourg au coeur religieux du seizième siècle.* Edited by Georges Livet and Francis Rapp. Strasbourg, France, 1977. Pages 111–141.

MIRIAM USHER CHRISMAN

BRUNI, LEONARDO (c. 1370–1444), Italian humanist and historian, chancellor of Florence (1427–1444). Leonardo Bruni was the most important Italian humanist between Petrarch and Lorenzo Valla. He was born in the Tuscan town of Arezzo to Francesco (or Ceccho) and Bruna Bruni, probably in 1370.

Life. Bruni's father, Francesco Bruni, was a prosperous grain dealer with estates in the village of Marcena, north of Arezzo. But his death in 1386, followed by Bruna's in 1388, left the young Leonardo with few resources apart from the enviable command of Latin he had acquired in Arezzo's schools.

In the early 1390s Bruni went to study at the University of Florence with a view to following a career in law. In Florence he joined the circle of Coluccio Salutati, the humanist chancellor of Florence, of whose literary discussions Bruni gives a brilliant picture in his *Dialogi ad Petrum Histrum* (1405–1406; trans. *Dialogues Dedicated to Pier Paolo Vergerio*). His closest literary associate in this group was the scholar and book collector Niccolò Niccoli. During the same period in Florence he also studied Latin literature with Giovanni Malpaghini of Ravenna, an early exponent of Ciceronianism, and Greek with Manuel Chrysoloras, a Byzantine diplomat and educator. Bruni belonged to the first generation of Italian humanists to acquire a real command of the Greek language and was ultimately recognized as among the finest Latin stylists of his time.

In 1405 Bruni abandoned his legal studies and went to Rome, where, on Salutati's recommendation, he was appointed apostolic secretary to Pope Innocent VII. With the exception of a three-month period early in 1411, when he held the post of chancellor of Florence, Bruni stayed with the papal Curia for nearly a decade, serving a succession of popes, including Gregory XII, Alexander V, and John XXIII. When John XXIII was deposed by the Council of Constance (1414), Bruni returned to Florence to take up the life of a private citizen and man of letters. In 1416 he was granted Florentine citizenship and a tax privilege in recognition of his work on the *Historiarum Florentini populi libri XII* (Histories of the Florentine people in twelve books; composed between 1415 and 1444). In this period of literary retirement, Bruni also undertook numerous translation projects and composed his most important treatises, including *De recta interpretatione* (On correct translation; c. 1420), *De militia* (On knighthood; 1421), *De studiis et literis* (On literary study; 1422–1429), and the *Isagogicon moralis philosophiae* (Introduction to moral philosophy; 1424–1425).

In December 1427 the Florentine Signoria appointed Bruni chancellor of Florence, in which capacity he was responsible for overseeing the public correspondence of the Florentine government. By this date, as Florentine tax documents show, Bruni had become immensely wealthy. By one estimate, he ranked seventy-second among all Florentine taxpayers in 1427 and thus fell easily within the top one percent of the city's population in terms of net assets. To his professional and economic successes, Bruni added numerous civic honors. Since the 1420s he had served on many civic boards and delegations as well as on guild committees. But in the late 1430s, thanks presumably to the favor of the Medici party, he began to be chosen for major public offices. In 1437 he was made a member of the Twelve Good Men, one of the three main executive councils of state. Between 1439 and 1441 he was elected three times to serve on the Ten of War, the most powerful civic body in Florence. In 1443 he was drawn for the Priorate. Poggio Bracciolini reports that, had Bruni not died, he would in due course have been selected to serve as Standard-Bearer of Justice, Florence's highest civic dignity. Bruni died in March 1444, loaded with wealth, honors, and fame, and was voted a magnificent public funeral by the Signoria. Some years later, an elegant tomb, the work of Bernardo Rossellino, was erected in the church of Santa Croce as a memorial.

Bruni's fame extended beyond Florence. He was undoubtedly the best-known literary man of his day and the best-selling author of the fifteenth century. Thanks to his connections in the papal Curia, as well as to Florence's position at the center of the book trade, Bruni's writings began to circulate widely from the time of the Council of Constance. Over 3,200 manuscript books and nearly 200 incunabla editions containing his works survive from the quattrocento (fifteenth century), an extraordinary number. In contrast, the works of Lorenzo Valla survive in fewer than one hundred manuscripts and a handful of printed editions. Valla is far better known to modern students of the Renaissance, but Bruni was much more famous during the period itself.

Translations from the Greek. Bruni's fame during the Renaissance derived primarily from his historical writings and his translations from the Greek. As a translator Bruni's chief interests were in ancient Greek oratory, biography, history, and moral philosophy. In his first decade of literary activity Bruni produced a series of Latin versions from the Greek orators, illustrating the struggle of the Greek city-states against Philip of Macedon in the fourth century B.C. This included Demosthenes's four *Philippic Orations* (1405–1412), the *Oration for Diopeithes* (1406), the *Oration for Ctesiphon* or *On the Crown* (1407), and Aeschines's *Oration against Ctesiphon* (1412). Around the same time he translated a corpus of biographies of Greek and Roman heroes from Plutarch, including the lives of Marc Antony (before March 1405), Cato the Younger (1405–1413), Aemilius Paullus (before August 1409), the Gracchi (before March 1410), Sertorius (1410), Pyrrhus (1412), and Demosthenes (1412). Owing partly to the encouragement of Salutati and Chrysoloras, in this period Bruni also undertook to translate all the dialogues of Plato into Latin, though in the end he translated only four dialogues, the pseudo-Platonic *Epistulae* (Letters; 1427), and parts of two other dialogues. The four dialogues completely translated were the *Phaedo* (1404–1405), the *Apology* (first version 1404–1409; second version 1424–1427), the *Crito* (first version 1404–1409; second version 1424–1427), and the *Gorgias* (1409). In 1424 he translated the parts of the *Phaedrus* dealing with poetic inspiration and in 1435 "Alcibiades's Speech" from the *Symposium*. Bruni's interest in Socrates and Plato also led to his early translations of the *Hiero* (1401–1403) and the *Apology of Socrates* (soon after April

1407) by the fourth-century soldier and oligarch Xenophon.

Bruni's most popular translation—and, indeed, the most popular humanist text of the early Renaissance—was his version of St. Basil of Caesarea's *Epistula ad adolescentes* (Letter to young men; 1400–1401). St. Basil's letter encourages his young nephews to study the best works of pagan literature, especially the poets and Plato, and argues, citing the Bible, that Christians can benefit morally from knowledge of such literature. Bruni undertook his translation of this letter to support Salutati in the latter's controversies with clerical conservatives who opposed the study of the classics by Christian youth. This text became a kind of manifesto for the humanist movement in the fifteenth century and continued to be used in humanist polemics well into the seventeenth century. The work survives in nearly 450 manuscripts and in 91 printed editions.

If his translation of St. Basil's short letter was Bruni's most successful work, his most laborious was his project to retranslate the moral philosophy of Aristotle into humanistic Latin. Bruni worked on this for more than two decades, producing versions of the *Nicomachean Ethics* (1416), the pseudo-Aristotelian *Economics* (1420), and the *Politics* (1436–1438). Bruni's new versions were a direct challenge to the scholastic traditions inherited from the Middle Ages, which in Florence were represented chiefly by houses of study maintained by the various religious orders. Bruni's new *Ethics* translation, which emphasized correct classical diction and eloquence, was repeatedly attacked by the mendicants and their allies for its smooth ambiguity and lack of philosophical rigor. They compared it unfavorably with the thirteenth-century version of Robert Grosseteste, an English scholastic philosopher. These attacks led Bruni to compose his treatise *De recta interpretatione,* the first theoretical discussion of translation in European history. In this work he defended his method of translation *ad sententiam* (according to the sense) against his critics, who preferred the traditional technique of word-for-word translation (*ad verbum*).

Historical Writings. Thanks to Bruni's leading role in reviving political and military history in the ancient manner, he is generally regarded by students of historiography as the first modern historian. His historical writings range in subject matter from ancient Greece and Rome to modern Italy. His compositions in ancient history were mostly intended, in his words, to supplement "from the treasuries of the

Leonardo Bruni. Tomb by Bernardo Rossellino (1409–1464) in the church of Santa Croce, Florence. SCALA/ART RESOURCE

Greeks" the Latin histories that were available in his day. Thus, his *De primo bello punico commentarius* (History of the First Punic War; 1418–1422), based on Polybius's Greek histories, was intended to fill the gap left by the loss of the second decade of Livy's Roman histories. It celebrated the imperial expansion of the Roman republic, hinting at numerous parallels with recent Florentine history. Bruni's *De bello italico adversus Gothos* (Italian war against the Goths; 1441), based on Procopius, covers the history of Italy in late antiquity, a period neglected in the surviving Latin historiography. The *Rerum graecarum commentarius* (Commentary on Greek affairs; 1439), based on Xenophon's *Hellenica,* provides a narrative history of Greece in the early fourth century B.C. The latter two works also had a political message, evidently directed at the delegates attending the Council of Florence (1439). The first pointed out that the Greek empire had come to the aid of the Italians when Italy had been threatened by barbarians in the sixth century, while the second taught the oligarchic lesson that disaster follows when decisions are not made by prudent and educated citizens but are instead left to the rash judgment of the multitude. All of these works were translated into Italian during Bruni's lifetime and in some cases had a larger circulation in Italian than in the original Latin.

There is no doubt, however, that Bruni's masterpiece was *Historiarum Florentini populi,* a work that immediately achieved the status of an official history. It was composed over a period of more than a quarter century, from 1415 to 1444, and was translated into Italian by Donato Acciaiuoli in 1473 at the request of the Florentine Signoria. Book 1 ranges widely from the foundation of Florence in the first century B.C. down to the thirteenth century and is remarkable for its crisp and critical dismissal of the luxuriant founding myths so eagerly embraced in earlier Florentine chronicles. Books 2–12 cover the history of Florence from the death of Emperor Frederick II to the death of Giangaleazzo Visconti of Milan in 1402. They move at a much slower pace, chronicling each year's important events in the manner of Livy and Tacitus, who are also used as models of diction. These books concentrate primarily on the military affairs and institutional development of the republic, neglecting, especially in the later books, its internal political struggles. The work's major themes are the maintenance of Florentine liberty against foreign powers and the expansion of Florence's empire in Tuscany. In the history, Bruni aims to teach prudence in the conduct of foreign affairs, to provide models of good conduct, and to celebrate the achievements of the city in war and peace. Much admired throughout Italy as well as within Florence, the work inspired a host of imitators in the fifteenth and sixteenth centuries.

In 1440 Bruni also wrote a memoir of the first four decades of the fifteenth century, the *Rerum suo tempore gestarum commentarius* (Commentary on the events of his time), a work that includes some vignettes of his youth and career in the papal Curia, as well as an account of recent Italian history seen from a Florentine perspective. In the same year he published his *Epistolae familiares* (Familiar letters) in eight books (enlarged to nine books after his death), which further illustrated the political and cultural history of his lifetime.

Bruni composed four biographies, two in Latin and two in Italian. All four were of men he admired deeply. His purpose in writing their lives was to celebrate their achievements and to revise existing accounts of which he disapproved. The earliest was his biography of Cicero, the *Cicero novus* (New Cicero; 1412–1413), so called because it was intended to supplant the biography by Plutarch, which Bruni considered insufficiently laudatory. In 1429–1430 Bruni wrote a biography of his philosophical hero,

Aristotle, a work that emphasized the Greek philosopher's devotion to literature and praised him for his elegance of style. In Italian Bruni wrote parallel biographies of Petrarch and Dante (1436); these are probably the most widely read of his works in modern times. In the life of Petrarch Bruni emphasized the great poet's efforts to revive the literary Latin of classical antiquity, an achievement that Bruni believed had not been fully appreciated by his fellow citizens. The life of Dante aimed to correct the "frivolous" life by Boccaccio, which (according to Bruni) presents Dante as a lovesick poet. Bruni's life, by contrast, emphasizes Dante's merits as a soldier, a statesman, and a scholar.

Civic Humanism. During the Renaissance itself Bruni was best known as a translator, orator, and historian, but in modern times his fame has rested on his role as the first civic humanist in the modern republican tradition. This role was assigned to him by the great German-American scholar Hans Baron in his famous work *The Crisis of the Early Italian Renaissance* (1955), as well as in numerous other publications by Baron and his followers. According to Baron, the era of the Visconti wars between the duchy of Milan and the republic of Florence (1388–1402) led to a fusion between the republican folklore of the medieval Florentine commune and the literary tradition of Petrarchan humanism, which until then had been politically quietist. The 1402 crisis engendered a new breed of civic humanists who overturned traditional medieval values and forged a rich new ideology of republican liberty, civic participation, self-sacrifice, and devotion to the common good. This ideological transformation had broad effects and led to a new, more positive evaluation of family life, wealth, military service, and secular activities in general. Its influence could even be glimpsed, Baron claimed, in the new historical writing and the artistic languages of the early fifteenth century. According to other scholars, principally J. G. A. Pocock (*The Machiavellian Moment,* 1975), the Florentine republican tradition founded by Bruni was taken up and transformed by Machiavelli in the early sixteenth century and from there transmitted to early modern Britain and colonial America, where it inspired a republican ideology that found expression in such documents as the Declaration of Independence.

The Baron thesis remains widely influential, though it has also sustained a great deal of criticism in the half century since its major elements were formulated. Critics have charged that the period of the

Visconti wars did not have the transformative effects attributed to them by Baron and point out that theoretical defenses of republicanism were in circulation for a century before Bruni (for example, in the writings of Ptolemy of Lucca [c. 1237–1327]). Other critics have faulted Baron for his failure to recognize the narrow limits of *Florentina libertas* and the extent to which Florence's defense of Tuscan liberties was motivated by imperial ambitions. For such critics, civic humanism is often little more than oligarchic or imperialistic propaganda. Still others have denied that civic humanists were in fact deeply committed to the republican ideology they espoused (as Baron insisted they were) and have maintained that men like Bruni should be seen as "professional rhetoricians" rather than as civic humanists.

Few of Baron's critics have examined Bruni's political writings in detail, and even fewer have sought to place these writings in the broader context of Bruni's life and works or to analyze them in terms of the rhetorical practices of the time. Modern assessments of Bruni's political thought have been based on the *Laudatio Florentinae urbis* (Panegyric of the city of Florence; 1403–1404), the treatise *De militia* (On knighthood; 1421), the *Oratio in funere Ioannis Strozzae* (Oration for the funeral of Nanni Strozzi; 1428), and a treatise in Greek, *Peri tēs tōn Flōrentinōn politeias* (On the Florentine constitution; 1439). These compositions are very different from one another in character and scope. The first and third are examples of epideictic (or demonstrative) rhetoric where (according to Bruni's own statement) the orator is expected to employ a certain degree of embellishment and exaggeration. The second is a polemical assault on medieval, especially French, notions of chivalry that attempts to reinterpret knighthood as a special form of public service rooted in Greek political theory and Roman political practice. The last was a description of the Florentine constitution modeled on similar descriptions in Aristotle's *Politics* and was intended for the information of Greek visitors to the Council of Florence (as we know from a copy that ended up in the possession of Gemistus Pletho).

The *Panegyric* (modeled on an oration of Aelius Aristides) and the *Funeral Oration* (modeled on Pericles's funeral oration in Thucydides) both present an idealized image of Florence in which the Arno city is praised for its beauty, its military achievements, its virtuous behavior in peace and war, its cultural contributions, its well-ordered institutions, and its free way of life. Bruni emphasizes that Florentine citizens are equal under the law and have "equal hope of participating in public life." He paints Florence as a competitive meritocracy where the virtuous and well-educated rule and vie for honor. At first glance a number of statements in both orations seem remarkably populist. Read carefully in their rhetorical context, however, they do not really depart from the oligarchic ideology that Bruni promotes elsewhere in his writings. In these speeches, as well as in his histories and public letters, Bruni elaborates a "negative" conception of liberty that stresses political autonomy abroad and freedom from arbitrary power at home. Nowhere does he endorse a "positive" conception of liberty as self-rule, such as he might have found exemplified in Thucydides's account of Athenian democracy or in the corporatist traditions of the medieval Florentine commune.

A clearer glimpse of Bruni's own ideological profile is visible in his treatise *On the Constitution of the Florentines,* a late work less constricted by rhetorical imperatives than the above two orations. In this treatise Bruni describes Florence as a mixed polity in the Aristotelian sense, that is, a combination of democracy and aristocracy. Although the Florentine constitution has some democratic features, such as short terms of office, election by lot, and free speech, its predominant character is aristocratic. The power of "the best and the wealthy" (*hoi aristoi kai plousiotatoi*) is guaranteed by the infrequency of popular assemblies, by advisory bodies confined to honorable citizens, and by the prohibition of mechanics (those who worked with their hands) and the lower classes from participation in politics. Florence was at one time more democratic than it is now, says Bruni, but this changed when mercenary troops replaced popular militias. This situation naturally empowered the class who paid for them: the aristocracy of wealth and merit. Bruni displays no sign that he disapproves of this state of affairs. It is sometimes thought that the late treatise reflects Bruni's disillusionment with the decline of Florentine liberty under the rule of Cosimo de' Medici. But no real evidence supports this, and much contrary evidence indicates that Bruni accepted, and indeed flourished, under Medicean rule. As a political thinker Bruni, like most humanists of the fifteenth century, was throughout his life a conservative whose writings provided ideological support for the princely and oligarchic regimes he served. At the same time, he aimed to improve the character of those regimes by holding up a standard of wise and virtuous conduct derived from the example and teachings of classical antiquity.

See also Humanism, *subentry on* Italy; Renaissance, **Interpretations of the,** *subentry on* **Hans Baron.**

BIBLIOGRAPHY

Primary Works

Bruni, Leonardo. *Epistularum libri VIII* (Familiar letters in eight books). Edited by Laurentius Mehus. 2 vols. Florence, 1741.

Bruni, Leonardo. *Historiarum Florentini populi libri XII* (History of the Florentine people in twelve books). Edited by Emilio Santini. Vol. 19, Rerum italicarum scriptores. Città di Castello, Italy, 1926.

Bruni, Leonardo. *Humanistisch-philosophische Schriften.* Edited by Hans Baron. Leipzig, Germany, 1928. Still useful for the texts of the prefaces to Bruni's translations.

Bruni, Leonardo. *Opere letterarie e politiche.* Edited by Paolo Viti. Turin, Italy, 1996. Text editions with Italian translations of all of Bruni's works, excluding only the histories, familiar and public letters, and the prefaces.

The Humanism of Leonardo Bruni: Selected Texts. Edited by Gordon Griffiths, James Hankins, and David Thompson. Binghamton, N.Y., 1987. A representative sample of Bruni's works in English translation.

Secondary Works

Baron, Hans. *The Crisis of the Early Italian Renaissance: Civic Humanism and Republican Liberty in an Age of Classicism and Tyranny.* 2 vols. Princeton, N.J., 1955. Rev. ed. in one vol. 1966. Classic work on the origins of Florentine civic humanism.

Baron, Hans. *From Petrarch to Leonardo Bruni: Studies in Humanistic and Political Literature.* Chicago, 1968.

Baron, Hans. *In Search of Florentine Civic Humanism: Essays on the Transition from Medieval to Modern Thought.* 2 vols. Princeton, N.J., 1988. Baron's collected articles, expanded and revised.

Baron, Hans. "The Year of Leonardo Bruni's Birth and Methods for Determining the Ages of Humanists Born in the Trecento." *Speculum* 52 (1977): 582–625.

Hankins, James. "The Baron Thesis after Forty Years and Some Recent Studies on Leonardo Bruni." *Journal of the History of Ideas* 56 (1995): 1–30. Surveys recent Bruni scholarship.

Hankins, James. *Repertorium Brunianum: A Critical Guide to the Writings of Leonardo Bruni.* Vol. 1: *Handlist of Manuscripts.* Fonti per la Storia dell'Italia medievale, subsidia, vol. 5. Rome, 1997. Catalogue raisonné of Bruni's writings and their textual tradition, with full bibliographies; two more volumes are in progress.

Hankins, James, ed. *Renaissance Civic Humanism: Reappraisals and Reflections.* Cambridge, U.K., forthcoming. Revisionist essays on Bruni and civic humanism.

Luiso, Francesco Paolo. *Studi su l'Epistolario di Leonardo Bruni.* Edited by Lucia Gualdo Rosa. Rome, 1980. Indispensable for Bruni's biography.

Pocock, J. G. A. *The Machiavellian Moment: Florentine Political Thought and the Atlantic Republican Tradition.* Princeton, N.J., 1975.

Viti, Paolo. *Leonardo Bruni e Firenze: Studi sulle lettere pubbliche e private.* Florence, 1992. Pioneering work on Bruni's public correspondence.

Viti, Paolo, ed. *Leonardo Bruni Cancelliere della Repubblica di Firenze, Convegno di Studi, Firenze, 27–29 ottobre 1987.* Florence, 1990.

JAMES HANKINS

BRUNO, GIORDANO (1548–1600), Italian philosopher and Dominican friar, burned at the stake in Rome for his heretical teachings on 17 February 1600. Bruno was born in Nola (Campania), the son of a military officer. He was baptized Filippo but changed his name to Giordano when he entered the Dominican order in 1565. He was ordained a subdeacon in early 1570 and a deacon in early 1571 and was a priest by February 1572. Until 1576 he studied in various priories of the order, where he acquired a vast knowledge of philosophy, theology, and science, and became well versed in Latin and Italian letters. He had a prodigious memory, for which he was well known even in his youth. Suspected of heresy around 1575, presumably for reading the works of Erasmus when these were prohibited within the order, he fled from the priory in Naples on 30 January 1576 while awaiting trial on the charges. Thus began a long series of travels that occupied much of his adult life.

Travels in Europe. Bruno first went to Rome and then to various cities in northern Italy, including Venice, where he apparently published a lost work, *De' segni de' tempi* (On the signs of the times). In 1578 he journeyed to Chambéry in Savoy and was hosted there in a Dominican convent. He then moved on to Geneva, where he matriculated as professor of theology at the university on 20 May 1579. He soon quarreled with the Calvinists and was charged with defamation in a lawsuit a few months later. He quickly left Geneva for Lyon and then Toulouse. There he received the M. A. and lectured on Aristotle, mathematics, and Ramon Lull (c. 1232–1316) until 1581, when he departed for Paris in the summer or autumn. While at Toulouse he wrote another work, subsequently lost, *Clavis magna* (The great key).

In Paris Bruno gave "una lezione straordinaria," a course of thirty lectures on Thomas Aquinas that became the basis for his *De' predicamenti di Dio* (On God's predicaments), which remained unpublished and was lost. He did publish, however, three works, *De umbris idearum* (On the shadows of ideas), *Ars memoriae* (The art of memory), and *De compendiosa architectura et complementa artis Lullij* (On architecture and additions to Lull's art). The first of these works he organized around the number thirty, presenting five sets of thirty images that could be arranged in a memory wheel and that, in a magical way, would unlock the whole universe of knowledge for the reader. The second disparaged Aristotle and other honored philosophies, for which Bruno

Giordano Bruno. HULTON GETTY/LIAISON AGENCY

favored substituting his own method of learning. In this work and the third, he developed a new method for memorization and further extended the combinative art projected by Lull.

Bruno left Paris for England, arriving in London around April 1583. In June he traveled to Oxford and engaged in theological and philosophical debate with John Underhill, who became the vice-chancellor of the university the following year. During the summer Bruno returned to the university and began lecturing in Latin on the Copernican theory. When he was suspected of plagiarizing the lectures from a work of Marsilio Ficino, Bruno terminated the series and returned to London, where over the next two years he published an important sequence of works.

The first of these was a 1583 volume containing *Ars reminiscendi* (The art of remembering), *Explicatio triginta sigillorum* (An explanation of the thirty seals), and *Sigillus sigillorum* (The seal of seals), continuing the project begun in Paris. After this came a dialogue in Italian, *La cena de le ceneri* (The Ash Wednesday supper) of 1584, in which he developed a new cosmological scheme arising from Copernicus's critique of Ptolemy's geocentric system. In Bruno's view, space is infinite, with neither center nor boundary. In 1584 he also published three other works in Italian, *De la causa, principio, et uno* (On cause, principle, and one), *De l'infinito, universo, e mondi* (On the infinite universe and worlds), and *Spaccio della bestia trionfante* (Expulsion of the triumphant beast). In these works Bruno expounds the concepts that underlie his monistic view of life, his view of the universe as an image of, and emanation from, God, and his rationalist critique of traditional religion as based largely on superstition. These were complemented in 1585 by his *Cabala del cavallo pegaso* (Cabala of the horse Pegasus) and his *De gli eroici furori* (On heroic frenzies), which continued these themes and exalted Platonic love as leading to the contemplation of God.

Bruno returned to France in October 1585, where he began frequenting the library of the Abbey of Saint-Victor and published a work on Aristotle's *Physics,* as well as a dialogue on the differential compass, recently developed by Fabrizio Mordente. He left there for Germany in June 1586, where he visited various cities, including Wittenberg, took a side trip to Prague, then went to Helmstedt, and by June 1590 ended his travels in Frankfurt, from which he made a brief visit to Zürich.

At Wittenberg Bruno converted to Lutheranism, lectured on Aristotle's *Organon,* and wrote commentaries on Aristotle's physical works that were unpublished until 1891. He also continued work on Lull's combinatory logic and his own system of thought. At Prague he published the fruits of these labors in two Latin treatises, then left in 1588 for Helmstedt. Here, already excommunicated by the Catholics and the Calvinists, he was excommunicated by the Lutherans for his ideas. He also wrote a series of works on magic, also unpublished until 1891.

In Frankfurt Bruno published a series of poems in classical Latin entitled *De triplici minimo et mensura* (On the threefold minimum and measure). In these he expounded a type of atomism and explored concepts of the infinitely small and the infinitely large in the cosmos [*see* Matter, Structure of]. At Zurich in 1591 he taught scholastic philosophy. His lectures were an attempt at metaphysical synthesis and were published in Latin, partially at Zurich in 1596, in their entirety at Marburg in 1609. He then went back to Frankfurt, where he was invited by the Venetian patrician Giovanni Mocenigo to come to Venice and teach him the art of memory.

Trial and Death. Bruno arrived in Venice in late August 1591. Within a year Mocenigo became

307

dissatisfied with Bruno's teaching and on 21 May 1592 foiled his attempt to return to Frankfurt. A few days later Mocenigo brought charges against Bruno to the Venetian Inquisition. In these charges, he accused Bruno of disparaging religion, of not recognizing the three Persons in the Trinity, of blaspheming Christ, of not believing in transubstantiation, of claiming that the world is eternal and that there are infinite worlds, of believing in metempsychosis, of practicing magical arts, of denying the virginity of Mary, and other heresies.

At first it appeared that the Venetian Inquisitors would throw out the charges against Bruno. But the Roman Inquisition became involved in the case and arranged to extradite him. On 17 February 1593 Bruno arrived in Rome and was incarcerated by the Holy Office. His trial was long and drawn out. Additional charges were brought against him. On 8 February 1600 Bruno was sentenced to be burned at the stake. And in the early hours of Thursday 17 February he was put to death in Rome's Campo dei Fiori.

Bruno's focus on memory and its symbolic representations shows a great debt to the thought of the Catalan polymath Ramon Lull. Bruno also sought to develop a materialist naturalism indebted in many ways to the new philosophy of nature advanced by Bernardino Telesio (1509–1588). But in the end he opted for a monism that would comprehend both the finite and the infinite, along the lines of the coincidence of opposites earlier taught by Nicholas of Cusa (circa 1401–1464). To these elements must be added Bruno's personal fascination with magic and pantheism, which drove him in the direction of idolatry and even demonolatry. The key to his thought may well have been hermeticism, as Frances Yates has argued cogently. But behind it all was his irresistible urge to be a free-thinker, to cast aside the revealed religion of Jews and Christians for a natural religion of his own devising, to question all traditional philosophies except the overarching materialism of a Lucretius (c.95–c.55 B.C.). Perhaps that is why Bruno's death at the hands of the Roman Inquisition has made him, for many, a martyr for the cause of freedom of thought [see Libertinism].

Yet Bruno's brilliance and original thought has to be counterbalanced by his volatile personality, which combined an intense love of wisdom with a temperament that could be violent and intolerant. At a time when Europe was faced with religious crises and was undergoing painful and complex changes, Bruno refused to accept any societal responsibility in either church or state. His teachings were cryptic, suffused with polemics, and strongly influenced by his individual circumstances. Nevertheless, he did incorporate in his vision many themes that are characteristic of Renaissance thought, and for this his writings are worthy of serious study.

BIBLIOGRAPHY

Primary Works

Bruno, Giordano. *The Ash Wednesday Supper.* Translated by Edward A. Gosselin and Lawrence S. Lerner. Toronto, 1995.

Bruno, Giordano. *The Ash Wednesday Supper.* Translated by Stanley Jaki. The Hague, 1975.

Bruno, Giordano. *Dialoghi italiani.* Edited by Giovanni Aquilecchia. Florence, 1958.

Bruno, Giordano. *The Infinite in Giordano Bruno, with a Translation of His Dialogue* Concerning the Cause, Principle, and One. Translated by Sidney T. Greenberg. New York, 1950.

Bruno, Giordano. *The Expulsion of the Triumphant Beast.* Translated by Arthur Imerti. New Brunswick, N.J., 1964.

Bruno, Giordano. *Giordano Bruno: His Life and Thought with an Annotated Translation of* On the Infinite Universe and Worlds. Translated by Dorothea Waley Singer. New York, 1968.

Bruno, Giordano. *The Heroic Frenzies.* Translated by Paul E. Memmo Jr. Chapel Hill, N.C., 1965.

Bruno, Giordano. *On the Composition of Images, Signs, and Ideas.* Translated by Charles Doria. Edited by Dick Higgins. New York, 1991.

Bruno, Giordano. *Opera latine conscripta.* Edited by F. Fiorentino. Naples and Florence, 1879–1881.

Secondary Works

Aquilecchia, Giovanni. *Giordano Bruno.* Rome, 1971.

Atanasijevic, Ksenija. *The Metaphysical and Geometrical Doctrine of Bruno. As Given in His Work* De Triplici Minimo. Translated from the French by George Vid Tomashevich. St. Louis, Mo., 1972.

Ciliberto, M. *Giordano Bruno.* Rome, 1990.

Copenhaver, Brian, and Charles B. Schmitt. *Renaissance Philosophy.* A History of Western Philosophy, 3. Oxford and New York, 1992. Chapter 5.

Firpo, Luigi. *Il proceso de Giordano Bruno.* Edited by Diego Quaglioni. Rome, 1993.

Yates, Frances A. *The Art of Memory.* Chicago, 1966.

Yates, Frances A. *Giordano Bruno and the Hermetic Tradition.* London, 1964.

Yates, Frances A. *Lull and Bruno: Collected Essays.* Vol. 1. London, 1982.

PAUL COLILLI

BRUNSWICK-WOLFENBÜTTEL. The dukes of Brunswick-Wolfenbüttel were the last of the north German princes to introduce the Lutheran faith into their territories. In 1568 the accession of Duke Julius (1528–1589) marked both the end of Catholicism and an upsurge in humanist learning focused on the Wolfenbüttel court.

Patrons of Learning. Julius, who had studied in Louvain and traveled through France, founded the University of Helmstedt in 1576 with the main intention of schooling Lutheran clergy. The university statutes, however, stressed the need for a broad humanist program and paved the way for the independent-minded teachers of later decades, such as the political theorist Johannes Caselius, the professor of law Herman Conring, and the philosopher Giordano Bruno.

The building activity of Julius's stepmother, Sophia of Poland (1522–1575), and of his son, Heinrich Julius (1564–1613), introduced Italianate Renaissance architecture into the region, both in Wolfenbüttel (the church, arsenal, and chancellery) and Helmstedt (the university). The Wolfenbüttel court was also an important center of musical culture, with composers such as Michael Praetorius, Heinrich Schütz, and Johann Rosenmüller acting as court musicians.

Founding the Library. It was Duke Julius who founded the first court library in Wolfenbüttel in 1572, when he issued a decree regulating the use of his collection and appointed the composer Leonhart Schröter as its first librarian. The treasures collected by Julius include the only extant copy of the first illustrated printed book in the French language, *Le livre de Melusine* (The book of Melusine; Geneva, 1478), and several valuable medieval collections that were incorporated into the Wolfenbüttel library as a result of the secularization of local monasteries that accompanied his introduction of the Reformation. Books belonging to Sophia of Poland, who had a library of approximately 450 imprints, were clearly also added to the collection after her death in 1575.

Heinrich Julius, successor to Julius, was a dramatist and a great patron of the arts who spent much time as a councilor at the court of Rudolf II (ruled 1576–1612) in Prague. He was also responsible for significant additions to the Wolfenbüttel library, including the acquisition of books from the Aurifaber collection and books and manuscripts belonging to Matthias Flacius Illyricus, the proponent of orthodox Lutheranism and adversary of Philipp Melanchthon. In 1618 Heinrich Julius's son donated the Wolfenbüttel court library to the University of Helmstedt. The books returned to Wolfenbüttel, however, after the dissolution of the university in the nineteenth century.

Duke August the Younger. In 1635, after the duchy had fallen vacant, Duke August the Younger (1579–1666) acceded at the age of fifty-six. He was not actually able to take up residence in Wolfenbüttel until 1643, after he had concluded the Peace of Goslar in 1642, effectively taking the duchy

out of the Thirty Years' War (1618–1648). The duke was an avid collector of books and manuscripts. In 1644 he had his books transferred to Wolfenbüttel, where they were housed in the stables building on the castle square. August brought fifty thousand imprints with him, and over the next thirty years his collection grew to over 135,000 works, becoming one of the largest libraries in Europe. The library reflects his universal interests, with a strong bias toward Lutheran theology. As a young man, August had received a humanist education, studying at the universities of Rostock and Tübingen, after which he traveled extensively in Germany, France, and Italy.

The duke retained a passion for the Italian language and its literature throughout his life. He was a member of the Fruchtbringende Gesellschaft (Fruitbearing Society), a German academy founded in 1617, based on the model of the Florentine Accademia della Crusca (Academy of the Chaff), which promoted the Tuscan language. The main aim of the Fruchtbringende Gesellschaft was to promote the development of vernacular German into a poetic language by encouraging the translation of models from French and Italian Renaissance literature, such as the works of Ludovico Ariosto or Giovanni Boccaccio. August corresponded with a network of agents throughout Europe who sent him books, objects of art, and political news.

In contrast to other bibliophile aristocrats, the duke was not just a collector but also a librarian. At a time when, even in university libraries, cataloging was rare, he organized and cataloged his library in twenty subject categories. Each book was accorded a shelf mark with the possibility of using a decimal point, which allowed the collection to be augmented without problems. This was a unique system, and it reflected the duke's concept of a working library that served as a scholarly instrument rather than an object of princely ostentation.

In the course of his collecting life, August managed to acquire innumerable treasures of medieval and Renaissance book art, including nine of the famous late-fifteenth-century illuminated manuscripts from the collection of Matthias Corvinus, king of Hungary, among them three works by the Florentine Neoplatonist philosopher Marsilio Ficino (1433–1499).

The Library after Duke August. Dukes and duchesses of succeeding generations donated valuable collections to the library, although there was no continuation of the systematic acquisitions practiced by Duke August. An important library with holdings from the late Renaissance is the collection of twelve thousand imprints belonging to the Alvensleben family, on permanent loan to the library since 1975. The central figure responsible for this collection is Joachim von Alvensleben (1514–1588), a widely traveled member of the landed gentry who had studied law in France, the Low Countries, and Italy for a total of fifteen years. His library is distinguished by his humanist interests and by the dictates of administrative and ecclesiastical reforms confronting the German aristocracy in the sixteenth century.

At the beginning of the eighteenth century, Duke August's successor commissioned a library building to house the collection, the famous Bibliotheca Rotunda, the first freestanding secular library building in Europe in the modern age. The philosopher Gottfried Wilhelm Leibniz, librarian in Wolfenbüttel from 1691 to 1716, oversaw planning for the Rotunda, which was later taken as a model for James Gibbs's Radcliffe Camera (1749) at Oxford and Anthony Panizzi's British Museum reading room (1857).

See also Libraries.

BIBLIOGRAPHY

Arnold, Werner. "Adelsbildung in Mitteldeutschland. Joachim von Alvensleben und seine Bibliothek." In *Bibliotheken und Bücher im Zeitalter der Renaissance*. Edited by Werner Arnold. Wolfenbütteler Abhandlungen zur Renaissanceforschung, 16. Wiesbaden, Germany, 1997. Pages 167–194.

Heinemann, Otto von. *Die Herzogliche Bibliothek zu Wolfenbüttel, 1550–1893*. 2d ed. Wolfenbüttel, Germany, 1894. Reprint, Amsterdam, 1969.

Katte, Maria von. "Die 'Bibliotheca Selenica' von 1586 bis 1612. Die Anfänge der Bibliothek des Herzogs August zu Braunschweig und Lüneburg." *Wolfenbütteler Beiträge* 3 (1978): 135–153.

Katte, Maria von. "Herzog August und die Kataloge seiner Bibliothek." *Wolfenbütteler Beiträge* 1 (1972): 168–199.

Pirozynski, Jan. *Die Herzogin Sophie von Braunschweig-Wolfenbüttel aus dem Hause der Jagiellonen (1522–1575) und ihre Bibliothek*. Wolfenbütteler Schriften zur Geschichte des Buchwesens, 18. Wiesbaden, Germany, 1992.

JILL BEPLER

BRUSSELS. If a single date marks the start of the Renaissance in Brussels, it is 1531. In that year the governess of the Low Countries, Mary of Hungary, moved her court from Mechelen to Brussels, while her brother, the emperor Charles V, established three collateral councils there to promote more centralized rule. The presence of the court and these administrative institutions stimulated the business of art. Under the dukes of Burgundy, Brussels had already experienced an early bloom, but the definitive establishment of this city of 35,000 as a political and social center brought a luxuriant flowering.

Tangible evidence of the city's medieval prosperity, made possible by its internationally celebrated cloth industry, included the Gothic church of Saint Gudule (thirteenth to fifteenth centuries) and a magnificent town hall (1402–1454). By the end of the fifteenth century, the cloth guilds were replaced as the leading lights in Brussels by the carpet and tapestry weavers, renowned for their depictions of greenery in all manner of plant and flower motifs. But in the sixteenth century Italian influences came to dominate wall tapestries, especially in the work of Pieter van Aelst, who in 1516 was commissioned by Pope Leo X to fashion a series of tapestries for the walls of the Sistine Chapel.

A similar evolution toward the Italian style could be found in the painting guilds. While Rogier van der Weyden and his fifteenth-century school represented the high point of the Flemish Primitives, from the sixteenth century onward the influence of the Italian Renaissance held sway in both technique and theme, as reflected in the work of Barend van Orley (c. 1488–1541), Pieter Coecke van Aelst (1502–1550), Michiel Coxcie (1499–1592), and Anthonis Mor (1517/19–1576), the court painter of both Charles V and Philip II. Of special importance was Pieter Brueghel the Elder (1525–1569), who fabricated a highly original oeuvre in which human beings, in all their deeds and slothfulness, stood central, and who became the progenitor of a famous painting dynasty active in Brussels and elsewhere.

The Renaissance also influenced the architecture of Brussels. The presence of the court prompted many nobles to build residences there: the Egmonts, Brederodes, Croy, and other leading families saw to the construction of spacious "hôtels" for themselves, especially in the neighborhood of the church of Our Lady of the Zavel. The shining example of a Renaissance palace (now ruined) was surely that of Antoine Perrenot de Granvelle, later a cardinal. However, genuine Renaissance churches were not to be found in Brussels. Many long-standing Gothic projects received their finishing touches only in the sixteenth century, and any churches begun after that date were influenced more by the baroque.

Despite its strong role in the plastic arts, Brussels was no great center of humanism. The influence of the printing industry was rather limited, especially in comparison to Antwerp. Writers worthy of note included the rhetorician Jan Baptiste Houwaert (1533–1599) and Philips van Marnix van Sint Aldegonde (1540–1598) in Dutch and French literature. In the field of education, the Latin school of the chapter of St. Gudule (the "Great School") and the Latin school

The Royal Palace, Brussels. Anonymous drawing, sixteenth century. JOHNNY VAN HAEFTEN GALLERY, LONDON, U.K./THE BRIDGEMAN ART LIBRARY

of the Brethren of the Common Life (1504) deserve mention. For higher education interested Brusselaars had to travel to nearby Leuven (Louvain), where the medical faculty included Andreas Vesalius (1514–1564), a native of Brussels who achieved his fame outside the city, especially through his pathbreaking *De humani corporis fabrica libri septem* (Seven books on the structure of the human body; Basel, 1543). Brussels played no great role in the development of polyphonic music either, despite the prominence of other southern Netherlanders in that field.

The revolt that broke out during the reign of Philip II of Spain dragged Brussels and all the Netherlands into the bog of civil war for eighty years (1568–1648) and dampened the newfound glory and power of the capital city. Though the impact of early religious troubles caused by the Reformation had been limited for decades, the perceived inflexibility of the Spanish king, in both religious and political matters, led to the outbreak of genuine war in the 1560s. The execution of the local counts Egmont and Hoorne at the Grand Market of Brussels on 5 June 1568 marked the height of the repression effected by the king's new commander in chief in the Netherlands, the duke of Alba. The last quarter of the sixteenth century was a tumultuous and unstable period for the Netherlands, as many provinces de-

clared independence from Spain. Only after the successful recovery of the southern provinces during the 1580s, achieved by the gifted general Alessandro Farnese, did Brussels (1585) and other great cities return to Spanish rule, while the northern provinces became known as the new Dutch Republic.

When Philip II ceded the Spanish Netherlands in 1598 to his daughter Isabella and her new husband, Archduke Albert of Austria, yet another turning point was reached. Especially during the period of the Twelve Years' Truce (1609–1621), the new state enjoyed a moment of economic prosperity and well-being. Brussels under the archdukes became once again a capital city of great international allure and diplomatic importance. The patronage of the archdukes and the beginning of strong Catholic reform helped to resurrect all artistic endeavors. Peter Paul Rubens and Anthony van Dyck were not native Brusselaars, but both worked as court painters in the city. Other leading painters of the early period included Wenceslas Coebergher (1557/61–1634) and Theodore van Loon (1581–1667).

The relative peace afforded by the Twelve Years' Truce led to another feverish period of building in the city, resulting in countless baroque churches and monasteries, often with the financial support of the archdukes. The colleges of the Augustinians (1601) and Jesuits (1604) expanded and in a short time overwhelmed the old Latin schools. The churches of both colleges, built respectively by Wenceslas Coebergher and Jacques Francquart (1583–1651) and later destroyed, were quintessential examples of the early baroque. Most of the baroque buildings that still survive date from after 1650.

The artistic guilds continued to profit during the seventeenth century from the presence of the court. The tapestry industry also remained important, though foreign competition increased as the century wore on. The lace industry even experienced a significant expansion during this time.

The foremost buildings still surviving from the period between 1450 and 1650 include the Town Hall, the Broodhuis (1512–1536; razed and rebuilt in 1873–1885), the Nassau Chapel, the Clèves-Ravensteinhof (fifteenth to sixteenth centuries), the church of Our Lady of the Zavel (fifteenth to sixteenth centuries), the Kapellekerk (twelfth to sixteenth centuries), and Saint Gudule church (thirteenth to fifteenth centuries; now a cathedral). Brilliant examples of Renaissance painting are housed in the Museum voor Oude Kunst (Museum of Fine Art).

See also Netherlands, *subentries on* Netherlands in the Renaissance *and* Art in the Netherlands.

BIBLIOGRAPHY

Martiny, V. G. *Bruxelles: L'architecture des origines à 1900.* Brussels, 1980.

Saintenoy, P. *Les arts et les artistes à la cour de Bruxelles.* 3 vols. Brussels, 1932–1935.

Stengers, J., ed. *Brussel: groei van een hoofdstad.* Antwerp, Belgium, 1979.

EDDY PUT

Translated from Dutch by Craig Harline

BUCER, MARTIN (also Butzer, Bucerus; 1491–1551), German Protestant Reformer, theologian, and polemicist. Born to a family of artisans in Sélestat in central Alsace, Bucer entered the Dominican order around 1507 and attended the town's famous Latin school. At Heidelberg, where he matriculated in January 1517, he studied Greek and developed an interest in Erasmian humanism. His theology evolved under the dual influence of Erasmus and Luther. Secularized in April 1521, he joined the circle around Franz von Sickingen, married, briefly attempted a church reform at Wissembourg in northern Alsace, and arrived, an excommunicated refugee, at Strasbourg in May 1523.

His first published writing, *Das ym selbs niemant sonder anderen leben soll* (That no one should live for himself, but rather for others; 1523), formulated his theology in a recognizably Bucerian form: Christ's death on the cross enables the believer, with the aid of the Holy Spirit, to live and act in accordance with God's original divine order. Through all subsequent twists and turns, Bucer's theology retained its relative emphasis on ethics, love, the action of the Holy Spirit, and sanctification. Together with Huldrych Zwingli (1484–1531) of Zurich, he became a leading adapter of Luther's teachings to the German burghers. In the mounting quarrel between Zwingli and Luther, he took Zwingli's side at the Disputation of Bern in 1528 and at the Marburg Colloquy in 1529.

During the civic struggles over the reform at Strasbourg during the 1520s, Bucer played a supporting role to the leading civic reformer, Wolfgang Capito. At the Imperial Diet of Augsburg in 1530, he and Capito drafted the Four-Cities' Confession (Tetrapolitana), which restated their Zwinglian ("spiritualist") understanding of the Eucharist. Subsequently, Bucer was recruited for Strasbourg's policy of military alliance with the Lutheran princes and cities, and his tireless work for this cause made him a Protestant churchman of the first rank. Unity was reached at Wittenberg in 1536 on the basis of Luther's understanding of a "sacramental union" between Christ's presence and the elements of the Eucharist. This removed barriers to religious unity and political collaboration, though at the price of cutting political ties to Strasbourg's Swiss allies at Basel, Bern, and Zurich. In the following years, Bucer became one of the empire's leading Evangelical churchmen through his work to reform churches at Ulm, Frankfurt am Main, Augsburg, and—somewhat later—Hamburg and Cologne.

In 1533 Bucer engaged in a struggle to rid Strasbourg of Anabaptists and other sectarian separatists and to establish a system of compulsory religious discipline there. With the magistrates' backing he achieved the first goal in 1534 with the proclamation of Strasbourg's first Evangelical church order, but the second goal eluded him then, again during a second synod in 1539, and once more during the early 1540s. Bucer became very close to John Calvin during the latter's Strasbourg period (1538–1541). He also published his commentary on Romans and expanded the commentaries on the synoptic Gospels and other biblical books he had composed and published during the late 1520s. His most important programmatic writing, *Von der waren Seelsorge und dem rechten Hirtendienst* (Concerning true pastoral care; 1538), gave definite shape to the doctrine that put him most at odds with Strasbourg's magistrates:

authority over the local church was given by God to the faithful, that is, to the true Christians, not to the heads of the civic community.

The 1540s brought the collapse of nearly everything Bucer had helped to build during the previous decade. By this time he stood emotionally closer to Landgrave Philip of Hesse than to his Strasbourg partner, the magistrate Jacob Sturm, and he was one of the few public defenders of Philip's bigamous second marriage in 1539–1540. He tried but failed to persuade the Protestant princes to consign the ecclesiastical properties to support the churches and schools. His participation in the reformation of the electorate of Cologne in the early 1540s came to naught, and he quarreled with Sturm over the Evangelicals' seizure of Brunswick-Wolfenbüttel in 1542. Following the Schmalkaldic League's defeat by Charles V in 1546–1547, Bucer defied Sturm by agitating against the emperor's temporary religious settlement, the Interim of Augsburg, but failed to raise Strasbourg against its magistrates. Beaten on all sides, Bucer was expelled from Strasbourg in January 1549. He and Paul Fagius accepted Archbishop Thomas Cranmer's invitation to England, where he received a Cambridge professorship. There he drafted his most famous work, *De regno Christi* (The kingdom of Christ; 1550), and there he died. Originally buried with honor, his remains, along with his books, were publicly burned under Queen Mary; he was ceremonially rehabilitated under Queen Elizabeth I in 1560.

BIBLIOGRAPHY

Brady, Thomas A., Jr. *Protestant Politics: Jacob Sturm (1489–1553) of Strasbourg and the German Reformation.* Atlantic Highlands, N.J., 1995.

Eells, Hastings. *Martin Bucer.* New Haven, Conn., 1931. The standard biography in English.

Greschat, Martin. *Martin Bucer: Ein Reformator und seine Zeit, 1491–1551.* Munich, 1990.

Hammann, Gottfried. *Entre la secte et la cité: Le projet d'église du réformateur Martin Bucer (1491–1551).* Geneva, 1984.

THOMAS A. BRADY JR.

BUDÉ, GUILLAUME (c. 1467–1540), French scholar and diplomat. Budé was born into a family with a tradition of royal service dating from the late fourteenth century. At his father's urging he began to study law at the tender age of fifteen, but after three years became engrossed with hunting and allied pursuits. At twenty-three he underwent a conversion to humanist studies and began to study law on his own. Through family connections he obtained the office of secretary to the king from 1497 until 1515.

Guillaume Budé. Portrait by Jean Clouet (c. 1485–c. 1540). Oil on wood; 39.7 × 34.3 cm (16 × 13.5 in.). THE METROPOLITAN MUSEUM OF ART, MARIA DEWITT JESUP FUND, 1946

After study with the Greek scholar Janus Lascaris, Budé published Latin translations of Greek works by Plutarch. His first major work, *Annotationes in quatuor & viginti Pandectarum libros* (Annotations on twenty-four books of the Pandects; 1508), was the first extensive humanist study of Justinian's *Digest,* the most important section of the Eastern Roman Emperor's sixth-century compilation of Roman law, the *Corpus iuris civilis* (Body of civil law). Budé, building upon the philological methods of Lorenzo Valla and Angelo Poliziano, was among the first in France to make sophisticated use of humanist philology. He set aside the medieval glosses and sought rather to establish the meanings of key terms in numerous passages from the Western Roman jurists excerpted in the *Digest,* many of which had long puzzled medieval legal scholars, by referring them to the usage of jurists' contemporaries as evidenced primarily in literary and historical Roman writings. He thus applied the new humanist philological methods to problems long debated by medieval legal scholars, who themselves were thoroughly familiar with the texts included in the *Corpus iuris*—the charges leveled against them by humanists and subsequent scholars notwithstanding. Budé revealed a strong awareness of historical change from the time of the jurists to that of Justinian, as well as of the pitfalls involved in the transmission of texts over several centuries. Thus he presented a list of contradictory passages, the *antinomiae,* long known to the scholastics, not as problems for resolution but as evidence of the corruption of the *Corpus iuris* and the failings of its editor, Tribonian. Yet Budé's interpretation was colored by his preference for classical Latin literature and his aversion to the legal profession of his own time, and so he often criticized as corruptions legal terms used by Roman jurists but rare or absent in nonlegal writings and showed little interest in critically engaging the analyses of particular legal problems preserved in the *Digest.*

In his next major work, *De asse* (c. 1515), Budé surpassed such immediate humanist (and Italian) predecessors as Ermolao Barbaro and Poliziano in seeking to understand money systems and units of measure of antiquity, a problem of central concern to humanists as they sought to reconstruct the life and society of Greece and Rome. This project involved the innovative use of Roman coins as historical sources, as well as a sophisticated critical approach to written sources that unraveled their many internal contradictions and corrupt passages.

Budé was a strong advocate of the French "genius" and often criticized the court for its excessive admiration of things Italian. His works, including the *Annotationes* and *De asse,* are filled with glowing praise for France and the French crown and rather unhistorical comparisons of the king to Roman emperors. With the accession of Francis I in 1515 Budé placed his hopes for humanism in France on the king's patronage. Budé's blend of fervid humanism, Francophilia, and French monarchism was rewarded with the king's creation in 1530 of the Royal Lecturers—professorships in Greek, Hebrew, Latin, and mathematics—which led directly to the Collège de France. Budé himself was also rewarded with several royal appointments, most notably as master of requests from 1522.

In Budé's final major work, *De transitu Hellenismi ad Christianismum* (The passage from Hellenism to Christianity; 1535), he sought to distance humanism from nascent Protestantism. While continuing his long practice of criticizing the excesses and corrupt practices of the clergy, he staunchly opposed Luther and sacramentarian reformers and defended the legitimacy of the established church, its basic teachings and sacramental practices (although he leaned toward a Gallican and conciliarist view of the church). Budé rebuked many of his humanist con-

temporaries for ascribing to Greco-Roman philosophy a status equal or superior to that of the Christian faith. Yet he insisted upon the value of classical mythology when read allegorically through a Christian lens, an approach he had long practiced, and he presented classical Latin, humanism, and philology, when properly subordinated to Christian ends, as virtuous handmaidens to Christian theology.

See also **Humanism,** *subentries on* **France** *and* **Legal Humanism.**

BIBLIOGRAPHY

Kelley, Donald R. *Foundations of Modern Historical Scholarship: Language, Law, and History in the French Renaissance.* New York, 1970.

La Garanderie, Marie Madeleine de. *Christianisme et lettres profanes: Essai sur l'humanisme français (1515–1535) et sur la pensée de Guillaume Budé.* 2d ed. Paris, 1995.

McNeil, David O. *Guillame Budé and Humanism in the Reign of Francis I.* Geneva, 1975.

MICHAEL L. MONHEIT

BUONAMICI, FRANCESCO (1533–1603), Italian physician. Buonamici was a professor of natural philosophy at the University of Pisa (1565–1603) and teacher of Galileo Galilei. His most important work is *De motu* (On motion), completed in 1587 and published at Florence in 1591, which exposes, in ten books, Aristotle's teachings on the four causes of motion, the types of motion, and their relation to the heavenly bodies. Other works by him include *Discorsi poetici* (Poetic discourses; Florence, 1597) and *De alimento* (On food; Florence, 1603; Venice, 1604).

Similarities between Buonamici's *De motu* and Galileo's early Latin treatises on the universe, the elements, and motion have long been recognized. (Koyré, 1978; Drabkin, 1969). More revealing is Buonamici's statement that his *De motu* was occasioned by controversies on the motion of the elements that had arisen at Pisa among students and professors (Helbing, 1989). Galileo was undoubtedly one of the students, and the other professors were Girolamo Borro (1512–1592) and Filippo Fantoni (d. 1591), both of whom wrote on the subject.

Buonamici's project in *De motu* was to write a definitive treatise on motion in general, using all available resources of philological research on Greek texts. Galileo's project, by way of opposition, was to concentrate on only one motion, that of heavy bodies, and to use mainly mathematical techniques to disclose its nature. Rather than recover the past and be an apologist for Aristotle, as Buonamici was, Galileo was intent on discovery and innovation, on finding a new science that went beyond Aristotle's. Yet Buonamici provided Galileo with much knowledge that the latter would find useful, mainly Greek and medieval teachings on motion, and criticisms of Archimedes, the second of which provoked strong reactions from Galileo.

Galileo's polemic with his one-time teacher over Archimedes continued to the end of his life. Yet in three areas there were positive elements in Buonamici's influence on Galileo. The first was the autonomy they both granted to the natural sciences, separating them from metaphysics and religion; the second was their shared commitment to a method of resolution and composition in their search for causes; and the third was the status each accorded to mathematics as a science in its own right and as an aid in investigating the secrets of nature.

See also **Mechanics**; *and biography of Galileo Galilei.*

BIBLIOGRAPHY

Drake, Stillman, and I. E. Drabkin, eds. *Mechanics in Sixteenth-Century Italy.* Madison, Wis., and London, 1969. Selections from Tartaglia, Benedetti, Guido Ubaldo, and Galileo, translated and annotated by the editors.

Helbing, Mario. *La filosofia di Francesco Buonamici, professore di Galileo a Pisa.* Pisa, Italy, 1989. See page 54.

Koyré, Alexandre. *Galileo Studies.* Translated by John Mepham. Atlantic Highlands, N.J., 1978.

Wallace, William A. "Buonamici, Francesco." In *Dictionary of Scientific Biography.* Vol. 2. New York, 1970. Pages 590–591.

WILLIAM A. WALLACE

BURCHIELLO (Domenico di Giovanni; 1404–1449), Florentine poet. A Florentine barber and autodidact who achieved a remarkable reputation as one of the Renaissance's greatest composers of satiric and surrealistic poetry, Burchiello penned approximately 150 *sonetti caudati* that allude to vernacular authors (ranging from the comico-realistic poets to Dante and Giovanni Boccaccio) as well as to the classical encomiastic tradition of "things without honor." Before he was forced into exile following Cosimo de' Medici's takeover of Florence in 1434, his shop on Via Calimala became a famous gathering place for leading poets and humanists such as Leon Battista Alberti. His lyrics fall into four categories: moralistic political works (usually attacking the Medici), *tenzoni* (disputes) exchanged with other poets, autobiographical poems describing his destitute and dissolute life, and "nonsense" verse. Characterized by hallucinatory, kaleidoscopic imagery and a virtuosic handling of alliteration and wordplay, the latter includes sonnets such as "Nom-

inativi fritti e mappamondi" (Fried nominatives and maps of the world) and "Sospiri azzurri di speranze bianche" (Azure sighs of white hopes). According to Jean Toscan, such poems contain highly coded references to homosexual mores and discourse. This code inflects much of his poetic output. Burchiello's satire targets academic and humanistic ideologies as well as Petrarchan conventions. Despite his popularity with and influence on leading fifteenth- and sixteenth-century figures such as Lorenzo de' Medici, Luigi Pulci, Francesco Berni, Niccolò Machiavelli, and Anton Francesco Doni, no complete, critical edition of his poetry exists.

BIBLIOGRAPHY

Primary Works

Burchiello (Domenico di Giovanni). *I Sonetti del Burchiello e d'altri poeti fiorentini alla burchiellesca.* London, 1757.

Giovannetti, Eugenio, ed. *Le più belle pagine del Burchiello e dei burchielleschi.* Milan, 1940. Largely based on the "London, 1757" edition.

Lanza, Antonio. *Polemiche e berte letterarie nella Firenze del primo rinascimento (1375–1449).* Rome, 1991. Documents the tense climate of rivalry and competition that shaped the ambient culture.

Messina, Michele. *Domenico di Giovanni detto il Burchiello: Sonetti inediti.* Florence, 1952. A philological study that expands the poet's oeuvre.

Secondary Works

Smith, Alan K. "Fraudomy: Reading Sexuality and Politics in Burchiello." In *Queering the Renaissance.* Edited by Jonathan Goldberg. Durham, N.C., and London, 1993. Pages 84–106.

Toscan, Jean. *Le carnaval du langage. Le lexique érotique de Burchiello à Marino (quinzième–dix-septième siècles).* 4 vols. Lille, France, 1981. An indispensable, massively documented resource for understanding Burchiello's highly coded references and figurative stratagems.

ALAN SMITH

BURCKHARDT, JAKOB. *See* **Renaissance, Interpretations of the,** *subentry on* **Jakob Burckhardt.**

BURGUNDY. The Renaissance state of Burgundy was the product of several historical accidents. When Philip of Rouvres, the last Capetian duke of Burgundy, died heirless in November 1361, the duchy of Burgundy reverted back to the French crown. King John the Good then assigned it to his youngest son, Philip the Bold, who became the first Valois duke of Burgundy (1364–1404). More fortuitously, Philip also added to his empire when he married Margaret of Flanders, sole heiress to the wealthy county of Flanders along the North Sea. Thus Philip's son and heir, John the Fearless (1404–1419), became

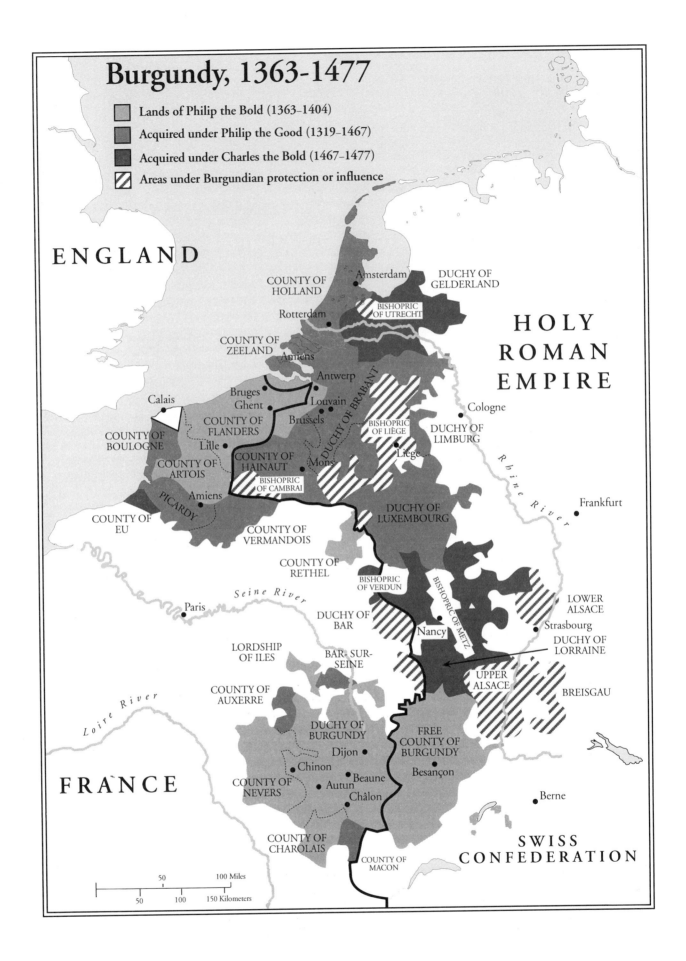

Burgundy, 1363-1477

Lands of Philip the Bold (1363–1404)

Acquired under Philip the Good (1319–1467)

Acquired under Charles the Bold (1467–1477)

Areas under Burgundian protection or influence

ENGLAND

HOLY ROMAN EMPIRE

FRANCE

SWISS CONFEDERATION

COUNTY OF HOLLAND

Amsterdam

DUCHY OF GELDERLAND

Rotterdam

BISHOPRIC OF UTRECHT

COUNTY OF ZEELAND

Amiens

Antwerp

Cologne

Calais

Bruges

Ghent

Louvain

DUCHY OF BRABANT

BISHOPRIC OF LIÈGE

DUCHY OF LIMBURG

COUNTY OF FLANDERS

Brussels

COUNTY OF BOULOGNE

Lille

Mons

Liège

COUNTY OF ARTOIS

COUNTY OF HAINAUT

BISHOPRIC OF CAMBRAI

Rhine River

Amiens

PICARDY

DUCHY OF LUXEMBOURG

Frankfurt

COUNTY OF EU

COUNTY OF VERMANDOIS

COUNTY OF RETHEL

BISHOPRIC OF VERDUN

Seine River

Paris

DUCHY OF BAR

BISHOPRIC OF METZ

LOWER ALSACE

Strasbourg

LORDSHIP OF ILES

BAR-SUR-SEINE

Nancy

DUCHY OF LORRAINE

COUNTY OF AUXERRE

UPPER ALSACE

BREISGAU

Loire River

DUCHY OF BURGUNDY

FREE COUNTY OF BURGUNDY

Dijon

Chinon

Beaune

Besançon

FRANCE

COUNTY OF NEVERS

Autun

Châlon

Berne

COUNTY OF CHAROLAIS

COUNTY OF MACON

SWISS CONFEDERATION

50   100 Miles

50   100   150 Kilometers

Philip the Good of Burgundy. Jean Wauquelin presents the *Chroniques de Hainaut* to Duke Philip the Good, 1446. The boy between them is Philip's son and heir, Charles the Bold. 1448. BIBLIOTHÈQUE ROYALE ALBERT IER, BRUSSELS. MS 9242, FOL. 1R

duke of the duchy of Burgundy, count of the Free County of Burgundy (Franche-Comté), as well as count of Flanders. His son and heir, Philip the Good (1419–1467), not only consolidated the Burgundian state but increased its territory once again. Within a decade of his coming to power in 1419, the various marital alliances arranged by his grandfather Philip the Bold resulted in the acquisition of the counties of Holland, Zeeland, Hainaut, and Namur, as well as the duchies of Brabant and Limburg. The duchy of Luxembourg was also added to the Burgundian state in 1443, though a military presence was required to make good on the claim.

There was nothing inevitable about the creation of the Burgundian state. It did acquire a degree of institutional centralization from Philip the Good and his successor, Charles the Bold (1467–1477). There was a single chancellor and a single chancery that served as the highest law court, but there was never any permanent notion of unity or coherence to its political structures. The various counties, duchies, and lordships that made up the Burgundian state were simply component parts of a larger whole. Linguistically, culturally, politically, and economically, the Dutch-speaking Hollanders had no more in common with the German-speaking Luxembourgers than they did with the French-speaking Burgundi-

ans: they all simply shared a common suzerain. Geographically, however, the Renaissance state of Burgundy stretched from the North Sea right down to the Franco-Swiss border, and it served as a useful buffer between France and the Holy Roman Empire.

This very new state quickly acquired a powerful court culture and international significance out of proportion to its accidental beginnings. The Valois dukes of Burgundy took advantage of the Hundred Years' War (1337–1453) and the dynastic tensions between England and France to promote their own interests. When John the Fearless sided with the English King Henry V, the result was the defeat of the French at Agincourt in 1415. When John's son, Philip the Good, switched sides and supported the French dauphin (later Charles VII), the result was the eventual defeat of England and the end of the English occupation of much of France. In just three generations, the Valois dukes of Burgundy turned their state into a European power of some consequence, roughly comparable to the much older states of England and France.

Culturally, the Burgundian court also came to rival the courts of Renaissance Italy in both splendor and display. The Burgundian dukes, in fact, regularly maintained two courts: one in Brussels in the north and one in Dijon in the duchy of Burgundy in the

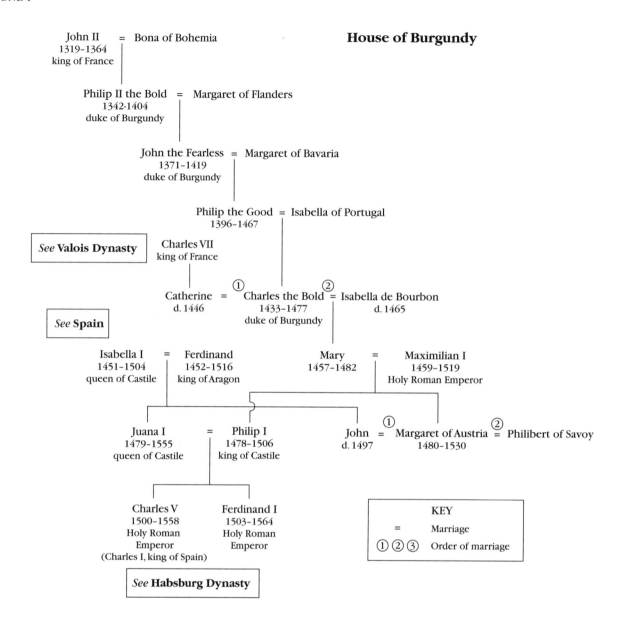

House of Burgundy

John II
1319–1364
king of France
= Bona of Bohemia

Philip II the Bold
1342–1404
duke of Burgundy
= Margaret of Flanders

John the Fearless
1371–1419
duke of Burgundy
= Margaret of Bavaria

Philip the Good
1396–1467
= Isabella of Portugal

See **Valois Dynasty**

Charles VII
king of France

Catherine
d. 1446
= ① Charles the Bold ②
1433–1477
duke of Burgundy
= Isabella de Bourbon
d. 1465

See **Spain**

Isabella I
1451–1504
queen of Castile
= Ferdinand
1452–1516
king of Aragon

Mary
1457–1482
= Maximilian I
1459–1519
Holy Roman Emperor

Juana I
1479–1555
queen of Castile
= Philip I
1478–1506
king of Castile

John
d. 1497
= ① Margaret of Austria ②
1480–1530
= Philibert of Savoy

Charles V
1500–1558
Holy Roman
Emperor
(Charles I, king of Spain)

Ferdinand I
1503–1564
Holy Roman
Emperor

See **Habsburg Dynasty**

KEY	
=	Marriage
① ② ③	Order of marriage

south. Although one was Flemish and the other French, both became sites of artistic recognition and achievement, and the two-way traffic of artists between the two capitals became commonplace by the reign of Philip the Good. That so many works of Flemish artists, such as the painters Jan van Eyck and Rogier van der Weyden or the sculptor Claus Sluter, still survive in Dijon and other Burgundian towns today is a direct result of this artistic legacy. Philip the Good also founded the chivalric Order of the Golden Fleece in 1430, made up of an exclusive group of aristocrats who served as great patrons of the arts. Thus the Burgundian court functioned as the greatest source of artistic patronage in northern Europe, much like the Renaissance courts did in Italy.

The state whose historical gestation was founded on accident came to a sudden demise via the same route. When the last Valois duke of Burgundy, Charles the Bold, was killed on the battlefield at Nancy in January 1477, his only heir was his daughter Mary. He had been at war with the French king Louis XI, and Louis wasted little time in seizing control of the capital Dijon within weeks of Charles's death. Mary herself, however, favored the Habsburg prince Maximilian of Austria (who later became Holy Roman Emperor), whom she married later that spring. The result was a tug of war between the French and German states over who would inherit Burgundy. In the end, it was almost inevitable that the state would be divided, with the duchy of Burgundy becoming part of the kingdom of France, but with the Free County as well as all the Netherlands territories reverting to the Habsburgs.

This Franco-Habsburg rivalry would intensify just a decade later when the French king invaded Italy in a dispute over the emperor's claim to the vacant duchy of Milan, starting the Habsburg-Valois Wars (1491–1559). Maximilian's grandson and heir, Charles V, later tried to reunite the duchy to the rest of the Burgundian state under Habsburg control. Having captured the king of France, Francis I, on the battlefield at Pavia in Italy in 1525, he succeeded in getting Francis to renounce the duchy of Burgundy as part of the deal to release him. Francis reneged on his promise once he acquired his freedom, however, and the duchy remained in French hands.

The legacy of the Burgundian state during the Renaissance was one of political, military, and artistic achievement. Although formed by historical accident and surviving only four generations, it played an important role in the distribution of power in western Europe in the fifteenth century.

BIBLIOGRAPHY

Huizinga, Johan. *The Autumn of the Middle Ages.* Translated by Rodney J. Payton and Ulrich Mammitzsch. Chicago, 1996.

Vaughan, Richard. *Valois Burgundy.* London, 1975.

MACK P. HOLT

BURTON, ROBERT (1577–1640), English scholar, writer, divine, author of *The Anatomy of Melancholy.* Born in Leicestershire, Burton was educated in the local grammar schools and later at Oxford, taking his first degree at Christ Church College in 1602. He remained as a resident "student" of the college until the end of his life, a fact reflected in the bookish nature of the *Anatomy.*

The *Anatomy* was first published in 1621 and then in five editions that incorporated the author's revisions and additions, four in his own lifetime (1624, 1628, 1632, 1638, and 1651). It is an encyclopedic work of roughly half a million words. The subject of melancholy, the roots of which went back to ancient humoral medicine, had important dimensions in Burton's period—philosophical, astrological, and literary, as well as scientific—and he set out to "anatomize" every aspect of it. He claimed that his interest in the subject was personal: "I write of Melancholy, by being busie to avoid Melancholy." While some Renaissance writers and artists exalted melancholy as the affliction of gifted spirits "born under Saturn," Burton saw it as a debilitating condition to which everybody was vulnerable.

The *Anatomy* is divided into three "partitions": the first on the causes and symptoms of melancholy, the second on cures, and the third on two important types of melancholy—those associated with love and religion. The comprehensive nature of Burton's project is clear from the outset in his long satiric preface entitled "Democritus Junior to the Reader." It describes a universal panorama of human frailty under the rubric of melancholy and madness and has been compared to Erasmus's *Praise of Folly,* a work Burton mentions. The preface also contains a utopia notable for its practical concerns. Other celebrated sections of the *Anatomy* include the "Digression on the Misery of Scholars" and the "Digression of Air," in which Burton takes an imaginary flight through the cosmos, discussing various contradictory explanations for natural and cosmic phenomena, including some that were debated at the time he wrote.

Burton called the *Anatomy* a "cento," a work culled from the writings of others but ultimately his own. He claimed (perhaps speciously) that he would have preferred to write it in Latin if he had found a printer for it. Instead, he developed one of the most individual English prose styles of the period, "extemporean" rather than preplanned, according to his own description, copious and energetic, peppered with Latin allusions and tags, many of which are followed in the text by his own translations. He made little effort to conceal disagreements among the sources on which he depended, such contradictions being themselves symptomatic of the melancholy of learning. Burton's lifelong devotion to the study of melancholy and the inscription on his tomb in Christ Church stating that melancholy gave him his life and his death have caused some scholars to wonder if he committed suicide. There is no evidence, however, to support this conclusion.

The *Anatomy* has influenced subsequent writers, including John Milton, Samuel Johnson, Lawrence Sterne (the author of *Tristram Shandy*), and John Keats, who got the plot of "Lamia" from it.

BIBLIOGRAPHY

Primary Work

Burton, Robert. *The Anatomy of Melancholy.* Edited by Thomas C. Faulkner, Nicholas K. Kiessling, and Rhonda L. Blair. 3 vols. Oxford and New York, 1989–1994. The authoritative modern edition with an informative introduction about the author and his work by J. B. Bamborough.

Secondary Works

O'Connell, Michael. *Robert Burton.* Boston, 1986.

Vicari, Eleanor Patricia. *The View from Minerva's Tower: Learning and Imagination in "The Anatomy of Melancholy."* Toronto, 1989.

BRIDGET GELLERT LYONS

BUSCHE, HERMANN VON DEM (c. 1468–1534), German humanist. Busche (Busch, Buschius) was one of the last "wandering apostles" of humanism in Germany. He was born around 1468 in the castle of Sassenberg near Münster in Westphalia. As a youth he studied in Münster with his relative Rudolf von Langen, a cathedral provost and humanist. Busche continued his studies with Alexander Hegius at Deventer and Rudolf Agricola in Heidelberg. Traveling with Langen to Italy in 1485, he spent nearly five years at the Roman Academy of Pomponio Leto. He then studied briefly with the older Filippo Beroaldo in Bologna. Imbued with the new spirit of Italian humanism, Busche returned to his homeland, joining the court of Heinrich von Schwarzberg, bishop of Münster. In 1495 the restless scholar matriculated at Cologne, where he taught poetry and took courses in law. By the turn of the century, his wanderlust led him to teach and study in a number of north and west German towns.

Between 1501 and 1508 Busche continued to publish his collections of poetry and other writings and to participate in literary controversies, while falling into a dissolute lifestyle. In 1502 he was appointed as the first salaried humanist at Wittenberg. Only a year later he received his bachelor's degree in law at Leipzig, where he also became the university's first regularly paid poet. However, his boasting and insulting behavior led to his ouster at Leipzig and, several years later, at Erfurt. While in Erfurt, he probably came into contact with members of the humanist circle of Conrad Mutian. They included Ulrich von Hutten and Crotus Rubeanus, with whom he later collaborated on the *Epistolae obscurorum virorum* (Letters of obscure men).

From 1508 to 1516 Busche was again in Cologne lecturing on poetry and classical prose authors. He was part of the circle of Count Hermann von Neuenahr, who was a promoter of humanist reform at the university and a supporter of Johann Reuchlin, who had become embroiled in a controversy over the merit of Hebrew literature. Busche engaged in several such conflicts, coming out in Reuchlin's favor in 1514. The next year he met Erasmus, who cautioned moderation in the growing conflict between the humanist defenders of Reuchlin and the scholastic opposition in Cologne. In 1516 Busche left Cologne to become headmaster of the Latin school in Wesel. Although relieved of his duties after a year, he continued to write his most important defense of humanist study, *Vallum humanitatis* (Fortress of humanity), published in 1518.

Busche soon became an active promoter of the new evangelical cause of Martin Luther. He took a leading role in supporting the religious reformer during the imperial diet at Worms in 1521. The following year he participated in a public demonstration against the Lenten fast in Basel. In 1523 he lectured on the humanities at Heidelberg. Between 1527 and 1533 he taught history and other humanistic subjects at the newly established Reformed university at Marburg. He died in Dülman in 1534, having carried the cause of humanism into the early Reformation.

See also **Reuchlin Affair.**

BIBLIOGRAPHY

Liessem, Hermann Joseph. *Hermann van dem Busche: Sein Leben und seine Schriften.* Köln, 1884–1908. Reprint, Nieuwkoop, Netherlands, 1965. This older study unfortunately traces events only to around 1509, but does contain a thorough, annotated bibliography of Busche's publications.

Mehl, James V. "Hermann von dem Busche's *Vallum humanitatis* (1518): A German Defense of the Renaissance *Studia Humanitatis.*" *Renaissance Quarterly* 42 (1989): 480–506.

JAMES V. MEHL

BUSSA DE' PONZIANI, FRANCESCA (Frances of Rome; 1384–1440), laywoman, foundress, mystic, patroness of Rome. Born into an aristocratic Roman family, Francesca Bussa de' Ponziani married at the age of thirteen, and though she displayed signs of piety and asceticism, her spiritual life unfolded across forty years of marriage and worldly immersion in the turbulence of Rome during the early years of the fifteenth century. The mother of several children—two of whom died at a young age—Francesca lived through a series of crises, culminating in the pillaging of her house by the antipapal troops of Ladislas of Naples in 1409, and the subsequent forced banishment of her husband, who after a time returned as a broken man. Long used to acts such as selling her jewels to aid plague victims, in 1425 she organized with other Roman ladies a society committed to good works and self-denial, and eight years later established in association with Benedictine monks a community known as the Oblates of Tor de' Specchi, consisting primarily of aristocratic women and other female members of the rising commercial classes.

Throughout her life Francesca experienced tormenting visions of hellfire and the apocalypse, with demons appearing to her in the form of lions, snakes, humans, and corpses. Her intense religiosity impelled her to whip herself and undertake other self-woundings, to confront a priest celebrating mass with the claim that she saw him rotting with leprosy, to miraculously heal the sick, and to make prophecies that foretold, for example, the end of the Great Schism, that is, the period of rival popes (1378–1417). These and other behaviors were recorded by her confessor, Giovanni Mattiotti, in a biography that spread her name throughout Italy as one who counseled both the poor and the renowned—the latter including Pope Eugenius IV (reigned 1431–1447). She died in 1440, four years after her husband's death, and was canonized in 1608, leaving behind a community that flourished through the twentieth century.

BIBLIOGRAPHY

Primary Work
Romagnoli, Alessandra Bartolomei, ed. *Santa Francesca Romana: Edizione critica dei trattati latini di Giovanni Mattiotti.* Vatican City, 1994.

Secondary Works
Esch, Arnold. "Die Zeugenaussagen im Heiligsprechungsverfahren für S. Francesca Romana als Quelle zur Sozialgeschichte Roms im frühen Quattrocento." *Quellen und Forschungen aus italienischen Archiven und Bibliotheken* 53 (1973): 93–151.
Esposito, Anna. "St. Francesca and the Female Religious Communities of Fifteenth-Century Rome." In *Women and Religion in Medieval and Renaissance Italy.* Edited by Daniel Bornstein and Roberto Rusconi. Translated by Margery J. Schneider. Chicago, 1996. Pages 196–218.

SARAH COVINGTON

BYRD, WILLIAM (c. 1540–1623), English composer. Born in London to Thomas and Margery Byrd, William Byrd probably served as a chorister in the Chapel Royal, where the composer Thomas Tallis was his principal teacher. In 1563 he became organist and master of the choristers at Lincoln Cathedral, and in 1568 married Julian Birley, a marriage that lasted forty years. Byrd retained the position at Lincoln until 1572, when he was formally appointed gentleman of the Chapel Royal as a singing man and coorganist with Tallis and others. In 1575 Elizabeth I granted Byrd and Tallis a twenty-one-year privilege for the printing and sale of music, commemorated by the composers' *Cantiones . . . Sacrae* (Sacred songs) dedicated to the queen in that year. This patent was scarcely exercised again until Byrd's publication of his own accumulated songs (1588 and 1589) and motets (1589 and 1591). During the 1560s, 1570s, and 1580s Byrd also composed several services and anthems for the Anglican rite, though the Byrd family remained Catholic and its members were repeatedly indicted as recusants. Byrd seems to have ceased his regular Chapel Royal duties in the early 1590s and to have gone into semiretirement at Stondon Massey, Essex, by 1594. He continued to compose, however, publishing three Masses (c. 1592–1595), two books of Mass Propers (*Gradualia,* 1605–1607), and a further book of songs (1611). His pupils included the composers Thomas Morley, Thomas Tomkins, John Bull, and probably Peter Philips.

Byrd composed extensively in all genres current in England apart from the madrigal and lute ayre. His Latin works were the first in England to master thoroughly the flexibly imitative textures of the continental motet, combined with consistent and intense textual expression. Although the intended use of the expansive *Cantiones Sacrae* of the 1570s and 1580s remains ambiguous, the more concise settings of *Gradualia* clearly offered music for the Catholic church year. Byrd's Anglican services range from the simple textures of the "short" service to the highly complex "great" service; the largely syllabic, imitative, undemonstrative idiom of his anthems became a primary model for subsequent Anglican composers. Although most of Byrd's secular songs were conceived for solo voice and viol consort, he published many of them with words in all parts. The songs largely abjured the word-painting of the madrigal in favor of a more generally expressive, intricately contrapuntal style. Byrd's impressive body of consort and keyboard music is notable for contrapuntal ingenuity, brilliant figuration, and a carefully conceived sense of overall shape.

BIBLIOGRAPHY

Primary Works
Brett, Philip, ed. *The Byrd Edition.* 17 vols. London, 1976–. Replaces *The Collected Vocal Works of William Byrd,* edited by Edmund H. Fellowes.
Brown, Alan, ed. *Musica Britannica.* Vols. 27–28, *William Byrd: Keyboard Music.* London, 1969–1971.

Secondary Works
Harley, John. *William Byrd: Gentleman of the Chapel Royal.* Aldershot, U.K., 1997.
Kerman, Joseph. *The Music of William Byrd.* Vol. 1, *The Masses and Motets of William Byrd.* Berkeley and Los Angeles, 1981.
Monson, Craig. "Authenticity and Chronology in Byrd's Church Anthems." *Journal of the American Musicological Society* 35 (1982): 280–305.
Neighbour, Oliver. *The Music of William Byrd.* Vol. 3, *The Consort and Keyboard Music of William Byrd.* London, 1978.
Turbet, Richard. *William Byrd: A Guide to Research.* New York, 1987.

CRAIG A. MONSON

CABALA. *See* **Kabbalah.**

CAJETAN, THOMAS DE VIO (1469–1534), Dominican philosopher, theologian, and cardinal, important for his role in "second scholasticism." Generally known by the place of his birth, Gaeta, Italy (whence his latinized name Gaietanus), he was baptized James de Vio but changed his name to Thomas on entering the Dominican order in 1485. He studied philosophy at Naples and theology at Bologna, then went to Padua, teaching metaphysics at the priory and the *Sentences* of Peter Lombard at the university (1493). In 1494 Cajetan held a disputation with Giovanni Pico della Mirandola at Ferrara; he then taught at Pavia (1497–1499), lecturing on the *Summa* of St. Thomas Aquinas. While serving as procurator general of his order from 1501 to 1508 he taught at the University of Rome.

Elected master general in 1508, Cajetan served in that capacity until 1518, promoting studies and reform and sending the first Dominican missionaries to the New World. From 1512 to 1517 he participated in the Fifth Lateran Council, where he defended papal supremacy and played a major part in discussions of Averroism. On 6 July 1517 he was made a cardinal and served as a legate of Pope Leo X to Germany; while there he promoted a crusade against the Turks, had discussions with Martin Luther at Augsburg (1518), and represented the pope in the election of Charles V as the new German emperor (1519). Cajetan took part in the consistory of 1520, which condemned Luther, and the conclave of 1522, which elected Adrian VI as pope. He served as Adrian's legate to Hungary, Poland, and Bohemia in 1523, but on Adrian's death in September of that year returned to Rome. He spent the remainder of his life in study and writing, focusing mainly on the Scriptures and their interpretations by the Reformers.

Cajetan's philosophical works date from his teaching years (1493–1507) and include commentaries on Aristotle (the *Organon, On the Soul,* and the *Metaphysics*) and Aquinas (*On Being and Essence*), and several short treatises, the most important being *On the Analogy of Names.* While master general and papal legate, his works were theological and consisted mainly of a lengthy commentary on Aquinas's *Summa* (1507–1520), reprinted in the Leonine critical edition of that work (1888–1906). This replaced his earlier unpublished commentary on the *Sentences* (1493–1494). His writings on Scripture followed; these include a translation of the Psalms from the Hebrew (1527) plus commentaries on the Gospels (1527–1528), Epistles (1528–1529), Pentateuch (1530–1531), historical books (1531–1532), Job (1533), and Ecclesiastes (1534).

Cajetan's philosophical positions were basically Thomistic but influenced by his polemics with Averroists and Scotists. He held distinctive positions on existence and analogy and on the relationship between nature and grace. In his early writings he held that the soul's immortality was demonstrable by reason, but he reversed that position in his later writings. He was sympathetic to the humanists and their work in textual exegesis. Convinced that the Latin Vulgate was inadequate for serious biblical studies, he used the Greek text of Erasmus (1467–1536) for his commentaries on the New Testament.

Cajetan and Luther. Cardinal Cajetan meets with Martin Luther at Augsburg in October 1518. Wood engraving from *Historien der heyligen ausserwaehlten Gottes Zeugen* by Ludwig Robus (Strasbourg, 1557).

BIBLIOGRAPHY

Doherty, Dennis. *The Sexual Doctrine of Cardinal Cajetan.* Regensburg, Germany, 1966.

Janz, Denis R. *Luther and Late Medieval Thomism: A Study in Theological Anthropology.* Waterloo, Canada, 1983.

McInerny, Ralph. *Aquinas and Analogy.* Washington, D.C., 1996.

Reilly, John P. *Cajetan's Notion of Existence.* The Hague, Netherlands, 1971.

Wicks, Jared, ed. and trans. *Cajetan Responds: A Reader in Reformation Controversy.* Washington, D.C., 1977.

WILLIAM A. WALLACE

CALDERÓN DE LA BARCA, PEDRO

(1600–1681), Spanish dramatist, poet, and librettist. Calderón was born and raised in Madrid in a family of the lower nobility, educated in the Jesuit Colegio Imperial, and enrolled in the University of Alcalá in 1614. He left his studies in 1615 when his apparently despotic father died, stipulating in his will that Pedro should continue his studies toward the priesthood and assume a chaplaincy endowed by his maternal aunt. Pedro did study canon law at the University of Salamanca between 1615 and 1619, but then he turned toward a literary career, writing plays, poetry for literary competitions, and entering the service of the Constable of Castile in Madrid in 1621, the same year the theater-loving Philip IV ascended the throne.

Calderón's dramatic career began with the 1623 performance at court of *Amor, honor y poder* (Love, honor, and power). That play and title mark preoccupations that would persist throughout his career: the conflicting claims of personal desires, the public exigencies of the honor code, and the demands—and limits—of royal and paternal power. The clash frequently involves a father-son conflict and a double plot, as in his most famous work, *La vida es sueño* (Life is a dream; first version before 1630, second version 1635), a philosophical drama questioning knowledge, faith, freedom, and political power. Calderón wrote approximately 120 three-act plays, the majority of his most famous by 1642. In delightful comedies such as *La dama duende* (The phantom lady; 1629), *Casa con dos puertas, mala es de guardar* (A house with two doors is difficult to guard; 1629), *No hay burlas con el amor* (Love is no laughing matter; c. 1635), and *Guárdate de agua mansa* (Still waters run deep; 1649), his intellectual, self-conscious art laughs at its own conventions as well as at social customs. "Wife-murder" tragedies like *El médico de su honra* (The surgeon of his honor; 1635) and *El pintor de su deshonra* (The painter of his own dishonor; c. 1648) invite audiences to judge the lethal effects of the honor code. Calderón dramatizes the power of Catholic faith in religious dramas such as *El príncipe constante* (The constant prince; 1629), *La devoción de la cruz* (Devotion to the cross; c. 1625), and his Faustian story of two Christian martyrs, *El mágico prodigioso* (The wonder-working magician; 1637). *El alcalde de Zalamea* (The mayor of Zalamea; 1642) pits civilian justice and honor as classless moral integrity against military law and aristocratic privilege.

Calderón was made a Knight of the Military Order of Santiago by Philip IV in 1637, and between 1640 and 1642 he served in two campaigns during the Catalonian revolt. In that dark decade his two brothers died and war and royal mourning closed the theaters (1644–1645 and 1646–1649). Calderón then chose to become a priest (1651) and take up the endowed family chaplaincy. Thereafter he wrote less for the public theaters but composed numerous court productions. In elaborate court spectacle-plays like *El mayor encanto, amor* (Love, the greatest enchantment; 1635), *Las fortunas de Andrómeda y Perseo* (The fortunes of Andromeda and Perseus; 1653), *Eco y Narciso* (Echo and Narcissus; 1661), and *La estatua de Prometeo* (The statue of Prometheus; c. 1670), he wrote tragicomedies on mythological themes making lavish and effective use of music, dance, scenery, and stage effects that simultaneously entertained, exalted, and instructed the reigning monarch. He contributed to the beginnings of opera in Spain with two fully sung spectacle plays and to the semioperatic zarzuela that mixed song with declamation.

From 1648 until his death, Calderón was the exclusive author of the Madrid *autos sacramentales* (allegorical religious dramas), one-act, open-air performances for the annual Corpus Christi festival. Drawing on his wealth of scriptural, scholastic, and patristic learning and his mastery of the polyphonic codes of theater, he turned abstract moral and dogmatic concepts into dramatic sermons in exquisite verse, employing music and stage effects to great didactic effect: *El gran teatro del mundo* (The great theater of the world; c. 1635), *La cena de Baltasar* (Belshazzar's feast; c. 1630); *El divino Orfeo* (The divine Orpheus; first version before 1635, second version 1663). In many of his eighty *autos,* he incorporated a political discourse that sanctified the institutions of the Habsburg monarchy. He also wrote short burlesque interludes performed with *autos* or between the acts of dramas, often using them to poke fun at the conventions of the works they accompanied. He penned a brief but aesthetically significant prose preface to the 1677 edition of his *autos* and dramatic prologues that explain the artistic principles he followed in *autos* and court spectacles.

Pedro Calderón de la Barca. BIBLIOTECA NACIONAL, MADRID/ORONOZ

Calderón, the last of the triad of great Spanish dramatists, perfected the three-act polymetric *comedia* form developed by Lope de Vega and furthered by Tirso de Molina. Often rewriting his own plays and those of others, he excised extraneous elements and made plot, character, theme, and poetic imagery a synergistic unity. Calderón turned the sensual brilliance and dense syntax of the poetry of Luis de Góngora into dramatic conceits that enact in language the tensions of baroque aesthetics and Counter-Reformation court life.

Outside Spain, translations of his works or adaptation of his plots spread Calderón's influence within decades to Italy, France, England, the Spanish Netherlands, Holland, and Germany. In Germany they would become central in the Romantic renewal of appreciation of the genius of Spanish golden age drama and its master craftsman, Calderón.

BIBLIOGRAPHY

Primary Works

Calderón de la Barca, Pedro. *Calderón Plays.* Translated and introduced by Gwynne Edwards. London, 1991. Includes *The*

Surgeon of Honour, Life Is a Dream, and *Three Judgments in One.*

Calderón de la Barca, Pedro. *Comedias.* Prepared by D. W. Cruickshank and J. E. Varey. Facsimile edition. 19 vols. Farnborough, U.K., 1973. Volume 1, *The Textual Criticism of Calderón's Comedias.* Edited by D. W. Cruickshank. Volume 19, *Critical Studies of Calderón's Comedias.* Edited by J. E. Varey. London, 1973.

Calderón de la Barca, Pedro. *Four Comedies.* Translated and with an introduction by Kenneth Muir. Notes by Ann L. Mackenzie. Lexington, Ky., 1980. Includes *From Bad to Worse, The Secret Spoken Aloud, The Worst Is Not Always Certain,* and *The Advantages and Disadvantages of a Name.*

Calderón de la Barca, Pedro. *Love Is No Laughing Matter/No hay burlas con el amor.* Translated by Don Cruickshank and Sean Page. Warminster, U.K., 1986.

Calderón de la Barca, Pedro. *Obras completas.* Edited by Angel Valbuena Prat and Angel Valbuena Briones. 3 vols. Madrid, 1991.

Calderón de la Barca, Pedro. *The Painter of His Dishonour/El pintor de su deshonra.* Edited and translated by A. K. G. Paterson. Warminster, U.K., 1991. Also translated by David Johnston as *The Painter of Dishonour.* Bath, U.K., 1995.

Calderón de la Barca, Pedro. *The Prodigious Magician.* Edited, translated, and annotated by Bruce Wardropper. Madrid and Potomac, Md., 1982.

Calderón de la Barca, Pedro. *The Schism in England/La cisma de Inglaterra.* Edited by Ann L. Mackenzie. Translated by Kenneth Muir and Ann L. Mackenzie. Warminster, U.K., 1990.

Calderón de la Barca, Pedro. *Six Plays.* Translated by Denis Florence MacCarthy. New York, 1961. Includes *Life Is a Dream, The Wonder-Working Magician, The Constant Prince, The Devotion of the Cross, Love after Death,* and *Belshazzar's Feast.*

Calderón de la Barca, Pedro. *Six Plays by Calderón.* Translated and with introductions by Edwin Honig. New York, 1993. Includes *Secret Vengeance for Secret Insult, Devotion to the Cross, The Mayor of Zalamea, The Phantom Lady, Life Is a Dream,* and *The Crown of Absalom.*

Calderón de la Barca, Pedro. *Three Comedies.* Translated by Kenneth Muir and Ann L. Mackenzie. Lexington, Ky., 1985. Includes *A House with Two Doors Is Difficult to Guard, Mornings of April and May,* and *No Trifling with Love.*

Calderón de la Barca, Pedro. *Three Mythological Plays of Calderón.* Translated by Pedro León and John Warden. Toronto, 1990. Includes translations of *Eco y Narciso* and two versions of the *auto The Divine Orpheus.*

Calderón de la Barca, Pedro. *Three Plays.* Translations by Adrian Mitchell and John Barton. Bath, U.K., 1990 Includes *The Mayor of Zalamea, Life's a Dream, Great Theatre of the World.*

For other translations, see Kurt Reichenberger and Roswitha Reichenberger. *Bibliographisches Handbuch der Calderón-Forschung. Manual Bibliográfico Calderoniano.* Vol. 1. Kassel, Germany, 1979.

Secondary Works

Cascardi, Anthony J. *The Limits of Illusion: A Critical Study of Calderón.* Cambridge, U.K., and New York, 1984.

De Armas, Frederick A., ed. *The Prince in the Tower: Perceptions of* La vida es sueño. Lewisburg, Pa., 1993.

Delgado Morales, Manuel, ed. *The Calderonian Stage: Body and Soul.* Lewisburg, Pa., and London, 1997.

Greer, Margaret R. *The Play of Power: Mythological Court Dramas of Calderón de la Barca.* Princeton, N.J., 1991.

Kurtz, Barbara E. *The Play of Allegory in the* Autos Sacramentales *of Pedro Calderón de la Barca.* Washington, D. C., 1991.

Parker, Alexander A. *The Allegorical Drama of Calderón.* Oxford, U.K., 1943.

Rupp, Stephen. *Allegories of Kingship: Calderón and the Anti-Machiavellian Tradition.* University Park, Pa., 1996.

Tyler, Richard W., and Sergio G. Elizondo. *The Characters, Plots, and Settings of Calderón's Comedias.* Lincoln, Nebr., 1981.

Wardropper, Bruce, ed. *Critical Essays on the Theatre of Calderón.* New York, 1965.

MARGARET RICH GREER

CALENDARS. The term "calendar" derives from the Latin *Kalendae,* the first day of every Roman month, when the order of days was proclaimed for religious feasts, market days, payment of taxes, and other important matters. Various calendars have been used throughout history, all depending on the basic units of time: the day, the month, and the year. The length of these units depends on astronomical phenomena to which they are linked. The day is determined by the earth's rotation, the month by the moon's phases, and the year by the sun's return to the same point in the heavens, say, at the vernal (spring) equinox. The main difficulty for the calendar maker is that the year, so defined, does not have a whole number of days, which, for practical affairs, it should have. Each attempted calendar offers a different and pragmatic solution to this problem.

The Julian Calendar. At the suggestion of the Alexandrian astronomer Sosigenes (fl. first century B.C.), in 45 B.C. the Roman statesman Julius Caesar introduced the calendar that carries his name. It has been in use since A.D. 8. The Julian calendar is based on the sun's cyclical return, which Sosigenes assumed was completed in a year composed of 365¼ days. This led him to suggest that an extra day be added every fourth year. The year with the extra day is what we know as leap year, one whose date is exactly divisible by four. The Julian calendar is thus divided into twelve months that alternate approximately between thirty and thirty-one days, except that February has only twenty-eight days, or twenty-nine in leap year. Originally months were determined by the moon's phases, but this mode of determination was lost in the Julian calendar.

The week or interval of seven days is not a natural unit. Each day has long been associated with the heavenly bodies in the order: Sun, Moon, Mars, Mercury, Jupiter, Venus, and Saturn. The week's association with a seven-day sequence has never been questioned or interrupted.

Christianity has many religious feasts with a fixed date in the Julian calendar. Its most important feast, however, is Easter, which has no fixed date. Like the Jewish Passover, its determination depends on the moon; unlike Passover, Easter is always celebrated on a Sunday. The rule for its calculation is that Easter is the first Sunday after the first full moon after the vernal equinox. Other feast days, such as Ash Wednesday and Pentecost, are then reckoned from the date of Easter.

In the year 325 the Council of Nicaea was concerned about a lack of uniformity in the celebration of Easter. The council suggested that the practice of Alexandria, because of the city's reputation in astronomy, should be followed in calculating its date. In accordance with this recommendation, the late-fifth-century canonist Dionysius Exiguus gave the final method of Easter calculation. He took advantage of the fact that the moon phases repeat themselves in a period of nineteen years, called the Metonic cycle. He also provided a table of paschal dates up to the year 626, but used the year of the Incarnation as his point of departure. He was the first to date the Christian era by the birth of Christ, although he made an error of four to seven years in its determination.

Marking the beginning of the year has not been uniform throughout history. In the old Roman calendar the year began on 1 March, and only later was it changed to 1 January. Different dates were used in various countries. In Florence the year began on 25 March, the date of Christ's Incarnation (the feast of the Annunciation), whereas in Pisa it began the previous day. In England the year began on Christmas Day, 25 December, up to the fourteenth century, when it was superseded by the Florentine style.

The Gregorian Reform. We now know that the length of the year used for the Julian calendar was 11 minutes and 14 seconds too long. The result was that the vernal equinox calculated on its basis drifted about one day in 314 years. Through the use of the Alfonsine astronomical tables, called such because they were sponsored by Alfonso of Castile (1221–1284), a closer approximation to the year's actual length was determined at the beginning of the fourteenth century. But by the sixteenth century the true equinox was ten days ahead of the "official" equinox, then fixed on 21 March.

The more pressing problem for churchmen was determining the date of Easter Sunday as prescribed by the Council of Nicaea. Robert Grosseteste (c. 1175–1253), bishop of Lincoln, had urged a correction of the calendar, and so had Pierre d'Ailly

In octo libros De emendatione temporum Index.

A

AB
Aban
Abyssini
Achos siue Ochos
Actiaca victoria
A. D. IIII. EID.
Adar
Adarpahascht
Adeser
Adorare de geniculis
Adrianus Imper.
Adu
Aegon
Aequatio anni Graecorum
Aera quid
Aera Hispanica
Aera tres technica
Aerae Coptica vel martyrum
Aequinoctium
Aequinoctialia puncta non iisdem stellis semper affixa
Aequinoctiorum epoche immobilis
Aequinoctium autumnale obseruatum a Muhamede Albateni ab Hipparcho
Aequinoctium tempore Niceni consessus 21. Martij
Aethiopum lingua proxime abest a Chaldaea & Assyria
Aethiopes quando ineunt ieiunia
Agon Capitolinus
Ahaschuueros
Abeli
Alalcomenios
Αλεκτρυφωνία
Alexander, Imperator Asiae salutatus
eius subtile commentum
quo anno Darium vicit
eius obitus
Alliensis pugna
Amalek i copia delete
Amistris & Ester, idem
Amschir
ασαρχι ημεραι

76.c.165.d.179.b.378.b
145 d.378.d.379.c
338 c
214.c
237.d
117.b
76.c.165.d.378.d.379.c
145.c.378.d.379.d
250.c
346.b
244.d
316.d
171.a.379.c
23.c
235.d.236.a.313.b
234.d
367.b
245.b
190.c

181.b
181.a

192.d
193.c

193.c

338 d
342 d
344 d
243.c
285.a
378.d
ibid.
303.c
226.a
41.a.42.a
209.b
42.b.209.c
225.b
204.a.383.d
284.d
164.d.379.c
48.c

Annas pontifex
Annius Viterbiensis notatur
Annus
Annus Saturni
Annus Luna
Anni duo praecipua genera apud veteres
Anni principium naturale & populare
Annus non ab ea die institutus qua mundus conditus est, sed ab ea qua Sol & Luna
Annus defectiuus, abundans, communis & aequabilis
Annus cauus & plenus
Annus embolimaeus
Annus solaris
Anni solaris genera
Annus solaris ante Caesarem cognitus
Annus solaris Iudaicus
Annus solaris Hipparchi
Annus Lunaris periodicus & simplex
Annus Lunaris aequabilis in duas partes aequales diuiditur
Anno lunari quo tempore Iudaei vti caeperunt
Annus caelestis
eius examinatio
Anni caelestis hemerologium
Annus caelestis Dionysianus Orientalium
Annus caelestis προςεμπλώσεως ισημεραῆς duo genera
Annus aequabilis minor Graecorum
Annus Atticus 362. dierum
eius initium incurrit in tempus bruma
principium populare ab Hecatombaeone, naturale à Gamelione
Annus totius Graeciae modus
Anno Graeco aequabili duae castigationes adhibitae
Annus Romanorum Iulianus
Annus Iulianus est fundamentum instituti auctoris
Annus Romanorum vetus
ab initio duodecim mensium fuit
Annus Lilianus

253.b
215 d
7.d.294.c
7.d
ibid.
8.b
25.a.b

199.a

10.a.11.d.86.c.127.a.315.c
9.d.315.c
298.c
7.d
11.d
59.a
167.d
11.b
9.d.70.b
9

317.d

79.a
11.d.180.c
190.b
382
170.a
172.a
180.a
ibid.c
15.a
27.c
25.a

ibid.
17.b

8.d
155.a.& inde

14.b
116.c.117.d
ibid.
429.c

o*

Scaliger on the Calendar. Index to *De emendatione temporum* by Joseph Justus Scaliger (1593). COURTESY OF THE UNIVERSITY OF ILLINOIS, URBANA-CHAMPAIGN

(1350–1420) at the Council of Constance in 1414. Nicholas of Cusa (1401–1464) made the same point at the Council of Basel in 1434. At the request of Pope Sixtus IV, the astronomer Johannes Regiomontanus (1436–1476) spent some time in Rome working on the problem, but died soon after he began the task. In his 1533 edition of the liturgical books, Pope Pius V adjusted the calendar by four days to correct errors in the calculation of Easter. Then, in its session of 1562–1563, the Council of Trent decreed that the pope should carry out the needed calendar reform. Some ten years later Pope Gregory XIII appointed a commission to study the question.

In 1560, Pietro Petati had proposed a key calculation for the reform of the civil part of the Julian calendar. He pointed out that 3 times 134 is roughly 400, and thus three leap years should be removed in 400 years. He proposed the rule that any year divisible by 100, which in the Julian calendar would be a leap year, should instead be an ordinary year of 365 days, except when the year is divisible by 400. According to this rule, which was then adopted by the Gregorian reformers, the year 1900 was not a leap year but the year 2000 was.

The Gregorian calendar was actually promulgated in 1582. It included the provision that ten days be dropped from the calendar to bring the vernal equinox back to where it had been in the time of Caesar. As a result the day after 4 October became 15 October. According to this method of calculation the average length of the year became 365.2425 days. Notably, the Gregorian rule is the inverse of the Julian rule, using centuries instead of years.

When the reform commission compared the adopted length of the year in the Gregorian calendar with the value found in the Alfonsine tables, the members thought that its adopted value still left an excess of approximately one day in 22,000 years. Although they were aware even at that time that 365.2425 days was not the best astronomical value, the commissioners judged with good common sense that the figure was close enough and left further adjustment to later generations.

Reception of the Gregorian Reform.
Whether the calendar reformers used the Alfonsine or the Copernican astronomical data has been controversial. Both are mentioned in the literature. The reform commission did object strongly, however, to the proposal that astronomically true data be used to calculate Easter. Instead they kept the traditional Metonic lunar cycle and suppressed ten days to bring the equinox back to 21 March, as it was at the time of the Council of Nicaea. Christopher Clavius (1537–1612), the Jesuit astronomer, pointed out that the available astronomical tables were not entirely reliable and themselves did not agree. Thus, he believed, their use would become a source of disagreement and division instead of unity.

Since the final reform of the calendar was done in Rome, most Protestant countries initially resisted it for religious and political reasons. Scholars and astronomers, including Michael Maestlin (1550–1631) and Justus Scaliger (1540–1609), found fault with the new calendar. As a member of the reform commission, Clavius was asked to write in its defense. His

Explanatio remains the official reference work for anyone wishing to study the details of the reform. (The *Explanatory Supplement,* published in 1961, gives the official date of adoption for every state or region.) Most Catholic countries adopted the new calendar immediately or shortly after it was promulgated. Little by little the Protestant countries accepted the reform, but the Orthodox Church did not. England and its dominions introduced the Gregorian calendar on 3 September 1752; at the same time they changed the beginning of the year from 25 March to 1 January.

The Gregorian calendar had the merit of being simple and well adapted for computation. Its civil part is still the worldwide standard as a reference calendar. Though the original reformers estimated the calendar's error as one day in excess in 22,000 years, we now know that the error is actually one day in about 2,500 years. Astronomers now also know that the length of the day is in fact slightly variable in a way not fully understood. In any event, it would be labor lost to attempt to improve on the Gregorian civil year when our understanding of the astronomical problems still remains incomplete.

See also **Astronomy**.

BIBLIOGRAPHY

Clavius, Christoph. *Explicatio romani calendarii a Gregorio XIII restituti* (Explanation of the Roman calendar restored by Gregory XIII). Rome, 1603.

Coyne, G. V., M. A. Hoskin, and O. Pedersen, eds. *Gregorian Reform of the Calendar.* Vatican City, 1983. Contains essays by the editors and by O. Gingerich, G. Moyer, H. M. Nobis, and J. D. North.

Explanatory Supplement to the Astronomical Ephemeris. London, 1961.

Explanatory Supplement to the Astronomical Almanac. Mill Valley, Calif., 1992.

Ginzel, F. K. *Handbuch der mathematischen und technischen Chronologie.* 3 vols. Leipzig, Germany, 1906–1911.

Kluepfel, Charles. "How Accurate Is the Gregorian Calendar?" *Sky and Telescope,* November 1982: 417–418.

Moyer, Gordon. "Luigi Lilio and the Gregorian Reform of the Calendar." *Sky and Telescope,* November 1982: 418–419.

JUAN CASANOVAS

CALLIGRAPHY. Renaissance writing was characterized by a heightened concern for clarity and elegance, and an ideological commitment to the notion that this clarity reflected that of ancient writing. A crucial turning point in the history of Latin script came with the contributions of two Florentine humanists, Poggio Bracciolini (1380–1459) and Niccolò Niccoli (c. 1364–1437). They gave forceful momentum to a self-conscious effort that was already under way among humanists to clarify and beautify writing by using what they looked upon as ancient models.

Late Medieval Background. Despite the negative image of the medieval world that one can glean from the writings of many humanists, the intellectual environment of the high and late Middle Ages was vigorous and thriving. It simply tended to be broken up into a number of separate, intradisciplinary traditions. Manuscript production reflected this. Different areas of documentary and literary culture had their own styles and traditions of writing, and many of these continued well into the Renaissance. The physical form of writing, like all forms of cultural expression, continued to evolve; but for quite some time scholastic philosophical scripts as well as notarial and chancery scripts evolved organically and in a self-contained manner.

However, the evolution of humanism and the eventual turn toward the *studia humanitatis* (humanistic studies) did represent something new: a disciplinary tradition that fell into the interstices created by the differentiation of the traditional medieval disciplines. Humanists wanted to define their movement as something separate and apart; part of this meant the evolution of a new means of calligraphic expression. It did not happen overnight. We hear the first well-defined laments about the unclear penmanship of scribes—a favorite humanist target—from Petrarch (1304–1374), the first great exponent of Italian humanism. He states that scribes often write in such an unclear, compressed, and unreadable manner that "the scribe himself, if he returned soon after to his work, could scarcely read what he had written, and the buyer of the book would purchase not so much a book as blindness by means of a book" (Ullman, p. 13, n. 7). Elsewhere, Petrarch writes to Giovanni Boccaccio that he is having a copy made of his own letters in a hand that is "trim and clear . . . and in which [Boccaccio] will say that nothing orthographical and absolutely nothing pertaining to the art of grammar has been left out" (Ullman, p. 13, n. 6). Petrarch's greatest immediate successor in the humanist movement, Coluccio Salutati (1331–1406), had similar complaints and goals with respect to manuscript production. It is significant that both men complained most when they were of advancing age and when, by their own admission, their eyes were not what they had used to be. But whatever their initial personal motivations may have been, their thoughts about scribal practice soon became an arrow in the quiver of typical humanist anti-

Calligraphy. Title page of Horace's works by two Paduan calligraphers, c. 1480. SPENCER COLLECTION, THE NEW YORK PUBLIC LIBRARY, ASTOR, LENOX AND TILDEN FOUNDATIONS

scholastic complaints. Moreover, Salutati himself was an important part of the experiments in writing that Poggio Bracciolini brought to maturity.

Renaissance Evolution. In fact it was two members of the school of Coluccio Salutati—Poggio Bracciolini and Niccolò Niccoli—who were largely responsible for the shift toward a well-defined and recognizable humanist handwriting. Poggio, who rose from poverty to become a notary, papal secretary, and eventually chancellor of Florence, evolved a script known variously as humanist round hand, humanist book script, or, in his own day, *lettera antica.* If we compare it to the Gothic book hand that preceded it, we notice a number of differences, both in writing and in layout. Where the Gothic hand has words close together, the humanist hand uses more uniform spacing; where the Gothic is heavily abbreviated, the humanist hand tends to use fewer abbreviations; where the Gothic employs a number of straight strokes that can be hard to distinguish, the humanist hand differentiates the letters more clearly; where the Gothic hand will use a round final *s,* the humanist hand writes a long *s;* and where the Gothic page is laid out in two columns, the humanist layout is straight across the page.

From a cultural perspective, perhaps the most interesting aspect of the story is that in creating this script Poggio copied from preexisting exemplars that he seems to have believed, perhaps encouraged by Salutati, were written in an ancient Roman script. In fact the script he copied was a late example (eleventh or twelfth century) of Caroline minuscule, a script that owed its clarity and organization to another, earlier Renaissance, the Carolingian. Poggio and others assumed that because the script seemed clear it must be ancient, since the ancients were the masters of clarity of expression in all things.

We can also note that Poggio's imitation of his model was not complete. It owed, unsurprisingly, a number of debts to Italian medieval practice; its rotundity, for instance, was as much indebted to the Italian Gothic script known as the Bolognese round hand as it was to Caroline minuscule. Whether this and other differences from his exemplars should properly be seen as "failures" to imitate correctly or as self-conscious creative choices is a question scholarship has yet to answer. In any case, the humanist round hand was influential. With the introduction of printing with movable type, eventually it became one of the most widely used fonts and is the basis for the type you are reading now.

The other important humanist innovator was Niccolò Niccoli, the well-known Florentine antiquarian. He quickly learned Poggio's new script; then, by 1423, he adopted the letter forms of the new humanist hand into his own cursive script. His personal book hand, commonly known as humanist cursive, was the origin of what we now know as italic script. Eventually these two elements of humanist writing permeated the rest of Italy and much of Europe. They were an important influence in the development of European book hand during the Renaissance.

BIBLIOGRAPHY

Bischoff, Bernhard. *Latin Palaeography: Antiquity and the Middle Ages.* Translated by Dáibhí Ó. Cróinín and David Ganz. Cambridge, U.K., 1990. Sweeping account of Latin scripts from antiquity through the Middle Ages. See pp. 145–149 for Renaissance developments and for recent literature on the subject.
Black, R. "Humanism." In *The New Cambridge Medieval History: Volume Seven.* Edited by Christopher Allmand. Cambridge, U.K., 1998. Pages 243–277 and 906–915.
Davies, Martin. "Humanism in Script and Print in the Fifteenth Century." In *The Cambridge Companion to Renaissance Humanism.* Edited by Jill Kraye. Cambridge, U.K., 1996. Pages 47–62.
De la Mare, Albinia. *The Handwriting of the Italian Humanists.* Oxford, 1973. Masterful comparative study of the scripts of a number of important early Italian humanists, with a wealth of visual examples.
De la Mare, Albinia. "Humanistic Script—The First Ten Years." In *Das Verhältnis der Humanisten zum Buch.* Edited by Fritz Krafft and Dieter Wuttke. Boppard, Germany, 1977. Pages 89–108.
De la Mare, Albinia. "New Research on Humanistic Scribes in Florence." In *Miniatura fiorentina del Rinascimento, 1440–1525: Un primo censimento.* 2 vols. Edited by Annarosa Garzelli. Florence, 1985. Vol. 1, pp. 393–600. An excellent and detailed survey, with many scribal identifications.
Kirchner, Joachim. *Scriptura latina libraria a saeculo primo usque ad finem medii aevi.* 2d ed. Munich, 1970. A good collection of plates illustrating the development of Latin script.
Petrucci, Armando. *Writers and Readers in Medieval Italy.* Translated by Charles M. Radding. New Haven, Conn., 1995.
Ullman, Berthold L. *The Origin and Development of Humanistic Script.* Rome, 1960. The standard and classic account of the roles of Poggio and Niccoli, though now it should be supplemented with the work of de la Mare.

CHRISTOPHER S. CELENZA

CALVIN, JOHN (Jean Chauvin; 1509–1564), French humanist, rhetorician, and Protestant reformer. Calvin was best known as the most prominent intellectual spokesman for the Reformed (as opposed to the Evangelical or Lutheran) version of Protestantism.

He was born in Noyon, where his father, a notary, worked for the local bishop. He got his earliest education there and was awarded a benefice while still a boy, to finance his education for a clerical career. In 1523, he moved to Paris, where he studied first at the Collège de la Marche, with Mathurin Cordier, and then at the Collège Montaigu. After he completed his studies in the arts, his father decided to have him study law rather than theology. He moved to the University of Orléans in 1528 and studied with Pierre de l'Estoile. In 1529 he studied with Andrea Alciati at the University of Bourges. After returning to Paris in 1531, Calvin studied with several of the royal lecturers newly appointed by the king to introduce new humanistic disciplines into the intellectual community there. He came to know particularly well the great classicist Guillaume Budé, a specialist in the Greek texts of Roman law.

Calvin's first significant publication was his *Commentary on Seneca's* De clementia (1532). It was designed to display his skills as a young humanist and to show that he could improve on points of detail in the recent edition of Seneca's text by the great Erasmus. It revealed Calvin to be a fluent Latin stylist in the Ciceronian tradition, capable of using Greek sources when indicated, although without the real mastery of that language displayed by Budé and Erasmus. Clearly he was thoroughly informed on the writers of antiquity and their contemporary humanist commentators, and he was especially sensitive to Seneca's use of formal rhetorical devices. A reading of Calvin's commentary suggests that in the great intellectual quarrel then going on between scholastic dialecticians and humanist rhetoricians, Calvin was firmly on the side of the rhetoricians.

At about this time, in circumstances that remain obscure, Calvin became a Protestant and began associating with other Protestants in and around Paris. Late in 1533 after a general crackdown by the royal government on all Protestants, Calvin fled Paris. He spent the next two years in private study, voraciously reading Protestant theologies, primarily those of Luther, and editions of the church fathers, primarily Augustine. The end result was his *Institutes of the Christian Religion (Christianae religionis institutio)*, published in 1536. Designed to be an expanded catechism, it explained the essentials of the Christian faith from a Protestant perspective, for common pious readers, not professional theologians. The *Institutes* avoided formal syllogistic logic and most technical theological terms. It was a work of epideictic (demonstrative), deliberative, and forensic rhetoric, with the deliberative element predominating, designed to persuade readers to embrace this new vision of the Christian faith. It used rhetorical proof in the form of examples and figures of speech that are truncations of traditional proofs. It became the single most widely read and influential work of theology published in the entire period of the Reformation. Luther was more prolific but never reduced his ideas to a single book. Only Philipp Melanchthon's *Common Places (Loci communes rerum theologicarum*; 1521) approaches Calvin's *Institutes* in popularity and influence. No single Roman Catholic work of theology won similarly wide readership. Calvin spent much of the rest of his life revising, translating, and expanding this single book. Final versions appeared in 1559 in Latin and in 1560 in French.

It was on the strength of the *Institutes* that Calvin was invited by Guillaume Farel to become a public lecturer in Geneva in 1536. He and Farel were ex-

John Calvin. Anonymous portrait. BIBLIOTHÈQUE NATIONALE, PARIS/SNARK/ART RESOURCE

pelled from the city in 1538, but Calvin was invited back in 1541, now as a pastor as well as a teacher. He was given powers that made it possible for him to create an entirely new Reformed Church. He proceeded to use Geneva as a base to spread his version of Christianity to France and to many other countries in Europe, making it the chief Protestant alternative to Lutheranism.

Among the reforms that Calvin introduced in Geneva were changes in the educational system that made it thoroughly humanistic. In 1537, he invited his old teacher Cordier to reform the elementary school system. Cordier, too, was expelled from Geneva in 1538; he returned during the period of Calvin's ascendancy, but only toward the end of his (Cordier's) career. In 1559, Calvin helped create an academy that introduced humanist studies on an advanced level. Designed primarily to train Protestant pastors, it was the forerunner of the present University of Geneva. Calvin may well be the most powerful example of the contribution of Renaissance humanism to Protestant religion.

See also **Humanism,** *subentry on* **France; Protestant Reformation.**

BIBLIOGRAPHY

Primary Works
Calvin, John. *Commentary on Seneca's* De Clementia. Introduction, translation, and notes by Ford Lewis Battles and Andre Malan Hugo. Leiden, Netherlands, 1969.
Calvin, John. *Institutes of the Christian Religion.* Translation by Henry Beveridge. London, 1949.

Secondary Works
Battles, Ford Lewis. *Interpreting John Calvin.* Grand Rapids, Mich., 1996. A collection of articles, valuable particularly for information on Calvin's classical education and his use of classical sources.
Breen, Quirinus. *Christianity and Humanism: Studies in the History of Ideas.* Grand Rapids, Mich., 1968. A collection of Breen's articles on the debates between rhetoricians and dialecticians in the period, including one on rhetoric in Calvin's *Institutes.*
Bouwsma, William J. *John Calvin: A Sixteenth-Century Portrait.* New York and Oxford, 1988. An acute and thoughtful essay on Calvin and his thought, expertly set in its intellectual context.
Doumergue, Émile. *Jean Calvin: Les hommes et les choses de son temps.* 7 vols. Lausanne and Neuilly-sur-Seine, France, 1899–1927. The most detailed and documented account, though consistently hagiographic.

ROBERT M. KINGDON

CAMBRAI, LEAGUE OF. The League of Cambrai was a military alliance formed in the French city of Cambrai on 10 December 1508. Its member states joined forces ostensibly to ward off a threat of Turkish invasions, but their primary purpose was to stay Venetian expansionism. The treaty's signatories, each intent on recovering individual losses to Venice, included Emperor Maximilian I; Pope Julius II; King Louis XII of France; King Ferdinand II of Aragon; Francesco Gonzaga, the marquis of Mantua; Charles III, the duke of Savoy; and Alfonso d'Este, the duke of Ferrara.

After a century of successful conquests, the Republic of Venice extended on *terraferma* (the mainland) west to Bergamo, north to Trent, and east along the Dalmatian coast. But at the Battle of Agnadello in northern Italy near Milan on 14 May 1509, in a crushing defeat under the French armies of the League of Cambrai, Venice rapidly began to forfeit those mainland gains, all except Treviso. Fortunately for the Venetians, the allied interests that held the League together soon weakened with internal distrust and competing allegiances. By October 1511, Julius and Ferdinand had organized a new military alliance, a "Holy League," which included Venice. Although defeated by the French at Ravenna in April

1512, the Holy League advanced when French troops withdrew from their pyrrhic Italian victory. For the Venetians, that development marked a military change of tide, as Venice reconquered its entire mainland state by 1517.

See also **Wars of Italy.**

BIBLIOGRAPHY
Gilbert, Felix. "Venice in the Crisis of the League of Cambrai." In *Renaissance Venice.* Edited by J. R. Hale. London, 1973. Pages 274–292.
Sherman, Michael A. "Political Propaganda and Renaissance Culture: French Reaction to the League of Cambrai, 1509–1510." *Sixteenth Century Journal* 8 (1977): 97–128.

MICHAEL MILWAY

CAMBRIDGE, UNIVERSITY OF. The University of Cambridge owes its origin to Oxford, following on the suspension of studies there in 1209 as a consequence of the papal interdict on England of 1208 and, in 1209, the hanging of two or three Oxford students in reprisal for the killing of a townswoman. The university masters withdrew with their students, some to Cambridge, probably led by masters who had local connections and influence. After the resumption of teaching at Oxford in 1214, at least some of the migrants stayed behind to found England's second university in the East Anglian market town. The university developed rapidly, the regents securing the right to elect their own chancellor by 1225. By 1233 the university was a juridical entity; the first official act promulgated by the chancellor and regent masters dates from 1246. By about 1250 a set of organized, if rather elementary, statutes had appeared.

Government. The medieval constitution of Cambridge naturally resembled that of Oxford, but it was not a slavish copy. "Convocation" in Cambridge meant the body of regent masters—that is, masters of arts engaged in lecturing—acting in concert, although by 1304 it included nonregents (as it did at Oxford), and the body of regents (regent masters), who did most of the day-to-day business of the university, was henceforth (as in Oxford) called "congregation." The head of convocation was the chancellor. He might delegate his powers to a commissary. If the chancellor was absent for two weeks or more, his powers would be exercised by an official elected by congregation called the "vice chancellor," a term later adopted in Oxford. It was convocation (at Cambridge later called the "senate") that made statutes and university appointments and granted dispensations from statutory requirements.

As a training ground of clerics and civil servants, Cambridge, like Oxford, was protected by the crown, its jurisdiction over both scholars and the town being ensured by royal charters. Its students were drawn largely from the eastern counties, reaching into the north. Modern estimates place the numbers in the mid-fourteenth century at some seven hundred against Oxford's fifteen hundred, but a century later the numbers were much closer—about thirteen hundred to seventeen hundred. Throughout the fifteenth century the university gathered strength in patronage and endowments as well as numbers, and the vitality it was to exhibit in the Tudor period was already evident under the Yorkist kings.

Tudor government affected Cambridge's medieval constitution as it did that of Oxford. Most information about the successive royal visitations of 1535, 1549, and 1556 comes from Cambridge, the Oxford materials having disappeared. In place of the earlier polity of regent masters, a new estate in government was created, based on the growing wealth and influence of the undergraduate colleges. The Elizabethan statutes of 1570 centralized authority through the heads of the colleges, usually nominees of the crown. Where before their official influence scarcely extended outside their own foundations, the heads now nominated two men for the post of vice chancellor annually and, with the doctors and other senior members, shared in the annual selection of a new steering committee, known as the *caput senatus* (head of convocation), to vet the business placed before the assembly of regents and nonregents. In conjunction with the vice chancellor, the heads secured virtual control over the officials and legislative powers of the entire university and acquired the right of veto over elections held within their own colleges.

Renaissance Influences.

At neither Cambridge nor Oxford was there a sharp disjunction between late-medieval scholastic culture and the early influences of Renaissance humanism. Owing to the fortunes of dynastic politics, the last part of Duke Humphrey of Gloucester's library intended for Oxford was granted instead to King's College, Cambridge. Cambridge scholars began to travel to Italy to acquire humanistic Latin and Greek and left their libraries within the university for the use of others. More significant from the standpoint of university teaching was the step taken in 1488, when the regent masters changed the requirements for undergraduates in arts. Henceforth, students were to follow a new sequence of lectures, the first two years being devoted to humane letters, the third to logic, and

the fourth to philosophy. These lectures were to be given by salaried professors, not by ordinary regents—that is, recent graduates earning their seniority. Three regents were also to be chosen annually to provide ordinary lectures in each of those subjects.

This alteration foreshadowed the provision of new studies through the establishment of endowed chairs attached to the colleges; and it was at Cambridge that the pioneering measures were taken. They resulted from the decisive collaboration of John Fisher, the future bishop of Rochester, with Lady Margaret Beaufort (d. 1509), countess of Richmond and Derby and, as mother of Henry VII, the last representative of the Lancastrian line to wield royal authority. Fisher, a graduate of the university and a member of the Faculty of Theology, became Beaufort's spiritual and academic adviser and a powerful figure in Cambridge, having been made chancellor for life in 1514.

In 1497 Lady Margaret endowed readerships in theology at both Oxford and Cambridge to provide free instruction to the universities. The first holder at Cambridge was John Fisher; his successor from 1511 to 1514 was Erasmus of Rotterdam. In subsequent years this collaboration was responsible for the conversion of a Lancastrian foundation intended to produce schoolmasters into Christ's College (1505), which was created to supply a new generation of educated clergy. More significant was the foundation of St. John's College (1511) to the design of John Fisher, who made provision for readers in Greek and Hebrew and insisted that theology be approached through a preliminary grounding in the humanities. Whatever the state of Hebrew teaching at St. John's may have been—and in the early years this is by no means clear—a chair in Hebrew came to the university as a consequence of Thomas Cromwell's injunctions of 1535, and, as at Oxford, it was paid for by the colleges. In the foundation of Trinity College (1546, statutes 1552), King Henry VIII gave Cambridge a counterpart to Oxford's Christ Church, with similar provision of regius chairs (chairs of royal foundation) in theology, Hebrew, Greek, civil law, and medicine, established in a college on a scale surpassing even Thomas Wolsey's original dream.

Colleges continued to foster new studies quite independently of such initiatives. Dr. John Caius, the second founder of Gonville and Caius College, encouraged medical and scientific studies, and St. John's endowed lectures in arithmetic, geometry, perspective, and cosmography. John Dee, the celebrated Elizabethan scientist and mathematician, was

King's College, Cambridge. Interior, showing the fan vaulting of the ceiling and the organ. The chapel was begun in the reign of King Henry VI in 1446 under the direction of Robert Ely; work was suspended in 1461 after the defeat of Henry in the Wars of the Roses. Work resumed in 1506 under the direction of John Wastell and the exterior was completed in 1515. The interior decoration was undertaken by Henry VIII. The organ case dates from 1686–1688. JOHN BETHELL/THE BRIDGEMAN ART LIBRARY

the university. Thus, Cambridge seems to have led the way in the reception of the criticism by Petrus Ramus of Aristotle's logic in the 1570s, as well as of Niccolò Machiavelli and Jean Bodin, as it had done earlier in the reception of Protestantism.

Indeed, religion and religious controversy largely dominated the debates of the university in the later years of Elizabeth I and those of James I, a fact that has influenced the university's historiography. The esteem in which Cambridge was held by Protestant Tudor governments is best indicated by the powerful laymen chosen as chancellors: Thomas Cromwell, after the execution of John Fisher in 1535; Edward Seymour, duke of Somerset, and John Dudley, first duke of Northumberland (both under Edward VI); and (under Elizabeth I), William Cecil, Lord Burghley, who died in 1598 after forty years in office, Robert Devereux, second earl of Essex, until his execution in 1601, and Robert Cecil, later earl of Salisbury (d. 1612). At the same time, the violent religious controversies associated with the names of John Whitgift, William Fulke, and Thomas Cartwright, like those surrounding the Cambridge advocates of presbyterianism and "godly" ministry or the debates on grace and predestination, disturbed the reformed church of England and occupied the national spotlight.

Social Change. The social impact of the laicization of the university, as of the new emphasis on humanistic and scientific studies, was readily apparent by the turn of the seventeenth century. Robert Cecil, as chancellor, wrote in 1602 that among disorders in the university "tending to the decay of learning, and other dissolute behaviour," was the fact that "scholars now go in their silks and velvets, liker to courtiers than scholars." In the present state of information about Renaissance Cambridge, it is not possible to quantify the change, but it is amply clear that, whereas in medieval times it would have been exceptional to find men of high birth in Cambridge or Oxford, by the time of Elizabeth's reign so widespread was the search for literacy and the accomplishments that would favor a career in politics, at court, or in diplomacy that the sons of the gentry and nobility had become the dominant element in the student body. And a Cambridge man produced one of the most notable schemes for the creation of a noble academy for young Englishmen of good birth: Sir Nicholas Bacon (d. 1579) of Corpus Christi College.

Finally, if its graduates define a university's culture, for unmistakable representatives of the Euro-

known at both universities and migrated from St. John's, Cambridge, to the new royal foundation of Trinity as a founding fellow. Fulke Greville, Lord Brooke (d. 1628), left provision in his will to found a chair in history, corresponding to that of Camden in Oxford, dedicated to the instruction of the young in the "knowledge and use" of the past with an eye on public affairs in the present.

Although Cambridge lagged behind Oxford in the formal establishment of chairs in the sciences, the adaptability of college teaching allowed for innovations that were not visible in the formal provision of

pean Renaissance at Cambridge we need look no further than Gabriel Harvey (d. 1631) and Francis Bacon (d. 1626) for philosophical innovation; Lancelot Andrewes (d. 1626) and Jeremy Taylor (d. 1667), among scholar churchmen; Sir Edward Coke (d. 1634), among lawyers; and George Herbert (d. 1633) and John Milton (d. 1674), among poets. And, although he came up to the university at a date outside the limits of this volume, matriculating at Trinity College on 6 June 1661, it would seem illogical not to conclude with the name of one Cambridge man of unquestionable genius who perhaps more than any other individual exemplifies the achievement of Renaissance learning in the world of the university, Sir Isaac Newton (d. 1727).

See also **Oxford, University of; Universities.**

BIBLIOGRAPHY

Primary Work

Hackett, M. B. *The Original Statutes of Cambridge University: The Text and Its History.* Cambridge, U.K., 1970. Edition with historical introduction of the statutes of c. 1250. See also the review by Walter Ullmann in *Journal of Ecclesiastical History* 22 (1971): 134–139, questioning their official status.

Secondary Works

Aston, T. H., G. D. Duncan, and T. A. R. Evans. "The Medieval Alumni of the University of Cambridge." *Past and Present* 86 (February 1980): 9–86. A systematic study of the limited evidence.

Cobban, Alan B. *The King's Hall within the University of Cambridge in the Later Middle Ages.* London, 1969.

Curtis, Mark. *Oxford and Cambridge in Transition, 1558–1642.* Oxford, 1959. Still the standard work on the social and intellectual developments at Cambridge.

Leader, Damian Riehl. *A History of the University of Cambridge.* Vol. 1, *The University to 1546.* Cambridge, U.K., 1988. Exemplary first volume of a series.

Mullinger, J. Bass. *The University of Cambridge from the Earliest Times to the Royal Injunctions of 1535.* Cambridge, U.K., 1873. Still the only general history of the university, in some respects severely dated but generally reliable.

Mullinger, J. Bass. *The University of Cambridge from the Royal Injunctions of 1535 to the Accession of Charles the First.* Cambridge, U.K., 1884.

JAMES MCCONICA

CAMERARIUS, JOACHIM (Kammermeister; 1500–1574), German humanist polymath, classical scholar, and pedagogue. Camerarius was born in the episcopal city of Bamberg, in Franconia, where his father, a member of the lesser nobility, served as councillor to the local bishop. After early studies at the University of Leipzig (1513–1517), where he learned Greek under the tutelage of such humanists as the Englishman Richard Crocus and later Peter Mosellanus, he moved to the University of Erfurt

(1517–1521), where he received his master of arts degree and taught Greek. He left in 1521 to escape the plague and unrest in that city and matriculated at the University of Wittenberg, where he struck up a lifelong friendship with Philipp Melanchthon. Under Melanchthon and Martin Luther's influence he became a supporter of the Reformation. On a trip with Melanchthon to southern Germany in 1523, he traveled on alone to Basel and met Erasmus of Rotterdam. Having left Wittenberg to return to his hometown in 1524, he served with his father and brother as go-between in negotiations with peasants during the Peasants' War of 1525.

When Melanchthon declined to move to Nürnberg to oversee the newly founded Latin school there, he nominated instead Camerarius, who served as the school's first rector from 1526 until 1535. He represented Nürnberg at the second Diet of Speyers (1529) and at the Diet of Augsburg (1530), where he encouraged Melanchthon's work on the Augsburg Confession, a statement of faith presented to the emperor by the Lutheran estates, including Nürnberg. In 1535 Camerarius became professor of Greek literature at the University of Tübingen. In 1541, again through the offices of Melanchthon, Camerarius became professor of Latin and Greek at the (now Lutheran) University of Leipzig, where he remained until his death. During this time he represented Protestant interests at the 1555 Diet of Augsburg and at the 1557 religious colloquy in Worms. He invariably defended theological positions taken by Melanchthon. Following the latter's death, he published heavily edited versions of Melanchthon's letters and the first, and most influential, biography of him, *De Philippi Melanchthonis ortu, totius vitae curriculo et morte . . . narratio* (An account of the birth, life, and death of Philipp Melanchthon; 1566), which was in part a defense of Melanchthon's theology against certain Lutheran detractors.

Camerarius was a humanist par excellence. Throughout his career he concerned himself with the classical *progymnastica,* preparatory work in grammar and rhetoric, even translating the *Libellus progymnasmatum* of Aphthonius Sophista (1570). He wrote textbooks on rhetoric, figures of speech, and orthography and edited works on Greek grammar and syntax. He provided students with original texts and Latin translations and commentary for a variety of Greek authors, including Demosthenes, Sophocles, Aesop, and Homer. Camerarius also edited and commented upon Latin classics by such writers as Cicero and Plautus. He was so committed to the humanist ideal of imitation in language that he strongly objected to Erasmus's 1528 attack on the concept in *Ciceronianus* and finally published a refutation of that work ten years later in a commentary on Cicero.

Camerarius practiced what he taught, producing a variety of speeches, funeral orations, and poems. His eclogues, which included veiled references to his failed attempts at negotiating an end to the Peasants' War, were published by his son in 1568. He also wrote biographical sketches (notably of Albrecht Dürer, the Nürnberg painter) and full-length biographies (on the Lutheran bishop, Count Georg von Anhalt; on the German poet and fellow teacher in Nürnberg, Helius Eobanus Hessus; and on Melanchthon and Aesop). His stoic ideal of properly controlled emotions colored his depictions, and his strict adherence to the principles of rhetoric made them models for his students.

In religious literature, too, his goal was imitation in theology (particularly Melanchthon's) and emphasis on instruction. Thus, Camerarius composed basic catechetical materials, including a Greek poem in hexameter and a popular Greek catechism. In line with his commitment to humanist ideals, he cultivated particular interest in church history, producing (in addition to the biographies listed above) a life of Jesus, entitled *Historiae Jesu Christi . . . expositio* (1566), a history of the Moravian church Unitas Fratrum, and a history of the ecumenical councils. In this connection, he was among the first to question the authorship of the so-called Athanasian Creed. He analyzed apostolic figures of speech and translated Sirach into Latin. Like Melanchthon, Camerarius was interested in astrology, especially after the 1531 appearance of Halley's Comet. He wrote works on comets, translated Ptolemy's *Tetrabiblos* and other classic texts, cast horoscopes, and dabbled in divination. He also published and translated medical and pharmacological texts and translated Euclid into Latin.

BIBLIOGRAPHY

Baron, Frank, ed. *Joachim Camerarius (1500–1574), Beiträge zur Geschichte des Humanismus im Zeitalter der Reformation / Essays on the History of Humanism during the Reformation.* Munich, 1978. This bilingual collection of essays traces the wide-ranging scholarly contributions of Camerarius and includes a bibliography of his publications.

Wengert, Timothy J. " 'With Friends Like This . . .': The Biography of Philip Melanchthon by Joachim Camerarius." In *The Rhetorics of Life-Writing in Early Modern Europe: Forms of Biography from Cassandra Fedele to Louis XIV.* Edited by Thomas F. Mayer and D. R. Woolf. Ann Arbor, Mich., 1995. Pages 115–131. An examination of Camerarius's biography of his friend Melanchthon in the context of the theological disputes of the 1560s.

Woitkowitz, Torsten. "Die Freundschaft zwischen Philipp Melanchthon und Joachim Camerarius." In *Philipp Melanchthon und Leipzig: Beiträge und Katalog zur Ausstellung.* Edited by Günther Wartenberg. Leipzig, Germany, 1997. Pages 29–39. An examination of Melanchthon's influence in Camerarius's life, especially in connection with the professorship at the University of Leipzig.

TIMOTHY J. WENGERT

CAMÕES, LUÍZ VAZ DE (1524/25–1580), Portuguese poet. A signal example of the Renaissance soldier-poet, Camões is known principally as the author of *Os Lusíadas,* an epic of discovery in ten cantos.

The son of Simão Vaz de Camões and Ana de Sá, members of the lower nobility who lived in the Mouraria district of Lisbon, Camões may have attended the University of Coimbra. He served as a simple soldier in North Africa, where he lost an eye. He returned to Lisbon in 1549, but his involvement in a street brawl led to his imprisonment and a one-way ticket to India in 1553, again as a common soldier. He spent nearly twenty years in the colonies, serving eight viceroys and giving part of his time to writing plays and satiric verse. He was eventually sent to Macao in 1556 but in 1559 was relieved of his duties and sent back to Goa. He was shipwrecked off Cambodia in 1559 and just managed to save the manuscript of his epic.

Ambitious, he struggled desperately to return to Lisbon to get his poems printed. After many incidents he arrived in 1570, when the boy king Sebastião was on the throne; to him Camões dedicated his epic, printed in 1572. It merited a modest pension, which did not relieve his poverty. In 1578 Sebastião, who was childless, was killed at the battle of Alcázarquivir in Morocco. Camões did not live to see Philip II of Spain invade Portugal, but he knew that tragedy was imminent. On his deathbed he wrote: "All will see that so dear to me was my country that I was content to die not only in it but with it."

The title of his epic, *Os Lusíadas* (trans. *The Lusiads,* or the sons of Lusus), points to Camões's attitude toward his classical model, the *Aeneid* of Virgil. The title has a Latin ring yet does not evoke a single protagonist as does the *Aeneid, Orlando Furioso, La Franciade,* or a single epic voyage like the *Odyssey.* Although the fulcrum of the poem is the voyage of Vasco da Gama from Lisbon to Calicut (8 July 1497–20 May 1498), Camões makes this historic trajectory bear the weight of Portuguese history from its mythical beginnings to a point far beyond the conclusion of Gama's voyage of discovery.

The objectives of Virgil and Camões were remarkably similar: to write a national poem, embodying the pageant of Roman and Portuguese history, pivoted on a single issue; to establish and vindicate the link, on the one hand, between Greece and Rome and, on the other, between Rome and Christianity; to show that Rome was distinct from Greece, which it absorbs and supersedes, and that Christian Portugal was distinct from Rome but through Rome's culture and language was a true inheritor of its greatness; to exalt the new regime, the family of Augustus and the House of Aviz, and its chosen policies; and to connect all this with a supernatural conflict between rival powers—on the one hand, Juno and Venus, and, on the other, Venus and Bacchus, the representative deities of West and East, of wisdom and wine. In both poems past and present are constantly interwoven; both begin in medias res, in the historic present, and oscillate rhythmically between retrospect and prophecy, earth and heaven.

Juxtaposing past and present was a major challenge for all Renaissance epic poets. For both Virgil and Camões human history includes and is justified by a divine plan. In Os Lusíadas this plan manifests itself through a pagan supernatural inserted between Gama and the Christian God. Camões was determined to carry the whole panoply of Greco-Roman culture into the modern Christian world, creating the only dramatically successful European literary epic on a contemporary theme. But his eulogy is by no means uninterrupted. The hard edge of history is never absent, but this edge is honed by the poetry into matter for reflection on the flawed human condition and its potential for good and evil.

Although Camões also wrote extensively in a range of poetic genres in both Spanish and Portuguese, nothing else of his work was published until 1595, when his lyric and elegiac poetry was printed. It took some eighty years before Os Lusíadas was translated into English by Sir Richard Fanshawe (1655), an English diplomat who had long served in Spain. In 1776 William Julius Mickle produced a version that placed Camões in a different context, since he saw the poem as an epic of commerce. In the nineteenth century Camões's fame, not only as an epic poet but also as a writer of lyric love poetry, spread quickly among the great figures of English literature. Lord Viscount Strangford (1780–1855), another diplomat, translated *Poems, from the Portuguese of Luis de Camões* (1803), which awakened the reverence of the British explorer Richard Burton, who published translations of Camões's work in 1881, and of the poet Elizabeth Barrett Browning,

who published *Sonnets from the Portuguese* in 1850. By the mid-nineteenth century Camões's name began to circulate in North America, creating enthusiasm in Edgar Allan Poe, Henry Wadsworth Longfellow, and Herman Melville. The best modern translation is by Leonard Bacon (1950), and, to mark the quincentenary of Gama's arrival in Calicut, the Calouste Gulbenkian Foundation commissioned a translation by Landeg White (1997).

See also **Portuguese Literature and Language.**

BIBLIOGRAPHY

Primary Works
Camões, Luíz Vaz de. *Obras completas.* Lisbon, 1946. With preface and notes by Hernani Cidade.
Camões, Luíz Vaz de. *Os Lusíadas.* Edited with introduction and notes by Frank Pierce. Oxford, 1973. With selected bibliography.
The Lusiads of Luíz de Camões. Translated by Leonard Bacon with introduction and notes. New York, 1950. A rendering in octaves.
Camões, Luíz Vaz de. *The Lusíads.* Translated by Landeg White. London, 1997. With introduction, maps, select bibliography, chronology, and notes.

Secondary Works
Bell, Aubrey F. G. *Luís de Camões.* Oxford, 1923.
Freitas, William John. *Camoëns and His Epic: A Historic, Geographic, and Cultural Survey.* Stanford, Calif., 1963.
Hart, Thomas R. "Luís Vaz de Camoens." In *Petrarch to Renaissance Short Fiction.* Vol. 2 of *European Writers: The Middle Ages and the Renaissance.* Edited by William T. H. Jackson and George Stade. New York, 1983. Pages 747–767.
Monteiro, George. *The Presence of Camões: Influences on the Literature of England, America, and Southern Africa.* Lexington, Ky., 1996.

ROBERT BRIAN TATE

CAMPANELLA, TOMMASO (1568–1639), Italian poet, philosopher, and utopian.
[This entry includes three subentries:

The Life of Campanella
Campanella the Philosopher
Campanella the Literary Figure]

The Life of Campanella

The son of an illiterate shoemaker in the town of Stilo, in the Calabria region of southern Italy, Giovanni Dominico Campanella entered the Dominican order in 1582; in 1583 he took his vows under the name Tommaso because of his admiration for Saint Thomas Aquinas. A gifted student, he quickly mastered the more traditional authors but showed an early dissatisfaction with Aristotelianism, the predominant philosophy in the schools. He therefore decided to develop a new philosophical synthesis based on Christian sources rather than on Aristotle.

When in 1588 he discovered Bernardino Telesio's *De rerum natura* (On the nature of things), he converted to the new Renaissance philosophy, proclaiming the importance of the senses in the apprehension of knowledge. The earliest result of his new way of thinking was his first philosophical work, completed less than a year later, *Philosophia sensibus demonstrata* (Philosophy proven by the senses; 1591), a defense of Telesio's philosophy against his Aristotelian adversaries. In order to better discuss his ideas with fellow philosophers, Campanella moved to Naples.

Philosophia sensibus demonstrata and similar writings and activities caused him problems with the authorities, especially the Inquisition, and earned him a brief jail sentence. He was subsequently ordered to return to his convent in Calabria, but Campanella instead embarked on an extended journey through Italy, visiting Tuscany, Bologna, and Padua, where he was arrested again. Upon his release he began publishing, defending, and expanding on Telesio's philosophy. In 1594 he was again imprisoned, brought to Rome by the Inquisition, and forced to recant in the Church of Santa Maria sopra Minerva on 16 May 1595.

Campanella was arrested again in 1597 and ordered to return to Calabria. There he became the leader of a political conspiracy to overthrow the Spanish dominion of the Kingdom of Naples and found a new state inspired by utopian ideals of freedom of conscience, abolition of private property, and pursuit of knowledge. He was betrayed by one of the conspirators and arrested on 6 September 1599. Transferred to Naples, he was tortured, forced to confess, and condemned to death, both as a heretic and conspirator against the Spanish state. In order to escape the death sentence, Campanella pretended to be mad, well aware that canon law forbade the execution of insane people. He was spared but remained in jail for nearly thirty years until 23 May 1626. He wrote voluminously during these years, in part to maintain his sanity. He had few books at his disposal and had to depend on his prodigious memory. Liberated due to the intervention of Pope Urban VIII, Campanella went to Rome, disguised and under false name, in order to escape the Spanish viceroy of Naples.

After eight years in Rome, perceiving the mounting hostility of the Jesuits and the lessening of the Pope's protective efforts, Campanella fled to France with the help of the French envoy de Noailles in

Tommaso Campanella. Woodcut made at Paris by Balthasar Moncornet, 1638–1639.

October 1634. The fame of his works and the persecution by the Spanish authorities had preceded him, and in December 1634 he was received by Cardinal Richelieu in Paris. In February 1635 King Louis XIII granted him a pension. In May he was received by the Faculty of the Sorbonne, where his works were discussed and approved. Still opposed by the Spanish Inquisition and Spanish government, Campanella continued writing until his death in Paris on 21 May 1639.

RICHARD J. BLACKWELL *and* STELIO CRO

Campanella the Philosopher

Campanella was one of the great literary figures and philosophical thinkers in Italy in the early seventeenth century. He is especially noteworthy for his development of a philosophical synthesis, his utopian writings, and his role in the Galileo affair.

Philosophical Synthesis. The central idea that unifies Campanella's philosophical system is that everything that exists contains three different components, or "primalities," as he calls them. These three components, in the order of their origination, are power (to exist and to act), knowledge (of the self and others), and love (of the self and others). Knowledge presupposes that an entity exists and acts, and love presupposes that one is aware of the object of attraction. These three primalities are distinct and of equal value, and they interpenetrate each other in such a way as to constitute the unity of each individual thing and of all things as a whole. Everything in existence, from God down to the smallest pieces of matter, contains these three principles.

These primalities constitute the trinitarian nature of God the Father as power, God the Son as knowledge, and God the Holy Spirit as love. When God created the world, this same triadic structure was communicated to creatures in progressively weaker and more finite forms.

In keeping with this system, human beings must be composed of three substances: body, spirit, and mind, in contrast to the much more common dualistic notion of humans as composed of body and soul so prevalent in the Aristotelian-Thomistic philosophy of Campanella's day. Campanella's human spirit is a physical, and not immaterial, component of the human being. While the human body is composed of dense matter, the spirit is composed of imperceptible matter (thinner than air) that is mobile, bright, warm, and endowed with causal power, sensation, and desire—further reflection of the three primalities. The human spirit resides primarily in the brain but also travels through the neural system and the blood of the body, as it respectively vivifies the body and senses objects in the physical world. The latter cause sensations directly in the spirit residing in the sense organs of the body, which are merely conduits for this causal action. The spirit thus mediates between the body and the mind or intellectual soul, bridging the gap between the material and immaterial in humans. The mind is created by God and infused in the body, already organized and permeated by the spirit. It is the mind that elevates humans far above the animals, and that is open to religious communication and reunion with God, who is the object of human love and happiness.

Campanella's three primalities also extend below the human level to all animals, plants, and inanimate objects. As a result, there runs throughout Campanella's writings an obscure but persistent presence of the occult in the form of magical and astrological explanations and predictions. These explanations at times seem to amount to an animism in his thought, and at other times to an intimation of pantheism, doctrines that were very suspect to the church officials of that day. The overall unity of Campanella's philosophical synthesis was imperfect and harbored inconsistencies that he was unable to resolve.

Campanella's ethical system is derived from the ontology sketched above. The highest moral good for humans is the conservation of one's own being. Whatever contributes to self-conservation is morally good; whatever impedes it is morally evil, and moral virtues are the instruments to attain the moral good. The highest form of self-conservation can be attained only by existing with God and becoming like God in the next life. In this way the human share of power, knowledge, and love reaches fulfillment by participation in these same primalities as they exist in God, thereby completing the circle of creation.

The Ideal State. By far the most popular and best known of Campanella's voluminous writings is *La città del sole* (*The City of the Sun;* written in 1602, first published in 1623), a classic example of Renaissance utopian literature. Although imprisoned by the Spanish state and the Catholic church at the time he wrote this treatise, Campanella nevertheless envisioned a society in which these two great institutions, each significantly reformed and purged of abuses, would be merged into one universal theocratic society without distinction between church and state, and ruled by a philosophical and princely pope. This society would be totalitarian, although not authoritarian since it would be ruled by reason. It would be communistic in its work requirements, property laws, and sexual practices. It would be egalitarian in that all positions in the society would be assigned on the basis of merit alone; women as well as men would qualify based on merit for any and all positions not requiring unusual physical strength in public office, in the military, and in civil life in general. Like Francis Bacon's *New Atlantis* (1627), Campanella's ideal state placed a heavy emphasis on education, science, and technology, which would be responsible for maintaining the stability and improving the lives of the Solarians, as the citizens would be called. Although this society would not have received the Christian revelation yet, the Solarians would have been able to use their powers of reason to comprehend the trinitarian nature of the world and of God. When the religious revelation would come later, it would add not much more than the sacraments, which was Campanella's way of saying that much of the institutional Christianity of his day was merely an accidental accretion to the essential message of the religious revelation. According to Campanella a significant part of theology could be derived from science, in keeping with his basic view

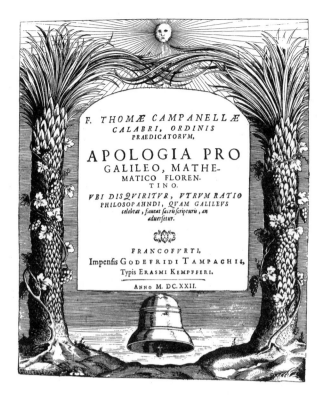

Campanella's Defense of Galileo. Title page of *Apologia pro Galileo,* (Frankfurt, 1622).

that the world exhibits the three primalities of power, knowledge, and love found first in God. His optimism about his ideal City of the Sun was almost unbounded, despite the harsh treatment he had received at the hands of both church and state. It was only later in his life that he became much less sanguine about the possibility of actually implementing the Solarian society on earth.

The Galileo Affair. The preliminary phase of the trial of Galileo Galilei (1564–1642) occurred in 1616 and centered on the question of whether Copernicus's new heliocentric theory of the world was contrary to the revealed truths of the Bible. At that time Campanella himself had already been in prison for seventeen years on charges of heresy. Nevertheless he was asked by Cardinal Boniface Caetani, a member of the church tribunal considering the matter, to submit his theological assessment of the issues involved. This in itself was an extraordinary recognition of Campanella's reputation as a theologian in the church.

Campanella was not a close friend of Galileo, having met him only briefly years earlier; he personally believed that the commonsense geocentric view of the structure of the world was accurate and that Ga-

lileo had not proven his case for heliocentrism. However, he wrote a very strong brief in support of Galileo. After considering in detail the scientific and the biblical arguments at issue, Campanella sided with Galileo primarily because the well-being of the church itself was at stake, since any restrictions on freedom of inquiry in general would be a serious betrayal of its genuine interests.

Campanella's treatise, *Apologia pro Galileo* (A defense of Galileo; written in 1616, first published in 1622), has become a classic appeal for freedom of thought. Given the threatening circumstances under which he had to work, his courage in writing this stirring defense of intellectual freedom was remarkable. Unfortunately he failed to influence the decision of the court.

See also **Political Thought; Utopias;** *and biography of Galileo Galilei.*

BIBLIOGRAPHY

Primary Works

Campanella, Tommaso. *A Defense of Galileo, the Mathematician from Florence.* Translated by R. J. Blackwell. Notre Dame, Ind., 1994. Translation of *Apologia pro Galileo, mathematico florentino* (1622).

Campanella, Tommaso. *La città del sole: Dialogo poetica. The City of the Sun: A Poetical Dialogue.* Translated by Daniel J. Donno. Berkeley, Calif., 1981. Text in English and Italian.

Secondary Works

Amabile, Luigi. *Fra Tommaso Campanella: La sua congiura, i suoi processi e la sua pazzia.* 3 vols. Naples, Italy, 1882.

Blanchet, Léon. *Campanella.* Paris, 1920. Reprint, New York, 1964.

Bonansea, Bernardino. *Tommaso Campanella: Renaissance Pioneer of Modern Thought.* Washington, D.C., 1969. The best comprehensive study of Campanella in English.

Firpo, Luigi. *Bibliografia degli scritti de Tommaso Campanella.* Turin, Italy, 1940.

Headley, John M. *Tommaso Campanella and the Transformation of the World.* Princeton, N.J., 1997. Another excellent study.

Langford, James R. "Science, Theology, and Freedom." In *On Freedom.* Edited by Leroy S. Rouner. Notre Dame, Ind., 1989. Pages 108–125.

RICHARD J. BLACKWELL

Campanella, the Literary Figure

Most of Campanella's literary works—the utopian *La città del sole* (*The City of the Sun*) and his poetry—were written while he was in jail in Naples.

Utopian Work. By far the best known and most influential of his works was *La città del sole,* first published in 1623. It was inspired by the rational philosophy of the Renaissance, epitomized by Bernardino Telesio's *De rerum natura* (On the nature of things), which Campanella had read in 1588. Campanella envisioned an original pedagogical system in which children were taught through play using audiovisual means and encouraged to experiment in shops and laboratories, a concept that may not seem new to us but was in fact far ahead of its time. He also describes futuristic machines, self-propelled vessels, and a medical science that would eradicate all illness and increase the human life span.

Poetry. The initial publication of Campanella's poetry came about through the efforts of a German scholar, Tobia Adami, who had visited him in the Neapolitan jail and smuggled out several of Campanella's manuscripts, among them a manuscript of his poetry. From this manuscript Adami selected verses and published them in 1622 under the title of *Scelta* (Selection).

Two themes dominate this work: Campanella's sorrow at his unjust imprisonment, torture, and mistreatment; and the reconciliation of faith and science, the Bible and the new science of Galileo. His scientific discussion was founded on the certitude that the discovery of America and Galileo's astronomical discoveries had changed the world forever, and that it was a mistake to argue that the authority of the Bible ought also to be considered as a scientific principle. For Campanella the Bible and nature were both divine codes with different purposes. He criticized poets who clung to classical mythology and medieval superstitions without recognizing the great historical events that occurred in their time. According to Campanella only historical events should be the dominion of poetry; epic poetry ought to address significant events like Columbus's voyage. In his view poetry must speak a universal language based on facts, not theories; on nature, not abstract notions.

Campanella stated his view in the "Proemio" (Introduction), which he composed for the publication of the *Scelta*. In it he presents himself as "sagace amante del bene, vero e bello" (wise lover of goodness, truth, and beauty). In order to apprehend these notions people must free themselves of the false school of thought that spreads "doglia, superbia e l'ignoranza" (sorrow, arrogance, and ignorance). This false school of thought is Aristotelianism. Campanella defended Galileo when the great scientist was condemned in 1516, writing, while still in jail, *Apologia pro Galileo* (A defense for Galileo). The function of science, in Campanella's view, was to imitate nature, to respect the natural order of things, and to oppose vices and falsehoods. In a poem entitled *Del mondo e sue parti* (Of the world and its parts), Campanella imagines the universe as a "large, perfect animal" and humankind as "imperfect worms and despicable race," in order to distance himself from the rationalist conviction spread during the Renaissance of humanity as center and master of the universe, and to remind mankind of the majesty of nature and creation.

The rationalist philosophy of the Renaissance was superseded by a series of revolutionary discoveries and developments that caused a radical shift in the way the world and humans were conceived. This change, involving the Protestant Reformation, the discovery of the New World by Columbus, and Galileian and Copernican astronomy, found its way into Campanella's poetry and evolved into a modern view of humanity. This evolution caused in Campanella a disquieting sense of the inadequate pedagogical principles guiding the teaching of the younger generation. His poetry anticipated many baroque authors who felt a similar uneasiness, as well as more modern movements, including romanticism, with its valuation of the beauty and purity of nature over the excesses of reason.

See also **Galilei, Galileo; Political Thought; Utopias.**

BIBLIOGRAPHY

Primary Works

Campanella, Tommaso. *The City of the Sun.* Translated by A. M. Elliott and R. Millnor. Introduction by A. L. Morton. London and West Nyack, N.Y., 1981.

Campanella, Tommaso. *Poetica e poesia di Tommaso Campanella.* Edited by Pasquale Tuscano. Milan, 1969.

Campanella, Tommaso. *Tutte le opere. I scritti letterari.* Edited by Luigi Firpo. Milan, 1954.

Secondary Works

Cro, Stelio. "Tommaso Campanella and the Poetry of the Baroque." *Romance Notes* 22, no. 1 (1981): 88–93.

Cro, Stelio. *Tommaso Campanella e i prodromi della civiltà moderna.* Hamilton, Pa., 1979.

STELIO CRO

CANTER, JACOB (1469–1529), Dutch poet and prose writer. Jacob Canter was born in Groningen into a leading patrician family. His father, Johannes Canter, a lawyer, who was influenced by Italian humanism, made sure that Jacob mastered Latin at a very young age. He enrolled in the law faculty of the University of Cologne in 1487, but did not finish his law studies. He continued his study of the liberal arts and read the Latin classics and humanist writers like Petrarch. It is not clear where and when Canter received his doctorate in the liberal arts.

In 1489 Canter went to Antwerp, where he gave private lessons in Latin to a small number of students. There he met the publisher and printer Gerard de Leeuw, for whom he prepared three Latin text editions, most notably an edition of Petrarch's autobiographical dialogue *Secretum.* Canter was convinced—mistakenly—that his was the first printed edition of this work. The preface testifies that Canter was familiar with the opinions of fifteenth-century Italian humanists: he regarded Petrarch's style as old-fashioned, although he admired him as the founder of humanism. Canter's humanistic interest led him to Italy in 1489 and 1490. On his travels he met a number of German humanists, above all Conrad Celtis. In Antwerp in 1494 Canter was crowned poet laureate by the emperor Maximilian II. In 1495–1496 Canter stayed in Mainz, where he edited two Latin texts, the most prominent being Rudolf Agricola's Latin translation of Plato's *Axiochus.* In 1497 he became court poet of the Rosenberg family at Český Krumlov in Czechia.

Canter's most important works are the *Rosa Rosensis* (The rose of the Rosenbergs), a small Latin love-drama of 851 verses, and the prose treatise *Dyalogus de solitudine* (Dialogue on solitude). *Rosa Rosensis* displays an interesting fusion of genres, combining elements of ancient Latin comedy with various forms of hexametric poetry. The plot is dominated by the theme of courtly love between the "young lover" Eutychus and princess Calliroë. One may suppose that the *Rosa Rosensis* was performed (or recited) at the court of the Rosenbergs.

Even more important is Canter's *Dyalogus de solitudine,* probably written between 1497 and 1504. It displays an interesting fusion of elements of Latin comedy and various types of Latin dialogues. It testifies to Canter's mastery of Neo-Latin prose style, which is all the more noteworthy given that hardly any prose works by Dutch humanists survive from before 1500. Judging from its title, contemporary readers would certainly have expected a treatise about monastic life, but they can hardly be more deceived. Ignoring religious questions almost entirely, the work offers a fundamental criticism of contemporary urban civilization, putting forward the argument that the lifestyle of prehistoric man was to be preferred and unfolding a discussion of extreme cultural pessimism versus cultural optimism. As the author hides himself behind the mask of his dialogue persons, his personal stand in the dilemma must elude our grasp. The work, an enticing thought experiment, belongs to the *genus ioco-serium* and can, in this respect, be compared to Erasmus's *Laus stultitiae.* Sometime between 1498 and 1505 he was ordained as a priest; in 1505 he was appointed vicar at

Emden. Toward the end of his life he returned to Groningen, where he died.

BIBLIOGRAPHY

Enenkel, Karl A. E. *Kulturoptimismus und Kulturpessimismus in der Renaissance. Studie zu Jacobus Canters "Dyalogus de solitudine" mit kritischer Textausgabe und deutscher Übersetzung.* Frankfurt am Main and New York, 1995.

K. A. E. ENENKEL

CANTI CARNASCIALESCHI. *See* **Parades, Processions, and Pageants.**

CAPITO, WOLFGANG (Wolfgang Köpfel; 1478–1541), theologian, Hebrew scholar. Born in Haguenau, Capito attended the universities of Ingolstadt (1501–1504; B.A.), Heidelberg (May 1504–1505), and Freiburg im Breisgau (M.A., 1506; Doctor of Theology, July 1515). From 1512 to 1515 he was a canon and was appointed preacher of the Benedictine foundation in Bruchsal, near Karlsruhe; he then became cathedral preacher in Basel, where he spent five years, taught theology at the university, and entered the circle of humanists gathering at the Froben Press. Capito published a Hebrew handbook (2 vols.; 1516, 1518) and was involved in the edition of Martin Luther's collected writings, published by Johann Froben in October 1518. On 28 April 1520 he left Basel for Mainz, where he had been appointed preacher of Saint Martin's Cathedral, and soon (October 1520) became counselor to Archbishop Albert, at whose instigation the emperor granted to the Köpfel family an armorial bearing (7 February 1523). After a legal action started in June 1519, Capito managed (25 August 1521) to be appointed provost of Saint Thomas in Strasbourg (where he withdrew only in March 1523), yet without having gotten rid of his opponents.

In July 1523, when he was confirmed as provost of the collegiate church of Saint Thomas in Strasbourg, Capito openly joined the Reformation. That meant an end to his friendship with Erasmus; he nevertheless translated Erasmus's *Liber de sarcienda ecclesiae concordia* into German in 1533, not without distorting somewhat the author's aim in his dedication to the archbishop of Mainz. In 1524 he married and became pastor of Saint Peter the Younger, lecturing for several years on biblical books. In the following years he published commentaries on Habakkuk (1526) and Hosea (1528), as well as a Latin and a German catechism (1527). In 1528 he was only present at the disputation between Catholics and Reformers in Bern, but in January 1532 he had an important influence on the second Synod of Bern, since he was the main author of the normative theological text produced at this meeting. In 1530 he went with Martin Bucer to the Diet of Augsburg and was probably involved in the writing of the *Confessio Tetrapolitana*. In May 1536 he signed the Concord of Wittenberg, and in the 1540s he attended the conferences between Protestants and Catholics.

Several of Capito's actions demonstrate his interest in the French Reformation: in 1525 and 1526 he received at his home French religious refugees such as Jacques Lefèvre d'Étaples, Gérard Roussel, Michel d'Arande, Guillaume Farel, and Simon Robert; he dedicated his commentary on Hosea to Margaret of Navarre (22 March 1528); and in 1535 he signed one of the preliminary pieces to the Olivetan Bible, the French translation of the Bible, under the initials "V. F. C." He is also known for extolling the experience of faith in the Holy Spirit, for which fraternity and unity among believers are more important than doctrines, outward ceremonies, or the literal Word. Capito is thus a forerunner of Pietism. In spite of his estrangement from Erasmus, Capito continued to reflect his influence, both in his love of peace and abhorrence of civil unrest and in his belief that education is the mainstay of religion and society. He died on 3 November 1541 in Strasbourg.

BIBLIOGRAPHY

Primary Work

Millet, Olivier. *Correspondance de Wolfgang Capiton (1478–1541): Analyse et index.* Strasbourg, France, 1982.

Secondary Works

Kittelson, James M. *Wolfgang Capito: From Humanist to Reformer.* Leiden, Netherlands, 1975.
Scholl, Hans. "Wolfgang Fabricius Capitos reformatorische Eigenart." *Zwingliana,* vol. 16. Zurich, Switzerland, 1986. Pages 126–141.
Stierle, Beate. *Capito als Humanist.* Gütersloh, Germany, 1974.

REINHARD BODENMANN

CARAVAGGIO, MICHELANGELO MERISI DA

(1571–1610), Italian painter. Michelangelo Merisi was probably born in Milan but lived in nearby Caravaggio, where his father was steward to Marchese Francesco I Sforza. Apprenticed in 1584–1588 to the conservative Milanese painter Simone Peterzano, he is intermittently recorded in Caravaggio until 1592, when he arrived in Rome. Certain aspects of Caravaggio's north Italian heritage were clearly influential throughout his career. Beyond figural and compositional borrowings from local artists such as Giovanni Girolamo Savoldo and Peterzano, he more importantly absorbed the north Italian traditions of naturalism and dramatic chiaroscuro (contrasts of light and dark), using the latter, like Leonardo da Vinci and his Milanese followers, to enhance the sculptural relief of figures. This lyrical, naturalistic tradition emphasized still life painting, portraiture, and genre scenes; meanwhile, the towering figures of Counter-Reformation Milan, archbishops Carlo and Federico Borromeo, who later owned Caravaggio's *Basket of Fruit,* encouraged naturalism and simplicity in Milanese religious art.

Roman Period. Caravaggio's early Roman production (c. 1593–1595) is notable both for its reliance on the Lombard naturalist tradition and, conversely, for its failure to imitate respected artistic models from antiquity and the high Renaissance. These earliest canvases, not done on commission, are technical demonstration pieces intended to highlight Caravaggio's insistent, sharp naturalism taken directly from life study. Yet the contrived system of lighting and affected pose of models betray a refined atmosphere and sophisticated design process. The *Sick Little Bacchus, Boy with a Basket of Fruit, Boy Peeling a Fruit,* and the *Boy Bitten by a Lizard* are characterized by the depiction of a single half-length figure, an androgynous youth clad in classicizing garments, who addresses the viewer. Eschewing a defined background setting and any sense of atmosphere or depth, Caravaggio focuses on still life objects with an exaggerated, tactile literalness. Objects tend to be placed against, and sometimes beyond, the picture plane, allowing for virtuoso displays of foreshortening.

In these early works Caravaggio attempts to capture momentary gesture, expression, and emotion, qualities best seen in the *Boy Bitten by a Lizard.* In the *Magdalene,* a full-length figure placed away from the plane, the mood is quiet and introspective, a feeling enhanced by the dark background shadow, two features important to his later religious images. In a horizontal format, the *Cardsharps* and *Fortuneteller* are Caravaggio's first essays in multifigure narrative composition. Duplicity is the theme of these genre scenes, which represent foolish youths in contemporary clothing, yet the blank, bright backgrounds reveal Caravaggio's staged, studio realism.

From 1595 to 1601, Caravaggio joined the household of the Florentine Cardinal Francesco del Monte, a well-known patron of music and art, who influenced Caravaggio's imagery by commissioning canvases of musical subjects. Although Caravaggio depended on north Italian precedents for composition,

Caravaggio. *The Fortune Teller.* Oil on canvas; 1594–1595; 99 × 131 cm (39 × 51.5 in.). MUSÉE DE LOUVRE, PARIS/ART RESOURCE

the instruments and various scores belonged to his patrons and were studied with consummate skill. It has recently been hypothesized that the seemingly erotic, androgynous model in the musical images is a Spanish castrato singer in Del Monte's retinue.

Religious Works. Caravaggio's contemporary religious works, such as the *Rest on the Flight into Egypt* and *St. Francis in Ecstasy,* signal a change in style and mood from his secular scenes. Both canvases include landscapes, which contribute to the quiet, intimate atmosphere, and androgynous angels, adopted from the secular pictures. Caravaggio begins to concentrate on spiritual meaning and initiates his famous exploitation of the effects of strong chiaroscuro, especially in the nocturnal *St. Francis,* where light is employed as the sole indicator of divinity. The introspective feeling of the tender *St. Francis* is a precocious intimation of Caravaggio's extraordinary ability to communicate images of spiritual profundity. *St. Catherine* demonstrates Cara-

vaggio's development by depicting a monumental, full-length figure comfortably situated in space by the dramatic contrast of light and dark. Likewise, the *Judith and Holofernes* and *Conversion of the Magdalene* elaborate the narrative format of the *Cardsharps* and *Fortune-teller,* although here chiaroscuro enhances drama and the sharp, sculptural relief of figures.

In 1599 Caravaggio received his first public commission, to paint the lateral canvases depicting the *Calling of St. Matthew* and the *Martyrdom of St. Matthew* in the Contarelli Chapel of San Luigi dei Francesi, Rome. This project secured Caravaggio a lasting reputation and much notoriety. Completed by 1600, the Contarelli canvases successfully synthesized diverse elements from both his early secular and sacred images. Apparently, two systems of lighting are employed: directed sunlight entering at an angle from a window and diffuse, overhead light from an artificial source such as a lamp. Light conveys sculptural form to figures while simultaneously serving as a metaphor for the divine. Dramatic gesture and movement also gain significance. Furthermore, sacred figures are depicted as unidealized, realistic human beings while secular actors are identified by a closer attention to costume, appearing as contemporary dandies. After the original version of the altarpiece was rejected, Caravaggio executed a more dignified, corrected replacement with a stately Matthew and distant angel.

Caravaggio was next commissioned, in 1601, to paint the two lateral canvases in the Cerasi Chapel of Santa Maria del Popolo, in direct competition with Annibale Carracci, who executed the altarpiece. Caravaggio's original versions of the *Conversion of Paul* and *Crucifixion of St. Peter* were rejected (only the *Paul* survives), but he quickly completed two astounding replacements. Hereafter, Caravaggio's religious works tend to convey deep concentration and utter seriousness enhanced by dark, contemplative shadow; yet, through the foregrounding of figures, they still appeal directly to the viewer. The deeply moving *Death of the Virgin* was also refused because, although touching and emotional, the scene was devoid of heavenly apparitions and resembled too much a common, realistic ceremony of mourning. Yet Caravaggio never lacked for private patrons.

Naples. In 1606, after committing a murder, Caravaggio fled Rome under the protection of the Colonna family, painting a *Supper at Emmaus* (Milan, Brera; for the version in the National Gallery, London, see the color plates in this volume) and a *Magdalene in Ecstasy* while in exile. He is next recorded in Spanish Naples, safe from papal jurisdiction and a capital sentence.

Between 1606 and his death in 1610, Caravaggio rapidly moved from Naples to Malta, where he spent a year, was knighted and later imprisoned, only to escape to Sicily and return again to Naples. In July 1610, on his way to Rome to receive the Pope's pardon, Caravaggio stopped at Port'Ercole, where he became ill and died of fever. Throughout this period Caravaggio, although a fugitive, continued to receive patronage at the highest levels of society. His brushwork becomes more rapid and broader, causing greater visibility of the red-brown middle ground, which now acts almost as a middle tone contributing to greater pictorial unity and evocative atmosphere. Precise naturalism yields to softer, more expressive forms as the mood of these predominantly religious images is one of melancholy, sobriety, and humility. Figures are reduced in scale, placed in a middle ground, and arranged in geometrical groups and

clear compositions. A dark, open space or void, which occupies the top portion of the canvas, contributes to the contemplative, tragic atmosphere. Gestures are subdued and posture restrained as Caravaggio concentrates on simple, intense inner emotion. The *Beheading of St. John, Burial of St. Lucy,* and *Raising of Lazarus* demonstrate well the geometrical organization of space and figural grouping. Massive architecture also gains significance in these canvases, for it contributes monumentality and solemnity while lending intimacy to the humble figures.

Style and Influence. Caravaggio and Annibale Carracci were the two major opponents of mannerism and exponents of a return to naturalism at Rome from the decade of the 1590s. Both wished to clarify the subject matter and intensify the message of religious art through the realistic depiction of figures and legible composition, initiating the baroque by emphasizing the appeal to sensory perception and directly engaging the viewer. Yet Annibale's idealized naturalism was tempered through the study of artistic tradition, of antiquity and the high Renaissance, and laborious preparatory drawing. His highly selective realism utilized and combined only what was most beautiful in nature.

Caravaggio, however, while frequently availing himself of artistic precedent, always remained far more devoted to direct, observable naturalism. In his singular experimentation with the dramatic effects of light and chiaroscuro, he employed light to increase the solidity of form, add pictorial or expressive interest, and represent the presence of the divine, sometimes all simultaneously in a single image. Yet Caravaggio consistently subordinated realist practices to a comprehensive sense of design; his famed naturalism was clearly regulated and studio-based. He achieved such stunning immediacy and presence from his figures by skipping the intermediary drawing process and instead painting from posed studio models directly onto the canvas. But perhaps Caravaggio's greatest achievement was his unparalleled communication of profound spiritual meaning and a searching exploration of human nature. His uncompromising realism dictated that sacred figures be depicted as unidealized and common human types, so that frequently, the witnesses to supernatural, divine events are clearly destitute members of the lower classes. Some patrons rejected these humble examples of faith, devotion, and piety; for other groups and audiences, they seemed to embody Counter-Reformation ideals.

Ironically, Caravaggio's spirituality was also the least understood and imitated feature of his output. Giovanni Battista Caracciolo, the Neapolitan painter, was possibly the only follower of Caravaggio to comprehend the style and mood of his mature spiritual sentiment. The majority of the Caravaggisti, as his imitators are called, in the first two decades of the seventeenth century focused on genre scenes, figural naturalism, and chiaroscuro, with little grasp of underlying content. As a group they lacked his sense of composition and subtle, sophisticated atmosphere. His most important Italian emulators were Orazio Gentileschi, Orazio Borgianni, and Carlo Saraceni; French followers include Valentin de Boulogne and Georges de la Tour; Dirck van Baburen, Gerrit van Honthorst, and Hendrick ter Brugghen reinterpreted his style in the north.

See also **Carracci Family**; **Naples**, *subentry on* **Art in Naples**.

BIBLIOGRAPHY

The Age of Caravaggio. New York, 1985. Exhibition catalog with information on Caravaggio and his contemporaries.

Cinotti, Mia. *Caravaggio*. Rev. ed. Bergamo, Italy, 1991. Meticulous, thorough, and reliable study.

Gregori, Mina, ed. *Caravaggio: Come nascono i capolavori*. Milan, 1992. An exploration of Caravaggio's technique and method.

Hibbard, Howard. *Caravaggio*. New York, 1983. Excellent introduction to Caravaggio's personality and art.

Puglisi, Catherine. *Caravaggio*. London, 1998. Balanced study that includes discoveries of archival documents and canvases relating to Caravaggio.

MARIO PEREIRA

CARDANO, GIROLAMO (1501–1576), Italian mathematician and physician. A man of contrasts, combining naive superstition with outstanding ability in the mathematical, medical, and physical sciences, Cardano also wrote prolifically on astronomy, astrology, philosophy, and probability. Born in Pavia, the illegitimate son of lawyer Fazio Cardano, he studied medicine at the universities of Pavia and Padua, supplementing his income by gambling. After graduating, he practiced in Saccolongo, a small town near Padua, where he married and subsequently had two sons and a daughter. He later described this period as the happiest in his life.

Cardano's repeated applications to the Milanese College of Physicians were for many years turned down, but in 1534 he secured an appointment teaching mathematics in the Piatti Foundation in Milan, where his lectures were very popular. At the same time he practiced medicine with such success that

Girolamo Cardano. Portrait from the title page of the first edition of his *Practica arithmeticae* (1539).

he eventually secured entry to the college (1539) and soon became one of the most eminent physicians in Europe. Among his most famous patients was John Hamilton, archbishop of St. Andrews, whom he successfully treated for asthma in 1552.

Cardano was a professor of medicine at the University of Pavia from 1543 to 1560 (with a break from 1552 to 1559). In 1560 his elder son was executed for poisoning his wife, and shortly afterward Cardano, who never recovered from this incident, moved to Bologna. Although he was imprisoned by the Inquisition for some months in 1570, he spent his last years in Rome, on a pension from the pope.

Cardano made notable contributions to mechanics, geology, and hydrodynamics, and his suspension device still bears his name. He observed that the trajectory of a projectile takes the form of a parabola, and made studies of the conditions for mechanical equilibrium and of methods of estimating the rate of flow of streams. From the presence of marine fossils on land Cardano deduced that an ocean floor could rise and dry out, and he is responsible for the idea that streams are fed from rainwater, which runs down to the sea to evaporate and fall again as rain.

Cardano's mathematical ability is apparent in his first mathematical work, the *Practica arithmeticae* (Mathematical practice; 1539), which was influenced by the *Summa* of Luca Pacioli (1494) and its vernacular Italian predecessors. Cardano demonstrated great skill in the manipulation of equations, exploiting the technique of adding expressions to both sides to enable reduction of the degree by factorization, and also that of the rationalization of denominators containing cube roots.

Cardano's gambling experiences led him to write an account of probability, the *Liber de ludo aleae* (Book on games of chance). His analytical ability is amply demonstrated by his understanding of the concept of probability, the power law for the repetition of an event, and what is now called the Law of Large Numbers. Unfortunately, this treatise, published posthumously (1663), came too late to have any influence on the subject.

Cardano is famous for the bitter dispute between him and his contemporary Niccolò Tartaglia (1499–1557) over the general solution to the cubic equation (an equation that involves the cubic and no higher power of the unknown), a problem that had occupied mathematicians for centuries. This conflict marks the contrast between an older tradition of mathematicians whose livelihoods depended on their success at public contests and who needed to keep their discoveries secret, and a newer school whose adherents sought like Cardano to build their reputations through publishing. In one of these public contests Tartaglia was challenged with a number of problems that all reduced to one form of the cubic equation, which he managed to solve just in time to win. After much persuasion he passed the solution to Cardano in the form of some verses that he had composed as a mnemonic. But Cardano himself supplied the demonstration and developed solutions for other cases of the equation with the help of his pupil Ludovico Ferrari, who devised a solution for the quartic equation (an equation that involves the fourth and no higher power of the unknown). When Cardano learned that Tartaglia's technique had been formulated many years before by Scipione dal Ferro of Bologna, he considered himself free to publish his research, and his *Ars magna* (Great art; 1545) gave Tartaglia full credit for his part. However, Tartaglia responded angrily the following year in his *Quesiti et inventioni diverse* (Sundry problems and discoveries), and there followed a bitter public dispute be-tween Tartaglia and Ferrari, with the publication of a series of abusive broadsheets.

Apart from the solutions mentioned, *Ars magna* contains some remarkable mathematical achievements. Among the ideas treated are the reduction of the general cubic equation to one without the second degree term, an idea of the expected number of roots in higher degree equations, symmetric functions, an account of the relations between the values and signs of the coefficients of an equation and those of its roots, and methods of obtaining successive approximations to the roots. Cardano also stumbled upon complex numbers, although he did not appreciate their importance. These first steps towards a theory of equations inspired fruitful mathematical study in the following centuries.

BIBLIOGRAPHY

Primary Works
Cardano, Girolamo. *The Book of My Life (De vita propria liber)*. Translated by Jean Stoner. New York, 1930. Reprint, New York, 1962.
Cardano, Girolamo. *The Great Art, or The Rules of Algebra*. Translated and edited by T. Richard Witmer. Cambridge, Mass., and London, 1968. Good biographical introduction and balanced account of the controversy with Tartaglia. Clear translation of the *Ars magna*.

Secondary Works
Fierz, Markus. *Girolamo Cardano, 1501–1576: Physician, Natural Philosopher, Mathematician, Astrologer, and Interpreter of Dreams*. Boston, 1983. Another good biographical account, which concentrates on Cardano's nonmathematical achievements.
Gliozzi, Mario. "Girolamo Cardano." In *Dictionary of Scientific Biography*. Vol. 3. New York, 1971. Pages 64–67. Good survey article.
Ore, Oystein. *Cardano, the Gambling Scholar*. Princeton, N.J., 1953. Detailed account of Cardano's life and times, with a full study of his account of probability.
Siraisi, Nancy G. *The Clock and the Mirror: Girolamo Cardano and Renaissance Medicine*. Princeton, N.J., 1997.

FENELLA K. C. SMITH

CARNIVAL. The most universally popular lay festival in Renaissance Europe, Carnival was a day and a season of widespread gaiety and taboo-breaking. The day of Carnival occurred just before Lent, the forty days of penance and fasting preceding Easter Sunday, and could fall at any time between early February and the middle of March. In Italy, Carnival fell on Fat Thursday (*giovedì grasso*), the Thursday before Ash Wednesday, the first day of Lent, but elsewhere it was usually the day before Ash Wednesday (Shrove Tuesday, mardi gras, Fastnacht). The length of the entire Carnival season varied according to the locality, stretching in some places as far back as Christmas. Carnival was more popular in southern than in northern Europe, where carnival-like festivals were celebrated during the spring (May Day) and summer (Midsummer Night). Christian Carnival paralleled Jewish Purim, and in areas where the two communities lived in proximity to one another, such as Spain, Provence, and Rome, each influenced the other.

According to the standard etymology, "carnival" derives from *carne,* meaning "meat," and *levare,* "to take away," and the festival celebrated the consumption of meat, which observant Christians renounced during Lent. Meat and other rich foods provided the symbolic core of Carnival. As Emmanuel Le Roy Ladurie put it, the motto of Carnival might be, "say it with meat." Festive companies adopted animal totems, and Carnival was a time for killing pigs, making sausages, and indulging in gluttonous banquets. In the famous Nürnberg Carnival, the butchers' guild played the central role in organizing festivities.

Since the Lenten fast also required abstention from sexual intercourse, Carnival became a period of sexual license. Carnival season was one of the most popular times to marry, and historical demographers have demonstrated that conceptions increased during Carnival and declined during Lent. Carnival's potential for violence in rough sports, gang fights, riots, and revolts was proverbial.

The unifying theme in Carnival festivity was the "world turned upside down," or the land of Cockaigne, in which the normal rules of the social order and the Christian pieties were inverted, disputed, and mocked. Carnival themes were improvised in popular pantomimes and explored in comic theater: artisans masquerading as kings; choirboys pretending to be bishops; servants giving orders to their masters; poor men offering alms to the rich; boys whipping their schoolmasters; and both men and women cross-dressing. Carnival typically involved the temporary, symbolic triumph of the weak over powerful elites, the young over the old, and the profane over the sacred.

There have been three principal interpretive schools of Carnival. The first, deriving from social anthropology, sees Carnival as a "safety valve," which released tensions produced by the hierarchic, status-driven society of Renaissance Europe. The paradoxes and illicit behavior of Carnival provided an emotional release for participants, but since such behavior was restricted to a defined day or season, Carnival actually reinforced the social order rather than subverted it. The second school, based on the work of the Russian literary theorist Mikhail Bakhtin, argues that Carnival possessed a logic of its own by presenting a reality that was separate from official society. From this point of view, Carnival was a source of liberation and creativity, evoked through the "grotesque realism" of the lower parts of the human body in images of defecation, sex, and violence. The liberating lower body of Carnival imagery subverted the authoritarian upper body, the dominion of reason and morality. The third school, derived from detailed historical studies of actual festivals, insists that Carnival did not function in any single way, either reinforcing or subverting authority. Carnival revolved around an ongoing improvised social drama, played out in a highly creative and elastic fashion that evoked multiple meanings, which depended on changing local contexts and conditions. The festival that one year served to keep the peasants in their place could in another induce a rebellion.

The fifteenth and sixteenth centuries witnessed the great age of creative, spontaneous, popular festivity in which the roles of actors and audience were completely interchangeable. The comic and satirical sensibilities of Renaissance culture can largely be traced to Carnival festivity. By the seventeenth century, under persistent criticism from moralists and Protestant reformers, Carnival had either been abolished, had begun to wither, or had become commercialized, with professional actors, acrobats, and opera singers replacing spontaneous, festive crowds.

BIBLIOGRAPHY

Bakhtin, Mikhail. *Rabelais and His World.* Translated by Helene Iswolsky. Cambridge, Mass., 1968.

Kinser, Samuel. *Rabelais's Carnival: Text, Context, Metatext.* Berkeley and Los Angeles, 1990.

Le Roy Ladurie, Emmanuel. *Carnival in Romans.* Translated by Mary Feeney. New York, 1979.

EDWARD MUIR

CARO, JOSEPH BEN EPHRAIM (also Karo; 1488–1575), last great codifier of Jewish law. After the expulsion of the Jews from Portugal, Caro and his family left for the Ottoman Empire, where he lived in Anatolia and Greece for about forty years. His teachers in halakah (Jewish law) were his father and his uncle Isaac. He was influenced by the Kabbalists Solomon Alkabetz and Joseph Taitazak and their groups of pietists. He was deeply influenced by Solomon Molcho, who was nurturing messianic expectations and died a martyr's death at 1532. Throughout his life Caro expressed his yearning to meet the same fate. Caro left for Safed in 1536, where he was one of four scholars ordained by Jacob Beirav. This act was laden with messianic hopes, but due to the opposition of other authorities, these had to be abandoned. In Safed he headed the Jewish religious court and a large yeshiva.

Caro's magnum opus, *Beit Yosef* (House of Joseph), written between 1522 and 1542, took the form of a commentary on the *Arba'ah turim* (Four columns) of Jacob ben Asher (fourteenth century, Spain). Its goals were to cite all sources for the legal decisions of the *Turim,* to clarify their rationale and the talmudic and later debates on them, and to add as much as possible of the legal decisions and customs left unmentioned in the *Turim* or created since, among Ashkenazic as well as Sephardic Jews. Caro attributed special importance to the customs and laws defined by the Kabbalists, mostly the holy *Safer ha-Zohar* (Book of splendor). When contradictions arose in this vast number of sources, Caro's rule (applied with some flexibility) was to go by the majority from among the three major halakists (codifiers of Jewish law)—Moses Maimonides, Isaac Alfasi, and Asher ben Jehiel.

In 1558 Caro started writing the *Shulhan 'arukh* (The well-laid table), a digest of the *Beit Yosef* intended to provide a popular version of that text, citing only the laws laymen should know for practical purposes. He also wrote *Kesef Mishneh,* a commentary on Maimonides's *Mishneh Torah,* as well as hundreds of *responsa* (a rabbinic term denoting an exchange of letters in which one party consults another on halakic matters).

Through his two major books Caro reached the uncommon status of a halakist accepted by Jewish communities everywhere. He emerged as such in his lifetime, and his status was later maintained by some other halakists who added a whole literature of glosses, adjusting its opinions to the changing needs of different communities, especially Ashkenazic ones.

In his halakic books, as well as in other aspects of life, Caro revealed himself as a thinker in the tradition of the Middle Ages who happened to live in the time of the Renaissance. Thus he was not interested in the revival of classical knowledge, nor did he rebel against the legacy of the Middle Ages; on the contrary, he saw himself as the culmination of the continuous chain of knowledge from antiquity through the Middle Ages to his own time.

Like most of Safed's scholars Caro was deeply engaged in Kabbalah, its doctrines, its spiritual and ascetic way of life, and its mystical techniques. In his diary (printed under the title of *Maggid mesharim*),

which he probably started writing in 1533, he described nocturnal visitations by a maggid, which revealed itself through automatic speech. This maggid, a personification of the Mishnah, evoked by its recitation, was at times feminine, at times masculine; on the one hand it was his own soul and on the other the feminine part of the divinity, the Shekhina; an angel, a mother, and a lover. It rebuked Caro for his sins, such as not fasting enough, and it praised him for his asceticism. It soothed his soul by promising him the status of a spiritual leader of all Jewry.

See also **Kabbalah.**

BIBLIOGRAPHY

Primary Works

Caro, Joseph. *Beit Yosef.* Jerusalem, 1990. Caro's greatest halakic work.

Caro, Joseph. *Maggid mesharim.* Petah-Tikvah, Israel, 1990. Caro's popular halakic work.

Caro, Joseph. *Shulhan arukh.* Jerusalem, 1958. Caro's mystical diary.

Secondary Works

Katz, Jacob. "Post-Zoharic Relations between Halakhah and Kabbalah." In *Jewish Thought in the Sixteenth Century.* Edited by Bernard Dov Cooperman. Cambridge, Mass., 1983. Pages 283–307. The first research to show that Caro was influenced in his halakic decisions by the book of *Zohar.*

Werblowsky, R. J. Zwi. *Joseph Karo: Lawyer and Mystic.* 2d ed. Philadelphia, 1977. Brilliant research about his life and mystical experiences as well as his Kabbalah.

RONIT MEROZ

CARPACCIO, VITTORE (Carpathius; Carpatio; Scarpaza; Scharpaza; Scarpazza; Scarpatia; 1465?–c. 1525), Venetian painter, son of a furrier. Little is known of Carpaccio's work prior to his first major commission—nine large canvases painted for the Scuola di Sant' Orsola (c. 1490–1500; Venice, Accademia), narrating the life of its patron saint, which made his reputation. The *Arrival of St. Ursula at Cologne* (1490) is his earliest dated work; subsequently he often dated and signed his important creations.

Following the success of the St. Ursula series, Carpaccio produced narrative scenes for other *scuole* (lay devotional confraternities). For the *Miracles of the True Cross* cycle commissioned by the Scuola Grande di San Giovanni Evangelista to extol its miraculous relic, he painted the *Healing of the Possessed Man* (1494; Venice, Accademia), which presents in rich and anecdotal detail a Venetian cityscape bustling with commercial activity. The painting showcases Carpaccio's talent for capturing many facets of contemporary life and integrating sacred events into local reality, thereby endowing

Carpaccio. *St. Augustine in His Study.* Scuola di San Giorgio degli Schiavoni, Venice; c. 1502. ALINARI/ART RESOURCE

them with credibility and his city with sacral and historic importance.

Carpaccio also completed a narrative program for the Scuola di San Giorgio degli Schiavoni (c. 1502–1507, in situ), which comprised two scenes pertaining to the life of Christ, three to the exploits of St. George, one to St. Tryphon, and three to St. Jerome, including St. Augustine experiencing a vision of his death. This picture depicts the saint in a spacious study filled with objects of contemporary humanistic interest, among them ancient pottery and bronzes. For the Scuola di Santa Maria degli Albanesi, Carpaccio painted six scenes from the life of the Virgin (c. 1502–1508); for the Scuola di Santo Stephano a narrative cycle devoted to St. Stephen (c. 1511–1520). Carpaccio was gifted at organizing great numbers of participants and spectators peopling his canvases by combining them into groups and conveying animation and variety without sacrificing balance and orderliness. He enhanced his narratives by drawing inspiration from local architecture and spectacle as well as books illustrating diverse geographic locales and national costumes. His large workshop assisted him in carrying out his multiple commissions.

Carpaccio also served the city of Venice. In 1501 he contracted to paint a canvas of unknown subject for the Senate Hall and in 1507 to assist Giovanni Bellini in completing the *Alexander III* cycle in the Sala del Maggior Consiglio in the Doge's Palace; in 1508 he sat on a committee evaluating the recently completed Fondaco de' Tedeschi frescoes by Giorgione.

Carpaccio produced altarpieces for clientele within and outside the city. For Venetian churches he painted *St. Thomas Aquinas Enthroned* (1507; Stuttgart, Staatsgalerie), the *Presentation of Christ in the Temple* (1510; Venice, Accademia), and the *Martyrdom of the Ten Thousand* (1515; Venice, Accademia). From 1510 onward he sent increasingly more works to customers in Treviso, Capodistria, Pirano, Brescia, and Pozzale di Cadore in the Dolomites. He was admired as a portraitist, and one delighted patroness, Girolama Corsi Ramos, a poetess of noble lineage and wife of a condottiere in the service of the Venetian Republic, wrote a sonnet in his praise.

Carpaccio was regarded by subsequent generations as the most important of Giovanni Bellini's Venetian contemporaries. The contemporary Venetian

Carpaccio. *Knight in a Landscape.* The knight is Francesco Maria della Rovere (1490–1538), who became duke of Urbino in 1508. Painted c. 1510. THYSSEN-BORNEMISZA COLLECTION, MADRID/ERICH LESSING/ART RESOURCE

351

chronicler Marin Sanudo listed only three programs of painting among the "notable things" of Venice, Carpaccio's St. Ursula cycle being one of them. Giorgio Vasari grouped lesser north Italian artists under the umbrella of Carpaccio's biography.

See also **Bellini Family**; **Venice**, *subentry on* **Art in Venice**.

BIBLIOGRAPHY

Primary Work

Sansovino, Francesco. *Venetia città nobilissima et singolare* (Venice, the most noble and singular city). Venice, 1581. Reprint in enlarged form 1604, 1663, 1968.

Secondary Works

Fortini Brown, Patricia. *Venetian Narrative Painting in the Age of Carpaccio.* London and New Haven, Conn., 1988.
Lauts, Jan. *Carpaccio: Paintings and Drawings.* London, 1962.
Molmenti, Pompeo, and Gustav Ludwig. *The Life and Works of Vittorio Carpaccio.* Translated by Robert H. Hobart. London, 1907. Translation of *Vittore Carpaccio: La vita e le opere* (1906).
Sgarbi, Vittore. *Carpaccio.* Milan and New York, 1994.
Zampetti, Pietro, ed. *Vittore Carpaccio.* Venice, 1963. Exhibition catalog.

MARINA BELOZERSKAYA

CARRACCI FAMILY. The Carracci of Bologna were a family of painters, draftsmen, and printmakers active in the later sixteenth and early seventeenth centuries. Their extraordinary art historical importance lies in their project of "reforming" the art of painting, then dominated by the highly artificial stylistic tendency now known as mannerism, and their successful institution of a new and more naturalistic pictorial style known since the eighteenth century as the baroque. The Carracci also founded an important art academy whose pupils included some of the most acclaimed artists of the seventeenth century, for example, Guido Reni, Francesco Albani, and Domenichino, and whose theoretical teachings influenced countless other artists. The many individual styles that developed within this new naturalistic tendency were imitated not only within Italy but also across Europe. Thus among connoisseurs and collectors of art the Carracci and their school achieved widespread fame that lasted until the end of the eighteenth century.

Principal Family Members. A drawing made around 1600, probably by Agostino Carracci and now preserved at the British Museum, represents the Carracci family tree, founded on the line of Giovanni Carracci in 1364. The family came to Bologna from Cremona in the mid-fifteenth century, es-

tablishing themselves as tradesmen, and it was not until the later sixteenth century that three members of the family, Ludovico Carracci (1555–1619) and his two cousins, Agostino (1557–1602) and Annibale (1560–1609), abandoned their families' traditional professions and achieved fame as the greatest painters of their day. Agostino's natural son Antonio Carracci (1583–1618) also became a painter of some distinction. Paolo Carracci (1568–1625), Ludovico's younger brother, and Francesco Carracci, sometimes called "Franceschino" (1595–1622), son of Agostino's and Annibale's brother Giovanni Antonio, both became painters, but their works have not been regarded as historically significant.

Education and Artistic Foundations. Ludovico was the son of Vincenzo, a butcher. He studied painting under the Bolognese mannerist Prospero Fontana and petitioned for acceptance into the Corporazione dei Pittori (corporation of painters) at Bologna on 23 March 1578. Agostino and Annibale, whose father was a tailor, had first been sent to study at a *scuola di grammatica* (a school in which Latin grammar and rhetoric are taught), and Agostino in particular appears to have profited in his studies, achieving mastery of Latin grammar and composition. With Ludovico's encouragement, Agostino and Annibale eventually became artists, but these early humanistic studies, particularly the study of rhetoric, must certainly have helped to shape their understanding of humanistic pictorial theory. Agostino subsequently studied painting with Ludovico's teacher, Fontana, with the Bolognese painter Bartolomeo Passarotti, with the architect and engraver Domenico Tibaldi, and perhaps also with the sculptor Alessandro Menganti, but it is clear from the early sources that both he and Annibale also received instruction from Ludovico himself.

The earliest and most important biographer of the Carracci is the seventeenth-century Bolognese writer Count Carlo Cesare Malvasia. In his *Felsina pittrice* (The paintress Bologna; 1678), Malvasia says that following his admission to the Corporazione dei Pittori, Ludovico traveled extensively in northern Italy, studying the great pictorial traditions of Florence, Venice, Parma, and Mantua. In Florence, Ludovico probably came into contact with a circle of artists associated with the Florentine art academy, called the Accademia del Disegno, who were then initiating their own "reform" of the art of painting. These Florentine reformers, including such artists as Santi di Tito and Lodovico Cigoli, rejected the artificiality of the mannerists in favor of a more naturalistic style

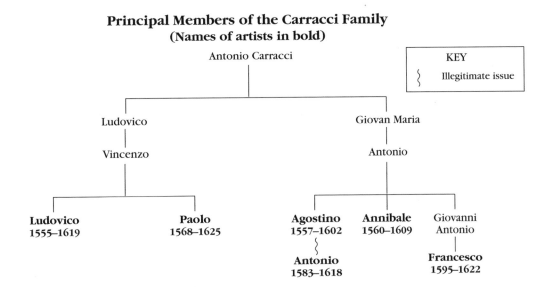

Principal Members of the Carracci Family
(Names of artists in bold)

modeled on such sixteenth-century Emilian masters as Correggio and Niccolò dell'Abate and on the Umbrian painter Federico Barocci.

Ludovico returned to Bologna and by about 1580 his own works reveal a careful analysis and imitation of these same artistic models, and an equal appreciation for the naturalistic styles of such Venetian masters as Veronese and Titian. By the later 1580s Ludovico was producing such works as the *Flagellation of Christ,* now in the Musée de la Chartreuse (Douai, France), which vies with the most naturalistic works of Titian, Tintoretto, or Veronese with respect to its powerful illusion of three-dimensional form. Ludovico sent Annibale and Agostino on similar journeys to Parma and Venice in order to study the great works of Correggio and of the Venetians. In Parma in April 1580, Annibale wrote letters to Ludovico expressing his enthusiasm for the works of Correggio. Indeed, since Correggio was from Emilia, the same region of Italy to which Bologna belonged, the Carracci found in him a native Emilian precedent for the type of naturalistic style they themselves were trying to develop.

The Carracci Academy. Ludovico evidently had been impressed not only by the Florentines' stylistic experimentations, but also by their academy and its pedagogical program. Founded in 1563, the Accademia del Disegno was the first officially recognized educational institution for artists, an organ of the Florentine grand ducal government that encompassed both the traditional functions of a guild and those of a liberal arts institution devoted specifically to the theoretical training of painters, sculptors,

and architects. Ludovico was elected to the council of the painters' guild in Bologna on 28 June 1582, but around that same time he and his two cousins founded an art academy of their own, known variously as the Accademia dei Desiderosi (the academy of those who desire [virtue]), the Accademia degli Incamminati (the academy of those who have set out on the road [to virtue]) and the Accademia dei Carracci (the Carracci academy). Evidence also strongly suggests that after Agostino's death in 1602, Ludovico attempted to merge the academy with the Corporazione dei Pittori, thus creating an institution similar to the Florentine academy in its form and functions.

The pedagogical program of the Carracci academy, described by its secretary Lucio Faberio in his *Il funerale d'Agostin Carracci* (The funeral of Agostino Carracci; 1603), closely resembled that of the Florentine academy. While the Florentine program included the study of anatomy, life drawing, mathematics, natural philosophy, cosmology, and architecture, the Carracci program included anatomy, proportion, life drawing, perspective (including a wide variety of illusionistic techniques), and the invention of literary subject matter. These disciplines are essentially identical to the traditional elements of humanistic art theory as described in treatises from Leon Battista Alberti's *Della pittura* (On painting; 1435) to Franciscus Junius's *De pictura veterum* (On the painting of the ancients; 1637), and beyond.

However, like the artists of the Florentine reform, the Carracci perceived that the mannerists had painted on the basis of pure, rote practice, without internalizing or acting upon theoretical principles. Since the components of humanistic pictorial theory may all ultimately be seen as tools that enable the artist to analyze and imitate nature, and thus to discover the universal verities concealed within natural forms and human actions, the Carracci understood the artificiality of mannerist style as the result of a failure to acquire the intellectual means with which to discover such profound natural truths. The purpose of the Carracci academy was thus not merely to teach artists a new and different style, but rather to teach them how to unify theory with practice, to produce works that embody a kind of truth rooted in the intelligent observation of nature rather than in pure fantasy, and thus to perfect the arts themselves.

The Carracci therefore emphasized practice of life drawing. Indeed, pupils were encouraged not only to draw from models but also to keep their sketchbooks constantly by their side and to draw everything they encountered in their daily experience. However, this kind of "life drawing" is not to be understood as a simple copying of what the eye sees. Rather, the goal was to see nature analytically, breaking down visual experience through the application of theoretical principles, and thus discovering the essence of any given thing. Annibale Carracci is also widely believed to have invented the art of caricature, a type of drawing that presupposes the perception of an abstract, "normative" form from which the deliberately distorted image may deviate.

By these pedagogical means, the Carracci and their pupils developed a powerful new style characterized by an idealized naturalism that contrasted forcefully with what they viewed as the lifeless and bloodless artifice of contemporary Bolognese mannerists such as Ercole Procaccini and Denys Calvaert, or of central Italian mannerists like the Florentine Giorgio Vasari. A volume of Vasari's famous biographical work, *The Lives of the Most Excellent Painters, Sculptors, and Architects* (second revised edition, 1568), once belonging to the Carracci still survives, and its margins are filled with annotations bitterly and often sarcastically rebutting Vasari's underestimations of northern Italian painters and his excessive praises for Michelangelo and other central Italian artists. Although it has proven difficult to identify the hands responsible for each individual utterance, it is now generally agreed that all of the Carracci contributed annotations, and that these writings express a uniformly anti-Vasarian attitude. These marginalia, along with the known epistolary and poetical writings of the Carracci, have been published in a critical edition by Giovanna Perini (1990).

Collaborative Works and Individual Achievements. The Carracci established their fame through several collaborative projects that brilliantly displayed the striking illusionism of their new style, and also served to attract talented young pupils to their academy. Around 1583–1584, Ludovico, Agostino, and Annibale painted a series of frescoes, representing the myths of Europa and Jason, in the Palazzo Fava at Bologna, and returned in 1586 to add a further series representing the story of Aeneas. Around 1589–1590, they received a commission to portray the myth of the founding of Rome in the Palazzo Magnani-Salem (now Credito Romagnolo). When asked which of them was responsible for this latter cycle, their now famous reply was: "It is by the Carracci; we all made it." However, each of the Carracci also worked independently, thus revealing individual personalities and artistic strengths. For example, all three Carracci made prints, but Agostino is especially well known as an extraordinarily talented engraver whose works were admired and collected throughout Europe.

In 1593, Ranuccio Farnese, duke of Parma and Piacenza, invited Ludovico and Agostino to enter his service at the court of Parma, while the duke's younger brother Cardinal Odoardo Farnese extended a similar invitation for Annibale (considered the most talented of the three Carracci) to serve him in Rome. Ultimately it was Annibale and Agostino who went to Rome, in 1594, while Ludovico remained behind in Bologna, taking sole responsibility for the academy. In Rome, Annibale and Agostino undertook numerous projects, the most important being the decoration of two rooms in the Farnese Palace: the Camerino Farnese (the cardinal's private study, painted in 1595–1597) and the Galleria Farnese (1597–1601). These works represented an extremely important stylistic development, in which the two artists digested the stylistic essences of antique statuary, of Michelangelo, and of Raphael. Departing from their early attachment to Correggesque and Venetian models, the two artists now synthesized a breathtakingly new style that reflects a study of Michelangelo's heroic grandeur and of Raphael's idealizing beauty while remaining within the bounds of natural decorum.

However, this does not contradict their earlier theoretical principles. Indeed, this tendency to select and appropriate artistic perfections from disparate sources is now viewed within the context of Renaissance pictorial theory as an attempt to assimilate the practices of rhetorical imitation, in which literary authors similarly sought to perfect their works by ex-

Carracci Family. Ceiling of the gallery of the Palazzo Farnese, Rome, by Annibale and Agostino Carracci. 1595–1604.
SCALA/ART RESOURCE

tracting and synthesizing the perfections of the most excellent prior models. Viewed in this light, the stylistic changes accompanying Annibale's and Agostino's work in Rome are simply an extension of the same mimetic processes by which the Carracci had synthesized their earlier Correggesque styles.

The Galleria Farnese is generally regarded as Annibale's masterpiece, and it is clear that Agostino's role was secondary. The two brothers argued constantly over the work and Agostino finally left Rome in 1599, entering the service of Duke Ranuccio II at Parma, where his major work, the decoration of the camerino of the Palazzo del Giardino, remained unfinished at the time of his death on 22 March 1602. Annibale remained in Rome, but soon after completing his work on the Farnese Gallery began suffering from a debilitating illness whose exact nature remains unknown. His major accomplishment during this period was the design and supervision of the fresco decorations for the Herrera chapel in the church of San Giacomo degli Spagnuoli, executed by his pupils (1607). He died in Rome on 15 July 1609. Meanwhile, Ludovico had continued to supervise the academy in Bologna, visiting Rome only briefly between 31 May and 13 June 1602. His most important later projects include the supervision of academy pupils in decorating the cloister of San Michele in Bosco, Bologna (1604–1605), and his fresco cycles in the courtyard and vault of the cathedral of Piacenza (1606–1609). He died in Bologna on 13 November 1619.

See also **Baroque, Concept of the; Emilia, Art in; Mannerism.**

BIBLIOGRAPHY

Bohlin, Diane De Grazia. *Prints and Related Drawings by the Carracci Family: A Catalogue Raisonné.* Bloomington, Ind., 1979.
Dempsey, Charles. *Annibale Carracci and the Beginnings of Baroque Style.* Glückstadt, Germany, 1977.
Dempsey, Charles. *Annibale Carracci: The Farnese Gallery, Rome.* New York, 1995.
Emiliani, Andrea, ed. *The Age of Correggio and the Carracci: Emilian Painting of the Sixteenth and Seventeenth Centuries.* Washington, D.C., 1986. Exhibition catalog.
Emiliani, Andrea, ed., and Gail Feigenbaum, cataloger. *Ludovico Carracci.* Bologna, Italy, and Fort Worth, Tex., 1993. Exhibition catalog.
Negro, Emilio, and Massimo Pirondini, eds. *La scuola dei Carracci: dall'accademia alla bottega di Ludovico.* Modena, Italy, 1994.
Perini, Giovanna, ed. *Gli scritti dei Carracci: Ludovico, Annibale, Agostino, Antonio, Giovanni Antonio.* Introduction by Charles Dempsey. Bologna, Italy, 1990. Dempsey's and Perini's essays are now the essential sources on the interpretation of primary sources on the Carracci.
Posner, Donald. *Annibale Carracci: A Study in the Reform of Italian Painting around 1590.* 2 vols. London and New York, 1971. To be read with Charles Dempsey's 1977 study.

ANTHONY COLANTUONO

CARTOGRAPHY. *See* **Geography and Cartography.**

CARVAJAL Y MENDOZA, LUISA DE (1566–1614), religious poet and missionary to England. Born to a branch of the influential Mendoza family, Carvajal was orphaned at age five and raised for a time at court with her great aunt, governness to Philip II's daughters. As a ward of her uncle, the Marquis of Almazán, viceroy of Navarra, she moved with his family to Pamplona, where the marquis's harsh physical discipline and religious exercises prompted a religious zeal that culminated in her missionary trip to England to reconvert the Anglicans to Catholicism. Unusual for most Spanish Renaissance women, Carvajal refused to wed or profess as a nun; instead, after her uncle's death in 1592, she moved with a few servants to an abandoned house where she lived openly in poverty. There, as part of her mortifications, she joined the poor in breadlines and ministered to the sick.

Carvajal's 1605 mission to England was approved and facilitated by the Jesuit order. While in London, she was twice imprisoned for preaching Catholic dogma in the streets and for attempting to establish a convent in her home. Proving a political liability to the Spanish cause after the Gunpowder Plot, an alleged conspiracy to blow up the English Parliament, she nevertheless obtained permission through family connections to remain in England. After her death from an illness contracted in jail, her body was shipped to Spain, where proceedings for her beatification began but were never finalized.

Although her poetry has received little attention, the Spanish bibliographer Manuel Serrano y Sanz deems her "the most illustrious female religious poet of the seventeenth century" (1975). Written in both sonnet and ballad form and unpublished during her lifetime, Carvajal's religious poems often follow the dialogue form preferred by medieval visionaries, assigning the poetic voice the anagram of "Silva." Their recurrent tropes of bonds, chains, and desire for martyrdom evoke the sufferings experienced by her as a child and reveal a lyrical sense of intimacy with Christ.

See also **Spirituality, Female.**

BIBLIOGRAPHY

Primary Works

Carvajal y Mendoza, Luisa de. *Epistolario y poesías.* Edited by Jesús González Marañon and Camilo María Abad. Madrid, 1965.

Carvajal y Mendoza, Luisa de. *Escritos autobiográficos.* Edited by Camilo María Abad. Vol. 1. Barcelona, 1966.

Muñoz, Luis. *Vida y virtudes de la venerable virgen doñ Luisa de Carvaial y Mendoza.* Madrid, 1632.

Secondary Works

Abad, Camilo Maria. *Una misionera española en la Inglaterra del siglo XVII. Doña Luisa de Carvajal y Mendoza (1566–1614).* Santander, Spain, 1966.

Cruz, Anne J. "Chains of Desire: Luisa de Carvajal y Mendoza's Poetics of Penance." In *Studies on Hispanic Women Writers in Honor of Georgina Sabat Rivers.* Edited by Lou Charnon-Deutsch. Madrid, 1992. Pages 97–112.

Ortega Costa, Milagros. "Spanish Women in the Reformation." In *Women in Reformation and Counter-Reformation Europe.* Edited by Sherrin Marshall. Bloomington, Ind., 1989. Pages 89–119.

ANNE J. CRUZ

CASAUBON, ISAAC (1559–1614), French classical scholar and Protestant polemicist. Casaubon was professor of Greek at the Academy of Geneva (1582–1596) and at the University of Montpellier (1596–1599). In 1600, by then the leading Greek scholar in Europe, he migrated to Paris at the invitation of King Henry IV, who hoped that he might be induced to convert to Catholicism. Though Casaubon refused the strong inducement, he was made keeper of the royal library, a trove of manuscripts whose riches he exploited. Casaubon continued to work on classical Greek authors, but his interests were shifting to Christian antiquities, for the intellectual climate of the age was dominated by research into and controversy about Christian history and doctrine. Casaubon lived in England from 1610 until his death, where he was supported by King James I (serving as the king's frequent interlocutor), and was employed to defend the Anglican position. Like others, he was the target of a campaign of abuse by the Jesuits, but hard-line Calvinists also viewed him as a waverer, if not a defector.

Casaubon's reputation was built on his annotated editions of a number of Greek authors. His last and best-known work was his *De rebus sacris et ecclesiasticis exercitationes* (Exercises on sacred and ecclesiastical matters; 1614), a severe critique of the scholarship of Cardinal Cesare Baronio in his *Annales* of church history. One famous chapter demonstrated that the hermetic corpus, Greek texts venerated in the Italian Renaissance as a mysterious revelation of universal religious truth imparted to the ancient Egyptians centuries before the birth of Christ, was no more than a forgery of late antiquity.

BIBLIOGRAPHY

Grafton, Anthony. *Defenders of the Text: The Traditions of Scholarship in an Age of Science, 1450–1800.* Cambridge, Mass., 1991. See especially chapters 5 and 6.

Pattison, Mark. *Isaac Casaubon, 1559–1614.* 2d ed. Oxford, 1892.

WILLIAM McCUAIG

CASTAGNO, ANDREA DEL. *See* **Florence,** *subentry on* **Art of the Fifteenth Century.**

CASTIGLIONE, BALDASSARE (1478–1529), Italian writer and diplomat. Baldassare Castiglione is one of the most influential writers of the Italian Renaissance, and he stands along with Shakespeare and Montaigne among the important literary figures of Renaissance Europe.

While his primary occupation was that of diplomat, his fame rests on *Il cortegiano* (trans. *The Book of the Courtier*), his dialogue-treatise on the "perfect" courtier. First published in 1528, *The Courtier* enjoyed enormous publishing success in Italy for most of the century. It also soon became a European success, translated into Spanish by Juan Boscán (1534) with a preface by Garcilaso de la Vega, into French by Jacques Colin (1537; revised by Étienne Dolet and Mellin de Saint-Gelais in 1538) and again by Gabriel Chappuis (1580), into English by Thomas Hoby (1561), and even into Latin by Bartholomew Clerke (1571). For centuries it served as the model "courtesy" book, a guide, both ethical and aesthetic, for interpersonal social relations.

Life and Career. Baldassare Castiglione was born in Casatico, near Mantua, on 6 November 1478, the son of Cristoforo, a professional soldier in the service of the marquis of Mantua, and Aloisa Gonzaga, who was related to the ruling family. In 1490 he was sent to Milan to pursue humanistic studies. When his father died in 1499, Castiglione returned to Mantua and entered the service of Francesco Gonzaga as a military officer and diplomat. He represented the marquis at the court of the Pio family in Carpi in 1501, and he accompanied him to Rome and Naples in 1503; in that same year Castiglione took part in the battle of Garigliano. In Rome shortly thereafter he met Guidobaldo da Montefeltro, who had recently regained the duchy of Urbino; in 1504 Castiglione entered Guidobaldo's service. In 1506 he was sent by the duke to England to the court of Henry VII to accept the Order of the Garter in the duke's name; later he represented Guidobaldo at the Milanese court of the French king Louis XII.

From 1506 until 1516 he remained in the service of Urbino, whose court he would immortalize in his famous dialogue. He wrote a dramatic eclogue, *Tirsi,* for carnival at Urbino in 1506, and in it he recited the role of the enamored shepherd Iola. The eclogue is a celebration of the court, of Guidobaldo, the duchess and her entourage, and of many friends who would figure prominently in *The Courtier.* After Guidobaldo's death in 1508, Castiglione remained in the service of his successor Francesco Maria della Rovere, participating in the duchy's military actions against Venice, at Mirandola, and in Bologna. At home in Urbino he organized the first performance of *Calandria* (Follies of Calandro), the comedy written by Bibbiena (Bernardo Dovizi; 1470–1520), for which he wrote a prologue, now lost. He also continued to travel, representing the duchy first in France and then in Rome from 1513 until 1516. When the Medici took Urbino from the della Rovere family, Castiglione followed his patron in exile to Mantua.

In 1516 he married a Bolognese noblewoman, Ippolita Torelli, and in 1516 he returned to the service of the duke of Mantua, whom he accompanied to Venice in that year and represented at the papal court in Rome. In 1520 his wife died giving birth to their third child. The next year he took minor orders but continued his diplomatic activities, returning to Rome as the Mantuan ambassador in 1523. In 1524 Clement VII named him papal nuncio to the court of Charles V in Spain, where he was received in 1525 and where he spent the rest of his life. Castiglione died of plague in Toledo on 8 February 1529.

Writing *The Courtier*. Besides *The Courtier* (1528), *Tirsi* (1506), a Latin letter in praise of his patron (*De vita et gestis Guidubaldi Urbini Ducis* [The life and deeds of Guidobaldo, duke of Urbino; 1508]), and the prologue to Bibbiena's *Calandria* (1513), Castiglione also wrote conventional poetry in the Petrarchist mode and humanistic verse in Latin. He left a large and important correspondence, both official and personal, which allows us some insight into his personal life and convictions.

Castiglione had begun writing *The Courtier* by 1513–1514, and it occupied him for most of the rest of his life. Ghino Ghinassi has identified three important stages in the composition of the text: a first (concluded in 1515), in which the perfect courtier, his language, and the court lady are the three subjects treated in books 2, 3, and 4, respectively, while book 1 served as preface; a second stage (1515–

1518), in which the political material was introduced as well as a consideration of Platonic love; a third and final stage (1520–1524, with continued revisions up until the year of publication) produced the book as we know it, in which the discussions of politics and love, introduced in the second redaction, developed into what is now book 4.

It seems clear that Castiglione originally had in mind a work quite different from the dialogue he published in the end, and the long discussion of women and of love places his earlier redactions close to a tradition that flourished in the northern courts of Castiglione's youth and was represented by the *De laudibus mulierum* (In praise of women; 1487) of Bartolommeo Goggio, the *Defensio mulierum* (Defense of women; 1501) of Agostino Strozzi, and the *De mulieribus* (On women; 1501) of Mario Equicola. *The Courtier* was finished by 1518, and Castiglione sent it to close friends for suggestions and corrections as he made revisions. In 1525 he took a copy with him to Spain, planning to continue refining his work, but when he got word that Vittoria Colonna was circulating parts of the text, fearing a pirated edition, he sent his book to Venice, where Giovanni Battista Ramusio and Pietro Bembo prepared it to be published by the Aldine press in 1528.

The Courtier follows the classical models of Plato and Cicero, both in its proposal of an ideal type to be imitated, the perfect courtier, and in its choice of dialogic form, for which it is especially indebted to the Ciceronian model. Like Cicero, Castiglione chooses as interlocutors contemporary historical figures, who are known for the attitudes and actions they represent and who take different sides in the discussion of subjects of contemporary debate (arms versus letters, painting versus sculpture, republics versus monarchies, the language question, the virtues and defects of women, Neoplatonism, and so on), thus lending verisimilitude to the dialogue and giving the conversations a lively, dramatic quality. In addition to discussing specific issues, the dialogue also dramatizes the act of communication and persuasion. It seeks to persuade through a process of argument and counterargument that progresses toward a conclusion proffered by one of the authoritative interlocutors, typically a known expert in the subject at hand. Often the interlocutors both present their opinions verbally and, through their actions, provide an illustration.

The Courtier is also an autobiographical text. The conversations it depicts are set at the court of Urbino in 1506, and the interlocutors are courtiers and ladies, many of whom Castiglione met during the years he spent there. In the letter that opens the book, the author looks back to those days with nostalgia, remembering with admiration and love those friends who have since died. He calls his book a "portrait of the court of Urbino," intended to preserve their memory. He imagines that the conversations took place during his absence in 1506, when Pope Julius II and his entourage had stopped at Urbino—a device that allows the author to include in the assembled group courtiers who were not part of the Urbino court at the time and to absent himself from the discussions, which he claims to narrate as they were reported to him.

In the opening letter Castiglione defends his use of a language that is not the literary Tuscan of Petrarch or Boccaccio but the language currently in use by educated persons throughout the peninsula. This emphasis on language may explain why the letter is addressed to Don Michel de Silva, a Portuguese diplomat and friend of Castiglione's who took an interest in the contemporary discussions of the Italian vernacular. The work is dedicated to Alfonso Ariosto, a cousin of Ludovico Ariosto and close friend of the author, who urged him on behalf of Francis I of France to undertake a work on the subject of the perfect courtier.

Content of *The Courtier*. In book 1 the assembled courtiers and ladies propose games for their entertainment and decide to "portray in words a perfect courtier," with the provision that "everyone will be permitted to contradict the speaker as in the schools of the philosophers." Ludovico da Canossa (1476–1532), a Veronese nobleman, diplomat, bishop, and relative of Castiglione, is chosen to lead the evening's discussions of the physical and moral qualities of the perfect courtier. He must be a nobleman whose principal profession is arms and who excels in physical activities, always maintaining his dignity. He must also be well versed in the arts and letters, a connoisseur and a practitioner. Most important, he must pursue moderation in all he does, perform with grace (*grazia*) and seemingly without effort (with *sprezzatura*). At all costs he must avoid affectation. Outward appearance is of the utmost importance. Book 1 includes digressions on the current debates regarding the vernacular language, on the relative importance of arms and of letters for the courtier, and on the question of the preeminence of painting or sculpture.

Book 2 treats the ways and circumstances in which the ideal courtier might demonstrate his qualities and argues the importance of decorum and of conversational skills. Federico Fregoso (d. 1541), cardinal and archbishop of Salerno, presides at first, but when the topic turns to humorous, entertaining language, it is Bibbiena, famous wit and comic author, who takes over, quoting, often verbatim, from the *De oratore* of Cicero; examples are given that constitute a collection of humorous stories, pleasantries, and practical jokes.

Book 3 sets out to define a suitable female companion for the perfect courtier. The virtue of women is both discussed and demonstrated through examples, ancient and modern, which provide another collection of entertaining stories; among the most famous are those of Camma and of the peasant girl from Gazuolo. Leading the discussions and defending women against misogynist attacks is Giuliano de' Medici (1479–1516), duke of Nemours, son of Lorenzo the Magnificent, and brother of Pope Leo X. To the lady of the palace are attributed many of the same qualities and talents as the courtier, though physical beauty is more important to her, and she must always be more discreet in order to preserve her good reputation. In this book the voices of the assembled ladies begin to be heard more often, but here as elsewhere the women only ask questions and moderate the discussions; they are never active participants.

Book 4 begins with a long treatment of the courtier's raison d'être, his service to his prince. As adviser to the prince, the courtier must earn favor through his accomplishments and win his master's trust so completely that he can always speak to him truthfully without fear and even correct him if necessary. The subject leads to debate on the relative merits of republics and monarchies. The topic of conversation turns finally to love, picking up the theme introduced in book 3. Here the discussion centers on how the courtier, who is no longer young, should love. Pietro Bembo (1470–1547), as author of *Asolani* (1505) a noted authority on the subject, instructs the assembled party in the theory of Neoplatonic love, following closely Marsilio Ficino's Christianizing commentary on Plato's *Symposium*. As Bembo explains step by step the way to ascend from a vision of human beauty to an internalized understanding of the idea of beauty and from there to God, he seems to lose touch with his surroundings and must be awakened from his *raptus* by Emilia Pia with a tug at his shirt. This is the most obvious example of how the participants in the game both expound upon their theories and confirm through example.

Modern critical debate on *The Courtier* has centered on the ethics of its excessive concern with outward appearance, on the faith it expresses in the individual's ability to fashion a public self, and on the author's unwillingness to discuss, except in the last book, the courtier's primary function, his service to his prince, and the depressing political realities of the time that are at the center of attention of his contemporary Niccolò Machiavelli. Issues of coherence have also been raised, especially in regard to the relationship of book 4 to the rest of the dialogue. But no one disputes the status of *The Courtier* as a masterpiece, a brilliant original that was never surpassed by any of its many imitators, and a portrait of the culture of Italian Renaissance court society in the early sixteenth century.

[Raphael's portrait of Castiglione appears in the color plates in this volume.]

BIBLIOGRAPHY

Editions of The Courtier
The Book of the Courtier. Translated by George Bull. Harmondsworth, U.K., 1967 and 1976. A British translation.
The Book of the Courtier. Translated by Charles S. Singleton. New York, 1959. An American translation.
The Courtier. Translated by Sir Thomas Hoby. London, 1561. Reprint, London, 1928, 1967, 1975.
Libro del cortegiano. 4th ed. Edited by Vittorio Cian. Florence, 1947. A classic, unsurpassed for the historical information in its notes.
Libro del cortegiano. Edited by Bruno Maier. Turin, Italy, 1955. With a selection of minor works. The most commonly used edition.
La seconda redazione del "Cortegiano" di Baldassare Castiglione. Edited by Ghino Ghinassi. Florence, 1968.

Other Works by Castiglione
"Dieci lettere inedite di Baldassare Castiglione." Edited by Maria Luisa Doglio. *Lettere italiane* 23 (1971): 559–569.
Lettere. Edited by Guido La Rocca. Milan, 1978.
Lettere del conte Baldesar Castiglione. 2 vols. Edited by Pierantonio Serassi. Padua, Italy, 1769–1771.
Lettere inedite e rare. Edited by Guglielmo Gorni. Milan, 1969.
Poesie volgari e latine. Edited by Pierantonio Serassi. Rome, 1760.

Secondary Works
Burke, Peter. *The Fortunes of the Courtier: The European Reception of Castiglione's* Cortegiano. University Park, Pa., 1996.
Cian, Vittorio. *Un illustre nunzio pontificio del Rinascimento: Baldassar Castiglione.* Vatican City, 1951. See also the review of Cian's article by Carlo Dionisotti in the *Giornale storico della letteratura italiana* 129 (1952): 31–57.
Cox, Virginia. *The Renaissance Dialogue: Literary Dialogue in Its Social and Political Contexts, Castiglione to Galileo.* Cambridge, U.K., and New York, 1992.
Finucci, Valeria. *The Lady Vanishes: Subjectivity and Representation in Castiglione and Ariosto.* Stanford, Calif., 1992. Contains an important feminist reading of *The Courtier.*
Ginassi, Ghino. "Fasi dell'elaborazione del 'Cortegiano.'" *Studi di filologia italiana* 25 (1967): 155–196.
Hanning, Robert W., and David Rosand, eds. *Castiglione: The Ideal and the Real in Renaissance Culture.* New Haven, Conn., and London, 1983.
Ossola, Carlo. *Dal "Cortegiano" all' "Uomo di mondo": Storia di un libro e di un modello sociale.* Turin, Italy, 1987.
Ossola, Carlo, and Adriano Prosperi, eds. *La corte e il cortegiano.* 2 vols. Rome, 1980.
Quondam, Amedeo. "Introduction to Baldassare Castiglione." In *Il libro del cortegiano.* Milan, 1981. Pages vii–xlv. A thorough and perceptive interpretation of the book.
Rebhorn, Wayne A. *Courtly Performances: Masking and Festivity in Castiglione's* Book of the Courtier. Detroit, Mich., 1978.
Woodhouse, J. R. *Baldesar Castiglione: A Reassessment of "The Courtier."* Edinburgh, 1978.

ELISSA B. WEAVER

CASTLES. *See* **Fortifications; Villas.**

CATALAN LITERATURE AND LANGUAGE.

Some scholars claim that there never was a Catalan Renaissance in literature; the truth, however, is a little more complicated, and it seems more accurate to speak of a "Pre-Renaissance" followed by what is usually known as a "Decadence."

Pre-Renaissance. Toward the end of the fourteenth century, the reform of the chancellory under Pere III, king of Catalonia (ruled 1336–1387), had literary consequences that could hardly have been foreseen at the time. The formation of a group of royal notaries, skilled in writing Latin, Catalan, and Aragonese, coincided with a growing demand for translations from classical Latin. At first such classics were valued chiefly for their moral content; eventually, however, in the early 1380s, certain stylistic tendencies began to emerge, notably, the attempt to adapt Ciceronian prose to the vernacular. This aesthetic revaluation of prose on the part of a group of professional writers with a taste for classical culture led to a new type of humanism that is often referred to as the Catalan Pre-Renaissance.

The outstanding figure in this movement was Bernat Metge (before 1346–1413), himself a member of the royal chancellory, whose translation of the story of Walter and Griselda from Giovanni Boccaccio's *Decameron,* via the Latin version of Petrarch (1388), marks the appearance of a new kind of Catalan prose and contains the first eulogy of Petrarch by a Peninsular writer. Metge's masterpiece, however, is *Lo somni* (The dream; 1399), in which a patchwork of other authors—Cicero, Valerius Maximus, Boccaccio, and the church fathers—is given coherence by the author's own intellectual attitude. It is this skeptical persona, symbolized in the work by the phrase "I believe what I see and pay no attention to the rest," that raises *Lo somni* above the level of a literary exercise. If its tone is at times similar to that of Montaigne, this merely indicates the real, though limited, extent to which it anticipates the Renaissance.

Metge's example, however, remains unique. Although he was followed by a series of minor humanists and translators whose work extended almost to the end of the fifteenth century, and although Petrarch—the Latin Petrarch—remained at the center of their enterprise, they present a curiously neutralized version of the Italian writer, adapting him to their medieval coordinates and apparently remaining unaware of his importance as a precursor of the Renaissance.

What strikes one most forcibly is the contrast between these glimmerings of the Renaissance and the late medieval character of the outstanding literary productions of the period. The major authors of the time, Jordi de Sant Jordi (1397?–1424), Ausiàs March (1397–1459), and Roiç de Corella (1438?–1497), were all late-medieval poets. The two fictional masterpieces of the time, the anonymous *Curial e Güelfa* (written 1443–1460; published 1901) and Joanot Martorell's *Tirant lo blanc* (1490) both have strong medieval features. Certainly there are times when such writers seem on the point of breaking into something different: Roiç de Corella shows a quite unmedieval taste for fine writing in his reworkings of the fables of Ovid; in *Curial e Güelfa* there is a curious episode in which the hero visits Mount Parnassus, where he is asked to adjudicate between Hector and Achilles; and in *Tirant* the oscillation between formal and colloquial speech is unprecedented. Yet none of this variance is enough to indicate a new sensibility, and, despite claims for the "modernity" of *Tirant,* there is no reason to attempt to relate it to the Renaissance.

Decadence. From the death of Roiç de Corella in 1497 until the second half of the nineteenth century, there were no major writers in Catalan, and until the later 1700s the literary scene was one of almost unrelieved mediocrity. The reasons for this mediocrity are complex, but there are several important points to bear in mind. First, the decline in literature was one of standards, not of quantity, and the decline was specifically literary; other kinds of art, for example, painting and architecture, did not suffer to nearly the same extent, and the eighteenth century in particular produced a number of outstanding intellectuals who wrote in Castilian. Furthermore, the literary situation in Catalonia did not correspond in any precise way to the pattern of economic prosperity and decline, nor did the literary situation reflect a change in the status of the Catalan language. Catalan remained the official language of the country until 1714, and the teaching of Catalan in schools was not prohibited until 1768.

It is only when one considers the apparent abruptness of the literary decline that a different kind of factor begins to emerge. The fifteenth century was clearly a period of considerable achievement, but even then there were signs that the situation was changing for the worse. After 1412, the country was ruled by the Castilian dynasty of the Trastámaras; Castilian became the familiar language at the court, as evidenced by the number of writers in the second half of the fifteenth century who wrote in both Castilian and Catalan. The situation was confirmed by the union of Castile and Aragon in 1479, and in the sixteenth century, the court withdrew still further from the Aragonese territories. As a result, the Catalan aristocracy was attracted more and more to the Castilian-speaking court, while the mercantile classes failed to create a genuine culture of their own. When one considers that practically any writer of importance before 1500 was connected in some way with the court, it becomes apparent how serious the consequences were for literature. With the disappearance of the chancellory, the chief source of literary criteria was also removed; the desertion of the nobility and a succession of Castilian viceroys helped to complete the process.

Two qualifications need to be made to this picture. One is that Valencia, where bilingualism had deeper roots, tended to pull away from Barcelona and produced a series of outstanding writers in Castilian. The other is the persistence of popular, as opposed to sophisticated, poetry, although its existence was only fully recognized in the nineteenth century. It would be wrong, of course, to suppose that the vitality of popular traditions was sufficient in itself to ensure the renewal of literary values. What was needed was a serious awareness of these cultural resources, the grounds for which were prepared in the eighteenth century by a series of minor writers and scholars who could scarcely have realized how important their work would be for the future of Catalan literature.

See also Spanish Literature and Language.

BIBLIOGRAPHY

Primary Works
Curial and Guelfa. Translated by Pamela Waley. London, 1982.
March, Ausiàs. *A Key Anthology.* Edited by Robert Archer. Sheffield, U.K., 1992.

Martorell, Joanot, and Galba, Martí Joan de. *Tirant lo blanc*. Translated by David Rosenthal. Reprint, Baltimore, 1996.

Secondary Works

Riquer, Martin de. *Història de la literatura catalana*. Vols. 2 and 3. Barcelona, Spain, 1964.
Terry, Arthur. *Catalan Literature*. London and New York, 1972.

ARTHUR TERRY

Catherine de Médicis. Portrait by an anonymous French artist. PALAZZO PITTI, FLORENCE/THE BRIDGE-MAN ART LIBRARY

CATHERINE DE MÉDICIS (1519–1589), queen consort of Henry II of France (1547–1559), regent of France (1560–1574), mother of three kings of France—Francis II, Charles IX, and Henry III—and one of the most important participants in the French Wars of Religion (1562–1598). The orphaned daughter of Lorenzo de' Medici, duke of Urbino, and the Bourbon princess Madeleine de La Tour d'Auvergne, Catherine was educated by nuns in Florence and Rome before her uncle, Pope Clement VII, arranged her marriage to Henry, duc d'Orléans (October 1533). With the death of his father, Francis I (April 1547), Henry ascended to the French throne as Henry II.

Catherine's first important foray into politics occurred on the occasion of Henry's untimely death in July 1559. The reign of his successor, the fifteen-year-old Francis II, was strongly influenced by the ultramontane (conservative Catholic) Guise family. Catherine's efforts to counteract their control forged the enduring policy of her political life: to steer France on a path of religious moderation between Catholics and Huguenots in order to preserve the independence and integrity of the French monarchy. Catherine's moderating influence was first seen in the Edict of Amboise (March 1560), which pardoned the king's subjects for religious offenses if they would live as good Catholics. The Edict of Romorantin (May 1560), which transferred the prosecution of heresy cases from royal to ecclesiastical courts, thus creating a distinction between heresy and sedition, shows a continuation of her policy.

Catherine assumed the regency for Charles IX upon the premature death of Francis II (December 1560). With the support of the chancellor Michel de L'Hôpital, she continued her efforts to resolve the growing religious conflict in France. After the failure of the Colloquy of Poissy (September–November 1561), called to effect religious reconciliation, Catherine issued the Edict of January (1562), which allowed for a qualified Calvinist coexistence in France. Protestants welcomed the edict; the Catholic rejection of it ultimately led France into four decades of civil war (often called the Wars of Religion) in 1562.

Catherine's policy of moderation allowed her to oversee negotiations to end the first civil war with a second Edict of Amboise (March 1563), a reworking of the Edict of January. However, the Huguenots and the Guise family provoked renewed hostilities in France—the second and third civil wars. Although Catherine was able to end the second one (September 1567–March 1568) with the Peace of Longjumeau (a renewal of Amboise), the peace was fleeting; fighting resumed in August 1568. After the conclusion of the third civil war in August 1570, Catherine continued her efforts to effect a permanent peace between Catholics and Protestants with the marriage of her daughter, Margaret of Valois, to the young Protestant leader Henry of Navarre (later Henry IV, the first Bourbon king of France).

Catherine's attempts at religious reconciliation were again thwarted, however, as the worst atrocity of the civil wars, the Saint Bartholomew's Day massacre (24 August 1572), put an end to the wedding festivities and led to a fourth war. The massacre began in Paris two days after an unsuccessful attempt of unknown origins on the life of Gaspard de Coligny, head of the Protestant faction. Fearing Protestant reprisals for the attempt on Coligny, Catherine, along with Charles and the royal council, decided on a preemptive strike—the murder of Coligny and a few of his principal followers. What was conceived as selective assassination ended as a general massacre, however, as French Catholics murdered thousands of Protestants. Catherine's reputation as the wicked Machiavellian queen stems from this cataclysmic event. Polemical pamphleteers blamed Catherine not only for the initial unsuccessful attempt on Coligny, as well as his and his followers' deaths, but also for the general slaughter of Huguenots throughout France that followed.

After the Saint Bartholomew's Day massacre, Catherine's focus shifted from the civil war in France to her successful diplomatic efforts to gain the throne of Poland for her favorite son, Henry, duc d'Anjou (May 1573). With the death of Charles in May 1574, Catherine again assumed the regency until the king of Poland could return to France to take his place as Henry III. During the reign of Henry III, Catherine's power was in decline, although she was ultimately successful in her lifelong quest to preserve the integrity of the French throne. Although the majesty of the French throne appeared to weaken under the reign of Henry III, his assassination eight months after Catherine's death led to the reign of Henry IV and a return to stability for France and the monarchy.

Catherine's influence in politics was paralleled by the impact that she had on French culture, across the spectrum of the arts, as a result of her wide-ranging interests. Chief among the fields she affected was architecture, beginning with the development of monumental Paris in 1564 when she commissioned Philibert Delorme (and later Jean Bullant) to build the Palais des Tuileries (destroyed by fire in 1871). Catherine also initiated construction of the Louvre's Galerie du Bord de l'Eau (Waterside Gallery) in an attempt to connect the Tuileries with the old Louvre; Henry IV completed that project.

Catherine helped to transplant a new Italian art form, the ballet, to France. Under her patronage the *ballet de cour,* a predecessor of modern ballet that mixed theatrics, voices, and instruments, took root.

In 1581, Joyeuse's *Ballet de la Royne,* the first known French example of the *ballet de cour,* appeared.

Researchers through the ages have benefited from Catherine's scholarly interests as well. Her personal library contained numerous rare manuscripts, manuscripts that eventually enriched the collection of the Bibliothèque Royale (now the Bibliothèque Nationale). Through her influence in politics and the arts, Catherine left an indelible mark on French history and culture.

See also **Valois Dynasty; Wars of Religion.**

BIBLIOGRAPHY

Héritier, Jean. *Catherine de Médicis.* Paris, 1959.

Knecht, R. J. *Catherine de' Medici.* London and New York, 1998.

Sutherland, N. M. *The Huguenot Struggle for Recognition.* New Haven, Conn., 1980.

Barbara J. Whitehead

CATHERINE OF ARAGON (1485–1536), queen of England, first wife of Henry VIII. Catherine of Aragon was born to Isabella of Castile and Ferdinand of Aragon on 16 December 1485. Besides the usual female education in domestic arts, she was taught to read and write in Castilian and in Ciceronian Latin. In 1501 she wed Arthur, prince of Wales, only to be

Catherine of Aragon. Portrait by an unknown artist. NATIONAL PORTRAIT GALLERY, LONDON/SUPERSTOCK

widowed the following April. Remaining in England, she was betrothed in 1503 to Henry, her husband's brother, after a papal bull had dispensed with certain impediments to their marriage.

At Henry's accession in 1509, they were wed and crowned in a double coronation ceremony. From 1510 to 1518 she suffered several miscarriages and was delivered of fragile children who died in infancy, but in 1516 she gave birth to a surviving daughter named Mary. Shortly thereafter, hoping to persuade God to bless her with a son, she began to wear under her gowns the habit of the third order of St. Francis.

Her life is noteworthy for her loyalty to her family and lineage. Early in her husband's reign, she represented Spanish interests in England as her father's unofficial ambassador. Although Henry and his chief minister, Thomas Cardinal Wolsey, appointed the household of her young daughter, who lived away from court but visited her parents regularly at major church festivals, Catherine demonstrated an avid interest in the progress of Mary's classical studies. Along with the king, she patronized poets and translators, such as Sir Thomas Wyatt, and humanists, such as Juan Luis Vives, who dedicated works to her. Vives also composed an educational handbook for the princess.

By 1527 Henry considered illegal the dispensation that had permitted their marriage on the grounds that the pope lacked the power to override biblical law as stated in Leviticus 20:21, which forbids a man to take his brother's wife. For this verse even to apply to their marriage, Catherine's union with Arthur had to have been consummated, but until her death she maintained that she was still a virgin when she became Henry's bride.

Refusing to agree that she had been his mistress for almost twenty years and attempting to preserve the inheritance of her daughter, who would be recognized as illegitimate if the marriage were invalidated, Catherine appealed the case to the papal curia. In 1529 the papal legates Lorenzo Cardinal Campeggio and Cardinal Wolsey convened a court at Blackfriars to inquire into the legality of the union but adjourned it before a verdict could be given. She continued to live as the king's consort while pressuring Pope Clement VII to hear her appeal, but at the same time Henry, who planned to wed Anne Boleyn, was seeking to have their marriage dissolved. From 1531 Catherine resided apart from her husband, who approved an appeals statute that authorized Thomas Cranmer, archbishop of Canterbury, to dispose of the marital inquiry.

Catherine adamantly refused to accept the subsequent annulment and her concurrent demotion to princess dowager of Wales in 1533 or to recognize the validity of the Act of Succession of 1534 that ignored her daughter Mary's claim to the throne. Remaining intransigent on these issues until her death on 7 January 1536 of natural causes, not of the rumored poisoning, she was buried at Peterborough Abbey.

BIBLIOGRAPHY

Loades, David. *The Politics of Marriage: Henry VIII and His Queens.* Dover, N.H., 1994.

Mattingly, Garrett. *Catherine of Aragon.* Boston, 1941. The traditional, sympathetic view of her life.

RETHA M. WARNICKE

CATHERINE OF BOLOGNA (Caterina Vegri; 1413–1463), Clarist sister, writer, artist, mystic, and abbess. Raised as a lady-in-waiting to Margaret d'Este at the court of Ferrara, Catherine received a good upbringing, which was offset, however, by intense spiritual struggles that manifested themselves in doubts, torments, and visions of attacking demons and other diabolic struggles for her soul. While still in her teens, and upon the marriage of Margaret, Catherine adopted the Rule of St. Clare and joined the beguinage of Corpus Domini, a community of women devoted to piety, charity, and worship, founded originally in 1406 by Bernardina Sedazzari. The Corpus Domini ultimately claimed Catherine as its most illustrious member, based in part on her reformist influence and on writings that included accounts of her demonic attacks and struggles, descriptions of her visions—the most famous being a visitation by the Virgin Mother, who placed the newborn Jesus in her arms—and an important treatise describing what she called the seven spiritual weapons. On the basis of her work, Catherine was transferred to Bologna to start a new chapter of the Corpus Domini, and remained there until her death in 1463. Canonized by Clement XI in 1712 and honored as the patron saint of artists, her remains are preserved sitting in a chair and richly garbed, her body undecayed but blackened with age, in the chapel of the convent at Bologna.

BIBLIOGRAPHY

Primary Work

Berrigan, Joseph R. "Catherine of Bologna." In *Women Writers of the Renaissance and Reformation.* Edited by Katharina M. Wilson. Athens, Ga., and London, 1987. Pages 81–95.

Secondary Works

Craveri, Marcello. *Sante e streghe: biografie e documenti dal quattordicesimo al diciassettesimo secolo.* Milan, 1981.

McLaughlin, Mary Martin. "Creating and Recreating Communities of Women: The Case of Corpus Domini, Ferrara, 1406–1452." *Signs* 14 (1989): 293–320.

SARAH COVINGTON

CATHERINE OF GENOA (Caterina Fieschi Adorno; 1447–1510), Italian mystic, hospital administrator, "theologian of purgatory," and central figure of an important group of reformist clergy. Born into the ancient and noble family of the Fieschi, Catherine sought from an early age to enter the religious life, but was forced by political expediency into marriage with the dissipated and extravagant Giuliano Adorno. Ten years of isolation and unhappiness ensued, compounded by Catherine's already melancholy disposition, until she reached a spiritual crisis in 1473 that culminated in revelations she experienced in a chapel and, two days later, a vision of Christ dripping with blood and bearing the cross. Other visions followed, of paradise resplendent and Genoa aflame, and were accompanied by penitential acts that included wearing a hairshirt, embarking on extreme fasts, placing thorns in her bed, and praying six hours a day. When her husband, now bankrupt, reformed his life a few years later, the childless couple moved to a small house in a poor district near the hospital of Pammatone to devote the rest of their lives to the sick, the orphaned, and the dying.

It was during this period of plague and poor relief that Catherine began to attract a circle of friends, most notably the young lawyer Ettore Vernazza who acted as her amanuensis, compiling with her protégé Cattaneo Marabotto the *Vita della serafica s. Caterina da Genova* (Life and doctrine of Saint Catherine of Genoa; published 1737). From this record of her ecstasies and revelations came a doctrine that focused especially on the idea of purgatory as an act of holy cleansing that moved one toward ultimate unification with God. Her otherworldliness and theological inspirations did not interfere with a good head for business, however, and in 1490 she became director of the hospital, supervising doctors, priests, and nuns, setting up tent cities outside the hospital in times of plague, and serving as spiritual mother to a new generation of reforming clergy. The death of her husband in 1497 did not slow these activities, though she became increasingly debilitated by illness, until she died in 1510. She was formally canonized in 1737.

BIBLIOGRAPHY

Primary Work
Catherine of Genoa. *Purgation and Purgatory: The Spiritual Dialogue.* Translated by Serge Hughes. New York, 1979.

Secondary Works
Hügel, Friedrich von. *The Mystical Element of Religion as Studied in Saint Catherine of Genoa and Her Friends.* 2 vols. London, 1923.
Kaye-Smith, Sheila. *Quartet in Heaven.* Freeport, N.Y., 1970.
Nugent, Donald Christopher. "Saint Catherine of Genoa: Mystic of Pure Love." In *Women Writers of the Renaissance and Reformation.* Edited by Katharina M. Wilson. Athens, Ga., and London, 1987. Pages 67–80.

SARAH COVINGTON

CATHERINE OF SIENA (1347–1380), mystic, saint. Catherine, the twenty-fourth of twenty-five children, was born the year the Black Death swept Europe to a Sienese wool dyer, Giacomo Benincasa, and his wife, Lapa di Puccio di Piacenti. The family belonged to a powerful trade faction known as the Party of Twelve, which dominated the political scene of Siena from 1355 to 1368. Catherine was remarkably gifted and revered in her lifetime as a religious reformer, teacher, theologian, and ardent adviser to both secular and ecclesiastical leaders. Canonized at the height of the Renaissance in 1461, she was named a patron saint of Italy in 1939 and declared a doctor of the church in 1970.

Throughout her life, Catherine was devoted to the church, to the authority of the papacy, and to restoring and securing peace among the feuding city-states of Italy. After a particularly spiritual childhood, at sixteen she became a Dominican tertiary (*mantellata*) and, after three years of self-imposed solitude, ministered to the sick and the poor. A number of years later she experienced a spiritual marriage to Christ and in 1375 received the stigmata (the wounds of the crucified Christ), the signs of which by her own request were to remain invisible. Her influence was felt far beyond her convent. Concerned with the instability of the church in Italy, she visited Pope Gregory XI in Avignon to seek reconciliation between Florence and the Holy See. Influenced by her mission and heeding her prophecies, he returned to Rome in 1376, only to flee to Avignon again in 1378. (The papal elections after his death in 1378 began the Great Schism.) Catherine gained many followers, and her disciples, both men and women, formed a spiritual community or *brigata* around her called the Catarinati. In the last years of her life Catherine actively supported the pope's plea for a crusade, worked for reform of the Dominican order, and served as one of Pope Urban VI's trusted advisers. Shortly before her death at the age of thirty-three, weakened by a long period of fasting, her final contribution to ecclesiastical stability was the reconciliation of Pope Urban VI with the Roman republic.

Catherine of Siena. *St. Catherine Receiving the Stigmata* by Giovanni di Paolo (c. 1400–1482). Tempera and gold on wood; 27.9 × 20 cm (11 × 7.9 in.). THE METROPOLITAN MUSEUM OF ART, ROBERT LEHMAN COLLECTION, 1975.

can be divided broadly into three genres: a collection of 382 letters to popes, monarchs, prisoners, and secular leaders; a mystical treatise, *Libro della divina dottrina* (known in English as *The Dialogue of St. Catherine of Siena* or *A Treatise on Divine Providence;* or both as title and subtitle), which was written in 1377–1378 and is regarded as a classic of fourteenth-century Italian literature; and a collection of twenty-six prayers. Her works, directed at the full range of laity and clergy, reveal an intense interest in the concept of selfhood as well as familiarity with biblical sources, Augustine, Gregory the Great, Bernard of Clairvaux, and Thomas Aquinas. But it is her collected correspondence, the *Epistolario,* that is particularly notable for a study of the Renaissance. Edited and published in 1500 by the Venetian humanist, printer, and publisher Aldus Manutius, the *Epistolario* was later included in the sixteenth-century literary canon of Anton Francesco Doni's *Libraria* (1550). Even though Catherine lacked formal schooling, her letters are characterized by a religious zeal and have a definitive and vivid didactic tone. The letters—many of them exhortations for peace and reconciliation—gave her access to the public sphere. Catherine used the epistolary genre with the intent to shape religious politics and to influence the powerful for the benefit of the church. For many historians today, Catherine's letters and *Dialogue* evoke questions of how she garnered the authority necessary for the success of her secular and religious activism.

See also **Spirituality, Female.**

BIBLIOGRAPHY

Primary Works

Catherine of Siena. *The Dialogue.* Translated by Suzanne Noffke. New York, 1980. The translation is largely based on Giuliana Cavallini's 1968 critical edition of *Biblioteca Casanatense,* MS 292.

Catherine of Siena. *The Letters of St. Catherine of Siena.* Translated by Suzanne Noffke. Vol. 1 (of four projected). Binghamton, N.Y., 1988.

Catherine of Siena. *The Prayers of Catherine of Siena.* Translated by Suzanne Noffke. New York, 1983.

Raymond of Capua. *The Life of Catherine of Siena.* Translated by Conleth Kearns. Wilmington, Del., 1980.

Secondary Works

Berrigan, Joseph. "The Tuscan Visionary: Saint Catherine of Siena." In *Medieval Women Writers.* Edited by Katharina M. Wilson. Athens, Ga., 1984. Pages 252–268.

Noffke, Suzanne. *Catherine of Siena: Vision through a Distant Eye.* Collegeville, Minn., 1996.

Parks, M. Carola. "Social and Political Consciousness in the Letters of Catherine of Siena." In *Western Spirituality: Historical Roots, Ecumenical Routes.* Edited by Matthew Fox. Notre Dame, Ind., 1979. Pages 258–267.

With a spiritually motivated determination ever present, Catherine's remarkable political influence in a time of great distress between church and state is indicative of her unique and dynamic leadership.

The many paintings of Catherine by Renaissance artists follow the hagiographic depiction of her in the *Legenda major* written by her principal disciple and biographer, Raymond of Capua. Typical of the artistic renditions are Andrea Vanni's fresco in the Church of San Domenico painted shortly after her death, Giovanni di Paolo's altarpiece for the guild of the Pizzicaiuoli commissioned around 1449, and Bernadino Fungai's altar panel of her stigmatization from 1497 in the Santa Casa de Caterina in Siena. Renaissance artists drew on an aggregate of hagiographic images associated with Catherine, including her mystical marriage to Christ and her coronation, and frequently incorporated her symbols, a crown of thorns, the lily, and the book.

That Catherine was the first woman to write in the Tuscan dialect, dictating all her works to secretaries, is of immeasurable significance. Her extant writings

Scott, Karen. "*Io Catarina*': Ecclesiastical Politics and Oral Culture in the Letters of Catherine of Siena." In *Dear Sister: Medieval Women and the Epistolary Genre.* Edited by Karen Cherewatuk and Ulrike Wiethaus. Philadelphia, 1993. Pages 87–121.

ROSEMARY DRAGE HALE

CATHOLIC REFORMATION AND COUNTER-REFORMATION.

The Catholic Reformation and Counter-Reformation are terms used sometimes interchangeably to designate changes in Catholicism that occurred in the early modern period somehow in relationship to the Protestant Reformation; they are also often used to cover all aspects of early modern Catholicism, especially from about 1555 on.

The Concepts. By the mid-seventeenth century the term "Reformation" was well on its way into historians' vocabulary to indicate the movement begun by Martin Luther in 1517, but no correlative term was current that might indicate a Catholic counterpart. In the 1760s Johann Stephan Pütter, a German Lutheran jurist, coined *Gegenreformationen* (Counter-Reformations) to mean the forced return to the practice of Catholicism in areas once Lutheran. By the term he meant both a phenomenon—military, political, and diplomatic coercion against Lutherans by Catholics—and a period of time, from the Peace of Augsburg (1555) until the end of the Thirty Years' War (1648). Leopold von Ranke mediated the concept into the historical mainstream in *Deutsche Geschichte im Zeitalter der Reformation* (*History of the Reformation in Germany,* 1842–1847), understanding by it the same period of European history: "After the era of the Reformation [1517–1555] came the era of the Counter Reformations." Ranke also initiated a pan-European trend toward using the term, in the singular form, to cover all aspects of Catholicism during that period.

In 1880 the Lutheran Wilhelm Maurenbrecher introduced *katholische Reformation* (Catholic Reformation) to indicate reform initiatives that predated 1517. This term avoided the negative connotations of Counter-Reformation and hence was more acceptable to some Catholic historians. By the early twentieth century other terms were in circulation, such as Catholic Renaissance and Evangelism, while Counter-Reformation and Catholic Reformation were themselves being variously defined.

In 1946 Hubert Jedin, the great historian of the Council of Trent, tried to bring order out of the confusion by defining Catholic Reformation as the positive impulses toward reform that began in the late Middle Ages, reached a decisive codification at the Council of Trent, and continued beyond it. Counter-Reformation meant the measures the Catholic Church took to defend itself after about 1555, which included the doctrinal decrees of Trent directed against Protestant teaching. The proper designation was, therefore, "Catholic Reformation and Counter-Reformation."

Jedin's remains the classic statement on the subject, but it has been increasingly challenged. Moreover, his distinction between the two terms is often not observed, with Counter-Reformation predominating especially in Mediterranean countries as the catch-all designation for the situation after the Council of Trent. Alternatives have yet to gain widespread acceptance. The terms here will be understood in their most comprehensive sense as designations of all aspects of early modern Catholicism, that is, from the fifteenth into the eighteenth centuries. These disputes about naming, it must be noted, are the surface manifestation of profound differences among historians in perspective and method.

The Late Medieval Situation. How bad was it? This is the question, a leading question, that still lurks in many minds and is often still addressed by historians. While a fully satisfying answer will always elude us, some clarity is possible by distinguishing between the ecclesiastical situation and the religious situation, meaning by the former official church offices and officers like popes, bishops, and pastors of parishes.

The ecclesiastical situation. Complaints about such offices, especially the papacy, began to swell in the fourteenth century and reached a grand crescendo at the time of the Great Schism (1378–1417). They would continue to be heard until the Council of Trent. The venality of the papacy, the luxurious households of the cardinals, the absenteeism of bishops, the ignorance of the diocesan clergy, and, underneath these and similar abuses, the self-serving dispensations from canonical procedures were some of the typical and persistent grievances that resounded in preaching and in tracts and treatises. Measures dealing with abuses like these were what was generally meant by "reform of the church." They received their most famous formulation in Luther's "Open Letter to the Christian Nobility of the German Nation" (1520).

Even granted the hyperbole that often marked such cries of outrage, later-twentieth-century research while marking many exceptions, has confirmed how badly the situation deviated from canonical norms and from what thoughtful people expected of these official leaders. Beginning with the Council of Constance (1414–1418) and continuing until the Fifth Lateran Council (1512–1517), several attempts were made at the official level to remedy the situation, but the will to carry through was lacking, especially in the popes, until the pressure generated by the Reformation left no alternative.

The religious situation. The general religious situation is much more difficult to assess. Earlier historians were aware of what they considered isolated instances of godliness amid encircling corruption, but today many see the general situation more positively. There is good evidence that in many localities Christians were well instructed in basic beliefs and striving to lead devout lives. Research on confraternities, especially in Italy and Iberia, has suggested this positive reassessment, and research in other areas has corroborated it. A general concern for more effective catechesis was widespread, for instance, by the beginning of the sixteenth century. Movements like the *devotio moderna* (modern devotion) promoted greater inwardness and advocated practices like more frequent reception of the Eucharist. Women like Catherine of Siena (1347–1380) and Catherine of Genoa (1447–1510), both later canonized, took active roles in the society of their day and at the same time left documents testifying to their mystical experiences. Ignatius Loyola (1491–1556) and his companions, who originally had no further aim than "to help souls" by conversation and works of mercy, seem to have been symptomatic of a widespread and high level of religious concern that was not propelled by a desire "to reform the church." In this the origins of the Jesuits were similar to those of the future Barnabites and Ursulines. The humanist movement, even in fifteenth-century Italy, where earlier humanism was once thought to be essentially pagan, was strongly moral in its inspiration, and often its practitioners deliberately intended to promote an upright and devout life among those they addressed.

While many humanists went no further than that, Erasmus (c. 1466–1536) was notable for calling for changes in theological method, styles of piety, and pastoral practice. In other words there were persons and movements that, without addressing "reform of the church" as such, issued explicit calls for systemic changes of one kind or another that, it was expected, would lead to a further flowering of Christian fervor and devotion. Among these were the great penitential preachers like Bernardino of Siena (1380–1444) and John of Capistrano (1386–1456), who acted like nineteenth-century revivalists for the communities they addressed. The Observantist movements within the mendicant orders, which gained momentum after the end of the Great Schism, aimed at restoration of earlier commitment. Among Benedictine monks a similar impulse was felt, which led to the formation of congregations to establish groupings of monasteries pursuing similar goals, among which those of Santa Giustina (Italy), Valladolid (Spain), and Chézal-Benoît (France) and the unions of Melk (Austria) and Bursfeld (Germany) were the most important. The preaching of Girolamo Savonarola (1452–1498) is a good example of how calls for reform of the church and for a more general renewal could meet and overlap. The same is true for many of the apocalyptic and millenarian prophecies, including the prophecy of an "angelic pope," widely heard in the fifteenth century.

The Council of Trent. The rapid spread of various forms of Protestantism after 1517 caused alarm, even panic, and demands swelled that the papacy deal with the situation especially through a council. After the disastrous procrastination of Pope Clement VII (1523–1534), Pope Paul III (1534–1549) held a series of consistories nominating professed reformers as cardinals, established the Roman Inquisition in 1542, and finally, responding in part to pressure from the emperor Charles V, convoked the Council of Trent. The council lasted, with two long adjournments, for eighteen years, from 1545 to 1563. It was a watershed.

The agenda of the council soon fell into two distinct categories—doctrinal responses to Protestant teaching, which was the uppermost concern of the papal faction, and legislation to effect a thoroughgoing reform of the church, especially of the papal curia, which was the concern of the imperial faction. Shaken frequently by vicissitudes of papal, French, Spanish, and imperial policies, torn by internal controversies, and faced with a seemingly impossible agenda, the council declared its work done in December 1563 and received approval of its decrees from Pope Pius IV (1559–1565) the following month.

The comprehensive nature of Protestant abjuration of standard Catholic teaching on matters as central as the sacraments required an equally comprehensive response. Nonetheless, the council recognized the central importance of the doctrine of justification and expended its longest and best efforts in constructing that decree. Sometimes considered the masterpiece of the council, the decree affirmed the utter primacy of grace while insisting on some degree of human responsibility. It did not satisfy the Protestants, of course, and its interpretation would later cause bitter and violent disagreement among Catholics, especially manifest in the Jansenist controversy of the seventeenth and early eighteenth centuries.

Reformers at the council focused on three offices—papacy, episcopacy, and pastorates. Their efforts to reform the papal curia, considered by many to be the key to broader church reform, was essentially unsuccessful, blocked in one way or another by the papal legates. They were able finally to pass strong legislation requiring that bishops reside in their dioceses. Although sometimes later ignored, this legislation helped create a more pastorally committed episcopacy in the post-Tridentine period. In requiring residency of pastors in their parishes and in requiring every diocese to operate a seminary for the training of future priests, the council moved in the same direction for the diocesan clergy.

Any assessment of Trent must bristle with ironies. Every Protestant church and sect denied papal primacy in the church and most wanted the office obliterated, yet Trent, because the precise extent of papal authority was so contentious an issue, had no decree concerning it. However, the papacy, which so feared and resisted a council, ended up gaining great benefit and new power from it, as it assumed responsibility for interpreting and implementing the conciliar decrees. While pastoral in intent, the reform decrees were framed in juridical language and carried punitive consequences, which in insensitive hands would render the decrees into crude forms of social discipline. The council had nothing to say about the role of women in the church except to insist on the strict cloistering of nuns, but within a few generations women would assume a massive role in active ministry. Finally, the scope of the council, which at first glance looks so comprehensive, in fact had important limitations. Few things were more characteristic of Catholicism during this period than the efforts at evangelization that followed upon the Iberian discoveries, settlements, and conquests in Asia and Latin America, but of this phenomenon not a word was issued at Trent.

The New Situation. Trent was but one factor that contributed to significant changes in the Catholic Church, whose origins are clearly discernible by the mid-sixteenth century. Among the most remarkable were the roles the papacy now assumed and that were attributed to it.

The papacy. Pope Paul IV (1555–1559) was a zealot who asserted by his deeds an uncompromising understanding of papal authority that empowered him to run the church single-handedly. He brought Cardinal Giovanni Morone (1509–1580) to trial for heresy and published in 1559 the first papal Index of Prohibited Books, the most extreme such list ever put together. Although many of his actions were for the most part repudiated or drastically modified by his successors, he was symptomatic of a new rigor and energy in religious matters that would affect even some of the more genial among them. In the many religious wars that Europe suffered beginning in 1546, the papacy readily provided moral support and comfort to the Catholic parties but often also provided, directly or indirectly, men and munitions. Within the papal curia itself, while many of the old abuses continued, they were somewhat curtailed and, by a kind of tacit agreement, criticism throughout the Catholic world became muted, in solidarity against Protestants. Under Pope Sixtus V (1585–1590) the curia was reorganized from its older consistorial, or consultative, form into a precocious state bureaucracy that, in tandem with developments in secular monarchies, signified a step toward the age of absolutism.

Of even more profound significance was the position the papacy began to achieve in the configuration of Catholic teachings and in the belief-system of even the illiterate. Before the Reformation, for instance, catechisms made no mention of the papacy, and most Christians of Europe probably had no idea that the office held particular significance for their religious faith. The controversies with Protestants changed that situation, and beginning in mid-century the papacy figured explicitly in catechisms in the definition of church. From oblivion or, at best, periphery it gradually moved to the center, as Catholics began to define themselves as indeed essentially papists. This development was symptomatic on the Catholic side of the more general phenomenon described as confessionalization, that is, the construction by all churches and sects of particular rituals, creeds, and practices that set them off from each other, almost in denial of their common Christian heritage.

Local authorities. The activities of the papacy, nonetheless, rarely touched directly the lives of the faithful. Even the implementation of Trent fell to local authorities, clerical and lay. Among the latter none was more important than King Philip II of Spain (1556–1598), who acted almost completely in-

Catholic Reformer. Carlo Borromeo (1538–1584), archbishop of Milan, at supper. Portrait (detail) by Daniele Crespi (c. 1595–1630) in the church of the Passion, Milan. ALINARI/ART RESOURCE

dependently of the papacy in the affairs of the Spanish church and its overseas dominions, where he directly appointed all the bishops and collected all the revenues. In all Catholic countries, as the decades wore on into the seventeenth century, a partnership between the higher clergy and the monarchies devolved into the marriage between throne and altar that would be a hallmark of the ancien régime.

Still, by the turn of the century, the local bishop had in many places assumed a much stronger religious role, fulfilling the aim of the Tridentine decrees. Those decrees might have become a dead letter, however, had not a few bishops seized the moment to assert their authority with dramatic force and shaken off the old image of feudal potentate. The most important among these prelates was Carlo Borromeo, archbishop of Milan from 1560 until his death in 1584. A nephew of Pope Pius IV, Borromeo studied the decrees of the council with the intention of carrying them out in the minutest detail. In compliance with the decrees, he convened a number of archdiocesan and provincial synods that touched on every aspect of ecclesiastical life. Uncompromising in his approach, he made many enemies but soon attained a reputation for sanctity that, at least after his death, gave his ideas momentum. The decrees of his synods were, meanwhile, codified in a monument of regulation called the *Acta ecclesiae Mediolanensis* (Acts of the church of Milan; 1582). It began

to be considered such an authentic interpretation of the Council of Trent that it was forwarded to harried bishops in Poland and Germany. In France, where the publication of the decrees of Trent were long delayed for political reasons, the *Acta* provided a means to smuggle them in, and they later assumed almost canonical status. The *Acta* constructed new codes of conduct for clergy and laity alike, often accompanied by penalties for failure to comply, which would be administered sometimes by ecclesiastical, sometimes by secular officials.

Changes and continuities. Besides changes like these on the official and juridical level, many of which were the direct or indirect result of the Council of Trent, others took place almost independently of Catholic officialdom, whether clerical or lay. Some were continuations, but with new emphases, of earlier traditions. The proliferation of books on the devout life was one of the most obvious. Spain enjoyed almost a monopoly in this area in the sixteenth century, beginning with Francisco de Osuna (c. 1497–1542) and culminating with great classics of Christian mysticism by Teresa of Ávila (1515–1582) and John of the Cross (1542–1591). In the seventeenth century leadership passed to Francophone culture, with Francis de Sales's (1567–1622) *Introduction to the Devout Life* (1609) and *Treatise on the Love of God* (1616) the best known and most widely read. Hagiography got a new lease on life, influenced now by the literary and source-critical norms advocated by Renaissance humanists.

The late sixteenth century initiated a golden age of Catholic preaching. Perhaps never before or since was so much thought and preparation given to this ministry, as occasions to preach increased through the creation of new observances like novenas and the *Quarante ore* (Forty hours 'devotion). In this development humanism played a crucial role, both in the value it set on the power of the spoken word and in the changes in form, content, and purpose that the adaptation of classical rhetoric to preaching entailed.

The most massive and systematic instrument for the transmission of the humanist legacy was, however, the network of schools established first by the Jesuits and later by other religious orders. In this new era and context the tradition underwent changes, to be sure, but the essential ideals and program did not get swamped by them. The canons of textual criticism developed by the humanists, especially as they applied to the Bible, were cautiously, sometimes defensively, applied.

Although often viewed with suspicion, women emerged during this period with a much more prominent and activist profile. Teresa of Ávila was not only a great writer but also the founder of many convents and, in effect, a whole new branch of the Carmelite order. Barbe-Jeanne Acarie (Mary of the Incarnation; 1566–1618) was instrumental in bringing the Carmelites to France, the Ursulines and the Oratory to Paris, and in creating in her house a religious salon that nurtured the vocations of Sales, Pierre de Bérulle (1575–1629), and many others. Most astounding, however, was the sudden proliferation in seventeenth-century France of congregations of women pursuing organized and active ministry. By mid-century the running of schools for girls, often more or less copying the Jesuit model for boys, emerged as perhaps their most important activity, with the Ursulines being especially important. But with the Daughters of Charity of Vincent de Paul (1581–1660) and Louise de Marillac (1591–1660), women now worked outside their convents nursing the sick and, soon, in running hospitals and similar institutions.

Catholicism in this period experienced a proliferation of new ministries and an intensification of older ones only adumbrated earlier. With the *Spiritual Exercises* of Loyola, the religious retreat, usually guided by a cleric, assumed almost classic contours. Its equivalent on the more popular level was the so-called missions, elaborate pastoral strategies running for several days or weeks and directed to the whole population of a hamlet or, eventually, of an urban quarter.

The Schools of Christian Doctrine, organized catechism classes begun in Italy in the early sixteenth century, spread widely in one form or another, and in them laymen and laywomen taught boys and girls the basics of their religion on a scale heretofore unknown. This zeal for better catechesis was but one manifestation of a more general war against ignorance and superstition that marked both Catholicism and Protestantism. In this phenomenon can be noted the beginnings of an important shift in mentality. Whereas early catechesis placed its emphasis on orthopraxis, learning one's religion to practice it, the later now subtly began to place it on orthodoxy, learning about one's religion in order to understand or defend it.

Shaken to its core by the Reformation, Catholicism had begun by the early seventeenth century to reassert itself confidently in traditional ways. Scholasticism revived as a legitimate theological form, and in its great practitioners like Francisco Suárez

(1548–1617) can be detected modifications that suggest attention being paid to humanists' earlier criticisms of the enterprise. The older religious orders like the Dominicans and Franciscans doubled their membership between 1540 and 1700, and especially in seventeenth-century France new orders of men and women continued to spring up. Confraternities, abolished by Protestant reformers, flourished as never before, even as they now began to fall ever more under the authority of the clergy. The cult of the saints gained new vigor, and canonizations resumed. Pilgrimages and similar practices derided by Protestants and by humanists like Erasmus regained their popularity. The veneration of images, whose legitimacy Trent confirmed, took on new life, as Catholic prelates and princes commissioned artists for works intended to satisfy their devotion. The new religious orders of men constructed an impressive number of new churches throughout Europe in building programs that culminated in a number of mannerist and baroque masterpieces. They and the older orders did the same in their missions in Asia and America.

While religion remained essentially a local affair during this period, interest in overseas missions and commitment to them seized significant portions of the Catholic population in an utterly unprecedented degree. The great discoveries had opened the way for a massive export of missionaries and for impressive, often disastrously destructive efforts at evangelization fired by religious enthusiasm. In this situation the defense of the Amerindians by Bartolomé de las Casas (1474–1566) and others is all the more impressive. The Jesuit missions to Japan and China mark a significant moment of recognition by Europeans of the dignity of cultures other than their own. But, despite its mighty expansion around the globe, Catholicism remained both in Europe and abroad essentially a western European phenomenon.

See also Confraternities; Constance, Council of; Devotio Moderna; Hagiography; Humanism, *subentry on* The Definition of Humanism; Index of Prohibited Books; Lateran V, Council of; Papacy; Pilgrimage; Preaching and Sermons; Protestant Reformation; Religious Literature; Religious Orders; Religious Piety; Scholasticism; Seminaries; Spirituality, Female; Trent, Council of; *and biographies of figures mentioned in this entry.*

BIBLIOGRAPHY

Primary Works

The Jesuit Relations and Allied Documents: Travels and Explorations of the Jesuit Missionaries in New France, 1610–1791.

Edited by Reuben Gold Thwaites. 73 vols. Cleveland, Ohio, 1896–1901. Original text with English translation.

Olin, John C., ed. *Catholic Reform: From Cardinal Ximenes to the Council of Trent, 1495–1563*. New York, 1990. A collection of primary documents in translation.

Tanner, Norman P., ed. *Decrees of the Ecumenical Councils*. 2 vols. London and Washington, D.C., 1990. Original text established by Giuseppe Alberigo et al. An edition of the texts of the conciliar decrees in the original language with English translation.

Secondary Works

Bossy, John. *Christianity in the West, 1400–1700*. Oxford and New York, 1985. Sweeping vision and provocative interpretation.

Châtellier, Louis. *The Europe of the Devout: The Catholic Reformation and the Formation of a New Society*. Translated by Jean Birrell. Cambridge, U.K., 1989. A study of the Jesuits' Marian congregations.

Del Col, Andrea, and Giovanna Paolin, eds. *L'Inquisizione Romana in Italia nell'età moderna: Archivi, problemi di metodo e nuove ricerche*. Rome, 1991. Collection of papers addressing various aspects of, especially, the Roman Inquisition.

DeMolen, Richard L., ed. *Religious Orders of the Catholic Reformation*. New York, 1994. A collection of studies on nine such orders.

Flynn, Maureen. *Sacred Charity: Confraternities and Social Welfare in Spain, 1400–1700*. Ithaca, N.Y., 1989. Laity and clergy interacting in a variety of ways.

Hudon, William V. "Religion and Society in Early Modern Italy—Old Questions, New Insights." *American Historical Review* 101 (1996): 783–804. A judicious review of historiographical and terminological issues.

Jedin, Hubert. *A History of the Council of Trent*. Translated by Ernest Graf. 2 vols. London, 1957–1961. Translation of two (of four) volumes of *Geschichte des Konzils von Trient*.

McGinness, Frederick J. *Right Thinking and Sacred Oratory in Counter-Reformation Rome*. Princeton, N.J., 1995. Depicts the change in mentality and vocabulary after Trent.

O'Malley, John W. *The First Jesuits*. Cambridge, Mass., 1993. A comprehensive overview, 1540–1565.

O'Malley, John W. "Was Ignatius Loyola a Church Reformer? How to Look at Early Modern Catholicism." *Catholic Historical Review* 77 (1991): 177–193. A discussion of interpretative categories that argues in favor of early modern Catholicism.

Prodi, Paolo. *The Papal Prince: One Body and Two Souls: The Papal Monarchy in Early Modern Europe*. Translated by Susan Haskins. Cambridge, U.K., 1987. Describes the evolution of papal government after Trent.

Rapley, Elizabeth. *The Dévotes: Women and Church in Seventeenth-Century France*. Montreal and Buffalo, N.Y., 1990. Important study of how nuns were finally able to do active ministry.

Reinhard, Wolfang. "Disciplinamento sociale, confessionalizzazione, modernizzazione: Un discorso storigrafico." In *Disciplina dell'anima, disciplina del corpore e disciplina della società tra medioevo et età moderna*. Edited by Paolo Prodi and Carla Penuti. Bologna, Italy, 1994. Pages 101–123. Analysis of the newer categories of interpretation.

Soergel, Philip M. *Wondrous in His Saints: Counter-Reformation Propaganda in Bavaria*. Berkeley and Los Angeles, 1993. Describes the revival of traditional piety to confute the Reformation.

Venard, Marc. *Réforme protestante, réforme catholique dans la province d'Avignon au XVIᵉ siècle*. Paris, 1993. An exceptionally important study of a given locality.

JOHN W. O'MALLEY

CAVENDISH, MARGARET (c. 1624–1673), English writer and intellectual. Margaret Cavendish, the first duchess of Newcastle, was born to a wealthy gentry family from the Colchester area. Her father was Thomas Lucas, and she was the youngest of eight children in an extraordinarily close family. Even as adults her brothers and sisters were often together when in London. In predicting her later career, her childhood was most significant for her siblings' encouragement of her juvenilia and her mother's management of the family's property after the father's death, of which Cavendish stated in her autobiography: "And though she would often complain that her family was too great for her weak management . . . yet I observe she took a pleasure and some little pride, in the governing thereof." Her long writing career, and her questioning of the concept of a female nature or sphere, were the most significant characteristics of her own life.

At age twenty Margaret joined Queen Henrietta Maria's court in Oxford in 1643 and accompanied her into exile to Paris in 1644. By 1645 she had met William Cavendish, who unsuccessfully led troops at Marston Moor, but came to court as a royalist hero and eligible bachelor given the recent death of his first wife in childbirth. Over the objections of the queen and William's friends the couple wed within six months, remaining in exile until the Restoration of Charles II in 1660. Margaret published the first of her many works (*Poems and Fancies*) in 1653.

Her works received a mixed reception during her lifetime, more negative than positive, and have continued to gain mixed reviews ever since. More recent scholars have approached her as a writer of fantasy, autobiography, and biography, and as an idiosyncratic author of early scientific works. Margaret Cavendish wrote more substantial works than any other mid-seventeenth-century woman, and she wrote in the greatest variety of genres of any woman (and most men) during the century. Her works consist of natural and physical philosophy, two volumes of plays, poetry, fantasies, essays, letters, a biography of her husband, and an autobiography. She was known in her lifetime as "Mad Madge"; contemporary and later assessments of her work have always been tied to the general bias against women publishing their works or having them appear in print.

Contemporary and later critics note her lack of training (she knew no foreign languages and lacked any classical or scholarly education), her failure to produce polished works, her writing in areas—especially scientific—where she could claim no expertise, her arrogance in making her identity public, her willingness to debate important thinkers such as Descartes, and, above all, her criticism of intellectual elites and of women's lack of serious education, or recognition of their ideas and writings. Those who acknowledge her contributions point to the originality of much of what she wrote, the breadth of her subjects, her representation of a scientific tradition outside of the patriarchal, experimental direction established by Francis Bacon, her strong feminist views, and the quality of some of her poetry. As a duchess she had advantages over middle-class authors, but the comments against her by contemporary men and women make clear that she was consistently a subject of ridicule and a social isolate.

Margaret Cavendish was a complex figure. While a strong royalist, she had few ties to the Anglican Church and published essays and letters critical of England's social hierarchy and royal rule. She offered radical critiques of women's social, political, intellectual, and legal standing, yet often painted women as weak, emotional creatures dependent upon the goodness and competence of men. While others have seen her as privileged, she often portrayed herself as an intellectual and social outcast, isolated from the intellectual discourse and debates of universities and scholarly correspondence, her views and writings little respected, even by other women. Isolated in a family in which only her husband seemed to care for her, and mistress of an isolated estate, she found fulfillment in her study. Yet she sought fame through her works, and while during her lifetime she may have only been infamous, in the late twentieth century her works gained serious attention from literary scholars, historians of science, women's historians, and those studying women philosophers.

BIBLIOGRAPHY

Primary Work

Newcastle, Margaret Cavendish, Duchess of. *The Description of a New World, Called the Blazing World and Other Writings.* Edited by Kate Lilley. New York, 1992.

Secondary Works

Grant, Douglas. *Margaret the First: A Biography of Margaret Cavendish, Duchess of Newcastle, 1623–1673.* Toronto, 1957.

Smith, Hilda L. " 'A General War amongst the Men but None amongst the Women': Political Differences between Margaret and William Cavendish." In *Politics and the Political Imagination in Later Stuart Britain: Essays Presented to Lois Green Schwoerer.* Edited by Howard Nenner. Rochester, N.Y., 1997. Pages 143–160.

HILDA SMITH

CAXTON, WILLIAM (c. 1420–1491), first English printer, first printer of English, first printer in England. Caxton was born in Kent and apprenticed by 1438 to the wealthy London mercer Robert Large (lord mayor, 1439). In the 1440s he served out his apprenticeship and became a freeman of the Mercers' Company. For some thirty years from the mid-1440s Caxton resided primarily on the Continent, as a member of the Merchant Adventurers trading from Bruges. He prospered, and in 1462 he was elected governor of the Adventurers. In 1470 Caxton resigned the governorship and lived for the next year and a half in Cologne, where he set up—or took control of—the printing shop of Johann Schilling. The first of its three productions was the large encyclopedia of Bartholomaeus Anglicus, *De proprietatibus rerum* (On the properties of things; 1472). In 1473 Caxton returned to Bruges and set up a new printing shop. The first of some half-dozen books he printed there was his translation from the French of the historical romance *Recuyell of the Histories of Troy,* completed late 1473 or early 1474. He dedicated the *Recuyell* to Margaret, duchess of Burgundy, and sister of King Edward IV. She had, Caxton wrote, commanded the translation from him. This was the first of a number of royal or noble dedications in his books.

In 1476 Caxton moved back to England and lived the rest of his life in Westminster near the royal court, renting shops from the abbey. He produced there some hundred editions, ranging in size from single-leaf printed indulgences to his most substantial translation, Jacobus de Voragine's collection of saints' lives, the *Golden Legend* (1484), a large folio of almost nine hundred pages. Caxton's publishing program ranged widely, but its central emphasis lay in vernacular literature, chronicles, and works of edification. The discursive prologues and epilogues he wrote for many of his books give them a lively actuality that remains attractive. No other early printer spoke so directly to his intended audience. Caxton produced the first editions of Chaucer's *Canterbury Tales* (1477, reprinted 1483 with woodcuts), of works by John Lydgate and John Gower, and of Sir Thomas Malory's *Morte d'Arthur* (1485). Among his many translations are *The Game and Play of Chess* (1474, reprinted 1483), *Aesop's Fables* (1484), *Charles the Great* (a history of Charlemagne; 1485),

Caxton's Printer's Mark.

and *Reynard the Fox* (1481, reprinted 1489). His successor Wynkyn de Worde printed Caxton's translation of the lives of the desert saints, *Vitas patrum* (1495), recording that his former master had "finished it at the last day of his life."

In Caxton's age and for generations after, the major Latin works of learning and literature were imported to England from continental shops. For English readers, however, Caxton was the dominant figure of his time with regard to both number and quality of publication. Concurrent English printing shops in London, Oxford, and Saint Albans, 1478 and after, all died out in the mid-1480s, and their combined output was little over half of Caxton's.

See also **Printing and Publishing.**

BIBLIOGRAPHY

Hellinga, Lotte. *Caxton in Focus.* London, 1982.

Needham, Paul. *The Printer and the Pardoner: An Unrecorded Indulgence Printed by William Caxton for the Hospital of St. Mary Rounceval, Charing Cross.* Washington, D.C., 1986.

Painter, George D. *William Caxton: A Quincentenary Biography of England's First Printer.* London and New York, 1976.

PAUL NEEDHAM

CECCHI, GIOVANNI MARIA (1518–1587), Florentine gentleman, notary, wool trader, playwright.

Guided by a sense of family pride and tradition, Giovanni Maria Cecchi joined the guild of judges and notaries and became a notary in the city of Florence, holding various public offices of secondary political significance. He also engaged in the wool trade in partnership with other Florentine families of old stock. His true vocation, however, was literature. His writings include *Dichiarazione di molti proverbi* (A digest of many proverbs; no date), a useful philological commentary on Florentine proverbs and popular sayings; *Compendio di più ritratti* (A compendium of cultural portraits; 1575), a travelogue replete with cultural facts and amusing anecdotes about foreign countries, especially France, Germany, and Spain; *Cicalamento di Maestro Bartolino* (Rigamarole of Master Bartolino; 1582), a parody of pedantic sessions typically held at contemporary academies; and *Ragionamenti spirituali* (Religious discourses; 1558), an effort to retell in the vernacular lessons from the Gospels and other religious teachings in order to make them easily accessible to the least-educated faithful.

It was in the theater, however, that Cecchi truly distinguished himself. His more than sixty dramatic works made him the most prolific playwright in the Italian Renaissance and earned him the appreciation of his contemporaries, who called him "Il Comico." Although critical attempts to divide the dramas into various categories have proved unsatisfactory, one may safely distinguish between the erudite comedies, written mostly before 1560, and the religiously oriented plays that Cecchi wrote in the later part of his life. This division notwithstanding, Cecchi's contribution to the history of theater lies in his vast theatrical production, which helped to stereotype characters such as the old man in love, the miser, the pedant, the braggart, and many others that became regular masks in the commedia dell'arte.

BIBLIOGRAPHY

Primary Works

Cecchi, Giovanni Maria. *Commedie di Giovanmaria Cecchi.* Edited by Gaetano Milanesi. 2 vols. Florence, 1899.

Cecchi, Giovanni Maria. *Dei proverbi Toscani.* Edited by Luigi Fiacchi. Florence, 1838.

Cecchi, Giovanni Maria. *Drammi spirituali inediti di Giovanmaria Cecchi.* Edited by Raffaello Rocchi. 2 vols. Florence, 1895–1900.

Cecchi, Giovanni Maria. *The Horned Owl.* Translated by Konrad Eisenbichler. Waterloo, Canada, 1981. Translation of *L'assivolo.*

Secondary Works

Di Maria, Salvatore. "Linguaggio teatrale nelle commedie di Giovan Maria Cecchi." *Italian Quarterly* 104 (1986): 5–16.

Radcliff-Umstead, Douglas. *Carnival Comedy and Sacred Play: The Renaissance Dramas of Giovan Maria Cecchi.* Columbia, Mo., 1986.

SALVATORE DI MARIA

CECIL, WILLIAM (1520–1598), first Baron Burghley (1571), principal secretary to Edward VI of England, principal secretary and lord treasurer to Elizabeth I. Cecil was born in Lincolnshire in 1520, the son of Richard Cecil, a yeoman of the robes at the court of Henry VIII. William was educated at the Stamford grammar school and matriculated at St. John's College, Cambridge, in 1535. He studied and taught classical Greek at St. John's until 1540. Cecil was part of the avant-garde group of classicists led by John Cheke, Thomas Smith, Roger Ascham, and Walter Haddon. In 1541 Cecil married Cheke's sister Mary, but she soon died. Cecil remarried four years later: his second wife was Mildred, daughter of the humanist scholar and courtier Sir Anthony Cooke. Mildred, like William, was a talented Greek scholar.

In 1540 Cecil left Cambridge without a degree and (possibly influenced by his father) entered Gray's Inn in London to train as a lawyer in common law. Cecil remained at the inn until 1547, when he entered the service of Edward Seymour, duke of Somerset, the protector of the realm during the early minority of Edward VI. Cecil acted as Seymour's master of requests, dealing with subjects' suits for property and requests for favor. His political career developed rapidly. Cecil became Seymour's private secretary in 1548 and assumed wider responsibilities in London and his home county of Lincolnshire. A court coup against Seymour in 1549—and the seizure of power by John Dudley, earl of Warwick, later duke of Northumberland—was the only setback in an otherwise meteoric rise. Although he spent just over two months in the Tower of London between 1549 and 1550, Cecil was very quickly readmitted into political life. Dudley recognized Cecil's abilities, and he was appointed a principal secretary in 1550 and knighted a year later.

Cecil's political position depended on the stability of Dudley as de facto protector; it is clear from the archives that Cecil was one of Dudley's most trusted and effective political managers. But the success of the regime—and its radically Protestant policies—rested on the fragile health of Edward VI. The death of Edward meant two things: the accession of Mary, his Catholic half sister, and effective political retirement for Cecil. Still, he sat as a member of Parliament in 1555 and traveled on diplomatic missions in 1554 and 1555. The key change came in 1558 with the death of Mary and the accession of Henry VIII's other daughter, Elizabeth. Some of Cecil's friends from the Edwardian years were part of Princess Elizabeth's household, and this may help to explain his prominence in 1558. Cecil engineered a smooth transfer of power and became a privy councillor and Elizabeth's principal secretary. Between 1558 and 1598 Cecil's influence was immense. He was appointed master of the Court of Wards in 1561 and lord treasurer in 1572.

Cecil has often been dismissed as a loyal, moderate, and rather uninspiring bureaucrat. This idea is fundamentally wrong. Cecil was part of a Protestant and humanist group at Cambridge in the late 1530s and early 1540s. He helped important Protestants in the 1540s and 1550s, and protected puritans during the push for conformity in the Church of England in the 1580s. He was at the center of a network of correspondence and conciliar action that had to react to fears of a European Catholic conspiracy against England. This led Cecil to consider some radical policies. In 1559 he argued for English military support for the Protestant Scottish Lords of the Congregation. Cecil was also conscious of the threat posed by Mary Stuart, queen of Scots, a woman with a good claim to the English throne and backed by the Catholic powers of continental Europe. In response, in 1563 Cecil devised a plan for interregnum government by the Privy Council in the event of Elizabeth's death. In 1584 he worked with Sir Francis Walsingham to involve subjects in a "bond of association" to take action in the event of Elizabeth's assassination.

Cecil was a councillor who consciously acted the part of the humanist-classical *vir civilis,* the civil man prepared for political life by a classical education and rhetorical and legal training. This shaped Cecil's political consciousness and led him, at times, to press Elizabeth on important issues he thought were crucial to the preservation and protection of the commonwealth. Even his handwriting—a crafted italic, a humanist script—is a key to his educational background, influenced by John Cheke in his formative years. Cecil was a classical scholar of some renown. He used English diplomats in Europe to purchase books, and his collection was impressive: a library catalog from 1568 lists multiple editions of Greek, Latin, and Italian texts. Genealogy was another favorite subject, reflecting, in part, his aspiration to acquire the ancestry and status of nobility. One manifestation of this desire was architectural. Cecil built three great houses: Cecil House in London, Theobalds in Hertfordshire, and Burghley House in Lincolnshire.

William Cecil. BY COURTESY OF THE MARQUESS OF SALISBURY

Two portraits of Cecil hang in the collection of the marquess of Salisbury at Hatfield House in Hertfordshire. Both are Elizabethan. The first was possibly painted before his appointment as lord treasurer in 1572; the second portrays an elderly Cecil riding his mule. There is another impressive painting of Cecil in old age in the collection of the National Portrait Gallery in London.

BIBLIOGRAPHY

Primary Works

Burghley, William Cecil. *Collection of State Papers . . . Left by William Cecil, Lord Burghley.* Edited by Samuel Haynes. London, 1740.

Murdin, William, ed. *Collection of State Papers Relating to Affairs in the Reign of Queen Elizabeth from the Year 1571 to 1596.* London, 1759.

Secondary Works

Alford, Stephen. *The Early Elizabethan Polity: William Cecil and the British Succession Crisis 1558–1569.* New York, 1998.

Alford, Stephen. "Reassessing William Cecil in the 1560s." In *The Tudor Monarchy.* Edited by John Guy. London, 1997. Pages 233–253.

Read, Conyers. *Lord Burghley and Queen Elizabeth.* London, 1960.

STEPHEN ALFORD

CELLINI, BENVENUTO (1500–1571), Florentine writer, goldsmith, and sculptor.

[This entry includes two subentries, the first on Cellini the writer, the second on Cellini the artist.]

Cellini the Writer

Benvenuto Cellini's development as a writer can be traced to his loss of favor in the late 1550s in the court of Cosimo I de' Medici. No longer steadily employed by the duke, of whom he had made a bronze bust and for whom he had made other sculptures, the artist replaced his chisel with the pen and became his own image maker: "da poi che m'è impedito il fare, così io mi son messo a dire" (since my work has been disallowed, I started writing). Realizing that writing about himself could be judged a sign of pride, Cellini decided to dictate the adventures of his life to a fourteen-year-old apprentice, Michele di Goro Vestri, but eventually completed the work himself between 1558 and 1566. Cellini believed that "all individuals who have performed something worthwhile . . . should write the story of their own life." This was particularly true for an artist who so boastfully described himself in the introductory sonnet of his manuscript: "Molti io passo e chi mi passa arrivo" (I outdo many rivals and can equal the ones who outdid me), a line that the playwright Vittorio Alfieri (1749–1803) judged "worthy of a great poet." Cellini portrayed himself as the most eminent figure of the sixteenth-century art world, God's gift to the arts, and characterized the mass of hostile pseudo-artists who surrounded him as jealous *bestioni* and buffoons. He described honors and favors bestowed on him by kings, such as Francis I, who called him "mon ami" (my friend), and popes, such as Paul III, who considered him so "unique in [his] profession" that he could not be compelled to follow the law; yet Cellini, honestly and shamelessly, admitted to his liaisons, murders, and petty crimes.

Antonio Cocchi (1695–1758), a physician and writer, published Cellini's manuscript under the generic title *Vita* (Life, or autobiography) because of its wealth of information on sixteenth-century fellow artists. Since it appeared in print only in 1728, *Vita* had no direct influence on other Renaissance writers. Yet despite, or perhaps because of, its author's biases and overwhelmingly self-absorbed disposition,

Vita was an immediate success in the eighteenth century.

Cellini's prose has the vitality of the spoken Florentine language and at times the incoherence of a tall tale. His writing reflects so closely the spoken Florentine dialect that a literal translation is practically impossible. Giorgio Vasari's description of Cellini as a man could be applied to his writing style: "courageous, proud, lively, ready, and terrible."

Thomas Nugent's English translation of *Vita* (1771) ran to several editions and was followed by numerous other versions: those of Thomas Roscoe (1822), John Addington Symonds (1888), Anne Macdonell (1907), Robert H. Hobart Cust (1910), and George Bull (1956). Eighteenth-century Italian literati showed great interest in Cellini's spontaneity and ebullient individualism. Johann Wolfgang von Goethe liked his combination of civility and barbarism and saw him as a forerunner of European romanticism. Francesco De Sanctis, with other leading nineteenth-century Italian critics, admired Cellini's *Vita* as a violation of Renaissance rhetorical conventions and a forerunner of preromantic virtues. Cellini portrayed himself as an individualistic hero who was gifted with extraordinary *virtù* (virtue), yet who, after serving the world's most powerful popes and princes, was almost forgotten in the small, provincial court of Florence, where he struggled to please Cosimo I de' Medici, who, he complained, was "more of a businessman than a duke." Late-twentieth-century scholarship considered *Vita* a forerunner of the modern novel. Cellini's narrative unfolds as the self-appraisal of an artist determined to deal with his past successes and failures in order to seek meaning in his life.

Cellini's only published treatises, *Dell'oreficeria* (On goldsmithing) and *Della scultura* (On sculpture), were published in 1568 and dedicated to Cardinal Bernardo de' Medici. Although primarily of technical interest, they mix long and tedious discussions on craft with many autobiographical details written with the same emotional and frantic style of *Vita*. These treatises provided Cellini's contemporaries with glimpses of the writing style that otherwise emerged only posthumously with the publication of *Vita*.

Cellini's poetry is an uneven body of hastily written sonnets and *canzoni* (songs) directed to friends and patrons. Written in a tame, subdued language, it reflects mostly contemporary Petrarchan trends and images. Cellini met with great difficulty in his attempts to conform his style to the strict require-

ments of meter. Now and then, however, a burst of antagonism for fellow artists or a rush of bitterness against unfair criticism of his work gives his poetry the unbridled and arrogant eloquence of *Vita*.

BIBLIOGRAPHY

Primary Works

Cellini, Benvenuto. *The Autobiography of Benvenuto Cellini.* Translated by George Anthony Bull. Harmondsworth, U.K., 1956.

Cellini, Benvenuto. *The Autobiography of Benvenuto Cellini.* Translated by John Addington Symonds, with an introduction and illustrations by John Pope-Hennessy. London, 1949.

Cellini, Benvenuto. *The Life of Benvenuto Cellini, a Florentine Artist . . . Written by Himself and Translated by Thomas Nugent.* London, 1771; Philadelphia, 1812.

Cellini, Benvenuto. *Opere: Vita, Trattati, Rime, Lettere.* Edited by Bruno Maier. Milan, 1968.

Cellini, Benvenuto. *The Treatises of Benvenuto Cellini on Goldsmithing and Sculpture.* Translated by C. R. Ashbee. London, 1888. Reprint, New York, 1967.

Secondary Work

Cervigni, Dino S. *The* Vita *of Benvenuto Cellini: Literary Tradition and Genre.* Ravenna, Italy, 1979.

LUIGI MONGA

Cellini the Artist

Benvenuto Cellini (1500–1571) was a Florentine goldsmith, sculptor, medallist, and writer who is generally considered to be one of Italy's greatest mannerist artists. He led an itinerant life in his early years and worked for various illustrious patrons, including Popes Clement VII and Paul III in Rome, Cosimo I de' Medici in his native Florence, and Francis I in France. Cellini chronicled many of the events from his brilliant career in his highly engaging autobiography, the *Vita di Benvenuto Cellini,* begun in 1558 but not published until the eighteenth century. His own account of his life gives invaluable insights into his volatile personality, his turbulent relations with his patrons, his views on art and fellow artists, and the working processes linked to his craft.

The Early Years: 1500–1527. Cellini was born into a family of prosperous, well-respected craftsmen: his grandfather was a mason and his father, Giovanni Cellini, was a master carpenter who constructed scaffolding for one of Leonardo da Vinci's Florentine artistic projects. In 1513 Cellini began to train in the art of the goldsmith with Michelangelo de' Brandini in Florence and two years later moved to the workshop of Andrea di Sandó Marcone, but in 1516 he was forced to leave the city following a brawl and moved to Siena. Subsequently

Benvenuto Cellini. *Perseus with the Head of Medusa.* In the Loggia dei Lanzi, Florence. ALINARI/ART RESOURCE

he traveled to and worked in Bologna, Pisa, and Rome while periodically visiting his native city. In the early 1520s, he returned to Florence, where he worked or was associated with the artists Francesco Salimbeni and Giovanbattista Sogliani. But in 1523 Cellini was prosecuted for sodomy, and he fled Florence after he had a violent confrontation with fellow goldsmiths. The following year in Rome he worked for several goldsmiths, then opened his own shop at the end of the same year. In this period he worked in precious metals for important members of the church and the nobility; none of the items for these patrons is thought to have survived. This successful and productive phase of his career came to an abrupt end in May 1527 with the Sack of Rome by imperial troops.

After the Sack of Rome: 1527–1540. Cellini left Rome in 1527 and returned to Florence and then, after a short stay, made his way to Mantua, where he worked for the Gonzaga family. In 1529 he was again in Rome, where he entered the service of Pope Clement VII and was employed in the papal mint. Among his works of this moment are two silver gilt medals (1533–1534 and 1534; Florence, Bargello) with the bust of the pope on the obverse, or front. Although small in scale, Cellini's designs are extremely effective as portraits and are characterized by psychological suggestiveness and an attention to minute detail. The reverse of the earlier of the two medals depicts an allegory of Peace; the other shows Moses striking water from the rock. Both testify to Cellini's skill in organizing a complex composition within a restricted area. For the pope he also worked on a splendid jewel-encrusted morse or clasp, which is now lost but was fortunately recorded in 1729 in Francesco Santi Bartoli's watercolors (London, British Museum).

Following the death of Clement VII, Cellini was charged with the murder of a fellow goldsmith, but was pardoned by the newly elected Pope Paul III, who also commissioned him to work on a die for a gold coin depicting Saint Paul. Despite papal intervention, Cellini left Rome in 1535 to avoid arrest, and he traveled first to Florence and then to Venice. Back in Florence later in the same year, he was employed by Alessandro de' Medici to work on coin dies. The artist returned to Rome in 1536, but left the city the following year and headed for Padua, where he worked on a portrait medal of Pietro Bembo (Florence, Bargello). He then went to Paris, where he may have designed a bronze portrait medal of King Francis I (Florence, Bargello). After a brief stay in France he returned to Rome at the close of 1537 via Ferrara. In Rome, however, his earlier misdeeds caught up with him, and in October 1538 he was imprisoned in the Castel Sant' Angelo, from which he managed to escape. By 1540 Cellini had decided to return to France, but before leaving Italy he stopped in Ferrara, where he worked for members of the Este family.

France: 1540–1545. Throughout his second stay in France Cellini carried out a variety of projects for Francis I. Among the earlier commissions (1542) was the decoration for the Porte Dorée at the château of Fontainebleau, which consisted of two bronze Satyrs (never cast), and a bronze lunette of the Nymph of Fontainebleau (Paris, Louvre; cast before March 1543), his first surviving monumental sculpture. The iconography of the relief is partly connected to a now-destroyed fresco by Rosso on the Fontainebleau legend (a hunting dog discovered a spring and its goddess). The style of Cellini's reclining nymph, in the pose of an ancient river-god, resembles that of the mannerist sculptures designed in the 1530s by Primaticcio and Rosso Fiorentino for Fontainebleau. Accordingly, the nymph's anatomy is defined by elongated limbs that create the effect of perfect poise and studied elegance. But her languid sophistication contrasts with the vibrant naturalism of the stag (an emblem of the French king), dogs, and boars, which have all been designed with the goldsmith's eye for detail and finish. The relief, however, was never placed on the Porte Dorée; it was instead set up in the entrance to the château of Anet by Philibert de L'Orme.

While in the service of Francis I, Cellini occupied the post of goldsmith to the king and executed the Salt Cellar (1540–1543; Vienna, Kunsthistorisches Museum), the most celebrated work in gold to have survived from the Renaissance. With Earth and Neptune, the two principal figures of the piece, Cellini successfully communicated a sense of the monumentality of sculpture, although he was working in the more delicate scale of the goldsmith's art. With their abstracted anatomical forms and composed manners, both figures are characterized by a mannerist refinement typical of the Fontainebleau school. Decorating the base are personifications of Morning, Day, Evening, and Night, which reflect Cellini's interest in Michelangelo's sculptures in the new sacristy of San Lorenzo, Florence. Cellini, however, transformed Michelangelo's expressive force into sheer delicacy and grace. Alongside the four times of day are the four winds or seasons and, beneath

the principal figures, allusions to Francis I, such as the salamander and the elephant. Furthermore, colored enameling enriches the already gleaming, finely detailed surfaces of the work and is to be found on the miniature Ionic temple (for the peppercorns) and the boat (for the salt).

Despite the privilege of being granted French citizenship, Cellini was forced to leave Paris in July 1545 after he was accused of embezzling a quantity of silver given to him by the king to make a set of candlesticks.

Florence: ***Perseus*** **and Other Works; 1545–1553.** Cellini returned to Florence in the summer of 1545 and entered the service of duke Cosimo I, received the commission for a bronze statue of Perseus with the head of Medusa (1545–1553; Florence, Loggia dei Lanzi) in August. Positioned close to Donatello's *Judith* (c. 1446–1460; Piazza della Signoria), the *Perseus* was conceived as an emblem of Florentine civic pride, and it may also have been intended to symbolize the strength of Cosimo's leadership. The commission also gave Cellini the opportunity to establish his reputation in monumental sculpture in his home city. He is thought to have used an Etruscan statuette as the basis for the pose of his triumphant figure. But the poise, graceful forms, and eight intended points of view of Cellini's statue are typical of mannerist works of art. Although large, the *Perseus* displays all the intricately wrought surfaces found in the artist's small-scale works in precious metals. The hand of the goldsmith is especially evident in the base, which is encrusted with a wide range of decorative motifs and is adorned with four bronze statuettes of Mercury, Danaë, Jupiter, and Minerva, and a bronze relief of Perseus and Andromeda (all now in Florence, Bargello).

In 1545 Cellini also set to work on a bronze portrait bust of Cosimo I (Florence, Bargello). He intended the design to compete with a marble bust by Bandinelli, Cellini's great rival in Florence. Cellini's engaging and vibrantly characterized portrait evokes a sense of nervous energy that is, in part, also created by the turn of the head, deeply drilled eyes (once silvered or enamelled), and windswept locks of hair. The bust clearly displays the artist's skill in differentiating surface textures, especially in the precious and elegant effects of Cosimo's cuirass, or upperbody armor, which is embellished with carefully chiseled emblems of the duke. In 1557 Cellini's work was sent to Portoferraio on the island of Elba and replaced by a portrait by Bandinelli, who had closely modeled his design on an antique bust and, as a result, presented a less revealing and more conventional public image of Cosimo.

While working on the Cosimo I bust, Cellini executed the bronze bust of the Florentine banker resident in Rome, Bindo Altoviti (c. 1550; Boston, Isabella Stewart Gardner Museum). A successful design in the field of portraiture, the work was apparently praised by Michelangelo. The degree of psychological introspection and careful rendering of detail (see, for example, the furrowed brow, wrinkles around the eyes, and thick eyebrows) suggest that Cellini may have modeled the portrait from life. Like the Cosimo I work, the Altoviti bust displays the sitter caught in a moment of action. In the case of the latter, the head is gently inclined to the left, and the chest and shoulders appear to move beneath the tunic and cloak.

On his return to Florence, Cellini was also involved in restoring works of antiquity in marble and bronze from Cosimo's collections. Some time after 1548 the artist designed a marble *Ganymede* (Florence, Bargello) which incorporated an antique torso given to the duke by Stefano Colonna (Cellini carved the remaining sections). Inspired by the pose of Jacopo Sansovino's *Bacchus* (1511–1518; Florence, Bargello), the *Ganymede* exhibits subtly carved surfaces that define delicate areas of flesh and the gentle feathers of the eagle. Aiming to establish a reputation as a marble sculptor, and in direct competition with Bandinelli, Cellini designed two other statues on mythological subjects: the *Apollo and Hyacinth* and the *Narcissus* (c. 1548–1557; both Florence, Bargello). He carved the former work from an imperfect block of marble presented by Bandinelli, and, despite its unfinished state and weathered surfaces (it was placed in the Boboli Gardens in the eighteenth century with the *Narcissus* and only rediscovered in 1940), it displays a careful arrangement of lithe, gracefully moving forms. With the languorous *Narcissus,* Cellini manifests his concerns with elegant outline, the poised body, and more than one intended viewpoint.

The Final Phase: 1553–1571. With the completion of the *Perseus* in 1553, Cellini reached the high point of his career. In the subsequent years his relations with the Medici administration became strained, and he experienced personal problems that eventually led to his imprisonment. During this difficult period Cellini carved a life-size *Crucifix* (Madrid, Escorial; dated 1562) from a single block of white marble, and this is considered to be the masterpiece of his last years. Originally intended for his own tomb, the *Crucifix* was presented to Cosimo I, but in 1576 Francesco I de' Medici gave it to Philip II of Spain, who installed it in the Escorial. Characterized by a masterful handling of the marble, the *Crucifix* displays the crisply delineated facial features and anatomical forms of a deeply moving Christ.

In 1565 Cellini started writing his treatises on sculpture and the art of the goldsmith, which were printed in 1568. He died on 3 February 1571 and was interred in the Chapel of the Accademia del Disegno in the Florentine church of the SS. Annunziata.

See also **Mannerism**.

BIBLIOGRAPHY

Primary Work
Barbaglia, S. *L'opera completa del Cellini.* Milan, 1981.

Secondary Works
Arnaldi, I. *La vita violenta di Benvenuto Cellini.* Rome, 1986.
Avery, Charles. "Benvenuto Cellini's Bust of Bindo Altoviti." *Connoisseur* 198 (1978): 62–72.
Baldini, Gianni. "Un ricordo del Cellini a Reggio Emilia." *Mitteilungen des Kunsthistorischen Institutes in Florenz* 32 (1988): 554–556.
Heil, Walter. "A Rediscovered Marble Portrait of Cosimo I de' Medici by Cellini." *Burlington Magazine* 109 (1967): 4–12.
Pope-Hennessy, John. "A Bronze Satyr by Cellini." *Burlington Magazine* 134 (1982): 406–412.
Pope-Hennessy, John. *Cellini.* London, 1985.

FLAVIO BOGGI

CELTIS, CONRAD (1459–1508), German Neo-Latin poet, editor, founder of humanist sodalities. Celtis was born as Konrad Pickel or Bickel (the Latin equivalent is Celtis) in the small village of Wipfeld near Würzburg, the son of a vintner. He studied the liberal arts in Cologne, receiving a bachelor of arts degree in 1479. After a short stay in Buda, where he had contacts with the scholars at the court of King Matthias Corvinus, Celtis enrolled at the University of Heidelberg in 1484, drawn there by the presence of Rudolf Agricola (1443–1485), the eminent Frisian humanist. There he acquired the fundamentals of Greek and some Hebrew. After completing his studies with a master of arts degree in 1485, Celtis taught poetry for the following two years at the universities of Erfurt, Rostock, and Leipzig. At Leipzig he published his first work, *Ars versificandi et carminum* (The art of making verses and of poems; 1486).

The year 1487 marks the beginning of his "*decennalis peregrinatio*" (ten years of wandering), as he called this decade of extensive travel and uncertain employment. His journey first took him to Italy, the cradle of humanism, where he visited Venice, Padua,

Ferrara, Bologna, Florence, and Rome and had contacts with such well-known humanists as Marsilio Ficino and Pomponio Leto. In the spring of 1489 he moved to Cracow to devote himself to the study of the natural sciences, astronomy, and mathematics. Upon his return to Germany, Celtis obtained a temporary appointment—upgraded in 1494 to a regular faculty position—in poetry at the University of Ingolstadt, an occasion he celebrated with his inaugural lecture *Oratio in gymnasio Ingolstadensi habita* (Speech given at the University of Ingolstadt; 1492). In it he programmatically outlined the themes that inform his later work: the cultural rivalry between Italy and Germany; the praise of Germany's cultural past (which he later would find gloriously confirmed by the discovery of the Latin dramas of the tenth-century canoness Hrosvitha von Gandersheim); the necessity and usefulness of humanist studies; and the centrality of *philosophia* as the integrating universal discipline. The outbreak of the plague, which closed the university, provided him with the opportunity for a lengthy stay in Heidelberg, where he served as a tutor for the sons of the Elector Philip of the Palatinate. From 1497 to his death in 1508, Celtis was professor of poetry at the University of Vienna. There, at Celtis's urgings, the Collegium Poetarum et Mathematicorum (College of poets and mathematicians) was established in 1501 by the emperor Maximilian. Complementing the curricular offerings of the university, its mission was to train an elite for leading positions in the state.

Celtis's most important work, and the only major one that was published during his life, is his *Quattuor libri amorum* (Four books of love poetry; 1502), known as the *amores*. Much more than a collection of amorous poems, the *amores* are also a description of Germany from a geographical point of view. These two aspects, the erotic and geographical, are combined in such a way that each of the poet's four love affairs takes place in one of the four major regions of Germany. But Celtis's fascination with numbers goes further. Each of the four books is associated with nine—the number of the Muses—different phenomena, which in turn occur in fours: the seasons, the ages of man, the times of the day, the cardinal points, the temperaments, the signs of the zodiac, the four basic colors, the winds, and the elements. Praised by critics as the most original contribution of German humanism to literary Renaissance culture, the *amores,* for all their schematic organization, struck a new, refreshing chord with their vivid descriptions of the poet's amorous, albeit largely fictional, adventures.

Conrad Celtis. Woodcut by Hans Burgkmair the Elder (1473–c. 1531). © THE BRITISH MUSEUM, LONDON

Five years after his death, his former students edited and published *Libri odarum quattuor cum epodo et saeculari Carmine* (Four books of odes with the epode and the hymn for the saeculum; 1513). Patterned after the collection of the Roman poet Horace (whose German successor Celtis aspired to be) the odes follow the same principle of organization as the *amores:* each of the four books is devoted to one of Germany's major regions. Although the odes also include poems about love, these recede into the background in favor of verses on humanist friends. Celtis's early death prevented him from publishing a collection of his epigrams. Written in the tradition of the Roman poets Persius, Juvenal, and Martial, these clever and often cutting poems cover a variety of topics. Satirical poems on foes and detractors alternate with flattering verses on fellow humanists and nobles; lines addressed to Saints Catherine and Anna are found next to those dedicated to lovers.

Although Celtis was also unable to realize his ambitious project of the *Germania illustrata,* which was intended to combine geographical, historical, and ethnographical perspectives, his book on Nürnberg, the *Norinberga* (1502), can be considered a preliminary work to that undertaking. Written in lively Latin prose, it is a splendid portrait of the topography, architecture, customs, religious and cultural life, economic situation, and civic government of early-sixteenth-century Nürnberg.

Celtis's importance for German humanism lies not only in his literary works but also in his role as initiator of a number of humanist societies. Inspired by the academies of Marsilio Ficino and Pomponio Leto, which he had visited in Florence and Rome, Celtis founded, or proposed the formation of, such *sodalitates* (sodalities). In these circles members, regardless of their social background or professional affiliations, found a sense of belonging to a larger intellectual movement. Sodalities embarked on cooperative scholarly projects, such as editions of Latin works, and gave mutual assistance by explaining difficult philological projects and obtaining manuscripts. The best documented sodalities are those in Heidelberg, the so-called *sodalitas litteraria Rhenana* (founded 1495) and the *sodalitas Danubiana* centered in Vienna (1497). Inspired by Celtis, other groups formed in Augsburg, Ingolstadt, and Olmütz.

Celtis is considered the best Neo-Latin poet of the pre-Reformation era in Germany. Through his various activities, he devoted his entire life to the cause of Renaissance humanism in Germany, leading the nineteenth-century critic David Friedrich Strauss to call him "the German arch-humanist."

BIBLIOGRAPHY

Primary Works
An Anthology of Neo-Latin Poetry. Edited and translated by Fred J. Nichols. New Haven, Conn., 1979. Pages 436–461.
Celtis, Conrad. *Selections.* Edited and translated by Leonard Forster. Cambridge, U.K., 1948.
Der Briefwechsel des Konrad Celtis. Edited by Hans Rupprich. Munich, 1934.

Secondary Works
Price, David. "Conrad Celtis." In *Dictionary of Literary Biography.* Vol. 179, *German Writers of the Renaissance and Reformation, 1280–1580.* Edited by James Hardin and Max Reinhart. Detroit, Mich.; Washington, D.C.; and London; 1997. Pages 23–33. A concise article in English on Celtis.
Spitz, Lewis W. *Conrad Celtis: The German Arch-Humanist.* Cambridge, Mass., 1957. The only full-length biography of Celtis in English.
Wuttke, Dieter. "Conradus Celtis Protucius." In *Deutsche Dichter der frühen Neuzeit (1450–1600).* Edited by Stephan Füssel. Berlin, 1993. Pages 173–199. Excellent article written by Germany's foremost Celtis scholar.

ECKHARD BERNSTEIN

CENSORSHIP.
[This entry includes two subentries, the first on censorship on the European continent, the second on censorship in England.]

Censorship on the Continent

Neither state nor church in the Renaissance—or at any other time in history—believed in complete freedom of expression. Both tried to suppress ideas considered dangerous and to promote those judged to be beneficial. But the extent and nature of censorship depended on whether leaders and society believed that different ideas seriously threatened the religious doctrines, moral values, and political structure held dear. Shaped by the humanistic confidence in the individual and openness to new ideas, continental Europe in the Renaissance had little censorship until the Protestant Reformation divided Europe religiously and politically. Then rulers and churches imposed religious, moral, and philosophical censorship. Political censorship, on the other hand, existed throughout the Renaissance.

The Question of Pagan Literature. The major censorship question of the fifteenth century was whether adults and schoolchildren should read the Latin and Greek classics of pagan antiquity, some of which praised multiple gods and portrayed vice attractively. The humanists believed that everyone should read the pagan classics because they inspired virtuous behavior. Surface impieties were to be interpreted allegorically; readers would profit from the underlying truths. Thus, they concluded that no censorship was necessary, although they allowed that a few immoral passages might be excluded from a child's reading.

Humanists and other readers took a similar approach toward immoral vernacular literature read for pleasure. Beginning with the racy stories of Giovanni Boccaccio's *Decameron* (written c. 1350), an enormous quantity of vernacular literature described men and women exuberantly fornicating and committing multiple adulteries, all passed off with witticisms. Monks and nuns cheerfully ignored their vows of chastity in these works. Some authors, such as Pietro Aretino (1492–1556), wrote pornography with clever banter. No attempts were made to censor any of this until the second half of the sixteenth century.

At the same time, an unannounced, but understood, political censorship existed. Subjects did not openly criticize their rulers with voice or pen because governments often viewed criticism as sedition and reacted accordingly. So critics went to the next political jurisdiction to speak or write, or they published anonymously.

Philosophical Freedom and Censorship.

Little philosophical censorship occurred before 1500. An isolated example was the ban by King Louis XI on teaching philosophical nominalism at the University of Paris from 1474 to 1481. And the papacy condemned a handful of the nine hundred theses of Giovanni Pico della Mirandola (1463–1494) as heretical or likely to give scandal to the faithful.

An important issue of philosophical freedom arose at the end of the fifteenth century: Could philosophers teach that the human soul was mortal? If they did, they could be accused of denying life after death, a fundamental tenet of Christianity. Around 1500 some philosophers in Italian universities taught that, according to reason alone, the human soul could not be shown to be immortal. Following Aristotle as interpreted by the Arab philosopher Averroes (Ibn Rushd; 1126–1198), they argued that the intellective soul died when the body died. The Catholic Church affirmed at the Fifth Lateran Council in 1513 that the human soul was immortal and established guidelines for teaching on the subject.

The council did not demand, however, that philosophers must prove philosophically that the soul was immortal. It only asserted that reason supported by Christian revelation in the New Testament could know that the soul was immortal. Philosophy acting alone might reach a different, erroneous conclusion. Hence, the practical effect of the council's decree was to separate theology and philosophy, or to bring them into an uneasy collaboration. Philosophers might speculate as they saw fit, so long as they asserted that the truth of philosophy could not contradict the truth of faith. Some Italian philosophers held the position that faith and philosophy might reach different conclusions, each valid in its own sphere, and had no difficulties with ecclesiastical or civil authorities.

The celebrated incident of Galileo Galilei's punishment by the Holy Office in Rome in 1633 was a case of alleged disobedience and a form of philosophical censorship. The Holy Office concluded that Galileo had been ordered not to teach as physical truth that the earth revolved around the sun; it punished him for disobeying the order. But Galileo contended that he had not been so ordered, and that he had treated heliocentrism as a hypothesis, not as physical truth, even though his claim seems a little disingenuous.

Religious Censorship.

The Protestant Reformation produced a significant change in censorship. Since Protestants promulgated their views through the printing press, and Catholics replied in the same medium, it was inevitable that both sides would try to control the press. But it took several decades before effective press censorship became a reality.

Civil and ecclesiastical authorities initially tried to halt the spread of what they considered to be heretical ideas by means of limited, isolated actions. On the Catholic side, the emperor Charles V, the French and Spanish monarchies, and Italian states sought to halt the publication and diffusion of Protestant books. Protestant Europe did the same to Catholic works. For example, in 1523 the city council of Zurich, under the influence of the Protestant Huldrych Zwingli (1484–1531), established a committee of laymen and ministers to examine all manuscripts before they might be printed. These tentative, unsystematic attempts to censor the press had limited effect. Moreover, the leaders of church and state did not yet endorse extensive censorship, because they hoped for reconciliation between Catholics and Protestants. By the middle of the century, however, civil and ecclesiastical authorities on both sides moved toward coordinated press censorship.

Effective press censorship was a complicated three-step process. First, someone had to determine which books, authors, and ideas were dangerous; a commission of experts had to prepare a list of previously published banned books. Second, governments established committees of readers, perhaps a clergyman and a civic official, to read all manuscripts before issuing permissions to print. This prepublication censorship sought to ensure that nothing heretical, seditious, or offensive to good morals was printed. Censorship committees had the power to demand textual changes. Third, heretical books printed elsewhere had to be barred entry. This was done by inspecting goods entering the city or state, usually at the custom house. All books coming in were checked against a list or catalog of banned authors and books, a control directed primarily at booksellers who imported large quantities of books. It was not always possible to stop travelers from smuggling a few banned books. Church and state officials could make surprise visits to local bookstores looking for prohibited books.

The papacy fulfilled the first requirement by promulgating the Tridentine Index of Prohibited Books (1564). The basic document of Catholic press censorship, it listed authors and titles that could not be printed, read, or held. Major Protestant religious figures headed this list. Second, it listed some titles that contained errors but whose "chief matter" was good. Such books might be owned and read after the offending passages were eliminated. Many extant sixteenth-century books with passages inked out by hand document this form of expurgation. In time, new printings quietly omitted or altered offending passages. Boccaccio's *Decameron* and other racy vernacular titles were expurgated in this way.

Finally, the Tridentine Index promulgated rules with which to judge new books coming from foreign presses and to guide those doing prepublication censorship. The rules mostly banned heretical ideas and those contrary to Christian morality. For example, the Tridentine Index banned the books of Niccolò Machiavelli because he argued that princes were permitted to lie to their subjects and murder opponents in order to hold on to political power. The rules of the Tridentine Index also banned works of magic and the occult arts that argued that fate or fortune could overcome free will. To enforce the Tridentine Index and its rules, the papacy depended on the support of civil governments.

Protestant censorship followed the same path, except that no universal religious authority existed to guide and coordinate censorship, and Protestants did not publish lists of forbidden books. Each Protestant state had to formulate its own censorship policies. Moreover, since Protestant religious leaders invested the state with substantial authority over the church, the state assumed the leading role in censorship. Protestant states banned the publication, importation, and ownership of Catholic works, and sometimes the works of other Protestants. They also condemned works considered immoral. For example, Calvinist Geneva banned chivalric romances and the works of François Rabelais (1494?–1553) on these grounds. Geneva probably had a more effective press censorship than any other continental Protestant state. In general, Catholic and Protestant states exercised quite effective prepublication censorship. But the controls over the movement of books were less successful, as book smuggling was widespread.

Both Catholic and Protestant churches and states regulated what was preached in the pulpit and taught in universities. One could not preach or publish what religious and civil authorities judged to be heretical. Publishing scholars sometimes had to accept unwelcome changes that prepublication censors demanded. They obviously exercised some degree of self-censorship in areas deemed sensitive. Investigation into the history of the early Christian church was such an area, because both Catholics and Protestants claimed to be the true heirs of primitive Christianity.

Many Catholic areas insisted that professors make a profession of the Catholic faith, as ordered by Pope Pius IV in 1564. Protestant churches and states also insisted on adherence to confessional statements, but the divisions within Protestantism made the situation more complicated. Censorship in the German Lutheran states illustrates the point.

After Martin Luther's death in 1546, German Lutheran theologians divided initially into the "true Lutherans" led by Matthias Flacius Illyricus (1520–1575), and Philippists, a moderate party that followed the lead of Philipp Melanchthon (1497–1560) on some doctrinal points. The spread of Calvinism into Germany further complicated matters. Each Lutheran party sought to convince the rulers of Lutheran states to support its side in doctrinal disputes. When they made a decision, princes enforced confessional obedience on their subjects and sometimes dismissed those with different views. The most extreme result occurred in 1574, when Elector August (reigned 1553–1586), the ruler of Albertine Saxony, jailed four Philippist Lutheran theologians, two of whom died in prison. Moreover, a few professors, mostly theologians, lost their positions at the University of Wittenberg, as it shifted Lutheran allegiances, and at the University of Heidelberg, as it oscillated between Lutheranism and Calvinism in the 1570s and 1580s.

Political censorship also became more obvious and severe in the late sixteenth century, which saw a flood of vitriolic political pamphlets criticizing rulers and endorsing rebellion, especially in France. Civil authorities sought to punish those who wrote them. Professors at the University of Paris had to stop teaching theories of tyrannicide when King Henry IV, whom they opposed, entered Paris in 1594. One luckless librarian was caught with pamphlets favoring tyrannicide and hanged.

Religious, philosophical, and political censorship was stronger in 1600 than it had been in 1500, and the penalties more severe. Nevertheless, censorship did not prevent the spread of heterodox ideas.

See also Immortality; Index of Prohibited Books.

BIBLIOGRAPHY

Primary Work

Index des livres interdits. Edited by J. M. de Bujanda et al. 10 vols. Sherbrooke, Canada, and Geneva, 1984–1996. The basic source for texts and history of the sixteenth-century Catholic Indexes of Prohibited Books.

Secondary Works

Brockliss, L. W. B. *French Higher Education in the Seventeenth and Eighteenth Centuries: A Cultural History.* Oxford, 1987. See pages 298–299 for the prohibition against teaching tyrannicide.

Eisenhardt, Ulrich. *Die kaiserliche Aufsicht über Buchdruck, Buchhandel, und Presse im Heiligen Römischen Reich Deutscher Nation (1496–1806).* Karlsruhe, Germany, 1970. Censorship in the Holy Roman Empire.

Grendler, Paul F. "Intellectual Freedom in Italian Universities: The Controversy over the Immortality of the Soul." In *Le contrôle des idées à la Renaissance.* Edited by J. M. de Bujanda et al. Geneva, 1996. Pages 31–48. Study of the circumstances and results for Italian philosophers of the decree of the Fifth Lateran Council.

Grendler, Paul F. *The Roman Inquisition and the Venetian Press, 1540–1605.* Princeton, N.J., 1977. Book censorship in the major Italian publishing center.

Grendler, Paul F. *Schooling in Renaissance Italy: Literacy and Learning, 1300–1600.* Baltimore and London, 1989. See pages 236–238 for humanist defenses of reading pagan poetry.

Maag, Karin. *Seminary or University? The Genevan Academy and Reformed Higher Education, 1560–1620.* Aldershot, U.K., 1995. See pages 156, 160–161, and 168 for the imposition of Lutheran and Calvinist religious oaths on professors at Heidelberg University.

Peterson, Luther D. "Philippists." In *Oxford Encyclopedia of the Reformation.* Edited by Hans Hillerbrand et al. Vol. 3. New York, 1996. Pages 255–262. A succinct account of the Philippist controversy.

Santschi, Catherine. *La censure à Genève au XVIIe siècle.* Geneva, 1978. The best study of Genevan censorship.

PAUL F. GRENDLER

Censorship in England

Censorship emerged in Renaissance England in conjunction with the establishment of a national church with its concomitant religious and political dissension. The principal measures taken to control the press during the reigns of the Tudor monarchs Henry VIII, Edward VI, Mary, and Elizabeth related directly or indirectly to the crown's interest in ensuring a particular religious settlement. The Stuart monarchs James I and Charles I, while still concerned about their religious agendas, also employed censorship to protect the prestige of the monarchy. Both printed and dramatic works were suppressed by parliamentary statute and by various forms of royal authority, including proclamation, Privy Council action, and the prerogative Court of High Commission. In addi-

tion, varied measures repeatedly required that plays, pamphlets, and books be approved (allowed) prior to receiving a license for performance or publication. Influenced by the documents that sought to establish censorship, historians and literary critics have found in these multiple mechanisms a repressive system of theatrical and press censorship. In practice, however, the multiple entities that were created formed a loose web of authority that, although it might be tightened by official will, rarely achieved a censorship as thorough or ruthless as the language that the documents of control imply.

Statutory Censorship. The most enduring acts of censorship came from statutes passed by Parliament. After Henry VIII's break with Rome and a temporary warming toward Protestant theology, Henry's strongly conservative religious advisers in 1540 and again in 1542 pressed for statutory censorship that abolished any books contrary to the Henrician articles of faith that articulated traditional Catholic doctrine (without papal authority). The act strictly controlled religious publication by prohibiting the printing or possession of all kinds of writings by Continental Protestants and requiring that books printed in England receive government approval (authorization) prior to receiving a license for publication. The act did, however, permit printing and possession of law books, chronicles, biographies, the works of the poets Geoffrey Chaucer and John Gower, and plays, songs, and interludes that did not meddle with interpretation of scripture. When Edward VI came to the throne in 1547, his more reform-minded government repealed Henrician religious statutes, including those that called for censorship, and the next five years saw an explosion of all kinds of printing.

Mary's accession was marked by the repeal of Edward's Protestant religious reforms, and the strong opposition to this and to her marriage to Philip II of Spain turned her government's interest to the treason laws. Since the pre-Tudor laws made no mention of printed treason, Parliament passed a statute that extended the definition of treason—acting to overthrow the monarch—to include writing and described as seditious in any form of language "any false Matter Clause or Sentence of Slander Reproche and Dishonor of the King and Queenes Majesties."

When Elizabeth came to the throne, although Parliament repealed Mary's religious program and in 1559 passed the acts of Uniformity and Supremacy, which established a national Protestant church and placed it under the monarch's authority, it retained the Marian statute on seditious rumor. Between 1558 and 1603, while Parliament passed no statutes with the express purpose of controlling the English press or theater, it did pass eleven statutes addressing treason and sedition that included in their definitions some form of the words or phrase "by Writing Preaching Speache expresse Wordes or Sayinges." The statutory ground for censorship was clear: speaking, writing, or printing anything denying the monarch's political or ecclesiastical authority, advocating the right of anyone else to that authority (including writing on the succession), advocating rebellion, and "compassing" bodily harm to or slandering the monarch came within the definition of treason. Furthermore, in establishing Elizabeth's religious settlement, Parliament gave the monarch the authority to visit and reform the "ecclesiastical state" as well as the means to execute this—an ecclesiastical commission. To this body, the Court of High Commission, Elizabeth assigned the responsibility for assuring that the printed word did not challenge the religious settlement. At the accession of James I, Parliament repealed neither Elizabeth's religious settlement nor her treason laws but in 1606 imposed censorship on the theater by passing an act to "Restrain Abuses of Playes," which restricted jests and profanity in plays.

Royal Proclamations. Statutory censorship, effective as it was because it could impose sanctions within the judicial system, was too slow to respond to offenses not already defined. In the Renaissance world of shifting religion and politics, where print and playing were highly innovative and responsive to their immediate culture, statutes could rarely foresee the kinds of transgressions that might arise. The royal proclamation proved a more useful measure for ad hoc response. Every English Renaissance monarch used the royal proclamation to specify books or classes of books that ought to be suppressed or to institute government licensing conditioned upon official approval. In 1538, Henry VIII required the pre-print approval by ecclesiastical officials of all religious printing to control debate on transubstantiation (the doctrine that bread and wine are transformed into the body and blood of Christ at mass). In 1551, after five years of unrestricted printing, Edward VI, anxious over perceived moral excesses, ordered prelicensing approval by the king or six of his privy councillors of plays and all printed texts—not just religious works. In 1555 Mary's proclamation authorized bishops and local civil officials

"to inquire and search out" Protestant writings and "for this purpose to enter into the house or houses, closets, and secret places of every person whatsoever degree." In 1556 she issued letters patent by proclamation to establish a special commission to "inquire concerning all heresies, heretical and seditious books" and "to seize all such books and writings in printers' houses or shops or elsewhere."

Queen Elizabeth's 1559 Injunctions, issued by proclamation to direct her religious settlement, contained one item (Item 51) that required licensing for print of "any manner of boke or paper, of what sort, nature, or in what language soever it be" by the allowance of the queen (in writing), by six privy councillors, by the chancellors of the universities, or by the High Commission. It also called for the High Commission to decide whether or not works previously printed, both in London and abroad, were acceptable. The queen's anxiety about the religious settlement extended from print to the theater, and in April 1559 Elizabeth issued a proclamation restraining playing that continued until November. She also issued a proclamation in 1559 that prohibited plays that were unlicensed by local justices or the chief officers of the towns. The proclamation clearly specified the grounds upon which licenses could be granted: "that they permytt none to be played wherein either matters of religion or of the governaunce of the estate of the common weale shalbe handled or treated."

Proclamations also attempted to suppress books already printed. Elizabeth, for example, issued eleven censorship proclamations that called for the suppression of religio-political writings (both Catholic and Protestant) that opposed her ecclesiastical or political authority. Some of these were for classes of books (papist writings from the Continent, writings by the religious sects the Family of Love and the Brownists); others were for specific texts (the Martin Marprelate pamphlets of the late 1580s, the anonymous *Leicester's Commonwealth* of 1584, Robert Parson's *A Conference on the Next Succession* of 1594, and John Stubbs's *A Gaping Gulf* of 1579). James I prohibited John Cowell's *The Interpreter* (1607) by proclamation and employed this device twice (in 1623 and 1624) in attempts to quell opposition to his pro-Spanish policy by reiterating press licensing requirements. Charles I's 1629 proclamation suppressed Richard Montagu's *Apello Caesarem* (1625) and called for an end to publications that participated in the debate between Arminians and Calvinists. Generally, however, Stuart monarchs relied less than their forebears on proclamations and more on the administrative authority of their Privy Councils. James's Privy Council, for example, interrogated authors or restrained playing when such plays as Samuel Daniel's *Philotas* (1605); Ben Jonson's *Sejanus* (performed 1603; published 1605); George Chapman, John Marston, and Ben Jonson's *Eastward Hoe* (1605); and Thomas Middleton's *A Game at Chess* (1604); or books such as Walter Ralegh's *History of the World* (1614) and George Wither's *Motto* (1621) offended the king or proved embarrassing to his government.

While royal proclamations could readily respond to immediate situations, they were relatively ineffective as censorship tools. Proclamations had to institute their own measures of enforcement, and by common law they could not create felonies or in their penalties touch life or limb. Books censored in this manner were not eliminated from circulation unless the proclamation provided a means to recall them (and few did). *Leicester's Commonwealth* and *A Conference on the Next Succession* circulated widely despite proclamations against them, and *The Interpreter* was even reprinted after it was prohibited. Since censorship proclamations were printed and widely disseminated, they were effective more as tools of propaganda than of repression.

The High Commission.   From its inception in 1559, the ecclesiastical Court of High Commission was clearly the means by which Elizabeth's regime expected to control opposition to the religious settlement—including printed opposition. From all available evidence, although the High Commission did on several occasions exert its authority over printing, it never enforced invasive and inclusive licensing of all printed matter. It was most effective when an offending writer or printer was a cleric who could be summoned before the commission for opposing the ecclesiastical state.

Over the years, the jurisdiction over printing given to the High Commission devolved to its principal clerics, the archbishop of Canterbury and the bishop of London. By a decree of the Court of Star Chamber in 1586, this informal governance of printing was formalized; the archbishop and bishop were designated as responsible for pre-print authorization, and the former received authority to approve requests for establishing new printing presses. By extension of this authority, in 1599 Archbishop John Whitgift and Bishop Richard Bancroft issued a unique order banning satires and requiring that histories be licensed by a member of the Privy Council. In the early seventeenth century the common law lawyers, led by

Edward Coke, repeatedly challenged the High Commission's authority: this resulted in James I issuing new letters patent for the High Commission in 1611, which upheld its authority to imprison and gave it wide authority to search out and seize books that opposed the political and religious establishment. Subsequent to this both James I and Charles I called upon the High Commission on several occasions to suppress oppositional writing by questioning and imprisoning writers and printers.

The London Company of Stationers.   Although the ultimate responsibility for approving books for the press rested with the High Commission, the administration of press licensing fell to the masters and wardens of the London Company of Stationers. The Stationers' Company, created by royal charter in 1557, exercised a monopoly on printing that it shared with small university presses at Oxford and Cambridge. The charter gave the company privileges and practices common among the older guilds: the right to property ownership, self-regulation, keeping apprentices, and engaging in searches to protect the trade from nonmembers and poor workmanship. The Stationers enjoyed one benefit beyond other companies: while the custom of the city of London allowed members of one company to engage in the trade of another, the Stationers' Company charter reserved to its members the exclusive practice of the trade of printing.

The Stationers' Company's principal business was protecting its members' copyrights, which was accomplished first by requiring company licenses, and then by bringing those who printed against license before the company's Court of Assistants. In exchange for the economic benefits derived from its monopoly, it was understood that the Stationers' Company would not countenance seditious printing by its members. The Stationers were enjoined repeatedly to require official approval, which they often did, especially for religious, political, and foreign texts.

This, however, did not mean that the Stationers were the government's agents in licensing. The company's license was distinct from official approbation, and despite repeated official demands that all books be allowed (especially in times of political or religious crisis), rarely did more than half the books printed receive official authorization. Nor, as has often been thought, did the Stationers search out and confiscate illegal or seditious books and presses for the government. (Both the Privy Council and the High Commission employed their own agents.)

The Stationers' Company did, however, have the authority to confiscate books and presses of non-member printers or of members who printed another's copyrighted work. Since illegal (non-Stationers) presses often printed transgressive books, this meant that the Stationers might be employed to destroy offending presses, as they were in the case of the Marprelate tracts. While not all illegal presses sought to obfuscate prepress censorship (many sought only to be free of the economic constraints imposed by the company's membership and copyright regulations), their existence and the kind of texts they printed (political libels and radical religious treatises) suggest that company licensing placed boundaries on the printed word.

The Master of the Revels. Just as the administration of press licensing in London devolved from the High Commission to the Stationers' Company, the administration of theatrical censorship became the responsibility of the master of the revels, an appointee of the lord chamberlain (a member of the royal household). While there had been restraints on interludes and plays from the time of Henry VIII, theatrical censorship became significant only after the emergence of the public theater during the reign of Elizabeth. Influenced by Protestant religious reform, civic authorities viewed plays as a threat to peace and moral order. In 1572 they helped to secure an act that deemed common players "vagabonds" unless they belonged to the household of a "Baron of the Realm . . . or other honorable Personage of greater Degree," which led the acting companies to seek out patronage among the aristocracy. Acting companies under such patronage could receive licenses to perform on the condition that prior to performance they be "sene and allowed" by the royal master of the revels. The players thus became adjuncts to the court even though no permanent master with licensing authority was appointed until 1579, when Edmund Tilney was confirmed.

In 1581 a royal patent officially created the Revels Office and conferred the office of master on Tilney. This patent gave him authority to license acting companies, to censor and license plays, and to charge fees for doing so. While the office's interests were primarily directed to court performance, Tilney and his successors gradually translated their powers into authority over the commercial theater.

No evidence has been found for fixed standards of censorship, but it appears that the master's review generally prevented the presence of blasphemous language and the representation of living monarchs on the stage. Even though Elizabeth's 1559 proclamation would seem to have prevented theatrical representation of politics and religious issues (and indeed probably did preclude representation of such sensitive issues as the religious settlement and Elizabeth's legitimacy and succession), the masters appear to have allowed the expression of those political differences that were part of the court's usual spectrum of opinion.

When James I came to the throne, the increased authority of the Revels Office came more from the restrictions imposed on the playing companies than from changes in the office itself. In 1597, in response to a performance of *The Isle of Dogs,* the mayor and aldermen of London petitioned the Privy Council to suppress all playing, and although the council ordered the theaters closed, nothing happened. City officials subsequently issued a series of restrictions on companies and playing because they threatened moral order. As a consequence of this, theatrical companies were restructured and their number reduced. When James came to the throne only two companies remained, and what had been the Lord Chamberlain's Men became the King's Men. Such constraints effectively kept the theater within the realm of power and privilege, and as an agent of this power, the master of the revels continued to assure that the theater conformed to the tastes and interests of the court. Whatever freedom of speech James I and Charles I extended to their advisers, their masters of the revels extended in a suitably codified version to the theater.

This did not mean, however, that the master of the revels always prevented anything offensive. In 1624, for example, Henry Herbert, who proactively protected the right of the master of the revels to license plays and players, granted a license to Thomas Middleton's *Game at Chess,* a veiled satire on court politics that encoded the English as white chess pieces and the Spanish as black. The allegorical veil that was adequate enough in the manuscript for Herbert to license the play was dropped in performance, provoking the Spanish ambassador vehemently to protest. The Privy Council suspended the play's performance. The case of *A Game at Chess* illustrates how fine a line the master of revels drew between a liberty of playing topical enough to engage the sensibilities of the Renaissance court and careful enough to prevent offenses to those same sensibilities and interests.

See also **Drama, English; Printing and Publishing.**

BIBLIOGRAPHY

Clegg, Cyndia Susan. *Press Censorship in Elizabethan England.* Cambridge, 1997.

Dutton, Richard. *Mastering the Revels.* London, 1991.

Hunt, Arnold, Giles Mandelbrote, and Alison Shell, eds. *The Book Trade and Its Customers, 1450–1900.* Winchester, U.K., 1997.

Loades, David H. *Politics, Censorship, and the English Reformation.* London and New York, 1991.

Myers, Robin, and Michael Harris, eds. *Censorship and the Control of Print in England and France, 1600–1910.* Winchester, U.K., 1992.

Sharpe, Kevin. *The Personal Rule of Charles I.* New Haven, Conn., and London, 1992.

CYNDIA SUSAN CLEGG

CENSUS. A census is a statistical survey that constitutes the primary source of information about the total number of a population as well as its principal structural characteristics, including the gender, age, civil status, level of instruction, and profession of those surveyed.

In several western European countries (and especially Italy) sporadic census-related documentation exists from as early as the second half of the thirteenth century but becomes more frequent in the fourteenth and fifteenth centuries. Most of this documentation relates to taxes or food taxes and can yield estimates of the total population of urban centers and sometimes of the surrounding rural areas. It is rarer to find sources that permit an estimate of the demographic characteristics of entire states or of large territorial areas before the beginning of the sixteenth century. (See table 1 for estimated populations of European states during the Renaissance.)

The documentation available today for demographic investigations of past ages exists in the form of individual data (i.e., of individuals identified by their name) but more frequently in the form of aggregate statistics which can sometimes be derived

TABLE 1. Population of European Countries (in millions)

	c. 1400	c. 1500	c. 1600
Balkans	4	4.5	6
British Isles	3.5	5	7
France	11	16	18
Germany	6.5	9	12
Italy	7	11	13
Low Countries	1	2	3
Poland	3	4	5
Russia	9	12	15
Spain and Portugal	7	9	11
Scandinavian Countries	1	2	2
Switzerland	0.8	0.8	1

Sources: Cipolla, *Before the Industrial Revolution,* p. 4; McEvedy and Jones, *Atlas of World Population History.*

from the lists of individuals for which basic documentation has been lost. Simple enumerations of the population counted the total number of families or of the inhabitants of each community, parish, or other administrative entity. The people surveyed were sometimes distinguished by their gender or their age, if the original purpose of the survey was for military conscription. These cases indicate that we should reserve the term "census" for surveys of an individual or nominative character. Even these enumerations of population (for the late medieval and Renaissance period), however, are often simply lists of heads of families or of hearths, which only sometimes include other information, such as the total number of people living in the household or, more rarely, all the names of members of the household.

Especially in the case of surveys taken for fiscal or food purposes, it is necessary to evaluate sources critically to determine whether the surveys were extended over the entire population. Often people categorized as exempt from tax payments were not included. Children under the ages of two or three were usually excluded from early censuses taken to determine the number of grain consumers because they were too young to be considered consumers. Very young children were occasionally excluded from documentation until the sixteenth and seventeenth centuries.

It is possible to apply a household "multiplier" (the average household size) in order to estimate the total population in the frequent cases in which surviving documentation only exists in the form of simple lists of heads of households or of enumerations of fiscal hearths without additional information on members of these groups. This operation is risky, especially when no other information is available to permit evaluation of the margin of error of the estimate.

From at least the fourteenth century, taking a census of the population was practiced especially in the cities of central and western Europe. Within Europe, Italy is the country (with significant differentiations among Italian states) for which demographic sources are the most numerous and, due to their degrees of thoroughness and reliability, the most interesting.

A source of exceptional relevance is the Florentine *catasto* (land register) of 1427. A survey with a fiscal aim, it describes the personal property and real estate of each taxpayer as well as that of the entire population under the jurisdiction of the Florentine republic. The land register examines 60,000 families and over 260,000 individuals and is entirely preserved in the State Archives of Florence and Pisa. It took place in a time of demographic and economic crises that concerned Florence, all of Italy, and most of Europe after the great catastrophes provoked by the plague, from the middle of the fourteenth century. An attempt was made to remedy the republic's financial crisis through fiscal reform—by executing a land register—which would establish more equitable and efficient criteria for levying taxes. The complete implementation of the land register took about three years (1427–1430), but the declarations of the taxpayers were taken in a fairly short period (from June to July of 1427). David Herlihy and Christiane Klapisch-Zuber, who thoroughly analyzed the land register, maintain that it is a fairly complete survey of the population of the Florentine state, but note several absences. Very young children living within the family or placed in the care of wet nurses in other homes, single widows, vagabonds and poor people, patients in welfare institutions, and those belonging to religious orders or to the secular clergy are all categories that are probably undercounted. For the city of Florence, it is certain that the 37,246 inhabitants listed in the 1427 register represent an underestimated population.

In the principal countries of western Europe (France, Spain, and England), as a consequence of early political-administrative unity, some surveys exist that are fairly old (dating from 1328 in France and 1377 in England). However, these cases represent exceptions; they were compiled randomly and for declaredly fiscal reasons (as lists of hearths, lists of taxable adults, and so on). France and England completely lack continuity in the documentation available for demographic investigations. In Spain, on the other hand, due to early consolidation of territory, a series of statistical surveys date from the fifteenth century in the territories of Castile and Aragon. In the second half of the sixteenth century, a series of statistical initiatives were enacted by Philip II, the true founder of Spanish statistics. His important general statistical survey of 1574 is held in eight volumes in the Escorial Library.

Until the middle of the sixteenth century, the most detailed and interesting documentation concerns cities. The Republic of Venice is an excellent example. In 1338 the first direct, nominative, and universal survey of the population of the city of Venice was taken. In 1440 a statistically modern project was designed (but never fully carried out) that anticipated classifying people according to age, sex, profession, social condition, and nationality. In the course of the sixteenth century, Venetian censuses presented organized information according to well-defined schemes, which facilitate comparison between different surveys. In 1607 parishes (which were in charge of compiling surveys) received, for the first time, printed forms on which to report required statistical information. And in 1624 the principle of compiling surveys on a quinquennial basis was established, although it was not respected until the second half of the eighteenth century.

See also **Demography.**

BIBLIOGRAPHY

Beloch, Julius. *Bevölkerungsgeschichte Italiens.* 3 vols. Berlin, 1937–1961.

Cipolla, Carlo M. *Before the Industrial Revolution: European Society and Economy, 1000–1700.* New York, 1976.

Contento, Aldo. *Il censimento della popolazione sotto la Repubblica Veneta.* Venice, 1900.

Dupaquier, Jaques, and Michel Dupaquier. *Histoire de la démographie.* Paris, 1985.

Herlihy, David, and Christiane Klapisch-Zuber. *Tuscans and Their Families: A Study of the Florentine Catasto of 1427.* New Haven, Conn., and London, 1985.

McEvedy, Colin, and Richard Jones. *Atlas of World Population History.* New York, 1978.

Mols, Roger. *Introduction à la démographie historique des villes d'Europe du XIVe au XVIIIe siècle.* 3 vols. Louvain, Belgium, 1954–1956.

LORENZO DEL PANTA

Translated from Italian by Elizabeth Bernhardt

CERAMICS. Inspired by imported Eastern and Near Eastern ceramics, Renaissance potters elevated their craft from the mere production of utilitarian ware to the level of a high art. The principal ceramic types of the period were earthenware with either a lead or tin glazing, made throughout Europe, and stoneware, localized to Germany and parts of France.

Ceramic Making. Dug from pits, the basic clays could be transported from one region to another but were usually refined and prepared locally. After shaping the clay—by hand, on a wheel, or in a mold—potters hardened it by firing in a kiln. To make vessels impervious to liquids or to enhance visual appeal, craftsmen applied a glassy coating, called a glaze, and fired this at a low temperature. Lead glazes, mixed with various colors, created smooth, glossy surfaces. Tin glazes produced a dense white that masked the color of the clay and served as an ideal background for painted decoration; this ware is known as maiolica in Italy or faience in France. Some potting centers, notably Deruta and Gubbio in Italy, finished with the applica-

Ceramic Piece. Wine cistern made by Francesco Durantino. Tin-glazed earthenware (maiolica); 1553. ART INSTITUTE OF CHICAGO, MARY WAILER LANGHORNE FUND, 1966/PHOTOGRAPH BY ROBERT HASHIMOTO

tion of a thin metallic coating, known as a luster. The most informative Renaissance ceramic treatise concerns maiolica: Cipriano Piccolpasso of Casteldurante's *Li tre libri dell'arte del vasaio* (The three books of the potter's art), a manuscript dating about 1556–1559, is the source of much of our knowledge of Renaissance ceramic technique. A final ceramic type, stoneware, is composed of clays requiring a higher firing temperature than earthenware. These clays were well suited to incised or relief decoration and were often glazed with salt, since their firing temperatures were too high for lead glazes.

Distinctive regional styles developed. Although every corner of Europe made pottery of some kind, the most renowned and influential work during the fifteenth and sixteenth centuries centered in Spain, Italy, France, and Germany.

Spain. The Moorish kingdom in Grenada introduced to Europe the tin-glazed technique and decorative forms of ceramics originating in the Near East. By the fourteenth and fifteenth centuries potters in Malaga were blending the geometric or floral interlace patterns of Islamic art with European motifs. Red-gold lusters distinguished these wares, which were often painted in blues and browns. Drug jars, wing-handled vases, and tiles are characteristic forms of Spanish pottery. By 1540 pottery from Manises (a suburb of Valencia) became popular in Italy; numerous plates featuring European coats of arms surrounded by blue and gold vines or other foliate decoration indicate how extensively these wares were commissioned from abroad. Hispano-Moresque ware, as it is sometimes called, in its turn inspired potters in other countries, above all, Italy. Most of these wares were imported to Italy from Valencia via Majorca, the likely derivation of the name "maiolica" that was given to tin-glazed earthenware produced in Italy.

Italy. From the late medieval into the early Renaissance period, various ceramic traditions coexisted in Italy. A type prevalent in the north, particularly along the Po River, was an incised slipware, sometimes called "sgraffito," in which the design was scratched through a liquid clay covering to reveal a darker clay beneath. Despite a limited palette and simple decoration, this ware continued to enjoy popularity through the sixteenth century. One of the earliest centers to be influenced by Near Eastern tin-glazed ware was at Orvieto in the thirteenth to fifteenth centuries. Sculptural and thickly potted forms painted in green and brown hues in a rustic manner issued from Orvieto kilns. Among the most elegant early Renaissance ceramics are the so-called "oak leaf jars," produced in Florence in the fifteenth century. An abstract leaf pattern, painted in a thickly applied cobalt blue against white tin glaze, unifies other motifs around the generally ovoid shapes.

As the imported Hispano-Moresque wares spread, Italian potting became finer, the decoration more varied, and the colors more brilliant. Islamic-derived geometric or Gothic foliation evolved into more complex patterns. Some towns developed particular patterns, such as the overlapping scales that characterize Deruta ware, often surrounding bold female or male busts on large plates called *piatti di pompa* (display plates). Rediscovered ancient wall paintings inspired some of the most distinctive maiolica decorations, the grotesques, featuring fantastic creatures whimsically combined with swirling linear shapes. The most sophisticated of these grotesques, produced in Urbino in the mid-sixteenth century, follow designs by Raphael and his atelier painted at the Vatican Logge and elsewhere in Rome.

One of the distinctions of maiolica was, in fact, its capacity to incorporate designs by the great painters of the era. Through the intermediary of engraving, Nicola Pellipario (active c. 1520–1537/38) often adapted the paintings of Raphael to the bright colors and circular shapes of maiolica plates. In the same years, the 1530s and 1540s in Urbino, another master, Francesco Xanto Avelli (active 1529–1542; for an example of his work, see the color plates in this volume), created series of subjects—most famously drawn from Ovid—often based on compositions by Raphael and his school. Maiolica that focuses on biblical or mythological scenes is called *istoriato*.

An important ceramic tradition that existed alongside maiolica but belongs more properly in the realm of sculpture is the molded, glazed terra-cotta of the della Robbia workshops. Luca della Robbia (1399–1482), his family, and followers produced large-scale altarpieces, architectural decoration, and smaller devotional works well into the sixteenth century. By contrast, a courtly production of limited scope is the "Medici porcelain." In Florence between 1575 and 1587, under the patronage of Francesco de' Medici, potters experimented with blue painting under the glaze on high-fired paste in an attempt to imitate Chinese porcelain. By the last quarter of the sixteenth century maiolica had become increasingly repetitive and lost the prestige it had once enjoyed.

France. While maiolica influenced French ceramics, local traditions of lead-glazed earthenware and stoneware continued and startling new types developed. Following Italian example, the Rouen master Masséot Abaquesne created sophisticated faience, notably tile floors for châteaus in and around the Ile-de-France. Provincial centers, such as in Saintonge, produced green glazed earthenware with decoration in relief toward the end of the fifteenth and beginning of the sixteenth centuries. The pilgrim's flask—a flattened jug with loops for attaching to saddle or bag—is a characteristic form. These works were so refined that they sometimes bear the coats of arms of noble families. At Beauvais the hard nonporous pottery known as stoneware was produced in a blue glaze.

The most famous French potter, Bernard Palissy (1510–1590), invented an astonishing new type of pottery. Drawing on his extensive knowledge of the natural world, Palissy arranged clay forms molded from actual flora and fauna on vessels and plates. From experiments with colors in his early stained-glass training, he developed brilliant hues to enhance his clay works. Palissy called his plates *rustiques figulines,* or rustic figures, on which snakes, lizards, shells, ferns, and other motifs appeared to represent a naturalistic slice of riverbank life but were arranged, in fact, in highly sophisticated decorative patterns on oval platters. Anne de Montmorency and Catherine de Médicis, the most discerning patrons in France, supported his work, commissioning grottoes that were to be entirely covered with glazed ceramics of natural forms, sadly never completed. Palissy's followers continued to produce similar work though in a more decorative vein into the seventeenth century; a center at Avon, near Fontainebleau, issued figurines of genre subjects in Palissy's manner.

A fascinating if still mysterious ceramic is known as Saint-Porchaire. In a complex fabrication, a white pipe clay is stamped with patterns that are then inlaid with dark clay to form geometric and knot patterns;

these are combined with molded decorations to form ewers, *biberons* (nursing jugs), salts, and other vessels. This extremely rare and refined ware has been associated with the town of Saint-Porchaire in the Poitou (Deux-Sèvres), possibly under the patronage of the Montmorency-Laval family based in that region. Some scholars suspect, however, that the sophisticated range of sources of this ware could only have been possible in a Parisian base, rather than in the provinces, and archaeological findings in the late twentieth century appear to support this position.

Germany. Germany created its own distinct ceramic tradition. The need for tiled stoves drove a considerable industry to produce lead-glazed earthenware with high three-dimensional decoration. The Preunring family in Nürnberg produced more refined ware with figures in relief on tankards and jugs glazed in a variety of colors, usually against a dark blue ground. Germany's significant contribution to ceramic making was in the area of stoneware. The rich deposits of clay in the Westerwald made the Rhineland the center of stoneware production. Since finely detailed incised or stamped work suits the dense clay, such decoration typifies German stoneware, often painted in somber tones of brown or blue. Lead-glazed earthenware and stoneware dominated German ceramics through the seventeenth century until the discovery of porcelain at Meissen in 1708/10.

BIBLIOGRAPHY

Amico, Leonard N. *Bernard Palissy: In Search of Earthly Paradise.* Paris and New York, 1996. The best overall study of the man in context of his times.

Barbour, Daphne, and Shelley Sturman, eds. *Saint Porchaire Ceramics.* Washington, D.C., 1996. Papers from symposium proposing new ideas and presenting new technical information.

Charleston, Robert J., and John Ayers, eds. *World Ceramics: An Illustrated History.* London and New York, 1968. Chapters on Renaissance ceramics by various authors constitute an excellent survey.

Frothingham, Alice Wilson. *Lustreware of Spain.* New York, 1951.

Hetjens-Museum/Deutsche Keramikmuseum. *Deutsches Steinzug der Renaissance- und Barokzeit.* Dusseldorf, 1979. Exhibition catalog by Ekhart Klinge. Exhibition organized by manufacturing center.

Wilson, Timothy. *Ceramic Art of the Italian Renaissance.* Austin, Tex., 1987. Catalog of an important exhibition reflecting new research in this area.

IAN WARDROPPER

CERETA, LAURA (Cereto, Cereti; 1469–1499), Brescian writer and humanist scholar. Laura Cereta

Laura Cereta.

was the first of six children born to Silvestro Cereta, an attorney and magistrate in Brescia, and Veronica di Leno, whose family claimed the trappings of a noble lineage. She was educated at home and at the nearby convent in Chiari. At age fifteen, Laura left home to marry. Eighteen months later, her young husband died of the plague.

Widowed and childless, Cereta spent her days and nights alone writing essays in letter form addressed to prominent churchmen, scholars, and citizens. She met frequently with humanist scholars in Chiari and Brescia to whom she presented her epistolary essays. Although she failed in attempts to befriend the leading woman humanist in Italy, Cassandra Fedele, Cereta sustained friendships with a number of learned women, among them the nuns Nazaria Olympica, Veneranda (the abbess at Chiari), and Santa Pelegrina. The fierce invectives she sent several male humanists in Brescia testify to her willingness to enter into combat with scholars who attacked her work. Unlike Fedele, Cereta refused to play a merely ornamental role in the all-male literary circles.

When Cereta died she left behind a single unpublished volume containing a dialogue and eighty-two Latin letters, many of them explicitly autobiographical. The self-portrait Cereta fashions for herself is unparalleled in quattrocento (fifteenth century) humanist letters. She paints herself alternately as a compliant daughter of demanding parents, a war protester, a frustrated bride, a woman humanist in search of fame in a man's world, and, finally, a widow contemplating a life of religious seclusion. Among letters to her family are essays on political and philosophical themes: the German and Venetian incursions into Brescia, a narrative of her ascent of Mount Isola imitating Petrarch's famous letter about climbing Mount Ventoux, an essay warning against the teachings of the Epicureans. In Cereta's only work in dialogue form, *Asinarium Funus Oratio* (A discourse on the death of an ass), she herself plays the leading interlocutor in an intriguing murder mystery indebted to Apuleius's *Metamorphoses*.

Cereta's most important legacy to the writers who followed her lies in her articulation of concerns that impacted women as a class. Her letters laid the groundwork for the feminist polemics of such later Renaissance writers as Modesta da Pozzo, Lucrezia Marinella, and Arcangela Tarabotti. Her work also anticipated themes associated with the Enlightenment feminism of Germaine de Staël and Mary Wollstonecraft, themes including Cereta's enshrinement of the emotions in a genre (the humanist letterbook) in which rationality was regarded as the guide for all action, her quarrel with traditional views of sex and gender roles, her depiction of women's history as an imaginary community of women, her construction of housework as a barrier to women's intellectual aspirations, her portrayal of marriage as slavery, and her use of the culture of the "salon" (in Cereta's time the convent or urban residence) as a means for women writers to enter the civic arena without injury to their reputations.

So widespread was her fame as a writer at the time of her death that all Brescia was said to have mourned her passing. A redacted version of her book of Latin letters finally was published in Padua in 1640 as *Laurae Ceretae Brixiensis Feminae Clarissimae Epistolae* (The letters of the illustrious Laura Cereta).

See also Fedele, Cassandra.

BIBLIOGRAPHY

Primary Works

Cereta, Laura. *Collected Letters of a Renaissance Feminist*. Edited and translated by Diana Robin. Chicago, 1997. Includes interpretative introductions and commentaries to each letter.
Cereta, Laura. *Divae Laurae in Asinarium Funus Oratio* and selected letters. In *Laura Cereta: Quattrocento Humanist*. Edited by Albert Rabil Jr. Binghamton, N.Y., 1981. Contains the Latin texts of eleven letters not included in the 1640 edition, pp. 118–163.

Secondary Works

King, Margaret L., and Albert Rabil Jr., eds. *Her Immaculate Hand: Selected Works by and about the Women Humanists of Quattrocento Italy*. Binghamton, N.Y., 1983. Includes selected letters by Cereta in translation, pp. 77–86.
Rabil, Albert, Jr. *Laura Cereta. Quattrocento Humanist*. Binghamton, N.Y., 1981.
Rabil, Albert, Jr. "Laura Cereta (1469–1499)." In *Italian Women Writers: A Bio-Bibliographical Sourcebook*. Edited by Rinaldina Russell. Westport, Conn., 1994. Pages 57–75.
Robin, Diana. "Woman, Space, and Renaissance Discourse." In *Sex and Gender in Medieval and Renaissance Texts: The Latin Tradition*. Edited by Barbara K. Gold, Paul Allen Miller, and Charles Platter. Albany, N.Y., 1997. Pages 165–187.

DIANA ROBIN

CERVANTES SAAVEDRA, MIGUEL DE (1547–1616), Spanish novelist, playwright, poet. Cervantes was born in the university town of Alcalá de Henares, the second son of Rodrigo de Cervantes and his wife, Leonor de Cortinas. He had three sisters and three brothers, one of whom died before Miguel was born.

Biography. Although Miguel's paternal grandfather had been a prominent and successful lawyer, his father always had trouble making ends meet with his surgeon's skills of barbering and bloodletting. The liaisons of Miguel's sisters Andrea and Magdalena were crucial in keeping the family afloat. Because the family traveled all over Spain in search of a decent living, Miguel had no access to formal university training, but he did receive an amazing exposure to Spanish geography and society.

Travels beyond Spain. Probably as the result of a nocturnal scuffle with a certain Antonio de Sigura that produced a warrant for Cervantes's arrest and the removal of his right hand, he fled to Italy in 1569. Italy was the capital of culture, and the Italian experience was crucial for Cervantes's development as an artist. He was a member of the household staff of Cardinal Giulio Acquaviva in Rome until he enlisted in the Spanish army in the summer of 1570. He served with distinction in the naval battle of Lepanto (7 October 1571), losing the use of his left hand.

En route from Italy to Spain in 1575, Miguel and his brother Rodrigo were captured by Muslim pirates and sold into captivity in Algiers. The ransom of captives seized at sea was big business in the sixteenth century, practiced both by Muslims in North Africa and by Christians in Italy and Malta. Because Cervantes was carrying letters of commendation from high-ranking officials, he appeared to be an important personage and his ransom was consequently set at a figure hopelessly out of the reach of his lower middle-class family. Rodrigo was ransomed in 1577, but Miguel did not return to Spain until 1580.

His first work of narrative prose dates from just before his departure from Algiers. It is a document he prepared that recounts his heroic conduct and steadfast Christian devotion during his captivity, which thirteen of his friends and acquaintances then confirmed with their own testimony. In this document, known as the *Información de Argel,* Cervantes chronicles the four unsuccessful escape attempts he organized, his refusal to implicate any of his fellow captives, and his near-miraculous escape from the severe punishments normally meted out for these offenses by the notoriously cruel Hassan Pasha. Most of what we know about Cervantes's experience of captivity is derived from this document.

Early literary career. When Cervantes returned to Spain he hoped to parlay his heroism at Lepanto, together with the record of his extraordinary service to God and country collected in the *Información de Argel,* into a government position that would provide a secure and dignified living. In this he was unsuccessful. He did land a job requisitioning provisions for the 1588 armada against England, and another job collecting taxes. His duties took him frequently from Castile to Andalucia and brought him into contact with the most varied elements of Spanish society, but he lived from hand to mouth and was twice imprisoned for irregularities in his accounts.

During this time Cervantes began to write for the theater. Two patriotic plays date from this period: *El cerco de Numancia* (The siege of Numantia) and another one derived from his Algerian experience and entitled *El trato de Argel* (The business of Algiers). In 1585 he published his first work of avowed narrative fiction, a pastoral romance entitled *La Galatea.*

Around 1587 he began to use the name Saavedra in place of his mother's Cortinas. The name is probably adapted from an old ballad about a heroic Christian named Sayavedra captured by Muslims who chooses death before conversion. There is a similarly heroic Christian captive named Sayavedra in *El trato de Argel,* and another in *Don Quixote.* In 1584 Cervantes had married Catalina Salazar Palacios, a native of Esquivias, a little town on the edge of La Mancha. Almost immediately he absented himself to take up his duties as requisitioner and tax collector. This fact, together with the absence of any children resulting

Miguel de Cervantes. LIBRARY OF CONGRESS

from the union, has led to widespread speculation that the couple was incompatible or that Cervantes preferred the company of men. In 1590 he applied for any of several vacant government positions in America. His petition was refused with the famous annotation "let him look for something here."

Valladolid and Madrid. When Philip III moved the court from Madrid to Valladolid in 1601 Cervantes established a household there with his wife, his sister Andrea and her illegitimate daughter Constanza, his other sister Magdalena, and his illegitimate daughter Isabel. The whole ménage was briefly jailed following the murder of a certain Gaspar de Ezpeleta in the street outside their house. During the proceedings allegations were made concerning the virtue of all the Cervantes women and their many gentleman callers.

In 1605 Cervantes published *Don Quixote,* part 1. It was his first real literary success and established him, at age fifty-eight, as an important writer. In 1606 the king moved the capital back to Madrid and the Cervantes family followed. Cervantes spent the remaining years of his life living and writing in Madrid.

Most of his literary production dates from this period: a collection of twelve short narratives called *Novelas ejemplares* (Exemplary tales; 1613); a long poem that combines literary criticism and autobiography entitled *Viaje del Parnaso* (Journey to Parnassus; 1614); *Ocho comedias y ocho entremeses nunca representados* (Eight plays and eight interludes never performed; 1615); *Don Quixote,* part 2 (1615). Following his death, his widow published his last work, a neo-Byzantine romance entitled *Los trabajos de Persiles y Sigismunda* (The travails of Persiles and Sigismunda; 1617).

Cervantes's Writings. By any standards, but especially considered within the ideological straitjacket imposed by his society, Cervantes's works are audacious and innovative. He refers again and again to his own originality, but he generally limits himself to matters of strictly literary theory and practice. He was the first, he says in the *Viaje del Parnaso,* to give voice to internal psychic conflicts through allegorical personages in the theater; he was the first to write original short narrative in Spain; he showed "how the Castilian language can depict moral deviance (*desatino*) with propriety." He invented Don Quixote. He calls himself "the one who exceeds most in his capacity for invention," and he adds that "those who lack that capacity must perforce be lacking in fame as well."

Theater. Cervantes began to write plays at a time when there was as yet no established national form of theater. Along with such now-minor dramatists as Cristóbal de Virués (1550–1609) and Juan de la Cueva (c. 1550–c. 1610), he attempted to create such a theater, of a generally neoclassical inspiration and form, with a division into four acts, a clear distinction between comedy and tragedy, and with appropriately lofty diction and serious national themes. The tragedy of the destruction of the Celtiberian city of Numantia in 133 B.C.E., seen retrospectively as a part of the Spanish national experience (*El cerco de Numancia*), and the first Algerian play (*El trato de Argel*) follow this pattern. Although *Numancia* has become a classic and has been performed at various tense moments of Spanish history such as the Napoleonic invasion (1808) and the Spanish Civil War (1936–1939), Cervantes's attempt to create a national theater was unsuccessful. This was due to the sudden and definitive triumph of the theatrical formula introduced by Lope de Vega (1562–1635) and known simply as the *comedia:* a division into three acts, no distinction between comedy and tragedy, a predominance of rapid octosyllabic verse forms, and

an exuberant celebration of the official national values that eclipsed Cervantes's more nuanced vision.

Cervantes did not abandon the theater altogether, however. In 1615 he published a collection of eight full-length plays in the three-act *comedia* format, accompanied by eight farcical interludes. Jean Canavaggio has demonstrated that even though Cervantes adopted the format, his plays question both the theatrical and the ideological underpinnings of the national theater. These plays were never performed in his lifetime.

Narrative prose. Cervantes's appeal is always to the solitary and potentially thoughtful reader, alone at home with his book, in contradistinction to the spectator at the theater, whose reactions to the play are subject to the scrutiny of his peers. His greatest achievements are clearly his narrative prose fictions: *La Galatea, Don Quixote,* parts 1 and 2, the *Novelas ejemplares,* and the posthumous *Los trabajos de Persiles y Sigismunda.* Posterity has tended to downplay *La Galatea* and *Persiles y Sigismunda* generally because nineteenth-century positivism frowned on the artificiality of pastoral and Byzantine romance. More recent readings have concentrated on other aspects. It will be instructive to consider these "peripheral" works, the beginning and the end respectively of Cervantes's narrative production, before addressing *Don Quixote* and the *Novelas ejemplares.*

La Galatea *and* Persiles y Sigismunda. In 1559 Jorge de Montemayor (c. 1520–1561) had published a work entitled *Los siete libros de la Diana* (The seven books of Diana), in which he discovered how to combine the intensely personal lyricism of pastoral with the dynamism of narrative. A new narrative genre was born. In *La Galatea,* Cervantes confronts the generic norms and expectations of the recently invented and wildly popular pastoral romance. He also considers the relation of pastoral to epic as it was understood in Renaissance literary theory, and he offers an anatomy and prognosis for the future of Spanish poetry in particular.

At just about the same time that Montemayor was inventing pastoral romance, the Renaissance rediscovery of Byzantine Greek romance and the reeditions of Heliodorus and Achilles Tatius began to yield new narratives in Spanish. In 1552 a Spanish Marrano in exile in Italy named Alonso Núñez de Reinoso published *Los amores de Clareo y Florisea y los trabajos de la sin ventura Isea* (The loves of Clareo and Florisea, with the travails of the unfortunate Isea), a work largely inspired by Lodovico

EL INGENIOSO
HIDALGO DON QVI-
XOTE DE LA MANCHA,

Compuesto por Miguel de Ceruantes
Saauedra.

DIRIGIDO AL DVQVE DE BEIAR,
Marques de Gibraleon, Conde de Benalcaçar, y Baña-
res, Vizconde de la Puebla de Alcozer, Señor de
las villas de Capilla, Curiel, y
Burguillos.

Año, 1605.

CON PRIVILEGIO,
EN MADRID Por Iuan de la Cuesta.

Vendese en casa de Francisco de Robles, librero del Rey nro señor.

Don Quixote. Title page of the 1605 edition. BIBLIOTECA NACIONAL, MADRID/INSTITUT AMATLLER D'ART HISPÀNIC, BARCELONA

Dolce's adaptation of Achilles Tatius. By the end of the sixteenth century, Byzantine romance had been given the stamp of approval by both humanistic scholars and literary theorists. Alonso López Pinciano's *Filosofía antigua poética* (1596), the most influential neo-Aristotelian commentary in Spanish, elevated Byzantine romance to the status of epic and opened the way for a new genre of narrative prose conceived as epic and partaking of the prestige of epic. In 1604 Lope de Vega published a modern, Spanish version of Byzantine romance entitled *El peregrino en su patria* (The pilgrim in his own country). In *Don Quixote,* part 1, two characters discuss the possibilities offered by this new narrative form.

Cervantes's *Los trabajos de Persiles y Sigismunda* gathers up this revival and relegitimation of Byzantine romance, adds his own conception of pastoral as the apprenticeship for epic already expressed in

La Galatea, and responds to the stimulus of Lope's recent *Peregrino.* The work is conceived as a grandiose semiallegorical pilgrimage from the outer edges to the center of civilization and of the True Religion, from Virgil's *Ultima Thule* to Counter-Reformation Rome. This is Cervantes's attempt to incorporate Heliodorus into Virgil, to bring Virgil up to date, and to outdo him at his own game. Cervantes considered *Persiles y Sigismunda* his most ambitious work, a book "that dares to compete with Heliodorus, if its boldness doesn't earn it a whack on the head," as he wrote in the prologue. In addition to its obvious engagement with literary history and theory, *Persiles y Sigismunda* also suggests critical reflection on the structures and institutions of Spanish society and on the universality of Roman Catholicism.

The Novelas ejemplares *and* Don Quixote. In the central narrative works of his canon Cervantes repeatedly engages the ruling orthodoxies, both literary and cultural. The *Novelas ejemplares* systematically challenge the poetics of every existing narrative genre. In particular, "El coloquio de los perros" (The dialogue of the dogs) and the story "Rinconete y Cortadillo" deconstruct the picaresque and its most influential representative, Mateo Alemán's *Guzmán de Alfarache* (1599 and 1604). Alemán's powerful but simplistic insistence on a single narrative and existential point of view is undone by Cervantes's presentation of a plurality of viewpoints that relativize reality and make questionable our relation to it. "El amante liberal" (The generous lover) and "La española inglesa" (The English Spanish woman) demonstrate how international commerce and banking undercut and overcome the religious and political differences between Spaniards and both English Protestants and Ottoman Muslims.

The two novels of *Don Quixote,* constructed as a road narrative, tell the tale of a nameless minor aristocrat who suddenly turns psychotic in about his fiftieth year. Attempting to model his life on late-medieval romances of chivalry he has read, he wills himself into a new existence as an old-fashioned knight-errant. He and his squire, Sancho Panza, who is his opposite in every way, sally forth to battle evil and defend women, interpreting modern society in terms of fanciful and anachronistic readings. In part 2, Don Quixote suffers a series of defeats and is forced to come to terms with the way the world is. He returns to his village and dies an exemplary Christian death.

In the work, Cervantes again engages every existing narrative form as well as the most prestigious and advanced literary theory and the consecrated values of his society. He deconstructs the very foundation of Aristotelian literary theory, the distinction between history and fiction insisted upon by Ludovico Castelvetro, Sebastiano Minturno, Francesco Robortello, and other Renaissance commentators, by taking into account the phenomenon of textualization, which was discovered by theorists only toward the end of the twentieth century. Cervantes reveals himself as the poet of intertextuality, the first writer to have understood that literature is made out of and engages in dialogue with other literature: late medieval chivalric romance, chivalric material in the Spanish ballad tradition and in the Renaissance epics of Boiardo and Ariosto, pastoral romance, neo-Byzantine romance, the Spanish novel of Moors and Christians, and the picaresque. These questions of literary theory and practice are not merely adumbrated in the text; they are fully thematized and incorporated into the lives of the characters. The religious orthodoxy defined at Trent falls victim to stinging jabs such as ridicule of religious processions (part 1, chapters 19 and 52), a toilet-paper rosary (part 1, chapter 25), mortification of the flesh (part 2, chapter 8), and to the sustained parody of purgatory that is the disenchantment of Dulcinea by Sancho's self-inflicted lashing.

The meaning of this book has been the subject of endless speculation and affirmation. Until the end of the eighteenth century, readers tended to identify with society and reason, and to view Don Quixote as a more or less amusing or dangerous deviant who needs to be brought under control. This reading celebrates his return to sanity and Christian death as the triumph of right thinking and social conformity. The Romantics inverted the paradigm and made Don Quixote the locus of positive values, a misunderstood genius engaged in a hopeless struggle with an uncomprehending society that finally wears him down. Most current interpretations are based on this reading. The Spanish philosopher and poet Miguel de Unamuno (1864–1936), for whom Don Quixote becomes the Spanish national Christ, is its most extreme proponent. Anthony Close has argued to the contrary, that all post-Romantic readings betray Cervantes's intention and (therefore) the work's true meaning.

Most readers agree that *Don Quixote* presents a dialectic of the ideal and the real, the universal and the particular. Many agree that it anticipates our post-Romantic conception of existence as a dialectic of individual and environment in the course of which an identity is forged. However, because of the per-

vasive recourse to irony, *Don Quixote*'s most enduring feature is perhaps its simultaneous susceptibility to diametrically opposed interpretations.

Evaluations of Cervantes. Traditional biographies present Cervantes as a minor aristocrat (*hidalgo*), a heroic soldier, and exemplary Christian captive, that is, as a paradigm of the official national virtues. A significant body of more recent work tends to focus on his position on the margins of Spanish society. In all likelihood he was a converso, or descendant of Jews, and as such excluded (de facto and de jure) from full participation in society. He was also the product of a semidysfunctional family dominated by assertive women who challenged the patriarchal social order by trading more or less discreetly on their feminine charms.

His heroism in captivity has been called into question, and hypotheses of a homosexual relation with Hassan Pasha have been advanced to explain the Algerian ruler's strange refusal to impale or behead him for the repeated escape attempts. This trend is in part a manifestation of a general tendency to deconstruct consecrated hagiographic narratives, and in part the result of attempts to explain or account for certain concrete features of Cervantes's writings. His works are populated, for example, by a galaxy of passive male characters dominated by assertive females. He holds Muslim social organization and institutions in high regard. He repeatedly calls the official values of Spanish society into question: He makes fun of the official mania of "purity of blood" (*limpieza de sangre*) as the prime requisite for access to the power structure; he ridicules the Roman Catholic orthodoxy established at the Council of Trent (1545–1563) and written into the Spanish civil code by Philip II; he pits vigorous bourgeois entrepreneurs against parasitic aristocrats.

In his own age and social context, Cervantes belongs to a minority of Spaniards who lined up with the ideals and values of the European Renaissance. Américo Castro demonstrated in 1925 that he keeps company with the subjective introspection of Montaigne, the sly mockery of Erasmus, the exuberance of Rabelais, and with Ariosto's simultaneous celebration and deconstruction of medieval chivalry and heroic literature. In Cervantes, the values that would come to define modern western civilization confront tradition. Reason challenges revelation, bourgeois capitalism challenges feudo-agrarianism, and audacity challenges authority. In contrast to the rest of Europe, however, the new mentality did not prevail in Spain. Cervantes and those like him were not at liberty to challenge the established order directly. Recourse to irony became the indispensable strategy for intellectual and artistic survival.

See also Spanish Literature and Language; Vega Carpio, Lope Félix de.

BIBLIOGRAPHY

Primary Works

Cervantes, Miguel de. *Don Quixote.* Edited by Diana de Armas Wilson. New York, 1998.

Cervantes, Miguel de. *Exemplary Stories.* Edited by C. A. Jones. London, 1972. Translation of six *Novelas ejemplares* (1613).

Cervantes, Miguel de. *Interludes.* Edited by Edwin Honig. New York, 1964. Translation of *Entremeses* (1615).

Cervantes, Miguel de. *Journey to Parnassus.* Edited by James Y. Gibson. London, 1883. Translation of *Viaje del Parnaso* (1614).

Cervantes, Miguel de. *Obras completas.* Edited by Angel Valbuena Prat. Madrid, 1960.

Cervantes, Miguel de. *The Trials of Persiles and Sigismunda: A Northern Story.* Edited by Celia R. Weller and Clark A. Colahan. Berkeley, Calif., 1989.

Secondary Works

Astrana Marín, Luis. *Vida heroica y ejemplar de Miguel de Cervantes Saavedra.* 7 vols. Madrid, 1948–1958. The most detailed and copiously documented biography.

Canavaggio, Jean. *Cervantes.* New York, 1990. A scholarly biography.

Castro, Américo. *El pensamiento de Cervantes.* Madrid, 1925. 2d ed., Barcelona, Spain, 1972. The starting point for all serious work on Cervantes. Situates Cervantes in the European Renaissance and, in the 1972 edition, in the Spanish social context as well.

Combet, Louis. *Cervantès ou les incertitudes du désir.* Lyon, France, 1980. An alternative to the official biography.

El Saffar, Ruth, ed. *Critical Essays on Cervantes.* Boston, 1986. A collection of classic studies, including pertinent excerpts from books by Michel Foucault and Marthe Robert.

Flores, Angel, and M. J. Bernardete, eds. *Cervantes across the Centuries.* New York, 1947. Fundamental essays by Américo Castro and Leo Spitzer, among others.

Forcione, Alban K. *Cervantes and the Humanist Vision: A Study of Four "Exemplary Novels."* Princeton, N.J., 1982. The presence of Erasmian humanism in the *Novelas.*

Forcione, Alban K. *Cervantes, Aristotle, and the "Persiles".* Princeton, N.J., 1970. Situates Cervantes and the *Persiles* in Renaissance literary theory.

Johnson, Carroll B. *Don Quixote: The Quest for Modern Fiction.* Boston, 1990. Concise introduction.

Márquez Villanueva, Francisco. *Personajes y temas del Quijote.* Madrid, 1975. Erudite and sensitive essays on several much-discussed episodes of *Don Quixote.*

McGaha, Michael D., ed. *Cervantes and the Renaissance.* Easton, Pa., 1980. Essays by American scholars.

Sears, Theresa Ann. *A Marriage of Convenience: Ideal and Ideology in the "Novelas ejemplares."* New York, 1993. Iconoclastic feminist readings of the *Novelas.*

Wilson, Diana de Armas. *Allegories of Love: Cervantes's "Persiles y Sigismunda."* Princeton, N.J., 1991. Erudite comparatist-feminist reading of the *Persiles.*

CARROLL B. JOHNSON

CESALPINO, ANDREA (Andreas Caesalpinus; 1525–1603), Italian physician, botanist, mineralogist, philosopher. Cesalpino's father was a mason wealthy enough to send his son to the University of Pisa and leave him a sizable property in his native city of Arezzo. At Pisa, Cesalpino studied under the anatomists Andreas Vesalius, Realdo Colombo, and Guido Guidi, as well as under the botanist Luca Ghini, taking his degrees in philosophy and medicine in 1551.

From Ghini, Cesalpino learned the new art of preserving plant specimens on sheets of paper; his herbarium survives in the Botanical Museum of Florence. In 1556 Cesalpino succeeded Ghini as professor of medicinal plants and director of the Pisa botanical garden, founded in 1545. In 1569 he was appointed professor of medicine. In 1592 Cesalpino accepted Clement VIII's call to a chair of medicine at the University of Rome and the post of papal physician.

Cesalpino signaled his deep allegiance to Aristotelianism with the term "peripatetic" in the titles of his *Questionum peripateticarum libri V* (Peripatetic questions; Venice, 1571) and *Daemonum investigatio peripatetica* (Peripatetic investigation of demons; Florence, 1580; revised 1593, consulting on a case of demonic possession in nuns) and, throughout his work, by his use of Aristotelian methods and principles to propose novel solutions to both old and new problems in astronomy, physics, medicine, mineralogy, and botany.

Cesalpino's most original contributions lay in botany. His *De plantis libri XVI* (Sixteen books on plants; Florence, 1583) introduced a method of classifying plants based primarily on the characteristics of fruits. In both his method and his choice of morphological characters, he explicitly adopted the taxonomic principles followed by Aristotle in his zoological works and by Theophrastus in his botanical books. Cesalpino's focus on plant parts that were key to growth, nutrition, and reproduction (the primary functions of the plant soul, according to Aristotle) led him to group together plants that were later considered to be in the same genus or family. Unlike the great majority of Renaissance herbals, *De plantis* provided no illustrations and rarely discussed medicinal properties. Cesalpino's firsthand botanical knowledge—he described some fifteen hundred kinds of plants—was held in high regard by his contemporaries. However, they complained that his taxonomy, which he never summarized in an outline, was difficult to grasp. From the seventeenth-century botanists Joachim Jung and John Ray, Carolus Linnaeus learned to admire Cesalpino and in *Species plantarum* (Species of plants; 1753) named the genus *Caesalpinia* in his honor.

Cesalpino is probably best known as the first person to use the phrase "circulation of the blood" (*Peripatetic Questions,* folio 111v). In trying to reconcile Aristotelian and Galenic doctrine on the movements of the heart and blood, Cesalpino argued from anatomical evidence and teleology that blood leaves the arteries and moves through "anastomoses" to enter the veins, whence it flows back to the heart. The short discussion, followed by somewhat ambiguous passages in *De plantis* and *Artis medicae liber VII* (Art of medicine, book seven; 1603), foreshadowed William Harvey's *De motu cordis* (On the motion of the heart; 1628) and gave rise to four centuries of nationalist controversy over priority of discovery of the circulation of the blood.

BIBLIOGRAPHY

Primary Works
"Andrea[e] Cesalpini, *Questionum peripateticarum,* libri V, liber V, quaestio IV." Edited and translated by Mark Edward Clark, Stephen A. Nimis, and George R. Rochefort. *Journal of the History of Medicine and Allied Sciences* 33 (1978): 185–213. Gives context of "circulation of blood" phrase.
Morton, A. G. "A Letter of Andrea Cesalpino." *Archives of Natural History* 14 (1987): 169–173. Translates a 1563 letter in which Cesalpino outlines his classificatory methods and describes his herbarium.

Secondary Works
Bylebyl, Jerome J. "Cesalpino and Harvey on the Portal Circulation." In *Science, Medicine, and Society in the Renaissance: Essays to Honor Walter Pagel.* Edited by Allen G. Debus. Vol. 2. New York, 1972. Pages 39–52. Surveys Harvey's acquaintance with Cesalpino's work.
Greene, Edward Lee. *Landmarks of Botanical History.* Edited by Frank N. Egerton, with contributions by Robert P. McIntosh and Rogers McVaugh. 2 vols. Stanford, Calif., 1983. Chapter 22 includes key to Cesalpino's taxonomic groups.
Viviani, Ugo. *Vita e opere di Andrea Cesalpino.* Arezzo, Italy, 1922. Uses documentary sources to correct 1519 birthdate, still found in many sources.

KAREN MEIER REEDS

CHAMPIER, SYMPHORIEN (1472–1539), French poet, physician, historian, humanist. Born into a bourgeois family at Saint-Symphorien-sur-Coise, near Lyon, Champier studied arts in Paris and medicine at Montpellier, where he qualified in 1496. He taught liberal arts in Grenoble for the next two years, took a doctorate in theology in 1502, and thereafter practiced medicine in Lyon until 1509. In 1503 he married Marguerite de Terrail, a cousin of the celebrated chevalier Bayard, on whom he published a

eulogy. From 1509 to 1519 he served as physician to Antoine, duc de Lorraine, in the Italian wars, being present at the battles of Agnadello (1509) and Marignano (1515). For the last twenty years of his life he was at the center of the cultural Renaissance of Lyon, while simultaneously promoting the study of medicine by helping to found the College of the Holy Trinity and sponsoring translations of, and writing commentaries on, the works of Hippocrates and Galen. He took an active part in city government, being twice elected to the municipal council.

Champier's early publications criticized sorcery and the occult. They also included *La nef des princes* (The ship of princes; 1502) and *La nef des dames vertueuses* (The ship of virtuous ladies; 1503), written in prose and verse and showing the influence of Italian Neoplatonism. Among his prolific later writings were comparisons of French and Italian literature. His historical works were influenced by the school of Rhétoriqueurs and took particular interest in ancient Gaul, a theme continued by his son, Claude Champier. A nephew, Jean Champier, who also practiced medicine at Lyon, extended his uncle's work on the relationship between ancient Greek and Arab science.

See also Humanism, *subentry on* France; Rhétoriqueurs.

BIBLIOGRAPHY

Primary Work
Condamnation des sciences occultes / Dyalogus in magicarum artium destructionem (Condemnation of the occult sciences / A dialogue intended to destroy the magical arts). Edited and translated by Annie Rijper. Paris, 1974.

Secondary Works
Allut, P. *Étude biographique et bibliographique sur Symphorien Champier.* Paris, 1859.
Tricou, Jean. "Le testament de Symphorien Champier." *Bibliothèque d'Humanisme et Renaissance* 18 (1956): 101–109.

J. H. M. SALMON

CHAPMAN, GEORGE. *See* **Drama, English,** *subentry on* **Jacobean Drama.**

CHARITY. *See* **Poverty and Charity.**

CHARIVARI. Charivaris were ritual modes of censorship, regulation, and folk justice exercised by village and urban communities across Europe from the British Isles to the Holy Roman Empire. They were practiced in many forms and contexts and changed over time. It was common for youth abbeys—institutionalized groups of young male peasants or artisans who had passed the age of puberty but were not yet married—to stage charivaris in their local communities.

Participants in the rituals aimed to produce discomfort in the people subject to censure through verbal, visual, and physical ridicule. According to Natalie Zemon Davis, the charivari had a typical form. It began in a comic mood that might include mocking songs and noise made by beating pots and pans (rough music, *Katzenmusik, mattinata*). Normally it included a procession or parade, perhaps with costuming. Victims were dunked in water, chased, paraded backward on an ass, and so on. The performances moved toward a reckoning with victims, who could sometimes negotiate their way out by paying a fine or buying a round of drinks. If successful, the charivari ended in the withdrawal of the crowd, drinking, and festivity. If not successful, it could result in physical violence, especially when the community failed to achieve consensus on the issues of contention.

Charivaris were staged to act out social, political, and cultural dissonance. Perceived violators of community norms—wives who beat their husbands, widows who remarried, older men who married younger women or vice versa, adulterers, and barren couples—were common subjects of social ridicule, as were abusive power holders. On the surface the mood was carnivalesque, yet underneath the charivaris were attempts to work through difficult problems and achieve satisfying resolutions: among them, to integrate or reject violators of community traditions; to protest the abusive powers of tax collectors, landlords, mayors, or opposing religious groups; to negotiate honor and reputation; to regulate sexual access to young women; and to placate the spirits of the dead. Charivaris served to reinforce the bonds uniting communities, but at times they furthered conflict.

BIBLIOGRAPHY

Cashmere, John. "The Social Uses of Violence in Ritual: *Charivari* or Religious Persecution?" *European History Quarterly* 21, no. 3 (1991): 291–319.

Davis, Natalie Zemon. "Charivari, Honor, and Community in Seventeenth-Century Lyon and Geneva." In *Rite, Drama, Festival, Spectacle: Rehearsals toward a Theory of Cultural Performance.* Edited by John MacAloon. Philadelphia, 1984. Pages 42–57.

Davis, Natalie Zemon. *Society and Culture in Early Modern France.* Stanford, Calif., 1975. See the chapters "The Reasons of Misrule," pages 97–123, and "The Rites of Violence," pages 152–187.

Klapisch-Zuber, Christiane. *Women, Family, and Ritual in Renaissance Italy.* Translated by Lydia G. Cochrane. Chi-

cago, 1985. See the chapter "The 'Mattinata' in Medieval Italy," pp. 261–282.

JOANNE M. FERRARO

CHARLES V (1500–1558), Holy Roman Emperor (as Karl V, 1519–1556), king of Spain (as Carlos I, 1515–1556). Born in Ghent in 1500 to Philip I (the Handsome), archduke of Austria, and Joanna (the Mad) of Castile, Charles was the heir to a glittering collection of European titles and lands; his grandparents were Ferdinand and Isabella of Spain and Holy Roman Emperor Maximilian I and Mary of Burgundy. By the time he reached young adulthood, Charles's heritage had become the biggest empire assembled on the continent since the days of Charlemagne. He spent his life defending this inheritance and Europe from the threats of heresy and invasion.

Education and Inheritance. Charles was raised in the Netherlands largely without parental influence. His father, frequently absent in Spain, died in 1506, and his mother's mental problems, growing worse after Philip's death, forced her to remain a prisoner in her native land. His father's sister, the twice-widowed Margaret of Austria, took responsibility for Charles's upbringing and that of three of his sisters in the court at Brussels. Here he learned piety from the Christian humanist cleric Adrian of Utrecht (later Pope Adrian VI), although he seems to have preferred hunting and military training to book learning. Statecraft he learned from his governor Guillaume de Croy, the sieur de Chièvres, who was to serve Charles for the rest of his life.

On his father's death, Charles inherited the Burgundian lands of the Netherlands and Franche-Comté. In 1516 his maternal grandfather Ferdinand died, and Charles became king of Spain, as well as ruler of Spanish possessions in Italy and much of the New World. When his other grandfather, Maximilian, died in 1519, Charles bid for the vacant throne of the Holy Roman Empire, which his Habsburg ancestors had ruled for centuries. Although he was opposed by Francis I of France and England's Henry VIII, Charles was able to count on vast sums in bribe money (500,000 florins of which had been borrowed from the Fuggers) and military blackmail to sway the electors. In June 1519 Charles was unanimously elected emperor and was crowned at Aix-la-Chappelle in October 1520. As the head of a vast agglomeration of holdings around the world, Charles's choices in how he viewed his role and used his power would affect millions in the years to come.

Mercurino Gattinara, his grand chancellor, had told Charles that God had set him on the path to world monarchy and that he who sat on the imperial throne was the leader of Christendom, ordained by God himself. There is no doubt that Charles had come to see himself in this light, the defender of his religion against Islamic aggressors (a crusading role his Spanish ancestors had played throughout the centuries of the *Reconquista*) and later the bulwark against the rise of Protestant heretics.

Government and Policies. This exalted role did not sit well with many of Charles's Spanish subjects, who believed that he ought to be spending his time and effort on the throne of Spain. Already unpopular with Spaniards because of the influence he allowed his foreign-born councillors, Charles found that they now resented him for his leaving the country so precipitously to seek a German title (he had arrived in Spain only in 1517) and the financial burdens that imperial policy levied on them. In 1520 the towns of Castile rose in revolt. Though the Spanish nobility put down this *comunero* movement, the rebellion foreshadowed how Charles would be tugged in conflicting directions by his differing responsibilities.

With Spain once more at peace, Charles faced two immediate problems: the growing Lutheran heresy in Germany and the threat from France to his possessions in Italy. The first he met with the assertion of his orthodoxy and a desire to see that a well-reformed church offer no occasion for heresy. His statement to Luther at the 1521 Diet of Worms was as uncompromising in its way as was Luther's. He was, he said, the descendant of a long line of kings dedicated to the defense of the Christian faith and the honor of God. On this he would stake his lands, friends, body, blood, life, and soul, and he would oppose even the suspicion of heresy in Germany. However, his desire to see the Catholic Church reformed aroused enmity in Rome, which mistrusted his power in Italy and resisted his calls for a general council to settle the vexing questions of religion. Rather than support the emperor, the papacy would ally itself with his French enemies.

Before his death, his grandfather Ferdinand had warned Charles of the dangers of war with France. Such a conflict, he said, would be long and costly and detract from the far more important struggle with the forces of Islam. An "eternal war within Christendom" was what Ferdinand predicted; certainly what ensued in the Habsburg-Valois rivalry was very close to that for the rest of Charles's reign. Chièvres too had always advised his master to follow a conciliatory policy with the French, but his death

in 1521 and France's maneuvering against Habsburg ascendancy in Italy led the emperor to conspire with England and the dissident constable Charles of Bourbon. At first things went badly for Charles: the English invasion was a failure, and the rebellion that Bourbon was to lead soon sputtered out. At the Battle of Pavia, however, the situation was reversed. In February 1525, on the emperor's twenty-fifth birthday, the imperial army smashed the French forces in Lombardy and took King Francis I himself captive.

What would Charles do with such an advantage? Gattinara proposed the dismemberment of France by forcing it to yield all its old Burgundian acquisitions and giving Navarre to Bourbon; the French would also have to abandon their claims to Naples and Milan; the pope could be forced to accede to the call for a council and for church reform. In the end Charles achieved almost nothing from the windfall of Pavia. In the 1526 Peace of Madrid, Francis agreed to return his Burgundian holdings and renounce French claims in Italy, but once safely across the border, he repudiated its terms, stating that they had been extorted by duress and against fundamental French law. The war resumed, and it was the pope who paid for his alliance with France. On 6 May 1527 a rampaging imperial army entered Rome, laid waste to the city, and took Clement VII prisoner. This phase of the Habsburg-Valois struggle ended in 1530 with the compromise Peace of Cambrai (sometimes called the "Ladies' Peace" for the role played in it by Francis's mother and Charles's aunt Margaret of Austria).

Meanwhile, central Europe was becoming more of a concern for Charles. The Lutheran movement had grown since the meeting at Worms and had attracted a number of cities and princes to its cause. Attempts at various Diets to solve the schism were unsuccessful (in fact only hardening positions on both sides), and any thought that military force might be useful against his German subjects was illusory as long as the Turkish forces of Süleyman the Magnificent continued their pressure on Austria. Vienna had been besieged in 1529, and in 1532 a Turkish army, following up on its successes in Hungary, launched another attack against Vienna, forcing Charles to adopt a softer position toward the Protestant princes in the Peace of Nürnberg in return for troops to fight the Muslim invaders. After helping force the Turks to withdraw, Charles returned to Spain to carry out a naval campaign against them, taking the war to North Africa. Although his forces under Andrea Doria of Genoa captured Tunis in 1535, he failed to thwart the activities of the corsair

Charles V Victorious. Seated between the Pillars of Hercules, the emperor holds captive his defeated enemies, from left, Süleyman the Magnificent, Pope Clement VII, Francis I of France, Duke William V of Jülich-Cleves, Duke John Frederick of Ernestine Saxony, and Landgrave Philip of Hesse. Illuminated manuscript by Giulio Clovio, mid-sixteenth century. BY PERMISSION OF THE BRITISH LIBRARY. ADD 33733, PAGE 5

Barbarossa (Khayr ad-Dīn, d. 1546), who continued to serve the Ottomans as an effective admiral in the central Mediterranean. Despite an anti-Turkish Holy League with Venice and the papacy, Charles's fleet failed to capture Algiers.

Throughout all this Christendom was scandalized by the support that France gave to the Turks. Combined Franco-Ottoman fleets were the scourge of the Spanish and Italian coasts, and the renewed war between Charles and Francis kept the emperor from using his full strength against either the Turks or the German heretics. Imperial finances were stretched beyond the breaking point, which led to the 1544 Peace of Crépy, where Charles agreed to extremely generous concessions to France if only he could have their support against the Protestants and the Turks. The price he was willing to pay for a chance to unite Catholic Europe was a high one—a Habsburg marriage alliance with a French prince, with the Netherlands or Milan as a wedding present—but in the end the plan fell through.

Religious Policies. Peace with France did allow the General Council Charles had long hoped for to be summoned to Trent in 1545 by Pope Paul III. This halt in the fighting with France and a truce with the Turks also gave the emperor the luxury of con-

templating a military solution to the problem of religious division in Germany. Striking at the Schmalkaldic League of Protestant princes and cities would, he hoped, bring them to a state of mind where they could agree to a reasonable compromise. Accusing two leading Lutheran princes, Elector John Frederick of Saxony and Landgrave Philip of Hesse, of rebellion, Charles launched a campaign that was crowned with success at the Battle of Mühlberg in April 1547. The league capitulated, and it seemed for a moment as if Charles had achieved something of lasting significance. Charles had enough political capital in the short term to gain the separation of the Netherlands from the Holy Roman Empire and to impose the religious Interim of Augsburg on German Protestants, but before too long events again turned against him.

In 1551 the pope reconvened the Council of Trent in Bologna to lessen the imperial influence that had pressed for a religious compromise that would work in Germany. Meanwhile, Charles was unable to convince his brother to resign the inheritance of the empire to his son Philip of Spain; the Turks, the French, and Protestant princes resumed their wars on Charles. In 1552 Maurice of Saxony betrayed Charles and forced him to flee for his life from Innsbruck while Henry II of France seized the imperial cities of

Metz, Toul, and Verdun. Discouraged by these setbacks he tried to strengthen Philip's future by arranging a marriage between his son and Mary I of England, which took place in 1554, but even there Charles was frustrated when the English agreed only on very advantageous terms and even then refused to crown Philip. Unwilling to countenance the consequences of the peace that Ferdinand worked out with German Protestants whereby the principle of *cuius regio eius religio* (whose the reign, his the religion) would enshrine religious division, the frustrated, angry, and increasingly ineffective Charles began to contemplate retirement.

Abdication. At a moving ceremony in Brussels in 1555, where he recounted the struggles of his life, Charles abdicated the rule of the Netherlands to Philip; in 1556 he handed over his Spanish possessions to his son and stepped down from the imperial throne in favor of Ferdinand. By September 1556 he was back in Spain preparing to spend his final years next to the Hieronymite monastery at Yuste in the Estremadura. He had prepared for himself and the little court who accompanied him a comfortable villa filled with art, clocks (a passion of his), music, and books (one of which was a translation of the Bible in French for which he had to secure the permission of the Inquisition to possess). Here the irascible old man continued to besiege his relations with advice but also came to find in his devotions a measure of the peace he sought. He died on 21 September 1558.

It is tempting to judge Charles V by the gap between his lofty inheritance and ambitions and the lack of success that too often attended his efforts. The unity of his empire on which he had built such hopes never lived up to the dreams that men such as Gattinara had had for it. Frustrated by the religious divisions he was unable to heal in Germany, by the everlasting war with the French that his grandfather had warned him of, by the paltry results of his crusade against the Turks, by the machinations of a Hispanophobe pope (Paul IV), and by the truncation of the empire he had wished to pass on whole to his son, he was in his last years a man who felt he had outlived his usefulness. Yet if he was not the world emperor that Dante had called for, he was still a man who could point to a life of honor and some accomplishment. If he had not succeeded in utterly repressing heresy in Germany, he had at least helped to limit its progress in the empire and made sure that it gained no foothold in Spain or Italy. His forces in the Mediterranean had blunted the power of the Turks and taken the war into Islamic territory. He

had thwarted French ambitions in Italy and preserved his inheritance there. Charles encouraged the conquistadors and their creation of vast holdings in the Americas for Spain, but he had also decreed just laws for the humane treatment of the native population. His commissioning of Ferdinand Magellan had resulted in the first circumnavigation of the globe. He had pressed for the church council that, when held, would eventually define Catholicism for the next four centuries. Perhaps most importantly Charles had participated in the creation of Spain as Europe's next great power. Funded by American gold and silver (and the taxes of Castile) the Spain of his successor, Philip II, would soon show how the balance of power on the continent had shifted from its center to the Atlantic.

If his reputation as a ruler is not what it might have been, Charles nonetheless remains an attractive personality. He was a loving family man, especially in his devotion to his wife, Isabella of Portugal, who died in 1539, and in the care he took to educate Philip. He was careful of his honor, as illustrated by his safe-conduct to Luther and his anachronistic challenge of Francis I to trial by single combat. His Erasmian reformism contrasts well with Philip's more ruthless Counter-Reformation zeal. His memoirs and political testaments are among the most interesting of their kind, showing a keen eye for both the problems he faced and the circumstances that would oppose him.

Patron of Music and Art. Charles was a lover of the arts, especially music, and he was not the easiest of patrons to please. He took his famous chapel singers with him when he traveled and kept them by him even after he had abdicated. The group's fame helped maintain the reputation of Flemish music for the rest of the sixteenth century. Charles also formed a chapel for his wife and gave his son Philip, when he reached the age of twelve, a suite of musicians that included singers, instrumentalists, and composers. The composers who served Charles V included Josquin des Prez, Nicolas Gombert, and Arnolt Schlick.

Charles admired the work of Titian so much that he conferred on him the title of Count Palatine. He summoned the painter to Augsburg in 1548, where he produced the most famous of his portraits—*Charles V at the Battle of Mühlberg* [see the color plates in this volume], where he is depicted as a triumphant knight, the seated portrait of 1548, and the beginnings of the wonderful *Gloria* of 1554, which shows a kneeling Charles and wife among a throng in adoration of the Trinity and the Virgin. Accompanying Charles to the conquest of Tunis were the poet Garcilaso de la Vega and the painter Vermeyen, from whose sketches tapestries depicting the victory were made. His commissioning of Leone Leoni and his son Pompeo produced works including the striking bronze sculpture (with removable armor) *Charles V Triumphs over Savagery,* now in the Prado. Ironically, one of the greatest contributions the career of Charles V made to the course of the Renaissance was the Sack of Rome in 1527 by his unpaid mercenaries—a devastation that shifted the focus of patronage from papal Rome to Venice and northern Italian cities.

See also **Comuneros, Revolt of the; Habsburg Dynasty; Holy Roman Empire; Pavia, Battle of; Rome, Sack of; Trent, Council of;** *and biographies of Adrian VI; Francis I; Gattinara, Mercurino; Süleyman I.*

BIBLIOGRAPHY

Primary Works

Fernandez Alvarez, Manuel, ed. *Corpus documental de Carlos V.* Salamanca, Spain, 1973–1981. Five volumes of Charles's correspondence with his Spanish family; includes the emperor's memoirs.

Lanz, K., ed. *Correspondenz des Kaisers Karls V.* Leipzig, Germany, 1844–1846.

Morel-Fatio, A., ed. *Historiographie de Charles-Quint, 1e partie, suivi des mémoires de Charles-Quint.* Paris, 1913. Texts in French and Portuguese.

Secondary Works

Brandi, Karl. *The Emperor Charles V: The Growth and Destiny of a Man and a World-Emperor.* Translated by C. V. Wedgwood. Reprint, New York, 1980. Still the standard biography but dated.

Fernandez Alvarez, Manuel. *Charles V, Elected Emperor and Hereditary Ruler.* Translated by J. A. Lalaguna. London, 1975. Short and politically focused with more material on the Spanish point of view.

Headley, J. M. *The Emperor and His Chancellor.* Cambridge, U.K., 1983. Charles V, Gattinara, and the imperial civil service.

Koenigsberger, H. G. *The Habsburgs and Europe, 1516–1660.* London, 1971. Charles V in a dynastic context.

Lutz, Heinrich. *Das römisch-deutsche Reich im politischen System Karls V.* Munich, 1982. Concentrates on Charles V in his imperial role.

Rodríguez Salgado, M. J. *The Changing Face of Empire: Charles V, Philip II, and Habsburg Authority, 1551–1559.* Cambridge, U.K., 1988. Revisionist view of Charles's last years and the transfer of power.

Seibt, Ferdinand. *Karl V: Der Kaiser und die Reformation.* Berlin, 1990. Focuses on the German Reformation.

GERRY BOWLER

CHARLES I (1600–1649), king of Great Britain and Ireland (1625–1649). Born in Dunfermline Castle, on 19 November 1600, he was the second son of James VI of Scotland and Anne, princess of Denmark. His childhood and adolescence were unhappy. When his father inherited the English throne as James I on 22 March 1603, following the death of Queen Elizabeth I, Charles was left behind in Scotland. As a young child he suffered from rickets and a severe stammer that bedeviled him almost until his death. On moving to England in 1604 he was entrusted to the guardianship of Sir Robert and Lady Elizabeth Carey. His parents had little to do with him, while his elder brother Prince Henry, the charismatic heir, teased him mercilessly.

On 6 November 1612 Henry died unexpectedly from typhoid fever, making the insecure Charles heir. He took the bereavement badly, and was almost as upset when in 1613 his elder sister Elizabeth married Frederick V, the ruler of the Palatinate, and left England to live with her husband in Germany. The death of his mother in March 1619 and the fact that his father, James I, found him a prudish irritation, preferring the company of homosexual lovers, did nothing to help the adolescent's self-confidence.

Ironically it was one of those lovers, George Villiers, later duke of Buckingham, who liberated the heir from his insecure youth. Realizing that the aging James I was reaching the end of his life, and that he needed his heir's support to maintain his power, Villiers befriended Charles, who responded avidly.

In the spring of 1623 the pair went to Spain to woo Philip IV's sister, the Infanta Donna Maria, in an escapade that was as farcical as it was historically significant. The idea of a marriage alliance to Catholic Spain went back to 1604, and was in part an attempt to balance Princess Elizabeth's marriage to Frederick, a leading German Protestant prince. Fancying himself in love with the Infanta and deciding to cut through more than a decade of diplomatic dilly-dallying, Charles, with Buckingham in tow, set off in disguise for Madrid, where they arrived unexpectedly at the home of the British ambassador. After the Spanish rejected his terms humiliatingly—notwithstanding major secret concessions on his part—Charles angrily left Spain. He returned to England the hero of the hour, and more under Buckingham's influence than ever. The public was relieved that Charles had not sold out to the Spanish, but Buckingham knew how politically damaging were the concessions he had secretly offered. The trip to Spain did serve to expose Charles to the work of artists such as Titian, Michelangelo, and Raphael, but it also augmented the authoritarian side of his character. A year later he told Bishop William Laud, "I cannot defend a bad, nor yield in a good cause."

Attempts to Work with Parliament.

Charles succeeded to the throne on 27 March 1625, and for three years Buckingham dominated English politics. He and Charles became involved in a number of military expeditions, first against Spain, to revenge themselves for the slights they felt they had suffered in Madrid, and then against France. In 1625 they sent a fleet to Cádiz to capture the Spanish treasure fleet, but crippled by poor leadership and bad luck, the campaign was an utter failure. So too was the expedition that Buckingham personally commanded in the summer of 1627 to the French island of Ré.

To pay for these military adventures the king asked Parliament to vote for taxes, which the Commons refused unless he would first dismiss Buckingham. To protect his friend, Charles dissolved Parliament and collected the taxes anyway through a "Forced Loan," so called because of the degree of coercion used to collect the tax. In July 1628 the constitutional crisis reached a climax, when Parliament passed the Petition of Right, a statement of major grievances. Charles assented to the petition with such ill grace that relations between king and Commons continued to deteriorate.

A month later, on 23 August 1628 in Portsmouth, John Felton, a deranged army officer, assassinated Buckingham, who was about to lead a fleet against the French port of La Rochelle. Charles was devastated (unlike the overwhelming majority of his subjects, who raucously welcomed the murder). The fleet was ignominiously defeated, further poisoning the relationship between the king and Parliament. On 2 March 1629, defying the king's orders to adjourn, the House of Commons locked its chamber doors and, as two members literally sat on the speaker to prevent him and the house from rising, passed three resolutions condemning those who supported Catholicism and Arminianism (a Dutch school of theology that rejected the strict Calvinist doctrine of predestination), as well as all who had paid illegal taxes such as the Forced Loan. Outraged by this open defiance of his authority, Charles determined to rule on his own.

The next eleven years, from 1629 to 1640, formed Charles's "Personal Rule." In many ways the king retreated from the world of politics to that of his court. He fell in love with his wife, Henrietta Maria, the French princess whom he had wed in March 1625. Due to Buckingham's influence their marriage

had at first been unhappy. But after his murder the two found affection; children followed, and their eldest surviving son, later Charles II, was born on 29 May 1630.

Charles's Art Collection.

Charles used this time to create one of the finest art collections ever assembled by a British monarch. His interest in art went back to childhood. He was eleven when he inherited Henry's collection, which was particularly strong in the works of Venetian Masters. His mother left him 161 paintings, while Philip IV of Spain gave him Titian's *Venus of Prado* and Correggio's *Holy Family* when he was in Madrid. His greatest coup as a collector was the acquisition in 1628 of the collection that the dukes of Mantua had assembled over a century and a half, which included some of the best works by Raphael, Titian, Correggio and Mantegna. Six years later he bought one-quarter of the works collected by the Venetian Bartolomeo della Nova, his share being determined by a roll of dice. An inventory of the king's paintings listed some 546 works in Whitehall Palace alone, and by the time of his death the collection had grown to include some 1,760 paintings. In addition, Charles had a large sculpture collection, including some 210 pieces in Greenwich Palace and its gardens.

Charles used diplomats, artists, and agents to acquire individual works. Rubens purchased the Raphael tapestry cartoons (which now hang in the Victoria and Albert Museum in London) on the king's behalf. Knowing Charles's weakness for art, diplomats and foreign potentates presented him with works to influence England's foreign policy, while courtiers and politicians did the same to further their careers. Archbishop Laud commissioned the French sculptor Hubert Le Sueur to cast a bronze of Charles on horseback (it now stands in Trafalgar Square), tactfully instructing the artist to make the short monarch a foot taller.

Charles's taste and judgment were superb. At the age of twenty he knew enough about painting to return the *Judith and Holofernes* he had commissioned from Rubens because he detected it was largely the work of an apprentice. He could also drive a hard bargain, reducing the price of Van Dyck's *Le Roi à la chasse,* which portrayed Charles about to go hunting, from £200 to £100. Nonetheless, Charles's art collection did not come cheap. The Mantua collection cost £18,280, the Nova purchases, £800. When Parliament sold off his collection in 1649, reserving the choicest pieces for leaders of the new republic, the paintings fetched £31,913 and the

Charles I. *Le roi à la chasse* by Anthony van Dyck (1599–1641). MUSÉE DU LOUVRE, PARIS/LAUROS-GIRAUDON/ART RESOURCE

sculptures another £17,990. Their worth in modern terms is staggering to contemplate; the puritan who criticized the king for "squandering away millions of pounds in rotten pictures and broken nosed marbles" may have been as financially correct as he was aesthetically wrong.

Charles's art collection not only revealed his connoisseurship, but also shed light on his personality and policies. Take, for instance, the massive set of three paintings which Rubens did on the ceiling of the Banqueting House at Whitehall. Designed by Inigo Jones in the Palladian style, this building was the most important piece of architecture erected in England during the first half of the seventeenth century. Intended for the most important state occasions, such as the reception of ambassadors, its main

themes were order and harmony. The interior's clean straight lines climaxed where the king sat in his throne. The central panel, *The Apotheosis of James I,* shows Charles's father ascending into heaven. It sanctifies not only the former king, but all kings, who as divine-right rulers went directly to Paradise. The second panel praises James for uniting the crowns of England and Scotland, while the third acclaims him as a peacemaker, and by implication supports Charles's refusal to get involved with the Thirty Years' War, which was ravaging the Continent.

These themes are explicit in another great painting that Charles commissioned from Rubens, *St. George and the Dragon*. It depicts Charles as England's patron saint who has just rescued the fair maiden (who looks just like Henrietta Maria) from

Charles I, Patron of the Arts. *Apotheosis of James I* by Peter Paul Rubens (1577–1640) on the ceiling of Banqueting House, London. REPRODUCED BY PERMISSION OF HISTORIC ROYAL PALACES UNDER LICENSE FROM THE CONTROLLER OF HER MAJESTY'S STATIONERY OFFICE

the horrors of war, which are symbolized by ravaged women and massacred corpses, all in contrast with the peaceful English countryside in the background.

Perhaps the most important portrait the king commissioned was Van Dyck's *Charles I on Horseback,* which today hangs in the National Gallery in London. Its theme was a familiar one. Both classical and Holy Roman Emperors had portrayed themselves on horseback. Van Dyck's masterpiece shows the king not only as a divine-right monarch, but also as an absolutist who brooks no limits on his power. He is the knight-errant whose sword could be unsheathed at any time to right wrongs, punish the evil, and bring law and order to the realm. Fully in control of his powerful stallion, this happy warrior also has the

wise mien of a philosopher king, the confident master of all he surveys.

The Civil War. The self-confident king was probably not looking north toward Scotland when Van Dyck completed this picture in 1639, for by then his policies were coming apart. In spite of general complaints during the eleven years of the Personal Rule, for the most part things were not as bad as some parliamentarians later alleged. To raise money without parliamentary approval, the king resurrected old taxes, such as knighthood fines, or extended them, by, for example, making all counties, not merely those beside the sea, pay ship money to raise a fleet for coastal defense. Although far from popular, the king's taxes were not oppressive enough to make his subjects rebel.

But his religious policies were. Apart from their king, the English and Scots had little in common. The Scottish church, unlike the English, was largely Calvinistic. So when in 1637 Charles, after extensive consultations, introduced into Scotland a new prayer book that was thought there to be idolatrous and papist, the results were explosive. Riots broke out north of the border. When the dean of Saint Giles's Cathedral first used it for Sunday morning service on 23 July 1637, the congregation rioted, pelting him and the bishop with cudgels and three-legged stools. Hundreds of thousands of Scots signed a covenant, some using their own blood as ink, vowing to fight to keep their religion and resist the imposition of bishops. Convinced that the Scots were determined to abolish not only bishops, but the monarchy itself—and thus turn England into a republic as inconsequential as that which ruled Venice—on 11 June 1638 the king vowed, "I will rather die than yield to their impertinent and damnable demands."

Charles fought two wars against the Scots. Although politically inconclusive, the First Bishops' War of 1639 forced the king to call the Short Parliament in April 1640. After impulsively dismissing this parliament on 5 May, Charles fought the Second Bishops' War, which he lost, and thus had to call the Long Parliament, which opened on 3 November. For over a year king and Commons tried to compromise. Parliament wanted to control the crown; the king would accept no real limits on his powers. On 4 January 1642 Charles led a company of armed soldiers to the House of Commons to arrest the five ringleaders of parliamentary opposition, but just before he entered the house they escaped. The breach between king and Parliament was irreparable. As they fought to control the army, which was being raised to put down the revolt that had broken out in Ireland the previous October, both sides collected arms and courted public opinion.

Soon after declaring war against his rebellious subjects on 22 August, Charles raised an army, which beat the parliamentary forces at Edgehill on 23 October. But he failed to follow up the advantages he had gained at Edgehill by promptly moving against London. By the time he did so, resistance had grown so great that on 13 November he had to retreat from Turnham Green to spend the winter at Oxford.

During 1643 the two sides sparred. On 21 August Charles failed to lift the Siege of Gloucester, but beat the parliamentarians at the First Battle of Newbury on 20 September. During 1644 royalist forces under the king's nephew, Prince Rupert, were routed at the Battle of Marston Moor (2 July), while in a brilliant maneuver Charles forced the Roundheads to surrender at Lostwithiel on 31 August. The decisive year was to be 1645, for on 14 June, at the Battle of Naseby, Oliver Cromwell's New Model Army defeated the king's forces.

Although fighting continued for over a year, on 6 May 1646 Charles surrendered to the Scots army, who, the following 30 January, handed him over to Parliament. On 3 June 1647 the army seized the king, but on 11 November he escaped from their custody, ending up in Carisbrooke Castle on the Isle of Wight. For the next two years Charles bargained in bad faith with the Scots, the army, and Parliament, hoping to divide and thus rule. Instead he produced a second civil war, which was far more brutal than the first. As a result, on 19 December 1648 the army arrested the king and brought him to London, where they put him on trial for treason. The result was inevitable. Condemned to death, Charles was executed outside the Banqueting House at Whitehall on 30 January 1649.

In a way the site was sublimely appropriate. The Banqueting House, with its magnificent Rubens ceiling, symbolized Charles's exquisite artistic tastes, which in turn were an excellent guide to his personality. The product of an oppressive childhood, Charles I was too much an authoritarian to deal with his subjects in good faith, and too insecure to take decisive action. Archbishop Laud had earlier commented that he was "a mild and gracious prince, who knew not how to be, or be made great." For Charles, character was indeed fate.

BIBLIOGRAPHY

Carlton, Charles. *Charles I: The Personal Monarch*. London, 1983. 2d ed., 1995.

Cogswell, Thomas. *The Blessed Revolution: English Politics and the Coming of the War, 1621–1624*. Cambridge, U.K., 1989.

Gregg, Pauline. *King Charles I*. London, 1981.

Russell, Conrad. *The Fall of the British Monarchies, 1637–1642*. Oxford, 1991.

Sharpe, Kevin. *The Personal Rule of Charles I*. New Haven, Conn., and London, 1992.

Smuts, Robert M. *Court Culture and the Origin of a Royalist Tradition in Early Stuart England*. London, 1987.

Young, Michael B. *Charles I: King of England*. Basingstoke, U.K., 1997.

CHARLES CARLTON

CHARLES VIII (1470–1498), king of France (1483–1498). The only son of Louis XI and Charlotte of Savoy, Charles, a fragile child, was kept isolated at Amboise and had little formal education or train-

CARLO VIII·RE DI FRANCIA

Charles VIII, King of France. Engraving from Aliprando Capriolo's *Ritratti di cento capitani illustri,* Rome, 1596. © THE BRITISH MUSEUM, LONDON

reconstruction of the château of Amboise after 1495. He brought the famed engineer Fra Giovanni Giocondo to France to design it and the sculptor Guido Mazzoni to decorate it. He extended patronage to several early French humanists, especially Robert Gaguin. Charles's only child died in 1497, and when Charles died the next year, the throne passed to Louis XII.

BIBLIOGRAPHY

Bridge, John. *A History of France from the Death of Louis XI to 1515.* 5 vols. Oxford, 1921–1936.
Labande-Mailfert, Yvonne. *Charles VIII et son milieu (1470–1498).* Paris, 1975.

FREDERIC J. BAUMGARTNER

CHARLES IX (1550–1574), king of France (1560–1574). Succeeding to the throne as a small boy when his elder brother Francis II died suddenly in December 1560, Charles IX required a regent to govern in his stead until he came of age (the beginning of a king's fourteenth year, in France). His mother, Catherine de Médicis, served in the capacity of regent, and she attempted with varying degrees of success to influence her son long after the regency government came to a formal end in 1563. The lack of an adult king, coupled with growing religious tensions in the kingdom as a result of the Reformation, led to the outbreak of the French Wars of Religion at the beginning of Charles's reign, and he spent his entire career attempting to resolve these disputes.

Neither a military figure like his father Henry II nor a particularly adept politician, Charles was destined to stand in the shadow of both his mother and other leading nobles at court. His historical reputation is tied inevitably to the Saint Bartholomew's Day massacres, in which up to two thousand French Protestants—called Huguenots in France—were slain in Paris and perhaps four thousand others were killed elsewhere in the provinces in August and September 1572. Although Charles was not personally responsible for causing all these deaths, he certainly should have realized the consequences of ordering the murder and execution of the Huguenot leader, Gaspard de Coligny, and a couple dozen of his fellow nobles who had gathered in the capital for the wedding of Charles's sister Margaret to a leading Huguenot aristocrat, Henry of Navarre. In the midst of a seething religious cauldron, Charles ought to have known that this bloodshed would set off a wave of popular violence.

Charles's foreign policy was no more efficacious than his domestic policy. He became involved in se-

ing when he succeeded his father in 1483. He was not ready to rule, and his older sister Anne and her husband, Pierre de Beaujeu, were named his guardians and took control of the government. His cousin Louis of Orléans (later Louis XII), objecting to the power of the Beaujeu, led a revolt called the "Fools War" along with the duke of Brittany. The rebels were defeated at Saint-Aubin in Brittany in 1488. The victory paved the way for Charles to marry Anne of Brittany in 1491 and bring the last autonomous province under royal authority. Breaking free of his sister's tutelage, Charles led French forces in the first French invasion of Italy in 1494. He hoped to make good the Angevin claim to the kingdom of Naples and use Italy to stage a crusade against the Turks. Although he easily occupied Naples, Ferdinand of Aragon organized a league against him. Charles returned homeward but fought a bloody battle at Fornovo in 1495 before making good his retreat.

Italian Renaissance culture impressed Charles, and he took the first steps toward introducing it to France. His principal cultural achievement was the

Charles IX, King of France. Portrait by François Clouet. 1560. MUSÉE DU LOUVRE, PARIS/LAUROS-GIRAUDON/ART RESOURCE

cretly aiding both the Dutch rebels who were revolting against Philip II of Spain in the Netherlands, as well as Sultan Selim II of the Ottoman Turks. Both projects were designed to undercut Spanish hegemony in Europe, but both nearly proved disastrous. Philip II came close to declaring war on France on several occasions as a result of French aid to the Dutch rebels, and the Ottoman Turks were only narrowly defeated at Lepanto in 1571—by forces raised by Spain and the pope—when the sultan decided to attempt to invade the Christian West. Moreover, Charles's aid was not nearly enough to prevent Spain

from remaining the dominant power in Europe throughout Charles's lifetime.

Charles was neither a scholar nor a particularly serious patron of the arts. Compared with some of his predecessors, particularly Francis I (1515–1547), Charles left a rather meager record of intellectual and artistic achievement, a record that even his younger brother and successor, Henry III (1574–1589), managed to surpass. All in all, he is remembered primarily for his power struggles with his mother and for the blood shed on Saint Bartholomew's Day.

BIBLIOGRAPHY

Holt, Mack P. *The French Wars of Religion, 1562–1629.* Cambridge, U.K., 1995.

Salmon, J. H. M. *Society in Crisis: France in the Sixteenth Century.* New York, 1975.

MACK P. HOLT

CHARLES THE BOLD (1433–1477), duke of Burgundy (1467–1477). The last of the great Burgundian dukes, Charles ruled over a patchwork of territories that had been cobbled together over the previous century through strategic marriages, inheritance, and warfare. Arguably the most powerful of the emerging Renaissance states, certainly possessing the most magnificent court, Burgundy precariously straddled the border between France and the Holy Roman Empire. Charles the Bold's desire to expand the territories acquired by his immediate predecessors, preferably at the expense of his hated rival Louis XI (ruled 1461–1483), led him to engage in several risky military enterprises; his sobriquet "le Téméraire" is often translated not as "the Bold" but as "the Rash."

The son of Philip the Good and Isabella of Portugal, Charles was born at Dijon on 10 November 1433. Although he was the third son, Charles was the only one to survive infancy, thus becoming the focus of all Philip's hopes. At a very early age Charles was named count of Charolais and made a knight of the Golden Fleece. He was first married to Catherine de Bourbon (the daughter of the French king Charles VII) in 1446, but she died before the marriage was consummated. In 1454 Charles married Isabella de Bourbon, with whom he had his only child, Marie.

Early on Charles was moderately pro-French, even receiving the office of governor of Normandy from Louis XI upon the latter's succession in 1461. Very quickly, however, Charles saw that his Burgundian aspirations could only be achieved by thwarting Louis XI's own attempts to expand French territory and consolidate monarchical authority. Charles assumed the leadership of a noble coalition called the

League of the Public Weal, which launched a rebellion against Louis XI in 1464. The first phase of Charles's ongoing battle with Louis XI ended with the Treaty of Conflans, which gave back to Burgundy territories on the Somme River that Louis XI had previously annexed. When Louis XI subsequently reneged on many of the promises made to the nobles, Charles hoodwinked the French king by luring him to a meeting at Péronne. There Charles made Louis XI his captive and forced the king, by way of punishment, to participate in the sacking of Liège, whose inhabitants Louis had previously encouraged to rebel against Burgundian overlordship.

Charles's anti-French orientation led him to conclude an alliance with Edward IV of England, whose daughter Margaret became his third wife in 1468. After receiving assurances of English support, Charles continued to harass Louis XI, driving troops into the heart of French territory and ravaging parts of Île-de-France before concluding a truce in November 1472. In his bid to enlarge the Burgundian patrimony, Charles proceeded to acquire Alsace in 1469 and Gelderland in 1473. He then turned his attention to Lorraine, but by this time Louis XI had convinced Edward IV to abandon the Anglo-Burgundian alliance; Charles was forced to take on Lorraine, the last piece to his territorial puzzle, alone. Between 1475 and 1477 Charles fought the combined armies of the Swiss cantons, Sigismund of Austria, and René of Lorraine. He was killed on the battlefield outside Nancy on 5 January 1477.

Charles's dreams of a magnificent "middle kingdom" did not outlive him. Without a male heir, by Salic law the province of Burgundy reverted to France. Charles's daughter, Marie, initially courted by Louis XI as a wife for the dauphin, Charles, was instead married to Maximilian of Austria, thereby delivering the rest of the Burgundian lands into the hands of the Habsburgs. Charles's death also signaled the end of the golden age of Burgundian art. Although Charles's artistic patronage appears to have been less enthusiastic and sustained than that of his forebears, during his reign the International Gothic style continued to flourish. Works such as the St. Columba altarpiece by Rogier van der Weyden, on which the figure of Charles the Bold as the third of the Three Magi figures prominently, bear testimony to the cultural importance of the last Valois duke of Burgundy.

[For an image of Charles and his father, Philip the Good, see the entry on Burgundy.]

See also **Burgundy.**

BIBLIOGRAPHY

Bittmann, Karl. *Ludwig XI und Karl der Kühne: Die Memoiren des Philippe de Commynes als historische Quelle.* Göttingen, Germany, 1964.
Soisson, Jean-Pierre. *Charles le Téméraire.* Paris, 1997.
Vaughan, Richard. *Charles the Bold: The Last Valois Duke of Burgundy.* New York, 1974.

ADRIANNA E. BAKOS

CHARRON, PIERRE (1541–1603), French theologian and moral philosopher. Son of a Parisian bookseller, Pierre Charron studied at the University of Paris, where he was exposed to both scholastic and humanistic influences. He then pursued law at the universities of Orléans and Bourges, the latter while Jacques Cujas taught the philological approach to Roman law there. After his ordination to the priesthood, he completed his legal education at Montpellier in 1571, when he obtained degrees in both civil and canon law. He then established himself as a popular preacher in the Bordeaux region (a Protestant stronghold), where he was befriended by Margaret, queen of Navarre, who made him her household priest, and by Michel de Montaigne, who influenced the development of his moral thought.

Charron is sometimes caricatured as systematizing the moral lessons scattered throughout Montaigne's *Essais,* although in reality the priest had more ambitious goals. Writing during the last and most violent phase of the French Wars of Religion, Charron sought to diffuse religious hatred by distinguishing faith from reason while maintaining the presence of the divinity in both realms. His major works, *Les trois veritez* (The three truths) and *De la sagesse* (Of wisdom), form complementary halves of this project. *Trois veritez* (1593) establishes three fundamental truths of Christianity while *Sagesse* (1601; revised 1604), using the same tripartite structure, establishes the fundamental qualities of the human condition as separate from, yet subordinate to, religion. One of the most popular works of late Renaissance moral philosophy, *Sagesse* was widely viewed by admirers and critics alike as sanctioning a morality entirely apart from religion. Thus, ironically, this work of a devout priest garnered the sobriquet "breviary of the libertines."

BIBLIOGRAPHY

Belin, Christian. *L'oeuvre de Pierre Charron, 1541–1603: Littérature et théologie de Montaigne à Port-Royal.* Paris, 1995.
Kogel, Renée. *Pierre Charron.* Geneva, 1972.
Sabrié, J. B. *De l'humanisme au rationalisme: Pierre Charron (1541–1603).* Paris, 1913. Still the standard analysis of Charron's life and work.

Schiffman, Zachary Sayre. *On the Threshold of Modernity: Relativism in the French Renaissance*. Baltimore, 1991. See chapter 4.

ZACHARY S. SCHIFFMAN

CHÂTEAUX. The Renaissance château retained traces of its early origins as the defensive château-fort, the medieval fortress and seat of seigniorial power. Even in these earlier residences, builders and owners were also interested in elements of comfort and elegance, whether in the arrangement of rooms or in the furnishings and decorations. The later history of the château continues to carry forth these two elements: the buildings' role in military power and defense, and the desire to create a residence that would reflect changing ideals of luxury. The high point of the medieval châteaux was in the schemes developed during the reign of Philip-Augustus in the first half of the thirteenth century with their simple and effective plans based on the study of ancient forts (as reflected by Coucy, rebuilt c. 1225–1250, and later by the Louvre, begun by King Charles V in 1370).

The pattern of building during the later Middle Ages and the Renaissance was uneven; there was a flurry of building during the Hundred Years' War (1337–1453), then under Charles V and Charles VI, and again during the second half of the fifteenth century and through the Renaissance, when many of the earlier fortresses were transformed into châteaux de plaisance (country retreats).

The Châteaux of Francis I.

King Francis I (ruled 1515–1547) was a prodigious builder and began work at Blois soon after his accession. The asymmetry of the new Francis I wing and subsequent additions derive from the use of existing foundations for the new construction and the traditional French propensity for additive architecture. Classical ornament, pilasters, and grotesque work are applied to the surface of the facade. Against this rich treatment of the surface of the building, the monumental staircase (1515–1524) in the inner court is a highly sculptural interpretation of the spiral form popular in earlier French building. The new facade over the town (1520–1524) projects off the cliff in a series of open loggias built on a vast substructure, comparable to the contemporary loggias by Donato Bramante at the Vatican Palace in Rome.

Work at Chambord (1519–1550) spans the reign of Francis I and was eventually completed after his death. The overall plan derives from medieval châteaux—especially the model of Vincennes (completed by Charles V in 1370) with a square keep surrounded by round towers with connecting buildings—though here the keep is divided into a Greek cross around a vast double-helix staircase. There are similarities to Giuliano da Sangallo's designs for the Medici villa at Poggio a Caiano, a possible result of the work of Domenico da Cortona (perhaps a student of Sangallo) at Chambord. Any Italian influence, however, is overshadowed by the essentially French character of the massive towers and highly original roof, filled with chimneys and turrets that continue the inventive spirit of flamboyant Gothic design.

Gilles de Breton's Porte Dorée at Fontainebleau (1528–1540) transforms a medieval fortified gate with vertically stacked windows into a triumphal arch, a French interpretation of classical prototypes. At the Château de Madrid (Paris, begun 1523), towers of apartments were connected by open loggias decorated with glazed and colored terra-cotta, designed by Girolamo della Robbia. According to contemporary observers (the château was destroyed) the effect was that of a glittering and ethereal surface, a fantastic combination of French aesthetics and Italian details.

Architectural innovations can also be seen in the châteaux for private individuals such as Azay-le-Rideau (1518–1529), built for Gilles Berthelot, who rose from the middle classes to become the general of finances for Normandy, one of the four treasurers of France under Francis I. His château in the Loire Valley gave him an unimpeachable architectural pedigree: a newly built and grand house, yet closely resembling the earlier traditions of castle architecture. While Azay-le-Rideau uses the architectural language of fortresses—corner towers, moat, and even the medieval plan with one room leading directly into the next—it includes the most up-to-date features: a tower of the classical orders set off against a symmetrical facade, and leading to a grand Italianate staircase.

Classicism and Experimentation.

Since the Italian wars of 1494 to 1559, French culture had close contacts with Italy. Italian artists and architects were employed by the French court, and information on Italian arts and letters was available through the dissemination of printed and manuscript material. Yet even the most avid observers of Italian style sought to adapt it to a French context. Thus classical principles and planning were always mediated by the traditions of French building practice and the variations of climate, available materials, and social habits.

Château of Chambord. The château (near Blois, France) was designed for Francis I, probably by Domenico da Cortona, around 1519. It was constructed between 1519 and 1550. GIRAUDON/ART RESOURCE

When the Venetian architect Sebastiano Serlio (1475–1554) arrived in France (in 1540 or 1541) he was in charge of the building projects and renovations at Fontainebleau. Ancy-le-Franc, however, gives the clearest demonstration of his use of pilasters on all exterior surfaces and a flattened triumphal arch motif on the two main levels of the courtyard. These Italian motifs ultimately have an entirely different effect in combination with the steeply pitched roof and strongly vertical arrangement of all elements.

During the reign of Henry II (1547–1559), Henry's longtime mistress Diane de Poitiers commissioned the architect Philibert de l'Orme (Delorme; c. 1515–1570) to design her château of Anet. Drawing on his experience as an engineer and his training in Italy, de l'Orme composed a highly original scheme. Of the surviving elements, the entrance (c. 1552) recalls military architecture in its block forms and bastions, with the stag, emblem of Diane, appearing as part of the elaborate clock mechanism. The chapel is an investigation of centrally planned structures, reminiscent of Bramante's Tempietto in Rome, though with a more complex structural geometry of projected curves on the surface of a cylinder.

In the second half of the sixteenth century the use of classical details became more pronounced, yet always interpreted through the filter of French aesthetics and building practice. At Écouen, Jean Bullant (c. 1520–1578) used a giant order on the south wing, a more monumental statement than the expected use of superimposed orders. The spacing of the columns and alignment of the dormer windows continue to emphasize the vertical, thus giving a fully French feel even to this more archaeological study of classicism.

Developments and Destruction. The political significance of the French châteaux cannot be overemphasized. Even when they were no longer intended for defensive purposes but for the pleasures of hunting and the profits of land ownership, châteaux denoted the political power of owners and residents. Wary of their symbolic associations, Cardinal Richelieu waged a systematic campaign in the seventeenth century to destroy fortified castles. The French Revolution brought about even more destruction of the great residences, often in order to reuse the stone and building materials.

Major châteaux continued to be built, however, through the seventeenth century. The châteaux built by Salomon de Brosse early in the seventeenth century (Blérancourt, 1612–1619, destroyed; Coulommiers, 1613; and Montceaux, completed 1615) explored the possibilities of architectural massing within the frame of the traditional building types.

Much of what we know about French Renaissance architecture and the history of the châteaux is preserved in the two volumes of Jacques Androuet Du Cerceau's *Les plus excellents bastiments de France* (1576–1579). Intended as a testimony to the excellence of French architecture, the buildings are arranged in a hierarchy based on the status of the owner, with royal buildings coming first. Information about the sites, building materials, symbolism, and current condition are included in the text that accompanies the plans, elevations, perspective views, and details. Du Cerceau's book gave a heightened status to the craze for building in the sixteenth century and allowed armchair travelers, and competitive patrons, the opportunity to visit the great houses of France.

BIBLIOGRAPHY

Primary Work

Du Cerceau, Jacques Androuet. *Les plus excellents bastiments de France.* Paris, 1576–1579.

Secondary Works

Babelon, Jean-Pierre. *Les Châteaux de France au siècle de la Renaissance.* Paris, 1989.

Blunt, Anthony. *Art and Architecture in France, 1500–1700.* New Haven, Conn., and London, 1953.

Gebelin, François. *Les châteaux de la Renaissance.* Paris, 1927.

Pérouse de Montclos, Jean-Marie. *Histoire de l'architecture française de la Renaissance à la Revolution.* Paris, 1989.

Zerner, Henri. *L'art de la Renaissance en France: L'invention du classicisme.* Paris, 1996.

CHRISTY ANDERSON

CHEMISTRY. Chemistry is a discipline concerned with the principles and elements of which substances are composed and into which they can be decomposed. During the Renaissance chemistry did not exist as a science in the modern sense, although beginnings were made in a "chemical philosophy" from which the science emerged in the seventeenth and eighteenth centuries. The proximate foundation of this philosophy was the alchemical work of Paracelsus (1493–1541), and only gradually did chemical philosophy differentiate itself from Paracelsian alchemy. With hindsight one might say that Renaissance chemistry is alchemy considered without its magical and mystical elements, but such a consideration would be more in the minds of historians than in the minds of the discipline's early practitioners.

We shall regard the early practitioners as basically concerned with the elemental constituents of things, working in the fields of metallurgy and medical chemistry and adumbrating later laboratory and quantitative techniques. The investigators were mainly Paracelsian, but in some cases anti-Paracelsian, in their outlooks. Paracelsus himself is usually characterized as an alchemist, yet his main interest was in the invention of new and nontoxic metals for medicinal uses, not in their transmutation into gold. And, prescinding from his spiritual and magical views, he would also qualify as a chemical philosopher. He devised new laboratory methods for concentrating alcohol by detoxification and freezing, described many new preparations arising from the combination of metals, developed a new way to prepare nitric acid, and was the first to group chemicals according to their susceptibility to similar chemical processes.

Metallurgy. The Italian Vannoccio Biringuccio (1480–c. 1539), a contemporary of Paracelsus, made significant contributions to the chemistry of metals. These are all documented in a single work, his *De la pirotechnia* (On pyrotechnics) published posthumously in 1540. Biringuccio's theoretical framework was Aristotelian, but his practice with metals and ores was more modern. He wrote extensively on metallic ores and on assaying and preparing them for smelting; on "semiminerals" such as mercury, sulfur, alum, arsenic, vitriol, gems, and glass; on the parting of gold and silver with nitric acid and with antimony sulfide; and on alloys of gold, silver, copper, lead, and tin. He also experimented with furnaces; with the distillation of acids and alcohol; and with the making of saltpeter, gunpowder, and fireworks for various purposes. The *Pirotechnia* contains eighty-three woodcuts, some depicting furnaces for distillation, mechanisms used in bellows, and other devices.

Similar work with metals and ores was done by the Germans Georgius Agricola (1494–1555) and Lazarus Ercker (c. 1530–1594). Agricola's *De re metallica* (1556), though mainly concerned with mining, presented a systematic survey of metallurgical knowledge, including techniques for working with metals and the laboratories and apparatus this work employed. Ercker, also a mining expert, built on Agricola's foundation. His *Beschreibung* (Description; 1574), regarded by some as the first manual of analytical and metallurgical chemistry, is a systematic study of silver, gold, copper, antimony, mercury, bismuth, and lead. It treats ways of obtaining and refining these metals, and then of obtaining acids, salts, and other compounds from them.

Medical Chemistry. Germans were also leaders in developing Paracelsus's iatrochemistry, or therapeutic chemistry, along fuller lines. Among the earlier group, Adam of Bodenstein (1528–1577) and Andreas Libavius (c. 1560–1616) are worthy of mention. Adam edited and translated Paracelsus's works, concentrating on the relationship between minerals and medicine and advocating the use of metallic compounds by physicians. Also interested in the writings of Arnaldus of Villanova (c. 1240–1311), Adam propounded the medieval teaching that mercury is the primary matter of metallic bodies and that sulfur and mercury can be transmuted into gold by processes going on in the bowels of the earth. Libavius, by way of opposition, was anti-Paracelsian and Aristotelian in outlook. His chief work was *Alchymia,* which appeared in several forms between 1597 and 1606. The last, a folio edition, contains more than two hundred designs and pictures of chemical glassware, apparatuses, and furnaces, along with plans for building a chemical laboratory. Libavius was especially interested in the analysis of mineral waters. Although he took much of his material from the books of Agricola and Ercker, Libavius is commonly seen as a founder of chemical analysis.

A slightly different development is seen in the writings of Oswald Croll (c. 1560–1609) and Johannes Hartmann (1568–1631). Croll was more Paracelsian in orientation, considering the harmony of microcosm and macrocosm as the foundation of medicine. He performed practical chemical experiments in the attempt to determine the properties of his chemical remedies, which he recorded in his *Basilica chymica* (Chemical edifice; 1609). In contrast to Paracelsus's vagueness, Croll described in detail his individual preparations, their composition, and their application. *Basilica* became the first textbook of medical chemistry, being used by Hartmann on its publication when he introduced pharmaceutical chemistry in a course he taught at the University of Marburg. There he gave lectures and laboratory instruction on the chemical and mineralogical preparation of medicines. He himself avoided alchemical speculation and sought instead to mediate between the Galenists and iatrochemists of his time.

In France Guy de La Brosse (c. 1586–1641) combined expertise in botany with an interest in medicine and chemistry. He was the founder and in 1626 the first director ("intendant," but not "superintendant") of the Royal Botanical Garden in Paris. Guy admired Paracelsus because of the latter's stress on experience and experiment and his opposition to Aristotle and Galen. The third of his five books on the nature of plants (1628) he regarded as "a general treatise on chemistry," which he saw as an important adjunct to both medicine and botany. Chemistry, for him, is based on the assumption that every body can be reduced to the entities from which it is formed. Only when substances have been reduced to their principles and elements, he said, can we truly understand them. All natural composed bodies, he held, can be reduced to five simple bodies of different natures—the three principles of the Paracelsians (salt, sulfur, and mercury) and only two of the traditional elements (water and earth). Guy rejected fire and air as elements, air because of the large number of substances it contains, fire because it is the "universal instrument" of chemical change, not a substance itself.

Modern Innovations. In Belgium Jan Baptista van Helmont (1579–1644), despite his strong mystical inclinations, made notable contributions in chemistry and medicine. His scientific methodology included extensive use of the balance, quantification, and experiment. His chemical analysis of smoke led him to call it a "gas" with properties specific to the substance of its origin, thus different from air and water vapor. Helmont identified a number of such gases, including carbon dioxide and carbon monoxide from burning charcoal, chlorine gas from the reaction of nitric acid and sal ammoniac, sulfur dioxide from burning sulfur, and "explosive gas" from an ignited gunpowder mixture of charcoal, sulfur, and saltpeter. He also designed methods for preparing sulfuric acid, nitric acid, and hydrochloric acid, the last from sea salt and potter's clay. Helmont studied a variety of alkali salts and was familiar with the neutralizing effect of alkali on acid. Further, he recognized specific gravity as a good diagnostic indicator, and was acquainted with, and used, the pendulum for the measurement of time.

In theoretical chemistry the most significant advances were made by Daniel Sennert (1572–1637), professor of medicine at the University of Wittenberg from 1602 to his death. These are recorded in his works on *chymia,* which Paracelsus had placed in the service of medicine. Principal among these is his *De chymicorum cum Aristotelicis et Galenicis consensu ac dissensu* (The agreement and disagreement of chemists with Aristotelians and Galenists), published at Wittenberg in 1619, with an expanded edition in 1629. Sennert himself was an Aristotelian in natural philosophy and a Galenist in humoral pathology, and his aim was to reconcile the teachings of Aristotle, Galen, and Paracelsus with ancient atomic theorists. He accepted the three Paracelsian principles of sulfur, salt, and mercury, but thought of them as *mista* (mixed), composed of the four traditional elements, fire, air, water, and earth. In his view the forms of the elements persist in compounds, but they do so under a superior form that accounts for the new properties that the compound manifests.

Sennert's principle of analysis was that natural bodies consist of the things into which they can be decomposed, and so of those of which they are composed. He thought of these components as *minima,* or very small particles. Chemical reaction, for him, consists in a body's splitting up into specific *minima,* which then move about and reform as a new body. The end product is not a mere assemblage of the particles, however, but a new substance with its own nature and distinctive attributes. In 1629 he saw this type of reaction at work in such chemical processes as distillation, sublimation, coagulation, the melting of the gold-silver alloy, and the solution of silver in nitric acid and of common salt in water. By 1636 he advocated the inalterable persistence of the particles themselves. And finally, for Sennert chemistry was not merely an art auxiliary to medicine, but a discipline in its own right whose goal is to decompose natural substances and prepare them for use.

See also Alchemy; Matter, Structure of.

BIBLIOGRAPHY

Debus, Allen G. *The Chemical Philosophy: Paracelsian Science and Medicine in the Sixteenth and Seventeenth Centuries.* 2 vols. New York, 1977.

Debus, Allen G. *The English Paracelsians.* London, 1965; New York, 1966.

Debus, Allen G. *Science and History: A Chemist's Appraisal.* Coimbra, Portugal, 1984.

Debus, Allen G., ed. *Science, Medicine, and Society in the Renaissance: Essays to Honor Walter Pagel.* New York, 1972.

Hannaway, Owen. *The Chemists and the Word: The Didactic Origins of Chemistry.* Baltimore and London, 1975.

Multhauf, Robert P. *The Origins of Chemistry.* London, 1966.

WILLIAM A. WALLACE

CHILDHOOD. Children were important primarily because there were so many of them. During the Renaissance more than half the population was under twenty-five, an age distribution not unlike that of many developing countries in the twentieth century. They were also the instruments of one of the fundamental organizing principles of Renaissance society—inheritance.

Young people were treated in contradictory ways. They were expected to be obedient and respectful, yet once they had survived infancy the difficulty of taming their rebelliousness and transforming them into moral beings proved a constant challenge.

The Meaning of Childhood.
Childhood was commonly thought to begin at age seven and end at fourteen. Children under seven, the stage labeled "infancy," belonged to the world of women. After seven, children were regarded as capable of being instructed. In some places the laws considered children under fourteen to be capable of committing adult crimes. Confirmation and first communion took place between seven and fourteen. Many children started to work before age fourteen; some boys were legally declared released from parental control ("emancipated") as young as nine, and some were required to bear arms when they were even younger. The upper boundary of fourteen seems to have meant little.

Historians have disagreed about the experience of childhood in this period. Some have emphasized the constraints imposed on children and the apparent absence of warmth and playfulness. Others claim there is abundant evidence of real love and tender care. The controversy is far from settled, since it is difficult to apply this spotty data to all social groups and all types of households.

Childhood was considered a state of powerlessness, which required adults to assert control, as children left to themselves might not lose their animal impulses. Great effort was needed to tame their wildness, which was seen as evidence of original sin. Dealing with children was assumed to be a battle of wills, in which the only good outcome was their capitulation to authority.

Children also needed protection against the forces of evil. The devil's work was closely associated with sexuality. Some scholars have suggested that children were not protected from exposure to coarse and blasphemous language or gambling and excessive drinking. Such behavior was impossible to avoid in the ordinary life of village and town and in the close confines of most houses, but there was nevertheless general agreement that precocious sexuality should not be encouraged. Apart from the household, most institutions intended for children were sexually segregated.

Upbringing.
Generalizations about upbringing are difficult because of class differences and the absence of regulation and standardization, but it can be said that play had a part in childhood at all social levels. The few toys that have survived look much like the balls, sticks, hoops, dolls, and marbles of later times. There were occasional references in writing to games, as well as to improvised horseplay. Pieter Brueghel the Elder's painting *Children's Games* (1560) gives some hints. It is unlikely that there was much solitary play. Children who lived in the very small houses of the poor probably did most of their playing out of doors.

Young Reader. *Young Cicero Reading* by Vincenzo Foppa (c. 1427–c. 1516). Fresco; c. 1464. WALLACE COLLECTION, LONDON/THE BRIDGEMAN ART LIBRARY

While scholars have speculated about the cold atmosphere surrounding children in their homes, this notion is somewhat challenged by the frequency with which writers on education chastised parents for overindulging their children. This was thought to deprive children of necessary control and was associated primarily with the lower classes. A distinguished man like Thomas More (c. 1478–1535) however, proudly confessed to unbounded affection for his children.

Many children were motherless, fatherless, or completely orphaned. Relatives took orphans into their homes, sometimes reluctantly. It remains uncertain whether life for orphans was more difficult than life for other children. Rich orphans were sometimes shamelessly exploited by their guardians. The most deprived children were those who were abandoned and left to be raised in foundling homes like the Ospedale degli Innocenti (Hospital of the Holy Innocents) in Florence, some run by religious orders, some by municipalities.

Children started learning about religion in the household at a very early age, often from women. The heads of larger households led regular morning and evening prayers; in wealthy households, a chaplain or an almoner led prayers. The pressure to do this became even greater after the Reformation. Humanist advisers of women held that the reading of stories distracted from religion and morality. After the Reformation the disapproval of superstitious stories intensified under both Catholics and Protestants, but their appeal remained undiminished, probably because adults remembered how stories had moved and sometimes frightened them.

The serious training that started around the age of seven almost always took place in a household. Peasant children of both sexes started helping around the house even before they were seven. One form of early work was looking after younger children. In wealthy households children were likely to pass from wet nurses into the hands of governesses and tutors. As in peasant households, gender differentiation was pronounced. Girls learned needlework and something of household management, while boys were taught horsemanship and hunting. At the age of five, six, or seven, fortunate boys and girls began formal schooling, either inside or outside the home. The form (whether Latin or vernacular) and quantity of education varied according to the economic and social status of the family, the sex of the pupils, the expectations of their parents, and the availability of schooling.

In northwestern Europe children of both town and country commonly left home. Peasant children

Pieter Brueghel the Elder. *Children's Games.* Wood; 1560; 118 × 161 cm (46.5 × 63.4 in.). KUNSTHISTORISCHES MUSEUM, VIENNA/ARTOTHEK

of both sexes often went to live in other peasant households and sometimes to great country houses or to better-off urban ones. Some children became apprentices with craftsmen or, if they were of the appropriate social rank, with merchants or professionals like physicians and lawyers. At the very highest social levels children entered the houses of great nobles or princes. There was no set age at which children left home, and the length of time away from home varied as much as the age at which it happened. Peasant children might return after a year or two, spend some time working at home, and then leave again. Apprenticeships usually lasted for several years and generally meant a permanent separation from home. The people who took in children also took on the educational and disciplinary roles of the children's parents. Arrangements with masters were usually made by the children's parents. In one

guise or another this experience was common up and down the social scale.

In Italy, upper-class families were less likely to send their children away from home during the Renaissance. Even craft apprentices in Italy tended to work with their own fathers or with masters in the same town and continued to live at home. The Venetian ambassador to England, Daniele Barbaro, commented about the English practice in his *Relazione* (Italian relations) of 1551. Barbaro's comments reveal not only his incomprehension but also hint at the benefits of the practice, so widespread in Europe. He speaks of "the want of affection in the English" and of "hard service in the houses of other people" starting "at the age or seven or nine years at the utmost. . . . And on inquiring their reason for this severity, they answered that they did it in order that their children might learn better manners" (translated and quoted in Molly Harrison and O. M. Royston, eds., *How They Lived,* Oxford, 1962–1969, pp. 167–168).

Books of courtesy and etiquette give us an idea of the elaborate code of behavior expected of those who frequented the courts of powerful people. These books were directed at young boys and stressed the acquisition of both good manners and the skills of serving a noble lord at table. The sons and daughters of gentlemen learned a great deal at court. They also forged links between their families and the families they served and made valuable contacts for their own later careers. Fathers who chose not to give their sons this experience were thought to have done them them a disservice.

Youth. The transition to youth from childhood was imperceptible, variable, and ambiguous. Almost everything that has been said about childhood also pertains to youth. The same juridical conditions applied, and the same deferential behavior to adults. In spite of this, the signs of physical maturation made a difference. These seem to have appeared fairly late, past the conventional age marker of fourteen. Research suggests that this was true not only of menstruation in girls but also of voice change and facial hair in boys.

Strength, health, and beauty were youthful characteristics that were praised and envied. Adults tended to be nostalgic about their own youth. Many remembered it as a carefree time rather than one of subservience and hard work, although some master craftsmen took advantage of apprentices by having them do full-scale productive work without paying them regular wages. Another characteristic of youth was irresponsibility, encouraged by the absence of autonomy. Sports and games might become rambunctious, especially when combined with drinking and gambling, activities specifically forbidden in apprenticeship contracts. Some youthful activities were semiautonomous, following old village traditions. Youth groups organized seasonal celebrations and supervised courtship behavior. Membership in such groups was generally limited to unmarried males—the functional definition of "youth."

For most people of both sexes being a servant was equated with youth. The conventional view was that servants were both young and single. If they had not left home before age fourteen, they were likely to do so shortly afterward. Especially in the countryside the period of service could go on for many years and usually consisted of a series of relatively short stays with different masters. Servants had considerable geographical mobility, moving from village to village, town to town, and, for females particularly, from country to town. The wandering was not considered a sign of independence but rather a movement from one quasi-paternal dependent relationship to another. Some highborn young men and women served in noble houses in their teens and twenties, as some had started to do when they were younger. Apprenticeship sometimes continued well into the twenties and was the form of service with the most well defined rules. Stereotypes of apprentices—that they were abused by masters or that they were difficult to control—repeated the stereotypes of youth in general.

The end of youth came only with a change in legal status. Not surprisingly, youth was the time for courtship. The primary entry into adulthood was marriage, which brought with it a degree of autonomy. It usually coincided with the end of apprenticeship and other kinds of service, for men and women alike. Women, however, did not achieve the same legal autonomy. They passed from childhood to the dependency of wifehood. Some men passed from childhood to an adulthood of partial dependency in monasteries. Some men became technically autonomous without getting married if their fathers chose to emancipate them. Age did not define adulthood, but marriage certainly terminated childhood and youth.

See also **Birth and Infancy; Education; Family and Kinship; Life Stages; Literacy; Motherhood.**

BIBLIOGRAPHY

Ariès, Philippe. *Centuries of Childhood: A Social History of Family Life.* Translated by Robert Baldick. New York, 1962. Translation of *L'enfant et la vie familiale sous l'ancien régime* (1960). An influential work, which has been criticized on many counts since its publication.

Boswell, John. *The Kindness of Strangers: The Abandonment of Children in Western Europe from Late Antiquity to the Renaissance.* New York, 1988.

Cunningham, Hugh. *Children and Childhood in Western Society since 1500.* New York, 1995.

Davis, Natalie Zemon. *Society and Culture in Early Modern France; Eight Essays.* Stanford, Calif., 1975. See "The Reasons of Misrule," pp. 97–123, about youth groups.

Kussmaul, Ann. *Servants in Husbandry in Early Modern England.* Cambridge, U.K., 1981.

Mitterauer, Michael. *A History of Youth: Family, Sexuality, and Social Relations in Past Times.* Oxford and Cambridge, Mass., 1993.

Orme, Nicholas. *From Childhood to Chivalry: The Education of the English Kings and Aristocracy, 1066–1530.* London, 1984.

Trexler, Richard C. *Power and Dependence in Renaissance Florence.* Vol. 1, *The Children of Renaissance Florence.* Binghamton, N.Y., 1993.

BEATRICE GOTTLIEB

CHINA. *See* Asia, East.

CHIVALRY. [This entry includes four subentries:

Knighthood and Chivalric Orders
Romance of Chivalry
English Arthurian Romance
Chivalry in Renaisssance Art]

Knighthood and Chivalric Orders

Chivalry (from the French *chevalier*) referred to the heavily armed men on horseback, the knights, who gave medieval warfare its special character and formed the nucleus of an evolving hereditary aristocracy. The word also signified the ethos and culture of chivalry, which, particularly in its Renaissance phase, is the subject of this article.

Medieval Chivalry. Chivalric ideals and values derived from a variety of sources, including Christian ethical teachings, troubadour poetry, and romance literature. Feudal relationships, with their demands of personal loyalty and service, were a practical school of chivalry, while the Crusades harnessed the ideal of the Knight of Christ to the pursuit of land and treasure. Calatrava, Santiago, the Hospitallers, Templars, and other orders fused monastic austerity, crusading ardor, and military skill. In Spain and the Holy Land Christian knights observed, and may have borrowed from, Moorish and Saracen models of refined comportment. In the households of their lords peacetime warriors read and modeled themselves after the Rolands, El Cids, and Sir Gawains of Carolingian and Arthurian romance, elaborating rules for conducting love affairs, devising norms of etiquette and style, and dreaming deeds of knight errantry. The culture of these feudal courts still resonates in such terms as "courtly," "courtship," and "courtesy."

While the chansons de geste (medieval epic poems) and other romances celebrated the peerless chivalry of legendary heroes, John of Salisbury and other twelfth-century critics ridiculed real knights and courtiers as vainglorious and faithless. More practically, thirteenth-century chivalric manuals tried to educate Christian warriors to the ideals and obligations of their creed. The first of these was the anonymous *L'Orden de Chivalrie,* followed by the more expansive and enduringly popular *Libro de la orden de Caballeria* by Ramon Llull, the Catalan cleric, philosopher, former knight, and courtier who dreamed of a crusade in North Africa. Many others followed.

Whatever self-improving effects the handbooks may have had, they did not silence the perennial complaints that chivalry was dead or dying—nor could they do so, since nostalgia for a mythical heroic past was part of chivalric culture. Historians have tended to view late medieval chivalry as an outmoded institution, citing the growing disenchantment with crusading, the demise of the Templars, the decline of the Teutonic Knights and other orders, the displacement of heavily armed cavalry by infantry and artillery, the growth of urban commercial life, and the end of feudalism itself. Johan Huizinga recognized that chivalric values and perceptions continued to rule the minds of fourteenth- and fifteenth-century nobles and princes, but he regarded their way of thinking as increasingly outmoded and fantastic, causing them to mistake the ideal world of chivalry for the real world of politics, business, and military science.

Such views, according to critics, are moral judgment disguised as historical fact. Maurice Keen maintains that chivalry "retained its vigour [to the end of the fifteenth century] because it remained relevant to the social and political realities of the time" (p. 219). In part, its continued relevance can be accounted for by the continued influence of the military aristocracy. Even in Renaissance Italy the blue blood of the old feudal *magnati* (magnates) flowed in the veins of many of the urban patricians and *signori* (lords) who dominated the political and social life of the urban communes. A noble lineage and aristocratic style continued to be important assets for men who aspired to become prelates or diplomats—or to marry wealthy brides. Urban governments were as preoccupied with war and the threat of war as feudal princes, and scarcely less dependent on skilled, mounted warriors. Magnanimity, courage, service, loyalty, Christian faith, and erotic grace—the essentials of chivalric honor—were extolled in princely and civic pageantry and tournaments, while a growing reading public devoured the old Carolingian and Arthurian romances and the new works they inspired.

Chivalry in a Changing Society. Knightly orders and brotherhoods were formed with even greater frequency in the fourteenth and fifteenth

A Procession of Knights. *Procession of the Knights of the Garter* by Marcus Gheeraerts the Elder, 1576. © THE BRITISH MUSEUM, LONDON

centuries than in the heyday of the Crusades. While many nobles continued to cultivate military traditions and to demonstrate their prowess in tournaments and war, they were now likely to do so under the auspices or in the service of a reigning prince—or, in communal Italy, of a sovereign republic. These orders were made up of lay knights, and the most important of them, including Hungary's Fraternal Society of St. George (1325–1326), Castile's Order of the Banda (1330), England's Order of the Garter (1344–1349), and Burgundy's Order of the Golden Fleece (1431) were commanded by their princely founders largely for secular purposes. By 1469, according to D'Arcy Boulton, "virtually every major court in Europe had a knightly order adequate to its needs" (p. 448). This, together with the consolidation of princely courts by marital unions, not a decline in chivalry's appeal, explains the absence of new foundations for another century.

Chivalric culture thus continued to be viable in the late Middle Ages and Renaissance because it expressed the values and stirred the emotions of powerful and influential elites in a society that still had strong ties to its feudal past. But the nature of political power and social relations was changing and the code of chivalry was beginning to serve different people and different ends. Nobility came to signify a hereditary social status, while men who had never shattered a lance in battle were claiming the dignity of knighthood. Military lineage, possession of a landed estate, and an aristocratic lifestyle continued to define a family as noble. The taint of trade, manual labor, or "new money" in one's parentage remained serious obstacles. But a crooked limb on an otherwise noble family tree might be made straight if the pretender to nobility was a distinguished jurist, a high princely functionary or a rich man who knew how to use his wealth to good purpose. Parvenus adopted the symbols and manners of chivalry, sought the title of knight, and devised coats of arms. Wearing a sword in public marked the wearer as a member of an ancient chivalric community where knights settled questions of honor among themselves.

The Duel of Honor. The preoccupation with dignity, reputation, and family standing—all subsumed under the rubric of "honor"—was most dramatically expressed in the rise of the duel of honor toward the end of the fifteenth century. Unlike the

medieval judicial duel in which, typically, two proxy champions were engaged to determine a third party's guilt or innocence in a criminal matter, the personal duel was fought by two antagonists on their own behalf over a question of honor. The rampant spread of the duel of honor in the sixteenth century is symptomatic of the insecurity that accompanied social mobility and the permeability of social boundaries. Fostered by dozens of duel treatises (a virtual Italian monopoly), the punctilio (careful observance of form) of the duel took on a life of its own. Whether or not they actually crossed swords, antagonists who could afford the expense published elegant printed copies of the *cartelli,* the written messages and opinions that had passed between them. The aim was to prove to "the world" that they had scrupulously observed the protocol of honor. At the middle of the sixteenth century the most renowned exponent of "chivalric science" was the man of letters Girolamo Muzio, whose genius, Claudio Donati remarks, "was to realize that the matter of the duel was no longer the exclusive concern of a restricted circle of knights dedicated to the military profession, but had come to assume a much wider social and ideological relevance" (p. 95). Pride and anger, the besetting sins of a warrior society, had become the defining virtues of Renaissance gentlemen.

Churchmen assiduously denounced the duel of honor as unchristian, and rulers banned it as destructive of the peace. Antidueling treatises poured forth. In 1563 the Council of Trent decreed excommunication for duelists and their supporters. The effectiveness of these measures is difficult to estimate since they were unevenly and inconsistently applied. At most the craze abated, but dueling did not disappear. Princes themselves reflected the general ambivalence: keepers of the public peace and arbiters of justice on one hand, they were also leaders and models of the honor culture. Some princes, like Duke Cosimo I de' Medici of Tuscany (1519–1574; ruled 1537–1574), banned it from their territories while acting as consultants for duels elsewhere. Even monarchs fought duels—or tried to do so—as in the famous case of the challenge to the emperor Charles V by King Francis I in 1528.

In 1561, after a hiatus of more than a century during which no new military orders appeared, Duke Cosimo I of Tuscany founded the Order (or *Religione* as it was frequently called) of Santo Stefano, and in 1572 Prince Emanuele Filiberto of Savoy founded the Order of San Maurizio e San Lazzaro. With the Mediterranean and eastern Europe under attack by the Ottoman Turks, these orders, unlike those of the fifteenth century, reached back to the crusading tradition, their *cavalieri* obliged to abide by chivalric statutes and to live under monastic discipline while training for war. If their inspiration was medieval, however, they served the purposes of Renaissance statecraft and Counter-Reformation religious politics. By providing opportunities for glory and preferment they attracted young nobles to the service of their princes. By providing skilled knights for the defense of Christendom they gave the small states of Tuscany and Savoy leverage vis-à-vis Spain and the papacy, Italy's dominant powers. Santo Stefano's marine-carrying galleys won distinction at the relief of Malta in 1565 and the Battle of Lepanto in 1571.

Chivalric Literature of the Renaissance.

Fostered by princes as an ethos of military and civil service, and cultivated by old nobles, gentlemen, and Johnny-come-latelies alike, chivalry also supplied the context for some of the masterpieces of Renaissance literature. In Baldassare Castiglione's classic, *Il libro del Cortegiano* (The book of the courtier; 1528), the medieval Christian knight reemerges as the ideal courtier, and in Stefano Guazzo's *La civile conversazione* (1574) as the cultured Renaissance gentleman. Giovanni Della Casa's *Galateo* (1558) reduced the knightly moral tradition to a matter of refined comportment—and achieved European popularity. Matteo Boiardo's *Orlando innamoroso* (1487) and Ludovico Ariosto's *Orlando furioso* (1516) reworked the Arthurian and Carolingian romances in the light of current psychological, comic, and ironic sensibilities. Luís de Camões' *Os Lusíadas* (The Lusiads; 1572) employed the medieval epic style to celebrate the Portuguese discovery of the ocean route to India, while in *Gerusalemme liberata* (Jerusalem delivered; 1581) Torquato Tasso invested the First Crusade with Counter-Reformation fervor. In *Don Quixote* (1605) Miguel Cervantes tells the story of a gentleman of La Mancha who, his mind affected by reading chivalric romances, embarked on a disastrous career of knight errantry. Don Quixote's misadventures were hugely comic, but it was irony, not ridicule, that Cervantes was after, and he treated his hero with tender sympathy. The novel is a profound commentary on the interplay of realism and idealism that characterized chivalry from the onset. By parodying the medieval romance, *Don Quixote* wrote finis to the genre. And, more effectively than any amount of censure or scorn, the story of the bemused knight brought home the exhaustion of chivalry itself as a guide to life. Huizinga's picture of the chivalric ethos as an anachronism was not so much wrong in its features as premature by three centuries.

Chivalry could not indefinitely survive the rise of sovereign states, knight-errantry the cold opportunism of Machiavellian statecraft, noblesse oblige the logic of capitalist self-interest, or chivalric honor the materialist calculus of success. New institutions and social goals demanded different standards of behavior and decorum and new measures of human worth. Egalitarianism and democracy, ushered in by the French, American, and industrial revolutions, swept away the old aristocracies that were the mainstays of chivalry and thus, seemingly, delivered its coup de grâce. The irony of the popular cliché declaring that "the Age of Chivalry is not dead" lies in its defiance of common sense. Still, such diverse manifestations as the recrudescence of the duel of honor in the antebellum American South, Wilhelmine Germany, and twentieth-century France, the cult of John Wayne and the cowboy western, and the currency of violent honor codes among the street gangs of Los Angeles, New York, and Mexico City all demonstrate that centuries after the death of medieval and Renaissance chivalry modern culture does not lack for inventiveness in idealizing aggressive male impulses.

See also **Duel; Honor; Tournaments.**

BIBLIOGRAPHY

Primary Works

Ariosto, Ludovico. *Orlando Furioso.* Translated by Barbara Reynolds. New York, 1975.

Camões, Luís de. *The Lusiads.* Translated by Leonard Bacon. New York, 1950.

Castiglione, Baldassare. *The Book of the Courtier.* Translated by George Bull. Baltimore, 1967.

Cervantes Saavedra, Miguel de. *The Adventures of Don Quixote.* Translated by J. M. Cohen. Baltimore, 1950.

Guazzo, Stefano. *The Civile Conversation of M. Steeven Guazzo.* Translated by Edward Sullivan. London, 1925.

Tasso, Torquato. *Gerusalemme Liberata.* Translated by Edward Fairfax. London, 1851.

Secondary Works

Anglo, Sydney, ed. *Chivalry in the Renaissance.* Woodbridge, U.K., 1990.

Barber, Richard. *The Knight and Chivalry.* Woodbridge, U.K., 1995.

Boulton, D'Arcy Jonathan Dacre. *The Knights of the Crown: The Monarchical Orders of Knighthood in Later Medieval Europe 1325–1520.* Woodbridge, U.K., 1987.

Donati, Claudio. *L'Idea di nobiltà in Italia: secoli xiv–xviii.* Rome, 1988.

Huizinga, Johan. *The Waning of the Middle Ages.* Translated by F. Hopman. London, 1924. New revised translation as *The Autumn of the Middle Ages.* Chicago, 1996. Translation of *Herfsttij der middeleeuwen.*

Keen, Maurice. *Chivalry*. London, 1984.

Morgan, David. "From Death to a View: Louis Robessart, Johan Huizinga, and the Political Significance of Chivalry," In *Chivalry in the Renaissance*. Edited by Sydney Anglo. Woodbridge, U.K., 1990.

Vale, Malcolm G. A. *War and Chivalry: Warfare and Aristocratic Culture in England, France, and Burgundy at the End of the Middle Ages*. Athens, Ga., 1981.

DONALD WEINSTEIN

Romance of Chivalry

Medieval Origins. Romance, as a literary form, should be distinguished from the modern idea of a love story. The first romances were adaptations, written in twelfth-century France, of Latin works. For example, the *Roman d'Eneas* (after 1130) derived from Virgil's *Aeneid* (19 B.C.), the story of the founding of Rome. The *Roman de Thèbes* (1155) was based on Statius's *Thebiad* (c. A.D. 90), describing the war fought at Thebes between the sons of Oedipus. The anonymous authors of such romances were undoubtedly clerics who could read Latin. They turned Latin hexameter verse into French eight-syllable couplets and adapted their material to a medieval audience: classical foot soldiers become mounted knights; the camp of Aeneas's soldiers becomes a medieval castle, complete with crenellations. The genre they invented was called *roman* (romance) because they were translating from Latin to French, a Romance language, spoken by the common people.

Chivalry refers both to a moral code of conduct and mode of existence for knights-errant in literature. As a set of ethical ideals, chivalry is a fusion of military, social, and Christian ethics that developed during the Middle Ages and into the Renaissance. Its values included piety, honor, valor, courtesy, chastity, and loyalty to a lord, a cause, or a noblewoman. Over the centuries, what began as a system of virtues appropriate to crusaders protecting military fortresses in foreign lands, like the Knights Templar or Knights Hospitaler, adapted to the changing social conditions of Renaissance courtiers who continued to conduct tournaments long after gunpowder outmoded their need to fight in armor on horseback.

The literary sources of chivalry may be found in the earliest form of medieval French literature, the chansons de geste, or songs of great deeds. The first and greatest of these is *The Song of Roland* (1098), which tells how Roland, Charlemagne's greatest warrior, died at Roncesvalles due to treachery as he protected the rear guard of the French army while crossing the Pyrenees from Spain to France. The chief conflict in later chansons de geste is either between Christians and Saracens or between the great barons and their king, Charlemagne. The military themes of the chansons tended to be lost during the Middle Ages as Arthurian romance became the dominant form but were revived in the Renaissance by Matteo Maria Boiardo (1441–1494), who invented the romance epic, the form that shaped the greatest Renaissance romances of chivalry.

Major Thematic Lines. It would be difficult to overestimate the impact on chivalry of Arthurian romance, which developed out of the work of Chrétien de Troyes. Stories about Lancelot and Guinevere, Gawain, Percival, the Holy Grail, and the related stories of Tristan and Isolde established the pattern of action still followed by Don Quixote in the last great Renaissance romance of chivalry: A knight sets out on a quest—whether for Guinevere in peril or Dulcinea, to right a wrong, complete a task, uproot an enchantment, slay a dragon, or find the way to Heaven. On the way he meets adventure, for which his strength is usually sufficient but his luck, or Fortune, may be good or bad.

These adventures, which threaten to defeat the knight's quest, often require action according to a code of conduct. The ethics involved may be no more than that knights must be strong to win and women must be beautiful or suffer the consequences. But even this most basic formula is morally ambiguous because it is patently unfair. Any joust is a gauge of good and evil in a system where right is supposed to triumph. Good knights try to do the right thing, but they are often at a loss. Values may conflict. How does one remove the foul custom of the castle that one is obligated to defend? How can Tristan or Lancelot remain loyal to their kings and their ladies when each knight loves the king's wife? The best romance authors, like Chrétien, Boiardo, Ludovico Ariosto, and Edmund Spenser, are aware of this problem and create ironic narratives that leave their heroes morally bewildered. The characteristic and endlessly repeated plot devices of romances of chivalry—jousts, tournaments, strange customs, enchantments, giants, pilotless ships, flying horses—justify themselves because they create subtle comparisons between similar situations, allowing readers to register slight changes in moral temperature. Cervantes's joke is that Don Quixote cites unreliable rules from romances of chivalry as he decides how to handle an enchantment or other bad situation. Fredric Jameson has suggested that enchantments are the romance's expression of moral contradictions. Ann Astell argues that the physical combat of the romance quest unveils the allegorical meaning of epic, whose goal is not earthly empire but the struggle of the soul to attain self-knowledge and return to its spiritual home in heaven. Whatever the interpretation, the possibility of moral meanings helps explain the popularity of romances of chivalry for five hundred years.

Italy. Romances tend to be formless and to lack resolution, in contrast to epic, the story of victory told by history's winners. The romance epic as it emerged in Italy, however, complicates this separation of genres and their identification with winners and losers. The new genre may be traced to Giovanni Boccaccio, who recast the Trojan War from a romantic perspective in his *Filostrato* by giving prominence to the tragic love story of Troilus and Cressida, the source of Chaucer's *Troilus* and Shakespeare's *Troilus and Cressida*.

During the course of its development, the romance of chivalry was a protean form, absorbing minor genres like the novella (the short-story form Boccaccio used in his *Decameron*) or the lyric, transforming them into its own likeness. The romance epic multiplied this capability. Boiardo, for example, combined the love and magic of Arthurian romance with the military adventures of Charlemagne's knights. His eight-line stanzas imitated Boccaccio's verse style but also the lyricism of Dante and Petrarch.

Love and the magic, usually associated with Arthurian romance, entered the more military chansons de geste in thirteenth- and early fourteenth-century French romances like *Huon de Bordeaux,* Adenet le Roi's *Berte au grand pied* (Big-foot Bertha), and *La Belle Hélène de Constantinople* (Beautiful Helen of Constantinople). Orlando chases a princess through the East in the *Entrée d'Espagne* (Expedition into Spain), one of the early fifteenth-century romances composed in a combination of French and the Venetian dialect of Italy. Renaissance romances of chivalry continued this mixed tradition in order to preserve the old virtues of chivalry—like friendship, piety, and loyalty—in a world where individual military valor was being replaced by gunpowder wars and the pressures of the Turkish advance in the Mediterranean.

Later Renaissance Italians were also influenced by the prose romances of Andrea de Barberino (c. 1370–after 1431). His stories about the early years of Orlando and the royal house of Charlemagne reached a broad readership in Italy in works like *I*

Reali di Francia (The royal house of France), *Aspramonte, Le storie nerbonesi,* the *Storia di Ajolfo del Barbicone e di altri valorosi cavalieri,* and *Guerino detto il Meschino.* Shorter verse romances called *cantari,* some associated with the name of Antonio Pucci (d. 1388), presented episodes about chivalric knights or ladies (*Cantari di Fiorio e Biancifiore, Il bel Gherardino, Pulzella gaia*). Among the earliest printed books were chivalric romances like *Altobello* (1480), *Trabisonda* (1483), and stories about Troy, Alexander the Great, Rinaldo of Montalbano, and the siege of Pamplona.

Boiardo wrote for an aristocratic audience in Ferrara, where chivalry remained an element of society, along with an interest in Arthurian romance. A few years earlier, Luigi Pulci (1432–1484) composed *Il Morgante Maggiore* (Morgante the giant; 1481) for a more mercantile audience in Florence, a city of bankers. In contrast to Boiardo's ideal world, Pulci's poem, which ends with Orlando's death at Roncesvalles, features comic language, puns, and proverbial sayings still waiting for a full exposition in English. Perhaps no other poem before Ariosto's *Orlando furioso* (Mad Roland; 1516) reveals such a fully self-conscious, ironic narrator.

Boiardo left his story unfinished when he died in 1494. It was brilliantly continued and completed by Ludovico Ariosto (1474–1533). His *Orlando furioso* tells the story of how madness afflicts the warrior Orlando, as a result of his love for Angelica that began in Boiardo's poem.

Like the French romance *Melusine,* which told the fabulous origins of the French House of Lusignan, Boiardo's *Orlando innamorato* (Orlando in love; 1482) and Ariosto's *Orlando furioso* include the dynastic origins of the Este family, rulers of Ferrara. (Boiardo dedicated his poem to Ercole I d'Este, duke of Ferrara, while Ariosto dedicated his to Hippolytus, the brother of Ercole's son Duke Alfonso I.) The success of the Orlando poems touched off an explosion of romances based on minor characters such as Bradamante, Angelica, and Dragontina.

Spain. The vast outpouring of chivalric romances in sixteenth-century Spain coincided with the years of discovery and conquest in the New World. *Reinaldos de Montalván, Melunsina, Santo Gral, Flores y Blancaflor, Paris y Viana, Guarino Mesquino, Lanzarote del Lago,* and *Orlando* were Spanish translations of standard French and Italian romances. Although *Amadís de Gaula,* an original Spanish romance, has been traced to the thirteenth century, its new popularity began with the version of Garcia Rodríguez de Montalvo, first printed in 1508. The first two parts of this often reprinted romance soon included a fifth book, titled *Sergas de Esplandián* (1510); a sixth, titled *Florisando* (1510); a seventh and an eighth, called *Lisuarte de Grecia* (1514 and 1526); a ninth, *Amadís de Grecia* (1530); a tenth, *Florisel de Niquea* (1532); and an eleventh book, *Rogel de Grecia* (1535). Part 3 appeared in 1535, and part 4 was published in Salamanca in 1551. Meanwhile, the first two parts of another popular romance, *Belianís de Grecia* came out in Seville in 1545. Don Alonso de Ercilla y Zuñiga wrote a romance epic about the Spanish conquest of Chile, *La Araucana* (1590).

Popularity of Chivalric Romances. Romances tended to decline in quality, but not in popularity, until the form was revived during the Renaissance. They served as models for real careers and for the stories subsequently told about real people. An Anglo-Norman poet celebrated the life of the Black Prince, son of England's King Edward III, in the fourteenth century, and others similarly celebrated Richard Beauchamp (1382–1439) and the Chevalier Bayard (died 1524).

During the fourteenth and fifteenth centuries, medieval French romances were expanded, altered, and translated into English, Spanish, and Italian. These stories were usually in prose. They typically imitate plot devices created by Chrétien, divide right and wrong between heroes and villains without regard for moral ambiguity, and often seem to echo the rigid pride and codes of honor of the military aristocracies, who could often read French. Romances like *Ponthus et Sidoine, Les quatre fils Aimon,* and *Perceforest*—three volumes that the earl of Shrewsbury gave to Margaret, Henry VI's queen—indicate the literary taste of the English aristocracy in the mid-fifteenth century.

Chivalric romances were the most popular form of fiction in England after the introduction of printing. William Caxton (c. 1422–1491), the first English printer, whose patrons included Queen Margaret, published expensive folio editions, which only the wealthy could afford. In addition to Thomas Malory's *Le Morte Darthur* (1485), Caxton's output included *The Recuyell of the Historyes of Troye* (1471), *The Siege of Jerusalem* (1480–1481), *Charles the Grete* (1485), and *The Four Sons of Aymon* (1489), as well as translations of Ramon Lull's *Book of the Order of Chivalry* (1483–1485) and Christine de Pisan's *The Book of the Fayttes of Armes and of Chyvalrie* (1489). Wynkyn de Worde, who inherited Caxton's busi-

ness, added *The History of King Ponthus* (1511) and Robert Copland's translation *Helyas, Knight of the Swan* (1512), a story about the supposed ancestor of Godfrey of Bouillon, leader of the First Crusade, whose brothers are turned into swans by their evil grandmother in a story unrelated to Lohengrin. He also printed Henry Watson's translations of *Oliver of Castile* (1518) and *Valentine and Orson,* the story of two brothers, one of whom is brought up by a bear. (Some of these romances cannot be dated with precision.)

In addition to prose romances, de Worde published metrical romances: *Bevis of Hampton, Sir Degore, Sir Eglamour,* and *Guy of Warwick.* He also printed *Ipomydon, Richard Coeur de Lion* (1509, 1528), and *The Squire of Low Degree,* whose hero appears in Spenser's *Faerie Queene.* At the same time, in the first half of the century, English romances circulated in manuscript, along with printed French romances such as the prose *Merlin* (published 1498) and *Lancelot of the Lake.*

Works before 1575 were generally translations from French; later Renaissance translations were from Spanish. The fame of Spanish romances peaked in the 1570s. Many were translated from French intermediaries. In the 1580s and 1590s, Anthony Munday, a draper's son, translated the first two or three parts of *Palmerin of England,* two parts of *Palmerin d'Oliva, Palladine of England, Palmendos,* two parts of *Primaleon of Greece,* and three of four parts of *Amadis of Gaul.* There was also a version of *The Mirror of Knighthood* (1578), an influence on Robert Greene's *Pandosto,* the source of Shakespeare's *Winter's Tale.* After 1601 there were no other translations until mid-century.

Critical Reception. The vogue of chivalric romance died with Elizabeth I, but not before producing two original masterpieces, Sir Philip Sidney's *Arcadia* (1590) and Edmund Spenser's *Faerie Queene* (1590 and 1596). The most popular chivalric romances belonged not to England, however, but to Italy. Ariosto's *Orlando furioso* had enormous influence and prompted competing poetic theories over what Italian critics called the heroic poem. The *Furioso* did not employ the single action that Aristotle recommended in his newly recovered *Poetics.* Instead of a unity of action like the wrath of Achilles or heroic burden of leadership assumed by Aeneas, the *Furioso* showed a unity of well-linked parts, so that what seemed like digressions were not. The action of the poem is multiple, based on the deeds of several illustrious heroes and heroines, although the multiple plot lines are interlaced, weaving in and out of each other in the fashion developed by medieval writers of chivalric romance. The critic Giovanni Battista Giraldi Cinthio (1504–1573) said Ariosto invented a new form, unknown to the ancients, and he called it the *romanzo*.

Torquato Tasso disagreed on the issue of unity. He said that no difference existed between a romance and a heroic poem, because the rules of poetry were fundamental. He proved his point by giving unity to his *Gerusalemme Liberata* (1580; trans. *Jerusalem Delivered*), the other Italian masterpiece of the sixteenth century. But Tasso did agree that the romance of chivalry provided or was capable of adopting most of the elements necessary for a well-constructed poem. Besides a proper plot, a poem should please audiences by its use of marvels. Homer introduced the supernatural through his gods. A modern poet could not, because no one would believe him, but he could use Christian marvels, like angels or magic. Further, the poet could learn the elements of imitation, or mimesis, from the good writers like Virgil, and he could seek an aesthetic style, one that gave pleasure to the reader, particularly in his elocution. Indeed, it is the verse of Ariosto, Tasso, and their follower Spenser that keeps the chivalric romance alive for readers today.

Later poets were not able to sustain the pretense of chivalry or the artistry that these writers achieved. In Italy, long after the decline of that country's Renaissance, Alessandro Tassoni claimed to have created a new genre, the comic epic in prose: his *La secchia rapita* (Rape of the bucket; 1622) mocks the military aspects of chivalry even as Cervantes, in Spain, had mocked the amatory enchantments of the form earlier in the century. Another successful long Italian poem, Giambattista Marino's *L'Adone* (Adonis; 1623), barely simulated the elements of chivalric romance. Only Milton, in England, maintained something of the beauty of the form. His *Paradise Lost* (1667) is no quest. It is an epic, yet its villains and enchantresses, dragons, and single combats recall the old romances. Milton, however, was an exception to the general trend. During most of the seventeenth century, the emerging form of the novel absorbed and domesticated the formerly dominant ethos of chivalry and the romance form that once embodied it.

BIBLIOGRAPHY

Astell, Ann. *Job, Boethius, and Epic Truth*. Ithaca, N.Y., 1994. Argues that romance represents an allegorical reading of epic as a Christian pilgrimage through life.

Brownlee, Kevin, and Maria Scordilis Brownlee, eds. *Romance: Generic Transformation from Chrétien de Troyes to Cervantes*. Hanover, N.H., 1985.

Crane, R. S. *The Vogue of Medieval Chivalric Romance During the English Renaissance*. Menasha, Wis., 1919.

Eisenberg, Daniel. *Spanish Romances of Chivalry in the Spanish Golden Age*. Newark, Del., 1982.

Giamatti, A. Bartlett. *The Earthly Paradise and the Renaissance Epic*. Princeton, N.J., 1966. Symbolic scenes that tend to attract romance knights.

Jameson, Fredric. *The Political Unconscious: Narrative as a Socially Symbolic Act*. Ithaca, N.Y., 1980.

Murrin, Michael. *The Allegorical Epic: Essays in Its Rise and Decline*. Chicago, 1980. Classic essays on the allegorical meaning of the poems of Virgil, Boiardo, Tasso, Spenser, and Milton.

Murrin, Michael. *History and Warfare in the Renaissance Epic*. Chicago, 1994. Examines how poetic theory and various poets' actual experience of war influenced their literary art.

Quint, David. *Epic and Empire: Politics and Generic Form from Virgil to Milton*. Princeton, N.J., 1993. Explores the interrelationship between ideology, romance, and epic from Virgil's *Aeneid* and Lucan's *Civil Wars* through the Italian Renaissance to Spanish poets in the New World.

Ross, Charles. *The Custom of the Castle: From Malory to Macbeth*. Berkeley, Calif., 1997. The moral dilemma of a common romance feature, the foul custom of a castle that a knight may be required to defend.

Ross, Charles. Introduction. In *Orlando Innamorato*. Berkeley, Calif., 1989. Pages 1–27. Surveys the medieval background of the romance epic, the role of allegorical enchantresses, biblical influences, and the court of Ferrara, where romances of chivalry found new life during the Renaissance.

Scaglione, Aldo. *Knights at Court: Courtliness, Chivalry, & Courtesy from Ottonian Germany to the Italian Renaissance*. Berkeley, Calif., 1991.

Snuggs, Henry L. *Giraldi Cinthio on Romances*. Lexington, Ky., 1968. Snuggs's introduction summarizes the features of romance according to Renaissance theory.

Vinaver, Eugène. *The Rise of Romance*. Oxford, 1971. Compares the intricate interlaced plots of romances to medieval art.

Weinberg, Bernard. *A History of Literary Criticism in the Italian Renaissance*. 2 vols. Chicago, 1961. Describes the Ariosto-Tasso controversy and the debate in sixteenth-century Italy over Aristotle's *Poetics*.

Zink, Michel. *Medieval French Literature: An Introduction*. Translated by Jeff Rider. Binghamton, N.Y., 1995. Introduction to medieval French romances of chivalry, whose influence lasted throughout the Renaissance.

CHARLES ROSS

English Arthurian Romance

In an effort to revive chivalry and to co-opt it for political uses, English royalty staged chivalric tournaments and other chivalric theatricals. Chivalry preserved the glamour of aristocrats, who feared they were being domesticated into "carpet knights" (knights who stayed indoors and did no fighting).

In its interest in chivalry, England was partly following the lead of the Netherlands, where Burgundian chivalric pageantry had been revived to lend

King Arthur and the Knights of the Round Table. The Holy Grail appears to Arthur and his knights. From a manuscript of *Lancelot du Lac*. Bibliothèque Nationale, Paris, MS. fr. 112. BIBLIOTHÈQUE NATIONALE, PARIS/GIRAUDON/ART RESOURCE

vigor to a revolt against Catholic Spain. England traded heavily with the Netherlands and sympathized with its embattled Protestants. In the 1580s most English Protestants became militant, and in 1585 the earl of Leicester (against the preferences of Queen Elizabeth) mobilized an anti-Catholic crusade in the Netherlands.

English sympathy with the Protestant cause in the Netherlands manifested itself in the poetry of the period, as did the renewed interest in chivalry. Sir Philip Sidney (1554–1586), who would later die as an enthusiastic soldier for the Protestant cause in the Netherlands, wrote a romance, the *Arcadia,* which is in many respects chivalric. He explicitly affirmed the connection between chivalric romance and a military career when he wrote in *The Defence of Poesie* (1595), "Honest King Arthur [of *Le Morte Darthur*] will never displease a soldier." Edmund Spenser (1552 or 1553–1599) allegorized the struggle over the Netherlands between England and Roman Catholic Spain in his chivalric romance *The Faerie Queene* (V.x–xi). He also contributed sonnets and epigrams to the English version of a book by the Burgundian Jan Van der Noot, *A Theatre for Worldlings* (1569); and some of his love sonnets imitate those of the Flemish poet and chronicler Jean Lemaire de Belges (1473–1525). Spenser owes certain static allegorical tableaux in books 1 and 2 of *The Faerie Queene* and the very idea of inserting such tableaux throughout the romance to the Burgundian allegorical romancers Olivier de La Marche (c. 1425–1502), the author of *Le chevalier délibéré,* and La Marche's imitator Jean de Cartigny (1520?–1578), the author of *Le voyage du chevalier errant.*

Arthuriana. Elizabeth's Order of the Garter was modeled ultimately on Arthur's Knights of the Round Table. St. George, the Garter's patron saint, is the "real name" of Spenser's Red Cross Knight. The Tudors were Welsh, and so was Arthur; they claimed to be emperors, and Geoffrey of Monmouth in his *Historia regum Britanniae* (c. 1135–1139)—containing the first account of King Arthur as we know him—traced Arthur's lineage and kingdom to a Roman, Brutus, the supposed founder of Britain. Henry VII named his firstborn (and unfortunately short-lived) son Arthur and invented for him the title Prince of Wales. Spenser named his hero Arthur and incorporated chunks of Geoffrey of Monmouth's *Historia* into *The Faerie Queene* (II.x., III.iii, and III.x).

Genre. Besides these social values, the some-times frivolous genre of chivalric romance had ac-quired a classical luster and hence new prestige among the literate from the vogue of the pastoral (especially the work of the newly recovered Greek pastoralist Theocritus), which influenced Sidney's *Arcadia* (1590) and *The Faerie Queene* (VI.ix–x); and from the popular new Italian romance epics, which influenced Spenser's romance throughout, es-pecially books III and IV.

BIBLIOGRAPHY

Geoffrey of Monmouth. *History of the Kings of Britain*. Trans-lated by Sebastian Evans. Revised by Charles W. Dunn. New York, 1958. Translation of *Historia regum Britanniae*.

Kipling, Gordon. *The Triumph of Honour: Burgundian Origins of the Elizabethan Renaissance*. The Hague, Netherlands, 1977.

Millican, Charles B. *Spenser and the Table Round: A Study in the Contemporaneous Background for Spenser's Use of the Arthurian Legend*. Cambridge, Mass., 1932. Reprint, New York, 1967.

Prescott, Anne Lake. "Spenser's Chivalric Restoration: From Bateman's *Travayled Pylgrime* to the Redcrosse Knight." *Studies in Philology* 86, no. 2 (1989): 166–197.

Rovang, Paul R. *Refashioning "Knights and Ladies Gentle Deeds": The Intertextuality of Spenser's* Faerie Queene *and Malory's* Morte Darthur. Madison, Wis., 1996.

Sidney, Sir Philip. "The Defense of Poesie" in *Miscellaneous Prose*. Edited by Katherine Duncan-Jones and J. A. van Dor-sten. Oxford, 1973.

Yates, Frances A. *Astraea: The Imperial Theme in the Sixteenth Century*. London, 1975.

CAROL V. KASKE

Chivalry in Renaissance Art

In the late Middle Ages and early Renaissance, in Italy as in northern Europe, the adventures of such heroes as Lancelot and Tristan in chivalric romance resonated with the same significance that would, by the sixteenth century, adhere to the exploits of such heroes as Scipio and Alexander in classical texts. In-deed, admiration for chivalric and classical heroes overlapped during much of the fifteenth century, and the two classes of literature should not be per-ceived as standing in a chronological antithesis, with a new enthusiasm replacing an old one. A fifteenth-century patron, especially a northern Italian ruler, saw no intellectual conflict between the continuing lure of French romance and his emerging interest in humanist studies.

The chivalric stories that were favored for the dec-oration of material culture were those deriving from Britain and Brittany, of presumed Celtic ancestry, featuring King Arthur and the knights of the Round Table, that were known as the *matière de Bretagne* (matter of Britain).

Chivalric stories were used to adorn the secular minor arts; such a table decoration as the Burghley Nef, a ship model in silver made in Paris in the late fifteenth century (London, Victoria and Albert Mu-seum), shows Tristan and Isolde clasping hands and playing chess on their voyage to Cornwall. Other small personal possessions, made of leather, box-wood, ivory, bone, and paper, such as small caskets, combs, hair parters, mirror cases, writing tablets, and decks of playing cards, were decorated with epi-sodes from the romances of Tristan, Lancelot, and Gawain, as were the manuscripts recounting these tales. The most interesting Italian codex of this kind is the 1446 *Tavola ritonda* (Round table), illustrated with 289 drawings attributed to Bonifazio Bembo (Florence, Biblioteca Nazionale).

If the names of rooms in castle inventories are anything to go by, an entire corpus of large-scale late medieval secular murals has disappeared in Italy and elsewhere: the fourteenth-century palace in Mantua, for instance, boasted a *camera Lanzaloti* (Lancelot's room) and a *camera Paladinorum* (room of the pal-adins), and the fifteenth-century palace in Ferrara in-cluded a *camera de Lanziloto;* all were named for the stories with which they were decorated. Other halls were hung with lavish and expensive tapes-tries. The two chivalric heroes most frequently de-picted in tapestries in fourteenth-century France were Tristan and Chrétien de Troyes's Perceval; such hangings were in the possession of the duke of Bur-gundy in 1379, 1390, and 1395, Philip the Bold in 1404, Margaret of Flanders in 1405, and Philip the Good in 1420. Inventories confirm the enormous popularity of such tapestries with chivalric subjects at fifteenth-century Italian courts.

Most of the few monumental paintings on chival-ric subjects that survive from the fifteenth century do so in remote centers and are therefore provincial in character. The Sommerhaus at Castel Roncolo (near Bolzano) was frescoed around 1400 with chivalric stories: tales of Wigalois, based on the poem written around 1210 by Wirnt von Grafenberg, were painted in green earth in an open loggia, and rooms on the *piano nobile* (second floor) were frescoed with sto-ries of Tristan and Isolde, based on the poem by Gottfried von Strassburg (d. c. 1210), and with twenty-two scenes based on Der Pleier's thirteenth-century *Garel von dem blühenden Tal* (Garel of the flowering valley).

Early fifteenth-century frescoes in a room on the *piano nobile* of the castle of La Manta near Saluzzo in Piedmont represent two well-known subjects that were also often depicted on tapestries: one of these is the *Neuf Preux*, the Nine Worthies (supreme heroes), deriving from an early fourteenth-century poem in French by the patron's father, together with the *preuses*, nine illustrious women; the other is the Fountain of Youth. The *preux* comprise three champions of chivalry of the Jewish law (Joshua, David, and Judas Maccabeus), three champions of the pagan law (Hector, Alexander, and Caesar), and three champions of the new Christian law (Arthur, Charlemagne, and Godefroy de Bouillon). Such triads became popular subjects for castle decoration: the exterior balcony of the Sommerhaus in Castel Roncolo, for instance, was painted with an Arthurian adaptation of the Worthies, comprising triads of knights of the Round Table (Perceval, Gawain, and Ivain), famous pairs of lovers (including Tristan and Isolde), and the three strongest giants and three wildest giantesses.

Opposite the Nine Worthies in the La Manta hall, the Fountain of Youth, a subject derived from the Matter of Rome (the romances of antiquity) that was particularly popular in France, depicts the gnarled, aged, and infirm who haul themselves with difficulty into a fountain, in whose waters they immediately regain their youthful vigor and cavort naked with members of the opposite sex. The frescoes were commissioned, probably around 1420–1430, by Valerano of Saluzzo, who, together with his wife, can be identified among the Worthies. The many inscriptions throughout the cycle are in French, each of the Worthies being identified by several lines of French verse, and the Fountain of Youth being punctuated by banderoles (scrolls) bearing the protagonists' speeches in the same language. Inventories confirm important holdings of chivalric romance in French prose in Italian princely libraries.

The only surviving Italian cycle depicting an Arthurian romance that can be characterized as Renaissance in style—especially figure style—is that left unfinished by Antonio Pisanello in the Gonzaga stronghold of the Ducal Palace in Mantua, dated variously from the 1420s through the 1440s. The frescoes in the Sala del Pisanello illustrate an episode from the prose *Lancelot,* a thirteenth-century romance in French that was printed in as many as seven editions in the late fifteenth and early sixteenth centuries. The Mantuan court library possessed a particularly rich collection of such codices: in 1407, out of 392 volumes, 67 were in French, compared with 32 in Italian.

Visual references to chivalric romance continued into the sixteenth century: among others, Rosso Fiorentino depicted the Fountain of Youth in King Fran-

cis I's palace at Fontainebleau, and at the court of Ferrara the Dossi brothers may have illustrated several episodes from Ludovico Ariosto's poem *Orlando furioso.*

BIBLIOGRAPHY

Lacy, Norris J., ed. *The New Arthurian Encyclopedia.* Rev. ed. New York, 1991.
Loomis, Roger Sherman, and Laura Hibbard Loomis. *Arthurian Legends in Medieval Art.* London and New York, 1938.
Woods-Marsden, Joanna. *The Gonzaga of Mantua and Pisanello's Arthurian Frescoes.* Princeton, N.J., 1988.

JOANNA WOODS-MARSDEN

CHRIST IN RENAISSANCE ART. *See* **Religious Themes in Renaissance Art.**

CHRISTIAN HUMANISM. *See* **Humanism,** *subentry on the* **Definition of Humanism.**

CHRISTIANITY. [This entry includes two subentries, the first on the Western Church, the second on Orthodox Christianity. For further discussion of Christianity, see Catholic Reformation and Counter-Reformation; Clergy; Papacy; Protestant Reformation; Religious Orders; Religious Piety; and Spirituality, Female.]

The Western Church

At the beginning of the Renaissance the Western Church was in schism, not only with the churches of the Christian East, but also within itself; and at the end of the Renaissance it was in schism once again. The second Western schism, which was brought on by the Protestant Reformation, proved to be more lasting, and probably even more serious, than the first. The place of the Renaissance in this process— or the place of Christianity as an institution and system of faith in the Renaissance movement—may properly be seen as a crucial question for the historical understanding of the Renaissance and of the Christian religion.

The Renaissance and the Medieval Church. Despite the emphasis of many modern historians (and of many Renaissance humanists themselves) on the novelty of Renaissance Christianity in relation to the medieval church and on its greater spiritual affinities with the remote than with the more recent Christian past, historical hindsight permits us to recognize the Renaissance of the fourteenth and fifteenth centuries as a legitimate heir to the traditions of medieval Christianity. The church and the papacy were often its patrons, the Bible and the lives of the saints its artistic themes, the prayers and canons of the Mass the texts for its music, the questions of Christian faith and morals its issues. Beyond those obvious connections, the Renaissance was—and frequently saw itself to be—the flowering of a long-standing spiritual and intellectual tradition. It was not an accident that Jerome (c. 347–419/20), the leading scholar of the ancient church in the West and the humanist among the church fathers, became the patron saint for so many Renaissance figures. In 1516 his works were edited and published in nine volumes by Erasmus.

The recent discovery of various "Renaissances before the Renaissance" ("Carolingian Renaissance," "Renaissance of the twelfth century," "Byzantine Renaissance") has not always been helpful in clarifying the medieval heritage on which the Renaissance drew. But it is evident, for example, that there were in the life and faith of St. Francis of Assisi (c. 1182–1226) and in the movement that he founded important anticipations of many ways of believing, thinking, and speaking that we associate with the Renaissance, including the drive for a Christian personalism and the renewed relation to the natural world, the two themes that Jakob Burckhardt, as part of his definition of the Renaissance in *The Civilization of the Renaissance in Italy,* called "the discovery of the world and of humanity." The artist for whom Francis provided both an inspiration and a major subject, Giotto (c. 1267–1337), was in turn an inspiration to other early Renaissance artists, so that Francis could be seen by the early twentieth-century art historian Henry Thode, with some exaggeration, as the fountainhead of Renaissance art. And Dante Alighieri (1265–1321) was simultaneously the embodiment of much of medieval Christianity and the harbinger of the spirit of the Renaissance; as Burckhardt himself said of the Renaissance, "in all essential points, the first witness to be called is Dante." Beginning with Augustine (354–430) and Boethius (c. 480–524), and even much earlier, the scholars and thinkers of the Middle Ages in the West had been no less concerned than were those of the Renaissance with the relation between Christianity and the pagan classical tradition, even though the recovery of Greek, made possible in considerable measure by the renewal of contact with the Eastern Church, enabled the Renaissance to grasp the full range of that tradition.

Nevertheless, in the history of Christianity as in the history of art or of politics, the age of the Renaissance did mark a new departure and open a new period. Even when one grants that the knowledge and the use of the Bible were far more profound in the Middle Ages than later (especially Protestant) partisans acknowledged, the fact remains that the Renaissance was responsible for a major biblical revival in the West, both in Italy, above all through the scholarship of Lorenzo Valla (1407–1457), and in northern Europe, through the work of humanists like Johann Reuchlin (1455–1522) for the Old Testament and Desiderius Erasmus (c. 1466–1536) for the New Testament. Although many Renaissance figures, including Valla and Michelangelo (1475–1564), were the beneficiaries of papal and ecclesiastical sponsorship, the Renaissance witnessed a quantum increase in lay, secular patronage of learning and of the arts, thus anticipating the modern development. Renaissance academies and, increasingly, universities fostered an intellectual coming-of-age that encouraged the members of the church, now that more and more of them were beginning to read for themselves, also to think and eventually to believe for themselves, even when what they believed was in fact still the faith of the Catholic Church.

The Renaissance and Catholic Reform. Throughout much of the fifteenth century the life and preaching—and the prayers—of the Western Church were dominated by a call for authentic and thoroughgoing reform "in head and members." In 1377 the papacy had returned to Rome from its "Babylonian Captivity" in Avignon, where it had gone in 1309, but the net result of this long-desired action was that there were now (and would be until 1417) two claimants to the throne of Peter, one in Avignon, the other in Rome. The Great Schism is entitled to the dubious honor of being called "great" only if one ignores the schism between East and West going back to 1054 (the mutual excommunication of the patriarch of Constantinople and the pope of Rome) or to 1204 (the sack of Orthodox Constantinople by Western Crusaders). The calls for reform voiced by John Wycliffe at Oxford (c. 1330–1384) and Jan Hus at Prague (c. 1373–1415) eventually led to the separation of the Hussites from the Roman Catholic Church, and thus, even before the Reformation of the sixteenth century, to a "church outside the church"; and the apocalyptic summons to repentance issued by Girolamo Savonarola (1452–1498) in Florence led to his excommunication. A series of church councils (Pisa, 1409; Constance, 1414–1418; Basel-Ferrara-Florence, 1431–1449) strove to address the crisis. Agenda items for all of them, as formulated at Constance, were reunion and the healing of the schism both within the West and between East

Palace of the Popes, Avignon. The palace was constructed during the pontificates of Benedict XII (1334–1342) and Clement VI (1342–1352). GIAN BERTO VANNI/ART RESOURCE, NY

and West (*causa unionis*), reform (*causa reformationis*), and the renewal of the faith and teaching of the church (*causa fidei*).

The contribution of the Renaissance to each of these three "causes" is well epitomized in the career of the humanist and churchman Cardinal Nicholas of Cusa (called Cusanus; 1401–1464). He worked with others for the reconciliation of the Hussites with the church and served as papal legate in Constantinople to heal the East-West separation. Both these efforts achieved short-term success, but failed in the long run. The temporary armistice between the church and the followers of Hus in 1433 did not gain permanent support on either side, and the understanding between East and West represented by *Laetentur coeli,* the decree of union proclaimed at the Council of Florence on 6 July 1439, was repudiated by various Eastern churches, including the increasingly powerful Orthodox Church of Moscow. Cusanus took the lead as bishop and cardinal in rooting out immorality and simony among the clergy both within his own diocese and beyond, and called upon the church and the papacy to purge themselves of corruption. And he used his immense speculative and literary talents to urge a fundamental reconsideration of the assumptions of scholastic philosophy and theology.

Belying the common caricature of the Renaissance as an elite movement indifferent to the needs and beliefs of the common people, other Renaissance leaders also made these causes of Catholic reform their own. Among these, pride of place must be awarded to Erasmus, even though his reformatory zeal was often effectively concealed under a masterful irony. His lampooning of monastic corruption, as in *Moriae encomium* (The praise of folly; 1509), proceeded from a deep sense of the gospel's summons to self-denial, which applied to all Christian believers and not only to professional ascetics; and the bitter satire *Julius exclusus* (Julius excluded; 1517), published anonymously but certainly written by Erasmus, expressed, behind its harsh attack on Pope Julius II (reigned 1503–1513), an almost wistful longing for a genuinely spiritual and pastoral papacy to lead and reform the church. The *Enchiridion militis Christiani* (Handbook of a Christian knight; 1503) looked to an informed, biblically literate, and mature laity as the hope of the church and of the faith. Erasmus's edition of the Greek New Testament of 1516, dedicated to Pope Leo X, followed the precedent of Valla in urging that a better and more accurate knowledge of the Bible was the path to genuine reform, not only for the institutional church and its clergy but also for Christian men and women everywhere.

The Renaissance and the Reformations.
The agitation for radical reform and the campaign to carry it out in every area of Christian life and worship came to be taken up in the sixteenth century by Mar-

Burning of Jan Hus. On 6 July 1415, Hus, wearing a hat with the inscription "heresiarch," was burned *(above)* and his ashes scattered *(below)*. Wood engraving from Ulrich von Reichental's account of the Council of Constance (Augsburg, 1483). BIBLIOTHÈQUE NATIONALE DE FRANCE, PARIS

tin Luther (1483–1546), John Calvin (1509–1564), and the other Protestant Reformers. As was suggested by the contemporary bon mot that Erasmus had laid the egg but that Luther had hatched it, the relation of the Protestant Reformation to the Renaissance was complex and subtle, for in many individuals such as Luther's colleague at the University of Wittenberg, Philipp Melanchthon (1497–1560), Renaissance humanism and Reformation doctrine were inseparable. Without the tools that had been provided by humanism, such as Erasmus's Greek New Testament and the Hebrew grammar of Johann Reuchlin, published in 1506, neither the biblical exegesis that was the foundation of the Reformation's

program nor the biblical preaching and translation of the scriptures into the several vernaculars that were at the core of its reformatory strategy would have been conceivable.

On the other hand, the emphases that the Protestant Reformers found in the newly available Greek New Testament and their readiness to break with the church and its institutions in the name of the authority of the Bible convinced Erasmus and others that Luther had gone too far, so that in his *De libero arbitrio* (On the freedom of the will; 1524), to which Luther replied the following year in *De servo arbitrio* (On the bondage of the will), Erasmus charged the Protestants with isolating divine grace from human freedom and with severing the moral nerve. By a reversal of the caricature, it was, Erasmus and his supporters claimed, not the Renaissance but the Reformation that was elitist, by preaching a doctrine of sin and salvation that would promote smugness and ethical indifference in the hearers.

These professions of loyalty to the church and to the essence of Catholicism, which the Renaissance scholarship of the twentieth century has largely vindicated, did not protect Erasmus and other Renaissance leaders from the censure of the Catholic Counter-Reformation. The polemical attacks on the Protestant Reformers by the defenders of the faith sometimes seemed to equate Renaissance criticism and Reformation criticism, Catholic reform and Protestant Reformation. Although the Council of Trent (1545–1563) did not go to these extremes and may even be seen as fundamentally "Erasmian" in emphasis, the writings of Erasmus and other Renaissance texts were still condemned by Pope Paul IV in 1557 and 1559 and went on being included on the Index of Prohibited Books even after the period of the Counter-Reformation. Yet the critical loyalty epitomized in such writings as these perpetuated itself within the Western Church also after the Reformation, so that Blaise Pascal (1623–1662), as scientist and man of letters, as Catholic philosopher and Christian apologist, may rightly be seen as an heir of the Renaissance.

The Renaissance and the Secularization of the West. Wherever one may choose to locate the cutoff point of the history of the Renaissance in its relation to the history of Western Christianity— with the publication of the Authorized (King James) Version of the English Bible in 1611, or the death of William Shakespeare in 1616, or the outbreak of the Thirty Years' War in 1618, or the condemnation of Galileo by the Inquisition in 1633—the question still

Divided Christianity. *Fishing for Souls* by Adriaen van de Venne. Protestants stand on the left, Catholics on the right. Oil on panel; 1614. RIJKSMUSEUM, AMSTERDAM

remains whether, by the law of unintended consequences, the Renaissance may have helped to bring on the secularization of the West. That was how the Renaissance was viewed by the Enlightenment of the seventeenth and eighteenth centuries, whose own major role in that process of secularization seems undeniable. If, in the classic definition of the Enlightenment by Immanuel Kant, its central motto was the imperative formulated by Horace, "Dare to do your own thinking!" (*Sapere aude*), it does seem legitimate to see in the Renaissance an important anticipation of that theme.

From the condemnation of Galileo by the Roman Catholic Inquisition and, even earlier, Luther's attack on Copernicus, to the Scopes trial of 1925 and the defense of the literal accuracy of the biblical account of creation by Protestant fundamentalism in the United States, organized Christianity has often been seen as fighting a rearguard action against the spirit of free inquiry that was symbolized, and in some sense pioneered, by the Renaissance. But it would be simplistic to concentrate exclusively on that historical succession and to ignore the lasting importance of Renaissance ideas and methods for the history of modern Christianity in the West. On the Protestant side, those who see themselves as heirs of Luther and Calvin are to a great degree heirs of Erasmus and the Renaissance as well, pressing for

the recognition of the results of critical biblical scholarship even when these seem to be in conflict with cherished practices and teachings of the churches. On the Roman Catholic side, it is possible to read the decrees of the Second Vatican Council (1962–1965) in the light of the programmatic ideas of the Christian Renaissance: the spirit of openness and free inquiry, a greater lay participation in worship, the Mass as the supreme expression of Christian community and not only as "unbloody sacrifice," the freedom of conscience and the recognition of diversity. It is not a coincidence that these developments in Western Christianity since the nineteenth century have been accompanied by a new and deeper appreciation of the Renaissance and of its contributions, as the condemnations of Erasmus and the Renaissance by both Luther and Pope Paul IV have faded, in favor of the recognition that both for the history of Christianity and for the history of the Renaissance the close connection between the two is an indispensable insight.

See also **Bible; Catholic Reformation and Counter-Reformation; Conciliarism; Constance, Council of; Humanism; Middle Ages; Protestant Reformation; Trent, Council of;** *and biographies of figures mentioned in this entry.*

BIBLIOGRAPHY

Bainton, Roland H. *Erasmus of Christendom.* New York, 1969. Renaissance humanism as church reform.

Orthodox Christianity. *Old Testament Trinity* attributed to Andrey Rublyov (1360/1370–c. 1430) painted for the monastery of the Trinity in Zagorsk, Russia, c. 1410–1420. The icon depicts the visit of the Lord to Abraham by the oaks of Mamre (Genesis 18:1–15). TRETYAKOV GALLERY, MOSCOW/SCALA/ART RESOURCE

thereby assuming the leadership of eastern Christendom.

Russian Orthodoxy. From an organizational standpoint, the ecclesiastical hierarchy of Kiev, whose metropolitan (bishop) was for a while subject to Moscow, ended up being closely tied to civil authority, but investiture had to be granted by the patriarch of Constantinople. The Greek metropolitan, Isidore of Kiev (later a cardinal of the Roman Church), was imprisoned by the grand duke of Muscovy when he attempted to proclaim the so-called Florentine Union in Moscow in 1441. In 1448, a council of Russian bishops presided over by Grand Duke Basil II elected Bishop Jonas as metropolitan of Moscow, without requesting confirmation from Constantinople, thereby initiating an autonomous and self-governing Russian Church. However, the church of Kiev, during the period in which it remained within the confines of the Polish-Lithuanian state, had, along with Constantinople, accepted the union adopted at the Council of Florence.

Russian Orthodoxy emphasized the liturgy, and service books were brought into conformity with those of Byzantium, while writings such as patristic works, lives of the saints, and chronicles were translated from Greek into Old Slavonic to produce more accurate and literary translations. The founder of this movement was Euthymius, patriarch of Trnovo (1375–1393). His principal disciple in Russia was Cyprian of Samblack, metropolitan of Moscow (1390–1406). Maxim the Greek (Michael Trivolis; c. 1470–1556), who had studied in Italy between 1492 and 1506 and who had even been a Dominican friar in Florence from 1502 to 1504 before entering an Orthodox monastery on Mount Athos, was sent to Moscow in 1516. There he translated Greek works into Russian and propagated the Renaissance synthesis between ancient secular learning and Christian piety in his numerous literary and religious writings.

The spiritual foundation of the Russian Church, like that of Byzantium, resided in its monastic traditions. The monasteries, centers of uniquely Russian Orthodox culture, became increasingly influential, through receipt of generous donations and, beginning in the fifteenth century, attracted the interest of those wielding political power. In reaction to the monasteries' wealth, St. Nil Sorsky (c. 1433–1508) supported the tsar's confiscation of monastic lands, while Abbot Joseph of Volokalamsk (1439–1515) is reported to have successfully defended continued ownership at the church councils of 1503 and 1504. A resolution of the conflict between Possessors and Nonpossessors was found in the prohibition against further increases in monastic land holdings.

Monastic life emphasized the liturgy, which had enormous importance for the religious education of the populace. Within the Russian tradition, the liturgy's sacred nature—the hieratic sense of the celebrants hidden behind the iconostasis (the icon screen in front of the altar), where the icons instructed the people with graphic representations of devotional themes—developed unique cosmic, eschatological, and christological accents. Greek was replaced by Slavic languages, although the issue of "Greekness" persisted through the centuries, with all the problems of dependency and autonomy related to ritual, use of liturgical books, and monastic regulations.

Geographically beyond the Turkish threat, the eastern Slavs developed a sense of Byzantine tradition in their own fashion. Lacking a direct connection to the tradition of the Greek or Latin church fathers, although aware of various important works, the Slavs did not develop the distinct Christian speculation—whether theological, moral, or ascetic—that was known in Byzantium or in the West. Instead,

Russian Orthodoxy remained anchored to the liturgical life practiced in monasteries and churches.

Relations with the Catholic West. In 1589, with the consent of the ecumenical patriarch of Constantinople, Jeremias II, then visiting Moscow, Tsar Fyodor I chose Job to be the first patriarch of Moscow and all Russia. (The Moscow patriarchate lasted for little more than a century, until the reign of Peter the Great.) While there was dissension with the other Eastern patriarchs, the patriarch of Moscow gave new prestige to the capital of Muscovy, now called Russia, a community largely composed of eastern Slavic peoples. Another significant event for the relationship between the Roman Catholic and Orthodox churches was the synod of Brest in 1596, which officially approved the union of a group of Ruthenian bishops and churches with the Roman Catholic Church. The Ruthenian bishops preferred Rome, depending on a centralized but distant church rather than the local Orthodox metropolitan or the Russian patriarch, who was subject to the tsar. The Russian Orthodox Church remained subject to the political realities of Russia and dependent on the tsars and their increasingly forceful interventions in church life. When the patriarchate of Moscow annexed the see of Kiev, new problems were created, in part because of Kiev's different culture, which was more open to Western influences.

The question of the Orthodox Church's relationship with the West has always been complex. Martin Luther and other Reformers explored the example of the Eastern Church, different as it was from the Western Church. By the middle of the sixteenth century there had already been attempts at dialogue between the Protestants of the University of Tübingen and the patriarch of Constantinople. The unsuccessful correspondence highlighted the divergence of Orthodoxy from Lutheran teachings on authority, faith, grace, and the sacraments. There were other attempts at dialogue in the seventeenth century, such as the initiative by Patriarch Cyril Lucaris (c. 1572–1638) supported by Western ambassadors to Constantinople, this time Calvinists, but again there was no progress toward reconciliation. The synod of Jerusalem (1672) formally condemned Protestant teachings and issued an official Orthodox profession of faith.

Orthodoxy in the Ottoman Empire. The emperor Justinian had given stability and hierarchy to the institution of the patriarchate by bestowing primacy on Rome, followed by Constantinople, Alexandria, Antioch, and Jerusalem. In subsequent centuries, various attempts to create other patriarchates—as in Bulgaria (at Ochrid and Trnovo), Serbia (at Pec), or Moscow—weakened the institutions' importance of the five ancient patriarchates. Other aspects of self-government or independence from the original patriarchates developed later.

Over the centuries numerous attempts were made by the Eastern churches to unify among themselves or with the Roman Catholic Church. Missionaries from western European religious orders, especially during the second half of the sixteenth century, tried to convince Eastern Christians to look upon the Western churches with less suspicion. Thus various Eastern churches were united with the Western Church: a branch of the Nestorians known as the Chaldeans (1553), the Melchite Church of Antioch (c. 1560), and the Maronite Church (1445, 1516, and 1574). The same phenomenon occurred along the Malabar Coast of southwestern India, where, at the synod of Diamper (1599), the St. Thomas Christians achieved a close union with the Syro-Malabar Church, subject to the Roman Catholic Church. The Ethiopian Church was briefly united with Rome (1624–1632) by order of the ruler Susneyos (1607–1632), but the union failed due to a reaction against excessive latinization.

Meanwhile, in Constantinople the position of the patriarch was compromised, since his functions were clearly determined by the sultan, who could depose him at will. In the early seventeenth century the patriarch's legal situation differed little from what it had been during the second half of the fifteenth century: his spiritual jurisdiction extended to the Christians of the patriarchate, but under Mehmed II (d. 1481) he was also considered the civil head of all Christians who resided within the borders of the Ottoman Empire, although Christians were still dependent in religious matters on the individual patriarchates.

The historiographic debate about the cultural position of the Byzantine world under Turkish rule, particularly the role of the Orthodox Church, is a fascinating study. During the Renaissance there was considerable literary production by Greek émigré scholars. For the most part ecclesiastical, these writings covered a broad area of inquiry and maintained the high standards of Greek scholarship. While links to the fathers of the Western Church were significant, the Eastern Church had never forgiven the sack of Constantinople in 1204 by a combined force of Franks and Venetians during the Fourth Crusade (1198–1205). During the Renaissance period, the Roman Catholic Church organized missionary activities in traditionally Orthodox areas of the Balkan Peninsula, and the Turks took full advantage of the increasing breach between the Orthodox and Roman Catholic churches.

Orthodox Christians who had not been forcibly converted to Islam, but were nonetheless subjects of the sultan, were organized in a semiautonomous community known as the *Rum Millet* (Roman nation). Although the Ottomans introduced many hated policies, including an onerous tax system and the buying of ecclesiastical positions, Orthodox communities of the former Byzantine Empire remained faithful to their religious traditions and preserved the use of the Greek language. Despite formidable odds, the Orthodox Church was thus able to preserve itself.

See also **Florence, Council of**; **Greek Émigrés**; **Ottoman Empire**; **Russia**.

BIBLIOGRAPHY

Primary Works
Darrouzès, Jean, ed. *Les regestes des actes du patriaracat de Constantinople*. Vol. 1: *Les actes des patriarches*. Fasc. 5: *Les regestes de 1310 à 1376*. Paris, 1977. Fasc. 6: *Les regestes de 1377 à 1410*. Paris, 1979. Fasc. 7: *Les regestes de 1410 à 1453*. Paris, 1991.
Fedalto, Giorgio, ed. *Hierarchia ecclesiastica orientalis*. 2 vols. Padua, Italy, 1988.
Herman Aemilius, ed. *De fontibus iuris ecclesiastici Russorum commentarius historico-canonicus*. Eastern Canonical Codification. Sources. Series 2, fasc. 6. Vatican City, 1936.
Welykyj, Athanasius G., ed. *Documenta Pontificum Romanorum historiam Ucrainae illustrantia (1075–1953)*. Analecta OSBM. Sectio 3: Documenta Romana ecclesiae unitae in terris Basilianorum collecta et edita. Documenta Pontificum Romanorum. Vol. 1, pages 1075–1700. Vol. 2, pages 1700–1953. Rome, 1953–1954.

Secondary Works
Ammann, A. M. *Storia della chiesa russa e dei paesi limitrofi*. Turin, Italy, 1948.
Atiya, Aziz S. *A History of Eastern Christianity*. London, 1968. 2d ed. Millwood, Wash., 1980.
Fedalto, Giorgio. *Le chiese d'Oriente*. 3 vols. Milan, 1991. 2d ed., 1995.
Handy, Jack V. *From Italy to Muscovy: The Life and Works of Maxim the Great*. Munich, 1973.
Janin, R. *La géographie ecclésiastique de l'empire byzantin*. Vol. 1: *Le siège de Constantinople et le patriarcat oecuménique*. Vol. 3: *Les églises et les monastères*. Paris, 1969.
Müller, C., and G. Detlef. *Geschichte der orientalischen Nationalkirchen*. Die Kirche in ihrer Geschichte, vol. 1, pt. 2. Göttingen, Germany, 1981.
Podskalsky, Gerhard. *Griechische Theologie in der Zeit der Türkenherrschaft, 1453–1821*. Munich, 1988.
Runciman, Steven. *The Great Church in Captivity: A Study of the Patriarchate of Constantinople from the Eve of the Turkish Conquest to the Greek War of Independence*. Cambridge, U.K., 1968.

Setton, Kenneth M. *The Papacy and the Levant (1204–1571).* 4 vols. Philadelphia, 1976–1984.

Sherrard, Philip. *The Greek East and Latin West: A Study of the Christian Tradition.* Oxford, 1959. Reprint, Limni (Evia), Greece, 1992.

Ware, Timothy. *The Orthodox Church.* Harmondsworth, U.K., 1963.

GIORGIO FEDALTO

Translated from Italian by Marguerite Shore

CHRISTIAN THEMES IN RENAISSANCE ART. *See* **Religious Themes in Renaissance Art.**

CHRISTIAN THEOLOGY. The Renaissance was a major force in the development of Christian theology, even though many modern historians of the Renaissance and of theology have chosen to ignore or to neglect the close connection between them. The historical movements of individual doctrines and of entire theological systems during the Renaissance make a thematic overview preferable to a more strictly chronological treatment.

Theological Pluralism in the Later Middle Ages.

The dominant impression left by the Christian theology of the later Middle Ages on the eve of the Renaissance, not only upon later generations of theologians and historians but even upon its contemporaries, was pluralism and diversity, if not sometimes downright chaos. Even during the high Middle Ages, the age of Thomas Aquinas (1225–1274) and Bonaventure (c. 1217–1274), there had been many profound differences of theological method and doctrine within the theoretical unity of the "one, holy, catholic, and apostolic church," so that unity in the faith had never been identical with uniformity in theological teaching; but those differences became both more acute and more visible in the century that followed.

A significant reason for the change was that the theoretical unity, and therefore the visible authority of the church as an institution, was itself being negated, first by the "Babylonian Captivity" of the papacy in Avignon from 1309 to 1377, then even more drastically by the Great Schism between Avignon and Rome from 1378 to 1417. Of particular importance was the issue of whether, as the proponents of the "conciliarist" theory were insisting, the way to deal with both of these crises was by subjecting the authority of the papacy to the authority of an ecumenical council of the church. Theological defiance of the authority both of the pope and of the general council came into the open in the thought of John Wycliffe at Oxford (c. 1330–1384) and of Jan Hus at

Prague (c. 1373–1415), who was put to death by the Council of Constance, which declared its supremacy over the papacy.

Various other doctrines of the faith were likewise the subject of vigorous disagreement among theologians throughout the fourteenth and fifteenth centuries, as the nominalism coming from William of Ockham (c. 1285–1349) and leading to Gabriel Biel (c. 1420–1495) called into question many scholastic views. One of the most prominent and divisive questions was the immaculate conception of the Virgin Mary—not whether she had conceived Christ immaculately, which had been the orthodox Catholic consensus since the apostolic age, but whether she herself had been immaculately conceived. Franciscan theologians, led by John Duns Scotus (c. 1266–1308), contended that by a unique privilege of divine grace Mary had been preserved by God from ever having incurred the taint of original sin in the first place; Dominican theologians, following Thomas Aquinas, insisted that she had been conceived in original sin as had all human beings, but that immediately thereafter she was purified of sin by divine grace, so that she too had been saved by Christ. The question would not be settled officially until 1854, when Pope Pius IX made the immaculate conception, which by then was all but universally accepted within Roman Catholic teaching, a binding dogma of the church.

The Renaissance Critique of Scholasticism.

Thus it was into a welter of already existing doctrinal controversy that the Renaissance brought its distinctive theological emphases. The monumental intellectual achievement carried out by the *Summa theologica* of Thomas Aquinas (in which the power of natural human reason, as represented by the thought of Aristotle, received consideration as a prolegomenon to the discussion of divine revelation in holy scripture as "sacred science" or theology) was criticized by Renaissance philosophers for its treatment of Aristotle and by Renaissance biblical theologians for its treatment of holy scripture. It was, above all, the scholastic penchant for abstract ideas, definitions, and formulas that drew this criticism. When Erasmus, in his *Enchiridion militis Christiani* (Handbook of a Christian knight; 1503), set forth the *philosophia Christi* (philosophy of Christ) as the alternative to Scholasticism, he was aligning himself with the emphases of such late medieval works of devotion as the *Imitation of Christ,* usually attributed to Thomas à Kempis (1379/80–1471), in which the imperative of obeying the example and the teaching

Thomas Aquinas. *The Triumph of St. Thomas Aquinas* by Benozzo Gozzoli (1420–1497) summarizes the role of theology in the Western Church. Above, God, SS. Paul and Peter, and the four evangelists (Mark with his lion, John with his eagle, Matthew with his winged human figure, and Luke with his ox) provide the subject matter of the theologian. God says, "You have written well of me, Thomas." Thomas (1225–1274) sits between the representatives of worldly knowledge, Aristotle and Plato; the Muslim philosopher Ibn Rushd (Averroes; 1126–1198), whose ideas he took pains to refute in the thirteenth century, lies at his feet. Below, the church, including the pope, prelates, and theologians, is enlightened by Thomas's teaching. MUSÉE DU LOUVRE, PARIS/ALINARI/ART RESOURCE

able agreement with Aquinas. The eventual outcome of the controversy over Scholasticism, therefore, was the rehabilitation of Thomism. At the Council of Trent (1545–1563), the redefinition of Roman Catholic doctrine in response to the Reformation (and, in some measure, also in response to the Renaissance) gave new authority to the classic formulations of that doctrine by the scholastic theologians on such central issues as the relation of faith and works in justification, the authority of tradition, and the divine institution of the seven sacraments.

The Christian East. The age of the Renaissance was simultaneously a period of renewed negotiations between the Eastern and the Western churches, beginning with the Council of Lyon in 1274 and climaxing with the Councils of Basel and Ferrara-Florence in the 1430s and 1440s. In addition to the contribution that these negotiations made to a growing awareness of the Greek church fathers, they also broadened the horizon of Western theologians in other ways, many of which came together in the remarkable career of Bessarion (1403–1472), metropolitan of Nicaea. Bessarion was a product of the final flowering of the humanistic culture and theology of the Byzantine Empire, uniting in his thought an openness toward the Greek classics with a loyalty to the Catholic orthodoxy of Eastern Christianity, and thus embodying the very combination of the best in Christian doctrine with the best in humanistic thought to which the Western theologians of the Renaissance aspired.

The negotiations at the Council of Florence brought Bessarion to Italy as a spokesman for the Eastern position, but he became a supporter of the Union of Florence, documented in *Laetentur coeli* of 6 July 1439, and therefore of Western teaching on

of the Jesus of the Gospels took precedence over the systems and definitions of the scholastic doctors.

In this attack upon Scholasticism the thinkers of the Renaissance were joined by the Protestants of the Reformation, who objected to some of the very doctrines, such as the freedom of the human will in relation to God, on which Erasmus shared consider-

such controverted doctrines as the double procession of the Holy Spirit. As a result, he returned to the West, where he had been named a cardinal in 1439, and continued his dual role in vindicating the essential unity of Eastern and Western teaching and defending Plato against his "calumniators." His patronage of refugee Greek scholars in Italy was a major force in the Greek revival.

The Sources of Theology: Biblical.

Most scholars of the Renaissance would probably agree that its greatest contribution to Christian theology—and to the Christian church—lay in its study of the Bible, which participated in and benefited from the campaign of the humanists to recover the other primary sources of Western civilization such as the Greek and Latin classics. For most of its history the Christian theology of the West had been obliged to content itself with translations of scripture. In place of the Hebrew of the Old Testament the Eastern Church was dependent on the Greek version of the Septuagint, which was the work of Alexandrian Jews and was the source for most of the biblical quotations in the Greek New Testament. In place of the Greek of the New Testament most Western theologians from Augustine (354–430) to Aquinas used the Latin Vulgate rather than the original.

The Latin Vulgate was a flawed masterpiece whose translations and mistranslations had determined theological thought and vocabulary, for example the Latin *sacramentum* (sacrament) as a translation of the Greek *mystērion* (mystery) in Ephesians 5:32 ("Sacramentum hoc magnum est"), which thus became a proof text for the definition of matrimony as one of the seven sacraments, and indeed as the only one of the seven so identified in the Bible. The critical examination of such mistranslations by Lorenzo Valla (1407–1457) was made possible by his study of the Greek New Testament, but he did not publish this work in his lifetime. Instead, Valla's manuscript was discovered and published by Desiderius Erasmus (c. 1466–1536), whose edition of the Greek text of the New Testament, the *Novum instrumentum* of 1516, inadequate though it was in many technical respects, truly became a "new instrument" for theology to establish a direct contact with the most primary of all its primary sources.

Meanwhile, the recovery of biblical Hebrew, which had begun during the later Middle Ages with the help of rabbinical learning, produced, in the Franciscan Nicholas of Lyra (c. 1270–1349), a new concern with the literal, grammatical interpretation of the Old Testament. It also claimed the attention of the Augustinian reformer Giles of Viterbo (c. 1469–1532) and of other Christian humanistic scholars, whom the new tools of printed grammars, lexicons, and critical editions of the Hebrew text equipped to explore with unprecedented illumination what modern theologians call "the strange new world within the Bible."

The Sources of Theology: Patristic.

Although it is often overlooked in the textbooks, the recovery of the patristic sources of theology from the Greek East as well as the Latin West was a contribution of the Renaissance to Christian theology second in importance only to the biblical revival. For in the history of Western theology during the Middle Ages, every major development had been accompanied by a fresh look at the thought of the fathers of the church—Augustine above all but also other Latin fathers, such as Ambrose of Milan (339–397). The reopening of constructive dialogue with the theologians of the Eastern churches added the riches of the Greek church fathers to the library of Western theologians, more and more of whom could now read in the original the theological works of Athanasius of Alexandria (c. 293–373) or of the "Three Hierarchs"—Basil of Caesarea (c. 329–379), Gregory of Nazianzus (c. 330–c. 389), and John Chrysostom (c. 347–407)—who had long been venerated as saints also by the Latin West but whose books were available only in fragmentary and inadequate Latin translations.

Believing that they could serve as an antidote to medieval Scholasticism and, when the divisions of the Reformation were growing more bitter, also as a counterbalance to the extremes on both sides, Erasmus made use of the new power of the printing press to publish *editiones principes* (first editions) of writings of John Chrysostom, as well as of Jerome (1516), Cyprian (1520), Arnobius (1522), Hilary of Poitiers (1523), Irenaeus (1526), Ambrose (1527), Augustine (1528–1529), Basil of Caesarea (1532), and Origen of Alexandria (1536). The patristic theology of the Renaissance thus laid the foundation for the great critical editions of the church fathers by the Benedictine Maurists in the seventeenth and eighteenth centuries and then by Protestant as well as Roman Catholic scholars in the nineteenth and twentieth centuries, and for the quantum leap made by the study of the history of Christian doctrine during the modern period.

The Sources of Theology: Neoplatonic.

All these factors—the growing knowledge of Greek, the invention of printing, the heightened contact with Greek Orthodox theologians, and the broadened study of the church fathers from both East and West—helped to shape one of the most distinctive theological phenomena of the Renaissance, the Platonic (or, more precisely, Neoplatonic) theology of the fifteenth and sixteenth centuries. One of its fountainheads was the Byzantine scholar and mentor of Bessarion, George Gemistus (c. 1355–1452), who in his reverence for Plato adopted the surname "Pletho" and who traveled to Florence as a member of the Eastern delegation at the union negotiations of 1438–1439. Partly under Gemistus's inspiration, the most dramatic expression of Renaissance Neoplatonism came in the thought of Marsilio Ficino (1433–1499). He undertook a fresh translation, from the original Greek into Latin, of the works of Plato, all but *Timaeus* having been unknown to the Western Middle Ages.

Although the hostility of many Renaissance thinkers to the theology of Thomas Aquinas was based in part on their charge that he had misunderstood the philosophy of Aristotle, Ficino and other Christian Neoplatonists, such as the English biblical humanist John Colet (1466/67–1519), advocated the replacement of Aristotle by Plato, and thus the reinstatement of the philosophical orientation that had been characteristic both of Augustine and of the Greek church fathers. One of these Greek church fathers wrote under the pseudonym of Dionysius the Areopagite, the Athenian convert of Saint Paul (see Acts 17:34). He blended Neoplatonism and Eastern Christian theology in a reinterpretation of liturgy and dogma that had been known throughout the Latin Middle Ages in several successive translations but that now became, in its original Greek text and in Ficino's translation, a source of greater theological experimentation and renewal.

Mystical Theology in the Renaissance.
The upsurge of interest in the Pseudo-Dionysius also contributed to the deepening of mystical theology in the Renaissance. When it was linked with biblical faith, mystical theology concentrated on certain figures, events, and symbols in the history of Israel and in the history of Christ. One of the richest cases of such a linkage was the Kabbalah (Cabala).

The Kabbalah had originated as a Jewish system of speculation in which certain mysteries of biblical interpretation—such as the Tetragrammaton of the Divine Name, YHWH, revealed to Moses from the burning bush (Exodus 3:14)—were seen as fraught with symbolic meanings of far-reaching metaphysical import. Many Renaissance humanists acquired,

Augustine the Theologian. *St. Augustine* by Sandro Botticelli. Mural in the church of Ognissanti, Florence. ALINARI/ ART RESOURCE

with their newfound knowledge of Hebrew, a fascination with the arcane method and spiritual vocabulary of the Kabbalah. Pressing this method far beyond its original rabbinical provanence and borrowing extensively also from the recent revival of Neoplatonism, Christian Neoplatonic philosophers like Giovanni Pico della Mirandola (1463–1494) and Giordano Bruno (1548–1600) were joined by Christian Hebraists such as Johann Reuchlin (1455–1522) in exploring the mystical depths of the Kabbalah for the more profound meaning of such traditional Christian doctrines as the Trinity and the Incarnation. But even beyond these roots in Neoplatonism and the Kabbalah, the mystical theology of the Renaissance had a right to claim orthodox Christian legitimacy by its association with the thought of saints like Augustine and, in the Middle Ages, Bernard of Clairvaux (1090–1153), who had found in the imagery of the Song of Songs a description of the union of the soul with Christ the Beloved.

The Renaissance and the Theology of the Reformation.
The history of Christian theology

in the Renaissance, which is the subject of this article, is not the same as the history of Christian theology during the Renaissance. The latter has, however, received far more attention than the former, largely because it is part of the history of the Reformation, which is one of the most heavily studied periods in the entire history of Christianity and especially in the history of Christian doctrine, with a scholarly literature that continues to burgeon.

Nevertheless the question of the relation between Renaissance theology and Reformation theology remains unavoidable. Geography may be a partial answer to the question, but it is an answer that begs or compels another question of historical causation: Reformation theology was largely confined to northern Europe and the British Isles, while the Renaissance, and therefore Renaissance theology, was initially an Italian phenomenon. Statistics is a second partial answer: when the dust had settled after all the theological controversies of the sixteenth and seventeenth centuries, most of the major figures of Renaissance theology, those whose biographies are important enough to appear in this encyclopedia, had ended up remaining (more or less) comfortably within the institutional boundaries of the Roman Catholic Church, while the term "Reformation theology" is usually, and arbitrarily, reserved for those who voluntarily broke with that institution or who were excommunicated from it. Despite the elements of determinism and fatalism that appeared in some Renaissance figures, it seems valid to suggest that the Reformation theology of Lutheranism and Calvinism did diverge from much of the mainstream of the Renaissance when it intensified—or, as Erasmus would have put it, exaggerated—the Augustinian emphasis on the total depravity wrought by the fall of Adam and original sin, and therefore the bondage of the human will in relation to the sovereignty of the grace of God.

It does seem clear, nevertheless, that Reformation theology as we know it would not have been possible if it had not been for the humanism of the Renaissance. To the extent that Luther and Calvin were right in their claim that the Reformation had elevated the authority of the Bible as *sola scriptura* (scripture alone) over the authority of church and tradition, the *scriptura* that was, whether *sola* or not, the bearer of that authority was the inspired original text in Hebrew and Greek—as that text had been recovered and made accessible by the biblical "sacred philology" of the Renaissance and its theologians.

See also **Aristotle and Aristotelianism; Augustine of Hippo; Bible,** *subentries on* **Texts and Textual Criticism** *and* **Christian Interpretation of the Bible; Christianity,** *subentry on* **Orthodox Christianity; Conciliarism; Florence, Council of; Greek Émigrés; Kabbalah; Patristics; Plato and Platonism; Protestant Reformation; Scholasticism;** *and biographies of figures mentioned in this entry.*

BIBLIOGRAPHY

Bentley, Jerry H. *Humanists and Holy Writ: New Testament Scholarship in the Renaissance.* Princeton, N.J., 1983. The biblical Renaissance and its significance for the definition of "the" Renaissance.

Blau, Joseph L. *The Christian Interpretation of the Cabala in the Renaissance.* New York, 1944.

Cassirer, Ernst. *The Individual and the Cosmos in Renaissance Philosophy.* Translated by Mario Damandi. Oxford, 1963.

Cassirer, Ernst, Paul Oskar Kristeller, and John Herman Randall, Jr., eds. *The Renaissance Philosophy of Man.* Chicago, 1948.

Colish, Marcia L. *Medieval Foundations of the Western Intellectual Tradition, 400–1400.* New Haven, Conn., 1997. The intellectual and theological heritage on which the Christian thought of the Renaissance drew.

Kristeller, Paul Oskar. *Renaissance Thought: The Classic, Scholastic, and Humanist Strains.* New York, 1961. Magisterial redefinition of continuity and change in Renaissance thought.

Oberman, Heiko A. *The Harvest of Medieval Theology.* Cambridge, Mass., 1963. Discusses nominalism as a defining force in the theology of the period.

O'Malley, John W. *Giles of Viterbo on Church and Reform: A Study in Renaissance Thought.* Leiden, Netherlands, 1968. Linguist, scholar, humanist, and Catholic reformer.

Pelikan, Jaroslav. *The Christian Tradition: A History of the Development of Doctrine.* 5 vols. Chicago, 1971–1989.

Skinner, Quentin, and Eckhard Kessler, eds. *The Cambridge History of Renaissance Philosophy.* Cambridge, U.K., 1988.

Southern, Richard W. *Medieval Humanism.* New York, 1970. What was new, and what was not, in the "humanism" of the Renaissance humanists.

Spitz, Lewis W. *The Religious Renaissance of the German Humanists.* Cambridge, Mass., 1963. Distinctive religious emphases of the Renaissance in northern Europe.

Trinkaus, Charles. *In Our Image and Likeness: Humanity and Divinity in Italian Humanist Thought.* 2 vols. Chicago, 1970. A veritable *Summa* of Renaissance theologies.

JAROSLAV PELIKAN

CHRISTINA OF SWEDEN (1626–1689), queen of Sweden (1644–1654) and patron of the arts. Called the "Minerva of the North" for her erudition, Christina shocked Europe by abdicating and converting to Roman Catholicism.

The daughter of King Gustavus Adolphus, who died in battle when she was six, Christina became the sole heir to the throne of Sweden. To prepare her to rule—and to counter what was seen as the problem of her gender—Christina was raised in the manner of a male prince, learning politics from chancellor-regent Axel Oxenstierna while becoming educated in theology, mathematics, and astronomy and skilled in horsemanship and hunting. In 1644, eighteen-year-old Christina assumed the crown of Sweden and proceeded over the next few years to oversee the peace negotiations that ended the Thirty Years' War and to exert shrewd control over Sweden's political structure, previously dominated by Oxenstierna and a strongly wayward noble class. By 1649 she had attained the power of an absolute monarch, at which point she announced, to the alarm of many, "it is impossible for me to marry," giving as the reason, "I am not so inclined."

After solving the succession problem by securing the future throne for her cousin Charles Gustav (later King Charles X Gustavus), Christina continued to preside over a brilliant court, with artists, musicians, and scholars dedicating innumerable works to her. Despite the somewhat libertine atmosphere at court, however, she was disciplined in the pursuit of her own studies, awakening at five o'clock each morning to read, write, or consult her library, one of the largest in Europe. Eminent intellectuals came to tutor her, the most famous being the philosopher René Descartes, whom she had persuaded to come to Sweden and draft the statutes for a new academy, which he did not live to see.

In 1654, at the height of her power, Christina renounced the crown, having secretly embraced the Roman Catholic faith. She had never been very interested in the Lutheranism of her country, and her conversion had been encouraged over the years by visiting Jesuits and emissaries. Knowing that she could not be both queen of Sweden and a Catholic, however, Christina chose the latter course, left Sweden, and headed south with her manuscripts and entourage. An ebullient Pope Alexander VII greeted her in Rome, but Christina, neither an ascetic person nor retiring, soon disappointed him by living lavishly and involving herself in secret machinations. The most notorious scheme involved a secret plan to become queen of Naples, with the help of Cardinal Jules Mazarin of France—a plan that backfired when her secretary revealed it and was executed on Christina's orders. Although the incident tarnished her name somewhat, she nevertheless spent the rest of her life maintaining a highly influential court in Rome, where she amassed books, paintings (including the greatest works of the Venetian school), friends (such as Giovanni Bernini), and beneficiaries of her often strained largesse (including the composer Alessandro Scarlatti). In 1689 she died and was buried in Saint Peter's Basilica, a woman who—in the words of a contemporary—had to the end "freely followed her own genius . . . and car'd not what anybody said."

BIBLIOGRAPHY

Masson, Georgina. *Queen Christina*. New York, 1968.
Stolpe, Sven. *Christina of Sweden*. London, 1966.

SARAH COVINGTON

CHRISTINE DE PISAN. *See* **Pisan, Christine de.**

CHRONICLE, ELIZABETHAN. The Elizabethan chronicle was both a serious genre of historical writing and a source of plots and themes for popular dramatists. During the Tudor period, chronicles assembled by printers from manuscript and print sources combined ancient, medieval, and contemporary materials without regard to their veracity or stylistic incompatibility. For example, medieval legends of England's Trojan origins and a contemporary description of Elizabeth's coronation appear together in Richard Grafton's *An Abridgement of the Chronicles of England* (1562). John Stow, whose *Survey of London* (1598) remains an important historical source, accused Grafton of sloppy methodology; the debate between them shaped conversation in the period about the historian's professional responsibility as purveyor of fact.

Dramatists were less interested in factual accuracy than in the wealth of material provided by chronicles and in the moral shapes imposed on that material. Four kinds of chronicle are prevalent in the Tudor period. City chronicles, which list names and events, are relatively unimportant for the drama. Humanist historiography, introduced into England by Polydore Vergil (*Anglica historia;* 1534), places people and events within a providential pattern of human triumph and divine retribution. Thomas More's *Life of Richard III* (1514–1518; printed 1543) and Edward Hall's *The Union of the Two Noble and Illustre Families of Lancaster and York* (1548) were popular examples of providential history. Humanist historiography influenced drama from Thomas Sackville and Thomas Norton's *Gorboduc* (first performed 1561, printed 1565) to William Shakespeare's two tetralogies concerning the Wars of the Roses (c. 1591–1600) and is especially important to plays about the royal succession, which occur at both the beginning and end of Elizabeth's reign. National chronicles, such as John Stow's *Chronicles of England* (1580), tell the patriotic story of England's rise as a nation and celebrate its female sovereign. The influence of national chronicles is most evident in later history

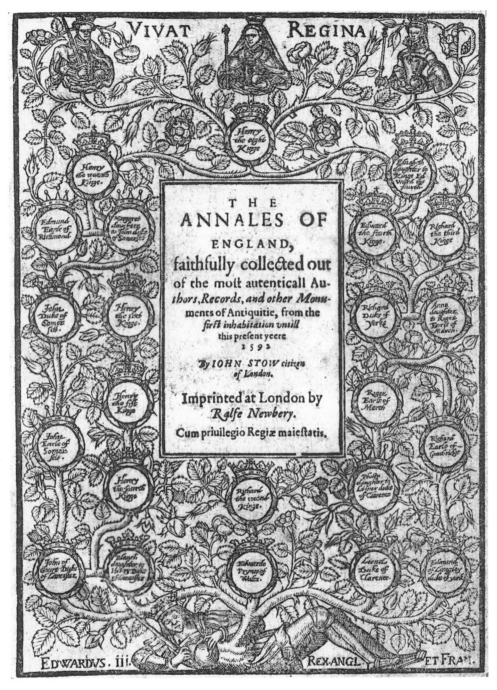

An Elizabethan Chronicle. Title page of *The Annales of England* by John Stow, printed at London in 1592. The illustration around the title shows the lineage of King Edward VI, Queen Mary I, and Queen Elizabeth I *(top)* from King Edward III *(bottom)*. HENRY E. HUNTINGTON LIBRARY AND ART GALLERY

plays, such as Thomas Heywood's *If You Know Not Me, You Know Nobody* (Part 1, 1606; Part 2, 1632), and in late Shakespearean histories-as-romance, such as *Cymbeline* (1609–1610) and *Henry VIII*

(1613). Raphael Holinshed's *Chronicles of England, Scotland, and Ireland* (1577 and 1587), the single most important source for English dramatists, represents a fourth kind of chronicle, a corporate production by multiple authors with conflicting religious and political perspectives. With Holinshed, the historical chronicle becomes once again an encyclopedia that juxtaposes what Annabel Patterson calls competing stories and motives.

While *Gorboduc* might be considered the first English history play, the genre flourished on stage in the 1590s and declined rapidly after the accession of James I. Discussion of why and how English dramatists used chronicle sources has centered around the example of Shakespeare. While Henry Ansgar Kelly argues that Shakespeare consulted a wide range of historical sources, attention has focused on Shakespeare's use of Holinshed as a source and his ideological attraction to Hall and providential history. At the end of World War II, Lily Bess Campbell argued that Shakespeare's histories were cautionary "mirrors" for Elizabethan politics; E. M. W. Tillyard saw them as celebrating an official "Tudor myth." More recent critics argue either that Shakespeare's plays embrace the ideological pluralism that Patterson attributes to Holinshed or that they subvert the "official" history of his chronicle sources. D. R. Woolf notes that the English historical chronicle declined when newspapers began to disseminate cheaply cultural information that previously was provided by chronicles. Why the history play died out is still a matter of debate.

See also **Shakespeare, William; Vergil, Polydore.**

BIBLIOGRAPHY

Primary Works
Hall, Edward. *Hall's Chronicle.* Edited by Henry Ellis. London, 1809.
Holinshed, Raphael. *Holinshed's Chronicles.* Edited by Henry Ellis. 6 vols. London, 1807–1808.
Hosley, Richard, ed. *Shakespeare's Holinshed: An Edition of Holinshed's Chronicles, 1587.* New York, 1968.
Stow, John. *A survey of London: written in the year 1598.* Edited by Antonia Fraser. Phoenix Mill, U.K., and Dover, N.H., 1994.

Secondary Works
Campbell, Lily B. *Shakespeare's "Histories": Mirrors of Elizabethan Policy.* San Marino, Calif., 1947.
Kelly, Henry Ansgar. *Divine Providence in the England of Shakespeare's Histories.* Cambridge, Mass., 1970.
Patterson, Annabel. *Reading Holinshed's Chronicles.* Chicago, 1994.
Ribner, Irving. *The English History Play in the Age of Shakespeare.* London, 1957.
Tillyard, E. M. W. *Shakespeare's History Plays.* New York, 1946.
Woolf, D. R. "Genre into Artifact: The Decline of the English Chronicle in the Sixteenth Century." *Sixteenth-Century Journal* 19 (1988): 321–354.

CHRISTY DESMET

CHRYSOLORAS, MANUEL (c. 1349–1415), Greek diplomat and teacher. Chrysoloras was the single most important teacher of Greek in the Renaissance, but we know almost nothing about the first forty years of his life except that he was born into an aristocratic family in Constantinople about 1349, that he had a reputation as a scholar, and that he enjoyed the friendship of the Byzantine emperor Manuel II. When the emperor sent him and the Roman Catholic convert Demetrius Cydones on a mission to Venice from 1390 to 1391 to gather forces against the Turks, they were visited by two young humanists eager to learn Greek, Roberto de' Rossi and Jacopo Angeli da Scarperia. Rossi and Angeli had traveled from Florence, where they belonged to the intellectual circle of the chancellor Coluccio Salutati. Four years later, in 1395, when Angeli traveled to Constantinople to learn Greek with Chrysoloras, he also acted as the agent of Salutati, who had persuaded the Florentines to pay a generous salary to bring Chrysoloras to Florence. By February 1397, Chrysoloras had arrived in Florence.

Over the next three years, by teaching Salutati's talented protégés Greek, Chrysoloras broadened the intellectual range of Renaissance humanism. By 1397 the humanist reacquisition of classical Latin and classical Latin literature was well under way, but until the humanists learned Greek, their recovery of the classical heritage would continue to be significantly limited. Petrarch, the first great humanist, had clearly understood the importance of learning Greek a generation earlier, but his attempts to learn the language had come to naught. The Salutati circle achieved Petrarch's aspiration.

Chrysoloras also taught his pupils a theory of translation. Medieval translations were notorious for their tendency toward literal renderings that at times followed the original Greek so closely as to be incomprehensible. Chrysoloras himself also used literal translation as a teaching device for beginners. As a classroom exercise, Chrysoloras produced for his students what amounted to a literal translation of some dialogues of Lucian. However, a true translation, he explained, must translate the sense and not simply the words of the original. Chrysoloras's theory would become the dominant one among humanists in the Renaissance. His teaching while in Florence produced the Renaissance's first group of translators, including not only Angeli and Rossi, but also Pier Paolo Vergerio and, perhaps most notably, Leonardo Bruni, the first truly major translator of the Renaissance.

During his stay in Florence, Chrysoloras also wrote at Salutati's request a brief grammatical piece on Greek breathings, which he eventually incorporated into the final chapter of his popular Greek grammar, the *Erotemata* ("Questions," because it was in catechetical question-and-answer form). Numerous generations learned Greek from the *Erotemata,* which was still being printed as late as 1584.

In March 1400 Chrysoloras left Florence and traveled to Pavia and to the court of Giangaleazzo Visconti, the duke of Milan. The following month, in Milan, he greeted the emperor Manuel II, who had come to the Latin West seeking aid. After the emperor left, Chrysoloras remained in Lombardy until returning to Constantinople with the emperor in 1403. While at the ducal court of Milan, Chrysoloras tutored the humanist chancellor Uberto Decembrio in Greek, the most notable result of that instruction being Decembrio's somewhat primitive translation of Plato's *Republic.*

Returning to Constantinople, Chrysoloras continued his school in cooperation with his nephew John Chrysoloras. One of their students was Guarino da Verona, already a prominent humanist teacher, who had come to Constantinople to learn Greek. Guarino lived with the Chrysoloras family for five years; once he returned to Italy he not only reestablished himself as one of the country's premier humanist teachers, but also became a leading translator and teacher of Greek at Ferrara. Chrysoloras himself was absent from Constantinople for much of the time that Guarino was studying there because he had in effect become Byzantium's main emissary to the Latin West.

Chrysoloras returned to Venice in 1404 and then again in 1406. Sometime before this last visit he converted to Roman Catholicism. In 1405 he wrote to Pope Innocent VII asking permission to be ordained a priest and to be allowed to celebrate the Latin rite in Greek. There in fact exists a translation by Chrysoloras of the Latin Mass into Greek. He returned once again to Venice in 1407 and then continued on to northern Europe before returning to the papal court in Bologna in 1410. He followed the papal court to Rome, where he stayed for two years (1411 to 1413) in the vain hope of facilitating a Greek and Latin religious union. In Rome he tutored another significant early humanist translator in Greek: the papal secretary Cencio de' Rustici. The Roman stay was also the occasion of his most genial work, a comparison of the old and new Romes (Constantinople being the new Rome) in the form of a letter to the Byzantine co-emperor John VII. While he admired

Manuel Chrysoloras. Département des Arts Graphiques, Collection Rothschild, Musée du Louvre, Paris

the classical remains of the old Rome, he nonetheless preferred the landscape and architecture of Constantinople, in particular the church of Hagia Sophia.

In 1414, after traveling to Venice and other Italian cities, Chrysoloras made his way to the Council of Constance with the papal entourage, and it was there that he died of fever the following year. He was buried in the Dominican church in Constance.

In addition to the writings already mentioned, Chrysoloras left behind a modest literary correspondence as well as a lengthy eulogy of the despot Theodore I of Mistra. His greatest achievement, however, was his inauguration of Greek studies in Renaissance Italy.

See also **Greek Émigrés.**

BIBLIOGRAPHY

Barker, John W. *Manuel II Palaeologus (1391–1425): A Study in Late Byzantine Statesmanship.* New Brunswick, N.J., 1969.

Cammelli, Giuseppe. *I dotti bizantini e le origini dell'Umanesimo.* Vol. 1, *Manuele Crisolora.* Florence, 1941.

Patrinelis, C. G. "An Unknown Discourse of Chrysoloras Addressed to Manuel II Palaeologus." *Greek, Roman, and Byzantine Studies* 13 (1972): 497–502.

Thomson, Ian. "Manuel Chrysoloras and the Early Italian Renaissance." *Greek, Roman, and Byzantine Studies* 7 (1966): 63–82.

Weiss, Roberto. *Medieval and Humanist Greek: Collected Essays*. Padua, Italy, 1977. Pages 232–241.

JOHN MONFASANI

CICERO (106–43 B.C.), Roman statesman, orator, writer whose work influenced Renaissance thought and literature. B. L. Ullman, an expert on Neo-Latin literature, once remarked: "If Petrarch was the father of humanism, Cicero was its grandfather" (*Studies*, p. 35). One might add, if the Renaissance remade Western culture, it also remade Cicero, for the Cicero the Middle Ages knew and admired was not the same Cicero the Renaissance knew and admired.

The Discovery of Cicero. For the Middle Ages, Cicero was primarily the author of philosophical dialogues. His *De officiis* (On duties), *De natura deorum* (On the nature of the gods), *De finibus bonorum et malorum* (On the chief goods and evils), *De senectute* (On old age), *De amicitia* (On friendship), *De divinatione* (On divination), *Somnium Scipionis* (The dream of Scipio), *Paradoxa, De legibus* (On laws), and *Tusculan disputations* were widely available (the *Academica* much less so). He was secondarily a teacher of rhetorical lore. His *De inventione* (On invention), *Topica* (Topics), and the pseudo-Ciceronian *Rhetorica ad Herennium* (Textbook of rhetoric addressed to Herennius) were read and commented upon in the schools. The *Partitiones Oratoriae* (Divisions of oratory) also had some circulation.

However, the Renaissance discovered the oratorical and private Cicero. Petrarch's first classical "find" was his discovery of Cicero's oration *Pro Archia* (Defense of Archias) in 1333. For the medieval scholars Cicero hardly existed as an orator. John of Salisbury (c. 1120–1180) was the most distinguished humanist of the "Renaissance of the Twelfth Century." Yet, in the *Metalogicon*, his celebrated defense of eloquence, he did not refer to a single Ciceronian oration. In contrast, Renaissance humanists scoured libraries looking for copies of unknown Ciceronian orations. By the time the humanist Giovanni Andrea Bussi printed the first edition of Ciceronian orations at Rome in 1471 he had at his disposal all but one of Cicero's fifty-eight extant orations.

Petrarch also made another great find. In 1345, in the chapter library of Verona, he discovered a portion of Cicero's extant letters, namely, the three collections, *Ad Atticum* (Letters to Atticus), *Ad Brutum* (To Brutus), and *Ad Quintum fratrem* (To his brother Quintus). Before the end of the century, others had discovered the sixteen books of Cicero's letters *Ad familiares* (Letters to his friends). In less than seventy years, the humanists had recovered the corpus of Cicero's correspondence—the largest extant group of letters from classical antiquity.

In the next century, Cicero's mature rhetorical works were unearthed. His *De optimo genere oratorum* (On the best kind of orator; the preface to his lost translation of Demosthenes's oration *On the Crown*) became available, and in 1421 Gerardo Landriani found Cicero's *Brutus* (his history of rhetoric), *Orator* (his description of the complete orator and views on style), and *De oratore* (his largest and most thoughtful work on rhetoric) in the chapter library of Lodi. In short, one of the earliest achievements of the Renaissance was the recovery of virtually all the extant works of Cicero, the only large work missing being the *De Republica* (On the commonwealth), discovered in 1820 in a Vatican palimpsest.

The Imitation of Cicero. The Renaissance discovered a "New Cicero" (the title of Leonardo Bruni's revision of Plutarch's biography). The humanists sought eloquence as well as wisdom from antiquity, and for them Cicero was first and foremost an orator, a man who united eloquence and wisdom in his leadership of society. Petrarch had put Cicero at the head of his list of favorite authors before he made any of his discoveries; he was therefore dismayed to learn from Cicero's letters how crass a politician his hero really was. He even wrote Cicero a letter of complaint, which if nothing else shows how much his beloved classical authors were "alive" for him. Later generations of humanists admired Cicero more because of his political involvement. Bruni's *Cicero novus* of 1415 was in a sense a response to Petrarch. In the 1390s, Antonio Loschi inaugurated the Renaissance tradition of detailed commentaries on Cicero's orations. George of Trebizond's massive *Rhetoric* of 1433–1434 was in large part an explication of Cicero's speeches, and Lorenzo Valla's argument in his *Repastinatio dialecticae* (Reworking of logic) that rhetoric subsumes logic was in essence a restatement of Cicero's portrayal in the *De oratore* of the supreme orator encompassing the knowledge of the philosopher.

Cicero was by far the classical author most imitated during the Renaissance, a fact reflected in the genres humanists preferred for their own writings:

the oration, the letter, and the dialogue. Although Petrarch's prose was not especially Ciceronian, he considered Cicero Rome's greatest prose author. By the end of the fourteenth century, the itinerant teacher Giovanni Conversini of Ravenna achieved fame as an apostle of Cicero. Indeed, in 1381–1382 Filippo Villani could think of no better compliment to pay Coluccio Salutati, the chancellor of Florence, than to call him "an ape of Cicero." By the first half of the fifteenth century all the leading humanist stylists (Gasparino Barzizza, Pietro Paolo Vergerio, Leonardo Bruni, Poggio Braccciolini, Vittorino da Feltre, Francesco Filelfo, and George of Trebizond) modeled their Latin after Cicero's. They were working on the premise that if classical Latin is the only proper Latin, and if classical Latin had reached a high point in Cicero, then it would be foolish for those reviving classical eloquence to imitate anyone but the best classical author. The early Ciceronians were not rigidly exclusive in their imitation, but Cicero was unquestionably the dominant model and became for some later humanists the only model; thus was born the Ciceronian controversy.

Critics of Cicero.

Lorenzo Valla scandalized contemporaries in the first half of the fifteenth century by preferring Quintilian to Cicero as his model of Latinity. Angelo Poliziano caused a stir at the end of the century by condemning the Ciceronians and issuing his celebrated dictum in a letter to the Ciceronian Paolo Cortese: *non sum Cicero; me exprimo* (I am not Cicero; I express myself). At the start of the sixteenth century, the philosopher Gianfrancesco Pico della Mirandola also criticized Ciceronianism. It was in response to Pico that in 1512 the literary theorist Pietro Bembo gave one of the Renaissance's best defenses of Ciceronianism. For Bembo, Cicero provided the highest standard in Latin, and since imitation was an utterly natural human tendency, one should imitate the best. For imitation to be successful, however, one must capture the style and temperament of the model, not merely repeat the model's favorite words and constructions. In imitation, Bembo explained, one does not seek merely to follow, but rather to surpass. *Imitatio,* he insisted, is always joined to *emulatio* (competition).

The most enduring text of the controversy is Erasmus's *Ciceronianus* (The Ciceronian) of 1528. Erasmus first encountered Italian Ciceronians in his visit to Italy in 1506–1509. After returning north, he playfully criticized them in several writings. When they began to attack him in return, his revenge was the *Ciceronianus*. A fellow Netherlander named Christophe Longueil had gone to Rome a decade earlier and, with the encouragement of Bembo, had dedicated himself to becoming the living embodiment of pure Ciceronian style. Erasmus caricatured Longueil in *Ciceronianus* as Nosoponus, an obsessive pedant, whom Bulephorus, Erasmus's persona in the dialogue, cures of the disease of Ciceronianism. Erasmus portrayed Ciceronians as insanely anachronistic, trying to express in the vocabulary of first-century B.C. pagan Rome the radically different material and spiritual conditions of sixteenth-century Christian Europe.

The Dominance of Cicero.

Although Erasmus's *Ciceronianus* had its detractors and supporters, it is evident that Ciceronianism itself thrived throughout the Renaissance. The sheer number of Ciceronian editions, commentaries, epitomes, abstracts, lexica, citations in manuals, and prescriptions in curricula prove that Cicero dominated Latin and rhetorical instruction well into the seventeenth century. There were some three hundred print editions of Ciceronian texts before 1500, and almost three thousand more were printed during the sixteenth century, making Cicero one of the most published authors of the Renaissance. Even Longueil's orations and letters were best-sellers. At least sixty-eight editions of Mario Nizzoli's Ciceronian dictionary were completed in the hundred years after its publication in 1535. Philipp Melanchthon, Martin Luther's close assistant at Wittenberg, was a proponent of Ciceronianism, as were other leading Protestant educators such as Joachim Camerarius and Johann Sturm. Ciceronianism was a powerful current in sixteenth-century Spain. A whole string of Spanish cultural leaders, such as Juan Maldonado, Francisco Sánchez de las Brozas, Juan Ginés de Sepúlveda, Jerónimo Zurita, and Antonio Agustín, placed themselves in the Ciceronian camp. An even more powerful current of Ciceronianism was the Society of Jesus. The Jesuits ensured the continuance of Cicero's dominance in the traditional humanist educational curriculum educational curriculum. Although not all Jesuits were Ciceronians, the unique imitation of Cicero was written into the Jesuits' *Regulae praeceptorum* (Rules for teachers) of 1558. Even into the eighteenth century, Ciceronianism remained a viable option among German Protestants. In 1726 Friedrich Andreas Hallbauer found enough interest to issue an excellent collection of treatises for and against Ciceronianism. Nizzoli's Ciceronian lexicon also continued to find an audience into the eighteenth century.

During the Renaissance Cicero never ceased to be what he had been in the Middle Ages: a philosophical authority. Petrarch based his views of Plato in part on what he learned from Cicero. Lorenzo Valla's knowledge of Epicureanism was very much derived from reading Cicero's dialogues *De finibus* and *De natura deorum*. Together with Seneca, Cicero was the most important Latin source for Stoicism. Cicero's *Academica* played a role in the rising interest in scepticism in the sixteenth century. When not attacking the Ciceronians, Erasmus several times acknowledged his admiration of Cicero as a moral philosopher. Cicero's *De officiis* was the first of his works to be printed, and throughout the Renaissance his philosophical works were immensely popular.

See also Classical Scholarship; Epicurus and Epicureanism; Neo-Latin Literature and Language; Rhetoric; Stoicism.

BIBLIOGRAPHY

Fumaroli, Marc. *L'âge de l'éloquence: Rhétorique et "res literaria" de la Renaissance au seuil de l'époque classique.* Geneva, 1980.

Monfasani, John. "Humanism and Rhetoric." In *Renaissance Humanism: Foundations, Forms, and Legacy.* Vol 3. Edited by Albert Rabil Jr. Philadelphia, 1991. Pages 171–235. Reprinted in *Language and Learning in Renaissance Italy* by John Monfasani. Aldershot, U.K., 1994.

Mouchel, Christian. *Cicéron et Sénèque dans la rhétorique de la Renaissance.* Marburg, Germany, 1990.

Schmitt, Charles B. *Cicero Scepticus: A Study of the Influence of the* Academica *in the Renaissance.* The Hague, Netherlands, 1972.

Ullman, B. L. *Studies in the Italian Renaissance.* Rome, 1973.

Ward, John. *Ciceronian Rhetoric in Treatise, Scholion, and Commentary.* Turnhout, Belgium, 1995.

Ward, John. "Renaissance Commentators on Ciceronian Rhetoric." In *Renaissance Eloquence: Studies in the Theory and Practice of Renaissance Rhetoric.* Edited by James J. Murphy. Berkeley, Calif., 1983. Pages 126–173.

JOHN MONFASANI

CIRUELO, PEDRO (c. 1470–1548), Castilian theologian. Ciruelo expounded Thomas Aquinas, translated the Old Testament, and published tracts in Spanish on pastoral topics. His significance for the Renaissance lies in his combination of humanist and scholastic methods and structures.

By 1502 Ciruelo was teaching at the College of Saint Antonio de Portaceli, in Sigüenza; after 1508 he held the chair of Thomistic theology at the University of Alcalá de Henares. In the 1530s he assumed teaching positions at the cathedrals of Segovia and Salamanca. He learned Hebrew from the conversos, or Catholic converts from Judaism, who handled the Hebrew and Aramaic materials for the Complutensian Polyglot Bible (the Old Testament was printed 1515–1517). Ciruelo was a converso himself; his grandparents were burned for Judaizing—that is, for following Jewish rituals after conversion to Christianity—but he still pursued the study of Hebrew. He was never indicted by the Spanish Inquisition.

Ciruelo produced word-for-word translations of the Pentateuch, the first five books of Mosaic Law, in 1526, 1533, and 1536; he dedicated these texts to notable individuals and institutions, such as the archbishop of Toledo, the cathedral chapter of Segovia, and the University of Salamanca. In 1537 he translated Job, Psalms, Proverbs, Ecclesiastes, the Song of Songs, Esther, and Ruth in the same fashion, and dedicated this manuscript to the University of Salamanca as well. Ciruelo's biblical translations have never been studied in depth. His prologues to those translations mix conspicuous submission to the Vulgate—the common Latin Bible ascribed to St. Jerome (c. 347–420)—with a willingness to critique it. In fact, in all his musings on translation practice, Ciruelo demonstrated the value of textual criticism and an awareness of Jewish history. Such elements make him a Renaissance humanist, albeit one who frequently wrote dialectically.

Ciruelo evinced the same compound of humanism and Scholasticism in his vernacular pastoral treatises, which often were extremely popular in Spain in the sixteenth century. His tracts in Castilian were indebted to medieval genres but also drew from philology and history. Ciruelo's *Arte de bien confessar* (Art of confessing well; Alcalá, 1514) descended from thirteenth-century manuals on penance but repeated the First Commandment according to the Hebrew; his *Reprobación de las superticiones y hechicerías* (Reprobation of superstitions and sorceries; Alcalá, 1530) arose from the fifteenth-century development of the witch stereotype but tied its male and female culprits to Old Testament idolaters. Ciruelo thus owed as many of his emphases to humanism as to Scholasticism, and late-twentieth-century scholarship highlights his participation in the Spanish Renaissance.

BIBLIOGRAPHY

Bataillon, Marcel. *Érasme et l'Espagne.* Edited by Daniel Devoto and Charles Amiel. 3 vols. Travaux d'Humanisme et Renaissance, no. 250. Geneva, 1991.

Homza, Lu Ann. *Religious Authority in the Spanish Renaissance.* Baltimore, 1999. Chapter 3 relates Ciruelo's converso ancestry, writings on biblical exegesis, and invocation of humanist methodology.

Homza, Lu Ann. "Religious Humanism, Pastoral Reform, and the Pentateuch: Pedro Ciruelo's Journey from Grace to Law." Ph.D. diss., University of Chicago, 1992.

LU ANN HOMZA

CISNEROS, FRANCISCO JIMÉNEZ DE (1436–

1517), Castilian prelate, reformer, patron, statesman. Born into an impoverished *hidalgo* (lower nobility) family in New Castile, Cisneros was early destined for a career in the church. After private tutoring with an uncle, he was sent to school at Alcalá de Henares and then to the University of Salamanca, where he graduated as a bachelor of laws around 1460. By the early 1480s Cisneros was a wealthy and successful churchman on the threshold of high office, but in 1484 he seems to have experienced a change of heart and entered the Franciscan Observance, the leading reform movement within the order. Here he began a life of eremitical retreat, yet without severing his contacts with the circle of Cardinal Mendoza, or with the court. Through these contacts he was made confessor of Isabella the Catholic in 1492, an appointment which marks the beginning of his rise to the summit of power and influence in the Spanish kingdoms.

At court Cisneros impressed not only with his personal asceticism but also with the driving sense of mission which he brought to the office of royal confessor. The spring of 1493 found him in Barcelona with Ferdinand and Isabella, supervising the attempted reform of Catalan monastic life. In Castile, where he was elected vicar-provincial of the Franciscan Observance in May 1494, Cisneros was instrumental in establishing the primacy of this congregation over the Conventuals, and two years later was appointed visitor of the entire order in Spain. In 1495 Isabella saw to his elevation as archbishop of Toledo, the wealthiest diocese in Christendom, in which he immediately began an energetic program of clerical reform. A papal bull of 1495 authorized the visitation and reform of the regular clergy in the archdiocese, while another in 1499 entrusted him with that of the mendicants throughout Spain. As in his own order—though often with rather less success—Cisneros wished to strengthen Observant movements against their Conventual counterparts, while taking steps to ensure that nunneries were properly funded and attached to the reformed congregations of their respective orders. Influential as these and other measures were on a generation of reformers, the ruthlessness of their execution often provoked great bitterness and ensured that they would be of short duration, and consequently Cisneros's work remained largely incomplete until after the Council of Trent (1545–1563).

The crusading fervor that characterizes the turn of the sixteenth century in Spain is accurately reflected in Cisneros's own policies and career. He is believed

Francisco Jiménez de Cisneros. *Cisneros Disembarking in Oran* by Juan de Borgona. Mural in the Mozarabic Chapel, Toledo Cathedral. TOLEDO CATHEDRAL/ORONOZ

to have played a key role in Isabella's decision to expel the Jews in 1492, and thereafter he followed a notably intolerant policy toward the newly conquered Granadine Moors. Impatient at the slow progress of evangelization, from 1499 Cisneros began a policy of enforced conversion of the Muslim population which provoked rebellions in the kingdom of Granada and presaged the slow and painful demise of Spanish Islam over the following century. For Cisneros, however, the evangelizations recalled the apostolic fervor of the early church, and it was in this cast of mind that he extended the Isabelline Reconquista to Africa with crusading campaigns on the Barbary Coast, culminating in his personal conquest of Oran in 1509.

The death of Isabella in 1504 and then of her heir, Philip of Austria, in 1506 triggered a serious dynastic crisis. Ferdinand the Catholic, who had been forced to renounce his title of king of Castile at Isabella's death, was now installed as regent until Philip's son

Charles of Ghent reached his majority. It was Cisneros who engineered this agreement against the opposition of a significant sector of the Castilian nobility, in token of which Ferdinand saw him made a cardinal and appointed inquisitor general in 1507. This collaboration continued until Ferdinand's death in January 1516, when Cisneros assumed the regency on behalf of Charles, heir to the Aragonese and Castilian crowns. Until Charles reached Spain in September 1517, the government was faced by serious unrest and noble faction, though the cardinal proved equal to the challenge. A permanent militia of some thirty thousand men was established and a series of rebellions ruthlessly crushed. Although the burning political issues of Castile were only temporarily assuaged, the smooth transition of power to Charles's Flemish court owed much to Cisneros's statesmanship. He was on his way to meet the young king when he died at Roa on 8 November 1517.

Central as Cisneros's political role undoubtedly was in the last twenty years of his life, it is as a Renaissance patron and founder that he is chiefly remembered. In 1499 he began the construction of the University of Alcalá de Henares, which opened its doors in 1508. The first and greatest enterprise undertaken here was the so-called Complutensian Polyglot, a consolidation of the Latin, Greek, Hebrew, and Aramaic texts of the Bible. Carried out by a team of humanists, philologists, and orientalists gathered by Cisneros, the result was both a monument of scholarship and the apogee of the printer's art in Spain, appearing in six volumes between 1513 and 1517. Cisneros also sponsored the publication of the devotional writings of Vincent Ferrer, Catherine of Siena, Angela da Foligno, and Girolamo Savonarola, along with many of the leading works of Northern piety and the *Devotio moderna* (Modern devotion), which were to have such an impact on Spanish spirituality. Plans to produce scholarly editions of classical and theological texts along the lines of the Complutensian Bible were, however, curtailed by his death. Even so, his accomplishments formed an immensely varied contribution to the religious culture of Renaissance Spain before the Reformation foreshadowed the onset of a more dogmatic climate in the peninsula.

See also Complutensian Polyglot Bible; Alcalá de Henares, University of.

BIBLIOGRAPHY

Bataillon, Marcel. *Erasmo y España: Estudios sobre la historia espiritual del siglo XVI*. Translated by Antonio Alatorre. 2d Spanish ed. Mexico City, 1966. Also *Erasme et l'Espagne*. 2d

French ed. 3 vols. Geneva, 1991. Essential for Cisneros's work and legacy in the spiritual field.

Cedillo, Conde de. *El Cardenal Cisneros, gobernador del reino*. 3 vols. Madrid, 1921–1928. One of the chief sources for Cisneros's political role in Castile.

Escandell Bonet, Bartolomé. *Estudios cisnerianos: In honorem B. Escandell Bonet collectanea dicata*. Alcalá de Henares, Spain, 1990. A collection of studies on all aspects of Cisneros's life and work.

García Oro, José. *El Cardenal Cisneros: Vida y empresas*. 2 vols. Madrid, 1992–1993. Perhaps the definitive biography.

García Oro, José. *Cisneros y la reforma del clero español en tiempo de los Reyes Católicos*. Madrid, 1971.

Gómez de Castro, Alvar. *De las hazañas de Francisco Jiménez de Cisneros*. Edited and translated by José Oroz Reta. Madrid, 1984. Translation of *De rebus gestis a Francisco Ximenio Cisnerio, Archiepiscopo Toletano*. Alcalá de Henares, Spain, 1569. The fundamental biography which provides essential information on what remains a comparatively poorly documented career.

Sainz Rodríguez, Pedro. *La siembra mística del Cardenal Cisneros y las reformas en la Iglesia*. Madrid, 1979. A development of themes advanced by Bataillon, but seen in broader compass.

BRUCE TAYLOR

CITIES AND URBAN LIFE.

Around one in four western Europeans lived in urban centers during the Renaissance. The proportion was even higher if they lived in the densely populated regions of northern and central Italy, southern Germany, and the Low Countries. The size of the towns and cities in which they lived varied enormously, from settlements of fewer than five hundred inhabitants, some of which in France and Germany had their own fortifications, to major centers like Venice, which had a population of 190,000 at the end of the sixteenth century, and Paris, which counted 220,000 inhabitants in 1600. In principle, the larger the urban center, the more complex was its economic and social structure, but there were major variations between one part of Europe and another, as well as changes over time. Much depended on a town's place in international and regional networks. The European urban network that was in place at the beginning of the Renaissance remained largely unchanged in its overall distribution, although the experience of individual centers varied sharply over time.

Many urban centers shared characteristics that helped to distinguish them visibly and constitutionally from their rural hinterlands. The height of their buildings—whether church towers, domes or steeples, government offices, or private residences—could be seen from afar. Coming closer, a traveler became aware of fortifications, which, whether they were older towers and curtain walls or the more advanced earthworks and bastions pioneered in fifteenth-century Italy, fulfilled the common role of establishing a barrier between the town and an often menacing outside world. The physical separateness of many centers was matched by their constitutional status as corporate bodies, whose members had the right to elect representative assemblies to govern their affairs and to represent them elsewhere. These characteristics were balanced by others that make it less easy to use them to distinguish urban centers in this way. Not all towns had fortifications. Others lost them during the Renaissance, or saw their utility decline as suburban settlement fueled by migration expanded beyond old established borders. Even larger towns had a considerable agricultural character. Agricultural workers often lived in towns, while working outside them. In mid-sixteenth-century Aix-en-Provence, they represented the largest occupational group. Pigs and geese were a common sight in the streets and tended to be among the first casualties of measures taken at the outbreak of plague. Even within walled areas, large spaces devoted to crops and orchards were common. The influx of migrants brought patterns of rural behavior that shaped urban society, particularly among the poor.

Chartered towns were more common in France and Germany than in England, where competition among established urban centers for incorporation became a useful source of income for the monarchy. And yet contemporaries were all in agreement that they could distinguish urban from rural. Whether, like Giovanni Botero, they were writing about existing sixteenth-century towns, or planning new centers in the abstract like Sebastiano Serlio, urban functions were the center of their focus. The importance of these functions varied from one center to another. Towns were above all centers of exchange and production. A small minority also concentrated on specialist activities such as large-scale industrial production, military training and provisioning, and maritime services for entrepôt ports. Administrative and ecclesiastical functions remained the preserve of the few, but were subject to sweeping religious and political changes. Renaissance Europe was marked less by the splendor of its new capital cities than by the loss of this status by many formerly independent city-states.

Diversity.　Urban life was marked above all by its diversity. The range of economic activities in all but the smallest of towns meant that there was constant interaction between individuals with differing dress, training, and traditions. The main points of entry, often gates or barriers in fortifications, admit-

ted a constant flow of people and goods in both directions throughout the day, bringing contacts with the outside world, considerable diversity in goods for sale, and a certain level of dynamism and instability to the lives of many residents, who needed to accommodate the presence of temporary visitors and migrants. Individual experience was also mediated by different kinds of solidarities. Townspeople had loyalties to their town; they also belonged to parishes, guilds, neighborhoods, and unofficial personal networks linked by kinship, marriage, the mutual exchange of loans, godparenthood, and the guardianship of widows and children. Male and female solidarities also played their part.

The diversity of urban life remained. If anything, this increased and consequently became more confusing as time passed. Economic, political, and religious forces, particularly in the sixteenth century, brought about changes both to the place of towns in the larger context and to the organization of urban life itself. Rapid demographic expansion, interrupted by major loss of life in outbreaks of epidemic disease, enabled most economies to expand and prosper until the late 1500s. Thereafter, the effects of economic slowdown were intensified particularly in the Mediterranean area by a general shift in the control of international trade and shipping toward the Dutch and the English, leaving major commercial centers such as Venice and Genoa, and industrial centers like Florence, struggling against outside competition. Even north of the Alps, the main reasons for urban growth and renewal owed more to the expansion of state power than to the commercial market, while the economic difficulties of larger towns in Italy and the Holy Roman Empire compounded their slow loss of political autonomy or independence to stronger entities, a process that had begun in the mid-fifteenth century.

Where this was accompanied by a sharp decline in "popular" participation in urban government, the result was a dilution in the ways in which many of the population identified with their native town. Residents retained more focused loyalties, but also developed new solidarities. The presence of substantial religious minorities, particularly after the Reformation, encouraged positive acts of identification with particular districts, buildings, and rituals as a way of emphasizing difference, as well as laying the foundation for suspicion and bitterness that sometimes led to violence and armed conflict. In centers with substantial confessional uniformity, religious institutions formed a renewed cultural focus.

The diversity of Protestant belief offered townspeople in the largest cities, such as London and Amsterdam, a choice of religious practice. The sharp reduction in the numbers of clergy after the Reformation, the closure of convents and monasteries, the ending of priestly celibacy, and the integration of the clergy into the civic corpus all brought about a new dimension to the nature of urban life. This was symbolized on both sides of the religious divide by changes to the urban landscape, characterized by the construction or reconstruction of churches and other religious buildings by Catholics, and the demolition or transformation of redundant religious buildings by Protestants. Changes in warfare and the new imperatives of the territorial state alike contributed to the shape of the urban landscape by transforming traditional fortifications into complex geometrical earthworks in militarily sensitive areas, and tree-lined boulevards where there was no perceived threat.

Contemporaries divided up urban society in several ways: citizens and noncitizens, nobles and people, merchants and artisans, householders and tenants. Definitions that depended on membership of the civic body effectively excluded the poor and anyone who lacked financial independence. Although citizen status persisted, and in so doing promoted an artificial civic solidarity that was at odds with political reality, it ceased to have much meaning on its own. The number of citizens often became too large to assemble in one place to take collective oaths or to endorse the election of councillors. Even service in the militia came to be the preserve of a minority. Modern historians portray a more complex picture of urban society in which a wealth hierarchy, reflected in tax assessments, cut across a social pyramid dependent on the nature of a man's occupation or source of revenue.

Women derived much of their social status from male relatives, but are also increasingly recognized to have had solidarities of their own that did not necessarily correspond to the social gradations applied to men. Groups of immigrant origin often retained a separate identity, reinforced by intermarriage and certain occupations, such as the French water carriers of Madrid and the great Italian families of long-distance merchants in Lyon. There is little evidence of class solidarity in cases of urban conflict during the period, other than the justifiable fear of the wealthy for their property during riots. By contrast, much politically inspired conflict took place between loosely defined deference networks, such as the factions that clashed in early seventeenth-century Marseille, and sometimes between stronger party-groupings as in fifteenth-century Florence.

Government. There was a marked contrast between the persistence in the outward forms of urban government, many of which had been established during the Middle Ages, and the scale and nature of the tasks that faced the urban authorities. While they continued to legislate the conditions in which markets were held, the level of taxes to be raised, and the nuisance of clutter in the streets, they were also faced with unprecedented levels of immigration, economic fluctuations of some importance, and the need to come to terms with external authorities. There was also a growing recognition that the diversity of problems required more specialized handling. Committees were set up to deal with matters such as public health, fire prevention, provisioning, defense, the maintenance of order, and poor relief, leading to the development of more specialized expertise on the one hand, and greater opportunities for corruption on the other. It is doubtful whether urban governments would have operated as smoothly as they did without the mediation of gifts and other forms of bribery. Their effectiveness was further limited in the later sixteenth century by the effects of rising government expenditure on new fortifications, more organized forms of poor relief, the construction or maintenance of ostentatious public buildings, and falling fiscal income. The latter was a reflection of the combined effects of the diversion of tax revenue to the central authorities, and of a decline in the overall productivity of urban economies.

With the exception of a shrinking number of city-states, most urban centers lost political autonomy to territorial rulers. In some states, parallel authorities were appointed by the center to oversee tax collection, defense, the courts, and the general implementation of policy decisions. Elsewhere, territorial rulers made increasing use of their powers to nominate members of urban ruling bodies to ensure that policies would be adopted that would be received with favor at the center. On the other hand, urban governments were able to use their new position within the territorial state to lobby for economic and political advantage over their neighbors. State-building was a long and complicated business, and many townsmen turned this to their own advantage. The capital cities were most affected by this process. The end of the peripatetic court and the growth in the numbers of administrators altered the existing relationship between rulers and their capitals. The presence of a princely court created an alternative focus to traditional oligarchies and fueled a substantial wave of construction. New symbols of authority such as princely palaces in Turin, Madrid, or Vienna, or citadels such as the one built to overlook Florence in the sixteenth century by its early Medici dukes, expressed their dominance over their capitals in no uncertain terms.

Economy. As a whole, urban economies were not marked by consistent dynamism. Population levels experienced sharp fluctuations, and while commercial success continued to motivate economic development, some of the most consistent urban growth took place in administrative centers. All towns shared the common economic functions of exchange, production, and some kind of associated services, whether innkeeping, domestic service, fetching and carrying, prostitution, or the professions. However, the prosperity of towns and their inhabitants was closely linked to more passive sources of income, such as investments in municipal funds, rents from houses, and the ownership of property outside the town. Where demand rose, commercial activity ranging from itinerant peddlers to merchants who found it more convenient to do business in inns and taverns spilled over into locations beyond the control of the guilds or market authorities. The number of different occupations in a town was directly related to its size and its position in the regional urban hierarchy. In Strasbourg, for example, there were ninety-nine individual occupations, in each of which more than ten people were engaged.

As a rule, craft production remained small in scale throughout the period, even in the textile industry, and the attempts by entrepreneurs to alter working practices and increase production levels were often frustrated, not so much by the restrictive policies of guilds as by the unwillingness of the urban authorities to alter long-standing statutes.

Life in the City. The increasing numbers of people and goods moving around public spaces not designed for such a volume of traffic exacerbated the ways in which many aspects of urban life were an assault on the senses in general and on individual sensibilities in particular. Deciding who had the right of way where wheeled vehicles carrying goods or passengers had to compete with artisans whose work spilled outside their houses was a frequent source of conflict, particularly when carriages came into fashion for persons of importance during the later sixteenth century. King Henry IV of France was

Life in the City. A Florentine merchant from *De sphaera* (detail), fourteenth century. By permission of the Ministero per i Beni e le Attività Culturali, Biblioteca Estense Universitaria, Modena, Italy

assassinated in his coach in 1610 during one of the many Parisian traffic jams. Legislative action to reduce congestion was often only a temporary palliative. A one-way system was introduced in Amsterdam in 1615. Attempts were also made in London to license hackney carriages in order to keep down their numbers, but in both cases the rising demand for wheeled transport only compounded the problem. The rich sought construction of new residential quarters with wide streets and squares in order to distance themselves from the noise, congestion, and unpleasant odors of everyday life.

Foreign visitors frequently recorded in their journals the spectacle of urban life. They commented on the relative freedom with which women circulated in public, the color and theatricality of the many religious and civic processions, often accompanied by music and dancers, and the contrasts in dress and comportment between townspeople and peasants and individuals of differing social status. Even if some of these accounts are exaggerated, the rhythm of urban life was constantly interrupted by both official and unofficial spectacle. People were free to stop and stare. All spectacle had a serious purpose, but its entertainment value was not underestimated by participants and spectators alike. The mountebanks who sold quack medicines, perfumes, and other fripperies in Saint Mark's Square in Venice and in other public places relied on their capacity to entertain a crowd of passersby in order to make sales. Carnival was a widespread invitation to townspeople to engage in extreme behavior, but in some ways it was just an extension of the daily promenade in Mediterranean towns in which people moved around in order to see and to be seen.

The entertainment of the street was increasingly supplanted by forms of indoor diversion that were directed at a more limited clientele who used them to reinforce their social exclusiveness. Members of urban elites were joined by courtiers in capital cities, and elsewhere by visiting gentry, for whom the town had become a social magnet with opportunities for both business and distraction. Some entertainments paralleled those of the street. Dances were held in town halls. In Nürnberg, the list of those who were permitted to take part became the legal basis for membership of the elite. Gambling could take place in comfortable and attractive surroundings, from which the poor and the disreputable who played cards in taverns were excluded. New forms of entertainment also developed, particularly at the end of the Renaissance: opera, theater, private poetry readings, and discussion groups.

Organized religion was a major part of urban life. Ecclesiastical buildings dominated the skyline. Parish churches functioned as social and cultural centers. Guild membership offered spiritual as well as secular benefits. Much educational and charitable provision was in the hands of the church. Independent from the urban authorities, the church offered alternative forms of jurisdiction. While relations between the two were often cordial and mutually supportive, they could also be competitive and occasionally acrimonious. By the end of the sixteenth century, much had changed. The introduction of Protestant forms of worship in most of northern Europe not only secularized the clergy and removed their assets, it also moved the emphasis of popular piety away from communal worship to individual expression in private. Control of education and poor relief passed to secular groups and institutions.

Elsewhere in Europe, in the south, in France, and in parts of Germany, urban Catholicism remained, but religious practice was marked by the Reformation. As a result of the Tridentine reforms, better-informed and better-trained priests were complemented by members of the new religious orders, the Jesuits in particular. New buildings were inserted into the urban fabric to emphasize the centrality of belief. Existing churches were refurbished. The earlier importance of parish churches and guilds as a focus for lay religious activity declined in the face of new confraternities, whose members came from many different districts, and whose activities emphasized key elements of Catholic dogma in preference to the veneration of individual saints. In all cities, whether Protestant or Catholic, the ecclesiastical and secular authorities worked together to assert a common religious and political orthodoxy to underwrite the primacy of both urban and territorial rulers.

Towns were centers of education of all kinds, ranging from dames' schools to ensure minimum literacy levels for the purposes of doing business and understanding religious principles, to Latin grammar schools and universities, to vocational training schools providing instruction in spinning for paupers, to craft and trade apprenticeships and preparation for the legal professions. An educational hierarchy developed in which larger towns were able to offer more advanced forms of education. Smaller university towns, such as Bologna, Padua, Wittenberg, Oxford, Cambridge, and Glasgow, rarely exhibited other attributes of urban importance. As centers of education and training rather than commercial, industrial, or administrative centers, towns frequently attracted young people from outside, who used these opportunities as a means of social improvement. Education and training were offered to boys and girls alike, but the latter were rarely given the opportunity to progress very far. The development of educational provision was also marked by the religious changes of the sixteenth century. The Jesuits became the key to educational expansion. The quality of the experience they offered attracted even the sons of some Protestants and was seen as a dual weapon in the fight to maintain the strength of the church. In Protestant towns, control of education passed to the urban authorities, who wished to emphasize the godly nature of their activities while giving full rein to the humanist educational model exported across the Alps in the early sixteenth century.

See also **City-State**.

BIBLIOGRAPHY

General

Clark, Peter, ed. *The Early Modern Town*. New York, 1976.
Cowan, Alexander. *Urban Europe, 1500–1700*. New York, 1998.
Friedrichs, Christopher R. *The Early Modern City, 1450–1750*. New York, 1995.
Vries, Jan de. *European Urbanization, 1500–1800*. London, 1984.

Urban Histories

Barry, Jonathan, ed. *The Tudor and Stuart Town, 1530–1688: A Reader*. New York, 1990.
Benedict, Philip, ed. *Cities and Social Change in Early Modern France*. London, 1989.

Society

Cowan, Alexander Francis. *The Urban Patriciate: Lübeck and Venice, 1580–1700*. Cologne, Germany, and Vienna, 1986.
Farr, James R. *Hands of Honor: Artisans and Their World in Dijon, 1550–1650*. Ithaca, N.Y., 1988.
Mackenney, Richard. *Tradesmen and Traders: The World of the Guilds in Venice and in Europe, c. 1250–c. 1650*. London and Sydney, Australia, 1987.

Government

Pullan, Brian. *Rich and Poor in Renaissance Venice: The Social Institutions of a Catholic State, to 1620*. Oxford, 1971.
Schneider, Robert A. *Public Life in Toulouse, 1463–1789: From Municipal Republic to Cosmopolitan City*. Ithaca, N.Y., 1989.
Strauss, Gerald. *Nuremberg in the Sixteenth Century*. Bloomington, Ind., 1976.

Economy

Van der Wee, H., ed. *The Rise and Decline of Urban Industries in Italy and in the Low Countries*. Leuven (Louvain), Belgium, 1988.

Religion

Black, Christopher. *Italian Confraternities in the Sixteenth Century*. Cambridge, U.K., 1989.
Châtellier, Louis. *The Europe of the Devout: The Catholic Reformation and the Formation of a New Society*. Cambridge, U.K., 1989.

ALEXANDER COWAN

CITY-STATE. In the context of Renaissance Italy, a city-state is understood to be a largely independent city that, in the fourteenth and fifteenth centuries, had extended its authority over its hinterland, the *contado,* and in some cases over other cities to create a larger territorial state. The phenomenon was particularly marked in regions in the north of the peninsula—Lombardy, the Veneto, Tuscany—nominally subject to the Holy Roman Empire. The city-state also emerged in the Lands of Saint Peter, the Papal States, nominally subject to the papacy. In the south and the islands the city-state did not appear. Despite the economic, political, and strategic importance of such cities as Naples and Palermo, they never broke from their royal overlords sufficiently to attain the status of city-states. Nor did regions of the north—Piedmont, for example—where economic conditions were not so flourishing and the authority of the feudal overlord remained.

Independence and Sovereignty. That city-states were pivotal to the Renaissance has long been recognized. Politically they challenged the medieval order presided over by the Western emperor and the papacy. This challenge appeared particularly acute and significant in Italy, where the claimants to the inheritance of ancient Rome—the Holy Roman Empire and the papacy—were most engaged in terms of territory and support. Out of this conflict emerged a new type of state, one that owed scant allegiance to either of the medieval world powers and that depended on its own resources rather than on privileges and concessions conferred from on high. Authority and legitimacy were based on the concept and practice of popular sovereignty; they rested with the community (commune), which created its own magistrates and officials. Hence, for example, the ducal title claimed by Francesco Sforza (1401–1466), lord of Milan and formerly a mercenary commander, was derived in large measure from the acclamation of his subjects in 1450 rather than from imperial grant. Moreover, some of these new city-states also proved to be expansionist, seeking to take their frontiers beyond the *contado,* ignoring the older rights and claims of other legitimate rulers. For example, from the late fourteenth to early sixteenth centuries the Republic of Venice expanded into territories nominally subject to the empire, the papacy, and the crowns of Hungary and Naples.

Related to this is the idea that the Italian city-states comprised a new social and economic order. Status and citizenship were determined by the community itself. In the feudal order of society of the medieval era, wealth and power were closely linked to the land and the rights, obligations, and revenues associated with it. The Italian city-state, however, drew on sources of wealth more familiar to a modern, capitalist world. Employment and wealth increasingly came from trade, industry, and a proliferating range of financial activities: money changing, banking, credit transactions, and insurance. The wealth of the state and its citizens was no longer narrowly local or regional in origin, but international. The commercial world described in the trading manual of the Florentine merchant Francesco Pegolotti (1315–1340) stretched from Peking to Dunfermline (Scotland). A merchant such as Francesco Datini from Prato (c. 1335–1410) had business interests encompassing the Mediterranean and northern Europe. Hence, society was dominated not by feudal landlords but by an emerging bourgeoisie of merchants, bankers, entrepreneurs, and lawyers. They challenged the wealth and power of the medieval order, and, being literate and appreciating the value of education, they also deprived the clergy of its once near monopoly of learning.

The impact of the emerging city-states could be seen in various ways. They sought, often aggressively, to defend their own authority while reducing that of their likely opponents. City governments directed resources at the construction of walls and gates and often fortified their own seats of government while taking steps to ensure the surrender and destruction of private fortresses within the city and its *contado*. The fresco dedicated to the theme of good government painted by Ambrogio Lorenzetti in one of the council chambers in the Palazzo Pubblico of Siena depicts nobles submitting themselves and their castles to the commune, while the ideal city itself is free of fortifications other than its protective walls. More generally, from the thirteenth century, city-states compiled their own statutes, organized their own courts, appointed their own magistrates and officials, signed treaties, declared war and peace, and raised taxes. The range of government action became increasingly ambitious, taking in such activities as the supply of food and the control of disease, the latter prompted by the impact of the Black Death (1348) and later outbreaks of plague.

Despite the persistence of traditional medieval doubts as to the worthiness of material wealth, the church became thoroughly reconciled to the new city-state. To be sure, hermitages, monasteries, and shrines were found in the hinterland, as in the case of the retreat of Saint Francis of Assisi (1181–1226) at La Verna in the Casentino north of Arezzo. But the church was organized from the cities where the principal shrines and churches—the cathedrals and the churches and convents of the orders of friars—were located. Despite the claims of the papacy and the canonical procedures of the church itself, the governments of Italian city-states tried to influence ecclesiastical appointments, tax the clergy, concern themselves with issues of reform, and control church building, as the efforts made by the Venetian government to limit the temporal influence of the church while proclaiming the piety of the Venetians in ceremonial and stone well testify. As Venice also demonstrates, it was in the cities that lay piety manifested

itself with increasing vigor from the thirteenth century, encouraged there by the preaching of the friars. Hence the city-states of Renaissance Italy are noted for their devotional activity, as seen in the *scuole,* the confraternities of Venice, and in the foundation of welfare institutions such as the foundling hospital, Ospedale degli Innocenti, in Florence (1445).

Medieval Origins. It is important to realize that the Italian city-states were not a product of the Renaissance. The cities at their core—for example, Milan, Siena, Florence—were of Roman, if not earlier, origin; Venice was founded early in the Middle Ages. Their period of greatest economic and population growth was during the commercial revolution of the Middle Ages, from the tenth to the thirteenth centuries. By contrast, in the Renaissance, with the emergence of the northern and Atlantic powers and the Ottoman Empire, Italian entrepreneurs no longer enjoyed an ascendancy in Europe and the Mediterranean. Population levels only gradually returned to those reached in the thirteenth century, before the onslaught of the Black Death and the establishment of plague as an endemic disease. Hence the physical extent and layout of the cities of Renaissance Italy had been largely established in the Middle Ages.

The period from the eleventh to the thirteenth centuries had also been one of intense rivalry in Italy between the empire and the papacy, which had assisted in the emergence of the cities of the north and center as states. The decline of effective imperial power was signaled in the Treaty of Constance of 1183 with the emperor Frederick I recognizing the liberties of the northern cities. The political weakness of the papacy was prolonged during the residence of the popes at Avignon (1309–1376), and even more so by the events of the Great Schism (1378–1417) and the conciliar movement that followed.

However, the weakness of these two powers in the Renaissance should not be exaggerated. Their sovereign status remained; even the Republic of Venice, which was the only Italian city-state to be acknowledged as sovereign in the Middle Ages, sought recognition for the territories it acquired in the imperial kingdom of Italy. From the mid-fifteenth century, the papacy gradually began to recover its political authority in the Papal States, as the "Liberty of the Church," meaning in effect the authority of the church, was extended so that the liberties of its subject cities were checked. This can be seen most clearly in the case of Rome, where aspirations for wider autonomy for the city government in the fourteenth and early fifteenth centuries were effectively stifled. The papal court replaced the Capitol, the seat of Roman city government, as the center of power, and the city's lordship over the surrounding countryside became largely ceremonial. In the case of the empire, effective imperial authority had largely been reduced in the fourteenth and fifteenth centuries to sporadic military expeditions and the sale of titles and privileges, but when the imperial crown was joined to the enlarged Habsburg empire in the sixteenth century, its authority and influence in Italy recovered. For example, the duchy of Milan was incorporated into the empire in 1535.

Republics and Princedoms. These developments, taken together with the fact that some city-states—Venice, for example—had emerged as territorial states in the fifteenth century, meant that in the Renaissance the number of independent city-states was in decline. In decline even earlier was the number of city-states with communal or republican forms of government. Historians in the nineteenth century could see the rise of the Italian communes in terms of democracy, and if their interpretation was influenced more by wishful thinking than historical accuracy, they were undoubtedly correct to see the later Middle Ages and Renaissance in terms of narrowing regimes. Large citizen bodies, representing the entire community, were either manipulated—like the Florentine *parlamento*—or abandoned—like the *arengo* of Venice. Citizenship, which was the key to high public office and always seen as a privileged status enjoyed by a minority, became more strictly defined. In a few cases, such as Venice, the right to participate in government became the preserve of a hereditary nobility. More generally, access to public office was controlled by an elite of lawyers, landowners, and entrepreneurs. Attempts to overthrow this situation were short-lived, as when the *ciompi,* the unenfranchised laborers in the Florentine textile industry, rebelled in 1378 and were put down by 1382.

Indeed the social and economic changes often associated with the Italian city-states were not as great as once was thought. Although new areas of economic activity certainly did develop, land remained central to the economy. Even in relatively highly urbanized areas—Lombardy, the Veneto, Tuscany— the vast majority of the population had no rights to citizenship and lived and worked on the land. The rise of the communes had not destroyed the power of the nobility; indeed, the reverse was probably true. The bourgeoisie displayed a fascination for the culture of the aristocracy: its titles, its taste for chivalric values and literature. It respected the military skills of the nobility and shared its belief in the value of landed wealth. Marriage to and association with noble families were much prized. On the other hand, the wealth and opportunities for political influence offered by the city-states of Italy made them magnets for ambitious noble families, and it is partly for these reasons that the majority of the cities of northern and central Italy surrendered from the thirteenth century onward to the *signoria,* the lordship, of a powerful local noble family, as in the case of the Visconti of Milan (late 1200s–1447), the Carrara of Padua (1318–1405), and the Varano of Camerino (late 1200s–1527). Venice was the only major city-state with the resources and political stability to retain its independence and republican constitution throughout the Renaissance era. Florence retained its republican regime, but from 1434 its government was increasingly manipulated by the Medici family. After republican interludes (1494–1512; 1527–1530), the Medici were recognized as rulers of the city, being awarded the title of duke in 1532.

Champions of the republican tradition both at the time and since have cast these developments—confirmed by the citadels that signorial regimes began to install in the cities under their rule—in a negative light. Others have seen signorial regimes an answer to the ills allegedly suffered by the republican form of city-state: indecision, military unpreparedness, factionalism, corruption, even elitist government. However, modern research tends to show that both forms of city-state were much less effective in terms of government and administration than the Swiss historian Jakob Burckhardt's description of the Renaissance state as "a work of art" would suggest. Both found it difficult to raise revenues and organize defense. Both found it hard to achieve probity in administration and maintain law and order. Both found it impossible to ignore the pleas—rather, the demands—for special privileges from the church, leading families, *contado* communities, and subject cities. Both failed to solve the problems posed by famine and disease.

Art and Architecture. If the city-states of Renaissance Italy were not as numerous, independent, republican, socially distinct, and powerful as was once thought, their contribution to the Renaissance in cultural terms is still undoubted. The reasons are partly economic. Although Italy had lost the leadership it had once enjoyed, there was still sufficient wealth to fund what today is called "patronage of the arts and letters," although at the time, most of these patrons would have understood their support as expressions of piety, of civic or family utility and pride, or of magnificence; only for a few was such largesse a matter of intellectual curiosity and connoisseurship. Economic conditions in the cities provided the resources in terms of finance, skills, and materials needed to sustain such massive projects as the construction of the cathedral of Milan (from 1386), projects which in turn contributed to economic activity. The same is also true of one of the major innovations of the Renaissance: the introduction of the printing press. From the later fifteenth century, the city-states—Venice above all—provided the materials, skills, money, markets, and patronage to ensure the rapid development of this invention.

Otherwise the contribution of the Italian city-state to the Renaissance had much to do with the legacy of the Middle Ages. The cathedral library in Verona, where Francesco Petrarch found Cicero's letters to Atticus (1345), had been founded early in the Middle Ages. The universities of Italy, which provided the governments of the city-states with legal expertise, prestige, and economic benefits, began with the University of Bologna in the late twelfth century, with other Italian universities founded in the thirteenth, fourteenth, and fifteenth centuries.

Pride in a city's founding, its saints and relics, history, and heroes, was also medieval in origin. In Venice, for example, myths concerning its founding fathers (Trojan and Roman) and its close association with Saint Mark were well established by the Renaissance. A city's sense of identity can also be measured in its architecture, seen in the palazzi that house its council chambers, archives, courts, prisons; in the layout of its piazzas, the construction of roads and bridges, the installation of aqueducts and fountains; and in the provision of markets and merchants' halls. Siena provides a good example of such developments, and one that can be readily appreciated to this day. Its government offices were housed in the Palazzo Pubblico (begun in the late thirteenth century). It faced onto the central piazza, the Piazza del Campo, paved in the fourteenth century. An aqueduct was completed in 1344 and an elaborate fountain, the Fonte Gaia, was commissioned from Jacopo della Quercia in 1409. Close to the Campo and the city's commercial and banking houses, the Loggia dei Mercanti was erected in the early fifteenth century to house the merchants' tribunal.

One of the later architectural features added to the Palazzo Pubblico in Siena was an open chapel erected in thanksgiving for the passing of the Black Death; this introduces the point that civic pride could also lead to the building and decoration of religious buildings. This is well illustrated by the Basilica of San Marco in Venice. This was not the city's cathedral before 1807, but rather its principal church, shrine, and the doge's chapel. Begun in the ninth century, the building was carefully maintained and embellished by the state to celebrate the conquests, wealth, and piety of the Venetians—the rewards of their devotion to Saint Mark. Similarly, in 1390, the commune of Bologna sought to honor its patron saint, San Petronio. Again, not the city's cathedral but very much its church, San Petronio became the largest church in Bologna as a consequence of building campaigns that lasted into the seventeenth century.

From Law to Culture. The cultural implications of civic pride and the workings of the city-state went beyond secular and religious architecture and the decorative programs that went with it. The city-states needed literate and legally trained administrators to draft statutes, preside over the courts, keep minutes (*atti* or *ricordanze*), conduct diplomacy and correspondence, and manage the accounts. The basis of the statutes and legal procedures in most city-states was Roman law, and historians have long argued that the professionals needed to master this source stimulated a familiarity with the language and ideas of Roman, and subsequently Greek, authorities. This produced a number of political thinkers and civic humanists who drew on the writings of antiquity to make the case for the existence and aims of the city-state.

Key figures in this development were the political thinker Marsiglio of Padua (c. 1275–1343), the jurist Bartolus of Sassoferrato (1314–1357), and the Florentine chancellors Coluccio Salutati (1331–1406) and Leonardo Bruni (1370–1444). The nature and longevity of the Venetian Republic created a long tradition of native and foreign commentators, while the courts of the signorial city-states produced political thinkers and propagandists who drew on ancient models to justify princely rule. The historical epics written in praise of such dynasties as the Sforza of Milan or the Montefeltro of Urbino are good examples of this kind of literature, an equivalent to the civic chronicles and histories written in Venice or Florence. The Medici, probably the most prominent princely dynasty to survive the Renaissance in power, used an impressive galaxy of talents to hail their greatness and the benefits brought to Florence and Tuscany by their rule. The artist, architect, and art historian Giorgio Vasari (1511–1574) is a good example of the gifted and influential sycophancy encouraged at the Medici court in sixteenth-century Florence.

It must be noted that the Medici had valued the importance of "magnificence" in the fifteenth century, when they were ostensibly private citizens, and this introduces the point that the cultural impact of the city-state on the Renaissance stemmed from more than the needs of the state—republican or princely—and the church. Contributions came from the guilds, as demonstrated by the Florentine shrine of Orsanmichele embellished by the guilds of the city in the course of the fifteenth century. Confraternities made their mark, as seen, for example, in the paintings commissioned from Carpaccio (1460–1525) by the greater and lesser confraternities—the *scuole grandi* and *scuole piccoli*—of Venice. The environment of the city-state also stimulated contributions from individuals and families. For example, the Greek cardinal Bessarion (1403–1473) left his collection of manuscripts to Venice, seeing the republic as a bulwark against Islam. Venetian noble families vied with one another in the construction of palaces on the Grand Canal and villas on the mainland, as well as in the patronage of churches and the collection of works of art and antiquities.

The Example of Verona. By way of conclusion, many of the points raised above can be illustrated by the case of Verona. An important Roman city, its development in the Middle Ages had much to do with its situation on the navigable river Adige and the resources of its hinterland; both encouraged the growth of a flourishing textile industry. The commune's search for independence began in the late eleventh century and in the twelfth it participated in urban leagues against imperial power. However, the ambitions and rivalries of powerful local and regional families helped ensure that Verona would not survive for long as a republic. The *signoria* of the della Scala family began in 1260 and lasted until 1387, when the city passed under foreign rule, especially that of the Venetian Republic (1405–1796).

Therefore, during the Middle Ages, Verona had only fleeting periods as a free, republican city-state. Under the della Scala, however, in the early fourteenth century it was the capital of one of the extensive territorial states of northern Italy. The della Scala also established one of the most brilliant and cosmopolitan courts of the fourteenth century, and they continued to advance civic projects—a new circuit of the city's walls, another bridge across the Adige, a new edition of the commune's statutes—as well as

embellishing their own palaces, constructing a citadel (the Castelvecchio) and erecting for some of their number monumental tombs.

But the della Scala *signoria* and the centuries of Venetian rule did not end Verona's sense of identity as a city-state. Communal institutions survived—indeed, a new council hall, the Loggia del Consiglio, was built in the late fifteenth century—and a citizen elite sought, not without success, to preserve its own authority in the government of Verona and its *contado* while contesting the demands imposed by Venice in areas like taxation.

In cultural terms the ending of political independence and the lack of a resident court perhaps encouraged some men of talent to move elsewhere: the humanist and educator Guarino Guarini (1374–1460) settled under the Este patronage at Ferrara from 1429; the architect Michele Sanmicheli (1484–1559) worked extensively in Venice, as did the painter Paolo Veronese (1528–1588). However, Verona did not see itself as a "provincial" city in the Renaissance. Local noble families not only dominated the government but also built themselves palaces and villas, endowed the church, entered into scholarly debate and correspondence, and supported (from the sixteenth century) a musical academy, the Accademia Filarmonica. Pride and a growing interest were taken in Verona's Roman heritage and, from the sixteenth century, in the della Scala *signoria*. In turn, this encouraged local scholars and antiquarians to preserve and copy archives, record inscriptions, compile family trees, describe buildings, collect medals and other antiquities, and write Verona's history. Hence a rich record of a Renaissance city has been left for the modern historian.

See also **Republicanism.**

BIBLIOGRAPHY

Ady, Cecelia M. *The Bentivoglio of Bologna: A Study in Despotism*. Oxford, 1937.

Brucker, Gene A. *Renaissance Florence*. New York, 1969.

Chambers, David S. *The Imperial Age of Venice, 1380–1580*. London, 1970.

Clarke, M. V. *The Medieval City-State: An Essay on Tyranny and Federation in the Later Middle Ages*. London, 1926. Still valuable study of the subject.

Cochrane, Eric W. *Historians and Historiography in the Italian Renaissance*. Chicago, 1981. A comprehensive treatment of history writing in the context of the Italian city-state.

Gundersheimer, Werner L. *Ferrara: The Style of a Renaissance Despotism*. Princeton, N.J., 1973.

Jones, P. J. *The Italian City-State: From Commune to Signoria*. Oxford and New York, 1997. The first volume of a dense, magisterial treatment.

Kohl, Benjamin G. *Padua under the Carrara, 1318–1405*. Baltimore and London, 1998.

Martines, Lauro. *Power and Imagination: City-States in Renaissance Italy*. New York and London, 1979. A stimulating comparison of republican and signorial regimes.

Waley, David Philip. *The Italian City Republics*. 3d ed. London and New York, 1988. A clear, accessible introduction to the subject.

JOHN E. LAW

CIVIC HUMANISM. *See* Renaissance, Interpretations of the, *subentry on* Hans Baron.

CIVIC RITUAL. *See* Ritual, Civic.

CIVILITY.

During the Renaissance, "civility" was the subject of several books of conduct, which outlined proper behavior in courtly and urban settings. The most important of these works were Baldassare Castiglione's *Il cortegiano* (1508–1528; trans. *The Book of the Courtier*), Giovanni della Casa's *Galateo ovvero de' costumi* (1558, posthumous), and Stefano Guazzo's *La civil conversatione* (The civil conversation; 1574). Castiglione and Guazzo aimed to define the qualities and education of the ideal high bureaucrat of court, whereas della Casa focused more specifically on manners, including table manners. These treatises were immediately popular and became broadly influential in England and elsewhere in Europe where the educated public could read Italian easily. All three were also translated into English in the sixteenth century, and Castiglione certainly influenced Thomas Elyot's *The Boke Named the Governour* (1531) and Roger Ascham's *The Scholemaster* (1570).

As shown in the much-quoted *Civilizing Process* by sociologist Norbert Elias, the lemma, or common theme, of civility was not new. These treatises were preceded by numerous medieval books of conduct, which were partly based on ancient models. Later developments relied mainly on the Italian Renaissance texts, which introduced the more specific notions of *cortegianeria* (courtliness) and *cortegiano* (courtier); these terms were in due course transformed into the French *honnête homme* (man of breeding) and *gentilhomme* (gentleman) and the English derivative, "gentleman." This last term echoed the Italian use of the word *gentile* (gentle) to replace "high born," "noble," and "aristocratic"; the term avoided an emphasis on social status, which the Italians (most vocally and authoritatively Dante) tended to downplay, generally obeying their militant self-consciousness as burghers of the mercantile city-states.

Civility in the City-State. Woodcut from the *Nürnberg Institutes,* 1564. BY PERMISSION OF THE BRITISH LIBRARY. 123313

In Italy, civility remained closely related both to the ancient, especially Ciceronian, doctrine of the civil servant, as interpreted and modified in the numerous medieval treatises on courtliness (that is, the education and behavior of the high ecclesiastic and high lay civil servants of the episcopal and secular courts). Guazzo also popularized the notion of sociability as the truest form of morality as well as the use of the term "conversation" to mean "civilized, pleasant social intercourse."

Transformation of the Concept. The English term "civility" derives from the Italian *civiltà,* and the French *civilité,* and later *civilisation,* all of which stem from Erasmus's enormously successful *De civilitate morum puerilium* (1530; trans. *On Good Manners for Boys*); all of these terms replaced the

Italian *cortigianeria,* which was the equivalent of the Latin *curialitas* (courtliness), the virtue of the court. This replacement followed the spread of the ideal of civility from the original, socially restricted role models of nobility to the broader classes of their emulators. This shift can be seen in the topics encompassed in the seven chapters of Erasmus's treatise: bodily cleanliness, care of the body, and manners at church, at the table, in public gatherings, at games, and in the bedchamber.

In French, *honnête* echoed Cicero's *honestas,* the broad virtue of the civil servant, broader, that is, than moral uprightness, and including elegance and personal charm, a concept that in the Middle Ages had been coupled with some Christian virtues to make up *curialitas.* As early as 1675 Dominique Bouhours noticed that *civil* and *civilité,* along with *poli* (polite) and *politesse* (politeness), and *honnête* and *honnêteté* (honesty, decency), had replaced the more medieval (court- and aristocratic-centered) *courtois* (courtly) and *courtoisie* (courtesy), just as in English "courteous" replaced "courtly." In Italy, also, *gentiluomo* (gentleman) was replacing *cortegiano* (courtier), as in Girolamo Muzio's *Il gentiluomo* (1571). A parallel evolution is also noticeable in other languages: in German *Höfischkeit* (courtesy) replaced the etymologically and semantically related *Höflichkeit* (courtliness) and the even earlier, medieval *Hofzucht* (courtly manners or customs), referring to the comportment of the *hübsche Leute* (the fine people), meaning the court nobles.

The Virtues of Civility. Just as Castiglione addresses nobles of the court as his principal audience, so do his courtier's virtues hark back to the knightly virtues of the medieval courtier, collectively, *curialitas.* Those virtues, which combined Aristotelian and Ciceronian dictates with those of Christian ethics, were chiefly: fortitude, measure, moderation, decorousness and elegance, affability and urbanity (*urbanitas*), wit (*facetia*), magnanimity, gracefulness, and naturalness. This last one, which became Castiglione's vaunted *sprezzatura* (nonchalance or poise), was meant to avoid envy by dissimulating and hiding one's extraordinary talents and acquired arts. Education is therefore essential for the courtier, and civility, the sign of true humanity, the sign that distinguishes humans from animals, is acquired through humane education, or education in the (classical) humanities.

The social impact of this ideology derived from the Platonic mentality of the Renaissance, whereby all value was based on the imitation of high models (the closest available to the divine idea). The preferred models were ancient classical masterpieces in literature and art, authoritative documents in religion and thinking (philosophical and scientific), and the most educated leadership of society. The Renaissance codes of conduct called for changes that affected thinking, feeling, and everyday habits. For example, all over Europe it gradually became imperative to use forks and handkerchiefs, which did not exist before they were introduced in the Venetian polite society in the early sixteenth century.

On a deeper level, the notion of civility is an extension of the ancient, even pre-Greek, conception of civilization as urban, in opposition to the beastly state of country life of subhuman "villains." The encounter of the civilized, civilizing hero and the brutish woodsman is first articulated in the complementary couple of Gilgamesh and Enkidu, the former conquering and befriending the latter, in the Sumerian epic *Gilgamesh,* the earliest versions of which date to the third millennium B.C.E. At least through the end of the nineteenth century the whole of a nation was not conceived as having a chance at cultural unity unless the lower social strata looked up to the members of the ruling class as role models and agreed to become civilized by imitating them.

See also **Castiglione, Baldassare; Erasmus, Desiderius.**

BIBLIOGRAPHY

Primary Work

Erasmus, Desiderius. *On Good Manners for Boys.* Translated by Brian McGregor. In *Collected Works of Erasmus.* Edited by J. K. Sowards. Toronto; Buffalo, N.Y.; and London, 1985. Vol. 25, pp. 269–289, and vol. 26, pp. 562–567. Translation of *De civilitate morum puerilium* (1530).

Secondary Works

Elias, Norbert. *The Civilizing Process.* Vol. 1: *The Development of Manners: Changes in the Code of Conduct and Feeling in Early Modern Times.* 2 vols. New York, 1978 and 1982. Translation of *Über den Prozess der Zivilisation,* 2 vols. (1939).

Jaeger, C. Stephen. *The Origins of Courtliness: Civilizing Trends and the Formation of Courtly Ideals, 939–1210.* Philadelphia, 1985.

Scaglione, Aldo. *Knights at Court: Courtliness, Chivalry, and Courtesy from Ottonian Germany to the Italian Renaissance.* Berkeley, Calif., 1991.

ALDO SCAGLIONE